Table of Titles

TITLE
1. General Provisions.
2. Agriculture.
3. Animals.
4. Aviation.
5. Banks and Financial Institutions.
6. Civil Practice.
7. Commercial Code.
8. Commercial Law and Consumer Protection.
9. Conservation and Natural Resources.
10. Corporations, Partnerships and Associations.
11. Counties and Municipal Corporations.
12. Courts.
13. Repealed.
13A. Criminal Code.
14. Criminal Correctional and Detention Facilities.
15. Criminal Procedure.
16. Education.
17. Elections.
18. Eminent Domain.
19. Fiduciaries and Trusts.
20. Food, Drugs and Cosmetics.
21. Handicapped Persons.
22. Health, Mental Health and Environmental Control.
23. Highways, Roads, Bridges and Ferries.
24. Housing.
25. Industrial Relations and Labor.
26. Infants and Incompetents.
27. Insurance.
28. Intoxicating Liquor, Malt Beverages and Wine.
29. Legislature.
30. Marital and Domestic Relations.
31. Military Affairs and Civil Defense.
32. Motor Vehicles and Traffic.
33. Navigation and Watercourses.
34. Professions and Businesses.
35. Property.
36. Public Officers and Employees.
37. Public Utilities and Public Transportation.
38. Public Welfare.
39. Public Works.
40. Revenue and Taxation.

TITLE
41. State Government.
42. United States.
43. Wills and Decedents' Estates.
44. Youth Services.

In Addition, This Publication Contains

Constitution of the United States of 1787.
Constitution of Alabama of 1875.
Constitution of Alabama of 1901. 0 0;0 Rules of the Alabama Supreme Court.
Table of Comparative Sections.
Table of Acts.

CODE OF ALABAMA
1975

With Provision for Subsequent Pocket Parts

Prepared Under the Supervision of

The Code Revision Subcommittee of
The Legislative Council

Robert H. Harris, Chairman

by

The Editorial Staff of the Publishers

Under the Direction of

A. D. Kowalsky, S. C. Willard, W. L. Jackson, P. R. Roane
and S. S. West

VOLUME 16

1986 REPLACEMENT VOLUME

---

*Including Acts of the 1986 Regular Session and
annotations taken through Southern Reporter,
Second Series, Volume 484, Page 365*

THE MICHIE COMPANY
Law Publishers
Charlottesville, Virginia
1986

Table of Contents

VOLUME 16

Title 27.

Insurance.

CHAPTER	PAGE
1. General Provisions, §§ 27-1-1 through 27-1-18	3
2. Department and Commissioner of Insurance, §§ 27-2-1 through 27-2-55	12
3. Authorization of Insurers, §§ 27-3-1 through 27-3-29	35
4. Fees and Taxes, §§ 27-4-1 through 27-4-11	56
5. Kinds of Insurance; Limits of Risk; Reinsurance, §§ 27-5-1 through 27-5-13	67
6. Administration of Deposits, §§ 27-6-1 through 27-6-16	75
7. Property, Casualty and Surety Insurance Representatives, §§ 27-7-1 through 27-7-38	83
8. Life and Disability Insurance Representatives, §§ 27-8-1 through 27-8-28	107
9. Adjusters, §§ 27-9-1 through 27-9-8	126
10. Unauthorized Insurers and Surplus Lines, §§ 27-10-1 through 27-10-56	130
11. Mail Order Insurance, §§ 27-11-1 through 27-11-7	147
12. Trade Practices Law, §§ 27-12-1 through 27-12-24	152
13. Rates and Rating Organizations, §§ 27-13-1 through 27-13-105	166
14. The Insurance Contract, §§ 27-14-1 through 27-14-32	196
15. Life Insurance and Annuity Contracts, §§ 27-15-1 through 27-15-29	225
16. Industrial Life Insurance, §§ 27-16-1 through 27-16-17	254
17. Burial Insurance Policies, §§ 27-17-1 through 27-17-16	261
18. Group Life Insurance, §§ 27-18-1 through 27-18-16	268
19. Disability Insurance Policies, §§ 27-19-1 through 27-19-58	275
19A. Dental Care Services, §§ 27-19A-1 through 27-19A-11	298
20. Group and Blanket Disability Insurance, §§ 27-20-1 through 27-20-7	302
20A. Alcoholism Treatment in Group Plans, §§ 27-20A-1 through 27-20A-4	308
21. Alabama Health Care Plan, §§ 27-21-1 through 27-21-6	310
21A. Health Maintenance Organizations, §§ 27-21A-1 through 27-21A-32	313
22. Property Insurance Contracts, §§ 27-22-1, 27-22-2	337

CHAPTER PAGE

23. Casualty Insurance Contracts, §§ 27-23-1 through 27-23-28 339
24. Surety Insurance Contracts, §§ 27-24-1 through 27-24-8 352
25. Title Insurance, § 27-25-1 355
26. Medical Liability Insurance, §§ 27-26-1 through 27-26-43 356
27. Organization and Corporate Procedures of Stock and Mutual
    Insurers, §§ 27-27-1 through 27-27-61 367
28. Holding Companies, §§ 27-28-1 through 27-28-5 400
29. Insurance Holding Company Systems, §§ 27-29-1 through 27-29-14 406
30. Mutual Aid Associations, §§ 27-30-1 through 27-30-33 423
31. Reciprocal Insurers, §§ 27-31-1 through 27-31-29 440
32. Rehabilitation, Reorganization, Conservation and Liquidation of
    Insurers, §§ 27-32-1 through 27-32-41 452
33. Trusteed Assets of Alien Insurers, §§ 27-33-1 through 27-33-16 472
34. Fraternal Benefit Societies, §§ 27-34-1 through 27-34-54 477
35. Conversion of Fraternal Benefit Societies, §§ 27-35-1 through
    27-35-11 509
36. Liabilities, §§ 27-36-1 through 27-36-7 514
37. Assets, §§ 27-37-1 through 27-37-9 530
38. Separate Accounts and Variable Annuities, §§ 27-38-1 through
    27-38-6 535
39. Automobile Clubs and Associations, §§ 27-39-1 through 27-39-8 ... 539
40. Insurance Premium Finance Companies, §§ 27-40-1 through
    27-40-18 543
41. Investments of Life, Disability and Burial Insurance Companies,
    §§ 27-41-1 through 27-41-41 553
42. Insurance Guaranty Association, §§ 27-42-1 through 27-42-20 572
43. Legal Expense Insurance, §§ 27-43-1 through 27-43-23 584
44. Life and Disability Insurance Guaranty Association, §§ 27-44-1
    through 27-44-21 596

Title 28.

Intoxicating Liquor, Malt Beverages and Wine.

1. General Provisions, §§ 28-1-1 through 28-1-5 611
2. Elections as to Sale and Distribution of Alcoholic Beverages Within
    Counties, §§ 28-2-1 through 28-2-25 616
2A. Elections as to Sale and Distribution of Alcoholic Beverages
    Within Municipalities, §§ 28-2A-1 through 28-2A-4 621
3. Regulation and Control of Alcoholic Beverages in Wet Counties,
    §§ 28-3-1 through 28-3-286 625
3A. Alcoholic Beverage Licensing Code, §§ 28-3A-1 through 28-3A-26 703
4. Regulation and Control of Alcoholic Beverages in Dry Counties and
    Dry Municipalities, §§ 28-4-1 through 28-4-326 727
5. Regulation of Manufacture, Sale, etc., of Industrial Alcohol,
    §§ 28-5-1 through 28-5-14 833

CHAPTER   PAGE

6. Regulation of Production, Sale, etc., of Native Farm Wine, §§ 28-6-1
   through 28-6-6 839
7. Importation, Distribution and Sale of Table Wine, §§ 28-7-1 through
   28-7-24 842
8. Exclusive Sales Territories and Wholesalers, §§ 28-8-1 through
   28-8-8 854

TITLE 27.

INSURANCE.

Chap. 1. General Provisions, §§ 27-1-1 through 27-1-18.
2. Department and Commissioner of Insurance, §§ 27-2-1 through 27-2-55.
3. Authorization of Insurers, §§ 27-3-1 through 27-3-29.
4. Fees and Taxes, §§ 27-4-1 through 27-4-11.
5. Kinds of Insurance; Limits of Risk; Reinsurance, §§ 27-5-1 through 27-5-13.
6. Administration of Deposits, §§ 27-6-1 through 27-6-16.
7. Property, Casualty and Surety Insurance Representatives, §§ 27-7-1 through 27-7-38.
8. Life and Disability Insurance Representatives, §§ 27-8-1 through 27-8-28.
9. Adjusters, §§ 27-9-1 through 27-9-8.
10. Unauthorized Insurers and Surplus Lines, §§ 27-10-1 through 27-10-56.
11. Mail Order Insurance, §§ 27-11-1 through 27-11-7.
12. Trade Practices Law, §§ 27-12-1 through 27-12-24.
13. Rates and Rating Organizations, §§ 27-13-1 through 27-13-105.
14. The Insurance Contract, §§ 27-14-1 through 27-14-32.
15. Life Insurance and Annuity Contracts, §§ 27-15-1 through 27-15-29.
16. Industrial Life Insurance, §§ 27-16-1 through 27-16-17.
17. Burial Insurance Policies, §§ 27-17-1 through 27-17-16.
18. Group Life Insurance, §§ 27-18-1 through 27-18-16.
19. Disability Insurance Policies, §§ 27-19-1 through 27-19-58.
19A. Dental Care Services, §§ 27-19A-1 through 27-19A-11.
20. Group and Blanket Disability Insurance, §§ 27-20-1 through 27-20-7.
20A. Alcoholism Treatment in Group Plans, §§ 27-20A-1 through 27-20A-4.
21. Alabama Health Care Plan, §§ 27-21-1 through 27-21-6.
21A. Health Maintenance Organizations, §§ 27-21A-1 through 27-21A-32.
22. Property Insurance Contracts, §§ 27-22-1, 27-22-2.
23. Casualty Insurance Contracts, §§ 27-23-1 through 27-23-28.
24. Surety Insurance Contracts, §§ 27-24-1 through 27-24-8.
25. Title Insurance, § 27-25-1.
26. Medical Liability Insurance, §§ 27-26-1 through 27-26-43.
27. Organization and Corporate Procedures of Stock and Mutual Insurers, §§ 27-27-1 through 27-27-61.
28. Holding Companies, §§ 27-28-1 through 27-28-5.

1

29. Insurance Holding Company Systems, §§ 27-29-1 through 27-29-14.
30. Mutual Aid Associations, §§ 27-30-1 through 27-30-33.
31. Reciprocal Insurers, §§ 27-31-1 through 27-31-29.
32. Rehabilitation, Reorganization, Conservation and Liquidation of Insurers, §§ 27-32-1 through 27-32-41.
33. Trusteed Assets of Alien Insurers, §§ 27-33-1 through 27-33-16.
34. Fraternal Benefit Societies, §§ 27-34-1 through 27-34-54.
35. Conversion of Fraternal Benefit Societies, §§ 27-35-1 through 27-35-11.
36. Liabilities, §§ 27-36-1 through 27-36-7.
37. Assets, §§ 27-37-1 through 27-37-9.
38. Separate Accounts and Variable Annuities, §§ 27-38-1 through 27-38-6.
39. Automobile Clubs and Associations, §§ 27-39-1 through 27-39-8.
40. Insurance Premium Finance Companies, §§ 27-40-1 through 27-40-18.
41. Investments of Life, Disability and Burial Insurance Companies, §§ 27-41-1 through 27-41-41.
42. Insurance Guaranty Association, §§ 27-42-1 through 27-42-20.
43. Legal Expense Insurance, §§ 27-43-1 through 27-43-23.
44. Life and Disability Insurance Guaranty Association, §§ 27-44-1 through 27-44-21.

The business of insurance has historically been treated by legislatures and courts with a view to the public interest. Brown-Marx Assocs. v. Emigrant Sav. Bank, 527 F. Supp. 277 (N.D. Ala. 1981), aff'd, 703 F. 2d 1361 (11th Cir. 1983).

Insurance companies and insurance contracts are subject to strict regulation. Brown-Marx Assocs. v. Emigrant Sav. Bank, 527 F. Supp. 277 (N.D. Ala. 1981), aff'd, 703 F. 2d 1361 (11th Cir. 1983).

For application of tort of outrage in insurance claims, see Sexton v. Liberty Nat'l Life Ins. Co., 405 So. 2d 18 (Ala. 1981).

The plaintiff in a "bad faith refusal to pay a valid insurance claim" has the burden of proving: (a) an insurance contract between the parties and a breach thereof by the defendant; (b) an intentional refusal to pay the insured's claim; (c) the absence of any reasonably legitimate or arguable reason for that refusal (the absence of a debatable reason); (d) the insurer's actual knowledge of the absence of any legitimate or arguable reason; (e) if the intentional failure to determine the existence of a lawful basis is relied upon, the plaintiff must prove the insurer's intentional failure to determine whether there is a legitimate or arguable reason to refuse to pay the claim. In short, plaintiff must go beyond a mere showing of nonpayment and prove a bad faith nonpayment, a nonpayment without any reasonable ground for dispute. Or, stated differently, the plaintiff must show that the insurance company had no legal or factual defense to the insurance claim. National Sav. Life Ins. Co. v. Dutton, 419 So. 2d 1357 (Ala. 1982).

The law to be applied in a case involving the tort of outrage has been clearly stated: the behavior of a defendant must be so outrageous in character, and so extreme in degree, as to go beyond all possible bounds of decency, and to be regarded as atrocious, and utterly intolerable in a civilized community. Barrett v. Farmers & Merchants Bank, 451 So. 2d 257 (Ala. 1984).

For history and analysis of tort of bad faith, see Berry v. United of Omaha, 719 F.2d 1127 (11th Cir. 1983).

For present status of the tort of bad faith, see Sprowl v. Ward, 441 So. 2d 898 (Ala. 1983).

The tort of bad faith refusal to pay a valid insurance claim is in the embryonic stage, and the Alabama supreme court has not had occasion to address every issue that might arise in these cases. National Sav. Life Ins. Co. v. Dutton, 419 So. 2d 1357 (Ala. 1982).

In order for a plaintiff to make out a prima facie case of bad faith refusal to pay an insurance claim, the proof offered must show that the plaintiff is entitled to a directed verdict on the contract claim, and, thus, entitled to recover on the contract claim as a matter of law. Ordinarily, if the evidence produced by either side creates a fact issue with regard to the validity of the claim and, thus, the legitimacy of the denial thereof, the tort claim must fail and should not be submitted to the jury. National Sav. Life Ins. Co. v. Dutton, 419 So. 2d 1357 (Ala. 1982).

In first party insurance claims, the intentional tort of bad faith is viable cause of action if insurer intentionally refused to settle where there was: (1) no lawful basis for refusal coupled with actual knowledge of that fact; or, (2) intentional failure to determine whether or not there was a lawful basis for such refusal. Chavers v. National Sec. Fire & Cas. Co., 405 So. 2d 1 (Ala. 1981).

The tort of bad faith does not apply where insurer has paid a substantial part of the claim as the failure to pay another part could well be a clerical error. Sexton v. Liberty Nat'l Life Ins. Co., 405 So. 2d 18 (Ala. 1981).

The Alabama supreme court has rejected the tort of bad faith in noninsurance contexts. Lawrence v. Lackey, 451 So. 2d 278 (Ala. 1984).

Collateral references.
Liability of premium finance agency to insurer for consequences of ineffectual cancellation of policy. 26 ALR4th 346.

What constitutes bad faith on part of insurer rendering it liable for statutory penalty imposed for bad faith in failure to pay, or delay in paying, insured's claim. 33 ALR4th 579.

CHAPTER 1.

GENERAL PROVISIONS.

Sec.
27-1-1. Short title.
27-1-2. Definitions.
27-1-3. Applicability of title — Generally.
27-1-4. Same — Exemptions.
27-1-5. Compliance requirement.
27-1-6. Prevalence of particular over general provisions.
27-1-7. Effect of captions or headings.
27-1-8. Life insurance companies may invest in notes secured by mortgages or deeds of trust.
27-1-9. Life insurance companies may invest in loans guaranteed under Service Men's Readjustment Act.
27-1-10. Payment for health services of chiropractor; insured to have exclusive right to select practitioner of healing arts.
27-1-11. Dentists and dental hygienists as "physicians" under health or accident insurance policies.
27-1-11.1. Appropriations to certain universities not to be considered in patient care reimbursement.
27-1-12. Penalty for violation of title.
27-1-13. Existing forms and filings.
27-1-14. Preservation of prior rights, obligations, etc.
27-1-15. Payment for services of podiatrist.
27-1-16. Standard health insurance claim form; format for health insurance claims submitted by electronic, etc., means.
27-1-17. Limitation period for payment of claims under health and accident insurance policies; payment of interest; right of action for recovery of unpaid benefits.
27-1-18. Contract providing for mental health services to entitle insured to reimbursement for outpatient and inpatient services by qualified psychiatrist or psychologist.

Cross references. — As to any person or activity subject to this title being exempt from the Deceptive Trade Practices Act, see § 8-19-7. As to authority of local boards of education to form groups of employees for purpose of obtaining group insurance, see § 16-22-5. As to disposition of unclaimed funds held by insurance corporations, see § 35-12-23.

As to duty of fire insurance companies to report fire losses to state fire marshal, see § 36-19-24. As to requiring insurers to furnish to certain fire officials information relating to their investigations of various types of property fire losses, see §§ 36-19-40 to 36-19-44. As to state insurance fund, see § 41-15-1 et seq.

Collateral references. — Liability insurance coverage as extending to liability for punitive or exemplary damages. 16 ALR4th 11.

Misrepresentation or concealment by insured or agent avoiding liability by title insurer. 17 ALR4th 1077.

Revocation or suspension of insurance agent's license for withholding or misappropriation of premiums. 17 ALR4th 1106.

Insurer's tort liability for consequential or punitive damages for wrongful failure or refusal to defend insured. 20 ALR4th 23.

§ 27-1-1. Short title.

This title constitutes the Alabama Insurance Code. (Acts 1971, No. 407, p. 707, § 1.)

A tort of bad faith is permissible in this state in insurance contracts. Bad faith is the intentional failure by an insurer to perform the duty implied by law of good faith in fair dealing. Gulf Atl. Life Ins. Co. v. Barnes, 405 So. 2d 916 (Ala. 1981).

The tort of bad faith refusal to pay a valid insurance claim is in the embryonic stage, and the Alabama supreme court has not had occasion to address every issue that might arise in these cases. National Sav. Life Ins. Co. v. Dutton, 419 So. 2d 1357 (Ala. 1982).

The plaintiff in a "bad faith refusal to pay a valid insurance claim" has the burden of proving: (a) an insurance contract between the parties and a breach thereof by the defendant; (b) an intentional refusal to pay the insured's claim; (c) the absence of any reasonably legitimate or arguable reason for that refusal (the absence of a debatable reason); (d) the insurer's actual knowledge of the

absence of any legitimate or arguable reason; (e) if the intentional failure to determine the existence of a lawful basis is relied upon, the plaintiff must prove the insurer's intentional failure to determine whether there is a legitimate or arguable reason to refuse to pay the claim. In short, plaintiff must go beyond a mere showing of nonpayment and prove a bad faith nonpayment, a nonpayment without any reasonable ground for dispute. Or, stated differently, the plaintiff must show that the insurance company had no legal or factual defense to the insurance claim. National Sav. Life Ins. Co. v. Dutton, 419 So. 2d 1357 (Ala. 1982).

Collateral references. — Construction and effect of clause in fidelity bond or insurance policy excluding from coverage losses proved by "inventory computation" or "profit and loss computation". 45 ALR4th 1049.

§ 27-1-2. Definitions.

For the purposes of this title, the following terms shall have the meanings respectively ascribed to them by this section.

(1) INSURANCE. A contract whereby one undertakes to indemnify another or pay or provide a specified amount or benefit upon determinable contingencies.

(2) INSURER. Every person engaged as indemnitor, surety or contractor in the business of entering into contracts of insurance.

(3) PERSON. An individual, insurer, company, association, organization, Lloyd's insurer, society, reciprocal insurer or interinsurance exchange, partnership, syndicate, business trust, corporation and every legal entity.

(4) COMMISSIONER. The commissioner of insurance of this state.

(5) DEPARTMENT. The department of insurance of this state.

(6) DOMESTIC INSURER. One formed under the laws of this state.

(7) FOREIGN INSURER. One formed under the laws of any jurisdiction other than this state. Except where distinguished by context, "foreign" insurers includes also "alien" insurers.

(8) ALIEN INSURER. One formed under the laws of any country other than the United States of America, its states, district, territories and commonwealths.

(9) STATE. Such term, when used in context signifying a jurisdiction other than the state of Alabama, means any state, district, territory, commonwealth or possession of the United States of America.

(10) AUTHORIZED INSURER; UNAUTHORIZED INSURER. An "authorized" insurer is one duly authorized, by a subsisting certificate of authority issued by the commissioner, to transact insurance in this state. An "unauthorized" insurer is one not so authorized.

(11) TRANSACT. Such term, with respect to insurance, includes any of the following:

　　a. Solicitation and inducement;

　　b. Preliminary negotiations;

　　c. Effectuation of a contract of insurance; or

　　d. Transaction of matters subsequent to effectuation of a contract of insurance and arising out of it. (Acts 1971, No. 407, p. 707, §§ 2-9.)

§ 27-1-3. Applicability of title — Generally.

No provision of this title shall apply with respect to:

(1) Domestic mutual aid associations, as identified in chapter 30, except as stated in chapter 30; or

(2) Fraternal benefit societies, as identified in chapter 34, except as stated in chapters 34 and 35. (Acts 1971, No. 407, p. 707, § 11.)

§ 27-1-4. Same — Exemptions.

This title shall not apply as to:

(1) Any fraternal or other organization or activity which is exempted from the provisions of chapter 34 under section 27-34-5, except to the extent provided in such section;

(2) Nonprofit corporations for establishment of hospitalization plan under section 10-4-100 et seq., except to the extent now or hereafter provided in such laws;

(3) The insurance department of a brotherhood or labor union, the members of which are subject to the act of congress known as the Railway Labor Act; or

(4) The establishment, maintenance, administration and operation of any trust established pursuant to section 22-21-240 by agreement of any hospitals, other health care units or dental practitioners licensed as such by the state of Alabama. (Acts 1971, No. 407, p. 707, § 12; Acts 1977, No. 166, p. 226, § 1; Acts 1978, 2nd Ex. Sess., No. 24, p. 1703, § 1.)

Code commissioner's note. — Acts 1986, No. 86-196 (House Joint Resolution 74) requests the attorney general and the insurance commissioner of this state to see that the provisions of this section are fully enforced against any health service insurance carrier doing business in this state and to take appropriate action against any such carrier refusing or failing to obey the laws of this state.

U.S. Code. — For the Railway Labor Act, see 45 U.S.C. § 151 et seq.

§ 27-1-5. Compliance requirement.

No person shall transact a business of insurance in Alabama, or relative to a subject resident, located or to be performed in Alabama, without complying with the applicable provisions of this title. (Acts 1971, No. 407, p. 707, § 10.)

§ 27-1-6. Prevalence of particular over general provisions.

Provisions of this title relative to a particular kind of insurance, a particular type of insurer or a particular matter shall prevail over provisions in this title relating to insurance in general, insurers in general or such matters in general. (Acts 1971, No. 407, p. 707, § 13.)

§ 27-1-7. Effect of captions or headings.

The scope and meaning of any provision shall not be limited or otherwise affected by the caption or heading of any chapter, section or provision. (Acts 1971, No. 407, p. 707, § 14.)

§ 27-1-8. Life insurance companies may invest in notes secured by mortgages or deeds of trust.

(a) Any life insurance company of this state, for the purpose of investing its capital, surplus and other funds, or any part thereof, other than the deposit fund, may invest in notes secured by mortgages or trust deeds on unencumbered real estate located within the United States whose principal amount shall not be more than three fourths of the value of said real estate. For the purposes of this section, real estate shall not be deemed to be encumbered within the meaning of this section by reason of the existence of taxes or assessments that are not delinquent, instruments creating or reserving mineral, oil or timber rights, rights-of-way, joint driveways, sewer rights, public utility easements, rights in walls, nor by reason of building restrictions or other restrictive covenants nor when such real estate is subject to lease in whole or in part whereby rents or profits are reserved to the owner; provided, that the security created by the mortgage or trust deed on such real estate securing such note is a first lien upon such real estate and that there is no condition or right of reentry or forfeiture under which such lien can be cut off, subordinated or otherwise disturbed.

(b) Nothing contained in this section shall be construed to affect or limit the right heretofore granted to life insurance companies to invest funds in mortgages insured by the federal housing commissioner or his successors or to loans guaranteed or insured by the veterans administration; nor shall anything contained in this section apply to purchase money obligations. (Acts 1943, No. 438, p. 403; Acts 1961, Ex. Sess., No. 86, p. 2003.)

§ 27-1-9. Life insurance companies may invest in loans guaranteed under Service Men's Readjustment Act.

(a) In addition to all other investments now authorized by law, life insurance companies of this state are hereby authorized to invest in any loan or loans which may be guaranteed in whole or in part under the act of congress known as the Service Men's Readjustment Act of 1944, or any amendments thereto.

(b) Any portion of any such loan which is not either insured by the federal housing commissioner or guaranteed under said Service Men's Readjustment Act shall be subject to the provisions of law now in existence with respect to uninsured mortgage loans.

(c) This section is remedial in its nature and shall be liberally construed. (Acts 1945, No. 37, p. 44.)

§ 27-1-10. Payment for health services of chiropractor; insured to have exclusive right to select practitioner of healing arts.

Any contract or policy of insurance or any plan or agreement for health services providing for reimbursement or payment for health services performed by a medical doctor or physician or upon the certification of a medical doctor, surgeon, osteopath or physician, shall also reimburse or pay for such health services performed by a doctor of chiropractic or upon his certificate; provided, that the health services performed by the doctor of chiropractic are within the scope of his license and he is duly licensed by the state of Alabama.

The insured or such other person entitled to benefits under such contract or policy of insurance or plan or agreement for health services shall have the exclusive right to choose or select any practitioner or member of the healing arts of Alabama to perform such services, notwithstanding any provisions of such contract or policy of insurance or plan or agreement for health services to the contrary. (Acts 1975, No. 1101, p. 2172, § 1.)

§ 27-1-11. Dentists and dental hygienists as "physicians" under health or accident insurance policies.

Whenever the terms "physician" and/or "doctor" are used in any policy of health or accident insurance issued in this state or in any contract for the provision of health care, services or benefits issued by any health, medical or other service corporation existing under, and by virtue of any laws of this state, said terms shall include within their meaning those persons licensed under and in accordance with chapter 9 of Title 34 in respect to any care, services, procedures or benefits covered by said policy of insurance or health care contract which the said persons are licensed to perform, any provisions in any such policy of insurance or health care contract to the contrary notwithstanding. This section shall be applicable to all policies in this state, regardless of date of issue, on October 10, 1975. (Acts 1975, No. 1241, p. 2607, § 1.)

§ 27-1-11.1. Appropriations to certain universities not to be considered in patient care reimbursement.

Any appropriations made by the legislature of Alabama to the University of Alabama in Birmingham and to the University of South Alabama shall be for the unrestricted support of the activities of the said university and therefore insurance companies, whether operated for profit or not for profit, licensed under the laws of the state of Alabama, whether acting on their own behalf or for others, are prohibited from applying or taking into account in any manner whatsoever, any portion of those appropriations in determining reimbursement for patient care activities. (Acts 1980, No. 80-445, p. 690.)

§ 27-1-12. Penalty for violation of title.

Each willful violation of this title for which a greater penalty is not provided by another provision of this title or by other applicable laws of this state shall, in addition to any applicable prescribed denial, suspension or revocation of certificate of authority or license, be punishable as a misdemeanor, upon conviction, by a fine of not more than $1,000.00 or by imprisonment in the county jail, or by sentence to hard labor for the county, for a period not to exceed one year or by both such fine and imprisonment or hard labor in the discretion of the court. Each instance of violation shall be considered a separate offense. (Acts 1971, No. 407, p. 707, § 15.)

§ 27-1-13. Existing forms and filings.

Every form of insurance document and every rate or other filing lawfully in use immediately prior to January 1, 1972, may continue to be so used or be effective until the commissioner otherwise prescribes pursuant to this title. (Acts 1971, No. 407, p. 707, § 809.)

§ 27-1-14. Preservation of prior rights, obligations, etc.

This title shall not impair or affect any act done, offense committed or right accruing, accrued or acquired or liability, penalty, forfeiture or punishment incurred prior to January 1, 1972, but the same may be enjoyed, asserted, enforced, prosecuted or inflicted, as fully, and to the same extent, as was possible prior to January 1, 1972. (Acts 1971, No. 407, p. 707, § 810).

Cited in Hilgeman v. State ex rel. Payne, 374 So. 2d 1327 (Ala. 1979).

§ 27-1-15. Payment for services of podiatrist.

Notwithstanding any other provision of law, when any contract of health insurance or any plan or agreement for health services provides for the reimbursement or payment for services which are within the scope of a podiatrist's professional license as defined in the general laws of Alabama, such policy shall be construed to include payment to a podiatrist who has performed such procedures. (Acts 1976, No. 678, p. 927.)

Cross references. — As to licensing and regulation of podiatrists, see § 34-24-230 et seq.

§ 27-1-16. Standard health insurance claim form; format for health insurance claims submitted by electronic, etc., means.

(a) (1) The commissioner of the department of insurance shall prescribe a standard health insurance claim form to be used by all hospitals. Such forms shall be prescribed in a format which allows for the use of generally accepted diagnosis and treatment coding systems by providers of health care and payors. Such standard form shall be accepted and used by all insurers doing business in the state of Alabama and by all state agencies which pay providers of health care for hospital services.

(2) The commissioner of the department of insurance shall also prescribe a format for all health insurance claims transmitted or submitted for payment by electronic or electro-mechanical means. Such a format shall be used by all insurers doing business in the state of Alabama and by all state agencies which pay providers of health care for hospital services.

(b) An advisory committee of five persons, two appointed by the Alabama Hospital Association, two by the Health Insurance Association of America and one by an Alabama nonprofit corporation which markets health insurance, shall advise the commissioner on an acceptable standard health insurance claim form and an electronic or electro-mechanical claims form no later than 60 days prior to January 1, 1982. If changes in the forms need to be made at any future time, the commissioner of the department of insurance shall inform the advisory committee and the committee will make recommendations as to the changes.

(c) All insurers doing business in Alabama and all state agencies shall accept, for services from physicians licensed to practice medicine, the Uniform Health Insurance Claim Form approved by the Council on Medical Service of the American Medical Association. Nothing in this section shall be construed to prohibit an insurer or state agency from accepting any other health insurance claim form for services provided by a physician licensed to practice medicine. (Acts 1981, No. 81-292, p. 374.)

Collateral references. — 44 C.J.S., Insurance, §§ 56, 59.

43 Am. Jur. 2d, Insurance, §§ 51, 52, 55.

§ 27-1-17. Limitation period for payment of claims under health and accident insurance policies; payment of interest; right of action for recovery of unpaid benefits.

(a) All persons, firms, corporations or associations issuing health and accident insurance policies within this state shall consider claims made thereunder and, if found to be valid and proper, shall pay such claims within 45 days after the receipt of proof of loss under such policies. Benefits due under the policies and claims are to be considered overdue if not paid within 45 days after the insurer receives reasonable proof of the fact and amount of loss sustained. If reasonable proof is not supplied as to the entire claim, the amount supported by reasonable proof shall be considered overdue if not paid within 45 days after such proof is received by the insurer. Any part or all of the remainder of the claim that is later supported by reasonable proof shall be considered overdue if not paid within 45 days after such proof is received by the insurer. For the purposes of calculating the extent to which any benefits are overdue, payment shall be treated as made on the date a draft or other valid instrument was placed in the United States mail to the last known address of the claimant or beneficiary in a properly addressed, postpaid, envelope, or, if not so posted, on the date of delivery.

(b) If the claim is not denied for valid and proper reasons by the end of said 45 day period, the insurer must pay the insured one and one-half percent per month on the amount of said claim until it is finally settled or adjudicated.

(c) In the event that the insurer fails to pay such benefits when due, the person entitled to such benefits may bring an action to recover them. (Acts 1981, No. 81-371, p. 539.)

Collateral references. — Modern status of rules requiring liability insurer to show prejudice to escape liability because of insured's failure or delay in giving notice of accident or claim, or in forwarding suit papers. 32 ALR4th 141.

§ 27-1-18. Contract providing for mental health services to entitle insured to reimbursement for outpatient and inpatient services by qualified psychiatrist or psychologist.

(a) Whenever any group, or blanket hospital or medical expense insurance policy or hospital or medical service contract issued for delivery in this state provides for the reimbursement of health or health related services which includes mental health services, and such services are within the lawful scope of practice of a duly qualified psychiatrist or psychologist, the insured or other person entitled to benefits under such policy or contract shall be entitled to reimbursement for outpatient services, and inpatient services if requested by the attending physician, performed by a duly qualified psychiatrist or psychologist notwithstanding any provisions of the policy or contract to the contrary.

(b) For purposes of this section, a duly qualified psychologist means, one who is duly licensed or certified at the doctorate level in the state by the licensing board for psychologists of the state where the service is rendered, has had at least two years post-doctoral, clinical experience in a recognized health setting or has met the standards of the National Register of Health Service Providers in Psychology which require two years post-doctoral, clinical experience.

(c) Nothing in this section shall be construed to mandate or require an insurance company to include mental health services in a policy or contract which does not include such services, nor shall it be construed to expand the scope or nature of benefits provided when mental health services are included in a policy or contract.

(d) This section shall become effective immediately upon its passage and approval by the governor, or upon its otherwise becoming law and shall apply to policies or contracts covered by the section delivered or issued for delivery in this state on and after such effective date and to group and blanket policies and contracts issued prior to the effective date on the next anniversary or renewal date or the expiration of the applicable collective bargaining agreement, if any, whichever date is the later. (Acts 1982, No. 82-628, p. 1182, §§ 1, 2, 5.)

CHAPTER 2.

DEPARTMENT AND COMMISSIONER OF INSURANCE.

Article 1.

General Provisions.

Sec.
27-2-1. Department of insurance.
27-2-2. Commissioner of insurance — Appointment; term; qualifications.
27-2-3. Same — Oath; bond.
27-2-4. Same — Salary; duty generally.
27-2-5. Same — Official seal.
27-2-6. Same — Offices.
27-2-7. Same — Powers and duties generally.
27-2-8. Same — Delegation of powers, etc.
27-2-9. Same — Annual report.
27-2-10. Appointment, etc., of state fire marshal, assistants, etc.; compensation and bond thereof; contracting for professional services.
27-2-11. Assignment of assistant attorney general.
27-2-12. Travel expenses.
27-2-13. Conflicts of interest; additional compensation, etc.
27-2-14. Records, documents and files — Custody; inspection; reproduction; destruction.
27-2-15. Same — Use as evidence.
27-2-16. Publication of materials relating to insurance.
27-2-17. Rules and regulations.
27-2-18. Orders and notices of commissioner.
27-2-19. Enforcement of insurance code.
27-2-20. Examinations — Power generally.
27-2-21. Same — Affairs, etc., of insurers and surplus line brokers.
27-2-22. Same — Examiners.
27-2-23. Same — How conducted.
27-2-24. Same — Report.
27-2-25. Same — Expenses.
27-2-26. Witnesses and evidence for examina-

Sec.
tion, investigation or hearing — Generally.
27-2-27. Same — Compelling testimony or production of documents, etc.; immunity from prosecution.
27-2-28. Hearings — Power to hold.
27-2-29. Same — Notice.
27-2-30. Same — How conducted.
27-2-31. Same — Order.
27-2-32. Same — Appeals.
27-2-33. Order of supervision — Authority of commissioner; reasons for issuance.
27-2-34. Same — Appointment of supervisor; acts which may be prohibited during period of supervision.
27-2-35. Same — Withdrawal of order; duration of order.
27-2-36. Same — Effect on rehabilitation, liquidation and delinquency proceedings.
27-2-37. Same — Form and content; appeal.
27-2-38. Same — Notice and hearing as to issuance.

Article 2.

Receivership Division.

27-2-50. Established; appointment, term of office and compensation of chief.
27-2-51. Bond of chief.
27-2-52. Offices, equipment and personnel; operating expenses.
27-2-53. Appointment of chief as receiver — Generally.
27-2-54. Same — Existing receiverships.
27-2-55. Assumption by receiver of certain former powers, duties, etc., of commissioner.

Collateral references. — Insurer's tort liability for consequential or punitive damages for wrongful failure or refusal to defend insured. 20 ALR4th 23.

ARTICLE 1.

GENERAL PROVISIONS.

§ 27-2-1. Department of insurance.

(a) There shall be a department of insurance of the state of Alabama with such subordinate bureaus and divisions as the commissioner determines to be necessary.

(b) The expenses of operating the department shall be paid out of funds appropriated to it by the legislature or otherwise made available for the purpose. (Acts 1951, No. 234, p. 504, §§ 1, 8; Acts 1971, No. 407, p. 707, § 16.)

Collateral references. — 44 C.J.S., Insurance, § 57. 81 C.J.S., States, § 50.

§ 27-2-2. Commissioner of insurance — Appointment; term; qualifications.

(a) A commissioner of insurance shall be chief executive officer of the department. The commissioner shall be appointed by the governor. He shall serve for a term concurrent with that of the governor by whom he is appointed, or for the unexpired portion thereof.

(b) The commissioner shall be selected with special reference to his training, experience and capacity. He shall not be a candidate for, nor hold, any other public office of trust nor be a member of any political committee. If he becomes a candidate for public office or becomes a member of a political committee, his office as commissioner shall be immediately vacated. (Acts 1951, No. 234, p. 504, §§ 4, 5; Acts 1971, No. 407, p. 707, § 17.)

Collateral references. — 81 C.J.S., States, §§ 67-71, 76-78.

§ 27-2-3. Same — Oath; bond.

Before entering upon the duties of his office the commissioner shall take and subscribe to the oath prescribed by article 16, section 279 of the state Constitution and give bond in favor of the state of Alabama in the penal sum of $50,000.00. The surety on the bond shall be a corporate surety authorized to transact such business in this state. The form of the bond and surety shall be subject to the governor's approval. The bond and oath shall be filed with the secretary of state. (Acts 1951, No. 234, p. 504, § 6; Acts 1971, No. 407, p. 707, § 18.)

Collateral references. — 81 C.J.S., States, § 76.

§ 27-2-4. Same — Salary; duty generally.

(a) The commissioner shall receive such annual salary as fixed by the governor in the same manner as the salaries of other appointive department heads. Such salary shall be payable in the same manner as other state employees are paid.

(b) The commissioner shall devote his entire time to the duties of his office. (Acts 1951, No. 234, p. 504, § 8; Acts 1971, No. 407, p. 707, § 19.)

Cross references. — As to salaries of public officers and employees generally, see § 36-6-1 et seq.

Collateral references. — 81 C.J.S., States, §§ 88-99.

§ 27-2-5. Same — Official seal.

(a) The commissioner shall have an official seal as heretofore provided him by the state of Alabama.

(b) All certificates executed by the commissioner, other than licenses of agents, brokers, solicitors, adjusters and similar licenses, shall bear his seal.

(c) Every such certificate so executed and sealed under the authority conferred upon the commissioner by law may be recorded in the proper recording office in this state in the same manner and with the same effect as a deed regularly acknowledged or proven.

(d) Every certificate and other document or paper executed by the commissioner pursuant to any authority conferred upon him by law and sealed with the seal of his office and all copies or photographic copies of papers certified by him and authenticated by such seal shall, in all cases, be evidenced equally and in like manner as the original thereof and shall have the same force and effect as the original would in any action or proceeding in any court of this state.

(e) The commissioner shall collect such fees and charges for the use of his official seal as are provided for under section 27-4-2. (Acts 1923, No. 464, p. 607; Acts 1971, No. 407, p. 707, § 20.)

§ 27-2-6. Same — Offices.

(a) The commissioner's offices shall be located at the state capitol. The commissioner may have a service office at Birmingham and in such other cities of this state as he may deem necessary.

(b) The commissioner shall keep his offices open at all reasonable times for the transaction of public business. (Acts 1951, No. 234, p. 504, § 7; Acts 1971, No. 407, p. 707, § 21.)

§ 27-2-7. Same — Powers and duties generally.

The commissioner shall:

(1) Organize, supervise and administer the department of insurance so that it will perform its lawful functions efficiently and effectively;

(2) Enforce the provisions of this title;

(3) Execute the duties imposed upon him by this title;

(4) Have the powers and authority expressly conferred upon him by, or reasonably implied from, the provisions of this title;

(5) Sign and execute in the name of the state, by "the state department of insurance," all contracts or agreements with the federal government or its agencies, other states or political subdivisions thereof, political subdivisions of this state or with private persons;

(6) Conduct such examinations and investigations of insurance matters, in addition to examinations and investigations expressly authorized, as he may deem proper to determine whether any person has violated any provision of this title or to secure information useful in the lawful administration of any such provision. The cost of such additional examinations or investigations shall be borne by the state except as otherwise expressly provided;

(7) Invoke any legal, equitable or special remedy for the enforcement of orders or the provisions of this title;

(8) Have such powers and perform such duties as may be granted to or required of the "superintendent of insurance" of this state under laws remaining in force after the effective date of this title; and

(9) Have such additional powers and duties as may be provided by other laws of this state. (Acts 1951, No. 234, p. 504, § 9; Acts 1971, No. 407, p. 707, § 27.)

Jurisdiction of courts not displaced. — Nowhere in the statute enacted with reference to the department of insurance does there appear to be any intention on the part of the legislature to displace the jurisdiction and duty of the courts which have been established as a resort for trusting principals against unfaithful agents. American Armed Servs. Underwriters, Inc. v. Atlas Ins. Co., 268 Ala. 637, 108 So. 2d 687 (1958) (decided under former Code 1940, T. 28, § 47(9), appearing in the 1958 Revision).

Regulations. — See § 27-2-17 and notes thereto.

Collateral references. — 81 C.J.S., States, §§ 57-66.

43 Am. Jur. 2d, Insurance, § 56.

§ 27-2-8. Same — Delegation of powers, etc.

(a) The commissioner may delegate to any deputy, assistant, examiner or employee of the department the exercise or discharge in the commissioner's name of any power, duty or function, whether ministerial, discretionary or of whatever character, vested by this title in the commissioner.

(b) The commissioner is responsible for the official acts of his deputy, assistant, examiner or employee acting in the commissioner's name and by his authority. (Acts 1951, No. 234, p. 504, § 11; Acts 1971, No. 407, p. 707, § 26.)

§ 27-2-9. Same — Annual report.

As early as consistent with full and accurate preparation, the commissioner shall annually make a report to the governor of his official transactions during the preceding calendar year. He shall include in the report:

(1) A statement of the receipts and expenditures of the department for the preceding year;

(2) An exhibit of the financial condition and business transactions during the preceding year of insurers authorized to transact business in this state, as disclosed by the financial statements of the insurers filed with the commissioner;

(3) Names of insurers whose business was closed during the year, the cause thereof and amount of assets and liabilities as ascertainable;

(4) Names of insurers against whom delinquency or similar proceedings were instituted and a concise statement of the circumstances and results of each such proceeding;

(5) His recommendations as to amendments or supplementation of laws affecting insurance;

(6) His recommendations concerning the condition, operation and functioning of the department; and

(7) Such other pertinent information and matters as he deems to be in the public interest. (Code 1940, T. 28, § 72; Acts 1971, No. 407, p. 707, § 34.)

§ 27-2-10. Appointment, etc., of state fire marshal, assistants, etc.; compensation and bond thereof; contracting for professional services.

(a) Subject to the Merit System Act and rules and regulations issued pursuant thereto, the commissioner shall prescribe the qualifications and duties of and appoint, employ, bond and remove a state fire marshal and such other assistants, deputies, actuaries, examiners and other employees as he deems necessary for the efficient performance of his duties under this Code.

(b) The commissioner shall fix the compensation of all such personnel in accordance with the Merit System Act and the pay plan of the state personnel department.

(c) The commissioner may contract for and procure on a basis of fee, and without giving such persons any status in the classified service of the state, such independently contracting actuarial, technical and other similar professional services as he may from time to time require for the discharge of his duties.

(d) Before entering upon the duties of their respective offices, the chief deputy fire marshal, the deputy fire marshal and the chief clerk shall execute to the state of Alabama a bond, to be approved by the governor, in amounts to be fixed by the insurance commissioner, for the faithful performance of their duties. (Acts 1943, No. 122, p. 123; Acts 1951, No. 234, p. 504, § 10; Acts 1961, Ex. Sess., No. 208, p. 2190; Acts 1971, No. 407, p. 707, § 22.)

Cross references. — As to state fire marshal generally, see § 36-19-1 et seq. As to merit system, see § 36-26-1 et seq.

Collateral references. — 81 C.J.S., States, §§ 59, 69, 77, 78, 90.

§ 27-2-11. Assignment of assistant attorney general.

The attorney general shall assign to the department an assistant attorney general who shall render to the commissioner such legal services as may be required. (Acts 1951, No. 234, p. 504, § 12; Acts 1971, No. 407, p. 707, § 23.)

§ 27-2-12. Travel expenses.

In addition to compensation for their services, the commissioner and deputy commissioners shall receive actual expenses for travel on official business in accordance with article 2, chapter 7 of Title 36 of this Code. Assistants and employees of the department shall be paid expenses for travel on official business as may be authorized by the commissioner and incurred by them in the performance of their duties in the same manner and in the same amounts as such expenses are paid to all other state employees. (Acts 1951, No. 234, p. 504, § 8; Acts 1971, No. 407, p. 707, § 24.)

Collateral references. — 81 C.J.S., States, § 92.

§ 27-2-13. Conflicts of interest; additional compensation, etc.

(a) The commissioner or any deputy, examiner, assistant or employee of the commissioner shall not be financially interested, directly or indirectly, in any insurer, insurance agency or insurance transaction except as a policyholder or claimant under a policy; except, that as to such matters wherein a conflict of interests does not exist on the part of any such individual, the commissioner may employ or retain, from time to time, insurance actuaries, accountants or other professional personnel who are independently practicing their professions even though similarly employed or retained by insurers or others.

(b) The commissioner or any deputy, examiner, assistant or employee of the commissioner shall not be given, nor receive, any fee, compensation, loan, gift or other thing of value in addition to the compensation and expense allowance provided by law for any service rendered, or to be rendered, as such commissioner, deputy, assistant, examiner or employee or in connection therewith. This section shall not apply to any person who is holding office or position on date of enactment of this title. (Acts 1971, No. 407, p. 707, § 25.)

Collateral references. — 81 C.J.S., States, § 133.

§ 27-2-14. Records, documents and files — Custody; inspection; reproduction; destruction.

(a) The commissioner shall keep and preserve in permanent form accurate and complete records of his proceedings, including also a concise statement of the result of such examination of insurers by the commissioner, record and file all bonds and contracts and shall file such records in the department. The commissioner is responsible for the custody and preservation of all records, documents and files of the department.

(b) The records of the commissioner and insurance filings in his office shall be open to public inspection, except as otherwise provided by this title.

(c) The commissioner may photograph, microphotograph or reproduce on film, whereby each page will be reproduced in exact conformity with the original, all financial records, financial statements of domestic insurers, reports of business transacted in this state by foreign insurers, reports of examination of domestic insurers and such other records and documents on file in his office as he may in his discretion select.

(d) To facilitate efficient use of floor space and filing equipment in his offices the commissioner may destroy records and documents as follows:

(1) General correspondence files over three years old;

(2) Agent, broker, solicitor, adjuster and similar license files over two years old;

(3) Insurer certificate of authority files over two years old;

(4) All documents and records which have been photographed or otherwise reproduced as provided in subsection (c) of this section, and such reproduction has been filed and after audit of the commissioner's office has been completed for the period embracing the dates of such documents and records; and

(5) All other records, documents and files not expressly provided for in subdivisions (1) through (4) of this subsection. (Code 1940, T. 28, § 72; Acts 1971, No. 407, p. 707, § 31.)

Collateral references. — 73 C.J.S., Public Administrative Bodies & Procedure, § 22.

§ 27-2-15. Same — Use as evidence.

(a) Photographs or microphotographs in the form of film or prints of documents and records made under subsection (c) of section 27-2-14 shall have the same force and effect as the originals thereof and shall be treated as originals for the purpose of their admissibility in evidence. Duly certified or authenticated reproductions of such photographs or microphotographs shall be as admissible in evidence as the originals.

(b) Upon request of any person and payment of the applicable fee, the commissioner shall give a certified copy of any record in his office which is then subject to public inspection.

(c) Copies of original records or documents in his office certified by the commissioner shall be received in evidence in all courts as if they were originals.

(d) If at any time the commissioner or any deputy, assistant, examiner or other employee of the department is required by subpoena duces tecum to produce in any court or proceeding in this state any record of the department or copy thereof for the purpose of offering the same in evidence in such court or proceeding, the commissioner may designate any deputy, assistant or other full-time employee of the department, who is competent for the purpose, to respond to such subpoena with the record or copy thereof so required and in lieu of the individual to whom the subpoena is directed. (Acts 1971, No. 407, p. 707, § 32.)

§ 27-2-16. Publication of materials relating to insurance.

(a) The commissioner shall have printed or otherwise published for public distribution:

(1) The insurance laws of this state;

(2) The rules and regulations of the commissioner;

(3) A directory, annually, of all insurers and of all resident insurance agents and brokers authorized or licensed by this state;

(4) A booklet, annually, containing each and every question and the correct answer thereto from which shall be taken the questions to be used in any written examination of applicants for license under chapters 7 and 8 of this title; and

(5) Such other material as he deems relevant and suitable for the more effective administration of the laws relating to insurance.

(b) The commissioner shall fix at a price at not less than cost of printing and distribution, to be paid by persons requesting copies of the insurance laws, booklets containing questions and answers for examination for licenses and such other publications as he deems proper to sell on behalf of the state rather than distribute free of charge; except that the commissioner may furnish, without charge, copies of any such publication to the legislature or to officials and departments of government or political subdivisions of this state or of other states, of the federal government or of foreign countries. The commissioner shall promptly deposit all moneys so received in the state treasury to the credit of the state general fund. (Acts 1951, No. 234, p. 504, § 15; Acts 1971, No. 407, p. 707, § 33.)

Collateral references. — 73 C.J.S., Public Administrative Bodies & Procedure, § 101.

§ 27-2-17. Rules and regulations.

(a) The commissioner may make reasonable rules and regulations necessary for the effectuation of any provision of this title. No such rule or regulation shall extend, modify or conflict with any law of this state or the reasonable implications thereof.

(b) Any such rule or regulation affecting persons or matters other than the personnel or the internal affairs of the commissioner's office shall be made or amended only after a hearing thereon of which notice was given as required by section 27-2-29. If reasonably possible the commissioner shall set forth the proposed rule, regulation, amendment or summary in or with the notice of hearing.

(c) No such rule or regulation as to which a hearing is required under subsection (b) of this section above shall be effective until after it has been on file as a public record in the commissioner's office and in the office of the secretary of state for at least 10 days.

(d) Upon request and payment of the reasonable cost thereof, if required and fixed by the commissioner, the commissioner shall furnish a copy of any such rule or regulation to any person so requesting.

(e) The willful failure to comply with or willful violation of any material provision of a rule or regulation may be treated by the commissioner in the same manner as the willful failure to comply with or willful violation of any material provision of this title, but such action taken by the commissioner shall not be in the nature of a criminal penalty and shall be limited to suspension or revocation of licenses of agents or insurers doing business in Alabama. (Acts 1951, No. 234, p. 504, § 13; Acts 1971, No. 407, p. 707, § 28; Acts 1975, No. 215, p. 739, § 1.)

Regulations to be given effect of law. — The official regulations of the state fire marshal are to be given the effect of law. Standard Oil Co. v. City of Gadsden, 263 F. Supp. 502 (N.D. Ala. 1967) (decided under former Code 1940, T. 28, § 47(13)).

And ordinance restrictions in conflict therewith are void. — The restrictions of an ordinance on the size and number of underground tanks installed for the storage of gasoline are rendered null, void and of no effect by the Constitution of 1901, § 89, where such restrictions are in conflict with regulations of the fire marshal of the state of Alabama, which regulations were approved and adopted pursuant to legislative authority and which have the effect of law. Standard Oil Co. v. City of Gadsden, 263 F. Supp. 502 (N.D. Ala. 1967)

(decided under former Code 1940, T. 28, § 47(13)).

Regulation conflicting with former § 10-2-31 and § 27-27-41 void under this section. — A departmental insurance regulation that proscribes reduction of the par value of stock below one dollar per share without approval of the commissioner conflicts with former § 10-2-31 and § 27-27-41(b), and is therefore void under this section. Assured Investors Life Ins. Co. v. Payne, 356 So. 2d 144 (Ala. 1978).

Cited in Blue Cross & Blue Shield of Ala., Inc. v. Hendrix, 385 So. 2d 63 (Ala. Civ. App. 1980).

Collateral references. — 73 C.J.S., Public Administrative Bodies & Procedure, §§ 92-113.

§ 27-2-18. Orders and notices of commissioner.

(a) Orders and notices of the commissioner shall be effective only when in writing signed by him or by his authority.

(b) Every such order shall state its effective date, and shall concisely state:

(1) Its intent or purpose;

(2) The grounds on which based; and

(3) The provisions of this title pursuant to which action is taken or proposed to be taken; but failure to so designate a particular provision shall not deprive the commissioner of the right to rely thereon.

(c) Except as may be provided in this title respecting particular procedures, an order or notice may be given by delivery to the person to be ordered or notified or by mailing it, postage prepaid, addressed to him at his principal place of business as last of record in the department. Notice so mailed shall be deemed to have been given when deposited in a letter depository of a United States post office. (Acts 1971, No. 407, p. 707, § 29.)

Collateral references. — 73 C.J.S., Public Administrative Bodies & Procedure, §§ 142-151.

§ 27-2-19. Enforcement of insurance code.

The commissioner may institute such actions or other proceedings as may be required for enforcement of any provisions of this title. If the commissioner has reason to believe that any person has violated any provision of this title for which criminal prosecution would be in order, he shall give the information relative thereto to the attorney general or the district attorney having jurisdiction of any such violation. The attorney general shall promptly institute such action or proceeding against such person as the information may require or justify. (Acts 1971, No. 407, p. 707, § 30.)

§ 27-2-20. Examinations — Power generally.

(a) If he has reason to believe that any such person has violated or is violating any provision of this title or upon complaint by any resident of this state indicating that any such violation may exist, the commissioner may examine the accounts, records, documents and transactions pertaining to or affecting the insurance affairs of any:

(1) General agent, agent, broker, surplus line broker, solicitor or adjuster;

(2) Person having a contract or power of attorney under which he enjoys in fact the exclusive or dominant right to manage or control an insurer; or

(3) Person engaged in or proposing to be engaged in or assisting in the promotion or formation of a domestic insurer, insurance holding corporation or corporation to finance a domestic insurer or the production of its business.

(b) The commissioner may examine the insurance affairs and transactions of the attorney-in-fact of a reciprocal insurer in the same manner and on the same basis as examination of such an insurer.

(c) When he deems it necessary for determination of the value of such securities or compliance with any provision of this title, the commissioner may, in his discretion, examine the transactions and affairs of any corporation of which a domestic insurer owns shares of stock or other securities under which it has, or effectively participates in, the control of such corporation. (Acts 1971, No. 407, p. 707, § 36.)

§ 27-2-21. Same — Affairs, etc., of insurers and surplus line brokers.

(a) For the purpose of determining its financial condition, ability to fulfill its obligations and compliance with the law, the commissioner shall examine the affairs, transactions, accounts, records and assets of each authorized insurer, and the records of surplus line brokers restricted to those matters under section 27-10-29 as often as he deems advisable, including the attorney-in-fact of a reciprocal insurer insofar as insurer transactions are involved. Except as otherwise expressly provided, he shall so examine each domestic insurer not less frequently than every three years. Examination of an alien insurer shall be limited to its insurance transactions, assets, trust deposits and affairs in the United States except as otherwise required by the commissioner.

(b) The commissioner shall in like manner examine each insurer applying for an initial certificate of authority to transact insurance in this state.

(c) In lieu of making his own examination, the commissioner may, in his discretion, accept a full report of the last recent examination of a foreign or alien insurer, certified to by the insurance supervisory officials of another state.

(d) As far as practical, the examination of a foreign or alien insurer shall be made in cooperation with the insurance supervisory officials of other states in which the insurer transacts business. (Acts 1915, No. 730, p. 834; Acts 1939, No. 527, p. 818; Acts 1965, No. 571, p. 1056; Acts 1971, No. 407, p. 707, § 35; Acts 1980, No. 80-774, p. 1608, § 1.)

Collateral references. — 44 C.J.S., Insurance, §§ 56, 57, 59, 60, 75, 79, 82.
43 Am. Jur. 2d, Insurance, §§ 56-59, 72-84.

§ 27-2-22. Same — Examiners.

(a) The commissioner may conduct any such examination in person or by examiners regularly employed and commissioned by him in writing for the purpose. No person shall be eligible for designation as an examiner to examine an insurer unless by reason of experience as an accountant, auditor or examiner of financial institutions or other special experience, education or

training he is capable of adequately discharging the responsibilities of such an examiner.

(b) At any time, when examiners who are regular officers or employees of the department are not available for the purpose, the commissioner may specially appoint and employ a competent examiner, or examiners, for the purpose of making a particular examination. The special examiner shall be compensated and reimbursed for expenses in the same manner as provided for regular examiners under section 27-2-25, but shall not have any status in the classified service of the state. (Acts 1971, No. 407, p. 707, § 37.)

§ 27-2-23. Same — How conducted.

(a) The examination may be conducted by the commissioner or his accredited examiners at the offices wherever located of the person being examined and at such other places as may be required for determination of matters under examination.

(b) Every person being examined, its officers, attorneys, employees, agents and representatives, shall make freely available to the commissioner or his examiners the accounts, records, documents, files, information, assets and matters in his possession or control relating to the subject of the examination.

(c) If the commissioner or examiner finds any account or record of an insurer being examined to be inadequate or inadequately kept or posted for proper examination of the condition and affairs of the examinee, he shall give written notice to such examinee specifying:

(1) The deficiencies to be corrected; and

(2) A reasonable period within which to correct the stated deficiencies.

If the examinee fails to maintain, complete or correct such accounts or records within the period specified, the commissioner may employ experts to reconstruct, rewrite, post or balance such accounts or records in accordance with recognized accounting principles and procedures.

(d) If the commissioner deems it necessary to value any asset involved in such an examination, he may make written request of the person being examined to appoint one or more competent appraisers approved by the commissioner for the purpose of appraising such property. If no such appointment is made within 10 days after such request was delivered to such person, the commissioner may appoint the appraiser or appraisers. Any such appraisal shall be promptly made, and a copy of the report thereof shall be furnished to the commissioner. The reasonable expense of the appraisal shall be borne by the person being examined.

(e) Neither the commissioner nor any examiner shall remove any record, account, document, file or other property of the person being examined from the offices of such person except with the written consent of such person given in advance of such removal or pursuant to an order of court duly obtained.

(f) Any individual who obstructs the commissioner or his examiner in the examination of an insurer shall be guilty of a misdemeanor and, upon conviction, shall be punished as provided in section 27-1-12. (Acts 1971, No. 407, p. 707, § 38.)

§ 27-2-24. Same — Report.

(a) The commissioner or his examiner shall make a full and true written report of each examination. The report shall contain only information obtained from examination of the records, accounts, files and documents of, or relative to, the person examined or from testimony of individuals under oath, together with recommendations of the examiner based thereon. The commissioner shall furnish a copy of the proposed report to the person examined not less than 20 days prior to filing the report in his office. If such person so requests in writing within such 20-day period, the commissioner shall grant a hearing with respect to the report and shall not so file the report until after the hearing and after such modifications have been made therein as the commissioner deems proper.

(b) The report, when so filed, shall be admissible in evidence in any action or proceeding brought by the commissioner against the person examined, or against its officers, employees or agents. The commissioner or his examiners may, at any time, testify and offer other proper evidence as to information secured or matters discovered during the course of an examination, whether or not a written report of the examination has been either made, furnished or filed in the department.

(c) The commissioner may withhold from public inspection any examination or investigation report for so long as he deems necessary to protect the person examined from unwarranted injury or to be in the public interest.

(d) After the examination report has been filed, as provided in this section, the commissioner may publish the results of any such examination in one or more newspapers published in this state whenever he deems it to be in the public interest. (Acts 1971, No. 407, p. 707, § 39.)

§ 27-2-25. Same — Expenses.

(a) Each person being examined shall pay to the commissioner the travel expense to and from such examination, a living expense allowance at such reasonable rates customary for such examination in which state the examination takes place and established or adopted by the commissioner and the compensation of the examiners making the examination, upon presentation by the commissioner of a detailed account of such allowances and expenses. Such an account may be so presented periodically during the course of the examination or at the termination of the examination, as the commissioner deems proper.

(b) The commissioner shall deposit all funds received under subsection (a) of this section in the state treasury to the credit of a fund to be known as the special examination revolving fund. The expenses incurred by the commissioner and his examiners in the making of examinations under this title, together with the compensation of such examiners, shall be paid from such revolving fund and the amount necessary to make such payments is hereby appropriated from such fund. (Acts 1939, No. 527, p. 818; Acts 1943, No. 416, p. 381; Acts 1953, No. 776, p. 1047; Acts 1971, No. 407, p. 707, § 40.)

§ 27-2-26. Witnesses and evidence for examination, investigation or hearing — Generally.

(a) As to the subject of any examination, investigation or hearing being conducted by him, the commissioner may subpoena witnesses and administer oaths or affirmations and examine any individual under oath or take depositions and, by subpoena duces tecum, may require and compel the production of records, books, files, documents and other evidence.

(b) Witness fees and mileage, if claimed, shall be allowed the same as for testimony in a circuit court: Witness fees, mileage and the actual expense necessarily incurred in securing attendance of witnesses and their testimony shall be itemized and shall be paid by the person being examined if in the proceedings in which such witness is called such person is found to have been in violation of the law or by the person, if other than the commissioner, at whose request the hearing is held.

(c) Subpoenas of witnesses shall be served in the same manner and at the same cost as if issued by a circuit court. If any individual fails to obey a subpoena issued and served under this section with respect to any matter concerning which he may be lawfully interrogated or required to produce for examination, on application of the commissioner, the circuit court of the county in which is pending the proceeding at which such individual was so required to appear or the circuit court of the county in which such individual resides may issue an order requiring such individual to comply with the subpoena and to testify or produce the evidence subpoenaed. Any failure to obey such order of the court may be punished by the court as a contempt thereof.

(d) Any person willfully testifying falsely under oath as to any matter material to any such examination, investigation or hearing shall, upon conviction thereof, be guilty of perjury and punished accordingly. (Acts 1939, No. 527, p. 818; Acts 1971, No. 407, p. 707, § 41.)

§ 27-2-27. Same — Compelling testimony or production of documents, etc.; immunity from prosecution.

(a) If any individual asks to be excused from attending or testifying or from producing any books, papers, records, contracts, correspondence or other documents in connection with any examination, hearing or investigation being conducted by the commissioner or his examiner on the ground that the testimony or evidence required of him may tend to incriminate him or subject him to a penalty or forfeiture and shall, by the attorney general, be directed to give such testimony or produce such evidence, he must nonetheless comply with such direction; but he shall not thereafter be prosecuted or subjected to any penalty or forfeiture for, or on account of, any transaction, matter or thing concerning which he may have so testified or produced evidence, and no testimony so given or evidence produced shall be received against him upon any criminal action, investigation or proceeding; except, that no such individual so testifying shall be exempt from prosecution or punishment for any perjury committed by him in such testimony, and the testimony or evidence so given or produced shall be admissible against him upon any criminal action, investigation or proceeding concerning such perjury; nor shall such individual be exempt from the refusal, suspension or revocation of any license, permission or authority conferred, or to be conferred, pursuant to this title.

(b) Any such individual may execute, acknowledge and file in the department a statement expressly waiving such immunity or privilege in respect to any transaction, matter or thing specified in such statement, and thereupon, the testimony of such individual or such evidence in relation to such transaction, matter or thing may be received or produced before any judge, court, tribunal, grand jury or otherwise; and, if so received or produced, such individual shall not be entitled to any immunity or privileges on account of any testimony he may so give or evidence so produced. (Acts 1971, No. 407, p. 707, § 42.)

§ 27-2-28. Hearings — Power to hold.

(a) The commissioner may hold hearings for any purpose within the scope of this title deemed by him to be necessary.

(b) The commissioner shall hold a hearing if required by any provision, or upon written demand therefor by a person aggrieved by any act, threatened act or failure of the commissioner to act or by any report, rule, regulation or order of the commissioner, other than an order for the holding of a hearing or an order on hearing or pursuant thereto. Any such demand shall specify the grounds to be relied upon as a basis for the relief to be demanded at the hearing, and unless postponed by mutual consent, the hearing shall be held within 30 days after receipt by the commissioner of demand therefor.

(c) Pending such hearing and decision thereon, the commissioner may suspend or postpone the effective date of his previous action.

(d) This section does not apply as to hearings provided for in chapter 13 of this title. (Acts 1971, No. 407, p. 707, § 43.)

Collateral references. — 73 C.J.S., Public Administrative Bodies & Procedure, §§ 114-159.

§ 27-2-29. Same — Notice.

(a) Except where a longer period of notice is provided by other provisions of this title relative to particular matters, not less than 10 days in advance the commissioner shall give notice of the time and place of the hearing, stating the matters to be considered thereat. If the persons to be given notice are not specified in the provision pursuant to which the hearing is held, the commissioner shall give such notice to all persons whose pecuniary interests are to be directly and immediately affected by such hearing.

(b) If any such hearing is to be held for consideration of rules and regulations of the commissioner or for the consideration of other matters which under subsection (a) of this section would otherwise require separate notices to more than 50 persons, in lieu of the notice required under such subsection the commissioner may give notice of the hearing by publication thereof in two or more newspapers of general circulation in this state at least once each week during the four weeks immediately preceding the week in which the hearing is to be held. The published notice shall state the time and place of the hearing and shall specify the matters to be considered thereat.

(c) All such notices, other than published notices, shall be given as provided in section 27-2-18.

(d) This section does not apply as to hearings provided for in chapter 13 of this title. (Acts 1971, No. 407, p. 707, § 44.)

Collateral references. — 73 C.J.S., Public Administrative Bodies & Procedure, §§ 130-138.

§ 27-2-30. Same — How conducted.

(a) A hearing may be held in the department at Montgomery, Alabama, or at any other place in this state more convenient to parties and witnesses, as the commissioner determines. The commissioner or his deputy or examiner shall preside at the hearing and shall expedite the hearing and all procedures involved therein.

(b) Hearings may be closed to the public at the commissioner's discretion; except that a hearing shall be open to the public if so requested in writing by any party to the hearing.

(c) The commissioner shall allow any party to the hearing to appear in person and by counsel to be present during the giving of all evidence, to have a reasonable opportunity to inspect all documentary and other evidence, to examine and cross-examine witnesses, to present evidence in support of his interest and to have subpoenas issued by the commissioner to compel attendance of witnesses and production of evidence in his behalf. The testimony may be taken orally or by deposition, and any party shall have such right of introducing evidence by deposition as may obtain in the circuit courts.

(d) Upon good cause shown, the commissioner shall permit to become a party to the hearing by intervention, if timely, only such persons who were not original parties thereto and whose pecuniary interests are to be directly and immediately affected by the commissioner's order made upon the hearing.

(e) Formal rules of pleading or evidence need not be observed at any hearing.

(f) Upon written request seasonably made by a party to the hearing and at such person's expense, the commissioner shall cause a full stenographic record of the proceedings to be made by a competent reporter. If transcribed, a copy of such stenographic record shall be furnished to the commissioner without cost to the commissioner or the state and shall be a part of the commissioner's record of the hearing. If so transcribed, a copy of such stenographic record shall be furnished to any other party to such hearing at the request and expense of such other party. If no stenographic record is made or transcribed, the commissioner shall prepare an adequate record of the evidence and of the proceedings.

(g) Upon written request setting forth the reasons therefor of a party to a hearing filed with the commissioner within 30 days after any order made pursuant to a hearing has been mailed or delivered to the persons entitled to receive the same, the commissioner may, in his discretion, grant a rehearing or reargument of any matter involved in such hearing. Notice of such rehearing or reargument shall be given as provided in section 27-2-29.

(h) This section does not apply as to hearings provided for in chapter 13 of this title. (Acts 1971, No. 407, p. 707, § 45.)

Right of party to notice of right to counsel or appointment of counsel. — The legislature has provided that a party to a hearing before the insurance commissioner or his agent is entitled to be represented by counsel, but it did not require the commissioner to specifically inform a party of his right to counsel nor to appoint counsel to represent him. DeRamus v. Winfield, 388 So. 2d 1215 (Ala. Civ. App. 1980).

License revocation proceedings conducted by the insurance commissioner are civil in nature and do not require the appointment of counsel nor the advice that employed counsel may be used in order to satisfy sixth amendment rights as guaranteed by the fourteenth amendment to the United States Constitution. DeRamus v. Winfield, 388 So. 2d 1215 (Ala. Civ. App. 1980).

Collateral references. — 73 C.J.S., Public Administrative Bodies & Procedure, §§ 114, 135, 136.

Sufficiency of express finding of fact to support administrative determinations. 146 ALR 209.

Administrative decision on finding based on evidence secured outside of hearing, and without presence of interested party or counsel. 18 ALR2d 552.

Hearing and decision by different officers; change of personnel. 18 ALR2d 613.

Counsel's absence because of attendance on legislature as ground for continuance in case before quasi-judicial officer or board. 49 ALR2d 1073, Later Case Serv., § 4.

Reopening decision: power of administrative agency to reopen and reconsider final decision as affected by lack of specific statutory authority. 73 ALR2d 939.

Assistance of counsel: right to assistance by counsel in administrative proceedings. 33 ALR3d 229.

Hearsay evidence in proceedings before state administrative agencies. 36 ALR3d 12.

§ 27-2-31. Same — Order.

(a) In the conduct of hearings under this title and making his order thereon, the commissioner shall act in a quasi-judicial capacity.

(b) Within 30 days after termination of the hearing, or of any rehearing thereof or reargument thereon, or within such other period as may be specified in this title as to particular proceedings, the commissioner shall make his order on hearing, covering matters involved in such hearing and in any such rehearing or reargument, and shall give a copy of such order to the same persons given notice of the hearing and to all parties to the hearing.

(c) The order shall contain a concise statement of the facts as found by the commissioner, his conclusions therefrom and the matters required by section 27-2-18.

(d) The order may affirm, modify or rescind action theretofore taken or may constitute the taking of new action within the scope of the notice of hearing.

(e) This section does not apply as to hearings provided for in chapter 13 of this title. (Acts 1971, No. 407, p. 707, § 46.)

Collateral references. — 73 C.J.S., Public Administrative Bodies & Procedure, §§ 142-151.

§ 27-2-32. Same — Appeals.

(a) An appeal from the commissioner shall be taken only from an order on hearing, or as to a matter on which the commissioner has refused or failed to hold a hearing after demand therefor under section 27-2-28 or as to a matter as to which the commissioner has refused or failed to make his order on hearing as required by section 27-2-31. Any person who was a party to such hearing or whose pecuniary interests are directly and immediately affected by any such refusal or failure to grant or hold a hearing and who is aggrieved by such order, refusal or failure may appeal from such order or as to any such matter within 30 days after:

(1) The order on hearing has been mailed or delivered to the persons entitled to receive the same;

(2) The commissioner's order denying rehearing or reargument has been so mailed or delivered;

(3) The commissioner has refused or failed to make his order on hearing as required under section 27-2-31; or

(4) The commissioner has refused or failed to grant or hold a hearing as required under section 27-2-28.

(b) The appeal shall be granted as a matter of right, and shall be taken to the circuit court of Montgomery county, Alabama, or in the case of denial, suspension or revocation of a license as agent, broker, solicitor, adjuster and other licensed insurance representatives, the appeal may at the appellant's option be taken to the circuit court of the county in Alabama of the appellant's residence or principal place of business. The appeal shall be taken by filing notice of appeal or on writ of certiorari by filing petition therefor with the register or clerk of the court, together with a bond, with good and sufficient sureties to be approved by such register or clerk, conditioned to pay all costs which may be assessed against the appellant or petitioner in such proceedings and by service upon or delivery to the commissioner of a copy of such notice or petition.

(c) Upon receiving the notice of appeal or petition for review, the commissioner shall prepare, or cause to be prepared, an official record certified by him which shall contain a copy of all proceedings, findings and orders of the commissioner and any transcript of testimony and exhibits or record thereof made as provided in subsection (f) of section 27-2-30. Within 30 days after the notice of appeal or petition was filed, the commissioner shall file such official record with the court in which the appeal is pending.

(d) Upon filing of the notice of appeal or petition for review, the court shall have full jurisdiction of the proceeding and shall determine, and may so determine ex parte, whether such filing shall stay the enforcement of the commissioner's decision or order appealed from.

(e) In hearing the appeal by the circuit court and by the court of civil appeals of Alabama on appeal to it as provided in subsection (g) of this section, the commissioner's decision or order shall be taken as prima facie just and reasonable. No new or additional evidence may be introduced in the circuit court except as to fraud or misconduct of some person engaged in the administration of this title and affecting the decision or order appealed from, but the court shall otherwise hear the case upon the certified record. The court shall reverse, vacate or modify the commissioner's decision or order in whole or in part if it finds that:

(1) The commissioner erred to the prejudice of appellant's substantial rights in his application of the law;

(2) The decision or order was procured by fraud or was based upon a finding of facts contrary to the weight of the evidence; or

(3) The commissioner's action was arbitrary or capricious.

(f) Instead of reversing, vacating or setting aside the commissioner's decision or order or part thereof, the court may remand the case to the commissioner for further proceedings in accordance with the court's directions, or, in advance of judgment and upon a sufficient showing, the court may remand the case to the commissioner for the purpose of taking additional testimony or other proceedings.

(g) From the judgment of the circuit court, either the commissioner or the interested party taking the appeal may appeal directly to the court of civil appeals of Alabama by taking such appeal within 42 days after the date of the making and entering of its judgment by the circuit court. The interested party so appealing to the court of civil appeals of Alabama shall give security for the costs of such appeal to be approved by the register or clerk of the circuit court. No such security shall be required of the commissioner. (Acts 1971, No. 407, p. 707, § 47.)

Determination as to whether commissioner's order is arbitrary and capricious must be made on basis of record. — Under subsection (e) of this section, a determination on whether the insurance commissioner's order is arbitrary or capricious must be made on the basis of the evidence set out in the record compiled at the hearing before the commissioner or his representative. If the commissioner's ultimate decision on the matter before his agency is unsupported by the evidence documented by record taken at the hearing before the commissioner (or facts surrounding the proceedings out of which the commissioner's order arose warrant it), then the circuit court may, upon appeal, reverse the commissioner's order on the grounds that it was arbitrary or capricious. Payne v. Overton, 352 So. 2d 1139 (Ala. Civ. App. 1977).

Where there is no allegation or evidence of fraud or misconduct, only the certified record compiled before the insurance commissioner is available as a basis for determining whether the order of the commissioner should be affirmed, reversed or modified. Payne v. Overton, 352 So. 2d 1139 (Ala. Civ. App. 1977).

Independent or extraneous evidence should not be considered on appeal. — "Independent" or "extraneous" evidence should not be admitted to determine if the commissioner's action in revoking a license is "arbi-

trary" or "capricious." Payne v. Overton, 352 So. 2d 1139 (Ala. Civ. App. 1977).

Cited in Roussel v. Payne, 352 So. 2d 1364 (Ala. Civ. App. 1977).

Collateral references. — 44 C.J.S., Insurance, § 58. 73 C.J.S., Public Administrative Bodies & Procedure, §§ 160-255.

Effect of court review on administrative decision. 79 ALR2d 1141.

§ 27-2-33. Order of supervision — Authority of commissioner; reasons for issuance.

The commissioner of insurance is empowered to place an insurance company under supervision, after a hearing thereon, by appropriate order, for the following reasons:

(1) When an insurance company has been notified under the provisions of section 27-27-41 of impairment or deficiency of assets and given 60 days to make good the impairment;

(2) A determination by the commissioner that an insurer is impaired or insolvent;

(3) A determination by the commissioner that an insurer's condition is such as to render the continuation of its business hazardous to its policyholders following an examination of the operations and financial condition of an insurer by the commissioner;

(4) Any of the grounds for rehabilitation or liquidation of domestic insurers set forth in sections 27-32-6 and 27-32-7. (Acts 1975, No. 217, p. 742, § 1; Acts 1977, No. 409, p. 547, § 1.)

§ 27-2-34. Same — Appointment of supervisor; acts which may be prohibited during period of supervision.

During the period of supervision the commissioner may appoint a supervisor and may provide that the insurer may not do the following things during the period of supervision without the prior approval of the commissioner or his duly appointed supervisors:

(1) Dispose of, convey or encumber any of its assets or its business in force;

(2) Withdraw any of its bank accounts;

(3) Lend any of its funds;

(4) Invest any of its funds;

(5) Transfer any of its property;

(6) Incur any debt, obligation or liability;

(7) Enter into any new reinsurance contract or treaty;

(8) Issue to the public policies of insurance. (Acts 1975, No. 217, p. 742, § 2; Acts 1977, No. 409, p. 547, § 3.)

§ 27-2-35. Same — Withdrawal of order; duration of order.

The commissioner shall withdraw the supervision order immediately upon determination that the reasons for the supervision set forth in section 27-2-33 have been corrected or no longer exist, but in no event shall the supervision order last longer than 180 days without another notice and hearing being conducted in the same manner as set out in section 27-2-38. (Acts 1975, No. 217, p. 742, § 3; Acts 1977, No. 409, p. 547, § 4; Acts 1982, 2nd Ex. Sess., No. 82-788, p. 293.)

§ 27-2-36. Same — Effect on rehabilitation, liquidation and delinquency proceedings.

The provisions of chapter 32 of this title concerning rehabilitation and liquidation shall not be stayed during the period of supervision and the commencement of delinquency proceedings under section 27-32-4, may commence either before, during or after a supervision order or period of supervision. (Acts 1975, No. 217, p. 742, § 4; Acts 1977, No. 409, p. 547, § 5.)

§ 27-2-37. Same — Form and content; appeal.

The order of supervision issuing after the hearing shall follow the provisions of section 27-2-18, and may be appealed in the same manner as orders falling under the provisions of section 27-2-32. (Acts 1975, No. 217, p. 742, § 5; Acts 1977, No. 409, p. 547, § 6.)

§ 27-2-38. Same — Notice and hearing as to issuance.

No order of supervision shall be issued by the commissioner until the insurance company has been given notice of the commissioner's intentions to place the company under supervision, the appropriate reasons for supervision set out in section 27-2-33 and a hearing held thereon. The notice and hearing shall conform to the requirements set forth in sections 27-2-26 through 27-2-31. (Acts 1977, No. 409, p. 547, § 2.)

ARTICLE 2.

RECEIVERSHIP DIVISION.

§ 27-2-50. Established; appointment, term of office and compensation of chief.

There is hereby established within the department of insurance a receivership division to be managed and headed by a chief of said division. The chief of said receivership division shall be appointed by the commissioner of insurance and shall serve at his pleasure. The compensation of said chief shall be fixed by the commissioner; except, that said compensation shall not exceed that of the highest paid division chief in the insurance department under the merit system. (Acts 1975, No. 1039, p. 2083, § 1.)

Cross references. — As to merit system, see § 36-26-1 et seq.

§ 27-2-51. Bond of chief.

The chief of the receivership division shall make bond payable to the state of Alabama in the amount of $75,000.00, conditioned upon faithful performance of his duties, the premiums of which shall be borne by the state. In addition each receivership court may require adequate bond of said receiver if the court deems it necessary, the premiums of which shall be paid from funds of the receivership. (Acts 1975, No. 1039, p. 2083, § 6.)

§ 27-2-52. Offices, equipment and personnel; operating expenses.

The commissioner of insurance shall furnish offices, equipment, operating expenses and necessary personnel to maintain and operate the receivership division. The operating expenses of said division shall as far as practical be paid from the receiverships as administrative expenses on a pro rata basis, such expenses to be verified by the receiver to the receivership court having jurisdiction and paid on order of said court into the special examination revolving fund provided for in section 27-2-25. To the extent of and limited to the funds paid into said revolving fund from receiverships, the commissioner of insurance is hereby authorized to draw upon said revolving fund on proper voucher, to pay for salaries, expenses, rent or equipment, or portion thereof, for the proper operation of the receivership division. Expenses and salaries not recoverable from receivership funds may be paid from funds appropriated to the insurance department. The commissioner of insurance is hereby authorized to assign one or more insurance examiners to the receivership division from time to time and to pay their salaries and expenses and to provide necessary equipment from the special examination revolving fund hereinabove mentioned. (Acts 1975, No. 1039, p. 2083, § 5.)

§ 27-2-53. Appointment of chief as receiver — Generally.

Upon the commissioner of insurance bringing delinquency proceedings against any insurer pursuant to this title, or other insurance laws of the state, the proper circuit court having jurisdiction thereof shall appoint the chief of the receivership division as receiver of such impaired or insolvent insurer, or ancillary receiver if a foreign insurer is found to be impaired or insolvent. (Acts 1975, No. 1039, p. 2083, § 2.)

§ 27-2-54. Same — Existing receiverships.

The commissioner of insurance, as receiver in any existing receivership, may petition the proper receivership court to name as receiver thereof the chief of the receivership division as provided for in this article, and upon making an accounting of the assets of such receivership by the commissioner, the court shall so change receivers or ancillary receivers by releasing and discharging the commissioner from such duty and responsibility and shall name the chief of the receivership division as receiver or ancillary receiver. (Acts 1975, No. 1039, p. 2083, § 3.)

§ 27-2-55. Assumption by receiver of certain former powers, duties, etc., of commissioner.

All duties, rights, power, authority and responsibility placed upon the commissioner of insurance by sections 27-32-15 through 27-32-36, or by future law, as receiver of an insurer shall be vested in and assumed by the receiver appointed pursuant to this article, however, nothing herein shall divest the commissioner of the authority to examine insurers for solvency and to institute delinquency proceedings pursuant to law. (Acts 1975, No. 1039, p. 2083, § 4.)

CHAPTER 3.

AUTHORIZATION OF INSURERS.

Sec.
27-3-1. Certificate of authority — Requirement.
27-3-2. Same — Exceptions — Generally.
27-3-3. Same — Same — Investment in real estate or securities secured thereby.
27-3-4. Authority to transact insurance — Eligibility.
27-3-5. Same — Use of name by insurer.
27-3-6. Same — Kind or combinations of kinds — Restrictions.
27-3-7. Same — Same — Minimum paid-in capital stock and surplus.
27-3-8. Same — Same — Special surplus.
27-3-9. Minimum capital and surplus for new domestic stock life insurance company.
27-3-10. Application of capital surplus to reduction or elimination of deficit by domestic stock insurers.
27-3-11. Deposit requirements — Generally.
27-3-12. Same — Special deposit — Surety insurers.
27-3-13. Same — Same — Title insurers.
27-3-14. Same — Alien insurers — Generally.
27-3-15. Same — Same — Trusteed assets.
27-3-16. Lloyd's insurers.
27-3-17. Application for certificate of authority — Filing.
27-3-18. Same — Issuance or refusal; ownership of certificate.

Sec.
27-3-19. Continuance, expiration, reinstatement and amendment of certificates.
27-3-20. Suspension or revocation of certificates — Mandatory grounds; notice and hearing.
27-3-21. Same — Additional grounds; notice and hearing.
27-3-22. Same — Order and notices.
27-3-23. Same — Duration of suspension; obligations of insurer during suspension; reinstatement.
27-3-24. Service of process on insurers — Appointment of commissioner as agent.
27-3-25. Same — How served; time to answer or plead.
27-3-26. Annual statement of insurers; furnishing of other information on request.
27-3-27. Insurers to do business through licensed agents, etc.; exceptions.
27-3-28. Execution of contracts through countersigning resident agent; exceptions.
27-3-29. Protection of state insurers against foreign discriminatory or onerous requirements.

Collateral references. — 44 C.J.S., Insurance, § 69.

43 Am. Jur. 2d, Insurance, §§ 51, 52.

Public regulation or control of insurance agents or brokers. 10 ALR2d 950.

Performance by one insurer of its duty to defend as excusing failure of other insurers equally obligated to defend. 90 ALR3d 1199.

§ 27-3-1. Certificate of authority — Requirement.

(a) No person shall act as an insurer and no insurer shall transact insurance in this state unless so authorized by a subsisting certificate of authority issued to it by the commissioner, except as to such transactions as are expressly otherwise provided for in this title.

(b) No insurer shall from offices or by personnel or facilities located in this state solicit insurance applications or otherwise transact insurance in another state or country unless it holds a subsisting certificate of authority issued to it by the commissioner authorizing it to transact the same kind or kinds of insurance in this state. (Acts 1971, No. 407, p. 707, § 48.)

§ 27-3-2. Same — Exceptions — Generally.

A certificate of authority shall not be required of an insurer with respect to the following:

(1) Transactions relative to its policies lawfully written in this state or liquidation of assets and liabilities of the insurer, other than collection of new premiums, all as resulting from its former authorized operations in this state;

(2) Transactions thereunder subsequent to issuance of a policy covering only subjects of insurance not resident, located or expressly to be performed in this state at time of issuance and lawfully solicited, written or delivered outside this state;

(3) Transactions pursuant to surplus lines coverages lawfully written under chapter 10 of this title; and

(4) Reinsurance. (Acts 1971, No. 407, p. 707, § 49.)

Cited in Dutton v. Chester F. Raines Agency, Inc., 475 So. 2d 545 (Ala. 1985).

§ 27-3-3. Same — Same — Investment in real estate or securities secured thereby.

A foreign insurer may transact business in this state without certificate of authority for the purpose, and to the extent only, of investing its funds in real estate located in this state, or in securities secured thereby, by complying with the requirements of amendment 154 of the Constitution of Alabama. Such an insurer shall not be subject to any other provisions of this title. (Acts 1971, No. 407, p. 707, § 50.)

Collateral references. — 44 C.J.S., Insurance, § 79.

§ 27-3-4. Authority to transact insurance — Eligibility.

To qualify for and hold authority to transact insurance in this state, an insurer must be otherwise in compliance with this title and with its charter powers and must be an incorporated stock insurer or an incorporated mutual insurer or a reciprocal insurer, all of the same general type as may be formed as a domestic insurer under this title; except that:

(1) No foreign insurer shall be authorized to transact insurance in this state which does not maintain reserves as required by chapter 36 of this title applicable to the kind, or kinds, of insurance transacted by such insurer, wherever transacted in the United States, or which transacts insurance in the United States on the assessment premium plan, stipulated premium plan, cooperative plan or any similar plan;

(2) Any foreign insurer which has transacted insurance as an authorized insurer in its state or country of domicile for less than five years shall not be

authorized to transact insurance in this state unless it is otherwise qualified for such authority under this code and is:

    a. The wholly owned subsidiary of an insurer authorized to transact insurance in this state;

    b. The continuing corporation resulting from a merger or consolidation of insurers at least one of which insurers has been an authorized insurer in its state or country of domicile for at least five years; or

    c. Is in compliance with the requirements as to capital and surplus provided therefor under sections 27-3-7 and 27-3-8;

    (3) The commissioner shall not grant or continue authority to transact insurance in this state as to any insurer the management of which is found by him, after thorough investigation, to be incompetent or untrustworthy, or so lacking in insurance company managerial experience as to make the proposed operation hazardous to the insurance-buying public or which, after thorough examination or investigation, he has good reason to believe is affiliated directly or indirectly through ownership, control, reinsurance transactions or other insurance or business relations with any person, or persons, whose business operations are, or have been, marked to the injury of insurers, stockholders, policyholders, creditors or the public by manipulation of assets, of accounts or of reinsurance or by bad faith;

    (4) No insurer the voting control of which is held, in whole or substantial part, by any government or governmental agency shall be authorized to transact insurance in this state. Membership in a mutual insurer or subscribership in a reciprocal insurer shall not be deemed to be either an ownership or control of the insurer for the purposes of this subdivision; and

    (5) Lloyd's plan insurers may be authorized to transact insurance in this state as provided in section 27-3-16. (Acts 1971, No. 407, p. 707, § 51.)

Collateral references. — 44 C.J.S., Insurance, § 69.

43 Am. Jur. 2d, Insurance, §§ 93-119.

§ 27-3-5. Same — Use of name by insurer.

(a) No insurer shall be authorized to transact insurance which has or uses a name so similar to that of another insurer already so authorized as likely to mislead the public.

(b) No life insurer shall be so authorized which has or uses a name deceptively similar to that of another insurer authorized to transact insurance in this state within the preceding 10 years if life insurance policies originally issued by such other insurer are still outstanding in this state.

(c) No insurer shall be so authorized which has or uses a name which tends to deceive or mislead as to the type of organization of the insurer.

(d) In case of conflict of names hereafter between two insurers, or a conflict otherwise prohibited under the foregoing subsections of this section, the commissioner may permit or require, as a condition to the issuance of an original certificate of authority to an applicant insurer, that such insurer shall use in Alabama such supplementation or modification of its name or such business name as may reasonably be necessary to avoid such conflict. No such name, supplementation or modification shall contain the principal identifying factor contained in the name of any other insurer already authorized to transact insurance in this state. (Acts 1971, No. 407, p. 707, § 52.)

§ 27-3-6. Same — Kind or combinations of kinds — Restrictions.

An insurer which otherwise qualifies therefor may be authorized to transact any one kind or combination of kinds of insurance as defined in chapter 5 of this title, except:

(1) A life insurer may grant annuities and shall be authorized to transact in addition only disability insurance, and no insurer shall be authorized to transact life insurance in this state which transacts anywhere any kind of insurance in addition to life and disability insurances and annuities; except, that the commissioner shall, if the insurer otherwise qualifies therefor, continue to so authorize any life insurer which, immediately prior to the effective date of this title, was lawfully authorized to transact in this state a kind or kinds of insurance in addition to life and disability;

(2) A reciprocal or Lloyd's plan insurer shall not transact life insurance; and

(3) A title insurer shall be a stock insurer and shall transact no other kind of insurance; except, that the commissioner may continue to so authorize any insurer which immediately prior to the effective date of this title was lawfully authorized to transact and was lawfully writing in this state a kind, or kinds, of insurance in addition to title insurance. (Acts 1971, No. 407, p. 707, § 53.)

§ 27-3-7. Same — Same — Minimum paid-in capital stock and surplus.

(a) To qualify for authority to transact any one kind of insurance, as defined in chapter 5 of this title, or combination of kinds of insurance as shown below, an insurer applying for its original certificate of authority in this state after the effective date of this title or continuing such original certificate of authority shall possess and thereafter maintain unimpaired paid-in capital stock, if a stock insurer, or unimpaired surplus, if a foreign mutual or foreign reciprocal insurer, in amount not less than as applicable under the schedule below and shall possess when first so authorized such additional funds as surplus as are required under section 27-3-8:

Kind or kinds of insurance	Minimum capital or surplus required
Life	$800,000.00
Disability	500,000.00

Kind or kinds of insurance	Minimum capital or surplus required
Life and disability	$800,000.00
Property	300,000.00
Marine	300,000.00
Casualty	400,000.00
Surety	350,000.00
Title	200,000.00
Multiple lines — Any two or more: Property, marine, casualty, surety; and all kinds of insurance other than title and life insurance	500,000.00

(b) An insurer holding a valid certificate of authority to transact insurance in this state immediately prior to the effective date of this title may continue to be authorized to transact the same kinds of insurance as permitted by such certificate of authority by maintaining thereafter not less than the same amount of paid-in capital stock, if a stock insurer, or not less than the same amount of surplus, if a mutual or reciprocal insurer, as required by the laws of this state for such authority immediately prior to such effective date; but such insurer shall not thereafter be granted authority to transact any other or additional kind of insurance unless it then fully complies with the requirements as to capital and surplus, as applied to all kinds of insurance it then proposes to transact, as provided by this title with respect to insurers applying for original certificates of authority under this title.

(c) Capital and surplus requirements shall be based upon all the kinds of insurance actually transacted, or to be transacted, by the insurer in any and all areas in which it operates, whether or not only a portion of such kinds are to be transacted in this state.

(d) As to surplus required for qualification to transact one or more kinds of insurance and thereafter to be maintained, domestic mutual insurers shall be governed by chapter 27 of this title, and domestic reciprocal insurers shall be governed by chapter 31 of this title.

(e) A life insurer may also grant annuities without additional capital or additional surplus.

(f) A casualty insurer may be authorized to transact also disability insurance without additional capital or additional surplus. (Code 1940, T. 28, § 1; Acts 1965, 2nd Ex. Sess., No. 143, p. 194; Acts 1971, No. 407, p. 707, § 54; Acts 1975, No. 1041, p. 2086, § 1.)

Former minimum capital requirements preserved. — This section preserves the $100,000.00 minimum capital requirement for those insurance companies which were holding valid certificates of authority prior to October 2, 1965. Assured Investors Life Ins. Co. v. Payne, 356 So. 2d 144 (Ala. 1978).

§ 27-3-8. Same — Same — Special surplus.

(a) In addition to the minimum paid-in capital stock (stock insurers) or minimum surplus (mutual and reciprocal insurers) required by section 27-3-7, special surplus shall be possessed by insurers hereafter applying for original certificates of authority in this state as follows:

(1) All stock insurers and foreign mutual and foreign reciprocal insurers which have actively transacted insurance in their states or countries of domicile as an authorized insurer for less than five years and which do not meet the requirements of paragraphs (2) a or (2) b of section 27-3-4, when first authorized to transact insurance in this state shall have a surplus or additional surplus equal to 150 percent of the paid-up capital stock, if a stock insurer, or surplus, if a foreign mutual or foreign reciprocal insurer, otherwise required under section 27-3-7 for the kinds of insurance to be transacted; and

(2) An insurer that has actively transacted insurance as an authorized insurer in its state or country of domicile for more than five years, or which meets the requirements of paragraphs (2) a or (2) b of section 27-3-4, shall possess when first authorized in this state surplus, if a stock insurer, or additional surplus, if a mutual or reciprocal insurer, equal to 100 percent of the paid-in capital stock, if a stock insurer, or surplus, if a foreign mutual or foreign reciprocal insurer, otherwise required under section 27-3-7.

(b) If within five years after date of its original certificate of authority to transact insurance in this state such an insurer requests authority to transact an additional kind or kinds of insurance, it shall not be so authorized unless it then possesses surplus, if a stock insurer, or additional surplus, if a mutual or reciprocal insurer, in such an amount as would be required under this section as for an original certificate of authority covering all the kinds of insurance the insurer then proposes to transact.

(c) After issuance of its original certificate of authority the insurer may use the special surplus required under this section in the normal course of its business only.

(d) Execution by a mutual or reciprocal surety insurer as sole surety of certain bonds or undertakings required or permitted by law or by certain political subdivisions, public bodies or public officers is subject further to surplus requirement as provided in section 27-24-3. (Acts 1971, No. 407, p. 707, § 55.)

§ 27-3-9. Minimum capital and surplus for new domestic stock life insurance company.

The minimum capital required to form and organize a new domestic stock life insurance company shall be $1,000,000.00, and in addition thereto the minimum surplus to form such a company shall be $1,000,000.00. (Acts 1973, No. 643, p. 953.)

Cited in Roussel v. Payne, 352 So. 2d 1364 (Ala. Civ. App. 1977).

§ 27-3-10. Application of capital surplus to reduction or elimination of deficit by domestic stock insurers.

(a) For the purposes of this section, the following words and phrases shall have the following meanings:

(1) DOMESTIC STOCK INSURER. A corporation incorporated under the laws of the state of Alabama with its capital divided into shares and owned by its stockholders which is engaged as indemnitor, surety or contractor in the business of entering into contracts of insurance.

(2) CAPITAL SURPLUS. Such term shall have the meaning given thereto in the statutes of this state relating to the powers and procedures of domestic private corporations formed for profit.

(3) EARNED SURPLUS. Such term shall have the meaning given thereto in the statutes of this state relating to the powers and procedures of domestic private corporations formed for profit.

(b) A domestic stock insurer which has the minimum unimpaired paid-in capital stock required for the transaction of insurance by such domestic stock insurer by the statutes of this state governing domestic stock insurers may, by resolution of its board of directors, apply any part, or all, of its capital surplus to the reduction or elimination of any deficit, however incurred, but only after first eliminating the then earned surplus, if any, of the domestic stock insurer by applying such earned surplus against such deficit. Each such application of capital surplus shall, to the extent thereof, effect a reduction of capital surplus. (Acts 1973, No. 825, p. 1292.)

§ 27-3-11. Deposit requirements — Generally.

(a) The commissioner shall not issue or permit to exist a certificate of authority as to any insurer, other than an alien insurer, unless it has deposited and maintains deposited in trust with the treasurer of this state cash or securities eligible under section 27-6-3 and having a value at all times of not less than $100,000.00 or the minimum paid-in capital stock, if a stock insurer, or surplus, if a mutual or reciprocal insurer, required to be maintained by the insurer under this title for authority to transact the kinds of insurance to be transacted, whichever is the smaller amount.

(b) The deposit shall be for the general benefit and protection of the insurer's policyholders or its policyholders and creditors.

(c) In lieu of such deposit, or part thereof, in this state of a foreign insurer, the commissioner shall, subject to the retaliatory law, section 27-3-29, accept the current certificate in proper form of the public official having supervision over insurers in any other state to the effect that a like deposit, or part thereof, of such insurer, comprised of cash or securities of substantially the same character as required under subsection (a) of this section, of similar deposits in this state, is being maintained under law in public custody or control in such state in trust for the purpose, among other reasonable purposes of protection of policyholders or policyholders and creditors, of the protection of all the insurer's policyholders or of its policyholders and creditors in this state.

(d) All such deposits in this state shall be subject to the applicable provisions of chapter 6 of this title.

(e) Any insurance company, with respect to its general account or separate accounts, is authorized to deposit or arrange for the deposit of securities which it may own in a clearing corporation, as defined in section 7-8-102(3), or in a federal reserve bank under the book-entry system. When such securities are so deposited, certificates representing securities of the same class of the same insurer may be merged and held in bulk in the name of the nominee of such clearing corporation with any other securities deposited in such clearing corporation by any person, regardless of the ownership of such securities, and securities of small denominations may be merged into one or more certificates of larger denominations. Title to such securities may be transferred by bookkeeping entry on the books of such clearing corporation or federal reserve bank without physical delivery of certificates representing such securities. Any company making deposits by means of such securities shall provide to the commissioner evidence customarily issued by federal reserve banks and clearing corporations establishing that the securities are actually recorded in a book-entry account or actually held in safekeeping by a clearing corporation. Securities deposited in a clearing corporation or in a book-entry account and used to meet the deposit requirements under the insurance laws of this state shall be under the control of the commissioner and shall not be withdrawn by the insurance company without the approval of the commissioner. (Acts 1909, No. 43, p. 29; Acts 1915, No. 87, p. 132; Acts 1966, Ex. Sess., No. 241, p. 363, § 2; Acts 1967, No. 97, p. 436, § 2; Acts 1971, No. 407, p. 707, § 56; Acts 1981, No. 81-541, p. 904, § 1.)

Collateral references. — 44 C.J.S., Insurance, § 72.

43 Am. Jur. 2d, Insurance, § 63.

§ 27-3-12. Same — Special deposit — Surety insurers.

(a) In addition to the deposit required under sections 27-3-11 or 27-3-14, a surety insurer shall deposit and maintain deposited with the treasurer of this state in trust for the benefit of holders, resident in this state, of the obligations of the insurer cash or securities eligible under section 27-6-3 having a value at all times of at least $50,000.00; except, that a domestic surety insurer may take credit for the amount of such special deposit against the deposit otherwise required of it under section 27-3-11, and except that a foreign insurer showing a deposit pursuant to subsection (c) of section 27-3-11 in the amount of $200,000.00 shall not be required to comply with this section.

(b) Such deposits shall be subject to the applicable provisions of chapter 6 of this title. (Acts 1909, No. 43, p. 29; Acts 1971, No. 407, p. 707, § 57.)

§ 27-3-13. Same — Same — Title insurers.

(a) For authority to transact such insurance in this state, a foreign title insurer shall have and maintain on deposit in this state for the better protection of its guaranty holders and creditors, resident in this state, under its contracts of title insurance, cash and securities eligible under section 27-6-3 having a value at all times of not less than $50,000.00. The deposit shall be so made and maintained in trust with a bank or trust company located in this state, approved by the commissioner, having a capital and surplus of not less than $500,000.00.

(b) At its option, a domestic title insurer may maintain a deposit in like manner, amount, character and for like purposes as required for foreign insurers under subsection (a) of this section.

(c) Such deposits shall be subject to the applicable provisions of chapter 6 of this title. (Acts 1923, No. 485, p. 635; Acts 1971, No. 407, p. 707, § 58.)

§ 27-3-14. Same — Alien insurers — Generally.

(a) An alien insurer shall not have authority to transact insurance in this state unless it has and maintains within the United States as deposits with trustees, public depositaries or in trust institutions approved by the commissioner under section 27-3-15 assets available for discharge of its United States insurance obligations, which assets shall be in amount not less than the outstanding liabilities of the insurer arising out of its insurance transactions in the United States together with the greater of the following sums:

(1) The largest deposit required by section 27-3-11 to be made by foreign insurers transacting like kinds of insurance; or

(2) $300,000.00.

(b) Of the amount deposited by an alien insurer, an amount not less than that required under subdivisions (a)(1) or (a)(2) of this section shall be deposited and maintained on deposit in cash or securities eligible for deposit under section 27-6-3 with the treasurer of this state or with or through the public official having supervision of insurance in another state and shall be held in trust exclusively for the benefit and protection of the insurer's policyholders or policyholders and creditors in the United States.

(c) The amount so held on deposit under subdivisions (a)(1) or (a)(2) of this section shall, for the purposes of this title, be deemed to be the paid-in capital, if a stock insurer, or minimum surplus, if a mutual insurer, of the insurer required to be maintained.

(d) If the insurer transacts surety insurance in this state, it shall make and maintain in this state the special deposit required under section 27-3-12.

(e) Any such deposit made in this state shall be subject to the applicable provisions of chapter 6 of this title; except, that if this state is the state of entry into the United States of the alien insurer the deposit shall be subject to the provisions of chapter 33 of this title. (Code 1940, T. 28, § 68; Acts 1967, No. 97, p. 436, § 1; Acts 1971, No. 407, p. 707, § 59.)

Collateral references. — 44 C.J.S., Insurance, § 81.

§ 27-3-15. Same — Same — Trusteed assets.

(a) In order to comply with the requirements of section 27-3-14, an alien insurer shall appoint citizens of the United States of America or public depositaries or trust institutions located in the United States, all as approved by the commissioner, as trustee, or trustees, to hold its funds and assets in trust for the benefit of its policyholders or policyholders and creditors in the United States. Any such trustee, or trustees, shall be named by the board of directors or comparable directive body of the insurer, and a certified copy of the record of the appointment and of the deed of trust shall be filed with the commissioner.

(b) Funds and assets so held, to the extent that they consist of cash, securities and other assets of the same general character as are eligible for the investment of like funds of a domestic insurer, under sections 27-1-8 and 27-1-9, shall constitute the assets of the insurer for the purposes of this title.

(c) Such trustees and assets, and all accounts and records relating thereto, shall be subject to examination by the commissioner in the same manner as the officers, agents, assets and affairs of insurers.

(d) Trusteed assets of an alien insurer using this state as its state of entry into the United States shall be subject to chapter 32 of this title. (Code 1940, T. 28, § 69; Acts 1971, No. 407, p. 707, § 60.)

§ 27-3-16. Lloyd's insurers.

Aggregations of individuals as underwriters, whether domestic, foreign or alien, assuming insurance risks upon the plan known as "Lloyd's," whereby each underwriter is liable for the proportionate part assumed by him of the whole amount so insured by a policy issued by such underwriters, may be authorized to transact any kind, or kinds, of insurance in this state other than life or title insurances if the insurer is otherwise in compliance with this title, subject to the following conditions:

(1) If a foreign or alien insurer, it must have successfully been in business as an authorized insurer in the state or country of domicile for at least 10 years.

(2) If a domestic insurer, it must file with the commissioner evidence, satisfactory to him, that it has been soundly organized and that its insurance operations will, at all times, be competently conducted by individuals having the necessary experience in insurance underwriting and management to do so, that at all times it will be comprised of not less than 30 individual "underwriters," that no such underwriter shall retain risk as to any one subject of insurance in amount exceeding two percent of his total net worth and that the liability of such underwriter, as to any such risk within the extent and amount of coverage provided by the amount of insurance, is unlimited. For the purpose of determining compliance with this provision, the commissioner may at any time require any and all such underwriters to file with him their individual financial statements, duly certified and sworn to under oath, in such form and scope of contents as the commissioner may reasonably require. The assets and insurance transactions of any or all such underwriters shall be subject to examination by the commissioner under the same conditions as apply to domestic insurers in general under chapter 2 of this title.

(3) Such an insurer shall otherwise be subject to the same applicable requirements and obligations as apply under this title to a stock insurer transacting like kinds of insurance; and for the purposes of this title such an insurer's deposit made and maintained as required under section 27-3-11 or subdivision (a)(1) or (a)(2) of section 27-3-14 shall be deemed to be the minimum capital required to be maintained by such an insurer, but subject to the requirements of section 27-3-8 as to surplus. (Code 1940, T. 28, § 71; Acts 1971, No. 407, p. 707, § 61.)

Collateral references. — 46 C.J.S., Insurance, §§ 1410-1434.

43 Am. Jur. 2d, Insurance, §§ 55, 113.

§ 27-3-17. Application for certificate of authority — Filing.

To apply for an original certificate of authority an insurer shall file with the commissioner its application therefor, accompanied by the applicable fees as specified in section 27-4-2, showing its name, location of its home office or, if an alien insurer, principal office in the United States, kinds of insurance to be transacted, state or country of domicile and such additional information as the commissioner may reasonably require, together with the following documents, as applicable:

(1) A copy of its corporate charter, articles of incorporation or other charter documents with all amendments thereto, certified by the public officer with whom the originals are on file in the state or country of domicile;

(2) If a mutual insurer, a copy of its bylaws, as amended, certified by its secretary or other officer having custody thereof;

(3) If a foreign reciprocal insurer, copies of the power of attorney of its attorney-in-fact or its subscribers' agreement, certified by its attorney-in-fact, and if a domestic reciprocal insurer, the declaration provided for by section 27-31-7;

(4) A copy of its financial statement as of December 31, next preceding, on the "convention" form as then currently in general use for similar insurers, sworn to by at least two executive officers of the insurer or certified by the public insurance supervisory official of the insurer's state of domicile or of entry into the United States;

(5) Copy of report of last examination, if any, made of the insurer, certified by the insurance supervisory official of its state of domicile or of entry into the United States;

(6) Appointment of the commissioner pursuant to section 27-3-24 as its attorney to receive service of legal process;

(7) If a foreign or alien insurer, a certificate of the public official having supervision of insurance in its state, or state of entry into the United States or country of domicile showing that it is legally organized and is authorized to transact the kinds of insurance proposed to be transacted in this state;

(8) If an alien insurer, a copy of the appointment and authority of its United States manager, certified by its officer having custody of its records;

(9) Evidence satisfactory to the commissioner of any deposit required under sections 27-3-11, 27-3-12, 27-3-13 or 27-3-14; and

(10) If other than a life insurer, the affidavit, on a form furnished by the commissioner, of the insurer's president or other chief officer that it has not violated any of the provisions of section 27-3-27 during the preceding 12 months and an agreement that the insurer accepts the terms and the obligations of such section as part of the consideration for authority to transact insurance in this state. (Acts 1935, No. 194, p. 256; Acts 1955, 2nd Ex. Sess., No. 77, p. 193, § 2; Acts 1971, No. 407, p. 707, § 62.)

§ 27-3-18. Same — Issuance or refusal; ownership of certificate.

(a) If upon completion of the application for a certificate of authority the commissioner finds that the insurer has met the requirements for and is entitled thereto under this title, he shall issue to the insurer a proper certificate of authority; if he does not so find, the commissioner shall issue his order refusing such certificate. The commissioner shall act upon an application for a certificate of authority within a reasonable period after its completion.

(b) The certificate, if issued, shall specify the kind, or kinds, of insurance the insurer is authorized to transact in this state. At the insurer's request, the commissioner may issue a certificate of authority limited to particular types of insurance or insurance coverages within the scope of a kind of insurance as defined in chapter 5 of this title.

(c) Although issued to the insurer, the certificate of authority is at all times the property of the state of Alabama. Upon any expiration, suspension or termination thereof, the insurer shall promptly deliver the certificate of authority to the commissioner. (Acts 1971, No. 407, p. 707, § 63.)

Collateral references. — 44 C.J.S., Insurance, § 69.
Right of person wrongfully refused license upon proper application therefor to do act for which license is required. 30 ALR2d 1006.

§ 27-3-19. Continuance, expiration, reinstatement and amendment of certificates.

(a) Certificates of authority issued or renewed under this title shall continue in force as long as the insurer is entitled thereto under this title and until suspended, revoked or terminated at the request of the insurer; subject, however, to continuance of the certificate by the insurer each year by:

(1) Payment prior to March 1 of the continuation fee provided in section 27-4-2; and

(2) Due filing by the insurer of its annual statement for the calendar year preceding as required under section 27-3-26.

(b) If not so continued by the insurer, its certificate of authority shall expire at midnight on the May 31, next following, such failure of the insurer so to continue it in force. The commissioner shall promptly notify the insurer of the occurrence of any such failure resulting in impending expiration of its certificate of authority.

(c) The commissioner may, in his discretion, reinstate a certificate of authority which the insurer has inadvertently permitted to expire, after the insurer has fully cured all its failures which resulted in such expiration and upon payment by the insurer of the fee for reinstatement, in addition to the current continuation fee, in the amounts provided in section 27-4-2. Otherwise, the insurer shall be granted another certificate of authority only after filing application therefor and meeting all other requirements as for an original certificate of authority in this state.

(d) The commissioner may amend a certificate of authority at any time to accord with changes in the insurer's charter or insuring powers. (Acts 1971, No. 407, p. 707, § 64.)

§ 27-3-20. Suspension or revocation of certificates — Mandatory grounds; notice and hearing.

(a) The commissioner shall suspend or revoke an insurer's certificate of authority:

(1) If such action is required by any provision of this title;

(2) If the insurer no longer meets the requirements for the authority originally granted on account of deficiency of assets or otherwise; or

(3) If the insurer's authority to transact insurance is suspended or revoked by its state of domicile or state of entry into the United States if an alien insurer.

(b) Except in cases of insolvency or impairment of required capital or surplus or suspension or revocation by another state as referred to in subdivision (a) (3) of this section, the commissioner shall give the insurer at least 10 days' notice in advance of any such suspension or revocation under this section and of the particulars of the reasons therefor. If the insurer requests a hearing thereon within such 10 days, such request shall automatically stay the commissioner's proposed action until his order is made on such hearing. (Acts 1971, No. 407, p. 707, § 65.)

Collateral references. — 44 C.J.S., Insurance, § 74.

Actual receipt of cancellation notice mailed by insurer as prerequisite to cancellation of insurance. 40 ALR4th 867.

§ 27-3-21. Same — Additional grounds; notice and hearing.

(a) The commissioner may, in his discretion, suspend or revoke an insurer's certificate of authority if, after a hearing thereon, he finds that the insurer has willfully violated any material provision of this title other than those for which suspension or revocation is mandatory or has failed to pay applicable taxes with respect to a preceding calendar year as required by this title.

(b) The commissioner shall, after a hearing thereon, suspend or revoke an insurer's certificate of authority if he finds that the insurer:

(1) Is in unsound condition, or is in such condition or is using such methods and practices in the conduct of its business as to render its further transaction of insurance in this state hazardous to its policyholders or to the public;

(2) Has refused to be examined or to produce its accounts, records and files for examination or if any of its officers or agents have refused to perform any legal obligation relative thereto or have refused to give information with respect to its affairs when required by the commissioner;

(3) Has failed to pay any final judgment entered against it in this state within 30 days after the judgment became final, or within 30 days after the

time for taking an appeal has expired or within 30 days after dismissal of appeal before final termination, whichever date is later;

(4) With such frequency as to indicate its general business practice in this state:

a. Has, without just cause, refused to pay proper claims arising under coverages provided by its policies, whether the claim is in favor of an insured or is in favor of a third person with respect to liability of an insured to such third person; or

b. With like frequency and without just cause, compels insureds or claimants in this state to accept less than the amount due them or compels them to employ attorneys or to bring an action against the insurer or such an insured to secure full payment or settlement of such claims; provided, that as a condition precedent to a revocation or suspension of the insurer's certificate of authority under this subsection there has been a prior determination that the insured has engaged in an unfair method of competition or an unfair act or practice in the business of insurance; or

(5) Is affiliated with and under the same general management or interlocking directorate or ownership as another insurer which transacts direct insurance in this state without having a certificate of authority therefor, except as permitted as to surplus line insurers under chapter 10 of this title.

(c) The commissioner may, in his discretion and without advance notice on a hearing thereon, immediately suspend the certificate of authority of any insurer as to which proceedings for receivership, conservatorship, rehabilitation or other delinquency proceedings have been commenced in any state by the insurance supervisory official of such state. (Acts 1971, No. 407, p. 707, § 66.)

Cited in Assured Investors Life Ins. Co. v. Payne, 356 So. 2d 144 (Ala. 1978).

Collateral references. — Sufficiency of express finding of fact to support administrative determinations. 146 ALR 209.

Administrative decision on finding based on evidence secured outside of hearing, and without presence of interested party or counsel. 18 ALR2d 552.

Hearing and decision by different officers; change of personnel. 18 ALR2d 613.

Applicability of stare decisis doctrine to decisions of administrative agencies. 79 ALR2d 1126.

Assistance of counsel: right to assistance by counsel in administrative proceeding. 33 ALR3d 229.

Hearsay evidence in proceeding before state administrative agencies. 36 ALR3d 12.

§ 27-3-22. Same — Order and notices.

(a) Suspension or revocation of an insurer's certificate of authority shall be by the commissioner's order given to the insurer as provided by section 27-2-18. The commissioner shall promptly also give notice of such suspension or revocation to the insurer's agents in this state of record in the commissioner's office. The insurer shall not solicit or write any new coverages in this state during the period of any such suspension or revocation.

(b) In his discretion, the commissioner may cause notice of any such revocation to be published in one or more newspapers of general circulation published in this state.

(c) Upon revocation or suspension of the certificate of authority of a surety insurer, the commissioner shall so notify each officer in this state authorized to approve official bonds by circular letter stating the grounds of such suspension or revocation. (Acts 1971, No. 407, p. 707, § 67.)

Collateral references. — Actual receipt of cancellation notice mailed by insurer as pre- requisite to cancellation of insurance. 40 ALR4th 867.

§ 27-3-23. Same — Duration of suspension; obligations of insurer during suspension; reinstatement.

(a) Suspension of an insurer's certificate of authority shall be for such period as is fixed by the commissioner in the order of suspension, but not to exceed one year from the date of suspension, unless the commissioner shortens or rescinds such suspension or the order upon which the suspension is based is modified, rescinded or reversed.

(b) During the period of suspension the insurer shall file its annual statement, pay fees, licenses and taxes as required under this title as if the certificate had continued in full force, and it may service its outstanding policies and adjust losses thereunder.

(c) Upon expiration of the suspension period, if within such period the certificate of authority has not otherwise terminated, the insurer's certificate of authority shall automatically reinstate unless the commissioner finds that the causes of the suspension have not been removed or that the insurer is otherwise not in compliance with the requirements of this title, of which the commissioner shall give the insurer notice not less than 30 days in advance of the expiration of the suspension period. If not so automatically reinstated, the certificate of authority shall be deemed to have expired as of the end of the suspension period or upon failure of the insurer to continue the certificate during the suspension period, whichever event first occurs.

(d) Upon reinstatement of the insurer's certificate of authority, the authority of its agents in this state to represent the insurer shall likewise reinstate. The commissioner shall promptly notify the insurer and its agents in this state of record in the department of such reinstatement. (Acts 1971, No. 407, p. 707, § 68.)

§ 27-3-24. Service of process on insurers — Appointment of commissioner as agent.

(a) Each insurer applying for a certificate of authority to transact business in this state shall file with the commissioner an appointment of the commissioner and his successors in office, on a form as furnished by the commissioner, as its attorney upon whom may be served all lawful process in any action or proceeding against it in this state and therein shall agree that any such process served upon such attorney shall be of the same force and validity as if served on the insurer. The appointment shall be irrevocable, shall bind the insurer and any successor in interest or to the assets or liabilities of the insurer and shall remain in effect as long as there is outstanding in this state any obligation or liability of the insurer resulting from its transactions therein.

(b) At the time of such appointment of the commissioner as its process agent, the insurer shall file with the commissioner designation of the name and address of the person to whom process against it served upon the commissioner is to be forwarded. The insurer may change such designation by a new filing. (Code 1940, T. 28, § 65; Acts 1971, No. 407, p. 707, § 69.)

Collateral references. — 44 C.J.S., Insurance, § 84.

19 Am. Jur. 2d, Corporations, § 1462 et seq. 36 Am. Jur. 2d, Foreign Corporations, § 516 et seq.

Cessation by foreign corporation of business within state as affecting designation of agent for service of process. 45 ALR 1447.

Statute providing for service of process upon statutory agent in action against foreign corporation as regards communications to corporation of fact of service. 89 ALR 658.

§ 27-3-25. Same — How served; time to answer or plead.

(a) Service of process upon the commissioner as process agent of the insurer under section 27-3-24 shall be made by the proper officer of Montgomery county by serving copies in triplicate of the process upon the commissioner or upon his assistant, deputy or other person in charge of his office. Upon receiving such service, the commissioner shall promptly forward a copy thereof by certified mail or registered mail, with return receipt requested, to the person last designated by the insurer to receive the same, as provided under subsection (b) of section 27-3-24, return one copy with his admission of service and retain one copy in the files of the department. The commissioner shall keep a record of all actions filed against insurers wherein process is served on the commissioner, noting the name of the insurer, the date of service and the type of action.

(b) Where process is served upon the commissioner as an insurer's process agent, the insurer shall not be required to answer or plead except within 30 days after the date upon which the insurer's designee received the copy of the process mailed by the commissioner, as shown by the return receipt therefor referred to in subsection (a) of this section.

(c) Process served upon the commissioner, and copy thereof forwarded as in this section provided, shall for all purposes constitute valid and binding service thereof upon the insurer.

(d) This section shall not be deemed to prohibit service of process upon an insurer by any other method provided for by law. (Code 1940, T. 28, § 65; Acts 1971, No. 407, p. 707, § 70.)

§ 27-3-26. Annual statement of insurers; furnishing of other information on request.

(a) Each authorized insurer shall, annually on or before March 1, or within such extension of time not exceeding 30 days after March 1 as the commissioner for good cause shown may grant as to a particular insurer, file with the commissioner a full and true statement of its financial condition, transactions and affairs as of the December 31, preceding. The statement shall be in such general form and context as is in current use for similar reports to states in general with respect to the type of insurer and kinds of insurance to be reported upon and as supplemented by additional information required by the commissioner. The statement shall be verified by the oath of the insurer's president or vice-president and secretary or actuary as applicable or, if a reciprocal insurer, by the oath of the attorney-in-fact or its like officers if a corporation.

(b) The statement of an alien insurer shall be verified by the insurer's United States manager or other officer duly authorized and shall relate only to its transactions and affairs in the United States, unless the commissioner requires otherwise. If the commissioner requires a statement as to the alien insurer's affairs throughout the world, the insurer shall file such statement with the commissioner as soon as reasonably possible.

(c) The commissioner may in his discretion suspend or revoke the certificate of authority of an insurer failing to file its annual statement when due. In addition the insurer shall be subject to a penalty of $250.00, such penalty to be collected by the commissioner, if necessary, by a civil action therefor brought by the commissioner in the circuit court of Montgomery county, unless waived by the commissioner upon a showing by the insurer of good cause for its failure to file its report on or before the date due.

(d) At time of filing, the insurer shall pay the fee for filing its annual statement as prescribed by section 27-4-2.

(e) In addition to information called for and furnished in connection with its annual statement, an insurer shall furnish promptly to the commissioner such information with respect to any of its transactions or affairs as the commissioner may, from time to time, request in writing. (Acts 1971, No. 407, p. 707, § 71.)

Collateral references. — 44 C.J.S., Insurance, § 73.

43 Am. Jur. 2d, Insurance, § 61.

§ 27-3-27. Insurers to do business through licensed agents, etc.; exceptions.

(a) No insurer shall, in this state, directly or indirectly, accept applications for insurance, negotiate for or issue any policy or contract of insurance or assume direct liability as to a subject of insurance resident, located or to be performed in this state unless through insurance agents, solicitors or brokers duly licensed under the provisions of this title.

(b) This section shall not apply to title insurance or insurance of the rolling stock, vessels or aircraft of any common carrier in interstate or foreign commerce or covering any liability or other risks incident to the ownership, maintenance or operation thereof. This section shall not apply as to life or disability insurance not delivered or issued for delivery in this state and lawfully solicited outside this state. (Acts 1936-37, Ex. Sess., No. 224, p. 267; Code 1940, T. 28, § 66; Acts 1971, No. 407, p. 707, § 72.)

Collateral references. — 44 C.J.S., Insurance, § 85.

43 Am. Jur. 2d, Insurance, § 84.

Provisions of insurance company's contract with independent insurance agent restricting competitive placements by agent as illegal restraint of trade under state law. 42 ALR4th 1072.

§ 27-3-28. Execution of contracts through countersigning resident agent; exceptions.

(a) To assure the validity and construction of contracts according to the laws of this state and to facilitate the collection of privilege taxes and fees, all property, surety and casualty insurers doing business in this state shall execute all contracts upon property or risks in this state through a resident agent of the insurer, duly licensed under this title, who shall execute or countersign all such contracts. Each such agent regularly compensated on a commission basis shall collect and retain the usual commission paid by the insurer; except, that not over one half of such commission may be paid to a licensed nonresident agent or broker.

(b) Each such agent shall keep a true record of all contracts thus executed or countersigned by him and shall, upon request, furnish a verified copy thereof to the commissioner to aid him in the collection of all privilege taxes due in this state.

(c) No such countersignature may be made by any solicitor, managing general agent or service representative, nor by any servant or employee thereof nor by any servant or employee of the insurer; except, that this provision shall not prevent any servant or employee of a direct-writing insurer from being licensed under this title as a resident insurance agent of the insurer to countersign contracts of insurance.

(d) As to policies covering property or risks located in more than one state, the insurer may, in its discretion, use a countersignature endorsement thereon showing the policy to which attached and information in respect to such policy, including full premium information sufficient for the countersigning agent's records. Such endorsement shall be signed by the countersigning agent in lieu of countersignature of the original policy.

(e) No countersigning resident agent shall countersign a policy or counter-signature endorsement in blank.

(f) This section shall not apply to:

(1) Insurance of the rolling stock, vessels or aircraft of any common carrier in interstate or foreign commerce or of any vehicle principally garaged and used in another state, or covering any liability or other risks incident to the ownership, maintenance or operation thereof;

(2) Insurance of property received for shipment or delivery or in transit while in the possession and custody of railroads or other common carriers;

(3) Wet marine and transportation insurance;

(4) Reinsurance contracts between insurers; or

(5) Bid bonds issued in connection with any public or private contracts.

(Acts 1935, No. 194, p. 256; Acts 1971, No. 407, p. 707, §§ 73, 74.)

Collateral references. — 44 C.J.S., Insurance, § 256.
43 Am. Jur. 2d, Insurance, § 226.
Stipulated period of time coverage of insurance policy as affected by counter-signing subsequent to specified commencement date. 22 ALR2d 984.

§ 27-3-29. Protection of state insurers against foreign discriminatory or onerous requirements.

(a) The purpose of this section is to aid in the protection of insurers formed under the laws of Alabama and transacting insurance in other states or countries against discriminatory or onerous requirements under the laws of such states or countries or the administration thereof.

(b) When by or pursuant to the laws of any other state or foreign country, any taxes, licenses and other fees, in the aggregate, and any fines, penalties, deposit requirements or other material obligations, prohibitions or restrictions are, or would be, imposed upon Alabama insurers, or upon the agents or representatives of such insurers, which are in excess of such taxes, licenses and other fees, in the aggregate, or which are in excess of the fines, penalties, deposit requirements or other obligations, prohibitions or restrictions directly imposed upon similar insurers, or upon the agents or representatives of such insurers, of such other state or country under the statutes of this state, so long as such laws of such other state or country continue in force or are so applied, the same taxes, licenses and other fees, in the aggregate, or fines, penalties or deposit requirements or other material obligations, prohibitions or restrictions, of whatever kind, shall be imposed by the commissioner upon the insurers, or upon the agents or representatives of such insurers, of such other state or country doing business or seeking to do business in Alabama. Any tax, license or other fee or other obligation imposed by any city, county or other political subdivision or agency of such other state or country on Alabama insurers, or their agents or representatives, shall be deemed to be imposed by such state or country within the meaning of this section.

(c) This section shall not apply as to personal income taxes, nor as to ad valorem taxes on real or personal property nor as to special purpose obligations or assessments imposed by another state in connection with particular kinds of insurance, other than property insurance; except, that deductions from premium taxes or other taxes otherwise payable allowed on account of real estate or personal property taxes paid shall be taken into consideration by the commissioner in determining the propriety and extent of retaliatory action under this section.

(d) For the purposes of this section, the domicile of an alien insurer, other than insurers formed under the laws of Canada or a province thereof, shall be that state designated by the insurer in writing filed with the commissioner at time of admission to this state or within six months after the effective date of this title, whichever date is the later, and may be any one of the following states:

(1) That in which the insurer was first authorized to transact insurance;

(2) That in which is located the insurer's principal place of business in the United States; or

(3) That in which is held the larger deposit of trusteed assets of the insurer for the protection of its policyholders or policyholders and creditors in the United States.

If the insurer makes no such designation its domicile shall be deemed to be that state in which is located its principal place of business in the United States.

(e) In the case of an insurer formed under the laws of Canada or a province thereof, its domicile shall be deemed to be that province in which is located its head office. (Acts 1935, No. 194, p. 256; Acts 1971, No. 407, p. 707, § 75.)

Collateral references. — 44 C.J.S., Insurance, § 76.

43 Am. Jur. 2d, Insurance, § 85.

CHAPTER 4.

FEES AND TAXES.

Sec.
27-4-1. Definitions.
27-4-2. Advance fees, licenses and miscellaneous charges.
27-4-3. Annual tax statement of insurers; exception.
27-4-4. Annual tax — Foreign insurers.
27-4-5. Same — Domestic insurers.
27-4-6. Same — Wet marine and transportation insurance.

Sec.
27-4-7. Penalty for violation of sections 27-4-3 through 27-4-6.
27-4-8. Annual license fee of life insurers organized to aid nonprofit educational and scientific institutions.
27-4-9. Taxation by counties not allowed.
27-4-10. Exemption from other fees, taxes or licenses.
27-4-11. Refund of taxes or licenses paid by mistake.

§ 27-4-1. Definitions.

For the purposes of this chapter, unless otherwise stated, the following terms shall have the meanings respectively ascribed to them by this section.

(1) INSURER. Such term shall include every insurer as defined in section 27-1-2 and shall include nonprofit corporations organized pursuant to the provisions of section 10-4-100 et seq. or any other insurance company or association or society charging a premium for contracts entered into by such companies, associations or societies; provided, however, that the exemptions granted in chapter 34 of this title are applicable hereto.

(2) FOREIGN INSURER. Such term shall include any insurance company organized under the laws of any country or of any state of the United States other than the state of Alabama and shall also include insurance companies organized under the laws of Alabama which maintain their principal office or chief place of business outside the state of Alabama.

(3) DOMESTIC INSURER. Such term shall include any insurance company organized under the laws of the state of Alabama which maintains its principal office and chief place of business in the state of Alabama.

(4) PREMIUMS. Such term shall include all amounts received in cash or otherwise on risks in this state as consideration for insurance contracts, less:

a. Insurance premiums returned;

b. Reinsurance premiums from insurance companies authorized to do business in Alabama and subject to the premium tax provided for in this chapter; and

c. Dividends paid, applied or left with the company to accumulate at interest.

With respect to title insurers, the term "premium" shall not include charges for abstracting, record searching, certificates as to the record title, escrow and closing services and other related services which may be offered or furnished or the costs and expenses of examinations of title.

(5) ANNUITY CONSIDERATIONS. All sums received as consideration for annuity contracts. (Acts 1935, No. 194, p. 256; Code 1940, T. 51, § 812; Acts

1955, 2nd Ex. Sess., No. 77, p. 193, § 1; Acts 1969, Ex. Sess., No. 28, p. 74, § 1; Acts 1971, No. 407, p. 707, § 77; Acts 1971, No. 2106, p. 3375, § 1.)

Cited in Metropolitan Life Ins. Co. v. Forrester, 437 So. 2d 535 (Ala. Civ. App. 1983); Metropolitan Life Ins. Co. v. Ward, 469 U.S. 810, 105 S. Ct. 1676, 84 L. Ed. 2d 751 (1985).

Collateral references. — 44 C.J.S., Insurance, § 49.

71 Am. Jur. 2d, State & Local Taxation, §§ 433, 434.

§ 27-4-2. Advance fees, licenses and miscellaneous charges.

(a) The commissioner shall collect in advance fees, licenses and miscellaneous charges as follows:

(1) Certificate of authority:

a. Initial application for original certificate of authority, including the filing with the commissioner of all documents incidental thereto .... $ 25.00

b. Issuance of original certificate of authority 20.00

c. Annual continuation or renewal fee 200.00

d. Reinstatement fee 50.00

(2) Charter documents, filing with the commissioner amendment to articles of incorporation or of association, or of other charter documents or to bylaws 5.00

(3) Solicitation permit, filing application and issuance 25.00

(4) Annual statement of insurer, except when filed as part of application for original certificate of authority, filing 10.00

(5) Agent's license (resident or nonresident agents):

a. Property, casualty and surety agents:

1. Filing application for license 10.00

2. Appointment of agent by insurer, property and casualty, each insurer 5.00

3. Annual continuation of appointment, property and casualty, each insurer 5.00

b. Life and disability insurance agents (resident agents):

1. Original license, each insurer 5.00

2. Annual continuation of license, each insurer 5.00

c. Life and disability nonresident agents:

1. Original license, each insurer 26.00

2. Annual continuation of license, each insurer 26.00

d. Each vending machine licensed under section 27-8-23, each year 5.00

(6) Broker's license (resident or nonresident brokers):

a. Filing application for license 10.00

b. Issuance of license 26.00

c. Annual continuation of license 26.00

(7) Solicitor's license:

a. Filing application for license 10.00

b. Issuance of license 5.00

c. Annual continuation of license .... $ 5.00
(8) General agent's license:
   a. Filing application for license 10.00
   b. Issuance of license, property and casualty, each insurer ... 5.00
   c. Annual continuation of license, each insurer 5.00
(9) Service representative's license:
   a. Filing application for license 10.00
   b. Issuance of license, property and casualty, each insurer ... 5.00
   c. Annual continuation of license, property and casualty, each
insurer 5.00
(10) Temporary license:
   a. As resident agent, each insurer, property, casualty and life 5.00
   b. As resident broker 26.00
   c. As solicitor 5.00
(11) Examination for agent, broker or solicitor license, resident
and nonresident, filing application for examination or reexamination, each classification of examination 5.00
(12) Surplus line broker license, each license year 26.00
(13) Adjusters:
   a. License 26.00
   b. Annual continuation of licenses 26.00
(14) Miscellaneous services:
   a. For copies of documents, records on file in insurance
department, per page .... .50
   b. For each certificate of the commissioner under his seal,
other than agent licenses 1.00
(15) The commissioner is hereby authorized and directed to collect a fee
of $5.00 when, in acting as agent or attorney for any insurance company,
fraternal benefit society, mutual aid association or credit union, he accepts
the service of legal process as provided by the laws of this state. He shall
refuse to receive and file or serve any process unless such process is
accompanied by the aforementioned fee, which shall be taxed as costs in the
action.

(b) The commissioner shall promptly pay all fees and licenses collected
under this section into the state treasury to the credit of the general fund.
(Acts 1935, No. 194, p. 256; Acts 1957, No. 598, p. 848, § 4; Acts 1971, No.
407, p. 707, § 76.)

§ 27-4-3. Annual tax statement of insurers; exception.

Each authorized insurer shall annually, on or before March 1, file with the commissioner a statement, in form as furnished or approved by him, setting forth the total amount of premiums and annuity considerations received by it for business done in this state during the preceding calendar year ending December 31, except as to wet marine and transportation insurance as defined in section 27-5-8. The statement shall be verified by the affidavit of an officer of the insurer having knowledge of the facts. (Acts 1935, No. 194, p. 256; Acts 1955, 2nd Ex. Sess., No. 77, p. 193, § 2; Acts 1971, No. 407, p. 707, § 78.)

Collateral references. — 44 C.J.S., Insurance, § 73.

§ 27-4-4. Annual tax — Foreign insurers.

(a) Every foreign insurer, except foreign life insurers, shall pay an annual premium tax amounting to four percent of the premiums received by such foreign insurer for business done in this state except as to wet marine and transportation insurance as defined in section 27-5-8, whether the same are actually received by said insurer in this state or elsewhere, during the year ending December 31, preceding. Every foreign life insurer shall pay an annual premium tax amounting to one percent of annuity considerations and an annual premium tax of three percent of any other premiums received by such foreign life insurer for business done in this state, whether the same are actually received by said insurer in this state or elsewhere, during the year ending December 31, preceding. The rate of tax on premiums shall be subject to reduction as provided in this section. Any foreign insurer beginning business in the state of Alabama after January 1, of any calendar year shall, on or before March 1, of the year succeeding the year of its entry, remit with its statement to the commissioner the taxes as required by this chapter on business written in Alabama for the preceding calendar year or fraction thereof in which it began business as a tax for such first year or fractional year; provided, that after any such insurer has been operating in this state for one complete calendar year, it shall compute its business done in this state during said year, and upon this basis, it shall pay its taxes for that and the succeeding year. Each succeeding year the tax shall be based and paid upon business done in Alabama for the preceding calendar year, it being the intent and meaning of this section that such insurers shall pay their premium taxes on March 1, for such current year; except, that the premium taxes for the first and second year shall be paid in the manner specifically provided in this section.

The premium taxes collected in this section shall be deposited in the state treasury and credited in accordance with the following tabulation:

(1) To the credit of the state general fund, from which the legislature may appropriate funds for old age assistance purposes:

    a. One hundred percent of premium tax on foreign life insurers;

b. Sixty-two and one-half percent of premium tax on all foreign property insurers; and

c. Seventy-five percent of premium tax on all other foreign insurers; and

(2) To the credit of the Alabama special educational trust fund:

a. Thirty-seven and one-half percent of premium tax on foreign property insurers; and

b. Twenty-five percent of premium tax on all other foreign insurers.

(b) If the annual statement or other report required to be made by such foreign insurer to the Alabama department of insurance, whose premiums are taxed under this chapter, for the preceding calendar year shows such insurer to have invested at the close of said year in Alabama investments, as defined in this section, the requisite percentages of its total admitted assets, the rate of premium tax hereby levied on premiums shall be that shown in the following schedules:

Percentage of Insurer's Admitted Assets Invested in Alabama Investments	Applicable Rate of Premium Tax for Foreign Life Insurers	Applicable Rate of Premium Tax for All Other Foreign Insurers
Less than 1%	3.0%	4.0%
1% and above but less than 2%	2.9%	3.9%
2% and above but less than 3%	2.8%	3.8%
3% and above but less than 4%	2.7%	3.7%
4% and above but less than 5%	2.6%	3.6%
5% and above but less than 6%	2.5%	3.5%
6% and above but less than 7%	2.4%	3.4%
7% and above but less than 8%	2.3%	3.3%
8% and above but less than 9%	2.2%	3.2%
9% and above but less than 10%	2.1%	3.1%
10% and above	2.0%	3.0%

(c) Alabama investments, as used in this section, shall mean any of the following investments:

(1) Real estate in this state;

(2) Bonds or interest-bearing warrants or other evidences of indebtedness of the state of Alabama or of any county, city, town, school district, state educational institution, municipality or other subdivision of the state, or of any duly authorized agency, board or authority of the state of Alabama or of any political subdivision thereof whether such agency, board or authority now exists or is hereafter created;

(3) Stocks, bonds or other evidences of indebtedness of any housing or redevelopment authority organized under the Housing Authorities Law or Redevelopment Law of the state of Alabama, as from time to time established and amended;

(4) Notes or bonds secured by mortgages or other liens on real estate or on leasehold interests in real estate in the state of Alabama;

(5) Stocks, bonds, debentures, notes or other evidences of indebtedness of any corporation organized under the laws of the state of Alabama;

(6) Notes, debentures or other evidences of any indebtedness of any business operated as a sole proprietorship, partnership or other legal entity having its principal office and place of business in the state of Alabama;

(7) Notes, bonds or other evidences of indebtedness secured by mortgage or other lien upon real estate situated in the state of Alabama and insured or guaranteed, in whole or in part, by the United States or any agency or instrumentality thereof, together with any bonds, debentures or other evidences of indebtedness of the United States or any agency or instrumentality thereof received and retained in whole or partial settlement of any such insurance or guaranty;

(8) Collateral loans to Alabama residents or to others where at least one half of the value of the collateral so pledged constitutes an Alabama investment as defined in this section;

(9) Cash deposits in regularly established national or state banks in this state on the basis of the average monthly deposits throughout the calendar year;

(10) Loans secured by policies on the lives of residents of the state of Alabama;

(11) Share or share accounts of building and loan associations organized under the laws of the state of Alabama or in the share or share accounts of federal savings and loan associations having their principal office in the state of Alabama;

(12) Stocks, bonds, notes, debentures or other evidences of indebtedness of any corporation organized under the laws of any other state of the United States, to the extent that the assets of such corporation located in the state of Alabama bear to the total assets of the corporation issuing such stocks, bonds, notes or other evidences of indebtedness;

(13) Stocks, bonds, notes or other evidences of indebtedness issued by railroad companies, public carriers or transportation companies, to the extent that its trackage or mileage in Alabama bears to the total trackage or mileage of such railroad, public carrier or other transportation company;

(14) That percentage of such insurer's investments in stocks, bonds, notes or other evidences of indebtedness of any telegraph, telephone, electric power company or other public utility to the extent that the revenue of any such company from Alabama bears to the total of such telegraph, telephone, electric power company or other public utility; and

(15) That percentage of the insurer's investments held as of December 31, in direct obligations of the United States of America as the total premiums received by the company for direct insurance of subjects located, resident or to be performed in Alabama relate to the total premiums received by the insurer.

(d) Any such tax so determined shall be subject to credit and deduction of the full amount of:

(1) All ad valorem taxes paid by the insurer for the tax year next preceding the filing of the return required by this section upon any real estate and the improvements thereon in the state of Alabama owned and at least 50 percent occupied by the insurer for the full period of such tax year;

(2) All license fees and taxes paid to any county in this state during the year preceding the filing of the return required by this section for the privilege of engaging in the business of insurance within said county;

(3) All franchise taxes paid by the insurer under the provisions of sections 40-14-40 or 40-14-41 for the tax year preceding the filing of the return required by this section; and

(4) All expense of examination of the insurer by the commissioner. (Acts 1935, No. 194, p. 256; Code 1940, T. 51, § 816; Acts 1955, 2nd Ex. Sess., No. 77, p. 193, § 3; Acts 1969, Ex. Sess., No. 28, p. 74, § 2; Acts 1971, No. 407, p. 707, § 79; Acts 1971, No. 2106, p. 3375, § 2.)

Domestic preference tax violative of equal protection clause. — Alabama's domestic preference tax statute (§§ 27-4-4 and 27-4-5) taxes out-of-state insurance companies at a higher rate than domestic insurance companies, violates the equal protection clause. Metropolitan Life Ins. Co. v. Ward, 469 U.S. 810, 105 S. Ct. 1676, 84 L. Ed. 2d 751 (1985).

Cited in Metropolitan Life Ins. Co. v. Ward, 447 So. 2d 142 (Ala. 1983); Alabama Farm Bureau Mut. Cas. Ins. Co. v. City of Hartselle, 460 So. 2d 1219 (Ala. 1984).

Collateral references. — 44 C.J.S., Insurance, § 80.

What constitutes doing business within state by foreign insurance corporation. 137 ALR 1128.

Foreign corporations: validity, under federal constitution, of state tax measured by income of foreign corporation. 67 ALR2d 1322.

Construction, application, and operation of state "retaliatory" statutes imposing special taxes or fees on foreign insurers doing business within the state. 30 ALR4th 873.

§ 27-4-5. Same — Domestic insurers.

(a) Every domestic life insurer shall pay to the commissioner on or before March 1, 1970, and annually thereafter, a premium tax equal to one percent of the premiums and annuity considerations received by such insurer for business done in this state during the preceding calendar year ending December 31, whether the same are actually received by said insurer in this state or elsewhere. Every other domestic insurer and every nonprofit corporation organized pursuant to the provisions of section 10-4-100 et seq. shall pay to the commissioner on or before March 1, 1970, and annually thereafter, a premium tax equal to one percent of the premiums received by such insurer for business done in this state during the preceding calendar year ending December 31, whether the same are actually received by said company in this state or elsewhere. Any domestic insurer beginning business after January 1, of any calendar year, on or before March 1, of the year following the year beginning business, shall remit with its statement to the commissioner the taxes as required by this section on business written in Alabama for the preceding calendar year or fraction thereof in which it began business as a tax for such first year or fractional year; provided, that after any domestic insurance company has been operating in this state for one complete calendar year, it shall compute its business done in this state during said year, and upon this basis, it shall pay its taxes for that and the succeeding year. Each succeeding year the tax shall be based and paid on business done in Alabama for the preceding calendar year as provided in this section, it being the meaning and intent of this section that domestic insurers shall pay their premium taxes on March 1, for such current year; except, that premium taxes for the first and second year shall be paid in the manner specifically provided in this section.

(b) Any such tax so determined shall be subject to credit and deduction of the full amount of:

(1) All ad valorem taxes paid by the insurer for the tax year preceding the filing of the return required by this section upon any building and real estate in the state of Alabama owned and occupied, in whole or in part, by the insurer for the full period of such tax year as its principal office in the state of Alabama;

(2) All ad valorem taxes paid by the insurer for the tax year preceding the filing of the return required by this section upon all other real estate and improvements thereon in this state owned and at least 50 percent occupied by the insurer for the full period of such tax year;

(3) All license fees and taxes paid to any county in this state during the year preceding the filing of the return required by this section for the privilege of engaging in the business of insurance within said county;

(4) All expenses of examination of the insurer by the commissioner;

(5) All license or privilege taxes on lists of securities paid by the insurer under the provisions of section 40-24-8 during the tax year preceding the filing of the return required by this section; and

(6) All franchise taxes paid by the insurer under the provisions of section 40-14-40 for the tax year preceding the filing of the return required by this section.

(c) The premium taxes collected under this section shall be deposited in the state treasury and credited as follows:

(1) To the credit of the state general fund:

a. Fifty percent of premium tax on domestic life insurers;

b. No part of premium tax on nonprofit corporations organized pursuant to the provisions of section 10-4-100 et seq.; and

c. Twenty-five percent of premium tax on all other domestic insurers; and

(2) To the credit of the Alabama special educational trust fund:

a. Fifty percent of premium tax on domestic life insurers;

b. One hundred percent of premium tax on nonprofit corporations organized pursuant to the provisions of section 10-4-100 et seq.; and

c. Seventy-five percent of premium tax on all other domestic insurers.

(d) Every domestic insurer, anything in this chapter to the contrary notwithstanding, shall be exempt from and not required to pay any premium tax for or on account of any premiums or annuity considerations for hospital, medical, surgical or other health care benefits supplementary to Medicare and

Medicaid received by it for or on account of business done in this state, whether the same are actually received in this state or elsewhere. (Acts 1935, No. 194, p. 256; Code 1940, T. 51, § 819; Acts 1945, No. 156, p. 196; Acts 1955, 2nd Ex. Sess., No. 77, p. 193, § 4; Acts 1969, Ex. Sess., No. 28, p. 74, §§ 3, 3½; Acts 1971, No. 407, p. 707, § 80; Acts 1971, No. 2106, p. 3375, §§ 3, 3½.)

Domestic preference tax violative of equal protection clause. — Alabama's domestic preference tax statute (§§ 27-4-4 and 27-4-5) taxes out-of-state insurance companies at a higher rate than domestic insurance companies, violates the equal protection clause. Metropolitan Life Ins. Co. v. Ward, 469 U.S. 810, 105 S. Ct. 1676, 84 L. Ed. 2d 751 (1985).

Tax on renewal premiums. — Since the state does not base its tax on premiums from policies issued during the preceding year, but on all premiums received, renewal premiums are included in the computation of the tax. Alabama Farm Bureau Mut. Cas. Ins. Co. v. City of Hartselle, 460 So. 2d 1219 (Ala. 1984).

§ 27-4-6. Same — Wet marine and transportation insurance.

(a) On or before March 1 of each year, each insurer shall file with the commissioner, on forms prescribed and furnished by him, a report of its gross underwriting profit on wet marine and transportation insurance, as defined in section 27-5-9, written in this state during the calendar year next preceding, and shall at the same time pay to the commissioner a tax of three quarters of one percent of such gross underwriting profit.

(b) Such gross underwriting profit shall be ascertained by deducting from the net premiums (i.e. gross premiums less all return premiums and premiums for reinsurance) on such wet marine and transportation insurance contracts the net losses paid (i.e. gross losses paid less salvage and recoveries on reinsurance ceded) during such calendar year under such contracts. In the case of insurers issuing participating contracts, such gross underwriting profit shall not include for computation of the tax prescribed by this subsection the amounts refunded or paid as participation dividends by such insurers to the holders of such contracts.

(c) The commissioner shall deposit all taxes collected under this section in the state treasury to the credit of the state general fund. (Acts 1971, No. 407, p. 707, § 81.)

Cited in Metropolitan Life Ins. Co. v. Ward, 469 U.S. 810, 105 S. Ct. 1676, 84 L. Ed. 2d 751 (1985).

§ 27-4-7. Penalty for violation of sections 27-4-3 through 27-4-6.

Every insurer failing to comply with the requirements of sections 27-4-3 through 27-4-6 shall be subject to a penalty of not less than $100.00 nor exceeding $1,000.00, recoverable in an action brought by the attorney general for the commissioner. Upon any such violation, the commissioner may, in his discretion, suspend or revoke the insurer's certificate of authority. Penalties recovered under this section shall be paid into the state treasury to the credit of the general fund. (Acts 1955, 2nd Ex. Sess., No. 77, p. 193, § 5; Acts 1971, No. 407, p. 707, § 82.)

§ 27-4-8. Annual license fee of life insurers organized to aid nonprofit educational and scientific institutions.

Annuity considerations and premiums received by a life insurer licensed to transact business in this state and which is organized and operated without profit to any private shareholder or individual and exclusively for the purpose of aiding nonprofit education and scientific institutions by issuing insurance or annuity contracts only for the benefit of such institutions and individuals employed in the services thereof at the time such policy or contract is issued shall not be subject to the payment of a privilege tax based upon premiums or annuity considerations under the provisions of this chapter or any other law of this state. In lieu of such privilege tax upon premiums and annuity considerations, such nonprofit company shall pay an annual license fee of $5,000.00 to the commissioner for the privilege of transacting an insurance business in this state. The initial payment of such shall be due on the date that such insurer is licensed to do business in the state of Alabama and upon March 1, of each year succeeding that of admission, so long as such insurer shall be licensed to transact an insurance business in this state. (Acts 1971, No. 407, p. 707, § 83.)

§ 27-4-9. Taxation by counties not allowed.

No license or privilege tax shall be charged any insurer by or on behalf of any county. (Acts 1935, No. 194, p. 256; Code 1940, T. 51, § 826; Acts 1971, No. 407, p. 707, § 84.)

Cross references. — As to licensing of insurance companies by municipalities, see §§ 11-51-120 through 11-51-123.

§ 27-4-10. Exemption from other fees, taxes or licenses.

Nothing in this title shall be construed to repeal any existing laws or statutes of Alabama which exempt or exclude insurers from the payment of fees, taxes or licenses. Without limiting the generality of the preceding sentence, insurers upon which the statutes of Alabama impose a tax upon their premium income shall continue to be exempt from income taxes imposed by the state of Alabama under the provisions of chapter 18 of Title 40 of this Code or under any other similar law; and the shares of domestic insurers shall continue to be exempt from ad valorem tax as provided by section 40-14-70. (Acts 1971, No. 407, p. 707, § 85.)

§ 27-4-11. Refund of taxes or licenses paid by mistake.

(a) Where any taxpayer in the payment of taxes or payments of licenses which are paid directly to the commissioner and where by a mistake of fact or law has paid an amount in excess of the amount due or has made an erroneous payment, the comptroller is authorized to draw his warrant on the treasurer in favor of such taxpayer and the treasurer is authorized to pay such warrant for the amount of such overpayment or erroneous payment.

(b) Before any refund under this section can be made the taxpayer, his heirs, successors or assigns shall file, in duplicate, a petition directed to the commissioner, setting up the fact relied on to procure the refunding of the money erroneously paid. Such application must be made within three years from the date of such payment.

(c) The commissioner shall examine said petition and the records of the department of insurance, and if the facts set forth in the petition are such as to entitle the petitioner to the refunding of the money as requested and the commissioner, upon the evidence adduced is satisfied that the petitioner is entitled to the refund as requested, he shall so certify to the comptroller, stating the amount to be refunded by the state, the particular fund on which such warrant shall be drawn, including both the special revolving fund and the general fund, and he shall forward to the comptroller a copy of the petition with the certificate attached. If the comptroller shall be satisfied that the petition is in form required by law, he shall draw his warrant on the treasurer as provided in this section for the amount certified to him by the commissioner. (Acts 1971, No. 407, p. 707, § 86.)

Collateral references. — Interest on tax refund or credit in absence of specific controlling statute. 88 ALR2d 823.

CHAPTER 5.

KINDS OF INSURANCE; LIMITS OF RISK; REINSURANCE.

Sec.
27-5-1. Definitions not mutually exclusive; exceptions to applicability of chapter.
27-5-2. "Life insurance" defined.
27-5-3. "Annuity" defined.
27-5-4. "Disability insurance" defined.
27-5-5. "Property insurance" defined.
27-5-6. "Casualty insurance" defined.
27-5-7. "Surety insurance" defined.

Sec.
27-5-8. "Marine insurance" defined.
27-5-9. "Wet marine and transportation insurance" defined.
27-5-10. "Title insurance" defined.
27-5-11. Limits of risk.
27-5-12. Reinsurance.
27-5-13. Denial of health or disability insurance coverage upon diagnosis of sickle-cell anemia prohibited.

Collateral references. — Insurer's tort liability for consequential or punitive damages for wrongful failure or refusal to defend insured. 20 ALR4th 23.

Apportionment of payments of no-fault (personal injury protection) benefits between insurers providing coverage to same insured under policies covering different vehicles. 34 ALR4th 374.

§ 27-5-1. Definitions not mutually exclusive; exceptions to applicability of chapter.

(a) It is intended that certain insurance coverages may come within the definitions of two or more kinds of insurance as defined in this chapter, and the inclusion of such coverage within one definition shall not exclude it as to any other kind of insurance within the definition of which such coverage is likewise reasonably includable.

(b) The definitions contained in this chapter shall not be applicable to the construction of sections 11-51-120 and 11-51-121. (Acts 1971, No. 407, p. 707, § 87.)

Cited in State Farm Mut. Auto. Ins. Co. v. Board of Trustees of Firemen's Pension & Relief Fund, 291 Ala. 250, 279 So. 2d 512 (1973).

§ 27-5-2. "Life insurance" defined.

"Life insurance" is insurance on human lives. The transaction of life insurance includes also the granting of endowment benefits, additional benefits in event of death or dismemberment by accident or accidental means, additional benefits in event of the insured's disability, burial insurance and optional modes of settlement of proceeds of life insurance. Life insurance does not include workmen's compensation coverages. (Acts 1971, No. 407, p. 707, § 88.)

Collateral references. — 44 C.J.S., Insurance, § 25.

Death during or allegedly resulting from surgery as within the accidental death benefit provisions of health, accident, or life insurance policies. 91 ALR3d 1042.

§ 27-5-3. "Annuity" defined.

For the purpose of this title, an "annuity" is a contract under which obligations are assumed with respect to periodic payments for a specific term, or terms, or where the making or continuance of all or of some of such payments or the amount of any such payment is dependent upon the continuance of human life, except payments made pursuant to optional modes of settlement under the authority of section 27-5-2. Such a contract, which includes extra benefits of the kinds set forth in sections 27-5-2 and 27-5-3, shall, nevertheless, be deemed to be an annuity if such extra benefits constitute a subsidiary or incidental part of the entire contract. (Acts 1971, No. 407, p. 707, § 88.1.)

§ 27-5-4. "Disability insurance" defined.

"Disability insurance" is insurance of human beings against bodily injury, disablement or death by accident or accidental means, or the expense thereof, or against disablement or expense resulting from sickness and every insurance appertaining thereto. Disability insurance does not include workmen's compensation coverages. (Acts 1971, No. 407, p. 707, § 89.)

Sickness has been defined to embrace injury. Globe Life Ins. Co. v. Howard, 41 Ala. App. 621, 147 So. 2d 853 (1962) (decided under former Code 1940, T. 28, § 418).

Cited in Moses v. American Home Assurance Co., 376 So. 2d 656 (Ala. 1979).

Collateral references. — 44 C.J.S., Insurance, § 12.

What conditions constitute "disease" within terms of life, accident, disability or hospitalization insurance policy. 61 ALR3d 822.

Death during or allegedly resulting from surgery as within the accidental death benefit provisions of health, accident, or life insurance policies. 91 ALR3d 1042.

What constitutes total disability within coverage of disability insurance policy issued to lawyer. 6 ALR4th 422.

§ 27-5-5. "Property insurance" defined.

"Property insurance" is insurance on real or personal property of every kind and of every interest therein, whether on land, water or in the air, against loss or damage from any and every hazard or cause and against loss consequential upon such loss or damage other than noncontractual legal liability for any such loss or damage. (Acts 1971, No. 407, p. 707, § 90.)

§ 27-5-6. "Casualty insurance" defined.

(a) "Casualty insurance" includes:

(1) VEHICLE INSURANCE. — Insurance against loss of, or damage to, any land vehicle or aircraft, or any draft or riding animal or to property while contained therein or thereon or being loaded or unloaded therein or therefrom from any hazard or cause and against any loss, liability or expense resulting from, or incidental to, ownership, maintenance or use of any such vehicle, aircraft or animal, together with insurance against accidental death or accidental injury to individuals, including the named

insured, while in, entering, alighting from, adjusting, repairing, cranking or caused by being struck by a vehicle, aircraft or draft or riding animal, if such insurance is issued as an incidental part of insurance on the vehicle, aircraft or draft or riding animal;

(2) LIABILITY INSURANCE. — Insurance against legal liability for the death, injury or disability of any human being or for damage to property, and provision of medical, hospital, surgical and disability benefits to injured persons and funeral and death benefits to dependents, beneficiaries or personal representatives of persons killed, irrespective of legal liability of the insured, when issued as an incidental coverage with, or supplemental to, liability insurance;

(3) WORKMEN'S COMPENSATION AND EMPLOYER'S LIABILITY. — Insurance of the obligations accepted by, imposed upon or assumed by employers under law for death, disablement or injury of employees;

(4) BURGLARY AND THEFT. — Insurance against loss or damage by burglary, theft, larceny, robbery, forgery, fraud, vandalism, malicious mischief, confiscation, or wrongful conversion, disposal or concealment or from any attempt at any of the foregoing, including supplemental coverage for medical, hospital, surgical and funeral expense incurred by the named insured or any other person as a result of bodily injury during the commission of a burglary, robbery or theft by another; also, insurance against loss of or damage to moneys, coins, bullion, securities, notes, drafts, acceptances or any other valuable papers and documents resulting from any cause;

(5) PERSONAL PROPERTY FLOATER. — Insurance upon personal effects against loss or damage from any cause under a personal property floater;

(6) GLASS. — Insurance against loss or damage to glass, including its lettering, ornamentation and fittings;

(7) BOILER AND MACHINERY. — Insurance against any liability and loss, or damage to, property or interest resulting from accidents to, or explosions of, boilers, pipes, pressure containers, machinery or apparatus and to make inspection of and issue certificates of inspection upon boilers, machinery and apparatus of any kind, whether or not insured;

(8) LEAKAGE AND FIRE EXTINGUISHING EQUIPMENT. — Insurance against loss or damage to any property or interest caused by the breakage or leakage of sprinklers, hoses, pumps and other fire-extinguishing equipment or apparatus, water pipes or containers or by water entering through leaks or openings in buildings and insurance against loss or damage to such sprinklers, hoses, pumps and other fire-extinguishing equipment or apparatus;

(9) CREDIT. — Insurance against loss or damage resulting from failure of debtors to pay their obligations to the insured;

(10) MALPRACTICE. — Insurance against legal liability of the insured and against loss, damage or expense incidental to a claim of such liability and including medical, hospital, surgical and funeral benefits to injured persons, irrespective of legal liability of the insured, arising out of the

death, injury or disablement of any person or arising out of damage to the economic interest of any person as the result of negligence in rendering expert, fiduciary or professional service;

(11) LIVESTOCK. — Insurance against loss or damage to livestock and services of a veterinarian for such animals;

(12) ELEVATORS. — Insurance against loss of, or damage to, any property of the insured resulting from the ownership, maintenance or use of elevators, except loss or damage by fire, and to make inspections of and issue certificates of inspection upon elevators;

(13) ENTERTAINMENTS. — Insurance indemnifying the producer of any motion picture, television, radio, theatrical, sport, spectacle, entertainment or similar production, event or exhibition against loss from interruption, postponement or cancellation thereof due to death, accidental injury or sickness of performers, participants, directors or other principals; and

(14) MISCELLANEOUS. — Insurance against any other kind of loss, damage or liability properly, a subject of insurance and not within any other kind of insurance as defined in this chapter, if such insurance is not disapproved by the commissioner as being contrary to law or public policy.

(b) Provision of medical, hospital, surgical and funeral benefits and of coverage against accidental death or injury, as incidental to and part of other insurance as stated under subdivisions (a) (1), (a) (2), (a) (4) and (a) (10) of this section shall, for all purposes, be deemed to be the same kind of insurance to which it is so incidental and shall not be subject to provisions of this title applicable to life or disability insurances. (Acts 1971, No. 407, p. 707, § 91.)

Collateral references. — 44 C.J.S., Insurance, § 6.

Theft coverage of losses sustained through payment of extortion demands at a place other than insured premises. 85 ALR3d 1103.

Rights or liabilities of a debtor for loss upon failure of creditor to secure credit insurance. 88 ALR3d 794.

Exchange of labor by farmers as creating an employment relationship for liability insurance purposes. 89 ALR3d 834.

Apportionment of payments of no-fault (personal injury protection) benefits between insurers providing coverage to same insured under policies covering different vehicles. 34 ALR4th 374.

Automobile fire, theft, and collision insurance: insurable interest in stolen motor vehicle. 38 ALR4th 538.

§ 27-5-7. "Surety insurance" defined.

"Surety insurance" includes:

(1) Fidelity insurance, which is insurance guaranteeing the fidelity of persons holding positions of public or private trust;

(2) Insurance guaranteeing the performance of contracts, other than insurance policies, and guaranteeing and executing bonds, undertakings and contracts of suretyship; and

(3) Insurance indemnifying banks, bankers, brokers, financial or moneyed corporations or associations against loss, resulting from any cause, of bills of exchange, notes, bonds, securities, evidences of debt, deeds,

mortgages, warehouse receipts or other valuable papers, documents, money, precious metals and articles made therefrom, jewelry, watches, necklaces, bracelets, gems, precious and semiprecious stones, including any loss while the same are being transported in armored motor vehicles or by messenger, but not including any other risks of transportation or navigation; also, insurance against loss or damage to such an insured's premises or to his furnishings, fixtures, equipment, safes and vaults therein caused by burglary, robbery, theft, vandalism or malicious mischief, or any attempt thereat. (Acts 1971, No. 407, p. 707, § 92.)

Collateral references. — 44 C.J.S., Insurance, § 13.

§ 27-5-8. "Marine insurance" defined.

"Marine insurance" includes:

(1) Insurance against any and all kinds of loss or damage to:

a. Vessels, craft, aircraft, cars, automobiles and vehicles of every kind, as well as all goods, freights, cargoes, merchandise, effects, disbursements, profits, moneys, bullion, precious stones, securities, choses in action, evidence of debt, valuable papers, bottomry and respondentia interests and all other kinds of property and interests therein in respect to, appertaining to or in connection with any and all risks or perils of navigation, transit or transportation, including war risks, on or under any seas or other waters, on land or in the air, or while being assembled, packed, crated, baled, compressed or similarly prepared for shipment or while awaiting the same or during any delays, storage, transshipment or reshipment incident thereto, including marine builder's risks and all personal property floater risks;

b. Person or to property in connection with, or appertaining to, a marine, inland marine, transit or transportation insurance, including liability for loss of, or damage to, either, arising out of or in connection with the construction, repair, operation, maintenance or use of the subject matter of such insurance, but not including life insurance or surety bonds nor insurance against loss by reason of bodily injury to the person arising out of the ownership, maintenance or use of automobiles;

c. Precious stones, jewels, jewelry, gold, silver and other precious metals, whether used in business or trade or otherwise and whether the same be in course of transportation or otherwise; and

d. Bridges, tunnels and other instrumentalities of transportation and communication, excluding buildings, their furniture and furnishings, fixed contents and supplies held in storage, unless fire, tornado, sprinkler leakage, hail, explosion, earthquake, riot and/or civil commotion are the only hazards to be covered; piers, wharves, docks and slips, excluding the risks of fire, tornado, sprinkler leakage, hail, explosion, earthquake, riot and/or civil commotion; and other aids to navigation and transportation, including dry docks and marine railways, against all risks.

(2) "Marine protection and indemnity insurance," meaning insurance against, or against legal liability of the insured for, loss, damage or expense arising out of, or incident to, the ownership, operation, chartering, maintenance, use, repair or construction of any vessel, craft or instrumentality in use in ocean or inland waterways, including liability of the insured for personal injury, illness or death or for loss of, or damage to, the property of another person. (Acts 1971, No. 407, p. 707, § 93.)

Collateral references. — 44 C.J.S., Insurance, §§ 30-37.

§ 27-5-9. "Wet marine and transportation insurance" defined.

For the purposes of this title, "wet marine and transportation insurance" is that part of marine insurance which includes only:

(1) Insurance upon vessels, crafts, hulls and of interests therein or with relation thereto;

(2) Insurance of marine builder's risks, marine war risks and contracts of marine protection and indemnity insurance;

(3) Insurance of freights and disbursements pertaining to a subject of insurance coming within this section; and

(4) Insurance of personal property and interests therein in course of exportation from, or importation into, any country and in course of transportation coastwise or on inland waters, including transportation by land, water or air from point of origin to final destination, in respect to, appertaining to or in connection with any and all risks or perils of navigation, transit or transportation, and while being prepared for and while awaiting shipment and during any delays, storage, transshipment or reshipment incident thereto. (Acts 1971, No. 407, p. 707, § 93.)

Collateral references. — 44 C.J.S., Insurance, §§ 30-37.

§ 27-5-10. "Title insurance" defined.

"Title insurance" is insurance of owners of property, or others having an interest therein or liens or encumbrances thereon against loss by encumbrance, or defective titles, or invalidity or adverse claim to title. (Acts 1971, No. 407, p. 707, § 94.)

Cited in Childs v. Mississippi Valley Title Ins. Co., 359 So. 2d 1146 (Ala. 1978).

Collateral references. — 44 C.J.S., Insurance, § 46.

Construction of the words, "Created, suffered, assumed, or agreed to" as they are used in a title insurance policy clause. 87 ALR3d 515.

§ 27-5-11. Limits of risk.

(a) No insurer shall retain any risk on any one subject of insurance, whether located or to be performed in this state or elsewhere, in an amount exceeding 10 percent of its surplus to policyholders.

(b) A "subject of insurance," for the purposes of this section, as to insurance against fire and hazards other than windstorm, earthquake and other catastrophic hazards, includes all properties insured by the same insurer which are customarily considered by underwriters to be subject to loss or damage from the same fire or the same occurrence of such other hazard insured against.

(c) Reinsurance ceded as authorized by section 27-5-12 shall be deducted in determining risk retained. As to surety risks, deduction shall also be made of the amount assumed by any established incorporated cosurety and the value of any security deposited, pledged or held subject to the surety's consent and for the surety's protection.

(d) As to alien insurers, this section shall relate only to risks and surplus to policyholders of the insurer's United States branch.

(e) "Surplus to policyholders," for the purposes of this section, in addition to the insurer's capital and surplus, shall be deemed to include any voluntary reserves which are not required pursuant to law and shall be determined from the last sworn statement of the insurer on file with the commissioner or by the last report of examination of the insurer, whichever is the more recent at time of assumption of risk.

(f) This section shall not apply to life or disability insurance, title insurance, insurance of wet marine and transportation risks, workmen's compensation insurance, employers' liability coverages nor to any policy or type of coverage as to which the maximum possible loss to the insurer is not readily ascertainable on issuance of the policy.

(g) Limits of risk as to newly formed domestic mutual insurers shall be as provided in section 27-27-15. (Acts 1971, No. 407, p. 707, § 95.)

Insurers have the right to limit their liability and write policies with narrow coverage. Thus, although the presence of an ambiguity in an insurance contract requires construction of the policy in a manner most favorable to the insured, where there is no ambiguity in its terms, the supreme court must enforce the contract as written and cannot defeat express provisions in the policy, including exclusions, by making a new contract for the parties. Turner v. United States Fid. & Guar. Co., 440 So. 2d 1026 (Ala. 1983).

Collateral references. — Whether liability insurance coverage extends to losses incurred for violations of government antipollution laws. 88 ALR3d 182.

Apportionment of payments of no-fault (personal injury protection) benefits between insurers providing coverage to same insured under policies covering different vehicles. 34 ALR4th 374.

§ 27-5-12. Reinsurance.

(a) An insurer authorized under this title may accept reinsurance only of such risks and retain risk thereon within such limits as it is otherwise authorized to insure.

(b) An insurer authorized under this title may reinsure all, or any part, of any particular risk with any solvent insurer which has been authorized to transact insurance in one or more states for not less than three years and has:

(1) Unimpaired paid-in capital stock, if a stock insurer, or unimpaired surplus, if a mutual or reciprocal insurer, in amount not less than that required under this title of a foreign insurer transacting like kinds of insurance; or

(2) A trust fund, if a group of unincorporated alien insurers, maintained in a state of the United States for the benefit of American policyholders in a sum at least equal to $50,000,000.00.

(c) No credit shall be allowed, as an asset or as a deduction from liability to any ceding insurer for reinsurance placed with a reinsurer not qualified under subsection (b) of this section, nor unless the reinsurance is payable by the assuming insurer on the basis of the liability of the ceding insurer under the contracts reinsured without diminution because of the insolvency of the ceding insurer.

(d) Upon request of the commissioner, an insurer shall promptly inform the commissioner in writing of the cancellation or any other material change of any of its reinsurance treaties or arrangements.

(e) This section shall not apply to wet marine and transportation insurance. (Acts 1971, No. 407, p. 707, § 96.)

Collateral references. — 46 C.J.S., Insurance, §§ 1220-1242.

44 Am. Jur. 2d, Insurance, § 1857.

Right of reinsurer to question the insurable interest or eligibility of beneficiary. 18 ALR 1163.

Who may enforce liability of reinsurer. 35 ALR 1348, 103 ALR 1485.

Reinsurance by foreign insurance corporation as doing business within state. 137 ALR 1141.

§ 27-5-13. Denial of health or disability insurance coverage upon diagnosis of sickle-cell anemia prohibited.

Notwithstanding any other provision of law, any insurance company doing business within the state which offers health or disability insurance, is hereby prohibited from denying coverage to applicants because the applicant has been diagnosed as having sickle-cell anemia, and is hereby required to pay any valid claim made involving treatment or care of sickle-cell anemia in accordance with other policy provisions. (Acts 1982, No. 82-542, p. 893, § 1.)

CHAPTER 6.

ADMINISTRATION OF DEPOSITS.

Sec.
27-6-1. Deposits of insurers — Authorized deposits.
27-6-2. Same — Purposes for which held.
27-6-3. Same — Composition.
27-6-4. Same — State treasurer as custodian.
27-6-5. Same — Record of securities and assets.
27-6-6. Securities and assets — Assignment and reassignment, etc.; appraisal or valuation.
27-6-7. Same — Power of attorney to sell, etc.
27-6-8. Same — Authority to sell; exception.

Sec.
27-6-9. Power of attorney — Safekeeping; return.
27-6-10. Same — New power of attorney.
27-6-11. Excess deposits.
27-6-12. Rights of solvent insurers.
27-6-13. Sale of surety insurers' special deposit to pay outstanding judgment.
27-6-14. Curing of deficiency in market value of deposit.
27-6-15. Release of deposit — Generally.
27-6-16. Same — Filing of statement; authorization of release.

§ 27-6-1. Deposits of insurers — Authorized deposits.

The following deposits of insurers, when made through the commissioner, shall be accepted and held and shall be subject to the provisions of this chapter:

(1) Deposits required under this title for authority to transact insurance in this state;

(2) Deposits of domestic insurers when made pursuant to the laws of other states, provinces and countries as requirement for authority to transact insurance in such state, province or country;

(3) Deposits of reserves made by domestic life insurers under laws heretofore in force; and

(4) Deposits in such additional amounts as are permitted to be made under section 27-6-11. (Acts 1971, No. 407, p. 707, § 97.)

§ 27-6-2. Same — Purposes for which held.

Such deposits shall be held for purposes as follows:

(1) Deposits made in this state under sections 27-3-11, 27-3-12 and 27-3-14 of this title shall be held for the purposes stated in the respective sections;

(2) A deposit made in this state by a domestic insurer transacting insurance in another state, province or country and as required by the laws of such state, province or country shall be held for the protection of the insurer's policyholders or policyholders and creditors;

(3) Deposits of reserves made by domestic life insurers under laws heretofore in force shall be held for the purpose or purposes specified in such laws or in the policies or contracts by which such deposit was required or declared; and

(4) Deposits required pursuant to the retaliatory provision, section 27-3-29, shall be held for such purposes as are required by such laws and as specified by the commissioner's order by which the deposit is required. (Acts 1971, No. 407, p. 707, § 98.)

Collateral references. — 43 Am. Jur. 2d,
Insurance, §§ 63, 139.

§ 27-6-3. Same — Composition.

(a) All such deposits required under sections 27-3-11, 27-3-12 and 27-3-14 for authority to transact insurance in this state shall consist of certified checks, or certificates of deposit or any combination of securities, the market value of which is readily ascertainable, and, if negotiable by delivery or assignment, of the kinds described below:

(1) United States government obligations;

(2) State, county, municipal and school obligations;

(3) Public improvement obligations;

(4) Housing authority obligations;

(5) Obligations, stock of certain federal agencies;

(6) Canadian governmental obligations;

(7) International banks;

(8) Corporate obligations;

(9) Equipment trust obligations; and

(10) Railroad leased lines, terminal obligations.

(b) All such deposits required of a domestic insurer pursuant to the laws of another state, province or country shall be comprised of securities, if negotiable by delivery or assignment, of the kind, or kinds, required or permitted by the laws of such state, province or country, except common stocks, mortgages of any kind and real estate.

(c) Deposits of the reserves of a domestic life insurer under laws heretofore in force shall consist of securities, if negotiable by delivery or assignment, eligible for investment of the insurer's reserves.

(d) Deposits of foreign insurers made in this state under the retaliatory provision, section 27-3-29, shall consist of such securities or assets as are required by the commissioner pursuant to such provision.

(e) Any insurance company, with respect to its general account or separate accounts, is authorized to deposit or arrange for the deposit of securities which it may own in a clearing corporation, as defined in section 7-8-102(3), or in a federal reserve bank under book-entry system. When such securities are so deposited, certificates representing securities of the same class of the same issuer may be merged and held in bulk in the name of the nominee of such clearing corporation with any other securities deposited in such clearing corporation by any person, regardless of the ownership of such securities, and securities of small denominations may be merged into one or more certificates of larger denominations. Title to such securities may be transferred by bookkeeping entry on the books of such clearing corporation or federal reserve bank without physical delivery of certificates representing such securities. Any company making deposits by means of such securities shall provide to the commissioner evidence customarily issued by federal reserve banks and clearing corporations establishing that the securities are actually recorded in a book-entry account or actually held in safekeeping by a clearing corporation. Securities deposited in a clearing corporation or in a book-entry account and used to meet the deposit requirements under the insurance laws of this state shall be under the control of the commissioner and shall not be withdrawn by the insurance company without the approval of the commissioner. (Acts 1971, No. 407, p. 707, § 99; Acts 1981, No. 81-541, p. 904, § 2.)

§ 27-6-4. Same — State treasurer as custodian.

(a) Deposits made in this state under sections 27-3-11, 27-3-12 and 27-3-14, together with deposit of reserves of domestic life insurers under registered policies heretofore issued, shall be made through the commissioner with the treasurer of the state of Alabama.

(b) The state treasurer, in his official capacity, shall take receipt for and hold deposits made under this title as provided in subsection (a) of this section, subject to the provisions of this chapter.

(c) The state treasurer shall hold all such deposits in safekeeping in the vaults located in his offices or, if space in such vaults is not reasonably adequate and safe for all securities and property otherwise to be contained therein, the treasurer may keep such securities in safe deposit boxes rented by him for the purpose and under his control in established safe deposit institutions located in the city of Montgomery, Alabama.

(d) The treasurer shall be the custodian only of such deposits and shall have no powers or responsibility as to the character or amount thereof. He shall accept, permit substitutions and release securities or assets so deposited only upon written authorization of the commissioner and the insurer or upon order of the court and shall have no obligation to determine in any instance whether such authorization or order, if genuine, is otherwise lawful or proper.

(e) For all securities and assets deposited as provided in this section, the faith and credit of the state of Alabama is pledged that the same will be returned to the parties entitled to receive them or disposed of as provided in this chapter. (Code 1940, T. 28, § 73; Acts 1971, No. 407, p. 707, § 100.)

§ 27-6-5. Same — Record of securities and assets.

The commissioner shall keep a record of the securities and assets comprising each deposit, showing by item the amount and market value and of all his transactions relative thereto. (Acts 1971, No. 407, p. 707, § 101.)

§ 27-6-6. Securities and assets — Assignment and reassignment, etc.; appraisal or valuation.

(a) All securities not negotiable by delivery and deposited by an insurer shall be duly assigned to the commissioner and his successors in office. All other assets so deposited shall be duly transferred or conveyed to the commissioner. Upon release of any such security or asset to the insurer, the commissioner shall reassign, or transfer or reconvey the same to the insurer.

(b) The commissioner may, in his discretion, prior to acceptance for deposit of any security or asset or at any time thereafter while so deposited, have the same appraised or valued by competent appraisers. The reasonable costs of any such appraisal or valuation shall be borne by the insurer. (Acts 1971, No. 407, p. 707, § 102.)

§ 27-6-7. Same — Power of attorney to sell, etc.

In lieu of the assignment, transfer or conveyance of securities and assets to the commissioner as provided for in subsection (a) of section 27-6-6 and at all events in connection with any deposit heretofore or hereafter made through the commissioner, the commissioner may require or permit the depositing insurer to deliver to him a power of attorney, executed by the lawful owner of such securities or assets, authorizing the commissioner to transfer, sell or exchange the same for the purposes of the law under which the same are deposited or held on deposit. The power of attorney shall specifically describe each of the securities and assets covered thereby and shall not be a general power of attorney covering all securities and assets on deposit or thereafter deposited. (Acts 1953, No. 727, p. 981, § 1; Acts 1971, No. 407, p. 707, § 103.)

§ 27-6-8. Same — Authority to sell; exception.

The commissioner shall exercise the power granted by the power of attorney provided for in section 27-6-7 or otherwise sell any security or asset under any assignment, transfer or conveyance pursuant to section 27-6-6, only pursuant to, and in accordance with, an order of a court of competent jurisdiction in a proper proceeding or action to which the insurer owning such securities or assets is a party. This section shall not apply as to the special deposits of surety insurers which are subject to section 27-6-13. (Acts 1953, No. 727, p. 981, § 2; Acts 1971, No. 407, p. 707, § 104.)

§ 27-6-9. Power of attorney — Safekeeping; return.

The power of attorney provided for in section 27-6-7 shall be kept by the commissioner in a place of safekeeping and may be physically attached to the securities or assets described therein. Whenever such securities or assets, or any portion thereof, are returned to the insurer which deposited them, the power of attorney shall be returned to the insurer or to the trustee or other representative authorized for that purpose. (Acts 1953, No. 727, p. 981, § 3; Acts 1971, No. 407, p. 707, § 105.)

§ 27-6-10. Same — New power of attorney.

If less than all of the securities or assets covered by any such power of attorney is returned to the insurer or its trustee or agent, the commissioner may require the insurer to deliver to him, as a condition precedent to the return of such power of attorney, a new power of attorney covering the securities and assets not then being withdrawn. The new power of attorney shall be held and exercised under the same restrictions and upon the same conditions as prescribed in this chapter for the original power of attorney. (Acts 1953, No. 727, p. 981, § 4; Acts 1971, No. 407, p. 707, § 106.)

§ 27-6-11. Excess deposits.

An insurer may so deposit assets or securities in an amount exceeding its deposit required or otherwise permitted under this title by not more than 20 percent of such required or permitted deposit or $100,000.00, whichever is the larger amount, for the purpose of absorbing fluctuations in the value of securities and assets deposited and to facilitate the exchange and substitution of such securities and assets. During the solvency of the insurer, any such excess shall be released to the insurer upon its request. During the insolvency of the insurer, such excess deposit shall be released only as provided in subdivision (b) (3) of section 27-6-15. (Acts 1971, No. 407, p. 707, § 107.)

§ 27-6-12. Rights of solvent insurers.

So long as the insurer remains solvent and is in compliance with this title, it may:

(1) Demand, receive, maintain actions for and recover the income from the securities or assets deposited;

(2) Exchange and substitute for the deposited securities or assets, or any part thereof, other eligible securities and assets of equivalent or greater value; and

(3) At any reasonable time, inspect any such deposit. (Code 1940, T. 28, § 73; Acts 1971, No. 407, p. 707, § 108.)

§ 27-6-13. Sale of surety insurers' special deposit to pay outstanding judgment.

(a) If any surety insurer which has made the deposit provided for in section 27-3-12 fails or refuses to pay any final judgment entered against it upon any bond or undertaking from which no appeal and supersedeas has been taken for 30 days after the entry of such judgment, the clerk or register of the court in which such judgment was entered shall certify a copy thereof to the commissioner, together with the fact that it remains unpaid, and the commissioner shall sell as many of the securities or other assets deposited by such insurer as may be necessary to pay such judgment, and the interest and costs thereon, and to pay to the clerk or register of the court, from the proceeds of the sale, the amount of the judgment, with interest and costs. The commissioner shall sell such securities or other assets at private or public sale, with or without notice, or so many as may be necessary for the best price he can obtain in the market, shall assign the same to the purchaser and shall apply the proceeds, or so much thereof as may be necessary, to the payment of such judgment, with interest and costs, the surplus, if any, remaining on deposit in lieu of the securities or other assets so sold.

(b) Of such sale, the commissioner must forthwith notify the insurer and require it to supply the deficiency, if any, in the deposit within 30 days as required in section 27-6-14; and, if the insurer fails to do so, the commissioner shall revoke its certificate of authority. (Acts 1909, No. 147, p. 329; Acts 1971, No. 407, p. 707, § 109.)

Collateral references. — 44 C.J.S., Insurance, § 72.

§ 27-6-14. Curing of deficiency in market value of deposit.

(a) If for any reason the market value of assets and securities of an insurer held on deposit in this state under this title falls below the amount so required, the insurer shall promptly deposit other or additional assets or securities eligible for deposit sufficient to cure such deficiency. If the insurer has failed to cure the deficiency within 30 days after receipt of notice thereof by registered or certified mail from the commissioner, the commissioner shall revoke the insurer's certificate of authority.

(b) If for any reason the market value of assets and securities of a domestic life insurer, representing deposit of the reserves of certain of its outstanding registered policies and registered annuity contracts under laws heretofore in force, falls below the amount so required and as determined from the insurer's most recent annual statement or most recent examination of the insurer by the commissioner, the insurer shall promptly deposit other or additional assets or securities eligible for deposit sufficient to cure such deficiency. If the insurer has failed to cure the deficiency, after the commissioner has given the insurer notice thereof by registered or certified mail, within such reasonable time not exceeding 90 days as may be allowed therefor by the commissioner and so specified in his notice, the insurer shall be deemed to be insolvent and the commissioner shall revoke its certificate of authority and institute delinquency proceedings against the insurer under chapter 31 of this title. (Acts 1971, No. 407, p. 707, § 110.)

§ 27-6-15. Release of deposit — Generally.

(a) All deposits in this state made under this title shall be held on deposit as long as there is outstanding any liability of the insurer with respect to which the deposit was made.

(b) Any such deposit shall be released and returned:

(1) To the insurer upon extinguishment by reinsurance in an insurer authorized to transact such insurance in this state, or otherwise, of all liability of the insurer for the security of which the deposit is held;

(2) To the insurer during solvency, to the extent such deposit is in excess of the amount required; or

(3) Upon proper order of a court of competent jurisdiction, to the receiver, conservator, rehabilitator or liquidator of the insurer or to any other properly designated official, or officials, who succeed to the management and control of the insurer's assets.

(c) The treasurer shall release any such deposit, or part thereof, upon written authorization of the commissioner and of the insurer or order of court, as provided in subsection (d) of section 27-6-4.

(d) In the case of deposits of title insurers made under section 27-3-13, the deposit or excess portion thereof shall be released by the trustee bank or trust company upon written authorization of the commissioner or upon order of a court of competent jurisdiction. If a foreign title insurer which has made such a deposit reincorporates under the laws of the state of Alabama and qualifies under this code as a domestic title insurer and if all of the liabilities of such foreign insurer in this state are assumed by such new domestic insurer and the foreign insurer does not thereafter transact business in this state, its deposit shall be delivered by such trustee to such new domestic insurer upon its application and the written authorization of the commissioner.

(e) This section shall not apply as to deposits held with respect to registered life insurance policies or registered annuity contracts insured under laws heretofore in force. Such deposits shall be released only as provided under the laws pursuant to which such policies and contracts were so issued and registered. (Acts 1971, No. 407, p. 707, § 111.)

Collateral references. — 43 Am. Jur. 2d, Insurance § 63.
Remedy of creditor of corporation to reach funds or securities deposited with state official as security for corporations' obligations. 101 ALR 496.

§ 27-6-16. Same — Filing of statement; authorization of release.

(a) Before authorizing the release of any deposit or excess portion thereof to the insurer, as provided in section 27-6-15, the commissioner shall require the insurer to file with him a statement under its seal and the oath of its chief executive officer, or of its United States manager in the case of an alien insurer, setting forth the facts upon which it bases its entitlement to such release.

(b) If release of the deposit is claimed by the insurer upon the ground that its liabilities in this state, as to which the deposit was originally made and is held, have been assumed by another insurer authorized to transact insurance in this state, the insurer shall file with the commissioner a copy of the contract or agreement of such reinsurance.

(c) Upon being satisfied by such statement and such other information and evidence as he may reasonably require and by such examination, if any, of the affairs of the insurer as he deems advisable to make that the insurer is entitled to the release of its deposits or excess portions thereof as provided in section 27-6-15, the commissioner shall authorize the treasurer or the trustee bank or trust company in the case of deposits of title insurers made under section 27-3-13 to release the deposit or excess portion thereof to the insurer or its authorized representative. The commissioner shall have no liability as to any such release so made by him in good faith. (Acts 1971, No. 407, p. 707, § 112.)

CHAPTER 7.

PROPERTY, CASUALTY AND SURETY INSURANCE REPRESENTATIVES.

Sec.
27-7-1. Definitions.
27-7-2. Applicability of chapter.
27-7-3. Applicability of provision on insurance vending machines.
27-7-4. Licenses — Requirement; forms.
27-7-5. Same — Qualifications.
27-7-6. Same — Artificial entities.
27-7-7. Same — Application — Generally; fees.
27-7-8. Same — Same — Statement of appointing insurer for agent.
27-7-9. Same — Same — Statement of appointing agent or broker for solicitor.
27-7-10. Same — Examination — Scope; notification; when given.
27-7-11. Same — Same — Study materials; contents; conduct; grading.
27-7-12. Same — Same — Renewal or continuation.
27-7-13. Same — Same — Exemptions; exception.
27-7-14. Same — Same — Consultations with experienced persons.
27-7-15. Same — Issuance or refusal.
27-7-16. Same — Reapplication or reexamination upon denial; fees therefor.
27-7-17. Same — Contents.
27-7-18. Same — Continuation and expiration; exception.
27-7-19. Same — Grounds for refusing to renew or continue or to suspend or revoke.

Sec.
27-7-20. Same — Proceedings to suspend or revoke.
27-7-21. Same — Notice of refusal to renew or of suspension or revocation.
27-7-22. Same — Return for cancellation; affidavit in lieu thereof.
27-7-23. Temporary license — Generally.
27-7-24. Same — Pending examination of agent.
27-7-25. Same — Agent properly licensed in another state.
27-7-26. Same — Apprentice solicitor.
27-7-27. Solicitors.
27-7-28. Nonresident agents or brokers — License; commissions.
27-7-29. Same — Service of process.
27-7-30. Filing of agent's appointment by insurer with commissioner of insurance; termination of such appointment.
27-7-31. Rights of agent following termination of appointment; exception.
27-7-32. Place of business; display of license.
27-7-33. Records.
27-7-34. Placing of insurance by agent not appointed or licensed.
27-7-35. Division or sharing of commissions by licensees.
27-7-36. Accounting for and payment of trust funds by licensees.
27-7-37. Complaints against licensees; notice, hearing and orders thereon.
27-7-38. Privileged information.

§ 27-7-1. Definitions.

(a) For the purposes of this chapter, the following terms shall have the meanings respectively ascribed to them by this section:

(1) AGENT. A natural person appointed by an insurer to solicit and negotiate insurance contracts on its behalf, and if authorized to do so by the insurer, to effectuate, issue and countersign such contracts. An agent may not delegate the countersignature authority by appointing another individual as his attorney-in-fact.

(2) BROKER. A natural person who, on behalf of the insured, for compensation as an independent contractor, for commission or fee and not being an agent of the insurer, solicits, negotiates or procures insurance or the renewal or continuance thereof, or in any manner aids therein, for insureds or prospective insureds other than himself. Brokers cannot bind the insurer and all business produced must be countersigned by a resident agent of the insurer accepting the risk.

(3) SOLICITOR. A natural person appointed and authorized by a licensed agent or broker to solicit applications for insurance as a representative of such agent or broker and to collect premiums thereon when expressly so authorized by the agent or broker. A solicitor may not bind the insurer, accept risks or countersign policies of insurance. The solicitor must be domiciled in the same city or town as the sponsoring agent and must be under the direct supervision of the agent. An individual employed by and devoting full time to clerical work with incidental taking of insurance applications and receiving premiums in the office of the agent or broker shall not be deemed to be a solicitor if his compensation is not related to the volume of such applications, insurances or premiums.

(4) MANAGING GENERAL AGENT. An individual, firm or corporation appointed as an independent contractor by one or more insurers for the principal purpose of exercising general supervision over the business of the insurer in Alabama, with authority to appoint agents for such insurer and to terminate such appointments. The authority of a managing general agent shall not include countersignature privileges. A managing general agent shall otherwise qualify and be licensed as such as provided in this chapter, but shall not be required to take and pass an examination nor be a resident of Alabama. A managing general agent must be licensed for each insurer represented and for each class of insurance handled by the insurer in this state.

(5) SERVICE REPRESENTATIVE. A natural person, other than an officer, manager or managing general agent of the insurer, employed on salary by an insurer or managing general agent to work for, with or through agents in soliciting, negotiating and effectuating insurance in such insurer or in the insurers represented by the managing general agent. Officers and salaried nonresident traveling representatives of a mutual insurer operating on the premium deposit plan or of a reciprocal insurer not using resident agents for the solicitation of business who inspect risks or solicit insurance in this state and who receive no commissions from the insurer shall be deemed also to be service representatives. A service representative shall otherwise qualify and be licensed as such under this chapter, but shall not be required to take and pass an examination nor be a resident of Alabama if he is qualified as a service representative in the state of his domicile. Service representatives are not authorized to countersign policies of insurance in the state of Alabama. The service representative must be licensed for each insurer represented and for each class of insurance handled by the insurer in this state.

(b) In addition to persons excluded by the terms thereof, the definition of an agent, broker, solicitor, managing general agent or service representative shall not be deemed to include any of the following:

(1) Salaried employees rendering solely clerical and administrative services in the office of the employer;

(2) Salaried administrative and clerical employees of agents and brokers performing any functions in the office and under the supervision of the employer and receiving no commissions;

(3) Salaried employees of insurers or organizations employed by insurers engaged in inspection, rating or classifying risks or in general supervision of agents and not in the solicitation or the writing of insurance;

(4) Officers of insurers or of an association of insurers engaged in the performance of their usual and customary executive duties, exclusive of field solicitation of insurance other than rendering assistance to, or on behalf of, a licensed agent but receiving no commission or other compensation directly, dependent upon the amount of business transacted;

(5) Persons completing or delivering declarations or certificates of coverage under running inland marine insurance contracts evidencing coverage thereunder, if:

a. Such persons receive no commissions directly or indirectly on such insurance; and

b. Such persons or their employers have an insurable interest in the risk evidenced by the certificate or declaration; and

(6) Persons who secure and furnish information for the purpose of group life insurance, group or blanket health insurance or annuity coverages, or for enrolling individuals under such plans or issuing certificates thereunder or otherwise assisting in administering such plans where no commission is paid for such services. (Acts 1957, No. 530, p. 726, § 2; Acts 1971, No. 407, p. 707, §§ 114-118.1.)

General agent. — Under Alabama and general insurance law, the test to determine whether a general agency exists is whether the agent has power to bind the insurer by his contract of insurance or to issue policies on his own initiative, or to accept risks; and if the agent has actual authority to do those things, he is a general agent, and he may then bind the company in other ways, such as by oral contract, by waiving certain policy or application provisions and the like. Fidelity & Cas. Co. v. Thomas, 315 F. Supp. 89 (M.D. Ala.

1970) (decided under former Code 1940, T. 28, § 85(21)).

Cited in Washburn v. Rabun, 755 F.2d 1404 (11th Cir. 1985).

Collateral references. — 44 C.J.S., Insurance, §§ 85, 136.

43 Am. Jur. 2d, Insurance, §§ 145, 149, 155, 159, 160.

Person to whom renewal premium may be paid or tendered so as to bind insurer. 42 ALR3d 751.

§ 27-7-2. Applicability of chapter.

This chapter applies only as to agents, brokers, solicitors and other insurance representatives, as defined in this chapter, transacting, or proposing to transact, as such representatives, any of the following kinds of insurance:

(1) Property insurance, except as to insurance of baggage or personal effects while in possession of a common carrier in connection with travel of the insured when such insurance is effectuated through ticket or transportation agencies selling tickets for such common carrier;

(2) Casualty insurance, except as to insurance of baggage or personal effects under the same circumstances as stated in subdivision (1) of this section;

(3) Surety insurance;

(4) Disability insurance when transacted by a casualty, property or surety insurer; and

(5) For the purposes of this chapter "property" insurance includes also "wet marine and transportation" insurance as defined in section 27-5-9. (Acts 1957, No. 530, p. 726, § 1; Acts 1971, No. 407, p. 707, § 113.)

Cited in Cincinnati Ins. Co. v. City of Talladega, 342 So. 2d 331 (Ala. 1977).
Collateral references. — Public regulation or control of insurance agents or brokers. 10 ALR2d 950.

§ 27-7-3. Applicability of provision on insurance vending machines.

Section 27-8-23, as to licensing of vending machines for the sale of personal travel accident insurance, shall also apply as to agents licensed under this chapter and appointed as such by any insurer authorized to transact disability insurance in this state. (Acts 1971, No. 407, p. 707, § 140.)

§ 27-7-4. Licenses — Requirement; forms.

(a) No person shall in this state be, act as, hold himself out as or claim to be or act as an agent, broker, solicitor, managing general agent or service representative unless then licensed as such agent, broker, solicitor, managing general agent or service representative under this chapter. Any insurer accepting business directly from a person not licensed by such insurer shall be liable to a fine up to three times the premium received from such unlicensed person.

(b) No agent, broker or solicitor shall solicit or take application for, procure or place for others any kind of insurance as to which he is not then licensed.

(c) No agent shall place any business, other than coverage of his own risks, with any insurer as to which he does not then hold an appointment as agent under this chapter.

(d) The commissioner shall prescribe and furnish on request all forms required in connection with application for, issuance, continuation or termination of licenses and appointments. (Acts 1957, No. 530, p. 726, § 3; Acts 1971, No. 407, p. 707, § 119.)

Cited in Alabama Ass'n of Ins. Agents v. Board of Governors of Fed. Reserve Sys., 533 F.2d 224 (5th Cir. 1976).
Collateral references. — 44 C.J.S., Insurance, § 85.
43 Am. Jur. 2d, Insurance, § 66.

Validity and enforceability of contract of agent failing to procure license. 30 ALR 866, 42 ALR 1226, 118 ALR 646.

Right of person wrongfully refused license upon proper application therefor to do act for which license is required. 30 ALR2d 1006.

§ 27-7-5. Same — Qualifications.

For the protection of the people of this state, the commissioner shall not issue, continue or permit to exist any agent, broker, solicitor, managing general agent or service representative license except in compliance with this chapter, or as to any individual not qualified therefor as follows:

(1) Must be a natural person 19 years or more of age, or be an individual whose disabilities of minority have been removed; except, that a managing general agent license may also be issued to a firm or corporation;

(2) Must be a citizen of the United States of America;

(3) Must be domiciled in and have been a bona fide resident of this state for not less than six months preceding the date of application for the license; except that this provision does not apply as to managing general agents or service representatives. Provided further, that the residence and domiciliary requirement may be waived upon determination by the commissioner that such waiver would be in the public interest and would prevent a hardship, if the applicant for a license:

a. Is a bona fide resident of and maintains an established office in a populous community lying partly in Alabama and partly in an adjoining state, which is composed of two or more contiguous cities, towns or villages not completely separated by a natural boundary;

b. Designates in writing the commissioner of insurance as his agent or attorney for acceptance of personal service of process in all actions involving matters connected with or arising out of his insurance business conducted in Alabama;

c. Agrees to keep like records, make similar reports and permit inspection of his records to the same extent as other licensees under this section; and

d. If the adjoining state by law or administrative action accords residents of Alabama a like waiver, benefit or privilege;

(4) Must be of good moral character and not have been convicted of a felony nor of any crime involving moral turpitude;

(5) Must intend to and, commencing immediately after issuance of such a license, shall, during the existence of the license, actively engage as to the general public in the business permitted under this license;

(6) If to be licensed as a broker, must have had experience either as an agent, solicitor, adjustor, managing general agent, broker or as an employee or special representative of an insurer, or insurers, or special education or training of sufficient duration and extent reasonably necessary for competence in fulfilling the responsibilities of a broker;

(7) Must not use, or intend to use, the license principally for the purpose of procuring insurance of his own risks or interests, or those of his relatives to the second degree or of his firm, corporation or employer;

(8) Must attend a pre-qualification course consisting of forty classroom hours or equivalent individual instruction on the general principles of insurance, such course to be taught only by those educational institutions,

junior or senior colleges, technical colleges, trade schools, insurance companies or insurance trade organizations which hold written authority from the commissioner to issue certificates of completion;

a. Each such authority holder must apply annually for the continued authority to issue certificates under rules and regulations to be prescribed by the commissioner;

b. Prior to writing the designated examination for license, the applicant must furnish a certificate of completion of the aforesaid pre-qualification course from the authorized educational institution, insurance company or insurance trade organization;

c. All applicants under this chapter who are holders of the professional designation Chartered Property Casualty Underwriter (CPCU) as conferred by the American Institute for Property and Liability Underwriters, Inc., shall be deemed to have completed the pre-qualification course as prescribed in this subdivision;

d. All applicants for license to transact only the following kinds of insurance shall be exempt from the requirements of this subdivision:

1. automobile physical damage insurance,

2. industrial fire (commonly known as debit fire) insurance, or

3. physical damage coverage on household goods;

e. All agents, brokers, solicitors, managing general agents and service representatives who are lawfully licensed as such immediately prior to the effective date of the 1979 amendment, are exempt from the requirements of this section unless, after such effective date, any such license is permitted to expire or is otherwise terminated and remains out of effect for a period of 24 consecutive months, the exemption from a pre-qualification course shall no longer be applicable.

(9) Must pass any written examination for the license required under this chapter. (Acts 1957, No. 530, p. 726, § 4; Acts 1959, 2nd Ex. Sess., No. 73, p. 250; Acts 1971, No. 407, p. 707, § 120; Acts 1971, 3rd Ex. Sess., No. 261, p. 4529; Acts 1979, No. 79-748, p. 1332.)

Collateral references. — 44 C.J.S., Insurance, § 85.

§ 27-7-6. Same — Artificial entities.

A corporation, partnership, firm, association or other artificial entity shall not be licensed as an agent, broker or solicitor, but may advertise its insurance business if such business is in charge of a duly licensed agent or broker. (Acts 1957, No. 530, p. 726, § 4; Acts 1959, 2nd Ex. Sess., No. 73, p. 250; Acts 1971, No. 407, p. 707, § 121.)

§ 27-7-7. Same — Application — Generally; fees.

(a) The commissioner shall not issue any license except upon application therefor as in this chapter provided. Each applicant for a license shall file with the commissioner his written application therefor signed by him and showing:

(1) His name, age and place of residence;

(2) The kinds of insurance to be transacted under the license and the insurer or insurers he proposes so to represent;

(3) The person, firm or corporation by whom he expects to be employed or associated with as such licensee and his status as an officer or representative thereof;

(4) Whether he proposes to write or solicit insurance of his own risks and interests, or those of his relatives, any firm or corporation in which he is financially interested or connected, directly or indirectly, or of his employer;

(5) A short business history of the applicant and the name and nature of any business enterprise with which he may be associated;

(6) The extent of his formal education and business experience or apprenticeship;

(7) Whether he has ever applied previously for license or been licensed to transact any kind of insurance business in this state or elsewhere and whether any such license was ever refused, suspended or revoked;

(8) Whether any insurer or managing general agent claims that he is in default as to premiums or other moneys collected and not accounted for and, if so, the details thereof and like information as to any member of his family who is then, or has theretofore been, engaged in the insurance business; and

(9) Any additional information reasonably required by the commissioner.

(b) At the time of filing his original application for license, the applicant shall pay to the commissioner the application fee and the fees for any examinations required under section 27-7-10 as specified in section 27-4-2. Such fees shall not be returnable. (Acts 1957, No. 530, p. 726, § 5; Acts 1971, No. 407, p. 707, § 122.)

§ 27-7-8. Same — Same — Statement of appointing insurer for agent.

At the time of application for license as agent, the insurer intending to appoint the applicant as its agent shall file with the commissioner its statement showing:

(1) The kind or kinds of insurance or classifications thereof as provided in section 27-7-11 it proposes to authorize the applicant to solicit or write;

(2) What investigation it has made of the applicant's qualifications, character and fitness for the duties to be assumed and the results of such investigation; and

(3) Such additional information as the commissioner reasonably requires. (Acts 1957, No. 530, p. 726, § 5; Acts 1971, No. 407, p. 707, § 123.)

§ 27-7-9. Same — Same — Statement of appointing agent or broker for solicitor.

At the time of application for license as solicitor, the agent or broker intending to appoint the applicant as a solicitor shall file with the commissioner his statement showing:

(1) The kind or kinds of insurance or classes thereof as provided in subsection (a) of section 27-7-11 the applicant is to handle under the license applied for and that the agent or broker is himself licensed to write the same such kinds and classes;

(2) What investigation he had made of the applicant's qualifications, character and fitness for the duties to be assumed and the results of such investigation;

(3) The extent to which insurance solicitation will constitute the activities of the applicant; and

(4) Such additional information as the commissioner reasonably requires. (Acts 1957, No. 530, p. 726, § 5; Acts 1971, No. 407, p. 707, § 124.)

§ 27-7-10. Same — Examination — Scope; notification; when given.

(a) After completion and filing of the application for license as required in sections 27-7-7 through 27-7-9, the commissioner shall give each applicant for license as agent, broker or solicitor, unless exempted from examination under section 27-7-13, a written examination of sufficient scope reasonably to test the applicant's knowledge relative to the kinds of insurance or classes thereof which may be dealt with under the proposed license and of the duties, responsibilities of and laws of this state applicable to such a licensee.

(b) Within 10 days after such completion of the application, the commissioner shall notify the applicant by letter addressed to him at his address as shown on his application of the time and place of the examination for license. The examination shall be given, within not more than 60 nor less than three days after the giving of the notice, at the office of the commissioner at Montgomery or at such other place in Alabama as the commissioner reasonably designates; except, that the commissioner shall schedule an examination at least once in each calendar month, and any applicant otherwise eligible to take the examination shall be allowed at his request to take at that time all examinations relative to licenses for which he has applied, including examinations for license as an agent for life and disability insurances under chapter 8 of this title. (Acts 1957, No. 530, p. 726, § 6; Acts 1971, No. 407, p. 707, § 125.)

§ 27-7-11. Same — Same — Study materials; contents; conduct; grading.

(a) An applicant for license as agent, broker or solicitor shall be so examined as to any one or more of the following kinds of insurance or insurance classifications, as applied for:

(1) Automobile physical damage insurance;

(2) Automobile liability insurance;

(3) General casualty insurances;

(4) Property insurance, from which questions dealing with wet marine and transportation insurance may be omitted in the commissioner's discretion;

(5) Fidelity and surety insurances; and

(6) Any other reasonable classification prescribed by order of the commissioner.

(b) The rules and regulations of the commissioner shall designate textbooks, manuals and other materials to be studied by applicants in preparation for examinations in each classification designated by the commissioner pursuant to this section. Such textbooks, manuals or other materials may consist of matter available to applicants by purchase from the publisher or may consist of matter prepared at the direction of the commissioner and distributed to applicants upon request and payment of the reasonable cost thereof. If textbooks, manuals or other materials are so designated or prepared by the commissioner, all examination questions shall be prepared from the contents of such textbooks, manuals or other materials. Prior to the examination, the commissioner shall value each question to be asked therein and the sum of such values shall total 100. Each of the answers given shall correspondingly be valued proportionately to its correctness, and the sum of such values totaling 70 shall constitute a passing grade. The commissioner may secure the assistance of the state personnel department in the preparation and analysis of the written portions of the examination.

(c) The commissioner shall give, conduct and grade all examinations in a fair and impartial manner and without unfair discrimination as between individuals examined.

(d) Upon the completion of the examination, the questions and answers of the applicant shall, by the person conducting the examination, be sealed in an envelope and forthwith delivered to the commissioner and be graded within the next 10 days.

(e) His graded examination papers shall be available for review by the applicant at the commissioner's office at Montgomery for a period of not less than six months after the date of the examination. (Acts 1957, No. 530, p. 726, § 6; Acts 1971, No. 407, p. 707, § 126; Acts 1982, No. 82-401, p. 606, § 1.)

§ 27-7-12. Same — Same — Renewal or continuation.

In every case where he has probable cause to find and does find that the applicant for renewal or continuation of a license does not possess the necessary qualifications of education, training and experience where prescribed by this chapter or reasonably required for the lawful discharge of his responsibilities under the license, the commissioner shall require the applicant to take and pass a written examination as a condition precedent to the renewal of the license. (Acts 1957, No. 530, p. 726, § 8; Acts 1971, No. 407, p. 707, § 127.)

§ 27-7-13. Same — Same — Exemptions; exception.

(a) Except as provided in section 27-7-12, an agent, broker or solicitor lawfully licensed as such immediately prior to January 1, 1972, shall not be required to take an examination as to any kind of insurance or classification thereof as to which he is so licensed. This section does not apply to agents, solicitors or brokers who presently hold a temporary license, pending written examination.

(b) If, after January 1, 1972, any such license is permitted to expire, or is otherwise terminated, and remains out of effect for a period of 24 consecutive months, the exemption from examination provided for in subsection (a) of this section shall no longer be applicable. (Acts 1957, No. 530, p. 726, § 6; Acts 1971, No. 407, p. 707, § 128.)

§ 27-7-14. Same — Same — Consultations with experienced persons.

The commissioner shall, from time to time as an aid to the efficient administration of this chapter, consult with individuals experienced in the fire, casualty and miscellaneous casualty insurance business, to include officers, employees, managing general agents, managers and licensed agents of insurers engaged in such business, to the end that an orderly and effective program be developed as to scope, type and conduct of written examinations and the times and places in the state when and where they shall be held. (Acts 1957, No. 530, p. 726, § 7; Acts 1971, No. 407, p. 707, § 129.)

§ 27-7-15. Same — Issuance or refusal.

(a) Within 10 days after receipt of the applicant's answers to examination questions, after examination for license as provided in this chapter, or within 10 days after completion of the application for license in the case of an applicant for license as managing general agent or service representative, the commissioner, if the applicant has passed any examination required and is otherwise qualified for the license pursuant to this chapter, shall notify the applicant that he is eligible for a license. Upon payment of the license issuance fee provided by subsection (a) of section 27-4-2, the filing, if for an agent's license, of an appointment of the agent by an insurer as provided in section 27-7-30, and payment of the appointment fee prescribed in paragraph (a) (5) a of section 27-4-2, the commissioner shall issue the license to which the applicant is so entitled.

(b) If the commissioner finds that the applicant is not entitled to receive any license applied for, he shall within 10 days after receiving the applicant's examination questions and answers, or within 10 days after completion of the application for license in the case of an applicant for license as managing general agent or service representative, give the applicant written notice that the license is refused, stating the grounds for refusal. (Acts 1957, No. 530, p. 726, § 6; Acts 1971, No. 407, p. 707, § 130.)

§ 27-7-16. Same — Reapplication or reexamination upon denial; fees therefor.

The failure of an applicant to be licensed by reason of any remediable cause upon application, examination or both shall not preclude a reapplication or reexamination one additional time within 30 days after the denial of a license, but thereafter, the commissioner shall not consider any further application from the same applicant within six months after the date upon which the issuance of a license was last denied. A new application fee shall not be charged for any reapplication properly made within 30 days from the date upon which the license was denied; however, the examination fees are again due. (Acts 1957, No. 530, p. 726, § 6; Acts 1971, No. 407, p. 707, § 131.)

§ 27-7-17. Same — Contents.

(a) The license of a managing general agent or service representative shall state the name and address of the licensee, the name of the insurer to be so represented, date of issue and of expiration and the general conditions of the license. The licensee shall have a separate and additional license as to each insurer so represented.

(b) The license of an agent shall state the name and address of the licensee, the name of the insurer represented, date of issue, general conditions relative to expiration or termination, the kinds of insurance or classifications thereof covered by the license, as classified under subsection (a) of section 27-7-11, and the general conditions of the license. The license shall state the name of the insurer to be so represented, and the agent shall be required to have a license for each insurer by whom he is appointed as an agent as to property, casualty and surety insurances and including disability insurance where transacted by an insurer also represented by the agent as to property, casualty or surety insurances.

(c) The license of a broker shall state the licensee's name and address, the kinds of insurance or classifications thereof covered by the license, as classified under subsection (a) of section 27-7-11, date of issuance, conditions relative to expiration or termination and the general conditions of the license.

(d) The license of a solicitor shall state the licensee's name and address, the name and address of the agent or broker by whom he is appointed, the kinds of insurance or classifications thereof covered by the license, as classified under subsection (a) of section 27-7-11, conditions relative to expiration or termination and the general conditions of the license. (Acts 1971, No. 407, p. 707, § 132.)

§ 27-7-18. Same — Continuation and expiration; exception.

(a) All agent, broker, solicitor, managing general agent and service representative licenses issued under this chapter shall continue in force until expired, suspended, revoked or otherwise terminated, but subject to payment to the commissioner annually on or before December 31, of the applicable continuation fee, as stated in section 27-4-2, accompanied by written request for such continuation. Request for continuation shall be made as follows:

(1) As to broker's license, request for continuation signed by the licensee;

(2) As to solicitor's license, request for continuation signed by the appointing agent or broker;

(3) As to managing general agent's license, request signed by the insurer to be so represented;

(4) As to service representative's license, request signed by the insurer or managing general agent to be so represented; and

(5) As to agent's licenses, request signed by the insurer to be represented.

(b) Any license as to which the request for continuation and fee is not received by the commissioner as required under subsection (a) of this section shall be deemed to have expired at midnight December 31, above mentioned. Request for continuation of any such license or payment of the continuation fee therefor which is received by the commissioner after such December 31, and prior to the next following February 15, may be accepted and effectuated by the commissioner, in his discretion, if accompanied by an annual continuation fee in twice the amount otherwise required.

(c) The license of an agent shall continue in force as long as there is in effect as to such agent, as shown by the commissioner's records, an appointment, or appointments, as agent of authorized insurers, covering collectively all of the kinds of insurance or classifications thereof included in the agent's license. Upon termination of all of such licensee's agency appointments as to a particular kind of insurance or classification thereof and failure to replace such appointment within 90 days thereafter, the licensee's license as agent shall automatically thereupon expire and terminate as to such kind of insurance or classification, and the licensee shall promptly deliver his license to the commissioner for reissuance, without fee or charge, as to the kinds of insurance or classifications thereof, if any, covered by the licensee's remaining agency appointments.

(d) This section does not apply to temporary licenses issued under sections 27-7-23 through 27-7-26. (Acts 1971, No. 407, p. 707, § 133.)

§ 27-7-19. Same — Grounds for refusing to renew or continue or to suspend or revoke.

The commissioner may refuse to renew or continue or may suspend or revoke the license of any licensee under this chapter upon any of the following grounds:

(1) For any cause for which issuance of the license could have been refused had it then existed and been known to the commissioner;

(2) For the willful misrepresentation of any material fact in any application or in any communication to the commissioner;

(3) For intentional, material, misrepresentation with respect to any insurance policy;

(4) For rebating;

(5) For inducing, persuading or advising any policyholder to surrender or cause to be cancelled any policy of insurance issued to such policyholder by any authorized insurer in exchange for a policy offered by the licensee where such surrender or cancellation shall proximately result to the financial detriment of such policyholder, unless such policyholder shall have been fully advised of that fact by such licensee;

(6) For fraudulent or dishonest practices in the conduct of business under a license;

(7) For being in default, for a period of 60 days or more, in remitting to any insurer premiums collected by such applicant or licensee, after receiving demand, accompanied by proof and justification, from such insurer;

(8) For the misappropriation, conversion or unlawful withholding of any moneys belonging to the insurers, insureds or others received by the licensee in the exercise of his license;

(9) For willful failure to comply with, or wilful violation of, any valid order, rule or regulation issued by the commissioner; or

(10) For willful violation of any provision of this title. (Acts 1957, No. 530, p. 726, § 8; Acts 1971, No. 407, p. 707, § 151.)

Collateral references. — 44 C.J.S., Insurance, § 85.
43 Am. Jur. 2d, Insurance, § 68.

Cancellation, suspension or renewal of license of insurance agent. 154 ALR 1146.

§ 27-7-20. Same — Proceedings to suspend or revoke.

The commissioner shall institute a proceeding to suspend or revoke a license by filing and serving a complaint as to the licensee, giving notice thereof to all interested parties the licensee is licensed or appointed to represent, and otherwise proceeding as provided in section 27-7-37. The commissioner is not required to swear to such a complaint. (Acts 1957, No. 530, p. 726, § 11; Acts 1971, No. 407, p. 707, § 152.)

§ 27-7-21. Same — Notice of refusal to renew or of suspension or revocation.

Upon refusal to renew or upon suspension or revocation of any license, the commissioner shall forthwith give written notice thereof to the licensee and all persons and insurers represented by the licensee and of record in the commissioner's office. The notice shall state the grounds for the commissioner's action. If a proceeding as provided for in section 27-7-37 has not already been had as to such action, upon written demand of any interested party feeling aggrieved and filed with the commissioner within 10 days after the above notice, the commissioner shall institute a complaint against the licensee under section 27-7-37 within 10 days after receipt of the demand. (Acts 1957, No. 530, p. 726, § 9; Acts 1971, No. 407, p. 707, § 153.)

§ 27-7-22. Same — Return for cancellation; affidavit in lieu thereof.

(a) All licenses issued under this chapter, though issued to a licensee, at all times are the property of the state of Alabama, and upon notice of any suspension, revocation, refusal to renew, expiration or other termination of the license, the licensee, or other person having possession or custody thereof, shall promptly deliver the license to the commissioner for cancellation.

(b) As to any license lost, stolen or destroyed while in the possession of any such licensee or person, the commissioner may accept in lieu of return of the license the affidavit of the licensee or other person responsible for, or involved in, the safekeeping of, such license concerning the facts of such loss, theft or destruction. (Acts 1971, No. 407, p. 707, § 154.)

§ 27-7-23. Temporary license — Generally.

(a) The commissioner may, in his discretion, issue a temporary license as agent or broker to a licensed agent's or broker's employee, family member, associate or personal representative or to the salaried employee of an insurer of which the agent was the sole licensed agent in Alabama, all subject to the following conditions:

(1) The agent or broker must have become deceased or unable to perform his duties as agent or broker because of military service, illness or other physical or mental disability;

(2) There must be no other person connected with the agent's or broker's business who is a licensed agent or broker and willing to act for the agent or broker;

(3) The proposed temporary licensee must be qualified as for an agent's or broker's license under this chapter, except as to residence, examination, education, training, experience and knowledge of insurance;

(4) Application for the temporary license must be made by the applicant by statement and affidavit filed with the commissioner on forms as prescribed and furnished by him;

(5) The temporary license shall be valid for a period of not over six months and, except as to one renewal in the case of disabling or confining illness or injury of the agent or broker, shall not be renewed either to the then holder of the temporary license or to any other person for, or on behalf of, the agent, agency or broker;

(6) As to a temporary license as agent issued on account of the death or disability of an agent, the licensee may so represent all of the insurers last represented by such deceased or disabled agent and without the making of new appointment of such licensee by such insurers; but the licensee shall not be appointed as to any additional kind or classification of insurance under a temporary license. This subdivision shall not be deemed to prohibit termination of its appointment by any insurer; and

(7) The holder of a temporary license may be granted a regular agent's or broker's license upon taking and passing an examination as required under this chapter, if then otherwise qualified for such a regular license.

(b) If the temporary licensee becomes entitled to receive a regular license prior to expiration of the temporary license, he shall surrender the temporary license to the commissioner at the time the regular license is issued.

(c) The applicant for a temporary license shall pay to the commissioner, prior to the issuance thereof, the applicable license fee as specified in section 27-4-2. (Acts 1957, No. 530, p. 726, § 12; Acts 1971, No. 407, p. 707, § 135.)

§ 27-7-24. Same — Pending examination of agent.

(a) The commissioner may, in his discretion, issue a temporary license as agent to an applicant for a regular agent's license who is qualified for such regular license except as to having taken and passed a written examination therefor, if the applicant is actively engaged in a course of study, instruction and field training approved by the commissioner and under the supervision of the insurer. The insurer shall be responsible for all acts and omissions of the licensee under the temporary license and within the scope of his employment or appointment.

(b) The temporary license shall be valid for six months, within which period the licensee shall submit to a written examination for a regular agent's license and for such further time until the commissioner has notified the applicant of the result of the examination.

(c) Subsections (a) and (b) of section 27-10-1 also shall apply as to such temporary licenses. (Acts 1957, No. 530, p. 726, § 12; Acts 1971, No. 407, p. 707, § 136.)

§ 27-7-25. Same — Agent properly licensed in another state.

(a) The commissioner may, in his discretion, issue a temporary license as agent to a resident of Alabama who was properly licensed as a resident agent or broker in another state under the laws of such state for the 12 consecutive months immediately prior to becoming a resident of Alabama, subject to the following conditions:

(1) The applicant must apply for the temporary license within 30 days after becoming a resident of Alabama;

(2) The applicant must take and pass a written examination covering the kinds of insurance or classifications thereof proposed to be transacted and be qualified as for a regular license as agent in all respects except as to the period of residence in Alabama;

(3) The state from which the applicant moved to Alabama must accord like privileges to former Alabama residents who move into that state;

(4) The insurance commissioner or other state official having supervision of insurance of such other state must certify, in writing filed with the commissioner, that the applicant had been a licensed resident agent or broker of such state during the period specified in subdivision (1) of this subsection; and

(5) The license shall be valid for a period of not more than six months.

(b) Subsections (b) and (c) of section 27-7-23 shall apply also as to such temporary licenses. (Acts 1957, No. 530, p. 726, § 12; Acts 1971, No. 407, p. 707, § 137.)

§ 27-7-26. Same — Apprentice solicitor.

(a) The commissioner may, in his discretion, issue a temporary license as solicitor to an individual who is a bona fide apprentice solicitor in the office of a licensed agent or broker, subject to the following conditions:

(1) The application for the license shall be by the apprentice and the agent or broker with whom he is to be so associated;

(2) The agent or broker must agree, in the application, diligently and faithfully to instruct the apprentice as to the insurance business and the laws, rules and regulations pertaining thereto, so that the apprentice may become qualified for a regular license as solicitor. The agent or broker must in good faith fulfill the terms of such agreement;

(3) The agent or broker shall be responsible for the acts and omissions of the apprentice within the scope of his authority as an apprentice solicitor;

(4) The temporary license shall state that it is an apprentice solicitor license and shall cover only the kinds of insurance or classifications thereof which the sponsoring agent or broker is licensed to transact; and

(5) The temporary license shall be valid for six months and shall not be renewed.

(b) Subsections (b) and (c) of section 27-7-23 shall apply also as to such temporary licenses. (Acts 1957, No. 530, p. 726, § 12; Acts 1971, No. 407, p. 707, § 138.)

§ 27-7-27. Solicitors.

(a) The same individual shall not be appointed or licensed as a solicitor as to more than one agent or broker.

(b) The solicitor's license shall cover all the kinds of insurance and classifications thereof, other than life and disability insurance, for which the appointing agent or broker is licensed; except, that the solicitor's license shall also cover disability insurance where written by an insurer also represented by the agent as to property or casualty or surety insurance.

(c) A solicitor shall not concurrently be licensed as broker nor as an agent except as to life or disability insurance.

(d) A solicitor shall not have authority to bind risks or countersign policies.

(e) The transactions of a solicitor under his license shall be in the name of the agent or broker by whom appointed, and the agent or broker shall be responsible for the acts or omissions of the solicitor within the scope of his appointment.

(f) The solicitor shall maintain his office with that of the appointing agent or broker, and records of his transactions under the license shall be maintained as part of the records of such agent or broker.

(g) The solicitor's license shall remain in the custody of the appointing agent or broker. Upon termination of the appointment, the agent or broker shall give written notice thereof to the commissioner and deliver the license to the commissioner for cancellation. (Acts 1971, No. 407, p. 707, § 139.)

§ 27-7-28. Nonresident agents or brokers — License; commissions.

(a) The commissioner may, upon written application made to him and payment of the license fee required under section 27-4-2, issue a license as a nonresident agent or nonresident broker to an individual otherwise qualified therefor under this chapter, but who is not a resident of this state, if by the laws of the state of his residence like licenses are granted to residents of this state.

(b) Any such licensing is also subject to the following conditions:

(1) The applicant must hold a license as an agent or broker in the state of his residence;

(2) The applicant or licensee must not have any direct or indirect pecuniary interest in any agent, insurance agency, broker or solicitor licensed as a resident of this state nor shall he establish or maintain any kind of office or place of business in this state; and

(3) The licensee must not enter this state for the purpose of inspecting any risk or property without the written advance permission of the insured or that of a countersigning Alabama agent on such risk, nor shall the licensee directly or indirectly in this state solicit, negotiate or effect insurance policies unless accompanied by a resident agent of Alabama who is the countersigning agent on any insurance policy or policies so solicited, negotiated or effectuated. This provision shall not be deemed to apply to a service representative as defined in section 27-7-1.

(c) A countersigning resident agent cooperating with a nonresident agent or broker shall collect and retain the usual commission paid, if any commissions be paid, by the insurer, except that not over one half of the commission may be paid by him to the licensed nonresident agent or broker. (Acts 1957, No. 530, p. 726, § 14; Acts 1971, No. 407, p. 707, § 141.)

Collateral references. — 44 C.J.S., Insurance, § 256.

§ 27-7-29. Same — Service of process.

(a) Each licensed nonresident agent and broker shall appoint the commissioner as his attorney to receive service of legal process issued against such agent or broker in this state upon causes of action arising within this state out of transactions under the nonresident agent's or broker's license. Service upon the commissioner as such attorney shall constitute effective legal service upon the nonresident agent or broker.

(b) The appointment shall be irrevocable for as long as there may be any such cause of action in this state against the nonresident agent or broker.

(c) Service of process under this section shall be made by leaving three copies of the summons and complaint, or other process, with the commissioner, and such service shall be sufficient service upon such nonresident if notice of the service and a copy of the summons and complaint or other process are forthwith sent by registered or certified mail to the defendant by the commissioner; and the defendant's return and the certificate of the commissioner certifying compliance herewith shall be filed in the office of the clerk of court, or in the court or tribunal wherein the action is pending. The certificate of the commissioner shall show the date of the mailing by registered or certified mail of the notice of the service and copy of the summons and complaint, or other process, to the nonresident defendant and the date of the receipt of the return card and shall be signed by the commissioner. The commissioner may give the nonresident defendant notice of such service upon him, in lieu of the notice of service hereinabove provided to be given by registered or certified mail, in the following manner:

(1) By having a notice of such service and a copy of the summons and complaint, or other process, served upon the nonresident defendant, if found within the state of Alabama, by any officer duly qualified to serve legal process within the state of Alabama or, if the nonresident defendant is found to be outside the state of Alabama, by a sheriff, deputy sheriff or United States marshal or deputy United States marshal or any duly constituted officer qualified to serve like process in the state or the jurisdiction where the nonresident defendant is found; and

(2) The officer's return showing such service, when made, shall be filed in the office of the clerk of the court, or in the court or tribunal wherein the action is pending, on or before the return day of the process or within such further times as the court or tribunal may allow, and the court or tribunal

in which the action is pending may order such continuance, or continuances, as may be necessary to afford the nonresident defendant reasonable opportunity to defend the action.

(d) The commissioner shall keep on file in his office a copy of the summons and complaint or other process so served upon him, together with a record of all such process and of the day, hour and manner of service. (Acts 1957, No. 530, p. 726, § 14; Acts 1971, No. 407, p. 707, § 142.)

Cross references. — As to rules of supreme court relative to service of process, see A.R.C.P., Rule 4 et seq.

Collateral references. — 46 C.J.S., Insurance, § 1270.

§ 27-7-30. Filing of agent's appointment by insurer with commissioner of insurance; termination of such appointment.

(a) Each insurer appointing an agent in this state shall file with the commissioner the appointment, specifying the kinds of insurance or classifications thereof as specified in section 27-7-11 to be transacted by the agent for the insurer, and pay the appointment fee as specified in section 27-4-2. If the insurer also transacts disability insurance, the agent may be appointed by the same insurer also as to disability insurance without requiring an additional appointment or appointment fee.

(b) Subject to annual continuation by the insurer not later than December 31, each appointment shall remain in effect until the agent's license is revoked or otherwise terminated, unless written notice of earlier termination of the appointment is filed with the commissioner by the insurer or agent.

(c) Annually, prior to December 31, each insurer shall file with the commissioner an alphabetical list of the names and addresses of all its agents whose appointments in this state are to remain in effect, accompanied by payment of the annual continuation of appointment fee as provided in section 27-4-2. At the same time, the insurer shall also file with the commissioner an alphabetical list of the names and addresses of all of its agents whose appointments in this state are not to remain in effect and shall give written notice thereof to all such agents where reasonably possible. Any appointment not so continued and not otherwise expressly terminated shall be deemed to have expired at midnight on December 31.

(d) Subject to the agent's contract rights, if any, an insurer may terminate an agent's appointment at any time. The insurer shall promptly give written notice of such termination to the commissioner and to the agent where reasonably possible. The commissioner may require of the insurer reasonable proof that the insurer has given such notice to the agent, whether upon termination of the appointment by affirmative action of the insurer or by failure of the insurer to continue the appointment as provided for in subsection (c) of this section.

(e) As part of the notice of termination given the commissioner and in connection with the insurer's list of agent's appointments not to be continued as provided for in subsection (c) of this section, the insurer shall file with the commissioner a statement of the facts relative to the termination or noncontinuance and the cause thereof. Any such information, or statement and information or statements supplemental thereto shall be privileged and shall not form the basis of, or be admitted as evidence in, any action or proceeding against the insurer, or any director, officer, employee or representative of the insurer by, or on behalf of, any person affected by such termination. (Acts 1971, No. 407, p. 707, § 134.)

Collateral references. — 44 C.J.S., Insurance, § 145.

§ 27-7-31. Rights of agent following termination of appointment; exception.

(a) Following termination of his agency appointment as to an insurer, the agent may continue to service and receive from the insurer commissions or other compensation relative to policies written by him for the insurer during the existence of the appointment. He may countersign all certificates or endorsements necessary to continue such policies, including renewal option periods, and collect and remit premiums due thereon, but shall not otherwise change or modify any such policy in any way nor increase the hazards insured against therein; except, that the limited authority hereinabove provided for shall cease as to any kind of insurance or classification thereof as to which the agent no longer holds a currently valid appointment as agent by any insurer, and such authority shall terminate altogether upon expiration or termination of the agent's license.

(b) This section does not apply as to agents of direct writing insurers or to agents and insurers between whom the relationship of employer and employee exists. (Acts 1957, No. 530, p. 726, § 3; Acts 1971, No. 407, p. 707, § 145.)

Collateral references. — Provisions of insurance company's contract with independent insurance agent restricting competitive placements by agent as illegal restraint of trade under state law. 42 ALR4th 1072.

§ 27-7-32. Place of business; display of license.

(a) Every managing general agent, resident agent and broker shall have and maintain in this state a place of business accessible to the public. The place of business shall be that wherein the licensee principally conducts transactions under his license. The address of such place shall appear upon the license, and the licensee shall promptly notify the commissioner of any change thereof. Nothing in this section shall be deemed to prohibit maintenance of such a place of business in the licensee's place of residence in this state.

(b) The licenses of the licensee and the licenses of solicitors appointed by and representing the licensee shall be conspicuously displayed by the licensee in his place of business in a part thereof customarily open to the public. (Acts 1957, No. 530, p. 726, § 13; Acts 1971, No. 407, p. 707, § 143.)

§ 27-7-33. Records.

(a) The agent or broker shall keep at his place of business complete records pertaining to transactions under his license and the licenses of his solicitors. If an agent, the licensee shall make and keep daily reports of all policies countersigned by him.

(b) The agent's records shall include also record of all policies executed or countersigned by him and representing coverages handled by a nonresident agent or nonresident broker. Upon the commissioner's request, the agent shall furnish a verified copy of such record to the commissioner to aid him in the collection of all privilege taxes due in this state.

(c) The licensee shall exhibit to an insured, at any reasonable time during business hours, records in his office pertaining to policies of the insured upon the insured's demand, and the agent and the insurer represented by him shall permit the insured or his representative to make copies of any such records. (Acts 1957, No. 530, p. 726, § 13; Acts 1971, No. 407, p. 707, § 144.)

§ 27-7-34. Placing of insurance by agent not appointed or licensed.

(a) An agent may place with an insurer for which he is not an appointed and licensed agent only a kind of insurance or classification thereof for which he is licensed by placing such insurance through a duly appointed and licensed agent of the insurer.

(b) In addition to any other penalties provided for, the licenses of any licensee violating or participating in the violation of this section may be suspended or revoked in the discretion of the commissioner; and, if so suspended or revoked, the licenses shall not be restored for a period of at least one year. (Acts 1957, No. 530, p. 726, § 15; Acts 1971, No. 407, p. 707, § 146.)

Collateral references. — Provisions of insurance company's contract with independent insurance agent restricting competitive placements by agent as illegal restraint of trade under state law. 42 ALR4th 1072.

§ 27-7-35. Division or sharing of commissions by licensees.

(a) No licensee shall divide with others or share in any commissions payable on account of the exercise of a license under this title except as follows:

(1) An agent may divide or share in the commissions with his own solicitors and with other resident agents or solicitors licensed as to the same kinds of insurance or classifications thereof; and

(2) An agent, broker or solicitor and a nonresident agent or broker, subject to the provisions of section 27-7-28, may divide between themselves commissions as to a kind of insurance or classification thereof as to which both are licensed.

(b) Violation of this section shall be punishable as provided in subsection (b) of section 27-7-34. (Acts 1957, No. 530, p. 726, § 15; Acts 1971, No. 407, p. 707, § 147.)

§ 27-7-36. Accounting for and payment of trust funds by licensees.

(a) All premiums, return premiums or other funds belonging to others received by an agent, broker or solicitor in transactions under his license shall be trust funds so received by the licensee in a fiduciary capacity, and the licensee in the applicable regular course of business shall account for and pay the same to the insurer, insured, agent, broker or other person entitled thereto.

(b) Any agent, broker or solicitor who, not being lawfully entitled thereto, diverts or appropriates such funds, or any portion thereof, to his own use shall, upon conviction, be guilty of embezzlement and shall be punished as provided by law as if he had stolen such funds. (Acts 1971, No. 407, p. 707, § 148.)

Cited in Washburn v. Rabun, 755 F.2d 1404 (11th Cir. 1985).

§ 27-7-37. Complaints against licensees; notice, hearing and orders thereon.

(a) Any person having an interest and feeling aggrieved may file a complaint with the commissioner against any licensed agent, solicitor, broker, managing general agent or service representative for the purpose of revocation or suspension of his license. The complaint shall be in writing and shall specify in reasonable detail the charge or charges made, the truth of which shall be sworn to by the complainant or some other person who has knowledge of the facts averred.

(b) If, upon reviewing the complaint, the commissioner finds that the charges made therein constitute grounds for the revocation or suspension of the license under section 27-7-19, he shall forthwith notify the licensee against whom the complaint has been made and serve him with a copy of the complaint. Service of the notice and copy of the complaint made shall be sent by registered or certified mail, addressed to the licensee at the address shown by the records of the commissioner, return receipt requested and marked "deliver addressee only."

(c) Within 30 days after service upon the licensee of the copy of the complaint made against him, the licensee shall file with the commissioner his answer in writing to the charges, either specifically admitting or denying or specifically confessing and avoiding each of the charges made. If the licensee against whom the complaint has been made stands in default for answer, the charges set forth in the complaint shall be taken as admitted.

(d) After receipt of the licensee's answer, the commissioner shall fix a time and place for the hearing of the complaint at his office or elsewhere as provided in section 27-2-30 and shall serve notice thereof upon the licensee and the complainant by registered or certified mail as provided in subsection (b) of this section with respect to service of the complaint upon the licensee; such notice shall be served at least 20 days before the date fixed for the hearing.

(e) At the time fixed by the commissioner for the hearing, the complaint shall be heard before the commissioner or a deputy appointed by him, and the complainant and licensee may each be represented by an attorney-at-law and may give the testimony and offer proof, documentary or ore tenus, as to the truth of the charges and any denial thereof.

(f) The commissioner shall have any power of subpoena, subpoena duces tecum or discovery obtaining in the circuit courts of this state, and any party shall have the right, upon request in writing filed with the commissioner, to cause a writ of subpoena to issue out of the office of the commissioner which shall be signed by him or his deputy and directed to the sheriff of any county of this state returnable to the office of the commissioner. The cost of issuing and serving subpoenas and witness fees shall be the same as such costs and fees in the circuit court and shall be recoverable by the prevailing party from the other party. The commissioner shall tax such costs, and, upon the same not being paid within a period of 10 days therefrom, payment thereof may be enforced in any court having jurisdiction over the person of the defaulting party.

(g) The testimony may be taken orally or by deposition, and any party shall have the right of introducing proof by deposition as may obtain in the circuit courts of this state.

(h) The commissioner or his deputy shall preside over the hearing and shall make a written finding of facts upon which his decisions shall be based.

(i) The commissioner shall, within 30 days after the conclusion of the hearing, make a ruling in writing fully disposing of the complaint and a copy of the ruling shall be served upon the complainant, the licensee and all interested parties represented by the licensee, by registered or certified mail, addressed to the licensee at the address shown by the records of the commissioner.

(j) Pursuant to such hearing, if the commissioner finds that the grounds therefor exist under section 27-7-19, he may suspend or revoke the licenses of the licensee complained against. (Acts 1957, No. 530, p. 726, § 10; Acts 1971, No. 407, p. 707, § 149; Acts 1975, No. 216, p. 740, § 1.)

Cross references. — As to rules of supreme court relative to service of process, see A.R.C.P., Rule 4 et seq.

Collateral references. — 44 C.J.S., Insurance, § 85.

Sufficiency of express finding of fact to support administrative determinations. 146 ALR 209.

Administrative decision on finding based on evidence secured outside of hearing, and with- out presence of interested party or counsel. 18 ALR2d 552.

Hearing and decision by different officers; change of personnel. 18 ALR2d 613.

Counsel's absence because of attendance on legislature as ground for continuance in case before quasi-judicial officer or board. 49 ALR2d 1073, Later Case Serv., § 4.

Reopening decision: power of administrative agency to reopen and reconsider final decision as affected by lack of specific statutory authority. 73 ALR2d 939.

Applicability of stare decisis doctrine to decisons of administrative agencies. 79 ALR2d 1126.

Disqualification, for bias or interest, of member of occupation or profession sitting in license revocation proceeding. 97 ALR2d 1210.

Assistance of counsel: right to assistance by counsel in administrative proceedings. 33 ALR3d 229.

Hearsay evidence in proceedings before state administrative agencies. 36 ALR3d 12.

§ 27-7-38. Privileged information.

(a) Any communications, complaint, evidence, testimony, document, deposition, affidavit, statement or other proof filed, given or proffered at the hearing provided for in section 27-7-37 shall be absolutely privileged to the same extent as in a court of law and shall never form the subject matter of any action, claim or proceeding against the person filing, giving or proffering the same nor against the principal or representative of such person.

(b) Reports of investigation, copies thereof and information furnished the commissioner by any insurer, agent, solicitor, broker, managing general agent or service representative and any other person shall be absolutely privileged communications, and no such report, copy, information or document, affidavit, statement, deposition or testimony so furnished to the commissioner shall ever form the subject matter of any action, claim or proceeding against any such person. (Acts 1957, No. 530, p. 726, § 10; Acts 1971, No. 407, p. 707, § 150.)

CHAPTER 8.

LIFE AND DISABILITY INSURANCE REPRESENTATIVES.

Sec.
27-8-1. "Agent" and "broker" defined; qualifications of applicants for broker's license; filing fee and annual fee for broker's license.
27-8-2. Applicability of chapter.
27-8-3. License — Requirements; forms.
27-8-4. Same — Qualifications of licensees; duties as to representation.
27-8-5. Same — Application; certificate of insurer; fees; bond.
27-8-6. Same — Examination — Requirement generally; educational prerequisite; exceptions.
27-8-7. Same — Same — Rules and regulations; preparation and administration; contracts with testing institutions.
27-8-8. Same — Same — Textbooks, manuals and other materials.
27-8-9. Repealed.
27-8-10. Same — Same — Reexamination; fee.
27-8-11. Same — Same — Agency advisory board.
27-8-12. Same — Issuance or refusal.
27-8-13. Same — Content; number of licenses generally.
27-8-14. Same — Issuance of additional licenses.

Sec.
27-8-15. Same — Continuation and expiration; filing of annual statements and fees.
27-8-16. Same — Refusal to renew or continue or suspension or revocation — Grounds.
27-8-17. Same — Same — Proceedings; appeal of order.
27-8-18. Same — Same — Privileged information.
27-8-19. Same — Return for cancellation; affidavit in lieu thereof.
27-8-20. Same — Relicensing after revocation.
27-8-21. Temporary licenses.
27-8-22. Nonresident agents.
27-8-23. Use of vending machines and credit facilities.
27-8-24. Termination of agency appointment by insurer.
27-8-25. Placement of excess or rejected risk by unlicensed agent.
27-8-26. Notice of change of business address or other changes.
27-8-27. Payment of commission or other valuable consideration to unlicensed persons not allowed; exceptions.
27-8-28. Accounting for and payment of trust funds by licensees.

Collateral references. — Public regulation or control of insurance agents or brokers. 10 ALR2d 950.

§ 27-8-1. "Agent" and "broker" defined; qualifications of applicants for broker's license; filing fee and annual fee for broker's license.

(a) An agent is a natural person, partnership or corporation appointed and authorized by an insurer to solicit applications or to negotiate for insurance or annuity contracts and to deliver policies or contracts on its behalf and, if authorized to do so by the insurer, to collect premiums in connection therewith.

(b) The term "agent" does not include any of the following:

(1) Any regular salaried officer or employee of an insurer or agent who does not solicit or accept from the public applications for any such insurance or contracts;

(2) A ticket-selling agent of a common carrier who sells accident insurance tickets to individuals;

(3) Any regular salaried officer or employee of an insurer who renders assistance to, or on behalf of, a licensed agent of the insurer, if such officer or employee devotes substantially all of his time to activities other than the solicitation of applications for insurance or annuity contracts and receives no commission or other compensation directly dependent upon the amount of business obtained; or

(4) Persons who secure and furnish information for the purpose of group life insurance, group or blanket health insurance or annuity coverages or for enrolling individuals under such plans or issuing certificates thereunder or otherwise assisting in administering such plans where no commission is paid for such services.

(c) An insurance broker is any individual, partnership or corporation who, for compensation, not being a licensed agent for the company in which a policy of insurance is placed, acts or aids in any manner in placing risks or effecting insurance for a party other than himself or itself. An individual, partnership or corporation not licensed as an insurance broker who solicits a policy of insurance to or on behalf of others or transmits for others an application for a policy of insurance to or from an insurance company or offers or assumes to act in the negotiations of such insurance shall be an insurance broker within the intent of this chapter, and shall thereby become liable for all the duties, requirements, liabilities and penalties to which such licensed brokers are subject.

(d) Each applicant for an insurance broker's license must have had not less than two years' experience as an insurance agent or in comparable employment for an insurance company, agency or brokerage firm during the three years immediately next preceding the date of application.

(e) An applicant for a broker's license shall pay an annual fee of $26.00 plus an initial filing fee of $10.00. (Acts 1957, No. 598, p. 848, § 1; Acts 1971, No. 407, p. 707, § 156; Acts 1981, No. 81-862, p. 1635, § 1.)

Cited in Cox v. State, 367 So. 2d 535 (Ala. Crim. App. 1978); American Pioneer Life Ins. Co. v. Sandlin, 470 So. 2d 657 (Ala. 1985).

Collateral references. — 44 C.J.S., Insurance, § 136.

43 Am. Jur. 2d, Insurance, § 145.

Meaning of term "solicit" in statute providing that any person who shall solicit insurance shall be regarded as agent of insurance company. 48 ALR 1173.

Provisions of insurance company's contract with independent insurance agent restricting competitive placements by agent as illegal restraint of trade under state law. 42 ALR4th 1072.

§ 27-8-2. Applicability of chapter.

This chapter applies only as to agents, and other insurance representatives and to brokers as defined in this chapter with respect to life insurance and annuity contracts and to disability insurance where written by an insurer authorized to transact disability insurance only or authorized to transact also life insurance, whether operating on a stock, mutual, reciprocal, fraternal, hospital or medical service plan. (Acts 1971, No. 407, p. 707, § 155; Acts 1981, No. 81-862, p. 1635, § 1.)

§ 27-8-3. License — Requirements; forms.

(a) No person shall in this state be, act as, hold himself out as or claim to be, or act as, an agent or broker unless then licensed as an agent or broker under this chapter.

(b) The commissioner shall prescribe and furnish on request all forms required in connection with application for, issuance or termination of licenses. (Acts 1957, No. 598, p. 848, §§ 3, 4; Acts 1971, No. 407, p. 707, § 157; Acts 1981, No. 81-862, p. 1635, § 1.)

Collateral references. — 44 C.J.S., Insurance, § 85.

Validity and enforceability of contract of agent failing to procure license. 30 ALR 866, 42 ALR 1226, 118 ALR 646.

§ 27-8-4. Same — Qualifications of licensees; duties as to representation.

(a) For the protection of the people of this state, the commissioner shall not issue, continue or permit to exist any agent or broker license for and on behalf of any natural person unless such person is in compliance with this chapter as follows:

(1) Must be a citizen of the United States of America, or Canada or a permanent resident under United States immigration laws and a resident of this state except as to licenses issued to nonresidents under section 27-8-22;

(2) Must be trustworthy, of good moral character and not have been convicted of a felony or of any crime involving moral turpitude, unless fully pardoned with restoration of civil rights;

(3) Must have had sufficient education, experience and training to make him reasonably competent to fulfill the responsibilities of a licensed agent or broker;

(4) Must intend to, and commencing after issuance of the license shall during the existence of the license, actively engage as to the general public in the business permitted under the license;

(5) Must not use, or intend to use, the license principally for the purpose of procuring insurance on his own risks or interests or those of his relatives, to the second degree, or the officers, directors, stockholders, partners or employees of any partnership, association or corporation of which he or a

member of his family is an officer, director, substantial stockholder, partner or employee;

(6) Must not use, or intend to use, the license principally for the purpose of procuring or assisting in the procurement of insurance on the lives of customers of a retail merchandise establishment or department store which does not maintain at least one place of business in this state where the credit facilities of such retail merchandise establishment or department store are used by the customer for the payment of premiums on such insurance and where such establishment or store, or the owners, officers, directors or employees thereof, receive, directly or indirectly, any commission or other valuable consideration for the writing of such insurance or the collecting of premiums thereon from the agent, broker or the insurer. This subdivision shall not apply to credit life or credit disability insurance;

(7) Must pass any written examination for the license required under this chapter; and

(8) Must, if a partnership or corporation, be organized under the laws of this state and the transaction of the insurance business under the license must be within the purposes stated in the partnership's partnership agreement or the corporation's articles.

(b) Every agent who solicits an application for insurance of any kind shall, in any controversy between the insured or his beneficiary and the insurer, be regarded as representing the insurer and not the insured or his beneficiary.

(c) Every insurance broker who solicits an application for insurance of any kind shall, in any controversy between the insured or his beneficiary and the insurer issuing any policy upon such application, be regarded as representing the insured or his beneficiary and not the insurer; except, that any company which directly or through its agents delivers in this state to any insurance broker a policy of insurance pursuant to the application or request of such broker, acting for an insured other than himself, shall be deemed to have authorized such broker to receive on its behalf payment of any premium which is due on such policy of insurance at the time of its issuance or delivery. (Acts 1971, No. 407, p. 707, § 158; Acts 1981, No. 81-862, p. 1635, § 1.)

Collateral references. — 44 C.J.S., Insurance, § 85.

43 Am. Jur. 2d, Insurance, § 66.

§ 27-8-5. Same — Application; certificate of insurer; fees; bond.

(a) The commissioner shall not issue any license except upon application therefor as provided in this section. Each applicant for a license as an agent or broker shall file with the commissioner his written application therefor signed by him, verified by his oath and showing:

(1) Applicant's full name, residence, age, occupation and place of business for five years next preceding the date of the application;

(2) Whether applicant has ever held a license to solicit insurance contracts in any state;

(3) Whether applicant has ever been refused or has had suspended or revoked any license to solicit insurance contracts in any state;

(4) What insurance experience, if any, he has had;

(5) What instruction in insurance and in the insurance laws of this state he has had or expects to have;

(6) Whether any insurer claims that applicant is indebted to the insurer under any agency contracts or otherwise and, if so, the name of the claimant, nature of the claim and applicant's defense thereto;

(7) Whether applicant has had any agency contract cancelled and, if so, when, by what insurer and the reason for the cancellation;

(8) Whether applicant will devote all, or part of, his efforts to acting as an insurance agent and, if part time only, how much time he expects to devote to work as an agent or broker and in what other business, or businesses, he is engaged or employed;

(9) Whether, if applicant is married, the spouse has ever applied for or held a license to solicit insurance in any state and whether any such license has ever been refused, suspended or revoked; and

(10) Such other information as the commissioner may reasonably require.

(b) The application for an agent's license shall be accompanied by a certificate on forms furnished by the commissioner and signed by an officer or duly authorized representative of the insurer stating, if true, that the insurer has investigated the character and background of the applicant and is satisfied that he is trustworthy and qualified to act as its agent and to hold himself out in good faith to the general public as an agent and that the insurer desires that the applicant be licensed as an agent of the insurer as defined in subsection (a) of section 27-8-1.

(c) If the applicant for an agent's or broker's license is a partnership or corporation, the application shall show, in addition, names of every member of the partnership and every officer, director, stockholder and employee of the corporation personally engaged in this state in soliciting or negotiating policies of insurance. Each such member, officer, director, stockholder or employee shall furnish information with respect to himself as part of the application, as though for an individual license, and shall otherwise meet the requirements for an individual license.

(d) Partnerships and corporations shall file their organizational documents with the commissioner accompanied by an initial filing fee of $25.00. The license shall continue in effect, subject to an annual fee of $25.00, unless cancelled, suspended or revoked. Each partnership and corporation shall file with the commissioner any change in its organization accompanied by a fee in the amount of $5.00.

(e) When filed, the application shall be accompanied by the examination filing fee specified in section 27-4-2 if the applicant is subject to an examination under this chapter. Any such fee shall not be subject to refund, whether or not the applicant in fact takes an examination. An additional license fee shall be paid as to each individual included in the application for a partnership or corporation license.

(f) Prior to issuance of a license as an insurance broker, the applicant shall file with the commissioner and, thereafter for as long as the license remains in effect, shall keep in force a bond in the penal sum of not less than $20,000.00 with an authorized corporate surety approved by the commissioner. The aggregate liability of the surety for any and all claims on any such bond shall in no event exceed the penal sum thereof. No such bond shall be terminated unless at least 30 days' prior written notice thereof is given by the surety to the licensee and the commissioner. Upon termination of the license for which the bond was in effect, the commissioner shall notify the surety within 10 working days.

(g) All surety protection under this section is to inure to the benefit of the aggrieved parties. (Acts 1957, No. 598, p. 848, § 4; Acts 1971, No. 407, p. 707, § 159; Acts 1981, No. 81-862, p. 1635, § 1.)

§ 27-8-6. Same — Examination — Requirement generally; educational prerequisite; exceptions.

(a) After completion of the educational requirements of subsection (c) of this section and filing of the application for license as required under section 27-8-5, each applicant for a license as agent or broker shall submit to a personal written examination to determine his competence to be an agent or broker and his familiarity with the pertinent provisions of the insurance laws of this state and shall pass the same to the satisfaction of the commissioner; except, that no such examination or initial educational requirements specified in subsection (c) of this section shall be required of:

(1) An applicant for renewal or continuation of a license, unless the commissioner determines that an examination is necessary to establish the competency of the applicant;

(2) An applicant whose license is limited to acting only as an agent with respect to life, health and accident insurance on borrowers or debtors, commonly known as credit life, health and accident insurance, if such applicant is a full-time employee of the institution granting the credit;

(3) An applicant whose license is limited to acting as an agent with respect to ticket travel accident policies;

(4) In the commissioner's discretion, an applicant whose license was suspended or otherwise terminated less than two years prior to the date of application;

(5) An applicant for a broker's license who holds a valid agent's license;

(6) An applicant for an agent's license who holds a valid broker's license; or

(7) An applicant holding the designation, Chartered Life Underwriter.

(b) If the applicant is a partnership or corporation, the examination shall be taken and initial educational requirements met by each individual who is to be designated in the license as having authority to act for the applicant under the license.

(c) An applicant for an agent's license, prior to examination, shall be required to complete successfully 40 hours of classroom instruction or the equivalent thereof, in the broad principles of insurance, no fewer than five hours of which shall be on the licensing and regulatory laws of the state and the obligations and duties of an agent. Said instruction may be offered by a school, college, university or bona fide educational school or program operated by an insurance company or by an insurance association. The insurance commissioner shall with the advice of the agency advisory board approve and certify any such course as being acceptable for the purposes of this section. (Acts 1957, No. 598, p. 848, § 5; Acts 1971, No. 407, p. 707, § 160; Acts 1981, No. 81-862, p. 1635, § 1.)

§ 27-8-7. Same — Same — Rules and regulations; preparation and administration; contracts with testing institutions.

(a) The commission shall establish rules and regulations with respect to:
(1) The classification of applicants according to the type of insurance to be effected by them;
(2) The scope, type and conduct of written examinations; and
(3) The times and places within the state for the holding of such examinations. An applicant shall be permitted to take an examination once in each two weeks in the principal office of the commissioner, and an examination shall be held at least as often as once in each three months in each congressional district.

(b) Such rules and regulations shall classify applicant for purposes of this section as follows:
(1) Those desiring to write life insurance;
(2) Those desiring to write disability insurance;
(3) Those desiring to write any combination of the above classifications; and
(4) Such other classifications as, in the opinion of the commissioner, are necessary or appropriate.

(c) Examination shall be prepared and given in those subjects only which pertain to the classification, or classifications, which apply to the applicant, and no applicant shall be required to take an examination on a subject, or subjects, pertaining to any other classification. Prior to the examination, the commissioner shall value each question to be asked therein, and the sum of such values shall total 100. Each of the answers given shall correspondingly be valued proportionately to its correctness, and the sum of such values totaling 70 shall constitute a passing grade. An applicant shall have the right to be examined as to all of such classifications in the same examination and shall be required to pay but one examination application filing fee therefor.

(d) The commissioner shall not contract with any qualified educational testing institutions for preparation, analysis or grading of the written portions of the examination. (Acts 1957, No. 598, p. 848, § 6; Acts 1971, No. 407, p. 707, § 161; Acts 1981, No. 81-862, p. 1635, § 1.)

§ 27-8-8. Same — Same — Textbooks, manuals and other materials.

The rules and regulations of the commissioner shall designate textbooks, manuals and other materials to be studied by applicants in preparation for examinations in each classification designated by the commissioner pursuant to section 27-8-7. Such textbooks, manuals or other materials may consist of matter available to applicants by purchase from the publisher or may consist of matter prepared at the direction of the commissioner and distributed to applicants upon request and payment of the reasonable cost thereof. If textbooks, manuals or other materials are so designated or prepared by the commissioner, all examination questions shall be prepared from the contents of such textbooks, manuals or other materials. (Acts 1957, No. 598, p. 848, § 6; Acts 1971, No. 407, p. 707, § 162; Acts 1981, No. 81-862, p. 1635, § 1.)

§ 27-8-9. Repealed by Acts 1981, No. 81-862, p. 1635, § 1, effective October 1, 1981.

§ 27-8-10. Same — Same — Reexamination; fee.

No person who has taken and failed to pass two examinations given pursuant to section 27-8-7 shall be entitled to take any further examination until after the expiration of six months from the date of the last examination in which he failed to pass. If such person thereafter fails to pass two more such examinations, he shall not be eligible to take any further examination until after the expiration of one year from the date of his last unsuccessful examination. An examination application filing fee shall be paid for each and every examination; except, that an applicant shall be permitted to take a single examination covering all classes of insurance contracts as defined in section 27-8-7. (Acts 1957, No. 598, p. 848, § 6; Acts 1971, No. 407, p. 707, § 164.)

§ 27-8-11. Same — Same — Agency advisory board.

The commissioner may appoint an agency advisory board, as an aid to the efficient administration of this chapter, to consult with individuals experienced in the life and disability insurance business, to include officers, employees, managers, and licensed agents of insurers engaged in such business and brokers, to the end that an orderly and effective program be developed as to scope, type and conduct of written examinations, as to the acceptability of courses of instruction under subsection (c) of section 27-8-6 and the times and places in the state where the examinations shall be held. (Acts 1957, No. 598, p. 848, § 6; Acts 1971, No. 407, p. 707, § 165; Acts 1981, No. 81-862, p. 1635, § 1.)

§ 27-8-12. Same — Issuance or refusal.

(a) If the commissioner finds, after the successful completion of the initial educational requirement, the completion of the application therefor and successful passing of any examination required under this chapter, that the applicant is fully qualified and entitled thereto under this chapter, and upon payment of the license fee specified in section 27-4-2, the commissioner shall promptly issue to the applicant the license to which he is so entitled.

(b) If the commissioner finds that the applicant is not qualified for, or entitled to, the license under the provisions of this chapter or that he failed to complete the initial educational requirement or to pass any examination required of him, he shall promptly give written notice to the applicant and, if applicable, the insurer by whom the applicant was sponsored that the license is refused, stating the reasons therefor. (Acts 1957, No. 598, p. 848, § 7; Acts 1971, No. 407, p. 707, § 166; Acts 1981, No. 81-862, p. 1635, § 1.)

§ 27-8-13. Same — Content; number of licenses generally.

(a) Licenses shall state the name and address of the licensee, the kinds of insurance or classifications thereof covered by the license, date of issue and of expiration and the general conditions of the license.

(b) An agent with a license in force may solicit applications for policies of life insurance on behalf of an insurer with respect to which he is not a licensed agent, provided that such agent submits an application for appointment as an agent of such insurer simultaneously with the submission to such insurer of the application for insurance solicited by him, and, provided further, that no commissions shall be paid by such insurer to the agent until such time as an additional license with respect to such insurer has been issued to the agent.

(c) The commissioner may, upon request, issue a single license covering all of the kinds of insurance and classifications thereof transacted by the same insurer. (Acts 1971, No. 407, p. 707, § 167; Acts 1981, No. 81-862, p. 1635, § 1.)

§ 27-8-14. Same — Issuance of additional licenses.

The commissioner may issue additional licenses to any agent when requested by an official or duly authorized representative of an insurer. Any such additional license shall be limited to the class, or classes, for which the agent holds a license. (Acts 1957, No. 598, p. 848, § 10; Acts 1971, No. 407, p. 707, § 168; Acts 1981, No. 81-862, p. 1635, § 1.)

§ 27-8-15. Same — Continuation and expiration; filing of annual statements and fees.

(a) All licenses issued under this chapter, other than temporary licenses issued under section 27-8-21, shall continue in force until expired, suspended, revoked or otherwise terminated, but subject to payment to the commissioner annually by the insurer, on or before December 31, of the applicable continuation fee, as stated in section 27-4-2 or subsection (d) of section 28-8-5 [27-8-5] and, with respect to an agent's license, accompanied by the insurer's written request and payment of the fee for such continuation.

(b) Any license as to which the request for continuation and fee is not received by the commissioner as required under subsection (a) of this section, shall be deemed to have expired at midnight on December 31, mentioned in subsection (a) of this section. Request for continuation of any such license or payment of the continuation fee therefor which is received by the commissioner after such December 31, and prior to the next following February 15, may be accepted and effectuated by the commissioner, in his discretion, if accompanied by a continuation fee in twice the amount otherwise required.

(c) Annually, prior to December 31, each insurer shall file with the commissioner an alphabetical list of the names and addresses of all its agents whose licenses in this state are to continue in effect, accompanied by payment of the annual continuation fee referred to in subsection (a) of this section. At the same time, the insurer shall also file with the commissioner an alphabetical list of the names and addresses of all its agents whose licenses in this state are not to remain in effect and shall give written notice thereof to all such agents where reasonably possible.

(d) If so requested by the commissioner, the insurer shall, as to each agent whose license is to be continued as provided in this section, file with the commissioner a statement, upon forms prescribed and furnished by the commissioner, showing whether the agent devotes all or part of his efforts to his work as agent and, if part only, how much time he devotes to such work and in what other business, or businesses, he is engaged or employed. (Acts 1957, No. 598, p. 848, § 11; Acts 1971, No. 407, p. 707, § 172; Acts 1981, No. 81-862, p. 1635, § 1.)

§ 27-8-16. Same — Refusal to renew or continue or suspension or revocation — Grounds.

(a) The commissioner may, after notice and hearing as provided in section 27-8-17, refuse to renew or continue or may suspend or revoke a license for any cause for which he could have refused to issue the license had such cause then existed and been known to the commissioner or if he finds that the licensee has:

(1) Willfully violated any provision of this title;

(2) Intentionally made a material misstatement in the application for license;

(3) Obtained or attempted to obtain the license by fraud or misrepresentation;

(4) Misappropriated or converted to his own use or illegally withheld money belonging to an insurer or an insured or beneficiary;

(5) Otherwise demonstrated lack of trustworthiness or competence to act as an agent or broker;

(6) Been guilty of fraudulent or dishonest practices;

(7) Materially misrepresented the terms or conditions of insurance policies or contracts;

(8) Made, issued or caused to be made or issued any statement misrepresenting or making incomplete comparisons regarding the terms or conditions of any insurance or annuity contract legally issued by any insurer for the purpose of inducing, or attempting to induce, the owner of such contract to forfeit, cancel or surrender such contract or allow it to lapse for the purpose of replacing such contract with another;

(9) Obtained such license not for the purpose of holding himself out to the general public as an agent or broker, but primarily for the purpose of soliciting, negotiating or procuring insurance or annuity contracts covering himself or members of his family or others, in violation of subdivision (5) of subsection (a) of section 27-8-4;

(10) Obtained such license not for the purpose of holding himself out to the general public as an agent or broker, but primarily for the purpose of soliciting, negotiating or procuring insurance on the lives of customers of a retail merchandise establishment or department store which does not maintain at least one place of business in this state where the credit facilities of such retail merchandise establishment or department store are used by the customer for the payment of premiums on such insurance and where such establishment or store or the owners, officers, directors or employees thereof receive, directly or indirectly, any commission or other valuable consideration for the procuring of such insurance or the collecting of premiums thereon from the agent or broker or from the insurer; except, that this subdivision shall not apply to credit life or credit disability insurance; or

(11) Does not possess cash and accounts receivable for insurance premiums owing the licensee in an amount equal to, or in excess of, the accounts payable by the licensee for insurance premiums. Such accounts receivable shall not include insurance premiums owing the licensee more than 120 days after the last day of the month in which the insurance was effective.

(b) The license of a partnership or corporation may be suspended, revoked or refused if the commissioner finds, after hearing, that an individual licensee's violation was known or should have been known by one or more of the partners, officers or managers acting on behalf of the partnership or corporation and such violation was not reported timely to the insurance department nor corrective action taken in relation thereto. (Acts 1957, No. 598, p. 848, § 14; Acts 1971, No. 407, p. 707, § 178; Acts 1981, No. 81-862, p. 1635, § 1.)

Cited in DeRamus v. Winfield, 388 So. 2d 1215 (Ala. Civ. App. 1980).

Collateral references. — 44 C.J.S., Insurance, § 85.

43 Am. Jur. 2d, Insurance, § 68.

Cancellation, suspension, or renewal of license of insurance agent. 154 ALR 1146.

Provisions of insurance company's contract with independent insurance agent restricting competitive placements by agent as illegal restraint of trade under state law. 42 ALR4th 1072.

Liability of insurance agent or broker to insured for misrepresentation of cash surrender value or accumulated value benefits of life insurance policy. 44 ALR4th 1030.

§ 27-8-17. Same — Same — Proceedings; appeal of order.

(a) Before any license shall be suspended or revoked or the renewal thereof refused, the commissioner shall give notice of his intention so to do and the reasons therefor by registered or certified mail to the licensee and the insurer whom he represents. The licensee may make written demand upon the commissioner within 30 days for a hearing before the commissioner to determine the reasonableness of the commissioner's action. Upon such a request, the commissioner shall set a date not less than 30 days from the date of receipt of the written demand when the licensee and, if applicable, a duly authorized representative of the insurer may appear to be heard and produce evidence. Upon termination of such hearing, findings shall be reduced to writing and, upon approval by the commissioner, shall be filed in his office and notice of the findings sent by registered or certified mail to the licensee and the insurer concerned.

(b) Any party to such a hearing who is aggrieved by any order of the commissioner suspending, revoking or refusing to renew a license may appeal therefrom as provided in section 27-2-32. (Acts 1957, No. 598, p. 848, §§ 14, 15; Acts 1971, No. 407, p. 707, § 179; Acts 1981, No. 81-862, p. 1635, § 1.)

Collateral references. — Sufficiency of express finding of fact to support administrative determinations. 146 ALR 209.

Administrative decision on finding based on evidence secured outside of hearing, and without presence of interested party or counsel. 18 ALR2d 552.

Hearing and decision by different officers; change of personnel. 18 ALR2d 613.

Counsel's absence because of attendance on legislature as ground for continuance in case before quasi-judicial officer or board. 49 ALR2d 1073, Later Case Serv., § 4.

Reopening decision: power of administrative agency to reopen and reconsider final decision as affected by lack of specific statutory authority. 73 ALR2d 939.

Applicability of stare decisis doctrine to decisions of administrative agencies. 79 ALR2d 1126.

Disqualification, for bias or interest, of member of occupation or profession sitting in license revocation proceeding. 97 ALR2d 1210.

Assistance of counsel; right to assistance by counsel in administrative proceedings. 33 ALR3d 229.

Hearsay evidence in proceedings before state administrative agencies. 36 ALR3d 12.

Liability of insurance agent or broker to insured for misrepresentation of cash surrender value or accumulated value benefits of life insurance policy. 44 ALR4th 1030.

§ 27-8-18. Same — Same — Privileged information.

All testimony, documents and other evidence required to be submitted to the commissioner in connection with any hearing held by him under section 27-8-17, or investigation made by the commissioner in connection therewith, or any act or thing done by the insurer or any director, officer, employee or representative of the insurer in connection with any such testimony, documents and other evidence shall be absolutely privileged and shall not be admissible in evidence in any other proceeding. (Acts 1957, No. 598, p. 848, § 18; Acts 1971, No. 407, p. 707, § 182.)

Collateral references. — Liability of insurance agent or broker to insured for misrepresentation of cash surrender value or accumulated value benefits of life insurance policy. 44 ALR4th 1030.

§ 27-8-19. Same — Return for cancellation; affidavit in lieu thereof.

(a) All licenses issued under this chapter, though issued to a licensee, at all times are the property of the state of Alabama, and, upon notice of any suspension, revocation, refusal to renew, expiration or other termination of the license, the licensee, or other person having possession or custody thereof, shall promptly deliver the license to the commissioner for cancellation.

(b) As to any license lost, stolen or destroyed while in the possession of any such licensee or person, the commissioner may accept in lieu of return of the license the affidavit of the licensee or other person responsible for, or involved in the safekeeping of, such license concerning the facts of such loss, theft or destruction. (Acts 1971, No. 407, p. 707, § 180.)

Collateral references. — Liability of insurance agent or broker to insured for misrepresentation of cash surrender value or accumulated value benefits of life insurance policy. 44 ALR4th 1030.

§ 27-8-20. Same — Relicensing after revocation.

No licensee whose license has been revoked shall be entitled to file another application for a license as an agent or broker within one year from the effective date of such revocation or, if judicial review of such revocation is sought, within one year from date of final court order or judgment affirming the revocation. Such application, when filed, may be refused by the commissioner unless the applicant shows good cause why the revocation of his license shall not be deemed a bar to the issuance of a new license. (Acts 1957, No. 598, p. 848, § 14; Acts 1971, No. 407, p. 707, § 181; Acts 1981, No. 81-862, p. 1635, § 1.)

Collateral references. — Liability of insurance agent or broker to insured for misrepresentation of cash surrender value or accumulated value benefits of life insurance policy. 44 ALR4th 1030.

§ 27-8-21. Temporary licenses.

(a) The commissioner, if satisfied that the applicant is otherwise qualified for a license under this chapter, shall issue a temporary license to an applicant for a license pending completion of the examination required under section 27-8-6. A temporary license shall not be effective for more than three months. The commissioner, in his discretion, may renew a temporary license issued under this section one time upon proper application and for good cause. A temporary license may be terminated for cause pursuant to the provisions of this chapter.

(b) The temporary license shall be issued immediately, upon receipt by the commissioner of an application executed by such person in the form required by section 27-8-5, together with the applicable license fee specified in section 27-4-2, and a certificate signed by an officer or properly authorized representative of the insurer stating, to the extent true:

(1) That the insurer has investigated the character and background of such person and is satisfied that he is trustworthy;

(2) That such person has been appointed, or is being considered for appointment by the insurer, as a full-time agent; and

(3) That the insurer desires that such person be issued a temporary license.

(c) The commissioner shall refuse to issue such license to applicants of any insurer where more than 25 percent of the applicants for a license for such insurer have repeatedly and without good cause failed to appear for the required examination during the preceding 12-month period.

(d) If a temporary license is not received from the commissioner within 10 days from the date on which the application and certificate were delivered to or placed in the United States mail properly addressed to the attention of the commissioner, the insurer may assume that the temporary license will be issued in due course and may continue such person in its employment until notified by the commissioner to the contrary.

(e) A temporary license shall be granted only to an applicant who intends to engage exclusively as an agent. (Acts 1957, No. 598, p. 848, § 12; Acts 1971, No. 407, p. 707, § 169; Acts 1981, No. 81-862, p. 1635, § 1.)

§ 27-8-22. Nonresident agents.

(a) The commissioner may issue a license as agent to an individual who is otherwise qualified for such license under this chapter, but is not a resident of this state, if the state in which such person resides accords the same privilege to residents of this state.

(b) The commissioner has authority to enter into reciprocal agreements with the appropriate official of any other state waiving the initial educational requirements or the written examination of any applicant resident in such other state if:

(1) A comparable initial educational requirement or written examination is required of applicants for an agent's license in such other state;

(2) The appropriate official of such other state certifies that the applicant holds a currently valid license as an agent in such other state and has passed a written examination or met the initial educational requirements or both or was the holder of an agent's license prior to the time a written examination was required; and

(3) In such other state, a resident of this state is privileged to procure an agent's license upon the foregoing conditions and without discrimination as to fees or otherwise in favor of the residents of such other state.

(c) No such applicant or licensee shall have a place of business within this state for the transaction of business as such an agent.

(d) If under the laws of the other state requirements as to countersignature, division of commissions, solicitation with a resident agent or as to other matter, other than amount of license fee, are imposed upon residents of this state transacting business as insurance agents in such state, then the commissioner shall impose similar requirements as to residents of such state soliciting business as nonresident agents in this state.

(e) Section 27-7-29, relative to service of process, shall apply also to nonresident agents licensed under this section.

(f) For the purposes of this section, the word "state" shall be construed as including any province of Canada. (Acts 1957, No. 598, p. 848, § 8; Acts 1971, No. 407, p. 707, § 170; Acts 1981, No. 81-862, p. 1635, § 1.)

§ 27-8-23. Use of vending machines and credit facilities.

(a) A licensed resident agent may solicit applications for and issue policies of personal travel accident insurance by means of mechanical vending machines supervised by him and placed at airports, railroad stations, bus stations and similar places where transportation tickets are sold and of convenience to the traveling public if the commissioner finds:

(1) That the policy to be so sold provides reasonable coverage and benefits, is reasonably suited for sale and issuance through vending machines and that use of such a machine therefor in a particular proposed location would be of material convenience to the public;

(2) That the type of vending machine proposed to be used is reasonably suitable and practical for the purpose;

(3) That reasonable means are provided for informing the prospective purchaser of any such policy of the coverage and restrictions of the policy; and

(4) That reasonable means are provided for refund to the applicant or prospective applicant of money inserted in defective machines and for which no insurance or a less amount than paid for is actually received.

(b) As to each machine to be so used, the commissioner shall issue to the agent a special vending machine license. The license shall specify the name and address of the insurer and agent, the name of the policy to be so sold, the serial number of the machine and the place where the machine is to be in operation. The license shall be subject to annual continuation, to expiration, suspension or revocation coincidentally with that of the agent. The commissioner shall also revoke the license as to any machine as to which he finds that the conditions upon which the machine was licensed, as referred to in subsection (a) of this section, no longer exist. The license fee shall be as stated in section 27-4-2 for each license year, or part thereof, for each respective vending machine. Proof of the existence of a subsisting license shall be displayed on, or about, each such vending machine in use in such manner as the commissioner may reasonably require.

(c) No person shall knowingly solicit or negotiate any contract of insurance, except credit life insurance and credit disability insurance and accidental death benefit insurance, or seek or accept applications for insurance, issue or deliver any policy for any insurance company, or otherwise transact insurance in this state, or relative to a subject of insurance, resident, located or to be performed in this state, through the arrangement or facilities of a credit card facility or organization or through the credit facilities of a retail merchandise establishment or department store; provided, however, that nothing contained in this title shall prohibit an insurer authorized to do business in this state, the representative of such insurer or an insurance agent, agency or broker from soliciting, negotiating, contracting or financing the sales of any such insurance, or the doing of any acts in relation thereto, as contemplated above where said solicitation is directed to the credit card holders or credit customers of any retail merchandise establishment or department store which maintains at least one business establishment in this state, provided, that the laws of this state requiring countersignature by a licensed agent resident in this state are complied with and said agent shall receive the applicable commission payable therefor. (Acts 1971, No. 407, p. 707, § 171.)

§ 27-8-24. Termination of agency appointment by insurer.

(a) Subject to the agent's contract rights, if any, an insurer may terminate an agency appointment at any time. The insurer shall promptly give written notice of such termination to the commissioner and to the agent, where reasonably possible. The commissioner may require of the insurer reasonable proof that the insurer has given such notice to the agent, whether upon termination of the appointment by affirmative action of the insurer or by failure of the insurer to continue the appointment as provided for in subsection (c) of section 27-8-15.

(b) Upon receipt of the insurer's notice of termination of the agency appointment, the commissioner shall terminate the license of the agent to represent the insurer.

(c) Upon termination of the appointment of an agent, or as soon thereafter as possible, and immediately upon completion of the insurer's investigation, the insurer shall file with the commissioner a written statement of the facts relative to the termination and the date and cause thereof, including a statement of the amount of indebtedness due the insurer or general agent.

(d) Any information, document, record or statement filed with or disclosed to the commissioner pursuant to subsection (c) of this section, or any information, document, record or statement supplemental thereto, is an absolutely privileged communication; and they and any act or thing done by the insurer or any director, officer, employee or representative of the insurer in connection with preparing and filing such information, record, document or statement with the commissioner shall not constitute basis of any action against the insurer or any director, officer, employee or representative of the insurer or against any other person and shall not be admissible as evidence in any court action or proceeding. (Acts 1957, No. 598, p. 848, § 13; Acts 1971, No. 407, p. 707, § 173.)

Collateral references. — 44 C.J.S., Insurance, § 148.

Duty of insurer to give notice of termination of agency. 14 ALR 846.

When is termination of insurance agency contract wrongful, so as to make insurer liable to agent. 5 ALR4th 1080.

§ 27-8-25. Placement of excess or rejected risk by unlicensed agent.

An agent may, from time to time, place, with an authorized insurer as to which he is not then a licensed agent, any portion of a risk which is in excess of the amount thereof acceptable to, or which has been rejected by, an insurer for which he is so licensed. The application for the insurance or annuity contract so placed must have been secured by the agent and must be within the kinds of insurance or classifications thereof for which the agent is licensed as to the insurer which so refused or rejected such business. (Acts 1957, No. 598, p. 848, § 10; Acts 1971, No. 407, p. 707, § 174.)

§ 27-8-26. Notice of change of business address or other changes.

(a) Every agent or broker shall promptly notify the commissioner in writing of any change of his principal business or residency address.

(b) A corporation or partnership licensee shall, within 10 working days, notify the commissioner of every change relative to the licensees associated with the corporation or partnership or of any change in the name of the corporation or of any change in the name or membership of the partnership. (Acts 1957, No. 598, p. 848, § 16; Acts 1971, No. 407, p. 707, § 175; Acts 1981, No. 81-862, p. 1635, § 1.)

Collateral references. — Actual receipt of cancellation notice mailed by insurer as pre-requisite to cancellation of insurance. 40 ALR4th 867.

§ 27-8-27. Payment of commission or other valuable consideration to unlicensed persons not allowed; exceptions.

(a) No insurer, agent or broker shall pay, directly or indirectly, any commission or other valuable consideration to any person for services as an agent or broker within this state unless such person holds a currently valid license as an agent or broker as to the kind or class of business involved as required by this chapter.

(b) Any insurer, agent or broker violating this section shall be liable for a fine in an amount of up to three times the amount of the commission paid. Such fine shall be levied and collected by the commissioner. Upon failure to pay such fine the commissioner may, in his discretion, revoke the license of the agent or broker, or the insurer's certificate of authority or both.

(c) The provisions of this section shall not prevent:

(1) Payment of renewal or other deferred commissions to any person solely because such person has ceased to hold a license to act as an agent or broker;

(2) Payment to the personal representative of a deceased agent or broker; and

(3) Payment of any commission or any other valuable consideration by an insurer, agent or broker to a person who has been appointed as its full-time agent and has applied for a temporary license pursuant to section 27-8-21, pending issuance of a permanent license.

(d) No insurer, agent or broker shall pay, directly or indirectly, any commission or other valuable consideration to any retail merchandise establishment or department store or to any of the owners, officers, directors or employees thereof for services in connection with procuring or assisting in the procurement of individual insurance on the lives of customers of such retail merchandise establishment or department store where the revolving credit facilities of such establishment or store are used by the customer for the payment of premiums on such insurance; except, that nothing contained in this title shall prohibit the payment of such commissions or other consideration where the contracting of said insurance and the financing thereof is not prohibited by the provisions of this title. This subsection shall not apply to credit life or credit disability insurance. (Acts 1957, No. 598, p. 848, § 3; Acts 1971, No. 407, p. 707, § 176; Acts 1981, No. 81-862, p. 1635, § 1.)

Collateral references. — 44 C.J.S., Insurance, §§ 141, 162.

Recovery back of money voluntarily paid to unlicensed person required by law to have occupational or business license or permit to make contract. 30 ALR2d 1233.

§ 27-8-28. Accounting for and payment of trust funds by licensees.

(a) All premiums, return premiums or other funds belonging to others received by an agent or broker in transactions under his license shall be trust funds so received by the licensee in a fiduciary capacity, and the licensee shall promptly account for and pay the same to the insurer, insured or other person entitled thereto.

(b) Any agent or broker who, not being lawfully entitled thereto, diverts or appropriates such funds, or any portion thereof, to his own use shall, upon conviction, be guilty of larceny by embezzlement and shall be punished as provided by law as if he had stolen such funds. (Acts 1971, No. 407, p. 707, § 177; Acts 1981, No. 81-862, p. 1635, § 1.)

Provision applicable where defendant's status as agent controlling. — Where no application for insurance would have been submitted and no money would have been received by defendant were it not for the defendant's agency and license as insurance agent, statute governing larceny by embezzlement by insurance agent was applicable to defendant's actions in failing to return funds received by him. Cox v. State, 367 So. 2d 535 (Ala. Crim. App. 1978), cert. denied, 367 So. 2d 542 (Ala. 1979).

Even repayment no defense to criminal charge. — It is no defense to a charge of embezzlement by an agent that after the offense was completed the agent promised to pay the money converted; a person taking money entrusted to him and using it even temporarily for his own benefit cannot avoid criminal responsibility by calling it a loan and even the fact that the funds have been repaid constitutes no defense. Cox v. State, 367 So. 2d 535 (Ala. Crim. App. 1978), cert. denied, 367 So. 2d 542 (Ala. 1979).

Collateral references. — 44 C.J.S., Insurance, § 157.

CHAPTER 9.

ADJUSTERS.

Sec.
27-9-1. "Adjuster" defined.
27-9-2. License — Requirement; application; issuance; fee; firms and corporations.
27-9-3. Same — Qualifications.
27-9-4. Same — Authority to act as adjuster without license.

Sec.
27-9-5. Same — Continuation and expiration.
27-9-6. Same — Suspension, revocation or refusal to continue.
27-9-7. Same — Return to commissioner; affidavit in lieu thereof.
27-9-8. Office and records of licensee.

Collateral references. — 45 C.J.S., Insurance, § 1102.

Activities of insurance adjusters as unauthorized practice of law. 29 ALR4th 1156.

§ 27-9-1. "Adjuster" defined.

(a) An "adjuster" is a person who, for compensation as an independent contractor, or as the employee of such an independent contractor or for fee or commission, investigates and negotiates settlement of claims arising under insurance contracts on behalf of the insurer.

(b) The definition of adjuster shall not include, nor require, a license of the following:

(1) A licensed attorney-at-law who is qualified to practice law in this state; or

(2) A salaried employee of an insurer. (Acts 1971, No. 407, p. 707, § 183.)

Collateral references. — 44 Am. Jur. 2d, Insurance, § 1701 et seq.

Activities of insurance adjusters as unauthorized practice of law. 29 ALR4th 1156.

§ 27-9-2. License — Requirement; application; issuance; fee; firms and corporations.

(a) No person shall in this state act as, or hold himself out to be, an adjuster unless then licensed therefor under this chapter. Application for license shall be made to the commissioner according to forms as prescribed and furnished by him.

(b) The commissioner shall promptly issue a license to each person who has properly completed application therefor and who is qualified for the license under this chapter.

(c) At time of application for the license, the applicant shall tender to the commissioner the license fee specified in section 27-4-2. If the license is refused, the commissioner shall refund the license fee to the applicant or person entitled thereto.

(d) Firms and corporations, as well as individuals, may be licensed as an adjuster. Each individual associated in such firm or corporation and who exercises, or proposes to exercise, license powers shall file application with the commissioner, pay the license fee and qualify as though for an individual license. The license issued to a firm or corporation shall list thereon all individuals who are thereby authorized to act as an adjuster or, in lieu thereof, the commissioner may issue a separate license as to each such individual.

(e) The license fee provided for in this section is payable to the state, as provided in section 27-4-2, and no license or fee shall be paid to the county. (Acts 1971, No. 407, p. 707, § 184.)

Collateral references. — Right of person wrongfully refused license upon proper application therefor to do act for which license is required. 30 ALR2d 1006.

§ 27-9-3. Same — Qualifications.

To be licensed as an adjuster, the applicant must be qualified therefor as follows:

(1) Must be an individual 19 years of age or more;

(2) Must be a resident in and of Alabama or resident of another state which will permit residents of Alabama regularly to act as adjusters in such other state;

(3) Must be a full-time salaried employee of a licensed adjuster, or a graduate of a recognized law school or must have had experience or special education or training as to the handling of loss claims under insurance contracts of sufficient duration and extent reasonably to make him competent to fulfill the responsibilities of an adjuster; and

(4) Must be trustworthy and of good character. (Acts 1971, No. 407, p. 707, § 185.)

§ 27-9-4. Same — Authority to act as adjuster without license.

No such adjuster's license, or qualifications therefor, shall be required as to any adjuster who is sent into this state by, and on behalf of, an insurer for the purpose of investigating or making adjustment of a particular loss of unique and unusual character under an insurance policy or for the adjustment of a series of losses resulting from a catastrophe common to all such losses and on behalf of, as authorized by, an insurer as to which he is licensed as agent under this title. An agent may, from time to time, act as an adjuster without a license as an adjuster, but no such agent shall act as an adjuster for an insurer with which he has a contract providing for compensation retrospectively contingent upon losses incurred under insurance sold or serviced by him. (Acts 1971, No. 407, p. 707, § 186.)

§ 27-9-5. Same — Continuation and expiration.

(a) An adjuster license shall continue in force until expired, suspended, revoked or otherwise terminated, but subject to payment to the commissioner annually, on or before December 31, of the continuation fee stated in section 27-4-2, accompanied by written request for such continuation.

(b) Any license as to which the fee and request for continuation is not received by the commissioner as required in subsection (a) of this section, shall be deemed to have expired at midnight on December 31, mentioned in subsection (a) of this section. Request for continuation of any such license and/or payment of the continuation fee therefor which is received by the commissioner after such December 31, but before the next following February 15, may be accepted and effectuated by the commissioner, in his discretion, if accompanied by a continuation fee of one and one-half times the continuation fee otherwise required. (Acts 1971, No. 407, p. 707, § 187.)

§ 27-9-6. Same — Suspension, revocation or refusal to continue.

(a) The commissioner may suspend for not more than 12 months or may revoke or refuse to continue any adjuster license if, after a hearing held on not less than 20 days' advance notice to the licensee of such hearing and of the charges against him by registered or certified mail as provided in subsection (c) of section 27-2-18, he finds that as to the licensee any one or more of the following causes exist:

(1) For any cause for which issuance of the license could have been refused had it then existed and been known to the commissioner;

(2) For obtaining or attempting to obtain any such license through misrepresentation or fraud;

(3) For violation of or noncompliance with any applicable provision of this title or for willful violation of any lawful rule, regulation or order of the commissioner;

(4) For misappropriation or conversion to his own use or illegal withholding of moneys or property belonging to policyholders, or insurers, or beneficiaries or others and received in conduct of business under the license;

(5) Conviction, by final judgment, of a felony involving moral turpitude; or

(6) If in the conduct of his affairs under the license the licensee has used fraudulent or dishonest practices or has shown himself to be incompetent or untrustworthy.

(b) The license of a firm or corporation may be suspended, revoked or refused also for any of such causes as relate to any individual designated in the license to exercise its powers.

(c) Any party to the hearing, referred to in subsection (a) of this section, who is aggrieved by the suspension, revocation or refusal to continue a license may appeal from the commissioner's order relative thereto as provided in section 27-2-32. (Acts 1971, No. 407, p. 707, § 189.)

§ 27-9-7. Same — Return to commissioner; affidavit in lieu thereof.

(a) All licenses issued under this chapter, although issued and delivered to the licensee, shall at all times be the property of the state of Alabama. Upon any expiration, termination, suspension or revocation of the license, the licensee, or other person having possession or custody of the license, shall forthwith deliver it to the commissioner either by personal delivery or by mail.

(b) As to any license lost, stolen or destroyed while in the possession of any such licensee or person, the commissioner may accept in lieu of return of the license the affidavit of the licensee or other person responsible for, or involved in, the safekeeping of such license concerning the facts of such loss, theft or destruction. (Acts 1971, No. 407, p. 707, § 190.)

§ 27-9-8. Office and records of licensee.

Each adjuster must have and maintain in this state an office accessible to the public and keep therein the usual and customary records pertaining to transactions under the license. Records relative to a particular transaction shall be so retained for not less than one year thereafter. This section shall not be deemed to prohibit maintenance of such an office in the home of the licensee. The license of the adjuster shall show the address of his office, and the licensee shall promptly give written notice to the commissioner of any change of such address. (Acts 1971, No. 407, p. 707, § 188.)

CHAPTER 10.

UNAUTHORIZED INSURERS AND SURPLUS LINES.

Article 1.

General Provisions.

Sec.
27-10-1. Representing or aiding unauthorized insurer not allowed; exceptions; validity of contracts.
27-10-2. Liability of persons violating section 27-10-1; liability of adjusters.
27-10-3. Actions by unauthorized insurers not allowed; exceptions.

Article 2.

Surplus Line Insurance.

27-10-20. Procuring of surplus lines from unauthorized insurers.
27-10-21. Report of surplus line broker.
27-10-22. Endorsement of surplus line contract.
27-10-23. Validity and enforceability of surplus line contracts.
27-10-24. Licensing of surplus line brokers.
27-10-25. Acceptance and placement of surplus line business from agents or brokers.
27-10-26. Eligibility of insurers for placement of surplus line insurance.
27-10-27. Evidence of surplus line insurance; changes; issuance of false certificate and failure to notify insured of material change.
27-10-28. Liability of insurer as to losses and unearned premiums.

Sec.
27-10-29. Records of surplus line brokers.
27-10-30. Annual statement of surplus line broker.
27-10-31. Annual tax of surplus line brokers.
27-10-32. Revocation or suspension of surplus line broker's license.
27-10-33. Service of process in action or proceeding against insurer.
27-10-34. Exemptions from surplus line insurance law.
27-10-35. Report of, and tax on, independently procured coverages; exceptions.
27-10-36. Production of policies, etc., for inspection by commissioner.
27-10-37. Penalty for violation of article.
27-10-38. Short title.

Article 3.

Unauthorized Insurers Process Act.

27-10-50. Purpose.
27-10-51. Acts constituting appointment of commissioner as agent for service of process on foreign or alien insurer.
27-10-52. Service of process upon insurer; judgment by default.
27-10-53. Defense of action or proceeding by insurer.
27-10-54. Transaction of insurance business not authorized by article.
27-10-55. Exemptions.
27-10-56. Short title; construction of article.

ARTICLE 1.

GENERAL PROVISIONS.

§ 27-10-1. Representing or aiding unauthorized insurer not allowed; exceptions; validity of contracts.

(a) No person shall in this state, directly or indirectly, act as agent for, or otherwise represent or aid on behalf of another, any insurer not then authorized to transact such insurance in this state in the solicitation, negotiation or effectuation of insurance or annuity contracts, forwarding of applications, delivery of policies or contracts, inspection of risks, fixing of rates, investigation or adjustment of losses, collection of premiums or in any other manner in the transaction of insurance with respect to subjects of insurance resident, located or to be performed in this state.

(b) This section shall not apply to:

(1) Acceptance of service of process by the commissioner under section 27-10-52;

(2) Surplus lines insurance or coverage specified in section 27-10-34 and other transactions as to which a certificate of authority is not required of an insurer;

(3) Adjustment of losses as authorized in section 27-10-35;

(4) Transactions for which a certificate of authority to do business is not required of an insurer under the laws of this state;

(5) Reinsurance effectuated in accordance with this title; or

(6) The property and operations of the shipbuilding and/or ship repair industry engaged in interstate or foreign commerce and vessels, cargoes, watercraft, piers, wharves, graven docks, drydocks, marine railways and building ways, commonly known as wet marine.

(c) This section shall not be deemed to render invalid, as between the parties thereto, any insurance contract entered into in violation of this section. (Acts 1963, No. 521, p. 1112, § 4; Acts 1971, No. 407, p. 707, § 191.)

Cited in Dutton v. Chester F. Raines Agency, Inc., 475 So. 2d 545 (Ala. 1985).

Collateral references. — 43 Am. Jur. 2d, Insurance, § 84.

Provisions of insurance company's contract with independent insurance agent restricting competitive placements by agent as illegal restraint of trade under state law. 42 ALR4th 1072.

§ 27-10-2. Liability of persons violating section 27-10-1; liability of adjusters.

(a) Any person who in this state willfully represents or aids an unauthorized insurer in violation of section 27-10-1 shall, in addition to any other applicable penalty, be liable for the full amount of any loss sustained by the insured under any such contract and for the amount of any premium taxes which may be payable under section 27-10-35 by reason of such contract.

(b) Any adjuster who, directly or indirectly, enters into an investigation or adjustment of any loss arising under a contract of insurance or annuity issued by an unauthorized insurer and covering at time of issuance a subject of insurance resident, located or to be performed in this state shall be liable for the full amount of any loss suffered by the insured under such contract. The commissioner may, after hearing, revoke the license of such an adjuster. This subsection does not apply as to surplus lines contracts lawfully written under this chapter, or exempted under section 27-10-34, or to insurance contracts procured by the insured on his own behalf and on which the tax is paid as required by section 27-10-35 or to transactions as to which the insurer is not required to have a certificate of authority. (Acts 1963, No. 521, p. 1112, § 5; Acts 1971, No. 407, p. 707, § 192.)

Cited in Dutton v. Chester F. Raines
Agency, Inc., 475 So. 2d 545 (Ala. 1985).

§ 27-10-3. Actions by unauthorized insurers not allowed; exceptions.

(a) No unauthorized insurer shall institute or file, or cause to be instituted or filed, any action or proceeding in this state to enforce any right, claim or demand arising out of any insurance transaction in this state until such insurer has obtained a certificate of authority to transact such insurance in this state.

(b) This section does not apply as to:

(1) Transactions for which a certificate of authority is not required;

(2) Surplus line coverages written under this chapter; or

(3) Coverages exempted from the surplus line law under section 27-10-34. (Acts 1963, No. 521, p. 1112, § 6; Acts 1971, No. 407, p. 707, § 193.)

ARTICLE 2.

SURPLUS LINE INSURANCE.

§ 27-10-20. Procuring of surplus lines from unauthorized insurers.

If certain insurance coverages cannot be procured on terms acceptable to the insureds from authorized insurers, such coverages, designated "surplus lines," may be procured from unauthorized insurers subject to the terms and conditions of either subdivisions (1) or (2) of this section:

(1) a. The insurance must be procured through a licensed surplus line broker;

b. The full amount of insurance required must not be procurable, after diligent effort has been made to do so, from among the insurers authorized to transact and actually transacting that kind and class of insurance in this state or has been procured to the full extent such insurers are willing to insure;

c. The insurance must not be procured for the purpose of securing advantages as to a lower premium rate than would be accepted by an authorized insurer; and

d. This section, and this surplus line law, does not apply as to life insurance or disability insurance.

(2) The contracts of insurance are issued to an industrial insured, defined as an insured:

a. Which procures the insurance of any risk by use of services of a full-time employee acting as an insurance manager or buyer or the services of a regularly and continuously retained, qualified insurance consultant;

b. Whose aggregate annual premiums for insurance on all risks other than workmen's compensation and group insurance total at least $25,000.00; and

c. Which has at least 25 employees. (Acts 1963, No. 521, p. 1112, § 7; Acts 1971, No. 407, p. 707, § 195.)

The duty of complying with this section is upon licensed surplus line broker in this case. Once the insurance agent with the consent of the insured authorized the surplus line broker to procure the surplus line coverage, and the agent authorized the surplus line broker to issue the policy, the court was authorized to find that no other statutory duties were placed on the agent. Dutton v. Chester F. Raines Agency, Inc., 475 So. 2d 545 (Ala. 1985).

The trial court did not err in finding that "the law places the duty of determining the financial soundness of an unauthorized insurance company upon the surplus line broker," because in Alabama the duty of determining the financial stability of a surplus line insurance carrier is placed upon the surplus line broker and the commissioner of insurance for the state of Alabama. Dutton v. Chester F. Raines Agency, Inc., 475 So. 2d 545 (Ala. 1985).

§ 27-10-21. Report of surplus line broker.

Within 30 days after the effective date of any such insurance, the surplus line broker shall file a written report with the commissioner setting forth facts from which it can be determined whether under section 27-10-20 the coverage has been lawfully placed as a surplus line. If so required by the commissioner, the report shall be in the form of the broker's affidavit. If so required by the commissioner, the report shall be accompanied by a written statement signed by the insured to the effect that the coverage was placed in an unauthorized insurer with the insured's knowledge and consent. (Acts 1963, No. 521, p. 1112, § 8; Acts 1971, No. 407, p. 707, § 196.)

§ 27-10-22. Endorsement of surplus line contract.

Every insurance contract procured and delivered as a surplus line coverage pursuant to this article shall be initialed by, or bear the name and license number of, the surplus line broker who procured it and shall have stamped upon it the following:

"This contract is registered and delivered as a surplus line coverage under the Alabama Surplus Line Insurance Law." (Acts 1963, No. 521, p. 1112, § 9; Acts 1971, No. 407, p. 707, § 197.)

§ 27-10-23. Validity and enforceability of surplus line contracts.

Insurance contracts procured as "surplus line" coverages from unauthorized insurers in accordance with this article shall be fully valid and enforceable as to all parties and shall be given acceptance and recognition in all matters and respects to the same effect and extent as like contracts issued by authorized insurers. (Acts 1963, No. 521, p. 1112, § 10; Acts 1971, No. 407, p. 707, § 198.)

§ 27-10-24. Licensing of surplus line brokers.

Any person, while licensed as a resident agent or broker of this state as to property, casualty and surety insurance and who is deemed by the commissioner to have had sufficient experience in the insurance business to be competent for the purpose may be licensed as a surplus line broker for the types and kinds of insurance that he as a resident agent or broker is licensed to handle as follows:

(1) Application to the commissioner for the license shall be made on forms as designated and furnished by the commissioner;

(2) License fee in the amount stated in section 27-4-2 shall be paid to the commissioner. The license shall expire on the first day of January next after its issue; and

(3) Prior to the issuance of the license, the applicant shall file with the commissioner, and thereafter for as long as any such license remains in effect he shall keep in force and unimpaired, a bond in favor of the state of Alabama in the penal sum of $5,000.00, aggregate liability, with authorized corporate sureties approved by the commissioner. The bond shall be conditioned that the broker will conduct business under the license in accordance with the provisions of the surplus line insurance law and that he will promptly remit the taxes as provided by such law. No such bond shall be terminated unless at least 30 days' prior written notice thereof is given to the broker and the commissioner. (Acts 1963, No. 521, p. 1112, § 11; Acts 1971, No. 407, p. 707, § 199.)

Collateral references. — 43 Am. Jur. 2d, Insurance, § 84.

§ 27-10-25. Acceptance and placement of surplus line business from agents or brokers.

A licensed surplus line broker may accept and place surplus line business for any insurance agent or broker licensed in this state for the kind and class of insurance involved and may compensate such agent or broker therefor. No such agent shall knowingly misrepresent to the broker any material fact involved in any such insurance or in the eligibility thereof for placement with an unauthorized insurer. (Acts 1963, No. 521, p. 1112, § 12; Acts 1971, No. 407, p. 707, § 200.)

§ 27-10-26. Eligibility of insurers for placement of surplus line insurance.

(a) A surplus line broker shall not knowingly place surplus line insurance with an insurer that is unsound financially, or that is ineligible under this section. The broker shall ascertain the financial condition of the unauthorized insurer before placing insurance therewith.

(b) The broker shall not so insure:

(1) With any insurer which is not an authorized insurer in at least one state of the United States for the kind of insurance involved, and with capital and/or surplus amounting to at least $1,500,000.00; or guaranteed trust fund amounting to at least $750,000.00; or

(2) With an alien insurer not authorized to transact insurance in at least one state of the United States, unless such insurer shall have established an effective trust fund of at least $750,000.00 within the United States administered by a recognized financial institution and held for the benefit of all its policyholders or policyholders and creditors in the United States; or

(3) With a foreign or alien insurer which has transacted insurance as an authorized insurer in its state or country of domicile for less than three years, unless it is a wholly owned subsidiary of an insurer authorized to transact insurance in this state; or

(4) With an insurer the voting control of which is held in whole or substantial part by any government or governmental agency; or

(5) In any insurer made ineligible as a surplus line insurer by order of the commissioner received by or known to the broker. The commissioner may issue such an order of ineligibility if he finds that the insurer:

a. Does not meet the financial requirements of this section;

b. Has without just cause refused to pay valid claims arising under its contracts in this state or has otherwise conducted its affairs in such a manner as to result in injury or loss to the insuring public of this state; or

c. Has conducted its affairs in such a manner as to result in the avoidance of payment of tax as required by sections 27-10-31 and 27-10-35. (Acts 1963, No. 521, p. 1112, § 13; Acts 1971, No. 407, p. 707, § 201; Acts 1975, No. 219, p. 746, § 1.)

The statute places on commissioner duty to determine ineligibility of an insurer to issue surplus line insurance coverage. Dutton v. Chester F. Raines Agency, Inc., 475 So. 2d 545 (Ala. 1985).

Duty to determine financial soundness of unauthorized insurance company. — The trial court did not err in finding that "the law places the duty of determining the financial soundness of an unauthorized insurance company upon the surplus line broker," because in Alabama the duty of determining the financial stability of a surplus line insurance carrier is placed upon the surplus line broker and the commissioner of insurance for the state of Alabama. Dutton v. Chester F. Raines Agency, Inc., 475 So. 2d 545 (Ala. 1985).

§ 27-10-27. Evidence of surplus line insurance; changes; issuance of false certificate and failure to notify insured of material change.

(a) Upon placing a surplus line coverage, the broker shall promptly issue and deliver to the insured evidence of the insurance, consisting either of the policy as issued by the insurer or, if such policy is not then available, the surplus line broker's certificate. Such a certificate shall be executed by the broker and shall show the description and location of the subject of the insurance, coverage, conditions and term of the insurance, the premium and rate charged and taxes collected from the insured and the name and address of the insured and insurer. If the direct risk is assumed by more than one insurer, the certificate shall state the name and address and proportion of the entire direct risk assumed by each such insurer.

(b) No broker shall issue any such certificate or any cover note or purport to insure or represent that insurance will be, or has been, granted by any unauthorized insurer unless he has prior written authority from the insurer for the insurance, or has received information from the insurer in the regular course of business that such insurance has been granted or an insurance policy providing the insurance actually has been issued by the insurer and delivered to the insured.

(c) If after the issuance and delivery of any such certificate there is any change as to the identity of the insurers, or the proportion of the direct risk assumed by an insurer as stated in the broker's original certificate or in any other material respect as to the insurance coverage evidenced by the certificate, the broker shall promptly issue and deliver to the insured a substitute certificate accurately showing the current status of the coverage and the insurers responsible thereunder.

(d) If a policy issued by the insurer is not available upon placement of the insurance and the broker has issued and delivered his certificate as provided in this section, upon request therefor by the insured, the broker shall, as soon as reasonably possible, procure from the insurer its policy evidencing such insurance and deliver such policy to the insured in replacement of the broker's certificate theretofore issued.

(e) Any surplus line broker who knowingly or negligently issues a false certificate of insurance or who fails promptly to notify the insured of any material change with respect to such insurance by delivery to the insured of a substitute certificate as provided in subsection (c) of this section shall, upon conviction, be subject to the penalties provided by section 27-1-12 or to any greater applicable penalty otherwise provided by law. (Acts 1963, No. 521, p. 1112, § 14; Acts 1971, No. 407, p. 707, § 202.)

§ 27-10-28. Liability of insurer as to losses and unearned premiums.

(a) As to a surplus line risk which has been assumed by an unauthorized insurer pursuant to this surplus line insurance law and if the premium thereon has been received by the surplus line broker who placed such insurance, in all questions thereafter arising under the coverage as between the insurer and the insured, the insurer shall be deemed to have received the premium due to it for such coverage and the insurer shall be liable to the insured as to losses covered by such insurance and for unearned premiums which may become payable to the insured upon cancellation of such insurance, whether or not in fact the broker is indebted to the insurer with respect to such insurance or for any other cause.

(b) Each unauthorized insurer assuming a surplus line direct risk under this surplus line insurance law shall be deemed thereby to have subjected itself to the terms of this section. (Acts 1963, No. 521, p. 1112, § 15; Acts 1971, No. 407, p. 707, § 203.)

§ 27-10-29. Records of surplus line brokers.

(a) Each surplus line broker shall keep in his office in this state a full and true record of each surplus line contract procured by him, including a copy of the policy, certificate, cover note or other confirmation of insurance and of the daily report, if any, and showing such of the following items as may be applicable:

(1) Amount of the insurance and risks insured against;

(2) Gross premium charged;

(3) Return premium paid, if any;

(4) Rate of premium charged upon the several items of property;

(5) Effective date of the contract and the terms thereof;

(6) Name and address of the insurer;

(7) Name and address of the insured;

(8) Brief general description of property insured and where located;

(9) Amount of tax and other sums collected from the insured; and

(10) Other information as may be required by the commissioner.

(b) The record shall at all times be open to examination by the commissioner and shall be kept available and open to the commissioner for five years next following the issuance of the contract. (Acts 1971, No. 407, p. 707, § 204.)

§ 27-10-30. Annual statement of surplus line broker.

(a) Each surplus line broker shall, on or before the first day of March of each year, file with the commissioner a verified statement of all surplus line insurance transacted by him during the preceding calendar year.

(b) The statement shall be on forms as prescribed and furnished by the commissioner and shall show:

(1) Gross amount of each kind of insurance transacted;

(2) Aggregate gross premiums charged, exclusive of sums collected to cover state or federal taxes;

(3) Aggregate of returned premiums and taxes paid to insureds;

(4) Aggregate of net premiums; and

(5) Additional information as required by the commissioner. (Acts 1963, No. 521, p. 1112, § 17; Acts 1971, No. 407, p. 707, § 205.)

§ 27-10-31. Annual tax of surplus line brokers.

(a) On or before the first day of March each year, the surplus line broker shall remit to the state treasurer through the commissioner, as a tax imposed for the privilege of transacting business as a surplus line broker in this state, a tax of four percent on the direct premiums, less return premiums and exclusive of sums collected to cover state or federal taxes, on surplus line insurance subject to tax transacted by him during the preceding calendar year as shown by his annual statement filed with the commissioner.

(b) If a surplus line policy covers risks or exposures only partially in this state, the tax so payable shall be computed on the proportion of the premium which is properly allocable to the risks or exposures located in this state.

(c) The tax under the provisions of this section shall be subject to deduction of the full amount of all expenses of examination of the surplus line broker by the commissioner in the same manner as that allowed for domestic insurers for examination expenses under the provisions of subdivision (4) of subsection (b) of section 27-4-5. (Acts 1963, No. 521, p. 1112, § 18; Acts 1971, No. 407, p. 707, § 206; Acts 1980, No. 80-774, p. 1608, § 2.)

Collateral references. — 44 C.J.S., Insurance, § 85.

43 Am. Jur. 2d, Insurance, § 84.

§ 27-10-32. Revocation or suspension of surplus line broker's license.

(a) The commissioner may revoke or suspend any surplus line broker's license:

(1) If the broker fails to file his annual statement or to remit the tax as required by law;

(2) If the broker fails to maintain an office in this state, or to keep the records or to allow the commissioner to examine his records as required by law; or

(3) For any of the causes for which an agent's license may be revoked.

(b) The commissioner may suspend or revoke the broker's license if he finds that the broker has, willfully or without exercise of due care, placed any insurance coverage with an unauthorized insurer in violation of any of the requirements or conditions of section 27-10-20.

(c) The procedures and rights provided by section 27-7-19 as for the suspension or revocation of agents' licenses shall be applicable to suspension or revocation of a surplus line broker's license.

(d) No broker whose license has been so revoked shall again be so licensed within one year thereafter nor until any fines or delinquent taxes owing by him have been paid. (Acts 1963, No. 521, p. 1112, § 19; Acts 1971, No. 407, p. 707, § 207.)

Collateral references. — 43 Am. Jur. 2d, Insurance, § 68.

§ 27-10-33. Service of process in action or proceeding against insurer.

(a) Any unauthorized insurer issuing a policy or assuming a direct insurance risk under this surplus line law shall be deemed thereby to have appointed the commissioner as its attorney upon whom may be served all lawful process in any action or proceeding against it in this state arising out of such insurance.

(b) Service of process upon the commissioner as process agent of the insurer shall be made by the proper officer of Montgomery county by serving copies in triplicate of the process upon the commissioner or upon his assistant, deputy or other person in charge of his office. Upon receiving such service, the commissioner shall promptly forward a copy thereof by certified mail or registered mail to the person last designated to receive the same, as provided in subsection (c) of this section, return one copy with his admission of service and retain one copy in the files of the department.

(c) Each such policy, or the certificate of insurance issued by the broker, shall contain a provision stating the substance of this section and designating the person to whom the commissioner shall mail process as provided for in subsection (b) of this section. The broker shall, likewise, file the name of such person with the commissioner. As to the same unauthorized insurer and all insurance coverages issued or accepted by it under this surplus line law, no more than one person shall at any one time be the designee to whom copies of process against the insurer, served upon the commissioner, shall be forwarded.

(d) Where process is served upon the commissioner as an insurer's process agent, the insurer shall not be required to answer or plead except within 30 days after the date upon which the commissioner mailed a copy of the process served upon him as required by subsection (b) of this section.

(e) Process served upon the commissioner, and copy thereof forwarded as in this section provided, shall for all purposes constitute valid and binding service thereof upon the insurer. (Acts 1963, No. 521, p. 1112, § 20; Acts 1971, No. 407, p. 707, § 208.)

Case must arise out of contracts of insurance. — For substituted service upon the commissioner of insurance pursuant to state law to be possible, the case must be one "arising out of" contracts of insurance. Hilgeman v. National Ins. Co. of Am., 444 F.2d 446 (5th Cir. 1971), (decided under former Code 1940, T. 28, § 417(20)).

Collateral references. — Statute providing for service of process upon statutory agent in action against foreign corporation as regards communications to corporation of fact of service. 89 ALR 658.

Requisites of service upon, or delivery to, designated public official, as a condition of substituted service of process on him. 148 ALR 975.

§ 27-10-34. Exemptions from surplus line insurance law.

The provisions of this surplus line insurance law controlling the placing of insurance with unauthorized insurers shall not apply to reinsurance or to the following insurances when so placed by licensed agents or brokers of this state:

(1) Wet marine and transportation insurance;

(2) Insurance on subjects located, resident or to be performed wholly outside of this state or on vehicles or aircraft owned and principally garaged outside this state;

(3) Insurance on property or operation of railroads engaged in interstate commerce;

(4) Insurance of aircraft owned or operated by manufacturers of aircraft or aircraft operated in scheduled interstate flight, or cargo of such aircraft or against liability, other than workmen's compensation and the employer's liability, arising out of the ownership, maintenance or use of such aircraft; and

(5) The property and operations of the shipbuilding and ship repair industry engaged in interstate or foreign commerce and vessels, cargoes, watercraft, piers, wharves, graving docks, drydocks, marine railways and building ways, commonly known as wet marine. (Acts 1963, No. 521, p. 1112, § 21; Acts 1971, No. 407, p. 707, § 209.)

§ 27-10-35. Report of, and tax on, independently procured coverages; exceptions.

(a) Anyone who may desire to place his insurance in a foreign insurer not authorized to do business in this state may place such insurance, and any insured who in this state procures, or causes to be procured, or continues or renews insurance in an unauthorized foreign insurer or any self-insurer who in this state so procures or continues excess loss, catastrophe or other insurance, upon a subject of insurance resident, located or to be performed within this state, other than insurance procured through a surplus line broker pursuant to the surplus lines law of this state or exempted from such law under section 27-10-34 shall, within 90 days after the date such insurance was so procured, continued or renewed, file a written report of the same with the commissioner on forms designated by the commissioner and furnished to such an insured upon request. The report shall show the name and address of the insured or insureds, name and address of the insurer, the subject of the insurance, a general description of the coverage, the amount of premium currently charged therefor and such additional pertinent information as is reasonably requested by the commissioner. If any such insurance covers also subjects of insurance resident, located or to be performed outside this state, a proper pro rata portion of the entire premium payable for all such insurance shall be allocated as to the subjects of insurance resident, located or to be performed in this state for the purposes of this section.

(b) Any insurance in an unauthorized insurer procured through negotiations or an application, in whole or in part, occurring or made within or from within this state or for which premiums, in whole or in part, are remitted, directly or indirectly, from within this state shall be deemed to be insurance procured, or continued or renewed in this state within the intent of subsection (a) of this section.

(c) For the general support of the government of this state, there is levied upon the obligation, chose in action or right represented by the premium charged or payable for such insurance a tax at the rate of four percent of the gross amount of such premium. The insured shall withhold the amount of the tax from the amount of premium charged by and otherwise payable to the insurer for such insurance; and, within 30 days after the insurance was so procured, continued or renewed and coincidentally with the filing with the commissioner of the report provided for in subsection (a) of this section, the insured shall pay the amount of the tax to the state treasurer through the commissioner.

(d) If the insured fails to withhold from the premium the amount of tax levied by this section, the insured shall be liable for the amount thereof and shall pay the same to the commissioner within the time stated in subsection (c) of this section.

(e) The tax imposed under this section, if delinquent, shall bear interest at the rate of six percent per annum, compounded annually.

(f) Payment of such tax shall be enforced by the commissioner by civil action against any person failing to pay the tax provided for in this section.

(g) A licensed adjuster may lawfully investigate and adjust any loss occurring or claim made under any such contract of insurance as to which the tax has been paid as provided in this section.

(h) This section does not apply as to life or disability insurances. (Acts 1963, No. 521, p. 1112, § 22; Acts 1971, No. 407, p. 707, § 210.)

§ 27-10-36. Production of policies, etc., for inspection by commissioner.

Every person as to whom insurance is placed with an unauthorized insurer, upon the commissioner's order, shall produce for his examination all policies and other documents evidencing the insurance and shall disclose to the commissioner the amount of gross premiums paid, or agreed to be paid, for the insurance. For each willful refusal to obey such order, such person shall be liable to a fine of not more than $500.00. (Acts 1963, No. 521, p. 1112, § 23; Acts 1971, No. 407, p. 707, § 211.)

§ 27-10-37. Penalty for violation of article.

(a) Any person who in this state represents or aids a nonadmitted insurer in willful violation of the provisions of this surplus lines insurance law shall, upon conviction thereof, be guilty of a misdemeanor and be subject to a fine not in excess of $1,000.00 or imprisonment for not more than one year, or by both such fine and imprisonment, in the discretion of the court.

(b) In addition to the penalties provided for in subsection (a) of this section, such violator shall be liable, personally, jointly and severally, with any other person, or persons, liable therefor for payment of taxes payable on account of such insurance.

(c) In addition to any other penalty provided for in this section or otherwise provided by law, including suspension, revocation or refusal to renew license, any person, firm, association or corporation willfully violating any provision of this article shall be liable to a penalty not exceeding $1,000.00 for the first offense and not exceeding $2,000.00 for each succeeding offense. (Acts 1963, No. 521, p. 1112, § 25; Acts 1971, No. 407, p. 707, § 212.)

Collateral references. — 44 C.J.S., Insurance, § 86.

§ 27-10-38. Short title.

This article constitutes, and may be referred to as, "the surplus line insurance law." (Acts 1971, No. 407, p. 707, § 194.)

ARTICLE 3.

UNAUTHORIZED INSURERS PROCESS ACT.

Cross references. — As to rules of supreme court relative to service of process generally, see A.R.C.P., Rule 4 et seq.

§ 27-10-50. Purpose.

The purpose of this article is to subject certain insurers to the jurisdiction of courts of this state in actions by, or on behalf of, insureds or beneficiaries under insurance contracts. The legislature declares that it is a subject of concern that many residents of this state hold policies of insurance issued or delivered in this state by insurers while not authorized to do business in this state, thus presenting to such residents the often insuperable obstacle of resorting to distant forums for the purpose of asserting legal rights under such policies. In furtherance of such state interest, the legislature provides in this article a method of substituted service of process upon such insurers and declares that in so doing it exercises its power to protect its residents and to define, for the purpose of this article, what constitutes doing business in this state and also exercises powers and privileges available to the state by virtue of the federal Insurance Regulation Act, which declares that the business of insurance and every person engaged therein shall be subject to the laws of the several states. (Acts 1951, No. 768, p. 1335, § 1; Acts 1971, No. 407, p. 707, § 214.)

Cited in Hilgeman v. National Ins. Co. of Am. 547 F.2d 298 (5th Cir. 1977).

Collateral references. — 44 C.J.S., Insurance, § 84. 46 C.J.S., Insurance, § 1270.

§ 27-10-51. Acts constituting appointment of commissioner as agent for service of process on foreign or alien insurer.

Any of the following acts in this state, effected by mail or otherwise, by an unauthorized foreign or alien insurer:

(1) The issuance or delivery of contracts of insurance to residents of this state or to corporations authorized to do business therein;

(2) The solicitation of applications for such contracts;

(3) The collection of premiums, membership fees, assessments or other considerations for such contracts; or

(4) Any other transaction of insurance business;

is equivalent to, and shall constitute, an appointment by such insurer of the commissioner and his successor or successors in office to be its true and lawful attorney, upon whom may be served all lawful process in any action or proceeding instituted by, or on behalf of, an insured or beneficiary arising out of any such contract of insurance; and any such act shall be signification of the insurer's agreement that such service of process is of the same legal force and validity as personal service of process in this state upon such insurer. (Acts 1951, No. 768, p. 1335, § 2; Acts 1971, No. 407, p. 707, § 215.)

Case must arise out of contracts of insurance. — For substituted service upon the commissioner of insurance pursuant to state law to be possible, the case must be one "arising out of" contracts of insurance. Hilgeman v. National Ins. Co. v. Am., 444 F.2d 446 (5th Cir. 1971) (decided under former Code 1940, T. 28, § 413).

Applicability of section to causes of action arising under federal securities laws. — See Hilgeman v. National Ins. Co. of Am., 547 F.2d 298 (5th Cir. 1977).

Collateral references. — 46 C.J.S., Insurance, § 1270, n. 72.

§ 27-10-52. Service of process upon insurer; judgment by default.

(a) Service of process upon an insurer pursuant to section 27-10-51 shall be made by delivering to, and leaving with, the commissioner, or some person in apparent charge of his office, two copies thereof and the payment to him of such fees as may be prescribed by law. The commissioner shall forthwith mail by registered mail one of the copies of the process to the defendant at its last known principal place of business and shall keep a record of all process so served upon him. Such service of process is sufficient, provided notice of the service and a copy of the process are sent promptly after such service by the commissioner by registered mail to the defendant at its last known principal place of business and the defendant's receipt, or receipt issued by the post office with which the letter is registered, showing the name of the sender of the letter and the name and address of the person to whom the letter is addressed, and the certificate of the commissioner showing a compliance herewith are filed with the clerk or register of the court in which such action is pending on, or before, the date the defendant is required to appear, or within such further time as the court may allow.

(b) Service of process in any such action or proceeding shall in addition to the manner provided in subsection (a) of this section, be valid if served in the manner provided by law upon any person within this state, who, in this state on behalf of such insurer, is:

(1) Soliciting insurance;

(2) Making, issuing or delivering any contract of insurance; or

(3) Collecting or receiving any premium, membership fee, assessment or other consideration for insurance; and a copy of such process is sent within 10 days thereafter by registered mail by the clerk or register of the court in which the action or proceeding is pending to the defendant at the last known principal place of business of the defendant, and the defendant's receipt, or the receipt issued by the post office with which the letter is registered, showing the name of the sender of the letter and the name and address of the person to whom the letter is addressed, are filed with the clerk or register of the court in which the action is pending on, or before, the date the defendant is required to appear, or within such further time as the court may allow.

(c) No plaintiff or complainant shall be entitled to a judgment by default under this section until the expiration of 30 days from date of the completion of service as provided in this section.

(d) Nothing in this section shall limit or abridge the right to serve any process, notice or demand upon any insurer in any other manner, now or hereafter, permitted by law. (Acts 1951, No. 768, p. 1335, § 2; Acts 1971, No. 407, p. 707, § 216.)

Case must arise out of contracts of insurance. — For substituted service upon the commissioner of insurance pursuant to state law to be possible, the case must be one "arising out of" contracts of insurance. Hilgeman v. National Ins. Co. of Am., 444 F.2d 446 (5th Cir. 1971), (decided under former Code 1940, T. 28, § 413).

§ 27-10-53. Defense of action or proceeding by insurer.

(a) Before an unauthorized insurer shall file, or cause to be filed, any pleading in any action or proceeding instituted against it under sections 27-10-51 and 27-10-52, such insurer shall:

(1) Procure a certificate of authority to transact insurance in this state; or

(2) Deposit with the clerk of the court in which such action or proceeding is pending cash or securities or file with such clerk a bond with good and

sufficient sureties, to be approved by the court, in an amount to be fixed by the court sufficient to secure the payment of any final judgment which may be entered in such action. The court may, in its discretion, make an order dispensing with such deposit or bond where the insurer makes a showing satisfactory to the court that it maintains in a state of the United States funds or securities, in trust or otherwise, sufficient and available to satisfy any final judgment which may be entered in such action or proceeding and that the insurer will pay any final judgment entered therein without requiring an action to be brought on such judgment in the state where such funds or securities are located.

(b) The court, in any action or proceeding in which service is made in the manner provided in section 27-10-52, may, in its discretion, order such postponement as may be necessary to afford the defendant reasonable opportunity to comply with the provisions of subsection (a) of this section, and to defend such action.

(c) Nothing in subsection (a) of this section is to be construed to prevent an unauthorized insurer from filing a motion to quash or to set aside the service of any process made in the manner provided in section 27-10-52 on the ground either:

(1) That such unauthorized insurer has not done any of the acts enumerated in section 27-10-51; or

(2) That the person on whom service was made pursuant to subsection (b) of section 27-10-52 was not doing any of the acts therein enumerated. (Acts 1951, No. 768, p. 1335, § 3; Acts 1971, No. 407, p. 707, § 217.)

Collateral references. — 44 C.J.S., Insurance, § 84.

§ 27-10-54. Transaction of insurance business not authorized by article.

Nothing in the Unauthorized Insurers Process Act shall be construed to authorize or permit the transaction of any insurance business in this state by any unauthorized insurer nor relieve any such insurer from any penalty provided by law in the transaction of business in this state. (Acts 1951, No. 768, p. 1335, § 5; Acts 1971, No. 407, p. 707, § 218.)

§ 27-10-55. Exemptions.

This Unauthorized Insurers Process Act shall not apply as to surplus line insurance lawfully effectuated under this title nor to any action or proceeding against an unauthorized insurer arising out of:

(1) Wet marine and transportation insurance;

(2) Insurance on, or with respect to, subjects located, resident or to be performed wholly outside this state or on, or with respect to, vehicles or aircraft owned and principally garaged outside this state;

(3) Insurance on property or operations of railroads engaged in interstate commerce; or

(4) Insurance on aircraft or cargo of such aircraft or against liability, other than employer's liability, arising out of the ownership, maintenance or use of such aircraft where the policy or contract contains a provision designating the commissioner as its attorney for the acceptance of service of lawful process in any action or proceeding instituted by, or on behalf of, an insured or beneficiary arising out of any such policy or contract or where the insurer enters a general appearance in any such action or proceeding. (Acts 1951, No. 768, p. 1335, § 6; Acts 1971, No. 407, p. 707, § 219.)

§ 27-10-56. Short title; construction of article.

(a) This article constitutes and may be cited as the Unauthorized Insurers Process Act.

(b) This article shall be so interpreted as to effectuate its general purpose to make uniform the law of those states which enact it. (Acts 1951, No. 768, p. 1335, § 7; Acts 1971, No. 407, p. 707, § 213.)

CHAPTER 11.

MAIL ORDER INSURANCE.

Sec.
27-11-1. Purpose of chapter; short title.
27-11-2. Prohibition against transaction of insurance business, etc., in state without license; exceptions.
27-11-3. Occurrences and acts deemed to constitute transacting of insurance business in state.
27-11-4. Actions and proceedings against violating or noncomplying insurers.

Sec.
27-11-5. Secretary of state as agent for service of process on insurer; service of process; attachment of jurisdiction; fees for service.
27-11-6. Validity of acts or contracts of unauthorized insurer; actions against or by same.
27-11-7. Penalty for violation of chapter.

Collateral references. — 43 Am. Jur. 2d, Insurance, § 89.

Liability insurance coverage as extending to liability for punitive or exemplary damages. 16 ALR4th 11.

§ 27-11-1. Purpose of chapter; short title.

The legislature declares its concern that insurers not licensed to transact the business of insurance in this state are soliciting the sale of insurance and selling insurance to residents of this state, thus presenting the commissioner with the problem of resorting to courts of foreign jurisdictions for the purposes of enforcing the insurance laws of this state for the protection of its residents. It is the purpose of this unauthorized insurers law to make it unlawful for insurers that are not licensed to transact the business of insurance in this state and to subject said insurers to the jurisdiction of the courts of this state in actions or proceedings brought by the commissioner in transactions involving unauthorized insurers or for the protection of insureds and claimants residing in this state and for the protection of the public. This chapter constitutes and may be referred to as the "Unauthorized Insurers Law." (Acts 1971, No. 407, p. 707, § 220.)

§ 27-11-2. Prohibition against transaction of insurance business, etc., in state without license; exceptions.

It shall be unlawful for any insurer to transact the business of insurance in this state or to enter into a contract for insurance in this state without first obtaining a license or certificate of authority from the commissioner. This unauthorized insurers law shall not apply to:

(1) Contracts of insurance procured pursuant to the surplus line insurance law;

(2) Transactions in this state involving contracts of insurance lawfully entered into, written and the policy delivered outside of this state covering subjects of insurance not resident, located or expressly to be performed in this state at the time of issuance and transactions subsequent to the making of such contract and the issuance of such policy;

(3) Reinsurance contracts;

(4) Transactions in this state involving group or blanket insurance and group annuities where the master policy or contract was lawfully issued and delivered in a state in which the insurer was authorized to transact business;

(5) Transportation insurance;

(6) Insurance on property or operation of railroads engaged in interstate commerce;

(7) Insurance of aircraft owned or operated by manufacturers of aircraft or aircraft operated in scheduled interstate flight or cargo of such aircraft or against liability, other than workmen's compensation and the employer's liability, arising out of the ownership, maintenance or use of such aircraft;

(8) The property and operations of shipbuilding and ship repair industry engaged in interstate or foreign commerce and vessels, cargoes, watercraft, piers, wharves, graving docks, dry docks, marine railways and building ways, commonly known as wet marine;

(9) Transactions in this state involving a policy or contract of insurance issued prior to 60 days after the effective date of this title; or

(10) Contracts of insurance issued to an industrial insured, defined as an insured:

a. Which procures the insurance of any risk by use or services of a full-time employee acting as an insurance manager or buyer or the services of a regularly and continuously retained, qualified insurance consultant;

b. Whose aggregate annual premiums for insurance on all risks other than workmen's compensation and group insurance, total at least $25,000.00; and

c. Which has at least 25 employees. (Acts 1971, No. 407, p. 707, § 221.)

Collateral references. — 44 C.J.S., Insurance, §§ 79, 88.

§ 27-11-3. Occurrences and acts deemed to constitute transacting of insurance business in state.

Any of the following occurrences or acts in this state, whether effected by mail or otherwise, by an insurer not licensed to do business in this state shall be included among those occurrences and acts deemed to constitute the transacting of the business of insurance in this state:

(1) The issuance or delivery of contracts or policies of insurance covering subjects resident, located or expressly to be performed in this state;

(2) The solicitation of applications for such insurance;

(3) The collection of premiums, membership fees, assessments or other considerations for such insurance; or

(4) The transacting of matters subsequent to the execution of such contracts and arising out of them or concerning them. (Acts 1971, No. 407, p. 707, § 222.)

Collateral references. — 44 C.J.S., Insurance, § 82.

§ 27-11-4. Actions and proceedings against violating or noncomplying insurers.

Whenever the commissioner believes, from evidence satisfactory to him, that any insurer is violating or not complying with the provisions of this unauthorized insurers law, the commissioner may, and is hereby empowered to, bring an action or proceeding against such insurer in the circuit court of Montgomery county, Alabama, to enjoin or restrain such violation or continuing noncompliance or the engaging therein or doing of any act in furtherance of such violation. The circuit court of Montgomery county, Alabama shall have jurisdiction of the proceedings and shall have the power and authority to make and enter such order or judgment as to such court shall be deemed proper. (Acts 1971, No. 407, p. 707, § 223.)

Collateral references. — 44 C.J.S., Insurance, §§ 83, 84.

§ 27-11-5. Secretary of state as agent for service of process on insurer; service of process; attachment of jurisdiction; fees for service.

(a) Any insurer not qualified under the laws of this state to transact the business of insurance as evidenced by a license or certificate of authority from the commissioner of insurance which shall transact, or attempt to transact, the business of insurance in this state or which shall do, or attempt to do, any of the acts and occurrences set out in section 27-11-3 shall, by the doing of such business or the performing or attempting to perform any of such acts, be deemed to have appointed the secretary of state, or his successor or successors in office, to be the true and lawful attorney or agent of such insurer whom process may be served in any action accrued or accruing from the transacting of such business or the performing of such act by any such insurer, or by its agent, servant or employee. Service of such process shall be made by serving three copies of the process on the said secretary of state, and such service shall be sufficient service upon the said insurer, provided, that notice of such service and a copy of the process are forthwith sent by registered or certified mail by the secretary of state to the defendant at its last known address, which shall be stated in the affidavit of the plaintiff or complainant, marked "deliver to addressee only" and "return receipt requested," and provided, further, that such return receipt shall be received by the secretary of state purporting to have been signed by said insurer, or the secretary of state shall be advised by the postal authority that delivery of said registered or certified mail was refused by said insurer; and the date on which the secretary of state receives said return receipt, or advice by the postal authority that delivery of said registered or certified mail was refused shall be treated and considered as the date of service of process on said insurer. The secretary of state shall make an affidavit as to the service of said process on him, and as to his mailing a copy of the same and notice of such service to the insurer and as to the receipt of said return receipt, or advice of the refusal of said registered or certified mail, and the respective dates thereof, and shall attach said affidavit, return receipt or advice from the postal authority to a copy of the process and shall return the same to the clerk or register who issued the same, and all of the same shall be filed in the action by the clerk or register. The commissioner, or his agent or attorney, desiring to obtain service upon an insurer under the provisions of this unauthorized insurers law shall make and file in the action an affidavit stating facts showing that this section is applicable and stating the last known address of the insurer, and the clerk or register of the court in which the action is filed shall attach a copy of the affidavit to the writ or process and a copy of the affidavit to each copy of the writ or process and forward the original writ or process and three copies thereof to the sheriff of Montgomery county, Alabama, for service on the secretary of state; and it shall be the duty of the sheriff to serve the same on the secretary of state and to make due return of such service. The court in which the action is pending may order such continuance of the action as may be necessary to afford the defendant, or defendants, reasonable opportunity to make defense. Any insurer who was licensed to transact the business of insurance in this state at the time of the doing of business or the performing of the act complained of, but which is not so licensed or authorized at the time of the pendency of an action involving the transacting of the business of insurance or the act or occurrence complained of, shall be deemed to be an unauthorized insurer within the meaning of this chapter, and service of process under such circumstances may be had as provided in this section.

(b) Service of summons when obtained upon any such insurer as provided in subsection (a) of this section for the service of process shall be deemed sufficient service of summons and process to give to the circuit court of Montgomery county, Alabama, jurisdiction over the cause of action and over such insurer and shall warrant and authorize personal judgment against such defendant, or defendants, in the event that the plaintiff prevails in the action. There shall be paid to the secretary of state for services under this section fees as may be provided for service of process on nonresidents doing business or performing work or service in this state. (Acts 1971, No. 407, p. 707, § 224.)

Cross references. — As to rules of supreme court relative to service of process generally, see A.R.C.P., Rule 4 et seq.

Collateral references. — 44 C.J.S., Insurance, § 84.

Cessation by foreign corporation of business within state as affecting designation of agent for service of process. 45 ALR 1447.

Statute providing for service of process upon statutory agent in action against foreign corporation as regards communications to corporation of fact of service. 89 ALR 658.

Manner of service of process upon foreign corporation which has withdrawn from state. 86 ALR2d 1000.

§ 27-11-6. Validity of acts or contracts of unauthorized insurer; actions against or by same.

The failure of an insurer to obtain a license or certificate of authority shall not impair the validity of any act or contract of such insurer and shall not prevent such insurer, its assigns or successors in interest, from defending any action in any court of this state; but no insurer transacting insurance business in this state without a license or certificate of authority shall be permitted to maintain an action in any court of this state to enforce any right, claim or demand arising out of the transaction of such business until such company, its assigns or successors in interest shall have:

(1) Obtained a license or certificate of authority; or

(2) Deposited with the clerk of the court in which such action or proceeding is pending cash or securities or file with such clerk a bond with good and sufficient sureties, to be approved by the court, in an amount to be fixed by the court sufficient to secure the payment of any final judgment which may be entered in such action; provided, that the court may, in its discretion and after reasonable notice to the opposing parties and upon a hearing, make an order dispensing with such deposit or bond where the insurer makes a showing satisfactory to such court that it maintains in a state of the United States funds or securities, in trust or otherwise, sufficient and available to satisfy any final judgment which may be entered in such action or proceeding.

No action shall be maintained, except upon the conditions provided in this section, in any court of this state by any successor or assignee or assumptor of such unauthorized insurer which has acquired all or substantially all of the assets of such unauthorized insurer. (Acts 1971, No. 407, p. 707, § 225.)

Collateral references. — Recovery back of money paid to unlicensed person required by law to have occupational or business license or permit to make contract. 74 ALR3d 637.

§ 27-11-7. Penalty for violation of chapter.

Any insurer which willfully violates the provisions of the unauthorized insurers law shall, upon proof thereof, forfeit and pay to the state of Alabama a sum of not less than $50.00 and not more than $500.00 for each offense, which may be recovered in a civil action brought by the commissioner under the provision of this unauthorized insurers law. (Acts 1971, No. 407, p. 707, § 226.)

Collateral references. — 44 C.J.S., Insurance, § 86.

CHAPTER 12.

TRADE PRACTICES LAW.

Sec.
27-12-1. Purpose of chapter; short title.
27-12-2. General prohibition against unfair
            competition, etc.
27-12-3 through 27-12-5. Repealed.
27-12-6. "Twisting."
27-12-7. False statements and entries.
27-12-8. Boycotts, coercion and intimidation.
27-12-9. Malicious statements on financial
            condition.
27-12-10. Financial inducements to purchase
            insurance.
27-12-11. Life, annuity and disability insur-
            ance — Unfair discrimination in
            rates, etc.
27-12-12. Same — Agreements not expressed
            in contract, rebates and other
            inducements.
27-12-13. Same — Exceptions to discrimina-
            tion, rebates or special induce-
            ments.
27-12-14. Inducements as to property, casualty
            or surety insurance.

Sec.
27-12-15. Purchase of insurance as condition
            precedent to sale or loan on prop-
            erty.
27-12-16. Common ownership, management
            and directorships.
27-12-17. Collection of premiums or charges
            when insurance not provided; ex-
            cess premium or charge.
27-12-18. Statement of charges; hearing, order
            and review thereon.
27-12-19. Service of statements, notices, or-
            ders and other processes.
27-12-20. Review of commissioner's cease and
            desist orders.
27-12-21. Proceedings on unfair competition,
            etc., not defined under chapter —
            Generally.
27-12-22. Same — Appeal by intervenor.
27-12-23. False statements, etc., in insurance
            application.
27-12-24. Refusal of insurer to pay or settle
            claims.

§ 27-12-1. Purpose of chapter; short title.

(a) The purpose of this chapter is to regulate trade practices in the business of insurance in accordance with the intent of congress as expressed in the Insurance Regulation Act by defining, or providing for the determination of, all such practices in this state which constitute unfair methods of competition or unfair or deceptive acts or practices and by prohibiting the trade practices so defined or determined.

(b) This chapter shall constitute, and may be referred to, as the "Trade Practices Law." (Acts 1957, No. 608, p. 865, § 1; Acts 1971, No. 407, p. 707, § 227.)

Cited in Crawford v. American Title Ins. Co., 518 F.2d 217 (5th Cir. 1975).

Collateral references. — Provisions of insurance company's contract with independent insurance agent restricting competitive placements by agent as illegal restraint of trade under state law. 42 ALR4th 1072.

§ 27-12-2. General prohibition against unfair competition, etc.

No person shall engage in this state in any trade practice which is defined in this chapter as, or determined pursuant to this chapter to be, an unfair method of competition or an unfair or deceptive act or practice in the business of insurance. (Acts 1957, No. 608, p. 865, § 3; Acts 1971, No. 407, p. 707, § 228.)

Collateral references. — 44 C.J.S., Insurance, §§ 90, 244.

Provisions of insurance company's contract with independent insurance agent restricting competitive placements by agent as illegal restraint of trade under state law. 42 ALR4th 1072.

§§ 27-12-3 through 27-12-5. Repealed by Acts 1977, No. 607, p. 812, § 9901, effective January 1, 1980.

✦§ 27-12-6. "Twisting." ✦

No person shall make or issue, or cause to be made or issued, any written or oral statement misrepresenting or making misleading incomplete comparisons as to the terms, conditions or benefits contained in any policy for the purpose of inducing, or attempting or tending to induce, the policyholder to lapse, forfeit, surrender, retain, exchange or convert any insurance policy. (Acts 1971, No. 407, p. 707, § 232.)

Collateral references. — 43 Am. Jur. 2d, Insurance, § 69.

§ 27-12-7. False statements and entries.

(a) No person shall file with any supervisory or other public official or make, publish, disseminate, circulate or deliver to any person or place before the public, or cause, directly or indirectly, to be made, published, disseminated, circulated, delivered to any person, or placed before the public, any false statement of financial condition of an insurer with intent to deceive.

(b) No person shall make any false entry in any book, report or statement of any insurer with intent to deceive any agent or examiner lawfully appointed to examine into its condition or into any of its affairs, or any public official to whom such insurer is required by law to report, or who has authority by law to examine into its condition or into any of its affairs or, with like intent, willfully omit to make a true entry of any material fact pertaining to the business of such insurer in any book, report or statement of such insurer.

(c) Any insurer willfully making a false annual or other statement required of it under this title and individuals knowingly making oath to and subscribing the same shall be punished by a fine of not less than $500.00 nor exceeding $5,000.00. (Acts 1957, No. 608, p. 865, § 4; Acts 1971, No. 407, p. 707, § 233.)

Collateral references. — 43 Am. Jur. 2d, Insurance, § 61.

§ 27-12-8. Boycotts, coercion and intimidation.

No person shall enter into any agreement to commit or, by any concerted action, commit any act of boycott, coercion or intimidation resulting in, or tending to result in, unreasonable restraint of, or monopoly in, the business of insurance. (Acts 1957, No. 608, p. 865, § 4; Acts 1971, No. 407, p. 707, § 234.)

§ 27-12-9. Malicious statements on financial condition.

No person shall make, publish, disseminate or circulate, directly or indirectly, or aid, abet or encourage the making, publishing, disseminating or circulating of any oral or written statement or any pamphlet, circular, article or literature which is false or maliciously critical of, or derogatory to, the financial condition of an insurer or of an organization proposing to become an insurer and which is calculated to injure any person engaged, or proposing to engage, in the business of insurance. (Acts 1957, No. 608, p. 865, § 4; Acts 1971, No. 407, p. 707, § 235.)

§ 27-12-10. Financial inducements to purchase insurance.

(a) No person shall issue or deliver, or permit its agents, officers or employees to issue or deliver, agency company stock or other capital stock, or benefit certificates or shares in any common-law corporation, or securities, or any special or advisory board contract or other contract of any kind promising returns and profits as an inducement to insurance. The commissioner shall refuse to issue certificate a of authority or license to any insurer or other person that is in violation of this section and shall revoke the certificate of authority or license of any such violating insurer or person if such authority or license is already outstanding.

(b) No person shall issue or deliver, or permit its agents, officers or employees to issue or deliver, in this state, any life insurance policy or contract of annuity in which are used such words as "investment plan," "expansion plan," "profit-sharing," "charter plan," "founders' plan," "surplus-sharing," or similar language in such context or under such circumstances or conditions as to have the capacity or tendency to mislead a purchaser or prospective purchaser of life insurance to believe that he will receive or that it is probable he will receive something other than an insurance policy, or contract, or some benefit not provided in the policy or contract or some benefit not available to other persons of the same class and equal expectation of life.

(c) No insurer shall issue or deliver, or permit its agents, officers or employees to issue or deliver, in this state a policy of life insurance containing benefits in the form of "coupons" or "guaranteed annual endowment" benefits unless the premium charged for the insurance coverage and the premium charged for the "coupons" or "guaranteed annual endowment" benefits are prominently specified in the policy separately from each other in dollar amounts. This shall not apply to any policy in which the amount of any pure endowment or periodic benefit, or benefits, payable during any policy year is greater than the total annual premium for such year. (Acts 1957, No. 608, p. 865, § 4; Acts 1971, No. 407, p. 707, § 236.)

Collateral references. — 43 Am. Jur. 2d, Insurance, §§ 734-743.

§ 27-12-11. Life, annuity and disability insurance — Unfair discrimination in rates, etc.

(a) No person shall make or permit any unfair discrimination between individuals of the same class and equal expectation of life in the rates charged for any contract of life insurance or of life annuity, or in the dividends or other benefits payable thereon or in any other of the terms and conditions of such contract.

(b) No person shall make or permit any unfair discrimination between amount of premium, policy fees or rates charged for any policy or contract of disability insurance, or in the benefits payable thereunder, or in any of the terms or conditions of such contract or in any other manner whatever. (Acts 1957, No. 608, p. 865, § 4; Acts 1971, No. 407, p. 707, § 237.)

Collateral references. — 44 C.J.S., Insurance, §§ 56, 60, 86, 245.
43 Am. Jur. 2d, Insurance, §§ 65, 535, 536.

§ 27-12-12. Same — Agreements not expressed in contract, rebates and other inducements.

(a) No person shall knowingly permit or offer to make, or make, any contract of life insurance, annuity or disability insurance or agreement as to such contract other than as plainly expressed in the contract issued thereon, or pay or allow, or give or offer to pay, allow or give, directly or indirectly, as an inducement to such insurance or annuity any rebate of premiums payable on the contract, or any special favor or advantage in the dividends or other benefits thereon, or any paid employment or contract for services of any kind, or any valuable consideration or inducement whatever not specified in the contract, or, directly or indirectly, give, or sell, or purchase or offer or agree to give, sell, purchase or allow as inducement to such insurance or annuity or in connection therewith, and whether or not to be specified in the policy or contract, any agreement of any form or nature promising returns and profits, or any stocks, bonds, or other securities, or interest present or contingent therein of any insurance company or other corporation, association or partnership or any dividends or profits accrued, or to accrue thereon, or offer, promise or give anything of value whatsoever not specified in the contract.

(b) The commissioner may, after hearing, revoke the certificate of authority of any insurer and the licenses of any agent or other licensed representative that has willfully violated this section. (Acts 1957, No. 608, p. 865, § 4; Acts 1971, No. 407, p. 707, § 238.)

Collateral references. — 44 C.J.S., Insurance, §§ 86, 342.

43 Am. Jur. 2d, Insurance, §§ 65, 535, 536. Construction and effect of state statute forbidding unfair trade practice or competition by discriminatory allowance of rebates, commissions, discounts, or the like. 54 ALR2d 1187.

§ 27-12-13. Same — Exceptions to discrimination, rebates or special inducements.

Nothing in sections 27-12-11 and 27-12-12 shall be construed as including within the definition of discrimination, rebates or special inducements any of the following practices:

(1) In the case of any contract of life insurance or annuity, paying bonuses to policyholders or otherwise abating their premiums in whole or in part out of surplus accumulated from nonparticipating insurance, provided, that any such bonuses or abatement of premiums is fair and equitable to policyholders and for the best interests of the insurer and its policyholders;

(2) In the case of life or disability insurance policies issued on the industrial debit or weekly premium plan, making allowance to policyholders who have continuously for a specified period made premium payments directly to an office of the insurer in an amount which fairly represents the saving in collection expense;

(3) Readjustment of the rate of premium for a group insurance policy based on the loss or expense experience thereunder, at the end of the first or any subsequent policy year of insurance thereunder, which may be made retroactive only for such policy year;

(4) In the case of life insurers, allowing its bona fide employees to receive a commission or reduction on the premiums paid by them on policies on their own lives or on the lives of their children or spouse;

(5) Issuing life or disability insurance policies on a salary savings, bank draft, preauthorized check or payroll deduction plan or other similar plan at a reduced rate reasonably related to the savings made by the use of such plan;

(6) In the case of life insurance, a written agreement between the parties for an extension of time for payment of a second or subsequent premium on the policy upon condition that the failure to pay the amount as and when so agreed shall lapse the policy; but no such agreement shall impair any right to extended or paid-up insurance which the insured may have under the policy nor any right to have the premiums, or any part thereof, or the amount payable for such extension charged against the policy under the terms of the policy. No such agreement need be attached to or made a part of the policy so affected; or

(7) Paying commissions or other compensation to duly licensed agents or allowing or returning to participating policyholders dividends or savings. (Acts 1957, No. 608, p. 865, § 4; Acts 1971, No. 407, p. 707, § 239.)

§ 27-12-14. Inducements as to property, casualty or surety insurance.

(a) No property, casualty or surety insurer, or any employee thereof, and no broker, agent or solicitor shall pay, allow or give, or offer to pay, allow or give, directly or indirectly, as an inducement to insurance or after insurance has been effected, any rebate, discount, abatement, credit or reduction of the premium named in a policy of insurance, or any special favor or advantage in the dividends or other benefits to accrue thereon or any valuable consideration or inducement whatever not specified in the policy except to the extent provided for in rating systems filed with the commissioner by, or on behalf of, the insurer and approved by the commissioner.

(b) No insured named in a policy nor any employee of such insured shall knowingly receive or accept, directly or indirectly, any such rebate, discount, abatement, credit or reduction of premium.

(c) Nothing in this section shall be construed as prohibiting the payment of commissions or other compensation to duly licensed agents, brokers or solicitors or as prohibiting any insurer from allowing or returning to its participating policyholders, members or subscribers, dividends, savings or the unused or unabsorbed portion of premiums and premium deposits.

(d) Nothing in this section or in this title shall be deemed to invalidate any insurance contract, or any amendment of, or agreement as to, such contract or the continuance or renewal of such contract which does not comply with chapters 12 or 14 of this title or any other provisions of this title, and no insured named in the policy and no officer or employee of such insured shall be deemed to have violated any provision of this title by knowingly receiving or accepting such contract, amendment, agreement, continuance or renewal, provided, that this subsection shall not be deemed to relieve any authorized insurer or licensed agent, broker, solicitor or surplus line broker of any forfeiture or penalty otherwise applicable under this title on account of any such violation, nor relieve any person otherwise liable therefor with respect to any tax payable on account of such insurance, nor relieve any insured named in the policy nor any employee of such insured who knowingly receives or accepts any rebate, discount, abatement, credit or reduction of the premium in violation of subsection (b) of this section, of any penalty otherwise applicable under this title on account of any such violation.

(e) No person in this state shall advertise, offer or provide free insurance as an inducement to the purchase or sale of real or personal property or of services, directly or indirectly, connected with such real or personal property.

(1) For the purposes of this subsection, "free insurance" is insurance for which no identifiable and additional charge is made to the purchase of such real property or personal property or services or insurance for which an identifiable or additional charge is made in an amount less than the cost of such insurance as to the seller or other person, other than the insurer providing the same.

(2) This subsection does not apply to:

   a. Insurance for loss of, or damage to, the real or personal property involved in any such sale or services under a policy covering the interests therein of the seller or vendor;

   b. Blanket disability insurance as defined in section 27-20-4;

   c. Credit life insurance or credit disability insurance;

   d. Any individual, isolated, nonrecurring, unadvertised transaction not in regular course of business; or

   e. Title insurance.

(3) No person shall use the word "free" to describe life or disability insurance in connection with the advertising or offering for sale of any kind of goods, merchandise or services. (Acts 1957, No. 608, p. 865, § 4; Acts 1971, No. 407, p. 707, § 240.)

Collateral references. — 44 C.J.S., Insurance, §§ 6, 16.

43 Am. Jur. 2d, Insurance, §§ 535, 536.

§ 27-12-15. Purchase of insurance as condition precedent to sale or loan on property.

No person, firm or corporation engaged in selling real or personal property or of lending money on the security of real or personal property and no trustee, director, officer, agent or other employee of any such person, firm or corporation shall require, or attempt or purport to require, as a condition precedent, concurrent or subsequent, to the sale or to financing the purchase of such property or to lending money upon the security of a mortgage thereon nor as a condition precedent, concurrent or subsequent, for the renewal or extension of any such loan or mortgage or for the performance of any other act in connection therewith that the person, firm or corporation purchasing such property, or for whom such purchase is to be financed, or to whom the money is to be loaned, or for whom such extension, renewal or other act is to be granted or performed negotiate any policy of insurance, or renewal thereof, covering such property or covering any liability arising from the ownership, maintenance or use thereof through a particular insurer, agent, solicitor or broker. This section shall not prevent the exercise by any person, firm or corporation of its right to designate reasonable and nondiscriminatory financial requirements as to insurer, the terms and provisions of the policy and the adequacy of the coverage with respect to insurance on property pledged or mortgaged to such person, firm or corporation; provided, however, that nothing in this section shall be construed as to prohibit the right of any person, firm or corporation from voluntarily negotiating for or soliciting the placing of such insurance. (Acts 1957, No. 608, p. 865, § 4; Acts 1971, No. 407, p. 707, § 241.)

§ 27-12-16. Common ownership, management and directorships.

(a) Any insurer may retain, invest in or acquire, the whole or any part of, the capital stock of any other insurer, or insurers, or have a common management with any other insurer, or insurers, unless such retention, investment, acquisition or common management is inconsistent with any other provision of this title or unless, by reason thereof, the business of such insurers with the public is conducted in a manner which substantially lessens competition generally in the insurance business.

(b) Any person otherwise qualified may be a director of two or more insurers which are competitors, unless the effect thereof is to lessen substantially competition between insurers generally. (Acts 1971, No. 407, p. 707, § 242.)

§ 27-12-17. Collection of premiums or charges when insurance not provided; excess premium or charge.

(a) No person shall willfully collect any sum as premium or charge for insurance which insurance is not then provided or is not in due course to be provided, subject to acceptance of the risk by the insurer, by an insurance policy issued by an insurer as permitted by this title.

(b) No person shall willfully collect as premium or charge for insurance any sum in excess of the premium or charge applicable to such insurance and as specified in the policy in accordance with the applicable classifications and rates as filed with, and approved by, the commissioner or, in cases where classifications, premiums or rates are not required by this title to be so filed and approved, such premiums and charges shall not be in excess of those specified in the policy and as fixed by the insurer. This section shall not be deemed to prohibit the charging and collection by surplus line brokers licensed under chapter 10 of this title of the amount of applicable state and federal taxes in addition to the premium required by the insurer; nor shall it be deemed to prohibit the charging and collection by a life insurer of amounts actually to be expended for medical examination of an applicant for life insurance or for reinstatement of a life insurance policy.

(c) Each violation of this section shall be punishable under section 27-1-12. (Acts 1971, No. 407, p. 707, § 243.)

§ 27-12-18. Statement of charges; hearing, order and review thereon.

(a) If the commissioner believes that any person has been engaged, or is engaging, in this state in any unfair method of competition or any unfair or deceptive act or practice expressly prohibited in this trade practices law and that a proceeding by him in respect thereto would be to the interest of the public, he shall issue and serve upon such person a statement of the charges in that respect and a notice of a hearing thereon to be held at a time and place fixed in the notice, which shall not be less than 10 days after the date of the service thereof.

(b) At the hearing, such person shall have an opportunity to be heard and to show cause why an order should not be made by the commissioner requiring such person to cease and desist from the acts, methods or practices so complained of. Upon good cause shown, the commissioner shall permit any person to intervene, appear and be heard at such hearing by counsel or in person.

(c) Provisions of chapter 2 of this title relative to the powers of the commissioner, witnesses, evidence and hearings shall apply as to procedures under this trade practices law, except where in conflict with the express provisions of this trade practices law.

(d) If, after such hearing, the commissioner finds that the method of competition, or the act or practice in question is defined in this chapter and that the person complained of has engaged in such method of competition, act or practice in violation of this chapter, he shall reduce his findings to writing and issue, and cause to be served upon such person, an order requiring such person to cease and desist from engaging in such method of competition, act or practice.

(e) Until the expiration of the time allowed under section 27-2-32 for filing a petition for review, if no such petition has been duly filed within such time, or if a petition for review has been filed within such time, then until the transcript of the record in the proceeding has been filed in the court, the commissioner may, at any time upon such notice and in such manner as he shall deem proper, modify or set aside, in whole or in part, any order issued by him under this section.

(f) After the expiration of the time allowed for filing such a petition for review, if no such petition has been duly filed within such time, the commissioner may, at any time after notice and opportunity for hearing, reopen and alter, modify or set aside, in whole or in part, any order issued by him under this section whenever in his opinion conditions of fact or of law have so changed as to require such action or if the public interest so requires.

(g) A cease and desist order issued by the commissioner under this section shall become final:

(1) Upon the expiration of the time allowed for filing of petition for review, if no such petition has been duly filed within such time; except, that the commissioner may thereafter modify or set aside his order to the extent provided in subsection (e) of this section; or

(2) Upon the final decision of the court if the court directs that the order of the commissioner be affirmed or the petition for review dismissed.

(h) No order of the commissioner pursuant to this trade practices law or order of court to enforce it shall in any way relieve or absolve any person affected by such order from any other liability, penalty or forfeiture under law.

(i) Violation of any such desist order shall be deemed to be, and shall be, punishable as a violation of this title.

(j) This section shall not be deemed to affect or prevent the imposition of any penalty provided by this title or by other law for violation of any other provision of this chapter, whether or not any such hearing is called or held or such desist order issued. (Acts 1957, No. 608, p. 865, § 7; Acts 1971, No. 407, p. 707, § 244.)

Collateral references. — Sufficiency of express finding of fact to support administrative determinations. 146 ALR 209.

Administrative decision on finding based on evidence secured outside of hearing, and without presence of interested party or counsel. 18 ALR2d 552.

Hearing and decision by different officers; change of personnel. 18 ALR2d 613.

Counsel's absence because of attendance on legislature as ground for continuance in case before quasi-judicial officer or board. 49 ALR2d 1073, Later Case Serv., § 4.

Reopening decision: power of administrative agency to reopen and reconsider final decision as affected by lack of specific statutory authority. 73 ALR2d 939.

Applicability of stare decisis doctrine to decisions of administrative agencies. 79 ALR2d 1126.

Disqualification, for bias or interest, of member of occupation or profession sitting in license revocation proceeding. 97 ALR2d 1210.

Assistance of counsel; right to assistance by counsel in administrative proceedings. 33 ALR3d 229.

Hearsay evidence in proceeding before state administrative agencies. 36 ALR3d 12.

§ 27-12-19. Service of statements, notices, orders and other processes.

Statements of charges, notices, orders and other processes of the commissioner under this trade practices law may be served by anyone duly authorized by the commissioner, either in the manner provided by law for service of process in civil actions or by registering or certifying and mailing a copy thereof to the person affected by such statement, notice, order or other process at his, or its, residence or principal office or place of business. The verified return by the person so serving such statement, notice, order or other process, setting forth the manner of such service, shall be proof of the same, and the return postcard receipt for such statement, notice, order or other process, registered or certified and mailed as aforesaid, shall be proof of the service of the same. (Acts 1957, No. 608, p. 865, § 6; Acts 1971, No. 407, p. 707, § 245.)

Collateral references. — 46 C.J.S., Insurance, § 1270.

§ 27-12-20. Review of commissioner's cease and desist orders.

Any person required by an order of the commissioner under section 27-12-18 to cease and desist from engaging in any unfair method of competition or any unfair or deceptive act or practice defined in this trade practices law may obtain a review of such order by filing an appeal therefrom in accordance with the provisions and procedures for appeals from the orders of the commissioner in general under section 27-2-32. To the extent that the commissioner's order is affirmed on such review, the court shall issue its own order commanding obedience to the terms of the commissioner's order. (Acts 1957, No. 608, p. 865, § 8; Acts 1971, No. 407, p. 707, § 246.)

Collateral references. — Effect of court review on administrative decision. 79 ALR2d 1141.

§ 27-12-21. Proceedings on unfair competition, etc., not defined under chapter — Generally.

(a) Whenever the commissioner has reason to believe that any person engaged in the business of insurance is engaging in this state in any method of competition, or in any act or practice in the conduct of such business which is not defined in this trade practices law, that such method of competition is unfair or that such act or practice is unfair or deceptive and that a proceeding by him in respect thereto would be to the interest of the public, he may issue and serve such person a statement of the charges in that respect and a notice of a hearing thereon to be held at a time and place fixed in the notice, which shall not be less than 10 days after the date of the service thereof. Each such hearing shall be conducted in the same manner as the hearings provided for in section 27-12-18. The commissioner shall, after such hearing, make a report in writing in which he shall state his findings as to the facts, and he shall serve a copy thereof upon such person.

(b) If such report charges a violation of this trade practices law and if such method of competition, act or practice has not been discontinued, the commissioner may, through the attorney general of this state, at any time after 30 days after the service of such report, cause a petition to be filed in the circuit court of this state, within the circuit wherein the person resides or has his principal place of business, to enjoin and restrain such person from engaging in such method, act or practice. The court shall have jurisdiction of the proceeding and shall have power to make and enter appropriate orders in connection therewith and to issue such writs as are ancillary to its jurisdiction or are necessary in its judgment to prevent injury to the public pendente lite.

(c) A transcript of the proceedings before the commissioner, including all evidence taken, and the report and findings shall be filed with such petition. If either party applies to the court for leave to adduce additional evidence and shows, to the satisfaction of the court, that such additional evidence is material and there were reasonable grounds for the failure to adduce such evidence in the proceeding before the commissioner, the court may order such additional evidence to be taken before the commissioner and to be adduced upon the hearing in such manner and upon such terms and conditions as to the court may seem proper. The commissioner may modify his findings of fact or make new findings by reason of the additional evidence so taken, and he shall file such modified or new findings with the return of such additional evidence.

(d) If the court finds that the method of competition complained of is unfair or that the act or practice complained of is unfair or deceptive, that the proceeding by the commissioner with respect thereto is to the interest of the public and that the findings of the commissioner are supported by the weight of the evidence, it shall issue its order enjoining and restraining the continuance of such method of competition, act or practice. (Acts 1957, No. 608, p. 865, § 9; Acts 1971, No. 407, p. 707, § 247.)

§ 27-12-22. Same — Appeal by intervenor.

If the report of the commissioner under section 27-12-21 does not charge a violation of this chapter, then any intervenor in the proceedings may, within 30 days after the service of such report, cause a notice of appeal to be filed in the circuit court of Montgomery county for a review of such report. Upon such review, the court shall have authority to issue appropriate orders and judgments in connection therewith, including, if the court finds that it is to the interest of the public, orders enjoining and restraining the continuance of any method of competition, act or practice which it finds, notwithstanding such report of the commissioner, constitutes a violation of this trade practices law. Subsection (c) of section 27-12-21 shall apply as to any such review. (Acts 1957, No. 608, p. 865, § 10; Acts 1971, No. 407, p. 707, § 248.)

§ 27-12-23. False statements, etc., in insurance application.

No agent, broker, solicitor, examining physician or other person shall knowingly make a false or fraudulent statement or representation in, or relative to, an application for insurance. Violations of this section shall be punishable under section 27-1-12. (Acts 1971, No. 407, p. 707, § 249.)

Collateral references. — 45 C.J.S., Insurance, § 473(4).

§ 27-12-24. Refusal of insurer to pay or settle claims.

No insurer shall, without just cause, refuse to pay or settle claims arising under coverages provided by its policies in this state and with such frequency as to indicate a general business practice in this state, which general business practice is evidenced by:

163

(1) A substantial increase in the number of complaints against the insurer received by the insurance department;

(2) A substantial increase in the number of lawsuits against the insurer or its insureds by claimants; and

(3) Other relevant evidence. (Acts 1971, No. 407, p. 707, § 249.1.)

For judicial recognition of tort of bad faith, see Chavers v. National Sec. Fire & Cas. Co., 405 So. 2d 1 (Ala. 1981) (intentional failure by insurer to perform duty to act in good faith in paying valid claim is actionable tort); and Gulf Atlantic Life Ins. Co. v. Barnes, 405 So. 2d 916 (Ala. 1981) (bad faith is the intentional failure by an insurer to perform the duty implied by law of good faith in fair dealing). Brown-Marx Assocs. v. Emigrant Sav. Bank, 703 F.2d 1361 (11th Cir. 1983).

Tort of bad faith is limited in application to bad faith by insurers failing to pay insurance claims. Brown-Marx Assocs. v. Emigrant Sav. Bank, 703 F.2d 1361 (11th Cir. 1983).

"Tort of bad faith," is a newly recognized Alabama theory of recovery. Brown-Marx Assocs. v. Emigrant Sav. Bank, 703 F.2d 1361 (11th Cir. 1983).

The plaintiff in a "bad faith refusal" case has the burden of proving: (a) an insurance contract between the parties and a breach thereof by the defendant; (b) an intentional refusal to pay the insured's claim; (c) the absence of any reasonably legitimate or arguable reason for that refusal (the absence of a debatable reason); (d) the insurer's actual knowledge of the absence of any legitimate or arguable reason; (e) if the intentional failure to determine the existence of a lawful basis is relied upon, the plaintiff must prove the insurer's intentional failure to determine whether there is a legitimate or arguable reason to refuse to pay the claim. National Sec. Fire & Cas. Co. v. Bowen, 417 So. 2d 179 (Ala. 1982).

Plaintiff must go beyond a mere showing of nonpayment and prove a bad faith nonpayment, a nonpayment without any reasonable ground for dispute. Or, stated differently, the plaintiff must show that the insurance company had no legal or factual defense to the insurance claim. National Sec. Fire & Cas. Co. v. Bowen, 417 So. 2d 179 (Ala. 1982); Madison County Sheriff's Posse, Inc. v. Horseman's United Ass'n, 434 So. 2d 1387 (Ala. 1983).

In the normal case in order for a plaintiff to make out a prima facie case of bad faith refusal to pay an insurance claim, the proof offered must show that the plaintiff is entitled to a directed verdict on the contract claim and, thus, entitled to recover on the contract claim

as a matter of law. Madison County Sheriff's Posse, Inc. v. Horseman's United Ass'n, 434 So. 2d 1387 (Ala. 1983).

Whether an insurance company is justified in denying a claim under a policy must be judged by what was before it at the time the decision was made. Madison County Sheriff's Posse, Inc. v. Horseman's United Ass'n, 434 So. 2d 1387 (Ala. 1983); Federated Guar. Life Ins. Co. v. Wilkins, 435 So. 2d 10 (Ala. 1983).

Where credit life policy expressly excluded coverage if the death of the insured resulted from suicide, and there was evidence from which it could be forcefully argued that the insured took his own life, the insurer had a right to have this issue determined, and also had a right to refuse payment of the claim, based upon the information it had, without subjecting itself to tort liability. Federated Guar. Life Ins. Co. v. Wilkins, 435 So. 2d 10 (Ala. 1983).

An insurer is liable for its refusal to pay a direct claim when there is no lawful basis for the refusal coupled with actual knowledge of that fact. No lawful basis "means that the insurer lacks a legitimate or arguable reason for failing to pay the claim." When a claim is "fairly debatable," the insurer is entitled to debate it, whether the debate concerns a matter of fact or law. National Sec. Fire & Cas. Co. v. Bowen, 417 So. 2d 179 (Ala. 1982).

"Debatable reason" means an arguable reason, one that is open to dispute or question. National Sec. Fire & Cas. Co. v. Bowen, 417 So. 2d 179 (Ala. 1982).

For discussion of tort of bad faith in insurance contracts if insurer intentionally refuses to settle, see Chavers v. National Security Fire & Cas. Co., 405 So. 2d 1 (Ala. 1981); Sexton v. Liberty Nat'l Life Ins. Co., 405 So. 2d 18 (Ala. 1981); Gulf Atl. Life Ins. Co. v. Barnes, 405 So. 2d 916 (Ala. 1981).

A counterclaim seeking damages for the bad faith refusal to pay an insurance claim is a compulsory counterclaim under A.R.C.P., Rule 13(a). Federated Guar. Life Ins. Co. v. Wilkins, 435 So. 2d 10 (Ala. 1983).

Waiver. — The substance of doctrine of waiver as applied in law of insurance is that if the insurer, with knowledge of facts which would bar an existing primary liability, recognizes such primary liability by treating the policy as in force, he will not thereafter be allowed to plead such facts to avoid his primary liability. McGee v. Guardian Life Ins. Co., 472 So. 2d 993 (Ala. 1985).

Collateral references. — Insurer's liability for consequential or punitive damages for wrongful delay or refusal to make payments due under contracts. 47 ALR3d 314.

Right of injured person recovering excess judgment against insured to maintain action against liability insurer for wrongful failure to settle claim. 63 ALR3d 677.

Punitive damages for an insurer's failure to settle another's claim against an insured. 85 ALR3d 1211.

Insured's right to recover from insurer prejudgment interest on amount of fire loss. 5 ALR4th 126.

What constitutes "other insurance" within meaning of insurance policy provisions prohibiting insured from obtaining other insurance on same property. 7 ALR4th 494.

When is automobile furnished or available for regular use within "drive other car" coverage of automobile liability policy. 8 ALR4th 387.

Nature and extent of insured's duty to seek retrieval of stolen automobile. 9 ALR4th 405.

Excess carrier's right to maintain action against primary liability insurer for wrongful failure to settle claim against insured. 10 ALR4th 879.

What constitutes "legal representative" or "personal representative" entitled to receive insurance proceeds on account of loss suffered by deceased. 40 ALR4th 255.

Reinsurer's liability for primary liability insurer's failure to compromise or settle. 42 ALR4th 1130.

CHAPTER 13.

RATES AND RATING ORGANIZATIONS.

Article 1.

General Provisions.

Sec.
27-13-1. Purpose of chapter; construction thereof.
27-13-2. Administration of laws relating to rates and rating systems.
27-13-3. Filing of data or information by insurers.
27-13-4. Rules and regulations.
27-13-5. Disposition of licenses collected from rating organizations.
27-13-6. Short title.

Article 2.

Fire, etc., and Inland Marine Insurance.

27-13-20. Definitions.
27-13-21. Applicability of article — Generally.
27-13-22. Same — Inland marine insurance.
27-13-23. Same — Exemptions.
27-13-24. Rating organizations — License; application therefor; renewal thereof; fee for same.
27-13-25. Same — Provisions for insurers to become members or subscribers.
27-13-26. Same — Withdrawal, expulsion and readmission of members or subscribers.
27-13-27. Rate-making and making rating systems.
27-13-28. Annual statistical reports of insurers.
27-13-29. Filing of rating systems with department by insurers — Requirement.
27-13-30. Same — Examination and approval or disapproval by commissioner.
27-13-31. Survey of risks rated upon schedule.
27-13-32. Hearings on applications to reduce rates.
27-13-33. Applications for uniform percentage increase or decrease of rates by insurers.
27-13-34. Approval of rates and forms for insuring special types or classes of risks.
27-13-35. Factors to be considered by commissioner in determining reasonableness, etc., of rates.
27-13-36. Examination of business, etc., of rating organizations and insurers making own rates.
27-13-37. Alteration, supplementation and amendment of rating systems.

Sec.
27-13-38. Prohibition against premiums not in accord with approved rating systems.
27-13-39. False or misleading information concerning rates.
27-13-40. Suspension of license or certificate of authority.
27-13-41. Order revoking or suspending licenses.
27-13-42. Notices, hearings and orders by commissioner.
27-13-43. Review of final orders of commissioner.
27-13-44. Delegation of authority by commissioner.
27-13-45. Penalty for violation of article.

Article 3.

Casualty and Surety Insurance.

27-13-60. Definitions.
27-13-61. Applicability of article.
27-13-62. Rating organizations — License; application therefor; renewal thereof; fee for same.
27-13-63. Same — Provisions for insurers to become members or subscribers.
27-13-64. Same — Admission, withdrawal, expulsion or readmission of members or subscribers.
27-13-65. Rate-making and making rating plans.
27-13-66. Annual statistical reports of insurers; exchange of information; rules and regulations.
27-13-67. Filing of rating plans with department by insurers — Requirement.
27-13-68. Same — Examination and approval or disapproval by commissioner.
27-13-69. Appeals from decisions of rating organizations.
27-13-70. Furnishing information as to rates.
27-13-71. Hearings on applications to reduce rates.
27-13-72. Application for uniform percentage increase or decrease in rates by insurers.
27-13-73. Factors to be considered in determining reasonableness, etc., of rates.
27-13-74. Examination of business, etc., of rating organizations and insurers making own rates.
27-13-75. Alteration, supplementation and amendment of rating plans.

Sec.
27-13-76. Prohibition against premiums not in accord with approved rating systems.
27-13-77. False or misleading information concerning rates.
27-13-78. Suspension of license or certificate of authority.
27-13-79. Order revoking or suspending license.
27-13-80. Notices, hearings and orders by commissioner.
27-13-81. Review of final orders of commissioner.
27-13-82. Delegation of authority by commissioner.
27-13-83. Penalty for violation of article.

Article 4.

Insurance Advisory Organizations.

Sec.
27-13-100. "Advisory organization" defined.
27-13-101. Compliance with article and rules, etc., of commissioner.
27-13-102. Filing with commissioner; orders by commissioner against unfair practices, etc., or violations.
27-13-103. Advisory organizations deemed subject to examination.
27-13-104. Enforcement and administration of article.
27-13-105. Construction of article.

ARTICLE 1.

GENERAL PROVISIONS.

Collateral references. — 44 C.J.S., Insurance, §§ 56, 60.

§ 27-13-1. Purpose of chapter; construction thereof.

The purpose of this chapter is to promote the public welfare by regulating insurance rates to the end that they shall not be excessive, inadequate or unfairly discriminatory and to authorize and regulate cooperative action among insurers in rate-making and in other matters within the scope of this chapter. Nothing in this chapter is intended:

(1) To prohibit or discourage reasonable competition; or

(2) Prohibit or encourage, except to the extent necessary to accomplish the aforementioned purpose, uniformity in insurance rates, rating systems, rating plans or practices.

This chapter shall be liberally interpreted to carry into effect the provisions of this section. (Acts 1971, No. 407, p. 707, § 250.)

Collateral references. — 43 Am. Jur. 2d, Insurance, § 64.

§ 27-13-2. Administration of laws relating to rates and rating systems.

The commissioner is charged with the duty of the administration of all laws now relating, or hereafter relating, to insurance rates and rating systems of all companies authorized to do business in the state of Alabama, with the exception of rates of life and health and accident business and rates of title insurance. (Acts 1945, No. 118, p. 111, § 2; Acts 1971, No. 407, p. 707, § 253.)

Cited in Crawford v. American Title Ins. Co., 518 F.2d 217 (5th Cir. 1975).

Collateral references. — 43 Am. Jur. 2d, Insurance, § 56.

§ 27-13-3. Filing of data or information by insurers.

The commissioner shall have authority to require any insurer engaged in any of the businesses in Alabama as enumerated in this article to file with the department any data or information required or necessary in the performance of the duties of the commissioner, said data or information to be filed in such manner and on such forms as may be prescribed by said commissioner. (Acts 1945, No. 118, p. 111, § 5; Acts 1971, No. 407, p. 707, § 254.)

§ 27-13-4. Rules and regulations.

The commissioner shall, from time to time, promulgate such rules and regulations as he may deem necessary to carry out the provisions of this article and, upon request, shall furnish to any interested party a copy of such rules and regulations. (Acts 1945, No. 118, p. 111, § 6; Acts 1971, No. 407, p. 707, § 255.)

§ 27-13-5. Disposition of licenses collected from rating organizations.

Any licenses collected from any rating organization by the commissioner shall be paid into the treasury of the state of Alabama. (Acts 1945, No. 118, p. 111, § 7; Acts 1971, No. 407, p. 707, § 256.)

§ 27-13-6. Short title.

This chapter may be referred to as "The Rating Law." (Acts 1971, No. 407, p. 707, § 251.)

ARTICLE 2.

FIRE, ETC., AND INLAND MARINE INSURANCE.

§ 27-13-20. Definitions.

For the purposes of this article, unless otherwise stated, the following terms shall have the meanings respectively ascribed to them by this section.

(1) RATE. The unit charge by which the measure of exposure or the amount of insurance specified in a policy of insurance or covered thereunder is multiplied to determine the premium.

(2) PREMIUM. The consideration paid, or to be paid, to an insurer for the issuance and delivery of any binder or policy of insurance.

(3) RATE-MAKING. The examination and analysis of every factor and influence related to, and bearing upon, the hazard and risk made the subject of insurance, the collection and collation of such factors and influences into rating systems and the application of such rating systems to individual risks.

(4) RATING SYSTEM. Every schedule, class, classification, rule, guide, standard, manual, table, rating plan, policy, policy form or compilation, by whatever name described, containing the rates used by any rating organization or by any insurer or used by any insurer or by any rating organization in determining or ascertaining a rate.

(5) RATING ORGANIZATION. Every person or persons, corporation, partnership, company, society, bureau or association, whether located within or outside this state, engaged in the business of rate-making for two or more insurers.

(6) INSURER. Any person or persons, corporation, association, partnership, reciprocal exchange or company authorized by the laws of this state to transact the business of insurance in this state.

(7) RISK. Any property, real or personal, described in any policy, exposed to any hazard or peril named in such policy.

(8) UNREASONABLY HIGH RATES. No rate shall be held to be unreasonably high unless:

a. Such rate is unreasonably high for the insurance provided; and

b. A reasonable degree of competition does not exist in the area with respect to the classification to which such rate is applicable.

(9) INADEQUATE RATE. No rate shall be held to be inadequate which upon reasonable assumptions of prospective loss and expense experience will produce an underwriting profit. (Acts 1945, No. 132, p. 133, § 1; Acts 1971, No. 407, p. 707, § 257.)

Collateral references. — 44 C.J.S., Insurance, §§ 49, 340.

§ 27-13-21. Applicability of article — Generally.

The provisions of this article shall apply to insurance against loss to property located in this state, or to any valuable interest therein, by fire, lightning, windstorm, explosion or by theft or physical damage to motor vehicles and all other kinds of insurance which fire insurance companies are authorized to write in this state, except this article shall not apply to reinsurance, aviation insurance and marine insurance, which term shall mean, and include, insurance and reinsurance against any, and all, kinds of loss or damage to the following subject matters of insurance and interests therein:

(1) Hulls, vessels and craft of every kind;

(2) Aids to navigation;

(3) Dry docks and marine railways, including marine builders' and repairers' risks, and whether complete or in process of, or awaiting, construction;

(4) All marine protection and indemnity risks; and

(5) All goods, freights, cargoes, merchandise, effects, disbursements, profits, moneys, bullion, precious stones, securities, choses in action,

evidences of debt, valuable papers, bottomry and respondentia interest and all other kinds of property and interests therein, in respect to, appertaining to or in connection with any and all risks or perils of navigation, transit or transportation on or under any seas, lakes, rivers or other waters, or in the air or on land in connection with, or incident to, export, import or waterborne risks, or while being assembled, packed, crated, baled, compressed or similarly prepared for such shipment, or while awaiting the same, or during any delays, storage, transshipment or reshipment incident thereto, including the insurance of war risks in respect to any or all of the aforesaid subject matters of insurance.

The provisions of this article shall, however, apply to inland marine insurance in the manner provided in section 27-13-22. (Acts 1945, No. 132, p. 133, § 2; Acts 1971, No. 407, p. 707, § 258.)

Collateral references. — Loss by heat, smoke, or soot without external ignition as within standard fire insurance policy. 17 ALR3d 1155.

Insured's right to recover from insurer prejudgment interest on amount of fire loss. 5 ALR4th 126.

§ 27-13-22. Same — Inland marine insurance.

The provisions of this section shall apply to all insurance which is now or hereafter defined by statute, by ruling of the commissioner or by lawful custom as inland marine insurance, but this article shall not apply to insurance of vessels or craft, their cargoes, marine builder's risks, marine protection and indemnity or other risks commonly insured under marine insurance policies:

(1) As to all classes of inland marine insurance for which class rates or rating plans are customarily fixed by rating organizations or associations of underwriters, rates or rating plans shall be filed by all authorized insurers writing such classes, with the department in such manner and form as it shall direct, and also special rates fixed by any such rating organization or association shall be similarly filed. All such rates shall be reasonable, adequate and not unfairly discriminatory. Due consideration shall be given to past experience within the state and outside the state when necessary, and due consideration may be given to prospective loss experience within the state and without when necessary, including catastrophe hazards, to a reasonable margin for profit and contingencies, to policyholders' dividends in the case of participating insurers and to all other relevant factors within the state and without the state when necessary;

(2) Any filing made pursuant to this section shall be approved by the commissioner unless he finds that such filing does not meet the requirements of this section. As soon as reasonably possible after the filing has been made, the commissioner shall in writing approve or disapprove the same; provided, however, that any filing of class rates, special rates or rating plans shall be deemed approved unless disapproved within 30 days. The commissioner may investigate rates not required to be filed under the

provisions of this section and may require the filing of any particular rate not otherwise required to be filed; and

(3) An insurer may satisfy its obligation to make such filings by becoming a member of, or a subscriber to, a licensed rating organization which makes such filings and by authorizing the department to accept such filings on its behalf. An insurer may belong or subscribe to an inland marine rating organization for inland marine insurance and also to other rating organizations for other types of insurance. (Acts 1945, No. 132, p. 133, § 3; Acts 1971, No. 407, p. 707, § 259.)

§ 27-13-23. Same — Exemptions.

Nothing in this article shall apply to any town or county farmers' mutual fire insurance association restricting their operations to not more than one county or to domestic insurance companies, associations, orders or fraternal benefit societies now doing business in this state on the assessment plan. (Acts 1945, No. 132, p. 133, § 25; Acts 1971, No. 407, p. 707, § 282.)

Collateral references. — 43 Am. Jur. 2d, Insurance, § 64.

§ 27-13-24. Rating organizations — License; application therefor; renewal thereof; fee for same.

(a) No rating organization shall do business in this state unless it shall have been licensed to do so by the commissioner. Application for such license shall be made on such forms as the commissioner shall prepare for that purpose. Upon applying for such license, every rating organization shall file with the department:

(1) A copy of its constitution, its articles of agreement or association or its certificate of incorporation and of its bylaws or rules governing the conduct of its business or such of the foregoing, if any, as such rating organization may have;

(2) A list of insurers who are, or who have agreed to become, members of, or subscribers to, such rating organization;

(3) The name and address of a person, or persons, in this state upon whom notices or orders of the commissioner affecting such rating organization may be served; and

(4) Such other information as the commissioner may require.

(b) If the commissioner finds that the applicant for a license:

(1) Has complied with the provisions of this article;

(2) Is equipped with an adequate staff of experts and clerks qualified in rate-making;

(3) Is otherwise qualified to function as a rating organization; and

(4) Maintains necessary service offices throughout Alabama beginning with at least three, viz: one in Mobile, Montgomery and Birmingham,

he shall issue a license to such rating organization authorizing it to engage in rate-making for the kinds of insurance specified in such license.

(c) The service offices described in the preceding sentence shall be adequately staffed and equipped and keep on hand a complete supply of all forms, clauses, permits, rules and such other information and data as the commissioner may prescribe for writing fire insurance in such territory. These service offices are, however, not to be required in the handling of any types of insurance serviced by special organizations. Such offices are to be kept open on all customary business days. Rating organizations having a membership of less than 25 members shall not be required to maintain such offices unless the department shall require same. If the commissioner shall determine that the applicant is not entitled to a license, he shall make an order denying its application, specifying his reasons for such denial. Licenses issued pursuant to this section shall be renewed on or before July 1, of each year in the manner provided by this article. Every rating organization doing business in the state on January 1, 1972, may continue to transact such business thereafter, subject to the provisions of this article, pending its application to the department, to be made within 180 days after January 1, 1972, for a license to do business as required by this section. A fee of $25.00 shall be paid annually to the department for such license issued under this section. (Acts 1945, No. 132, p. 133, § 4; Acts 1971, No. 407, p. 707, § 260.)

Collateral references. — 44 C.J.S., Insurance, § 92.

§ 27-13-25. Same — Provisions for insurers to become members or subscribers.

Every rating organization shall make reasonable provision in its bylaws, rules, constitution or otherwise to permit any insurer engaged in the kind of insurance for which rate-making is done by such rating organization to become a member or subscriber thereof upon application therefor by such insurer. An insurer may be a member of, or a subscriber to, more than one rating organization, but not for the purpose of rating the same risk. No insurer shall use any rate or rating systems made by a rating organization of which it is not a member or subscriber or by another insurer. No rating organization shall discriminate unfairly between insurers in the conditions imposed for admission as subscribers or in the services rendered to either members or subscribers. The refusal of any rating organization to admit an insurer as a subscriber shall, at the request of such insurer, be reviewed by the commissioner at a hearing held upon at least 10 days' notice to such rating organization and such insurer. If the commissioner shall find that the insurer has been refused admittance to such rating organization as a subscriber without justification, he shall make an order directing such rating organization to admit such insurer as a subscriber. If he shall find that the action of the rating organization in refusing admittance to an insurer as a subscriber is justified, he shall make an order affirming its action. (Acts 1945, No. 132, p. 133, § 5; Acts 1971, No. 407, p. 707, § 261.)

Collateral references. — 43 Am. Jur. 2d, Insurance, § 92.

§ 27-13-26. Same — Withdrawal, expulsion and readmission of members or subscribers.

Every rating organization shall notify the department within 10 days upon the withdrawal or expulsion therefrom of any member or subscriber. Should a rating organization expel or otherwise exclude a subscriber for the refusal or failure of such subscriber to pay such rating organization the subscribership fee agreed upon, such rating organization shall readmit such subscriber upon payment to it of any delinquent charges. No insurer shall, after expulsion or withdrawal from a rating organization, use any rate or rating system made by such rating organization during the period that such expulsion or withdrawal continues. (Acts 1945, No. 132, p. 133, § 16; Acts 1971, No. 407, p. 707, § 273.)

§ 27-13-27. Rate-making and making rating systems.

Every rating organization and every insurer which makes its own rates shall make rates that are not unreasonably high or inadequate for the safety and soundness of the insurer and which do not unfairly discriminate between risks in this state involving essentially the same hazards and shall, in rate-making and in making rating systems:

(1) Adopt basis classifications, which shall be used as the basis of all manual, minimum, class, schedule or experience rates;

(2) Adopt reasonable standards for construction, for protective facilities and for other conditions that materially affect the hazard or peril, which shall be applied in the determination or fixing of rates;

(3) Give consideration to past experience within the state and without the state when necessary, and due consideration may be given to prospective loss experience within the state and without the state when necessary, over such period of years as appears to be fairly representative of the frequency of the occurrence of the particular hazard or peril, including, where pertinent, the conflagration and catastrophe hazards, if any; and

(4) Give consideration to all factors reasonably related to the kind of insurance involved, including a reasonable profit for the insurer and, in the case of participating insurers, to policyholders' dividends. In the case of fire insurance, consideration shall be given to the latest available experience of the fire insurance business, other than fire insurance covering motor vehicles, during a period of not less than five years preceding the year in which rates are made or revised. (Acts 1945, No. 132, p. 133, § 6; Acts 1971, No. 407, p. 707, § 262.)

§ 27-13-28. Annual statistical reports of insurers.

Every insurer shall file annually, on or before July 1, with the rating organization of which it is a member or subscriber, or with such other common agency representing a group of insurers as the department may approve, and with the department a statistical report showing a classification schedule of its premiums and its losses on all kinds of insurance to which this article is applicable, together with such other information as the department may deem necessary for the proper determination of the reasonableness and adequacy of rates. Such statistical report filed with the rating organization may be consolidated and filed by such common agency. Such data shall be kept and reports made in such manner and on such forms as may be prescribed by the commissioner. All such annual filings with the department shall be kept under lock and key, and any official or employee of the department who shall divulge the contents or permit the examination thereof, except for the purpose of properly administering the provisions of this article or upon the order of court, shall be guilty of a misdemeanor and shall be subject to a fine of not more than $50.00, and shall thereafter be ineligible to be an employee or agent of said department. A mutual fire insurance company or reciprocal fire exchange which confines its business chiefly to the insurance of sprinklered risks and which pays no commission or brokerage for the acquisition of business shall be deemed to comply with the provisions of this section if it files its statistical reports of premium deposits and losses on the basis of comprehensive coverage. (Acts 1945, No. 132, p. 133, § 7; Acts 1971, No. 407, p. 707, § 263.)

Collateral references. — 44 C.J.S., Insurance, § 73.

§ 27-13-29. Filing of rating systems with department by insurers — Requirement.

Beginning 180 days after January 1, 1972, every insurer shall, before using or applying any rate to any kind of insurance coming within the scope of this article, file with the department a copy of the rating system upon which such rate is based or by which such rate is fixed or determined. The filing required in this section may be made on behalf of such insurer by a rating organization of which such insurer is a member or subscriber. The provisions of this section shall be deemed to have been complied with by any insurer which had, before January 1, 1972, been a member or subscriber of a rating organization doing business in the state. From and after the date of the filing of such rating systems, every insurer shall charge and receive rates fixed or determined in strict conformity therewith, except as in this article otherwise expressly provided. (Acts 1945, No. 132, p. 133, § 8; Acts 1971, No. 407, p. 707, § 264.)

§ 27-13-30. Same — Examination and approval or disapproval by commissioner.

If, after examination thereof, the commissioner shall find that such rating systems filed by, or on behalf of, an insurer provide for, result in or produce rates that are unreasonably high or excessive, or are not adequate for the safeness and soundness of the insurer or are unfairly discriminatory between risks in this state involving essentially the same hazards, he shall issue an order to such insurer, or to the rating organization of which such insurer is a member or subscriber, directing that such rating systems be altered in the manner, and to the extent, stated in such order to produce rates that are reasonable and adequate and not unfairly discriminatory. If the commissioner shall find that such rating systems provide for, result in or produce rates that are not unreasonably high, are not inadequate for the safeness and soundness of the insurer and are not unfairly discriminatory between risks in this state involving essentially the same hazards, he shall approve such rating systems, and such approval shall continue in effect until he shall, by order, direct that such rating systems be changed or modified as in this section provided. As soon as reasonably possible after the filing has been made the commissioner shall, in writing, approve or disapprove the same; provided, however, that unless disapproved within 30 days, such rating systems shall be deemed to be approved by him. Whenever the commissioner shall find that rating systems theretofore approved by him, or which pursuant to section 27-13-37 are effective without approval, provide for, result in or produce rates which are unreasonable or inadequate or which discriminate unfairly between risks in this state involving essentially the same hazards, he shall issue an order to all insurers employing such rating systems, or to the rating organizations of which such insurers are members or subscribers, directing that such rating systems be altered or revised in the manner, and to the extent, stated in such order to provide for, result in or produce rates which are reasonable, adequate and do not discriminate unfairly between risks in this state involving essentially the same hazards. Rating systems filed with the department on, or before, January 1, 1972, pursuant to the provisions of this section shall be deemed to have been approved by the commissioner, such approval to continue in effect until the commissioner shall, by order, direct that such rating system be altered or modified as in this section provided. Changes in rates resulting from an order of the commissioner directing or approving alterations or revisions in rating systems shall become effective following the date of such order as fixed by the commissioner and shall be applied to policies written on, or after, such effective date. Under such rules and regulations as he shall adopt, the commissioner may, by written order, suspend or modify the requirement of filing as to any kind of insurance subdivision, or combination thereof, or as to classes of risks, the rates for which cannot practicably be filed before they are used. Such orders, rules and regulations shall be made known to insurers and rating organizations affected thereby. The commissioner may make such examination as he may deem advisable to ascertain whether any rates affected by such order are excessive, inadequate or unfairly discriminatory. (Acts 1945, No. 132, p. 133, § 9; Acts 1971, No. 407, p. 707, § 265.)

Collateral references. — 43 Am. Jur. 2d,
Insurance, § 64.

§ 27-13-31. Survey of risks rated upon schedule.

Every rating organization, and every insurer which does its own ratemaking, shall keep in its office a written survey of every risk rated upon schedule after inspection and shall, upon request, furnish a copy of such survey to the interested insured or his duly authorized representative. (Acts 1945, No. 132, p. 133, § 10; Acts 1971, No. 407, p. 707, § 266.)

§ 27-13-32. Hearings on applications to reduce rates.

Every rating organization, and every insurer which does its own ratemaking, shall provide reasonable means within this state, to be approved by the department, whereby any person, or persons, affected by rate made by it may be heard on an application to reduce such rate. If such rating organization or such insurer shall refuse to reduce such rate, the person or persons affected thereby may make a like application to the commissioner within 30 days after receipt of notice in writing that the application for reduction of rate has been denied by such rating organization or by such insurer. If, upon the expiration of 20 days after application for the reduction of a rate, such rating organization or such insurer fails to grant or reject the application, the person, or persons, affected may make the application to the commissioner in the same manner as if the application had been rejected by such rating organization or by such insurer. The commissioner shall fix a time and place for hearing on such application, upon not less than 10 days' notice by registered or certified mail, for the applicant and such rating organization or such insurer to be heard. The commissioner shall make such order as he shall deem just and lawful upon the evidence placed before him at such hearing. (Acts 1945, No. 132, p. 133, § 11; Acts 1971, No. 407, p. 707, § 267.)

§ 27-13-33. Applications for uniform percentage increase or decrease of rates by insurers.

Any insurer may apply to the commissioner for permission to effect a uniform percentage increase or decrease in the rates applied to all risks of a particular class in the state in a particular kind, or kinds, of insurance. Upon the filing of such application, the commissioner shall give notice thereof by registered or certified mail to the rating organization, if any, of which such insurer is a member or subscriber and shall fix a time and place for a hearing upon the merits of such application. At such hearing, such insurer and such rating organization, or their representatives, shall be entitled to be heard and to present evidence in support of, or against, such application. The commissioner shall, upon the conclusion of such hearing, make such order as he shall deem consistent with the establishment and maintenance of reasonable, adequate and non- discriminatory rates. If the application is granted, such increase or decrease shall remain in force unless withdrawn by the insurer with the consent of, or by order of, the commissioner. If the commissioner shall find that such increase or decrease will result in rates that are unreasonable, inadequate or unfairly discriminatory, he shall make an order denying the application. Notwithstanding the foregoing, but subject to the provisions of section 27-13-30, to the extent not inconsistent therewith, when a filing of adjustments of rates for existing rating systems is made under this section and does not involve a change in the relationship between such rates and the expense portion thereof or does not involve a change of the element of expenses which are paid as a percentage of premiums and does not involve a change in rate relativities among such classifications on any basis other than loss experience, such filing shall become effective upon the date, or dates, specified in the filing and shall be deemed to meet the requirements of this title. A rate in excess of that promulgated by such rating organization may be charged on any specific risk provided such higher rate is charged with the knowledge and written consent of both the insured and the commissioner. (Acts 1945, No. 132, p. 133, § 12; Acts 1971, No. 407, p. 707, § 268.)

Collateral references. — 44 C.J.S., Insurance, § 343.

§ 27-13-34. Approval of rates and forms for insuring special types or classes of risks.

Any insurer, individually or as a member of a pool, group or association, engaged in the business of insuring special types or classes of risks in connection with a particular inspection or engineering service or with respect to which a set of standards has been maintained to the satisfaction of the commissioner may submit its loss experience data, forms and proposed rates and negotiate with the commissioner for his approval of such rates and forms either directly in its own behalf or through a unified facility of the group created, licensed as a rating organization and maintained entirely or in part for such purpose. In evaluating the forms and rates of such an insurer, or pool or association of insurers, the commissioner shall act with due regard for the previous record of such insurer or group of insurers and with due appreciation of previous and prospective loss trends, both within and outside the state, and to any other factors reasonably related to the classes or types of insurance written by such insurer or group of insurers. If approved, such forms and rates shall be filed with the rating organization, licensed to make rates on such types or classes of risks, of which such insurer is a member or subscriber. Nothing contained in this section shall be construed as exempting any insurer, pool, group or association of insurers from all other provisions of this article. (Acts 1945, No. 132, p. 133, § 13; Acts 1971, No. 407, p. 707, § 270.)

§ 27-13-35. Factors to be considered by commissioner in determining reasonableness, etc., of rates.

In every case where, pursuant to the provisions of this article, the commissioner is authorized or required to determine whether rates are reasonable and adequate and not unfairly discriminatory, he shall consider:

(1) The factors applied by insurers and rating organizations generally in determining the bases for rates;

(2) The financial condition of the insurer;

(3) The method of operation of such insurer;

(4) The past loss experience of the insurer within the state and without the state when necessary and may give consideration to prospective loss experience within the state and without the state when necessary, over such period of years as shall appear to be fairly representative of the frequency of the occurrence of the particular hazard or peril, including, where pertinent, the conflagration and catastrophe hazards, if any;

(5) All factors reasonably related to the kind of insurance involved; and

(6) A reasonable profit for the insurer and, in the case of participating insurers, to policyholders' dividends.

In the case of fire insurance, he shall consider the latest available experience of the fire insurance business, other than fire insurance covering motor vehicles, during a period of not less than five years preceding the year in which such rates are reviewed by him. (Acts 1945, No. 132, p. 133, § 14; Acts 1971, No. 407, p. 707, § 271.)

§ 27-13-36. Examination of business, etc., of rating organizations and insurers making own rates.

The commissioner may, whenever he deems it expedient, but at least once in every five years, make, or cause to be made, an examination of the business, affairs and method of operation of every rating organization doing business in this state and a like examination of an insurer making its own rates. The cost of such examination shall be fixed in the same manner as provided for in this title and shall be paid by the rating organization or insurer making its own rates being examined. The commissioner may, in his discretion, waive such examination upon proof that such rating organization has, within a reasonably recent period, been examined by a public official or department of another state pursuant to the laws of such state and upon the filing with the department of a certified copy of the report of such examination. The officers, managers, agents and employees of such rating organization or insurer making its own rates shall exhibit all its books, records, documents or agreements governing its method of operation, its rating systems and its accounts for the purpose of such examination. The commissioner, or his representative, may, for the purpose of facilitating and furthering such examination, examine, under oath, the officers, managers, agents and employees of such rating organization or insurer making its own rates. (Acts 1945, No. 132, p. 133, § 15; Acts 1971, No. 407, p. 707, § 272.)

§ 27-13-37. Alteration, supplementation and amendment of rating systems.

A rating organization, or any insurer making its own rates, may, with the approval of the commissioner, from time to time, alter, supplement or amend its rating systems, or any part thereof, by filing with the department copies of such alterations, supplements or amendments, together with a statement of the reason, or reasons, for such alteration, supplement or amendment. If such alteration, supplement or amendment shall have the effect of increasing or decreasing rates, the commissioner shall determine whether the rates as altered thereby are reasonable, adequate and not unfairly discriminatory. If the commissioner shall determine that the rates as so altered are not unreasonably high, or inadequate or unfairly discriminatory, he shall make an order approving them. If he shall find that the rates as altered are unreasonable, inadequate or unfairly discriminatory, he shall issue an order disapproving such alteration, supplement or amendment. Notwithstanding the foregoing, but subject to the provisions of section 27-13-30, to the extent not inconsistent with this section, when a filing of adjustments of rates for existing classifications of risks does not involve a change in the relationship between such rates and the expense portion thereof, or does not involve a change of the element of expenses which are paid as a percentage of premiums or does not involve a change in rate relativities among such classifications on any basis other than loss experience, such filing shall become effective upon the date, or dates, specified in the filing and shall be deemed to meet the requirements of this title. (Acts 1945, No. 132, p. 133, § 17; Acts 1971, No. 407, p. 707, § 274.)

§ 27-13-38. Prohibition against premiums not in accord with approved rating systems.

No insurer, or employee thereof, and no broker or agent shall knowingly charge, demand or receive a premium for any policy of insurance except in accordance with the respective rating systems on file with, and approved by, the commissioner. No insurer, or employee thereof, and no broker or agent shall pay, allow or give, or offer to pay, allow or give, directly or indirectly, as an inducement to insurance or after insurance has been effected, any rebate, discount, abatement, credit or reduction of the premium named in a policy of insurance, or any special favor or advantage in the dividends, or other benefits to accrue thereon or any valuable consideration or inducement whatever not specified in the policy of insurance, except to the extent that such rebate, discount, abatement, credit, reduction, favor, advantage or consideration may be provided for in rating systems filed by, or on behalf of, such insurer and approved by the commissioner. No insured named in a policy of insurance, nor any employee of such insured, shall knowingly receive or accept, directly or indirectly, any such rebate, discount, abatement or reduction of premium or any such special favor, or advantage, or valuable consideration or inducement. Nothing contained in this section shall be construed as prohibiting the payment of commissions or other compensation to regularly appointed and licensed agents and to brokers duly licensed by this state nor as prohibiting any participating insurer from distributing to its policyholders dividends, savings or the unused, or unabsorbed, portion of premiums and premium deposits. (Acts 1945, No. 132, p. 133, § 18; Acts 1971, No. 407, p. 707, § 275.)

§ 27-13-39. False or misleading information concerning rates.

No insurer, and no officer, agent or employee thereof, shall give false or misleading information to any rating organization of which it is a member or subscriber or to the department which will in any manner affect the proper determination of reasonable, adequate and nondiscriminatory rates. (Acts 1945, No. 132, p. 133, § 19; Acts 1971, No. 407, p. 707, § 276.)

§ 27-13-40. Suspension of license or certificate of authority.

Any rating organization which violates any provisions of this article shall be subject to suspension of its license, and any insurer making its own rates which violates any provision of this article shall be subject to suspension of its certificate of authority to do business in this state. Failure of a rating organization, or insurer making its own rates, to comply with the provisions of any order of the commissioner within 30 days after such order, or any extension thereof as the commissioner may, in his discretion, grant shall automatically suspend the license of such rating organization or insurer. (Acts 1945, No. 132, p. 133, § 20; Acts 1971, No. 407, p. 707, § 277.)

Collateral references. — 44 C.J.S., Insurance, § 74.

§ 27-13-41. Order revoking or suspending licenses.

If the commissioner shall find, after due notice and hearing, that any rating organization, insurer, officer, agent or representative thereof has willfully violated any of the provisions of this article, he may issue an order revoking or suspending the license of any such insurer, agent, broker or representative thereof. (Acts 1945, No. 132, p. 133, § 21; Acts 1971, No. 407, p. 707, § 278.)

§ 27-13-42. Notices, hearings and orders by commissioner.

The commissioner shall not make any order under the provisions of this article without giving every rating organization and insurer who may be affected thereby reasonable notice and a hearing, if hearing is requested. All hearings provided for in this article shall be held at such time and place as shall be designated in a notice which shall be given in writing by registered or certified mail to such rating organization and insurer, or the officers, agents and representatives thereof, which may be affected thereby, at least 30 days before the date designated therein, which notice shall state the subject of the order. At the conclusion of such hearing, or within 30 days thereafter, the commissioner shall make such order, or orders, as he may deem necessary in accordance with his findings. (Acts 1945, No. 132, p. 133, § 23; Acts 1971, No. 407, p. 707, § 280.)

§ 27-13-43. Review of final orders of commissioner.

Any final order made by the commissioner as provided by law may, upon appropriate petition filed by the attorney general on behalf of the state or by any interested party, at any time within 30 days from the date of said order, be reviewed by the circuit court of Montgomery county, Alabama, on a writ of certiorari. Upon the filing of such petition, the petitioner shall file with the register or clerk of said court a bond, with good and sufficient sureties, to be approved by the register or clerk, conditioned to pay all costs which may be assessed against the petitioner in such proceedings. The circuit court of Montgomery county, Alabama, or the court of civil appeals of Alabama, on appeal to it, may affirm said order or modify or repeal the same, in whole or in part. From the judgment of the circuit court of Montgomery county, Alabama, either the state or the interested party taking the appeal may appeal directly to the court of civil appeals of Alabama, within 42 days from the entry of the judgment; the interested party so appealing to the court of civil appeals shall give security for costs of such appeal to be approved by the register or clerk of said court. (Acts 1945, No. 132, p. 133, § 24; Acts 1971, No. 407, p. 707, § 281.)

Collateral references. — 44 C.J.S., Insurance, § 74.

§ 27-13-44. Delegation of authority by commissioner.

Whenever, under the provisions of this article, the commissioner is authorized or required to do any act, he may designate an assistant, or any salaried employee of the department, to act in his place and stead, who shall report to the commissioner and advise the commissioner on the nature of the matter delegated. The commissioner shall make such order, based upon such advice and report, as he shall, in his discretion, determine, and such order shall have the same force and effect as if the commissioner had acted thereon personally. (Acts 1945, No. 132, p. 133, § 26; Acts 1971, No. 407, p. 707, § 283.)

§ 27-13-45. Penalty for violation of article.

Any rating organization, any insurer, officer, agent or representative thereof failing to comply with, or otherwise willfully violating, any of the provisions of this article shall be guilty of a misdemeanor and, upon conviction, be punished by a fine of not less than $100.00 nor more than $500.00. (Acts 1945, No. 132, p. 133, § 22; Acts 1971, No. 407, p. 707, § 279.)

Collateral references. — 44 C.J.S., Insurance, § 86.

ARTICLE 3.

CASUALTY AND SURETY INSURANCE.

§ 27-13-60. Definitions.

For the purposes of this article, unless otherwise stated, the following terms shall have the meanings respectively ascribed to them by this section:

(1) RATE. The unit charge by which the measure of exposure or the amount of insurance specified in a policy of insurance or covered thereunder is multiplied to determine the premium.

(2) PREMIUM. The consideration paid or to be paid to an insurer for the issuance and delivery of any binder or policy of insurance.

(3) RATE-MAKING. The examination and analysis of every factor and influence related to and bearing upon the hazard and risk made the subject of insurance; the collection and collation of such factors and influences into rating plans; systems; and the application of such rating systems to individual risks.

(4) RATING PLAN. Every schedule, class, classification, rule, guide, standard, manual, table, rating plan, policy, policy form or compilation by whatever name described, containing the rates used by any rating organization or by any insurer, or used by any insurer or by any rating organization in determining and ascertaining a rate.

(5) RATING ORGANIZATION. Every person or persons, corporation, partnership, company, society, bureau or association, whether located within or outside this state, engaged in the business of rate-making for two or more insurers.

(6) INSURER. Any person or persons, corporation, association, partnership, reciprocal exchange or company authorized by the laws of this state to transact the business of insurance in this state.

(7) CASUALTY INSURANCE. As used herein this term is to be construed in its generally accepted trade sense.

(8) UNREASONABLY HIGH RATE. No rate shall be held to be unreasonably high unless

  a. Such rate is unreasonably high for the insurance provided and

182

b. A reasonable degree of competition does not exist in the area with respect to the classification to which such rate is applicable.

(9) INADEQUATE RATE. No rate shall be held to be inadequate which upon reasonable assumptions of prospective loss and expense experience will produce an underwriting profit. (Acts 1945, No. 133, p. 145, § 1; Acts 1971, No. 407, p. 707, § 284.)

Collateral references. — 44 C.J.S., Insurance, §§ 6, 49, 340.

§ 27-13-61. Applicability of article.

The provisions of this article shall apply to all lines of casualty insurance, including workmen's compensation, employer's liability, fidelity, surety and guaranty bonds, and all other kinds of insurance which casualty and surety insurance companies are authorized to write in this state, except reinsurance, aviation insurance and accident and health insurance. (Acts 1945, No. 133, p. 145, § 2; Acts 1971, No. 407, p. 707, § 285.)

§ 27-13-62. Rating organizations — License; application therefor; renewal thereof; fee for same.

No rating organization shall do business in this state until it shall have been licensed to do so by the commissioner. Application for such license shall be made on such forms as the commissioner shall prepare for that purpose. Upon applying for such license, every rating organization shall file with the department:

(1) A copy of its constitution, its articles of agreement or association or its certificate of incorporation and of its bylaws or rules governing the conduct of its business or such of the foregoing, if any, as such rating organization may have;

(2) A list of insurers who are or, who have agreed to, become members of, or subscribers to, such rating organization;

(3) The name and address of a person, or persons, in this state upon whom notices or orders of the commissioner affecting such rating organization may be served; and

(4) Such other information as the commissioner may require.

If the commissioner finds that the applicant for license:

(1) Has complied with the provisions of this article;

(2) Is equipped with an adequate staff of experts and clerks qualified in rate-making; and

(3) Is otherwise qualified to function as a rating organization, he shall issue a license to such rating organization authorizing it to engage in rate-making for the kinds of insurance or subdivision thereof specified in such license.

If the commissioner shall determine that the applicant is not entitled to a license, he shall make an order denying its application, specifying his reasons for such denial. Licenses issued pursuant to this section shall be renewed on, or before, July 1, of each year in the manner provided by this article. Every rating organization doing business in this state on January 1, 1972, may continue to transact such business thereafter, subject to the provisions of this article, pending its application to the department, to be made within 180 days after January 1, 1972, for a license to do business as required by this section. A fee of $25.00 shall be paid annually to the department for such license issued under this section. (Acts 1945, No. 133, p. 145, § 3; Acts 1971, No. 407, p. 707, § 286.)

Collateral references. — 44 C.J.S., Insurance, § 92.

§ 27-13-63. Same — Provisions for insurers to become members or subscribers.

Every rating organization shall make reasonable provision in its bylaws, rules, constitution or otherwise to permit any insurer engaged in the kind of insurance for which rate-making is done by such rating organization to become a member or subscriber to its rating services for any kind of insurance, or subdivisions thereof, upon application therefor by such insurer. No rating organization shall discriminate unfairly   ween insurers in the condition imposed for admission as subscribers or in   e services rendered to either members or subscribers. No rating organization shall adopt any rule the effect of which would be to prohibit or regulate the payment of dividends, savings or unabsorbed premium deposits allowed or returned by insurers to their policyholders, members or subscribers. The refusal of any rating organization to admit an insurer as a subscriber shall, at the request of such insurer, be reviewed by the commissioner at a hearing held upon at least 10 days' notice to such rating organization and such insurer. If the commissioner shall find that the insurer has been refused admittance to such rating organization as a subscriber without justification, he shall make an order directing such rating organization to admit such insurer as a subscriber. If he shall find that the action of the rating organization in refusing admittance to an insurer as a subscriber is justified, he shall make an order affirming its action. (Acts 1945, No. 133, p. 145, § 4; Acts 1971, No. 407, p. 707, § 287.)

Collateral references. — 43 Am. Jur. 2d, Insurance, § 92.

§ 27-13-64. Same — Admission, withdrawal, expulsion or readmission of members or subscribers.

Every rating organization shall notify the department within 10 days upon the admission, withdrawal or expulsion therefrom of any member or subscriber. Should a rating organization expel or otherwise exclude a subscriber for the refusal or failure of such subscriber to pay such rating organization the subscribership charges agreed upon, such rating organization shall readmit such subscriber upon payment to it of any delinquent charges. (Acts 1945, No. 133, p. 145, § 15; Acts 1971, No. 407, p. 707, § 298.)

§ 27-13-65. Rate-making and making rating plans.

Every rating organization and every insurer which makes its own rates shall make rates that are not unreasonably high or inadequate for the safety and soundness of the insurer and which do not unfairly discriminate between risks in this state and shall, in rate-making and in making rating plans:

(1) Adopt basis classifications, which shall be used as the basis of all manual, minimum, class, schedule or experience rates;

(2) Give consideration to past experience within the state and without the state, when necessary, and due consideration may be given to prospective loss experience within the state and without the state, when necessary, over such period of years as appears to be fairly representative of the frequency of the occurrence of the particular risk; and

(3) Give consideration to all factors reasonably related to the kind of insurance involved, including a reasonable profit for the insurer and, in the case of participating insurers, to policyholders' dividends.

The systems of expense provisions included in the rates for use by insurers or groups of insurers may differ from those of other insurers or groups of insurers to reflect the requirements of the operating methods of any such insurer or group with respect to any kind of insurance, or any subdivision or combination thereof, for which the commissioner approves the application of separate expense provisions. (Acts 1945, No. 133, p. 145, § 5; Acts 1971, No. 407, p. 707, § 288.)

§ 27-13-66. Annual statistical reports of insurers; exchange of information; rules and regulations.

Every insurer shall file annually on, or before, July 1, with the rating organization of which it is a member or subscriber, or with such other common agency representing a group of insurers as the department may approve, and with the department a statistical report showing its premiums and its losses on all kinds of insurance to which this article is applicable, together with such other information as the department may deem necessary for the proper determination of the reasonableness and adequacy of rates. Such statistical report filed with the rating organization may be consolidated and filed by such common agency. Such data shall be kept and reports made in such manner and on such forms as may be prescribed by the commissioner. All such annual filings with the department shall be kept under lock and key, and any official or employee of the department who shall divulge the contents or permit the examination thereof, except for the purpose of properly administering the provisions of this article or upon the order of court, shall be guilty of a misdemeanor and shall be subject to a fine of not more than $50.00 and shall thereafter be ineligible to be an employee or agent of said department. Reasonable rules and plans may be promulgated by the commissioner, after consultation with all insurers and rating organizations affected thereby, for the interchange of loss experience necessary for the application of rating plans. In order to further uniform administration of rating laws, the commissioner and every insurer and rating organization may exchange information and experience data with insurance supervisory officials, insurers and rating organizations in other states and may consult and cooperate with them with respect to rate-making and the application of rating systems. The commissioner may make reasonable rules and regulations necessary to effect the purposes of this article. (Acts 1945, No. 133, p. 145, § 6; Acts 1971, No. 407, p. 707, § 289.)

Collateral references. — 44 C.J.S., Insurance, § 73.

§ 27-13-67. Filing of rating plans with department by insurers — Requirement.

Beginning 180 days after January 1, 1972, every insurer shall, before using or applying any rate to any kind of insurance coming within the scope of this article, file with the department a copy of the rating plan upon which such rate is based or by which such rate is fixed or determined. The filing required in this section may be made on behalf of such insurer by a rating organization of which such insurer is a member or subscriber. From and after the date of the filing of such rating plans, every insurer shall charge and receive rates fixed or determined in strict conformity therewith, except as in this article otherwise expressly provided. (Acts 1945, No. 133, p. 145, § 7; Acts 1971, No. 407, p. 707, § 290.)

Cited in Yarbrough v. State Farm Mut. Auto. Ins. Co., 365 So. 2d 654 (Ala. 1978).

§ 27-13-68. Same — Examination and approval or disapproval by commissioner.

If, after examination thereof, the commissioner shall find that such rating plans filed by, or on behalf of, an insurer provide for, result in or produce rates that are unreasonably high or excessive, or are not adequate for the safeness and soundness of the insurer or are unfairly discriminatory between risks in this state involving essentially the same risks, he shall issue an order to such insurer, or to the rating organization of which such insurer is a member or subscriber, directing that such rating plans be altered in the manner, and to the extent, stated in such order to produce rates that are reasonable and adequate and not unfairly discriminatory. If the commissioner shall find that such rating plans provide for, result in or produce rates that are not unreasonably high, are not inadequate for the safeness and soundness of the insurer and are not unfairly discriminatory between risks in this state, he shall approve such rating plans and rates, and such approval shall continue in effect until he shall, by order, direct that such rating plans and rates be changed or modified as in this section provided. As soon as reasonably possible after the filing has been made, the commissioner shall, in writing, approve or disapprove the same; provided, however, that unless disapproved within 30 days such rating plans and rates shall be deemed to be approved by him. Whenever the commissioner shall find that rating plans theretofore approved by him or which pursuant to section 27-13-75 are effective without approval, provide for, result in or produce rates which are unreasonable or inadequate or which discriminate unfairly between risks in this state, he shall issue an order to all insurers employing such rating plans, or to the rating organizations of which such insurers are members or subscribers, directing that such rating plans be altered or revised in the manner, and to the extent, stated in such order to provide for, result in or produce rates which are reasonable, adequate and do not discriminate unfairly between risks in this state. Rating plans and rates filed with the department on, or before, January 1, 1972, pursuant to the provisions of this section, shall be deemed to have been approved by the department, such approval to continue in effect until the commissioner shall, by order, direct that such rating system be altered or modified as in this section provided. Changes in rates resulting from an order of the department directing or approving alterations or revisions in rating plans shall become effective following the date of such order as fixed by the commissioner and shall be applied to policies written on, or after, such effective date. Under such rules and regulations as he shall adopt, the commissioner may, by written order, suspend or modify the requirement of filing as to any kind of insurance, subdivision or combination thereof or as to classes of risks, the rates for which cannot practicably be filed before they are used. Such orders, rules and regulations shall be made known to insurers and rating organizations affected thereby. The commissioner may make examination as he may deem advisable to ascertain whether any rates affected by such order are excessive, inadequate or unfairly discriminatory. (Acts 1945, No. 133, p. 145, § 8; Acts 1971, No. 407, p. 707, § 291.)

Cited in Yarbrough v. State Farm Mut.   **Collateral references.** — 43 Am. Jur. 2d,
Auto. Ins. Co., 365 So. 2d 654 (Ala. 1978).   Insurance, § 64.

§ 27-13-69. Appeals from decisions of rating organizations.

Any member of, or subscriber to, a rating organization may appeal to the commissioner from the decision of such rating organization in approving or rejecting any proposed change in, or addition to, the filings of such rating organization; and the commissioner shall, after a hearing held on not less than 10 days' written notice to the appellant and to such rating organization, issue an order approving the decision of such rating organization or directing it to give further consideration to such proposal. If such appeal is based upon the failure of the rating organization to make a filing on behalf of such member or subscriber which is based on a system of expense provisions which differs, in accordance with the right granted in this article, from the system of expense provisions included in a filing made by the rating organization, the commissioner shall, if he grants the appeal, order the rating organization to make the requested filing for use by the appellant. (Acts 1945, No. 133, p. 145, § 9; Acts 1971, No. 407, p. 707, § 292.)

§ 27-13-70. Furnishing information as to rates.

Every rating organization and every insurer which makes its own rates shall, after receiving written request therefor from the department, furnish to any person affected by a rate made by it, or to the authorized representative of such person, all pertinent information as to such rate. (Acts 1945, No. 133, p. 145, § 10; Acts 1971, No. 407, p. 707, § 293.)

§ 27-13-71. Hearings on applications to reduce rates.

Every rating organization and every insurer which does its own rate-making shall provide reasonable means within this state, to be approved by the department, whereby any person, or persons, affected by a rate made by it may be heard on a written application to reduce such rate. If such rating organization or such insurer shall refuse to reduce such rate, the person, or persons, affected thereby may make a like application to the commissioner within 30 days after receipt of notice in writing that the application for reduction of rate has been denied by such rating organization or by such insurer. If, upon the expiration of 20 days after application for the reduction of a rate, such rating organization or such insurer fails to grant or reject the application, the person, or persons, affected may make the application to the commissioner in the same manner as if the application had been rejected by such rating organization or by such insurer. The commissioner shall fix a time and place for hearing on such application, upon not less than 10 days' notice by registered or certified mail, for the applicant and such rating organization or such insurer to be heard. The commissioner shall make such order as he shall deem just and lawful upon the evidence placed before him at such hearing. (Acts 1945, No. 133, p. 145, § 11; Acts 1971, No. 407, p. 707, § 294.)

§ 27-13-72. Application for uniform percentage increase or decrease in rates by insurers.

(a) Any insurer may apply to the commissioner for permission to effect a uniform percentage increase or decrease in the rates applied to all kinds of a particular class in the state in a particular kind, or kinds, of insurance. Upon the filing of such application, the commissioner shall give notice thereof by registered or certified mail to the rating organization, if any, of which such insurer is a member or subscriber and shall fix a time and place for a hearing upon the merits of such application. At such hearing, such insurer and such rating organization, or their representatives, shall be entitled to be heard and to present evidence in support of, or against, such application. The commissioner shall, upon the conclusion of such hearing, make such order as he shall deem consistent with the establishment and maintenance of reasonable, adequate and nondiscriminatory rates. If the application is granted, such increase or decrease shall remain in force unless withdrawn by the insurer with the consent of, or by order of, the commissioner. If the commissioner shall find that such increase or decrease will result in rates that are unreasonable, inadequate or unfairly discriminatory, he shall make an order denying the application.

(b) Notwithstanding the foregoing, but subject to the provisions of section 27-13-68, to the extent not inconsistent with this section, when a filing of adjustments of rates for existing classifications of risks is made under this section and does not involve a change in the relationship between such rates and the expense portion thereof, or does not involve a change of the element of expenses which are paid as percentage of premiums, and does not involve a change in rate relativities among such classifications on any basis other than loss experience, such filings shall become effective upon the date, or dates, specified in the filing and shall be deemed to meet the requirements of this article.

(c) A rate in excess of that promulgated by such rating organization may be charged on any specific risk, provided such higher rate is charged with the knowledge and written consent of both the insured and the commissioner.

(d) Subsection (b) of this section shall not apply to workmen's compensation or employer's liability insurance. (Acts 1945, No. 133, p. 145, § 12; Acts 1971, No. 407, p. 707, § 295.)

Collateral references. — 44 C.J.S., Insurance, § 343.

§ 27-13-73. Factors to be considered in determining reasonableness, etc., of rates.

In every case where, pursuant to the provisions of the article, the commissioner is authorized or required to determine whether rates are reasonable and adequate and not unfairly discriminatory, he shall consider the factors and standards set forth in section 27-13-65. (Acts 1945, No. 133, p. 145, § 13; Acts 1971, No. 407, p. 707, § 296.)

§ 27-13-74. Examination of business, etc., of rating organizations and insurers making own rates.

The commissioner may, whenever he deems it expedient, but at least once in every five years, make, or cause to be made, an examination of the business, affairs and method of operation of each rating organization doing business in this state and a like examination of each insurer making its own rates. The costs of such examination shall be fixed in the same manner as provided for in section 27-2-25 and shall be paid by the rating organization or insurer making its own rates examined. The commissioner may, in his discretion, waive such examination upon proof that such rating organization has, within a reasonably recent period, been examined by a public official or department of another state, pursuant to the laws of such state, and upon the filing with the department of a certified copy of the report of such examination. The officers, managers, agents and employees of such rating organization or insurer making its own rates shall exhibit all its books, records, documents or agreements governing its method of operation, its rating systems and its accounts for the purpose of such examination. The commissioner, or his representative, may, for the purpose of facilitating and furthering such examination, examine, under oath, the officers, managers, agents and employees of such rating organization or insurer making its own rates. (Acts 1945, No. 133, p. 145, § 14; Acts 1971, No. 407, p. 707, § 297.)

§ 27-13-75. Alteration, supplementation and amendment of rating plans.

A rating organization or any insurer making its own rates may, with the approval of the commissioner, from time to time, alter, supplement or amend its rating plans, or any part thereof, by filing with the department copies of such alterations, supplements or amendments, together with a statement of the reason, or reasons, for such alteration, supplement or amendment. If such alteration, supplement or amendment shall have the effect of increasing or decreasing rates, the commissioner shall determine whether the rates as altered thereby are reasonable, adequate and not unfairly discriminatory. If the commissioner shall determine that the rates as so altered are not unreasonably high, or inadequate or unfairly discriminatory, he shall make an order approving them. If he shall find that the rates as altered are unreasonable, inadequate or unfairly discriminatory, he shall issue an order disapproving such alteration, supplement or amendment. Notwithstanding the foregoing, but subject to the provisions of section 27-13-68, to the extent not inconsistent with this section, when a filing of adjustments of rates for existing classifications of risks does not involve a change in the relationship between such rates and the expense portion thereof, or does not involve a change of the element of expenses which are paid as a percentage of premiums or does not involve a change in rate relativities among such classifications on any basis other than loss experience, such filing shall become effective upon the date, or dates, specified in the filing and shall be deemed to meet the requirements of this article. The foregoing provisions shall not apply to workmen's compensation and employers' liability insurance. (Acts 1945, No. 133, p. 145, § 16; Acts 1971, No. 407, p. 707, § 299.)

§ 27-13-76. Prohibition against premiums not in accord with approved rating systems.

No insurer, or employee thereof, and no broker or agent shall knowingly charge, demand or receive a premium for any policy of insurance except in accordance with the respective rating systems on file with, and approved by, the commissioner. No insurer, or employee thereof, and no broker or agent shall pay, allow or give, or offer to pay, allow or give, directly or indirectly, as an inducement to insurance, or after insurance has been effected, any rebate, discount, abatement, credit or reduction of the premium named in a policy of insurance, or any special favor or advantage in the dividends or other benefits to accrue thereon or any valuable consideration or inducement whatever not specified in the policy of insurance, except to the extent that such rebate, discount, abatement, credit, reduction, favor, advantage or consideration may be provided for in rating systems filed by, or on behalf of, such insurer and approved by the commissioner. No insured named in a policy of insurance nor any employee of such insured shall knowingly receive or accept, directly or indirectly, any such rebate, discount, abatement or reduction of premium, or any such special favor or advantage, or valuable consideration or inducement. Nothing contained in this section shall be construed as prohibiting the payment of commissions or other compensation to regularly appointed and licensed agents and to brokers duly licensed by this state nor as prohibiting any participating insurer from distributing to its policyholders dividends, savings or the unused or unabsorbed portion of premiums and premium deposits. (Acts 1945, No. 133, p. 145, § 17; Acts 1971, No. 407, p. 707, § 300.)

Cited in Yarbrough v. State Farm Mut. Auto. Ins. Co., 365 So. 2d 654 (Ala. 1978).
Collateral references. — Dividends on poli- cies as violation of statutory prohibition of rebate, remission, refunds, or other discrimination in respect of premiums. 137 ALR 1029.

§ 27-13-77. False or misleading information concerning rates.

No insurer and no officer, agent or employee thereof shall give false or misleading information to any rating organization of which it is a member or subscriber or to the department which will in any manner affect the proper determination of reasonable, adequate and nondiscriminatory rates. (Acts 1945, No. 133, p. 145, § 18; Acts 1971, No. 407, p. 707, § 301.)

§ 27-13-78. Suspension of license or certificate of authority.

Any rating organization which violates any provision of this article shall be subject to suspension of its license, and any insurer making its own rates which violates any provisions of this article shall be subject to suspension of its certificate of authority to do business in this state. Failure of a rating organization or an insurer making its own rates to comply with the provisions of any order of the commissioner within 30 days after such order, or any extension thereof, as the commissioner may, in his discretion, grant shall automatically suspend the license of such rating organization or insurer. (Acts 1945, No. 133, p. 145, § 19; Acts 1971, No. 407, p. 707, § 302.)

Collateral references. — 44 C.J.S., Insurance, § 74.

§ 27-13-79. Order revoking or suspending license.

If the commissioner shall find, after due notice and hearing, that any rating organization, insurer, officer, agent or representative thereof has willfully violated any of the provisions of this article, he may issue an order revoking or suspending the license of any such insurer, agent, broker or representative thereof. (Acts 1945, No. 133, p. 145, § 20; Acts 1971, No. 407, p. 707, § 303.)

§ 27-13-80. Notices, hearings and orders by commissioner.

The commissioner shall not make any order under the provisions of this article without giving every rating organization and insurer who may be affected thereby reasonable notice and a hearing, if hearing is requested. All hearings provided for in this article shall be held at such time and place as shall be designated in a notice which shall be given in writing by registered or certified mail to such rating organization and insurer, or the officers and agents and representatives thereof, which may be affected thereby, at least 30 days before the date designated therein, which notice shall state the subject of the order. At the conclusion of such hearing, or within 30 days thereafter, the commissioner shall make such order, or orders, as he may deem necessary in accordance with his findings. (Acts 1945, No. 133, p. 145, § 22; Acts 1971, No. 407, p. 707, § 305.)

§ 27-13-81. Review of final orders of commissioner.

Any final order made by the commissioner as provided by law may, upon appropriate petition filed by the attorney general on behalf of the state or by any interested party at any time within 30 days from the date of said order, be reviewed by the circuit court of Montgomery county, Alabama, on a writ of certiorari. Upon the filing of such petition, the petitioner shall file with the register or clerk of said court a bond, with good and sufficient sureties, to be approved by the register or clerk, conditioned to pay all costs which may be assessed against the petitioner in such proceedings. The circuit court of Montgomery county, Alabama, or the court of civil appeals of Alabama, on appeal to it, may affirm said order or modify or repeal the same, in whole or in part. From the judgment of the circuit court of Montgomery county, Alabama, either the state or the interested party taking the appeal may appeal directly to the court of civil appeals of Alabama within 42 days from the entry of the judgment; the interested party so appealing to the court of civil appeals shall give security for the costs of such appeal to be approved by the register or clerk of said court. (Acts 1945, No. 133, p. 145, § 23; Acts 1971, No. 407, p. 707, § 306.)

Collateral references. — 44 C.J.S., Insurance, § 74.

§ 27-13-82. Delegation of authority by commissioner.

Whenever, under the provisions of this article, the commissioner is authorized or required to do any act, he may designate an assistant or any salaried employee of the department to act in his place and stead, who shall report to the commissioner and advise the commissioner on the nature of the matter delegated. The commissioner shall make such order, based upon such advice and report, as he shall, in his discretion, determine, and such order shall have the same force and effect as if the commissioner had acted thereon personally. (Acts 1945, No. 133, p. 145, § 24; Acts 1971, No. 407, p. 707, § 307.)

§ 27-13-83. Penalty for violation of article.

Any rating organization, and any insurer, officer, agent or representative thereof, failing to comply with, or otherwise willfully violating, any of the provisions of this article shall be guilty of a misdemeanor and, upon conviction, be punished by a fine of not less than $100.00 nor more than $500.00. (Acts 1945, No. 133, p. 145, § 21; Acts 1971, No. 407, p. 707, § 304.)

Collateral references. — 44 C.J.S., Insurance, § 86.

ARTICLE 4.

INSURANCE ADVISORY ORGANIZATIONS.

§ 27-13-100. "Advisory organization" defined.

"Advisory organization" means every group, association or other organization of insurers, whether located within or without this state, which assists insurers which make their own filings or rating organizations in rate-making by collection and furnishing of loss or expense statistics or by the submission of recommendations, but which does not make filings under articles 2 or 3 of this chapter. (Acts 1965, 2nd Ex. Sess., No. 120, p. 167, § 1; Acts 1971, No. 407, p. 707, § 308.)

§ 27-13-101. Compliance with article and rules, etc., of commissioner.

Every advisory organization assisting any rating organization or any insurer whose rates are subject to regulation under article 2 of this chapter or any rating organization or any insurer whose rates are subject to regulation under article 3 of this chapter, as a condition precedent to the rendering of such assistance, shall comply with the provisions of this article and any, and all, duly promulgated rules or regulations or orders of the commissioner relative to insurance rates, rate-making or assistance therein. (Acts 1965, 2nd Ex. Sess., No. 120, p. 167, § 2; Acts 1971, No. 407, p. 707, § 309.)

§ 27-13-102. Filing with commissioner; orders by commissioner against unfair practices, etc., or violations.

(a) Every advisory organization shall file with the commissioner:

(1) A copy of its constitution, its articles of agreement or association or its certificate of incorporation and its bylaws, rules and regulations governing its activities;

(2) A list of its members;

(3) The name and address of a resident of this state upon whom notices or orders of the commissioner or process issued at his direction may be served; and

(4) An agreement that the commissioner may examine such advisory organization in accordance with the provisions of this section.

(b) If, after a hearing, the commissioner finds that the furnishing of such information or assistance involves any act or practice which is unfair or unreasonable or otherwise inconsistent with the provisions of articles 2 or 3 of this chapter, as the case may be, he may issue a written order specifying in what respects such act or practice is unfair or unreasonable or otherwise inconsistent with the provisions of articles 2 or 3 of this chapter and requiring the discontinuance of such act or practice.

(c) No insurer which makes its own filings nor any rating organization shall support its filings by statistics or adopt rate-making recommendations furnished to it by an advisory organization which has not complied with this article or with an order of the commissioner involving such statistics or recommendations issued under subsection (b) of this section. If the commissioner finds such insurer or rating organization to be in violation of this subsection, he may issue an order requiring the discontinuance of such violation. (Acts 1965, 2nd Ex. Sess., No. 120, p. 167, § 3; Acts 1971, No. 407, p. 707, § 310.)

§ 27-13-103. Advisory organizations deemed subject to examination.

(a) Every advisory organization rendering assistance to a rating organization or to an insurer whose rates are subject to regulation under article 2 of this chapter shall agree to be subject to examination in the same manner, and upon the same terms and conditions, as rating organizations and insurers making their own rates are pursuant to section 27-13-36.

(b) Every advisory organization rendering assistance to a rating organization or to an insurer whose rates are subject to regulation under article 3 of this chapter shall agree to be subject to examination in the same manner, and upon the same terms and conditions, as rating organizations and insurers making their own rates are pursuant to section 21-13-74. (Acts 1965, 2nd Ex. Sess., No. 120, p. 167, § 4; Acts 1971, No. 407, p. 707, § 311.)

§ 27-13-104. Enforcement and administration of article.

The commissioner is authorized, and directed, to enforce this article, and he is hereby authorized to make such orders, rules and regulations as are reasonable and proper to facilitate the administration hereof. (Acts 1965, 2nd Ex. Sess., No. 120, p. 167, § 5; Acts 1971, No. 407, p. 707, § 312.)

§ 27-13-105. Construction of article.

The provisions of this article are supplemental and shall be construed in pari materia with other laws relating to insurance rates and rate-making. (Acts 1965, 2nd Ex. Sess., No. 120, p. 167, § 7; Acts 1971, No. 407, p. 707, § 313.)

CHAPTER 14.

THE INSURANCE CONTRACT.

Sec.
27-14-1. Definitions.
27-14-2. Applicability of chapter.
27-14-3. Insurable interest — Personal insurance.
27-14-4. Same — Property insurance.
27-14-5. Power to contract; purchase of insurance by or for minors.
27-14-6. Application for policy — Requirement; reliance by insurer; admissibility into evidence; alterations.
27-14-7. Same — Representations and misrepresentations, etc.
27-14-8. Forms — Filing and approval or disapproval.
27-14-9. Same — Grounds for disapproval or withdrawal of previous approval.
27-14-10. Standard or uniform provisions; waiver or substitution thereof.
27-14-11. Contents of policies — Generally.
27-14-11.1. Same — Denial or reduction of benefits due to medicaid eligibility void.
27-14-12. Same — Additional provisions.
27-14-13. Charter, bylaws, etc., of insurer as part of contract.
27-14-14. Execution of policies.
27-14-15. Underwriters' and combination policies.

Sec.
27-14-16. Noncomplying policies, riders and endorsements.
27-14-17. Construction of policies.
27-14-18. Binders.
27-14-19. Delivery of policies.
27-14-20. Renewal or extension of policies.
27-14-21. Assignment of policies.
27-14-22. Situs of contracts.
27-14-23. Effect of war on contracts of foreign insurer.
27-14-24. Effect of payments.
27-14-25. Receipt and giving of acquittance and discharge for payment by minors.
27-14-26. Forms for proof of loss.
27-14-27. Acts not deemed waiver of provisions or defenses.
27-14-28. Effect of misrepresentations in proof of loss.
27-14-29. Rights of beneficiaries, etc., under life insurance policies against creditors, etc.
27-14-30. Right to proceeds when same retained by life insurer.
27-14-31. Exemption from debt of proceeds — Disability.
27-14-32. Same — Annuity contracts.

For discussion of tort of bad faith in insurance contracts generally, see Gulf Atl. Life Ins. Co. v. Barnes, 405 So. 2d 916 (Ala. 1981).

Collateral references. — Unconscionability of insurance contracts or policies. 86 ALR3d 862.

Apportionment of payments of no-fault (personal injury protection) benefits between insurers providing coverage to same insured under policies covering different vehicles. 34 ALR4th 374.

§ 27-14-1. Definitions.

For the purposes of this chapter, the following terms shall have the meanings respectively ascribed to them by this section:

(1) POLICY. A written contract of, or written agreement for, or effecting, insurance, by whatever name called, and includes all clauses, riders, endorsements and papers attached, or issued, and delivered for attachment thereto and made a part thereof.

(2) PREMIUM. The consideration for insurance, by whatever name called. Any "assessment" or any "membership," "policy," "survey," "inspection," "service" or similar fee or charge in consideration for an insurance contract is deemed part of the premium. (Acts 1971, No. 407, p. 707, § 315.)

An insurance policy is a formal written contract containing all of the agreements pertaining to the insurance. Alabama Farm Bureau Mut. Cas. Ins. Co. v. City of Hartselle, 460 So. 2d 1219 (Ala. 1984).

Collateral references. — 44 C.J.S., Insurance, §§ 1, 340.

43 Am. Jur. 2d, Insurance, §§ 194, 530.

§ 27-14-2. Applicability of chapter.

This chapter applies as to all insurance contracts and annuity contracts other than:

(1) Reinsurance;

(2) Policies or contracts not issued for delivery in this state nor delivered in this state;

(3) Wet marine and transportation insurance; and

(4) Title insurance, except as to the following provisions:

    a. Section 27-14-5;

    b. Section 27-14-8;

    c. Section 27-14-9;

    d. Section 27-14-13;

    e. Section 27-14-14; and

    f. Section 27-14-17. (Acts 1971, No. 407, p. 707, § 314.)

§ 27-14-3. Insurable interest — Personal insurance.

(a) Insurable interest with reference to personal insurance is an interest based upon a reasonable expectation of pecuniary advantage through the continued life, health or bodily safety of another person and consequent loss by reason of his death or disability or a substantial interest engendered by love and affection in the case of individuals closely related by blood or by law.

(b) An individual has an unlimited insurable interest in his own life, health and bodily safety and may lawfully take out a policy of insurance on his own life, health or bodily safety and have the same made payable to whomsoever he pleases, regardless of whether the beneficiary so designated has an insurable interest.

(c) An insurable interest must exist at the time the contract of personal insurance becomes effective, but this requirement need not exist at the time the loss occurs.

(d) Any personal insurance contract procured, or caused to be procured, upon another individual is void unless the benefits under such contract are payable to the individual insured, or his personal representative, or to a person having, at the time when such contract was made, an insurable interest in the individual insured. In the case of such void contract, the insurer shall not be liable on the contract but shall be liable to repay to such person, or persons, who have paid the premiums, all premium payments without interest. (Acts 1971, No. 407, p. 707, § 316.)

Insurable interest necessary. — The long-standing rule that insurance is invalid unless the beneficiary has an insurable interest in the life of the insured is to the effect that a person has unlimited insurable interest in his own life and may designate any person as his beneficiary so long as the insurance was procured or taken out by the insured and the premiums paid by him, but one taking out a policy of insurance for his own benefit on the life of another person must have an insurable interest in the continuance of the life of such insured. Mutual Sav. Life Ins. Co. v. Noah, 291 Ala. 444, 282 So. 2d 271 (1973).

Reason for requirement. — Several reasons have been assigned as the basis for the insurable interest requirement, both of which are grounded upon public policy considerations: A policy taken out by one for his own benefit on the life of another in whom he has no insurable interest is, in substance, a wagering contract, and such a policy may hold out a temptation to the beneficiary to hasten by improper means the death of the insured. Mutual Sav. Life Ins. Co. v. Noah, 291 Ala. 444, 282 So. 2d 271 (1973).

Insured has unlimited insurable interest in his own life, so that any one may take out a policy on his own life and make it payable to whom he will. Afro-American Life Ins. Co. v. Adams, 195 Ala. 147, 70 So. 119 (1915).

And beneficiary of life policy need have no insurable interest. — Every person has an insurable interest in his own life, and where a beneficiary was not present when negotiations were made and a policy was taken out by insured on her own life, insured could make the benefit payable to such beneficiary, whether or not the beneficiary had an insurable interest, and the insurer having issued the policy with knowledge of the nature of the beneficiary's interest could not defeat recovery because of a want of insurable interest in such person. American Nat'l Ins. Co. v. Moore, 14 Ala. App. 413, 70 So. 190 (1915).

But policy of insurance taken out by one

person on life of another, in which he has no insurable interest is illegal and void on grounds of public policy. Helmetag v. Miller, 76 Ala. 183 (1884).

What will constitute an insurable interest in the life of another, such as will rescue such contracts from the imputation of being regarded as wager policies, is not easy to define by a general rule. It has been held, in some cases, that the interest must be, in some sense, a pecuniary one, not predicated merely upon the fact of existing relationship. In other cases, a contrary view has been intimated, which does not, however, seem to be sustained by the weight of authority. Helmetag v. Miller, 76 Ala. 183 (1884).

Brother-brother relationship will, in and of itself, support insurable interest. Mutual Sav. Life Ins. Co. v. Noah, 291 Ala. 444, 282 So. 2d 271 (1973).

Relationship of husband and wife has been held to be sufficiently close to give either an insurable interest in the life of the other. Mutual Sav. Life Ins. Co. v. Noah, 291 Ala. 444, 282 So. 2d 271 (1973).

Parent-child relationship has been accorded the same status as that given to husband and wife. Mutual Sav. Life Ins. Co. v. Noah, 291 Ala. 444, 282 So. 2d 271 (1973).

Relationships not creating insurable interest. — The following relationships have been held not to create an insurable interest on the basis of the relationship alone: Cousin and cousin; beneficiary has no interest in the life of the wife of his wife's brother; aunt and niece; aunt-in-law and niece; and niece and uncle. Mutual Sav. Life Ins. Co. v. Noah, 291 Ala. 444, 282 So. 2d 271 (1973).

Collateral references. — 44 C.J.S., Insurance, §§ 175-222.

43 Am. Jur. 2d, Insurance, §§ 460, 501 et seq., 529.

Partnership: insurable interest of partner or partnership in life of partner. 70 ALR2d 577.

Insurer's tort liability for wrongful or negligent issuance of life policy. 37 ALR4th 972.

§ 27-14-4. Same — Property insurance.

(a) No contract of insurance of property or of any interest in property, or arising from property, shall be enforceable as to the insurance except for the benefit of persons having an insurable interest in the things insured as at the time of the loss.

(b) "Insurable interest," as used in this section, means any actual, lawful and substantial economic interest in the safety or preservation of the subject of the insurance free from loss, destruction or pecuniary damage or impairment.

(c) The measure of an insurable interest in property is the extent to which the insured might be damnified by loss, injury or impairment thereof. (Acts 1971, No. 407, p. 707, § 317.)

Editor's note. — Many of the cases cited under this section were decided under former Code 1940, T. 28, § 2 or prior law.

Section is merely declaratory of long-standing Alabama rule governing insurable interest. National Security Fire & Cas. Co. v. Newman, 53 Ala. App. 614, 303 So. 2d 113 (1974); Brewton v. Alabama Farm Bureau Mut. Cas. Ins. Co., 474 So. 2d 1120 (Ala. 1985).

Insurable interest necessary. — The insurer must have an insurable interest or the policy will be void. Royal Exch. Assurance v. Almon, 206 Ala. 45, 89 So. 76 (1921), holding that bare possession of a barn will not suffice to give the husband of the owner an insurable interest. See also Burnett v. Eufaula Home Ins. Co., 46 Ala. 14 (1871).

A policy of insurance is void ab initio unless the insured has an insurable interest in the property. National Sec. Fire & Cas. Ins. Co. v. Brannon, 47 Ala. App. 319, 253 So. 2d 777 (1971).

The named insured in a policy of fire insurance must have an insurable interest in the property designated by the policy in order to recover under the insurance policy for a fire loss to the property. National Sec. Fire & Cas. Ins. Co. v. Brannon, 47 Ala. App. 319, 253 So. 2d 777 (1971).

This rule requires that the assured shall occupy such a relation to the property as would give him some sort of interest in its preservation, such as would relieve the contract of insurance from the merely gambling element which is offensive to public policy. National Sec. Fire & Cas. Co. v. Hester, 292 Ala. 592, 298 So. 2d 236 (1974).

"Factual expectation" theory of insurable interest, namely, that insurable interest exists if the insured will gain economic advantage from the continued existence of the property or will suffer economic disadvantage upon damage to or loss of the property, has been espoused in Alabama by statute and court decision. Granite State Ins. Co. v. Lowe, 362 So. 2d 240 (Ala. Civ. App.), cert. denied, 362 So. 2d 241 (Ala. 1978).

Reason for rule most commonly assigned for insurable interest requirement is that if the insured has no insurable interest in the property insured, the insured is wagering that a loss or damage to the property will occur and the insurer is wagering that it will not, thereby supplying the insured with an incentive to injure or destroy the insured property, which is against public policy. National Sec.

Fire & Cas. Ins. Co. v. Brannon, 47 Ala. App. 319, 253 So. 2d 777 (1971).

Insurable interest defined. — Whatever furnishes a reasonable expectation of pecuniary benefit from the continued existence of the subject of insurance is a valid insurable interest. National Sec. Fire & Cas. Ins. Co. v. Brannon, 47 Ala. App. 319, 253 So. 2d 777 (1971).

Whoever may fairly be said to have a reasonable expectation of deriving pecuniary advantage from the preservation of the subject-matter of insurance, whether that advantage inures to him personally or as the representative of the rights or interests of another, has an insurable interest. National Sec. Fire & Cas. Co. v. Hester, 292 Ala. 592, 298 So. 2d 236 (1974).

Doctrines of waiver and estoppel are integral part of concept of insurable interest. National Sec. Fire & Cas. Co. v. Hester, 292 Ala. 592, 298 So. 2d 236 (1974).

Recovery upon principles of waiver and estoppel or innocent misrepresentation made by the insurer's agent without fault of the insured requires that the insureds act in good faith and have some sort of pecuniary interest in the insured property at the time of the loss. National Sec. Fire & Cas. Co. v. Hester, 292 Ala. 592, 298 So. 2d 236 (1974); Brewton v. Alabama Farm Bureau Mut. Cas. Ins. Co., 474 So. 2d 1120 (Ala. 1985).

Insurer is bound by representation of full legal title placed in policy by its agent when it accepts the full premium and issues policy. National Sec. Fire & Cas. Co. v. Hester, 292 Ala. 592, 298 So. 2d 236 (1974).

If insurer has knowledge insureds do not own full legal title at the time a policy was issued, it is estopped to later question the sufficiency and the amount of the insurable interest. National Sec. Fire & Cas. Co. v. Hester, 292 Ala. 592, 298 So. 2d 236 (1974).

Person having equitable title has insurable interest in property. Home Protection v. Caldwell, 85 Ala. 607, 5 So. 338 (1889).

Mere qualified or legal interest in property is insurable interest. Home Protection v. Caldwell, 85 Ala. 607, 5 So. 338 (1889).

And owner of such interest in property can only insure to extent of that interest. Western Assurance Co. v. Stoddard, 88 Ala. 606, 7 So. 379 (1889). See also Commercial Fire Ins. Co. v. Capital City Ins. Co., 81 Ala. 320, 8 So. 222 (1886).

Love and affection for true owner not

insurable interest. — There is no case that holds that love and affection for the true owner of a piece of property constitutes an insurable interest in that property. National Sec. Fire & Cas. Ins. Co. v. Brannon, 47 Ala. App. 319, 253 So. 2d 777 (1971).

Mere love and affection for the true owner, though laudable, do not constitute the required insurable interest. Brewton v. Alabama Farm Bureau Mut. Cas. Ins. Co., 474 So. 2d 1120 (Ala. 1985).

Simple-contract creditor of deceased debtor, whose estate is sufficient to pay debts, has insurable interest in property of estate, since he has a right, by proceedings in rem, to subject it to the payment of his debt. Creed v. Sun Fire Office, 101 Ala. 522, 14 So. 323 (1893).

A person engaged in moving houses has an insurable interest in the houses which he is moving, to the extent of the compensation which he is to receive. Planters' & Merchants' Ins. Co. v. Thurston, 93 Ala. 255, 9 So. 268 (1891).

And stockholder has insurable interest in corporate property, which will sustain recovery on a fire insurance policy issued to him thereon. Aetna Ins. Co. v. Kennedy, 161 Ala. 600, 50 So. 73 (1909).

The interest of a stockholder to whom a fire insurance policy is issued on corporate property is not necessarily measured by the value thereof, for the reason that the property is liable first for the corporate debts, and the only interest held by him is his right to share in the distribution of the proceeds after payment thereof. Aetna Ins. Co. v. Kennedy, 161 Ala. 600, 50 So. 73 (1909).

And tenant may have insurable interest in leasehold, but this interest is only the value of the leasehold and not the monetary value of the property insured. Royal Exch. Assurance v. Almon, 206 Ala. 45, 89 So. 76 (1921).

A tenant must give notice to the insurer of the extent of his insurable interest. Royal Exch. Assurance v. Almon, 206 Ala. 45, 89 So. 76 (1921).

The insured having only a leasehold interest in premises insured is limited in his recovery for the loss of insured property to the value of that interest. National Sec. Fire & Cas. Co. v. Newman, 53 Ala. App. 614, 303 So. 2d 113 (1974).

Measure of damages for loss of leasehold interest may be the difference between the reasonable rental value of the property and the rental cost for the remainder of the term. Such a formula for measuring the damages due to a fire loss is not unreasonable. Especially is this so when one remembers that a policy of fire insurance merely indemnifies one against actual loss. National Sec. Fire & Cas. Co. v. Newman, 53 Ala. App. 614, 303 So. 2d 113 (1974).

One having care, custody or possession of property for another (or others) without liability and without any pecuniary interest therein may nevertheless obtain insurance thereon for the benefit of the owner. However, the custodian of the property must apply for the insurance in the name of the true owner or in his name as agent, trustee, executor or administrator of the true owner, and there must be a full disclosure to the insurer of the condition of the title. National Sec. Fire & Cas. Ins. Co. v. Brannon, 47 Ala. App. 319, 253 So. 2d 777 (1971).

Tenant in common with pecuniary interest in entire property. — Where a husband and wife were tenants in common, each of them owning an undivided interest in a mercantile building in which the husband conducted a store and delicatessen as a means of providing a livelihood for himself and family, the husband had a direct pecuniary interest; hence an insurable interest, in the entire property. National Sec. Fire & Cas. Ins. Co. v. Brannon, 47 Ala. App. 319, 253 So. 2d 777 (1971).

Trustees of school district have insurable interest in school building. — Where the trustees of a school district procured an insurance policy on a school building in their district, and the policy was issued to the trustees in their names, as such trustees and the action to collect the insurance was brought in their capacities as trustees of the school district, as such trustees they had a duty to care for the property and to look after the general interests of the school, and therefore, they had an insurable interest in the property insured. The company having issued to them the policy as such trustees, evidently had full notice and knowledge of the ownership of property. National Sec. Fire & Cas. Ins. Co. v. Brannon, 47 Ala. App. 319, 253 So. 2d 777 (1971).

Time interest should exist for fire insurance. — It is necessary that the party insured should have an interest or property at the time of insuring and at the time the fire happens. Burnett v. Eufaula Home Ins. Co., 46 Ala. 11 (1871); Loventhal v. Home Ins. Co., 112 Ala. 108, 20 So. 419 (1896); Pope v. Glens Falls Ins. Co., 136 Ala. 670, 34 So. 29 (1903).

Gratuitous agent has no insurable interest in property of undisclosed principal. — The gratuitous agent of an undisclosed principal, acting with full authority from his principal, may not procure in his own name a valid and enforceable policy of insurance on real estate, the title to which is in his undisclosed principal, because such an agent does not have such an interest in the property as amounts to an insurable interest. National Sec. Fire & Cas. Ins. Co. v. Brannon, 47 Ala. App. 319, 253 So. 2d 777 (1971).

Collateral references. — 43 Am. Jur. 2d, Insurance, §§ 460, 466 et seq., 529.

Husband and wife: insurable interest of husband or wife in other's property. 27 ALR2d 1059.

Corporations: insurable interest of stock-holder in corporation's property. 39 ALR2d 723.

Lessee: insurable interest of lessee in improvements and betterments made by him on leased premises. 97 ALR2d 1245.

Insurer's waiver of or estoppel to assert lack of insurable interest in property insured under a fire policy. 91 ALR3d 513.

Construction of clause in title insurance policy excepting defects resulting from the rights of parties in possession. 94 ALR3d 1188.

§ 27-14-5. Power to contract; purchase of insurance by or for minors.

(a) Any person of competent legal capacity may contract for insurance.

(b) Any minor of the age of 15 years or more, as determined by the nearest birthday, may, notwithstanding his minority, contract for annuities or for insurance upon his own life, body, health, property, liabilities or other interests or on the person of another in whom the minor has an insurable interest. Such a minor shall, notwithstanding such minority, be deemed competent to exercise all rights and powers with respect to, or under:

(1) Any contract for annuity or for insurance upon his own life, body or health; or

(2) Any contract such minor effected upon his own property, liabilities or other interests or on the person of another, as might be exercised by a person of full legal age, and may at any time surrender his interest in any such contracts and give valid discharge for any benefit accruing or money payable thereunder.

Such a minor shall not, by reason of his minority, be entitled to rescind, avoid or repudiate the contract nor to rescind, avoid or repudiate any exercise of a right or privilege thereunder; except, that such a minor, not otherwise emancipated, shall not be bound by any unperformed agreement to pay by promissory note or otherwise, any premium on any such annuity or insurance contract.

(c) Any annuity contract or policy of life or disability insurance procured by or for a minor under subsection (b) of this section, shall be made payable either to the minor or his estate or to a person having an insurable interest in the life of the minor. (Acts 1967, No. 96, p. 434, § 1; Acts 1971, No. 407, p. 707, § 318.)

Collateral references. — 43 C.J.S., Infants, § 76. 44 C.J.S., Insurance, §§ 241, 246. 46 C.J.S., Insurance, §§ 1156, 1157, 1159, 1161, 1166, 1173.

43 Am. Jur. 2d, Insurance, §§ 254, 255.

Minors: capacity of minor insured to effect a change of beneficiary. 14 ALR2d 375.

§ 27-14-6. Application for policy — Requirement; reliance by insurer; admissibility into evidence; alterations.

(a) No life or disability insurance contract upon an individual, except a contract of group life insurance or of group or blanket disability insurance, shall be made or effectuated unless at the time of the making of the contract the individual insured, being of competent legal capacity to contract, applies therefor or has consented thereto, except in the following cases:

(1) A spouse may effectuate such insurance upon the other spouse;

(2) Any person having an insurable interest in the life of a minor or any person upon whom a minor is dependent for support and maintenance may effectuate insurance upon the life of, or pertaining to, such minor; and

(3) Family policies may be issued insuring any two or more members of a family on an application signed by either parent, a stepparent or by a husband or wife;

(b) An insurer shall be entitled to rely upon all statements, declarations and representations made by an applicant for insurance relative to the insurable interest which such applicant has in the insured, and no insurer shall incur any legal liability except as set forth in the policy by virtue of any untrue statements, declarations or representations so relied upon in good faith by the insurer.

(c) As to kinds of insurance other than life or disability insurance, no application for insurance signed by, or on behalf of, the insured shall be admissible in evidence in any action between the insured and the insurer arising out of the policy so applied for if the insurer has failed, at expiration of 30 days after receipt by the insurer of written demand therefor by, or on behalf of, the insured, to furnish to the insured a copy of such application reproduced by any legible means.

(d) No alteration of any written application for any life or disability insurance policy shall be made by any person other than the applicant without his written consent, except that insertions may be made by the insurer, for administrative purposes only, in such manner as to indicate clearly that such insertions are not to be ascribed to the applicant. (Acts 1971, No. 407, p. 707, § 319.)

Collateral references. — 44 C.J.S., Insurance, §§ 232, 258, 301.

43 Am. Jur. 2d, Insurance, §§ 208, 209, 291-297.

Liability of insurer for damages resulting from delay in passing upon an application for life insurance. 1 ALR4th 1202.

§ 27-14-7. Same — Representations and misrepresentations, etc.

(a) All statements and descriptions in any application for an insurance policy or annuity contract, or in negotiations therefor, by, or in behalf of, the insured or annuitant shall be deemed to be representations and not warranties. Misrepresentations, omissions, concealment of facts and incorrect statements shall not prevent a recovery under the policy or contract unless either:

(1) Fraudulent;

(2) Material either to the acceptance of the risk or to the hazard assumed by the insurer; or

(3) The insurer in good faith would either not have issued the policy or contract, or would not have issued a policy or contract at the premium rate as applied for, or would not have issued a policy or contract in as large an amount or would not have provided coverage with respect to the hazard resulting in the loss if the true facts had been made known to the insurer as required either by the application for the policy or contract or otherwise.

(b) No plea of misrepresentation or fraud in connection with the issuance of a life insurance policy or annuity contract shall be filed unless accompanied by a payment into court of all premiums paid on the policy or contract. (Code 1940, T. 28, § 6; Acts 1971, No. 407, p. 707, § 320.)

I. General Consideration.
II. Misrepresentation.
    A. In General.
    B. Health of Insured.
    C. Automobile Insurance.
III. Bad Faith Refusal to Pay Claim.

I. GENERAL CONSIDERATION.

Editor's note. — Many of the cases cited under this section were decided under former Code 1940, T. 28, § 6 or prior law.

Section cannot be altered by any provision in contract. — Insured's agreement that falsity of any statement in application for accident policy shall bar recovery if statement materially affects acceptance of risk, held not to affect this section that no misrepresentation shall void policy unless made with intent to deceive or unless matters misrepresented increase risk of loss. General Accident, Fire & Life Assurance Corp. v. Jordan, 230 Ala. 407, 161 So. 240 (1935).

Former Title 28, section 6 was to be read into insurance contract. General Mut. Ins. Co. v. Ginn, 283 Ala. 470, 218 So. 2d 680 (1969).

Court should lean against construction of contract which will impose upon insured burden of warranty. National Life & Accident Ins. Co. v. Mixon, 291 Ala. 467, 282 So. 2d 308 (1973).

And where warranty is recognized it must be construed with other provisions of policy so as to modify it and give the insured the most favorable construction. National Life & Accident Ins. Co. v. Mixon, 291 Ala. 467, 282 So. 2d 308 (1973).

Representation is warranty, not condition precedent. — A representation, either in the application or policy, one or both, relating to the health of the insured at the time of the delivery of the policy, is a warranty, and not a condition precedent. National Life & Accident Ins. Co. v. Mixon, 291 Ala. 467, 282 So. 2d 308 (1973).

Therefore, it must be construed in connection with whole contract. National Life & Accident Ins. Co. v. Mixon, 291 Ala. 467, 282 So. 2d 308 (1973).

Insurance company is entitled to all material information bearing upon the obligation it undertakes in issuing a policy. Liberty Nat'l Life Ins. Co. v. Hale, 285 Ala. 198, 230 So. 2d 526 (1970); Bankers Life & Cas. Co. v. Long, 345 So. 2d 1321 (Ala. 1977).

Insurance company entitled to candid and truthful answers. — Where a candid and truthful answer would enable the insurer to discover the true facts with reference to an insured's health, insurance companies are entitled to candid and truthful answers, and when such candor is withheld and involves matters material to the risk, no just complaint can be raised when the falsity is discovered and the policies issued in reliance upon the truthfulness of the statements are avoided. Liberty Nat'l Life Ins. Co. v. Hale, 285 Ala. 198, 230 So. 2d 526 (1970).

An insurer has a right to expect applicants for insurance policies to tell the truth. An insurance company does not normally have a duty to inquire further to verify that an applicant has told it the truth. While the insurance company may have undertaken a duty to make inquiries of the doctor, the failure to do so does not support a bad faith action. Old S. Life Ins. Co. v. Spann, 472 So. 2d 987 (Ala. 1985).

Insurers are not required to investigate when the information furnished reveals nothing out of the ordinary. Stephens v. Guardian Life Ins. Co. of Am., 742 F.2d 1329 (11th Cir. 1984).

Policy not avoided if insurer knows true facts or falsity of statements. — The policy is not avoided if the insurer knows the true facts or the falsity of the statements, or has sufficient indications that would put a prudent person on notice so as to induce an inquiry which, if done with reasonable thoroughness, would reveal the truth. Bankers Life & Cas. Co. v. Long, 342 So. 2d 1321 (Ala. 1977).

The policy is not avoided if the insurer knows the true facts, or the falsity of the statements, or has sufficient indications that would put a prudent person on notice so as to induce an inquiry which, if done with reasonable thoroughness, would reveal the truth. Whether the particular information disclosed to an insurer would have prompted a reasonably prudent insurance company to investigate an applicant is an issue for the jury. Stephens v. Guardian Life Ins. Co. of Am., 742 F.2d 1329 (11th Cir. 1984).

Questions for jury. — There are some diseases which are commonly known to be of such serious consequences that the court will declare that they increase the risk of loss, without making a jury question, but the question is generally one for the jury. Sovereign Camp, W.O.W. v. Harris, 228 Ala. 417, 153 So. 870 (1934); Sovereign Camp, W.O.W. v. Sirten, 234 Ala. 421, 175 So. 539 (1937); New York Life Ins. Co. v. Zivitz, 243 Ala. 379, 10 So. 2d 276 (1942); National Sec. Ins. Co. v. Tellis, 39 Ala. App. 455, 104 So. 2d 483 (1958).

The Alabama courts have not yet held that every coronary occlusion increases the risk of loss to the insurance company as a matter of law. Until Alabama so declares the matter is inherently one of medical fact. As such it is properly one for the jury. Prudential Ins. Co. of Am. v. Gourley, 267 F.2d 156 (5th Cir. 1959).

Issue of whether particular fact increases risk of loss assumed by insurance company is generally one for jury. However, it has been held that there are some conditions which increase risk of loss as a matter of law. Clark v. Alabama Farm Bureau Mut. Cas. Ins. Co., 465 So. 2d 1135 (Ala. Civ. App. 1984); Thomas v. Liberty Nat'l Life Ins. Co., 368 So. 2d 254 (Ala. 1979); Inglish v. United Servs. Gen. Life Co., 394 So. 2d 960 (Ala. Civ. App. 1980).

Cited in Nall v. American Home Assurance Co., 486 F.2d 298 (5th Cir. 1973); Royal Indem. Co. v. Metzger Bros., 292 Ala. 624, 299 So. 2d 232 (1974).

Collateral references. — 45 C.J.S., Insurance, §§ 473(2)-473(4), 584, 585.

43 Am. Jur. 2d, Insurance, § 734 et seq.

Right of life insurer to restitution of payments made because of fraud as to death of insured. 59 ALR2d 1107.

Marital status or relationship: misrepresentation or misstatement as to insured's marital status, or as to his relationship to beneficiary, as ground for avoiding liability under life insurance policy. 14 ALR3d 931.

False answers: insured's responsibility for false answers inserted by insurer's agent in application following correct answers by insured, or incorrect answers suggested by agent. 26 ALR3d 6.

Marital status or name: insured's misrepresentation or misstatement as to his name or marital status as ground for avoiding liability insurance. 27 ALR3d 849.

Representations as to age or identity of persons who will drive vehicle, or as to extent of their relative use as avoiding coverage under automobile insurance policy. 29 ALR3d 1139.

Modern status of rules regarding materiality and effect of false statement by insurance applicant as to previous insurance cancellations or rejections. 66 ALR3d 749.

Automobile insurance: concealment or nondisclosure of physical defects or conditions as avoiding coverage. 72 ALR3d 804.

Exchange among insurers of medical information concerning insured or applicant for insurance as invasion of privacy. 98 ALR3d 561.

Liability insurance: misstatement by insured, later withdrawn or corrected, as breach of cooperation clause. 13 ALR4th 837.

Misrepresentation or concealment by insured or agent avoiding by title insurer. 17 ALR4th 1077.

II. MISREPRESENTATION.

A. In General.

Elements needed to defeat policy on ground of misrepresentations in application. — In order to defeat an insurance policy on the ground of misrepresentations in the application, it must appear: (1) the misrepresentations were false, (2) made with actual intent to deceive or the matter misrepresented increased the risk of loss and (3) the insurer relied on them to its prejudice. Bankers Life & Cas. Co. v. Long, 345 So. 2d 1321 (Ala. 1977); Federal Kemper Life Assurance Co. v. First Nat'l Bank, 712 F.2d 459 (11th Cir. 1983).

This section furnishes three separate grounds for the rescission of a policy. Stephens v. Guardian Life Ins. Co. of Am., 742 F.2d 1329 (11th Cir. 1984).

Actual fraud or increased risk must exist. — Neither warranty nor representation will avoid policy unless the conditions of this section are met, i.e., actual fraud or increased risk. National Life & Accident Ins. Co. v. Mixon, 291 Ala. 467, 282 So. 2d 308 (1973).

Misrepresentation voids the policy only if the matter misrepresented increases the risk of loss or was made with actual intent to deceive. National Ins. Underwriters v. King Craft Custom Prods., Inc., 368 F. Supp. 476 (N.D. Ala. 1973), aff'd, 488 F.2d 1393 (5th Cir. 1974).

"Material risk" is any previous affection which might reasonably have been considered a menace to the prolongation of the life of the insured and that, had it been revealed, the application would have been rejected. Metropolitan Life Ins. Co. v. Dixon, 226 Ala. 603, 148 So. 121 (1933); Liberty Nat'l Life Ins. Co. v. Trammell, 35 Ala. App. 300, 51 So. 2d 167 (1949).

Policy conditions which would void the policy because of misrepresentation by the insured are limited to "material" facts. National Ins. Underwriters v. King Craft Custom Prods., Inc., 368 F. Supp. 476 (N.D. Ala. 1973), aff'd, 488 F.2d 1393 (5th Cir. 1974).

Representations to be material need not be sole inducement to the contract, nor the chief influence leading to action. It is enough if, as a contributing influence, they operate upon the mind and conduct of the other party to any material extent. Associated Doctors Health & Life Ins. Co. v. Hanks, 44 Ala. App. 92, 203 So. 2d 148 (1967).

Good faith of party immaterial where matter misrepresented increases risk of loss. — Policy may be invalidated if matter was misrepresented and risk of loss was in-

creased though party making the representation was unaware of misrepresenting the true facts and was innocent of any bad motive. New York Life Ins. Co. v. Horton, 235 Ala. 626, 180 So. 277 (1938).

Intentional misrepresentation by applicant of material facts voids policy. — An intentional misrepresentation by the applicant of material facts relied on by the insurer permits the insurer to void the policy. Bankers Life & Cas. Co. v. Long, 345 So. 2d 1321 (Ala. 1977).

An intentional misrepresentation of material facts relied upon by the insurer permits the insurer to void the policy. Clark v. Alabama Farm Bureau Mut. Cas. Ins. Co., 465 So. 2d 1135 (Ala. Civ. App. 1984).

A representation does not have to be made with intent to deceive for the insurer to void an insurance policy. Clark v. Alabama Farm Bureau Mut. Cas. Ins. Co., 465 So. 2d 1135 (Ala. Civ. App. 1984).

The most innocent misrepresentation will afford a reason to rescind the policy if the truth is either material to the risk or, even if immaterial, would have caused the particular insurer acting in good faith to have declined coverage in the amount and at the rate obtained by the applicant. On occasion Alabama courts have held certain diseases material to the risk as a matter of law, but materiality is more commonly treated as a question of fact. Stephens v. Guardian Life Ins. Co. of Am., 742 F.2d 1329 (11th Cir. 1984).

Policy's effective date clause representation and not warranty. — Under this section a clause in insurance policy setting the effective date of the policy as the date of issue provided the insured is then alive and in sound health is a representation and not a warranty. Union-Mutual Stock Life Ins. Co. of Am. v. Wilkerson, 367 So. 2d 964 (Ala. Civ. App. 1978), aff'd, 367 So. 2d 971 (Ala. 1979).

As are statements and descriptions in application. — All descriptions and statements in an insurance policy application are considered representations, not warranties, and a misrepresentation does not prevent recovery under the policy unless it is fraudulent, it is material, or the insurer would not have issued the policy had the truth been disclosed. Lumbermens Mut. Cas. Co. v. Myrick, 596 F.2d 1313 (5th Cir. 1979).

Misrepresentations which are fault of insurance company's agent. — An insurance company cannot defend on the grounds of misrepresentations in the application, if the misrepresentations are the fault of its own agent without participation by the insured or the beneficiary, even where the application is a part of the policy. National Life & Accident

Ins. Co. v. Allen, 285 Ala. 551, 234 So. 2d 567 (1970).

Where an insurance agent does not ask questions of the insured, but writes answers as though he had done so, the insurer cannot deny coverage on this basis. National Life & Accident Inc. Co. v. Allen, 285 Ala. 551, 234 So. 2d 567 (1970).

When, without any fault on the part of the insured through neglect of the insurer's agent, misstatements are made in the application, the insurer cannot defend on this ground. National Life & Accident Ins. Co. v. Allen, 285 Ala. 551, 234 So. 2d 567 (1970).

Misrepresentations resulting solely from an act or oversight of the soliciting agent taking the application without the knowledge of the insured, are not available to the insurer although the company issuing the insurance acts on the application as presented and without knowledge of the agent's misfeasance. National Life & Accident Ins. Co. v. Allen, 285 Ala. 551, 234 So. 2d 567 (1970); Barnes v. Atlantic & Pac. Life Ins. Co. of Am., 295 Ala. 149, 325 So. 2d 143 (1975).

Misstatements or errors in insurance applications which occur due to the neglect or fault of the insurance company's agent are not a valid basis for denying coverage on the policy issued. Alabama Farm Bureau Mut. Ins. Co. v. Davis, 354 So. 2d 15 (Ala. Civ. App. 1978).

The failure of the agent to ask the questions necessary to correctly fill out inquiries in an insurance policy will not prevent the insurance company from being liable on the policy. Alabama Farm Bureau Mut. Ins. Co. v. Davis, 354 So. 2d 15 (Ala. Civ. App. 1978).

Misrepresentation of income. — An insurance company's failure to tell an insured that, on a disability insurance policy, "average earned monthly income" meant net income rather than gross income prevented it from avoiding coverage on the ground of misrepresentation of income. Nationwide Mut. Ins. Co. v. Clay, 469 So. 2d 533 (Ala. 1985).

Conviction of crime involving moral turpitude which is not disclosed to a prospective insurer increases the risk of loss as a matter of law. Clark v. Alabama Farm Bureau Mut. Cas. Ins. Co., 465 So. 2d 1135 (Ala. Civ. App. 1984).

Overstatement of extent of estate. — Where, as matter of law, ownership by assured of life estate only in property, in view of warranties in policy that his interest was unconditional and sole ownership, increased risk of loss. Gunn v. Palatine Ins. Co., 217 Ala. 89, 114 So. 690 (1927).

Occupant of dwelling misrepresented. — That dwelling warranted or represented to be occupied by tenant was in fact occupied by another, in disregard or denial of any possessory right claimed by insured, held to preclude recovery on fire policy, since status of possession was material and as matter of law increased risk of loss. Camden Fire Ins. Ass'n v. Landrum, 229 Ala. 300, 156 So. 832 (1934).

Proof of fraud. — The rule as to proof of fraud is not so strictly applied in Alabama as in some states where the application must be attached to the policy before it can be offered in evidence. Empire Life Ins. Co. v. Gee, 171 Ala. 435, 55 So. 166 (1911).

Policy provisions making fraud in application not attached to policy immaterial. — Where the policy provides that it "includes the endorsement and attached papers, if any, and contains the entire contract of insurance" and that "no statement made by the applicant not included herein shall avoid the policy or be used in any legal proceedings hereunder," these contractual provisions make fraud in an application not attached to the policy immaterial upon the issuance of the policy. The company had time before acceptance of the application to investigate. United Sec. Life Ins. Co. v. Wisener, 40 Ala. App. 350, 113 So. 2d 530 (1959).

B. Health of Insured.

"Sound health" provision in insurance contracts was "warranty" within meaning of former statute. To avoid the policy the unsound health must have been such as to increase the risk of loss. National Sec. Ins. Co. v. Tellis, 39 Ala. App. 455, 104 So. 2d 483 (1958).

Unsound health must increase risk. — To avoid the policy the unsound health must be such as to increase the risk of loss. Liberty Nat'l Life Ins. Co. v. Trammell, 33 Ala. App. 275, 33 So. 2d 479 (1947), cert. denied, 250 Ala. 159, 33 So. 2d 483 (1948); Liberty Nat'l Life Ins. Co. v. Trammell, 35 Ala. App. 300, 51 So. 2d 167 (1949); Liberty Nat'l Life Ins. Co. v. Winfield, 37 Ala. App. 575, 72 So. 2d 420 (1954).

If insured at the time of the issuance of policy was suffering from a disease which increased the risk of loss, the warranty in the policy as to sound health was breached, regardless of whether the insured knew of the presence of such disease. Liberty Nat'l Life Ins. Co. v. Trammell, 33 Ala. App. 275, 33 So. 2d 479 (1947), cert. denied, 250 Ala. 159, 33 So. 2d 483 (1948); Liberty Nat'l Life Ins. Co. v. Trammell, 35 Ala. App. 300, 51 So. 2d 167 (1949).

Unrevealed illness need not actually shorten life. — The phrase "unless the matter misrepresented increase the risk of loss" did not mean that the matter misrepresented, as omitted illness, must actually shorten the life of the insured. Prudential Ins. Co. of Am. v. Gourley, 267 F.2d 156 (5th Cir. 1959).

Significant matter is effect of insured's condition on probable reduction in life expectancy. — The significant matter is the effect of the insured's disease, illness or medical condition on the probable reduction in life expectancy rather than the general classification of that condition. The supreme court of Alabama has expressed it this way: "A material risk is any previous affection which might reasonably have been considered a menace to the prolongation of the life of the insured, and that, had it been revealed, the application would have been rejected."

Brotherhood of Ry. Clerks v. Riggins, 214 Ala. 79, 107 So. 44 (1925); Metropolitan Life Ins. Co. v. Dixon, 226 Ala. 603, 148 So. 121 (1933); Prudential Ins. Co. of Am. v. Gourley, 267 F.2d 156 (5th Cir. 1959).

Judicial notice that certain maladies increase risk of loss. — See Metropolitan Life Ins. Co. v. Chambers, 226 Ala. 192, 146 So. 524 (1932); Life Ins. Co. v. Mann, 28 Ala. App. 425, 186 So. 583 (1938); North Carolina Mut. Life Ins. Co. v. Coleman, 32 Ala. App. 287, 26 So. 2d 114 (1946); North Carolina Mut. Life Ins. Co. v. Coleman, 248 Ala. 32, 26 So. 2d 120 (1946).

Cancer is a disease which the courts judicially know increases the risk of loss and, if existing at the time of issuance of a policy containing a warranty as to sound health, per se breaches such warranty. Liberty Nat'l Life Ins. Co. v. Trammell, 33 Ala. App. 275, 33 So. 2d 579 (1947), cert. denied, 250 Ala. 159, 33 So. 2d 483 (1948); Liberty Nat'l Life Ins. Co. v. Trammell, 35 Ala. App. 300, 51 So. 2d 167 (1949); Liberty Nat'l Life Ins. Co. v. Winfield, 37 Ala. App. 575, 72 So. 2d 420 (1954).

There are types of fatal maladies, such as tuberculosis and cancer, of which the courts take judicial knowledge as being material to the risk of insurance, but the courts will not take judicial knowledge of the disease of insanity of insured so as to relieve defendant of the necessity of alleging that such fact was material to the risk, made with intent to deceive, and defendant, relying thereon, issued the policy and was thereby deceived. Booker T. Washington Ins. Co. v. Crocker, 36 Ala. App. 273, 56 So. 2d 353 (1951).

Court took judicial notice that pulmonary tuberculosis was a disease which was material to risk of burial insurance, as respects whether fact insured had had disease when policy was issued avoided policy under its terms. Booker T. Washington Burial Ins. Co. v. Williams, 27 Ala. App. 393, 173 So. 269 (1937); National Life & Accident Ins. Co. v. Cummings, 27 Ala. App. 355, 172 So. 353 (1937).

Judicial knowledge of fact certain disease increases risk of loss dispenses with proof. — In action on policy of life insurance, where insurer contended insured was not in sound health at time of issuance of policy, having tuberculosis, insurer was not required to specifically allege and prove that tuberculosis increased risk of loss or that misrepresentation was made with actual intent to deceive, since judicial knowledge of such fact dispenses with proof. Independent Life Ins. Co. v. Seale, 219 Ala. 197, 121 So. 714 (1929).

Court will not take judicial knowledge that syphilis increases risk of loss to insurer under life policy. Life Ins. Co. v. Mann, 28 Ala. App. 425, 186 So. 583 (1938).

Age of insured goes directly to risk in life insurance; hence, any substantial understatement of age is a material misrepresentation, because the matter misrepresented does increase the risk of loss. Ginsberg v. Union Cent. Life Ins. Co., 240 Ala. 299, 198 So. 855 (1940).

Hodgkin's disease is a malady which materially increases the risk of loss. Crumpton v. Pilgrim Health & Life Ins. Co., 35 Ala. App. 363, 46 So. 2d 848 (1950).

Pregnancy is not a condition affecting "good health" or "sound health," and a provision in the policy that the company's liability is limited to a return of the premiums paid if death results from pregnancy existing at the time of the issuance of the policy must be construed as a condition of the contract of insurance limiting the scope of liability, and not as a warranty or representation. Shinn v. Family Reserve Ins. Co., 33 Ala. App. 281, 33 So. 2d 741 (1947), cert. denied, 250 Ala. 194, 33 So. 2d 743 (1948).

Psychosis or nervous disease. — See Occidental Life Ins. Co. v. Nichols, 266 Ala. 521, 97 So. 2d 879 (1957).

Avoidance of policy on grounds insured not in good health at delivery of policy. — A condition of delivery in good health has the legal effect of a warranty, and by statute, a warranty is treated the same as a representation, so that avoidance of a policy on the grounds that the insured was not in good health at delivery of the policy would have to be based on actual fraud or an increased risk. National Life & Accident Ins. Co. v. Mixon, 291 Ala. 467, 282 So. 2d 308 (1973).

That sickness existing when policy was delivered proved fatal established sickness increased risk of loss. Life Ins. Co. v. Newell, 223 Ala. 401, 137 So. 16 (1931).

Representations as to treatment by physicians same as representations of good health. — As respects whether insurer could avoid life policy on ground that policy reinstatement application contained false representation that insured had not been treated by physician during the two years preceding the application, representations in regard to treatment by physicians stand on same footing as representations of good health made by the insured. New York Life Ins. Co. v. Hoffman, 238 Ala. 648, 193 So. 104 (1939).

Previous diseases or consultations with physicians. — The falsity of representations made in the application for life insurance as to previous diseases or touching consultation with or treatment by a physician will not defeat a recovery on a policy so issued, unless made with intent to deceive or unless the matter misrepresented increased the risk of loss. It must appear that they relate to some serious ailment material to the question of life expectancy. New York Life Ins. Co. v. Zivitz, 243 Ala. 379, 10 So. 2d 276 (1942); Liberty Nat'l Life Ins. Co. v. Trammell, 35 Ala. App. 300, 51 So. 2d 167 (1949).

To avoid life policies for insured's misrepresentation regarding his health, misrepresentation must have been made with intent to deceive or be material to the risk. National Life & Accident Ins. Co. v. Collins, 244 Ala. 182, 12 So. 2d 353 (1943).

Policy void when proven that insured procured policy on false statement. — While ordinarily what disease or sickness may be considered a material risk may present a jury question, there are some diseases of such known incurability and fatal character, commonly known to man to be material to the risk of insurance. The court of appeals and the supreme court have many times determined tuberculosis as one of these diseases, and when it is proven that an insured made a false statement that he had no such disease and upon such statement obtained policy contract of life insurance, the policy would be void. Miller v. Metropolitan Life Ins. Co., 214 Ala. 4, 106 So. 335 (1925); Brotherhood of Ry. Clerks v. Riggins, 214 Ala. 79, 107 So. 44 (1925); National Life & Accident Ins. Co. v. Cummings, 27 Ala. App. 355, 172 So. 353 (1937).

Statement in application for life policy that insured does not have disease of such known incurability and fatal character as tuberculosis, where false, will void policy issued thereunder. National Life & Accident Ins. Co. v. Cummings, 27 Ala. App. 355, 172 So. 353 (1937).

False information furnished by beneficiary. — The answer in an application that the applicant had not been attended by a physician in the last two years, based on information furnished by the beneficiary, was obviously untrue. Where misrepresentations are attributable to a beneficiary such misrepresentations defeat the rights of the beneficiary. Liberty Nat'l Life Ins. Co. v. Trammell, 35 Ala. App. 300, 51 So. 2d 167 (1949).

Application for life policy as evidence of misrepresentation. — Where answer to action on life policy is that insured made misrepresentations regarding his health, insured's application, although not made part of policy, is evidence of misrepresentations. Metropolitan Life Ins. Co. v. Chambers, 226 Ala. 192, 146 So. 524 (1932).

Incontestable provision in life policy held not to preclude pleading of fraud in procurement of reinstatement contract, since insurer's liability under original contract depended upon validity of reinstatement contract. New York Life Ins. Co. v. Ellis, 27 Ala. App. 113, 168 So. 200 (1936).

Burden on insurer to show disease where he relies on such circumstance. — In action on life policy, wherein defense was that insured's death resulted from syphilis, the insurer had burden of showing that the insured was afflicted with such disease or was not in sound health when the policy was issued. Life Ins. Co. v. Mann, 28 Ala. App. 425, 186 So. 583 (1938).

Where diseases pleaded as a breach of the alleged warranty were not, as a matter of common knowledge, such as would increase the risk, to sustain the pleading the defendant had the burden of showing that the insured was afflicted with the alleged diseases, that they were serious and such as affected the general soundness of his health. North Carolina Mut. Life Ins. Co. v. Coleman, 32 Ala. App. 287, 26 So. 2d 114 (1946).

C. Automobile Insurance.

DUI convictions. — It could not be said that insured, in absence of specific inquiry, was under affirmative duty to disclose existence of his DUI convictions when applying for automobile insurance. Allstate Ins. Co. v. Shirah, 466 So. 2d 940 (Ala. 1985).

Although an applicant's intentional misrepresentation of a material fact, which is relied upon by the insurer, permits the insurer to avoid the policy, where the testimony on the issue of whether insured had misrepresented his driving record was in direct conflict, the supreme court would not hold that judgment of the trial court was palpably wrong or manifestly unjust. Allstate Ins. Co. v. Shirah, 466 So. 2d 940 (Ala. 1985).

Driver's license. — Burden of proving materiality of risk involved in the representation as to whether insured had a driver's license was upon the insurer. Commercial Union Life Ins. Co. v. Security Gen. Ins. Co., 282 Ala. 344, 211 So. 2d 477 (1968).

Limiting principal use of car to place where garaged. — If an insurer intends to limit the principal use of a car to the place where it is garaged, it should so provide in plain and unequivocal language. Commercial Union Ins. Co. v. Security Gen. Ins. Co., 282 Ala. 344, 211 So. 2d 477 (1968).

Liability risk stems from use to which car is put, not where it is garaged. Commercial Union Ins. Co. v. Security Gen. Ins. Co., 282 Ala. 344, 211 So. 2d 477 (1968).

Representation as to place of garaging is a statement of expectation only. Commercial Union Ins. Co. v. Security Gen. Ins. Co., 282 Ala. 344, 211 So. 2d 477 (1968); Alabama Farm Bureau Mut. Ins. Co. v. Davis, 354 So. 2d 15 (Ala. Civ. App. 1978).

An incorrect declaration concerning the location where a vehicle is to be garaged shall not prevent recovery under the insurance policy unless it is demonstrated that the declaration was fraudulently made. Alabama Farm Bureau Mut. Ins. Co. v. Davis, 354 So. 2d 15 (Ala. Civ. App. 1978).

III. BAD FAITH REFUSAL TO PAY CLAIM.

Tort of bad faith refusal to pay a valid insurance claim is in the embryonic stage, and the Alabama supreme court has not had occasion to address every issue that might arise in these cases. National Sav. Life Ins. Co. v. Dutton, 419 So. 2d 1357 (Ala. 1982).

Prima facie case of bad faith refusal. — In order for a plaintiff to make out a prima facie case of bad faith refusal to pay an insurance claim, the proof offered must show that the plaintiff is entitled to a directed verdict on the contract claim, and, thus, entitled to recover on the contract claim as a matter of law. Ordinarily, if the evidence produced by either side creates a fact issue

with regard to the validity of the claim and, thus, the legitimacy of the denial thereof, the tort claim must fail and should not be submitted to the jury. National Sav. Life Ins. Co. v. Dutton, 419 So. 2d 1357 (Ala. 1982).

Insurer is liable for refusal to pay direct claim when there is no lawful basis for refusal coupled with actual knowledge of that fact. No lawful basis means that the insurer lacks a legitimate or arguable reason for failing to pay the claim. When a claim is "fairly debatable," the insurer is entitled to debate it, whether the debate concerns a matter of fact or law. National Sav. Life Ins. Co. v. Dutton, 419 So. 2d 1357 (Ala. 1982).

Burden of proof. — The plaintiff in a "bad faith refusal to pay a valid insurance claim" has the burden of proving: (a) an insurance contract between the parties and a breach thereof by the defendant; (b) an intentional refusal to pay the insured's claim; (c) the absence of any reasonably legitimate or arguable reason for that refusal (the absence of a debatable reason); (d) the insurer's actual knowledge of the absence of any legitimate or arguable reason; (e) if the intentional failure to determine the existence of a lawful basis is relied upon, the plaintiff must prove the insurer's intentional failure to determine whether there is a legitimate or arguable reason to refuse to pay the claim. In short, plaintiff must go beyond a mere showing of nonpayment and prove a bad faith nonpayment, a nonpayment without any reasonable ground for dispute. Or, stated differently, the plaintiff must show that the insurance company had no legal or factual defense to the insurance claim. National Sav. Life Ins. Co. v. Dutton, 419 So. 2d 1357 (Ala. 1982).

§ 27-14-8. Forms — Filing and approval or disapproval.

(a) No basic insurance policy or annuity contract form or application form where written application is required and is to be made a part of the policy, or contract, or printed rider, or endorsement form or form of renewal certificate shall be delivered or issued for delivery in this state unless the form has been filed with, and approved by, the commissioner. This subsection shall not apply to surety bonds or to specially rated inland marine risks, nor to policies, riders, endorsements or forms of unique character designed for, and used with, relation to insurance upon a particular subject or which relate to the manner of distribution of benefits or to the reservation of rights and benefits under life or disability insurance policies and are used at the request or with the consent of the individual policyholder, contract holder or certificate holder. As to group insurance policies effectuated and delivered outside this state, but covering persons resident in this state, the group certificates to be delivered or issued for delivery in this state shall be filed, for the commissioner's information only, with the commissioner at his request. As to forms for use in property, marine, other than wet marine and transportation insurance, casualty and surety insurance coverages, the filing required by this subsection may be made by rating organizations on behalf of its members and subscribers; but this subsection shall not be deemed to prohibit any such member or subscriber from filing any such forms on its own behalf.

(b) Every such filing shall be made not less than 30 days in advance of any such delivery. At the expiration of such 30 days, the form so filed shall be deemed approved unless prior thereto it has been affirmatively approved or disapproved by order of the commissioner. Approval of any such form by the commissioner shall constitute a waiver of any unexpired portion of such waiting period. The commissioner may extend, by not more than an additional 30 days, the period within which he may so affirmatively approve or disapprove any such form, by giving notice of such extension before expiration of the initial 30-day period. At the expiration of any such period as so extended, and in the absence of such prior affirmative approval or disapproval, any such form shall be deemed approved. The commissioner may, at any time, after notice and for cause shown, withdraw any such approval.

(c) Any order of the commissioner disapproving any such form or withdrawing a previous approval shall state the grounds therefor and the particulars thereof in such detail as reasonably to inform the insurer thereof.

(d) The commissioner may, by order, exempt from the requirements of this section for so long as he deems proper any insurance document or form, or type thereof, as specified in such order, to which, in his opinion, this section may not practicably be applied or the filing and approval of which are, in his opinion, not desirable or necessary for the protection of the public.

(e) Appeals from orders of the commissioner disapproving any such form or withdrawing a previous approval may be taken as provided in section 27-2-32. (Acts 1971, No. 407, p. 707, § 321.)

Cited in Utica Mut. Ins. Co. v. Tuscaloosa Motor Co., 295 Ala. 309, 329 So. 2d 82 (1976).
Collateral references. — 44 C.J.S., Insurance, §§ 249-254.

43 Am. Jur. 2d, Insurance, § 58.

§ 27-14-9. Same — Grounds for disapproval or withdrawal of previous approval.

The commissioner may disapprove any form filed under section 27-14-8 or withdraw any previous approval thereof only if the form:

(1) Is in any respect in violation of, or does not comply with, this title;

(2) Contains or incorporates by reference, where such incorporation is otherwise permissible, any inconsistent, ambiguous or misleading clauses or exceptions and conditions which deceptively affect the risk purported to be assumed in the general coverage of the contract;

(3) Has any title, heading or other indication of its provisions which is misleading;

(4) Is printed, or otherwise reproduced, in such manner as to render any provision of the form substantially illegible; or

(5) Contains provisions which are unfair, or inequitable or contrary to the public policy of this state or which would, because such provisions are unclear or deceptively worded, encourage misrepresentation. (Acts 1971, No. 407, p. 707, § 322.)

§ 27-14-10. Standard or uniform provisions; waiver or substitution thereof.

(a) Insurance contracts shall contain such standard or uniform provisions as are required by the applicable provisions of this title pertaining to contracts of particular kinds of insurance; however, the commissioner may waive the required use of a particular provision in a particular insurance policy form if:

(1) He finds such provision unnecessary for the protection of the insured or inconsistent with the purposes of the policy; and

(2) The policy is otherwise approved by him.

(b) No policy shall contain any provision inconsistent with, or contradictory to, any standard or uniform provision used or required to be used, but the commissioner may approve any substitute provision which is, in his opinion, not less favorable in any particular to the insured or beneficiary than the provisions otherwise required.

(c) In lieu of the provisions required by this title for contracts for particular kinds of insurance, substantially similar provisions required by the law of the domicile of a foreign or alien insurer may be used when approved by the commissioner. (Acts 1971, No. 407, p. 707, § 323.)

Collateral references. — 44 C.J.S., Insurance, §§ 274-277.

§ 27-14-11. Contents of policies — Generally.

(a) Every policy shall specify:

(1) The names of the parties to the contract;

(2) The subject of the insurance;

(3) The risks insured against;

(4) The time when the insurance thereunder takes effect and the period during which the insurance is to continue;

(5) The premium; and

(6) The conditions pertaining to the insurance.

(b) If under the policy the exact amount of premium is determinable only at stated intervals or termination of the contract, a statement of the basis and rates upon which the premium is to be determined and paid shall be included.

(c) This section shall not apply as to surety contracts or to group insurance policies. (Acts 1971, No. 407, p. 707, § 324.)

Insurer's right to limit liability. — The law in Alabama is clear that insurance companies have the right, in the absence of statutory provisions to the contrary, to limit their liability and write policies with narrow coverage; the insured has the option to purchase the policy or look elsewhere. Aetna Ins. Co. v. Pete Wilson Roofing & Heating Co., 289 Ala. 719, 272 So. 2d 232 (1972); Butler v. Michigan Mut. Ins. Co., 402 So. 2d 949 (Ala. 1981).

The law is clear that insurance companies, in the absence of statutory provisions to the contrary, have the right to limit their liability and write their policies with narrow coverage. These insurance contracts must be enforced as written and courts cannot defeat express provisions in a policy by judicial interpretation. Butler v. Michigan Mut. Ins. Co., 402 So. 2d 949 (Ala. 1981).

Collateral references. — 44 C.J.S., Insurance, § 255.

When is automobile "used under contract in behalf of, or loaned to," insured, within meaning of "hired automobile" provision of automobile insurance policy. 5 ALR4th 636.

Binding effects of limitations on or exclusions of coverage contained in master group insurance policy but not in literature given individual insureds. 6 ALR4th 835.

What constitutes "private passenger automobile" in insurance policy provisions defining risks covered or excepted. 11 ALR4th 475.

Liability insurer's waiver of right, or estoppel, to set up breach of co-operation clause. 30 ALR4th 620.

Construction and application of aviation exclusion clauses in public liability or homeowner's insurance policies. 39 ALR4th 201.

What is "aircraft" or the like within meaning of exclusion or exception clause of insurance policy. 39 ALR4th 214.

Construction and application of pollution exclusion clause in liability insurance policy. 39 ALR4th 1047.

Statutory or policy exclusion, from automobile no-fault coverage, of property damage covered by homeowner's policy of household member who is owner, registrant, or operator of vehicle involved. 41 ALR4th 973.

§ 27-14-11.1. Same — Denial or reduction of benefits due to medicaid eligibility void.

(a) For purposes of this section, "private insurer" is defined as:

(1) Any commercial insurance company offering health or casualty insurance to individuals or groups (including both experience-rated contracts and indemnity contracts);

(2) Any profit or nonprofit prepaid plan offering either medical services or full or partial payment for the diagnosis or treatment of an injury, disease or disability; and

(3) Any organization administering health or casualty insurance plans for professional associations, unions, fraternal groups, employer-employee benefit plans, and any similar organization offering these payments or services, including self-insured and self-funded plans.

(b) Any provision in an insurance contract issued or renewed after March 25, 1980 by a private insurer which denies or reduces benefits due to the eligibility of the insured to receive assistance under the medicaid program is null and void.

(c) The provisions of this section shall not be effective if they are found by a court of competent jurisdiction to contravene federal laws or federal regulations applicable to the medicaid program. (Acts 1980, No. 80-124, p. 188.)

Collateral references. — 44 C.J.S., Insurance, §§ 1, 2.

43 Am. Jur. 2d, Insurance, §§ 1-3.

§ 27-14-12. Same — Additional provisions.

A policy may contain additional provisions not inconsistent with this title and which are:

(1) Required to be inserted by the laws of the insurer's domicile;

(2) Necessary, on account of the manner in which the insurer is constituted or operated, in order to state the rights and obligations of the parties to the contract; or

(3) Desired by the insurer and neither prohibited by law nor in conflict with any provisions required to be included therein. (Acts 1971, No. 407, p. 707, § 325.)

Collateral references. — Liability insurance: failure or refusal of insured to attend trial or to testify as breach of cooperation clause. 9 ALR4th 218.

§ 27-14-13. Charter, bylaws, etc., of insurer as part of contract.

No policy shall contain any provision purporting to make any portion of the charter, bylaws or other constituent document of the insurer, other than the subscriber's agreement or power of attorney of a reciprocal insurer, a part of the contract unless such portion is set forth in full in the policy. Any policy provision in violation of this section shall be invalid. (Acts 1971, No. 407, p. 707, § 326.)

Collateral references. — 43 Am. Jur. 2d, Insurance, § 287.

§ 27-14-14. Execution of policies.

(a) Every insurance policy shall be executed in the name of and on behalf of the insurer by its officer, attorney-in-fact, employee or representative duly authorized by the insurer.

(b) A facsimile signature of any such executing individual may be used in lieu of an original signature.

(c) No insurance contract heretofore or hereafter issued and which is otherwise valid shall be rendered invalid by reason of the apparent execution thereof on behalf of the insurer by the imprinted facsimile of an individual not authorized so to execute as of the date of the policy. (Acts 1971, No. 407, p. 707, § 327.)

Collateral references. — 44 C.J.S., Insurance, § 256.

43 Am. Jur. 2d, Insurance, § 226 et seq.

§ 27-14-15. Underwriters' and combination policies.

(a) Two or more authorized insurers may jointly issue, and shall be jointly and severally liable on, an underwriters' policy bearing their names. Any one insurer may issue policies in the name of an underwriter's department, and such policy shall plainly show the true name of the insurer.

(b) Two or more insurers may issue a combination policy which shall contain provisions substantially as follows:

(1) That the insurers executing the policy shall be severally liable for the full amount of any loss or damage, according to the terms of the policy, or for specified percentages or amounts thereof, aggregating the full amount of insurance under the policy; and

(2) That service of process, or of any notice or proof of loss required by such policy, upon any of the insurers executing the policy, shall constitute service upon all such insurers.

(c) This section shall not apply to cosurety obligations. (Acts 1971, No. 407, p. 707, § 328.)

Collateral references. — Resolution of conflicts, in nonautomobile liability insurance policies, between excess or pro rata "other insurance" clauses. 12 ALR4th 993.

§ 27-14-16. Noncomplying policies, riders and endorsements.

Any insurance policy, rider or endorsement hereafter issued and otherwise valid which contains any condition or provision not in compliance with the requirements of this title shall not be thereby rendered invalid but shall be construed and applied in accordance with such conditions and provisions as would have applied had such policy, rider or endorsement been in full compliance with this title. (Acts 1971, No. 407, p. 707, § 329.)

§ 27-14-17. Construction of policies.

(a) Every insurance contract shall be construed according to the entirety of its terms and conditions as set forth in the policy and as amplified, extended or modified by any rider, endorsement or application which is a part of the policy.

(b) A clause in any policy of life insurance, including burial insurance, providing that such policy shall be incontestible after a specified period shall preclude only a contest of the validity of the policy and shall not preclude the assertion at any time of defenses based upon provisions in the policy which exclude or restrict coverage, whether or not such restrictions or exclusions are excepted in such clause. (Acts 1971, No. 407, p. 707, § 330.)

Editor's note. — Many of the cases cited under this section were decided under former Code 1940, T. 28, § 2 or prior law.

Same rules of construction by which all other instruments are construed will be **applied to policies of insurance.** Mobile Marine Dock, etc., Ins. Co. v. McMillan, 27 Ala. 77 (1855).

214

Hence, language in policy will be given its ordinary interpretation. Empire Life Ins. Co. v. Gee, 178 Ala. 492, 60 So. 90 (1912).

Conditions in a policy will not be extended by implication to cover matters not clearly and unmistakably within the meaning of the condition according to the usual and ordinary meaning of the words used. The insurer has a right to ingraft any lawful condition he sees fit upon the policy, but he must do so by the use of terms that leave no doubt as to the extent and purport of the condition and will receive no aid from forced inferences. Liverpool & London & Globe Ins. Co. v. Lavine, 5 Ala. App. 392, 59 So. 336 (1912).

The terms of a policy are construed in their plain, ordinary and popular usage and are to be given a rational and practical construction. Globe Life Ins. Co. v. Howard, 41 Ala. App. 621, 147 So. 2d 853 (1962).

In construing the provisions of an insurance policy, the language contained therein must be given its common interpretation. Green v. Merrill, 293 Ala. 628, 308 So. 2d 702 (1975).

It is well settled that the terms of an insurance policy are to be given a rational and practical construction. Green v. Merrill, 293 Ala. 628, 308 So. 2d 702 (1975).

Provisions of a policy which clearly indicate the parties' real intent are not to be given a strained construction to raise doubts where none exist. Green v. Merrill, 293 Ala. 628, 308 So. 2d 702 (1975).

And court cannot construct new agreement. — An insurance contract must be enforced according to its clear and unambiguous meaning, and the courts cannot construct a new agreement on the ground that the purposes which the parties intended to secure may have been unnecessary or as well secured by other means. Day v. Home Ins. Co., 177 Ala. 600, 58 So. 549 (1912).

Courts are not at liberty to make new contracts for parties, and where the language is unambiguous, and but one reasonable construction of the contract is possible, the court must expound it as made, however hard it may operate on the parties; for in contracts of insurance, as in other contracts, the rights of the parties are determined by the terms of the instrument as far as they are lawful. Continental Cas. Co. v. Ogburn, 175 Ala. 357, 57 So. 852 (1911).

It is also true that the courts must enforce insurance contracts as written and cannot defeat express provisions in a policy, including exclusions, by judicial interpretation. Aetna Ins. Co. v. Pete Wilson Roofing & Heating Co., 289 Ala. 719, 272 So. 2d 232 (1972).

The rule concerning ambiguities in insurance policies does not authorize the court to refine away the terms of the contract that are expressed with sufficient clarity to convey the intent and meaning of the parties. Green v. Merrill, 293 Ala. 628, 308 So. 2d 702 (1975).

But where ambiguity construction favors insured. — The lanauage in a policy will be given its ordinary common interpretation, but where a clause therein, when read in connection with the entire policy, is uncertain in its meaning and capable of two equally rational constructions, that construction which is most favorable to insured will be adopted. Empire Life Ins. Co. v. Gee, 178 Ala. 492, 60 So. 90 (1912).

While generally contracts of insurance are construed most strongly against the insurer, where there is no occasion for construction, the contract must be enforced according to its clear and unambiguous meaning, and the courts may not disregard its provisions and construct by implication or otherwise a new agreement, on the ground that the purposes which the parties intended to secure may have been unnecessary or as well secured by other means. Day v. Home Ins. Co., 177 Ala. 600, 58 So. 549 (1912).

In construing an insurance contract its terms, conditions, duties and obligations will be construed liberally in favor of the assured and strictly against the insurer. Mobile Marine Dock, etc., Ins. Co. v. McMillan, 27 Ala. 77 (1855); Piedmont, etc., Life Ins. Co. v. Young, 58 Ala. 476 (1877); Alabama Gold Life Ins. Co. v. Johnson, 80 Ala. 467, 2 So. 125 (1887); Royal Ins. Co. v. Lubelsky, 86 Ala. 530, 5 So. 768 (1889); Tubb v. Liverpool & London & Globe Ins. Co., 106 Ala. 651, 17 So. 615 (1894); Georgia Home Ins. Co. v. Allen, 119 Ala. 436, 24 So. 399 (1898); National Life & Accident Ins. Co. v. Lokey, 166 Ala. 174, 52 So. 45 (1910); Continental Cas. Co. v. Ogburn, 175 Ala. 357, 57 So. 852 (1911); Empire Life Ins. Co. v. Gee, 178 Ala. 492, 60 So. 90 (1912).

Insurance contracts are to be liberally construed in favor of the insured. Pennsylvania Fire Ins. Co. v. Draper, 187 Ala. 103, 65 So. 923 (1914); Mutual Life Ins. Co. v. Lovejoy, 201 Ala. 337, 78 So. 299 (1917); Southern Indem. Ass'n v. Hoffman, 16 Ala. App. 274, 77 So. 424 (1917).

When the language of an insurance policy is vague, uncertain and subject to two different interpretations, the court should adopt the interpretation most favorable to the insured, but where there is no ambiguity the court will not indulge in constructions favorable to the insured. Green v. Merrill, 293 Ala. 628, 308 So. 2d 702 (1975).

In case of any ambiguity in an insurance policy, the policy will be liberally construed in favor of the insured. Barnes v. Atlantic & Pac.

Life Ins. Co. of America, 295 Ala. 149, 325 So. 2d 143 (1975).

If the insurance policy is ambiguous, then the ambiguity must be construed against the insurer and in favor of the insured. Burton v. State Farm Fire & Cas. Co., 533 F.2d 177, rehearing denied, 540 F.2d 1084 (5th Cir. 1976).

Contracts of insurance are to be construed strictly when applied to insurer, and what insurer intends must be stated in its policy. Pennsylvania Fire Ins. Co. v. Draper, 187 Ala. 103, 65 So. 923 (1914); Southern Indem. Ass'n v. Hoffman, 16 Ala. App. 274, 77 So. 424 (1917).

Conditions in a policy of insurance prescribing duties upon the assured should be liberally construed in favor of the assured and strictly against the insurer. Robinson v. Aetna Ins. Co., 128 Ala. 477, 30 So. 665 (1901).

A contract of insurance will be construed strictly against the insurer and liberally in favor of the insured. Globe Life Ins. Co. v. Howard, 41 Ala. App. 621, 147 So. 2d 853 (1962).

Duty to enforce obvious intention of parties. — It is the duty of the court to interpret the contract of the parties as they have made it and to enforce it according to the obvious intention, legally expressed, so long, at least, as it offends no law or violates no principle of public policy. Alabama Gold Life Ins. Co. v. Thomas, 74 Ala. 578 (1883); Royal Ins. Co. v. Lubelsky, 86 Ala. 530, 5 So. 768 (1889).

The court will construe a fire policy and give such effect to the language used as the parties intended. Liverpool & London & Globe Ins. Co. v. Lavine, 5 Ala. App. 392, 59 So. 336 (1912).

And contract should be construed as a whole in order to ascertain the intention of the parties. Mutual Life Ins. Co. v. Lovejoy, 201 Ala. 337, 78 So. 299 (1917).

Where there are both written and printed words in a policy of insurance, both descriptions of words must be taken together. If there is a contradiction, the written words must control. Mobile Marine Dock, etc., Ins. Co. v. McMillan, 27 Ala. 77 (1855).

And surrounding circumstances should be considered. — In insurance contracts, the circumstances surrounding the parties must be taken into consideration, as in all other contracts. Royal Ins. Co. v. Lubelsky, 86 Ala. 530, 5 So. 768 (1889).

Usage may be considered part of contract. — Every usage of trade which is so well settled and generally known that all persons engaged in such trade may be considered as contracting with reference to it will be regarded as forming a part of a contract of insurance entered into to protect risks in such trade. Mobile Marine Dock, etc., Ins. Co. v. McMillan, 27 Ala. 77 (1855).

As may custom. — Where it is shown, or may be fairly presumed, that parties to a policy contracted with reference to a custom existing in the city where they had done business and where the policy was effected, the general law must give way to the custom. Fulton Ins. Co. v. Millner, etc., Co., 23 Ala. 420 (1853).

Life policy and application attached as part thereof must be construed as single contract. Satterfield v. Fidelity Mut. Life Ins. Co., 171 Ala. 429, 55 So. 200 (1911).

A policy of life insurance, and the application for it, must be construed together, and in the absence of something showing a contrary intention, words used in one must receive the same meaning when used in the other. Mobile Life Ins. Co. v. Walker, 58 Ala. 290 (1877).

Where a policy of life insurance contains a reference to other papers, such as a health certificate or an application, relating to the same transaction, such papers are to be construed with the policy, in determining the terms of the contract. Kelley v. Life Ins. Clearing Co., 113 Ala. 453, 21 So. 361 (1897).

Coverage under insurance policy cannot be created or enlarged by waiver or estoppel, and where there is no ambiguity it is the duty of the court to enforce the policy as written. Aetna Ins. Co. v. Pete Wilson Roofing & Heating Co., 289 Ala. 719, 272 So. 2d 232 (1972).

And where warranty is recognized it must be construed with other provisions of policy so as to modify it and give the insured the most favorable construction. National Life & Accident Ins. Co. v. Mixon, 291 Ala. 467, 282 So. 2d 308 (1973).

"Unconditional and sole ownership" clause waived. — Where an insurance policy was issued to the executor of an estate and the insurance policy contained an "unconditional and sole ownership" clause, but the insurer issued the policy in the name of the executor, as such, with full knowledge of an existing controversy as to whether or not the executor's testate had title to the property at the time of her death, the insurer waived the "unconditional and sole ownership" clause and was thereby estopped from denying the validity of the policy. National Sec. Fire & Cas. Ins. Co. v. Brannon, 47 Ala. App. 319, 253 So. 2d 777 (1971).

Forfeitures of insurance contracts are not favored by the law. Mutual Life Ins. Co. v. Lovejoy, 201 Ala. 337, 78 So. 299 (1917).

The rule that an insurance contract shall be construed strictly against the insurer is especially applicable to forfeiture clauses. Continental Cas. Co. v. Ogburn, 175 Ala. 357, 57 So. 852 (1911). See also Tubb v. Liverpool & London & Globe Ins. Co., 106 Ala. 651, 17 So. 615 (1894).

A stipulation authorizing cancellation of an insurance policy will be most strictly construed against the insurer, although, if there is nothing equivocal in it, the court cannot imply a meaning which the language does not warrant. American Auto. Ins. Co. v. Watts, 12 Ala. App. 518, 67 So. 758 (1914).

Cited in Utica Mut. Ins. Co. v. Tuscaloosa Motor Co., 295 Ala. 309, 329 So. 2d 82 (1976).

Collateral references. — 44 C.J.S., Insurance, §§ 24, 52, 54, 230, 285, 289-336, 344. 45 C.J.S., Insurance, §§ 473(5), 582, 587, 589, 592, 595, 614, 621, 639, 658, 747, 797, 835, 882, 939, 980, 982(1). 46 C.J.S., Insurance, §§ 1047, 1064, 1106, 1154, 1226, 1232, 1252, 1256, 1263, 1316, 1368, 1380, 1416.

43 Am. Jur. 2d, Insurance, § 257 et seq.

Construction of terms and ambiguities between various policy provisions relating to coverages or exclusions in aviation liability policies. 86 ALR3d 118.

What constitutes "operating," "riding in," and "descending from" as those terms are used in insurance policies relating to aeronautics. 88 ALR3d 1064.

Death during or allegedly resulting from surgery as within the accidental death benefit provisions of health, accident, or life insurance policies. 91 ALR3d 1042.

Who is a "named insured" under an automobile insurance policy provision extending or excluding coverage of "named insureds." 91 ALR3d 1280.

Heart attack following exertion or exercise as within terms of accident provision of insurance policy. 1 ALR4th 1319.

Division of opinion among judges on same court or among other courts or jurisdictions considering same question, as evidence that particular clause of insurance policy is ambiguous. 4 ALR4th 1253.

Construction and effect of provision excluding liability for automobile-related injuries or damage from coverage of homeowner's or personal liability policy. 6 ALR4th 555, 686, 835.

Scope of clause excluding from contractor's or similar liability policy damage to property in care, custody, or control of insured. 8 ALR4th 563.

Defect in, or condition of, adjacent land or way as within coverage of title insurance policy. 8 ALR4th 1246.

Construction, application, and effect of clause that liability insurance policy may be canceled by insured by mailing to insurer written notice stating when thereafter such cancellation shall be effective. 11 ALR4th 456.

Property damage resulting from inadequate or improper design or construction of dwelling as within coverage of "all risks" homeowner's insurance policy. 41 ALR4th 1095.

§ 27-14-18. Binders.

(a) Binders or other contracts for temporary insurance may be made orally or in writing and shall be deemed to include all the usual terms of the policy as to which the binder was given, together with such applicable endorsements as are designated in the binder, except as superseded by the clear and express terms of the binder.

(b) No binder shall be valid beyond the issuance of the policy with respect to which it was given or beyond 90 days from its effective date, whichever period is the shorter.

(c) If the policy has not been issued, a binder may be extended or renewed beyond such 90 days with the written approval of the commissioner or in accordance with such rules and regulations relative thereto as the commissioner may promulgate.

(d) This section shall not apply to life or disability insurances. (Acts 1971, No. 407, p. 707, § 331.)

Collateral references. — 44 C.J.S., Insurance, §§ 49, 230, 282, 283, 287.

43 Am. Jur. 2d, Insurance, § 216 et seq.

Temporary automobile insurance pending issuance of policy. 12 ALR3d 1304.

Temporary fire, wind, or hail insurance pending issuance of policy. 14 ALR3d 568.

§ 27-14-19. Delivery of policies.

(a) Subject to the insurer's requirements as to payment of premium, every policy shall be mailed or delivered to the insured or to the person entitled thereto within a reasonable period of time after its issuance, except where a condition required by the insurer has not been met by the insured.

(b) In event the original policy is delivered, or is so required to be delivered, to or for deposit with any vendor, mortgagee or pledgee of any motor vehicle, and in which policy any interest of the vendee, mortgagor or pledgor in or with reference to such vehicle is insured, a duplicate of such policy, setting forth the name and address of the insurer, insurance classification of vehicle, type of coverage, limits of liability, premiums for the respective coverages and duration of the policy, or memorandum thereof containing the same such information, shall be delivered by the vendor, mortgagee or pledgee to each such vendee, mortgagor or pledgor named in the policy or coming within the group of persons designated in the policy to be so included. If the policy does not provide coverage of legal liability for injury to persons or damage to the property of third parties, a statement of such fact shall be printed, written or stamped conspicuously on the face of such duplicate policy or memorandum. (Acts 1971, No. 407, p. 707, § 332.)

Payment of premium is generally necessary as a condition precedent to an enforceable contract of insurance. Johnson v. Dairyland Ins. Co., 398 So. 2d 317 (Ala. Civ. App. 1981).

Where an insurance premium check was returned by the bank after the accident due to insufficient funds in account, the court held that the insurance policy was not in effect at the time of an accident. Johnson v. Dairyland Ins. Co., 398 So. 2d 317 (Ala. Civ. App. 1981).

Collateral references. — 44 C.J.S., Insurance, §§ 263, 265, 266.

43 Am. Jur. 2d, Insurance, § 226 et seq.

§ 27-14-20. Renewal or extension of policies.

Any insurance policy terminating by its term at a specified expiration date and not otherwise renewable may be renewed or extended at the option of the insurer, and upon a currently authorized policy form and at the premium rate then required therefor for a specific additional period, or periods, by certificate or by endorsement of the policy and without requiring the issuance of a new policy. (Acts 1971, No. 407, p. 707, § 333.)

Collateral references. — 44 C.J.S., Insurance, § 287.

§ 27-14-21. Assignment of policies.

(a) A policy may be assignable or not assignable, as provided by its terms. Subject to its terms relating to assignability, any life or disability policy, whether heretofore or hereafter issued, under the terms of which the beneficiary may be changed upon the sole request of the owner, may be assigned either by pledge or transfer of title by an assignment executed by the owner alone and delivered to the insurer, whether or not the pledgee or assignee is the insurer. Any such assignment shall entitle the insurer to deal with the assignee as the owner or pledgee of the policy in accordance with the terms of the assignment until the insurer has received at its home office written notice of termination of the assignment or pledge or written notice by, or on behalf of, some other person claiming some interest in the policy in conflict with the assignment. No such written assignment is required in the case of a policy loan made by the insurer under the terms of the policy.

(b) A policy of life insurance, taken out by the insured himself or by a person having an insurable interest in the life of the insured, in good faith may, unless the policy provides otherwise, be assigned to anyone as any other chose in action without regard to whether the assignee has an insurable interest in the life insured or not. (Acts 1967, No. 98, p. 437; Acts 1971, No. 407, p. 707, § 334.)

Collateral references. — 45 C.J.S., Insurance, §§ 410, 411.

43 Am. Jur. 2d, Insurance, § 687 et seq.

Guardian and ward: power of guardian of incompetent to change beneficiary in ward's life insurance policy. 21 ALR2d 1191.

Pledge: effectiveness, as pledge, of transfer of insurance policy. 53 ALR2d 1404.

Obligation of insurer to give assignee of life policy notice of premiums due. 68 ALR3d 360.

§ 27-14-22. Situs of contracts.

All contracts of insurance, the application for which is taken within this state, shall be deemed to have been made within this state and subject to the laws thereof. (Code 1940, T. 28, § 10; Acts 1971, No. 407, p. 707, § 335.)

§ 27-14-23. Effect of war on contracts of foreign insurer.

No insurance contract issued to a citizen of this state by an insurer organized under the laws of a foreign country shall be invalidated by the occurrence of hostilities between such foreign country and the United States of America. (Code 1940, T. 28, § 8; Acts 1971, No. 407, p. 707, § 336.)

Collateral references. — 45 C.J.S., Insurance, §§ 473(5), 938.

§ 27-14-24. Effect of payments.

Whenever the proceeds of, or payments under, a life or disability insurance policy or annuity contract, heretofore or hereafter issued, become payable in accordance with the terms of such policy or contract, or the exercise of any right or privilege thereunder, and the insurer makes payment thereof in accordance with the terms of the policy or contract or in accordance with any written assignment thereof, the person then designated in the policy or contract, or by such assignment, as being entitled thereto shall be entitled to receive such proceeds or payments and to give full acquittance therefor; and such payments shall fully discharge the insurer from all claims under the policy or contract, unless, before payment is made, the insurer has received at its home office written notice by, or on behalf of, some other person that such other person claims to be entitled to such payment or some interest in the policy or contract. (Acts 1971, No. 407, p. 707, § 337.)

Collateral references. — 44 Am. Jur. 2d, Insurance, § 1791 et seq.
   Rights and remedies of insurer paying loss as against insured who has released or settled with third person responsible for loss. 51 ALR2d 697.

§ 27-14-25. Receipt and giving of acquittance and discharge for payment by minors.

(a) Any minor domiciled in this state who has attained the age of 18 years shall be deemed competent to receive and to give full acquittance and discharge for a payment, or payments, in aggregate amount not exceeding $3,000.00 in any one year, made by a life insurer under the maturity, death or settlement agreement provisions in effect or elected by such minor under a life insurance policy or annuity contract, provided such policy, contract or agreement shall provide for the payment, or payments, to such minor and if, prior to such payment, the insurer has not received written notice of the appointment of a duly qualified guardian of the property of such minor. No such minor shall be deemed competent to alienate the right to, or to anticipate, such payments. This section shall not be deemed to restrict the rights of minors set forth in section 27-14-5.

(b) This section shall not be deemed to require any insurer to determine whether any other insurer may be effecting a similar payment to the same minor. (Acts 1967, No. 96, p. 434; Acts 1971, No. 407, p. 707, § 338.)

Cited in Pittman v. Pittman, 419 So. 2d 1376 (Ala. 1982).
   Collateral references. — What constitutes "legal representative" or "personal representative" entitled to receive insurance proceeds on account of loss suffered by deceased. 40 ALR4th 255.

§ 27-14-26. Forms for proof of loss.

An insurer shall furnish, upon written request of any person claiming to have a loss under an insurance contract issued or assumed by such insurer, forms for proof of loss for completion by such person, but such insurer shall not, by reason of the requirement so to furnish forms, have any responsibility for, or with reference to, the completion of such proof or the manner of any such completion or attempted completion. (Acts 1971, No. 407, p. 707, § 339.)

Collateral references. — 44 Am. Jur. 2d, Insurance, § 1454 et seq.
   Depreciation as factor in determining actual cash value for partial loss under insurance policy. 8 ALR4th 533.

§ 27-14-27. Acts not deemed waiver of provisions or defenses.

Without limitation of any right or defense of an insurer otherwise, none of the following acts by, or on behalf of, an insurer shall be deemed to constitute a waiver of any provision of a policy or of any defense of the insurer thereunder:

(1) Acknowledgement of the receipt of notice of loss or claim under the policy;

(2) Furnishing forms for reporting a loss or claim, for giving information relative thereto, or for making proof of loss or receiving or acknowledging receipt of any such forms or proofs completed or uncompleted; or

(3) Investigating any loss or claim under any policy or engaging in negotiations looking toward a possible settlement of any such loss or claim. (Acts 1971, No. 407, p. 707, § 340.)

Coverage under insurance policy cannot be created or enlarged by waiver or estoppel, and where there is no ambiguity it is the duty of the court to enforce the policy as written. Aetna Ins. Co. v. Pete Wilson Roofing & Heating Co., 289 Ala. 719, 272 So. 2d 232 (1972).

Defense of insured by insurance company under reservation of rights. — An insurance company's assuming control of and defending a lawsuit against an insured under a reservation of rights does not estop the company from asserting an exclusory provision in a declaratory judgment action brought by the insured to establish coverage. Aetna Ins. Co. v. Pete Wilson Roofing & Heating Co., 289 Ala. 719, 272 So. 2d 232 (1972).

Waiver. — The substance of doctrine of waiver as applied in law of insurance is that if the insurer, with knowledge of facts which would bar an existing primary liability, recognizes such primary liability by treating the policy as in force, he will not thereafter be allowed to plead such facts to avoid his primary liability. McGee v. Guardian Life Ins. Co., 472 So. 2d 993 (Ala. 1985).

Collateral references. — 44 Am. Jur. 2d, Insurance, §§ 1507-1522.

Statutory requirements, theory of waiver as applicable where provisions of policy or acts of insurer are inconsistent with. 9 ALR2d 1436.

§ 27-14-28. Effect of misrepresentations in proof of loss.

No misrepresentation in any proof of loss under any insurance policy shall defeat or void the policy unless such misrepresentation is made with actual intent to deceive as to a matter material to the insured's rights under the policy. (Code 1940, T. 28, § 6; Acts 1971, No. 407, p. 707, § 341.)

Misrepresentation before and after loss compared. — There is a difference in the required elements of misrepresentation before loss and misrepresentation after loss. Before loss, a misrepresentation must be material to an increase in the risk of loss and must be relied on by the insurer to its prejudice. After loss, a misrepresentation need only be made with the actual intent to deceive and be related to a matter which is material. Risk of loss is not at issue after the loss has occurred since it

cannot be increased at that point. American Fire & Cas. Co. v. Archie, 409 So. 2d 854 (Ala. Civ. App. 1981).

Cited in Payne v. Nationwide Mut. Ins. Co., 456 So. 2d 34 (Ala. 1984).

Collateral references. — 45 C.J.S., Insurance, §§ 473(4), 488.

44 Am. Jur. 2d, Insurance, §§ 1501-1506.

Overvaluation in proof of loss of property insured as fraud avoiding fire insurance policy. 16 ALR3d 774.

§ 27-14-29. Rights of beneficiaries, etc., under life insurance policies against creditors, etc.

(a) If a policy of insurance, whether heretofore or hereafter issued, is effected by any person on his own life or on another life in favor of a person other than himself or, except in cases of transfer with intent to defraud creditors, if a policy of life insurance is assigned or in any way made payable to any such person, the lawful beneficiary, or assignee thereof, other than the insured or the person so effecting such insurance or his executors or administrators, shall be entitled to its proceeds and avails against the creditors, personal representatives, trustees in bankruptcy and receivers in state and federal courts of the person insured and of the person effecting the insurance, whether or not the right to change the beneficiary is reserved or permitted and whether or not the policy is made payable to the person whose life is insured, if the beneficiary or assignee shall predecease such person; provided, however, that, subject to the statute of limitations, the amount of any premiums for the insurance paid with intent to defraud creditors, with interest thereon, shall inure to their benefit from the proceeds of the policy; but the insurer issuing the policy shall be discharged of all liability thereon by payment of its proceeds in accordance with its terms, unless before such payment the insurer shall have written notice, by or in behalf of a creditor, of a claim to recover for transfer made or premiums paid with intent to defraud creditors, with specifications of the amount claimed.

(b) If a policy of insurance, whether heretofore or hereafter issued, is effected by any person on the life of another in favor of the person effecting the same or, except in cases of transfer with intent to defraud creditors, is made payable by assignment, change of beneficiary or otherwise to any such person, the latter shall be entitled to the proceeds and avails of the policy as against the creditors, personal representatives, trustees in bankruptcy and receivers in state and federal courts of the person insured. If the person effecting such insurance, or the assignee of such insurance, is the wife of the insured, she shall also be entitled to the proceeds and avails of the policy as against her own creditors, personal representatives, trustees in bankruptcy and receivers in state and federal courts.

(c) "Proceeds and avails," as used in this section, means death benefits, cash surrender and loan values, premiums waived and dividends, whether used in reduction of premiums or otherwise, excepting only where the debtor, subsequent to issuance of the policy, has actually elected to receive the dividends in cash.

(d) For the purposes of subsection (a) of this section, a policy shall also be deemed to be payable to a person other than the insured if, and to the extent that, a facility-of-payment clause, or similar clause, in the policy permits the insurer to discharge its obligations after the death of the individual insured by paying the death benefits to a person as permitted by such clause. (Acts 1971, No. 407, p. 707, § 342.)

Cited in Rau v. Rau, 429 So. 2d 593 (Ala. Civ. App. 1982).

Collateral references. — 46 C.J.S., Insurance, §§ 1155, 1162, 1165, 1179.

44 Am. Jur. 2d, Insurance, § 1727 et seq.

Rights of creditors of life insured as to options or other benefits available to him during his lifetime. 37 ALR2d 268.

Creditors of insured, loan value or loan proceeds of life insurance policy as subject to rights of. 37 ALR2d 309.

Testamentary direction for payment of debts or expenses of administration as affecting life insurance proceeds payable to estate. 56 ALR2d 865.

What constitutes "legal representative" or "personal representative" entitled to receive insurance proceeds on account of loss suffered by deceased. 40 ALR4th 255.

§ 27-14-30. Right to proceeds when same retained by life insurer.

If under the terms of any annuity contract or life insurance policy, or under any written agreement supplemental thereto, issued by any life insurer, the proceeds, or any part thereof, are retained by the insurer at maturity or otherwise, no person entitled to any part of such proceeds or any installments of interest due, or to become due thereon, shall be permitted to commute, anticipate, encumber, alienate or assign the same, or any part thereof, if such permission is expressly withheld by the terms of such contract, policy or supplemental agreement; and if such contract, policy or supplemental agreement so provides, no payment of interest or of principal shall be in any way subject to such person's debts, contracts or engagements nor to any judicial process to levy upon, or attach the same, for payment thereof. (Acts 1935, No. 231, p. 627; Code 1940, T. 28, § 4; Acts 1971, No. 407, p. 707, § 343.)

"Supplementary contract" prescribing disposition of policy proceeds pursuant to agreement between an insurer and a beneficiary must be sustained as valid and nontestamentary if its provisions are sufficiently close to those contemplated by the underlying insurance policy to warrant the conclusion that the "supplementary contract" is indeed "supplementary" to that policy, and not merely a totally unrelated document reflecting an agreement that could not reasonably be carried out under the terms of the policy. Zimmerman v. Mutual Life Ins. Co., 156 F. Supp. 589 (N.D. Ala. 1957) (decided under former Code 1940, T. 28, § 4).

§ 27-14-31. Exemption from debt of proceeds — Disability.

The proceeds or avails of all contracts or disability insurance and of provisions providing benefits on account of the insured's disability which are supplemental to life insurance or annuity contracts, heretofore or hereafter effected, shall be exempt from all liability for any debt of the insured and from any debt of the beneficiary existing at the time the proceeds are made available for his use. The exemption of income benefits payable as the result of disability shall not exceed an average of $250.00 of such benefits per month of the period of disability. (Acts 1971, No. 407, p. 707, § 344.)

Collateral references. — 46 C.J.S., Insurance, §§ 1155, 1173.

§ 27-14-32. Same — Annuity contracts.

(a) The benefits, rights, privileges and options which under any annuity contract, heretofore or hereafter issued, are due or prospectively due the annuitant shall not be subject to execution, nor shall the annuitant be compelled to exercise any such rights, powers or options, nor shall creditors be allowed to interfere with or terminate the contract, except:

(1) As to amounts paid for or as premium on any such annuity with intent to defraud creditors, with interest thereon, and of which the creditor has given the insurer written notice at its home office prior to the making of the payments to the annuitant out of which the creditor seeks to recover. Any such notice shall specify the amount claimed, or such facts as will enable the insurer to ascertain such amount, and shall set forth such facts as will enable the insurer to ascertain the insurance or annuity contract, the person insured or annuitant and the payments sought to be avoided on the ground of fraud;

(2) The total exemption of benefits presently due and payable to any annuitant periodically or at stated times under all annuity contracts under which he is an annuitant shall not at any time exceed $250.00 per month for the length of time represented by such installments, and such periodic payments in excess of $250.00 per month shall be subject to garnishment;

(3) If the total benefits presently due and payable to any annuitant under all annuity contracts under which he is an annuitant shall at any time exceed payment at the rate of $250.00 per month, then the court may order such annuitant to pay to a judgment creditor or apply on the judgment, in installments, such portion of such excess benefits as to the court may appear just and proper, after due regard for the reasonable requirements of the judgment debtor and his family, if dependent upon him, as well as any payments required to be made by the annuitant to other creditors under prior court orders.

(b) If the contract so provides, the benefits, rights, privileges or options accruing under such contract to a beneficiary or assignee shall not be transferable nor subject to commutation, and if the benefits are payable periodically or at stated times, the same exemptions and exceptions contained in this section for the annuitant shall apply with respect to such beneficiary or assignee. (Acts 1971, No. 407, p. 707, § 345.)

CHAPTER 15.

LIFE INSURANCE AND ANNUITY CONTRACTS.

Sec.
27-15-1. Applicability of chapter.
27-15-2. Life insurance policy provisions — Generally.
27-15-3. Same — Grace period.
27-15-4. Same — Incontestability.
27-15-5. Same — Entire contract; representations.
27-15-6. Same — Misstatement of age or sex.
27-15-7. Same — Dividends.
27-15-8. Same — Loans on policy.
27-15-8.1. Same — Maximum rates of interest on policy loans.
27-15-9. Same — Table of values and benefits.
27-15-10. Same — Table of installments.
27-15-11. Same — Reinstatement.
27-15-12. Same — Payment of premiums.
27-15-13. Same — Settlement of claims.
27-15-14. Same — Title.
27-15-15. Effect of incontestability clause.
27-15-16. Annuity and pure endowment contract provisions — Generally.

Sec.
27-15-17. Same — Grace period.
27-15-18. Same — Incontestability.
27-15-19. Same — Entire contract.
27-15-20. Same — Misstatement of age or sex.
27-15-21. Same — Dividends.
27-15-22. Same — Reinstatement.
27-15-23. Standard provisions in contracts for reversionary annuities.
27-15-24. Exclusions and restrictions in life insurance policies.
27-15-25. Contestability of reinstated policies.
27-15-26. Power of life insurer to hold proceeds of policy.
27-15-27. Deductions in determining amount due under life insurance.
27-15-28. Standard nonforfeiture law for life insurance.
27-15-28.1. Standard nonforfeiture law for individual deferred annuities.
27-15-29. Prohibited policy plans.

Cross references. — As to industrial life insurance, see § 27-16-1 et seq. As to group life insurance, see § 27-18-1 et seq.

§ 27-15-1. Applicability of chapter.

This chapter applies to contracts of life insurance and annuities other than reinsurance, group life insurance, group annuities, industrial life and burial insurance; except, that sections 27-15-15, 27-15-24, 27-15-25, 27-15-28 and 27-15-29 shall apply to industrial life insurance also. (Acts 1971, No. 407, p. 707, § 346.)

§ 27-15-2. Life insurance policy provisions — Generally.

(a) No policy of life insurance other than industrial, group and pure endowments, with or without return of premiums or of premiums and interest, shall be delivered or issued for delivery in this state unless it contains in substance all of the provisions required by sections 27-15-3 through 27-15-14. This section shall not apply to burial insurance, annuity contracts, to any provision of a life insurance policy, or contract supplemental thereto, relating to disability benefits or to additional benefits in the event of death or dismemberment by accident or accidental means or to any provision relating to waiver of premiums in the event of death or disability of the beneficiary or premium payer.

(b) Any of such provisions, or portions thereof not applicable to single premium or term policies, shall, to that extent, not be incorporated therein. (Acts 1971, No. 407, p. 707, § 347.)

§ 27-15-3. Same — Grace period.

There shall be a provision that a grace period of 30 days or, at the option of the insurer, of one month of not less than 30 days shall be allowed within which the payment of any premium after the first may be made, during which period of grace the policy shall continue in full force; but if a claim arises under the policy during such period of grace, the amount of any premium due or overdue may be deducted from the policy proceeds. (Acts 1971, No. 407, p. 707, § 348.)

Collateral references. — 44 C.J.S., Insurance, § 255, n. 16.

43 Am. Jur. 2d, Insurance, § 548.

§ 27-15-4. Same — Incontestability.

There shall be a provision that the policy, exclusive, at the option of the insurer, of provisions relating to disability benefits or to additional benefits in the event of death by accident or accidental means, shall be incontestable, except for nonpayment of premiums, after it has been in force during the lifetime of the insured for a period of two years from its date of issue. (Acts 1967, No. 181, p. 543; Acts 1971, No. 407, p. 707, § 349.)

Collateral references. — 45 C.J.S., Insurance, § 747.

43 Am. Jur. 2d, Insurance, § 1155 et seq.

Age adjustment clause of policy as affected by incontestable clause. 135 ALR 445.

Incontestable clause as applicable to suit to reform insurance policy. 7 ALR2d 504.

Suicide clause of life or accident insurance as affected by incontestable clause. 37 ALR2d 337.

What amounts to contest within contemplation of incontestable clause. 95 ALR2d 420.

§ 27-15-5. Same — Entire contract; representations.

There shall be a provision that the policy, or the policy and the application therefor, if a copy of such application is endorsed upon or attached to the policy when issued, shall constitute the entire contract between the parties and that all statements contained in the application shall, in the absence of fraud, be deemed representations and not warranties. (Acts 1935, No. 152, p. 194; Acts 1971, No. 407, p. 707, § 350.)

Collateral references. — 44 C.J.S., Insurance, § 250. 46 C.J.S., Insurance, § 1297.

43 Am. Jur. 2d, Insurance, § 281.

Oral contracts of insurance. 15 ALR 995, 69 ALR 559, 92 ALR 232.

Noncompliance with statutory requirement that insurance policy contain entire contract, or that application be attached to, incorporated in, endorsed upon, or delivered with, the policy as affecting right of insurer to show initial fraud or misrepresentation by insured. 93 ALR 374.

Failure to disclose terminal illness as basis for life insurer's avoidance of high-risk, high- premium policy requiring no health warranties or proof of insurability. 42 ALR4th 158.

§ 27-15-6. Same — Misstatement of age or sex.

There shall be a provision that if the age or sex of the insured or of any other person whose age or sex is considered in determining the premium has been misstated, any amount payable or benefit accruing under the policy shall be such as the premium would have purchased at the correct age or sex. (Acts 1971, No. 407, p. 707, § 351.)

Collateral references. — 45 C.J.S., Insurance, § 596.

§ 27-15-7. Same — Dividends.

There shall be a provision in participating policies that, beginning not later than the end of the third policy year, the insurer shall annually ascertain and apportion the divisible surplus, if any, that will accrue on the policy anniversary or other dividend date specified in the policy, provided the policy is in force and all premiums to that date are paid. Except as provided in this section, any dividend becoming payable shall, at the option of the party entitled to elect such option, be either:

(1) Payable in cash; or

(2) Applied to any one of such other dividend options as may be provided by the policy. If any such other dividend options are provided, the policy shall further state which option shall be automatically effective if such party shall not have elected some other option. If the policy specifies a period within which such other dividend option may be elected, such period shall be not less than 30 days following the date on which such dividend is due and payable. The annually apportioned dividend shall be deemed to be payable in cash within the meaning of subdivision (1) of this section, even though the policy provides that payment of such dividend is to be deferred for a specified period, provided such period does not exceed six years from the date of apportionment and that interest will be added to such dividend at a specified rate and provided, further, that upon the maturity, surrender or other expiry of the policy, any such dividend, and interest thereon, shall not be forfeited to the insurer. If a participating policy provides that the benefit under any paid-up nonforfeiture provision is to be participating, it may provide that any divisible surplus becoming payable or apportioned while the insurance is in force under such nonforfeiture provision shall be applied in the manner set forth in the policy. (Acts 1971, No. 407, p. 707, § 352.)

Collateral references. — 45 C.J.S., Insurance, § 940. 46 C.J.S., Insurance, § 1394.

43 Am. Jur. 2d, Insurance, §§ 120-123, 681-686.

Dividends: insurer's statements as to amount of dividends, accumulations, surplus, or the like as binding on insurer or merely illustrative. 17 ALR3d 777.

§ 27-15-8. Same — Loans on policy.

(a) In case of policies issued on and after the operative date of section 21-15-28, there shall be a provision that after the policy has a cash surrender value and while no premium is in default beyond the grace period for payment the insurer will advance, on proper assignment or pledge of the policy and on the sole security thereof, at a specified rate of interest not exceeding eight percent per annum, payable in advance, an amount equal to or, at the option of the party entitled thereto, less than the loan value of the policy. The loan value of the policy shall be at least equal to the cash surrender value at the end of the then current policy year, provided that the insurer may deduct, either from such loan value or from the proceeds of the loan, any existing indebtedness not already deducted in determining such cash surrender value including any interest then accrued but not due, any unpaid balance of the premium for the current policy year and interest on the loan to the end of the current policy year. The policy may also provide that if interest on any indebtedness is not paid when due it shall then be added to the existing indebtedness and shall bear interest at the same rate and that, if and when the total indebtedness on the policy, including interest due or accrued, equals or exceeds the amount of the loan value thereof, then the policy shall terminate and become void, but not until at least 30 days' notice shall have been mailed by the insurer to the last known address of the insured or policyowner and of any assignee of record at the home office of the insurer. The policy shall reserve to the insurer the right to defer the granting of a loan, other than for the payment of any premium to the insurer, for six months after application therefor. The policy, at the insurer's option, may provide for automatic premium loan, subject to an election of the party entitled to elect.

(b) This section shall not apply to term policies nor to term insurance benefits provided by rider or supplemental policy provision. (Acts 1971, No. 407, p. 707, § 353.)

Collateral references. — 44 C.J.S., Insurance, §§ 337-339.

43 Am. Jur. 2d, Insurance, §§ 649-653.

Right of beneficiary as against estate of insured who borrowed on the policy. 31 ALR2d 979.

Validity and effect of loan receipt or agreement between insured and insurer for a loan repayable to extent of insured's recovery from another. 13 ALR3d 42.

§ 27-15-8.1. Same — Maximum rates of interest on policy loans.

(a) For purposes of this section the "published monthly average" means:

(1) The Monthly Average of the Composite Yield on Seasoned Corporate Bonds as published by Moody's Investors Service, Inc. or any successor thereto; or

(2) In the event that the Monthly Average of the Composite Yield on Seasoned Corporate Bonds is no longer published, a substantially similar average, established by regulation issued by the commissioner.

(b) (1) Policies issued on or after May 15, 1981, shall provide for policy loan interest rates as follows:

a. A provision permitting a maximum interest rate of not more than eight percent per annum; or

b. A provision permitting an adjustable maximum interest rate established from time to time by the life insurer as permitted by law.

(2) The rate of interest charged on a policy loan made under subdivision (1) of this subsection shall not exceed the higher of the following:

a. The published monthly average for the calendar month ending two months before the date on which the rate is determined; or

b. The rate used to compute the cash surrender values under the policy during the applicable period plus one percent per annum.

(3) If the maximum rate of interest is determined pursuant to subdivision (2) of this subsection, the policy shall contain a provision setting forth the frequency at which the rate is to be determined for that policy.

(4) The maximum rate for each policy must be determined at regular intervals at least once every 12 months, but not more frequently than once in any three month period. At the intervals specified in the policy:

a. The rate being charged may be increased whenever such increase as determined under subdivision (2) of this subsection would increase that rate by one-half percent or more per annum;

b. The rate being charged must be reduced whenever such reduction as determined under subdivision (2) of this subsection would decrease that rate by one-half percent or more per annum.

(5) The life insurer shall:

a. Notify the policyholder at the time a cash loan is made of the initial rate of interest on the loan;

b. Notify the policyholder with respect to premium loans of the initial rate of interest on the loan as soon as it is reasonably practical to do so after making the initial loan. Notice need not be given to the policyholder when a further premium loan is added, except as provided in paragraph c. of this subdivision;

c. Send to policyholders with loans reasonable advance notice of any increase in the rate; and

d. Include in the notices required above the substance of the pertinent provisions of subdivisions (1) and (3) of this subsection.

(6) The loan value of the policy shall be determined in accordance with section 27-15-8, but no policy shall terminate in a policy year as the sole result of change in the interest rate during that policy year, and the life insurer shall maintain coverage during that policy year until the time at which it would otherwise have terminated if there had been no change during that policy year.

(7) The substance of the pertinent provisions of paragraphs (1) and (3) of this subsection shall be set forth in the policies to which they apply.

(8) For purposes of this subsection:

a. The rate of interest on policy loans permitted under this section includes the interest rate charged on reinstatement of policy loans for the period during and after any lapse of a policy.

b. The term "policy loan" includes any premium loan made under a policy to pay one or more premiums that were not paid to the life insurer as they fell due.

c. The term "policyholder" includes the owner of the policy or the person designated to pay premiums as shown on the records of the life insurer.

d. The term "policy" includes certificates issued by a fraternal benefit society and annuity contract which provide for policy loans.

(9) No other provisions of law shall apply to policy loan interest rates unless made specifically applicable to such rates.

(c) The provisions of this section shall not apply to any insurance contract issued before May 15, 1981, unless the policyholder agrees in writing to the applicability of such provisions.

(d) In the event of any conflicts between the provisions of this section and section 27-15-5, Code of Alabama 1975, the provisions of this section shall control. (Acts 1981, No. 81-542, p. 909.)

Collateral references. — 44 C.J.S., Insurance, §§ 65, 337.

43 Am. Jur. 2d, §§ 45, 64, 649, 650, 653.

§ 27-15-9. Same — Table of values and benefits.

In policies issued on and after the operative date of section 27-15-28, there shall be a table showing in figures the loan value and the cash surrender values and nonforfeiture benefits in accordance with subdivision (b) (5) of section 27-15-28, either during the first 20 policy years or during the term of the policy, whichever is shorter. (Acts 1971, No. 407, p. 707, § 354.)

§ 27-15-10. Same — Table of installments.

In case the policy provides that the proceeds may be payable in installments which are determinable at issue of the policy, there shall be a table showing the amounts of the guaranteed installments. (Acts 1971, No. 407, p. 707, § 355.)

Collateral references. — 46 C.J.S., Insurance, § 1394.

§ 27-15-11. Same — Reinstatement.

There shall be a provision that unless the policy has been surrendered for its cash value, or its cash surrender value has been exhausted or the period of any extended insurance provided by the policy has expired, the policy will be reinstated at any time within three years after the date of premium default upon written application therefor, the production of evidence of insurability satisfactory to the insurer, the payment of all overdue premiums and payment, or, within the limits permitted by the then cash value of the policy, reinstatement, of any other indebtedness to the insurer upon the policy, with interest as to both premiums and indebtedness at a rate not exceeding the rate of interest on policy loans specified in the policy in accordance with the provisions of § 27-15-8, as may be amended from time to time. (Acts 1971, No. 407, p. 707, § 356; Acts 1981, No. 81-381, p. 564.)

Collateral references. — 45 C.J.S., Insurance, §§ 667-671.

43 Am. Jur. 2d, Insurance, §§ 389-396.

Conflict of laws: choice of law in construction of insurance policy originally governed by law of one state as affected by modification, renewal, exchange, or replacement, or reinstatement in different state. 3 ALR3d 646.

Incontestable clause as affected by reinstatement of policy. 23 ALR3d 743.

§ 27-15-12. Same — Payment of premiums.

There shall be a provision relative to the payment of premiums. (Acts 1971, No. 407, p. 707, § 357.)

Collateral references. — 44 C.J.S., Insurance, §§ 344-351.

§ 27-15-13. Same — Settlement of claims.

There shall be a provision that when a policy shall become a claim by the death of the insured, settlement shall be made upon receipt of due proof of death and, at the insurer's option, surrender of the policy and proof of the interest of the claimant. If an insurer shall specify a particular period prior to the expiration of which settlement shall be made, such period shall not exceed two months from the receipt of such proofs. (Acts 1971, No. 407, p. 707, § 358.)

§ 27-15-14. Same — Title.

There shall be a title on the policy briefly describing the same. (Acts 1971, No. 407, p. 707, § 359.)

§ 27-15-15. Effect of incontestability clause.

A clause in any policy of life insurance or annuity contract providing that such policy or contract shall be incontestable after a specified period shall preclude only a contest of the validity of the policy or contract and shall not preclude the assertion at any time of defenses based upon provisions in the policy or contract which exclude or restrict coverage, whether or not such restrictions or exclusions are excepted in such clause. (Acts 1967, No. 181, p. 543; Acts 1971, No. 407, p. 707, § 360.)

Incontestability clause's principal function is to cut off defenses such as a breach of warranty or misrepresentation that go to the existence of the policy after the policy has been in force and effect for a period of time. National Life & Accident Ins. Co. v. Mixon, 291 Ala. 467, 282 So. 2d 308 (1973).

Incontestability clause does not operate to extend coverage of policy to a disease contracted before the issuance of the policy. National Life & Accident Ins. Co. v. Mixon, 291 Ala. 467, 282 So. 2d 308 (1973).

There is no conflict between incontestability clause and preexisting disease exclusion clause, as the latter constitutes an exception to the former, general clause; hence, the insurer's insistence that it is not liable under the policy by reason of its exclusion contained in the preexisting disease clause is not a "contest" of the policy within the meaning of the incontestable clause. National Life & Accident Ins. Co. v. Mixon, 291 Ala. 467, 282 So. 2d 308 (1973).

Proof of preexistence of disease not barred by clause. — It is necessary to distinguish between the preexistence of a disease, which has the effect of removing the subsequent disability from the coverage of the policy, and the concealment of such disease, contended to be a violation of the condition of the existence of good health at the time of the execution of the policy. As the former relates to the coverage, the proof of the preexistence of the disease is not barred by the incontestable period. National Life & Accident Ins. Co. v. Mixon, 291 Ala. 467, 282 So. 2d 308 (1973).

Collateral references. — 45 C.J.S., Insurance, §§ 747-752.

43 Am. Jur. 2d, Insurance, § 1159 et seq.

Defense predicated upon falsity of answer to question in original application for insurance, or in application for reinstatement, as to whether applicant has had any serious illness or disease. 153 ALR 709.

Incontestable clause as precluding insurer from defending on ground of particular clause in life policy limiting or precluding insurer's liability because of other life insurance. 22 ALR2d 809.

Suicide clause of life or accident insurance as affected by incontestable clause. 37 ALR3d 337.

§ 27-15-16. Annuity and pure endowment contract provisions — Generally.

(a) No annuity or pure endowment contract, other than reversionary annuities, survivorship annuities or group annuities and except as stated in this section, shall be delivered or issued for delivery in this state unless it contains in substance each of the provisions specified in sections 27-15-17 through 27-15-22. Any of such provisions not applicable to single premium annuities or single premium pure endowment contracts shall not, to that extent, be incorporated therein.

(b) This section shall not apply to contracts for deferred annuities included in, or upon the lives of beneficiaries under, life insurance policies. (Acts 1971, No. 407, p. 707, § 361.)

Collateral references. — 44 C.J.S., Insurance, § 18.

§ 27-15-17. Same — Grace period.

In an annuity or pure endowment contract, other than a reversionary, survivorship or group annuity, there shall be a provision that there shall be a period of grace of one month, but not less than 30 days, within which any stipulated payment to the insurer falling due after the first may be made, subject at the option of the insurer to an interest charge thereon at a rate to be specified in the contract but not exceeding six percent per annum for the number of days of grace elapsing before such payment, during which period of grace the contract shall continue in full force; but in case a claim arises under the contract on account of death prior to expiration of the period of grace before the overdue payment to the insurer or the deferred payments of the current contract year, if any, are made, the amount of such payments, with interest on any overdue payments, may be deducted from any amount payable under the contract in settlement. (Acts 1971, No. 407, p. 707, § 362.)

Collateral references. — 43 Am. Jur. 2d, Insurance, § 548.

§ 27-15-18. Same — Incontestability.

If any statements, other than those relating to age, sex and identity, are required as a condition to issuing an annuity or pure endowment contract, other than a reversionary, survivorship or group annuity and subject to section 27-15-20, there shall be a provision that the contract shall be incontestable after it has been in force during the lifetime of the person, or of each of the persons, as to whom such statements are required for a period of two years from its date of issue, except for nonpayment of stipulated payments to the insurer; and at the option of the insurer, such contract may also except any provisions relative to benefits in the event of disability and any provisions

233

which grant insurance specifically against death by accident or accidental means. (Acts 1971, No. 407, p. 707, § 363.)

Cited in Thomas v. Liberty Nat'l Life Ins. Co., 368 So. 2d 254 (Ala. 1979).

Collateral references. — 43 Am. Jur. 2d, Insurance, § 1155 et seq.

§ 27-15-19. Same — Entire contract.

In an annuity or pure endowment contract, other than a reversionary, survivorship or group annuity, there shall be a provision that the written contract shall constitute the entire contract between the parties or, if a copy of the application is endorsed upon or attached to the contract when issued, a provision that the written contract and the application therefor shall constitute the entire contract between the parties. (Acts 1935, No. 152, p. 194; Acts 1971, No. 407, p. 707, § 364.)

Collateral references. — 44 C.J.S., Insurance, § 250.
43 Am. Jur. 2d, Insurance, § 281.

§ 27-15-20. Same — Misstatement of age or sex.

In an annuity or pure endowment contract, other than a reversionary, survivorship or group annuity, there shall be a provision that if the age or sex of the person, or persons, upon whose life, or lives, the contract is made, or of any of them, has been misstated, the amount payable or benefits accruing under the contract shall be such as the stipulated payment, or payments, to the insurer would have purchased according to the correct age or sex and that if the insurer shall make, or has made, any overpayment, or overpayments, on account of any such misstatement the amount thereof, with interest at the rate to be specified in the contract but not exceeding six percent per annum, may be charged against the current or next succeeding payment, or payments, to be made by the insurer under the contract. (Acts 1971, No. 407, p. 707, § 365.)

§ 27-15-21. Same — Dividends.

If an annuity or pure endowment contract, other than a reversionary, survivorship or group annuity, is participating, there shall be a provision that the insurer shall annually ascertain and apportion any divisible surplus accruing on the contract. (Acts 1971, No. 407, p. 707, § 366.)

Collateral references. — 43 Am. Jur. 2d, Insurance, §§ 120-123.
Insurer's statements as to amount of dividends, accumulations, surplus, or the like as binding on insurer or merely illustrative. 17 ALR3d 777.

§ 27-15-22. Same — Reinstatement.

In an annuity or pure endowment contract, other than a reversionary, survivorship or group annuity, there shall be a provision that the contract may be reinstated at any time within one year from the default in making stipulated payments to the insurer unless the cash surrender value has been paid, but all overdue stipulated payments and any indebtedness to the insurer on the contract shall be paid or reinstated with interest thereon at a rate to be specified in the contract, but not exceeding six percent per annum payable annually, and, in cases where applicable, the insurer may also include a requirement of evidence of insurability satisfactory to the insurer. (Acts 1971, No. 407, p. 707, § 367.)

Collateral references. — 43 Am. Jur. 2d, Insurance, §§ 389-396.

Conflict of laws: choice of law in construction of insurance policy originally governed by law of one state as affected by modification, renewal, exchange, or replacement, or reinstatement in different state. 3 ALR3d 646.

§ 27-15-23. Standard provisions in contracts for reversionary annuities.

(a) Except as stated in this section, no contract for a reversionary annuity shall be delivered or issued for delivery in this state unless it contains in substance each of the following provisions:

(1) Any such reversionary annuity contract shall contain the provisions specified in sections 27-15-17 through 27-15-21 except that under section 27-15-20 the insurer may at its option provide for an equitable reduction of the amount of the annuity payments in settlement of an overdue or deferred payment in lieu of providing for deduction of such payments from an amount payable upon settlement under the contract; and

(2) In such reversionary annuity contracts, there shall be a provision that the contract may be reinstated at any time within three years from the date of default in making stipulated payments to the insurer upon production of evidence of insurability satisfactory to the insurer and upon condition that all overdue payments and any indebtedness to the insurer on account of the contract be paid or, within the limits permitted by the then cash values of the contract, reinstated with interest as to both payments and indebtedness at a rate to be specified in the contract, but not exceeding six percent per annum compounded annually.

(b) This section shall not apply to group annuities or to annuities included in life insurance policies, and any of such provisions not applicable to single premium annuities shall not to that extent be incorporated therein. (Acts 1971, No. 407, p. 707, § 368.)

§ 27-15-24. Exclusions and restrictions in life insurance policies.

(a) No policy of life insurance shall be delivered or issued for delivery in this state if it contains any of the following provisions:

(1) A provision for a period shorter than that provided by statute within which an action may be commenced on such a policy; and

(2) A provision which excludes or restricts liability for death caused in a certain specified manner or occurring while the insured has a specified status; except, that a policy may contain provisions excluding or restricting coverage as specified therein in the event of death under any one or more of the following circumstances:

a. Death as a result, directly or indirectly, of war, declared or undeclared, or of action by military forces, or of any act or hazard of such war or action, or of service in the military, naval or air forces or in civilian forces auxiliary thereto, or from any cause while a member of such military, naval or air forces of any country at war, declared or undeclared, or of any country engaged in such military action;

b. Death as a result of aviation or any air travel or flight;

c. Death as a result of a specified hazardous occupation or occupations, avocation or avocations;

d. Death while the insured is a resident outside continental United States and Canada; or

e. Death within two years from the date of issue of the policy as a result of suicide, while sane or insane.

(b) A policy which contains any exclusion or restriction pursuant to subsection (a) of this section shall also provide that in the event of death under the circumstances to which any such exclusion or restriction is applicable the insurer will pay an amount not less than a reserve determined according to the commissioner's reserve valuation method upon the basis of the mortality table and interest rate specified in the policy for the calculation of nonforfeiture benefits, or, if the policy provides for no such benefits, computed according to a mortality table and interest rate determined by the insurer and specified in the policy, with adjustment for indebtedness or dividend credit; except, that if the policy has been in force for not more than two years, the insurer shall pay the amount of the gross premiums charged on the policy less dividends paid in cash or used in the payment of premiums thereon and less any indebtedness to the insurer on the policy, including interest due or accrued.

(c) This section shall not apply to group life insurance, disability insurance, reinsurance or annuities, or to any provision in a life insurance policy or contract supplemental thereto relating to disability benefits or to additional benefits in the event of death or dismemberment by accident or accidental means or to any provision relating to waiver of premium in event of death or disability of the beneficiary or premium payer.

(d) Nothing contained in this section shall prohibit any provision which in the opinion of the commissioner is more favorable to the policyholder than a provision permitted by this section. (Acts 1971, No. 407, p. 707, § 369.)

Insurer's right to limit liability. — The law in Alabama is clear that insurance companies have the right, in the absence of statutory provisions to the contrary, to limit their liability and write policies with narrow coverage; the insured has the option to purchase the policy or look elsewhere. Aetna Ins. Co. v. Pete Wilson Roofing & Heating Co., 289 Ala. 719, 272 So. 2d 232 (1972).

Collateral references. — 45 C.J.S., Insurance, § 938.

Insurer's waiver of, or estoppel to assert contractual limitation provision. 29 ALR2d 636.

Construction and application of provision in liability policy limiting the amount of insurer's liability to one person. 13 ALR3d 1228.

§ 27-15-25. Contestability of reinstated policies.

A reinstated policy of life insurance or annuity contract may be contested on account of fraud or misrepresentation of facts material to the reinstatement only for the same period following reinstatement and with the same conditions and exceptions as the policy provides with respect to contestability after original issuance. (Acts 1967, No. 181, p. 543; Acts 1971, No. 407, p. 707, § 370.)

Collateral references. — 43 Am. Jur. 2d, Insurance, § 1174.

Reinstatement: incontestable clause as af-fected by reinstatement of policy. 23 ALR3d 743.

§ 27-15-26. Power of life insurer to hold proceeds of policy.

Any life insurer shall have the power to hold under agreement the proceeds of any policy issued by it upon such terms and restrictions as to revocation by the policyholder and control by beneficiaries and with such exemptions from the claims of creditors of beneficiaries other than the policyholder as set forth in the policy or as agreed to in writing by the insurer and the policyholder. Upon maturity of a policy, in the event the policyholder has made no such agreement, the insurer shall have the power to hold the proceeds of the policy under an agreement with the beneficiaries. The insurer shall not be required to segregate the funds so held but may hold them as part of its general assets. (Acts 1971, No. 407, p. 707, § 371.)

§ 27-15-27. Deductions in determining amount due under life insurance.

In determining the amount due under any life insurance policy heretofore or hereafter issued, deduction may be made of:

(1) Any unpaid premiums or installments thereof for the current policy year due under the terms of the policy; and

(2) The amount of principal and accrued interest of any policy loan or other indebtedness against the policy then remaining unpaid. (Acts 1971, No. 407, p. 707, § 372.)

§ 27-15-28. Standard nonforfeiture law for life insurance.

(a) This section shall be known as the standard nonforfeiture law for life insurance.

(b) In the case of policies issued on, or after January 1, 1972, no policy of life insurance, except as set forth in subsection (n) of this section, shall be delivered or issued for delivery in this state unless it shall contain in substance the following provisions, or corresponding provisions which, in the opinion of the commissioner, are at least as favorable to the defaulting or surrendering policyholder as are the minimum requirements specified in this subsection and are essentially in compliance with subsection (m) of this section:

(1) That, in the event of default in any premium payment, the insurer will grant, upon proper request not later than 60 days after the due date of the premium in default, a paid-up nonforfeiture benefit on a plan stipulated in the policy, effective as of such due date, of such amount as may be specified in this section. In lieu of such stipulated paid-up nonforfeiture benefit, the insurer may substitute, upon proper request not later than 60 days after the due date of the premium in default, in actuarially equivalent alternative paid-up nonforfeiture benefit which provides a greater amount or longer period of death benefits or, if applicable, a greater amount or earlier payment of endowment benefits;

(2) That, upon surrender of the policy within 60 days after the due date of any premium payment in default after premiums have been paid for at least three full years in the case of ordinary insurance and five full years in the case of industrial insurance, the insurer will pay, in lieu of any paid-up nonforfeiture benefit, a cash surrender value of such amount as may be specified in this section;

(3) That a specified paid-up nonforfeiture benefit shall become effective as specified in the policy unless the person entitled to make such election elects another available option not later than 60 days after the due date of the premium in default;

(4) That, if the policy shall have become paid up by completion of all premium payments, or if it is continued under any paid-up nonforfeiture benefit which became effective on, or after, the third policy anniversary in the case of ordinary insurance or the fifth policy anniversary in the case of industrial insurance, the insurer will pay, upon surrender of the policy within 30 days after any policy anniversary, a cash surrender value of such amount as may be specified in this section;

(5) In the case of policies which cause, on a basis guaranteed in the policy, unscheduled changes in benefits or premiums or which provide an option for changes in benefits or premiums other than a change to a new policy, a statement of the mortality table, interest rate and method used in calculating cash surrender values and the paid-up nonforfeiture benefits available under the policy. In the case of all other policies, a statement of the mortality table and interest rate used in calculating the cash surrender

values and the paid-up nonforfeiture benefits available under the policy, together with a table showing the cash surrender value, if any, and paid-up nonforfeiture benefit, if any, available under the policy on each policy anniversary, either during the first 20 policy years or during the term of the policy, whichever is shorter, such values and benefits to be calculated upon the assumption that there are no dividends or paid-up additions credited to the policy and that there is no indebtedness to the insurer on the policy; and

(6) A statement that the cash surrender values and the paid-up nonforfeiture benefits available under the policy are not less than the minimum values and benefits required by or pursuant to the insurance laws of this state; an explanation of the manner in which the cash surrender values and the paid-up nonforfeiture benefits are altered by the existence of any paid-up additions credited to the policy or any indebtedness to the insurer on the policy; and a statement of the method to be used in calculating the cash surrender value, and paid-up nonforfeiture benefit available under the policy on any policy anniversary beyond the last anniversary for which such values and benefits are consecutively shown in the policy.

(c) Any of the provisions, or portions thereof, set forth in subdivisions (1) through (6) of subsection (b) of this section which are not applicable by reason of the plan of insurance may, to the extent inapplicable, be omitted from the policy. The insurer shall reserve the right to defer the payment of any cash surrender value for a period of six months after demand therefor with surrender of the policy.

(d) Any cash surrender value available under the policy in the event of default in the premium payment due on any policy anniversary, whether or not required by subsection (b) of this section, shall be an amount not less than the excess, if any, of the present value on such anniversary of the future guaranteed benefits which would have been provided for by the policy, including any existing paid-up additions if there had been no default, over the sum of:

(1) The then present value of the adjusted premium as defined in subsections (f), (g), (h), (i) and (j) of this section, corresponding to premiums which would have fallen due on and after such anniversary; and

(2) The amount of any indebtedness to the insurer on account of or secured by the policy.

Provided, however, that for any policy issued on or after the operative date of subsection (j) of this section, as defined therein, which provides supplemental life insurance or annuity benefits at the option of the insured and for an identifiable additional premium by rider or supplemental policy provision, the cash surrender value referred to in the first paragraph of this subsection shall be an amount not less than the sum of the cash surrender value as defined in such paragraph for an otherwise similar policy issued at the same age without such rider or supplemental policy provision and the cash surrender value as defined in such paragraph for a policy which provides only the benefits otherwise provided by such rider or supplemental policy provision.

Provided, further, that for any family policy issued on or after the operative date of subsection (j) of this section, as defined therein, which defines a primary insured and provides term insurance on the life of the spouse of the primary insured expiring before the spouse's age 71, the cash surrender value referred to in the first paragraph of this subsection shall be an amount not less than the sum of the cash surrender value as defined in such paragraph for an otherwise similar policy issued at the same age without such term insurance on the life of the spouse and the cash surrender value as defined in such paragraph for a policy which provides only the benefits otherwise provided by such term insurance on the life of the spouse.

Any cash surrender value available within 30 days after any policy anniversary under any policy paid up by completion of all premium payments or any policy continued under any paid-up nonforfeiture benefits, whether or not required by subsection (b) of this section, shall be an amount not less than the present value, on such anniversary, of the future guaranteed benefits provided for by the policy, including any existing paid-up additions, decreased by any indebtedness to the insurer on account of or secured by the policy.

(e) Any paid-up nonforfeiture benefit available under the policy in the event of default in the premium payment due on any policy anniversary shall be such that its present value as of such anniversary shall be at least equal to the cash surrender value then provided for by the policy or, if none is provided for, that cash surrender value which would have been required by this section in the absence of the condition that premiums shall have been paid for at least a specified period.

(f) This subsection shall not apply to policies issued on or after the operative date of subsection (j) of this section, as defined therein. Except as provided in subsection (h) of this section, the adjusted premiums for any policy shall be calculated on an annual basis and shall be such uniform percentage of the respective premiums specified in the policy for each policy year, excluding extra premiums on a substandard policy, that the present value at the date of issue of the policy, of all such adjusted premiums shall be equal to the sum of:

(1) The then present value of the future guaranteed benefits provided for by the policy;

(2) Two percent of the amount of the insurance if the insurance be uniform in amount, or of the equivalent uniform amount, as defined in this section, if the amount of insurance varies with the duration of the policy;

(3) Forty percent of the adjusted premium for the first policy year; and

(4) Twenty-five percent of either the adjusted premium for the first policy year or the adjusted premium for a whole life policy of the same uniform or equivalent uniform amount with uniform premiums for the whole of life issued at the same age for the same amount of insurance, whichever is less; provided, however, that in applying the percentages specified in subdivisions (3) and (4) of this subsection, no adjusted premiums shall be deemed to exceed four percent of the amount of insurance or uniform amount equivalent thereto.

Whenever the plan or term of a policy has been changed, either by request of the insured or automatically in accordance with the provisions of the policy, the date of inception of the changed policy for the purposes of determining a nonforfeiture benefit or cash surrender value shall be the date as of which the age of the insured is determined for the purposes of the changed policy. The date of issue of a policy for the purpose of this subsection and subsections (g) and (h) of this section shall be the date as of which the rated age of the insured is determined.

(g) This subsection shall not apply to policies issued on or after the operative date of subsection (j) of this section, as defined therein. In the case of a policy providing an amount of insurance varying with the duration of the policy, the equivalent uniform amount thereof for the purposes of subsection (f) of this section shall be deemed to be the uniform amount of insurance provided by an otherwise similar policy containing the same endowment benefit, or benefits, if any, issued at the same age and for the same term, the amount of which does not vary with duration and the benefits under which have the same present value at the date of issue as the benefits under the policy; provided, however, that, in the case of a policy for a varying amount of insurance issued on the life of a child under age 10, the equivalent uniform amount may be computed as though the amount of insurance provided by the policy prior to the attainment of age 10 were the amount provided by such policy at age 10.

(h) This subsection shall not apply to policies to be issued on or after the operative date of subsection (j) of this section, as defined therein. The adjusted premiums for any policy providing term insurance benefits by rider or supplemental policy provision shall be equal to: (1) The adjusted premiums for an otherwise similar policy issued at the same age without such term insurance benefits increased, during the period for which premiums for such term insurance benefits are payable, by (2) the adjusted premiums for such term insurance, subdivisions (1) and (2) of this subsection being calculated separately, and as specified in subsections (f) and (g) of this section.

(i) This subsection shall not apply to ordinary or industrial policies to be issued on or after the operative date of subsection (j), as defined therein. The adjusted premiums and present values referred to in this section shall, for all policies of ordinary insurance, be calculated on the basis of the commissioners' 1958 standard ordinary mortality table, provided that, for any category of ordinary insurance issued on female risks, adjusted premiums and present values may be calculated according to an age not more than three years younger than the actual age of the insured and provided that, for any category of ordinary insurance issued on female risks on or after July 30, 1979, adjusted premiums and present values may be calculated according to an age not more than six years younger than the actual age of the insured. Such calculation for all policies of industrial insurance shall be made on the basis of the commissioners' 1961 standard industrial mortality table. All calculations shall be made on the basis of the rate of interest specified in the policy for calculating cash surrender values and paid-up nonforfeiture benefits; provided, that such rate of interest shall not exceed three and one-half percent per annum; provided further, that a rate of interest not exceeding four percent per annum may be used for policies issued on or after August 23, 1976, and prior to July 30, 1979, and a rate of interest not exceeding five and one-half percent per annum may be used for policies issued on or after July 30, 1979; provided, however, that, in calculating the present value of any paid-up term insurance with accompanying pure endowment, if any, offered as a nonforfeiture benefit, the rates of mortality assumed in the case of ordinary policies may not be more than those shown in the commissioners' 1958 extended term insurance table and, in the case of industrial policies, may not be more than those shown in the commissioners' 1961 industrial extended term insurance table; provided further, that, for insurance issued on a substandard basis, the calculation of any such adjusted premiums and present values may be based on such other table of mortality as may be specified by the insurer and approved by the commissioner.

(j) (1) This subsection shall apply to all policies issued on or after the operative date of this subsection as defined herein. Except as provided in subdivision (7) of this subsection, the adjusted premiums for any policy shall be calculated on an annual basis and shall be such uniform percentage of the respective premiums specified in the policy for each policy year, excluding extra premiums on a substandard policy and also excluding any uniform annual contract charge or policy fee specified in the policy in a statement of the method to be used in calculating the cash surrender values and paid-up nonforfeiture benefits, that the present value, at the date of issue of the policy, of all adjusted premiums shall be equal to the sum of:

a. The then present value of the future guaranteed benefits provided for by the policy;

b. One percent of either the amount of insurance, if the insurance be uniform in amount, or the average amount of insurance at the beginning of each of the first 10 policy years; and

c. One hundred twenty-five percent of the nonforfeiture net level premium, as hereinafter defined; provided, however, that in applying the percentage specified in this paragraph, no nonforfeiture net level premium shall be deemed to exceed four percent of either the amount of insurance, if the insurance be uniform in amount, or the average amount of insurance at the beginning of each of the first 10 policy years.

The date of issue of a policy for the purpose of this subsection shall be the date as of which the rated age of the insured is determined.

(2) The nonforfeiture net level premium shall be equal to the present value, at the date of issue of the policy, of the guaranteed benefits provided for by the policy divided by the present value, at the date of issue of the policy, of an annuity of one percent per annum, payable on the date of issue of the policy and on each anniversary of such policy on which a premium falls due.

(3) In the case of policies which cause, on a basis guaranteed in the policy, unscheduled changes in benefits or premiums or which provide an

option for changes in benefits or premiums other than a change to a new policy, the adjusted premiums and present values shall initially be calculated on the assumption that future benefits and premiums do not change from those stipulated at the date of issue of the policy. At the time of any such change in the benefits or premiums, the future adjusted premiums, nonforfeiture net level premiums and present values shall be recalculated on the assumption that future benefits and premiums do not change from those stipulated by the policy immediately after the change.

(4) Except as otherwise provided in subdivision (7) of this subsection, the recalculated future adjusted premiums for any such policy shall be such uniform percentage of the respective future premiums specified in the policy for each policy year, excluding extra premiums on a substandard policy and also excluding any uniform annual contract charge or policy fee specified in the policy in a statement of the method to be used in calculating the cash surrender values and paid-up nonforfeiture benefits, that the present value at the time of change to the newly defined benefits or premiums, or all such future adjusted premiums shall be equal to the excess of the sum of (i) the then present value of the then future guaranteed benefits provided for by the policy and (ii) the additional expense allowance, if any, over the then cash surrender value, if any, or present value of any paid-up nonforfeiture benefit under the policy.

(5) The additional expense allowance, at the time of the change to the newly defined benefits or premiums, shall be the sum of:

a. One percent of the excess, if positive, of the average amount of insurance at the beginning of each of the first 10 policy years subsequent to the change over the average amount of insurance prior to the change at the beginning of each of the first 10 policy years subsequent to the time of the most recent previous change, or, if there has been no previous change, the date of issue of the policy; and

b. One hundred twenty-five percent of the increase, if positive, in the nonforfeiture net level premium.

(6) The recalculated nonforfeiture net level premium shall be equal to the result obtained by dividing a. by b. where a. equals the sum of (i) the nonforfeiture net level premium applicable prior to the change times the present value of an annuity of one percent per annum payable on each anniversary of the policy on or subsequent to the date of the change on which a premium would have fallen due had the change not occurred; and (ii) the present value of the increase in future guaranteed benefits provided for by the policy, and b. equals the present value of an annuity of one percent per annum payable on each anniversary of the policy on or subsequent to the date of change on which a premium falls due.

(7) Notwithstanding any other provision of this subsection to the contrary, in the case of a policy issued on a substandard basis, which provides reduced graded amounts of insurance, so that, in each policy year, such policy has the same tabular mortality cost as an otherwise similar policy issued on the standard basis, which provides higher uniform amounts

243

of insurance, adjusted premiums and present values for such substandard policy may be calculated as if it were issued to provide such higher uniform amounts of insurance on the standard basis.

(8) All adjusted premiums and present values referred to in this subsection shall, for all policies of ordinary insurance, be calculated on the basis of the commissioners' 1980 standard ordinary mortality table or, at the election of the insurer for any one or more specified plans of life insurance, the commissioners' 1980 standard ordinary mortality table with 10-year select mortality factors; shall, for all policies of industrial insurance, be calculated on the basis of the commissioners' 1961 standard industrial mortality table; and shall, for all policies issued in a particular calendar year, be calculated on the basis of a rate of interest not exceeding the nonforfeiture interest rate, as defined in this subsection, for policies issued in that calendar year; provided, however, that:

a. At the option of the insurer, calculations for all policies issued in a particular calendar year may be made on the basis of a rate of interest not exceeding the nonforfeiture interest rate, as defined in this subsection, for policies issued in the immediately preceding calendar year.

b. Under any paid-up nonforfeiture benefit, including any paid-up dividend additions, any cash surrender value available, whether or not required by subsection (b) of this section, shall be calculated on the basis of the mortality table and rate of interest used in determining the amount of such paid-up nonforfeiture benefit and paid-up dividend additions, if any.

c. An insurer may calculate the amount of any guaranteed paid-up nonforfeiture benefit, including any paid-up additions, under the policy on the basis of an interest rate no lower than that specified in the policy for calculating cash surrender values.

d. In calculating the present value of any paid-up term insurance with accompanying pure endowment, if any, offered as a nonforfeiture benefit, the rates of mortality assumed may be not more than those shown in the commissioners' 1980 extended term insurance table for policies of ordinary insurance and not more than the commissioners' 1961 industrial extended term insurance table for policies of industrial insurance.

e. For insurance issued on a substandard basis, the calculation of any such adjusted premiums and present values may be based on appropriate modifications of the aforementioned tables.

f. Any ordinary mortality tables, adopted after 1980 by the National Association of Insurance Commissioners, that are approved by regulation promulgated by the commissioner for use in determining the minimum nonforfeiture standard may be substituted for the commissioners' 1980 standard ordinary mortality table with or without 10-year select mortality factors or for the commissioners' 1980 extended term insurance table.

g. Any industrial mortality tables, adopted after 1980 by the National Association of Insurance Commissioners, that are approved by regulation promulgated by the commissioner for use in determining the minimum nonforfeiture standard may be substituted for the commissioners' 1961 standard industrial mortality table or the commissioners' 1961 industrial extended term insurance table.

(9) The nonforfeiture interest rate per annum for any policy issued in a particular calendar year shall be equal to 125 percent of the calendar year statutory valuation interest rate for such policy as defined in the standard valuation law, rounded to the nearest one-quarter of one percent.

(10) Notwithstanding any other provision of this code to the contrary, any refiling of nonforfeiture values or their methods of computation for any previously approved policy form which involves only a change in the interest rate or mortality table used to compute nonforfeiture values shall not require refiling of any other provisions of that policy form.

(11) After the effective date of this subsection, any insurer may file with the commissioner a written notice of its election to comply with the provisions of this subsection after a specified date before January 1, 1989, which shall be the operative date of this subsection for such insurer. If an insurer makes no such election, the operative date of this subsection for such insurer shall be January 1, 1989.

(k) In the case of any plan of life insurance which provides for future premium determination, the amounts of which are to be determined by the insurer based on then estimates of future experience, or, in the case of any plan of life insurance which is of such a nature that minimum values cannot be determined by the methods described in subsection (b), (c), (d), (e), (f), (g), (h), (i) or (j) of this section, then:

(1) The commissioner must be satisfied that the benefits provided under the plan are substantially as favorable to policyholders and insureds as the minimum benefits otherwise required by subsection (b), (c), (d), (e), (f), (g), (h), (i) or (j) of this section;

(2) The commissioner must be satisfied that the benefits and the pattern of premiums of that plan are not such as to mislead prospective policyholders or insureds;

(3) The cash surrender values and paid-up nonforfeiture benefits provided by such plan must not be less than the minimum values and benefits required for the plan computed by a method consistent with the principles of this standard nonforfeiture law for life insurance, as determined by regulations promulgated by the commissioner.

(*l*) Any cash surrender value and any paid-up nonforfeiture benefit available under the policy in the event of default in a premium payment due at any time other than on the policy anniversary shall be calculated with allowance for the lapse of time and the payment of fractional premiums beyond the last preceding policy anniversary. All values referred to in subsections (d), (e), (f), (g), (h), (i) and (j) of this section may be calculated on the assumption that any death benefit is payable at the end of the policy year of death. The net value of any paid-up additions, other than paid-up term additions, shall not be less than the amounts used to provide such additions. Notwithstanding the provisions of subsection (d) of this section, additional benefits payable:

245

(1) In the event of death or dismemberment by accident or accidental means;

(2) In the event of total and permanent disability;

(3) As reversionary annuity or deferred reversionary annuity benefits;

(4) As term insurance benefits provided by a rider or supplemental policy provision to which, if issued as a separate policy, this section would not apply;

(5) As term insurance on the life of a child or on the lives of children provided in a policy on the life of a parent of the child, if such term insurance expires before the child's age is 26, is uniform in amount after the child's age is one and has not become paid-up by reason of the death of the parent of the child; and

(6) As other policy benefits additional to life insurance and endowment benefits,

and premiums for all such additional benefits shall be disregarded in ascertaining cash surrender values and nonforfeiture benefits required by this section, and no such additional benefits shall be required to be included in any paid-up nonforfeiture benefits.

(m) This subsection, in addition to all other applicable subsections of this section, shall apply to all policies issued on or after January 1, 1985. Any cash surrender value available under the policy in the event of default in a premium payment due on any policy anniversary shall be in an amount which does not differ by more than two-tenths of one percent of either the amount of insurance, if the insurance be uniform in amount, or the average amount of insurance at the beginning of each of the first 10 policy years, from the sum of (1) the greater of zero and the basic cash value hereinafter specified and (2) the present value of any existing paid-up additions, less the amount of any indebtedness to the insurer on account of or secured by the policy.

The basic cash value shall be equal to the present value, on such anniversary, of the future guaranteed benefits which would have been provided for by the policy, excluding any existing paid-up additions and before deduction of any indebtedness to the insurer, if there had been no default, less the then present value of the nonforfeiture factors, as defined in this subsection, corresponding to premiums which would have fallen due on and after such anniversary; provided, however, that the effects on the basic cash value of supplemental life insurance or annuity benefits or of family coverage, as described in subsection (d) or (h) of this section, whichever is applicable, shall be the same as are the effects specified in subsection (d) or (h) of this section, whichever is applicable, on the cash surrender values defined in that subsection.

The nonforfeiture factor for each policy year shall be an amount equal to a percentage of the adjusted premium for the policy year, as defined in subsection (f), (g), (h) or (j) of this section, whichever is applicable. Except as is required by the next succeeding sentence of this paragraph, such percentage: (1) Must be the same percentage for each policy year between the second policy anniversary and the later of (i) the fifth policy anniversary and (ii) the first policy anniversary at which there is available under the policy a cash surrender value in an amount, before including any paid-up additions and before deducting any indebtedness, of at least two-tenths of one percent of either the amount of insurance, if the insurance be uniform in amount, or the average amount of insurance at the beginning of each of the first 10 policy years; and (2) Must be such that no percentage after the later of the two policy anniversaries specified in the preceding item (1) may apply to fewer than five consecutive policy years.

Provided, that no basic cash value may be less than the value which would be obtained if the adjusted premiums for the policy, as defined in subsection (f), (g), (h), or (j) of this section, whichever is applicable, were substituted for the nonforfeiture factors in the calculation of the basic cash value.

All adjusted premiums and present values referred to in this subsection shall for a particular policy be calculated on the same mortality and interest bases as are used in demonstrating the policy's compliance with the other subsections of this section. The cash surrender values referred to in this subsection shall include any endowment benefits provided for by the policy.

Any cash surrender value available other than in the event of default in a premium payment due on a policy anniversary, and the amount of any paid-up nonforfeiture benefit available under the policy in the event of default in a premium payment, shall be determined in manners consistent with the manners specified for determining the analogous minimum amounts in subsections (b), (c), (d), (e), (j) and (*l*). The amounts of any cash surrender values and of any paid-up nonforfeiture benefits granted in connection with additional benefits such as those listed in items (1) through (6) in subsection (*l*) of this section shall conform with the principles of this subsection.

(n) This section shall not apply to any of the following:

(1) Reinsurance;

(2) Group insurance;

(3) Pure endowment;

(4) Annuity or reversionary annuity contract;

(5) Variable life insurance contract;

(6) Term policy of uniform amount, which provides no guaranteed nonforfeiture or endowment benefits, or renewal thereof, of 20 years or less, expiring before age 71, for which uniform premiums are payable during the entire term of the policy;

(7) Term policy of decreasing amount, which provides no guaranteed nonforfeiture for endowment benefits, on which each adjusted premium, calculated as specified in subsections (f), (g), (h), (i) and (j) of this section, is less than the adjusted premium so calculated on a term policy of uniform amount, or renewal thereof, which provides no guaranteed nonforfeiture or endowment benefits, issued at the same age and for the same initial amount of insurance and for a term of 20 years or less, expiring before age 71, for which uniform premiums are payable during the entire term of the policy; and

(8) Policy, which provides no guaranteed nonforfeiture or endowment benefits, for which no cash surrender value, if any, or present value of any paid-up nonforfeiture benefit, at the beginning of any policy year, calculated as specified in subsections (d), (e), (f), (g), (h), (i) and (j), exceeds two and one-half percent of the amount of insurance at the beginning of the same policy year.

(o) For purposes of determining the applicability of this section, the age at expiry for a joint term life insurance policy shall be the age at expiry of the oldest life.

(p) This section shall not apply to benefits provided in the form of funeral or monument merchandise and services under burial policies except to the extent provided in section 27-17-13. (Acts 1981, No. 407, p. 707, § 373; Acts 1979, No. 79-661, p. 1142, § 1; Acts 1981, No. 81-783, p. 1347, § 1.)

Collateral references. — 45 C.J.S., Insurance, §§ 634-636.

43 Am. Jur. 2d, Insurance, § 654 et seq.

Receipt of check for insurance premium as preventing forfeiture for nonpayment. 50 ALR2d 630.

Dividends as preventing lapse of policy for nonpayment of premiums. 8 ALR3d 862.

Remedies and measure of damages for wrongful cancellation of life, health and accident insurance. 34 ALR3d 245.

§ 27-15-28.1. Standard nonforfeiture law for individual deferred annuities.

(a) This section shall be known as the standard nonforfeiture law for individual deferred annuities.

(b) This section shall not apply to any reinsurance group annuity purchased under a retirement plan or plan of deferred compensation established or maintained by an employer (including a partnership or sole proprietorship) or by an employee organization, or by both, other than a plan providing individual retirement accounts or individual retirement annuities under section 408 of the Internal Revenue Code, as now or hereafter amended, premium deposit fund, variable annuity, investment annuity, immediate annuity, any deferred annuity contract after annuity payments have commenced or reversionary annuity, nor to any contract which shall be delivered outside this state through an agent or other representative of the company issuing the contract.

(c) In the case of contracts issued on or after the operative date of this section as defined in subsection (l) no contract of annuity, except as stated in subsection (b), shall be delivered or issued for delivery in this state unless it contains in substance the following provisions, or corresponding provisions which in the opinion of the commissioner are at least as favorable to the contract holder, upon cessation of payment of considerations under the contract:

(1) That upon cessation of payment of considerations under a contract, the company will grant a paid-up annuity benefit on a plan stipulated in the contract of such value as is specified in subsections (e), (f), (g), (h) and (j);

(2) If a contract provides for a lump sum settlement at maturity, or at any other time, that upon surrender of the contract at or prior to the commencement of any annuity payments, the company will pay in lieu of any paid-up annuity benefit a cash surrender benefit of such amount as is specified in subsections (e), (f), (h) and (j). The company shall reserve the right to defer the payment of such cash surrender benefit for a period of six months after demand therefor with surrender of the contract;

(3) A statement of the mortality table, if any, and interest rates used in calculating any minimum paid-up annuity, cash surrender or death benefits that are guaranteed under the contract, together with sufficient information to determine the amounts of such benefits; and

(4) A statement that any paid-up annuity, cash surrender or death benefits that may be available under the contract are not less than the minimum benefits required by any statute of the state in which the contract is delivered and an explanation of the manner in which such benefits are altered by the existence of any additional amounts credited by the company to the contract, any indebtedness to the company on the contract or any prior withdrawals from or partial surrenders of the contract.

Notwithstanding the requirements section, any deferred annuity contract may provide that if no considerations have been received under a contract for a period of two full years and the portion of the paid-up annuity benefit at maturity on the plan stipulated in the contract arising from considerations paid prior to such period would be less than $20.00 monthly, the company may at its option terminate such contract by payment in cash of the then present value of such portion of the paid-up annuity benefit, calculated on the basis of the mortality table, if any, and interest rate specified in the contract for determining the paid-up annuity benefit, and by such payment shall be relieved of any further obligation under such contract.

(d) The minimum values as specified in subsections (e), (f), (g), (h) and (j) of any paid-up annuity, cash surrender or death benefits available under an annuity contract shall be based upon minimum nonforfeiture amounts as defined in this subsection:

(1) With respect to contracts providing for flexible considerations, the minimum nonforfeiture amount at any time at, or prior to, the commencement of any annuity payments shall be equal to an accumulation up to such time at a rate of interest of three percent per annum of percentages of the net considerations (as hereinafter defined) paid prior to such time, decreased by the sum of:

a. any prior withdrawals from or partial surrenders of the contract accumulated at a rate of interest of three percent per annum; and

b. the amount of any indebtedness to the company on the contract, including interest due and accrued; and increased by any existing additional amounts credited by the company to the contract.

The net consideration for a given contract year used to define the minimum nonforfeiture amount shall be an amount not less than zero and shall be equal to the corresponding gross considerations credited to the

249

contract during that contract year less an annual contract charge of $30.00 and less a collection charge of $1.25 per consideration credited to the contract during that contract year. The percentages of net considerations shall be 65 percent of the net consideration for the first contract year and 87½ percent of the net considerations for the second and later contract years. Notwithstanding the provisions of the preceding sentence, the percentage shall be 65 percent of the portion of the total net consideration for any renewal contract year which exceeds by not more than two times the sum of those portions of the net considerations in all prior contract years for which the percentage was 65 percent.

(2) With respect to contracts providing for fixed scheduled considerations, minimum nonforfeiture amounts shall be calculated on the assumption that considerations are paid annually in advance and shall be defined as for contracts with flexible considerations which are paid annually with two exceptions:

a. The portion of the net consideration for the first contract year to be accumulated shall be the sum of 65 percent of the net consideration for the first contract year plus 22½ percent of the excess of the net consideration for the first contract year over the lesser of the net considerations for the second and third contract years.

b. The annual contract charge shall be the lesser of (i) $30.00 or (ii) 10 percent of the gross annual consideration.

(3) With respect to contracts providing for a single consideration, minimum nonforfeiture amounts shall be defined as for contracts with flexible considerations except that the percentage of net consideration used to determine the minimum nonforfeiture amount shall be equal to 90 percent and the net considerations shall be the gross consideration less a contract charge of $75.00.

(e) Any paid-up annuity benefit available under a contract shall be such that its present value on the date annuity payments are to commence is at least equal to the minimum nonforfeiture amount on that date. Such present value shall be computed using the mortality table, if any, and the interest rate specified in the contract for determining the minimum paid-up annuity benefits guaranteed in the contract.

(f) For contracts which provide cash surrender benefits, such cash surrender benefits available prior to maturity shall not be less than the present value as of the date of surrender of that portion of the maturity value of the paid-up annuity benefit which would be provided under the contract at maturity arising from considerations paid prior to the time of cash surrender reduced by the amount appropriate to reflect any prior withdrawals from or partial surrender of the contract, such present value being calculated on the basis of an interest rate not more than one percent higher than the interest rate specified in the contract for accumulating the net considerations to determine such maturity value, decreased by the amount of any indebtedness to the company on the contract, including interest due and accrued, and increased by any existing additional amounts credited by the company to the contract. In no event shall any cash surrender benefit be less than the minimum nonforfeiture amount at that time. The death benefit under such contracts shall be at least equal to the cash surrender benefit.

(g) For contracts which do not provide cash surrender benefits, the present value of any paid-up annuity benefit available as a nonforfeiture option at any time prior to maturity shall not be less than the present value of that portion of the maturity value of the paid-up annuity benefit provided under the contract arising from considerations paid prior to the time the contract is surrendered in exchange for, or changed to, a deferred paid-up annuity, such present value being calculated for the period prior to the maturity date on the basis of the interest rate specified in the contract for accumulating the net considerations to determine such maturity value, and increased by any existing additional amounts credited by the company to the contract. For contracts which do not provide any death benefits prior to the commencement of any annuity payments, such present values shall be calculated on the basis of such interest rate and mortality table specified in the contract for determining the maturity value of the paid-up annuity benefit. However, in no event shall the present value of the paid-up annuity benefit be less than the minimum nonforfeiture amount at that time.

(h) For the purpose of determining the benefits calculated under subsections (f) and (g) in the case of annuity contracts under which an election may be made to have annuity payments commence at optional maturity dates, the maturity date shall be deemed to be the latest date for which election shall be permitted by the contract, but shall not be deemed to be later than the anniversary of the contract next following the annuitant's seventieth birthday or the tenth anniversary of the contract, whichever is later.

(i) Any contract which does not provide cash surrender benefits or does not provide death benefits at least equal to the minimum nonforfeiture amount prior to the commencement of any annuity payments shall include a statement in a prominent place in the contract that such benefits are not provided.

(j) Any paid-up annuity, cash surrender or death benefits available at any time, other than on the contract anniversary under any contract with fixed scheduled considerations, shall be calculated with allowance for the lapse of time and the payment of any scheduled considerations beyond the beginning of the contract year in which cessation of payment of considerations under the contract occurs.

(k) For any contract which provides, within the same contract by rider or supplemental contract provisions, both annuity benefits and life insurance benefits that are in excess of the greater cash surrender benefits or a return of the gross considerations with interest, the minimum nonforfeiture benefits shall be equal to the sum of the minimum nonforfeiture benefits for the annuity portion and the minimum nonforfeiture benefits, if any, for the life insurance portion computed as if each portion were a separate contract. Notwithstanding the provisions of subsections (e), (f), (g), (h) and (j) additional benefits payable (1) in the event of total and permanent disability, (2) as reversionary annuity or deferred reversionary annuity benefits or (3) as other policy benefits additional to life insurance, endowment and annuity benefits, and considerations for all such additional benefits, shall be disregarded in ascertaining the minimum nonforfeiture amounts, paid-up annuity, cash surrender and death benefits that may be required by this section. The inclusion of such additional benefits shall not be required in any paid-up benefits, unless such additional benefits separately would require minimum nonforfeiture amounts, paid-up annuity, cash surrender and death benefits.

(*l*) After July 30, 1979, any company may file with the commissioner a written notice of its election to comply with the provisions of this section after a specified date before July 30, 1981. After the filing of such notice, then upon such specified date, which shall be the operative date of this section for such company, this section shall become operative with respect to annuity contracts thereafter issued by such company. If a company makes no such election, the operative date of this section for such company shall be July 30, 1981. (Acts 1979, No. 79-661, p. 1142, § 3.)

U.S. Code. — For section 408 of the Internal Revenue Code, see 26 U.S.C.A. § 408.

§ 27-15-29. Prohibited policy plans.

(a) No insurer shall hereafter deliver or issue for delivery in this state any policy or contract providing for the establishment of its policyholders or members into divisions and classes and for payment of benefits from special funds created for such purpose to the oldest member of the division and class or to the member of the division and class whose policy has been in force the longest period of time upon the death of a member in such division and class, or under any other similar plan; except, that any insurer heretofore operating on such a plan in this state, whether by conversion from a fraternal benefit society or otherwise, may continue to do so upon the condition that the insurer shall not hereafter establish its policyholders or members into any new divisions, classes or groupings of any kind, other than those heretofore established and containing subsisting policies heretofore issued, and that the insurer, if a stock insurer, shall have and maintain paid-in capital stock of at least $100,000.00 or, if a mutual insurer, a surplus of at least $25,000.00 and increase such surplus to, and thereafter maintain surplus in the amount of, at least $100,000.00 within six years from January 1, 1972.

(b) No insurer shall deliver, or issue for delivery, in this state as a part of, or in combination with, any insurance, endowment or annuity contract any agreement or plan which provides for the accumulation of profits over a period of years and for payment of all, or any part of, such accumulated profits only to policyholders or members of a designated group or class who continue as members or policyholders until the end of a specified period of time or under any other similar plan.

(c) This section shall not be deemed to prohibit the payment or allowance of regular annual dividends or "savings" under regular participating forms of policies or contracts. (Acts 1931, No. 687, p. 819; Acts 1936-37, Ex. Sess., No. 186, p. 221; Acts 1971, No. 407, p. 707, § 374.)

Collateral references. — 44 C.J.S., Insurance, §§ 241-243.

43 Am. Jur. 2d, Insurance, § 15.

CHAPTER 16.

INDUSTRIAL LIFE INSURANCE.

Sec.
27-16-1. "Industrial life insurance" defined.
27-16-2. Applicability of chapter.
27-16-3. Policy provisions — Generally.
27-16-4. Same — Grace period.
27-16-5. Same — Entire contract; repre-
            sentations.
27-16-6. Same — Incontestability.
27-16-7. Same — Misstatement of age or sex.
27-16-8. Same — Dividends.
27-16-9. Same — Reinstatement.
27-16-10. Same — Settlement of claims.
27-16-11. Same — Waiver, etc., of policy terms
            or conditions.

Sec.
27-16-12. Same — Beneficiaries; payment to
            other than designated benefi-
            ciary.
27-16-13. Same — Nonforfeiture benefits and
            cash surrender values.
27-16-14. Same — Title.
27-16-15. Same — Applicability to single pre-
            mium, etc., policies.
27-16-16. Same — Conversion to life insurance
            with less frequent premium pay-
            ments.
27-16-17. Same — Prohibited provisions.

Cross references. — As to life insurance and annuity contracts generally, see § 27-15-1 et seq.

§ 27-16-1. "Industrial life insurance" defined.

For the purposes of this title, "industrial life insurance" is that form of life insurance written under policies of face amount to $2,500.00 or less bearing the words "industrial policy" imprinted on the face thereof as part of the descriptive matter and under which premiums are payable monthly or more often. (Acts 1971, No. 407, p. 707, § 376.)

Collateral references. — 44 C.J.S., Insurance, § 20.

§ 27-16-2. Applicability of chapter.

The provisions of this chapter apply only to industrial life insurance policies. Sections 27-15-15, 27-15-24, 27-15-25, 27-15-28 and 27-15-29 shall also apply to industrial life insurance. (Acts 1971, No. 407, p. 707, § 375.)

Collateral references. — 44 C.J.S., Insurance, § 255.

§ 27-16-3. Policy provisions — Generally.

(a) No policy of industrial life insurance shall be delivered or be issued for delivery in this state unless it contains in substance the applicable provisions set forth in sections 27-16-4 through 27-16-14.

(b) This section does not apply to burial insurance policies as defined in section 27-17-1. (Acts 1971, No. 407, p. 707, § 377.)

§ 27-16-4. Same — Grace period.

There shall be a provision that the insured is entitled to a grace period of four weeks within which the payment of any premiums after the first may be made; except, that in policies the premiums for which are payable monthly, the period of grace shall be one month, but not less than 30 days, and that during the period of grace the policy shall continue in full force, but if during the grace period the policy becomes a claim, then any overdue and unpaid premiums may be deducted from any settlement under the policy. (Acts 1971, No. 407, p. 707, § 378.)

Collateral references. — 44 C.J.S., Insurance, § 255, n. 16. 45 C.J.S., Insurance, § 473(5).

43 Am. Jur. 2d, Insurance, § 548.

Receipt of check for insurance premium as preventing forfeiture for nonpayment. 50 ALR2d 630.

§ 27-16-5. Same — Entire contract; representations.

There shall be a provision that the policy shall constitute the entire contract between the parties or, if a copy of the application is endorsed upon or attached to the policy when issued, a provision that the policy and the application therefor shall constitute the entire contract. If the application is so made a part of the contract, the policy shall also provide that all statements made by the applicant in such application shall, in the absence of fraud, be deemed to be representations and not warranties. (1935, No. 152, p. 194; Code 1940, T. 28, § 6; Acts 1971, No. 407, p. 707, § 379.)

Collateral references. — 44 C.J.S., Insurance, § 250.

43 Am. Jur. 2d, Insurance, § 281.

§ 27-16-6. Same — Incontestability.

There shall be a provision that the policy, exclusive of provisions relating to disability or dismemberment benefits or to additional benefits in the event of death by accident or accidental means, shall be incontestable, except for nonpayment of premiums, after it has been in force during the lifetime of the insured for a period of two years from its date of issue. (Code 1940, T. 28, § 7; Acts 1967, No. 181, p. 543; Acts 1971, No. 407, p. 707, § 380.)

Editor's note. — The following cases were decided under former Code 1940, T. 28, § 7 or prior law.

Section is mandatory and controls policy of life insurance issued in state. First Nat'l Bank v. Equitable Life Assurance Soc'y, 31 F. Supp. 969 (N.D. Ala. 1940).

It is self-executing and part of every policy written in state. — This section is self-executing and is written or read into every policy of life insurance written in Alabama and has the effect of a statute of limitations against the defenses of fraud and misrepresentation. First Nat'l Bank v. Equitable Life Assurance Soc'y, 31 F. Supp. 969 (N.D. Ala. 1940).

This section is written into policies of life insurance and becomes a law-made stipulation, striking down all stipulations in the policy insofar as in conflict. Ginsberg v. Union Cent. Life Ins. Co., 240 Ala. 299, 198 So. 855 (1940).

And is in nature of statute of limitations. — This section is in the nature of a statute of limitations barring a contest of a policy on the grounds stated. It fixes a time while the insured is still living within which the insurer shall discover and institute appropriate proceedings to avoid the policy, such as rescission and cancellation. Ginsberg v. Union Cent. Life Ins. Co., 240 Ala. 299, 198 So. 855 (1940).

It is applicable only to written policy. — Statutes and decisions have virtually given to the terms "policy" and "policy of insurance" a meaning which makes them the written agreement of insurance in contradistinction to the parol agreement to insure. Prudential Cas. Co. v. Kerr, 202 Ala. 259, 80 So. 97 (1918).

Section limits period which reinstatement contract may be avoided for fraud. — This section limits the period in which a reinstatement contract of insurance may be avoided for fraud where the reinstatement contract is a new policy complete in all details. Jefferson Std. Life Ins. Co. v. Bomchel, 239 Ala. 135, 194 So. 156 (1940).

Reinstatement of lapsed life insurance contract is ordinarily continuation of original contract, but if there is fraud or breach of warranty in effecting the reinstatement the insurer is not barred of its right to make defense on ground of fraud or breach of warranty because two years have elapsed after date of original contract. Jefferson Std. Life Ins. Co. v. Bomchel, 239 Ala. 135, 194 So. 156 (1940).

Effect of misrepresentation in application for reinstatement. — Where application for reinstatement of life policy and contents of application were all made pursuant to reinstatement provision in old policy requiring satisfactory evidence of insurability, the appli-cation anticipated action by insurer on account of representation in application, and if it was materially false and induced action by insurer or if there was a breach of warranty in that connection, the misrepresentation and breach would be a good defense if sufficiently pleaded. Jefferson Std. Life Ins. Co. v. Bomchel, 239 Ala. 135, 194 So. 156 (1940).

Period of contestability dates from time warranty made. — The period of contestability of life policy on account of misrepresentation or warranty dates from the time when it was made and acted on and not some fictitious date in the past. Jefferson Std. Life Ins. Co. v. Bomchel, 239 Ala. 135, 194 So. 156 (1940).

Other cases construing former Code 1940, Title 28, section 7. — See Meridan Life Ins. Co. v. Dean, 182 Ala. 127, 62 So. 90 (1913); Massachusetts Mut. Life Ins. Co. v. Crenshaw, 186 Ala. 460, 65 So. 65 (1914); Life Ins. Co. v. Newell, 223 Ala. 401, 137 So. 16 (1931); Brown v. Supreme Lodge, 225 Ala. 114, 142 So. 388 (1932); North Carolina Mut. Life Ins. Co. v. Terrell, 227 Ala. 410, 150 So. 318 (1933); All States Life Ins. Co. v. Jaudon, 228 Ala. 672, 154 So. 798 (1934); Protective Life Ins. Co. v. Fischer, 234 Ala. 436, 175 So. 391 (1937); Ginsberg v. Union Cent. Life Ins. Co., 240 Ala. 299, 198 So. 855 (1940); Equitable Life Assurance Soc'y v. First Nat'l Bank, 113 F.2d 272 (5th Cir. 1940); Mutual Sav. Life Ins. Co. v. Brown, 245 Ala. 423, 17 So. 2d 164 (1944).

Collateral references. — 45 C.J.S., Insurance, § 747.

43 Am. Jur. 2d, Insurance, § 1155 et seq.

Incontestable clause as applicable to suit to reform insurance policy. 7 ALR2d 504.

What amounts to contest within contemplation of incontestable clause. 95 ALR2d 420.

§ 27-16-7. Same — Misstatement of age or sex.

There shall be a provision that if it is found that the age or sex of the individual insured or the age or sex of any other individual considered in determining the premium has been misstated, any amount payable or benefit accruing under the policy shall be such as the premium would have purchased at the correct age or ages, sex or sexes. (Acts 1971, No. 407, p. 707, § 381.)

Collateral references. — 45 C.J.S., Insurance, § 596.

§ 27-16-8. Same — Dividends.

If a participating policy, there shall be a provision that the insurer shall annually ascertain and apportion any divisible surplus accruing on the policy; except, that, at the option of the insurer, such participation may be deferred to the end of the fifth policy year. This provision shall not prohibit the payment of additional dividends on default of payment of premiums or termination of the policy. (Acts 1971, No. 407, p. 707, § 382.)

Collateral references. — 46 C.J.S., Insurance, § 1394.
43 Am. Jur. 2d, Insurance, §§ 120-123.
Insurer's statements as to amount of dividends, accumulations, surplus, or the like as binding on insurer or merely illustrative. 17 ALR3d 777.

§ 27-16-9. Same — Reinstatement.

(a) There shall be a provision that unless the policy has been surrendered for its cash value, or its cash surrender value has been exhausted or the period of any extended insurance provided by the policy has expired, the policy will be reinstated at any time within two years after the date of premium default upon written application therefor, the production of evidence of insurability satisfactory to the insurer, the payment of all overdue premiums and payment or, within the limits permitted by the then cash value of the policy, reinstatement of any other indebtedness to the insurer upon the policy with interest as to both premiums and indebtedness at a rate not exceeding six percent per annum compounded annually.

(b) If for the purpose of or toward reinstatement of a policy after its lapse the insurer receives a payment or tender of premium or other funds in amount less than as required to effectuate the reinstatement so as to place the policy currently in full force, then, within 60 days after the receipt of such payment or tender, the insurer shall either:

(1) Collect whatever amount is necessary to effectuate the reinstatement and place the policy in full force and effect currently;

(2) Refund to the person entitled thereto all such payments and amounts tendered and refuse the reinstatement; or

(3) In the absence of action referred to in subdivisions (1) or (2) of this subsection the insurer shall be deemed as a matter of law to have effectuated reinstatement of the policy so that it is in full force and effect currently as of the end of such 60-day period and to have forever waived the payment or collection of all premiums and amounts theretofore due and unpaid under the policy.

(c) The provisions made in subsection (b) of this section need not be contained in the policy. (Acts 1971, No. 407, p. 707, § 383.)

Collateral references. — 45 C.J.S., Insurance, §§ 667-671.

43 Am. Jur. 2d, Insurance, §§ 389-396.

Conflict of laws: choice of law in construction of insurance policy originally governed by law of one state as affected by modification, renewal, exchange, replacement, or reinstatement in different state. 3 ALR3d 646.

Incontestable clause as affected by reinstatement of policy. 23 ALR3d 743.

§ 27-16-10. Same — Settlement of claims.

There shall be a provision that, when the policy becomes a claim by the death of the insured, settlement shall be made upon receipt of due proof of death and, at the insurer's option, surrender of the policy and premium receipt book and proof of interest of the claimant. If the insurer specifies a particular period prior to the expiration of which settlement shall be made, such period shall not exceed two months from the receipt of such proofs. (Acts 1971, No. 407, p. 707, § 384.)

Collateral references. — 46 C.J.S., Insurance, § 1319.

44 Am. Jur. 2d, Insurance, §§ 1454 et seq., 1791 et seq.

§ 27-16-11. Same — Waiver, etc., of policy terms or conditions.

There shall be a provision that no agent shall have the power or authority to waive, change or alter any of the terms or conditions of any policy; except, that at the option of the insurer, the terms or conditions may be changed by an endorsement or rider signed by a duly authorized officer of the insurer. (Acts 1971, No. 407, p. 707, § 385.)

Collateral references. — 44 C.J.S., Insurance, §§ 281, 282.

Liability of insurance agent, for exposure of insurer to liability, because of issuance of policy beyond authority or contrary to instructions. 35 ALR3d 907.

§ 27-16-12. Same — Beneficiaries; payment to other than designated beneficiary.

(a) Each such policy shall have a space for the name of the beneficiary designated with a reservation of the right to designate or change the beneficiary after the issuance of the policy.

(b) The policy may also provide that no designation or change of beneficiary shall be binding on the insurer until endorsed on the policy by the insurer and that the insurer may refuse to endorse the name of any proposed beneficiary who does not appear to the insurer to have an insurable interest in the life of the insured.

(c) Such a policy may also provide that if the beneficiary designated in the policy does not make a claim under the policy or does not surrender the policy with due proof of death within the period stated in the policy, which shall be not less than 30 days after the death of the insured, or if the beneficiary is the estate of the insured, or is a minor, or dies before the insured or is not legally competent to give a valid release, then the insurer may make payment thereunder to the executor or administrator of the insured, or to any of the insured's relatives by blood or legal adoption or connection by marriage or to any person appearing to the insurer to be equitably entitled thereto by reason of having incurred expense for the maintenance, medical attention or burial of the insured. Such policy may also include a similar provision applicable to any other payment due under the policy. (Acts 1971, No. 407, p. 707, § 386.)

Collateral references. — 44 C.J.S., Insurance, § 255. 46 C.J.S., Insurance, § 1319.
44 Am. Jur. 2d, Insurance, § 1776 et seq.
Guardian and ward: power of guardian of incompetent to change beneficiary in ward's life insurance policy. 21 ALR2d 1191.
Gift of life insurance policy. 33 ALR2d 273.

§ 27-16-13. Same — Nonforfeiture benefits and cash surrender values.

There shall be provisions for nonforfeiture benefits and cash surrender values as required by section 27-15-28. (Acts 1971, No. 407, p. 707, § 387.)

§ 27-16-14. Same — Title.

There shall be a title on the face of each such policy briefly describing the same. (Acts 1971, No. 407, p. 707, § 388.)

§ 27-16-15. Same — Applicability to single premium, etc., policies.

Any of the provisions required by sections 27-16-4 through 27-16-14, or any portion thereof, which are not applicable to single premium or term policies or to policies issued or granted pursuant to nonforfeiture provisions shall, to that extent, not be incorporated therein. (Acts 1971, No. 407, p. 707, § 389.)

Collateral references. — 44 C.J.S., Insurance, § 48. 45 C.J.S., Insurance, §§ 634-636.

§ 27-16-16. Same — Conversion to life insurance with less frequent premium payments.

There may be a provision in the case of industrial policies granting to the insured, upon proper written request and upon presentation of evidence of insurability satisfactory to the insurer, the privilege of converting any industrial insurance policy to any form of life insurance with less frequent premium payments regularly issued by the insurer, in accordance with terms and conditions agreed upon with the insurer. The privilege of making such conversion need be granted only if the insurer's industrial policies on the life insured, in force as premium-paying insurance and on which conversion is requested, grant benefits in event of death, exclusive of additional accidental death benefits and exclusive of any dividend additions, in an amount not less than the minimum amount of such insurance, with less frequent premium payments issued by the insurer at the age of the insured on the plan of industrial or ordinary insurance desired. (Acts 1971, No. 407, p. 707, § 390.)

§ 27-16-17. Same — Prohibited provisions.

No policy of industrial life insurance shall contain any of the following provisions:

(1) A provision by which the insurer may deny liability under the policy for the reason that the insured has previously obtained other insurance from the same insurer;

(2) A provision giving the insurer the right to declare the policy void because the insured has had any disease or ailment, whether specified or not, or because the insured has received institutional, hospital, medical or surgical treatment or attention, except a provision which gives the insurer the right to declare the policy void if the insured has, within two years prior to the issuance of the policy, received institutional, hospital, medical or surgical treatment or attention and if the insured or claimant under the policy fails to show that the condition occasioning such treatment or attention was not of a serious nature or was not material to the risk; or

(3) A provision giving the insurer the right to declare the policy void because the insured has been rejected for insurance, unless such right be conditioned upon a showing by the insurer that knowledge of such rejection would have led to a refusal by the insurer to make such contract. (Acts 1971, No. 407, p. 707, § 391.)

CHAPTER 17.

BURIAL INSURANCE POLICIES.

Sec.
27-17-1. Applicability of chapter; "burial insurance" defined.
27-17-2. Policy provisions — Generally.
27-17-3. Same — Grace period.
27-17-4. Same — Entire contract; representations.
27-17-5. Same — Incontestability.
27-17-6. Same — Reinstatement.
27-17-7. Same — Authorized funeral director or monument dealer.
27-17-8. Same — Furnishing of merchandise and services — Generally.
27-17-9. Same — Same — Cash benefit in lieu thereof.
27-17-10. Same — Beneficiary.
27-17-11. Same — Payment of cash benefits.

Sec.
27-17-12. Same — Waiver, etc., of policy terms or conditions.
27-17-13. Same — Nonforfeiture benefits and cash surrender values.
27-17-14. Same — Title.
27-17-15. Applicability of other provisions to chapter.
27-17-16. Valuation of life insurance reserve liabilities for burial insurance policies; increase in amount of insurance; minimum standards for valuation; notice to commissioner as to change in valuation standards; increase in retail value, nonforfeiture value, and cash surrender value; construction with other laws.

Collateral references. — Validity of statutes regulating preneed contracts for the sale or furnishing of burial services and merchandise. 68 ALR2d 1251.

Funeral expenses which are necessary and thus covered under the medical payment and funeral expense provision of an insurance policy. 87 ALR3d 497.

§ 27-17-1. Applicability of chapter; "burial insurance" defined.

(a) This chapter applies only to burial insurance policies.

(b) For the purposes of this title, "burial insurance" is that form of life insurance under which:

(1) Benefits are provided in the form of merchandise and services incident to the burial of the insured or the furnishing of a monument to the insured;

(2) The specified retail value of such merchandise and services does not exceed $1,500.00; and

(3) The words "burial policy," "vault policy," "monument policy" or words of similar import are printed on the policy as a part of its description. (Acts 1971, No. 407, p. 707, § 392.)

Collateral references. — 43 Am. Jur. 2d, Insurance, § 8.

§ 27-17-2. Policy provisions — Generally.

No policy of burial insurance shall be delivered or issued for delivery in this state unless it contains in substance the provisions set forth in sections 27-17-3 through 27-17-14, or corresponding provisions, which in the opinion of the commissioner are not less favorable in any respect to the policyholder. Any of such provisions, or portions thereof, not applicable to single premium policies shall to that extent be omitted therefrom. (Acts 1971, No. 407, p. 707, § 393.)

Section does not violate section 6-5-410. — Where a restraint upon trade or monopolization is the result of valid governmental action, as in this section and § 27-17-7, as opposed to private action, no violation of § 6-5-410 can be made out. Twine v. Liberty Nat'l Life Ins. Co., 294 Ala. 43, 311 So. 2d 299 (1975).

Collateral references. — 44 C.J.S., Insurance, §§ 227-238.

§ 27-17-3. Same — Grace period.

There shall be a provision that the insured is entitled to a grace period of four weeks within which the payment of any premium after the first may be made, except, that, in policies the premiums which are payable monthly or less often, the period of grace shall be one month but not less than 30 days, and that during the period of grace the policy shall continue in full force, but if during the grace period the policy becomes a claim, then any overdue premiums may be deducted from any cash payment which may be due under the policy. (Acts 1971, No. 407, p. 707, § 394.)

Collateral references. — 44 C.J.S., Insurance, § 255, n. 16. 45 C.J.S., Insurance, § 473(5).

43 Am. Jur. 2d, Insurance, § 548.

Receipt of check for insurance premium as preventing forfeiture for nonpayment. 50 ALR2d 630.

§ 27-17-4. Same — Entire contract; representations.

There shall be a provision that the policy shall constitute the entire contract between the parties or, if a copy of the application is endorsed upon or attached to the policy when issued, a provision that the policy and the application therefor shall constitute the entire contract. If the application is so made a part of the contract, the policy shall also provide that all statements made by the applicant in such application shall, in the absence of fraud, be deemed to be representations and not warranties. (Acts 1935, No. 152, p. 194; Code 1940, T. 28, § 6; Acts 1971, No. 407, p. 707, § 395.)

Collateral references. — 44 C.J.S., Insurance, § 250.

43 Am. Jur. 2d, Insurance, § 281.

§ 27-17-5. Same — Incontestability.

There shall be a provision, with respect to benefits provided in the form of merchandise and services incident to the burial of the insured, that the policy shall be incontestable from its date of issue except for nonpayment of premiums and, with respect to benefits payable in cash, monuments, waiver of premium benefits and disability benefits, a provision that the policy shall be incontestable after it has been in force during the lifetime of the insured for a period of two years from its date of issue, except for nonpayment of premiums and except, at the option of the insurer, as to provisions relating to benefits in event of dismemberment or disability or to additional benefits for death by accident or accidental means. (Acts 1971, No. 407, p. 707, § 396.)

Collateral references. — 45 C.J.S., Insurance, § 747.

43 Am. Jur. 2d, Insurance, § 1155 et seq. Incontestable clause as applicable to suit to reform insurance policy. 7 ALR2d 504.

What amounts to contest within contemplation of incontestable clause. 95 ALR2d 420.

§ 27-17-6. Same — Reinstatement.

(a) There shall be a provision that the policy may be reinstated at any time within two years after the date of default in the payment of any premium unless the policy has been surrendered for its cash value or the period of any extended insurance provided by the policy has expired, upon evidence of insurability satisfactory to the insurer and the payment of all overdue premiums with interest at a rate not exceeding six percent per annum compounded annually.

(b) Subsections (b) and (c) of section 27-16-9 shall also apply as to burial insurance policies. (Acts 1971, No. 407, p. 707, § 397.)

Collateral references. — 45 C.J.S., Insurance, §§ 667-671.

43 Am. Jur. 2d, Insurance, §§ 389-396. Conflict of laws: choice of law in construction of insurance policy originally governed by law

of one state as affected by reinstatement in different state. 3 ALR3d 646.

Incontestable clause as affected by reinstatement of policy. 23 ALR3d 743.

§ 27-17-7. Same — Authorized funeral director or monument dealer.

There shall be a provision that the insurer has contracted with and appointed an authorized funeral director or monument dealer in this state to furnish the merchandise and services provided by the policy. The policy may also provide that the term "authorized funeral director" or "authorized monument dealer" shall mean a funeral director or monument dealer authorized by the insurer at the time of the insured's death. (Acts 1971, No. 407, p. 707, § 398.)

Section does not violate section 6-5-410. — Where a restraint upon trade or monopolization is the result of valid governmental action, as in this section and § 27-12-2, as opposed to

private action, no violation of § 6-5-410 can be made out. Twine v. Liberty Nat'l Life Ins. Co., 294 Ala. 43, 311 So. 2d 299 (1975).

§ 27-17-8. Same — Furnishing of merchandise and services — Generally.

There shall be a provision that if the death of the insured or, if a vault or monument policy, the burial of the insured occurs within the state of Alabama and within a specified distance from an authorized funeral director or monument dealer of the insurer, the merchandise and services provided by the policy shall be furnished by such authorized funeral director or monument dealer upon the request of the beneficiary or other person having authority to make funeral arrangements. (Acts 1971, No. 407, p. 707, § 399.)

Collateral references. — 44 C.J.S., Insurance, § 59.

§ 27-17-9. Same — Same — Cash benefit in lieu thereof.

There shall be a provision that if the death of the insured or, if a vault or monument policy, the burial of the insured occurs outside the state of Alabama or at a greater distance from an authorized funeral director or monument dealer of the insurer than that specified in section 27-17-8, the insurer will, in lieu of furnishing such merchandise and services, pay a cash benefit of not less than one half of the specified retail value of the merchandise and services provided in the policy; provided, however, that the insurer may provide for a reduced benefit as to an insured less than one year of age at death. The policy may contain a provision for the payment of such cash benefit at the option of the insurer under any other circumstances where it is impractical for any reason to furnish the merchandise and services provided by the policy. (Acts 1971, No. 407, p. 707, § 400.)

§ 27-17-10. Same — Beneficiary.

Each such policy shall have a space for the name of the beneficiary designated with a reservation of the right to designate or change the beneficiary after the issuance of the policy. The policy may also provide that no designation or change of beneficiary shall be binding on the insurer until endorsed on the policy by the insurer and that the insurer may refuse to endorse the name of any proposed beneficiary who does not appear to the insurer to have an insurable interest in the life of the insured. (Acts 1971, No. 407, p. 707, § 401.)

Collateral references. — 44 C.J.S., Insurance, § 255. 46 C.J.S., Insurance, § 1186.
44 Am. Jur. 2d, Insurance, § 1776 et seq.

§ 27-17-11. Same — Payment of cash benefits.

(a) There shall be a provision that any cash benefit provided by the policy upon the death of the insured will be payable upon receipt of due proof of death of the insured and, at the insurer's option, the surrender of the policy and premium receipt book.

(b) The policy may also provide for the payment of such benefit or any other cash benefit due under the policy to the beneficiary designated in the policy, or to the executor or administrator of the insured, or to any relative of the insured by blood, or legal adoption or connection by marriage or to any person appearing to the insurer to be equitably entitled thereto by reason of having incurred expense for the maintenance, medical attention or burial of the insured. (Acts 1971, No. 407, p. 707, § 402.)

Collateral references. — 46 C.J.S., Insurance, § 1186.

§ 27-17-12. Same — Waiver, etc., of policy terms or conditions.

There shall be a provision that no agent shall have the power or authority to waive, change or alter any of the terms or conditions of any policy; except, that, at the option of the insurer, the terms or conditions may be changed by an endorsement signed by a duly authorized officer of the insurer. (Acts 1971, No. 407, p. 707, § 403.)

Collateral references. — 44 C.J.S., Insurance, §§ 281, 282.

§ 27-17-13. Same — Nonforfeiture benefits and cash surrender values.

There shall be provisions for nonforfeiture benefits and cash surrender values as required by section 27-15-28; except, that, with respect to benefits provided in the form of funeral or monument merchandise and services, the required minimum cash surrender values shall be two thirds of the cash surrender values which would be required for a cash life insurance policy having a face amount equal to the cash benefit provided in accordance with section 27-17-9. (Acts 1971, No. 407, p. 707, § 404.)

Collateral references. — 45 C.J.S., Insurance, §§ 634-636.

§ 27-17-14. Same — Title.

There shall be a title on the face of the policy briefly describing the same. (Acts 1971, No. 407, p. 707, § 405.)

§ 27-17-15. Applicability of other provisions to chapter.

The following provisions of this title shall also apply as to burial insurance policies:

    (1) Section 27-15-15;
    (2) Section 27-15-24;
    (3) Section 27-15-25;
    (4) Section 27-15-29; and
    (5) Section 27-16-16. (Acts 1971, No. 407, p. 707, § 406.)

§ 27-17-16. Valuation of life insurance reserve liabilities for burial insurance policies; increase in amount of insurance; minimum standards for valuation; notice to commissioner as to change in valuation standards; increase in retail value, nonforfeiture value, and cash surrender value; construction with other laws.

(a) Except as hereinafter provided, any authorized insurer who issues or has heretofore issued "burial insurance" in this state shall value the life insurance reserve liabilities for such policies (hereinafter "burial reserves") in accordance with the provisions of section 27-36-7.

(b) An insurer shall increase the amount of insurance on which its burial reserves are based, not to exceed the retail value of such benefits as stated in the policies, when appropriate to reflect an increase in the costs to the insurer of providing the policy benefits. When an insurer shall increase the amount of insurance for this purpose, it shall be permitted to change the assumed interest rate and the valuation mortality table for computing such reserves, provided that the resulting reserves after such increase in amount of insurance and change in assumed interest rate or valuation mortality table, or both, shall not be less than the reserves before such changes, and provided further that the reserves shall not be less than those calculated using the minimum standards set forth below.

(c) The minimum standards for valuation of burial reserves under this chapter shall be:

(1) An assumed interest rate not exceeding six percent per annum;

(2) The commissioners 1961 standard industrial mortality table or any industrial mortality table, adopted after 1980 by the National Association of Insurance Commissioners, that is approved by the commissioner for use in determining the minimum standard of valuation for such policies; and

(3) The commissioners reserve valuation method as defined by section 27-36-7(e), as may be amended from time to time.

(d) Prior to the filing date of the annual statement for the year in which the insurer intends to change the assumed interest rate or the valuation mortality tables, or both, used in the valuation of burial reserves as permitted under this chapter, the insurer shall communicate in writing to the commissioner the valuation standards to be used in such calculation. The insurer shall as to each block of business specify the interest rate, mortality table, valuation method, and amount of insurance to be used in the reserve calculation. "Block of business" shall mean a logical and identifiable grouping of policies as specified by the insurer in its written notice to the commissioner.

(e) Nothing in this chapter shall be construed as authorizing or requiring an increase in the retail value of the policies or in the nonforfeiture values, including the cash surrender values of subject burial insurance policies.

(f) To the extent that other laws or parts of laws may be construed as being applicable to the calculation of burial reserves, the provisions of this chapter shall take precedence over and supersede said provisions to the extent necessary to effectuate the intent of this chapter. (Acts 1984, No. 84-326, p. 746.)

CHAPTER 18.

GROUP LIFE INSURANCE.

Sec.
27-18-1. Applicability of chapter.
27-18-2. Policy provisions — Generally.
27-18-3. Same — Grace period.
27-18-4. Same — Incontestability.
27-18-5. Same — Copy of application; representations; statements as evidence.
27-18-6. Same — Insurability.
27-18-7. Same — Adjustment of premiums and/or benefits.
27-18-8. Same — Furnishing of statement to debtors.

Sec.
27-18-9. Same — Payment of benefits.
27-18-10. Same — Individual certificates.
27-18-11. Same — Conversion — Termination of eligibility.
27-18-12. Same — Same — Termination of policy.
27-18-13. Same — Same — Death during conversion period.
27-18-14. Notice as to conversion rights.
27-18-15. Employee life insurance.
27-18-16. Assignment of rights and benefits under group policies.

Cited in Moses v. American Home Assurance Co., 376 So. 2d 656 (Ala. 1979).

Collateral references. — Conflict of laws as to group insurance. 72 ALR2d 695.

44 Am. Jur. 2d, Insurance, §§ 1868-1896.

§ 27-18-1. Applicability of chapter.

This chapter applies only as to group life insurance contracts hereafter issued and does not apply as to group life insurance contracts heretofore issued or to any amendment or renewal of such heretofore issued contracts. (Acts 1971, No. 407, p. 707, § 407.)

Cited in Moses v. American Home Assurance Co., 376 So. 2d 656 (Ala. 1979).

§ 27-18-2. Poiicy provisions — Generally.

No policy of group life insurance shall be delivered in this state unless it contains in substance the applicable provisions set forth in sections 27-18-3 through 27-18-13, or provisions which in the opinion of the commissioner are more favorable to the persons insured or at least as favorable to the persons insured and more favorable to the policyholder; except, however, that:

(1) Sections 27-18-9 and 27-18-13 inclusive shall not apply to policies issued to a creditor to insure debtors of such creditor;

(2) The standard provisions required for individual life insurance policies shall not apply to group life insurance policies; and

(3) If the group life insurance policy is on a plan of insurance other than the term plan, it shall contain a nonforfeiture provision, or provisions, which, in the opinion of the commissioner, is, or are, equitable to the insured persons and to the policyholder, but nothing in this section shall be construed to require that group life insurance policies contain the same nonforfeiture provisions as are required for individual life insurance policies. (Acts 1971, No. 407, p. 707, § 408.)

§ 27-18-3. Same — Grace period.

The group life insurance policy shall contain a provision that the policyholder is entitled to a grace period of not less than 30 days for the payment of any premium due except the first, during which grace period the death benefit coverage shall continue in force unless the policyholder shall have given the insurer written notice of discontinuance in advance of the date of discontinuance and in accordance with the terms of the policy. The policy may provide that the policyholder shall be liable to the insurer for the payment of a pro rata premium for the time the policy was in force during such grace period. (Acts 1971, No. 407, p. 707, § 409.)

Collateral references. — 44 C.J.S., Insurance, §§ 255, n. 16, 329. 45 C.J.S., Insurance, § 473(5).

43 Am. Jur. 2d, Insurance, § 548. 44 Am. Jur. 2d, Insurance, § 1890.

Receipt of check for insurance premium as preventing forfeiture for nonpayment. 50 ALR2d 630.

Termination of employee's individual coverage under group policy for nonpayment of premiums. 22 ALR4th 321.

§ 27-18-4. Same — Incontestability.

The group life insurance policy shall contain a provision that the validity of the policy shall not be contested, except for nonpayment of premium, after it has been in force for two years from its date of issue and that no statement made by any person insured under the policy relating to his insurability shall be used in contesting the validity of the insurance with respect to which such statement was made after such insurance has been in force prior to the contest for a period of two years during such person's lifetime nor unless it is contained in a written instrument signed by him. (Code 1940, T. 28, § 7; Acts 1967, No. 181, p. 543; Acts 1971, No. 407, p. 707, § 410.)

Collateral references. — 45 C.J.S., Insurance, §§ 747, 751.

43 Am. Jur. 2d, Insurance, § 1155 et seq.

Incontestable clause as applicable to suit to reform insurance policy. 7 ALR2d 504.

What amounts to contest within contemplation of incontestable clause. 95 ALR2d 420.

Misrepresentation as to employer-employee relationship as within incontestability clause of group insurance. 26 ALR3d 632.

§ 27-18-5. Same — Copy of application; representations; statements as evidence.

The group life insurance policy shall contain a provision that a copy of the application, if any, of the policyholder shall be attached to the policy when issued, that all statements made by the policyholder or by the persons insured shall be deemed representations and not warranties and that no statement made by any person insured shall be used in any contest unless a copy of the instrument containing the statement is or has been furnished to such person or to his beneficiary. (Code 1940, T. 28, § 6; Acts 1971, No. 407, p. 707, § 411.)

Effect of misdescription of beneficiary. — It is immaterial that the decedent incorrectly named the beneficiary as his "aunt" on the enrollment card. This misdescription does not act as a fraud by the decedent, nor has it any effect on the right of the beneficiary to receive the proceeds. Such a description is a representation, not a warranty. Outling v. Young, 398 So. 2d 256 (Ala. 1981).

Collateral references. — 44 C.J.S., Insurance, § 232.

Advertising of group insurance: waiver or estoppel on basis of statements in promotional or explanatory literature issued to insureds. 36 ALR3d 541.

Failure to disclose terminal illness as basis for life insurer's avoidance of high-risk, high-premium policy requiring no health warranties or proof of insurability. 42 ALR4th 158.

§ 27-18-6. Same — Insurability.

The group life insurance policy shall contain a provision setting forth the conditions, if any, under which the insurer reserves the right to require a person eligible for insurance to furnish evidence of individual insurability, satisfactory to the insurer as a condition to part or all of his coverage. (Acts 1971, No. 407, p. 707, § 412.)

Collateral references. — 44 C.J.S., Insurance, § 238.

§ 27-18-7. Same — Adjustment of premiums and/or benefits.

The group life insurance policy shall contain a provision specifying an equitable adjustment of premiums or of benefits, or of both, to be made in the event the age of a person insured has been misstated, such provision to contain a clear statement of the method of adjustment to be used. (Acts 1971, No. 407, p. 707, § 413.)

Collateral references. — 45 C.J.S., Insurance, § 596.

§ 27-18-8. Same — Furnishing of statement to debtors.

In the case of a policy issued to a creditor to insure debtors of such creditor, there shall be a provision that the insurer will furnish to the policyholder for delivery to each debtor insured under the policy a form which will contain a statement that the life of the debtor is insured under the policy and that any death benefit paid thereunder by reason of his death shall be applied to reduce or extinguish the indebtedness. (Acts 1971, No. 407, p. 707, § 414.)

§ 27-18-9. Same — Payment of benefits.

The group life insurance policy shall contain a provision that any sum becoming due by reason of the death of the person insured shall be payable to the beneficiary designated by the person insured, subject to the provisions of the policy in the event there is no designated beneficiary as to all, or any part, of such sum living at the death of the person insured, and subject to any right reserved by the insurer in the policy and set forth in the certificate to pay at its option a part of such sum not exceeding $500.00 to any person appearing to the insurer to be equitably entitled thereto by reason of having incurred funeral or other expenses incident to the last illness or death of the person insured. (Acts 1971, No. 407, p. 707, § 415.)

§ 27-18-10. Same — Individual certificates.

The group life insurance policy shall contain a provision that the insurer will issue to the policyholder for delivery to each person insured an individual certificate setting forth a statement as to the insurance protection to which he is entitled, to whom the insurance benefits are payable and the rights and conditions set forth in sections 27-18-11, 27-18-12 and 27-18-13. (Acts 1971, No. 407, p. 707, § 416.)

Cited in Moses v. American Home Assurance Co., 376 So. 2d 656 (Ala. 1979).

§ 27-18-11. Same — Conversion — Termination of eligibility.

The group life insurance policy shall contain a provision that if the insurance, or any portion of it, on a person covered under the policy ceases because of termination of employment or of membership in the class, or classes, eligible for coverage under the policy, such person shall be entitled to have issued to him by the insurer, without evidence of insurability, an individual policy of life insurance without disability or other supplementary benefits, provided application for the individual policy shall be made and the first premium paid to the insurer within 31 days after such termination and provided, further, that:

(1) The individual policy shall, at the option of such person, be on any one of the forms, except term insurance, then customarily issued by the insurer at the age and for the amount applied for;

(2) The individual policy shall be in an amount not in excess of the amount of life insurance which ceases because of such termination less the amount of any life insurance for which such person is, or becomes, eligible under any other group policy within 31 days after such termination, provided that any amount of insurance which shall have matured on, or before, the date of such termination as an endowment payable to the person insured, whether in one sum, or in installments or in the form of an annuity shall not, for the purposes of this provision, be included in the amount which is considered to cease because of such termination; and

(3) The premium on the individual policy shall be at the insurer's then customary rate applicable to the form and amount of the individual policy, to the class of risk to which such person then belongs and to his age attained on the effective date of the individual policy. (Acts 1971, No. 407, p. 707, § 417.)

Collateral references. — 43 Am. Jur. 2d, Insurance, § 388.

Group insurance: construction, application, and effect of policy provision extending conversion privilege to employee after termination of employment. 32 ALR4th 1037.

§ 27-18-12. Same — Same — Termination of policy.

The group life insurance policy shall contain a provision that if the group policy terminates, or is amended so as to terminate the insurance of any class of insured persons, every person insured thereunder at the date of such termination whose insurance terminates and who has been so insured for at least five years prior to such termination date shall be entitled to have issued to him by the insurer an individual policy of life insurance, subject to the same conditions and limitations as are provided by section 27-18-11; except, that the group policy may provide that the amount of such individual policy shall not exceed the smaller of:

(1) The amount of the person's life insurance protection ceasing because of the termination or amendment of the group policy, less the amount of any life insurance for which he is, or becomes, eligible under any group policy issued or reinstated by the same or another insurer, within 31 days after such termination; and

(2) $2,000.00. (Acts 1971, No. 407, p. 707, § 418.)

Collateral references. — 43 Am. Jur. 2d, Insurance, § 388.

Group insurance: construction, application, and effect of policy provision extending conversion privilege to employee after termination of employment. 32 ALR4th 1037.

§ 27-18-13. Same — Same — Death during conversion period.

The group life insurance policy shall contain a provision that if a person insured under the policy dies during the period within which he would have been entitled to have an individual policy issued to him in accordance with sections 27-18-11 and 27-18-12 and before such an individual policy shall have become effective, the amount of life insurance which he would have been entitled to have issued to him under such individual policy shall be payable as a claim under the group policy, whether or not application for the individual policy or the payment of the first premium therefor has been made. (Acts 1971, No. 407, p. 707, § 419.)

Collateral references. — Group insurance: construction, application, and effect of policy provision extending conversion privilege to employee after termination of employment. 32 ALR4th 1037.

§ 27-18-14. Notice as to conversion rights.

If any individual insured under a group life insurance policy hereafter delivered in this state becomes entitled under the terms of such policy to have an individual policy of life insurance issued to him without evidence of insurability, subject to making of application and payment of the first premium within the period specified in such policy, and if such individual is not given notice of the existence of such right at least 15 days prior to the expiration date of such period, then, in such event, the individual shall have an additional period within which to exercise such right, but nothing contained in this section shall be construed to continue any insurance beyond the period provided in such policy. This additional period shall expire 15 days next after the individual is given such notice, but in no event shall such additional period extend beyond 60 days next after the expiration date of the period provided in such policy. Written notice presented to the individual or mailed by the policyholder to the last known address of the individual or mailed by the insurer to the last known address of the individual as furnished by the policyholder shall constitute notice for the purpose of this section. (Acts 1971, No. 407, p. 707, § 420.)

Collateral references. — Group insurance: construction, application, and effect of policy provision extending conversion privilege to employee after termination of employment. 32 ALR4th 1037.

§ 27-18-15. Employee life insurance.

"Employee life insurance" is that plan of life insurance, other than salary savings life insurance or pension trust insurance and annuities, under which individual policies are issued to the employees of any employer and where such policies are issued on the lives of not less than three employees at date of issue. Premiums for such policies shall be paid by the employer or the trustee of a fund established by the employer either wholly from the employer's funds, or funds contributed by him, or partly from such funds and partly from funds contributed by the insured employees or from funds contributed wholly by the insured employees. (Acts 1971, No. 407, p. 707, § 421.)

§ 27-18-16. Assignment of rights and benefits under group policies.

Any person insured under a group insurance policy may, in accordance with section 27-14-21 and pursuant to the terms of such policy or an arrangement among the insured, the group policyholder and the insurer, make an assignment of the rights and benefits conferred by any provision of such policy or by law, including specifically, but not by way of limitation, the right to have issued to the insured an individual policy arising from conversion or otherwise and the right to name a beneficiary. Any assignment permitted in this section, whether made before or after January 1, 1972, shall be valid for the purpose of vesting in the assignee all such rights and benefits so assigned

273

and shall entitle the insurer to deal with the assignee as the owner of all rights and benefits conferred on the insured under the policy in accordance with the terms of the assignment without prejudice to the insurer on account of any payment it may make or any individual policy it may issue arising from conversion prior to receipt at its home office of written notice of such assignment. This section acknowledges, declares and codifies the right of assignment of interest under like insurance policies existing prior to the enactment of this title. (Acts 1971, No. 407, p. 707, § 421.1.)

Collateral references. — 45 C.J.S., Insurance, §§ 410-415.

CHAPTER 19.

DISABILITY INSURANCE POLICIES.

Article 1.

General Provisions.

Sec.
27-19-1. Applicability of article.
27-19-2. Scope and format of policy.
27-19-3. Mandatory policy provisions — Generally.
27-19-4. Same — Entire contract; changes.
27-19-5. Same — Time limit on certain defenses.
27-19-6. Same — Grace period.
27-19-7. Same — Reinstatement.
27-19-8. Same — Notice of claim; notice of disability continuance.
27-19-9. Same — Claim forms.
27-19-10. Same — Proofs of loss.
27-19-11. Same — Time of payment of claims.
27-19-12. Same — Payment of claims.
27-19-13. Same — Physical examination and autopsy.
27-19-14. Same — Legal actions.
27-19-15. Same — Change of beneficiary.
27-19-16. Optional policy provisions — Generally.
27-19-17. Same — Change of occupation.
27-19-18. Same — Misstatement of age.
27-19-19. Same — Other insurance in this insurer.
27-19-20. Same — Insurance with other insurers — Expense-incurred benefits.
27-19-21. Same — Same — Other benefits.
27-19-22. Same — Relation of earnings to insurance.
27-19-23. Same — Unpaid premiums.
27-19-24. Same — Conformity with state statutes.
27-19-25. Same — Illegal occupation.
27-19-26. Same — Intoxicants and narcotics.
27-19-27. Order of provisions in policy.
27-19-28. Exclusion of hospitalization benefits for mental patients in tax-supported institutions.

Sec.
27-19-29. Ownership in person other than insured.
27-19-30. Provisions of other jurisdictions.
27-19-31. Renewability.
27-19-32. Examination and return of policy.
27-19-33. Addition of endorsements or riders to existing policies.
27-19-34. Compliance with article by rider or endorsement.
27-19-35. Construction of policy provisions.
27-19-36. Age limit or date for termination of coverage.
27-19-37. Disability insurance on franchise plan.
27-19-38. Coverage of newly born children in health insurance policies.
27-19-39. Policies, etc., providing for reimbursement for visual service.

Article 2.

Medicare Supplement Policy Minimum Standards.

27-19-50. Short title.
27-19-51. Purpose of article.
27-19-52. Definitions.
27-19-53. Standards for policy provisions generally; policy provisions as to coverage of pre-existing conditions.
27-19-54. Minimum standards for benefits generally.
27-19-55. Standards for loss ratios.
27-19-56. Requirements as to provision in policy of outline of coverage and information relating to replacement of disability policies, subscriber contracts, etc.
27-19-57. Inclusion in policy of notice of right to return policy and receive refund of premium.
27-19-58. Applicability of provisions of title to regulations promulgated pursuant to article.

Cross references. — As to group and blanket disability insurance, see § 27-20-1 et seq.

Purpose of former Code 1940, Title 28, chapter 17. — By the former chapter the legislature sought to provide for uniform individual accident and sickness policy provisions in accident and sickness insurance policies.

National Sec. Ins. Co. v. Freeman, 281 Ala. 152, 199 So. 2d 851 (1967).

Collateral references. — Liability insurance coverage as extending to liability for punitive or exemplary damages. 16 ALR4th 11.

ARTICLE 1.

GENERAL PROVISIONS.

§ 27-19-1. Applicability of article.

Nothing in this article shall apply to or affect:

(1) Any policy of liability or workmen's compensation insurance, with or without supplementary expense coverage therein;

(2) Any group or blanket policy;

(3) Life insurance, endowment or annuity contracts, or contracts supplemental thereto which contain only such provisions relating to disability insurance as:

 a. Provide additional benefits in case of death or dismemberment or loss of sight by accident; or

 b. Operate to safeguard such contracts against lapse or to give a special surrender value, or special benefit or an annuity in the event that the insured or annuitant becomes totally and permanently disabled, as defined by the contract or supplemental contract;

(4) Reinsurance; or

(5) Industrial insurance, which is disability insurance issued under policies sold on a debit basis, bearing the words "industrial policy" imprinted on the face of the policy as part of the descriptive matter, and with premiums payable monthly or more often. (Acts 1953, No. 193, p. 247, § 8; Acts 1957, No. 597, p. 834; Acts 1971, No. 407, p. 707, § 422.)

§ 27-19-2. Scope and format of policy.

No policy of disability insurance shall be delivered, or issued for delivery, to any person in this state unless it otherwise complies with this title and complies with the following:

(1) The entire money and other considerations therefor shall be expressed therein;

(2) The time when the insurance takes effect and terminates shall be expressed therein;

(3) It shall purport to insure only one person, except that a policy may insure, originally or by subsequent amendment, upon the application of an adult member of the family, who shall be deemed the policyholder, any two or more eligible members of that family, including husband, wife, dependent children or any children under a specified age and any other person dependent upon the policyholder;

(4) The style, arrangement and overall appearance of the policy shall give no undue prominence to any portion of the text, and every printed portion of the text of the policy and of any endorsements or attached papers shall be plainly printed in lightfaced type of a style in general use, the size of which shall be uniform and not less than 10 point with a lower case

unspaced alphabet length not less than 120 point; the "text" shall include all printed matter except the name and address of the insurer, name or title of the policy, the brief description, if any, and captions and subcaptions;

(5) The exceptions and reductions of indemnity shall be set forth in the policy and, other than those contained in sections 27-19-4 through 27-19-26, shall be printed, at the insurer's option, either included with the benefit provision to which they apply or under an appropriate caption such as "Exceptions," or "Exceptions and Reductions;" except, that if an exception or reduction specifically applies only to a particular benefit of the policy, a statement of such exception or reduction shall be included with the benefit provision to which it applies;

(6) Each such form, including riders and endorsements, shall be identified by a form number in the lower left-hand corner of the first page thereof; and

(7) The policy shall contain no provision purporting to make any portion of the charter, rules, constitution or bylaws of the insurer a part of the policy unless such portion is set forth in full in the policy, except in the case of the incorporation of, or reference to, a statement of rates or classification of risks or short-rate table filed with the commissioner. (Acts 1953, No. 193, p. 247, § 2; Acts 1957, No. 597, p. 834; Acts 1971, No. 407, p. 707, § 423.)

Collateral references. — 44 C.J.S., Insurance, § 12.
Printing: validity and construction of statutes relating to style or prominence with which provisions must be printed in insurance policy. 36 ALR3d 464.

§ 27-19-3. Mandatory policy provisions — Generally.

(a) Except as provided in subsection (b) of this section, each such policy delivered, or issued for delivery, to any person in this state shall contain the provisions specified in sections 27-19-4 through 27-19-15, in the words in which the same appear; except, that the insurer may, at its option, substitute for one or more of such provisions corresponding provisions of different wording approved by the commissioner which are in each instance not less favorable in any respect to the insured or the beneficiary. Each such provision shall be preceded individually by the applicable caption shown or, at the option of the insurer, by such appropriate individual or group captions or subcaptions as the commissioner may approve.

(b) If any such provision is, in whole or in part, inapplicable to, or inconsistent with, the coverage provided by a particular form of policy, the insurer, with the approval of the commissioner, shall omit from such policy any inapplicable provision, or part of a provision, and shall modify any inconsistent provision, or part of a provision, in such manner as to make the provision as contained in the policy consistent with the coverage provided by the policy. (Acts 1953, No. 193, p. 247, § 3; Acts 1957, No. 597, p. 834; Acts 1971, No. 407, p. 707, § 424.)

§ 27-19-4. Same — Entire contract; changes.

There shall be a provision as follows:

"Entire Contract; Changes: This policy, including the endorsements and the attached papers, if any, constitutes the entire contract of insurance. No change in this policy shall be valid until approved by an executive officer of the insurer and unless such approval be endorsed hereon or attached hereto. No agent has authority to change this policy or to waive any of its provisions." (Acts 1953, No. 193, p. 247, § 3; Acts 1957, No. 597, p. 834; Acts 1971, No. 407, p. 707, § 425.)

§ 27-19-5. Same — Time limit on certain defenses.

There shall be a provision as follows:

"Time Limit on Certain Defenses: (1) After two years from the date of issue of this policy, no misstatements, except fraudulent misstatements, made by the applicant in the application for such policy shall be used to void the policy or to deny a claim for loss incurred or disability (as defined in the policy) commencing after the expiration of such two-year period."

(The foregoing policy provision shall not be so construed as to affect any legal requirement for avoidance of a policy or denial of a claim during such initial two-year period nor to limit the application of sections 27-19-17 through 27-19-21 in the event of misstatement with respect to age or occupation or other insurance.)

(A policy which the insured has the right to continue in force subject to its terms by the timely payment of premium:

(1) Until at least age 50; or

(2) In the case of a policy issued after age 44, for at least five years from its date of issue may contain in lieu of the foregoing the following provision, from which the clause in parentheses may be omitted at the insurer's option, under the caption "Incontestable":

"After this policy has been in force for a period of two years during the lifetime of the insured, excluding any period during which the insured is disabled, it shall become incontestable as to the statements contained in the application.)"

"(2) No claim for loss incurred or disability (as defined in the policy) commencing after two years from the date of issue of this policy shall be reduced or denied on the ground that a disease or physical condition not excluded from coverage by name or specific description effective on the date of loss had existed prior to the effective date of coverage of this policy." (Acts 1953, No. 193, p. 247, § 3; Acts 1957, No. 597, p. 834; Acts 1971, No. 407, p. 707, § 426.)

Collateral references. — 43 Am. Jur. 2d, Insurance, § 1170.

§ 27-19-6. Same — Grace period.

There shall be a provision as follows:

"Grace Period: A grace period of ... (insert a number not less than '7' for weekly premium policies, '10' for monthly premium policies and '31' for all other policies) days will be granted for the payment of each premium falling due after the first premium, during which grace period the policy shall continue in force."

A policy in which the insurer reserves the right to refuse any renewal shall have, at the beginning of the above provision,

"Unless not less than 30 days prior to the premium due date the insurer has delivered to the insured or has mailed to his last address as shown by the records of the insurer written notice of its intention not to renew this policy beyond the period for which the premium has been accepted." (Acts 1953, No. 193, p. 247, § 3; Acts 1957, No. 597, p. 834; Acts 1971, No. 407, p. 707, § 427.)

First premium not subject to grace period. — The statutory definition in § 27-19-3 and this section clearly indicates that a first premium is not subject to nor a part of the "grace period." Blue Cross-Blue Shield v. Caudle, 404 So. 2d 684 (Ala. Civ. App. 1981).

Collateral references. — 44 C.J.S., Insurance, § 255, n. 16. 45 C.J.S., Insurance, §§ 473(5), 625.

43 Am. Jur. 2d, Insurance, § 548.

Receipt of check for insurance premium as preventing forfeiture for nonpayment. 50 ALR2d 630.

Dividends as preventing lapse of policy for nonpayment of premiums. 8 ALR3d 862.

Cancellation: remedies and measure of damages for wrongful cancellation of life, health, and accident insurance. 34 ALR3d 245.

§ 27-19-7. Same — Reinstatement.

There shall be a provision as follows:

"Reinstatement: If any renewal premium be not paid within the time granted the insured for payment, a subsequent acceptance of premium by the insurer or by any agent duly authorized by the insurer to accept such premium, without requiring in connection therewith an application for reinstatement, shall reinstate the policy; provided, however, that if the insurer or such agent requires an application for reinstatement and issues a conditional receipt for the premium tendered, the policy will be reinstated upon approval of such application by the insurer or, lacking such approval, upon the forty-fifth day following the date of such conditional receipt unless the insurer has previously notified the insured in writing of its disapproval of such application. The reinstated policy shall cover only loss resulting from such accidental injury as may be sustained after the date of reinstatement and loss due to such sickness as may begin more than 10 days after such date. In all other respects, the insured and the insurer shall have the same rights thereunder as they had under the policy immediately before the due date of the defaulted premium, subject to any provisions endorsed hereon or attached hereto in connection with the reinstatement. Any premium accepted in connection with a reinstatement shall be applied to a period for which premium has not been previously paid, but not to any period more than 60 days prior to the date of reinstatement."

The last sentence of the above provision may be omitted from any policy which the insured has the right to continue in force subject to its terms by the timely payment of premiums:

(1) Until at least age 50; or

(2) In the case of a policy issued after age 44, for at least five years from its date of issue. (Acts 1953, No. 193, p. 247, § 3; Acts 1957, No. 597, p. 834; Acts 1971, No. 407, p. 707, § 428.)

Collateral references. — 45 C.J.S., Insurance, §§ 667-671.

43 Am. Jur. 2d, Insurance, §§ 389-396.

Conflict of laws: choice of law in construction of insurance policy originally governed by law of one state as affected by reinstatement in different state. 3 ALR3d 646.

Incontestable clause as affected by reinstatement of policy. 23 ALR3d 743.

§ 27-19-8. Same — Notice of claim; notice of disability continuance.

There shall be a provision as follows:

"Notice of Claim: Written notice of claim must be given to the insurer within 20 days after the occurrence or commencement of any loss covered by the policy, or as soon thereafter as is reasonably possible. Notice given by, or on behalf of, the insured or the beneficiary to the insurer at ... (insert the location of such office as the insurer may designate for the purpose), or to any authorized agent of the insurer, with information sufficient to identify the insured, shall be deemed notice to the insurer."

In a policy providing a loss-of-time benefit which may be payable for at least two years, an insurer may, at its option, insert the following between the first and second sentences of the above provision:

"Subject to the qualifications set forth below, if the insured suffers loss of time on account of disability for which indemnity may be payable for at least two years, he shall, at least once in every six months after having given notice of the claim, give to the insurer notice of continuance of the disability, except in the event of legal incapacity. The period of six months following any filing of proof by the insured or any payment by the insurer on account of such claim or any denial of liability, in whole or in part, by the insurer shall be excluded in applying this provision. Delay in the giving of such notice shall not impair the insured's right to any indemnity which would otherwise have accrued during the period of six months preceding the date on which such notice is actually given." (Acts 1953, No. 193, p. 247, § 3; Acts 1957, No. 597, p. 834; Acts 1971, No. 407, p. 707, § 429.)

Collateral references. — 45 C.J.S., Insurance, §§ 1066, 1067.
44 Am. Jur. 2d, Insurance, § 1454 et seq.
Disability insurance or provision: clause requiring notice of claim within specified time or as soon as reasonably possible, or the like. 17 ALR3d 530.

§ 27-19-9. Same — Claim forms.

There shall be a provision as follows:

"Claim Forms: The insurer, upon receipt of a notice of claim, will furnish to the claimant such forms as are usually furnished by it for filing proofs of loss. If such forms are not furnished within 15 days after the giving of such notice, the claimant shall be deemed to have complied with the requirements of this policy as to proof of loss upon submitting, within the time fixed in the policy for filing proofs of loss, written proof covering the occurrence, the character and the extent of the loss for which claim is made." (Acts 1953, No. 193, p. 247, § 3; Acts 1957, No. 597, p. 834; Acts 1971, No. 407, p. 707, § 430.)

§ 27-19-10. Same — Proofs of loss.

There shall be a provision as follows:

"Proofs of Loss: Written proof of loss must be furnished to the insurer at its said office in case of claim for loss for which this policy provides any periodic payment contingent upon continuing loss within 90 days after the termination of the period for which the insurer is liable and, in case of claim for any other loss, within 90 days after the date of such loss. Failure to furnish such proof within the time required shall not invalidate nor reduce any claim if it was not reasonably possible to give proof within such time, provided such proof is furnished as soon as reasonably possible and in no event, except in the absence of legal capacity, later than one year from the time proof is otherwise required." (Acts 1953, No. 193, p. 247, § 3; Acts 1957, No. 597, p. 834; Acts 1971, No. 407, p. 707, § 431.)

Collateral references. — 44 Am. Jur. 2d, Insurance, § 1454 et seq.

§ 27-19-11. Same — Time of payment of claims.

There shall be a provision as follows:

"Time of Payment of Claims: Indemnities payable under this policy for any loss, other than loss for which this policy provides periodic payment, will be paid immediately upon receipt of due written proof of such loss. Subject to due written proof of loss, all accrued indemnities for loss for which this policy provides periodic payment will be paid .... (insert period for payment which must not be less frequently than monthly) and any balance remaining unpaid upon the termination of liability will be paid immediately upon receipt of due written proof." (Acts 1953, No. 193, p. 247, § 3; Acts 1957, No. 597, p. 834; Acts 1971, No. 407, p. 707, § 432.)

§ 27-19-12. Same — Payment of claims.

There shall be a provision as follows:

"Payment of Claims: Indemnity for loss of life will be payable in accordance with the beneficiary designation and the provisions respecting such payment which may be prescribed herein and effective at the time of payment. If no such designation or provision is then effective, such indemnity shall be payable to the estate of the insured. Any other accrued indemnities unpaid at the insured's death may, at the option of the insurer, be paid either to such beneficiary or to such estate. All other indemnities will be payable to the insured."

The following provisions, or either of them, may be included with the foregoing provision at the option of the insurer:

"If any indemnity of this policy shall be payable to the estate of the insured or to an insured or beneficiary who is a minor or otherwise not competent to give a valid release, the insurer may pay such indemnity, up to an amount not exceeding $.... (insert an amount which shall not exceed $1,000.00), to any relative by blood or connection by marriage of the insured or beneficiary who is deemed by the insurer to be equitably entitled thereto. Any payment made by the insurer in good faith pursuant to this provision shall fully discharge the insurer to the extent of such payment."

"Subject to any written direction of the insured in the application or otherwise, all, or a portion of any, indemnities provided by this policy on account of hospital, nursing, medical or surgical services may, at the insurer's option and unless the insured requests otherwise in writing not later than the time of filing proof of such loss, be paid directly to the hospital or person rendering such services; but it is not required that the service be rendered by a particular hospital or person." (Acts 1953, No. 193, p. 247, § 3; Acts 1957, No. 597, p. 834; Acts 1971, No. 407, p. 707, § 433.)

§ 27-19-13. Same — Physical examination and autopsy.

There shall be a provision as follows:

"Physical Examinations and Autopsy: The insurer at its own expense shall have the right and opportunity to examine the person of the insured when, and as often as, it may reasonably require during the pendency of a claim hereunder and to make an autopsy in case of death where it is not forbidden by law." (Acts 1953, No. 193, p. 247, § 3; Acts 1957, No. 597, p. 834; Acts 1971, No. 407, p. 707, § 434.)

Collateral references. — 46 C.J.S., Insurance, § 1363.

Physical examination: validity, construction, and effect of provisions, in insurance policies allowing disability or accident benefits, which require insured to submit to physical examination. 5 ALR3d 929.

Autopsy: time for making autopsy or demand therefor under insurance policy. 30 ALR2d 837.

§ 27-19-14. Same — Legal actions.

There shall be a provision as follows:

"Legal Actions: No action shall be brought to recover on this policy prior to the expiration of 60 days after written proof of loss has been furnished in accordance with the requirements of this policy. No such action shall be brought after the expiration of three years after the time written proof of loss is required to be furnished." (Acts 1953, No. 193, p. 247, § 3; Acts 1957, No. 597, p. 834; Acts 1971, No. 407, p. 707, § 435.)

Collateral references. — 45 C.J.S., Insurance, § 751.

§ 27-19-15. Same — Change of beneficiary.

There shall be a provision as follows:

"Change of Beneficiary: Unless the insured makes an irrevocable designation of beneficiary, the right to change a beneficiary is reserved to the insured and the consent of the beneficiary, or beneficiaries, shall not be requisite to surrender or assignment of this policy or to any change of beneficiary, or beneficiaries, or to any other changes in this policy."

(The first clause of this provision, relating to the irrevocable designation of beneficiary, may be omitted at the insurer's option.) (Acts 1953, No. 193, p. 247, § 3; Acts 1957, No. 597, p. 834; Acts 1971, No. 407, p. 707, § 436.)

Collateral references. — 44 Am. Jur. 2d, Insurance, § 1776 et seq.

§ 27-19-16. Optional policy provisions — Generally.

Except as provided in subsection (b) of section 27-19-3, no such policy delivered, or issued for delivery, to any person in this state shall contain provisions respecting the matters set forth in sections 27-19-17 through 27-19-26 unless such provisions are in the words in which the same appear in the applicable section; except, that the insurer may, at its option, use in lieu of any such provision a corresponding provision of different wording approved by the commissioner which is not less favorable in any respect to the insured or the beneficiary. Any such provision contained in the policy shall be preceded individually by the appropriate caption or, at the option of the insurer, by such appropriate individual, or group captions or subcaptions as the commissioner may approve. (Acts 1953, No. 193, p. 247, § 3; Acts 1957, No. 597, p. 834; Acts 1971, No. 407, p. 707, § 437.)

§ 27-19-17. Same — Change of occupation.

There may be a provision as follows:

"Change of Occupation: If the insured be injured or contract sickness after having changed his occupation to one classified by the insurer as more hazardous than that stated in this policy or while doing for compensation anything pertaining to an occupation so classified, the insurer will pay only such portion of the indemnities provided in this policy as the premium paid would have purchased at the rates and within the limits fixed by the insurer for such more hazardous occupation. If the insured changes his occupation to one classified by the insurer as less hazardous than that stated in this policy, the insurer, upon receipt of proof of such change of occupation, will reduce the premium rate accordingly, and will return the excess pro rata unearned premium from the date of change of occupation or from the policy anniversary date immediately preceding receipt of such proof, whichever is the more recent. In applying this provision, the classification of occupational risk and the premium rates shall be such as have been last filed by the insurer prior to the occurrence of the loss for which the insurer is liable or prior to date of proof of change in occupation with the state official having supervision of insurance in the state where the insured resided at the time this policy was issued; but if such filing was not required, then the classification of occupational risk and the premium rates shall be those last made effective by the insurer in such state prior to the occurrence of the loss or prior to the date of proof of change in occupation." (Acts 1953, No. 193, p. 247, § 3; Acts 1957, No. 597, p. 834; Acts 1971, No. 407, p. 707, § 438.)

Collateral references. — 45 C.J.S., Insurance, § 610.

43 Am. Jur. 2d, Insurance, § 804 et seq.

§ 27-19-18. Same — Misstatement of age.

There may be a provision as follows:

"Misstatement of Age: If the age of the insured has been misstated, all amounts payable under this policy shall be such as the premium paid would have purchased at the correct age." (Acts 1953, No. 193, p. 247, § 3; Acts 1957, No. 597, p. 834; Acts 1971, No. 407, p. 707, § 439.)

§ 27-19-19. Same — Other insurance in this insurer.

There may be a provision as follows:

"Other Insurance in This Insurer: If an accident or sickness or accident and sickness policy, or policies, previously issued by the insurer to the insured be in force concurrently herewith, making the aggregate indemnity for .... (insert type of coverage or coverages) in excess of $.... (insert maximum limit of indemnity or indemnities), the excess insurance shall be void and all premiums paid for such excess shall be returned to the insured or to his estate."

Or, in lieu thereof:

"Insurance effective at any one time on the insured under a like policy, or policies, in this insurer is limited to the one such policy elected by the insured, his beneficiary or his estate, as the case may be, and the insurer will return all premiums paid for all other such policies." (Acts 1953, No. 193, p. 247, § 3; Acts 1957, No. 597, p. 834; Acts 1971, No. 407, p. 707, § 440.)

§ 27-19-20. Same — Insurance with other insurers — Expense-incurred benefits.

(a) There may be a provision as follows:

"Insurance with Other Insurers: If there be other valid coverage, not with this insurer, providing benefits for the same loss on a provision of service basis or on an expense-incurred basis and of which this insurer has not been given written notice prior to the occurrence or commencement of loss, the only liability under any expense-incurred coverage of this policy shall be for such proportion of the loss as the amount which would otherwise have been payable hereunder plus the total of the like amounts under all such other valid coverages for the same loss of which this insurer had notice bears to the total like amounts under all valid coverages for such loss, and for the return of such portion of the premiums paid as shall exceed the pro rata portion for the amount so determined. For the purpose of applying this provision when other coverage is on a provision of service basis, the 'like amount' of such other coverage shall be taken as the amount which the services rendered would have cost in the absence of such coverage."

(b) If the foregoing policy provision is included in a policy which also contains the policy provision set out in section 27-19-21 there shall be added to the caption of the foregoing provision the phrase "—Expense-Incurred Benefits." The insurer may, at its option, include in this provision a definition of "other valid coverage," approved as to form by the commissioner, which definition shall be limited in subject matter to coverage provided by organizations subject to regulation by insurance law or by insurance authorities of this, or any other, state of the United States or any province of Canada, and by hospital or medical service organizations and to any other coverage the inclusion of which may be approved by the commissioner. In the absence of such definition, such term shall not include group insurance, automobile medical payments insurance or coverage provided by hospital, or medical service organizations, or by union welfare plans or employer or employee benefit organizations. For the purpose of applying the foregoing policy provision with respect to any insured, any amount of benefit provided for such insured pursuant to any compulsory benefit statute, including any workmen's compensation or employer's liability statute, whether provided by a governmental agency or otherwise, shall, in all cases, be deemed to be "other valid coverage" of which the insurer has had notice. In applying the foregoing policy provision, no third party liability coverage shall be included as "other valid coverage." (Acts 1953, No. 193, p. 247, § 3; Acts 1957, No. 597, p. 834; Acts 1971, No. 407, p. 707, § 441.)

Insurer not relieved of obligation by other insurance. — Where the insurer contracted that "all benefits provided herein will be paid to the insured or beneficiary in addition to workmen's compensation or any other insurance the insured may have," the fact that the insured was indemnified for the same loss by another insurance company did not relieve the insurer of its obligation to pay. Globe Life Ins. Co. v. Howard, 41 Ala. App. 621, 147 So. 2d 853 (1962), decided under Title 28, § 420, appearing in the 1940 Code.

Collateral references. — 44 Am. Jur. 2d, Insurance, § 1814.

§ 27-19-21. Same — Same — Other benefits.

(a) There may be a provision as follows:

"Insurance with Other Insurers: If there be other valid coverage, not with this insurer, providing benefits for the same loss on other than an expense-incurred basis and of which this insurer has not been given written notice prior to the occurrence or commencement of loss, the only liability for such benefits under this policy shall be for such proportion of the indemnities otherwise provided hereunder for such loss as the like indemnities of which the insurer had notice (including the indemnities under this policy) bear to the total amount of all like indemnities for such loss and for the return of such portion of the premium paid as shall exceed the pro rata portion for the indemnities thus determined."

(b) If the foregoing policy provision is included in a policy which also contains the policy provision set out in section 27-19-20, there shall be added to the caption of the foregoing provision the phrase "—Other Benefits." The insurer may, at its option, include in this provision a definition of "other valid coverage," approved as to form by the commissioner, which definition shall be limited in subject matter to coverage provided by organizations subject to regulation by insurance law or by insurance authorities of this, or any other, state of the United States or any province of Canada and to any other coverage the inclusion of which may be approved by the commissioner. In the absence of such definition, such term shall not include group insurance or benefits provided by union welfare plans, or by employer or employee benefit organizations. For the purpose of applying the foregoing policy provision with respect to any insured, any amount of benefit provided for such insured pursuant to any compulsory benefit statute, including any workmen's compensation or employer's liability statute, whether provided by a governmental agency or otherwise, shall, in all cases, be deemed to be "other valid coverage" of which the insurer has had notice. In applying the foregoing policy provision, no third party liability coverage shall be included as "other valid coverage." (Acts 1953, No. 193, p. 247, § 3; Acts 1957, No. 597, p. 834; Acts 1971, No. 407, p. 707, § 442.)

Collateral references. — 44 Am. Jur. 2d, Insurance, § 1814.

§ 27-19-22. Same — Relation of earnings to insurance.

(a) There may be a provision as follows:

"Relation of Earnings to Insurance: If the total monthly amount of loss of time benefits promised for the same loss under all valid loss of time coverage upon the insured, whether payable on a weekly or monthly basis, shall exceed the monthly earnings of the insured at the time disability commenced or his average monthly earnings for the period of two years immediately preceding a disability for which claim is made, whichever is the greater, the insurer will be liable only for such proportionate amount of such benefits under this policy as the amount of such monthly earnings or such average monthly earnings of the insured bears to the total amount of monthly benefits for the same loss under all such coverage upon the insured at the time such disability commences and for the return of such part of the premiums paid during such two years as shall exceed the pro rata amount of the premiums for the benefits actually paid hereunder; but this shall not operate to reduce the total monthly amount of benefits payable under all such coverage upon the insured below the sum of $200.00 or the sum of the monthly benefits specified in such coverages, whichever is the lesser, nor shall it operate to reduce benefits other than those payable for loss of time."

(b) The foregoing policy provision may be inserted only in a policy which the insured has the right to continue in force subject to its terms by the timely payment of premiums:

(1) Until at least age 50; or

(2) In the case of a policy issued after age 44, for at least five years from its date of issue.

The insurer may, at its option, include in this provision a definition of "valid loss of time coverage," approved as to form by the commissioner, which definition shall be limited in subject matter to coverage provided by governmental agencies or by organizations subject to regulation by insurance law or by insurance authorities of this, or any other, state of the United States or any province of Canada, or to any other coverage the inclusion of which may be approved by the commissioner or any combination of such coverages. In the absence of such definition, such term shall not include any coverage provided for such insured pursuant to any compulsory benefit statute including any workmen's compensation or employer's liability statute, or benefits provided by union welfare plans or by employer or employee benefit organizations. (Acts 1953, No. 193, p. 247, § 3; Acts 1957, No. 597, p. 834; Acts 1971, No. 407, p. 707, § 443.)

§ 27-19-23. Same — Unpaid premiums.

There may be a provision as follows:
"Unpaid Premiums: Upon the payment of a claim under this policy, any premium then due and unpaid or covered by any note or written order may be deducted therefrom." (Acts 1953, No. 193, p. 247, § 3; Acts 1957, No. 597, p. 834; Acts 1971, No. 407, p. 707, § 444.)

§ 27-19-24. Same — Conformity with state statutes.

There may be a provision as follows:
"Conformity with State Statutes: Any provision of this policy which, on its effective date, is in conflict with the statutes of the state in which the insured resides on such date is hereby amended to conform to the minimum requirements of such statutes." (Acts 1953, No. 193, p. 247, § 3; Acts 1957, No. 597, p. 834; Acts 1971, No. 407, p. 707, § 445.)

§ 27-19-25. Same — Illegal occupation.

There may be a provision as follows:
"Illegal Occupation: The insurer shall not be liable for any loss to which a contributing cause was the insured's commission of, or attempt to commit, a felony or to which a contributing cause was the insured's being engaged in an illegal occupation." (Acts 1953, No. 193, p. 247, § 3; Acts 1957, No. 597, p. 834; Acts 1971, No. 407, p. 707, § 446.)

§ 27-19-26. Same — Intoxicants and narcotics.

There may be a provision as follows:
"Intoxicants and Narcotics: The insurer shall not be liable for any loss sustained or contracted in consequence of the insured's being intoxicated or under the influence of any narcotic unless administered on the advice of a physician." (Acts 1953, No. 193, p. 247, § 3; Acts 1957, No. 597, p. 834; Acts 1971, No. 407, p. 707, § 447.)

Collateral references. — 43 Am. Jur. 2d, Insurance, §§ 812, 813.

§ 27-19-27. Order of provisions in policy.

The provisions which are the subject of sections 27-19-4 through 27-19-26, or any corresponding provisions which are used in lieu thereof in accordance with such sections, shall be printed in the consecutive order of the provisions in such sections or, at the option of the insurer, any such provision may appear as a unit in any part of the policy with other provisions to which it may be logically related, provided that the resulting policy shall not be, in whole or in part, unintelligible, uncertain, ambiguous, abstruse or likely to mislead a person to whom the policy is offered, delivered or issued. (Acts 1953, No. 193, p. 247, § 3; Acts 1957, No. 597, p. 834; Acts 1971, No. 407, p. 707, § 448.)

§ 27-19-28. Exclusion of hospitalization benefits for mental patients in tax-supported institutions.

(a) No policy of health, sickness or accident insurance delivered, or issued for delivery, in this state, including both individual and group policies, which provide coverage for psychiatric treatment or mental illness shall exclude hospitalization benefits for mental patients in tax-supported institutions of the state of Alabama, or any county or municipality thereof.

(b) The provisions of this section shall not apply to any policy of insurance in effect prior to September 20, 1971, nor shall the provisions of this section apply to any employee benefit plan providing hospital benefits for mental patients where such employee benefit plan is established by the employer and contributions to the plan are provided by the employer and the employee, or either of them, and such plan is not evidenced by individual, or group or blanket policies of health, sickness or accident insurance issued by an insurance company. (Acts 1971, No. 1871, p. 3052.)

§ 27-19-29. Ownership in person other than insured.

The word "insured," as used in this article, shall not be construed as preventing a person other than the insured with a proper insurable interest from making application for and owning a policy covering the insured or from being entitled under such a policy to any indemnities, benefits and rights provided therein. (Acts 1953, No. 193, p. 247, § 3; Acts 1957, No. 597, p. 834; Acts 1971, No. 407, p. 707, § 449.)

§ 27-19-30. Provisions of other jurisdictions.

(a) Any policy of a foreign or alien insurer, when delivered or issued for delivery to any person in this state, may contain any provision which is not less favorable to the insured or the beneficiary than the provisions of this article and which is prescribed or required by the law of the state or country under which the insurer is organized.

(b) Any policy of a domestic insurer may, when issued for delivery in any other state or country, contain any provision permitted or required by the laws of such other state or country. (Acts 1953, No. 193, p. 247, § 3; Acts 1957, No. 597, p. 834; Acts 1971, No. 407, p. 707, § 450.)

Collateral references. — 44 C.J.S., Insurance, §§ 50-54.

§ 27-19-31. Renewability.

(a) Every individual policy of insurance providing hospital, medical or surgical benefits in which an insurer reserves the right to refuse renewal on an individual basis shall provide, in substance, in a provision thereof, or in an endorsement thereon or in a rider attached thereto that, subject to the right to terminate the policy upon nonpayment of premium when due, such right to refuse renewal shall not be exercised before the renewal date occurring on, or after and nearest, each policy anniversary or, in the case of lapse and reinstatement, before the renewal date occurring on, or after and nearest, each anniversary of the last reinstatement and that any refusal of renewal shall be without prejudice to any claim originating while the policy is in force. Subject to the right to terminate for nonpayment of premium, the right to refuse renewal by an insurer shall only be exercised after having given the insured no less than 30 days' notice in writing of the intent not to renew.

(b) Every individual disability insurance policy which is subject to renewal at the option of the insurer shall so indicate in a prominently captioned statement on the first page of such policy. (Acts 1957, No. 597, p. 834; Acts 1971, No. 407, p. 707, § 451.)

Collateral references. — 44 C.J.S., Insurance, §§ 283-288.
43 Am. Jur. 2d, Insurance, §§ 379-387.

Insurer's denial of renewal of policy. 85 ALR2d 1410.

§ 27-19-32. Examination and return of policy.

Every individual disability insurance policy, except single premium nonrenewable policies or contracts, issued for delivery in the state of Alabama shall have printed thereon, or attached thereto, a notice stating in substance that the person to whom the policy is issued shall be permitted to return the policy within 10 days of its delivery to such purchaser and to have the premium paid refunded if, after examination of the policy, the purchaser is not satisfied with it for any reason. If a policyholder or purchaser, pursuant to such notice, returns the policy or contract to the insurer at its home or branch office or to the agent through whom it was purchased, it shall be void from the beginning and the parties shall be in the same position as if no policy or contract has been issued. (Acts 1957, No. 597, p. 834; Acts 1971, No. 407, p. 707, § 452.)

§ 27-19-33. Addition of endorsements or riders to existing policies.

Any insurer writing disability insurance policies may, with approval of the commissioner, add endorsements or riders to existing policies of such insurance, with or without increase in premium, provided there is shown separately on the endorsement or rider a stated premium charge for additional coverage. (Acts 1957, No. 597, p. 834; Acts 1971, No. 407, p. 707, § 453.)

Collateral references. — 44 C.J.S., Insurance, §§ 281, 282.

§ 27-19-34. Compliance with article by rider or endorsement.

The requirements of this article may be complied with by the insurer by attaching to the policy such rider or endorsement as may be necessary for the purpose. (Acts 1957, No. 597, p. 834; Acts 1971, No. 407, p. 707, § 454.)

§ 27-19-35. Construction of policy provisions.

(a) No policy provision which is not subject to this article shall make a policy, or any portion thereof, less favorable in any respect to the insured or the beneficiary than the provisions thereof which are subject to this article.

(b) A policy delivered, or issued for delivery, to any person in this state in violation of this article shall be held valid but shall be construed as provided in this article. When any provision in a policy subject to this article is in conflict with any provision of this article, the rights, duties and obligations of the insurer, the insured and the beneficiary shall be governed by the provisions of this article. (Acts 1953, No. 193, p. 247, § 4; Acts 1957, No. 597, p. 834; Acts 1971, No. 407, p. 707, § 455.)

Collateral references. — 44 C.J.S., Insurance, §§ 289-336.

Heart attack following exertion or exercise as within terms of accident provision of insurance policy. 1 ALR4th 1319.

What constitutes total disability within coverage of disability insurance policy issued to lawyer. 6 ALR4th 422.

§ 27-19-36. Age limit or date for termination of coverage.

If any such policy contains a provision establishing, as an age limit or otherwise, a date after which the coverage provided by the policy will not be effective and if such date falls within a period for which premium is accepted by the insurer or if the insurer accepts a premium after such date, the coverage provided by the policy will continue in force subject to any right of cancellation until the end of the period for which premium has been accepted. In the event the age of the insured has been misstated and if, according to the correct age of the insured, the coverage provided by the policy would not have become effective or would have ceased prior to the acceptance of such premium, or premiums, then the liability of the insurer shall be limited to the refund, upon request, of all premiums paid for the period not covered by the policy. (Acts 1953, No. 193, p. 247, § 7; Acts 1957, No. 597, p. 834; Acts 1971, No. 407, p. 707, § 456.)

Ineffective age restrictions in policy granting indemnity for accidental death. — Where an insurance policy granted indemnity for accidental death of the insured prior to attaining age 50, but the policy itself showed that the insured was 53 at the time the policy was issued and the company had accepted premiums on the policy, the age restrictions were ineffective. National Sec. Ins. Co. v. Freeman, 281 Ala. 152, 199 So. 2d 851 (1967), (decided under former Code 1940, T. 28, § 428).

§ 27-19-37. Disability insurance on franchise plan.

Disability insurance on a franchise plan is hereby declared to be that form of disability insurance issued to:

(1) Three or more employees of any corporation, copartnership or individual employer, or any governmental corporation, agency or department thereof; or

(2) Ten or more members, employees or employees of members of any trade or professional association, or of a labor union or of any other association having had an active existence for at least two years where such association or union has a constitution or bylaws and is formed in good faith for purposes other than that of obtaining insurance where such persons, with or without their dependents, are issued the same form of an individual policy varying only as to amounts and kinds of coverage applied for by such persons under an arrangement whereby the premiums on such policies may be paid to the insurer periodically by the employer, with or without payroll deductions, or by the association for its members or by some designated person acting on behalf of such employer or association or union. The term "employees" as used in this section may be deemed to include the officers, managers, employees and retired employees of the employer and the individual proprietor or partners if the employer is an individual proprietor or partnership. (Acts 1971, No. 407, p. 707, § 457.)

§ 27-19-38. Coverage of newly born children in health insurance policies.

(a) All individual and group health insurance policies providing coverage on an expense-incurred basis and individual and group service or indemnity type contracts issued by a nonprofit service corporation which provide coverage for a family member of the insured or subscriber shall, as to such family members' coverage, also provide that the health insurance benefits applicable for children shall be payable with respect to a newly born child of the insured or subscriber from the moment of birth.

(b) The coverage for newly born children shall consist of coverage of injury or sickness including the necessary care and treatment of medically diagnosed congenital defects and birth abnormalities, but need not include benefits for routine well-baby care.

(c) The requirements of this section shall apply to all insurance policies and subscriber contracts renewed, delivered or issued for delivery in this state, 60 days after April 24, 1975. (Acts 1975, 3rd Ex. Sess., No. 82, p. 311, §§ 1-3.)

§ 27-19-39. Policies, etc., providing for reimbursement for visual service.

Whenever any policy of insurance or any medical service plan or hospital service contract or hospital and medical service contract provides for reimbursement for any visual service in Alabama which is within the lawful scope of practice of a duly licensed optometrist, as defined in section 34-22-1, the insured or other person entitled to benefits under such policy shall be entitled to reimbursement for such services, whether such services are performed by a duly licensed physician or by a duly licensed optometrist, whichever the insured selects, notwithstanding any provision to the contrary in any statute or in such policy, plan or contract. Duly licensed optometrists shall be entitled to participate in such policies, plans or contracts providing for visual services to the same extent as fully licensed physicians. (Acts 1967, No. 508, p. 1224.)

ARTICLE 2.

MEDICARE SUPPLEMENT POLICY MINIMUM STANDARDS.

§ 27-19-50. Short title.

This article shall be known and may be cited as the "Alabama Medicare Supplement Minimum Standards Act." (Acts 1981, No. 81-560, p. 940, § 1.)

§ 27-19-51. Purpose of article.

The purpose of this article is to establish certain definitions, policy provisions, anticipated loss ratio standards and disclosure requirements applicable to group and individual Medicare supplement disability policies and to authorize the implementation of these requirements through regulations promulgated by the commissioner of insurance consistent with the uniform standards developed by the National Association of Insurance Commissioners to meet the standards enacted in Public Law 96-265 (Laws 1980). (Acts 1981, No. 81-560, p. 940, § 2.)

§ 27-19-52. Definitions.

For purposes of this article, the following terms shall have the meaning indicated herein:

(1) APPLICANT. Such term means:

a. In the case of an individual Medicare supplement policy or subscriber contract, the person who seeks to contract for insurance benefits, and

b. In the case of a group Medicare supplement policy or subscriber contract, the proposed certificate holder.

293

(2) CERTIFICATE. Any certificate issued under a group Medicare supplement policy, which policy has been delivered or issued for delivery in this state.

(3) MEDICARE SUPPLEMENT POLICY. A group or individual policy of disability insurance or a nonprofit hospital and medical plan contract which is advertised, marketed or designed primarily as a supplement to reimbursements under Medicare for the hospital, medical or surgical expenses of persons eligible for Medicare. Such term does not include:

a. A policy or contract of one or more employers or labor organizations, or of the trustees of a fund established by one or more employers or labor organizations, or combination thereof, for employees or former employees, or combination thereof, or for members or former members, or combination thereof, of the labor organizations;

b. A policy or contract of any professional, trade or occupational association for its members or former or retired members, or combination thereof, if such association:

1. Is composed of individuals all of whom are actively engaged in the same profession, trade or occupation;

2. Has been maintained in good faith for purposes other than obtaining insurance; and

3. Has been in existence for at least two years prior to the date of its initial offering of such policy or plan to its members; or

c. Individual policies or contracts issued pursuant to a conversion privilege under a policy or contract of group or individual insurance when such group or individual policy or contract includes provisions which are inconsistent with the requirements of this article.

(4) MEDICARE. The "Health Insurance for the Aged Act", Title XVIII of the Social Security Amendments of 1965, as then constituted or later amended. (Acts 1981, No. 81-560, p. 940, § 3.)

§ 27-19-53. Standards for policy provisions generally; policy provisions as to coverage of pre-existing conditions.

(a) The commissioner shall issue reasonable regulations to establish specific standards for policy provisions of Medicare supplement policies. Such standards shall be in addition to and in accordance with applicable laws of this state, including article 1 of this chapter and chapter 20 of this title, and may cover but shall not be limited to:

(1) Terms of renewability;

(2) Initial and subsequent conditions of eligibility;

(3) Nonduplication of coverage;

(4) Probationary periods;

(5) Benefit limitations, exceptions and reductions;

(6) Elimination periods;

(7) Requirements for replacement;

(8) Recurrent conditions; and

(9) Definition of terms.

(b) The commissioner may issue reasonable regulations that specify prohibited policy provisions not otherwise specifically authorized by statute which, in the opinion of the commissioner, are unjust, unfair or unfairly discriminatory to any person insured or proposed for coverage under a Medicare supplement policy.

(c) Notwithstanding any other provisions of law, a Medicare supplement policy may not deny a claim for loss incurred more than six months from the effective date of coverage for a pre-existing condition. The policy may not define a pre-existing condition more restrictively than a condition for which medical advice was given or treatment was recommended by or received from a physician within six months before the effective date of coverage. (Acts 1981, No. 81-560, p. 940, § 4.)

§ 27-19-54. Minimum standards for benefits generally.

The commissioner shall issue reasonable regulations to establish minimum standards for benefits under Medicare supplement policies. (Acts 1981, No. 81-560, p. 940, § 5.)

§ 27-19-55. Standards for loss ratios.

(a) Medicare supplement policies shall be expected to return to policyholders benefits which are reasonable in relation to the premium charged. The commissioner shall issue reasonable regulations to establish minimum standards for loss ratios of Medicare supplement policies on the basis of incurred claims experience and earned premiums for the entire period for which rates are computed to provide coverage and in accordance with accepted actuarial principles and practices.

(b) For purposes of regulations issued pursuant to this section, Medicare supplement policies issued as a result of solicitation of individuals through the mail or mass media advertising, including both print and broadcast advertising, shall be treated as individual policies. (Acts 1981, No. 81-560, p. 940, § 6.)

§ 27-19-56. Requirements as to provision in policy of outline of coverage and information relating to replacement of disability policies, subscriber contracts, etc.

(a) In order to provide for full and fair disclosure in the sale of Medicare supplement policies to persons eligible for Medicare, the commissioner may require by regulation that no Medicare supplement policy may be delivered or issued for delivery in this state and no certificate may be delivered pursuant to a group Medicare supplement policy delivered or issued for delivery in this state unless an outline of coverage is delivered to the applicant at the time application is made.

(b) The commissioner shall prescribe the format and content of the outline of coverage required by subsection (a) of this section. For purposes of this section "format" means style, arrangements and overall appearance, including such items as the size, color and prominence of type and the arrangement of text and captions. Such outline of coverage shall include:

(1) A description of the principal benefits and coverage provided in the policy;

(2) A statement of the exceptions, reductions and limitations contained in the policy;

(3) A statement of the renewal provisions including any reservation by the insurer of a right to change the premiums; and

(4) A statement that the outline of coverage is a summary of the policy issued or applied for and that the policy should be consulted to determine governing contractual provisions.

(c) The commissioner may prescribe by regulation a standard form and the contents of an informational brochure for persons eligible for Medicare, which is intended to improve the buyer's ability to select the most appropriate coverage and improve the buyer's understanding of Medicare. Except in the case of direct response insurance policies, the commissioner may require by regulation that the information brochure be provided to any prospective insureds eligible for Medicare concurrently with delivery of the outline of coverage. With respect to direct response insurance policies, the commissioner may require by regulation that the prescribed brochure be provided upon request to any prospective insureds eligible for Medicare, but in no event later than the time of policy delivery.

(d) The commissioner may further promulgate reasonable regulations to govern the full and fair disclosure of the information in connection with the replacement of disability policies, subscriber contracts or certificates by persons eligible for Medicare, other than:

(1) Medicare supplement policies;

(2) Disability income policies;

(3) Basic, catastrophic, or major medical expense policies;

(4) Single premium, nonrenewable policies; or

(5) Other policies defined in paragraph (3) of section 27-19-52.

(e) The commissioner may further promulgate reasonable regulations to govern the full and fair disclosure of the information in connection with the replacement of accident and sickness policies, subscriber contracts or certificates by persons eligible for Medicare. (Acts 1981, No. 81-560, p. 940, § 7.)

§ 27-19-57. Inclusion in policy of notice of right to return policy and receive refund of premium.

(a) Medicare supplement policies or certificates, other than those issued pursuant to direct response solicitation, shall have a notice prominently printed on the first page of the policy, or attached thereto, stating in substance that the applicant shall have the right to return the policy or certificate within 10 days of its delivery and to have the premium refunded if, after examination of the policy or certificate, the applicant is not satisfied for any reason.

(b) Medicare supplement policies or certificates issued pursuant to a direct response solicitation to persons eligible for Medicare shall have a notice prominently printed on the first page, or attached thereto, stating in substance that the applicant shall have the right to return the policy or certificate within 30 days of its delivery and to have the premium refunded if, after examination, the applicant is not satisfied for any reason. (Acts 1981, No. 81-560, p. 940, § 8.)

§ 27-19-58. Applicability of provisions of title to regulations promulgated pursuant to article.

Regulations promulgated pursuant to this article shall be subject to the provisions of chapter 2 of this title. (Acts 1981, No. 81-560, p. 940, § 9.)

CHAPTER 19A.

DENTAL CARE SERVICES.

Sec.
27-19A-1. Scope of chapter.
27-19A-2. Definitions.
27-19A-3. Prohibited provisions.
27-19A-4. Required provisions.
27-19A-5. Provisions contrary to chapter.
27-19A-6. Dental benefits not required.
27-19A-7. Contracting directly with patient; distribution of information about policy or plan; payment and reimbursement procedures.

Sec.
27-19A-8. Plans not in conformance with chapter unlawful.
27-19A-9. Nonconforming policies and plans not to be approved by commissioner.
27-19A-10. Duty of commissioner to enforce chapter.
27-19A-11. Penalty for violations.

§ 27-19A-1. Scope of chapter.

This chapter shall apply to health insurance and employee benefit plans providing for dental care services. (Acts 1984, No. 84-411, p. 960, § 1.)

§ 27-19A-2. Definitions.

As used in this chapter, the following terms shall have the respective meanings herein set forth, unless the context shall otherwise require:

(1) ALABAMA INSURANCE CODE. Title 27 of the Code of Alabama 1975.

(2) INSURER. Such term shall have the meaning ascribed in section 27-1-2.

(3) PERSON. Such term shall have the meaning ascribed in section 27-1-2.

(4) COMMISSIONER AND DEPARTMENT. Such terms, respectively, shall have the meanings ascribed in section 27-1-2.

(5) CONTRACTUAL OBLIGATION. Any obligation under covered policies or employee benefit plans.

(6) COVERED POLICY or PLAN. Any policy, employee benefit plan or contract within the scope of this chapter.

(7) HEALTH INSURANCE POLICY. Any individual, group, blanket, or franchise insurance policy, insurance agreement, or group hospital service contract providing benefits for dental care expenses incurred as a result of an accident or sickness.

(8) EMPLOYEE BENEFIT PLAN. Any plan, fund, or program heretofore or hereafter established or maintained by an employer or by an employee organization, or by both, to the extent that such plan, fund, or program was established or is maintained for the purpose of providing for its participants or their beneficiaries, through the purchase of insurance or otherwise, dental care benefits in the event of accident or sickness.

(9) DENTAL CARE SERVICES. Any services furnished to any person for the purpose of preventing, alleviating, curing, or healing human dental illness or injury.

(10) DENTIST. Any person who furnishes dental care services and who is licensed as a dentist by the state of Alabama. (Acts 1984, No. 84-411, p. 960, § 2.)

§ 27-19A-3. Prohibited provisions.

No health insurance policy or employee benefit plan which is delivered, renewed, issued for delivery, or otherwise contracted for in this state shall:

(1) Prevent any person who is a party to or beneficiary of any such health insurance policy or employee benefit plan from selecting the dentist of his choice to furnish the dental care services offered by said policy or plan or interfere with said selection provided the dentist is licensed to furnish such dental care services in this state;

(2) Deny any dentist the right to participate as a contracting provider for such policy or plan provided the dentist is licensed to furnish the dental care services offered by said policy or plan;

(3) Authorize any person to regulate, interfere, or intervene in any manner in the diagnosis or treatment rendered by a dentist to his patient for the purpose of preventing, alleviating, curing, or healing dental illness or injury provided said dentist practices within the scope of his license; or

(4) Require that any dentist furnishing dental care services must make or obtain dental X rays or any other diagnostic aids for the purpose of preventing, alleviating, curing, or healing dental illness or injury; provided, however, that nothing herein shall prohibit requests for existing dental X rays or any other existing diagnostic aids for the purpose of determining benefits payable under a health insurance policy or employee benefit plan. Nothing herein shall prohibit the predetermination of benefits for dental care expenses prior to treatment by the attending dentist. (Acts 1984, No. 84-411, p. 960, § 2.)

§ 27-19A-4. Required provisions.

Any health insurance policy or employee benefit plan which is delivered, renewed, issued for delivery, or otherwise contracted for in this state shall, to the extent that it provides benefits for dental care expenses:

(1) Disclose, if applicable, that the benefit offered is limited to the least costly treatment;

(2) Define and explain the standard upon which the payment of benefits or reimbursement for the cost of dental care services is based, such as "usual and customary," "reasonable and customary," "usual, customary, and reasonable," fees or words of similar import or specify in dollars and cents the amount of the payment or reimbursement for dental care services to be provided. Said payment or reimbursement for a noncontracting provider dentist shall be the same as the payment or reimbursement for a contracting provider dentist; provided, however, that the health insurance policy or the employee benefit plan shall not be required to make payment or reimbursement in an amount which is greater than the amount so specified or which is greater than the fee charged by the providing dentist for the dental care services rendered. (Acts 1984, No. 84-411, p. 960, § 3.)

§ 27-19A-5. Provisions contrary to chapter.

Any provision in a health insurance policy or employee benefit plan which is delivered, renewed, issued for delivery, or otherwise contracted for in this state which is contrary to this chapter shall to the extent of such conflict be void. (Acts 1984, No. 84-411, p. 960, § 4.)

§ 27-19A-6. Dental benefits not required.

The provisions of this chapter do not mandate that any type of benefits for dental care expenses be provided by a health insurance policy or an employee benefit plan. (Acts 1984, No. 84-411, p. 960, § 5.)

§ 27-19A-7. Contracting directly with patient; distribution of information about policy or plan; payment and reimbursement procedures.

The provisions of this chapter do not prohibit the following conduct and shall be construed to provide that:

(1) A dentist may contract directly with a patient for the furnishing of dental care services to said patient as may be otherwise authorized by law;

(2) Any person providing a health insurance policy or employee benefit plan, or an employer, or an employee organization may:

a. Make available to its insureds, beneficiaries, participants, employees, or members information relating to dental care services by the distribution of factually accurate information regarding dental care services, rates, fees, location, and hours of service, provided such distribution is made upon the request of any dentist licensed by this state; or

b. Establish an administrative mechanism which facilitates payment for dental care services by insureds, beneficiaries, participants, employees, or members to the dentist of their choice; or

c. Pay or reimburse, on a nondiscriminatory basis, its insureds, beneficiaries, participants, employees, or members for the cost of dental care services rendered by the dentist of their choice. (Acts 1984, No. 84-411, p. 960, § 6.)

§ 27-19A-8. Plans not in conformance with chapter unlawful.

It shall be unlawful for any insurer or any person to provide any health insurance policy or employee benefit plan providing for dental care services that does not conform to the provisions of this chapter. (Acts 1984, No. 84-411, p. 960, § 7.)

§ 27-19A-9. Nonconforming policies and plans not to be approved by commissioner.

The commissioner of insurance shall not approve for sale in this state any health insurance policy or employee benefit plan providing for dental care services which does not conform to the provisions of this chapter or to the provisions of sections 27-14-8 and 27-14-9. (Acts 1984, No. 84-411, p. 960, § 8.)

§ 27-19A-10. Duty of commissioner to enforce chapter.

It shall be the duty and responsibility of the commissioner of insurance to enforce the provisions of this chapter. (Acts 1984, No. 84-411, p. 960, § 9.)

§ 27-19A-11. Penalty for violations.

Each willful violation of the provisions of this chapter shall be punishable as provided in section 27-1-12. (Acts 1984, No. 84-411, p. 960, § 10.)

CHAPTER 20.

GROUP AND BLANKET DISABILITY INSURANCE.

Sec.
27-20-1. Group disability insurance — Eligible groups.
27-20-2. Same — Mandatory policy provisions.
27-20-3. Same — Direct payment of those rendering services.
27-20-4. Blanket disability insurance — Eligible groups.

Sec.
27-20-5. Same — Power to issue; filing requirement; mandatory policy provisions.
27-20-6. Same — Applications and certificates.
27-20-7. Same — Payment of benefits.

Cross references. — As to disability insurance policies generally, see § 27-19-1 et seq.

Cited in Moses v. American Home Assurance Co., 376 So. 2d 656 (Ala. 1979).

Collateral references. — Liability insurance coverage as extending to liability for punitive or exemplary damages. 16 ALR4th 11.

§ 27-20-1. Group disability insurance — Eligible groups.

Group disability insurance is hereby declared to be that form of disability insurance covering groups of persons as defined in this section, with or without one or more members of their families or one or more of their dependents, or covering one or more members of the families or one or more dependents of such groups of persons, and issued upon the following basis:

(1) Under a policy issued to an employer or trustees of a fund established by an employer, who shall be deemed the policyholder, insuring employees of such employer for the benefit of persons other than the employer. The term "employees" as used in this subdivision shall be deemed to include the officers, managers and employees of the employer, the individual proprietor or partner if the employer is an individual proprietor or partnership, the officers, managers and employees of subsidiary or affiliated corporations and the individual proprietors, partners and employees of individuals and firms if the business of the employer and such individual or firm is under common control through stock ownership, contract or otherwise. The term "employees" as used in this subdivision may include retired employees. A policy issued to insure employees of a public body may provide that the term "employees" shall include elected or appointed officials. The policy may provide that the term "employees" shall include the trustees or their employees, or both, if their duties are principally connected with such trusteeship;

(2) Under a policy issued to an association, including a labor union, which shall have a constitution and bylaws and which has been organized and is maintained in good faith for purposes other than that of obtaining insurance, insuring members, employees or employees of members of the association for the benefit of persons other than the association or its officers or trustees. The term "employees" as used in this subdivision may include retired employees;

(3) Under a policy issued to the trustees of a fund established by two or more employers in the same or related industry, or by one or more labor unions, or by one or more employers and one or more labor unions or by an association as defined in subdivision (2) of this section, which trustees shall be deemed the policyholder, to insure employees of the employers, or members of the unions or of such association or employees of members of such association for the benefit of persons other than the employers, or the unions or such association. The term "employees" as used in this subdivision may include the officers, managers and employees of the employer and the individual proprietor or partners if the employer is an individual proprietor or partnership. The term "employees" as used in this subdivision may include retired employees. The policy may provide that the term "employees" shall include the trustees or their employees, or both, if their duties are principally connected with such trusteeship;

(4) Under a policy issued to any person or organization to which a policy of group life insurance may be issued or delivered in this state to insure any class, or classes, of individuals that could be insured under such group life policy;

(5) Under a policy issued to cover any other substantially similar group which, in the discretion of the commissioner, may be subject to the issuance of a group disability policy or contract; or

(6) Any group disability policy which contains provisions for the payment by the insurer of benefits for expenses incurred on account of hospital, nursing, medical or surgical services for members of the family or dependents of a person in the insured group may provide for the continuation of such benefit provisions or any part, or parts, thereof after the death of the person in the insured group. (Acts 1971, No. 407, p. 707, § 458.)

Cited in Moses v. American Home Assurance Co., 376 So. 2d 656 (Ala. 1979).
Collateral references. — 44 C.J.S., Insurance, § 15.

Temporary employees: provision excluding from coverage part-time or temporary employees. 41 ALR3d 1419.

§ 27-20-2. Same — Mandatory policy provisions.

Each such group disability insurance policy shall contain in substance the following provisions:

(1) A provision that, in the absence of fraud, all statements made by applicants, or the policyholders or by an insured person shall be deemed representations and not warranties and that no statement made for the purpose of effecting insurance shall void such insurance or reduce benefits unless contained in a written instrument signed by the policyholder or the insured person, a copy of which has been furnished to such policyholder or to such person or his beneficiary;

(2) A provision that the insurer will furnish to the policyholder for delivery to each employee, or member of the insured group, a statement in

summary form of the essential features of the insurance coverage of such employee or member and to whom benefits thereunder are payable. If dependents are included in the coverage, only one certificate need be issued for each family unit; and

(3) A provision that to the group originally insured may be added from time to time eligible new employees, or members or dependents, as the case may be, in accordance with the terms of the policy. (Acts 1971, No. 407, p. 707, § 459.)

Cited in Moses v. American Home Assurance Co., 376 So. 2d 656 (Ala. 1979).

Collateral references. — Misrepresentation as to employer-employee relationship as within incontestability clause of group insurance. 26 ALR3d 632.

§ 27-20-3. Same — Direct payment of those rendering services.

Any group disability policy may, on request by the group policyholder, provide that all, or any portion, of any indemnities provided by any such policy on account of hospital, nursing, medical or surgical services may, at the insurer's option, be paid directly to the hospital or person rendering such services. Payment so made shall discharge the insurer's obligation with respect to the amount of insurance so paid. (Acts 1971, No. 407, p. 707, § 460.)

§ 27-20-4. Blanket disability insurance — Eligible groups.

Blanket disability insurance is hereby declared to be that form of disability insurance covering groups of persons as enumerated in one of the following subdivisions:

(1) Under a policy or contract issued to any common carrier or to any operator, owner or lessee of a means of transportation, who or which shall be deemed the policyholder, covering a group of persons who may become passengers defined by reference to their travel status on such common carrier or such means of transportation;

(2) Under a policy or contract issued to an employer, who shall be deemed the policyholder, covering any group of employees, dependents or guests, defined by reference to specified hazards incident to an activity, or activities, or operations of the policyholder;

(3) Under a policy or contract issued to a college, school or other institution of learning, a school district or districts, or school jurisdictional unit or to the head, principal or governing board of any such educational unit, who or which shall be deemed the policyholder, covering students, teachers or employees;

(4) Under a policy or contract issued to any religious, charitable, recreational, educational or civic organization, or branch thereof, which shall be deemed the policyholder covering any group of members or participants defined by reference to specified hazards incident to an activity, or activities, or operations sponsored or supervised by such policyholder;

(5) Under a policy or contract issued to a sports team, camp or sponsor thereof, which shall be deemed the policyholder, covering members, campers, employees, officials or supervisors;

(6) Under a policy or contract issued to any volunteer fire department, first aid, civil defense or other such volunteer organization, which shall be deemed the policyholder, covering any group of members or participants defined by reference to specified hazards incident to an activity, or activities, or operations sponsored or supervised by such policyholder;

(7) Under a policy or contract issued to a newspaper or other publisher, which shall be deemed the policyholder, covering its carriers;

(8) Under a policy or contract issued to an association, including a labor union, which shall have a constitution and bylaws and which has been organized and is maintained in good faith for purposes other than that of obtaining insurance, which shall be deemed the policyholder, covering any group of members or participants defined by reference to specified hazards incident to an activity, or activities, or operations sponsored or supervised by such policyholder; or

(9) Under a policy or contract issued to cover any other risk or class of risks which, in the discretion of the commissioner, may be properly eligible for blanket disability insurance. The discretion of the commissioner may be exercised on an individual risk basis or class of risks, or both. (Acts 1971, No. 407, p. 707, § 461.)

Cited in Moses v. American Home Assurance Co., 376 So. 2d 656 (Ala. 1979).

Collateral references. — 44 C.J.S., Insurance, § 48.

§ 27-20-5. Same — Power to issue; filing requirement; mandatory policy provisions.

Any insurer authorized to write disability insurance in this state shall have the power to issue blanket disability insurance. No such blanket policy may be issued or delivered in this state unless a copy of the form thereof shall have been filed in accordance with section 27-14-8. Every such blanket policy shall contain provisions which, in the opinion of the commissioner, are at least as favorable to the policyholder and the individual insured as the following:

(1) A provision that the policy, including endorsements and a copy of the application, if any, of the policyholder and the persons insured shall constitute the entire contract between the parties, and that any statement made by the policyholder or by a person insured shall, in absence of fraud, be deemed a representation and not a warranty and that no such statements shall be used in defense to a claim under the policy unless contained in a written application. Such person, his beneficiary or assignee shall have the right to make written request to the insurer for a copy of such application, and the insurer shall, within 15 days after the receipt of such request at its home office or any branch office of the insurer, deliver or mail to the person making such request a copy of such application. If such copy shall not be so

delivered or mailed, the insurer shall be precluded from introducing such application as evidence in any action based upon, or involving, any statements contained therein;

(2) A provision that written notice of sickness or of injury must be given to the insurer within 20 days after the date when such sickness or injury occurred. Failure to give notice within such time shall not invalidate nor reduce any claim if it shall be shown not to have been reasonably possible to give such notice and that notice was given as soon as was reasonably possible;

(3) A provision that the insurer will furnish to the policyholder such forms as are usually furnished by it for filing proof of loss. If such forms are not furnished before the expiration of 15 days after the giving of such notice, the claimant shall be deemed to have complied with the requirements of the policy as to proof of loss upon submitting within the time fixed in the policy for filing proof of loss, written proof covering the occurrence, character and extent of the loss for which claim is made;

(4) A provision that in the case of claim for loss of time for disability, written proof of such loss must be furnished to the insurer within 30 days after the commencement of the period for which the insurer is liable, that subsequent written proofs of the continuance of such disability must be furnished to the insurer at such intervals as the insurer may reasonably require and that, in the case of claim for any other loss, written proof of such loss must be furnished to the insurer within 90 days after the date of such loss. Failure to furnish such proof within such time shall not invalidate nor reduce any claim if it shall be shown not to have been reasonably possible to furnish such proof and that such proof was furnished as soon as was reasonably possible;

(5) A provision that all benefits payable under the policy other than benefits for loss of time will be payable immediately upon receipt of due written proof of such loss, that, subject to due proof of loss, all accrued benefits payable under the policy for loss of time will be paid not later than at the expiration of each period of 30 days during the continuance of the period for which the insurer is liable and that any balance remaining unpaid at the termination of such period will be paid immediately upon receipt of such proof;

(6) A provision that the insurer, at its own expense, shall have the right and opportunity to examine the person of the insured when and so often as it may reasonably require during the pendency of claim under the policy and also the right and opportunity to make any autopsy in case of death where it is not prohibited by law; and

(7) A provision that no action shall be brought to recover under the policy prior to the expiration of 60 days after written proof of loss has been furnished in accordance with the requirements of the policy and that no such action shall be brought after the expiration of three years after the time written proof of loss is required to be furnished. (Acts 1971, No. 407, p. 707, § 462.)

Collateral references. — Disability insurance or provisions: clause requiring notice of claim within specified time or as soon as reasonably possible, or the like. 17 ALR3d 530.

Beneficiary's ignorance of existence of life or accident policy as excusing failure to give notice, make proofs of loss, or bring action within time limited by policy or statute. 28 ALR3d 292.

§ 27-20-6. Same — Applications and certificates.

An individual application shall not be required from a person covered under a blanket disability policy or contract, nor shall it be necessary for the insurer to furnish each person a certificate. (Acts 1971, No. 407, p. 707, § 463.)

Cited in Moses v. American Home Assurance Co., 376 So. 2d 656 (Ala. 1979).

§ 27-20-7. Same — Payment of benefits.

All benefits under any blanket disability policy shall be payable to the person insured, or to his employer, or to his designated beneficiary or beneficiaries or to his estate; except, that if the person insured be a minor or mental incompetent, such benefits may be made payable to his parent, guardian or other person actually supporting him, or, if the entire cost of the insurance has been borne by the employer, such benefits may be made payable to the employer; provided, however, that the policy may provide that all, or any portion, of any indemnities provided by such policy on account of hospital, nursing, medical or surgical services may, at the insurer's option, be paid directly to the hospital or person rendering such services; but the policy may not require that the service be rendered by a particular hospital or person. Payment so made shall discharge the insurer's obligation with respect to the amount of insurance so paid. (Acts 1971, No. 407, p. 707, § 464.)

Collateral references. — Minors: capacity of minor insured to effect a change of beneficiary. 14 ALR2d 375.

Power of guardian of incompetent to change beneficiary in ward's life insurance policy. 21 ALR2d 1191.

CHAPTER 20A.

ALCOHOLISM TREATMENT IN GROUP PLANS.

Sec.   Sec.
27-20A-1. Definitions.   27-20A-3. Benefits required.
27-20A-2. Chapter applicable to group, etc.,   27-20A-4. Extent of coverage.
           policies.

Collateral references. — 43 Am. Jur. 2d,
Insurance, § 1207.
  44 Am. Jur. 2d, Insurance, § 1289.

§ 27-20A-1. Definitions.

The following words and phrases used in this chapter, and others evidently intended as the equivalent thereof, shall, in the absence of clear implication otherwise, be given the following respective interpretations herein:

(1) ALCOHOLISM. A chronic disorder or illness in which the individual is unable, for psychological or physical reasons, or both, to refrain from the frequent consumption of alcohol in quantities sufficient to produce intoxication and, ultimately, injury to health and effective functioning.

(2) DETOXIFICATION. Supervised physical withdrawal from alcohol.

(3) INPATIENT TREATMENT FOR ALCOHOLISM. Care provided in a licensed hospital and is normally limited to detoxification where severe medical or psychiatric complications are present or may be anticipated.

(4) SHORT TERM RESIDENTIAL ALCOHOLISM TREATMENT FACILITY. A state certified facility which provides structured programs of intensive treatment services for people addicted to alcohol. Services may include supervised withdrawal from alcohol, backup emergency medical services for persons whose physical condition necessitates medical care, psychological and social evaluation, nutritional stabilization through proper dietary service, individual counseling, family counseling and referral to other providers who can provide additional services for continuity of care, aftercare and followup.

(5) OUTPATIENT TREATMENT. Treatment rendered in a nonresidential setting and using an intermittent, periodic schedule of visits. (Acts 1979, No. 79-436, p. 701, § 1.)

§ 27-20A-2. Chapter applicable to group, etc., policies.

No group, blanket, franchise or association health insurance policy providing coverage on an expense incurred basis, nor group, blanket, franchise or association service or indemnity type contract issued by a nonprofit corporation, nor group-type self insurance plan providing protection, insurance or indemnity against hospital, medical or surgical expenses, nor health maintenance organization plan shall be issued, delivered, executed or renewed in this state, or approved for issuance or renewal in this state by the commissioner of insurance after 90 days beyond the effective date of this chapter, unless such policy, contract or plan, at the option of the policyholder or sponsor, provides benefits to any insured, subscriber or other person covered under the policy, contract or plan for expenses incurred in connection with the treatment of alcoholism when such treatment is prescribed by a duly licensed doctor of medicine. (Acts 1979, No. 79-436, p. 701, § 2.)

Code commissioner's note. — The act which added this chapter indicated that it was signed by the governor on January 19, 1979. However, inasmuch as the senate passed the act on June 5, 1979, the house of representatives passed it on July 11, 1979 and the secretary of state received the act on July 23, 1979, it would appear likely that the act was, in fact, signed July 19, 1979, and as a result became effective on that date.

§ 27-20A-3. Benefits required.

The benefits to be offered under this chapter shall include inpatient or residential treatment rendered to the insured, subscriber or other person covered, at a state licensed hospital or at a short term residential alcoholism treatment facility or detoxification facility duly licensed or certified as such by the Alabama board of health or the Alabama mental health board. Benefits shall also include outpatient treatment rendered to the insured, subscriber or other person covered, by a duly licensed doctor of medicine or by an alcoholism treatment facility duly licensed or certified as such by the Alabama board of health or the Alabama mental health board. (Acts 1979, No. 79-436, p. 701, § 3.)

§ 27-20A-4. Extent of coverage.

When benefits are provided under this chapter, the benefits shall provide for a minimum of 30 days of inpatient treatment or its equivalent per calendar year with the equivalency to be computed based on a formula which equates two days of treatment in a short term residential alcoholism treatment facility to one day of inpatient treatment and which equates three sessions of outpatient treatment by a licensed doctor of medicine or an alcoholism treatment facility to one day of inpatient treatment. (Acts 1979, No. 79-436, p. 701, § 4.)

CHAPTER 21.

ALABAMA HEALTH CARE PLAN.

Sec.
27-21-1. Purpose of chapter.
27-21-2. Offering of insurance.
27-21-3. Premium rates and administration
          expenses.
27-21-4. Exemption from premium tax; de-
          duction of losses therefrom.

Sec.
27-21-5. Qualifications for plan; examina-
          tions; public hearings; employ-
          ment of consultants, etc.
27-21-6. Short title.

Collateral references. — Transsexual surgery as covered operation under state medical assistance program. 2 ALR4th 775.

Liability insurance coverage as extending to liability for punitive or exemplary damages. 16 ALR4th 11.

§ 27-21-1. Purpose of chapter.

The legislature of Alabama takes cognizance of the existence of many Alabama citizens who are unable to obtain adequate health care protection by reason of economic, physical or other related causes. It is the purpose of the legislature to provide adequate health care protection through this plan to those persons not otherwise able to obtain such protection by insurance companies or voluntary association on a nonprofit basis. (Acts 1971, No. 501, p. 1218.)

§ 27-21-2. Offering of insurance.

Any insurer authorized and licensed to engage in the business of health insurance in this state may join with one or more other such insurers to offer to any resident of this state, who meets the qualifications established by the commissioner, insurance against major financial loss from accident or disease. Such insurance may be offered by such insurers in their own names or in the name of a voluntary unincorporated association or other organization formed by such insurers solely for the purpose of this plan. The forms of applications, certifications and policies of such insurance, the applicable premium rates, annual statement and all other information required by the department under Alabama law for organizations in the business of health insurance shall be filed with the commissioner for his approval. Any other information which the commissioner deems necessary for the efficient operation of the plan may also be required. (Acts 1971, No. 501, p. 1218.)

Cross references. — As to incorporation of health care service plans, see § 10-4-100 et seq.

§ 27-21-3. Premium rates and administration expenses.

Each insurer or association electing to come under the provisions of this chapter shall charge the same premium for the same insurance coverage and be allowed the same percentage for expense of administration. Such premium rate and percentage for administration expense shall be determined and approved by the commissioner so as to maintain the nonprofit basis of the plan. (Acts 1971, No. 501, p. 1218.)

§ 27-21-4. Exemption from premium tax; deduction of losses therefrom.

The premiums collected under the provisions of the health care plan are hereby exempt from the payment of premium tax under chapter 4 of this title. Any losses suffered as a direct result of operation under the plan by those organizations electing to join and operate under the health care plan may be deducted from the premium tax submitted under the above-mentioned chapter 4 which would normally be paid on individual accident and health insurance premiums collected, but total loss deduction shall not exceed 50 percent of such premium tax normally payable on premiums from individual accident and health insurance. (Acts 1971, No. 501, p. 1218.)

§ 27-21-5. Qualifications for plan; examinations; public hearings; employment of consultants, etc.

(a) The commissioner shall set up standards and promulgate regulations concerning the qualifications of those Alabama citizens entitled to utilize this plan, and no insurer or association operating under the plan shall allow anyone to be insured under the plan unless that person meets these qualifications. Any willful material misrepresentation by a person attempting to qualify under the plan shall be a misdemeanor and, upon conviction thereof, shall be punishable as prescribed in section 13A-5-1.

(b) The commissioner may also make other necessary rules or regulations and may conduct any examination as to insurers at any reasonable time and may also, at his discretion, hold public hearings to determine qualifications of prospective insureds or rates and expenses of insurers in furtherance of this plan. The commissioner may also employ consultants, actuaries, attorneys or special investigators or examiners to assist him in the regulation of the plan and examination of the insurers, and the expense of these special assistants and consultants, along with any regular examination costs, will be borne by the concerned insurer. (Acts 1971, No. 501, p. 1218.)

§ 27-21-6. Short title.

This chapter shall be known as the Alabama health care plan and may be referred to by that designation. (Acts 1971, No. 501, p. 1218.)

CHAPTER 21A.

HEALTH MAINTENANCE ORGANIZATIONS.

Sec.
27-21A-1.   Definitions.
27-21A-2.   Establishment of health mainte-
            nance organizations.
27-21A-3.   Issuance of certificate of authority.
27-21A-4.   Powers of health maintenance or-
            ganizations.
27-21A-5.   Governing body.
27-21A-6.   Fiduciary responsibilities of direc-
            tors, officers, employees and part-
            ners.
27-21A-7.   Evidence of coverage and charges
            for health care services.
27-21A-8.   Reporting requirements.
27-21A-9.   Information to enrollees.
27-21A-10. Complaint system.
27-21A-11. Investments.
27-21A-12. Protection against insolvency.
27-21A-13. Prohibited practices.
27-21A-14. Regulation of agents.
27-21A-15. Powers of insurers and health care
            service plans.
27-21A-16. Examination.
27-21A-17. Suspension or revocation of certifi-
            cate of authority.
27-21A-18. Rehabilitation, liquidation, or con-

Sec.
            servation of a health maintenance
            organization.
27-21A-19. Regulations.
27-21A-20. Administrative procedures.
27-21A-21. Fees.
27-21A-22. Penalties and enforcement.
27-21A-23. Statutory construction and rela-
            tionship to other laws.
27-21A-24. Filings and reports as public docu-
            ments.
27-21A-25. Confidentiality of medical infor-
            mation.
27-21A-26. State health officer's and commis-
            sioner's authority to contract.
27-21A-27. Acquisition of control of or merger
            of a health maintenance organiza-
            tion.
27-21A-28. Taxes.
27-21A-29. Existing health maintenance orga-
            nizations.
27-21A-30. Coordination of benefits.
27-21A-31. Health maintenance organization
            advisory council.
27-21A-32. HMO enrollment requirements.

Effective date. — The act which added this chapter became effective May 29, 1986.

§ 27-21A-1. Definitions.

As used in this chapter, the following terms shall have the following meanings, respectively:

(1) AGENT. A person who is appointed or employed by a health maintenance organization and who engages in solicitation of membership in such organization. This definition does not include a person enrolling members on behalf of an employer, union or other organization.

(2) BASIC HEALTH CARE SERVICES. Emergency care, inpatient hospital and physician care, and outpatient medical services.

(3) COMMISSIONER. The commissioner of insurance.

(4) ENROLLEE. An individual who is enrolled in a health maintenance organization.

(5) EVIDENCE OF COVERAGE. Any certificate, agreement, or contract issued to an enrollee setting out the coverage to which he is entitled.

(6) HEALTH CARE SERVICES. Any services included in the furnishing to any individual of medical or dental care, or hospitalization or incident to the furnishing of such care or hospitalization, as well as the furnishing to any

person of any and all other services for the purpose of preventing, alleviating, curing or healing human illness, injury or physical disability.

(7) HEALTH MAINTENANCE ORGANIZATION. Any person that undertakes to provide or arrange for basic health care services through an organized system which combines the delivery and financing of health care to enrollees. The organization shall provide physician services directly through physician employees or under contractual arrangements with either individual physicians or a group or groups of physicians. The organization shall provide basic health care services directly or under contractual arrangements. When reasonable and appropriate, the organization may provide physician services and basic health care services through other arrangements. The organization may provide, or arrange for, health care services on a prepayment or other financial basis.

(8) INSURER. Every insurer authorized in this state to issue contracts of accident and sickness insurance. Hospital service nonprofit corporations, nonprofit medical service corporations, and nonprofit health care corporations are included within such term.

(9) PERSON. Any natural or artificial person including, but not limited to, individuals, partnerships, associations, trusts, or corporations.

(10) PROVIDER. Any physician, hospital, or other person which is licensed or otherwise authorized in this state to furnish health care services.

(11) SCHEDULE OF CHARGES. A statement of the method used by a health maintenance organization to establish rates;

(12) STATE HEALTH OFFICER. The executive officer of the state department of public health;

(13) UNCOVERED EXPENDITURES. The costs of health care services that are covered by a health maintenance organization, for which an enrollee would also be liable in the event of the organization's insolvency. (Acts 1986, No. 86-471, § 1.)

§ 27-21A-2. Establishment of health maintenance organizations.

(a) Notwithstanding any law of this state to be contrary, any person may apply to the commissioner for and obtain a certificate of authority to establish and operate a health maintenance organization in compliance with this chapter. No person shall establish or operate a health maintenance organization in this state without obtaining a certificate of authority under this chapter. A foreign corporation may qualify under this chapter, subject to its registration to do business in this state as a foreign corporation under the provisions of sections 10-2A-220, et seq.

(b) Health maintenance organizations licensed as of May 29, 1986, shall be issued a certificate of authority in accordance with section 27-21A-29.

(c) Each application for a certificate of authority shall be verified by an officer or authorized representative of the applicant, shall be in a form prescribed by the commissioner, and shall set forth or be accompanied by the following:

(1) A certified copy of the organizational documents of the applicant, such as the articles of incorporation, articles of association, partnership agreement, trust agreement, or other applicable documents, and all amendments thereto;

(2) A certified copy of the bylaws, rules and regulations, or similar document, if any, regulating the conduct of the internal affairs of the applicant;

(3) A list of the names, addresses, official positions, and such biographical information as may be required by the commissioner concerning the persons who are to be responsible for the conduct of the affairs of the applicant, including all members of the board of directors, board of trustees, executive committee, or other governing board or committee, the principal officers in the case of a corporation, and the partners or members in the case of a partnership or association;

(4) A copy of any contract made or to be made between any persons listed in subdivision (3) and the applicant;

(5) A copy of the form of evidence of coverage to be issued to the enrollees;

(6) A copy of the form or group contract, if any, which is to be issued to employers, unions, trustees, or other organizations;

(7) Financial statements showing the applicant's assets, liabilities, and sources of financial support. If the applicant's financial affairs are audited by independent certified public accountants, a copy of the applicant's most recent certified financial statement shall be deemed to satisfy this requirement unless the commissioner directs that additional or more recent financial information is required for the proper administration of this chapter;

(8) A description of the proposed method of marketing, a financial plan which includes a projection of operating results anticipated until the organization has had net income for at least one year, and a statement as to the sources of working capital as well as any other sources of funding;

(9) A power of attorney duly executed by such applicant, if not domiciled in this state, appointing the commissioner and his successors in office, and duly authorized deputies, as the true and lawful attorney of such applicant in and for this state upon whom all lawful process in any legal action or proceeding against the health maintenance organization on a cause of action arising in this state may be served;

(10) A statement reasonably describing the geographic area or areas to be served;

(11) A description of the complaint procedures to be utilized as required under section 27-21A-10;

(12) A description of the procedures and programs to be implemented to meet the health care requirements in subdivision (a)(2) of section 27-21A-3;

(13) The applicant's most recent report of examination and all annual reports and other periodic reports filed by the applicant within the past year in the applicant's state of domicile and state within which it maintains its principal place of business, if different from state of domicile; as well as any

similar reports which the applicant may be required to file under federal law, if applicable;

(14) Such other information as the commissioner or state health officer may require to make the determinations required in section 27-21A-3.

(d)(1) An applicant or a health maintenance organization holding a certificate of authority granted hereunder shall, unless otherwise provided for in this act, file a notice describing any material modification of the operation set out in the information required by subsection (c). Such notice shall be filed with the commissioner and the state health officer prior to modification. If the commissioner does not disapprove within (30) days of filing, such modification shall be deemed approved;

(2) The commissioner or state health officer may promulgate rules and regulations exempting from the filing requirements of subdivision (d)(1) those items he deems unnecessary.

(e) An applicant, or a health maintenance organization holding a certificate of authority granted hereunder shall file with the commissioner all contracts of reinsurance. Any agreement between the organization and an insurer shall be subject to the laws of this state regarding reinsurance. All reinsurance agreements and any modifications thereto must be approved by the commissioner. If the commissioner does not disapprove such agreements or modifications with 30 days of filing, such agreements or modifications shall be deemed approved. Reinsurance agreements shall remain in full force and effect for at least 90 days following written notice by registered mail or cancellation by either party to the commissioner. (Acts 1986, No. 86-471, § 2.)

§ 27-21A-3. Issuance of certificate of authority.

(a)(1) Upon receipt of an application for issuance of a certificate of authority, the commissioner shall forthwith transmit copies of such application and accompanying documents to the state health officer.

(2) The state health officer shall determine whether the applicant for a certificate of authority, with respect to health care services to be furnished:

a. Has demonstrated the willingness and potential ability to assure that such health care services will be provided in a manner to assure both availability and accessibility of adequate personnel and facilities and in a manner enhancing availability, accessibility and continuity of service;

b. Has arrangements, established in accordance with the regulations promulgated by the state health officer for an on-going quality assurance program concerning health care processes and outcomes; and

c. Has a procedure, established in accordance with regulations of the state health officer, to develop, compile, evaluate, and report statistics relating to the cost of its operations, the pattern of utilization of its services, the availability and accessibility of its services, and such other matters as may be reasonably required by the state health officer.

d. Has demonstrated that the health maintenance organization will effectively provide, or arrange for, the provision of health care services.

Such arrangements shall be established in accordance with rules promulgated by the state health officer for an on-going quality assurance/utilization review program concerning health care processes and outcomes.

e. Has demonstrated that a copy of the form or group contract which is to be issued to employers, unions, trustees, or other organizations or individuals is in compliance with rules promulgated by the state health officer; and

f. Has demonstrated that nothing in the proposed method of operation, as shown by the information submitted pursuant to section 27-21A-2, or by independent investigation is contrary to the public interest.

(3) Within 90 days of receipt of the application for issuance of a certificate of authority, the state health officer shall certify to the commissioner that the proposed health maintenance organization meets the requirements of subdivision (a)(2) or notify the commissioner that the health maintenance organization does not meet such requirements and specify in what respects it is deficient.

(b) After receipt of the certification from the state health officer, the commissioner shall issue or deny a certificate of authority to any person filing an application pursuant to section 27-21A-2. Issuance of a certificate of authority shall be granted upon payment of the application fee prescribed in section 27-21A-21 if the commissioner is satisfied that the following conditions are met:

(1) The ownership, control or management of the entity is competent and trustworthy and possesses managerial experience that would make the proposed health maintenance organization beneficial to the subscribers. The commissioner shall not grant or continue to license the business of a health maintenance organization in this state at any time the commissioner has good reason to believe that the ownership, control, or management of the organization is under the control of any person whose business operations are, or have been marked by business practices or conduct that is to the detriment of the public, stockholders, investors, or creditors; by the improper manipulation of assets or of accounts; or by bad faith;

(2) The state health officer certifies, in accordance with subdivision (a)(3), that the health maintenance organization's proposed plan of operation meets the requirements of subdivision (a)(2);

(3) Except to the extent of contractually required provisions for copayments, the health maintenance organization will effectively provide or arrange for the provision of basic health care services through insurance, written contractual agreements, or other existing arrangements; and

(4) The contracts for basic health care services contain a provision that providers shall hold the enrollee harmless for the payment of the cost of health care services in any event including, but not limited to, nonpayment of the health maintenance organization, or the health maintenance organization's insolvency. This provision shall not prohibit collection of supplemental charges or copayments on the health maintenance organiza-

tion's behalf made in accordance with terms of any applicable agreement between the health maintenance organization and the enrollee.

(5) The health maintenance organization is financially responsible and may reasonably be expected to meet its obligations to enrollees and prospective enrollees. In making this determination, the commissioner shall consider:

a. The financial soundness of the applicant and its arrangements for health care services and the schedule of charges used in connection therewith;

b. The adequacy of working capital;

c. Any agreement with an insurer or other organization for insuring the payment of the cost of health care services or the provision for automatic applicability of an alternative coverage in the event of discontinuance of the health maintenance organization;

d. Any agreement form or contract form with providers for the provision of health care services; and

e. Any deposit of cash or securities submitted in accordance with section 27-21A-12.

(6) Nothing in the proposed method of operation, as shown by the information submitted pursuant to section 27-21A-2 or by independent investigation, is contrary to the public interest;

(7) Any deficiencies identified by the state health officer have been corrected; and

(8) The form or group contract, if any, which is to be issued to employers, unions, trustees, or other organizations is in compliance with the rules and regulations of the state insurance department as such rules and regulations specifically apply to health maintenance organizations. Any provisions of this chapter to the contrary notwithstanding, no provision of this chapter shall exempt any HMO from compliance with the rules and regulations required for licensing or in any way exempt any HMO participant or enrollee from quality care standards and regulations as a condition for licensure. Any HMO under contract as of April 1, 1986, with the Alabama medicaid agency that has a grant with a national foundation and is licensed by the Alabama department of public health shall not be responsible for any of the fees, taxes, and other financial regulations so long as the grant is in existence. Any HMO which contracts with the medicaid agency shall be exempt from the financial responsibilities and taxes listed in this chapter for that percentage of enrollees that are medicaid recipients. These HMOs shall also be exempt from any provision necessary for the medicaid agency to comply with federal regulations. (Acts 1986, No. 86-471, § 3.)

§ 27-21A-4. Powers of health maintenance organizations.

(a) The powers of a health maintenance organization include, but are not limited to the following:

(1) The purchase, lease, construction, renovation, operation, or maintenance of hospitals, medical facilities, or both, and their ancillary equipment;

(2) The making of loans other than in the ordinary course of business, to providers under contract with it in furtherance of its program or the making of loans to a corporation or corporations in which it owns a majority interest for the purpose of acquiring or constructing medical facilities and hospitals or in furtherance of a program providing health care services to enrollees.

(3) The furnishing of health care services through providers which are under contract with or employed by the health maintenance organization.

(4) The contracting with any person for the performance on its behalf of certain functions such as marketing, enrollment and administration.

(5) The purchase, lease, construction, or renovation of property as may reasonably be required for its principal office or for such purposes as may be necessary in the transaction of the business of the organization;

(6) The contracting with an insurance company licensed in this state to do business in this state, or a health care service plan authorized to transact business in this state, for the provision of insurance, indemnity, or reimbursement against the cost of health care services provided by the health maintenance organization.

(7) The offering of other health care services, in addition to basic health care services or other required health care services.

(b)(1) A health maintenance organization shall file notice, assuring compliance with any applicable state or federal laws, with adequate supporting information, with the commissioner prior to the exercise of any power granted in subsections (a)(1), (a)(2), or (a)(4). The commissioner shall disapprove such exercise of power only if in his opinion it would substantially and adversely affect the financial soundness of the health maintenance organization and endanger its ability to meet its obligations. If the commissioner does not disapprove within 30 days of the filing, it shall be deemed approved.

(2) The commissioner may promulgate rules and regulations exempting from the filing requirement of subdivision (b)(1) those activities having a de minimis effect. (Acts 1986, No. 86-471, § 4.)

§ 27-21A-5. Governing body.

The governing body of any health maintenance organization may include providers, or other individuals, or both. (Acts 1986, No. 86-471, § 5.)

§ 27-21A-6. Fiduciary responsibilities of directors, officers, employees and partners.

(a) Any director, officer, employee or partner of a health maintenance organization who receives, collects, disburses, or invests funds in connection with the activities of such organization shall be responsible for such funds in a fiduciary relationship to the organization.

(b) A health maintenance organization shall maintain in force a fidelity bond on employees and officers in an amount not less than $25,000 or such other sum as may be prescribed by the commissioner. All such bonds shall be written with at least a one-year discovery period and if written with less than a three-year discovery period shall contain a provision that no cancellation or termination of the bond, whether by or at the request of the insured or by the underwriter, shall take effect prior to the expiration of 90 days after written notice of such cancellation or termination has been filed with the commissioner unless an earlier date of such cancellation or termination is approved by the commissioner.

(c) Any officer, or director, or any member of any committee or any employee of a health maintenance organization who is charged with the duty of investing or handling the organization's funds shall not deposit or invest such funds except in the organization's corporate name; except, that such health maintenance organization may for its convenience hold any equity investment in a street name or in the name of a nominee; shall not borrow the funds of such organization; shall not be pecuniarily interested in any loan, pledge or deposit, security, investment, sale, purchase, exchange, reinsurance or other similar transaction or property of such insurer except as a stockholder or member and shall not take or receive to his own use any fee, brokerage, commission, gift or other consideration for, or on account of, any such transaction made by, or on behalf of, such insurer.

(d) No health maintenance organization shall guarantee any financial obligation of any of its officers or directors.

(e) This section shall not prohibit such a director, or officer, or member of a committee or employee from becoming a member of the health maintenance organization and enjoying the usual rights so provided for its members, nor shall it prohibit any such officer, director, or member of a committee or employee from participating as a beneficiary in any pension trust, deferred compensation plan, profit-sharing plan or stock option plan authorized by the health maintenance organization and to which he may be eligible, nor shall it prohibit any director or member of a committee from receiving a reasonable fee for legal services actually rendered to such health maintenance organization.

(f) The commissioner may, by regulations from time to time, define and permit additional exceptions to the prohibition contained in subsection (c) of this section solely to enable payment of reasonable compensation to the director who is not otherwise an officer or employee of the health maintenance organization, or to a corporation or firm in which a director is interested, for necessary services performed or sales or purchases made to, or for, the health maintenance organization's business and in the usual private, professional or business capacity of such director or such corporation or firm. (Acts 1986, No. 86-471, § 6.)

§ 27-21A-7. Evidence of coverage and charges for health care services.

(a)(1) Every enrollee residing in this state is entitled to an evidence of coverage. If the enrollee obtains such coverage through an insurance policy or a contract issued by a health care service plan, the insurer or the health care service plan shall issue the evidence of coverage. Otherwise, the health maintenance organization shall issue the evidence of coverage.

(2) No evidence of coverage, or amendment thereto, shall be issued or delivered to any person in this state until a copy of the basic form of the evidence of coverage, or amendment thereto, has been filed with the commissioner and the state health officer, and approved by the commissioner.

(3) An evidence of coverage shall contain:

a. No provisions or statements which encourage misrepresentation, or which are untrue, misleading or deceptive as defined in subsection (a) of section 27-21A-13; and

b. A clear and concise statement, if a contract, or a reasonably complete summary, if a certificate, of:

1. The health care service and the insurance or other benefits, if any, to which the enrollee is entitled;

2. Any limitations on the services, kinds of services, benefits, or kinds of benefits, to be provided, including any deductible or copayment feature;

3. Where and in what manner information is available as to how services may be obtained;

4. The total amount of payments for health care services and the indemnity or service benefits, if any, which the enrollee is obligated to pay with respect to individual contracts; and

5. A clear and understandable description of the health maintenance organization's method for resolving enrollee complaints.

Any subsequent change may be evidenced in a separate document issued to the enrollee.

(b)(1) No schedule of charges for enrollee coverage for health care services, or amendment thereto, may be used until a copy of such schedule, or amendment thereto, has been filed with and approved by the commissioner.

(2) Such schedule of charges shall be established in accordance with actuarial principles for various categories of enrollees, provided that the charges applicable to any enrollee shall not be individually determined based on his health status. Charges shall not be excessive, inadequate, or unfairly discriminatory. A certification, by a qualified actuary or other qualified person acceptable to the commissioner as to the appropriateness of the use of the charges, based on reasonable assumptions, shall accompany the filing along with adequate supporting information.

(c) The commissioner shall within 30 days approve any form if the requirements of subsection (a) are met and the commissioner shall within 30 days approve any schedule of charges if the requirements of subsection (b) are met. It shall be unlawful to issue such form or to use such schedule of charges until approved. If the commissioner disapproves such filing, he shall notify the filer. In the notice, the commissioner shall specify the reasons for his disapproval. A hearing will be granted within 30 days after a request in writing by the person filing. If the commissioner does not approve any form or if the commissioner does not approve any schedule of charges within 30 days of the filing of such forms or schedule of charges, they shall be deemed approved.

(d) The commissioner may require the submission of whatever relevant information he deems necessary in determining whether to approve or disapprove a filing made pursuant to this section. (Acts 1986, No. 86-471, § 7.)

§ 27-21A-8. Reporting requirements.

Every health maintenance organization shall annually, on or before the first day of March, file a report verified by at least two principal officers with the commissioner, with a copy to the state health officer, covering the preceding calendar year. Such report shall be on forms prescribed by the commissioner, and shall include:

(1) A financial statement of the organization;

(2) Any material changes in the information submitted pursuant to subsection (c) of section 27-21A-2;

(3) The number of persons enrolled at the beginning and end of the year;

(4) A summary of information compiled pursuant to paragraph (a)(2)c of section 27-21A-3;

(5) The amount of uncovered and covered expenditures that are payable and more than 90 days past due; and

(6) Such additional information or reports as are deemed reasonably necessary and appropriate by the commissioner to enable him to carry out his duties under this chapter. (Acts 1986, No. 86-471, § 8.)

§ 27-21A-9. Information to enrollees.

Every health maintenance organization shall provide promptly to its enrollees notice of any material change in the operation of the organization that will affect them directly. (Acts 1986, No. 86-471, § 9.)

§ 27-21A-10. Complaint system.

(a)(1) Every health maintenance organization shall establish and maintain a complaint system which has been approved by the commissioner, after consultation with the state health officer, to provide reasonable procedures for the resolution of written complaints initiated by enrollees.

(2) Each health maintenance organization shall submit to the commissioner and the state health officer an annual report in a form prescribed by the commissioner, after consultation with the state health officer, which shall include:

a. A description of the procedures of such complaint system;

b. The total number of complaints handled through such complaint system and a compilation of causes underlying the complaints filed; and

c. The number, amount, and disposition of malpractice claims and other claims relating to the service or care rendered by the health maintenance organization made by enrollees of the organization that were settled during the year by the health maintenance organization. All such information shall be held in confidence by the commissioner.

(b) The commissioner or the state health officer may examine such complaint system. (Acts 1986, No. 86-471, § 10.)

§ 27-21A-11. Investments.

With the exception of investments made in accordance with subdivisions (a)(1), (a)(2), (a)(5) and subsection (b) of section 27-21A-4, the funds of a health maintenance organization shall be invested only in securities or other investments permitted by the laws of this state for the investment of assets constituting the legal reserves of life insurance companies or such other securities or investments as the commissioner may permit. (Acts 1986, No. 86-471, § 11.)

§ 27-21A-12. Protection against insolvency.

(a) Unless otherwise provided below, each health maintenance organization shall deposit with the commissioner, or with any organization or trustee acceptable to him through which a custodial or controlled account is utilized, cash, securities, or any combination of these or other measures acceptable to him in the amount set forth in this section.

(b) The amount for an organization that is beginning operation shall be the greater of: (1) five percent of its estimated expenditures for health care services for its first year of operation, (2) twice its estimated average monthly uncovered expenditures for its first year of operation, or (3) $100,000. At the beginning of each succeeding year, unless not applicable, the organization shall deposit with the commissioner, or organization, or trustee, cash, securities, or any combination of these or other measures acceptable to the commissioner, in an amount equal to four percent of its estimated annual uncovered expenditures for that year.

(c) Unless not applicable, an organization that is in operation on May 29, 1986, shall make a deposit equal to the larger of: (1) one percent of the preceding 12 months uncovered expenditures, or (2) $100,000 on the first day of the fiscal year beginning six months or more after May 29, 1986.

In the second fiscal year, if applicable, the amount of the additional deposit shall be equal to two percent of its estimated annual uncovered expenditures. In the third fiscal year, if applicable, the additional deposit shall be equal to three percent of its estimated annual uncovered expenditures for that year, and in the fourth fiscal year and subsequent years, if applicable, the additional deposit shall be equal to four percent of its estimated annual uncovered expenditures for each year. Each year's estimate, after the first year of operation shall reasonably reflect the prior year's operating experience and delivery arrangements.

(d) The commissioner may waive any of the deposit requirements set forth in subsections (a) and (b) above whenever satisfied that the organization has sufficient net worth and an adequate history of generating net income to assure its financial viability for the next year, or its performance and obligations are guaranteed by an organization with sufficient net worth and an adequate history of generating net income, or the assets of the organization or its contracts with insurers, health care service plants, governments, or other organizations are reasonably sufficient to assure the performance of its obligations; provided, however, that a minimum deposit of $100,000 shall be required in all cases.

(e) When an organization has achieved a net worth composed of investments authorized under section 27-21A-11, but not including land, buildings, and equipment, of at least $1 million or has achieved a net worth including direct investments in organization-related land, buildings, and equipment of at least $5 million, the annual deposit requirement shall not apply.

The annual deposit requirement shall not apply to an organization if the total amount of the accumulated deposit is equal to 25 percent of its estimated annual uncovered expenditures for the next calendar year, or the capital and surplus requirements for the formation for admittance of an accident and health insurer in this state, whichever is less.

If the organization has a guaranteeing organization which has been in operation for at least five years and has a net worth not including land, buildings and equipment of at least $1 million or which has been in operation for at least 10 years and has a net worth including direct investments in organization-related land, buildings, and equipment of at least $5 million, the annual deposit requirement shall not apply; provided, however, that if the guaranteeing organization is sponsoring more than one organization, the net worth requirement shall be increased by a multiple equal to the number of such organizations. This requirement to maintain a deposit in excess of the deposit required of an accident and health insurer shall not apply during any time that the guaranteeing organization maintains for each organization it sponsors a net worth of at least equal to the capital and surplus requirements for an accident and health insurer.

(f) All income from deposits shall belong to the depositing organization and shall be paid to it as it becomes available. A health maintenance organization that has made a securities deposit may withdraw that deposit or any part thereof after making a substitute deposit of cash, securities, or any combination of these or other measures of equal amount and value. Any securities shall be approved by the commissioner before being substituted.

(g) In any year in which an annual deposit is not required of an organization, at the organization's request the commissioner shall reduce the required, previously accumulated deposit by $100,000 for each $250,000 of net worth in excess of the amount that allows the organization not to make the annual deposit. If the amount of net worth no longer supports a reduction of its required deposit, the organization shall immediately redeposit $100,000 for each $250,000 of reduction in net worth, provided that its total deposit shall not exceed the maximum required under this section.

(h) Each health maintenance organization shall have and maintain a capital account of at least $100,000 in addition to any deposit requirements under this section. The capital account shall be net of any accrued liabilities and be in the form of cash, securities or any combination of these or other measures acceptable to the commissioner.

(i) There is created a nonprofit unincorporated legal entity to be known as the Alabama health maintenance organization guaranty association. All health maintenance organizations authorized to transact business in this state shall participate in this guaranty association which shall protect all enrollees of such organizations in this state against failure in the performance of obligations due to the impairment or insolvency of a health maintenance organization. The association shall be separate from, but shall be modeled on the Alabama life and disability guaranty association, sections 27-44-1, et seq. and the commissioner shall take such actions and promulgate, in accordance with the provisions of section 27-2-17, such regulations as he may deem necessary to effectuate the provisions of this subsection. (Acts 1986, No. 86-471, § 12.)

§ 27-21A-13. Prohibited practices.

(a) No health maintenance organization, or representative thereof, may cause or knowingly permit the use of advertising which is untrue or misleading, solicitation which is untrue or misleading, or any form or evidence of coverage which is deceptive. For purposes of this chapter:

(1) A statement or item of information shall be deemed to be untrue if it does not conform to fact in any respect which is or may be significant to an enrollee of, or person considering enrollment with a health maintenance organization;

(2) A statement or item of information shall be deemed to be misleading, whether or not it may be literally untrue, if, in the total context in which such statement is made or such item of information is communicated, such statement or item of information may be reasonably understood by a reasonable person, not possessing special knowledge regarding health care coverage, as indicating any benefit or advantage or the absence of any exclusion, limitation, or disadvantage or possible significance to an enrollee of, or person considering enrollment in a health maintenance organization, if such benefit or advantage or absence of limitation, exclusion or disadvantage does not in fact exist;

(3) An evidence of coverage shall be deemed to be deceptive if the evidence of coverage taken as a whole, and with consideration given to typography and format, as well as language, shall be such as to cause a reasonable person, not possessing special knowledge regarding health maintenance organizations and evidences of coverage therefor, to expect benefits, services, charges, or other advantages which the evidence of coverage does not provide or which the health maintenance organization issuing such evidence of coverage does not regularly make available for enrollees covered under such evidence of coverage.

(b) Sections 8-19-1, et seq. and 27-12-1, et seq. shall be construed to apply to health maintenance organizations and evidences of coverage except to the extent that such sections are clearly inappropriate in light of the nature of health maintenance organizations as set forth in this chapter.

(c) A health maintenance organization may not cancel or refuse to renew an individual enrollee, except for reasons stated in the organization's rules applicable to all enrollees, or for the failure to pay the charge for such coverage, or for such other reasons as may be promulgated by the commissioner; provided, however, that a health maintenance organization may not in any event cancel or refuse to renew an enrollee solely on the basis of the health of the enrollee.

(d) No health maintenance organization unless licensed as an insurer may refer to itself as a licensed insurer or use a name deceptively similar to the name or description of any insurance or surety corporation doing business in this state.

(e) Any person not in possession of a valid certificate of authority issued pursuant to this chapter may not use the phrase "health maintenance organization" or "HMO" in the course of operation. (Acts 1986, No. 86-471, § 13.)

§ 27-21A-14. Regulation of agents.

(a) Unless exempted pursuant to subsection (c) of this section, health maintenance organizations in this state shall only solicit enrollees or otherwise market their services through duly licensed agents. This requirement shall not apply to health maintenance organizations existing as of May 29, 1986, until six months after the promulgation of rules or regulations as provided in subsection (b) of this section.

(b) The commissioner shall, after notice and hearing, promulgate such reasonable rules and regulations as are necessary to provide for the licensing of agents.

(c) The commissioner may, by rule, exempt certain classes of persons from the requirement of obtaining a license:

(1) If the functions they perform do not require special competence, trustworthiness or the regulatory surveillance made possible by licensing; or

(2) If other existing safeguards make regulation unnecessary.

(d) Nothing in this section shall be deemed to prohibit a health maintenance organization from advertising. (Acts 1986, No. 86-471, § 14.)

§ 27-21A-15. Powers of insurers and health care service plans.

(a) An insurance company licensed in this state, or a health care service plan authorized to do business in this state, may either directly or through a subsidiary or affiliate organize and operate a health maintenance organization under the provisions of this chapter. Notwithstanding any other law which may be inconsistent herewith, any two or more such insurance companies, health care service plans, or subsidiaries or affiliates thereof, may jointly organize and operate a health maintenance organization. The business of insurance is deemed to include the providing of health care by a health maintenance organization owned or operated by an insurer or a subsidiary thereof.

(b) Notwithstanding any provision of insurance and health care service plan laws, Title 10, chapter 4, article 6 and Title 27, an insurer or a health care service plan may contract with a health maintenance organization to provide insurance or similar protection against the cost of care provided through health maintenance organizations and to provide coverage in the event of the failure of the health maintenance organization to meet its obligations. For such purposes, the enrollees of a health maintenance organization constitute a permissible group under such laws. Among other things, under such contracts, the insurer or health care service plan may make benefit payments to health maintenance organizations for health care services rendered by providers. (Acts 1986, No. 86-471, § 15.)

§ 27-21A-16. Examination.

(a) The commissioner may make an examination of the affairs of any health maintenance organization and providers with whom such organization has contracts or agreements as often as is reasonably necessary for the protection of the interests of the people of this state, but not less frequently than once every three years.

(b) The state health officer may make an examination concerning health care service of any health maintenance organization and providers with whom such organization has contracts, agreements, or other arrangements as often as is reasonably necessary for the protection of the interests of the people of this state, but not less frequently than once every three years.

(c) Every health maintenance organization shall submit its relevant books and records for such examinations and in every way facilitate these examinations. For the purpose of examinations, the commissioner and the state health officer may administer oaths to, and examine the officers and agents of the health maintenance organization and the principals of such providers concerning their business.

(d) The expenses of examinations under this section shall be assessed against the organization being examined and such assessment shall be remitted to the commissioner to be deposited to the credit of the special examination revolving fund in section 27-2-25, or the state health officer to be deposited to the credit of a fund to be known as the health maintenance organization revolving fund. The expenses incurred by the commissioner and his examiners in the making of examinations pursuant to the provisions of this chapter, together with the compensation of such examiners, shall be paid from the special examination revolving fund. The expenses incurred by the state health officer and his examiners in the making of examinations pursuant to the provisions of this chapter, together with the compensation of such examiners, shall be paid from the health maintenance organization revolving fund.

(e) In lieu of such examination, the commission or state health officer may accept the report of an examination made by the commissioner, state health officer or other appropriate agency of the state of domicile of the health maintenance organization. The health maintenance organization shall file a copy of any such report with the commissioner and the state health officer.

(f) All records necessary for the complete examination of a health maintenance organization domiciled in this state shall be maintained in a location approved by the commissioner. (Acts 1986, No. 86-471, § 16.)

§ 27-21A-17. Suspension or revocation of certificate of authority.

(a) The commissioner in consultation with and with the approval of the state health officer, where necessary, may suspend or revoke any certificate of authority issued to a health maintenance organization under this chapter if he finds that any of the following conditions exist:

(1) The health maintenance organization is operating significantly in contravention of its basic organizational document or in a manner contrary to that described in any other information submitted under section 27-21A-2, unless amendments to such submissions have been filed with the commissioner and the state health officer and approved by the commissioner;

(2) The health maintenance organization issues evidence of coverage or uses a schedule of charges for health care services which do not comply with requirements of section 27-21A-7;

(3) The health maintenance organization does not provide or arrange for basic health care services;

(4) The state health officer certifies to the commissioner that:

a. The health maintenance organization does not meet the requirements of subdivision (a)(2) of section 27-21A-3; or

b. The health maintenance organization is unable to fulfill its obligations to furnish health care services;

(5) The health maintenance organization is no longer financially responsible and may reasonably be expected to be unable to meet its obligations to enrollees or prospective enrollees:

(6) The health maintenance organization has failed to implement the complaint system required by section 27-21A-10 in a reasonable manner to facilitate the resolution of valid complaints;

(7) The health maintenance organization, or any person on its behalf, has advertised or merchandised its services in an untrue, misrepresentative, misleading, deceptive, or unfair manner;

(8) The continued operation of the health maintenance organization would be hazardous to its enrollees;

(9) The health maintenance organization has otherwise failed substantially to comply with this chapter.

(b) A certificate of authority shall be suspended or revoked only after compliance with the requirements of section 27-21A-20.

(c) When the certificate of authority of a health maintenance organization is suspended, the health maintenance organization shall not, during the period of such suspension, enroll any additional enrollees except newborn children or other newly acquired dependents of existing enrollees, and shall not engage in any advertising or solicitation whatsoever.

(d) When the certificate of authority of a health maintenance organization is revoked, such organization shall proceed, immediately following the effective date of the order of revocation, to wind up its affairs, and shall conduct no further business except as may be essential to the orderly conclusion of the affairs of such organization. It shall engage in no further advertising, solicitation or enrollment whatsoever. The commissioner may, by written order, permit such further operation of the organization as he may find to be in the best interest of enrollees, to the end that enrollees will be afforded the greatest practical opportunity to obtain continuing health care coverage. (Acts 1986, No. 86-471, § 17.)

§ 27-21A-18. Rehabilitation, liquidation, or conservation of a health maintenance organization.

(a) Any rehabilitation, liquidation or conservation of a health maintenance organization shall be deemed to be the rehabilitation, liquidation, or conservation of an insurance company and shall be conducted under the supervision of the commissioner pursuant to the law governing the rehabilitation, liquidation, or conservation of insurance companies. The commissioner may apply for an order directing him to rehabilitate, liquidate, or conserve a health maintenance organization upon any one or more grounds set out in section 27-32-6, or when in his opinion the continued operation of the health maintenance organization would be hazardous either to the enrollees or to the people of this state. Enrollees shall have the same priority in the event of liquidation or rehabilitation as the law provides to policyholders of an insurer.

(b) A claim by a health care provider for an uncovered expenditure has the same priority as a claim of an enrollee, provided such provider of services agrees not to assert such claim against any enrollee of the health maintenance organization.

(c) The state health officer shall provide to the commissioner or receiver of any financially troubled health maintenance organization advice and support to facilitate the expeditious rehabilitation, liquidation, conservation or dissolution of the health maintenance organization. (Acts 1986, No. 86-471, § 18.)

§ 27-21A-19. Regulations.

The commissioner may, after notice and hearing, promulgate reasonable rules and regulations, in accordance with section 27-2-17, as are necessary or proper to carry out the provisions of this chapter. The state health officer may promulgate such rules and regulations in accordance with the provisions of sections 41-22-1, et seq. (Acts 1986, No. 86-471, § 19.)

§ 27-21A-20. Administrative procedures.

(a) When the commissioner has cause to believe that grounds for the denial of an application for a certificate of authority exist, or that grounds for the suspension or revocation of a certificate of authority exist, he shall notify the health maintenance organization and the state health officer in writing specifically stating the grounds for denial, suspension, or revocation. If so requested in writing by the health maintenance organization, the commissioner shall set a hearing on the matter within 30 days of the receipt of such request.

(b) The state health officer or his designated representative, shall be in attendance at the hearing and shall participate in the proceedings. The recommendation and findings of the state health officer with respect to matters relating to the quality of health care services provided in connection with any decision regarding denial, suspension, or revocation of a certificate of authority, shall be conclusive and binding upon the commissioner. Within 30 days after such hearing, or upon the failure of the health maintenance organization to appear at such hearing, the commissioner shall take action as is deemed advisable on written findings which shall be mailed to the health maintenance organization with a copy thereof to the state health officer. The health maintenance organization can appeal the action of the commissioner and the recommendation and findings of the state health officer to the circuit court of Montgomery county by filing an appeal to such court within 30 days of the receipt of such findings. The court may, in disposing of the issue before it, modify, affirm or reverse the order of the commissioner in whole or in part.

(c) Those provisions of this title, relating to the suspension, denial or revocation of a certificate of authority, shall apply to proceedings under this section. (Acts 1986, No. 86-471, § 20.)

§ 27-21A-21. Fees.

(a) Every health maintenance organization subject to this chapter shall pay to the commissioner the following fees:

(1) For filing an application for certificate of authority or amendment thereto, $50.00;

(2) For filing an amendment to the organization documents that requires approval, $10.00;

(3) For filing each annual report, $20.00;

(4) For renewal of annual certificates of authority, $200.00.

(b) Fees charged under this section shall be deposited to the credit of the general fund. (Acts 1986, No. 86-471, § 21.)

§ 27-21A-22. Penalties and enforcement.

(a) The commissioner may, in lieu of suspension or revocation of a certificate of authority under section 27-21A-17, levy an administrative penalty in an amount not less than $500.00 nor more than $5,000.00, if reasonable notice in writing is given of the intent to levy the penalty and the health maintenance organization has a reasonable time within which to remedy the defect in its operations which gave rise to the penalty citation. The commissioner may augment this penalty by an amount equal to the sum that he calculates to be the damages suffered by enrollees or other members of the public. All moneys collected under this section shall be deposited to the credit of the general fund.

(b)(1) If the commissioner or the state health officer shall for any reason have cause to believe that any violation of this chapter has occurred or is threatened, the commissioner or state health officer may give notice to the health maintenance organization and to the representatives, or other persons who appear to be involved in such suspected violation, to arrange a conference with the alleged violators or their authorized representatives for the purpose of attempting to ascertain the facts relating to such suspected violation, and, in the event it appears that any violation has occurred or is threatened, to arrive at an adequate and effective means of correcting or preventing such violation.

(2) Proceedings under this subsection shall not be governed by any formal procedural requirements, and may be conducted in such manner as the commissioner or the state health officer may deem appropriate under the circumstances. However, unless consented to by the health maintenance organization, no rule or order may result from a conference until the requirements of this section or section 27-21A-20 of this chapter are satisfied.

(c)(1) The commissioner, after notice to the state health officer, may issue an order directing a health maintenance organization or a representative of a health maintenance organization to cease and desist from engaging in any act or practice in violation of the provisions of this chapter.

(2) Within 30 days after service of the cease and desist order, the respondent may request a hearing on the question of whether acts or practices in violation of this chapter have occurred. Such hearings shall be conducted and judicial review had in accord with the provisions of this title.

(d) In the case of any violation of the provisions of this chapter, if the commissioner elects not to issue a cease and desist order, or in the event of noncompliance with a cease and desist order issued pursuant to subsection (c), the commissioner may institute a proceeding to obtain injunctive or other appropriate relief in the circuit court of Montgomery county. (Acts 1986, No. 86-471, § 22.)

§ 27-21A-23. Statutory construction and relationship to other laws.

(a) Except as otherwise provided in this chapter, provisions of the insurance law and provisions of health care service plan laws shall not be applicable to any health maintenance organization granted a certificate of authority under this chapter. This provision shall not apply to an insurer or health care service plan licensed and regulated pursuant to the insurance law or the health care service plan laws of this state except with respect to its health maintenance organization activities authorized and regulated pursuant to this chapter.

(b) Solicitation of enrollees by a health maintenance organization granted a certificate of authority shall not be construed to violate any provision of law relating to solicitation or advertising by health professionals.

(c) Any health maintenance organization authorized under this chapter shall not be deemed to be practicing medicine and shall be exempt from the provisions of section 34-24-310, et seq., relating to the practice of medicine.

(d) No person participating in the arrangements of a health maintenance organization other than the actual provider of health care services or supplies directly to enrollees and their families shall be liable for negligence, misfeasance, nonfeasance or malpractice in connection with the furnishing of such services and supplies.

(e) Nothing in this chapter shall be construed in any way to repeal or conflict with any provision of the certificate of need law. (Acts 1986, No. 86-471, § 23.)

§ 27-21A-24. Filings and reports as public documents.

All applications, filings and reports required under this chapter, except those which are trade secrets or privileged or confidential commercial or financial information, other than any annual financial statement that may be required under section 27-21A-8, shall be treated as public documents. All testimony, documents and other evidence required to be submitted to the commissioner or state health officer in connection with enforcement of this chapter shall be absolutely confidential and shall not be admissible in evidence in any other proceeding. The commissioner or the state health officer may withhold from public inspection any examination or investigation report for so long as they deem necessary to protect the person examined from unwarranted injury or to be in the public interest. (Acts 1986, No. 86-471, § 24.)

§ 27-21A-25. Confidentiality of medical information.

Any data or information pertaining to the diagnosis, treatment, or health of any enrollee or applicant obtained from such person or from any provider by any health maintenance organization shall be held in confidence and shall not be disclosed to any person except to the extent that it may be necessary to carry out the purposes of this chapter; or upon the express consent of the enrollee or applicant; or pursuant to statute or court order for the production of evidence or the discovery thereof; or in the event of claim or litigation between such person and the health maintenance organization wherein such data or information is pertinent. A health maintenance organization shall be entitled to claim any statutory privileges against such disclosure which the provider who furnished such information to the health maintenance organization is entitled to claim. (Acts 1986, No. 86-471, § 25.)

§ 27-21A-26. State health officer's and commissioner's authority to contract.

The state health officer and the commissioner, in carrying out their obligations under this chapter, may contract with qualified persons to make recommendations concerning the determinations required to be made by them. Such recommendations may be accepted in full or in part by the state health officer or commissioner. (Acts 1986, No. 86-471, § 26.)

§ 27-21A-27. Acquisition of control of or merger of a health maintenance organization.

No person may make a tender for or a request or invitation for tenders of, or enter into an agreement to exchange securities for or acquire in the open market or otherwise, any voting security of a health maintenance organization or enter into any other agreement if, after the consummation thereof, that person would, directly or indirectly, (or by conversion or by exercise of any right to acquire) be in control of the health maintenance organization, and no person may enter into an agreement to merge or consolidate with or otherwise to acquire control of a health maintenance organization, unless at the time any offer, request, or invitation is made or any agreement is entered into, or prior to the acquisition of the securities if no offer or agreement is involved, the person has filed with the commissioner and has sent to the health maintenance organization, information required by section 27-29-3, and the offer, request, invitation, agreement or acquisition has been approved by the commissioner. Approval by the commissioner shall be governed by the provisions of said section 27-29-3. Control under this section shall be defined in the same manner as it is defined for the purposes of section 27-29-3, as amended from time to time. (Acts 1986, No. 86-471, § 27.)

§ 27-21A-28. Taxes.

(a) The same taxes and filing requirements applicable to life insurers under this title, shall apply to and shall be imposed upon each health maintenance organization licensed under the provisions of this chapter; and the organization shall also be entitled to the same tax deductions, reductions, abatements, and credits that life insurers are entitled to receive. All taxes collected hereunder shall be deposited to the credit of the general fund.

(b) As to health maintenance organizations doing business in this state as of May 29, 1986, the taxes imposed by this section shall not take effect until January 1, 1989, but on and after such date shall be payable in accordance with the provisions of sections 27-4-4 and 27-4-5. (Acts 1986, No. 86-471, § 28.)

§ 27-21A-29. Existing health maintenance organizations.

(a) Notwithstanding any other provision of this chapter, any health maintenance organization licensed by the state board of health and in operation on May 29, 1986, shall be granted a certificate of authority upon payment of the application fee prescribed in section 27-21A-21 and compliance with section 27-21A-12. Nothing in this section shall prohibit any such health maintenance organization from continuing to conduct business in this state until such certificate of authority is issued.

(b) Any health maintenance organization which was licensed in this state prior to January 1, 1986, may continue to operate under existing noncontractual provider arrangements (which have been approved by the state health officer) for three years.

(c) After issuance of a certificate of authority in accordance with subsection (a) of this section, the commissioner may require submission by the health maintenance organization of any additional information required in section 27-21A-2 which has not previously been submitted to the state health officer. (Acts 1986, No. 86-471, § 29.)

§ 27-21A-30. Coordination of benefits.

(a) A health maintenance organization is entitled to coordinate benefits on the same basis as an insurer. No such coordination shall be allowed against policies covering individuals on other than a group basis.

(b) A health maintenance organization providing medical benefits or payments to an enrollee who suffers injury, disease, or illness by virtue of the negligent act or omission of a third party is entitled to reimbursement from such third party for the reasonable value of the benefits or payments provided. (Acts 1986, No. 86-471, § 30.)

§ 27-21A-31. Health maintenance organization advisory council.

There shall be established a three member HMO advisory council to advise and consult with the commissioner and the state health officer in carrying out their duties under this chapter. The members of such advisory body shall be appointed annually by the Alabama association of health maintenance organizations. (Acts 1986, No. 86-471, § 31.)

§ 27-21A-32. HMO enrollment requirements.

(a) The state government, or any agency, board, commission, institution, or political subdivision thereof, and any city or county, or board of education, which offers its employees a health benefits plan may make available to and inform its employees or members of the option to enroll in at least one health maintenance organization holding a valid certificate of authority which provides health care services in the geographic areas in which such employees or members reside.

(b) The first time a health maintenance organization is offered by an employer, either public or private, each covered employee must make an affirmative written selection among the different alternatives included in the health benefits plan. Thereafter, those who wish to change from one plan to another will be allowed to do so annually, provided, that nothing in this section shall prevent any health maintenance organization or insurer from requiring evidence of insurability or imposing underwriting restrictions on the acceptance of any such employee. In addition to the annual group enrollment period, the employer shall make available the opportunity to select among different existing alternatives within a health benefits plan to eligible employees, who are new employees or have changed their place of residence resulting in eligibility for the plan.

(c) This section shall impose no responsibilities or duties upon any employer, either public or private, to offer health maintenance organization coverage as part of its health benefits plan.

(d) No employer shall in any way be required to pay more for health benefits as a result of the application of this section than would otherwise be required by a prevailing collective bargaining agreement or other legally enforceable contract or obligation for the provision of health benefits to its employees, or in any plan provided voluntarily by an employer. (Acts 1986, No. 86-471, § 32.)

CHAPTER 22.

PROPERTY INSURANCE CONTRACTS.

Sec.
27-22-1. Insurance of building in name of less than all owners.

Sec.
27-22-2. Industrial fire insurance policies.

Collateral references. — Liability policy providing coverage for damages because of injury to or destruction of property as covering injury to investments, anticipated profits, and goodwill. 92 ALR3d 525.

Obtaining new property insurance as cancellation of existing insurance. 14 ALR4th 781.

Insured's nondisclosure of information regarding value of property as ground for avoiding liability under property insurance policy. 15 ALR4th 1109.

§ 27-22-1. Insurance of building in name of less than all owners.

As to every insurance contract insuring any dwelling or other building and written in the name of less than all of the joint owners or tenants in common, with or without survivorship, if such joint tenants or tenants in common are husband and wife, it shall not be a defense against liability under the policy that all the joint owners or tenants in common were not named as the insured therein, nor will the amount due in event of loss be diminished on such account unless, by special endorsement of the policy, the insurer's liability is limited to the interest of the named insured. (Acts 1951, No. 781, p. 1376; Acts 1971, No. 407, p. 707, § 482.)

§ 27-22-2. Industrial fire insurance policies.

(a) Industrial fire insurance policies are policies issued by insurers writing fire and allied lines of insurance through agents operating on the debit agency system under which system a weekly or monthly collection percentage is paid based either on actual weekly or monthly premium collections or weekly or monthly increases of premium collections.

(b) No such policy, or such policies, covering any of the same subjects of insurance shall be issued which provides indemnity exceeding the limits set by the commissioner as to any one loss resulting from any, or all, of the hazards or perils insured against.

(c) No such policy shall be issued except upon a monthly or weekly premium payment basis. No discount for premiums paid in advance shall exceed five percent for premiums paid for six months in advance or 10 percent for premiums paid for 12 months in advance. In no event shall premiums be collected for more than 12 months in advance. (Acts 1971, No. 407, p. 707, § 483.)

Collateral references. — Insured's right to recover from insurer prejudgment interest on amount of fire loss. 5 ALR4th 126.

CHAPTER 23.

CASUALTY INSURANCE CONTRACTS.

Article 1.

General Provisions.

Sec.
27-23-1. When insurer's liability absolute.
27-23-2. Rights of judgment creditors.

Article 2.

Cancellation of Automobile Liability Insurance.

27-23-20. Definitions.

Sec.
27-23-21. Reasons for cancellation.
27-23-22. Effect of renewal.
27-23-23. Notice of cancellation — Time; reasons.
27-23-24. Same — Availability of assigned risk plan notification.
27-23-25. Same — Proof of notice.
27-23-26. Specification of reasons for cancellation upon insured's request.
27-23-27. Liability of insurer, etc., for statements, etc.
27-23-28. Applicability of article to nonrenewal.

Collateral references. — Liability of person, other than owner of animal or owner or operator of motor vehicle, for damage to motor vehicle or injury to person riding therein resulting from collision with domestic animal at large in street or highway. 21 ALR4th 132.

Liability of owner or operator of vehicle for damage to motor vehicle or injury to person riding therein resulting from collision with domestic animal at large in street or highway. 21 ALR4th 159.

What constitutes ownership of automobile within meaning of automobile insurance owner's policy. 36 ALR4th 7.

ARTICLE 1.

GENERAL PROVISIONS.

§ 27-23-1. When insurer's liability absolute.

As to every contract of insurance made between an insurer and any insured by which such insured is insured against loss or damage on account of the bodily injury or death by accident of any person for which loss or damage such insured is responsible, whenever a loss occurs on account of a casualty covered by such contract of insurance, the liability of the insurer shall become absolute and the payment of the loss shall not depend upon the satisfaction by the insured of a final judgment against him for loss, or damage or death occasioned by the casualty. No such contract of insurance shall be cancelled or annulled by any agreement between the insurer and the insured after the insured has become responsible for such loss or damage, and any such cancellation or annulment shall be void. (Code 1940, T. 28, § 11; Acts 1971, No. 407, p. 707, § 484.)

Editor's note. — Many of the following cases were decided under former Code 1940, T. 28, § 11 or prior law.

Constitutionality. — Former Code 1940, T. 28, § 11 did not violate due process and equal protection clauses of the U.S. Constitution, Amendment 14, § 1. Federal Automobile Ins. Ass'n v. Abrams, 217 Ala. 539, 117 So. 85 (1928).

Origin of former statute. — Former Code 1940, T. 28, § 11 had its origin in Massachusetts Statutes, 1914, ch. 464, §§ 1, 2. Insurance

Co. of N. Am. v. Davis, 274 Ala. 541, 150 So. 2d 192 (1962).

Former Code 1940, Title 28, sections 11 and 12, when construed together, were more than procedural in character and gave the injured party a vested interest (secondary) by way of hypothecation in the amount due the insured by the insurer after the entry of the judgment against the insured. Fleming v. Pan Am. Fire & Cas. Co., 495 F.2d 535 (5th Cir. 1974).

As to rights of judgment creditors, previously covered by former Code 1940, T. 28, § 12, see § 27-23-2.

Purpose of these former sections. — Former Code 1940, T. 28, §§ 11 and 12 were included in the 1923 Code to meet the decisions in Goodman v. Georgia Life Ins. Co., 189 Ala. 130, 66 So. 649 (1914), and Hollings v. Brown, 202 Ala. 504, 80 So. 792 (1919), wherein it was held that an injured judgment creditor could not proceed against the insurer when the policy required the insured to pay the loss before the insurer would become liable. Globe Indem. Co. v. Martin, 214 Ala. 646, 108 So. 761 (1926); Melco Sys. v. Receivers of Trans-America Ins. Co., 268 Ala. 152, 105 So. 2d 43 (1958).

They had to be read into contract. — Former Code 1940, T. 28, §§ 11 and 12, authorizing injured party to recover from insurer of party causing the injury, had to be read into contract of insurance. Employers Ins. Co. v. Brock, 233 Ala. 551, 172 So. 671 (1937).

Statutory provisions respecting indemnity policies are to be read into Alabama insurance contracts. Continental Auto Ins. Underwriters v. Menuskin, 222 Ala. 370, 132 So. 883 (1931).

Former Code 1940, T. 28, §§ 11 and 12 were read into, and became a part of, the insurance contract. Melco Sys. v. Receivers of Trans-America Ins. Co., 268 Ala. 152, 105 So. 2d 43 (1958).

Such provisions gave injured party vested interest. — Former Code 1940, T. 28, §§ 11 and 12 were held to give injured party vested interest in nature of hypothecation of amount, if any, due by insurer to insured, so that term of policy imposing obligations on insured, such as cooperation clauses, were effective against injured party. George v. Employers' Liab. Assurance Corp., 219 Ala. 307, 122 So. 175 (1929); Macey v. Crum, 249 Ala. 249, 30 So. 2d 666 (1947); State Farm Mut. Auto. Ins. Co. v. McClendon, 269 Ala. 456, 114 So. 2d 153 (1959).

They did no more than establish privity between judgment creditor and insurer. — Former Code 1940, T. 28, §§ 11 and 12 did not undertake to do more than establish privity between the injured judgment creditor and the insurer. Melco Sys. v. Receivers of Trans-

America Ins. Co., 268 Ala. 152, 105 So. 2d 43 (1958).

They did not apply to reinsurer. — It was never held in Alabama that former Code 1940, T. 28, §§ 11 and 12 applied to a reinsurer. Melco Sys. v. Receivers of Trans-America Ins. Co., 268 Ala. 152, 105 So. 2d 43 (1958).

Under Alabama law, the injured party acquires a vested interest (secondary) in the nature of a hypothecation of the insured's rights under the policy. Maness v. Alabama Farm Bureau Mut. Cas. Ins. Co., 416 So. 2d 979 (Ala. 1982).

Once an injured party has recovered a judgment against the insured, such party may compel the insurer to pay the judgment. The injured party, however, can bring an action against the insurer only after he has recovered a judgment against the insured and only if the insured was covered against the loss or damage at the time the injured party's right of action arose against the insured tort-feasor. Maness v. Alabama Farm Bureau Mut. Cas. Ins. Co., 416 So. 2d 979 (Ala. 1982).

Default judgment entered against insured in declaratory judgment action brought by insurer does not cut off all rights of the injured parties under the policy. Casualty Reciprocal Exch. v. Wallace, 280 Ala. 61, 189 So. 2d 861 (1966).

Where insured failed to appear in insurer's action for a declaratory judgment to determine coverage under an automobile liability policy, but the injured parties were called to litigate, the judge could properly order "coverage" for the injured parties and at the same time hold that because of the default judgment entered against insured, the insurer did not have to defend insured in actions; and such a holding does not do violence to the "derivative rights" theory. Casualty Reciprocal Exch. v. Wallace, 280 Ala. 61, 189 So. 2d 861 (1966).

Sufficient averment of due process to "final judgment". — Averments that judgment against insured was duly rendered and entered in accordance with jury's verdict, that it had not been satisfied and that more than 30 days had elapsed since its entry sufficiently averred due process to "final judgment" within this section, though not averring that neither motion for new trial nor appeal was pending when complaint to apply insurance money to satisfaction of judgment was filed. Federal Auto. Ins. Ass'n v. Abrams, 217 Ala. 539, 117 So. 85 (1928).

Clause of liability insurance policy requiring assured to render all reasonable cooperation and assistance in defending action was not affected by former Code 1940, T. 28, §§ 11 and 12, where conditions alleged did not justify an action under such statutes.

Metropolitan Cas. Ins. Co. v. Blue, 219 Ala. 37, 121 So. 25 (1929).

Conditions relating to insured's cooperation held not conditions precedent to liability, requiring injured person to plead compliance in action to reach insurance money. American Fid. & Cas. Co. v. Werfel, 230 Ala. 552, 162 So. 103 (1935).

Insurer's liability absolute when loss occurs. — Insurer's liability under terms of policy became absolute when loss occurred through casualty covered by automobile policy, and did not depend on satisfaction of judgment against insured. Indemnity Co. v. Bollas, 223 Ala. 239, 135 So. 174 (1931).

Insurer not released from liability for insured's failure to aid in defending case. — In action under former Code 1940, T. 28, §§ 11 and 12 against indemnity insurer, wherein policy required assured to render to insurer all cooperation and assistance in his power, defendant held not released from liability for insured's failure to aid in defending original case, notwithstanding that insured had removed to another city at time of trial and refused to come to court at his own expense, since such conduct was not lack of cooperation in any substantial respect and no effort was made to take his deposition. George v. Employers' Liab. Assurance Corp., 219 Ala. 307, 122 So. 175 (1929).

Right to collect by garnishment existed independently of former Code 1940, T. 28, §§ 11 and 12. Fleming v. Pan Am. Fire & Cas. Co., 495 F.2d 535 (5th Cir. 1974).

Foreign contract or nonresident parties. — As to a policy insuring the named insured against liability, as distinguished from indemnity against loss, former Code 1940, T. 28, §§ 11 and 12 applied without regard to whether the insurance contract was made in Alabama or not and without regard to whether the named parties to the contract of insurance were residents or nonresidents of Alabama. Fleming v. Pan Am. Fire & Cas. Co., 495 F.2d 535 (5th Cir. 1974).

Voluntary defense by insurer of uninsured codefendant entitles uninsured to protection of insurance. — Where indemnity insurer voluntarily defended insured primarily liable and also uninsured codefendant secondarily liable, codefendant by cross-claim against insurer could secure protection of insurance. United States Fid. & Guar. Co. v. Remond, 221 Ala. 349, 129 So. 15 (1930).

Reliance on agent's representations. — Where an agent makes representations within his apparent authority upon which an insured relies, an insurance company could be bound by the representations of the agent made within his apparent authority. National Sec.

Fire & Cas. Co. v. Reeves, 402 So. 2d 880 (Ala. 1981).

Matters within coverage of automotive liability policy. — Award for punitive damages, loss of time, hospital and doctor bills and other items of expenditures sustained by guest held within coverage of automobile liability policy insuring against loss from claims resulting from bodily injuries or death. Employers Ins. Co. v. Brock, 233 Ala. 551, 172 So. 671 (1937).

Effect of judgment against insured. — Judgment against insured gives injured person lien enforceable against liability insurer. Continental Auto Ins. Underwriters v. Menuskin, 222 Ala. 370, 132 So. 883 (1931).

Under former Code 1940, T. 28, §§ 11 and 12, injured party's complaint against automobile liability insurer was sufficient, though not specifically charging that automobile driven by insured was that covered by policy. Ft. Dearborn Ins. Co. v. Heaton, 224 Ala. 334, 140 So. 441 (1932).

Former Code 1940, T. 28, §§ 11 and 12 were inapplicable to judgment obtained in another state. Ft. Dearborn Ins. Co. v. Heaton, 224 Ala. 334, 140 So. 441 (1932).

Plaintiff's status derivative. — Under former Code 1940, T. 28, §§ 11 and 12, authorizing a plaintiff, with judgment for bodily injury or death against one insured against such loss, to have insurance money applied to satisfaction of judgment, a plaintiff's status is derivative and depends upon liability of insurer to insured under contract, provided that after accident and injury, insurer and insured cannot cancel or annul contract. Employers Ins. Co. v. Johnston, 238 Ala. 26, 189 So. 58 (1939); McDowell v. United States Fid. & Guar. Co., 260 Ala. 412, 71 So. 2d 64 (1954).

He does not have primary claim as contractee of contract. — The remedy provided by former Code 1940, T. 28, §§ 11 and 12, authorizing a plaintiff, with judgment for bodily injury or death against one insured against such loss, to have insurance money applied to satisfaction of judgment did not extend to plaintiff a primary claim as a contractee of such policy with a power to bring an action to enforce it independent of status created between insured, against whom judgment had been entered, and insurer. Employers Ins. Co. v. Johnston, 238 Ala. 26, 189 So. 58 (1939); McDowell v. United States Fid. & Guar. Co., 260 Ala. 412, 71 So. 2d 64 (1954).

Nor can he claim benefit where insured has breached cooperation clause. — Ordinarily, a plaintiff could not claim benefit of former Code 1940, T. 28, §§ 11 and 12, authorizing a plaintiff, with judgment for bodily injury or death against one insured against such loss, to have insurance money applied to satisfaction of judgment where insured had breached terms of cooperative clause requiring insured to cooperate with insurer in defending action, and such breach had not been waived. Employers Ins. Co. v. Johnston, 238 Ala. 26, 189 So. 58 (1939).

Burden on insurer to establish noncooperation by insured. — In guest's action on automobile liability policy for injuries sustained while riding in automobile of insured, burden was on insurer to establish noncooperation by insured so as to justify avoidance of liability by insurer on such grounds. American Fid. & Cas. Co. v. Werfel, 230 Ala. 552, 162 So. 103 (1935); Employers Ins. Co. v. Brock, 233 Ala. 551, 172 So. 671 (1937).

Evidence sufficient to sustain finding of no lack of cooperation. — In guest's action on liability policy for injuries sustained while riding in insured's automobile, evidence was sufficient to justify finding that there was no substantial lack of cooperation by insured which would entitle insurer to avoid policy on ground of noncooperation. Employers Ins. Co. v. Brock, 233 Ala. 551, 172 So. 671 (1937).

Question of fact for jury. — In guest's action on owner's automobile liability policy, question as to whether counsel for insurer was authorized to appear in action in which guest recovered judgment against owner and whether there was a waiver after knowledge of owner's alleged noncooperation with insurer held question of fact for trial court. Employers Ins. Co. v. Brock, 233 Ala. 551, 172 So. 671 (1937).

Cited in James & Hackworth v. Continental Cas. Co., 522 F. Supp. 785 (N.D. Ala. 1980); Baughman v. Harbor Ins. Co., 450 So. 2d 1090 (Ala. 1984).

Collateral references. — Insurer's liability for consequential or punitive damages for wrongful delay or refusal to make payments due under contracts. 47 ALR3d 314.

Right of innocent insured to recover under fire policy covering property intentionally burned by another insured. 11 ALR4th 1228.

Construction and application of provision of liability insurance policy expressly excluding injuries intended or expected by insured. 31 ALR4th 957.

Automobile fire, theft, and collision insurance: insurable interest in stolen motor vehicle. 38 ALR4th 538.

§ 27-23-2. Rights of judgment creditors.

Upon the recovery of a final judgment against any person, firm or corporation by any person, including administrators or executors, for loss or damage on account of bodily injury, or death or for loss or damage to property, if the defendant in such action was insured against the loss or damage at the time when the right of action arose, the judgment creditor shall be entitled to have the insurance money provided for in the contract of insurance between the insurer and the defendant applied to the satisfaction of the judgment, and if the judgment is not satisfied within 30 days after the date when it is entered, the judgment creditor may proceed against the defendant and the insurer to reach and apply the insurance money to the satisfaction of the judgment. (Acts 1953, No. 283, p. 350; Acts 1971, No. 407, p. 707, § 485.)

Editor's note. — Most of the following cases were decided under former Code 1940, T. 28, § 12 or prior law.

In general. — Former Code 1940, T. 28, § 12 made a statutory hypothecation of the claim of the insured defendant against his liability insurer to protect him against liability to the extent of the coverage. Ohio Cas. Ins. Co. v. Gantt, 256 Ala. 262, 54 So. 2d 595 (1951).

By virtue of the statute plaintiff in a judgment for personal injuries had the right to condemn to its satisfaction any matured claim which defendant as insured had by reason of his liability policy against the insurer. Ohio Cas. Ins. Co. v. Gantt, 256 Ala. 262, 54 So. 2d 595 (1951).

Origin of former statute. — Former Code 1940, T. 28, § 12 had its origin in Massachusetts Statutes, 1914, ch. 464, §§ 1, 2. Insurance Co. of N. Am. v. Davis, 274 Ala. 541, 150 So. 2d 192 (1962).

Procedure provided in former Code 1940, Title 28, section 12 was not exclusive. Southern Guar. Ins. Co. v. Jones, 279 Ala. 577, 188 So. 2d 537 (1966).

Procedure provided in that section impaired no contractual obligation and affected no substantive right under the contract of insurance pleaded.

Former Code 1940, Title 28, section 12 merely provided a remedy for enforcing agreement of the insurer to pay the damages contracted by the policy to be paid. Fleming v. Pan Am. Fire & Cas. Co., 495 F.2d 535 (5th Cir. 1974).

This section is procedural and applicable to foreign contracts of insurance. MacMillan-Bloedel, Inc. v. Firemen's Ins. Co., 558 F. Supp. 596 (S.D. Ala. 1983).

Adoption of interpretation by foreign court. — Former Code 1940, T. 28, § 12 was a replica of the Massachusetts statute, and following the customary canon of construction, the supreme court of Alabama adopted the interpretation accorded the statute by the Massachusetts supreme court. Macey v. Crum, 249 Ala. 249, 30 So. 2d 666 (1949); Fleming v. Pan Am. Fire & Cas. Co., 495 F.2d 535 (5th Cir. 1974).

Former Code 1940, Title 28, sections 11 and 12, when construed together, were more than procedural in character and gave the injured party a vested interest (secondary) by way of hypothecation in the amount due the insured by the insurer after the entry of the judgment against the insured. Fleming v. Pan Am. Fire & Cas. Co., 495 F.2d 535 (5th Cir. 1974).

As to when insurer's liability absolute, previously covered by former Code 1940, T. 28, § 11, see § 27-23-1.

Such provisions gave injured party vested interest. — Former Code 1940, T. 28, §§ 11 and 12 held to give injured party vested interest in nature of hypothecation of amount, if any, due by insurer to insured, so that term of policy imposing obligations on insured, such as cooperation clauses, were effective against injured party. George v. Employers' Liab. Assurance Corp., 219 Ala. 307, 122 So. 175 (1929); Macey v. Crum, 249 Ala. 249, 30 So. 2d 666 (1947); State Farm Mut. Auto. Ins. Co. v. McClendon, 269 Ala. 456, 114 So. 2d 153 (1959).

Former Code 1940, T. 28, § 12 gave to the plaintiff in judgment a vested interest by way of hypothecation in the amount due the insured by the insurer after the entry of the judgment against the insurer. Reed v. Hill, 262 Ala. 662, 80 So. 2d 728 (1955).

Either in connection with former Code 1940, T. 28, § 11, or alone, former Code 1940, T. 28, § 12 gave rise to a lien or vested interest on the part of the damaged or injured person by way of hypothecation in the amount due the insured under the terms of the policy. Fleming v. Pan Am. Fire & Cas. Co., 495 F.2d 535 (5th Cir. 1974).

Injured third party having acquired a lien or vested interest, the insurer cannot defeat his

right of action by settlement with the named insured. Fleming v. Pan Am. Fire & Cas. Co., 495 F.2d 535 (5th Cir. 1974).

Former Code 1940, Title 28, section 12 was not one merely of remedial character as to procedure, but one which affected the liability of the insurer and the rights of the insured, as well as one injured by the conduct, against loss from which the assured was insured in his policy. Insurance Co. of N. Am. v. Davis, 274 Ala. 541, 150 So. 2d 192 (1962).

But it was also procedural and related to the remedy, and, under certain conditions, authorized the proceeding to "reach and apply the insurance money to the satisfaction of the judgment." Macey v. Crum, 249 Ala. 249, 30 So. 2d 666 (1947); State Farm Mut. Auto. Ins. Co. v. McClendon, 269 Ala. 456, 114 So. 2d 153 (1959).

This section was more than a procedural statute. National Sur. Corp. v. Sanders, 53 Ala. App. 405, 301 So. 2d 93 (1974).

It did not enlarge or modify in any respect substantial liability created by contract of insurance. It merely enabled the person suffering the initial damages, out of which grew the loss to the insured, to acquire a lien against the loss and the right to damages or indemnity arising under the policy and to enforce it in his own name. Macey v. Crum, 249 Ala. 249, 30 So. 2d 666 (1947); State Farm Mut. Auto. Ins. Co. v. McClendon, 269 Ala. 456, 114 So. 2d 153 (1959).

Remedy partakes of nature of equitable garnishment. — The remedy afforded by former Code 1940, T. 28, § 12 to collect the judgment debt partook of the nature of an equitable garnishment, whereby the judgment creditor could collect his judgment from one who owes the judgment debtor and had agreed to pay the liability imposed by the judgment. Macey v. Crum, 249 Ala. 249, 30 So. 2d 666 (1947); State Farm Mut. Auto. Ins. Co. v. McClendon, 269 Ala. 456, 114 So. 2d 153 (1959).

It was said of this section, and of its parent, the Massachusetts statute, that it but adopted or amplified the familiar equitable process of creditor's bill or equitable attachment. Sansom v. New Amsterdam Ins. Co., 95 F. Supp. 6 (N.D. Ala. 1951).

A judgment creditor may properly utilize garnishment proceedings against a judgment debtor's liability insurer. Southern Guar. Ins. Co. v. Jones, 279 Ala. 577, 188 So. 2d 537 (1966).

And former Code 1940, Title 28, section 12 was applicable where insurance contract was not made in Alabama and the insurer as well as the defendant in judgment were nonresidents of Alabama. Macey v. Crum, 249 Ala. 249, 30 So. 2d 666 (1947).

Former Code 1940, T. 28, § 12 clearly transgressed no legal or constitutional barrier by providing a remedy for the enforcement of rights under a valid contract. The lex loci controls the validity and construction of the contract, but the lex fori operates on the remedy to enforce it. Macey v. Crum, 249 Ala. 249, 30 So. 2d 666 (1947).

Term "final judgment," referred to in former Code 1940, T. 28, § 12 could mean no more than a complete judgment which was then collectible by any and all means provided by law. Ohio Cas. Ins. Co. v. Gantt, 256 Ala. 262, 54 So. 2d 595 (1951).

The "final judgment" referred to in former Code 1940, T. 28, § 12 meant a complete judgment by a court having jurisdiction to enter it, and at a time when plaintiff in that judgment had a legal right to force its payment by such procedure as was available as though no appeal had been taken. An appeal without a stay suspended no right which the plaintiff in the judgment had to enforce its collection. Former Code 1940, T. 28, § 12 provided a proceeding for the collection which was not suspended by appeal without a stay, because it did not suspend the final effect of the judgment and, therefore, the liability stood at that time finally determined, as contemplated by the policy. Ohio Cas. Ins. Co. v. Gantt, 256 Ala. 262, 54 So. 2d 595 (1951); United States Cas. Co. v. Wilson, 262 Ala. 32, 76 So. 2d 506 (1954).

Term "right of action," refers to the right of action against the named insured instead of that against the insurer. Fleming v. Pan Am. Fire & Cas. Co., 495 F.2d 535 (5th Cir. 1974).

Word "may" not indicative of mere permissive joinder. — The use of the word "may" in former Code 1940, T. 28, § 12 was not indicative that the statute merely allowed a permissive joinder, but had to be read in connection with the immediately preceding phrase, i.e., "and if the judgment is not satisfied within 30 days after the date when it is rendered [now entered], the judgment creditor may proceed" which meant that if the judgment were left unsatisfied after the expiration of 30 days, the judgment creditor, should he so desire, could proceed in equity [now circuit court] against the defendant and the insurance company to collect the judgment. Insurance Co. of N. Am. v. Davis, 274 Ala. 541, 150 So. 2d 192 (1962).

Implied agreement by insurer. — The insurer, by issuing a policy of casualty insurance, impliedly agrees to be governed by the terms of this section and to consent that his obligation to the insured shall, to the extent of a judgment recovered by a third person against the assured for a casualty covered by the insurance, be hypothecated for the benefit of such third person. National Sur. Corp. v. Sanders, 53 Ala. App. 405, 301 So. 2d 93 (1974).

Injured third party's cause of action arises immediately upon the happening of accident, and such right cannot be destroyed by subsequent attempts between the insurer and insured to cancel, release or settle the claim. National Sur. Corp. v. Sanders, 53 Ala. App. 405, 301 So. 2d 93 (1974).

Remedy can be exercised only after judgment recovered against insured. — The remedy provided by this section can be exercised only after the injured party has recovered a judgment against the insured. MacMillan-Bloedel, Inc. v. Firemen's Ins. Co., 558 F. Supp. 596 (S.D. Ala. 1983).

Under Alabama law, the injured party acquires a vested interest (secondary) in the nature of a hypothecation of the insured's rights under the policy. Maness v. Alabama Farm Bureau Mut. Cas. Ins. Co., 416 So. 2d 979 (Ala. 1982).

This statute gives rise to a lien or vested interest on the part of the injured person by way of hypothecation in the amount due under the terms of insurance policy. MacMillan-Bloedel, Inc. v. Firemen's Ins. Co., 558 F. Supp. 596 (S.D. Ala. 1983).

Once an injured party has recovered a judgment against the insured, such party may compel the insurer to pay the judgment. The injured party, however, can bring an action against the insurer only after he has recovered a judgment against the insured and only if the insured was covered against the loss or damage at the time the injured party's right of action arose against the insured tort-feasor. Maness v. Alabama Farm Bureau Mut. Cas. Ins. Co., 416 So. 2d 979 (Ala. 1982).

Right to collect by garnishment existed independently of former Code 1940, T. 28, §§ 11 and 12. Fleming v. Pan Am. Fire & Cas. Co., 495 F.2d 535 (5th Cir. 1974).

Right of the judgment creditor relates back to the time when his right to action arose, but his right is, of course, limited to "the insurance money provided for in the contract of insurance." Fleming v. Pan Am. Fire & Cas. Co., 495 F.2d 535 (5th Cir. 1974).

Remedy of plaintiff dependent upon legal effect of contract rights. — The remedy provided by former Code 1940, T. 28, § 12, authorizing a plaintiff, with judgment for bodily injury or death against one insured against such loss, to have insurance money applied to satisfaction of judgment, was dependent upon legal effect of contract rights of injured party against insurer. Employers Ins. Co. v. Johnston, 238 Ala. 26, 189 So. 58 (1939).

Provision held applicable although rights of insured primary. — The remedy provided by former Code 1940, T. 28, § 12, authorizing a plaintiff, with judgment for bodily injury or death against one insured against such loss, to have insurance money applied to satisfaction of judgment, could be available although rights of insured party primary and not derivative. Employers Ins. Co. v. Johnston, 238 Ala. 26, 189 So. 58 (1939).

And provision held not applicable. — Former Code 1940, T. 28, § 12, authorizing action against insurer of judgment creditor in personal injury action, was not applicable where bank president gave indemnity to bank's liquidating agent to protect it against claim of landowner who had allegedly forwarded lease to bank with instructions to turn it over to president as her lessee on payment of a stipulated sum. Baker v. Baldwin County Bank, 232 Ala. 359, 168 So. 141 (1936).

Court properly dismissed complaint not bringing an action to compel insurer to pay judgment against insured within statute respecting enforcing liability against insurer after judgment. Franklin v. Georgia Cas. Co., 225 Ala. 58, 141 So. 702 (1932).

Complaint could only be dismissed since the jurisdiction conferred on courts by former Code 1940, T. 28, § 12 to enforce liability against insurer after judgment was statutory and limited. Franklin v. Georgia Cas. Co., 225 Ala. 58, 141 So. 702 (1932).

Joinder of insured. — Though the matter may be fraught with some doubt, and there was no intention of putting it to rest here, it would appear that former Code 1940, T. 28, § 12 did not require the joinder of the insured in every action brought under its authority. Sansom v. New Amsterdam Ins. Co., 95 F. Supp. 6 (N.D. Ala. 1951).

Foreign contract and nonresidency of parties immaterial. — As to a policy insuring the named insured against liability, as distinguished from indemnity against loss, former Code 1940, T. 28, §§ 11 and 12 applied without regard to whether the insurance contract was made in Alabama or not and without regard to whether the named parties to the contract of insurance were residents or nonresidents of Alabama. Fleming v. Pan Am. Fire & Cas. Co., 495 F.2d 535 (5th Cir. 1974).

Foreign judgment. — Where complaint in action under former Code 1940, T. 28, § 12 was objected to on grounds it did not allege that the original judgment was recovered in the courts of this state, nor allege with specificity that the nisi prius court had lost jurisdiction of the original judgment, to a point where it could no longer certify an appeal, these objections were affirmative defenses. United States Cas. Co. v. Wilson, 262 Ala. 32, 76 So. 2d 506 (1954).

Where Arkansas judgment was based on finding of fact that insured was physically present in the automobile directing the movements and directions and exhorting the driver to an unlawful rate of speed, Alabama trial court was correct in finding that the insured was "operating" the automobile within the meaning of the exclusive endorsement of policy providing coverages were in force only when insured was operating vehicle. Trans-Continental Mut. Ins. Co. v. Harrison, 262 Ala. 373, 78 So. 2d 917 (1955).

Insured is "necessary party" in an action to subject the proceeds of liability insurance to judgments secured against the insured in prior tort actions, under the rule that all persons having a material interest in the litigation, or who are legally or beneficially interested in the subject matter of the action and whose rights or interests are sought to be concluded thereby, are necessary parties. Insurance Co. of N. Am. v. Davis, 274 Ala. 541, 150 So. 2d 192 (1962); Alabama Farm Bureau Mut. Cas. Ins. Co. v. Crestman, 277 Ala. 410, 171 So. 2d 119 (1965).

Where provisions of policy render it a "claims-made" or "discovery" type of policy rather than an "occurrence" policy, that provision is not contrary to the public policy of the state. James & Hackworth v. Continental Cas. Co., 522 F. Supp. 785 (N.D. Ala. 1980).

When insurance company not party and not bound by previous judgment. — A party and his privies are generally bound by a previous judgment or decree, but there can be no privity where there is no identity of interest. Where a defendant insurance company was not a party to the previous action and that action did not address the question of whether the defamatory acts were excluded under the specific exclusionary clause, it cannot be bound by the previous action and can thus allege and prove that the offenses charged were either directly or indirectly related to a plaintiff's employment by the defendant's insured. Butler v. Michigan Mut. Ins. Co., 402 So. 2d 949 (Ala. 1981).

Where policy not renewed. — Where the record clearly shows without dispute that the insured architects did not renew their policy, neither they nor the plaintiff can claim benefit of the rider prohibiting cancellation change or lapse as to a mortgagee and the Secretary of the Department of Housing and Urban Development. James & Hackworth v. Continental Cas. Co., 522 F. Supp. 785 (N.D. Ala. 1980).

Automobile liability policy covering accidental personal injury or death held to cover punitive damages for bodily injuries, and hence, injured person's judgment against insured, even though including punitive damages, was for "bodily injury" within this sec-

345

tion. American Fid. & Cas. Co. v. Werfel, 230 Ala. 552, 162 So. 103 (1935).

No liability where insurance clause did not protect any person other than insured. — Automobile liability insurer held not liable to pay judgment against insured's son for injuries sustained through son's negligence in operating insured's automobile where general insuring clause of policy did not protect any person other than insured, though policy provided that insurer should not be liable unless automobile was being operated, among others, by members of insured's immediate family. State Farm Mut. Auto. Ins. Co. v. Burwell, 232 Ala. 11, 166 So. 598 (1936).

Proceedings must be brought against defendant and insurance company. — The legislature intended that proceedings under former Code 1940, T. 28, § 12 had to be brought against the defendant in the action and the insurance company as joint defendants. Insurance Co. of N. Am. v. Davis, 274 Ala. 541, 150 So. 2d 192 (1962).

The phraseology of former Code 1940, T. 28, § 12 which read "against the defendant and the insurance company" was connotative of the idea that the defendant was essential in the minds of the legislators in adopting the section. The two parties were joined in the conjunctive, and not in the disjunctive, which in statutory interpretation meant that both matters so joined must mutually coexist. Insurance Co. of N. Am. v. Davis, 274 Ala. 541, 150 So. 2d 192 (1962).

When remedy can be exercised. — The remedy provided by former Code 1940, T. 28, § 12 could be exercised only after the injured or damaged party had recovered final judgment against the insured, and only if the defendant in such action was insured against said loss or damage at the time when the right of action arose. Fleming v. Pan Am. Fire & Cas. Co., 495 F.2d 535 (5th Cir. 1974).

Cited in Dumas Bros. Mfg. Co. v. Southern Guar. Ins. Co., 431 So. 2d 534 (Ala. 1983); Baughman v. Harbor Ins. Co., 450 So. 2d 1090 (Ala. 1984); Thompson v. Hartford Accident & Indem. Co., 460 So. 2d 1264 (Ala. 1984).

Collateral references. — Limitation of actions against liability insurer for failure to settle claim or action against insured. 68 ALR2d 892.

Interest: liability insurer's liability for interest and costs on excess of judgment over policy limit. 76 ALR2d 983.

Conflicting interests: liability insurer's rights and duties as to defense and settlement as affected by its having issued policies covering parties who have conflicting interests. 18 ALR3d 482.

Insurer's failure to pay amount of admitted liability as precluding reliance on statute of limitations. 41 ALR3d 1111.

ARTICLE 2.

CANCELLATION OF AUTOMOBILE LIABILITY INSURANCE.

§ 27-23-20. Definitions.

For the purposes of this article, the following terms shall have the meanings respectively ascribed to them by this section.

(1) POLICY OF AUTOMOBILE LIABILITY INSURANCE. A policy delivered, or issued for delivery, in this state insuring a natural person as named insured or one or more related individuals, resident of the same household, and under which the insured vehicles therein designated are of the following types only:

a. A motor vehicle of the private passenger or station type that is not used as a public or livery conveyance for passengers nor rented to others; or

b. Any other four-wheel motor vehicle with a load capacity of 1,500 pounds or less which is not used in the occupation, profession or business of the insured; provided, however, that this article shall not apply:

1. To policies of automobile liability insurance issued under an automobile assigned risk plan;

2. To any policy insuring more than four automobiles; nor

3. To any policy covering garage, automobile sales agency, repair shop, service station or public parking place operation hazards and provided, further, that this article shall apply only to that portion of an automobile liability policy insuring against bodily injury and property damage liability and to the provisions therein, if any, relating to medical payments and uninsured motorists' coverage.

(2) NONPAYMENT OF PREMIUM. Failure of the named insured to discharge, when due, any of his obligations in connection with the payment of premiums on a policy of automobile liability insurance or any installment of such premium, whether the premium is payable directly to the insurer or its agent or indirectly under any premium finance plan or extension of credit. (Acts 1971, No. 407, p. 707, § 485.1.)

Notice requirement inapplicable where garage liability provision severable and excluded. — Under this section and section 27-23-23 requiring 20 days' notice of cancellation, unless, among other things, policy insured more than four automobiles or covered garage hazards, inasmuch as insured had five vehicles covered by policy, statutory notice requirement is inapplicable. Furthermore, even assuming notice requirement would be applicable where at least two of the vehicles were trucks, garage liability provision was clearly severable and therefore excluded by statute. Security Ins. Co. v. Smith, 360 So. 2d 280 (Ala. 1978).

Collateral references. — Who is "member" or "resident" of same "family" or "household," within no-fault or uninsured motorist provisions of motor vehicle insurance policy. 96 ALR3d 804.

Cancellation of compulsory or "financial responsibility" automobile insurance. 44 ALR4th 13.

§ 27-23-21. Reasons for cancellation.

(a) No notice of cancellation of a policy of automobile liability insurance shall be effective unless it is based on one or more of the following reasons:

(1) Nonpayment of premium;

(2) The policy was obtained through a material misrepresentation;

(3) Any insured violated any of the terms and conditions of the policy;

(4) The named insured failed to disclose fully his motor vehicle accidents and moving traffic violations for the preceding 36 months if called for in the application;

(5) The named insured failed to disclose in his written application or in response to inquiry by his broker, or by the insurer or its agent information necessary for the acceptance or proper rating of the risk;

(6) Any insured made a false or fraudulent claim or knowingly aided or abetted another in the presentation of such a claim;

(7) Failure to maintain membership in any group or organization when such membership is a prerequisite to the purchase of such insurance;

(8) The named insured or any other operator who either resides in the same household or customarily operates an automobile insured under such policy:

a. Has within the 36 months prior to the notice of cancellation had his driver's license under suspension or revocation;

b. Is, or becomes, subject to epilepsy or heart attacks, and such individual does not produce a certificate from a physician testifying to his unqualified ability to operate a motor vehicle safely;

c. Has an accident record, conviction record (criminal or traffic), physical, mental or other condition which is such that his operation of an automobile might endanger the public safety;

d. Has within the 36 months prior to the notice of cancellation been addicted to the use of narcotics or other drugs;

e. Uses alcoholic beverage to excess;

f. Has been convicted or forfeited bail during the 36 months immediately preceding the notice of cancellation for:

1. Any felony;

2. Criminal negligence resulting in death, homicide or assault arising out of the operation of a motor vehicle;

3. Operating a motor vehicle while in an intoxicated condition or while under the influence of drugs;

4. Being intoxicated while in, or about, an automobile or while having custody of an automobile;

5. Leaving the scene of an accident without stopping to report;

6. Theft or unlawful taking of a motor vehicle;

7. Making false statements in an application for a driver's license; or

g. Has been convicted of or forfeited bail for three or more violations, within the 36 months immediately preceding the notice of cancellation, of any law, ordinance or regulation limiting the speed of motor vehicle laws of any state, violation of which constitutes a misdemeanor, whether or not the violations were repetitions of the same offense or different offenses; or

(9) The insured automobile is:

a. So mechanically defective that its operation might endanger public safety;

b. Used in carrying passengers for hire or compensation; provided, however, that the use of an automobile for a car pool shall not be considered use of an automobile for hire or compensation;

c. Used in the business of transportation of flammables or explosives;

d. An authorized emergency vehicle;

e. Changed in shape or condition during the policy period so as to increase the risk substantially; or

f. Subject to an inspection law and has not been inspected or, if inspected, has failed to qualify.

(b) This section shall not apply to any policy of automobile liability insurance which has been in effect less than 60 days at the time notice of cancellation is mailed or delivered by the insurer unless it is a renewal policy. (Acts 1971, No. 407, p. 707, § 485.2.)

Policies may only be canceled in compliance with this section. — This statute does not permit a policy of insurance to be canceled for "any reason," but requires that a policy be canceled in compliance with this section. American Serv. Mut. Ins. Co. v. Grizzard, 356 So. 2d 191 (Ala. Civ. App. 1978).

Proof of valid cancellation. — In order to prove valid cancellation of automobile liability insurance policy plaintiff must prove that cancellation was based on one of the reasons listed in this section. Green v. Standard Fire Ins. Co., 398 So. 2d 671 (Ala. 1981).

Insurer does not have to meet the re- quirements of this section and § 27-23-23 when cancelling collision and comprehensive coverages since these sections specifically apply to automobile liability policies. Green v. Standard Fire Ins. Co., 398 So. 2d 671 (Ala. 1981).

Collateral references. — 45 C.J.S., Insurance, § 450, n. 3.

7 Am. Jur. 2d, Automobile Insurance, §§ 8-10.

Cancellation of compulsory or "financial responsibility" automobile insurance. 44 ALR4th 13.

§ 27-23-22. Effect of renewal.

Renewal of a policy shall not constitute a waiver or estoppel with respect to grounds for cancellation which existed before the effective date of such renewal. (Acts 1971, No. 407, p. 707, § 485.4.)

Collateral references. — Cancellation of compulsory or "financial responsibility" automobile insurance. 44 ALR4th 13.

§ 27-23-23. Notice of cancellation — Time; reasons.

No notice of cancellation of a policy to which section 27-23-21 applies shall be effective unless mailed or delivered by the insurer to the named insured at least 20 days prior to the effective date of cancellation; provided, however, that where cancellation is for nonpayment of premium, at least 10 days' notice of cancellation accompanied by the reason therefor shall be given. Unless the reason, or reasons, accompany or are included in the notice of cancellation, the notice of cancellation shall state, or be accompanied by a statement, that upon written request of the named insured, mailed or delivered to the insurer not less than 15 days prior to the effective date of cancellation, the insurer will specify the reason, or reasons, for such cancellation. (Acts 1971, No. 407, p. 707, § 485.3.)

Right of insurer to cancel insurance policy is strictly construed and the condition imposed upon it with respect to giving notice of cancellation must be strictly performed. Green v. Standard Fire Ins. Co., 398 So. 2d 671 (Ala. 1981).

A statement which gives notice that as soon as practicable after cancellation the insurance company would settle up with the policyholder is not a statement which gives notice of the reason for cancellation. Green v. Standard Fire Ins. Co., 398 So. 2d 671 (Ala. 1981).

Provision inapplicable where more than four cars or garage liability. — Under this section and section 27-23-20(1)(b) requiring 20 days' notice of cancellation, unless, among other things, policy insured more than four automobiles or covered garage hazards, inasmuch as insured had five vehicles covered by policy, statutory notice requirement is inapplicable. Furthermore, even assuming notice requirement would be applicable where at least two of the vehicles were trucks, garage liability provision was clearly severable and therefore excluded by statute. Security Ins. Co. v. Smith, 360 So. 2d 280 (Ala. 1978).

Cited in Yarbrough v. State Farm Mut. Auto. Ins. Co., 365 So. 2d 654 (Ala. 1978); Rolling "R" Constr., Inc. v. Dodd, 477 So. 2d 330 (Ala. 1985).

Collateral references. — 45 C.J.S., Insurance, §§ 440, 450, 458, n. 88.
Cancellation of compulsory or "financial responsibility" automobile insurance. 44 ALR4th 13.

§ 27-23-24. Same — Availability of assigned risk plan notification.

When a policy is cancelled other than for nonpayment of premium, the insurer shall notify the named insured of his possible eligibility for insurance through the automobile assigned risk plan. Such notice shall accompany, or be included in, the notice of cancellation and shall state that such notice of availability of the automobile assigned risk plan is given pursuant to this article. (Acts 1971, No. 407, p. 707, § 485.6.)

Collateral references. — Cancellation of compulsory or "financial responsibility" automobile insurance. 44 ALR4th 13.

§ 27-23-25. Same — Proof of notice.

Proof of mailing of notice of cancellation or of reasons for cancellation to the named insured at the address shown in the policy shall be sufficient proof of notice. (Acts 1971, No. 407, p. 707, § 485.5.)

Cited in Hilliar v. State Farm Mut. Auto. Ins. Co., 451 So. 2d 287 (Ala. 1984).
Collateral references. — Cancellation of compulsory or "financial responsibility" automobile insurance. 44 ALR4th 13.

§ 27-23-26. Specification of reasons for cancellation upon insured's request.

Where the reason, or reasons, for cancellation do not accompany or are not included in the notice of cancellation, the insurer shall, upon written request of the named insured, mailed or delivered to the insurer not less than 15 days prior to the effective date of cancellation, specify in writing the reason, or reasons, for such cancellation. Such reasons shall be mailed or delivered to the named insured within five days after nonpayment of premium. This section shall apply only to a cancellation to which section 27-23-21 applies. (Acts 1971, No. 407, p. 707, § 485.7.)

Collateral references. — Cancellation of compulsory or "financial responsibility" automobile insurance. 44 ALR4th 13.

§ 27-23-27. Liability of insurer, etc., for statements, etc.

There shall be no liability on the part of and no cause of action of any nature shall arise against any insurer, its authorized representative, its agents, its employees or any firm, person or corporation furnishing to the insurer information as to reasons for cancellation for any statement made by any of them in any written notice of cancellation, for the providing of information pertaining thereto or for statements made or evidence submitted at the hearings conducted in connection therewith. (Acts 1971, No. 407, p. 707, § 485.8.)

Collateral references. — Cancellation of compulsory or "financial responsibility" automobile insurance. 44 ALR4th 13.

§ 27-23-28. Applicability of article to nonrenewal.

Nothing in this article shall apply to nonrenewal. (Acts 1971, No. 407, p. 707, § 485.9.)

Collateral references. — Cancellation of compulsory or "financial responsibility" automobile insurance. 44 ALR4th 13.

CHAPTER 24.

SURETY INSURANCE CONTRACTS.

Sec.
27-24-1. Applicability of chapter.
27-24-2. Sole surety — Corporations.
27-24-3. Same — Mutual or reciprocal surety
          insurers.
27-24-4. Same — Cosureties on bond of state
          treasurer.
27-24-5. Additional bond upon insolvency,
          etc., of surety.

Sec.
27-24-6. Venue of actions on bonds or under-
          takings.
27-24-7. Estoppel of insurer to deny its
          power, etc.
27-24-8. Rights and remedies of insurers.

Collateral references. — 44 C.J.S., Insurance, § 16.

§ 27-24-1. Applicability of chapter.

This chapter shall not apply to any bond or undertaking which is not by law required to be approved by any state, county, municipal, precinct, township, district or other like office, officers, commissions, boards and similar governing bodies, or by any judge, clerk or register of any court of this state or to insurers engaged only in the business of becoming sureties on any such bond or undertaking. (Acts 1909, No. 147, p. 329; Acts 1971, No. 407, p. 707, § 486.)

§ 27-24-2. Sole surety — Corporations.

Except as provided in section 27-24-4, whenever any person or corporation is, or may be, required or permitted to execute bond or other undertaking, of whatsoever nature, with surety, or sureties, for the faithful discharge or performance of the duties of any state, county, municipal, precinct, township, district or corporate office or position or of any position of public or private trust or employment for the faithful discharge or performance of any duty or for the doing or not doing of anything in such bond or undertaking specified or when any person or corporation is required or permitted to execute any bond or other undertaking, of whatsoever nature, with surety or sureties, in any judicial proceeding or as guardian, executor, administrator, receiver, assignee or trustee, the court, officer or person having authority or charged with the duty of approving such bond or undertaking may, if such bond or undertaking is otherwise sufficient, approve the same when executed by a corporation having the power or authority under its charter to become surety on such bond or undertaking as surety and having complied with the provisions of this title. The execution by any such corporation as surety of any such bond or undertaking shall be, in all respects, upon the approval and acceptance of such bond, a full and complete compliance with the requirements of any law, ordinance, rule or regulation requiring that such bond or undertaking shall be executed by one surety, or by one or more sureties, or that such surety, or sureties, shall be residents of the state, or any county therein, or shall be householders or freeholders, or either or both, or shall possess any other qualification. (Code 1940, T. 41, § 98; Acts 1971, No. 407, p. 707, § 487.)

§ 27-24-3. Same — Mutual or reciprocal surety insurers.

An authorized mutual or reciprocal surety insurer which has and maintains a surplus over and above all of its liabilities of $500,000.00, upon meeting all of the requirements of this title, except as to capital stock, may become and be accepted as sole surety on bonds or undertakings required or permitted by the laws of this state or by the charters, ordinances, rules and regulations of any county, municipal corporation, board, body, organization or public officer; provided, however, that any such bond or undertaking executed by such insurer shall be nonassessable and shall not provide for any contingent liability. (Acts 1947, No. 533, p. 388; Acts 1971, No. 407, p. 707, § 488.)

§ 27-24-4. Same — Cosureties on bond of state treasurer.

No such corporation or insurer shall, however, be accepted as sole surety on the bond of the state treasurer but may become and be accepted as a cosurety with other persons or with other authorized surety insurers upon such bond, and in such event, its property or credit shall not be estimated to exceed $100,000.00. (Code 1940, T. 41, § 102; Acts 1971, No. 407, p. 707, § 489.)

§ 27-24-5. Additional bond upon insolvency, etc., of surety.

If the authority of a surety insurer to transact business in this state is revoked or otherwise terminated upon the ground that the insurer is insolvent or cannot be safely accepted as surety upon bonds and undertakings mentioned in section 27-24-2, it shall be the duty of any officer in this state authorized to approve official bonds, upon receiving the circular letter from the commissioner as provided for in subsection (c) of section 27-3-22 or upon otherwise being informed of such revocation or termination, to require the principal in any such bond upon which such insurer has become surety to give an additional bond as provided by law. (Acts 1909, No. 147, p. 329; Acts 1971, No. 407, p. 707, § 490.)

§ 27-24-6. Venue of actions on bonds or undertakings.

Any official bond or undertaking executed by a surety insurer may have an action maintained on it in the county of the residence of the principal or in which he resided at the time of the execution of the bond or undertaking, but actions by the state shall be brought in Montgomery county. (Code 1940, T. 41, § 104; Acts 1971, No. 407, p. 707, § 491.)

§ 27-24-7. Estoppel of insurer to deny its power, etc.

No corporation or insurer having signed any such official bond or undertaking shall be permitted to deny its corporate or other power to execute such instrument or incur such liability in any proceedings to enforce liability against the insurer thereunder. (Code 1940, T. 41, § 105; Acts 1971, No. 407, p. 707, § 492.)

§ 27-24-8. Rights and remedies of insurers.

Such an insurer as surety on any official bond, undertaking or obligation is entitled to all the rights and remedies of other sureties on such instruments; and any insurer becoming surety on any bond or undertaking, as authorized by this chapter, shall have the same right to be relieved from further liability thereon or to require the principal to give new or additional bonds or undertakings as is conferred by law upon the other sureties on like bonds or undertakings. (Code 1940, T. 41, § 107; Acts 1971, No. 407, p. 707, § 493.)

CHAPTER 25.

TITLE INSURANCE.

Sec.
27-25-1. Enjoining of certain acts; revocation
of charter for violating same.

§ 27-25-1. Enjoining of certain acts; revocation of charter for violating same.

If from any examination of a title insurer the commissioner finds that the insurer is violating any of the provisions of section 34-3-7, the commissioner shall so certify his findings in writing to the attorney general, and the attorney general shall forthwith bring an action in a court of competent jurisdiction in the state of Alabama to permanently enjoin the commission of such acts by the insurer. If the insurer violates any of the provisions of such an injunction, the attorney general shall forthwith bring an action in such court to revoke the corporate charter of such insurer, if a domestic corporation. (Acts 1923, No. 485, p. 635; Acts 1949, No. 168, p. 195; Acts 1971, No. 407, p. 707, § 494.)

Cited in Land Title Co. v. State ex rel. Porter, 292 Ala. 691, 299 So. 2d 289 (1974).

Collateral references. — Determination of what constitutes a charge, encumbrance, or lien within the contemplation of a title insurance policy. 87 ALR3d 764.

Title insurance company's rights in title information. 38 ALR4th 968.

CHAPTER 26.

MEDICAL LIABILITY INSURANCE.

Article 1.

General Provisions.

Sec.
27-26-1. Definitions.
27-26-2. Purpose of chapter.
27-26-3. When sale condition of doing business in state.
27-26-4. Annual reports of carriers.
27-26-5. Report of judgments and settlements; confidentiality; penalty.

Article 2.

Joint Underwriting Association.

27-26-20. Purpose.
27-26-21. Creation; composition.
27-26-22. Board of directors.
27-26-23. Powers and duties generally.
27-26-24. Cooperation with board and policyholders.
27-26-25. Plan of operation.
27-26-26. When underwriting operations commenced.

Sec.
27-26-27. Stabilization reserve fund — Generally.
27-26-28. Same — Charge.
27-26-29. Recoupment of shares of deficit.
27-26-30. Holding in trust and investing of funds.
27-26-31. Insufficiency of funds.
27-26-32. Application for coverage.
27-26-33. Policies generally.
27-26-34. Issuance of policy.
27-26-35. Cancellation of policies.
27-26-36. Rating plans.
27-26-37. Proration of participation in writings, expenses, etc.
27-26-38. Annual statements.
27-26-39. Examination of association's affairs.
27-26-40. Liability for statements made during proceedings, etc.
27-26-41. Effect of public officer's or employee's membership on board or directors of fund.
27-26-42. Appeal to commissioner.
27-26-43. Judicial review of commissioner's orders.

ARTICLE 1.

GENERAL PROVISIONS.

Cross references. — As to medical liability actions, see § 6-5-480 et seq. As to trusts for payment of liability claims against hospitals, etc., see § 22-21-240 et seq.

Collateral references. — 44 C.J.S., Insurance, §§ 94-114.

Public regulation or control of insurance agents or brokers. 10 ALR2d 950.

Coverage and exclusions of liability or indemnity policy on physicians, surgeons, and other healers. 33 ALR4th 14.

§ 27-26-1. Definitions.

For purposes of this chapter, the following words and phrases shall have the respective meanings ascribed by this section:

(1) MEDICAL PRACTITIONER. Anyone licensed to practice medicine or osteopathy in the state of Alabama, engaged in such practice, and shall include medical professional corporations, associations, and partnerships.

(2) DENTAL PRACTITIONER. Anyone licensed to practice dentistry in the state of Alabama, engaged in such practice, and such term includes professional dental corporations, associations and partnerships.

(3) MEDICAL INSTITUTION. Any licensed hospital, or any physicians' or dentists' offices or clinics containing facilities for the examination, diagnosis, treatment or care of human illnesses.

(4) PROFESSIONAL CORPORATION. Any medical or dental professional corporation or any medical or dental professional association.

(5) PHYSICIAN. Any person licensed to practice medicine in Alabama.

(6) DENTIST. Any person licensed to practice dentistry in Alabama.

(7) HOSPITAL. Such institutions as are defined in section 22-21-20 as hospitals.

(8) OTHER HEALTH CARE PROVIDERS. Any professional corporation or any person employed by physicians, dentists and hospitals who are directly involved in the delivery of health care services.

(9) MEDICAL LIABILITY. A finding by a judge, jury or arbitration panel that a physician, dentist, medical institution or other health care provider did not meet the applicable standard of care and that such failure was the proximate cause of the injury complained of, resulting in damage to the patient.

(10) BOARD. The board of directors of the joint underwriting association created by section 27-26-22. (Acts 1975, No. 513, p. 1148, § 3.)

Collateral references. — What constitutes a "hospital" within coverage or exclusionary clauses of hospitalization policy. 46 ALR3d 1244.

Acts in self-defense as within provision of liability insurance policy expressly excluding coverage for damage or injury intended or expected by insured. 34 ALR4th 761.

Criminal conviction as rendering conduct for which insured convicted within provisions of liability insurance policy expressly excluding coverage for damage or injury intended or expected by insured. 35 ALR4th 1063.

§ 27-26-2. Purpose of chapter.

It is hereby declared by the legislature of the state of Alabama that the availability of medical liability insurance at reasonable rates for the medical profession, medical institutions and other health care providers is essential to provide adequate health services to the people of Alabama, and without such insurance, medical services by the medical profession may be curtailed, and that while the need for such insurance is increasing, availability is limited and likely to become increasingly so, unless remedial legislation is enacted. The legislature further finds and declares that by reason of complicated and highly technical medical concepts, and the existence of sophisticated medical techniques, decisions with respect to optional procedures of diagnosis and treatment have become increasingly complex and are necessarily made on the basis of professional judgment, on which opinions may and often will reasonably vary. It is the purpose of this chapter to insure that the citizens of the state of Alabama are able to receive necessary health services by providing an environment in which the medical profession can be assured of medical liability insurance coverage and be afforded reasonable protection against personal liability for consequences proximately resulting from decisions with respect to diagnosis and treatment arrived at in the bona fide exercise of professional judgment. (Acts 1975, No. 513, p. 1148, § 2.)

§ 27-26-3. When sale condition of doing business in state.

Any insurance company writing casualty insurance in the state of Alabama which sells medical liability insurance in other states must make medical liability insurance available to Alabama physicians, hospitals and other health care providers as a condition of doing business in Alabama. (Acts 1975, No. 513, p. 1148, § 12.)

§ 27-26-4. Annual reports of carriers.

All insurance carriers writing medical liability insurance policies shall be required to make annual reports of the number of claims and cost incurred to the commissioner on such forms and in such manner as the commissioner may require. (Acts 1975, No. 513, p. 1148, § 9.)

§ 27-26-5. Report of judgments and settlements; confidentiality; penalty.

(a) Any insurance company which sells medical liability insurance to Alabama physicians, hospitals or other health care providers shall be required to report to the state licensing agency which issues the license of the physician, hospital or other health care provider any final judgment or any settlement in or out of court resulting from a claim or action for damages for personal injuries caused by an error, omission or negligence in the performance of professional services with or without consent rendered by its policy holder within 30 days after entry of a judgment in court or agreement to settle a claim in or out of court.

(b) The report rendered to the appropriate state agency shall consist of the name of the policyholder, the name of the claimant, a summary of the allegations made in the lawsuit, the injuries incurred by the claimant and the terms of the judgment or settlement.

(c) The report rendered pursuant to the requirements of this section, and any and all information, interviews, reports, statements, memorandum, or other documents produced by the licensing board as a result of any investigation of the subject matter of the report are declared to be privileged and confidential. All such records, reports, proceedings or other documents and any findings, conclusions, recommendations or actions of the licensing board shall be confidential and shall not be public records nor available for court subpoena or for discovery proceedings. Nothing contained herein shall apply to records made in the regular course of business of a physician, hospital or other health care provider and information, documents or records otherwise available from original sources are not to be construed as immune from discovery or use in civil proceedings merely because they were presented to or considered by the licensing board.

(d) The failure to make the reports required by this section within the time periods which are provided shall be punishable under section 27-1-12. (Acts 1986, No. 86-441.)

Effective date. — The act which added this section became effective April 29, 1986.

ARTICLE 2.

JOINT UNDERWRITING ASSOCIATION.

§ 27-26-20. Purpose.

The purpose of the joint underwriting association shall be to provide a market for medical liability insurance on a self-supporting basis without subsidy from its members. (Acts 1975, No. 513, p. 1148, § 7(2).)

§ 27-26-21. Creation; composition.

A joint underwriting association is hereby created, consisting of all insurers authorized to write and engage in writing, within this state on a direct basis, property and casualty insurance as defined in sections 27-5-5 and 27-5-6. Every such insurer shall be a member of the association and shall remain a member as a condition of its authority to continue to transact such kind of insurance in this state. (Acts 1975, No. 513, p. 1148, § 7(1).)

§ 27-26-22. Board of directors.

The association shall be governed by a board of 11 directors, to be appointed for one-year terms by the commissioner. Two of such 11 shall represent insurers which write property and casualty insurance in Alabama, as defined in sections 27-5-5 and 27-5-6 in Alabama and are members of the National Association of Independent Insurers, two shall represent insurers which write property and casualty insurance in Alabama, as defined in sections 27-5-5 and 27-5-6 and are members of the American Insurance Association, two shall represent insurers which write property and casualty insurance in Alabama, as defined in sections 27-5-5 and 27-5-6 and are members of the American Mutual Insurance Alliance, two shall represent insurers which write property and casualty insurance in Alabama, as defined in sections 27-5-5 and 27-5-6 but are not members of any of the foregoing trade associations. Three directors shall be appointed by the commissioner of insurance as representatives of accident and health insurers and prepaid medical, surgical and dental service plan providers. Directors shall be reimbursed out of the administrative funds of the joint underwriting association for necessary and actual expenses incurred for attending meetings of the governing board. (Acts 1975, No. 513, p. 1148, § 7(25).)

359

§ 27-26-23. Powers and duties generally.

The association shall, pursuant to the provisions of this chapter and the plan of operation with respect to medical liability insurance, have the power on behalf of its members to:

(1) Issue, or to cause to be issued, policies of insurance to applicants, including incidental coverages and subject to limits as specified in the plan of operation but not to exceed $1,000,000.00 for each claimant under one policy in any one year;

(2) Underwrite such insurance and adjust and pay losses with respect thereto, or appoint service companies to perform those functions;

(3) Assume reinsurance from its members; and

(4) Cede reinsurance. (Acts 1975, No. 513, p. 1148, § 7(4).)

§ 27-26-24. Cooperation with board and policyholders.

The association and its members are authorized and encouraged to cooperate with the board and the association's actual or prospective policyholders on all matters pertaining to the board's duties and the insurance issued or to be issued by the association. (Acts 1975, No. 513, p. 1148, § 7(5).)

§ 27-26-25. Plan of operation.

(a) Within 45 days following the creation of the association, the directors of the association shall submit to the commissioner, for his review, a proposed plan of operation, consistent with the provisions of this chapter.

(b) The plan of operation shall provide for economic, fair and nondiscriminatory administration and for the prompt and efficient provisions of medical liability insurance, and shall contain other provisions including but not limited to preliminary assessment of all members for initial expenses necessary to commence operations, establishment of necessary facilities, management of the association, assessment of members to defray losses and expenses, commission arrangements, reasonable and objective underwriting standards, acceptance and cession of reinsurance, appointment of servicing carriers or other servicing arrangements and procedures for determining amounts of insurance to be provided by the association.

(c) The plan of operation shall be subject to approval by the commissioner after consultation with the members of the association, representatives of the public and other affected individuals and organizations. If the commissioner disapproves all or any part of the proposed plan of operation, the directors shall within 15 days submit for review an appropriate revised plan of operation or part thereof. If the directors fail to do so, the commissioner shall promulgate a plan of operation or part thereof, as the case may be. The plan of operation approved or promulgated by the commissioner shall become effective and operational upon order by the commissioner.

(d) Amendments to the plan of operation may be made by the directors of the association, subject to the approval of the commissioner, or shall be made at the direction of the commissioner. (Acts 1975, No. 513, p. 1148, § 7(6)-(9).)

§ 27-26-26. When underwriting operations commenced.

The association shall not commence underwriting operations for physicians until the commissioner, after due hearing and investigation, has determined that medical liability insurance cannot be made available for physicians in the voluntary market. Upon such determination the association shall be an agency through which medical liability insurance may be written in this state on a primary basis for physicians. The association may also issue premises liability insurance to physicians, but need not be the exclusive agency through which either medical liability or premises liability insurance may be issued.

The association shall not commence underwriting operations for hospitals until the commissioner, after due hearing and investigation, has determined that medical liability insurance is not readily available for hospitals in the voluntary market. Upon such determination the association shall be authorized to issue policies of medical liability insurance and premises liability insurance to physicians, but need not be the exclusive agency through which such insurance may be written on a primary basis in this state.

The association shall not commence underwriting operations for other licensed health care providers until the commissioner, after due hearing and investigation, has determined that medical liability insurance cannot be made available for a specific type of licensed health care provider in the voluntary market. Upon such determination the association shall be the exclusive agency through which medical liability insurance may be written in this state on a primary basis for such specific type of health provider.

If the commissioner determines at any time that medical liability insurance can be made available in the voluntary market for either physicians, hospitals or any specific type of other licensed health care provider, the association shall thereby cease its underwriting operations for such medical liability insurance which he has determined can be made available in the voluntary market. (Acts 1975, No. 513, p. 1148, § 7(3); Acts 1976, No. 362, p. 446.)

§ 27-26-27. Stabilization reserve fund — Generally.

(a) There is hereby created a stabilization reserve fund. The fund shall be administered by three directors, one of whom shall be the commissioner or his deputy. The remaining two directors shall be appointed by the commissioner. One shall be a representative of the association, the other a representative of its policyholders.

(b) The directors shall act by majority vote with two directors constituting a quorum for the transaction of any business or the exercise of any power of the fund. The directors shall serve without salary, but each director shall be reimbursed for actual and necessary expenses incurred in the performance of his official duties as a director of the fund. The directors shall not be subject to any personal liability or accountability with respect to the administration of the fund. (Acts 1975, No. 513, p. 1148, § 7(17), (18).)

§ 27-26-28. Same — Charge.

(a) Each policyholder shall pay to the association a stabilization reserve fund charge equal to one third of each premium payment due for insurance through the association. Such charge shall be separately stated in the policy. The association shall cancel the policy of any policyholder who fails to pay the stabilization reserve fund charge.

(b) The association shall promptly pay to the trustee of the fund all stabilization reserve fund charges which it collects from its policyholders and any retrospective premium refunds payable under the group retrospective rating plan authorized by this chapter. (Acts 1975, No. 513, p. 1148, § 7(19), (20).)

§ 27-26-29. Recoupment of shares of deficit.

(a) The association shall certify to the commissioner the estimated amount of any deficit remaining after the stabilization reserve fund has been exhausted in payment of the maximum final premium for all policyholders of the association. Within 60 days after such certification the commissioner shall authorize the members of the association to commence recoupment of their respective shares of the deficit by one of the following procedures:

(1) Applying a surcharge to be determined by the association at a rate not to exceed two percent of the annual premiums on future policies affording those kinds of insurance which form the basis for their participation in the association under procedures established by the association; or

(2) Deducting their share of the deficit from past or future (franchise and/or premium) taxes due the state of Alabama.

(b) If the commissioner fails within 60 days to authorize one of the above procedures, each member of the association may commence recoupment of its deficit by the second procedure described above. The association shall amend the amount of its certification of deficit to the commissioner as the values of its incurred losses become finalized and the members of the association shall amend their recoupment procedure accordingly. (Acts 1975, No. 513, p. 1148, § 7(15).)

§ 27-26-30. Holding in trust and investing of funds.

All money received by the fund shall be held in trust by a corporate trustee selected by the directors. The corporate trustee may invest the money held in trust, subject to the approval of the directors. All investment income shall be credited to the fund. All expenses of administration of the fund shall be charged against the fund. The money held in trust shall be used solely for the purpose of discharging when due any retrospective premium charges payable by policyholders of the association under the group retrospective rating plan authorized by this chapter. Payment of retrospective premium charges shall be made by the directors upon certification to them by the association of the amount due. If all money accruing to the fund is finally exhausted in payment of retrospective premium charges, all liability and obligations of the association's policyholders with respect to the payment of retrospective premium charges have been paid shall be returned to policyholders upon procedures authorized by the directors. (Acts 1975, No. 513, p. 1148, § 7(21).)

§ 27-26-31. Insufficiency of funds.

In the event that sufficient funds are not available for the sound financial operation of the association, pending recoupment, as provided in subsection (a) of section 27-26-25, all members shall, on a temporary basis contribute to the financial requirements of the association in the manner provided for in section 27-26-37. Any such contribution shall be reimbursed to the members by recoupment as provided in section 27-26-29. (Acts 1975, No. 513, p. 1148, § 7(16).)

§ 27-26-32. Application for coverage.

Any licensed physician, hospital or other licensed health care provider shall, on or after the effective date of the plan of operation, be entitled to apply to the association for such coverage. Such application may be made on behalf of an applicant by a broker or agent authorized by the applicant. (Acts 1975, No. 513, p. 1148, § 7(22).)

§ 27-26-33. Policies generally.

All policies issued by the association shall be issued subject to the group retrospective rating plan for each of the groups described in section 27-26-26 and the stabilization reserve fund authorized by this chapter. All such policies shall be written so as to apply to injury which results from acts or omissions during the policy period, commonly designated as occurrence type policies. No policy form shall be used by the association unless it has been filed with the commissioner and either he has approved it or 30 days have elapsed and he has not disapproved it as misleading or violative of public policy. (Acts 1975, No. 513, p. 1148, § 7(10).)

§ 27-26-34. Issuance of policy.

If the association determines that the applicant meets the underwriting standards of the association as prescribed in the plan of operation and there is no unpaid, uncontested premium due from the applicant for prior insurance (as shown by the insured having failed to make written objection to premium charges within 30 days after billing) then the association, upon receipt of the premium, or such portion thereof as is prescribed in the plan of operation, shall cause to be issued a policy of medical liability insurance. (Acts 1975, No. 513, p. 1148, § 7(23).)

§ 27-26-35. Cancellation of policies.

Cancellation of the association's policies shall be governed by the same laws governing other insurance policies; except, that the association may also cancel any of its policies in the event of nonpayment of any stabilization reserve fund charge by mailing or delivering to the insured at the address shown on the policy written notice stating when, not less than 10 days after such notice, cancellation shall be effective. (Acts 1975, No. 513, p. 1148, § 7(11).)

Collateral references. — Wrongful cancellation of medical malpractice insurance. 99 ALR3d 469.

§ 27-26-36. Rating plans.

(a) The rates, rating plans, rating rules, rating classifications and territories applicable to the insurance written by the association and statistics relating thereto shall be subject to the same laws applicable to casualty policies, giving due consideration to the past and prospective loss and expense experience for medical liability insurance written and to be written in this state, trends in the frequency and severity of losses, the investment income of the association, and such other information as the commissioner may require. All rates shall be on an actuarially sound basis, giving due consideration to the group retrospective rating plan and the stabilization reserve fund, and shall be calculated to be self-supporting. The commissioner shall take all appropriate steps to make available to the association the loss and expense experience of insurers previously writing medical liability insurance in this state.

(b) All policies issued by the association shall be subject to a nonprofit group retrospective rating plan to be approved by the commissioner under which the final premiums for all policyholders of the association, as a group, will be equal to the administrative expenses, loss and loss adjustment expenses and taxes, plus a reasonable allowance for contingencies and servicing. Policyholders shall be given full credit on all investment income, net of expenses and a reasonable management fee, on policyholder supplied funds. The standard premium (before retrospective adjustment) for each policy period issued by the association shall be established for portions of the policy period coinciding with the association's fiscal year on the basis of the association's rates, rating plans, rating rules, rating classifications, and territories then in effect. The maximum final premium for all policyholders of the association, as a group, shall be limited as provided in section 27-26-30. Since the business of the association is subject to the nonprofit group retrospective rating plan required by this subsection, there shall be a strong presumption that the rates filed and premiums for the business of the association are not unreasonable or excessive.

(c) The commissioner shall examine the business of the association as often as he deems appropriate to make certain that the group retrospective rating plan is being operated in a manner consistent with this section. If he finds that it is not being so operated, he shall issue an order to the association specifying in what respects its operation is deficient and stating what corrective action shall be taken. (Acts 1975, No. 513, p. 1148, § 7(12)-(14).)

§ 27-26-37. Proration of participation in writings, expenses, etc.

All insurers which are members of the association shall participate in its writings, expenses, servicing allowance, management fees and losses in the proportion that the net direct premiums of each such member (excluding that portion of premium attributable to the operation of the association) written during the preceding calendar year bears to the aggregate net direct premiums written in this state by all members of the association. Each insurer's participation in the association shall be determined annually on the basis of such net direct premiums written during the preceding calendar year, as reported in the annual statements and other reports filed by the insurer with the commissioner. (Acts 1975, No. 513, p. 1148, § 7(24).)

§ 27-26-38. Annual statements.

The association shall file in the office of the commissioner annually on or before the first day of March, a statement which shall contain information with respect to its transactions, condition, operations and affairs during the preceding year. Such statement shall contain such matters and information as are prescribed and shall be in such form as is approved by the commissioner. The commissioner may, at any time, require the association to furnish additional information with respect to its transactions, condition or any matter connected therewith considered to be material and of assistance in evaluating the scope, operation and experience of the association. (Acts 1975, No. 513, p. 1148, § 7(28).)

§ 27-26-39. Examination of association's affairs.

The commissioner shall make an examination into the affairs of the association at least annually. (Acts 1975, No. 513, p. 1148, § 7(29).)

§ 27-26-40. Liability for statements made during proceedings, etc.

There shall be no liability on the part of, and no cause of action of any nature shall arise against, the board, the association, the commissioner or his authorized representatives or any other person or organization, for any statements made in good faith by them during any proceedings or concerning any matters within the scope of this chapter. (Acts 1975, No. 513, p. 1148, § 7(30).)

§ 27-26-41. Effect of public officer's or employee's membership on board or directors of fund.

No member of the board or the directors of the stabilization reserve fund who is otherwise a public officer or employee shall suffer a forfeiture of his office or employment or any loss or diminution in the rights and privileges appertaining thereto, by reason of membership on the board or serving as a director of the stabilization reserve fund. (Acts 1975, No. 513, p. 1148, § 7(31).)

§ 27-26-42. Appeal to commissioner.

Any applicant to the association, any person insured pursuant to this chapter or their representatives, or any affected insurer, may appeal to the commissioner within 30 days after any ruling, action or decision by or on behalf of the association, with respect to those items the plan of operation defines as appealable matters. (Acts 1975, No. 513, p. 1148, § 7(26).)

§ 27-26-43. Judicial review of commissioner's orders.

All orders of the commissioner made pursuant to this chapter shall be subject to judicial review; provided, that notwithstanding any other provisions of law, proceedings for review shall act as a stay of enforcement of any order or decision of the commissioner disapproving or ordering the withdrawal, adjustment or termination of the effectiveness of any rate filing made by or on behalf of the association on the ground that the rates or premiums for the business of the association are unreasonable or excessive, and the association may continue to charge rates pursuant to such filing pending final order of the court. (Acts 1975, No. 513, p. 1148, § 7(27).)

CHAPTER 27.

ORGANIZATION AND CORPORATE PROCEDURES OF STOCK AND MUTUAL INSURERS.

Sec.
27-27-1. Definitions.
27-27-2. Applicability of chapter.
27-27-3. Power of domestic insurers to indemnify directors, etc.
27-27-4. Solicitation permit — Requirement.
27-27-5. Same — Application.
27-27-6. Same — Approval or denial.
27-27-7. Same — Issuance; contents; compliance with terms.
27-27-8. Same — Effect of granting permit.
27-27-9. Same — Modification or revocation.
27-27-10. Same — Bond or deposit in lieu thereof; waiver of same.
27-27-11. Licensing of securities salesmen.
27-27-12. Deposit of solicitation permit funds in escrow — Requirement.
27-27-13. Same — Withdrawal and refund.
27-27-14. Solicitation permit for subsequent financing.
27-27-15. Domestic mutual insurers — Authorization to transact insurance.
27-27-16. Same — Bond or deposit in lieu thereof.
27-27-17. Same — Solicitation of qualifying applications for insurance.
27-27-18. Same — Deposit in trust of premiums or fees on qualifying applications.
27-27-19. Same — Failure to complete organization.
27-27-20. Same — Authorization to transact additional kinds of insurance.
27-27-21. Same — Membership.
27-27-22. Same — Bylaws.
27-27-23. Directors of domestic insurers — Number; election; qualifications.
27-27-24. Same — Removal; vacancies.
27-27-25. Corrupt or dishonest practices in meeting of stockholders or members.
27-27-26. Pecuniary interests of officers, etc., of domestic insurers.
27-27-27. Exclusive management and production of business contracts by domestic insurers.
27-27-28. Notice of change of directors, etc.
27-27-29. Principal place of business and home office of domestic insurers; maintenance of assets in state; removal of records or assets; exceptions.
27-27-30. Voucher or other document for disbursements.
27-27-31. Contingent liability of members of domestic mutual insurers — Generally.

Sec.
27-27-32. Same — Levy of assessments.
27-27-33. Collection of assessments by insurers.
27-27-34. Nonassessable policies in mutual insurers — Generally.
27-27-35. Same — Revocation of domestic insurers authority to issue.
27-27-36. Issuance of participating or nonparticipating policies by domestic insurers.
27-27-37. Dividends — Domestic stock insurers.
27-27-38. Same — Domestic mutual insurers.
27-27-39. Same — Liability for illegal dividends by domestic insurers.
27-27-40. Loans by domestic insurers.
27-27-41. Deficiencies in stock insurer's capital or assets of mutual insurers — Generally.
27-27-42. Same — Curing of deficiency.
27-27-43. Mutualization of stock insurers.
27-27-44. Conversion of mutual insurer into stock insurer.
27-27-45. Merger and consolidations — Domestic stock insurers.
27-27-46. Same — Domestic mutual insurers.
27-27-47. Bulk reinsurance — Domestic stock insurers.
27-27-48. Same — Domestic mutual insurers.
27-27-49. Distribution of assets upon liquidation of domestic mutual insurer.
27-27-50. Extinguishment and nullification of domestic insurers' corporate charter.
27-27-51. Rules and regulations as to securities of domestic stock insurers.
27-27-52. Insider trading of domestic stock insurer equity securities — Short title.
27-27-53. Same — Ownership statements.
27-27-54. Same — Recovery of certain profits by company.
27-27-55. Same — Unlawful sales.
27-27-56. Same — Exemptions from sections 27-27-54 and 27-27-55; prescription of terms and conditions thereon.
27-27-57. Same — Applicability of sections 27-27-53 through 27-27-55.
27-27-58. Same — Equity securities — Defined.
27-27-59. Same — Same — Applicability of sections 27-27-53 through 27-27-55.

Sec.
27-27-60. Same — Rules and regulations.
27-27-61. Applicability of corporation statutes
          to domestic insurers.

§ 27-27-1. Definitions.

For the purposes of this chapter, the following terms shall have the meanings respectively ascribed to them by this section:

(1) STOCK INSURER. An incorporated insurer with capital divided into shares and owned by its stockholders.

(2) DOMESTIC MUTUAL INSURER. An incorporated insurer without capital stock and the governing body of which is elected as provided in this chapter. (Acts 1971, No. 407, p. 707, §§ 496, 497.)

Collateral references. — 43 Am. Jur. 2d, Insurance, §§ 93, 101.

§ 27-27-2. Applicability of chapter.

This chapter shall apply only to domestic stock insurers and domestic mutual insurers; except, that:

(1) Sections 27-27-4 through 27-27-14, relative to sale of securities or other financing of insurers or insurance operations, and subsection (b) of section 27-27-24 shall also apply as to foreign and alien insurers; and

(2) This chapter shall be applicable as to mutual aid associations as stated in chapter 30 of this title and as to fraternal benefit societies as stated in chapters 34 and 35 of this title. (Acts 1971, No. 407, p. 707, § 495.)

§ 27-27-3. Power of domestic insurers to indemnify directors, etc.

Without limiting the powers and authorities of domestic insurers, as provided in section 27-27-61, a domestic insurer shall have the power and is hereby authorized to indemnify any director, officer or employee, or former director, officer or employee of the corporation, or any person who may have served at its request as a director or officer of another corporation in which it owns shares of capital stock or of which it is a creditor against expenses actually and reasonably incurred by him in connection with the defense of any action or proceeding, civil or criminal, in which he is made a party by reason of being, or having been, such director or officer, except in relation to matters as to which he shall be adjudged in such action or proceeding to be liable for negligence or misconduct in the performance of duty to the corporation and to make any other indemnification that shall be authorized by the articles of incorporation or by any bylaw or resolution adopted by the shareholders after notice or as may be authorized under any other statute of this state dealing with the right of a corporation to indemnify officers, directors and employees or to purchase insurance for such indemnification. (Acts 1971, No. 407, p. 707, § 499.)

§ 27-27-4. Solicitation permit — Requirement.

(a) No person forming, or proposing to form, in this state or secure funds in this state for the financing of an insurer, or insurance holding corporation or stock corporation to finance an insurer or corporation to be attorney-in-fact for a reciprocal insurer or a syndicate, association, firm, partnership or organization for any such purposes, whether domestic or foreign, shall advertise or solicit or receive any funds, subscription or membership on account thereof in this state except as authorized by a currently effective solicitation permit issued by the commissioner, in addition to complying with other applicable provisions of the law.

(b) Any person violating this section shall, upon conviction thereof, be subject to a fine of not more than $10,000.00 or imprisonment for not more than 10 years, or by both such fine and imprisonment.

(c) Any insurer violating this section, in addition to any other penalties provided by law, shall be forever barred from being authorized to transact insurance in this state. (Acts 1971, No. 407, p. 707, § 500.)

§ 27-27-5. Same — Application.

To apply for a solicitation permit, the person shall:

(1) File with the commissioner a request therefor showing:

a. Name, type and purpose of insurer, corporation, syndicate, association, firm, partnership or organization formed or proposed to be formed;

b. Names, addresses, business background and qualifications of each person associated, or to be associated, in the enterprise or in the formation of the proposed insurer, corporation, syndicate, association, firm, partnership or organization;

c. Full disclosure of the terms of all pertinent understandings and agreements existing or proposed among persons so associated; and copies of all such agreements, relative to the proposed financing of the insurer, corporation, syndicate, association, firm, partnership or organization, or the formation thereof;

d. The plan according to which solicitations are to be made; and

e. Such additional information as the commissioner may reasonably require;

(2) Submit to the commissioner:

a. The executed and acknowledged triplicate originals of the proposed articles of incorporation of any proposed domestic insurer, a certified copy of the articles of incorporation of any proposed domestic insurer, a certified copy of the articles of incorporation of any foreign insurer or of any other corporation proposing to sell its securities as referred to in section 27-27-4, and copy of any syndicate, association, firm, partnership, organization or other similar agreement, by whatever name called, if funds for any of the purposes referred to in section 27-27-4 are to be secured through the sale of any security, interest, or right in, or relative to, such syndicate, association, firm, partnership or organization and, if the proposed insurer is a domestic reciprocal insurer, an original and duplicate copy of the proposed power of attorney and of any other agreements proposed as affecting investors, subscribers, the attorney-in-fact and the insurer or proposed insurer;

b. Original and duplicate copy of any proposed bylaws;

c. Copy of any security, receipt or certificate proposed to be issued and copy of the proposed application or subscription agreement therefor;

d. Copy of any insurance contract proposed to be offered by a proposed domestic mutual or reciprocal insurer and copy of application therefor;

e. Copy of any prospectus, advertising or sales literature proposed to be used;

f. Copy of proposed form of any escrow agreement required; and

g. Irrevocable appointment of the commissioner as process agent to receive service of process issued in this state arising out of any transactions under a solicitation permit, if issued, the appointment to be on a form as prescribed and furnished by the commissioner;

(3) Deposit with the commissioner the fees required under section 27-4-2 and otherwise by law to be paid for the application, for filing of the articles of incorporation of an insurer, for filing the subscribers' agreement and attorney-in-fact agreement, if the proposed insurer is a reciprocal, and for the solicitation permit, if granted; and

(4) In lieu of a special filing of the information, or part thereof, called for in subdivision (1) of this section, the commissioner may, in his discretion, accept a duplicate copy of any filing made with any other state or federal agency relative to the same offering or proposed offering. (Acts 1971, No. 407, p. 707, § 501.)

§ 27-27-6. Same — Approval or denial.

(a) The commissioner shall expeditiously examine the application for a solicitation permit and make such investigation relative thereto as he deems necessary, subject to subsection (b) of this section, if he finds that:

(1) The application is complete;

(2) The documents therewith filed are proper in form; and

(3) The proposed articles of incorporation of any proposed domestic insurer comply with this title and are not in conflict with the Constitution and laws of the United States or of this state;

He shall give notice to the applicant that he will approve and file the articles of incorporation, if a proposed corporation, and issue a solicitation permit, stating the terms to be contained therein, upon the filing of any bond required by sections 27-27-10 or 27-27-16.

(b) If the commissioner does not so find, or finds that any proposed sale of securities would be, or tend to be, fraudulent or inequitable as to present or proposed security holders or investors, or if he finds that any of the individuals associated or to be associated in the insurer, corporation, snydicate, association, partnership, firm, organization or financing are not of good character, or that the insurer if formed or, if an applicant for a certificate of authority, would not be able to qualify for a certificate of authority by reason of the provisions of subdivision (3) of section 27-3-4, he shall give notice to the applicant that a solicitation permit will not be granted, stating the grounds therefor, return any proposed articles of incorporation to the applicant and refund to the applicant all sums so deposited, except the fee for application for a solicitation permit. (Acts 1971, No. 407, p. 707, § 502.)

§ 27-27-7. Same — Issuance; contents; compliance with terms.

(a) Upon the filing of any bond required by sections 27-27-10 or 27-27-16, after notice by the commissioner provided for in subsection (a) of section 27-27-6, or upon his decision to grant a solicitation permit if such a bond is not so required, the commissioner shall issue to the applicant or to the newly formed corporation, if the application is on behalf of a newly formed incorporated domestic insurer, a solicitation permit. Every solicitation permit issued by the commissioner shall contain provisions in substance as follows:

(1) State the securities or other rights or interests for which subscriptions are to be solicited, the number, classes, par value and selling price thereof, or identify the insurance contract, or contracts, for which applications and advance premiums or deposits of premium are to be solicited in the case of mutual or reciprocal insurers;

(2) Require that any particular class of securities, rights and interests proposed to be sold or offered under the permit shall be so sold and offered at the same price to all parties and that, if more than one class of securities, rights, or interests are to be offered, each subscriber shall have the right to acquire some of each such class in accordance with such reasonable combination of classes into subscription units as may be approved by the commissioner;

(3) Require that all such subscriptions and premiums shall be payable only in lawful money of the United States of America except where stock or other securities are to be issued in exchange for securities or rights thereto under a plan approved by the commissioner of merger, consolidation, recapitalization or refinancing of an insurer or other corporation;

(4) Limit the portion of funds received on account of stock or syndicate, association, partnership, firm or organization subscriptions which may be used for promotion, securities sales and organization expenses to such amount as the commissioner deems to be reasonably adequate under the proposed plan of solicitation, but in no event to exceed 15 percent of such funds as and when the funds are actually received;

(5) If to be a mutual or reciprocal insurer, limit the portion of funds received on account of applications for insurance which may be used for promotion, sales or organization expenses to a reasonable commission upon such funds, giving consideration to the kind of insurance and policy

involved and to the costs incurred by insurers generally in the production of similar business and provide that no such commission shall be deemed to be earned or paid until the insurer has received its certificate of authority and the policies applied for, upon which the commission is to be based, have been actually issued and delivered;

(6) Prohibit the granting of any options to subscribe to, buy or acquire, in any way, any securities, rights or interests other than options made a part of convertible securities constituting the proposed offering, in whole or in part, and made available on a uniform basis to all subscribers to any such securities, rights or interests;

(7) Prohibit, by any promoter or other person associated or to be associated in the proposed insurer, corporation, syndicate, firm, partnership or organization or in solicitations under the permit, the resale or transfer of his interest in any security, right or interest of the kind proposed to be offered under the solicitation permit or any other interest or right which he may have in, or as to, the same entity prior to the completion of sale of all securities, rights and interests proposed to be offered or sold under the solicitation permit. In connection with this subdivision, the commissioner may, in his discretion, require that any security, right or interest the resale or transfer of which is prohibited in this subdivision shall be deposited and held in escrow pending the completion of the sales or offering under the solicitation permit;

(8) State in boldface type that the permittee must comply with chapter 6 of Title 8 of this Code, if such chapter is applicable, and with other applicable laws of the state of Alabama;

(9) That the permit shall expire not more than two years from its date of issue, unless earlier terminated by the commissioner; if, however, in connection with a proposed offering of securities by a domestic insurer or corporation a registration thereof, or filing with respect thereto, is required by law to be made with any federal agency, the effective period of the permit may, in the commissioner's discretion, commence upon the effective date of such registration or filing if subsequent to the date of issuance of the permit; and

(10) Contain such other reasonable conditions relative to accounting, reports, deposits or other matters consistent with the provisions of this chapter as the commissioner deems advisable for the protection of existing or prospective investors.

(b) The holder of the solicitation permit and its directors, officers, employees, agents and representatives shall comply with the terms of the permit. (Acts 1971, No. 407, p. 707, § 503.)

§ 27-27-8. Same — Effect of granting permit.

The granting of a solicitation permit is permissive only and shall not constitute an endorsement by the commissioner of any person or thing related to any such insurer, corporation, syndicate, association, partnership, firm, organization or financing, and the existence of the permit shall not be advertised or used as an inducement in any solicitation. The commissioner shall place the substance of this section in boldface type at the top of each solicitation permit issued by him. (Acts 1971, No. 407, p. 707, § 504.)

§ 27-27-9. Same — Modification or revocation.

(a) The commissioner may, for cause, modify a solicitation permit theretofore issued or may, after a hearing, revoke any solicitation permit for violation of any provision of this title, or of the terms of the permit, or of any proper order of the commissioner or for misrepresentation in the offering or sale of securities or policies under the permit.

(b) The commissioner shall revoke the solicitation permit if requested in writing by a majority of the syndicate members, or by a majority of the incorporators and two-thirds of the subscribers to stock or applicants for insurance in the proposed incorporated insurer or corporation or if he is so requested by a majority of the subscribers of a proposed reciprocal insurer. (Acts 1971, No. 407, p. 707, § 505.)

§ 27-27-10. Same — Bond or deposit in lieu thereof; waiver of same.

(a) Except as to proposed domestic insurers which are subject to the requirements of section 27-27-16, the commissioner shall not issue a solicitation permit until the applicant therefor has filed with him a corporate surety bond in the penalty of $15,000.00 in favor of the state of Alabama and for the use and benefit of the state and of proposed Alabama investors in and creditors of the proposed organization.

(b) The bond shall be conditioned upon the payment of costs incurred by the state in event of any legal proceedings for liquidation or dissolution of the proposed organization before completion of organization or in event a certificate of authority is not granted and upon a full accounting for funds received until the proposed insurer has been granted its certificate of authority or until the proposed corporation, syndicate, organization or financing has been completed as defined in the solicitation permit.

(c) In lieu of filing such bond, the applicant may deposit with the state treasurer through the commissioner $15,000.00 in cash, or its equivalent, or in United States government bonds at par value, to be held in trust under the same conditions as required for the bond.

(d) The commissioner may, in his discretion, waive the requirement for a bond or deposit in lieu thereof if the solicitation permit provides that:

(1) The proposed securities are to be distributed solely and finally to those few persons who are the active promoters intimate to the formation of the insurer or other corporation, syndicate, or organization; or

(2) The securities are to be issued in connection with subsequent financing as provided in section 27-27-14.

(e) Any bond filed or deposited, or remaining portion thereof, held under this section shall be released and discharged upon settlement or termination of all liabilities against it. (Acts 1971, No. 407, p. 707, § 506.)

§ 27-27-11. Licensing of securities salesmen.

Solicitation for sale of securities under a solicitation permit shall be made only by individuals licensed as securities salesmen pursuant to the provisions of the Alabama Securities Act. (Acts 1971, No. 407, p. 707, § 507.)

Cross references. — As to Alabama Securities Act, see § 8-6-1 et seq.

§ 27-27-12. Deposit of solicitation permit funds in escrow — Requirement.

(a) All funds received in Alabama pursuant to a solicitation permit, other than advance premiums for insurance which are subject to section 27-27-18, shall, by the permit holder, be deposited and held in escrow in a bank or trust company located in this state under an agreement approved by the commissioner.

(b) No part of such funds shall be withdrawn from such deposit, except:

(1) For the payment of promotion, sales and organization expenses as authorized by the solicitation permit, and funds for such purposes may be withheld from the deposit;

(2) For the purpose of making any deposit with the commissioner required for the issuance of a certificate of authority to an insurer;

(3) If the proposed organization is not to be an insurer, upon completion of payments on securities subscriptions made under the solicitation permit and deposit or appropriation of such funds to the purposes specified in the solicitation permit; or

(4) For making of refunds as provided in section 27-27-13.

(c) When the commissioner has issued a certificate of authority to an insurer, any such funds remaining in escrow for its account shall be released to the insurer.

(d) The commissioner may waive compliance with this section as to funds required to be deposited in escrow or trust in similar institutions and for similar purposes as set forth in this section pursuant to any other law of this state. (Acts 1971, No. 407, p. 707, § 508.)

§ 27-27-13. Same — Withdrawal and refund.

The commissioner shall withdraw all funds held in escrow under section 27-27-12, and refund to securities subscribers or purchasers all sums paid in on securities subscriptions, less that part of such sums paid in as has been allowed and used for promotion, sales and organization expenses, and shall dissolve the proposed domestic insurer, corporation, syndicate or organization if:

(1) It fails to complete its organization or financing and obtain full payment for subscriptions and, if to be an insurer, it fails to secure its certificate of authority, all before expiration of the solicitation permit; or

(2) The commissioner revokes the solicitation permit. (Acts 1971, No. 407, p. 707, § 509.)

§ 27-27-14. Solicitation permit for subsequent financing.

(a) No insurer, or insurance holding corporation, or stock corporation for financing operations of a mutual insurer, or attorney-in-fact corporation, or a reciprocal insurer or any other type of organization existing for the same purpose, after:

(1) It has received a certificate of authority, if an insurer, in this or any other state; or

(2) It has completed its initial organization and financing, if a corporation, syndicate or other organization other than an insurer, shall in this state solicit or receive funds in exchange for its securities, other than when combining and selling, for the account of its stockholders entitled thereto, fractional shares to which they become entitled through a stock dividend to existing stockholders until it has applied to the commissioner for, and has been granted, a solicitation permit.

(b) The commissioner shall issue such a permit unless he finds:

(1) That the funds proposed to be secured are excessive in amount for the purposes intended;

(2) That the proposed securities or the manner of their distribution are inequitable; or

(3) That the offering or issuance of the securities would be unfair to existing or prospective holders of securities of the same insurer, corporation, syndicate or organization.

(c) Any such solicitation permit granted by the commissioner shall be for such duration and shall contain such terms, and be issued upon, such conditions as the commissioner may reasonably specify or require for the protection of existing or proposed policyholders or investors.

(d) This section is supplemental to other laws of this state applicable to the sale of securities. (Acts 1971, No. 407, p. 707, § 510.)

§ 27-27-15. Domestic mutual insurers — Authorization to transact insurance.

(a) When newly organized, a domestic mutual insurer may be authorized to transact any one of the kinds of insurance listed in the schedule contained in subsection (b) of this section.

(b) When applying for an original certificate of authority, the insurer must be otherwise qualified therefor under this title and must have received and accepted bona fide applications as to substantial insurable subjects for insurance coverage of a substantial character of the kind of insurance proposed to be transacted, must have collected in cash the full premium therefor at a rate not less than that usually charged by other insurers for comparable coverages, must have surplus funds on hand and deposited as of the date such insurance coverages are to become effective or, in lieu of such applications, premiums and surplus and may deposit surplus, all in accordance with that part of the following schedule which applies to the one kind of insurance the insurer proposes to transact:

(a) Kind of insurance	(b) Minimum no. of applicants accepted	(c) Minimum no. of subjects covered	(d) Minimum premium collected	(e) Minimum amount of insurance each subject	(f) Maximum amount of insurance each subject (5)	(g) Deposit of minimum surplus funds (6)	(h) Deposit of surplus in lieu (6)
Life (1)	500	500	annual	$1000	$2500	$50,000	$100,000
Disability (2)	500	500	quarterly	$10 (weekly indem.)	$25 (weekly indem.)	$50,000	$100,000
Property (3)	100	250	annual	$1000	$3000	$100,000	$200,000
Casualty (4)	250	500	annual	$1000	$10,000	$150,000	$200,000
Casualty with workmen's compensation	250	1500	quarterly	$1000	$10,000	$200,000	$300,000

The following provisos are respectively applicable to the foregoing schedule and provisions as indicated by like arabic numerals appearing in such schedule:

(1) No group insurance or term policies for terms of less than 10 years shall be included;

(2) No group, blanket or family plans of insurance shall be included. In lieu of weekly indemnity a like premium value in medical, surgical and hospital benefits may be provided. Any accidental death or dismemberment benefit provided shall not exceed $2,500.00;

(3) Only insurance of the owner's interest in real property may be included;

(4) Must include insurance of legal liability for bodily injury and property damage, to which the maximum and minimum insured amounts apply;

(5) The maximums provided for in column (f) are net of applicable reinsurance; and

(6) The deposit of surplus in the amount specified in columns (g) and (h) must thereafter be maintained unimpaired. The deposit is subject to the provisions of chapter 6 of this title. (Acts 1971, No. 407, p. 707, § 511.)

§ 27-27-16. Same — Bond or deposit in lieu thereof.

(a) Before soliciting any applications for insurance required under section 27-27-15, as qualification for the original certificate of authority, the incorporators of the proposed mutual insurer shall file with the commissioner a corporate surety bond in the penalty of $15,000.00 in favor of the state of Alabama and for the use and benefit of the state and of applicant members and creditors of the corporation. The bond shall be conditioned as follows:

(1) Upon payment of any loss suffered by applicants who have cancelled or lapsed existing insurance policies due to misrepresentation by the incorporators or by persons soliciting such applications under authorization by the corporation, to the effect that the making of such application for insurance and prepayment of premiums in such proposed insurer provides insurance protection prior to issuance of a certificate of authority to such insurer by the commissioner; and

(2) That in event the corporation fails to complete its organization and secure a certificate of authority issued by the commissioner within one year after the date of its certificate of incorporation, all premiums collected in advance from applicant members will be promptly returned to them, all other indebtedness of the corporation, other than any compensation to directors, officers or solicitors of insurance applications, will be paid and for payment of costs incurred by the state in event of any legal proceedings for liquidation or dissolution of the corporation.

(b) In lieu of such a bond, the incorporators may deposit with the commissioner $15,000.00 in cash, or its equivalent, or in United States government bonds at par value, to be held in trust upon the same conditions as required for the bond.

(c) Any such bond filed or deposit, or remaining portion thereof, held under this section shall be released and discharged upon settlement and termination of all liabilities against it under this section. (Acts 1971, No. 407, p. 707, § 512.)

§ 27-27-17. Same — Solicitation of qualifying applications for insurance.

(a) Upon receipt of the commissioner's approval of the bond or deposit as provided in section 27-27-16 the directors and officers of the proposed domestic mutual insurer may commence solicitation of such requisite applications for insurance policies as they may accept and may receive deposits of premiums thereon.

(b) All such applications shall be in writing signed by the applicant, covering subjects of insurance resident, located or to be performed in this state.

(c) All such applications shall provide that:

(1) Issuance of the policy is contingent upon the insurer qualifying for and receiving a certificate of authority;

(2) No insurance is in effect unless and until the certificate of authority has been issued; and

(3) The prepaid premium or deposit and membership or policy fee, if any, shall be refunded in full to the applicant if organization is not completed and the certificate of authority is not issued and received by the insurer before a specified reasonable date, which date shall be not later than one year after the date of the certificate of incorporation.

(d) All qualifying premiums collected shall be in cash.

(e) Solicitation for such qualifying applications for insurance shall be by licensed agents of the corporation, and the commissioner shall, upon the corporation's application therefor, issue temporary agent's licenses expiring on the date specified pursuant to subdivision (c) (3) of this section to individuals qualified as for a resident agent's license, except as to the taking or passing of an examination. The commissioner may suspend or revoke any such license for any of the causes and pursuant to the same procedures as are applicable to suspension or revocation of licenses of agents in general under chapter 7 of this title. (Acts 1971, No. 407, p. 707, § 513.)

§ 27-27-18. Same — Deposit in trust of premiums or fees on qualifying applications.

(a) All sums collected by a domestic mutual corporation as premiums or fees on qualifying applications for insurance therein shall be deposited in trust in a bank or trust company in this state under a written trust agreement approved by the commissioner and consistent with this section and with subdivision (c) (3) of section 27-27-17. The corporation shall file an executed copy of such trust agreement with the commissioner.

(b) Upon issuance to the corporation of a certificate of authority as an insurer for the kind of insurance for which such applications were solicited, all funds so held in trust shall become the funds of the insurer, and the insurer shall, thereafter in due course, issue and deliver its policies for which premiums had been paid and accepted. The insurance provided by such policies shall be effective as of the date of the certificate of authority or thereafter as provided by the respective policies. (Acts 1971, No. 407, p. 707, § 514.)

§ 27-27-19. Same — Failure to complete organization.

If the proposed domestic mutual insurer fails to complete its organization and to secure its original certificate of authority within one year from, and after, date of its certificate of incorporation, the corporation shall transact no further business, and the commissioner shall return, or cause to be returned, to the persons entitled thereto all advance deposits or payments of premiums held in trust under section 27-27-18. (Acts 1971, No. 407, p. 707, § 515.)

§ 27-27-20. Same — Authorization to transact additional kinds of insurance.

A domestic mutual insurer, after being authorized to transact one kind of insurance, may be authorized by the commissioner to transact such additional kinds of insurance as are permitted under section 27-3-6, while otherwise in compliance with this title and while maintaining unimpaired surplus funds in an amount not less than the amount of paid-in capital stock required of a domestic stock insurer transacting like kinds of insurance, subject further to the additional expendable surplus requirements of section 27-3-8 applicable to such a stock insurer. (Acts 1971, No. 407, p. 707, § 516.)

§ 27-27-21. Same — Membership.

(a) Each policyholder of a domestic mutual insurer, other than of a reinsurance contract, is a member of the insurer with all rights and obligations of such membership, and the policy shall so specify.

(b) Any individual, or firm or any public or private corporation, board or association in this state, or elsewhere, may make application, enter into agreements for and hold policies in any such mutual insurer. Any officer, stockholder, trustee or local representative of any such corporation, board, association or estate may be recognized as acting for, or on its behalf for, the purpose of such membership, but shall not be personally liable upon such contract of insurance by reason of acting in such representative capacity. The right of any corporation organized under the laws of this state to participate as a member of any such insurer is declared to be incidental to the purpose for which the corporation is organized and as much granted as the rights and powers expressly conferred.

(c) The right of certain governmental bodies or agencies of this state to become, and be, policyholders of mutual insurers shall be as provided by the laws of this state governing such bodies or agencies. (Acts 1971, No. 407, p. 707, § 517.)

Collateral references. — 43 Am. Jur. 2d,
Insurance, §§ 109-112.

§ 27-27-22. Same — Bylaws.

(a) A domestic mutual insurer shall have bylaws for the government of its affairs. The initial board of directors of a domestic mutual insurer shall adopt original bylaws, subject to the approval of the insurer's members at the next succeeding meeting. The members shall have power to make, modify and revoke bylaws.

(b) The bylaws shall provide:

(1) That each member is entitled to one vote upon each matter coming to a vote at meetings of members or to more votes in accordance with a reasonable classification of members as set forth in the bylaws and based upon the amount of insurance in force, number of policies held or upon the amount of the premiums paid by such member or upon other reasonable factors. A member shall have the right to vote in person or by his written proxy made not less than 30 days prior to the meeting. No such proxy shall be made irrevocable for longer than a period of three years;

(2) For election of directors by the members and the number, qualifications, terms of office and powers of directors;

(3) The time, notice, quorum and conduct of annual and special meetings of members and voting thereat. The bylaws may provide that the annual meeting shall be held at a place, date and time to be set forth in the policy and without giving other notice of such meeting;

(4) The number, designation, election, terms, powers and duties of the respective corporate officers;

(5) For deposit, custody, disbursement and accounting for corporate funds; and

(6) For any other reasonable provisions customary, necessary or convenient for the management or regulation of its corporate affairs.

(c) The insurer shall promptly file with the commissioner a copy, certified by the insurer's secretary, of its bylaws and of every modification thereof or addition thereto. The commissioner shall disapprove any bylaw provision deemed by him to be unlawful, unreasonable, inadequate, unfair or detrimental to the proper interests or protection of the insurer's members or any class thereof. The insurer shall not, after receiving written notice of such disapproval and during the existence thereof, effectuate any bylaw provision so disapproved. (Acts 1971, No. 407, p. 707, § 518.)

Collateral references. — 43 Am. Jur. 2d,
Insurance, § 103.

§ 27-27-23. Directors of domestic insurers — Number; election; qualifications.

(a) The affairs of every domestic insurer shall be managed by not less than three directors, and at least one-third of the directors shall be bona fide residents of this state.

(b) Directors must be elected by the members or stockholders of a domestic insurer at the annual meeting of stockholders or members. Directors may be elected for terms of not more than five years each and until their successors are elected and have qualified, and if to be elected for terms of more than one year, the insurer's bylaws shall provide for a staggered-term system under which the terms of a proportionate part of the members of the board of directors will expire on the date of each annual meeting of stockholders or members.

(c) If so provided in the insurer's bylaws, a director of a stock insurer shall be a stockholder thereof and a director of a mutual insurer shall be a policyholder thereof. (Acts 1971, No. 407, p. 707, § 519.)

§ 27-27-24. Same — Removal; vacancies.

(a) At a special meeting of stockholders or members called for that purpose, any director of a stock or mutual insurer may be removed from office by an affirmative vote of stockholders or members holding in the aggregate a majority of the voting power of all stockholders or members of an insurer entitled to vote at an election of directors. If the board of directors, or any member thereof, is so removed, new directors may be elected at the same meeting.

(b) Vacancies in the board of directors may be filled by the remaining members of the board, and each person so elected shall be a director until his successor is elected by the stockholders or members at the next annual meeting of stockholders or members or at any special meeting of stockholders or members called for that purpose and held prior thereto. (Acts 1971, No. 407, p. 707, § 520.)

§ 27-27-25. Corrupt or dishonest practices in meeting of stockholders or members.

No person shall buy, or sell or barter a vote or proxy relative to any meeting of stockholders or members of an insurer or engage in any corrupt or dishonest practice in, or relative to, the conduct of any such meeting. Violation of this section shall be punishable as provided in section 27-1-12. (Acts 1971, No. 407, p. 707, § 521.)

§ 27-27-26. Pecuniary interests of officers, etc., of domestic insurers.

(a) Any officer, or director, or any member of any committee or any employee of a domestic insurer who is charged with the duty of investing or handling the insurer's funds shall not deposit or invest such funds except in the insurer's corporate name; except, that such insurer may for its convenience hold any equity investment in a street name or in the name of a nominee; shall not borrow the funds of such insurer; shall not be pecuniarily interested in any loan, pledge or deposit, security, investment, sale, purchase, exchange, reinsurance or other similar transaction or property of such insurer except as a stockholder or member and shall not take or receive to his own use any fee, brokerage, commission, gift or other consideration for, or on account of, any such transaction made by, or on behalf of, such insurer.

(b) No insurer shall guarantee any financial obligation of any of its officers or directors.

(c) This section shall not prohibit such a director, or officer, or member of a committee or employee from becoming a policyholder of the insurer and enjoying the usual rights so provided for its policyholders, nor shall it prohibit any such officer, director, or member of a committee or employee from participating as beneficiary in any pension trust, deferred compensation plan, profit-sharing plan or stock option plan authorized by the insurer and to which he may be eligible, nor shall it prohibit any director or member of a committee from receiving a reasonable fee for legal services actually rendered to such insurer.

(d) The commissioner may, by regulations from time to time, define and permit additional exceptions to the prohibition contained in subsection (a) of this section solely to enable payment of reasonable compensation to a director who is not otherwise an officer or employee of the insurer, or to a corporation or firm in which a director is interested, for necessary services performed or sales or purchases made to, or for, the insurer in the ordinary course of the insurer's business and in the usual private professional or business capacity of such director or such corporation or firm. (Acts 1971, No. 407, p. 707, § 522.)

Cited in Bonner v. Disciplinary Bd., 401 So. 2d 734 (Ala. 1981).

§ 27-27-27. Exclusive management and production of business contracts by domestic insurers.

(a) No domestic insurer shall hereafter make any contract whereby any person is granted or is to enjoy in fact the management of the insurer to the substantial exclusion of its board of directors or to have the controlling or preemptive right to produce substantially all insurance business for the insurer, unless the contract is filed with, and approved by, the commissioner. The contract shall be deemed approved unless disapproved by the commissioner within 20 days after date of filing, subject to such reasonable extension of time as the commissioner may require by notice given within such 20 days. Any disapproval shall be delivered to the insurer in writing, stating the grounds therefor.

(b) Any such contract shall provide that any such manager or producer of its business shall, within 90 days after expiration of each calendar year, furnish the insurer's board of directors a written statement of amounts received under, or on account of, the contract and amounts expended thereunder during such calendar year, including the emoluments received therefrom by the respective directors, officers and other principal management personnel of the manager or producer, and with such classification of items and further detail as the insurer's board of directors may reasonably require.

(c) The commissioner shall disapprove any such contract if he finds that it:

(1) Subjects the insurer to excessive charges;

(2) Is to extend for an unreasonable length of time;

(3) Does not contain fair and adequate standards of performance; or

(4) Contains other inequitable provision, or provisions, which impair the proper interests of stockholders or members of the insurer.

(d) This section does not apply as to contracts entered into prior to January 1, 1972, nor to extensions or amendments to such contracts. (Acts 1971, No. 407, p. 707, § 523.)

§ 27-27-28. Notice of change of directors, etc.

An insurer shall promptly give the commissioner written notice of any change of personnel among the directors or principal officers of the insurer. (Acts 1971, No. 407, p. 707, § 524.)

§ 27-27-29. Principal place of business and home office of domestic insurers; maintenance of assets in state; removal of records or assets; exceptions.

(a) Every domestic insurer shall have, and maintain, its principal place of business and home office in this state and shall keep therein complete records of its assets, transactions and affairs in accordance with such methods and systems as are customary or suitable as to the kind, or kinds, of insurance transacted.

(b) Every domestic insurer shall have, and maintain, its assets in this state, except as to:

(1) Real property and personal property appurtenant thereto lawfully owned by the insurer and located outside this state; and

(2) Such property of the insurer as may be customary, necessary and convenient to enable and facilitate the operation of its branch offices and "regional home offices" located outside this state as referred to in subsection (d) of this section.

(c) Removal of all, or a material part of, the records or assets of a domestic insurer from this state except pursuant to a plan of merger or consolidation approved by the commissioner under this title, or for such reasonable purposes and periods of time as may be approved by the commissioner in writing in advance of such removal, or concealment of such records or assets, or material part thereof, from the commmissioner is prohibited. Any person who removes, or attempts to remove, such records or assets, or such material part thereof, from the home office or other place of business or of safekeeping of the insurer in this state with the intent to remove the same from this state or who conceals or attempts to conceal the same from the commissioner, in violation of this section, shall, upon conviction thereof, be guilty of a felony, punishable by a fine of not more than $10,000.00, or by imprisonment in the penitentiary for not more than five years or by both such fine and imprisonment in the discretion of the court. Upon any removal or attempted removal of such records or assets or upon retention of such records or assets, or material part thereof, outside this state beyond the period therefor specified in the commissioner's consent under which the records were so removed thereat or upon concealment of, or attempt to conceal, records or assets in violation of this section, the commissioner may institute delinquency proceedings against the insurer pursuant to the provisions of chapter 32 of this title.

(d) This section shall not be deemed to prohibit or prevent an insurer from:

(1) Establishing and maintaining branch offices or "regional home offices" in other states where necessary or convenient for the transaction of its business and keeping therein the detailed records and assets customary and necessary for the servicing of its insurance in force and affairs in the territory served by such an office, as long as such records and assets are made readily available at such office for examination by the commissioner at his request; or

(2) Having, depositing or transmitting funds and assets of the insurer in, or to, jurisdictions outside of this state required by the law of such jurisdiction or as reasonably and customarily required in the regular course of its business, including the retention of personal property or securities in a depository outside the state of Alabama for purposes of safekeeping or for the convenient operation of the insurer.

(e) For good cause shown and with the written permission of the commissioner, a domestic insurer may maintain its executive offices outside the state of Alabama, provided it keeps an office managed by one or more officers of the insurer and a complete duplicate set of records in Alabama and further agrees to make all records at the executive offices outside Alabama available to the commissioner of Alabama upon reasonable notice by him.

(f) This section shall not apply to those actions taken by insurance companies prior to January 1, 1972, but only applies to future actions of domestic insurance companies.

(g) Notwithstanding any other provision of this section, any company may evidence ownership of its assets by use of a clearing corporation or book-entry deposit system. (Acts 1971, No. 407, p. 707, § 525; Acts 1975, No. 218, p. 744, § 1; Acts 1981, No. 81-541, p. 904, § 3.)

§ 27-27-30. Voucher or other document for disbursements.

(a) No insurer shall make any disbursement of $25.00 or more unless evidenced by a voucher or other document correctly describing the consideration for the payment and support by a check or receipt endorsed or signed by, or on behalf of, the person receiving the money.

(b) If the disbursement is for services and reimbursement, the voucher or other document, or some other writing referred to therein, shall describe the services and itemize the expenditures.

(c) If the disbursement is in connection with any matter pending before any legislature or public body or before any public official, the voucher or other document shall also correctly describe the nature of the matter and of the insurer's interest therein. (Acts 1971, No. 407, p. 707, § 526.)

§ 27-27-31. Contingent liability of members of domestic mutual insurers — Generally.

(a) Each member of a domestic mutual insurer shall, except as otherwise provided in this chapter with respect to nonassessable policies, have a contingent liability, pro rata and not one for another, for the discharge of its obligations, which contingent liability shall be expressed in the policy and be in such maximum amount as is specified in the insurer's articles of incorporation.

(b) Termination of the policy of any such member shall not relieve the member of contingent liability for his proportion, if any, of the obligations of the insurer which accrued while the policy was in force.

(c) Unrealized contingent liability of members does not constitute an asset of the insurer in any determination of its financial condition. (Acts 1971, No. 407, p. 707, § 527.)

§ 27-27-32. Same — Levy of assessments.

(a) If at any time the assets of a domestic mutual insurer are less than its liabilities and the minimum amount of surplus required to be maintained by it under this title for authority to transact the kinds of insurance being transacted and the deficiency is not cured from other sources, its directors shall levy an assessment only upon its members who held policies providing for contingent liability at any time within the 12 months preceding the date notice of such assessment was mailed to them, and such members shall be liable to the insurer for the amount so assessed.

(b) The assessment shall be for such an amount as is required to cure such deficiency and to provide a reasonable amount of working funds above such minimum amount of surplus, but such working funds so provided shall not exceed five percent of the insurer's liabilities as of the date as of which the amount of such deficiency was determined.

(c) In levying an assessment on a policy providing for contingent liability, the assessment shall be computed on a basis of premium earned on such policy.

(d) No member shall have an offset against any assessment for which he is liable on account of any claim for unearned premium or loss payable.

(e) As to life insurance, any part of such an assessment upon a member which remains unpaid following notice of assessment, demand for payment and lapse of a reasonable waiting period as specified in such notice may, if approved by the commissioner as being in the best interests of the insurer and its members, be secured by placing a lien upon the cash surrender values and accumulated dividends held by the insurer to the credit of such member. (Acts 1971, No. 407, p. 707, § 528.)

§ 27-27-33. Collection of assessments by insurers.

(a) Any assessment made by an insurer under section 27-27-32 or 27-27-42 is prima facie correct. The amount of such assessment to be paid by each member as determined by the insurer is likewise prima facie correct.

(b) The insurer shall notify each member of the amount of the assessment to be paid by written notice mailed to the address of the member last of record with the insurer. Failure of the member to receive the notice so mailed, within the time specified therein for the payment of the assessment or at all, shall be no defense in any action to collect the assessment.

(c) If a member fails to pay the assessment within the period specified in the notice, which period shall not be less than 20 days after mailing, the insurer may institute an action to collect the same. (Acts 1971, No. 407, p. 707, § 529.)

§ 27-27-34. Nonassessable policies in mutual insurers — Generally.

(a) While possessing surplus funds in amount not less than the paid-in capital stock required of a domestic stock insurer transacting like kinds of insurance, a domestic mutual insurer may, upon receipt of the commissioner's order so authorizing, extinguish the contingent liability of its members as to all its policies in force and may omit provisions imposing contingent liability in all its policies currently issued.

(b) A foreign or alien mutual insurer may issue nonassessable policies to its members in this state pursuant to its articles of incorporation and the laws of its domicile. (Acts 1971, No. 407, p. 707, § 530.)

§ 27-27-35. Same — Revocation of domestic insurers authority to issue.

The commissioner shall revoke the authority of a domestic mutual insurer to issue policies without contingent liability if at any time the insurer's assets are less than the sum of its liabilities and the surplus required for such authority or if the insurer, by resolution of its board of directors approved by a majority of its members, requests that the authority be revoked. During the absence of such authority, the insurer shall not issue any policy without providing therein for the contingent liability of the policyholder nor renew any policy which is renewable at the option of the insurer without endorsing the same to provide for such contingent liability. (Acts 1971, No. 407, p. 707, § 531.)

§ 27-27-36. Issuance of participating or nonparticipating policies by domestic insurers.

Unless prohibited by its articles of incorporation, a domestic stock or domestic mutual insurer may issue any, or all, of its policies with, or without, participation in profits, savings or unabsorbed portions of premiums, may classify policies issued on a participating and nonparticipating basis and may determine the right to participate and the extent of participation of any class, or classes, of policies. Any such classification or determination shall be reasonable and shall not unfairly discriminate as between policyholders within the same such classifications. A life insurer may issue both participating and nonparticipating policies only if the right or absence of right to participate is reasonably related to the premium charged. (Acts 1971, No. 407, p. 707, § 532.)

§ 27-27-37. Dividends — Domestic stock insurers.

(a) A domestic stock insurer shall not pay any cash dividend to stockholders except out of that part of its available surplus funds which is derived from realized net profits on its business.

(b) A stock dividend may be paid out of any available surplus funds in excess of the aggregate amount of surplus loaned to the insurer under section 27-27-40.

(c) A dividend otherwise proper may be payable out of the insurer's surplus even though its total surplus is then less than the aggregate of its past contributed surplus resulting from issuance of its capital stock at a price in excess of the par value thereof. (Acts 1971, No. 407, p. 707, § 533.)

§ 27-27-38. Same — Domestic mutual insurers.

(a) The directors of a domestic mutual insurer may, from time to time, apportion and pay or credit to its members dividends only out of that part of its surplus funds which represents net realized savings and net realized earnings in excess of the surplus required by law to be maintained.

(b) A dividend otherwise proper may be payable out of such savings and earnings even though the insurer's total surplus is then less than the aggregate of its contributed surplus. (Acts 1971, No. 407, p. 707, § 534.)

§ 27-27-39. Same — Liability for illegal dividends by domestic insurers.

(a) Any director of a domestic stock or mutual insurer who knowingly votes for, or concurs in, declaration or payment of a dividend to stockholders or members except as authorized in sections 27-27-37 or 27-27-38 shall, upon conviction thereof, be guilty of a misdemeanor and shall be jointly and severally liable, together with other such directors likewise voting for or concurring, for any loss thereby sustained by the insurer.

(b) Any stockholder receiving such an illegal dividend shall be liable in the amount thereof to the insurer.

(c) The commissioner may revoke or suspend the certificate of authority of an insurer which has declared or paid such an illegal dividend. (Acts 1971, No. 407, p. 707, § 535.)

§ 27-27-40. Loans by domestic insurers.

(a) A domestic stock or mutual insurer may borrow money to defray the expenses of its organization, provide it with surplus funds or for any purpose of its business, upon a written agreement that such money is required to be repaid only out of the insurer's surplus in excess of that stipulated in such agreement. The agreement may provide for interest at a reasonable rate per annum, which interest shall, or shall not, constitute a liability of the insurer as to its funds other than such excess of surplus, as stipulated in the agreement. No commission or promotion expense shall be paid in connection with any such loan.

(b) Money so borrowed, together with the interest thereon if so stipulated in the agreement, shall not form a part of the insurer's legal liabilities except as to its surplus in excess of the amount thereof stipulated in the agreement or be the basis of any setoff, but, until repaid, financial statements filed or published by the insurer shall show as a footnote thereto the amount thereof then unpaid together with any interest thereon accrued but unpaid.

(c) Any such loan shall be subject to the commissioner's approval. The insurer shall, in advance of the loan, file with the commissioner a statement of the purpose of the loan and a copy of the proposed loan agreement. The loan and agreement shall be deemed approved unless, within 15 days after date of such filing, the insurer is notified of the commissioner's disapproval and the reasons therefor. The commissioner shall disapprove any proposed loan or agreement if he finds the loan is unnecessary or excessive for the purpose intended, or that the terms of the loan agreement are not fair and equitable to the parties and to other similar lenders, if any, to the insurer or that the information so filed by the insurer is inadequate.

(d) Any such loan, or substantial portion thereof, shall be repaid by the insurer when no longer reasonably necessary for the purpose originally intended. No repayment of such a loan shall be made, unless in advance approved by the commissioner.

(e) This section shall not apply to any loan other than one obtained upon a written agreement that such loan is required to be repaid only out of the insurer's surplus in excess of that stipulated in such agreement.

(f) The value of the surplus debenture issued under this section shall not be considered as the deciding authority for valuing the asset received for the above note, but shall only be taken into account with all other factors in determining admitted value. (Acts 1971, No. 407, p. 707, § 536; Acts 1980, No. 80-728, p. 1470.)

Collateral references. — 44 C.J.S., Insurance, § 110.

43 Am. Jur. 2d, Insurance, § 95.

§ 27-27-41. Deficiencies in stock insurer's capital or assets of mutual insurers — Generally.

(a) If a stock insurer's capital, as represented by the aggregated par value of its outstanding capital stock, becomes impaired or the assets of a mutual insurer are less than its liabilities and the minimum amount of surplus required to be maintained by it under sections 27-27-15 or 27-27-20 for authority to transact the kinds of insurance being transacted, the commissioner shall, at once, determine the amount of deficiency and serve notice upon the insurer to make good the deficiency within 60 days after service of such notice.

(b) The deficiency may be made good in cash or in assets eligible for the investment of the insurer's funds, or, if a stock insurer, by reduction of the insurer's capital to an amount not below the minimum required for the kinds of insurance thereafter to be transacted or, if a mutual insurer, by amendment of its certificate of authority to cover only such kind or kinds of insurance thereafter for which the insurer has sufficient surplus under this title.

(c) If the deficiency is not made good and proof thereof filed with the commissioner within such 60-day period, the insurer shall be deemed insolvent and the commissioner shall institute delinquency proceedings against it under chapter 32 of this title; except, that if such deficiency exists because of increased loss reserves required by the commissioner or because of disallowance by the commissioner of certain assets or reduction of the value at which carried in the insurer's accounts, the commissioner may, in his discretion and upon application and good cause shown, extend, for not more than an additional 60 days, the period within which such deficiency may be so made good and such proof thereof so filed. (Acts 1971, No. 407, p. 707, § 537.)

Departmental regulation conflicting with this section and former § 10-2-31 void. — A departmental insurance regulation that proscribes reduction of the par value of stock below one dollar per share without approval of the commissioner conflicts with this section and former § 10-2-31, and is therefore void under § 27-2-17(a). Assured Investors Life Ins. Co. v. Payne, 356 So. 2d 144 (Ala. 1978).

§ 27-27-42. Same — Curing of deficiency.

Any insurer receiving the commissioner's notice mentioned in section 27-27-41:

(1) If a stock insurer and if its articles of incorporation and laws of this state so permit, by resolution of its board of directors and subject to any limitations upon assessment contained in its articles of incorporation, may assess its stockholders for amounts necessary to cure the deficiency and provide the insurer with a reasonable amount of surplus in addition. If any stockholder fails to pay a lawful assessment after notice given to him in person or by advertisement in such time and manner as approved by the commissioner, the insurer may require the return of the original certificate of stock held by the stockholder and, in cancellation and in lieu thereof, issue a new certificate for such number of shares as the stockholder may then be entitled to, upon the basis of the stockholder's proportionate interest in the amount of the insurer's capital stock, as determined by the commissioner to be remaining at the time of determination of amount of impairment under section 27-27-41, after deducting from such proportionate interest the amount of such unpaid assessment. The insurer may pay for or issue fractional shares under this subdivision;

(2) If a mutual insurer, shall levy such an assessment upon members as is provided under section 27-27-32; and

(3) Neither this section nor section 27-27-41 shall be deemed to prohibit the insurer from curing any such deficiency through any lawful means other than those referred to in such sections. (Acts 1971, No. 407, p. 707, § 538.)

§ 27-27-43. Mutualization of stock insurers.

(a) A stock insurer other than a title insurer may become a mutual insurer under such plan and procedure as may be approved by the commissioner after a hearing thereon.

(b) The commissioner shall not approve any such plan, procedure or mutualization unless:

(1) It is equitable to stockholders and policyholders;

(2) It is subject to approval by the holders of not less than three fourths of the insurer's outstanding capital stock having voting rights and by not less

than three fourths of the insurer's policyholders who vote on such plan in person, by proxy or by mail pursuant to such notice and procedure as may be approved by the commissioner;

(3) If a life insurer, the right to vote thereon is limited to holders of policies other than term or group policies and whose policies have been in force for more than one year;

(4) Mutualization will result in retirement of shares of the insurer's capital stock at a reasonable price as specified in the plan;

(5) The plan provides for the purchase of the shares of any nonconsenting stockholder in the same manner and subject to the same applicable conditions as provided by the general corporation laws of the state as to rights of nonconsenting stockholders with respect to consolidation or merger of private corporations;

(6) The plan provides for definite conditions to be fulfilled by a designated early date upon which such mutualization will be deemed effective; and

(7) The mutualization leaves the insurer with surplus funds reasonably adequate for the security of its policyholders and to enable it to continue successfully in business in the states in which it is then authorized to transact insurance and for the kinds of insurance included in its certificates of authority in such states.

(c) This section shall not apply to mutualization under order of court pursuant to rehabilitation or reorganization of an insurer under chapter 32 of this title. (Acts 1971, No. 407, p. 707, § 539.)

§ 27-27-44. Conversion of mutual insurer into stock insurer.

(a) A mutual insurer may become a stock insurer under such plan and procedure as may be approved by the commissioner after a hearing thereon.

(b) The commissioner shall not approve any such plan or procedure unless:

(1) It is equitable to the insurer's members;

(2) It is subject to approval by vote of not less than three fourths of the insurer's current members voting thereon in person, by proxy or by mail at a meeting of members called for the purpose pursuant to such reasonable notice and procedure as may be approved by the commissioner; if a life insurer, right to vote may be limited to members who hold policies other than term or group policies and whose policies have been in force for not less than one year;

(3) The equity of each policyholder in the insurer is determinable under a fair formula approved by the commissioner, which such equity shall be based upon not less than the insurer's entire surplus, after deducting contributed or borrowed surplus funds, plus a reasonable present equity in its reserves and in all nonadmitted assets;

(4) The policyholders entitled to participate in the purchase of stock or distribution of assets shall include all current policyholders and all existing

persons who had been policyholders of the insurer within three years prior to the date such plan was submitted to the commissioner;

(5) The plan gives to each policyholder of the insurer, as specified in subdivision (b) (4) of this section a preemptive right to acquire his proportionate part of all of the proposed capital stock of the insurer, within a designated reasonable period, and to apply upon the purchase thereof the amount of his equity in the insurer as determined under subdivision (b) (3) of this section;

(6) Shares are so offered to policyholders at a price not greater than to be thereafter offered to others;

(7) The plan provides for payment to each policyholder not electing to apply his equity in the insurer for, or upon, the purchase price of stock to which preemptively entitled of cash in the amount of his equity not so used for the purchase of stock, and which cash payment, together with stock so purchased, if any, shall constitute full payment and discharge of the policyholder's equity as an owner of such mutual insurer; and

(8) The plan, when completed, would provide for the converted insurer paid-in capital stock in an amount not less than the minimum paid-in capital required of a domestic stock insurer transacting like kinds of insurance, together with surplus funds in amount not less than one half of such required capital. (Acts 1971, No. 407, p. 707, § 540.)

§ 27-27-45. Merger and consolidations — Domestic stock insurers.

(a) A domestic stock insurer may merge or consolidate with one or more domestic or foreign stock insurers by complying with the applicable provisions of the statutes of this state governing the merger or consolidation of stock corporations formed for profit, but subject to subsections (b) and (c) of this section.

(b) No such merger or consolidation shall be effectuated unless in advance thereof the plan and agreement therefor have been filed with the commissioner and approved in writing by him after a hearing thereon. The commissioner shall give such approval within a reasonable time after such filing unless he finds such plan or agreement:

(1) Is contrary to law;

(2) Inequitable to the stockholders of any domestic insurer involved; or

(3) Would substantially reduce the security of, and service to be rendered to, policyholders of the domestic insurer in this state or elsewhere.

(c) No director, officer, agent or employee of any insurer party to such merger or consolidation shall receive any fee, commission, compensation or other valuable consideration whatsoever for in any manner aiding, promoting or assisting therein except as set forth in such plan or agreement.

(d) If the commissioner does not approve any such plan or agreement, he shall so notify the insurer in writing, specifying his reasons therefor.

(e) If any domestic insurer involved in the proposed merger or consolidation is authorized to transact insurance also in other states, the commissioner may request the insurance commissioner, director of insurance, superintendent of insurance or other similar public insurance supervisory official of the two other such states in which such insurer has in force the larger amounts of insurance to participate in the hearing provided for under subsection (b) of this section, with full right to examine all witnesses and evidence and to offer to the commissioner such pertinent information and suggestions as they may deem proper.

(f) Any plan or proposal through which a stock insurer proposes to acquire a controlling stock interest in another stock insurer through an exchange of stock of the first insurer, issued by the insurer for the purpose, for such controlling stock of the second insurer is deemed to be a plan or proposal of merger of the second insurer into the first insurer for the purposes of this section and is subject to the applicable provisions of this section. (Acts 1911, No. 440, p. 623; Acts 1971, No. 407, p. 707, § 541.)

Two insurance companies may merge subject to second company becoming an approved company. — Nothing in the statute prohibits the commissioner from allowing an insurance company to merge with another insurance company, subject to the second insurance company becoming an approved insurance company. Roussel v. Payne, 352 So. 2d 1364 (Ala. Civ. App.), cert. denied, 352 So. 2d 1370 (Ala. 1977).

§ 27-27-46. Same — Domestic mutual insurers.

(a) A domestic mutual insurer may merge or consolidate with another insurer under the applicable procedures prescribed by the statutes of this state applying to corporations formed for profit, except as provided in this section.

(b) The plan and agreement for merger or consolidation shall be submitted to, and approved by, at least two thirds of the members of each mutual insurer voting thereon at meetings called for the purpose pursuant to such reasonable notice and procedure as has been approved by the commissioner. If a life insurer, right to vote may be limited to members whose policies are other than term and group policies and have been in effect for more than one year.

(c) No such merger or consolidation shall be effectuated unless in advance thereof the plan and agreement therefor have been filed with the commissioner and approved by him in writing after a hearing thereon. The commissioner shall give such approval within a reasonable time after such filing unless he finds such plan or agreement:

(1) Inequitable to the policyholders of any domestic insurer involved; or

(2) Would substantially reduce the security of, and service to be rendered to, policyholders of the domestic insurer in this state and elsewhere.

(d) If the commissioner does not approve such plan or agreement, he shall so notify the insurers in writing specifying his reasons therefor.

(e) Subsection (e) of section 27-27-45 shall also apply as to mergers and consolidations of such mutual insurers. (Acts 1971, No. 407, p. 707, § 542.)

§ 27-27-47. Bulk reinsurance — Domestic stock insurers.

(a) A domestic stock insurer may reinsure all, or substantially all, of its insurance in force or a major class thereof with another insurer by an agreement of bulk reinsurance, but no such agreement shall become effective unless filed with the commissioner and approved by him in writing after a hearing thereon.

(b) The commissioner shall approve such agreement within a reasonable time after such filing unless he finds that it is inequitable to the stockholders of the domestic insurer or would substantially reduce the protection or service to its policyholders. If the commissioner does not approve the agreement, he shall so notify the insurer in writing, specifying his reasons therefor. If the commissioner does not approve or disapprove such agreement and notify the insurer thereof in writing within 30 days after such filing, it shall conclusively be presumed that the agreement is approved by the commissioner. (Acts 1971, No. 407, p. 707, § 543.)

§ 27-27-48. Same — Domestic mutual insurers.

(a) A domestic mutual insurer may reinsure all, or substantially all, its business in force or all, or substantially all, of a major class thereof with another insurer, stock or mutual, by an agreement of bulk reinsurance after compliance with this section. No such agreement shall become effective unless filed with the commissioner and approved by him in writing after a hearing thereon.

(b) The commissioner shall approve such agreement within a reasonable time after filing if he finds it to be fair and equitable to each domestic insurer involved, and that such reinsurance if effectuated would not substantially reduce the protection or service to its policyholders. If the commissioner does not so approve, he shall so notify each insurer involved in writing, specifying his reasons therefor.

(c) The plan and agreement for such reinsurance must be approved by vote of not less than two thirds of each domestic mutual insurer's members voting thereon at meetings of members called for the purpose, pursuant to such reasonable notice and procedure as the commissioner may approve. If a life insurer, right to vote may be limited to members whose policies are other than term or group policies and have been in effect for more than one year.

(d) If for reinsurance of a mutual insurer in a stock insurer, the agreement must provide for payment in cash to each member of the insurer entitled thereto, as upon conversion of such insurer pursuant to section 27-27-44, of his equity in the business reinsured as determined under a fair formula approved by the commissioner, which equity shall be based upon such member's equity in the reserves, assets, whether or not "admitted" assets, and surplus, if any, of the mutual insurer to be taken over by the stock insurer. (Acts 1919, No. 443, p. 678; Acts 1971, No. 407, p. 707, § 544.)

§ 27-27-49. Distribution of assets upon liquidation of domestic mutual insurer.

(a) Upon any liquidation of a domestic mutual insurer, its assets remaining after discharge of its indebtedness, policy obligations, repayment of contributed or borrowed surplus, if any, and expenses of administration shall be distributed to existing persons who were its members at any time within 36 months next preceding the date such liquidation was authorized or ordered or date of last termination of the insurer's certificate of authority, whichever date is the earlier; except, that if the commissioner has reason to believe that those in charge of the management of the insurer have caused or encouraged the reduction of the number of members of the insurer in anticipation of liquidation and for the purpose of reducing thereby the number of persons who may be entitled to share in distribution of the insurer's assets, he may enlarge the 36-month qualification period provided for in this subsection by such additional period as he may deem to be reasonable.

(b) The distributive share of each such member shall be in the proportion that the aggregate premiums earned by the insurer on the policies of the member during the combined periods of his membership bear to the aggregate of all premiums so earned on the policies of all such members. The insurer may, and if a life insurer shall, make a reasonable classification of its policies so held by such members and a formula based upon such classification for determining the equitable distributive share of each such member. Such classification and formula shall be subject to the approval of the commissioner. (Acts 1971, No. 407, p. 707, § 545.)

§ 27-27-50. Extinguishment and nullification of domestic insurers' corporate charter.

(a) The corporate charter of any corporation formed under the laws of this state more than three years prior to January 1, 1972, for the purpose of becoming an insurer and which corporation within such three-year period has not actively engaged in business as a domestic insurer under a certificate of authority issued to it by the commissioner under laws then in force is hereby extinguished and nullified.

(b) The corporate charter of any other corporation formed under the laws of this state for the purpose of becoming an insurer and which corporation during any period of 36 consecutive months after January 1, 1972, is not actively engaged in business as a domestic insurer under a certificate of authority issued to it by the commissioner under laws currently in force is automatically hereby extinguished and nullified at the expiration of such 36-month period.

(c) The period during which any such corporation referred to in subsection (b) of this section is the subject of delinquency proceedings under chapter 32 of this title shall not be counted as part of any such 36-month period.

(d) Upon merger or consolidation of a domestic insurer with another insurer under this chapter, the corporate charter of such merged or consolidated domestic insurer shall thereby automatically be extinguished and nullified. (Acts 1971, No. 407, p. 707, § 546.)

§ 27-27-51. Rules and regulations as to securities of domestic stock insurers.

The commissioner shall have the power, and it shall be his duty, to prescribe, publish and disseminate to all domestic stock insurance companies uniform written rules and regulations of proxies, consents and authorizations, including the solicitation thereof, and information necessary, or appropriate to, such solicitation or to the authorization sought thereby, in respect of securities issued by such domestic stock insurance companies; and it shall be unlawful for any person to solicit or to permit the use of his name to solicit any proxy, consent or authorization in respect of any such securities in contravention of such rules and regulations as may be prescribed, published and disseminated pursuant to this section. (Acts 1971, No. 407, p. 707, § 547.)

§ 27-27-52. Insider trading of domestic stock insurer equity securities — Short title.

Sections 27-27-52 through 27-27-60 shall be known as the "Insider Trading of Domestic Stock Insurer Equity Securities Law." (Acts 1971, No. 407, p. 707, § 548.)

§ 27-27-53. Same — Ownership statements.

Every person who is, directly or indirectly, the beneficial owner of more than 10 percent of any class of any equity security of a domestic stock insurance company or who is a director or an officer of such company shall file in the office of the commissioner of insurance of Alabama on or before January 31, 1972, or within 10 days after he becomes such beneficial owner, director or officer, a statement, in such form as the commissioner may prescribe, of the amount of all equity securities of such company of which he is the beneficial owner and, within 10 days after the close of each calendar month thereafter, if there has been a change in such ownership during such month, shall file in the office of the commissioner a statement, in such form as the commissioner may prescribe, indicating his ownership at the close of the calendar month and such changes in his ownership as have occurred during such calendar month. (Acts 1971, No. 407, p. 707, § 549.)

§ 27-27-54. Same — Recovery of certain profits by company.

For the purpose of preventing the unfair use of information which may have been obtained by such beneficial owner, director or officer by reason of his relationship to such company, any profit realized by him from any purchase and sale or any sale and purchase, of any equity security of such company within any period of less than six months, unless such security was acquired in good faith in connection with a debt previously contracted, shall inure to, and be recoverable by, the company, irrespective of any intention on the part of such beneficial owner, director or officer in entering into such transaction of holding the security purchased or of not repurchasing the security sold for a period exceeding six months. An action to recover such profit may be instituted in any court of competent jurisdiction by the company or by the owner of any security of the company in the name, and in behalf, of the company if the company shall fail or refuse to bring such action within 60 days after request or shall fail diligently to prosecute the same thereafter; but no such action shall be brought more than two years after the date such profit was realized. This section shall not be construed to cover any transaction where such beneficial owner was not such both at the time of the purchase and sale or the sale and purchase of the security involved or any transaction or transactions which the commissioner, by rules and regulations, may exempt as not comprehended within the purpose of this section. (Acts 1971, No. 407, p. 707, § 550.)

§ 27-27-55. Same — Unlawful sales.

It shall be unlawful for any such beneficial owner, director or officer, directly or indirectly, to sell any equity security of such company if the person selling the security or his principal:

(1) Does not own the security sold; or

(2) If owning the security, does not deliver it against such sale within 20 days thereafter or does not within five days after such sale deposit it in the mails or other usual channels of transportation; but no person shall be deemed to have violated this section if he proves that, notwithstanding the exercise of good faith, he was unable to make such delivery or deposit within such time or that to do so would cause undue inconvenience or expense. (Acts 1971, No. 407, p. 707, § 551.)

§ 27-27-56. Same — Exemptions from sections 27-27-54 and 27-27-55; prescription of terms and conditions thereon.

The provisions of section 27-27-54 shall not apply to any purchase and sale or sale and purchase and the provisions of section 27-27-55 shall not apply to any sale of an equity security of a domestic stock insurance company not then, or theretofore, held by him in an investment account by a dealer in the ordinary course of his business and incident to the establishment, or maintenance by him, of a primary or secondary market, otherwise than on an exchange as defined in the Securities Exchange Act of 1934, for such security. The commissioner may, by such rules and regulations as he deems necessary or appropriate in the public interest, define and prescribe terms and conditions with respect to securities held in an investment account and transactions made in the ordinary course of business and incident to the establishment or maintenance of a primary or secondary market. (Acts 1971, No. 407, p. 707, § 552.)

§ 27-27-57. Same — Applicability of sections 27-27-53 through 27-27-55.

The provisions of sections 27-27-53 through 27-27-55 shall not apply to foreign or domestic arbitrage transactions unless made in contravention of such rules and regulations as the commissioner may adopt in order to carry out the purposes of this chapter. (Acts 1971, No. 407, p. 707, § 553.)

§ 27-27-58. Same — Equity securities — Defined.

The term "equity security," when used in this chapter, means any stock or similar security or any security convertible, with or without consideration, into such a security, or carrying any warrant or right to subscribe to or purchase such a security, or any such warrant or right or any other security which the commissioner shall deem to be of similar nature and consider necessary or appropriate, by such rules and regulations as he may prescribe in the public interest or for the protection of investors, to treat as an equity security. (Acts 1971, No. 407, p. 707, § 554.)

§ 27-27-59. Same — Same — Applicability of sections 27-27-53 through 27-27-55.

The provisions of sections 27-27-53 through 27-27-55 shall not apply to equity securities of a domestic stock insurance company if:

(1) Such securities shall be registered, or shall be required to be registered, pursuant to section 12 of the Securities Exchange Act of 1934, as amended; or

(2) Such domestic stock insurance company shall not have any class of its equity securities held of record by 100 or more persons on the last business day of the year next preceding the year in which equity securities of the company would be subject to the provisions of sections 27-27-53 through 27-27-55 except for the provisions of this subdivision. (Acts 1971, No. 407, p. 707, § 555.)

U.S. Code. — Section 12 of the Securities Exchange Act of 1934, referred to in subdivision (1), is codified as 15 U.S.C. § 78l.

§ 27-27-60. Same — Rules and regulations.

The commissioner shall have the power to make such rules and regulations as may be necessary for the execution of the functions vested in him by sections 27-27-53 through 27-27-59 and may for such purpose classify domestic stock insurance companies, securities and other persons or matters within his jurisdiction. No provision of sections 27-27-53 through 27-27-55 imposing any liability shall apply to any act done or omitted in good faith in conformity with any rule or regulation of the commissioner, notwithstanding that such rule or regulation may, after such act or omission, be amended or rescinded or determined by judicial or other authority to be invalid for any reason. (Acts 1971, No. 407, p. 707, § 556.)

§ 27-27-61. Applicability of corporation statutes to domestic insurers.

The applicable statutes of this state relating to the powers and procedures of domestic private corporations formed for profit shall apply to domestic stock insurers and to domestic mutual insurers, except where in conflict with the express provisions of this title and the reasonable implications of such provisions. (Acts 1971, No. 407, p. 707, § 498.)

Cited in Assured Investors Life Ins. Co. v. Payne, 356 So. 2d 144 (Ala. 1978).

CHAPTER 28.

HOLDING COMPANIES.

Sec.
27-28-1. Plan for exchange of stock, etc., between domestic stock insurer and holding company — Authority.
27-28-2. Same — Procedure for exchange.
27-28-3. Same — Fees, etc., for promotion of plan.

Sec.
27-28-4. Effect of chapter on powers of commissioner and authority to engage in insurance business.
27-28-5. Applicability of Alabama Business Corporation Act.

§ 27-28-1. Plan for exchange of stock, etc., between domestic stock insurer and holding company — Authority.

A domestic stock insurance company, hereinafter referred to in this chapter as "domestic company," may cause a corporation to be organized under the laws of this state or any other state of the United States of America to act as a holding company, hereinafter referred to in this chapter as "holding company," which may, or may not, be an insurance corporation, and the domestic company and holding company may adopt a plan for an exchange of stock or other securities in which stockholders of the domestic company exchange their stock for shares of stock or other securities issued by the holding company pursuant to the provisions of section 27-28-2. Such plan of exchange may provide for a direct exchange of stock or other securities between the stockholders of the domestic company and the holding company or may include provision for the merger of a wholly owned subsidiary of the holding company into the domestic company, in which stockholders of the domestic company receive shares of voting stock of the holding company in exchange for shares of stock of the domestic company and the holding company owns thereafter all of the outstanding stock of the domestic company. (Acts 1971, No. 1449, p. 2472.)

§ 27-28-2. Same — Procedure for exchange.

A plan of exchange shall be adopted and become effective in the following manner:

(1) APPROVAL OF THE BOARDS OF DIRECTORS. — The boards of directors of each corporate party to the plan of exchange by resolution shall adopt the plan of exchange which shall set forth the terms and conditions of the exchange and the mode of carrying the same into effect and such other provisions with respect to the exchange as may be deemed necessary or desirable.

(2) APPROVAL OF COMMISSIONER. — Every plan of exchange, before being submitted to vote of the stockholders pursuant to subdivision (3) of this section, shall be submitted for approval to the commissioner in accordance with the following procedure:

a. After the approval required by subdivision (1) of this section is obtained, the domestic company shall submit to the commissioner three copies of the plan of exchange and any other information which the commissioner may require with respect to such plan;

b. Upon the submission of the plan, the commissioner shall schedule a public hearing to determine if the terms and conditions of the plan of exchange are fair, to be held within 30 days after such submission. Each corporation which is a party to the plan shall give notice of the time and place of such hearing to each stockholder of record of the corporation, as of a date 15 days prior to the date of the hearing, by letter mailed not later than 10 days prior to the hearing. Each corporation which is a party to the plan shall further cause notice of the hearing to be published in a newspaper of general circulation in the city wherein is located the principal place of business of the corporation, once a week for two consecutive weeks, the last publication of such notice to be not more than two weeks prior to the hearing date. Each stockholder of any corporation which is a party to the plan and each policyholder of the domestic company or any other domestic insurance company which is a party to the plan shall be entitled to appear and be heard in said hearing and said notices shall so state; and

c. After conclusion of the hearing and not later than 60 days after submission of the plan, the commissioner shall issue a written order approving the terms and conditions of the plan of exchange as delivered to him and such modifications therein as the board of directors of each corporation which is a party to the plan shall approve, only if he finds:

1. That the terms and conditions of the plan, including modifications, if any, if effected, will not tend adversely to affect the financial stability or management of the domestic company or any other domestic insurance company which is a party to the plan;

2. That the interests of the policyholders of the domestic company and any other domestic insurance company which is a party to the plan are protected; and

3. That the terms and conditions of the plan and the proposed issuance and exchange are fair to all stockholders to whom it is proposed to issue stock or other securities of the holding company by the terms of the plan.

If the commissioner fails to approve the plan, he shall state his reasons therefor in writing. Any party in interest may appeal from the ruling of the commissioner to the circuit court in the circuit where the insurance company maintains its home office by giving notice of such appeal to the commissioner within two weeks after such ruling. All expenses of the commissioner relating to the hearing shall be paid by the domestic company.

(3) APPROVAL OF STOCKHOLDERS. — The plan of exchange as approved by the commissioner pursuant to the provisions of subdivision (2) of this section shall then be submitted to a vote of the stockholders of the domestic

company at an annual or special meeting of the stockholders. Written or printed notice shall be given to each stockholder of record entitled to vote at such meeting, not less than 20 days before such meeting, in the manner provided in the Alabama Business Corporation Act for the giving of notice of meetings of stockholders, and shall state the purpose of the meeting, whether the meeting be an annual or a special meeting. A copy or a summary of the plan of exchange shall be included in or enclosed with such notice. At such meeting, a vote of the stockholders shall be taken on the proposed plan of exchange. Each outstanding share of the domestic company shall be entitled to vote on the proposed plan of exchange, whether or not such share has voting rights under the provisions of the certificate of incorporation of the domestic company. The plan shall be approved upon receiving the affirmative vote of the holders of at least two thirds of the outstanding shares of the domestic company, unless any class of shares of the domestic company is entitled to vote as a class therein, in which event, the plan of exchange shall be approved upon receiving the affirmative vote of the holders of at least two thirds of the outstanding shares for each class of shares entitled to vote as a class thereon and of the total outstanding shares. Any class of shares of the domestic company shall be entitled to vote as a class if the plan of exchange contains any provision which, if contained in a proposed amendment to the certificate of incorporation, would entitle such class of shares to vote as a class. After such approval of the plan of exchange, and at any time prior to the filing of the certificate setting forth the plan of exchange pursuant to this subdivision, the plan of exchange may be abandoned pursuant to a provision for such abandonment, if any, contained in the plan of exchange. Stockholder approval by the stockholders of any other corporate party to the plan of exchange shall be governed by the laws otherwise applicable to the transactions involved in the plan.

(4) RIGHTS OF DISSENTING STOCKHOLDERS. — If any stockholder of the domestic company shall file with such corporation prior to, or at the meeting of, stockholders at which the plan of exchange is submitted to a vote a written objection to such plan and shall not vote in favor thereof and such stockholder, within 10 days after the date on which the vote was taken, shall make written demand on the domestic company for payment of the fair value of his shares as of the day prior to the date on which the vote was taken approving the plan, then, if the plan is effected, the domestic company or surviving corporation, if a merger is included in the plan, shall pay to such stockholder, upon surrender of his certificate, or certificates, representing such shares, the fair value thereof. Such demand shall state the number and class of the shares owned by such dissenting stockholder. Any stockholder failing to make demand within the 10-day period shall be bound by the terms of the plan of exchange.

Within 10 days after the plan is effected, the domestic company or surviving corporation, as the case may be, shall give notice thereof to each dissenting stockholder who has made demand as provided for in this subdivision the payment of the fair value of his shares.

If within 30 days after the date on which such plan was effected the value of such shares is agreed upon between the dissenting stockholder and the domestic company or surviving corporation, payment therefor shall be made within 90 days after the date on which such plan was effected from the fund established pursuant to the provisions of subdivision (5) of this section or, if the fund is not sufficient for such payment, from other cash assets, upon the surrender of the dissenting stockholder's certificate, or certificates, representing such shares. Upon payment of the agreed value, the dissenting stockholder shall cease to have any interest in such shares or in the corporation.

If within such period of 30 days the stockholder and the domestic company or the surviving corporation do not so agree, then the dissenting stockholder may, within 60 days after the expiration of the 30-day period, file a petition in any circuit court, asking for a finding and determination of the fair value of such shares, and shall be entitled to judgment against the domestic company or surviving corporation for the amount of such fair value as of the day prior to the date on which such vote was taken approving such plans, together with interest thereon to the date of such judgment. The judgment shall be payable only upon, and simultaneously with, the surrender to the domestic company or surviving corporation of the certificate or certificates representing such shares and shall be payable from the fund established pursuant to the provisions of subdivision (5) of this section or, if the fund is not sufficient for such payment, from other cash assets. Upon payment of the judgment, the dissenting stockholder shall cease to have any interest in such shares, or in the domestic company or surviving corporation. Unless the dissenting stockholder shall file such petition within the time limited in this subdivision, such stockholder and all persons claiming under him shall be bound by the terms of the plan of exchange.

Shares acquired by the domestic company or the surviving corporation pursuant to the payment of the agreed value thereof or of the judgment entered therefor, as in this subdivision provided, shall be treasury shares and may be held and disposed of by such corporation as in the case of other treasury shares.

A nominee of a corporate fiduciary holding shares of stock for more than one fiduciary account may dissent as to less than all of the shares registered in his name. In that event, his rights shall be determined as if the shares as to which he has dissented and his other shares were registered in the names of different stockholders.

The dissenting rights of stockholders of any other corporate party to the plan of exchange shall be governed by the laws otherwise applicable to the transactions involved in the plan.

(5) FILING PLAN OF EXCHANGE. — After the date of the meeting of stockholders of the domestic company at which the plan of exchange was submitted to such stockholders, a certificate setting forth:

a. The plan of exchange;

b. The vote by which such plan was adopted by the stockholders of the domestic company and any other corporate party to the plan whose stockholders approved the plan under the laws otherwise applicable;

c. The number of shares of the domestic company for which a dissenting right has been preserved and for which no payment has been made pursuant to subdivision (4) of this section; or

d. That the plan of exchange has been abandoned shall be executed on behalf of the domestic company by its president, or a vice-president, and attested by its secretary, or an assistant secretary, under the corporate seal, and shall then be presented in triplicate to the commissioner. If the certificate indicates that the plan of exchange has been approved by stockholders as required by subdivision (3) of this section and that the facts otherwise conform to the law, he shall require the domestic company, prior to the time the plan becomes effective, to create a fund in cash distinct from its other assets to provide for the payment for all shares with respect to which a dissenting right has been preserved and for which no payment has been made pursuant to subdivision (4) of this section. The amount of said fund shall not limit the amount to be paid to dissenting stockholders under the provisions of subdivision (4) of this section, nor shall the amount of the fund be used as evidence in any proceeding to establish the fair value of shares for which dissenting rights are asserted. Thereafter, upon the creation of such a fund, the commissioner shall endorse his approval on the certificate and the same shall then be filed in the office of the secretary of state. Upon such filing of such certificate, the plan of exchange shall become effective unless a later date and time is specified in the plan of exchange, in which event, the plan of exchange and issuance and exchange provided for therein shall become effective upon such later date and time.

(6) EFFECT OF EXCHANGE. — Upon the plan of exchange becoming effective, the exchange, or exchanges, provided for therein shall be deemed to have been consummated, each stockholder of the domestic company shall cease to be a stockholder of such company and the ownership of all shares of the issued and outstanding stock of the domestic company shall vest in the holding company automatically without any physical transfer or deposit of certificates representing such shares.

Certificates representing shares of the domestic company prior to the plan of exchange becoming effective shall after the plan of exchange becomes effective automatically represent shares of the issued and outstanding capital stock or other securities issued by the holding company, provided that the plan of exchange:

a. Shall specify that all certificates representing shares of stock of the domestic company may, after the plan of exchange becomes effective, be exchanged by any stockholder for shares of stock or other securities issued by the holding company; and

b. May require that all certificates representing shares of stock of the domestic company shall, after the plan of exchange becomes effective, represent only the right to receive shares of stock or other securities issued by the holding company as shall be specified in the plan of exchange. (Acts 1971, No. 1449, p. 2472.)

§ 27-28-3. Same — Fees, etc., for promotion of plan.

No director, officer, agent or employee of any corporation which is a party to the plan of exchange, except as is expressly provided by the plan filed with the commissioner. shall receive any fee, commission, other compensation or valuable consideration whatever for in any manner aiding, promoting or assisting in the promotion of the plan of exchange. (Acts 1971, No. 1449, p. 2472.)

§ 27-28-4. Effect of chapter on powers of commissioner and authority to engage in insurance business.

Nothing contained in this chapter shall affect the power of the commissioner to regulate, supervise and control insurance companies pursuant to the laws of the state of Alabama governing such companies, nor shall anything in this chapter be construed to authorize any insurance company to engage in any kind, or kinds, of insurance business not authorized by its charter or to authorize any holding company which is not an insurance corporation to engage directly in the business of insurance. Subsequent to the effective date of any plan of exchange, the commissioner, having due regard to the findings stated in subdivision (2) of section 27-28-2, shall have authority to require that the affairs of the domestic company be conducted in such manner as to assure the continued safe conduct and transaction of the business of insurance of the domestic company. (Acts 1971, No. 1449, p. 2472.)

§ 27-28-5. Applicability of Alabama Business Corporation Act.

This chapter shall be supplemental to, and construed with, the provisions of the Alabama Business Corporation Act, as amended, but in the event there exists any conflict between the provisions of this chapter and the provisions of that act, the provisions of this chapter shall control. (Acts 1971, No. 1449, p. 2472.)

Cross references. — As to Alabama Business Corporation Act, see § 10-2A-1 et seq.

CHAPTER 29.

INSURANCE HOLDING COMPANY SYSTEMS.

Sec.
27-29-1. Definitions.
27-29-2. Subsidiaries and affiliates of domes-
         tic insurers.
27-29-3. Acquisition of control of, or merger
         with, domestic insurers.
27-29-4. Registration of insurers.
27-29-5. Registered insurers — Standards for
         transactions with affiliates; ade-
         quacy of surplus; dividends and
         other distributions.
27-29-6. Same — Examination of records,
         etc., of insurer or affiliates.
27-29-7. Confidential treatment of informa-
         tion, etc., examined or reported.

Sec.
27-29-8. Rules, regulations and orders.
27-29-9. Injunctions; prohibitions against
         voting securities; sequestration of
         voting securities.
27-29-10. Criminal proceedings.
27-29-11. Delinquency proceedings and reha-
          bilitation.
27-29-12. Suspension, revocation or nonre-
          newal of insurer's license or au-
          thority to do business.
27-29-13. Judicial review of actions by com-
          missioner; petition for manda-
          mus against same.
27-29-14. Short title.

Cited in Roussel v. Payne, 352 So. 2d 1364 (Ala. Civ. App. 1977).

§ 27-29-1. Definitions.

For purposes of this chapter, unless otherwise stated, the following terms shall have the meanings respectively ascribed to them by this section:

(1) AFFILIATE. Such term shall include an "affiliate" of, or person "affiliated" with, a specific person, and shall mean a person that directly, or indirectly through one or more intermediaries, controls, or is controlled by, or is under common control with, the person specified.

(2) COMMISSIONER. The commissioner of insurance, his deputies or the insurance department as appropriate.

(3) CONTROL. Such term shall include "controlling," "controlled by" or "under common control with" and shall mean the possession, direct or indirect, of the power to direct or cause the direction of the management and policies of a person, whether through the ownership of voting securities, by contract other than a commercial contract for goods or nonmanagement services, or otherwise, unless the power is the result of an official position with or corporate office held by the person. Control shall be presumed to exist if any person, directly or indirectly owns, controls, holds with the power to vote or holds proxies representing five percent or more of the voting securities of any other person. Any person who, on April 15, 1982, directly or indirectly, owns, controls, holds with the power to vote or holds proxies representing five percent or more, but not as much as 15 percent, of the voting securities of any person shall not be presumed to be in control of such person but shall not acquire, otherwise than by stock dividends, additional voting securities of such other person without being presumed to have acquired control and without complying with the provisions of this chapter relating to acquisition of control. This presumption may be rebutted

by a showing made in the manner provided by subsection (i) of section 27-29-4 that control does not exist in fact. Such "control" as used in this section shall not be deemed to exist where proxies have been obtained by management of such insurer solely in connection with voting at an annual or other regular meeting of the shareholders of such insurer. The commissioner may determine, after furnishing all persons in interest notice and opportunity to be heard and making specific finding of fact to support such determination, that control exists in fact, notwithstanding the absence of a presumption to that effect.

(4) INSURANCE HOLDING COMPANY SYSTEM. A system which consists of two or more affiliated persons, one or more of which is an insurer.

(5) INSURER. An insurance company as set forth in section 27-1-2, except that it shall not include:

a. Agencies, authorities or instrumentalities of the United States, its possessions and territories, the Commonwealth of Puerto Rico, the District of Columbia or a state or political subdivision of a state;

b. Fraternal benefits societies; or

c. Nonprofit medical and hospital service associations.

Notwithstanding the foregoing, for purposes of section 27-29-3, a domestic insurer shall include any other person controlling a domestic insurer unless such other person is either directly or through its affiliates primarily engaged in business other than the business of insurance.

(6) PERSON. An individual, a corporation, a partnership, a limited partnership, an association, a joint-stock company, a trust, an unincorporated organization or any similar entity or any combination of the foregoing acting in concert, but shall not include any securities broker performing no more than the usual and customary broker's function.

(7) SECURITYHOLDER. One who owns any security of such person, including common stock, preferred stock, debt obligations and other security convertible into, or evidencing, the right to acquire any of the foregoing.

(8) SUBSIDIARY. An affiliate controlled by such person, directly or indirectly, through one or more intermediaries.

(9) VOTING SECURITY. Such term shall include any security convertible into, or evidencing, a right to acquire a voting security. (Acts 1973, No. 1042, p. 1636, § 2; Acts 1982, No. 82-230, p. 280, § 1.)

§ 27-29-2. Subsidiaries and affiliates of domestic insurers.

(a) *Authorization.* — Any domestic insurer, either by itself or in cooperation with one or more persons, may organize or acquire one or more subsidiaries or affiliates in accordance with the provisions contained in this section. Such subsidiaries or affiliates may conduct any kind of business, or businesses, permitted by the Constitution and the laws of this state, and their authority to do so shall not be limited by reason of the fact that they are subsidiaries or affiliates of a domestic insurer.

(b) *Additional investment authority.* — In addition to any other statute of this state, now existing or hereafter enacted, expressly authorizing investments in common stock, preferred stock, debt obligations and other securities, a domestic insurer, other than a life and health insurer, may also invest in common stock, preferred stock, debt obligations and other securities of one or more subsidiaries or affiliates. In the event any such investments shall be made after April 27, 1981, then all such investments of such domestic insurer, whether made prior to or subsequent to April 27, 1981, shall be stated in all financial statements of such insurer filed with the commissioner at values determined as follows:

(1) All investments in common stock, preferred stock and other equity securities in such subsidiaries or affiliates shall be valued at the net asset (book) value of such securities; and

(2) All debt obligations shall be valued in accordance with standards and procedures established by the commissioner, which shall be in reasonable accord with the procedures and rules for valuing such securities as may be recommended, from time to time, by the National Association of Insurance Commissioners.

(c) *Additional investment authority for life, disability and burial insurers.* — In addition to investments in common stock, preferred stock, debt obligations and other securities permitted under all other sections of this title, a domestic life, disability and burial insurer may also:

(1) Invest, in common stock, preferred stock, debt obligations and other securities of one or more subsidiaries or affiliates, amounts which do not exceed the lesser of 10 percent of such insurer's assets or 75 percent of the total of the insurer's capital and surplus as shown in the latest annual report of the insurer filed pursuant to subsection (a) of section 27-3-26, less the minimum capital and surplus required of said insurer for authority to transact insurance by sections 27-3-7 and 27-3-8, provided that after such investments the insurer's surplus as regards policyholders will be reasonable in relation to the insurer's outstanding liabilities and adequate to its financial needs. In calculating the amount of such investments, there shall be included:

a. Total net moneys or other consideration expended and obligations assumed in the acquisition or formation of a subsidiary or affiliate, including all organizational expenses and contributions to capital and surplus of such subsidiary or affiliate, whether or not represented by the purchase of capital stock or issuance of other securities; and

b. All amounts expended in acquiring additional common stock, debt obligations and other securities and all contributions to the capital or surplus of a subsidiary or affiliate subsequent to its acquisition or formation;

(2) If the insurer's total liabilities, as calculated for National Association of Insurance Commissioners annual statement purposes are less than 10 percent of assets, invest any amount in common stock, preferred stock, debt obligations and other securities of one or more subsidiaries or affiliates,

provided that after such investment the insurer's surplus as regards policyholders, considering such investment as if it were a disallowed asset, will be reasonable in relation to the insurer's outstanding liabilities and adequate to its financial needs;

(3) Invest any amount in common stock, preferred stock, debt obligations and other securities of one or more subsidiaries or affiliates, provided that each such subsidiary or affiliate agrees to limit its investments in any asset so that such investments will not cause the amount of the total investment of the insurer to exceed any of the investment limitations specified in subdivision (1) of this subsection or in sections 27-41-15 through 27-41-18 and 27-41-35. For the purpose of this subdivision, "the total investment of the insurer" shall include:

a. Any direct investment by the insurer in an asset; and

b. The insurer's proportionate share of any investment in an asset by any subsidiary or affiliate of the insurer, which shall be calculated by multiplying the amount of the subsidiary's investment by the percentage of the insurer's ownership of such subsidiary or affiliate;

(4) With the approval of the commissioner, invest any amount in common stock, preferred stock, debt obligations or other securities of one or more subsidiaries or affiliates, provided that after such investment the insurer's surplus as regards policyholders will be reasonable in relation to the insurer's outstanding liabilities and adequate to its financial needs; and

(5) Invest any amount in the common stock, preferred stock, debt obligations or other securities of any subsidiary or affiliate exclusively engaged in holding title to and managing or developing real or personal property, if after considering as a disallowed asset so much of the investment as is represented by subsidiary assets which if held directly by the insurer would be considered as a disallowed asset, the insurer's surplus as regards policyholders will be reasonable in relation to the insurer's outstanding liabilities and adequate to its financial needs, and if following such investment all voting securities of such subsidiary would be owned by the insurer.

(d) *Exemption from investment restrictions.* — Investments in common stock, preferred stock, debt obligations or other securities of subsidiaries or affiliates made pursuant to subsection (b) or (c) of this section shall not be subject to any of the otherwise applicable restrictions or prohibitions contained in this title applicable to such investments of insurers.

(e) *Qualification of investment; when determined.* — Whether any investment pursuant to subsection (b) or (c) of this section meets the applicable requirements thereof is to be determined immediately after such investment is made, taking into account the then outstanding principal balance on all previous investments in debt obligations and the value of all previous investments in equity securities as of the date they were made.

(f) *Cessation of control.* — If an insurer ceases to control a subsidiary, it shall dispose of any investment therein made pursuant to this section within three years from the time of the cessation of control or within such further time as the commissioner may prescribe, unless at any time after such investment shall have been made such investment shall have met the requirements for investment under any other section of this title, and the insurer has notified the commissioner. (Acts 1973, No. 1042, p. 1636, § 3; Acts 1980, No. 80-199, p. 276; Acts 1981, No. 81-314, p. 446.)

Collateral references. — 44 C.J.S., Insurance, §§ 100, 102.

43 Am. Jur. 2d, Insurance, § 95.

§ 27-29-3. Acquisition of control of, or merger with, domestic insurers.

(a) *Filing and approval requirements.* — No person other than the issuer shall make a tender offer for or a request or invitation for tenders of, or enter into any agreement to exchange securities for or acquire in the open market any voting security of a domestic insurer if, after the consummation thereof, such person would, directly or indirectly, or by conversion or by exercise of any right to acquire, be in control of such insurer, and no person shall enter into an agreement to merge with or otherwise to acquire control of a domestic insurer unless, at the time any such offer, request, or invitation is made or any such agreement is entered into, or prior to the acquisition of such securities if no offer or agreement is involved or within 15 days after any such offer, request or invitation is made or any such agreement is entered into, such person has filed with the commissioner and has sent to such insurer a statement containing the information required by this section and such offer, request, invitation, agreement or acquisition either:

(1) Has been approved by the commissioner in the manner prescribed in this section; or

(2) Expressly states that it is subject to approval by the commissioner in the manner prescribed in this section.

An offer, request, invitation, agreement or acquisition which contains such a condition and which is approved by the commissioner in the manner so prescribed shall be effective and binding according to its terms from the date on which it was made.

(b) *Content of statement.* — The statement to be filed with the commissioner under this section shall be made under oath or affirmation and shall contain the following information:

(1) The name and address of each person by whom, or on whose behalf, the merger or other acquisition of control referred to in subsection (a) of this section is to be effected (hereinafter called "acquiring party"), and

a. If such person is an individual, his principal occupation and all offices and positions held during the past five years, and any conviction of crimes other than minor traffic violations during the past 10 years; or

b. If such person is not an individual, a report of the nature of its business operations during the past five years or for such lesser period as such person and any predecessors thereof shall have been in existence; an informative description of the business intended to be done by such person and such person's subsidiaries; and a list of all individuals who are, or who have been selected to become, directors or executive officers of such person or who perform, or will perform, functions appropriate to such positions. Such list shall include for each such individual the information required by paragraph a of this subdivision;

(2) The source, nature and amount of the consideration used, or to be used, in effecting the merger or other acquisition of control, a description of any transaction wherein funds were, or are to be, obtained for any such purpose, and the identity of persons furnishing such consideration; provided, however, that where a source of such consideration is a loan made in the lender's ordinary course of business, the identity of the lender shall remain confidential if the person filing such statement so requests;

(3) Fully audited financial information as to the earnings and financial condition of each acquiring party for the preceding five fiscal years of each such acquiring party, or for such lesser period as such acquiring party and any predecessors thereof shall have been in existence, and similar unaudited information as of a date not earlier than 90 days prior to the filing of the statement; provided, however, that in the case of an acquiring party which is an insurer actively engaged in the business of insurance, the financial statements of such insurer need not be audited, except such audit may be required if the need therefor is determined by the commissioner;

(4) Any plans or proposals which each acquiring party may have to liquidate such insurer, to sell its assets or merge or consolidate it with any person or to make any other material change in its business or corporate structure or management;

(5) The number of shares of any security referred to in subsection (a) of this section which each acquiring party proposes to acquire, the terms of the offer, request, invitation, agreement or acquisition referred to in subsection (a) of this section and a statement as to the method by which the fairness of the proposal was arrived at;

(6) The amount of each class of any security referred to in subsection (a) of this section which is beneficially owned or concerning which there is a right to acquire beneficial ownership by each acquiring party;

(7) A full description of any contracts, arrangements or understandings with respect to any security referred to in subsection (a) of this section in which any acquiring party is involved, including, but not limited to, transfer of any of the securities, joint ventures, loan or option arrangements, puts or calls, guarantees of loans, guarantees against loss or guarantees of profits, division of losses or profits or the giving or withholding of proxies. Such description shall identify the persons with whom such contracts, arrangements or understandings have been entered into;

(8) A description of the purchase of any security referred to in subsection (a) of this section during the 12 calendar months preceding the filing of the statement by any acquiring party, including the dates of purchase, names of the purchasers and consideration paid, or agreed to be paid, therefor;

(9) A description of any recommendations to purchase any security referred to in subsection (a) of this section made during the 12 calendar months preceding the filing of the statement by any acquiring party or by anyone based upon interviews or at the suggestion of such acquiring party;

(10) Copies of all tender offers for, requests or invitations for tenders of, exchange offers for and agreements to acquire or exchange any securities referred to in subsection (a) of this section and, if distributed, or additional soliciting material relating thereto;

(11) The terms of any agreement, contract or understanding made with any broker-dealer as to solicitation of securities referred to in subsection (a) of this section for tender and the amount of any fees, commissions or other compensation to be paid to broker-dealers with regard thereto; and

(12) Such additional information as the commissioner may, by rule or regulation, prescribe as necessary or appropriate for the protection of policyholders and securityholders of the insurer or in the public interest.

If the person required to file the statement referred to in subsection (a) of this section is a partnership, limited partnership, syndicate or other group, the commissioner may require that the information called for by subdivisions (1) through (12) of this subsection shall be given with respect to each partner of such partnership or limited partnership, each member of such syndicate or group and each person who controls such partner or member. If any such partner, member or person is a corporation or the person required to file the statement referred to in subsection (a) of this section is a corporation, the commissioner may require that the information called for by subdivisions (1) through (12) of this subsection shall be given with respect to such corporation, each officer and director of such corporation and each person who is, directly or indirectly, the beneficial owner of more than 15 percent of the outstanding voting securities of such corporation. If any material change occurs in the facts set forth in the statement filed with the commissioner and sent to such insurer pursuant to this section, an amendment setting forth such change, together with copies of all documents and other materials relevant to such change, shall be filed with the commissioner and sent to such insurer within two business days after the person learns of such change. Such insurer shall send such amendment to its shareholders.

(c) *Alternative filing materials.* — If any offer, request, invitation, agreement or acquisition referred to in subsection (a) of this section is proposed to be made by means of a registration statement under the Securities Act of 1933, or in circumstances requiring the disclosure of similar information under the Securities Exchange Act of 1934, or under a state law requiring similar registration or disclosure, the person required to file the statement referred to in subsection (a) of this section may utilize such documents in furnishing the information called for by that statement.

(d) *Approval by commissioner; hearings.*

(1) The commissioner shall approve any merger or other acquisition of control referred to in subsection (a) of this section unless, after a public hearing thereon, he finds that:

a. After the change of control the domestic insurer referred to in subsection (a) of this section would not be able to satisfy the requirements for the issuance of a license to write the line, or lines, of insurance for which it is presently licensed;

b. The effect of the merger or other acquisition of control would be substantially to lessen competition in insurance in this state or to create a monopoly therein;

c. The financial condition of any acquiring party is such as might jeopardize the financial stability of the insurer or prejudice the interest of its policyholders;

d. The plans or proposals which the acquiring party has to liquidate the insurer, sell its assets or consolidate or merge it with any person or to make any other material change in its business or corporate structure or management are unfair and unreasonable to policyholders of the insurer and not in the public interest; or

e. The competence, experience and integrity of those persons who would control the operation of the insurer are such that it would not be in the interest of policyholders of the insurer and of the public to permit the merger or other acquisition of control.

(2) The public hearing referred to in subdivision (1) of this subsection shall be held within 45 days after the statement required by subsection (a) of this section is filed, and at least 20 days' notice thereof shall be given by the commissioner to the person filing the statement. Not less than 15 days' notice of such public hearing shall be given by the person filing the statement to the insurer and to such other persons as may be designated by the commissioner. The insurer shall give such notice to its securityholders. The commissioner shall make a determination within 30 days after the conclusion of such hearing. At such hearing, the person filing the statement, the insurer, any person to whom notice of hearing was sent and any other person whose interest may be affected thereby shall have the right to present evidence, examine and cross-examine witnesses and offer oral and written arguments and, in connection therewith, shall be entitled to conduct discovery proceedings in the same manner as is presently allowed in the circuit courts of this state. All discovery proceedings shall be concluded not later than five days prior to the commencement of the public hearing.

(e) *Mailings to stockholders; payments of expenses.* — All statements, amendments or other material filed pursuant to subsections (a) or (b) of this section and all notices of public hearings held pursuant to subsection (d) of this section shall be mailed by the insurer to its stockholders within 10 business days after the insurer has received such statements, amendments, other material or notices. The expenses of mailing shall be borne by the person making the filing. As security for the payment of such expenses, such person shall file with the commissioner an acceptable bond or other deposit in an amount to be determined by the commissioner.

(f) *Exemptions.* — The provisions of this section shall not apply to:

(1) Any offer, request, invitation, or agreement to acquire or the acquisition by a person referred to in subsection (a) of this section of any voting security referred to in said subsection (a) which, immediately prior to the consummation of such offer, request, invitation, agreement or acquisition, was authorized but not issued and outstanding; provided, however, that after the acquisition of voting securities by such person that person shall not, either directly or indirectly, own, control, vote, hold, or otherwise have the right to acquire in any manner, 10 percent or more of the total issued and outstanding voting securities of the domestic insurer after the completion of such transaction. Any person proposing to acquire authorized but not issued and outstanding voting securities of a domestic insurer whose total direct and indirect holdings, including the right to acquire voting securities, would, after such acquisition of voting securities, equal or exceed 10 percent of the total issued and outstanding voting securities of such insurer, shall be subject to the provisions of subsection (a) of this section;

(2) Any offer, request, invitation, agreement or acquisition which the commissioner by order shall exempt therefrom as:

a. Not having been made or entered into for the purpose and not having the effect of changing or influencing the control of a domestic insurer; or

(b) As otherwise not comprehended within the purposes of this section.

(g) *Violations.* — The following shall be violations of this section:

(1) The failure to file any statement, amendment or other material required to be filed pursuant to subsections (a) or (b) of this section; or

(2) The effectuation, or any attempt to effectuate, an acquisition of control of, or merger with, a domestic insurer unless the commissioner has given his approval thereto.

(h) *Jurisdiction; consent to service of process.* — The courts of this state are hereby vested with jurisdiction over every person not resident, domiciled or authorized to do business in this state who files a statement with the commissioner under this section and over all actions involving such person arising out of violations of this section, and each such person shall be deemed to have performed acts equivalent to and constituting an appointment by such a person of the commissioner to be his true and lawful attorney upon whom may be served all lawful process in any action or proceeding arising out of violations of this section. Copies of all such lawful process shall be served on the commissioner and transmitted by registered or certified mail by the commissioner to such person at his last known address. (Acts 1973, No. 1042, p. 1636, § 4; Acts 1986, No. 86-464, § 1.)

The 1986 amendment, effective April 30, 1986, rewrote subdivision (f)(1).

Cited in Roussel v. Payne, 352 So. 2d 1364 (Ala. Civ. App. 1977).

§ 27-29-4. Registration of insurers.

(a) *Registration.* — Every insurer which is authorized to do business in this state and which is a member of an insurance holding company system shall register with the commissioner, except a foreign insurer subject to disclosure requirements and standards adopted by statute or regulation in the jurisdiction of its domicile which are substantially similar to those contained in this section. Any insurer which is subject to registration under this section shall register within 60 days after September 3, 1973, or 15 days after it becomes subject to registration, whichever is later, unless the commissioner for good cause shown extends the time for registration and, then, within such extended time. The commissioner may require any authorized insurer which is a member of a holding company system which is not subject to registration under this section to furnish a copy of the registration statement or other information filed by such insurance company with the insurance regulatory authority of domiciliary jurisdiction.

(b) *Information and form required.* — Every insurer subject to registration shall file a registration statement on a form provided by the commissioner which shall contain current information about:

(1) The capital structure, general financial condition, ownership and management of the insurer and any person controlling the insurer;

(2) The identity of every member of the insurance holding company system;

(3) The following agreements in force, relationships subsisting and transactions currently outstanding between such insurer and its affiliates:

a. Loans, other investments or purchases, sales or exchanges of securities of the affiliates by the insurer or of the insurer by its affiliates;

b. Purchases, sales or exchanges of assets;

c. Transactions not in the ordinary course of business;

d. Guarantees or undertakings for the benefit of an affiliate which result in an actual contingent exposure of the insurer's assets to liability, other than insurance contracts entered into in the ordinary course of the insurer's business;

e. All management and service contracts and all cost-sharing arrangements, other than cost allocation arrangements based upon generally accepted accounting principles; and

f. Reinsurance agreements covering all, or substantially all, of one or more lines of insurance of the ceding company; and

(4) Other matters concerning transactions between registered insurers and any affiliates as may be included, from time to time, in any registration forms adopted or approved by the commissioner.

(c) *Materiality.* — No information need be disclosed on the registration statement filed pursuant to subsection (b) of this section if such information is not material for the purposes of this section. Unless the commissioner by rule, regulation or order provides otherwise, sales, purchases, exchanges, loans or extensions of credit or investments involving one half of one percent or less of an insurer's admitted assets as of December 31, next preceding, shall not be deemed material for purposes of this section.

(d) *Amendments to registration statements.* — Each registered insurer shall keep current the information required to be disclosed in its registration statement by reporting all material changes or additions on amendment forms provided by the commissioner within 15 days after the end of the month in which it learns of each such change or addition; provided, however, that subject to subsection (c) of section 27-29-5, each registered insurer shall so report all dividends and other distributions to shareholders within two business days following the declaration thereof.

(e) *Termination of registration.* — The commissioner shall terminate the registration of any insurer which demonstrated that it no longer is a member of an insurance holding company system.

(f) *Consolidated filing.* — The commissioner may require or allow two or more affiliated insurers subject to registration under this section to file a consolidated registration statement or consolidated reports amending their consolidated registration statement or their individual registration statements.

(g) *Alternative registration.* — The commissioner may allow an insurer which is authorized to do business in this state and which is part of an insurance holding company system to register on behalf of any affiliated insurer which is required to register under subsection (a) of this section and to file all information and material required to be filed under this section.

(h) *Exemptions.* — The provisions of this section shall not apply to any insurer, information or transaction if, and to the extent that, the commissioner by rule, regulation or order shall exempt the same from the provisions of this section.

(i) *Disclaimer.* — Any person may file with the commissioner a disclaimer of affiliation with any authorized insurer or such a disclaimer may be filed by such insurer or any member of an insurance holding company system. The disclaimer shall fully disclose all material relationships and bases for affiliation between such person and such insurer as well as the basis for disclaiming such affiliation. After a disclaimer has been filed, the insurer shall be relieved of any duty to register or report under this section which may arise out of the insurer's relationship with such person, unless and until the commissioner disallows such a disclaimer. The commissioner shall disallow such a disclaimer only after furnishing all parties in interest with notice and opportunity to be heard and after making specific findings of fact to support such disallowance.

(j) *Violations.* — The failure to file a registration statement or any amendment thereto required by this section within the time specified for such filing shall be a violation of this section. (Acts 1973, No. 1042, p. 1636, § 5.)

§ 27-29-5. Registered insurers — Standards for transactions with affiliates; adequacy of surplus; dividends and other distributions.

(a) *Transactions with affiliates.* — Material transactions by registered insurers with their affiliates shall be subject to the following standards:

(1) The terms shall be fair and reasonable;

(2) The books, accounts and records of each party will be so maintained as to clearly and accurately disclose the precise nature and details of the transactions; and

(3) The insurer's surplus as regards policyholders following any dividends or distributions to shareholder; affiliates shall be reasonable in relation to the insurer's outstanding liabilities and adequate to its financial needs.

(b) *Adequacy of surplus.* — For purposes of this chapter in determining whether an insurer's surplus as regards policyholders is reasonable in relation to the insurer's outstanding liabilities and adequate to its financial needs, the following factors, among others, shall be considered:

(1) The size of the insurer as measured by its assets, capital and surplus, reserves, premium writings, insurance in force and other appropriate criteria;

(2) The extent to which the insurer's business is diversified among the several lines of insurance;

(3) The number and size of risks insured in each line of business;

(4) The extent of the geographical dispersion of the insurer's insured risks;

(5) The nature and extent of the insurer's reinsurance program;

(6) The quality, diversification and liquidity of the insurer's investment portfolio;

(7) The recent past and projected future trend in the size of the insurer's surplus as regards policyholders;

(8) The surplus as regards policyholders maintained by other comparable insurers;

(9) The adequacy of the insurer's reserves; and

(10) The quality and liquidity of investments in subsidiaries made pursuant to section 27-29-2. The commissioner may treat any such investment as a disallowed asset for purposes of determining the adequacy of surplus as regards policyholders whenever in his judgment such investment so warrants.

(c) *Dividends and other distributions.* — No insurer subject to registration under section 27-29-4 shall pay any extraordinary dividend or make any other extraordinary distribution to its shareholders until:

(1) Thirty days after the commissioner has received notice of the declaration thereof and has not within such period disapproved such payment; or

(2) The commissioner shall have approved such payment within such 30-day period.

For purposes of this section, an extraordinary dividend or distribution includes any dividend or distribution of cash or other property whose fair market value, together with that of other dividends or distributions made within the preceding 12 months exceeds the greater of:

(1) Ten percent of such insurer's surplus as regards policyholders as of December 31, next preceding; or

(2) The net gain from operations of such insurer, if such insurer is a life insurer, or the net investment income, if such insurer is not a life insurer, for the 12-month period ending December 31, next preceding, but shall not include pro rata distributions of any class of the insurer's own securities.

Notwithstanding any other provision of law, an insurer may declare an extraordinary dividend or distribution which is conditional upon the commissioner's approval thereof, and such a declaration shall confer no rights upon shareholders until:

(1) The commissioner has approved the payment of such dividend or distribution; or

(2) The commissioner has not disapproved such payment within the 30-day period referred to above. (Acts 1973, No. 1042, p. 1636, § 6.)

§ 27-29-6. Same — Examination of records, etc., of insurer or affiliates.

(a) *Power of commissioner.* — Subject to the limitation contained in this section and in addition to the powers which the commissioner has under sections 27-2-7, 27-2-21, 27-2-23 and 27-2-26, relating to the examination of insurers, the commissioner shall also have the power to order any insurer registered under section 27-29-4 to produce such records, books or other information papers in the possession of the insurer, or its affiliates, as shall be necessary to ascertain the financial condition or legality of conduct of such insurer and to verify the information required to be contained in the insurer's registration statement and any additional information pertinent to transactions between the insurer and its affiliates. In the event such insurer fails to comply with such order, the commissioner shall have the power to examine such affiliates to obtain such information.

(b) *Purpose and limitation of examination.* — The commissioner shall exercise his power under subsection (a) of this section only if the examination of the insurer under sections 27-2-7, 27-2-21, 27-2-23 and 27-2-26 is inadequate or the interests of the policyholders of such insurer may be adversely affected.

(c) *Use of consultants.* — The commissioner may retain at the registered insurer's expense such attorneys, actuaries, accountants and other experts not otherwise a part of the commissioner's staff as shall be reasonably necessary to assist in the conduct of the examination under subsection (a) of this section. Any persons so retained shall be under the direction and control of the commissioner and shall act in a purely advisory capacity.

(d) *Expenses.* — Each registered insurer producing for examination records, books and papers pursuant to subsection (a) of this section shall be liable for and shall pay the expense of such examination as provided in section 27-2-25. (Acts 1973, No. 1042, p. 1636, § 7.)

§ 27-29-7. Confidential treatment of information, etc., examined or reported.

All information, documents and copies thereof obtained by or disclosed to the commissioner or any other person in the course of an examination or investigation made pursuant to section 27-29-6 and all information reported pursuant to section 27-29-4 shall be given confidential treatment, shall not be subject to subpoena and shall not be made public by the commissioner or any other person, except to insurance departments of other states, without the prior written consent of the insurer to which it pertains unless the commissioner, after giving the insurer and its affiliates who would be affected thereby not less than five days' written notice and opportunity to be heard, determines that the interests of policyholders, shareholders or the public will be served by the publication thereof, in which event he may publish all, or any part thereof, in such manner as he may deem appropriate. (Acts 1973, No. 1042, p. 1636, § 8.)

§ 27-29-8. Rules, regulations and orders.

The commissioner may issue such rules, regulations and orders as shall be necessary to carry out the provisions of this chapter. (Acts 1973, No. 1042, p. 1636, § 9.)

§ 27-29-9. Injunctions; prohibitions against voting securities; sequestration of voting securities.

(a) *Injunctions.* — Whenever it appears to the commissioner that any insurer or any director, officer, employee or agent thereof has committed, or is about to commit, a violation of this chapter or of any rule, regulation or order issued by the commissioner under this chapter, the commissioner may apply to the circuit court for the county in which the principal office of the insurer is located or if such insurer has no such office in this state, then to the circuit court for Montgomery county for an order enjoining such insurer or such director, officer, employee or agent thereof from violating, or continuing to violate, this chapter or any such rule, regulation or order and for such other equitable relief as the nature of the case and the interests of the insurer's policyholders, creditors and shareholders or the public may require.

(b) *Voting of securities; when prohibited.* — No security which is the subject of any agreement or arrangement regarding acquisition or which is acquired, or to be acquired, in contravention of the provisions of this chapter or of any rule, regulation or order issued by the commissioner under this chapter may be voted at any shareholders' meeting or may be counted for quorum purposes, and any action of shareholders requiring the affirmative vote of a percentage of shares may be taken as though such securities were not issued and outstanding; but no action taken at any such meeting shall be invalidated by the voting of such securities unless the action would materially affect control of the insurer or unless the courts of this state have so ordered. If an insurer or the commissioner has reason to believe that any security of the insurer has been, or is about to be, acquired in contravention of the provisions of this chapter or of any rule, regulation or order issued by the commissioner under this chapter, the insurer or the commissioner may apply to the circuit court for Montgomery county or to the circuit court for the county in which the insurer has its principal place of business to enjoin any offer, request, invitation, agreement or acquisition made in contravention of section 27-29-3 or any rule, regulation or order issued by the commissioner thereunder to enjoin the voting of any security so acquired, to void any vote of such security already cast at any meeting of shareholders and for such other equitable relief as the nature of the case and the interests of the insurer's policyholders, creditors and shareholders or the public may require.

(c) *Sequestration of voting securities.* — In any case where a person has acquired or is proposing to acquire any voting securities in violation of this chapter or any rule, regulation or order issued by the commissioner under this chapter, the circuit court for Montgomery county or the circuit court for the county in which the insured has its principal place of business may, on such notice as the court deems appropriate, upon the application of the insurer or the commissioner, seize or sequester any voting securities of the insurer owned, directly or indirectly, by such person and issue such orders with respect thereto as may be appropriate to effectuate the provisions of this chapter. Notwithstanding any other provision of law, for the purposes of this chapter the situs of the ownership of the securities of domestic insurers shall be deemed to be in this state. (Acts 1973, No. 1042, p. 1636, § 10.)

§ 27-29-10. Criminal proceedings.

Whenever it appears to the commissioner that any insurer or any director, officer, employee or agent thereof has committed a willful violation of this chapter, the commissioner may cause criminal proceedings to be instituted by the district attorney for the county in which the principal office of the insurer is located, or if such insurer has no such office in the state, then by the district attorney for Montgomery county, against such insurer or the responsible director, officer, employee or agent thereof. Any insurer which willfully violates this chapter may upon conviction be fined not more than $10,000.00. Any individual who willfully violates this chapter may upon conviction be fined not more than $1,000.00 or, if such willful violation involves the deliberate perpetration of a fraud upon the commissioner, imprisoned not more than two years, or both. (Acts 1973, No. 1042, p. 1636, § 11.)

§ 27-29-11. Delinquency proceedings and rehabilitation.

Whenever it appears to the commissioner that any person has committed a violation of this chapter which so impairs the financial condition of a domestic insurer as to threaten imminent insolvency or impairment as defined in subdivision (1) of section 27-32-1 or make the further transaction of business by it hazardous to its policyholders, creditors, shareholders or the public, then the commissioner may proceed as provided in sections 27-32-3 through 27-32-7 to take possession of the property of such domestic insurer and to conduct the business thereof. (Acts 1973, No. 1042, p. 1636, § 12.)

Collateral references. — What constitutes insolvency of insurance company justifying state dissolution proceedings and the like. 17 ALR4th 16.

§ 27-29-12. Suspension, revocation or nonrenewal of insurer's license or authority to do business.

Whenever it appears to the commissioner that any person has committed a violation of this chapter which makes the continued operation of an insurer contrary to the interests of policyholders or the public, the commissioner may, after giving notice and an opportunity to be heard, determine to suspend, revoke or refuse to renew such insurer's license or authority to do business in this state for such period as he finds is required for the protection of policyholders or the public. Any such determination shall be accompanied by specific findings of fact and conclusions of law. (Acts 1973, No. 1042, p. 1636, § 13.)

§ 27-29-13. Judicial review of actions by commissioner; petition for mandamus against same.

(a) Any person aggrieved by any act, determination, rule, regulation or order or any other action of the commissioner pursuant to this chapter may appeal therefrom within 30 days after such action, determination, rule or regulation is taken or issued, in accordance with the provisions of section 27-2-32, except that the court shall conduct its review without a jury and by trial de novo; provided, however, that all the parties, including the commissioner, may stipulate that the review shall be confined to the record. Portions of the record may be introduced by stipulation into evidence in a trial de novo as to those parties so stipulating.

(b) The filing of an appeal pursuant to this section shall stay the application of any such rule, regulation, order or other action of the commissioner to the appealing party unless the court, after giving such party notice and an opportunity to be heard, determines that such a stay would be detrimental to the interests of policyholders, shareholders, creditors or the public.

(c) Any person aggrieved by any failure of the commissioner to act or to make a determination required by this chapter may petition the circuit court for Montgomery county for a writ in the nature of a mandamus or a peremptory mandamus directing the commissioner to act or make such determination forthwith. (Acts 1973, No. 1042, p. 1636, § 14.)

§ 27-29-14. Short title.

This chapter may be cited as the Alabama Insurance Holding Company System Regulatory Act. (Acts 1973, No. 1042, p. 1636, § 1.)

CHAPTER 30.

MUTUAL AID ASSOCIATIONS.

Sec.
27-30-1. "Mutual aid association" defined.
27-30-2. Applicability of chapter — Generally.
27-30-3. Same — Exceptions.
27-30-4. Authorization to act as, or for, association — Generally.
27-30-5. Same — Requirements.
27-30-6. Capital stock or surplus requirements for existing associations.
27-30-6.1. Authority to increase paid-in capital stock and paid-in surplus; contracts or policies on any one life and accidental death benefits.
27-30-7. Name of association.
27-30-8. Certificate of authority — Application.
27-30-9. Same — Issuance or refusal.
27-30-10. Same — Expiration; renewal.
27-30-11. Same — Suspension or revocation — Grounds.
27-30-12. Same — Same — Procedure.
27-30-13. Commissioner as agent for process; service of process; notice of change of address.
27-30-14. Contracts — Issuance; contents; approval by commissioner.
27-30-15. Same — Limits of risk.

Sec.
27-30-16. Same — Annual valuation — Benefits payable in cash.
27-30-17. Same — Same — Benefits, aid or services other than cash.
27-30-18. Deposit — Amounts; purpose; kind.
27-30-19. Same — Administration.
27-30-20. Funds of association.
27-30-21. Accounts and records.
27-30-22. Annual statement; furnishing of other information.
27-30-23. Duty of officers and agents.
27-30-24. Examinations by commissioner.
27-30-25. Exemption of resident members', etc., interest from process.
27-30-26. Incorporation and financing of new associations.
27-30-27. Qualification of corporation for original certificate of authority.
27-30-28. Increase or decrease of capital stock.
27-30-29. Membership; meetings of members; voting rights.
27-30-30. Directors or trustees.
27-30-31. Applicability of fee and taxation provisions.
27-30-32. Applicability of chapter 8.
27-30-33. Applicability of other provisions.

§ 27-30-1. "Mutual aid association" defined.

For the purposes of this title, a "mutual aid association," whether otherwise known as a "benefit" or "industrial" company or by whatever other name called, is a corporation whose business is limited to the provision of any of the following payments, aid or benefits under certificates, policies or agreements issued to or made with members or policyholders and which payments, aid or benefits are derived from donations, fees, dues, assessments or premiums:

(1) Upon the birth of any child, or marriage, or sickness or physical disability of the policyholder or member, or of his dependent, to pay money or render aid;

(2) The provision of dental, medical or surgical attention, or hospital service or attention of any kind as to the member or policyholder or to his dependents; or

(3) Upon death of the policyholder or member or of his dependent, to pay money or render aid, including burial benefits or the furnishing of a complete funeral and including the payment of money and rendering aid to a beneficiary as designated by the policyholder or member becoming deceased. (Acts 1927, No. 548, p. 634; Acts 1935, No. 114, p. 165; Acts 1971, No. 407, p. 707, § 558.)

§ 27-30-2. Applicability of chapter — Generally.

(a) This chapter applies only to domestic mutual aid associations, as defined in section 27-30-1.

(b) No provision of this title shall apply to mutual aid associations except as contained or referred to in this chapter. (Acts 1971, No. 407, p. 707, § 557.)

§ 27-30-3. Same — Exceptions.

The designation "mutual aid association" and this chapter do not apply as to:

(1) Any secret or benevolent society, such as Masons, Odd Fellows, Knights and Ladies of Honor, Knights of Pythias, or like orders and societies, or any association organized and operating in good faith under the lodge system for purely benevolent purposes and with a ritualistic form of work;

(2) Agreements between hospitals and industrial corporations to provide for hospital services for the employees of such corporations, and the employment by such corporations of medical doctors, surgeons and dentists for the purpose of giving medical, surgical and dental attention to such employees; or

(3) Any insurer operating under, or subject to, the general insurance laws of this state. (Acts 1927, No. 548, p. 634; Acts 1935, No. 114, p. 165; Acts 1971, No. 407, p. 707, § 559.)

§ 27-30-4. Authorization to act as, or for, association — Generally.

(a) No person shall in this state be, act as or hold itself out to be a mutual aid association except in compliance with this chapter and as authorized by a subsisting certificate of authority therefor, issued by the commissioner under this chapter.

(b) No person shall act as solicitor, collector or otherwise as an agent or representative of any entity or organization acting as, or purporting to be, a mutual aid association unless such entity or organization is then authorized as a mutual aid association as required in subsection (a) of this section.

(c) Any person who violates this section shall, upon conviction thereof, be guilty of a misdemeanor and punished by a fine of not less than $200.00 nor more than $1,000.00, or by imprisonment in the county jail for not less than 10 days nor more than one year or by both such fine and imprisonment, in the discretion of the court. For the purposes of this section, each instance of such violation shall be deemed to constitute a separate offense. (Acts 1935, No. 114, p. 165; Acts 1971, No. 407, p. 707, § 560.)

§ 27-30-5. Same — Requirements.

No person shall hereafter be authorized or hold authority to transact business in this state as a mutual aid association unless it is otherwise in compliance with this chapter and meets the following requirements:

(1) Must be a corporation heretofore or hereafter lawfully formed under the laws of the state of Alabama;

(2) If a stock corporation, and except as provided in section 27-30-6, must have and maintain unimpaired paid-in capital stock of not less than $50,000.00 and, if newly organized, must have, in addition when first so authorized, a paid-in surplus of not less than $75,000.00;

(3) If a mutual corporation, and except as provided in section 27-30-6, must have applications for benefits and paid-in fees, dues, assessments or contributions, if required under section 27-30-27, and must thereafter have and maintain unimpaired surplus funds, representing the excess of its admitted assets over all its required reserves and incurred liabilities, of not less than $75,000.00;

(4) Its management and affairs must be conducted under the actual and active control, direction and supervision of directors or trustees, officers and other management personnel, each of whom has been found, by the commissioner after due investigation, to be an individual of good character and reputation and with sufficient education, training or experience to be reasonably competent in the fulfillment of his duties and responsibilities relative to the association;

(5) Must not be affiliated, directly or indirectly, with any person or persons whose business operations are, or have been, marked to the detriment of members, policyholders, stockholders, creditors or the public by manipulation of assets or accounts, or of reinsurance or by bad faith; and

(6) Must have and maintain in this state a principal office for the transaction of its business and must keep therein records and accounts of its affairs as required under section 27-30-21. (Acts 1939, No. 374, p. 502; Code 1940, T. 28, § 262; Acts 1947, No. 349, p. 229; Acts 1967, No. 99, p. 437; Acts 1971, No. 407, p. 707, § 561.)

§ 27-30-6. Capital stock or surplus requirements for existing associations.

Any domestic mutual aid association which immediately prior to January 1, 1972, lawfully held a certificate of authority or license to transact such business in this state and which is otherwise in compliance with the requirements of this chapter shall be entitled to have a certificate of authority while it has and maintains unimpaired paid-in capital stock, if a stock corporation, or surplus, if a mutual corporation, as follows:

(1) If it is a stock corporation, it must have and maintain capital stock of at least $25,000.00; except, that an association having unimpaired paid-in

capital stock on January 1, 1972, in less than such amount shall as of each December 31, following January 1, 1972, have increased its unimpaired paid-in capital stock by an amount equal to not less than 20 percent of such original deficiency, so that, and until not later than the fifth such December 31, the association shall have unimpaired paid-in capital stock of not less than $25,000.00. Such an association shall be entitled to have its certificate of authority continue in effect during such five-year period if it is otherwise entitled thereto under this chapter;

(2) If it is a mutual corporation, it must have and maintain unimpaired surplus funds in the amount of not less than $12,500.00; except, that an association having unimpaired surplus funds on January 1, 1972, in less than such amount shall as of each December 31, following January 1, 1972, have increased its unimpaired surplus funds by an amount equal to not less than 20 percent of such original deficiency, so that, and until not later than the fifth such December 31, the association shall have unimpaired surplus funds of not less than $12,500.00. Such an association shall be entitled to have its certificate of authority continue in effect during such five-year period if it is otherwise entitled thereto under this chapter; and

(3) The commissioner shall promptly revoke the certificate of authority of any such association that does not comply with the requirements of this section. (Acts 1971, No. 407, p. 707, § 562.)

§ 27-30-6.1. Authority to increase paid-in capital stock and paid-in surplus; contracts or policies on any one life and accidental death benefits.

(a) All mutual aid associations which have held valid certificates of authority under sections 27-30-1 through 27-30-33 for a period of five years prior to June 8, 1984, are hereby authorized to increase the paid-in capital stock and paid-in surplus of the association. Any association maintaining a minimum surplus of $100,000.00 is authorized to provide contracts or policies on any one life not to exceed five percent of the capital of such association, and to provide accidental death benefits on any one life so insured not to exceed the amount of life insurance provided.

(b) The provisions of subsection (a) of this section shall additionally apply to all mutual aid associations, after said associations have completed five years of operations and are in compliance with the Insurance Code of Alabama. (Acts 1984, 1st Ex. Sess., No. 84-729, p. 65.)

§ 27-30-7. Name of association.

Every mutual aid association shall have and use in its transactions a corporate name suited to the character and purposes of the association. No such name shall so closely resemble the name of any other corporation or organization doing business in Alabama or elsewhere as to tend to be confusing or deceptive, nor shall any such name be one which tends to confuse or mislead as to the character or plan of operation of the association. (Acts 1971, No. 407, p. 707, § 563.)

§ 27-30-8. Certificate of authority — Application.

(a) To apply for a certificate of authority, a mutual aid association shall file with the commissioner its application therefor, on forms as prescribed and furnished by him, and showing:

(1) Name of the association and the address of its principal office or place of business in this state;

(2) Name, identification and residence address of each director, trustee or officer of the association;

(3) The types of aid or benefits to be provided its members or policyholders;

(4) The general plan or plans according to which its business is, or will be, conducted; and

(5) Such other information as the commissioner may reasonably require.

(b) The applicant shall at the time of application for certificate of authority file with the commissioner such of the following as are not already on file with him:

(1) A copy of its articles of incorporation, its bylaws and other charter or constituent documents, certified by the public official having custody of the original or, in the case of documents not already of public record, certified by the officer of the association having custody thereof;

(2) A copy of each policy, certificate, contract and agreement it proposes to use in the conduct of its business and relating to aid and benefits to be provided its members or policyholders;

(3) A financial statement, upon the same form and with verification as required for its annual statement as provided for under section 27-30-22, showing its current financial condition;

(4) A schedule of fees, dues, contributions or other sums to be charged or received by the association in transactions under its certificate of authority, if granted;

(5) Appointment of the commissioner as its attorney to receive service of process, as required under section 27-30-13; and

(6) Such other documents and matters as the commissioner may reasonably require.

(c) At time of filing its application, the association shall pay to the commissioner the applicable fees prescribed in subdivision (a) (1) of section 27-4-2. (Acts 1935, No. 114, p. 165; Acts 1971, No. 407, p. 707, § 564.)

§ 27-30-9. Same — Issuance or refusal.

If, upon completion of the application for a certificate of authority, the commissioner finds:

(1) That the documents filed with the application are lawful and equitable in terms and have been properly executed and filed;

(2) That the applicant has the amount of unimpaired paid-in capital stock and/or surplus as required under this chapter and has made the deposit required under section 27-30-18;

(3) That the forms of contracts, policies or other agreements proposed to be used by the association in this state fulfill the requirements of section 27-30-14 and are not disapproved by him on any ground referred to in subsection (c) of section 27-30-14;

(4) That the proposed schedule of fees, dues, contributions or other sums to be charged or received by the association are provided for on a practical and feasible basis and would be adequate in amount to cover the risks and obligations to be assumed by the association under its certificates, policies and agreements, together with its reasonable expenses of operation;

(5) That the management and affairs of the association will be conducted under the actual and active control, direction and supervision of directors or trustees, officers and other management personnel, each of whom is an individual of good character and reputation and with sufficient education, training or experience to be reasonably competent in the fulfillment of his duties and responsibilities relative to the association; and

(6) That the applicant is otherwise entitled to a certificate of authority under this chapter,

he shall issue to the association a proper certificate of authority; if he does not so find, the commissioner shall issue his order refusing such certificate. The commissioner shall act upon an application for a certificate of authority within a reasonable period after its completion. (Acts 1935, No. 114, p. 165; Acts 1971, No. 407, p. 707, § 565.)

§ 27-30-10. Same — Expiration; renewal.

(a) The certificate of authority of a mutual aid association issued under this chapter shall expire annually at midnight on the May 31 next following the date of issuance or renewal.

(b) If the association has filed its annual statement for the preceding calendar year, has paid its taxes as provided for in this chapter and is otherwise entitled thereto under this chapter, the commissioner shall annually as of June 1, issue to the association a renewal certificate of authority if written request of the association therefor, accompanied by the annual renewal fee specified in section 27-4-2, is received by the commissioner not later than the preceding May 1. If such request for renewal and fee is received by the commissioner after such May 1, but prior to the next following

June 15, the commissioner may, in his discretion, issue to the association a renewal certificate of authority as of such June 1 if the request is also accompanied by a reinstatement fee in the amount specified in paragraph (a) (1) d of section 27-4-2. (Acts 1971, No. 407, p. 707, § 566.)

§ 27-30-11. Same — Suspension or revocation — Grounds.

(a) The commissioner shall suspend or revoke the certificate of authority of a mutual aid association if he finds, upon examination or other evidence, that any one or more of the following grounds exist:

(1) For any cause for which he could have refused to issue the certificate of authority under this chapter had it then existed and been known to the commissioner;

(2) If the association is in unsound condition or is in such condition or is using such methods and practices in the conduct of its business as to render its further transactions of insurance in this state hazardous to its members, policyholders, dependents, beneficiaries or to the public;

(3) If the association has refused to be examined or to produce its accounts, records and files for examination or if any of its officers or agents have refused to perform any legal obligation relative thereto or have willfully refused to give information with respect to its affairs, when required by the commissioner; or

(4) If the association has failed to pay any final judgment against it in favor of a citizen of this state.

(b) The commissioner may, in his discretion, suspend or revoke the certificate of authority of a mutual aid association if he finds, upon examination or other evidence, that any one or more of the following grounds exist:

(1) If the association has failed to keep adequate and proper records of its transactions or to give proper receipts and account for moneys paid to or received by it;

(2) If the association has, with such frequency as to indicate its general business practice in this state, without just cause, refused to pay proper claims arising under its policies, certificates, contracts or agreements or, without just cause, compels claimants to accept less than the amount due them or to employ attorneys or to bring an action against the association to secure full payment or settlement of such claims; or

(3) For violation of any provision of, or referred to in, this chapter. (Acts 1935, No. 114, p. 165; Acts 1971, No. 407, p. 707, § 567.)

§ 27-30-12. Same — Same — Procedure.

(a) If suspension or revocation of certificate of authority relates to grounds other than the financial condition of the association, the commissioner shall give the association written notice of his intention to so suspend or revoke not less than 10 days in advance of the effective date of the proposed order of suspension or revocation. The notice shall state the grounds of the commissioner's proposed action, together with such details as reasonably to inform the association thereof. Notice mailed to the association at its principal place of business last of record with the commissioner shall be deemed to have been given when so mailed. If within such 10-day period the association files with the commissioner its written request for a hearing with respect to the proposed suspension or revocation, setting forth the reasons why, in its opinion, the commissioner's proposed action is unlawful or should not be taken, the commissioner shall hold the hearing so requested, upon notice and under procedures as provided for in chapter 2 of this title, and shall not effectuate the proposed suspension or revocation pending the hearing and his order made thereon.

(b) Following any such suspension or revocation, the commissioner may cause notice thereof to be published in one or more newspapers of general circulation in this state.

(c) Upon such suspension or revocation becoming effective, the commissioner shall likewise suspend or revoke the licenses of all agents of the association. (Acts 1935, No. 114, p. 165; Acts 1971, No. 407, p. 707, § 568.)

§ 27-30-13. Commissioner as agent for process; service of process; notice of change of address.

(a) Every mutual aid association, at the time of filing application for its certificate of authority, shall, by a duly executed instrument filed with the commissioner, on a form as designated and furnished by the commissioner, designate the principal office of the association in this state and constitute and appoint the commissioner, and his successors in office, as its true and lawful attorney upon whom all lawful process in actions or legal proceedings against it may be served; and the association shall agree that any lawful process against it which may be served upon its said attorney shall be of the same force and validity as if served on the association itself and that the authority thereof shall continue in force irrevocably as long as any liability remains outstanding against it in this state.

(b) Two copies of any process issued by any court of record in this state and served upon the commissioner or the person in charge of the commissioner's office by the proper officer of Montgomery county shall be deemed a sufficient service on the association; and the commissioner, promptly after such service of process, shall forward by registered or certified mail one of the copies of such process to the association at its principal place of business referred to in subsection (a) of this section.

(c) Within 30 days after the change of address of its principal office in this state, the association shall file written notice thereof with the commissioner. (Code 1940, T. 28, § 262; Acts 1971, No. 407, p. 707, § 569.)

§ 27-30-14. Contracts — Issuance; contents; approval by commissioner.

(a) A mutual aid association shall issue to each member or policyholder a contract, in the English language, printed or reproduced by other easily legible means, and whether called a "certificate," "policy," "agreement" or by whatever name, setting forth the aid and benefits for which the association is liable as to the respective individuals covered by such contract and the terms and conditions thereof and the amounts payable to the association on account of such contract and the terms and conditions of such payments. Any contract providing for aid, service, funeral or other benefits payable otherwise than in cash shall set forth the reasonable cash value at retail of such aid, service, funeral and other benefits, together with the valuation of such benefits for the purpose of computation of the reserves as provided in section 27-30-17.

(b) No provision or agreement not contained in such contract shall be deemed to affect, in any manner, the terms and conditions of the contract. No provision contained, or to be contained, in any other document shall be made a part of the contract by reference unless the pertinent portions of such other document or an adequate summary thereof are set forth in the contract.

(c) An association shall not offer or use any form of contract until such form has been on file with the commissioner for at least 20 days, nor thereafter if the form has been disapproved by the commissioner. Within such 20 days, or at any time thereafter, the commissioner may disapprove any such form found by him to be unlawful, or unreasonable in its terms and conditions, or inequitable or that contains ambiguous and misleading clauses or clauses and conditions that tend to deceive as to the coverage and benefits purported to be given under the contract. The association shall not thereafter offer or use any such form which the commissioner has disapproved. The commissioner shall set forth the grounds thereof in any order of disapproval issued by him. (Acts 1971, No. 407, p. 707, § 570.)

§ 27-30-15. Same — Limits of risk.

(a) An association shall not, at any one time, have in force any contract, or any number of contracts, covering the same individual, whether such individual is so covered as a member, policyholder, dependent or in any other capacity, for benefits payable in cash, or having a reasonable cash value, aggregating in excess of amounts as follows:

(1) Death benefits payable upon the death of any one individual, for death by any cause, $1,000.00;

(2) Accidental death benefits payable only upon the accidental death of any one individual, and including any special or additional benefits for accidental death included in any other death benefit contract, $1,000.00; or

431

(3) Funeral benefits and other merchandise, aid and service benefits, $1,000.00.

(b) This section shall not be deemed to make illegal any contract or coverage lawfully issued prior to January 1, 1972, but the association shall not issue any new contract covering in any way any individual likewise covered under any such prior contract if after issuance of such new contract any such individual would be covered, under all contracts issued by the association and then in force, for amounts which exceed in aggregate amount the limits respectively provided for in subsection (a) of this section.

(c) Notwithstanding the limitations set forth in subsection (a) of this section, an association which maintains capital and surplus in amounts not less than that required by section 27-30-5, shall not, at any one time, have in force any contract, or any number of contracts, covering the same individual, whether such individual is so covered as a member, policyholder, dependent or in any other capacity for benefits payable in cash, or having a reasonable cash value, aggregating in excess of amounts as follows:

(1) Death benefits payable upon the death of any one individual, for death by any cause, $2,500.00; or

(2) Accidental death benefits payable only upon the accidental death of any one individual, and including any special or additional benefits for accidental death included in any other death benefit contract, $2,500.00. (Acts 1935, No. 114, p. 165; Acts 1947, No. 528, p. 386; Acts 1953, No. 646, p. 904; Acts 1971, No. 407, p. 707, § 571.)

§ 27-30-16. Same — Annual valuation — Benefits payable in cash.

(a) The commissioner shall each year compute the net value as of December 31 of the preceding year of all benefits payable in cash under all outstanding contracts or policies of each mutual aid association. Such valuation shall be made upon the basis of the "combined experience" or "actuaries table" or "the American experience table" rate of mortality (Illinois standard of valuation), with interest at the rate of four percent per annum. The aggregate net value so ascertained of such contracts or policies of the association shall be deemed its liability on account of such cash benefits, other than accrued claims, for the purpose of any determination of its financial condition.

(b) Funds of the association in amount not less than the value of such benefits, as valued under this section, shall be held by the association in cash or in investments as authorized under section 27-30-20. (Acts 1935, No. 114, p. 165; Acts 1947, No. 528, p. 386; Acts 1953, No. 643, p. 901; Acts 1953, No. 646, p. 904; Acts 1971, No. 407, p. 707, § 572.)

§ 27-30-17. Same — Same — Benefits, aid or services other than cash.

(a) The commissioner shall each year cause all outstanding contracts or policies of every mutual aid association to be carefully valued as of December 31 of the preceding year at 40 percent of the retail value of the benefits, aid or services provided under the terms of its contracts or policies or at the average wholesale cost of the funeral supplies, benefits, aid and services so provided for, whichever amount is the greater, as shown by the number of contracts or policies in force according to the books and records of the association, and shall at the time compute the net value of all such outstanding contracts or policies of every such association in the following manner:

(1) On all outstanding contracts or policies issued prior to September 16, 1953, the commissioner shall compute the net value thereof by the two following separate methods:

a. Method No. 1: On the basis of $1.50 for each $100.00 at risk; or

b. Method No. 2: On the basis of the "combined experience" or "actuaries table," or "the American experience table" rate of mortality (Illinois standard of valuation), with interest at the rate of four percent per annum.

On each December 31, the net value of all such outstanding contracts or policies issued prior to September 16, 1953, shall be the net value as computed by said method No. 1, plus as many times one tenth of the difference, if any there be, between the net value as computed by method No. 1 and the net value as computed by said method No. 2, as the number of full years elapsed since September 16, 1953; and said net value on each December 31 shall continue to be so computed until such time as said net value so computed shall be equal to the net value on such contracts or policies as computed exclusively by method No. 2, after which time the net value of all such outstanding contracts or policies shall be the net value as computed by method No. 2, exclusively; and

(2) On all outstanding contracts or policies issued on and after September 16, 1953, the commissioner shall compute the net value thereof on the basis set out in the method No. 2 in subdivision (1) of this subsection, and the net value of all such outstanding contracts or policies shall on each December 31 thereafter be the net value as so computed.

(b) The net value of all the outstanding contracts or policies of every such association as of each December 31, ascertained and computed in accordance with the provisions of subsection (a) of this section, shall be deemed its liability on account of the benefits, aid or services payable other than in cash of such outstanding contracts or policies, other than accrued claims, to provide for which; and for the protection of its contract or policyholders, each such association shall hold net assets of an amount equal to such net value, which reserve assets may consist of cash, and such investments as are authorized under section 27-30-20. (Acts 1935, No. 114, p. 165; Acts 1953, No. 643, p. 901; Acts 1971, No. 407, p. 707, § 573.)

§ 27-30-18. Deposit — Amounts; purpose; kind.

(a) Each mutual aid association shall, prior to issuance of its certificate of authority, deposit and thereafter maintain on deposit with the treasurer of the state of Alabama securities of the kind authorized under subsection (d) of this section, in the amount of not less than $5,000.00. If in any calendar year the gross premium receipts of the association from business done within this state exceed $50,000.00, the association shall, not later than the March 30 next following such calendar year, increase the amount of its deposit so made and maintained in accordance with the following schedule:

	Gross premium receipts during calendar year			Amount of deposit required
More than	$ 50,000	but less than	$ 150,000	$ 10,000
Equal to	150,000	but less than	250,000	15,000
Equal to	250,000	but less than	350,000	20,000
Equal to	350,000	but less than	500,000	25,000
Equal to	500,000	but less than	750,000	50,000
Equal to	750,000	but less than	1,000,000	75,000
Equal to	1,000,000	or more		100,000

(b) Any such deposit is so made and shall be so held by the state treasurer in trust for the benefit and protection of the contract or policyholders in this state of the depositing mutual aid association.

(c) The term "gross premium receipts" as used in this section shall include all sums received by the association as fees, dues, premiums, contributions or by whatever other name called from its contract or policyholders as consideration for, or in connection with, such contracts and policies.

(d) All such deposits shall consist of assets, approved by the commissioner, such as are eligible for deposit generally under subsection (a) of section 27-6-3. (Acts 1935, No. 114, p. 165; Acts 1971, No. 407, p. 707, § 574.)

§ 27-30-19. Same — Administration.

(a) Deposits of mutual aid associations, heretofore or hereafter made with the state treasurer under section 27-30-18 or under laws heretofore in force, shall be administered as provided by, be subject to withdrawal and release and otherwise be subject to the applicable provisions of chapter 6 of this title, other than the following sections:

(1) Section 27-6-2; and

(2) Section 27-6-13.

(b) A mutual aid association shall be deemed to be an "insurer" for the purposes and within the terms of chapter 6 of this title. (Acts 1935, No. 114, p. 165; Acts 1971, No. 407, p. 707, § 575.)

§ 27-30-20. Funds of association.

The funds of a mutual aid association shall be in cash or invested as provided by the laws of this state with respect to such associations and life insurers. (Code 1940, T. 28, § 253; Acts 1971, No. 407, p. 707, § 576.)

§ 27-30-21. Accounts and records.

(a) Every mutual aid association shall keep complete and accurate accounts and records of its affairs and transactions, in accordance with the usual and accepted methods and principles of insurance accounting and record keeping as applicable to the kind of business transacted by the association.

(b) All such accounts and records of a mutual aid association shall be kept in the principal offices of the association located in this state and be available for inspection thereat by the commissioner on any general business day.

(c) The commissioner may suspend or revoke the certificate of authority of any association found by him to be in violation of this section. (Acts 1971, No. 407, p. 707, § 577.)

§ 27-30-22. Annual statement; furnishing of other information.

(a) Each mutual aid association shall, annually on or before March 1, file with the commissioner a full and true statement of its financial condition, transactions and affairs as of the December 31 preceding. The statement shall be in such general form and content as is prescribed or approved by the commissioner and shall be reasonably adapted to the plans of operation of such associations. The statement shall be verified by an officer of the association having knowledge of the facts.

(b) In addition to information called for and furnished in connection with its annual statement, an association shall furnish promptly to the commissioner such information as to any of its transactions or affairs as the commissioner may, from time to time, request in writing.

(c) At the time of filing, the association shall pay the fee for filing its annual statement as prescribed by section 27-4-2.

(d) The commissioner may, in his discretion, suspend or revoke the certificate of authority of an association failing to file its annual statement when due. (Acts 1935, No. 114, p. 165; Acts 1971, No. 407, p. 707, § 578.)

§ 27-30-23. Duty of officers and agents.

Any officer or agent of a mutual aid association whose duty it is to maintain its accounts and records, or to make the annual report to the commissioner or to designate the principal place of business or agent for service of process of such association as required under this chapter and who fails so to do or who willfully makes a false account, record or report shall be guilty of a misdemeanor and, upon conviction, shall be fined not less than $200.00 nor more than $1,000.00 and may be imprisoned in the county jail for not fewer than 10 days nor longer than one year. (Acts 1971, No. 407, p. 707, § 579.)

§ 27-30-24. Examinations by commissioner.

The commissioner shall, at least once every three years and oftener whenever he deems it prudent to do so, examine each mutual aid association doing business in this state. Except as to frequency of examination, such examinations and the association shall be subject to the provisions of chapter 2 of this title as applicable to similar examinations of other insurers. (Acts 1935, No. 114, p. 165; Acts 1971, No. 407, p. 707, § 581.)

§ 27-30-25. Exemption of resident members', etc., interest from process.

The interest of resident members and policyholders of mutual aid associations therein, and of resident beneficiaries provided for thereby, is exempt from all process for the collection of debts or the enforcement of liabilities. (Code 1940, T. 28, § 276; Acts 1971, No. 407, p. 707, § 583.)

§ 27-30-26. Incorporation and financing of new associations.

New domestic mutual aid associations, whether stock corporations or mutual corporations, shall hereafter be incorporated and financed under the same provisions and procedures as apply to domestic legal reserve stock or mutual insurers under chapter 27 of this title, other than provisions made inapplicable under section 27-30-33 or in conflict with the express provisions of this chapter; except, that, if to be a mutual corporation, its articles of incorporation shall provide either for the contingent liability of its members for the payment of losses and expenses of the association or the general conditions under which such members may otherwise be required to pay assessments for the payment of such losses and expenses, and the liability of members to assessment shall be further detailed in the corporation's bylaws. (Acts 1971, No. 407, p. 707, § 584.)

§ 27-30-27. Qualification of corporation for original certificate of authority.

(a) When applying for an original certificate of authority, a domestic corporation formed to transact a mutual aid business on the mutual plan must be otherwise qualified therefor under this title, must have entered into bona fide agreements for insurance of the kind proposed to be transacted, with not less than 500 persons and must have received therefrom as initial premiums, fees or contributions at rates theretofore filed with, and approved by, the commissioner as being both adequate and reasonable, not less than $25,000.00 in cash.

(b) No such agreements shall be solicited, however, except pursuant to a solicitation permit granted by the commissioner as provided in sections 27-27-4 through 27-27-7. (Acts 1939, No. 374, p. 502; Acts 1971, No. 407, p. 707, § 585.)

§ 27-30-28. Increase or decrease of capital stock.

(a) A domestic mutual aid association incorporated on the stock plan, whether heretofore or hereafter formed, may increase or decrease the amount of its authorized capital stock by amendment of its articles of incorporation in the same manner, and subject to the same conditions and procedures, as apply to domestic stock insurers in general under this title.

(b) As to a corporation formed prior to January 1, 1972, no increase of authorized capital stock shall be made which does not bring the amount thereof up to at least $50,000.00, and no decrease of authorized capital stock shall be made which reduces authorized capital stock below $50,000.00. (Code 1940, T. 28, § 254; Acts 1971, No. 407, p. 707, § 586.)

§ 27-30-29. Membership; meetings of members; voting rights.

(a) Every holder of a policy, certificate or benefit agreement issued by the association and then in force shall be deemed to be a member of the association.

(b) Annual and special meetings of the members of a domestic mutual aid association formed on the mutual plan shall be held as provided by the laws of this state for stock insurers.

(c) Notwithstanding the provisions of subdivision (b) (1) of section 27-27-22, each member of the association shall be entitled to one vote upon each matter voted upon at the meeting. Each member shall have the right to attend and vote on all matters before the meeting in person or by written proxy executed at least 30 days prior to the meeting. (Acts 1971, No. 407, p. 707, § 587.)

§ 27-30-30. Directors or trustees.

(a) The affairs of every domestic mutual aid association shall be governed by a board of directors or board of trustees consisting of not less than seven members, each of whom must be a member or stockholder of the corporation.

(b) Directors shall be elected by the members or stockholders of the association at the annual meeting of stockholders or members. Directors may be elected for terms of not less than one nor more than five years each and until their successors are elected and have qualified, as provided in the association's bylaws. If to be elected for terms of more than one year, the bylaws shall provide for a staggered term system under which the terms of a proportionate part of the members of the board will expire on the date of each annual meeting of members or stockholders.

(c) A majority of the directors or trustees must at all times be residents of this state. (Code 1940, T. 28, §§ 251, 256, 258; Acts 1971, No. 407, p. 707, § 588.)

§ 27-30-31. Applicability of fee and taxation provisions.

(a) Mutual aid associations shall be subject to the applicable provisions of the following sections of this title:

(1) Section 27-4-1;

(2) Section 27-4-2;

(3) Section 27-4-3;

(4) Section 27-4-5;

(5) Section 27-4-7;

(6) Section 27-4-8; and

(7) Section 27-4-9.

(b) A mutual aid association shall be deemed to be an "insurer" for the purposes, and within the terms, of the sections referred to in subsection (a) of this section. (Acts 1971, No. 407, p. 707, § 580.)

§ 27-30-32. Applicability of chapter 8.

Persons representing or aiding a mutual aid association in the solicitation of business and the mutual aid association with respect thereto shall be subject to the provisions of chapter 8 of this title. (Acts 1935, No. 114, p. 165; Acts 1971, No. 407, p. 707, § 582.)

§ 27-30-33. Applicability of other provisions.

In addition to those contained or referred to in this chapter, the following chapters and sections of this title shall apply to mutual aid associations to the extent applicable and not in conflict with the express provisions of this chapter and the reasonable implications of such express provisions:

(1) Chapter 1;

(2) Chapter 2;

(3) The following sections:

a. Section 27-3-4;

b. Section 27-3-5;

c. Section 27-3-22;

d. Section 27-3-23;

e. Section 27-3-27;

f. Section 27-3-29; and

g. Section 27-4-2;

(4) The following section of chapter 5: section 27-5-12;

(5) The following sections of chapters 36 and 37:

a. Section 27-37-1;

b. Section 27-37-3;

    c. Section 27-37-2;

    d. Section 27-37-4;

    e. Section 27-36-1, except subdivision (4) thereof;

    f. Section 27-36-6; and

    g. Sections 27-37-5 through 27-37-9;

  (6) Chapter 10;

  (7) Chapter 12;

  (8) Chapter 14, except as to the following sections: sections 27-14-8, 27-14-9, 27-14-29 and 27-14-32;

  (9) Chapter 15;

  (10) Chapter 16;

  (11) Chapter 17;

  (12) Chapter 18;

  (13) Chapter 19;

  (14) Chapter 20;

  (15) Chapter 27, except the following sections:

    a. Section 27-27-15;

    b. Section 27-27-20;

    c. Section 27-27-23; and

    d. Sections 27-27-34 through 27-27-36.

  (16) Chapter 32. (Acts 1971, No. 407, p. 707, § 589.)

CHAPTER 31.

RECIPROCAL INSURERS.

Sec.
27-31-1. Definitions.
27-31-2. Applicability of chapter.
27-31-3. Powers generally.
27-31-4. Business name; actions.
27-31-5. Attorneys.
27-31-6. Surplus funds of domestic insurer.
27-31-7. Certificate of authority — Application by domestic insurer; contents of declaration.
27-31-8. Same — Issuance; refusal, suspension or revocation.
27-31-9. Power of attorney.
27-31-10. Modifications of subscribers' agreement or power of attorney of domestic insurer.
27-31-11. Bond of attorney of domestic insurer — Requirements.
27-31-12. Same — Deposit in lieu thereof.
27-31-13. Action on bond or deposit in lieu thereof.
27-31-14. Service of process on domestic insurer; judgment thereon.
27-31-15. Advancement of funds to domestic insurers.

Sec.
27-31-16. Annual statement; supplemental information.
27-31-17. Determination of financial condition.
27-31-18. Subscribers; exchange of insurance contracts; liability of representatives.
27-31-19. Subscribers' advisory committee of domestic insurer.
27-31-20. Liability of subscribers — Generally.
27-31-21. Same — Judgment.
27-31-22. Levy of assessments on subscribers of domestic insurers — Generally.
27-31-23. Same — Time limit.
27-31-24. Same — Aggregate liability.
27-31-25. Nonassessable policies.
27-31-26. Distribution of unused premiums, etc.
27-31-27. Distribution of assets upon liquidation of domestic insurer.
27-31-28. Merger or conversion of domestic insurer.
27-31-29. Proceedings when assets of insurer insufficient.

§ 27-31-1. Definitions.

For the purposes of this chapter, the following terms shall have the meanings respectively ascribed to them by this section.

(1) RECIPROCAL INSURANCE. Insurance resulting from an interexchange among persons, known as "subscribers," of reciprocal agreements of indemnity, the interexchange being effectuated through an "attorney-in-fact" common to all such persons.

(2) RECIPROCAL INSURER. An unincorporated aggregation of subscribers operating individually and collectively through an attorney-in-fact to provide reciprocal insurance among themselves. (Acts 1971, No. 407, p. 707, §§ 590, 591.)

Collateral references. — 46 C.J.S., Insurance, §§ 1410, 1412.

43 Am. Jur. 2d, Insurance, § 113.

§ 27-31-2. Applicability of chapter.

(a) All authorized reciprocal insurers shall be governed by those sections of this chapter not expressly made applicable to domestic reciprocals.

(b) Existing authorized reciprocal insurers shall, after January 1, 1972, comply with the provisions of this chapter and shall make such amendments to their subscribers' agreement, power of attorney, policies and other documents and accounts and perform such other acts as may be required for such compliance. (Acts 1971, No. 407, p. 707, § 592.)

Collateral references. — 43 Am. Jur. 2d, Insurance, § 114.

§ 27-31-3. Powers generally.

(a) A reciprocal insurer may, upon qualifying therefor as provided for by this title, transact any kind or kinds of insurance defined by this title, other than life or title insurances.

(b) Such an insurer may purchase reinsurance upon the risk of any subscriber and may grant reinsurance as to any kind of insurance it is authorized to transact directly. (Acts 1971, No. 407, p. 707, § 593.)

§ 27-31-4. Business name; actions.

A reciprocal insurer shall:

(1) Have and use a business name. The name shall include the word "reciprocal," or "interinsurer," or "interinsurance," or "exchange," or "underwriters" or "underwriting"; and

(2) Maintain actions and have actions maintained against it in its own name. (Acts 1971, No. 407, p. 707, § 594.)

§ 27-31-5. Attorneys.

(a) "Attorney," as used in this chapter, refers to the attorney-in-fact of a reciprocal insurer. The attorney may be an individual, firm or corporation.

(b) Contracts of the insurer, including its policies, shall be executed by the attorney, duly authorized and acting for the subscribers.

(c) The attorney of a foreign or alien reciprocal insurer, which insurer is duly authorized to transact insurance in this state, shall not, by virtue of discharge of its duties as such attorney with respect to the insurer's transactions in this state, be thereby deemed to be doing business in this state within the meaning of any laws of this state applying to foreign firms or corporations. (Acts 1915, No. 280, p. 315; Acts 1971, No. 407, p. 707, § 595.)

Collateral references. — 46 C.J.S., Insurance, §§ 1415, 1416.
  43 Am. Jur. 2d, Insurance, § 115.

§ 27-31-6. Surplus funds of domestic insurer.

(a) A domestic reciprocal insurer formed under this chapter, if it has otherwise complied with the applicable provisions of this title, may be authorized to transact insurance if it has, and thereafter maintains, surplus funds as follows:

(1) To transact property insurance, surplus funds of not less than $200,000.00; and

(2) To transact casualty insurance, surplus funds of not less than $300,000.00.

(b) In addition to surplus required to be maintained under subsection (a) of this section, the insurer shall have, when first so authorized, expendable surplus in amount as required of a like foreign reciprocal insurer under section 27-3-8.

(c) A domestic reciprocal insurer may be authorized to transact additional kinds of insurance if it has otherwise complied with the provisions of this title therefor and possesses and so maintains surplus funds in amount equal to the minimum capital stock required of a stock insurer for authority to transact a like combination of kinds of insurance, but subject to subsection (b) of section 27-3-8 as to additional kinds of insurance and surplus required therefor during the first five years. (Acts 1915, No. 280, p. 315; Acts 1971, No. 407, p. 707, § 596.)

Collateral references. — 46 C.J.S., Insurance, § 1417.

§ 27-31-7. Certificate of authority — Application by domestic insurer; contents of declaration.

(a) Twenty-five or more persons domiciled in this state may organize a domestic reciprocal insurer and make application to the commissioner for a certificate of authority to transact insurance.

(b) The proposed attorney shall fulfill the requirements of and shall execute and file with the commissioner when applying for a certificate of authority a declaration setting forth:

(1) The name of the insurer;

(2) The location of the insurer's principal office, which shall be the same as that of the attorney and shall be maintained within this state;

(3) The kinds of insurance proposed to be transacted;

(4) The names and addresses of the original subscribers;

(5) The designation and appointment of the proposed attorney and a copy of the power of attorney;

(6) The names and addresses of the officers and directors of the attorney, if a corporation, or its members, if a firm;

(7) The powers of the subscribers' advisory committee and the names and terms of office of the members thereof;

(8) That all moneys paid to the reciprocal shall, after deducting therefrom any sum payable to the attorney, be held in the name of the insurer and for the purposes specified in the subscribers' agreement;

(9) A copy of the subscribers' agreement;

(10) A statement that each of the original subscribers has in good faith applied for insurance of a kind proposed to be transacted and that the insurer has received from each such subscriber the full premium or premium deposit required for the policy applied for, for a term of not less than six months, at an adequate rate theretofore filed with and approved by the commissioner;

(11) A statement of the financial condition of the insurer, a schedule of its assets and a statement that the surplus as required by section 27-31-6 is on hand; and

(12) A copy of each policy, endorsement and application form it then proposes to issue or use.

Such declaration shall be acknowledged by the attorney in the manner required for the acknowledgment of deeds. (Acts 1915, No. 280, p. 315; Acts 1971, No. 407, p. 707, § 597.)

§ 27-31-8. Same — Issuance; refusal, suspension or revocation.

(a) The certificate of authority of a reciprocal insurer shall be issued to its attorney in the name of the insurer.

(b) The commissioner may refuse, suspend or revoke the certificate of authority, in addition to other grounds therefor, for failure of the attorney to comply with any provision of this title. (Acts 1915, No. 280, p. 315; Acts 1971, No. 407, p. 707, § 598.)

§ 27-31-9. Power of attorney.

(a) The rights and powers of the attorney of a reciprocal insurer shall be as provided in the power of attorney given it by the subscribers.

(b) The power of attorney must set forth:

(1) The powers of the attorney;

(2) That the attorney is empowered to accept service of process on behalf of the insurer in actions against the insurer upon contracts exchanged;

(3) The general services to be performed by the attorney;

(4) The maximum amount to be deducted from advance premiums or deposits to be paid to the attorney and the general items of expense in addition to losses, to be paid by the insurer; and

(5) Except as to nonassessable policies, a provision for a contingent several liability of each subscriber in a specified amount, which amount

shall be not less than one nor more than 10 times the premium or premium deposit stated in the policy.

(c) The power of attorney may:

(1) Provide for the right of substitution of the attorney and revocation of the power of attorney and rights thereunder;

(2) Impose such restrictions upon the exercise of the power as are agreed upon by the subscribers;

(3) Provide for the exercise of any right reserved to the subscribers directly or through their advisory committee; and

(4) Contain other lawful provisions deemed advisable.

(d) The terms of any power of attorney, or agreement collateral thereto, shall be reasonable and equitable. (Acts 1971, No. 407, p. 707, § 599.)

Collateral references. — 46 C.J.S., Insurance, § 1416.

§ 27-31-10. Modifications of subscribers' agreement or power of attorney of domestic insurer.

Modifications of the terms of the subscribers' agreement or of the power of attorney of a domestic reciprocal insurer shall be made jointly by the attorney and the subscribers' advisory committee. No such modification shall be effective retroactively nor as to any insurance contract issued prior thereto. (Acts 1971, No. 407, p. 707, § 600.)

§ 27-31-11. Bond of attorney of domestic insurer — Requirements.

(a) Concurrently with the filing of the declaration provided for in section 27-31-7, the attorney of a domestic reciprocal insurer shall file with the commissioner a bond in favor of this state for the benefit of all persons damaged as a result of breach by the attorney of the conditions of his bond as set forth in subsection (b) of this section. The bond shall be executed by the attorney and by an authorized corporate surety and shall be subject to the commissioner's approval.

(b) The bond shall be in the penal sum of $25,000.00, aggregate in form, conditioned that the attorney will faithfully account for all moneys and other property of the insurer coming into his hands and that he will not withdraw or appropriate to his own use from the funds of the insurer any moneys or property to which he is not entitled under the power of attorney.

(c) The bond shall provide that it is not subject to cancellation unless 30 days' advance notice in writing of cancellation is given both the attorney and the commissioner. (Acts 1971, No. 407, p. 707, § 601.)

§ 27-31-12. Same — Deposit in lieu thereof.

In lieu of the bond required under section 27-31-11, the attorney may maintain on deposit with the state treasurer, through the office of the commissioner, a like amount in cash or in value of securities qualified for deposit under section 27-6-3, and subject to the same conditions as the bond. (Acts 1971, No. 407, p. 707, § 602.)

§ 27-31-13. Action on bond or deposit in lieu thereof.

Action on the attorney's bond or to recover against any such deposit made in lieu thereof may be brought at any time by one or more subscribers suffering loss through a violation of its conditions, or by a receiver or liquidator of the insurer. Amounts recovered on the bond shall be deposited in, and become part of, the insurer's funds. The total aggregate liability of the surety shall be limited to the amount of the penalty of such bond. (Acts 1971, No. 407, p. 707, § 603.)

§ 27-31-14. Service of process on domestic insurer; judgment thereon.

(a) Legal process shall be served upon a domestic reciprocal insurer by serving the insurer's attorney at his principal offices or by serving the commissioner as the insurer's process agent under sections 27-3-24 and 27-3-25.

(b) Any judgment based upon legal process so served shall be binding upon each of the insurer's subscribers as their respective interests may appear, but in an amount not exceeding their respective contingent liabilities, if any, the same as though personal service of process was had upon each such subscriber. (Acts 1915, No. 280, p. 315; Acts 1971, No. 407, p. 707, § 604.)

Collateral references. — 46 C.J.S., Insurance, § 1430.

§ 27-31-15. Advancement of funds to domestic insurers.

The attorney or other parties may advance to a domestic reciprocal insurer, upon reasonable terms, such funds as it may require, from time to time, in its operations. Sums so advanced shall not be treated as a liability of the insurer and, except upon liquidation of the insurer, shall not be withdrawn or repaid except out of the insurer's realized earned surplus in excess of its minimum required surplus. No such withdrawal or repayment shall be made without the advance approval of the commissioner. This section does not apply to bank loans or to other loans made upon security. (Acts 1971, No. 407, p. 707, § 605.)

§ 27-31-16. Annual statement; supplemental information.

(a) The annual statement of a reciprocal insurer shall be made and filed by its attorney.

(b) The statement shall be supplemented by such information as may be required by the commissioner relative to the affairs and transactions of the attorney, insofar as they relate to the reciprocal insurer. (Acts 1915, No. 280, p. 315; Acts 1971, No. 407, p. 707, § 606.)

§ 27-31-17. Determination of financial condition.

In determining the financial condition of a reciprocal insurer, the commissioner shall apply the following rules:

(1) He shall charge as liabilities the same reserves as are required of incorporated insurers issuing nonassessable policies on a reserve basis;

(2) The surplus deposits of subscribers shall be allowed as assets, except that any premium deposits delinquent for 90 days shall first be charged against such surplus deposit;

(3) The surplus deposits of subscribers shall not be charged as a liability;

(4) All premium deposits delinquent less than 90 days shall be allowed as assets;

(5) An assessment levied upon subscribers and not collected shall not be allowed as an asset;

(6) The contingent liability of subscribers shall not be allowed as an asset; and

(7) The computation of reserves shall be based upon premium deposits, other than membership fees, and without any deduction for expenses and the compensation of the attorney. (Acts 1971, No. 407, p. 707, § 607.)

§ 27-31-18. Subscribers; exchange of insurance contracts; liability of representatives.

Individuals, partnerships and corporations of this state may make application, enter into agreement for, and hold, policies or contracts in, or with, and be a subscriber of any domestic, foreign or alien reciprocal insurer. Any corporation now or hereafter organized under the laws of this state shall, in addition to the rights, powers and franchises specified in its articles of incorporation, have full power and authority as a subscriber to exchange insurance contracts through such reciprocal insurer. The right to exchange such contracts is hereby declared to be incidental to the purposes for which such corporations are organized and to be as fully granted as the rights and powers expressly conferred upon such corporations. Government or governmental agencies, state or political subdivisions thereof, boards, associations, estates, trustees or fiduciaries are authorized to exchange nonassessable reciprocal interinsurance contracts with each other and with individuals, partnerships and corporations to the same extent that individuals, partnerships and corporations are authorized in this section to exchange reciprocal interinsurance contracts. Any officer, representative, trustee, receiver or legal representative of any such subscriber shall be recognized as acting for, or on its behalf for, the purpose of such contract, but shall not be personally liable upon such contract by reason of acting in such representative capacity. (Acts 1915, No. 280, p. 315; Acts 1971, No. 407, p. 707, § 608.)

§ 27-31-19. Subscribers' advisory committee of domestic insurer.

(a) The advisory committee of a domestic reciprocal insurer exercising the subscribers' rights shall be selected under such rules as the subscribers adopt.

(b) Not less than two thirds of such committee shall be subscribers other than the attorney or any person employed by, representing or having a financial interest in the attorney.

(c) The committee shall:

(1) Supervise the finances of the insurer;

(2) Supervise the insurer's operations to such extent as to assure conformity with the subscriber's agreement and power of attorney;

(3) Procure the audit of the accounts and records of the insurer and of the attorney at the expense of the insurer; and

(4) Have such additional powers and functions as may be conferred by the subscribers' agreement. (Acts 1971, No. 407, p. 707, § 609.)

§ 27-31-20. Liability of subscribers — Generally.

(a) The liability of each subscriber, other than as to a nonassessable policy, for the obligations of the reciprocal insurer shall be an individual, several and proportionate liability and not joint.

(b) Except as to a nonassessable policy, each subscriber shall have a contingent assessment liability, in the amount provided for in the power of attorney or in the subscribers' agreement, for payment of actual losses and expenses incurred while his policy was in force. Such contingent liability may be at the rate of not less than one nor more than 10 times the premium or premium deposit stated in the policy, and the maximum aggregate thereof shall be computed in the manner set forth in section 27-31-24.

(c) Each assessable policy issued by the insurer shall contain a statement of the contingent liability. (Acts 1971, No. 407, p. 707, § 610.)

Collateral references. — 46 C.J.S., Insurance, §§ 1413, 1418.

43 Am. Jur. 2d, Insurance, §§ 116, 117.

§ 27-31-21. Same — Judgment.

(a) No action shall lie against any subscriber upon any obligation claimed against the insurer until a final judgment has been obtained against the insurer and remains unsatisfied for 30 days.

(b) Any such judgment shall be binding upon each subscriber only in such proportion as his interests may appear and in amount not exceeding his contingent liability, if any. (Acts 1971, No. 407, p. 707, § 611.)

§ 27-31-22. Levy of assessments on subscribers of domestic insurers — Generally.

(a) Assessments may from time to time be levied upon subscribers of a domestic reciprocal insurer liable therefor under the terms of their policies by the attorney upon approval in advance by the subscribers' advisory committee and the commissioner or by the commissioner in liquidation of the insurer.

(b) Each subscriber's share of a deficiency for which an assessment is made, but not exceeding in any event his aggregate contingent liability as computed in accordance with section 27-31-24, shall be computed by applying to the premium earned on the subscriber's policy, or policies, during the period to be covered by the assessment, the ratio of the total deficiency to the total premiums earned during such period upon all policies subject to the assessment.

(c) In computing the earned premiums for the purposes of this section, the gross premium received by the insurer for the policy shall be used as base, deducting therefrom solely charges not recurring upon the renewal or extension of the policy.

(d) No subscriber shall have an offset against any assessment for which he is liable on account of any claim for unearned premium or losses payable. (Acts 1971, No. 407, p. 707, § 612.)

Collateral references. — 46 C.J.S., Insurance, §§ 1413, 1418.

§ 27-31-23. Same — Time limit.

Every subscriber of a domestic reciprocal insurer having contingent liability shall be liable for and shall pay his share of, any assessment, as computed and limited in accordance with this chapter, if:

(1) While his policy is in force or within one year after its termination, he is notified by either the attorney or the commissioner of his intentions to levy such assessment; or

(2) An order to show cause why a receiver, conservator, rehabilitator or liquidator of the insurer should not be appointed is issued while his policy is in force or within one year after its termination. (Acts 1971, No. 407, p. 707, § 613.)

§ 27-31-24. Same — Aggregate liability.

No one policy or subscriber as to such policy shall be assessed or charged with an aggregate of contingent liability as to obligations incurred by a domestic reciprocal insurer in any one calendar year in excess of the amount provided for in the power of attorney or in the subscribers' agreement, computed solely upon premium earned on such policy during that year. (Acts 1971, No. 407, p. 707, § 614.)

§ 27-31-25. Nonassessable policies.

(a) If a reciprocal insurer has a surplus of assets over all liabilities at least equal to the minimum capital stock required of a domestic stock insurer authorized to transact like kinds of insurance, upon application of the attorney and as approved by the subscribers' advisory committee, the commissioner shall issue his certificate authorizing the insurer to extinguish the contingent liability of subscribers under its policies then in force in this state and to omit provisions imposing contingent liability in all policies delivered, or issued for delivery, in this state for so long as all such surplus remains unimpaired.

(b) Upon impairment of such surplus, the commissioner shall forthwith revoke the certificate. Such revocation shall not render subject to contingent liability any policy then in force and for the remainder of the period for which the premium has theretofore been paid; but after such revocation, no policy shall be issued or renewed without providing for contingent assessment liability of the subscriber.

(c) The commissioner shall not authorize a domestic reciprocal insurer so to extinguish the contingent liability of any of its subscribers or in any of its policies to be issued unless it qualifies to and does extinguish such liability of all its subscribers and in all such policies for all kinds of insurance transacted by it; except, that if required by the laws of another state in which the insurer is transacting insurance as an authorized insurer, the insurer may issue policies providing for the contingent liability of such of its subscribers as may acquire such policies in such state and need not extinguish the contingent liability applicable to policies theretofore in force in such state. (Acts 1971, No. 407, p. 707, § 615.)

§ 27-31-26. Distribution of unused premiums, etc.

A reciprocal insurer may from time to time return to its subscribers any unused premiums, savings or credits accruing to their accounts. Any such distribution shall not unfairly discriminate between classes of risks or policies or between subscribers, but such distribution may vary as to classes of subscribers, based upon the loss experience of such subscribers. (Acts 1971, No. 407, p. 707, § 616.)

449

§ 27-31-27. Distribution of assets upon liquidation of domestic insurer.

Upon the liquidation of a domestic reciprocal insurer, its assets remaining after discharge of its indebtedness and policy obligations, the return of any contributions of the attorney or other persons to its surplus made as provided in section 27-31-15, and the return of any unused premium, savings or credits then standing on subscribers' accounts shall be distributed to its subscribers who were such within the 12 months prior to the last termination of its certificate of authority, according to such reasonable formula as the commissioner may approve. (Acts 1971, No. 407, p. 707, § 617.)

Collateral references. — 46 C.J.S., Insurance, § 1417.
43 Am. Jur. 2d, Insurance, § 119.

§ 27-31-28. Merger or conversion of domestic insurer.

(a) A domestic reciprocal insurer, upon affirmative vote of not less than two thirds of its subscribers who vote on such merger, pursuant to due notice and the approval of the commissioner of the terms therefor, may merge with another reciprocal insurer or be converted to a stock or mutual insurer.

(b) Such a stock or mutual insurer shall be subject to the same capital or surplus requirements and shall have the same rights as a like domestic insurer transacting like kinds of insurance.

(c) The commissioner shall not approve any plan for such merger or conversion which is inequitable to subscribers or which, if for conversion to a stock insurer, does not give each subscriber preferential right to acquire stock of the proposed insurer proportionate to his interest in the reciprocal insurer, as determined in accordance with section 27-31-27 and a reasonable length of time within which to exercise such right. (Acts 1971, No. 407, p. 707, § 618.)

§ 27-31-29. Proceedings when assets of insurer insufficient.

(a) If the assets of a reciprocal insurer are at any time insufficient to discharge its liabilities, other than any liability on account of funds contributed by the attorney or others, and to maintain the required surplus, its attorney shall forthwith make up the deficiency or levy an assessment upon the subscribers for the amount needed to make up the deficiency, but subject to the limitation set forth in the power of attorney or policy.

(b) If the attorney fails to make up such deficiency or to make the assessment within 30 days after the commissioner orders him to do so or if the deficiency is not fully made up within 60 days after the date the assessment was made, the insurer shall be deemed insolvent and shall be proceeded against as authorized by this title.

(c) If liquidation of such an insurer is ordered, an assessment shall be levied upon the subscribers for such an amount, subject to limits as provided by this chapter, as the commissioner determines to be necessary to discharge all liabilities of the insurer, exclusive of any funds contributed by the attorney or other persons, but including the reasonable cost of the liquidation. (Acts 1971, No. 407, p. 707, § 619.)

CHAPTER 32.

REHABILITATION, REORGANIZATION, CONSERVATION AND LIQUIDATION OF INSURERS.

Sec.
27-32-1. Definitions.
27-32-2. Purpose of chapter; construction thereof.
27-32-3. Delinquency proceedings — Jurisdiction; venue; appeal.
27-32-4. Same — Commencement; grant or denial of application.
27-32-5. Injunctions and restraining orders.
27-32-6. Grounds — Rehabilitation of domestic insurers.
27-32-7. Same — Liquidation of domestic or alien insurers.
27-32-8. Same — Conservation of assets — Foreign insurers.
27-32-9. Same — Same — Alien insurers.
27-32-10. Same — Ancillary liquidation of foreign insurers.
27-32-11. Orders — Rehabilitation of domestic insurers.
27-32-12. Same — Liquidation — Domestic insurers.
27-32-13. Same — Same — Alien insurers.
27-32-14. Conservation or liquidation of property.
27-32-15. Conduct of delinquency proceedings — Domestic and alien insurers.
27-32-16. Same — Foreign insurers.
27-32-17. Claims in delinquency proceedings — Nonresidents against domestic insurers.
27-32-18. Same — Residents against foreign insurers.
27-32-19. Same — Form; time; notice and hearing; order.

Sec.
27-32-20. Same — Priorities.
27-32-21. Attachment, garnishment and execution.
27-32-22. Uniform Insurers Liquidation Act.
27-32-23. Deposit of moneys collected.
27-32-24. Exemption of commissioner from fees.
27-32-25. Loans to facilitate rehabilitation, etc., of insurer.
27-32-26. Fixation of rights and liabilities on liquidation of insurer.
27-32-27. Voidable transfers and liens.
27-32-28. Priority of compensation owing employees of insurer.
27-32-29. Setoff of credits and debts.
27-32-30. Claims upon liquidation of insurer — Allowance.
27-32-31. Same — Time to file.
27-32-32. Assessments — Commissioner's report.
27-32-33. Same — Levy.
27-32-34. Same — Order to pay — Generally.
27-32-35. Same — Same — Publication and service.
27-32-36. Same — Same — Judgment.
27-32-37. Priority of claims of policyholders and beneficiaries — Established.
27-32-38. Same — Payment of claims.
27-32-39. Same — Reinsuring of policies.
27-32-40. Same — Classification of policyholders and beneficiaries.
27-32-41. Same — Liability of receiver.

Legislature intended commissioner to use own judgment in handling delinquency proceedings and not the judgment of the attorney general or anyone else. American Benefit Life Ins. Co. v. Ussery, 373 So. 2d 824 (Ala. 1979).

Cited in State, Dep't of Revenue v. Forrester, 419 So. 2d 231 (Ala. Civ. App. 1982).

Collateral references. — 43 Am. Jur. 2d, Insurance, §§ 124-143.

§ 27-32-1. Definitions.

For the purposes of this chapter, the following terms shall have the meanings respectively ascribed to them by this section:

(1) IMPAIRMENT or INSOLVENCY. The capital of a stock insurer, the net assets of a Lloyd's plan insurer or the surplus of a mutual or reciprocal insurer shall be deemed to be impaired and the insurer shall be deemed to be insolvent when such insurer is not possessed of assets at least equal to all

liabilities and required reserves, together with its total issued and outstanding capital stock, if a stock insurer, or the minimum surplus, if a Lloyd's plan, mutual or reciprocal insurer, required by this title to be maintained for the kind or kinds of insurance it is then authorized to transact.

(2) INSURER. Any person, firm, corporation, association or aggregation of persons doing an insurance business and subject to the insurance supervisory authority of, or to liquidation, rehabilitation, reorganization or conservation by, the commissioner, or the equivalent insurance supervisory official of another state.

(3) DELINQUENCY PROCEEDING. Any proceeding commenced against any insurer pursuant to this chapter for the purpose of liquidating, rehabilitating, reorganizing or conserving such insurer.

(4) STATE. Any state of the United States and also the District of Columbia and Puerto Rico.

(5) FOREIGN COUNTRY. Such term means territory not in any state.

(6) DOMICILIARY STATE. The state in which an insurer is incorporated or organized or, in the case of an insurer incorporated or organized in a foreign country, the state in which such insurer, having become authorized to do business in such state, has, at the commencement of delinquency proceedings, the largest amount of its assets held in trust and assets held on deposit for the benefit of its policyholders or policyholders and creditors in the United States, and any such insurer is deemed to be domiciled in such state.

(7) ANCILLARY STATE. Any state other than a domiciliary state.

(8) RECIPROCAL STATE. Any state other than this state in which in substance and effect the provisions of the Uniform Insurers Liquidation Act, as defined in section 27-32-22, are in force, including the provisions requiring that the commissioner of insurance or equivalent insurance supervisory official be the receiver of a delinquent insurer.

(9) GENERAL ASSETS. All property, real, personal or otherwise, not specifically mortgaged, pledged, deposited or otherwise encumbered for the security or benefit of specified persons or a limited class or classes of persons, and as to such specifically encumbered property, the term includes all such property or its proceeds in excess of the amount necessary to discharge the sum or sums secured thereby. Assets held in trust and assets held on deposit for the security or benefit of all policyholders or all policyholders and creditors in the United States shall be deemed general assets.

(10) PREFERRED CLAIM. Any claim with respect to which the law of the state or of the United States accords priority of payments from the general assets of the insurer.

(11) SPECIAL DEPOSIT CLAIM. Any claim secured by a deposit made pursuant to statute for the security or benefit of a limited class or classes of persons, but not including any general assets.

(12) SECURED CLAIM. Any claim secured by mortgage, trust deed, pledge, deposit as security, escrow or otherwise, but not including a special deposit

claim or claims against general assets. The term also includes claims which more than four months prior to the commencement of delinquency proceedings in the state of the insurer's domicile have become liens upon specific assets by reason of judicial process.

(13) RECEIVER. Such term means receiver, liquidator, rehabilitator or conservator as the context may require. (Acts 1971, No. 407, p. 707, § 621.)

Collateral references. — 44 C.J.S., Insurance, § 49.

§ 27-32-2. Purpose of chapter; construction thereof.

The purpose of this chapter is to promote effectiveness, economy and uniformity in the rehabilitation, reorganization, conservation and liquidation of insurers doing business in this state. It is intended that this chapter shall be liberally construed to the end so far as possible that the assets of such insurers shall be effectively conserved and that, in the case of insurers transacting business in more than one state, claimants against the insurer shall receive equal and uniform treatment irrespective of residence or the place of the acts or contracts upon which their claims are based. (Acts 1971, No. 407, p. 707, § 620.)

Cited in Myers v. Protective Life Ins. Co., 342 So. 2d 772 (Ala. 1977); Galloway v. State ex rel. Payne, 371 So. 2d 48 (Ala. Civ. App. 1979).

§ 27-32-3. Delinquency proceedings — Jurisdiction; venue; appeal.

(a) The circuit court shall have original jurisdiction of delinquency proceedings under this chapter, and any court with jurisdiction is authorized to make all necessary and proper orders to carry out the purposes of this chapter.

(b) The venue of delinquency proceedings against a domestic insurer shall be in the county of the insurer's principal place of business. The venue of such proceedings against foreign and alien insurers shall be in the circuit court of Montgomery county.

(c) At any time after the commencement of a proceeding under this chapter, the commissioner may apply to the court for an order changing the venue of and removing the proceedings to Montgomery county or to any other county of this state in which he deems that such proceeding may be most economically and efficiently conducted.

(d) Delinquency proceedings pursuant to this chapter shall constitute the sole and exclusive method of liquidating, rehabilitating, reorganizing or conserving an insurer. No person other than the commissioner and the attorney general representing him shall appear in the courts of this state requesting the appointment of a receiver or otherwise commence such delinquency proceedings to take over, liquidate, rehabilitate, reorganize or conserve an insurer, and no court shall entertain a petition for the commencement of such proceedings unless the same has been filed in the name of the state on the relation of the commissioner.

(e) An appeal shall lie to the supreme court of Alabama from an order granting or refusing rehabilitation, liquidation or conservation and from every order in delinquency proceedings having the character of a final order or judgment as to the particular portion of the proceedings embraced therein. (Acts 1971, No. 407, p. 707, § 622.)

Same criteria applicable to § 12-22-2 apply under subsection (e) of this section. — The same criteria applicable to § 12-22-2 are applicable to determine what has the character of a final order or decree within the purview of subsection (e) of this section. Moody v. State ex rel. Payne, 351 So. 2d 547 (Ala. 1977).

Cited in American Benefit Life Ins. Co. v. Ussery, 373 So. 2d 824 (Ala. 1979).

Collateral references. — 44 C.J.S., Insurance, §§ 133, 135.

§ 27-32-4. Same — Commencement; grant or denial of application.

The commissioner shall commence any such proceedings by application to the court for an order directing the insurer to show cause why the commissioner should not have the relief requested. On the hearing of such order to show cause, the court shall either deny the application or grant the application, together with such other relief as the nature of the case and the interests of the policyholders, creditors, stockholders, members, subscribers or the public may require. (Acts 1971, No. 407, p. 707, § 623.)

§ 27-32-5. Injunctions and restraining orders.

(a) Upon application by the commissioner for such an order to show cause, or at any time thereafter, the court may, without notice, issue an injunction restraining the insurer, its officers, directors, stockholders, members, subscribers, agents and all other persons from the transaction of its business or the waste or disposition of its property until the further order of the court.

(b) The court may, at any time during a proceeding under this chapter, issue such other injunctions or orders as may be deemed necessary to prevent interference with the commissioner or the proceeding, or waste of the assets of the insurer, or the commencement or prosecution of any actions, or the obtaining of preferences, judgments, attachments or other liens or the making of any levy against the insurer or against its assets or any part thereof.

(c) Notwithstanding any other provision of law, no bond shall be required of the commissioner as a prerequisite for the issuance of any injunction or restraining order pursuant to this section. (Acts 1971, No. 407, p. 707, § 624.)

Modification of permanent injunction by issuing court. — The court which has entered a final order in the form of a permanent or perpetual injunction in respect to future activities may open and modify it where the circumstances and situation of the parties are shown to have so changed as to make it just and equitable to do so. Moody v. State ex rel. Payne, 295 Ala. 299, 329 So. 2d 73 (1976).

The mere fact that an injunction was made permanent does not mean that such injunctions do not remain subject to clarification and modification by the trial court. Moody v. State ex rel. Payne, 295 Ala. 299, 329 So. 2d 73 (1976).

Appellate review of injunctions. — The general rule is that the appellate court, on review of injunction orders, will consider only such questions as are raised in the court below, and properly preserved and presented. Where that is not done, the court may refuse to consider an objection that the injunction is too broad in its operation. Moody v. State ex rel. Payne, 295 Ala. 299, 329 So. 2d 73 (1976).

Cited in Moody v. State ex rel. Payne, 351 So. 2d 547 (Ala. 1977).

§ 27-32-6. Grounds — Rehabilitation of domestic insurers.

The commissioner may apply to the court for an order appointing him as receiver of, and directing him to rehabilitate, a domestic insurer upon one or more of the following grounds. That the insurer:

(1) Is impaired or insolvent;

(2) Has refused to submit any of its books, records, accounts or affairs to reasonable examination by the commissioner;

(3) Has concealed or removed records or assets or otherwise violated section 27-27-29;

(4) Has failed to comply with an order of the commissioner to make good an impairment of capital or surplus, or both;

(5) Has transferred, or attempted to transfer, substantially its entire property or business or has entered into any transaction the effect of which is to merge substantially its entire property or business in that of any other insurer without having first obtained the written approval of the commissioner;

(6) Has willfully violated its charter or articles of incorporation or any law of this state;

(7) Has an officer, director or manager who has refused to be examined under oath concerning its affairs, for which purposes the commissioner is hereby authorized to conduct and to enforce by all appropriate and available means any such examination under oath in any other state or territory of the United States in which any such officer, director or manager may then presently be, to the full extent permitted by the laws of such other state or territory, this special authorization considered;

(8) Has been or is the subject of an application for the appointment of, a receiver, trustee, custodian or sequestrator of the insurer or its property otherwise than pursuant to the provisions of this title, but only if such appointment has been made or is imminent and its effect is, or would be, to oust the courts of this state of jurisdiction under this section;

(9) Has consented to such an order through a majority of its directors, stockholders, members or subscribers; or

(10) Has failed to pay a final judgment entered against it in this state upon any insurance contract issued or assumed by it, within 30 days after the judgment became final, or within 30 days after the time for taking an appeal has expired or within 30 days after dismissal of an appeal before final termination, whichever date is the later. (Acts 1971, No. 407, p. 707, § 625.)

§ 27-32-7. Same — Liquidation of domestic or alien insurers.

The commissioner may apply to the court for an order appointing him as receiver, if his appointment as receiver shall not be then in effect, and directing him to liquidate the business of a domestic insurer or of the United States branch of an alien insurer having trusteed assets in this state, regardless of whether or not there has been a prior order directing him to rehabilitate such insurer, upon any of the grounds specified in section 27-32-6, or if such insurer:

(1) Has ceased transacting business for a period of one year; or

(2) Is an insolvent insurer and has commenced voluntary liquidation or dissolution, or attempts to commence or prosecute any action or proceeding to liquidate its business or affairs, or to dissolve its corporate charter or to procure the appointment of a receiver, trustee, custodian or sequestrator under any law except this title. (Acts 1971, No. 407, p. 707, § 626.)

§ 27-32-8. Same — Conservation of assets — Foreign insurers.

The commissioner may apply to the court for an order appointing him as receiver, or ancillary receiver, and directing him to conserve the assets within this state of a foreign insurer upon any of the following grounds:

(1) Upon any of the grounds specified in sections 27-32-6 or 27-32-7; or

(2) Upon the ground that its property has been sequestrated in its domiciliary sovereignty or in any other sovereignty. (Acts 1971, No. 407, p. 707, § 627.)

§ 27-32-9. Same — Same — Alien insurers.

The commissioner may apply to the court for an order appointing him as receiver, or ancillary receiver, and directing him to conserve the assets within this state of any alien insurer upon any of the following grounds:

(1) Upon any of the grounds specified in sections 27-32-6 or 27-32-7;

(2) Upon the ground that the insurer has failed to comply, within the time designated by the commissioner, with an order made by him to make good an impairment of its trusteed funds; or

(3) Upon the ground that the property of the insurer has been sequestrated in its domiciliary sovereignty or elsewhere. (Acts 1971, No. 407, p. 707, § 628.)

§ 27-32-10. Same — Ancillary liquidation of foreign insurers.

The commissioner may apply to the court for an order appointing him as ancillary receiver of, and directing him to liquidate, the business of a foreign insurer having assets, business or claims in this state upon the appointment in the domiciliary state of such insurer of a receiver, liquidator, conservator, rehabilitator or other officer by whatever name called for the purpose of liquidating the business of such insurer. (Acts 1971, No. 407, p. 707, § 629.)

§ 27-32-11. Orders — Rehabilitation of domestic insurers.

(a) An order to rehabilitate a domestic insurer shall direct the commissioner forthwith to take possession of the property of the insurer and to conduct the business thereof and to take such steps toward removal of the causes and conditions which have made rehabilitation necessary as the court may direct.

(b) If at any time the commissioner deems that further efforts to rehabilitate the insurer would be useless, he may apply to the court for an order of liquidation.

(c) The commissioner or any interested person, upon due notice to the commissioner, at any time may apply to the court for an order terminating the rehabilitation proceedings and permitting the insurer to resume possession of its property and the conduct of its business, but no such order shall be made or entered except when, after a hearing, the court has determined that the purposes of the proceeding have been fully accomplished. (Acts 1971, No. 407, p. 707, § 630.)

§ 27-32-12. Same — Liquidation — Domestic insurers.

(a) An order to liquidate the business of a domestic insurer shall direct the commissioner forthwith to take possession of the property of the insurer, to liquidate its business, to deal with the insurer's property and business in his own name as commissioner of insurance or in the name of the insurer as the court may direct and to give notice to all creditors who may have claims against the insurer to present such claims.

(b) The commissioner may apply for and secure an order dissolving the corporate existence of a domestic insurer upon his application for an order of liquidation of such insurer or at any time after such order has been granted. (Acts 1971, No. 407, p. 707, § 631.)

§ 27-32-13. Same — Same — Alien insurers.

An order to liquidate the business of a United States branch of an alien insurer having trusteed assets in this state shall be in the same terms as those prescribed for domestic insurers, save and except only that the assets of the business of such United States branch shall be the only assets included therein. (Acts 1971, No. 407, p. 707, § 632.)

§ 27-32-14. Conservation or liquidation of property.

(a) An order to conserve the assets of a foreign or alien insurer shall require the commissioner forthwith to take possession of the property of the insurer within this state and to conserve it, subject to the further direction of the court.

(b) An order to liquidate the assets in this state of a foreign insurer shall require the commissioner forthwith to take possession of the property of the insurer within this state and to liquidate it, subject to the orders of the court and with due regard to the rights and powers of the domiciliary receiver as provided in this chapter. (Acts 1971, No. 407, p. 707, § 633.)

§ 27-32-15. Conduct of delinquency proceedings — Domestic and alien insurers.

(a) Whenever under this chapter a receiver is to be appointed in delinquency proceedings for a domestic or alien insurer, the court shall appoint the commissioner as such receiver. The court shall order the commissioner forthwith to take possession of the assets of the insurer and to administer the same under the orders of the court.

(b) As a domiciliary receiver, the commissioner shall be vested by operation of law with the title to all of the property, contracts and rights of action and all of the books and records of the insurer, wherever located, as of the date of entry of the order directing him to rehabilitate or liquidate a domestic insurer or to liquidate the United States branch of an alien insurer domiciled in this state, and he shall have the right to recover the same and reduce the same to possession; except, that ancillary receivers in reciprocal states shall have, as to assets located in their respective states, the rights and powers which are prescribed in this section for ancillary receivers appointed in this state as to assets located in this state.

(c) The recording of a certified copy of the order directing possession to be taken, or a certified copy thereof, in the office of the judge of probate of the county where the proceedings are pending shall impart the same notice as would be imparted by a deed, bill of sale or other evidence of title duly filed or recorded.

(d) The commissioner as domiciliary receiver shall be responsible for the proper administration of all assets coming into his possession or control. The court may at any time require a bond from him or his deputies if deemed desirable for the protection of such assets.

(e) Upon taking possession of the assets of an insurer, the domiciliary receiver shall, subject to the direction of the court, immediately proceed to conduct the business of the insurer or to take such steps as are authorized by this chapter for the purpose of rehabilitating, liquidating or conserving the affairs or assets of the insurer.

(f) In connection with delinquency proceedings, the commissioner may appoint one or more special deputy commissioners to act for him, and he may employ such counsel, clerks and assistants as he deems necessary. The compensation of the special deputies, counsel, clerks or assistants and all expenses of taking possession of the insurer and of conducting the proceedings shall be fixed by the receiver, subject to the approval of the court, and shall be paid out of the funds or assets of the insurer. Within the limits of duties imposed upon them, special deputies shall possess all the powers given to and, in the exercise of those powers, shall be subject to all of the duties imposed upon the receiver with respect to such proceedings. (Acts 1971, No. 407, p. 707, § 634.)

Employment of counsel authorized. — Subsection (f) of this section clearly authorizes commissioner to employ legal counsel to represent him in connection with delinquency proceedings as he deems necessary. American Benefit Life Ins. Co. v. Ussery, 373 So. 2d 824 (Ala. 1979).

Attorney general cannot be legal representative of receiver unless requested to act as such by him. American Benefit Life Ins. Co. v. Ussery, 373 So. 2d 824 (Ala. 1979).

Receiver charged with notice of pre-receivership investigation. — A receiver for an insurance company in Alabama is only appointed after an examination of the company reveals that it is "impaired," i.e., a finding that its liabilities exceed its assets. The product of that examination is in the hands of the Alabama department of insurance. It would be a gross admission of governmental inefficiency not to charge such a receiver with notice of facts determined by the pre-receivership investigation. Hunt v. American Bank & Trust Co., 606 F. Supp. 1348 (N.D. Ala. 1985), aff'd, 783 F.2d 1011 (11th Cir. 1986).

Collateral references. — Receiver's personal liability for negligence in failing to care for or maintain property in receivership. 20 ALR3d 967.

§ 27-32-16. Same — Foreign insurers.

(a) Whenever under this chapter an ancillary receiver is to be appointed in delinquency proceedings for an insurer not domiciled in this state, the court shall appoint the commissioner as ancillary receiver. The commissioner shall file a petition requesting the appointment on the grounds set forth in section 27-32-10:

(1) If he finds that there are sufficient assets of the insurer located in this state to justify the appointment of an ancillary receiver; or

(2) If 10 or more persons, resident in this state, having claims against such insurer, file a petition with the commissioner requesting the appointment of such ancillary receiver.

(b) The domiciliary receiver, for the purpose of liquidating an insurer domiciled in a reciprocal state, shall be vested by operation of law with the title to all of the property, contracts and rights of action and all of the books and records of the insurer located in this state, and he shall have the immediate right to recover balances due from local agents and to obtain possession of any books and records of the insurer found in this state. He shall also be entitled to recover the other assets of the insurer located in this state; except, that upon the appointment of an ancillary receiver in this state, the ancillary receiver shall during the ancillary receivership proceedings have the sole right to recover such other assets. The ancillary receiver shall, as soon as practicable, liquidate from their respective securities those special deposit claims and secured claims which are proved and allowed in the ancillary proceedings in this state and shall pay the necessary expenses of the proceedings. All remaining assets he shall promptly transfer to the domiciliary receiver. Subject to the foregoing provisions, the ancillary receiver and his deputies shall have the same powers and be subject to the same duties with respect to the administration of such assets as a receiver of an insurer domiciled in this state.

(c) The domiciliary receiver of an insurer domiciled in a reciprocal state may maintain an action in this state to recover any assets of such insurer to which he may be entitled under the laws of this state. (Acts 1971, No. 407, p. 707, § 635.)

§ 27-32-17. Claims in delinquency proceedings — Nonresidents against domestic insurers.

(a) In a delinquency proceeding begun in this state against a domestic insurer, claimants residing in reciprocal states may file claims either with the ancillary receivers, if any, in their respective states or with the domiciliary receiver. All such claims must be filed on or before the last date fixed for the filing of claims in the domiciliary delinquency proceedings.

(b) Controverted claims belonging to claimants residing in reciprocal states may either:

(1) Be proved in this state; or

(2) If ancillary proceedings have been commenced in such reciprocal states, may be proved in those proceedings. In the event a claimant elects to prove his claim in ancillary proceedings, if notice of the claim and opportunity to appear and be heard is afforded the domiciliary receiver of this state as provided in section 27-32-18 with respect to ancillary proceedings in this state, the final allowance of such claim by the courts in the ancillary state shall be accepted in this state as conclusive as to its amount and shall also be accepted as conclusive as to its priority, if any, against special deposits or other security located within the ancillary state. (Acts 1971, No. 407, p. 707, § 636.)

Collateral references. — 44 C.J.S., Insurance, § 134.

§ 27-32-18. Same — Residents against foreign insurers.

(a) In a delinquency proceeding in a reciprocal state against an insurer domiciled in that state, claimants against such insurer who reside within this state may file claims either with the ancillary receiver, if any, appointed in this state or with the domiciliary receiver. All such claims must be filed on or before the last date fixed for the filing of claims in the domiciliary delinquency proceedings.

(b) Controverted claims belonging to claimants residing in this state may either:

(1) Be proved in the domiciliary state as provided by the law of that state; or

(2) If ancillary proceedings have been commenced in this state, be proved in those proceedings. In the event that any such claimant elects to prove his claim in this state, he shall file his claim with the ancillary receiver and shall give notice in writing to the receiver in the domiciliary state, either by registered or certified mail or by personal service at least 40 days prior to the date set for hearing. The notice shall contain a concise statement of the amount of the claim, the facts on which the claim is based and the priorities asserted, if any. If the domiciliary receiver, within 30 days after the giving of such notice, shall give notice in writing to the ancillary receiver and to the claimant, either by registered or certified mail or by personal service, of his intention to contest such claim, he shall be entitled to appear or to be represented in any proceeding in this state involving adjudication of the claim. The final allowance of the claim by the courts of this state shall be accepted as conclusive as to its amount and shall also be accepted as conclusive as to its priority, if any, against special deposits or other security located within this state. (Acts 1971, No. 407, p. 707, § 637.)

§ 27-32-19. Same — Form; time; notice and hearing; order.

(a) All claims against an insurer against which delinquency proceedings have been begun shall set forth in reasonable detail the amount of the claim, or the basis upon which such amount can be ascertained, the facts upon which the claim is based and the priorities asserted, if any. All such claims shall be verified by the affidavit of the claimant, or someone authorized to act on his behalf and having knowledge of the facts, and shall be supported by such documents as may be material thereto.

(b) All claims filed in this state shall be filed with the receiver, whether domiciliary or ancillary, in this state on or before the last date for filing as specified in this chapter.

(c) Within 10 days of the receipt of any claim or within such further period as the court may, for good cause shown, fix, the receiver shall report the claim to the court, specifying in such report his recommendation with respect to the action to be taken thereon. Upon receipt of such report, the court shall fix a time for hearing the claim and shall direct that the claimant or the receiver, as the court shall specify, shall give such notice as the court shall determine to such persons as shall appear to the court to be interested therein. All such notices shall specify the time and place of the hearing and shall concisely state the amount and nature of the claim, the priorities asserted, if any, and the recommendation of the receiver with reference thereto.

(d) At the hearing, all persons interested shall be entitled to appear, and the court shall enter an order allowing, allowing in part or disallowing the claim. Any such order shall be deemed to be an appealable order. (Acts 1971, No. 407, p. 707, § 638.)

Cited in Myers v. Protective Life Ins. Co., 342 So. 2d 772 (Ala. 1977).

Collateral references. — Actual receipt of cancellation notice mailed by insurer as prerequisite to cancellation of insurance. 40 ALR4th 867.

§ 27-32-20. Same — Priorities.

(a) In a delinquency proceeding against an insurer domiciled in this state, claims owing to residents of ancillary states shall be preferred claims if like claims are preferred under the laws of this state. All such claims owing to residents or nonresidents shall be given equal priority of payment from general assets regardless of where such assets are located.

(b) In a delinquency proceeding against an insurer domiciled in a reciprocal state, claims owing to residents of this state shall be preferred if like claims are preferred by the laws of that state.

(c) The owners of special deposit claims against an insurer for which a receiver is appointed in this or any other state shall be given priority against their several special deposits in accordance with the provisions of the statutes governing the creation and maintenance of such deposits. If there is a deficiency in any such deposit so that the claims secured thereby are not fully discharged therefrom, the claimants may share in the general assets, but such sharing shall be deferred until general creditors and also claimants against other special deposits who have received smaller percentages from their respective special deposits have been paid percentages of their claims equal to the percentage paid from the special deposit.

(d) The owner of a secured claim against an insurer for which a receiver has been appointed in this or any other state may surrender his security and file his claim as a general creditor, or the claim may be discharged by resort to the security, in which case the deficiency, if any, shall be treated as a claim against the general assets of the insurer on the same basis as claims of unsecured creditors. If the amount of the deficiency has been adjudicated in ancillary proceedings as provided in this chapter or if it has been adjudicated by a court of competent jurisdiction in proceedings in which the domiciliary receiver has had notice and opportunity to be heard, such amounts shall be conclusive; otherwise, the amount shall be determined in the delinquency proceeding in the domiciliary state. (Acts 1971, No. 407, p. 707, § 639.)

Collateral references. — 44 C.J.S., Insurance, § 134.

§ 27-32-21. Attachment, garnishment and execution.

During the pendency of delinquency proceedings in this or any reciprocal state, no action or proceeding in the nature of an attachment, garnishment or execution shall be commenced or maintained in the courts of this state against the delinquent insurer or its assets. Any lien obtained by any such action or proceeding within four months prior to the commencement of any such delinquency proceeding, or at any time thereafter, shall be void as against any rights arising in such delinquency proceeding. (Acts 1971, No. 407, p. 707, § 640.)

§ 27-32-22. Uniform Insurers Liquidation Act.

(a) Subdivisions (2) through (13) of section 27-32-1, together with sections 27-32-4, 27-32-5 and 27-32-15 through 27-32-22 constitute, and may be referred to as, the Uniform Insurers Liquidation Act.

(b) The Uniform Insurers Liquidation Act shall be so interpreted and construed as to effectuate its general purpose to make uniform the law of those states that enact it. To the extent that its provisions when applicable conflict with other provisions of this chapter, the provisions of such act shall control. (Acts 1971, No. 407, p. 707, § 641.)

Collateral references. — 44 C.J.S., Insurance § 133.

Validity, construction, and effect of Uniform Insurers Liquidation Act. 46 ALR2d 1185.

§ 27-32-23. Deposit of moneys collected.

The moneys collected by the commissioner in a proceeding under this chapter shall be from time to time deposited in one or more state or national banks, savings banks or trust companies; and, in the case of the insolvency or voluntary or involuntary liquidation of any such depositary which is an institution organized and supervised under the laws of this state, such deposits shall be entitled to priority of payment on an equality with any other priority given by the banking laws of this state. The commissioner may, in his discretion, deposit such moneys, or any part thereof, in a national bank or trust company as a trust fund. (Acts 1971, No. 407, p. 707, § 642.)

§ 27-32-24. Exemption of commissioner from fees.

The commissioner shall not be required to pay any fee to any public officer in this state for filing, recording or issuing a transcript or certificate or authenticating any paper or instrument pertaining to the exercise by the commissioner of any of the powers or duties conferred upon him under this chapter, whether or not such paper or instrument be executed by the commissioner or his deputies, employees or attorneys of record and whether or not it is connected with the commencement of any action or proceeding by or against the commissioner or with the subsequent conduct of such action or proceeding. (Acts 1971, No. 407, p. 707, § 643.)

§ 27-32-25. Loans to facilitate rehabilitation, etc., of insurer.

For the purpose of facilitating the rehabilitation, liquidation, conservation or dissolution of an insurer pursuant to this chapter, the commissioner may, subject to the approval of the court, borrow money and execute, acknowledge and deliver notes, or other evidences of indebtedness therefor, and secure the repayment of the same by the mortgage, pledge, assignment, transfer in trust or hypothecation of any, or all, of the property, whether real, personal or mixed, of such insurer, and the commissioner, subject to the approval of the court, shall have power to take any and all other action necessary and proper to consummate any such loan and to provide for the repayment thereof. The commissioner shall be under no obligation personally or in his official capacity to repay any loan made pursuant to this section. (Acts 1971, No. 407, p. 707, § 644.)

§ 27-32-26. Fixation of rights and liabilities on liquidation of insurer.

The rights and liabilities of the insurer and of its creditors, policyholders, stockholders, members, subscribers and all other persons interested in its estate shall, unless otherwise directed by the court, be fixed as of the date on which the order directing the liquidation of the insurer is filed in the office of the clerk of the court which made the order, subject to the provisions of this chapter with respect to the rights of claimants holding contingent claims. (Acts 1971, No. 407, p. 707, § 645.)

Section 40-14-56 controls over this section as to liability for franchise taxes. — The specific language of § 40-14-56 as to the liability of a corporate receiver for franchise taxes controls over the provisions of this section which govern receivership debts in general. State, Dep't of Revenue v. Forrester, 419 So. 2d 231 (Ala. Civ. App. 1982).

Since corporate existence activates the imposition of franchise taxes upon a domestic corporation, the tax continues for as long as the corporation exists under the present laws. State, Dep't of Revenue v. Forrester, 419 So. 2d 231 (Ala. Civ. App. 1982).

Cited in Myers v. Protective Life Ins. Co., 342 So. 2d 772 (Ala. 1977).

§ 27-32-27. Voidable transfers and liens.

(a) Any transfer of, or lien upon, the property of an insurer which is made or created within four months prior to the granting of an order to show cause under this chapter with the intent of giving to any creditor a preference or of enabling him to obtain a greater percentage of his debt than any other creditor of the same class and which is accepted by such creditor, having reasonable cause to believe that such preference will occur, shall be voidable.

(b) Every director, officer, employee, stockholder, member, subscriber and any other person acting on behalf of such insurer who shall be concerned in any such act or deed and every person receiving thereby any property of such insurer of the benefit thereof shall be personally liable therefor and shall be bound to account to the commissioner.

(c) The commissioner, as receiver in any proceeding under this chapter, may avoid any transfer of, or lien upon, the property of an insurer which any creditor, stockholder, subscriber or member of such insurer might have avoided and may recover the property so transferred, unless such person was a bona fide holder for value prior to the date of the entering of an order to show cause under this chapter. Such property or its value may be recovered from anyone who has received it, except a bona fide holder for value as specified in this section. (Acts 1971, No. 407, p. 707, § 646.)

§ 27-32-28. Priority of compensation owing employees of insurer.

(a) Compensation actually owing to employees other than officers of an insurer, for services rendered within three months prior to the commencement of a proceeding against the insurer under this chapter, but not exceeding $500.00 for each employee, shall be paid prior to the payment of any other debt or claim and, in the discretion of the commissioner, may be paid as soon as practicable after the proceeding has been commenced; except, that at all times, the commissioner shall reserve such funds as will in his opinion be sufficient for the expenses of administration.

(b) Such priority shall be in lieu of any other similar priority which may be authorized by law as to wages or compensation of such employees. (Acts 1971, No. 407, p. 707, § 647.)

Collateral references. — 45 C.J.S., Insurance, § 634.

§ 27-32-29. Setoff of credits and debts.

(a) In all cases of mutual debts or mutual credits between the insurer and another person in connection with any action or proceeding under this chapter, such credits and debts shall be set off and the balance only shall be allowed or paid, except as provided in subsection (b) of this section.

(b) No offset shall be allowed in favor of any such person where:

(1) The obligation of the insurer to such person would not at the date of the entry of any liquidation order or otherwise, as provided in section 27-32-26, entitle him to share as a claimant in the assets of the insurer;

(2) The obligation of the insurer to such person was purchased by, or transferred to, such person with a view of its being used as an offset; or

(3) The obligation of such person is to pay an assessment levied against the members of a mutual insurer or against the subscribers of a reciprocal insurer or is to pay a balance upon the subscription to the capital stock of a stock insurer. (Acts 1971, No. 407, p. 707, § 648.)

§ 27-32-30. Claims upon liquidation of insurer — Allowance.

(a) No contingent and unliquidated claim shall share in a distribution of the assets of an insurer which has been adjudicated to be insolvent by an order made pursuant to this chapter; except, that such claim shall be considered, if properly presented, and may be allowed to share where:

(1) Such claim becomes absolute against the insurer on or before the last day for filing claims against the assets of such insurer; or

(2) There is a surplus and the liquidation is thereafter conducted upon the basis that such insurer is solvent.

(b) Where an insurer has been so adjudicated to be insolvent, any person who has a cause of action against an insured of such insurer under a liability insurance policy issued by such insurer shall have the right to file a claim in the liquidation proceeding, regardless of the fact that such claim may be contingent, and such claim may be allowed:

(1) If it may be reasonably inferred from the proof presented upon such claim that such person would be able to obtain a judgment upon such cause of action against such insured;

(2) If such person shall furnish suitable proof, unless the court for good cause shown shall otherwise direct, that no further valid claim against such insurer arising out of his cause of action other than those already presented can be made; and

(3) If the total liability of such insurer to all claimants arising out of the same act of its insured shall be no greater than its maximum liability would be were it not in liquidation.

(c) No judgment against such an insured taken after the date of entry of the liquidation order shall be considered in the liquidation proceedings as evidence of liability or of the amount of damages, and no judgment against an insured taken by default or by collusion prior to the entry of the liquidation order shall be considered as conclusive evidence in the liquidation proceedings, either of the liability of such insured to such person upon such cause of action or of the amount of damages to which such person is therein entitled.

(d) No claim of any secured claimant shall be allowed at a sum greater than the difference between the value of the claim without security and the value of the security itself as of the date of the entry of the order of liquidation or such other date set by the court for determining rights and liabilities as provided in section 27-32-26 unless the claimant shall surrender his security to the commissioner, in which event the claim shall be allowed in the full amount for which it is valued. (Acts 1971, No. 407, p. 707, § 649.)

"Contingent claim". — In insolvency cases, a contingent claim is one as to which it remains uncertain whether the insolvent party will ever become liable to pay. If liability is certain then the claim is not contingent but merely unliquidated. Hilgeman v. State ex rel. Payne, 374 So. 2d 1327 (Ala. 1979).

§ 27-32-31. Same — Time to file.

(a) If, upon the granting of an order of liquidation under this chapter or at any time thereafter during the liquidation proceedings, the insurer shall not be clearly solvent, the court shall, after such notice and hearing as it deems proper, make an order declaring the insurer to be insolvent. Thereupon, regardless of any prior notice which may have been given to creditors, the commissioner shall notify all persons who may have claims against the insurer and who have not filed proper proofs thereof to present the same to him at a place specified in such notice, within four months from the date of entry of such order or, if the commissioner certifies that it is necessary, within such longer time as the court shall prescribe. The last day for filing of proofs of claims shall be specified in the notice, and notice shall be given in a manner to be determined by the court.

(b) Proofs of claim may be filed subsequent to the date specified if filed during pendency of the proceedings, but no such claim shall share in the distribution of the assets until all allowed claims, proofs of which have been filed before said date, have been paid in full with interest. (Acts 1971, No. 407, p. 707, § 650.)

§ 27-32-32. Assessments — Commissioner's report.

Within three years from the date an order of rehabilitation or liquidation of a domestic mutual insurer or a domestic reciprocal insurer was filed in the office of the clerk of the court by which such order was made, the commissioner may make his report to the court setting forth:

(1) The reasonable value of the assets of the insurer;

(2) The insurer's probable liabilities; and

(3) The probable necessary assessment, if any, to pay all claims and expenses in full, including expenses of administration. (Acts 1971, No. 407, p. 707, § 651.)

§ 27-32-33. Same — Levy.

(a) Upon the basis of the report provided for in section 27-32-32, including any amendments thereto, the court may, of its own motion, order the commissioner to levy one or more assessments against all members of such insurer who, as shown by the records of the insurer, were members, if a mutual insurer, or subscribers, if a reciprocal insurer, at any time within one year prior to the date of issuance of the order to show cause under section 27-32-4.

(b) Such assessment or assessments shall cover the excess of the probable liabilities over the reasonable value of the assets, together with the estimated cost of collection and percentage of uncollectability thereof. The total of all assessments against any member or subscriber with respect to any policy, whether levied pursuant to this chapter or pursuant to any other provision of law, shall be for no greater amount than that specified in the policy or policies of the member or subscriber; except, that if the court finds that the policy was issued at a rate or premium below the minimum rate lawfully permitted for the risk insured, the court may determine the upper limit of such assessment upon the basis of such minimum rate.

(c) No assessment shall be levied against any member or subscriber with respect to any nonassessable policy issued in accordance with sections 27-27-34 or 27-31-25. (Acts 1971, No. 407, p. 707, § 652.)

§ 27-32-34. Same — Order to pay — Generally.

After levy of assessment as provided in section 27-32-33, upon the filing of a further detailed report by the commissioner, the court shall issue an order directing each member, if a mutual insurer, or each subscriber, if a reciprocal insurer, if he shall not pay the amount assessed against him to the commissioner on, or before, a day to be specified'in the order, to show cause why he should not be held liable to pay such assessment, together with costs, as provided in section 27-32-36, and to show cause why the commissioner should not have judgment therefor. (Acts 1971, No. 407, p. 707, § 653.)

§ 27-32-35. Same — Same — Publication and service.

The commissioner shall cause a notice of such assessment order, setting forth a brief summary of the contents of such order to be:
  (1) Published in such manner as shall be directed by the court; and
  (2) Enclosed in a sealed envelope, addressed and mailed postage prepaid to each member or subscriber liable thereunder at his last known address as it appears on the records of the insurer, at least 20 days before the return of the order, to show cause provided for in section 27-32-34. (Acts 1971, No. 407, p. 707, § 654.)

§ 27-32-36. Same — Same — Judgment.

(a) Upon the return day of the order to show cause provided for in section 27-32-34, if the member or subscriber does not appear and serve duly verified objections upon the commissioner, the court shall make an order adjudging that such member or subscriber is liable for the amount of the assessment against him, together with costs, and that the commissioner may have judgment against the member or subscriber therefor.

(b) If, on such return date, the member or subscriber appears and serves duly verified objections upon the commissioner, there shall be a full hearing before the court, which, after such hearing, shall make such order as the facts shall warrant.

(c) Any such order shall have the same force and effect, shall be entered and docketed and may be appealed from as if it were a judgment in an original action brought in the court in which the proceeding is pending. (Acts 1971, No. 407, p. 707, § 655.)

§ 27-32-37. Priority of claims of policyholders and beneficiaries — Established.

Upon the issuance of a proper court order placing a domestic insurer in receivership or placing a foreign insurer in ancillary receivership for rehabilitation or liquidation, pursuant to this chapter or other insurance laws of Alabama, all beneficiaries of and all persons holding or owning a contract of insurance with such insurer shall be a preferred creditor of said insurer to the extent of the equity, cash value or other benefit then accrued, arising under the terms of such contract. With the exception of costs of administration of said receiverships, recorded tax liens and judgments obtained prior to initiation of delinquency proceedings, and secured creditors' claims, no claim of a creditor shall be preferred over that of a policyholder of the insurer in receivership. Policyholders are hereby removed from the class of general creditors and all laws and court decisions in conflict herewith shall have no further application. This section and sections 27-32-38 through 27-32-41 shall apply to all policyholders of insurers in receivership on October 10, 1975, and to all future receiverships. (Acts 1975, No. 1040, p. 2085, § 1.)

The word "recorded" in this section modifies judgments as well as tax liens. Galloway v. State ex rel. Payne, 371 So. 2d 48 (Ala. Civ. App. 1979).

This section provides only three categories which have priority status over policyholders: (1) costs of administration of said receivership; (2) recorded tax liens and judgments obtained prior to initiation of delinquency proceedings; and (3) secured creditors' claims. Galloway v. State ex rel. Payne, 371 So. 2d 48 (Ala. Civ. App. 1979).

Collateral references. — Reinsurer's liability for primary liability insurer's failure to compromise or settle. 42 ALR4th 1130.

§ 27-32-38. Same — Payment of claims.

Upon proper filing of claims pursuant to this title and upon order of the appropriate circuit court having jurisdiction of such cause after hearing, the duly appointed receiver shall make payment of claims upon liquidation of the insurer giving preference to policyholder claims as set out in section 27-32-37 in strict conformity to said court order. (Acts 1975, No. 1040, p. 2085, § 2.)

§ 27-32-39. Same — Reinsuring of policies.

When, upon hearing, the circuit court having jurisdiction of a receivership shall determine it to be in the best interest of the policyholders and the public, said court may order and direct the receiver to reinsure the policies of such insurer with a solvent insurer to the extent of the assets available in said receivership. The circuit court is hereby empowered to place a lien or moratorium against policy benefits and values as necessary to reinsure all policyholders as fully as possible to the extent of assets available and to order the receiver to transfer such assets as determined adequate, necessary or available to reinsure policies of the insolvent insurer with a solvent insurer, to the exclusion of general creditors should no assets remain thereafter. (Acts 1975, No. 1040, p. 2085, § 3.)

§ 27-32-40. Same — Classification of policyholders and beneficiaries.

The circuit court having jurisdiction over a receivership for liquidation or rehabilitation pursuant to the insurance laws of this state may distinguish between classes of policyholders or beneficiaries and establish priorities for each such class for payment of claims, sharing in the assets remaining or for reinsurance purposes. In establishing priorities among classes of policyholders and beneficiaries, death claims payable on life insurance contracts, cash surrenders payable, annuity holders, paid up policies, single premium policies and other such classifications may be used by the court in establishing priorities for payment of claims or for reinsurance of policies. (Acts 1975, No. 1040, p. 2085, § 4.)

§ 27-32-41. Same — Liability of receiver.

A receiver of an insolvent insurer in liquidation or rehabilitation acting upon order of a circuit court having jurisdiction over said receivership shall not be liable to civil suit for obeying or carrying out the terms of such court order or in giving a preference to policyholders. Any such civil actions filed against a receiver shall be dismissed and barred upon a showing that the receiver was acting pursuant to court order or in conformity with sections 27-32-37 through 27-32-40. (Acts 1975, No. 1040, p. 2085, § 5.)

CHAPTER 33.

TRUSTEED ASSETS OF ALIEN INSURERS.

Sec.
27-33-1. Applicability of chapter.
27-33-2. Deposit of assets in trust.
27-33-3. Existing trusts.
27-33-4. Purpose and duration of trust.
27-33-5. Trust agreement — Requirement; approval by commissioner.
27-33-6. Same — Authority to make and execute.
27-33-7. Same — Amendment.
27-33-8. Same — Withdrawal of approval.

Sec.
27-33-9. Trusteed assets — Title.
27-33-10. Same — Separation; record.
27-33-11. Same — Trustee statements.
27-33-12. Same — Examination.
27-33-13. Same — Withdrawal.
27-33-14. Trustees — Substitution.
27-33-15. Same — Compensation and expenses.
27-33-16. Canadian insurers.

Collateral references. — 44 C.J.S., Insurance, § 81.

§ 27-33-1. Applicability of chapter.

This chapter applies to all alien insurers using Alabama as a state of entry to transact insurance in the United States. (Acts 1971, No. 407, p. 707, § 656.)

§ 27-33-2. Deposit of assets in trust.

(a) An alien insurer may use Alabama as a state of entry to transact insurance in the United States by making and maintaining in this state a deposit of assets in trust with a solvent bank or trust company approved by the commissioner.

(b) The deposit, together with other trust deposits of the insurer held in the United States for the same purpose, shall be in amount not less than the deposits required of an alien insurer under section 27-3-14 and shall consist of cash and/or securities eligible for the investment of the funds of like domestic insurers.

(c) Such a deposit may be referred to as "trusteed assets." (Acts 1971, No. 407, p. 707, § 657.)

§ 27-33-3. Existing trusts.

All trusts of trusteed assets heretofore created and now existing shall be continued under the instruments creating them, unless inconsistent with the provisions of this chapter. (Acts 1971, No. 407, p. 707, § 658.)

§ 27-33-4. Purpose and duration of trust.

The deposit required by section 27-33-2 shall be for the benefit, security and protection of the policyholders or policyholders and creditors of the insurer in the United States. It shall be maintained as long as there is outstanding any liability of the insurer arising out of its insurance transactions in the United States. (Acts 1971, No. 407, p. 707, § 659.)

§ 27-33-5. Trust agreement — Requirement; approval by commissioner.

(a) The deposit referred to in section 27-33-2 shall be made under a written trust agreement between the insurer and the trustee, consistent with the provisions of this chapter, and shall be authenticated in such form and manner as the commissioner may designate or approve.

(b) The agreement shall not be effective until filed with and approved in writing by the commissioner. The commissioner shall not approve any trust agreement found by him not to be in compliance with the law or the terms of which do not in fact provide reasonably adequate protection for the insurer's policyholders or policyholders and creditors in the United States. (Acts 1971, No. 407, p. 707, § 660.)

§ 27-33-6. Same — Authority to make and execute.

An alien insurer proposing to use Alabama as a state of entry to transact insurance in the United States, whether or not it is then authorized to transact insurance in this state, is authorized to make and execute any trust agreement required by this chapter. (Acts 1971, No. 407, p. 707, § 661.)

§ 27-33-7. Same — Amendment.

A trust agreement may be amended, but the amendment shall not be effective until filed with and approved in writing by the commissioner as being in compliance with this chapter. (Acts 1971, No. 407, p. 707, § 662.)

§ 27-33-8. Same — Withdrawal of approval.

The commissioner's approval of any trust agreement, or of any amendment thereof, may be withdrawn by the commissioner if he finds upon hearing, after notice thereof to the insurer and the trustee or trustees, that the requisites for such approval, as provided in this chapter, no longer exist. (Acts 1971, No. 407, p. 707, § 663.)

§ 27-33-9. Trusteed assets — Title.

Title to the trusteed assets is vested in the trustee or trustees and their successors for the purposes of the trust deposit, and the trust agreement shall so provide. (Acts 1971, No. 407, p. 707, § 664.)

§ 27-33-10. Same — Separation; record.

The trustee shall keep the trusteed assets separate from other assets and shall maintain a record thereof sufficient to identify trusteed assets at all times. (Acts 1971, No. 407, p. 707, § 665.)

§ 27-33-11. Same — Trustee statements.

(a) The trustee of trusteed assets shall from time to time file with the commissioner statements, in such form as he may designate and request in writing, certifying the character of such assets and the amounts thereof.

(b) If the trustee fails to file any such statement after request therefor and expiration of a reasonable time thereafter, the commissioner may suspend or revoke the certificate of authority of the insurer. (Acts 1971, No. 407, p. 707, § 666.)

§ 27-33-12. Same — Examination.

The commissioner may examine trusteed assets of any insurer at any time in accordance with the same conditions and procedures governing the examination of insurers in general under chapter 2 of this title. (Acts 1971, No. 407, p. 707, § 667.)

§ 27-33-13. Same — Withdrawal.

(a) The trust agreement shall provide, in substance, that no withdrawals of trusteed assets shall be made by the insurer or permitted by the trustee without the written authorization or approval of the commissioner in advance thereof except as follows:

(1) Any or all income, earnings, dividends or interest accumulations of the trusteed assets may be paid over to the United States manager of the insurer upon request of the insurer or the manager;

(2) For substitution, coincidentally with such withdrawal, of other securities or assets of value at least equal in amount to those being withdrawn, if such substituted securities or assets are likewise such as are eligible for investment of the funds of like domestic insurers and if such withdrawal is requested in writing by the insurer's United States manager pursuant to general or specific written authority previously given or delegated by the insurer's board of directors, or other similar governing body, and a copy of such authority has been filed with the trustee;

(3) For the purpose of making deposits required by law in any state in which the insurer is, or thereafter becomes, an authorized insurer for the protection of the insurer's policyholders or policyholders and creditors in such state or in the United States, if such withdrawal does not reduce the insurer's deposit in this state to an amount less than the minimum deposit required under subsection (a) of section 27-3-14. The trustee shall transfer any assets so withdrawn and in the amount so required to be deposited in the other state direct to the depositary required to receive such deposit in such other state, as certified in writing by the public official having supervision of insurance in the other state; and

(4) For the purpose of transferring the trusteed assets to an official liquidator, conservator or rehabilitator pursuant to the order of a court of competent jurisdiction.

(b) The commissioner shall so authorize or approve withdrawal of only such assets as are in excess of the amount of assets required to be so held in trust under section 27-33-2, or as may otherwise be consistent with the provisions of this chapter.

(c) If at any time the insurer becomes insolvent or if its assets held in the United States are less in amount than as required under subsection (a) of section 27-3-14, upon determination thereof, the commissioner shall in writing order the trustee to suspend the right of the insurer or any other person to withdraw assets as authorized under subdivisions (a) (1), (a) (2) and (a) (3) of this section, and the trustee shall comply with such order until the further order of the commissioner. (Acts 1971, No. 407, p. 707, § 668.)

Collateral references. — Trustee's power to exchange trust property for share of corporation organized to hold the property. 20 ALR3d 841.

Power of trustee of noncharitable trust to make gift of trust property. 21 ALR3d 801.

§ 27-33-14. Trustees — Substitution.

(a) A new trustee, or new trustees, may be substituted for the original trustee, or trustees, of trusteed assets in the event of a vacancy or for other proper cause. Any such substitution shall be subject to the commissioner's approval.

(b) If the trustees of any trusteed assets heretofore created are individuals, and if the number of such trustees is reduced to less than three by death, resignation or otherwise, the commissioner shall require that there be substituted for such trustees a bank or trust company in this state approved by him. (Acts 1971, No. 407, p. 707, § 669.)

§ 27-33-15. Same — Compensation and expenses.

The compensation and expenses of any trustee, or trustees, of assets of an alien insurer under this chapter shall be borne by the insurer in such amount, or on such basis, as may be agreed upon by the insurer and the trustees and as set forth in the trust agreement. (Acts 1971, No. 407, p. 707, § 671.)

§ 27-33-16. Canadian insurers.

The provisions of this chapter applicable to a United States manager shall, in the case of insurers domiciled in Canada, be deemed to refer to the president, vice-president, secretary or treasurer of such a Canadian insurer. (Acts 1971, No. 407, p. 707, § 670.)

CHAPTER 34.

FRATERNAL BENEFIT SOCIETIES.

Sec.
27-34-1. Definitions.
27-34-2. Societies deemed operating on lodge system.
27-34-3. When society deemed as having representative form of government.
27-34-4. Applicability of chapter — Generally.
27-34-5. Same — Exceptions.
27-34-6. License — Requirement; renewal; fee; evidence.
27-34-7. Same — Foreign or alien societies — Application; qualifications.
27-34-8. Same — Same — Suspension, revocation or refusal.
27-34-9. Articles of incorporation — Contents.
27-34-10. Same — Filing with other documents; bond; preliminary certificate.
27-34-11. Preliminary certificate — Time to complete organization.
27-34-12. Same — Initial solicitations and qualifications.
27-34-13. Certificate of compliance.
27-34-14. Constitution and laws; powers.
27-34-15. Existing incorporated societies.
27-34-16. Incorporation of existing unincorporated domestic voluntary associations.
27-34-17. Amendment of articles of incorporation, constitution or laws.
27-34-18. Waiver of societies' laws and constitution.
27-34-19. Principal office of domestic society; meetings of governing body and minutes thereof.
27-34-20. Creation, etc., of charitable, benevolent or educational institutions.
27-34-21. Members — Qualifications for membership.
27-34-22. Same — Payment of equitable part of deficiency.
27-34-23. Benefits — Generally.
27-34-24. Same — Lives of children.
27-34-25. Paid-up nonforfeiture benefits, cash surrender values and certificate loans, etc.

Sec.
27-34-26. Beneficiaries.
27-34-27. Exemption of benefits, etc., from attachment, garnishment or other process.
27-34-28. Personal liability for payment of benefits.
27-34-29. Issuance of certificate to each benefit member; matters constituting agreement.
27-34-30. Life benefit certificate — Filing with commissioner; standard provisions.
27-34-31. Same — Prohibited provisions.
27-34-32. Accident or health and total or permanent disability insurance contracts.
27-34-33. Reinsurance.
27-34-34. Assets; funds; expenses.
27-34-35. Investments.
27-34-36. Annual statements — Requirements.
27-34-37. Same — Valuation of certificates; reserves.
27-34-38. Same — Failure to file.
27-34-39. Examinations — Domestic societies.
27-34-40. Same — Foreign and alien societies.
27-34-41. Same — Publication of financial statement, report or finding.
27-34-42. Exemption from taxation.
27-34-43. Agents — Licensing.
27-34-44. Same — Solicitation without license.
27-34-45. Misrepresentations.
27-34-46. Discrimination, inducements and rebates.
27-34-47. Service of process.
27-34-48. Consolidation or merger — Procedure.
27-34-49. Same — Effect.
27-34-50. Actions to enjoin or in quo warranto; liquidation; receivership.
27-34-51. Applications for injunctions.
27-34-52. Review of decisions and findings of commissioner.
27-34-53. False statements.
27-34-54. Applicability of other provisions.

Cross references. — As to conversion of fraternal benefits societies into stock or mutual life insurance companies, see § 27-35-1 et seq.

Editor's note. — The following cases were decided under former Code 1940, T. 28, § 167 et seq., or prior law.

In general. — Under former Code 1940, T. 28, §§ 167, 172-226, 230 and 235, supreme master of society having a bylaw requiring signature of supreme master on all certificates with attestation by supreme secretary under corporate seal had no authority to insure life of member by parol and without the issuance of a written policy. Grand United Order of Eagles v. Workman, 218 Ala. 37, 117 So. 659 (1928).

Policyholder has right to invoke court's jurisdiction to conserve trust funds. — Policyholder and member of fraternal benefit society governed by former Code 1940, T. 28, §§ 167-235 had right to invoke court's jurisdiction for protection of trust fund which was being depleted and dissipated wrongfully, to irreparable injury of policyholders. McCall v.

Grand Lodge Knights of Pythias, 217 Ala. 194, 115 So. 254 (1928).

Cited in Robertson v. District Grand Lodge, 10 Ala. App. 408, 64 So. 647 (1914); Slaughter v. Grand Lodge, 192 Ala. 301, 68 So. 367 (1915); Rinehart v. Praetorian Mut. Life Ins. Co., 270 Ala. 498, 120 So. 2d 115 (1960).

Collateral references. — 36 Am. Jur. 2d, Fraternal Orders & Benefit Societies, § 1 et seq.

§ 27-34-1. Definitions.

For the purposes of this chapter, the following terms shall have the meanings respectively ascribed to them by this section:

(1) FRATERNAL BENEFIT SOCIETY. Any incorporated society, order or supreme lodge without capital stock, including one exempted under the provisions of subdivision (a) (2) of section 27-34-5, whether incorporated or not, conducted solely for the benefit of its members and their beneficiaries and not for profit, operated on a lodge system with ritualistic form of work, having a representative form of government and which makes provision for the payment of benefits in accordance with this chapter is hereby declared to be a fraternal benefit society.

(2) SOCIETY. Such term, unless otherwise indicated, means a fraternal benefit society.

(3) PREMIUMS. Premiums, rates or other required contributions by whatever name known. (Acts 1911, No. 476, p. 700; Acts 1971, No. 407, p. 707, §§ 672, 703.)

§ 27-34-2. Societies deemed operating on lodge system.

A society having a supreme legislative or governing body and subordinate lodges or branches, by whatever name known, into which members are elected, initiated or admitted in accordance with its constitution, laws, ritual and rules, which subordinate lodges or branches are required by the laws of the society to hold regular meetings at least once in each month shall be deemed to be operating on the lodge system. (Acts 1911, No. 476, p. 700; Acts 1931, No. 55, p. 71; Acts 1971, No. 407, p. 707, § 673.)

§ 27-34-3. When society deemed as having representative form of government.

A society shall be deemed to have a representative form of government when:

(1) It provides in its constitution or laws for a supreme legislative or governing body, composed of representatives elected either by the members or by delegates elected, directly or indirectly, by the members, together with such other members of such body as may be prescribed by the society's constitution and laws;

478

(2) The representatives elected constitute a majority in number and have not less than two thirds of the votes nor less than the votes required to amend its constitution and laws;

(3) The meetings of the supreme legislative or governing body and the election of officers, representatives or delegates are held as often as once in four calendar years;

(4) Each insured member shall be eligible for election to act or serve as a delegate to such meeting;

(5) The society has a board of directors charged with the responsibility for managing its affairs in the interim between meetings of its supreme legislative or governing body, subject to control by such body, and having powers and duties delegated to it in the constitution or laws of the society;

(6) Such board of directors is elected by the supreme legislative or governing body, except in case of filling a vacancy in the interim between meetings of such body;

(7) The officers are elected either by the supreme legislative or governing body or by the board of directors; and

(8) The members, officers, representatives or delegates shall not vote by proxy. (Acts 1911, No. 476, p. 700; Acts 1931, No. 55, p. 71; Acts 1971, No. 407, p. 707, § 674.)

Collateral references. — Remedies for determining right or title to office in unincorporated private association. 82 ALR2d 1169.

§ 27-34-4. Applicability of chapter — Generally.

Except as provided in this chapter, societies shall be governed by this chapter and shall be exempt from all other provisions of the insurance laws of this state, not only in governmental relations with the state, but for every other purpose. No law hereafter enacted shall apply to them unless they are expressly designated therein. (Acts 1911, No. 476, p. 700; Acts 1971, No. 407, p. 707, § 675.)

§ 27-34-5. Same — Exceptions.

(a) Nothing contained in this chapter shall be so construed as to affect or apply to:

(1) Grand or subordinate lodges of societies, orders or associations now doing business in this state which provide benefits exclusively through local or subordinate lodges;

(2) Orders, societies or associations which admit to membership only persons engaged in one or more crafts or hazardous occupations, in the same or similar lines of business, and the ladies' societies or ladies' auxiliaries to such orders, societies or associations;

(3) Domestic societies which limit their membership to employees of a particular city or town, designated firm, business house or corporation which provide for a death benefit of not more than $400.00 or disability benefits of not more than $350.00 to any person in any one year, or both; or

(4) Domestic societies or associations of a purely religious, charitable or benevolent description which provide for a death benefit of not more than $400.00 or for disability benefits of not more than $350.00 to any one person in any one year, or both.

(b) Any such society or association described in subdivisions (a) (3) or (a) (4) of this section which provides for death or disability benefits for which benefit certificates are issued and any such society or association included in subdivision (a) (4) of this section which has more than 1,000 members shall not be exempted from the provisions of this chapter, but shall comply with all requirements thereof.

(c) No society which, by the provisions of this section, is exempt from the requirements of this chapter, except any society described in subdivision (a) (2) of this section, shall give or allow, or promise to give or allow, to any person any compensation for procuring new members.

(d) Every society which provides for benefits in case of death or disability resulting solely from accident and which does not obligate itself to pay natural death or sick benefits shall have all of the privileges, and be subject to all the applicable provisions and regulations of this chapter; except, that the provisions thereof relating to medical examination, valuations of benefit certificates and incontestability shall not apply to such society.

(e) The commissioner may require from any society or association, by examination or otherwise, such information as will enable him to determine whether such society or association is exempt from the provisions of this chapter.

Societies, exempted under the provisions of this section, shall also be exempt from all other provisions of the insurance laws of this state. (Acts 1911, No. 476, p. 700; Acts 1931, No. 55, p. 71; Acts 1971, No. 407, p. 707, § 676.)

Collateral references. — 46 C.J.S., Insurance, § 1436.

§ 27-34-6. License — Requirement; renewal; fee; evidence.

(a) No fraternal benefit society shall transact business in this state unless authorized therefor under a subsisting license issued to the society by the commissioner.

(b) Societies authorized to transact business in this state as of immediately prior to January 1, 1972, may continue such business until the April 1 next succeeding January 1, 1972. The authority of such societies, and of all societies hereafter licensed, may thereafter be renewed annually, but in all cases to terminate on the succeeding April 1; however, a license so issued shall continue in full force and effect until the new license is issued or specifically refused.

(c) For each such license or renewal, the society shall pay the commissioner $50.00.

(d) A duly certified copy or duplicate of the license shall be prima facie evidence that the licensee is a fraternal benefit society within the meaning of this chapter.

(e) Any person who in this state solicits membership for, or in any manner assists in procuring membership in, any fraternal benefit society not currently licensed to do business in this state shall be guilty of a misdemeanor and, upon conviction thereof, shall be subject to the penalties prescribed by section 27-1-12. (Acts 1911, No. 476, p. 700; Acts 1971, No. 407, p. 707, § 677.)

Collateral references. — 46 C.J.S., Insurance, § 1436.

§ 27-34-7. Same — Foreign or alien societies — Application; qualifications.

(a) No foreign or alien society shall transact business in this state without a license issued by the commissioner. Any such society may be licensed to transact business in this state upon filing with the commissioner:

(1) A duly certified copy of its charter or articles of incorporation;

(2) A copy of its constitution and laws, certified by its secretary or corresponding officer;

(3) A power of attorney to the commissioner as prescribed in section 27-34-47;

(4) A statement of its business under oath of its president and secretary, or corresponding officers, in a form prescribed by the commissioner, duly verified by an examination made by the supervising insurance official of its home state or other state, territory, province or country satisfactory to the commissioner;

(5) A certificate from the proper official of its home state, territory, province or country that the society is legally incorporated and licensed to transact business therein;

(6) Copies of its certificate forms; and

(7) Such other information as he may deem necessary, and upon a showing that its assets are invested in accordance with the provisions of this chapter.

(b) Any foreign or alien society desiring admission to this state shall have the qualifications required of domestic societies organized under this chapter. (Acts 1911, No. 476, p. 700; Acts 1971, No. 407, p. 707, § 678.)

§ 27-34-8. Same — Same — Suspension, revocation or refusal.

(a) When the commissioner upon investigation finds that a foreign or alien society transacting or applying to transact business in this state:

(1) Has exceeded its powers;

(2) Has failed to comply with any of the provisions of this chapter;

(3) Is not fulfilling its contracts in good faith; or

(4) Is conducting its business fraudulently or in a manner hazardous to its members or creditors or the public,

he shall notify the society of his findings, state in writing the reasons for his dissatisfaction and require the society to show cause on a date named why its license should not be suspended, revoked or refused. If on such date the society does not show good and sufficient cause why its authority to do business in this state should not be suspended, revoked or refused, he may suspend or refuse the license of the society to do business in this state, until satisfactory evidence is furnished to him that such suspension or refusal should be withdrawn, or he may revoke the authority of the society to do business in this state.

(b) Nothing contained in this section shall be taken or construed as preventing any such society from continuing in good faith all contracts made in this state during the time such society was legally authorized to transact business herein. (Acts 1911, No. 476, p. 700; Acts 1971, No. 407, p. 707, § 679.)

§ 27-34-9. Articles of incorporation — Contents.

Seven or more citizens of the United States, a majority of whom are citizens of this state, who desire to form a fraternal benefit society, may make, sign and acknowledge before some officer, competent to take acknowledgment of deeds, articles of incorporation, in which shall be stated:

(1) The proposed corporate name of the society, which shall not so closely resemble the name of any society or insurance company as to be misleading or confusing;

(2) The purposes for which it is being formed and the mode in which its corporate powers are to be exercised. Such purposes shall not include more liberal powers than are granted by this chapter; provided, however, that any lawful, social, intellectual, educational, charitable, benevolent, moral, fraternal or religious advantages may be set forth among the purposes of the society; and

(3) The names and residences of the incorporators and the names, residences and official titles of all the officers, trustees, directors or other

persons who are to have and exercise the general control of the management of the affairs and funds of the society for the first year or until the ensuing election at which all such officers shall be elected by the supreme legislative or governing body, which election shall be held not later than one year from the date of the issuance of the permanent certificate. (Acts 1911, No. 476, p. 700; Acts 1971, No. 407, p. 707, § 680.)

Collateral references. — 46 C.J.S., Insurance, § 1437.

36 Am. Jur. 2d, Fraternal Orders & Benefit Societies, § 9.

§ 27-34-10. Same — Filing with other documents; bond; preliminary certificate.

Such articles of incorporation, duly certified copies of the constitution, laws and rules, copies of all proposed forms of certificates, applications therefor, and circulars to be issued by the society and a bond conditioned upon the return to applicants of the advanced payments, if the organization is not completed within one year, shall be filed with the commissioner, who may require such further information as he deems necessary. The bond, with sureties, approved by the commissioner shall be in such amount, not less than $5,000.00 nor more than $25,000.00, as required by the commissioner. All documents filed are to be in the English language. If the purposes of the society conform to the requirements of this chapter and all provisions of the law have been complied with, the commissioner shall so certify, retain and file the articles of incorporation and furnish the incorporators a preliminary certificate authorizing the society to solicit members as provided in this chapter. (Acts 1911, No. 476, p. 700; Acts 1971, No. 407, p. 707, § 681.)

§ 27-34-11. Preliminary certificate — Time to complete organization.

No preliminary certificate granted under the provisions of this section shall be valid after one year from its date or after such further period, not exceeding one year, as may be authorized by the commissioner upon cause shown, unless the 500 applicants required in this chapter have been secured and the organization has been completed as provided in this chapter. The articles of incorporation and all other proceedings thereunder shall become null and void in one year from the date of the preliminary certificate, or at the expiration of the extended period, unless the society shall have completed its organization and received a certificate of authority to do business as provided in this chapter. (Acts 1911, No. 476, p. 700; Acts 1971, No. 407, p. 707, § 682.)

§ 27-34-12. Same — Initial solicitations and qualifications.

Upon receipt of a preliminary certificate from the commissioner, the society may solicit members for the purpose of completing its organization, shall collect from each applicant the amount of not less than one regular monthly premium in accordance with its table of rates as provided by its constitution and laws and shall issue to each such applicant a receipt for the amount so collected. No society shall incur any liability other than for the return of such advance premium, nor issue any certificate, nor pay, allow or offer or promise to pay or allow any death or disability benefit to any person until:

(1) Actual bona fide applications for death benefits have been secured aggregating at least $500,000.00 on not less than 500 lives;

(2) All such applicants for death benefits shall have furnished evidence of insurability satisfactory to the society;

(3) Certificates of examinations or acceptable declarations of insurability have been duly filed and approved by the chief medical examiner of the society;

(4) Ten subordinate lodges or branches have been established into which the 500 applicants have been admitted;

(5) There has been submitted to the commissioner, under oath of the president or secretary, or corresponding officer of the society, a list of such applicants, giving their names, addresses, date each was admitted, name and number of the subordinate branch of which each applicant is a member, amount of benefits to be granted and premiums therefor; and

(6) It shall have been shown to the commissioner, by sworn statement of the treasurer, or corresponding officer of such society, that at least 500 applicants have each paid in cash at least one regular monthly premium as provided in this chapter, which premiums in the aggregate shall amount to at least $2,500.00, all of which shall be credited to the fund, or funds, from which benefits are to be paid and no part of which may be used for expenses. Such advance premiums shall be held in trust during the period of organization, and if the society has not qualified for a certificate of authority within one year, as provided in this chapter, the premiums shall be returned to the applicants. (Acts 1911, No. 476, p. 700; Acts 1971, No. 407, p. 707, § 683.)

§ 27-34-13. Certificate of compliance.

The commissioner may make such examination and require such further information as he deems advisable. Upon presentation of satisfactory evidence that the society has complied with all the provisions of law, he shall issue to the society a certificate to that effect and that the society is authorized to transact business pursuant to the provisions of this chapter. The certificate shall be prima facie evidence of the existence of the society at the date of such certificate. The commissioner shall cause a record of such certificate to be made. A certified copy of such record may be given in evidence with like effect as the original certificate. (Acts 1911, No. 476, p. 700; Acts 1971, No. 407, p. 707, § 684.)

§ 27-34-14. Constitution and laws; powers.

(a) Every society shall have the power to adopt a constitution and laws for the government of the society, the admission of its members, the management of its affairs and the fixing and readjusting of the rates of its members from time to time. It shall have the power to change, alter, add to or amend such constitution and laws.

(b) A society shall have such other powers as are necessary and incidental to carrying into effect the objects and purposes of the society. (Acts 1911, No. 476, p. 700; Acts 1971, No. 407, p. 707, § 685.)

Collateral references. — 46 C.J.S., Insurance, §§ 1438, 1441. 36 Am. Jur. 2d, Fraternal Orders & Benefit Societies, §§ 10-16.

§ 27-34-15. Existing incorporated societies.

Any incorporated society authorized to transact business in this state on January 1, 1973, may thereafter exercise all the rights, powers and privileges prescribed in this chapter and in its charter or articles of incorporation as far as consistent with this chapter. A domestic society shall not be required to reincorporate. (Acts 1911, No. 476, p. 700; Acts 1971, No. 407, p. 707, § 686.)

§ 27-34-16. Incorporation of existing unincorporated domestic voluntary associations.

(a) After January 1, 1973, no unincorporated or voluntary association shall be permitted to transact business in this state as a fraternal benefit society.

(b) Any domestic voluntary association now authorized to transact business in this state may incorporate and shall receive from the commissioner a permanent certificate of incorporation as a fraternal benefit society when:

(1) It has completed its conversion to an incorporated society not later than January 1, 1974;

(2) It has filed its articles of incorporation and has satisfied the other requirements described in sections 27-34-9 through 27-34-13; and

(3) The commissioner has made such examination and procured whatever additional information he deems advisable.

(c) Every voluntary association so incorporated shall incur the obligations and enjoy the benefits thereof the same as though originally incorporated, and such corporation shall be deemed a continuation of the original voluntary association. The officers thereof shall serve through their respective terms as provided in its original articles of association, but their successors shall be elected and serve as provided in its articles of incorporation. Incorporation of a voluntary association shall not affect existing actions, claims or contracts. (Acts 1971, No. 407, p. 707, § 687.)

§ 27-34-17. Amendment of articles of incorporation, constitution or laws.

(a) A domestic society may amend its articles of incorporation, constitution or laws in accordance with the provisions thereof by action of its supreme legislative or governing body at any regular or special meeting thereof or, if its articles of incorporation, constitution or laws so provide, by referendum. Such referendum may be held in accordance with the provisions of its articles of incorporation, constitution or laws by the vote of the voting members of the society, by the vote of delegates or representatives of voting members or by the vote of local lodges or branches. No amendment submitted for adoption by referendum shall be adopted unless, within six months from the date of submission thereof, a majority of all of the voting members of the society shall have signified their consent to such amendment by one of the methods specified in this subsection.

(b) No amendment to the articles of incorporation, constitution or laws of any domestic society shall take effect unless approved by the commissioner, who shall approve such amendment if he finds that it has been duly adopted and is not inconsistent with any requirement of the laws of this state or with the character, objects and purposes of the society. Unless the commissioner disapproves any such amendment within 60 days after the filing of same, such amendment shall be considered approved. The approval or disapproval of the commissioner shall be in writing and mailed to the secretary or corresponding officer of the society at its principal office. In case he disapproves the amendment, the reasons therefor shall be stated in the written notice.

(c) Within 90 days from the approval thereof by the commissioner, all such amendments, or a synopsis thereof, shall be furnished by the society to all members either by mail or by publication in full in the official organ of the society. The affidavit of any officer of the society, or of anyone authorized by it to mail any amendments, or synopsis thereof, stating facts which show that same have been duly addressed and mailed, shall be prima facie evidence that such amendments, or synopsis thereof, have been furnished the addressee.

(d) Every foreign or alien society authorized to do business in this state shall file with the commissioner a duly certified copy of all amendments of, or additions to, its articles of incorporation, constitution or laws within 90 days after the enactment of same.

(e) Printed copies of the constitution or laws as amended, certified by the secretary or corresponding officer of the society, shall be prima facie evidence of the legal adoption thereof. (Acts 1911, No. 476, p. 700; Acts 1971, No. 407, p. 707, § 688.)

Collateral references. — 36 Am. Jur. 2d, Fraternal Orders & Benefit Societies, §§ 17-24.

§ 27-34-18. Waiver of societies' laws and constitution.

The constitution and laws of the society may provide that no subordinate body, nor any of its subordinate officers or members, shall have the power or authority to waive any of the provisions of the laws and constitution of the society. Such provision shall be binding on the society and every member and beneficiary of a member. (Acts 1911, No. 476, p. 700; Acts 1971, No. 407, p. 707, § 689.)

Collateral references. — 46 C.J.S., Insurance, § 1436.

§ 27-34-19. Principal office of domestic society; meetings of governing body and minutes thereof.

(a) The principal office of any domestic society shall be located in this state. The meetings of its supreme legislative or governing body may be held in any state, district, province or territory wherein such society has at least five subordinate branches, and all business transacted at such meetings shall be as valid in all respects as if such meetings were held in this state.

(b) The minutes of the proceedings of the supreme or governing body and of the board of directors, or corresponding body of a society, shall be in the English language. (Acts 1911, No. 476, p. 700; Acts 1971, No. 407, p. 707, § 690.)

§ 27-34-20. Creation, etc., of charitable, benevolent or educational institutions.

(a) It shall be lawful for a society to create, maintain and operate charitable, benevolent or educational institutions for the benefit of its members and their families and dependents and for the benefit of children insured by the society. For such purpose, it may own, hold or lease personal property or real property located within or without this state, with necessary buildings thereon. Such property shall be reported in every annual statement, but shall not be allowed as an admitted asset of such society.

(b) Maintenance, treatment and proper attendance in any such institution may be furnished free or a reasonable charge may be made therefor, but no such institution shall be operated for profit. The society shall maintain a separate accounting of any income and disbursements under this section and report them in its annual statement.

(c) No society shall own or operate funeral homes or undertaking establishments. (Acts 1971, No. 407, p. 707, § 691.)

Collateral references. — Tort immunity of nongovernmental charities — modern status. 25 ALR4th 517.

§ 27-34-21. Members — Qualifications for membership.

(a) A society may admit to benefit membership any person not less than 15 years of age, nearest birthday, who has furnished evidence of insurability acceptable to the society. Any such member who shall apply for additional benefits more than six months after becoming a benefit member shall furnish additional evidence of insurability acceptable to the society.

(b) Any person admitted prior to attaining the full age of 19 years shall be bound by the terms of the application and certificate and by all the laws and rules of the society and shall be entitled to all the rights and privileges of membership therein to the same extent as though the age of majority had been attained at the time of application. A society may also admit general or social members who shall have no voice or vote in the management of its insurance affairs. (Acts 1911, No. 476, p. 700; Acts 1931, No. 55, p. 71; Acts 1971, No. 407, p. 707, § 692.)

Collateral references. — 46 C.J.S., Insurance, § 1440. 36 Am. Jur. 2d, Fraternal Orders & Benefit Societies, §§ 56, 57.

§ 27-34-22. Same — Payment of equitable part of deficiency.

A society shall provide in its constitution or laws that if its reserves as to all or any class of certificates become impaired, its board of directors, or corresponding body, may require that there shall be paid by the member of the society the amount of the member's equitable proportion of such deficiency as ascertained by its board and that, if the payment is not made, it shall stand as an indebtedness against the member's certificate and draw interest not to exceed five percent per annum, compounded annually. (Acts 1911, No. 476, p. 700; Acts 1971, No. 407, p. 707, § 693.)

§ 27-34-23. Benefits — Generally.

(a) A society authorized to do business in this state may provide for the payment of:

(1) Death benefits in any form;

(2) Endowment benefits;

(3) Annuity benefits;

(4) Temporary or permanent disability benefits as a result of disease or accident;

(5) Hospital, medical or nursing benefits due to sickness or bodily infirmity or accident; and

(6) Monument or tombstone benefits to the memory of deceased members not exceeding in any case the sum of $300.00.

(b) Such benefits may be provided on the lives of members or, upon application of a member, on the lives of a member's family, including the member, the member's spouse and minor children, in the same or separate certificates. (Acts 1911, No. 476, p. 700; Acts 1931, No. 55, p. 71; Acts 1949, No. 680, p. 1050, § 1; Acts 1971, No. 407, p. 707, § 694.)

§ 27-34-24. Same — Lives of children.

(a) A society may provide for benefits on the lives of children under the minimum age for adult membership but not greater than 19 years of age at time of application therefor, upon the application of some adult person, as its laws or rules may provide, which benefits shall be in accordance with the provisions of section 27-34-23. A society may, at its option, organize and operate branches for such children. Membership and initiation in local lodges shall not be required of such children, nor shall they have a voice in the management of the society.

(b) A society shall have power to provide for the designation and changing of designation of beneficiaries in the certificates providing for such benefits and to provide in all other respects for the regulation, government and control of such certificates and all rights, obligations and liabilities incident thereto and connected therewith. (Acts 1919, No. 10, p. 19; Acts 1949, No. 680, p. 1050, § 2; Acts 1971, No. 407, p. 707, § 695.)

§ 27-34-25. Paid-up nonforfeiture benefits, cash surrender values and certificate loans, etc.

(a) A society may grant paid-up nonforfeiture benefits, cash surrender values, certificate loans and such other options as its laws may permit. As to certificates issued on and after January 1, 1972, a society shall grant at least one paid-up nonforfeiture benefit, except in the case of pure endowment, annuity or reversionary annuity contracts reducing term insurance contracts or contracts of term insurance of uniform amount of 15 years or less expiring before age 66.

(b) In the case of certificates other than those for which reserves are computed on the commissioners 1958 standard ordinary mortality table or the 1961 standard industrial table, the value of every paid-up nonforfeiture benefit and the amount of any cash surrender value, loan or other option granted shall not be less than the excess, if any, of subdivision (1) over subdivision (2) of this subsection, as follows:

(1) The reserve under the certificate determined on the basis specified in the certificate; and

(2) The sum of any indebtedness to the society on the certificate, including interest due and accrued, and a surrender charge equal to two and one-half percent of the face amount of the certificate, which, in the case of insurance on the lives of children, shall be the ultimate face amount of the certificate if death benefits provided therein are graded.

(c) However, in the case of certificates issued on a substandard basis or in the case of certificates, the reserves for which are computed upon the American men ultimate table of mortality, the term of any extended insurance benefit granted including accompanying pure endowment, if any, may be computed upon the rates of mortality not greater than 130 percent of those shown by the mortality table specified in the certificate for the computation of the reserve.

489

(d) In the case of certificates for which reserves are computed on the commissioners 1958 standard ordinary mortality table or the 1961 standard industrial table, every paid-up nonforfeiture benefit and the amount of any cash surrender value, loan or other option granted shall not be less than the corresponding amount ascertained in accordance with the provisions of the laws of this state applicable to life insurers issuing policies containing like insurance benefits based upon such tables. (Acts 1911, No. 476, p. 700; Acts 1971, No. 407, p. 707, § 696.)

§ 27-34-26. Beneficiaries.

(a) The member shall have the right at all times to change the beneficiary, or beneficiaries, in accordance with the constitution, laws or rules of the society. Every society by its constitution, laws or rules may limit the scope of beneficiaries and shall provide that no beneficiary shall have or obtain any vested interest in the proceeds of any certificate until the certificate has become due and payable in conformity with the provisions of the insurance contract.

(b) A society may make provision for the payment of funeral benefits to the extent of such portion of any payment under a certificate as might reasonably appear to be due to any person equitably entitled thereto by reason of having incurred expense occasioned by the burial of the member, but the portion so paid shall not exceed the sum of $500.00.

(c) If, at the death of any member, there is no lawful beneficiary to whom the insurance benefits are payable, the amount of such benefits, except to the extent that funeral benefits may be paid as provided in this chapter, shall be payable to the personal representative of the deceased member. (Acts 1911, No. 476, p. 700; Acts 1931, No. 55, p. 71; Acts 1971, No. 407, p. 707, § 697.)

Editor's note. — The following cases were decided under former Code 1940, T. 28, § 173, which was similar to subsection (a) of the present section, or under prior law.

Purpose of former Code 1940, T. 28, § 173, allowing no vested rights in the beneficiary, was to protect subsequent beneficiaries selected by the insured, as well as the insurers. Parker v. Mosaic Templars of Am., 20 Ala. App. 479, 103 So. 63 (1924).

Knowledge of former statute was presumed. — See Summers v. Summers, 218 Ala. 420, 118 So. 912 (1928).

Beneficiary's right subordinate to that of assured. — The mere issuance of a policy does not vest in the beneficiary rights paramount to those of the assured; the assured may change beneficiary at any time. Royal Neighbors of Am. v. Fortenberry, 214 Ala. 387, 107 So. 846 (1926).

But it will afford basis for action. — Beneficiary of life policy has such substantial interest in policy as affords basis for right of action. Sovereign Camp, W.O.W. v. Feltman, 226 Ala. 390, 147 So. 396 (1933).

Interest of beneficiary not inheritable. — The interest of a beneficiary under former fraternal benefit societies provisions was only an expectancy and could not be inherited by the heirs of the beneficiary should he die before the insured. Ex parte Mosaic Templars of Am., 212 Ala. 471, 103 So. 65 (1925).

When no beneficiary designated, benefits of policy revert to insured. — In the absence of a designated beneficiary, the benefits of the policy revert to the insured as a lapsed trust upon the death of the named assignee, and these benefits pass to her estate upon her death. Mosaic Templars of Am. v. Raife, 21 Ala. App. 329, 110 So. 66 (1926).

Although the certificate specifies that a beneficiary be named it is not necessary. Parker v. Mosaic Templars of Am., 20 Ala. App. 479, 103 So. 63 (1924); Mosaic Templars of Am. v. Raife, 21 Ala. App. 329, 110 So. 66 (1926).

Compromise of claim by beneficiary. — There is sufficient consideration for a contract between a beneficiary and a fraternal benefit society for the payment of a part of the obligation and a surrender of the certificate for cancellation when the society has not sufficient funds to meet its obligations. Robertson v. District Grand Lodge No. 23, 10 Ala. App. 408, 64 So. 647 (1914).

Bylaw recognizing any beneficiary permitted by state law. — Where bylaws of fraternal benefit society provided for payment of benefits to any certain named classes of persons related to member and such other beneficiaries as might be permitted by laws of state and there were no statutory restrictions as to who might be made beneficiaries, a woman with whom insured was allegedly living in state of miscegenation and who was named as beneficiary by him in fraternal certificate was eligible to take as beneficiary, since there was no restriction as to whom insured could name as beneficiary. Mathews v. Stroud, 239 Ala. 687, 196 So. 885 (1940).

Change of beneficiary to illegitimate child. — Where bylaws of a fraternal benefit association permitted change of beneficiaries and included, among those eligible to benefits under its certificates, "children who by common knowledge are regarded as children . . . in the community where the member lived," member's designation of an illegitimate daughter in place of wife as beneficiary was authorized, the wife having no vested right therein. Adkinson v. Nearor, 243 Ala. 133, 8 So. 2d 816 (1942).

Divorce judgment held not to have given children vested equitable interest. — Divorce judgment embodying settlement provisions whereby husband named minor children irrevocable beneficiaries could not operate to give children vested equitable interest in certificate issued by fraternal insurance society when husband later undertook to change beneficiaries, in view of express provisions of former Code 1940, T. 28, § 173. Williams v. Williams, 276 Ala. 43, 158 So. 2d 901 (1963).

Insured could not by contract create vested right in beneficiary. — The effect of former Code 1940, T. 28, § 173 was construed to mean that the insured could not by contract create a vested right to any extent in a beneficiary of a policy within the operation thereof and exempted such contracts from the rule permitting an assignment thereof. Williams v. Williams, 276 Ala. 43, 158 So. 2d 901 (1963).

No reimbursement for dues paid in reliance of agreement that payor be retained as sole beneficiary. — Under former Code 1940, T. 28, § 173, original beneficiary was not entitled to reimbursement out of policy to extent of dues and assessments paid by her in reliance on agreement that she would be retained as sole beneficiary, such claim being as clearly within inhibition of statute as claim to entire fund. Summers v. Summers, 218 Ala. 420, 118 So. 912 (1928).

Court orders directing payment of certain expenses erroneous. — Court orders, directing receiver of fraternal benefit society to pay expenses of endowment department, salaries of officers thereof and debts of grand lodge from beneficiary mortuary fund, held erroneous. Carter v. Mitchell, 225 Ala. 287, 142 So. 514 (1932).

But court order, directing payment of expenses and compensation of receiver for fraternal benefit society, his attorney's fees, compensation of his auditors and actuary and court costs from beneficiary trust fund, sufficient to pay such charges without impairing security of certificate holders, held not abuse of discretion. Carter v. Mitchell, 225 Ala. 287, 142 So. 514 (1932).

Burden of proof. — Original beneficiary had burden of showing that insurer constituted a society limiting membership to any one hazardous occupation, so as to constitute it an exception within provision of former Code 1940, T. 28, § 173. Summers v. Summers, 218 Ala. 420, 118 So. 912 (1928).

Collateral references. — 46 C.J.S., Insurance, §§ 1547-1573.

36 Am. Jur. 2d, Fraternal Orders & Benefit Societies, §§ 129 et seq.

§ 27-34-27. Exemption of benefits, etc., from attachment, garnishment or other process.

No money or other benefit, charity, relief or aid to be paid, provided or rendered by any society shall be liable to attachment, garnishment or other process or to be seized, taken, appropriated or applied by any legal or equitable process or operation of law to pay any debt or liability of a member or beneficiary, or any other person who may have a right thereunder, either before or after payment by the society. (Acts 1911, No. 476, p. 700; Acts 1971, No. 407, p. 707, § 698.)

§ 27-34-28. Personal liability for payment of benefits.

The officers and members of the supreme, grand or any subordinate body of a society shall not be personally liable for payment of any benefits provided by a society. (Acts 1911, No. 476, p. 700; Acts 1971, No. 407, p. 707, § 699.)

Collateral references. — 46 C.J.S., Insurance, § 1441.

§ 27-34-29. Issuance of certificate to each benefit member; matters constituting agreement.

(a) Every society authorized to do business in this state shall issue to each benefit member a certificate specifying the amount of benefits provided thereby. The certificate, together with any riders or endorsements attached thereto, the charter or articles of incorporation, the constitution and laws of the society, the application for membership, and declaration of insurability, if any, signed by the applicant and all amendments to each thereof shall constitute the agreement, as of the date of issuance, between the society and the member, and the certificate shall so state. A copy of the application for membership and of the declaration of insurability, if any, shall be endorsed upon or attached to the certificate.

(b) All statements purporting to be made by the member shall be representations and not warranties. Any waiver of this subsection shall be void.

(c) Any changes, additions or amendments to the charter or articles of incorporation, constitution or laws duly made or enacted subsequent to the issuance of the certificate shall bind the member and the beneficiaries and shall govern and control the agreement in all respects the same as though such changes, additions or amendments had been made prior to, and were in force at the time of, the application for membership; except, that no change, addition or amendment shall destroy or diminish benefits which the society contracted to give the member as of the date of issuance.

(d) Copies of any of the documents mentioned in this section, certified by the secretary or corresponding officer of the society, shall be received in evidence of the terms and conditions thereof. (Acts 1911, No. 476, p. 700; Acts 1971, No. 407, p. 707, § 700.)

Collateral references. — 46 C.J.S., Insurance, §§ 1452-1474.

§ 27-34-30. Life benefit certificate — Filing with commissioner; standard provisions.

(a) After January 1, 1973, no life benefit certificate shall be delivered, or issued for delivery, in this state unless a copy of the form has been filed with the commissioner.

(b) The certificate shall contain in substance the following standard provisions or, in lieu thereof, provisions which are more favorable to the member:

(1) Title on the face and filing page of the certificate clearly and correctly describing its form;

(2) A provision stating the amount of rates, premiums or other required contributions, by whatever name known, which are payable by the insured under the certificate;

(3) A provision that the member is entitled to a grace period of not less than a full month, or 30 days at the option of the society, in which the payment of any premium after the first may be made. During such grace period the certificate shall continue in full force, but in case the certificate becomes a claim during the grace period before the overdue payment is made, the amount of such overdue payment, or payments, may be deducted in any settlement under the certificate;

(4) A provision that the member shall be entitled to have the certificate reinstated at any time within three years from the due date of the premium in default, unless the certificate has been completely terminated through the application of a nonforfeiture benefit, cash surrender value or certificate loan, upon the production of evidence of insurability satisfactory to the society and the payment of all overdue premiums and any other indebtedness to the society upon the certificate, together with interest on such premiums and such indebtedness, if any, at a rate not exceeding six percent per annum, compounded annually;

(5) Except in the case of pure endowment, annuity or reversionary annuity contracts reducing term insurance contracts or contracts of term insurance of uniform amount of 15 years or less expiring before age 66, a provision that, in the event of default in payment of any premium after three full years' premiums have been paid or after premiums for a lesser period have been paid if the contract so provided, the society will grant, upon proper request, not later than 60 days after the due date of the premium in default, a paid-up nonforfeiture benefit on the plan stipulated in the certificate, effective as of such due date, of such value as specified in this chapter. The certificate may provide, if the society's laws so specify or if the member shall so elect prior to the expiration of the grace period of any overdue premium, that default shall not occur so long as premiums can be paid under the provisions of an arrangement for automatic premium loan as may be set forth in the certificate;

(6) A provision that one paid-up nonforfeiture benefit as specified in the certificate shall become effective automatically unless the member elects

another available paid-up nonforfeiture benefit, not later than 60 days after the due date of the premium in default;

(7) A statement of the mortality table and rate of interest used in determining all paid-up nonforfeiture benefits and cash surrender options available under the certificate, and a brief general statement of the method used in calculating such benefits;

(8) A table showing in figures the value of every paid-up nonforfeiture benefit and cash surrender option available under the certificate for each certificate anniversary either during the first 20 certificate years or during the term of the certificate, whichever is shorter;

(9) A provision that the certificate shall be incontestable after it has been in force during the lifetime of the member for a period of two years from its date of issue except for nonpayment of premiums, violation of the provisions of the certificate relating to military, aviation or naval service and violation of the provisions relating to suspension or expulsion as substantially set forth in the certificate. At the option of the society, supplemental provisions relating to benefits in the event of temporary or permanent disability or hospitalization and provisions which grant additional insurance specifically against death by accident or accidental means may also be excepted. The certificate shall be incontestable on the ground of suicide after it has been in force during the lifetime of the member for a period of two years from date of issue. The certificate may provide, as to statements made to procure reinstatement, that the society shall have the right to contest a reinstated certificate within a period of two years from the date of reinstatement with the same exceptions as provided in this subdivision;

(10) A provision that in case the age of the member or of any other person is considered in determining the premium and it is found at any time before final settlement under the certificate that the age has been misstated and the discrepancy and premium involved have not been adjusted, the amount payable shall be such as the premium would have purchased at the correct age; but if the correct age was not an insurable age under the society's charter or laws, only the premiums paid to the society, less any payments previously made to the member, shall be returned or, at the option of the society, the amount payable under the certificate shall be such as the premium would have purchased at the correct age according to the society's promulgated rates and any extension thereof based on actuarial principles;

(11) A provision, or provisions, which recite fully, or which set forth the substance of, all sections of the charter, constitution, laws, rules or regulations of the society in force at the time of issuance of the certificate, the violation of which will result in the termination of, or in the reduction of, the benefit, or benefits, payable under the certificate; and

(12) If the constitution or laws of the society provide for expulsion or suspension of a member, any member so expelled or suspended, except for nonpayment of a premium or within the contestable period for material misrepresentations in such member's application for membership, shall have the privilege of maintaining his insurance in force by continuing payment of the required premium.

(c) Any of the provisions, or portions thereof, prescribed in subsection (b) of this section not applicable by reason of the plan of insurance or because the certificate is an annuity certificate may, to the extent inapplicable, be omitted from the certificate. (Acts 1971, No. 407, p. 707, § 701.)

§ 27-34-31. Same — Prohibited provisions.

After January 1, 1973, no life benefit certificate shall be delivered or issued for delivery in this state containing, in substance, any of the following provisions:

(1) Any provision limiting the time with which any action may be commenced to less than two years after the cause of action accrues;

(2) Any provision by which the certificate purports to be issued or to take effect more than six months before the original application for the certificate was made, except in case of transfer from one form of certificate to another in connection with which the member is to receive credit for any reserve accumulation under the form of certificate from which the transfer is made; or

(3) Any provision for forfeiture of the certificate for failure to repay any loan thereon or to pay interest on such loan which the total indebtedness, including interest, is less than the loan value of the certificate. (Acts 1971, No. 407, p. 707, § 702.)

§ 27-34-32. Accident or health and total or permanent disability insurance contracts.

(a) No domestic, foreign or alien society authorized to do business in this state shall issue or deliver in this state any certificate or other evidence of any contract of accident insurance or health insurance or of any total and permanent disability insurance contract unless and until the form thereof, together with the form of application and all riders or endorsements for use in connection therewith, shall have been filed with the commissioner.

(b) The commissioner shall have power, from time to time, to make, alter and supersede reasonable regulations prescribing the required, optional and prohibited provisions in such contracts, and such regulations shall conform, as far as practicable, to the provisions of chapter 19 of this title. Where the commissioner deems inapplicable, either in part or in their entirety, the provisions of chapter 19 of this title, he may prescribe the portions, or summary thereof, of the contract to be printed on the certificate issued to the member.

(c) Any filing made under this section shall be deemed approved unless disapproved within 60 days from the date of such filing. (Acts 1971, No. 407, p. 707, § 704.)

§ 27-34-33. Reinsurance.

A domestic society may, by a reinsurance agreement, cede any individual risk or risks, in whole or in part, to an insurer, other than another fraternal benefit society, having the power to make such reinsurance and authorized to do business in this state or, if not so authorized, one which is approved by the commissioner; but no such society may reinsure substantially all of its insurance in force without the written permission of the commissioner. It may take credit for the reserves on such ceded risks to the extent reinsured, but no credit shall be allowed as an admitted asset or as a deduction from liability to a ceding society for reinsurance made, ceded, renewed or otherwise becoming effective after January 1, 1972, unless the reinsurance is payable by the assuming insurer on the basis of the liability of the ceding society under the contract, or contracts, reinsured without diminution because of the insolvency of the ceding society. (Acts 1923, No. 596, p. 785; Acts 1971, No. 407, p. 707, § 705.)

Collateral references. — 46 C.J.S., Insurance, § 1444.

§ 27-34-34. Assets; funds; expenses.

(a) All assets shall be held, invested and disbursed for the use and benefit of the society, and no member or beneficiary shall have or acquire individual rights therein or become entitled to any apportionment or the surrender of any part thereof except as provided in the contract.

(b) A society may create, maintain, invest, disburse and apply any special fund or funds necessary to carry out any purpose permitted by the laws of such society.

(c) Every society, the admitted assets of which are less than the sum of its accrued liabilities and reserves under all of its certificates when valued according to standards required for certificates issued after January 1, 1973, shall, in every provision of the laws of the society for payments by members of such society, in whatever form made, distinctly state the purpose of the same and the proportion thereof which may be used for expenses, and no part of the money collected for mortuary or disability purposes, or the net accretions thereto, shall be used for expenses. (Acts 1911, No. 476, p. 700; Acts 1971, No. 407, p. 707, § 706.)

Collateral references. — 46 C.J.S., Insurance, §§ 1442, 1443, 1451.

§ 27-34-35. Investments.

A society shall invest its funds only in such investments as are authorized by the laws of this state for the investment of assets of life insurers and subject to the limitations thereon. Any foreign or alien society permitted or seeking to do business in this state which invests its funds in accordance with the laws of the state, district, territory, country or province in which it is incorporated shall be held to meet the requirements of this section for the investment of funds. (Acts 1911, No. 476, p. 700; Acts 1971, No. 407, p. 707, § 707.)

§ 27-34-36. Annual statements — Requirements.

(a) Report shall be filed and synopses of annual statements shall be published in accordance with the provisions of this section.

(b) Every society transacting business in this state shall annually, on or before March 1, unless for cause shown such time has been extended by the commissioner, file with the commissioner a true statement of its financial condition, transactions and affairs for the preceding calendar year and pay a fee of $10.00 for filing same. The statement shall be in general form and context as approved by the national association of insurance commissioners for fraternal benefit societies and as supplemented by additional information required by the commissioner.

(c) A synopsis of its annual statement providing an explanation of the facts concerning the condition of the society thereby disclosed shall be printed and mailed to each benefit member of the society not later than June 1 of each year, or, in lieu thereof, such synopsis may be published in the society's official publication. (Acts 1911, No. 476, p. 700; Acts 1971, No. 407, p. 707, § 708.)

§ 27-34-37. Same — Valuation of certificates; reserves.

(a) As a part of the annual statement required under section 27-34-36, each society shall, on or before March 1, file with the commissioner a valuation of its certificates in force on December 31 last preceding; provided, however, that the commissioner may, in his discretion for cause shown, extend the time for filing such valuation for not more than two calendar months. Such report of valuation shall show, as reserve liabilities, the difference between the present midyear value of the promised benefits provided in the certificates of such society in force and the present midyear value of the future net premiums as the same are in practice actually collected, not including therein any value for the right to make extra assessments and not including any amount by which the present midyear value of future net premiums exceeds the present midyear value of promised benefits on individual certificates. At the option of any society, in lieu of the above, the valuation may show the net tabular value. Such net tabular value as to certificates issued prior to one year after

January 1, 1972, shall be determined in accordance with the provisions of law applicable prior to January 1, 1972, and, as to certificates issued on or after January 1, 1973, shall not be less than the reserves determined according to the commissioners' reserve valuation method as defined in this section. If the premium charged is less than the tabular net premium according to the basis of valuation used, an additional reserve equal to the present value of the deficiency in such premiums shall be set up and maintained as a liability. The reserve liabilities shall be properly adjusted in the event that the midyear or tabular values are not appropriate.

(b) Reserves, according to the commissioners' reserve valuation method, for the life insurance and endowment benefits of certificates providing for a uniform amount of insurance and requiring the payment of uniform premiums shall be the excess, if any, of the present value, at the date of valuation, of such future guaranteed benefits provided for by such certificates over the then present value of any future modified net premiums therefor. The modified net premiums for any such certificate shall be such uniform percentage of the respective contract premiums for such benefits that the present value, at the date of issue of the certificate, of all such modified net premiums shall be equal to the sum of the then present value of such benefits provided for by the certificate and the excess of subdivision (1) over subdivision (2) of this subsection, as follows:

(1) A net level premium equal to the present value, at the date of issue, of such benefits provided for after the first certificate year, divided by the present value, at the date of issue, of an annuity of one per annum payable on the first and each subsequent anniversary of such certificate on which a premium falls due; provided, however, that such net level annual premium shall not exceed the net level annual premium on the 19 year premium whole life plan for insurance of the same amount at an age one year higher than the age at issue of such certificate; and

(2) A net one-year term premium for such benefits provided for in the first certificate year.

(c) Reserves according to the commissioners' reserve valuation method for:

(1) Life insurance benefits for varying amounts of benefits or requiring the payment of varying premiums;

(2) Annuity and pure endowment benefits;

(3) Disability and accidental death benefits in all certificates and contracts; and

(4) All other benefits, except life insurance and endowment benefits, shall be calculated by a method consistent with the principles of subsection (b) of this section.

(d) The present value of deferred payments due under incurred claims or matured certificates shall be deemed a liability of the society and shall be computed upon mortality and interest standards prescribed in subsections (e) and (f) of this section.

(e) Such valuation and underlying data shall be certified by a competent actuary or, at the expense of the society, verified by the actuary of the department of insurance of the state of domicile of the society.

(f) The minimum standards of valuation for certificates issued prior to one year from January 1, 1972, shall be those provided by the law applicable immediately prior to January 1, 1972, but not lower than the standards used in the calculating of rates for such certificates.

(g) The minimum standard of valuation for certificates issued after January 1, 1973, shall be three and one-half percent interest and the following tables:

(1) FOR CERTIFICATES OF LIFE INSURANCE. — American men ultimate table of mortality, with Bowerman's or Davis' extension thereof or, with the consent of the commissioner, the commissioner's 1958 standard ordinary mortality table, the commissioner's 1941 standard industrial table of mortality or the commissioner's 1961 standard industrial table of mortality;

(2) FOR ANNUITY CERTIFICATES, INCLUDING LIFE ANNUITIES PROVIDED OR AVAILABLE UNDER OPTIONAL MODES OF SETTLEMENT IN SUCH CERTIFICATES. — The 1937 standard annuity table;

(3) FOR DISABILITY BENEFITS ISSUED IN CONNECTION WITH LIFE BENEFIT CERTIFICATES. — Hunter's disability table, which, for active lives, shall be combined with a mortality table permitted for calculating the reserves on life insurance certificates, except that the table known as Class 3 disability table (1926) modified to conform to the contractual waiting period, shall be used in computing reserves for disability benefits under a contract which presumes that total disability shall be considered to be permanent after a specified period;

(4) FOR ACCIDENTAL DEATH BENEFITS ISSUED IN CONNECTION WITH LIFE BENEFIT CERTIFICATES. — The intercompany double indemnity mortality table combined with a mortality table permitted for calculating the reserves for life insurance certificates; and

(5) FOR NONCANCELLABLE ACCIDENT AND HEALTH BENEFITS. — The Class 3 disability table (1926) with conference modifications or, with the consent of the commissioner, tables based upon the society's own experience.

(h) The commissioner may, in his discretion, accept other standards for valuation if he finds that the reserves produced thereby will not be less in the aggregate than reserves computed in accordance with the minimum valuation standard prescribed in this section. The commissioner may, in his discretion, vary the standards of mortality applicable to all certificates of insurance on substandard lives or other extra hazardous lives by any society authorized to do business in this state. Whenever the mortality experience under all certificates valued on the same mortality table is in excess of the expected mortality according to such table for a period of three consecutive years, the commissioner may require additional reserves when deemed necessary in his judgment on account of such certificates.

(i) Any society, with the consent of the insurance supervisory official of the state of domicile of the society and under such conditions, if any, which he may impose, may establish and maintain reserves on its certificates in excess of the reserves required under this section, but the contractual rights of any insured member shall not be affected thereby. (Acts 1911, No. 476, p. 700; Acts 1971, No. 407, p. 707, § 709.)

Collateral references. — 46 C.J.S., Insurance, § 1443.

§ 27-34-38. Same — Failure to file.

A society neglecting to file the annual statement in the form and within the time provided by this chapter shall forfeit $100.00 for each day during which such neglect continues; and, upon notice by the commissioner to that effect, its authority to do business in this state shall cease while such default continues. (Acts 1971, No. 407, p. 707, § 710.)

§ 27-34-39. Examinations — Domestic societies.

(a) The commissioner, or any person he may appoint, shall have the power of visitation and examination into the affairs of any domestic society, and he shall make such examination at least once in every three years. He may employ assistants for the purpose of such examination, and he, or any person he may appoint, shall have free access to all books, papers and documents that relate to the business of the society.

(b) In making any such examination, the commissioner may summon and qualify as witnesses under oath and examine its officers, agents and employees or other persons in relation to the affairs, transactions and condition of the society.

(c) A summary of the report of the commissioner, and such recommendations or statements of the commissioner as may accompany such report, shall be read at the first meeting of the board of directors, or corresponding body of the society, following the receipt thereof and, if directed so to do by the commissioner, shall also be read at the first meeting of the supreme legislative or governing body of the society following the receipt thereof. A copy of the report, recommendations and statements of the commissioner shall be furnished by the society to each member of such board of directors or other governing body.

(d) The expense of each examination and of each valuation, including compensation and actual expense of examiners, shall be paid by the society examined or whose certificates are valued, upon statements furnished by the commissioner. (Acts 1911, No. 476, p. 700; Acts 1971, No. 407, p. 707, § 711.)

§ 27-34-40. Same — Foreign and alien societies.

The commissioner, or any person whom he may appoint, may examine any foreign or alien society transacting, or applying for admission to transact, business in this state. He may employ assistants and he, or any person he may appoint, shall have free access to all books, papers and documents that relate to the business of the society. He may, in his discretion, accept, in lieu of such examination, the examination of the insurance department of the state, territory, district, province or country where such society is organized. The compensation and actual expenses of the examiners making any examination or general or special valuation shall be paid by the society examined or by the society whose certificate obligations have been valued, upon statements furnished by the commissioner. (Acts 1911, No. 476, p. 700; Acts 1971, No. 407, p. 707, § 712.)

§ 27-34-41. Same — Publication of financial statement, report or finding.

Pending, during or after an examination or investigation of a society, either domestic, foreign or alien, the commissioner shall make public no financial statement, report or finding nor shall he permit to become public any financial statement, report or finding affecting the status, standing or rights of any society until a copy thereof shall have been served upon the society at its principal office and the society shall have been afforded a reasonable opportunity to answer any such financial statement, report or finding and to make such showing in connection therewith as it may desire. (Acts 1911, No. 476, p. 700; Acts 1971, No. 407, p. 707, § 713.)

Collateral references. — 46 C.J.S., Insurance, § 1652.

§ 27-34-42. Exemption from taxation.

Every society organized or licensed under this chapter is hereby declared to be a charitable and benevolent institution, and all of its funds shall be exempt from all and every state, county, district, municipal and school tax other than taxes on real estate and office equipment. (Acts 1911, No. 476, p. 700; Acts 1971, No. 407, p. 707, § 714.)

Collateral references. — 71 Am. Jur. 2d, State & Local Taxation, § 384.

§ 27-34-43. Agents — Licensing.

(a) A fraternal benefit society shall solicit applications for insurance or annuities only through agents of the society licensed as such agents by the commissioner under, and subject to, the same provisions and procedures as apply to life and disability insurers in general under chapter 8 of this title.

(b) For the purposes of this section, the term "agent" or "agents" shall not include:

(1) Any regular salaried officer or employee of a licensed society who devotes substantially all of his services to activities other than the solicitation of fraternal insurance contracts from the public and who receives for the solicitation of such contracts no commission or other compensation directly dependent upon the amount of business obtained; or

(2) Any agent or representative of a society who devotes, or intends to devote, less than 50 percent of his time to the solicitation and procurement of insurance contracts for such society. Any person who in the preceding calendar year has solicited and procured life insurance contracts on behalf of any society in an amount of insurance in excess of $50,000.00 or, in the case of any other kind or kinds of insurance which the society might write, on the persons of more than 25 individuals and who has received, or will receive, a commission or other compensation therefor, shall be presumed to be devoting, or intending to devote, 50 percent of his time to the solicitation or procurement of insurance contracts for such society. (Acts 1971, No. 407, p. 707, § 715.)

Collateral references. — 46 C.J.S., Insurance, § 1439.

§ 27-34-44. Same — Solicitation without license.

(a) Any person who in this state acts as insurance agent for a fraternal benefit society without having a currently effective license therefor issued by the commissioner shall, upon conviction thereof, be guilty of a misdemeanor and shall be subject to penalties as prescribed in section 27-1-12.

(b) No society shall pay any commission or other compensation to any person for services in this state in the solicitation of any application for insurance or an annuity except to an agent of the society licensed as provided in section 27-34-43. (Acts 1971, No. 407, p. 707, § 716.)

§ 27-34-45. Misrepresentations.

No person shall cause or permit to be made, issued or circulated in any form:

(1) Any misrepresentation or false or misleading statement concerning the terms, benefits or advantages of any fraternal insurance contract now issued, or to be issued, in this state or the financial condition of any society;

(2) Any false or misleading estimate or statement concerning the dividends or shares of surplus paid, or to be paid, by any society on any insurance contract; or

(3) Any incomplete comparison of an insurance contract of one society with an insurance contract of another society or insurer for the purpose of inducing the lapse, forfeiture or surrender of any insurance contract. A comparison of insurance contracts is incomplete:

a. If it does not compare in detail:

1. The gross rates and the gross rates less any dividend or other reduction allowed at the date of the comparison; and

2. Any increase in cash values and all the benefits provided by each contract for the possible duration thereof as determined by the life expectancy of the insured; or

502

b. If it omits from consideration:

1. Any benefit or value provided in the contract;

2. Any differences as to amount or period of rates; or

3. Any differences in limitations or conditions or provisions which directly or indirectly affect the benefits.

In any determination of the incompleteness or misleading character of any comparison or statement, it shall be presumed that the insured had no knowledge of any of the contents of the contract involved.

(4) Any person who violates any provision of this section or knowingly receives any compensation or commission by or in consequence of such violation shall, upon conviction, be punished by a fine not less than $100.00 nor more than $1,000.00 or by imprisonment in the county jail not less than 30 days nor more than 90 days, or by both fine and imprisonment, and shall, in addition, be liable for a civil penalty in the amount of three times the sum received by such violator as compensation or commission, which penalty an action may be maintained for and recovered by any person or society aggrieved for his, or its, own use and benefit in accordance with the provisions of civil practice. (Acts 1971, No. 407, p. 707, § 717.)

Collateral references. — 46 C.J.S., Insurance, § 1462.

Waiver or estoppel on basis of statements in promotional or explanatory literature issued to insured. 36 ALR3d 541.

§ 27-34-46. Discrimination, inducements and rebates.

(a) No society doing business in this state shall make or permit any unfair discrimination between insured members of the same class and equal expectation of life in the premiums charged for certificates of insurance in the dividends or other benefits payable thereon or in any other of the terms and conditions of the contracts it makes.

(b) No society, by itself, or any other party and no agent or solicitor, personally or by any other party shall offer, promise, allow, give, set off or pay, directly or indirectly, any valuable consideration or inducement to or for insurance on any risk authorized to be taken by such society which is not specified in the certificate. No member shall receive or accept, directly or indirectly, any rebate of premium, or part thereof, or agent's or solicitor's commission thereon payable on any certificate or receive or accept any favor or advantage or share in the dividends or other benefits to accrue on, or any valuable consideration or inducement not specified in, the contract of insurance. (Acts 1971, No. 407, p. 707, § 718.)

Collateral references. — 46 C.J.S., Insurance, § 1479.

Construction and effect of state statute forbidding unfair trade practice or competition by discriminatory allowance of rebates, commissions, discounts, or the like. 54 ALR2d 1187.

§ 27-34-47. Service of process.

(a) Every society authorized to do business in this state shall appoint, in writing, the commissioner and each successor in office to be its true and lawful attorney upon whom all lawful process in any action or proceeding against it shall be served and shall agree, in such writing, that any lawful process against it which is served on said attorney shall be of the same legal force and validity as if served upon the society and that the authority shall continue in force so long as any liability remains outstanding in this state. Copies of such appointment, certified by the commissioner, shall be deemed sufficient evidence thereof and shall be admitted in evidence with the same force and effect as the original thereof might be admitted.

(b) Service shall only be made upon the commissioner or, if absent, upon the person in charge of his office. It shall be made in duplicate and shall constitute sufficient service upon the society. When legal process against a society is served upon the commissioner, he shall forthwith forward one of the duplicate copies by registered or certified mail, prepaid, directed to the secretary or corresponding officer. No such service shall require a society to file its answer, pleading or defense in less than 30 days from the date of mailing the copy of the service to a society. Legal process shall not be served upon a society except in the manner provided in this section. At the time of serving any process upon the commissioner, the plaintiff or complainant in the action shall pay to the commissioner a fee of $2.00. (Acts 1911, No. 476, p. 700; Acts 1971, No. 407, p. 707, § 719.)

Collateral references. — 46 C.J.S., Insurance, § 1626.

§ 27-34-48. Consolidation or merger — Procedure.

(a) A domestic society may consolidate or merge with any other society by complying with the provisions of this section. It shall file with the commissioner:

(1) A certified copy of the written contract containing, in full, the terms and conditions of the consolidation or merger;

(2) A sworn statement by the president and secretary, or corresponding officers, of each society showing the financial condition thereof on a date fixed by the commissioner, but not earlier than December 31 next preceding the date of the contract;

(3) A certificate of such officers, duly verified by their respective oaths, that the consolidation or merger has been approved by a two-thirds vote of the supreme legislative or governing body of each society; and

(4) Evidence that at least 60 days prior to the action of the supreme legislative or governing body of each society, the text of the contract has been furnished to all members of each society, either by mail or by publication in full in the official organ of each society.

(b) The affidavit of any officer of the society, or of anyone authorized by it to mail any notice or document, stating that such notice or document has been duly addressed and mailed, shall be prima facie evidence that such notice or document has been furnished the addressees.

(c) If the commission finds that the contract is in conformity with the provisions of this section, that the financial statements are correct and that the consolidation or merger is just and equitable to the members of each society, he shall approve the contract and issue his certificate to such effect. Upon such approval, the contract shall be in full force and effect unless any society which is a party to the contract is incorporated under the laws of any other state. In such event, the consolidation or merger shall not become effective unless, and until, it has been approved as provided by the laws of such state and a certificate of such approval filed with the commissioner or, if the laws of such state contain no such provision, then the consolidation or merger shall not become effective unless, and until, it has been approved by the insurance supervisory official of such state and a certificate of such approval filed with the commissioner. (Acts 1923, No. 596, p. 785; Acts 1971, No. 407, p. 707, § 720.)

Collateral references. — 46 C.J.S., Insurance, § 1448.   36 Am. Jur. 2d, Fraternal Orders & Benefit Societies, § 8.

§ 27-34-49. Same — Effect.

Upon the consolidation or merger effective as provided in section 27-34-48, all the rights, franchises and interests of the consolidated or merged societies in, and to, every species of property, real, personal or mixed, and things in action thereunto belonging shall be vested in the society resulting from, or remaining after, the consolidation or merger without any other instrument; except, that conveyances of real property may be evidenced by proper deeds, and the title to any real estate, or interest therein, vested under the laws of this state in any of the societies consolidated or merged shall not revert, or be in any way impaired, by reason of the consolidation or merger, but shall vest absolutely in the society resulting from, or remaining after, such consolidation or merger. (Acts 1971, No. 407, p. 707, § 721.)

§ 27-34-50. Actions to enjoin or in quo warranto; liquidation; receivership.

(a) When the commissioner upon investigation finds that a domestic society:

(1) Has exceeded its powers; or

(2) Has failed to comply with any provision of this chapter; or

(3) Is not fulfilling its contracts in good faith; or

(4) Has a membership of less than 400 after an existence of one year or more; or

505

(5) Is conducting business fraudulently or in a manner hazardous to its members, creditors, the public or the business, he shall notify the society of his findings, state in writing the reasons for his dissatisfaction and require the society to show cause on a date named why it should not be enjoined from carrying on any business until the violation complained of shall have been corrected or why an action in quo warranto should not be commenced against the society.

(b) If on such date the society does not present good and sufficient reasons why it should not be so enjoined or why such action should not be commenced, the commissioner may present the facts relating thereto to the attorney general who shall, if he deems the circumstances warrant, commence an action to enjoin the society from transacting business or in quo warranto. The court shall thereupon notify the officers of the society of a hearing. If after a full hearing it appears that the society should be so enjoined or liquidated or a receiver appointed, the court shall enter the necessary order.

(c) No society so enjoined shall have the authority to do business until:

(1) The commissioner finds that the violation complained of has been corrected;

(2) The costs of such action have been paid by the society if the court finds that the society was in default as charged;

(3) The court has dissolved its injunction; and

(4) The commissioner has reinstated the society's license.

(d) If the court orders the society liquidated, it shall be enjoined from carrying on any further business, whereupon the receiver of the society shall proceed at once to take possession of the books, papers, money and other assets of the society and, under the direction of the court, proceed forthwith to close the affairs of the society and to distribute its funds to those entitled thereto.

(e) No action under this section shall be recognized in any court of this state unless brought by the attorney general upon request of the commissioner. Whenever a receiver is to be appointed for a domestic society, the court shall appoint the commissioner as such receiver.

(f) The provisions of this section relating to hearing by the commissioner, action by the attorney general at the request of the commissioner, hearing by the court, injunction and receivership shall be applicable to a society which voluntarily determines to discontinue business. (Acts 1911, No. 476, p. 700; Acts 1939, No. 525, p. 816; Acts 1939, No. 579, p. 936; Acts 1971, No. 407, p. 707, § 722.)

Collateral references. — 46 C.J.S., Insurance, §§ 1436, 1443, 1449-1451.

§ 27-34-51. Applications for injunctions.

No application or petition for injunction against any domestic, foreign or alien society, or branch thereof, shall be recognized in any court of this state unless made by the attorney general upon request of the commissioner. (Acts 1971, No. 407, p. 707, § 723.)

§ 27-34-52. Review of decisions and findings of commissioner.

All decisions and findings of the commissioner made under the provisions of this chapter shall be subject to review by the court in accordance with the provisions of section 27-2-32. (Acts 1971, No. 407, p. 707, § 724.)

§ 27-34-53. False statements.

Any person who willfully makes a false statement of any material fact or thing in a sworn statement as to the death or disability of a certificate holder in any fraternal benefit society, for the purpose of procuring payment of a benefit named in the certificate of such holder, and any person who willfully makes any false statement in any verified report or declaration under oath required or authorized by law as to fraternal benefit societies shall be guilty of perjury and shall be proceeded against and punished as provided by the statutes of this state in relation to the crime of perjury. (Acts 1911, No. 476, p. 700; Acts 1971, No. 407, p. 707, § 725.)

§ 27-34-54. Applicability of other provisions.

In addition to the provisions heretofore contained or referred to in this chapter, other chapters and provisions of this title shall apply to fraternal benefit societies, to the extent applicable and not in conflict with the express provisions of this chapter, and the reasonable implications thereof, as follows:
(1) Chapter 1;
(2) Chapter 2;
(3) The following sections of chapter 3:
a. Section 27-3-4; and
b. Section 27-3-5;
(4) The following sections of chapter 10:
a. Section 27-10-1;
b. Section 27-10-2; and
c. Section 27-10-3;
(5) Chapter 12;
(6) Section 27-15-29;
(7) The following sections of chapter 27:
a. Section 27-27-26;

    b. Section 27-27-27;

    c. Section 27-27-29; and

    d. Section 27-27-50; and

(8) Chapter 32. (Acts 1971, No. 407, p. 707, § 726.)

CHAPTER 35.

CONVERSION OF FRATERNAL BENEFIT SOCIETIES.

Sec.
27-35-1. Conversion into stock or mutual life insurance company — Authority; how effected.
27-35-2. Same — Plan of conversion; approval or disapproval thereof.
27-35-3. Same — Notice to subordinate lodges or branches.
27-35-4. Same — Ratification or amendment of articles of incorporation — Generally.
27-35-5. Same — Same — Filing.
27-35-6. Same — Certificates of incorporation and authority.

Sec.
27-35-7. Same — Provisions for certificate holders to subscribe to stock.
27-35-8. Same — Completion; effect.
27-35-9. Same — Preservation of debts, liabilities and duties.
27-35-10. Same — Obligation to holders of policies or certificates; pending actions.
27-35-11. Same — Separate record of premiums; exemption from premium taxes.

Cross references. — As to fraternal benefits societies generally, see § 27-34-1 et seq.

Collateral references. — 46 C.J.S., Insurance, § 1447.

§ 27-35-1. Conversion into stock or mutual life insurance company — Authority; how effected.

Any fraternal benefit society organized under the laws of this state may convert itself into a stock life insurance company or a mutual life insurance company, which may be a continuation of such society under an amended charter, if such society is then incorporated, or a new corporation formed for such purpose if such society is then unincorporated. In either event, the conversion of such society into a stock life insurance company or a mutual life insurance company shall be effected as provided in this chapter. (Acts 1927, No. 537, p. 624; Acts 1971, No. 407, p. 707, § 727.)

Authority of legislature. — Subject to constitutional limitations, the legislature of this state has full authority to regulate the insurance business, and once the legislature has established a constitutional statutory procedure for conversion and that procedure has been complied with, the matter is at an end. Ashurst v. Preferred Life Assurance Soc'y, 282 Ala. 119, 209 So. 2d 403 (1968).

§ 27-35-2. Same — Plan of conversion; approval or disapproval thereof.

(a) The proposed plan for the conversion of the society into a stock or mutual life insurer shall be prepared in writing, setting forth in full the terms and conditions thereof. After approval of the plan by the society's board of directors, the society shall file the plan of conversion with the commissioner.

(b) If, upon examination thereof, the commissioner is of the opinion that the plan is complete, is in compliance with the law, is fair and equitable to the certificate holders and interests of the society and that no reasonable objection thereto exists, he shall approve the plan; if he finds otherwise, the commissioner shall disapprove the plan. If not disapproved and written notice thereof given the society within 30 days after the date of filing with the commissioner, the plan shall be deemed to have been approved as of the expiration of such 30 days' period. In any such notice of disapproval, the commissioner shall state the reasons for disapproval.

(c) No society shall effectuate any plan of conversion which has been disapproved by the commissioner. (Acts 1971, No. 407, p. 707, § 728.)

§ 27-35-3. Same — Notice to subordinate lodges or branches.

After the plan of conversion has been approved by the commissioner, the society shall mail notice by registered or certified mail to all of its subordinate lodges or branches, by whatever name called, stating that a proposal will be made at a meeting of the supreme governing or legislative body of the society, to be held at least 90 days after the mailing of the notice, to convert the society into a stock or mutual life insurer and enclosing a copy of the proposed plan of conversion. (Acts 1927, No. 537, p. 624; Acts 1971, No. 407, p. 707, § 729.)

§ 27-35-4. Same — Ratification or amendment of articles of incorporation — Generally.

Pursuant to the notice provided for in section 27-35-3, the supreme governing or legislative body shall adopt a resolution authorizing the conversion of the society into a stock or mutual insurer, as the case may be, and shall ratify articles of incorporation, if the society is then unincorporated, or amend the society's articles of incorporation if it is then incorporated, to comply with the requirements of this title. (Acts 1927, No. 537, p. 624; Acts 1971, No. 407, p. 707, § 730.)

§ 27-35-5. Same — Same — Filing.

(a) The articles of incorporation so adopted or as so amended, as the case may be, shall be filed with the probate judge as required of domestic insurers under this title; except, that no bond or solicitation permit shall be required.

(b) At the time of filing of articles of incorporation or amended articles of incorporation with the commissioner, the society shall likewise file a report of the meeting of its supreme governing or legislative body referred to in sections 27-35-3 and 27-35-4, certified by the presiding officer thereof under the corporate seal, if the society has a corporate seal. (Acts 1927, No. 537, p. 624; Acts 1971, No. 407, p. 707, § 731.)

§ 27-35-6. Same — Certificates of incorporation and authority.

The society shall have corporate existence as a domestic stock or mutual life insurer upon issuance of the certificate of incorporation by the commissioner or approval of the amended articles of incorporation, as the case may be; but it shall not transact business as an insurer until all its authorized capital stock, if a stock insurer, has been subscribed and paid in full and it has otherwise qualified for, and received from the commissioner, a certificate of authority as provided in this title for legal reserve insurers. (Acts 1971, No. 407, p. 707, § 732.)

§ 27-35-7. Same — Provisions for certificate holders to subscribe to stock.

If the fraternal benefit society is to be converted into a stock life insurer, the plan of conversion shall make reasonable provisions under which each adult certificate holder of the society shall have the preemptive right to subscribe to and purchase that proportion of the total authorized capital which the amount of his insurance bears to the society's total insurance in force at a date to be specified in such plan; except, that if more than 75 percent of the society's adult certificate holders are residents of this state, such preemptive right may, in the commissioner's discretion, under the plan be limited to such residents. (Acts 1927, No. 537, p. 624; Acts 1971, No. 407, p. 707, § 733.)

§ 27-35-8. Same — Completion; effect.

(a) When a fraternal benefit society has complied with the provisions of this chapter and with the laws of this state relating to domestic stock life insurers or domestic mutual life insurers, as the case may be, and has received from the commissioner a certificate of authority to transact business in this state, its reorganization and conversion into such stock insurer or mutual insurer shall be complete.

(b) The reorganized and converted corporation shall be deemed in law to be a continuation of the fraternal benefit society, whether the reorganization and conversion shall have been accomplished by the formation of a new corporation or by the amendment of the certificate of incorporation of the former society; and such reorganized and converted corporation shall succeed to, and become invested with, all and singular, the rights, privileges, franchises, and all property, real, personal or mixed, and all debts due on any account and all other things in action theretofore belonging to such fraternal benefit society; and all property, rights, privileges, franchises and all and every other interest shall thereafter be as effectually the property of such reorganized and converted corporation as they were of the former fraternal benefit society; and the title to any real estate, by deed or otherwise vested in such former fraternal benefit society, shall vest in such reorganized and converted corporation and shall not in any way be impaired by reason of the conversion. (Acts 1927, No. 537, p. 624; Acts 1971, No. 407, p. 707, § 734.)

Assets of nonstock fraternal benefit society. — A nonstock fraternal benefit society as a whole holds assets of the society in trust for the benefit of the policyholders. Ashurst v. Preferred Life Assurance Soc'y, 282 Ala. 119, 209 So. 2d 403 (1968).

Interest of member-policyholders in surplus of nonstock fraternal benefit society. — Member-policyholders and the class they represent do not have a divisible and vested interest in the surplus of a nonstock fraternal benefit society. Ashurst v. Preferred Life Assurance Soc'y, 282 Ala. 119, 209 So. 2d 403 (1968).

Effect of conversion on surplus of nonstock fraternal benefit society. — Under former Code 1940, T. 28, § 242, after the conversion was completed, the surplus of nonstock fraternal benefit society became the property of the stock company and neither the former section nor any of the other conversion statutes provided for compensating the member-policyholders of the nonstock benefit society for any interest they may have had in the surplus before conversion. Ashurst v. Preferred Life Assurance Soc'y, 282 Ala. 119, 209 So. 2d 403 (1968).

§ 27-35-9. Same — Preservation of debts, liabilities and duties.

Rights of creditors and all liens upon the property of the former fraternal benefit society shall be preserved unimpaired after the society's conversion, and the former fraternal benefit society shall be deemed to continue in existence in order to preserve the same; and all debts, liabilities and duties of the former fraternal benefit society shall thenceforth attach to the reorganized and converted corporation and may be enforced against it to the same extent as if said debts, duties and liabilities had been incurred or contracted by it. (Acts 1927, No. 537, p. 624; Acts 1971, No. 407, p. 707, § 735.)

Distribution of surplus by fraternal benefit society not required. — Under the conversion statutes of this state, a fraternal benefit society is not required to distribute its surplus in cash or in stock to its member-policyholders upon conversion to a stock life insurance corporation. Ashurst v. Preferred Life Assurance Soc'y, 282 Ala. 119, 209 So. 2d 403 (1968).

Stock company could not use surplus of fraternal benefit society for dividends. — In view of former Code 1940, T. 28, §§ 243 and 244, the surplus and reserve funds of a nonstock fraternal benefit society were impressed with the trust for the protection of policyholders, and a stock company could not use the surplus which the nonstock fraternal benefit society had at the time of conversion for the purpose of paying dividends to its stockholders so long as policies or certificates of persons who were members of the benefit society at the time of conversion were in force. Ashurst v. Preferred Life Assurance Soc'y, 282 Ala. 119, 209 So. 2d 403 (1968).

§ 27-35-10. Same — Obligation to holders of policies or certificates; pending actions.

(a) The reorganized and converted corporation shall be obligated to carry out and perform all of the obligations of every kind and character owing by the former fraternal benefit society to the holders of its policies or beneficial certificates, and the same may be enforced against it to the same extent as if the policies and beneficial certificates had been issued by it after such conversion.

(b) Any pending actions wherein the former fraternal benefit society was a party shall be unaffected by the conversion thereof and shall be prosecuted by or against such reorganized and converted corporation the same as if the conversion had not taken place. (Acts 1927, No. 537, p. 624; Acts 1971, No. 407, p. 707, § 736.)

Cross references. — See notes to § 27-35-9.

§ 27-35-11. Same — Separate record of premiums; exemption from premium taxes.

The insurer, after conversion from a fraternal benefit society, shall maintain separate records of premiums received by it on account of policies and certificates originally issued while a fraternal benefit society and continuing in force without material change as to form or basis of premium. All such premiums shall be exempt from premium taxes to the same extent, if any, as to which exempted if currently received by a domestic fraternal benefit society. (Acts 1971, No. 407, p. 707, § 737.)

CHAPTER 36.

LIABILITIES.

Sec.
27-36-1. Liabilities generally.
27-36-2. Unearned premium reserve — Title insurance.
27-36-3. Same — Property, general casualty and surety insurance.
27-36-4. Same — Marine and transportation insurance.

Sec.
27-36-5. Active life reserve for disability insurance.
27-36-6. Increase of inadequate loss reserves.
27-36-7. Standard Valuation Law.

§ 27-36-1. Liabilities generally.

In any determination of the financial condition of an insurer, capital stock and liabilities to be charged against its assets shall include:

(1) The amount of its capital stock outstanding, if any;

(2) The amount, estimated consistent with the provisions of this title, necessary to pay all of its unpaid losses and claims incurred on or prior to the date of statement, whether reported or unreported, together with the expenses of adjustment or settlement thereof;

(3) With reference to life and disability insurance and annuity contracts:

a. The amount of reserves on life insurance policies and annuity contracts in force, valued according to the tables of mortality, rates of interest, and methods adopted pursuant to this title which are applicable thereto;

b. Reserves for disability benefits, for both active and disabled lives;

c. Reserves for accidental death benefits; and

d. Any additional reserves which may be required by the commissioner consistent with practice as last formulated or approved by the national association of insurance commissioners, or its successor organization, on account of such insurance;

(4) With reference to insurance other than specified in subdivision (3) of this section, and other than title insurance, the amount of reserves equal to the unearned portions of the gross premiums charged on policies in force, computed in accordance with this chapter;

(5) Taxes, expenses and other obligations due or accrued at the date of the statement; and

(6) In the case of life insurers, a securities valuation reserve calculated in accordance with the rules of the commissioner, which rules shall not be inconsistent with the rules and regulations promulgated by the national association of insurance commissioners or its successor organization. (Acts 1971, No. 407, p. 707, § 738.)

Collateral references. — Fact that passenger in negligently operated motor vehicle is owner as affecting passenger's liability to or rights against third person—modern cases. 37 ALR4th 565.

§ 27-36-2. Unearned premium reserve — Title insurance.

(a) In addition to an adequate reserve as to outstanding losses as required under section 27-36-1, a title insurer shall maintain an unearned premium reserve of not less than an amount computed as follows:

(1) Ten percent of the total amount of the risk premiums written in the calendar year for title insurance contracts shall be assigned originally to the reserve; and

(2) During each of the 20 years next following the year in which the title insurance contract was issued, the reserve applicable to the contract shall be reduced by five percent of the original amount of such reserve.

(b) The insurer may credit upon the reserve provided for by this section the amount of its deposit made under section 27-3-13.

(c) Title insurance risk premium shall not include charges for abstracting, record searching, certificates as to the record title, escrow and closing services, and other related services which may be offered or furnished, or the costs and expenses of examination of titles. (Acts 1971, No. 407, p. 707, § 743.)

§ 27-36-3. Same — Property, general casualty and surety insurance.

(a) As to insurance against loss or damage to property, except as provided in section 27-36-4, and as to all general casualty insurance and surety insurance, every insurer shall maintain an unearned premium reserve on all policies in force.

(b) The commissioner may require that such reserves shall be equal to the unearned portions of the gross premiums in force after deducting applicable reinsurance in solvent insurers as computed on each respective risk from the policy's date of issue. If the commissioner does not so require, the portions of the gross premium in force, less applicable reinsurance in solvent insurers, to be held as an unearned premium reserve, shall be computed according to the following table:

Term for Which Policy Was Written		Reserved for Unearned Premium
1 year or less		1/2
2 years	1st year	3/4
	2nd year	1/4
3 years	1st year	5/6
	2nd year	1/2
	3rd year	1/6
4 years	1st year	7/8
	2nd year	5/8

Term for Which Policy Was Written		Reserved for Unearned Premium
	3rd year	3/8
	4th year	1/8
5 years	1st year	9/10
	2nd year	7/10
	3rd year	1/2
	4th year	3/10
	5th year	1/10
Over 5 years	pro rata	

(c) In lieu of computation according to the table in subsection (b) of this section, the insurer, at its option, may compute all of such reserves on a monthly or more frequent pro rata basis.

(d) After adopting a method for computing such reserve, an insurer shall not change methods without approval of the insurance supervisory official of its state of domicile.

(e) This section does not apply to title insurance. (Acts 1971, No. 407, p. 707, § 739.)

§ 27-36-4. Same — Marine and transportation insurance.

As to marine and transportation insurance, the entire amount of premiums on trip risks not terminated shall be deemed unearned, and the commissioner may require the insurer to carry a reserve equal to 100 percent of premiums on trip risks written during the month ended as of the date of statement. (Acts 1971, No. 407, p. 707, § 740.)

§ 27-36-5. Active life reserve for disability insurance.

For all disability insurance policies, the insurer shall maintain an active life reserve which shall place a sound value on its liabilities under such policies and be not less than the reserve according to appropriate standards set forth in regulations issued by the commissioner and, in no event, less in the aggregate than the pro rata gross unearned premiums for such policies. (Acts 1971, No. 407, p. 707, § 741.)

§ 27-36-6. Increase of inadequate loss reserves.

If loss experience shows that an insurer's loss reserves, however computed or estimated, are inadequate, the commissioner shall require the insurer to maintain loss reserves in such increased amount as is needed to make them adequate. (Acts 1971, No. 407, p. 707, § 742.)

§ 27-36-7. Standard Valuation Law.

(a) This section shall be known as the standard valuation law.

(b) The commissioner shall annually value, or cause to be valued, the reserve liabilities (hereinafter called reserves) for all outstanding life insurance policies and annuity and pure endowment contracts of every life insurer doing business in this state and may certify the amount of any such reserves, specifying the mortality table or tables, rate or rates of interest and methods (net level premium method or others) used in the calculation of such reserves. In the case of an alien insurer, such valuation shall be limited to its insurance transactions in the United States. In calculating such reserves, the commissioner may use group methods and approximate averages for fractions of a year or otherwise. He may accept in his discretion the insurer's calculation of such reserves. In lieu of the valuation of the reserves required in this title of any foreign or alien insurer, he may accept any valuation made, or caused to be made, by the insurance supervisory official of any state or other jurisdiction when such valuation complies with the minimum standard provided in this section, and if the official of such state or jurisdiction accepts as sufficient and valid for all legal purposes the certificate of valuation of the commissioner when such certificate states the valuation to have been made in a specified manner according to which the aggregate reserves would be at least as large as if they had been computed in the manner prescribed by the law of that state or jurisdiction. Where any such valuation is made by the commissioner, he may use the actuary of the department or employ an actuary for the purpose, and the reasonable compensation and expenses of the actuary, at a rate approved by the commissioner, upon demand by the commissioner, supported by an itemized statement of such compensation and expenses, shall be paid by the insurer. When a domestic insurer furnishes the commissioner with a valuation of its outstanding policies as computed by its own actuary or by an actuary deemed satisfactory for the purpose by the commissioner, the valuation shall be verified by the actuary of the department without cost to the insurer.

(c) The minimum standard for the valuation of all such policies and contracts issued prior to January 1, 1972 shall be as required under laws in effect immediately prior to January 1, 1972, or the minimum provided in subsection (d) of this section, if less, except that the minimum standard for the valuation of annuities and pure endowments purchased under group annuity and pure endowment contracts issued prior to January 1, 1972 shall be that provided by the laws in effect prior to January 1, 1972 by replacing the interest rates specified in such laws by an interest rate of five percent per annum.

(d)(1) Except as otherwise provided in subdivisions (2) and (3) of this subsection, the minimum standard for the valuation of all such policies and contracts issued on or after January 1, 1972 shall be the commissioner's reserve valuation method defined in subsections (e) and (i) of this section, five percent interest for group annuities and pure endowment contracts and three and one-half percent interest for all other such policies and contracts or, in the case of policies and contracts, other than annuity and pure endowment contracts, issued on or after August 23, 1976, four percent interest, for such policies issued prior to July 30, 1979, and four and one-half percent interest for all other such policies issued on or after July 30, 1979, and the following tables:

a. For all ordinary policies of life insurance issued on the standard basis, excluding any disability and accidental death benefits in such policies, the commissioner's 1958 standard ordinary mortality table for such policies issued prior to the operative date of subsection (j) of the standard nonforfeiture law for life insurance, as amended; except, that for any category of such policies issued on female risks, modified net premiums and present values, referred to in subsection (e) of this section, may be calculated according to an age not more than three years younger than the actual age of the insured and for any category of such policies issued on female risks on or after July 30, 1979, modified net premiums and present values, referred to in subsection (e), may be calculated according to an age not more than six years younger than the actual age of the insured; and for such policies issued on or after the operative date of subsection (j) of the standard nonforfeiture law for life insurance, as amended:

1. The commissioner's 1980 standard ordinary mortality table; or

2. At the election of the insurer for any one or more specified plans of life insurance, the commissioner's 1980 standard ordinary mortality table with 10-year select mortality factors; or

3. Any ordinary mortality table, adopted after 1980 by the National Association of Insurance Commissioners, that is approved by regulation promulgated by the commissioner for use in determining the minimum standard of valuation for such policies.

b. For all industrial life insurance policies issued on the standard basis, excluding any disability and accidental death benefits in such policies, the commissioner's 1961 standard industrial mortality table or any industrial mortality table, adopted after 1980 by the National Association of Insurance Commissioners, that is approved by regulation promulgated by the commissioner for use in determining the minimum standard of valuation for such policies;

c. For individual annuity and pure endowment contracts, excluding any disability and accidental death benefits in such policies, the 1937 standard annuity mortality table or, at the option of the insurer, the annuity mortality table for 1949, ultimate, or any modification of either of these tables approved by the commissioner;

d. For group annuity and pure endowment contracts, excluding any disability and accidental death benefits in such policies, the group annuity mortality table for 1951, any modification of such table approved by the commissioner or, at the option of the insurer, any of the tables or modifications of tables specified for individual annuity and pure endowment contracts;

e. For total and permanent disability benefits in, or supplementary to, ordinary policies or contracts for policies or contracts issued on or after January 1, 1972, the tables of period 2 disablement rates and the 1930 to 1950 termination rates of 1952 disability study of the society of actuaries, with due regard to the type of benefit or any tables of disablement rates and termination rates, adopted after 1980 by the National Association of Insurance Commissioners, that are approved by regulation promulgated by the commissioner for use in determining the minimum standard of valuation for such policies; for policies or contracts issued prior to January 1, 1972, either such tables or, at the option of the insurer, the class (3) disability table (1926). Any such table shall, for active lives, be combined with a mortality table permitted for calculating the reserve for life insurance policies;

f. For accidental death benefits in or supplementary to policies, for policies issued on or after January 1, 1972, the 1959 accidental death benefits table or any accidental death benefits table, adopted after 1980 by the National Association of Insurance Commissioners, that is approved by regulation promulgated by the commissioner for use in determining the minimum standard of valuation for such policies; for policies issued prior to January 1, 1972, either such table or, at the option of the insurer, the intercompany double indemnity mortality table. Either table shall be combined with a mortality table permitted for calculating the reserves for life insurance policies;

g. For group life insurance, life insurance issued on the substandard basis and other special benefits, such tables as may be approved by the commissioner as being sufficient with relation to the benefits provided by such policies.

(2) Except as provided in subdivision (3) of this subsection, the minimum standards for the valuation of all individual annuity and pure endowment contracts issued on or after August 23, 1976, and for all annuities and pure endowments purchased on or after the operative date under group annuity and pure endowment contracts shall be the commissioner's reserve valuation method defined in subsection (e) of this section and the following tables and interest rates:

a. For individual annuity and pure endowment contracts issued on or after August 23, 1976 and prior to July 30, 1979, excluding any disability and accidental death benefits in such contracts, the 1971 individual annuity mortality table, or any modification of this table approved by the commissioner, and six percent interest for single premium immediate annuity contracts and four percent interest for all other individual annuity and pure endowment contracts;

b. For individual single premium immediate annuity contracts issued on or after July 30, 1979, excluding any disability and accidental death benefits in such contracts, the 1971 individual annuity mortality table or any individual annuity mortality table, adopted after 1980 by the National Association of Insurance Commissioners, that is approved by regulation promulgated by the commissioner for use in determining the minimum standard of valuation for such contracts, or any modification of these tables approved by the commissioner, and seven and one-half percent interest;

c. For individual annuity and pure endowment contracts issued on or after July 30, 1979, other than single premium immediate annuity contracts, excluding any disability and accidental death benefits in such contracts, the 1971 individual annuity mortality table or any individual annuity mortality table, adopted after 1980 by the National Association of Insurance Commissioners, that is approved by regulation promulgated by the commissioner for use in determining the minimum standard of valuation for such contracts, or any modification of these tables approved by the commissioner, and five and one-half percent interest for single premium deferred annuity and pure endowment contracts and four and one-half percent interest for all other such individual annuity and pure endowment contracts;

d. For all annuities and pure endowments purchased on or after August 23, 1976 and prior to July 30, 1979 under group annuity and pure endowment contracts, excluding any disability and accidental death benefits purchased under such contracts, the 1971 group annuity mortality table, or any modification of this table approved by the commissioner, and six percent interest;

e. For all annuities and pure endowments purchased on or after July 30, 1979 under group annuity and pure endowment contracts, excluding any disability and accidental death benefits purchased under such contracts, the 1971 group annuity mortality table or any group annuity mortality table, adopted after 1980 by the National Association of Insurance Commissioners, that is approved by regulation promulgated by the commissioner for use in determining the minimum standard of valuation for such annuities and pure endowments, or any modification of these tables approved by the commissioner, and seven and one-half percent interest.

After August 23, 1976, any insurer may file with the commissioner a written notice of its election to comply with the provisions of this subdivision after a specified date but before January 1, 1980, which shall be the operative date of this subdivision for such insurer; provided, that an insurer may elect a different operative date for individual annuity and pure endowment contracts. If an insurer makes no such election, the operative date of this subdivision for such insurer shall be January 1, 1980.

(3) a. The interest rates used in determining the minimum standard for the valuation of:

1. all life insurance policies issued in a particular calendar year, on or after the operative date of subsection (j) of the standard nonforfeiture law for life insurance;

2. all individual annuity and pure endowment contracts issued in a particular calendar year on or after January 1, 1982;

3. all annuities and pure endowments purchased in a particular calendar year on or after January 1, 1982 under group annuity and pure endowment contracts; and

4. the net increase, if any, in a particular calendar year after January 1, 1982, in amounts held under guaranteed interest contracts; shall be the calendar year statutory valuation interest rates as defined in this subdivision.

b. 1. The calendar year statutory valuation interest rates, I, shall be determined as follows and the results rounded to the nearest one-quarter of one percent:

(i) For life insurance,

$$I = .03 + W (R_1 - .03) + W/2 (R_2 - .09);$$

(ii) For single premium immediate annuities and for annuity benefits involving life contingencies arising from other annuities with cash settlement options and from guaranteed interest contracts with cash settlement options,

$$I = .03 + W (R - .03),$$

where R_1 is the lesser of R and .09, R_2 is the greater of R and .09, R is the reference interest rate defined in this subdivision, and W is the weighting factor defined in this subdivision;

(iii) For other annuities with cash settlement options and guaranteed interest contracts with cash settlement options, valued on an issue year basis, except as stated in item (ii) of this paragraph, the formula for life insurance stated in item (i) of this paragraph shall apply to annuities and guaranteed interest contracts with guarantee durations in excess of 10 years and the formula for single premium immediate annuities stated in item (ii) of this paragraph shall apply to annuities and guaranteed interest contracts with guarantee duration of 10 years or less;

(iv) For other annuities with no cash settlement options and for guaranteed interest contracts with no cash settlement options, the formula for single premium immediate annuities stated in item (ii) of this paragraph shall apply;

(v) For other annuities with cash settlement options and guaranteed interest contracts with cash settlement options, valued on a change in fund basis, the formula for single premium immediate annuities stated in item (ii) of this paragraph shall apply.

2. However, if the calendar year statutory valuation interest rate for any life insurance policies issued in any calendar year determined without reference to this sentence differs from the corresponding actual rate for similar policies issued in the immediately preceding calendar year by less than one-half of one percent, the calendar year statutory

valuation interest rate for such life insurance policies shall be equal to the corresponding actual rate for the immediately preceding calendar year. For purposes of applying the immediately preceding sentence, the calendar year statutory valuation interest rate for life insurance policies issued in a calendar year shall be determined for 1980 (using the reference interest rate defined for 1979) and shall be determined for each subsequent calendar year regardless of when subsection (j) of the standard nonforfeiture law for life insurance becomes operative.

c. The weighting factors referred to in the formulas stated in paragraph b. of this subsection are given in the following tables:

1. Weighting Factors for Life Insurance

Guarantee Duration (Years)	Weighting Factors
10 or less	.50
More than 10, but not more than 20	.45
More than 20	.35

For life insurance, the guarantee duration is the maximum number of years the life insurance can remain in force on a basis guaranteed in the policy or under options to convert to plans of life insurance with premium rates or nonforfeiture values or both which are guaranteed in the original policy;

2. Weighting factor for single premium immediate annuities and for annuity benefits involving life contingencies arising from other annuities with cash settlement options and guaranteed interest contracts with cash settlement options:

.80;

3. Weighting factors for other annuities and for guaranteed interest contracts, except as stated in subparagraph 2. of this paragraph, shall be as specified in tables in items (i), (ii), and (iii) below, according to the rules and definitions in items (iv), (v) and (vi) below:

(i) For annuities and guaranteed interest contracts valued on an issue year basis:

Guarantee Duration (Years)	Weighting Factor for Plan Type		
	A	B	C
5 or less:	.80	.60	.50
More than 5, but not more than 10:	.75	.60	.50
More than 10, but not more than 20:	.65	.50	.45
More than 20:	.45	.35	.35

(ii) For annuities and guaranteed interest contracts valued on a change in fund basis, the factors shown in item (i) of this subparagraph increased by:

Plan Type		
A	B	C
.15	.25	.05

(iii) For annuities and guaranteed interest contracts valued on an issue year basis (other than those with no cash settlement options) which do not guarantee interest on considerations received more than one year after issue or purchase and for annuities and guaranteed interest contracts valued on a change in fund basis which do not guarantee interest rates on considerations received more than 12 months beyond the valuation date, the factors shown in item (i) of this subparagraph or derived in item (ii) of this subparagraph increased by:

Plan Type		
A	B	C
.05	.05	.05

(iv) For other annuities with cash settlement options and guaranteed interest contracts with cash settlement options, the guarantee duration is the number of years for which the contract guarantees interest rates in excess of the calendar year statutory valuation interest rate for life insurance policies with guarantee duration in excess of 20 years. For other annuities with no cash settlement options and for guaranteed interest contracts with no cash settlement options, the guarantee duration is the number of years from the date of issue or date of purchase to the date annuity benefits are scheduled to commence.

(v) Plan type as used in the above tables is defined as follows:

Plan Type A: At any time policyholder may withdraw funds only (1) with an adjustment to reflect changes in interest rates or asset values since receipt of the funds by the insurer, or (2) without such adjustment but in installments over five years or more, or (3) as an immediate life annuity or (4) no withdrawal permitted.

Plan Type B: Before expiration of the interest rate guarantee, policyholder may withdraw funds only (1) with an adjustment to reflect changes in interest rates or asset values since receipt of the funds by the insurer, or (2) without such adjustment but in installments over five years or more or (3) no withdrawal permitted. At the end of interest rate guarantee, funds may be withdrawn without such adjustment in a single sum or installments over less than five years.

Plan Type C: Policyholder may withdraw funds before expiration of interest rate guarantee in a single sum or installments over less than five years either (1) without adjustment to reflect changes in interest rates or asset values since receipt of the funds by the insurer or (2) subject only to a fixed surrender charge stipulated in the contract as a percentage of the fund.

(vi) An insurer may elect to value guaranteed interest contracts with cash settlement options and annuities with cash settlement options on either an issue year basis or on a change in fund basis. Guaranteed interest contracts with no cash settlement options and other annuities with no cash settlement options must be valued on an issue year basis.

As used in this subdivision, an issue year basis of valuation refers to a valuation basis under which the interest rate used to determine the minimum valuation standard for the entire duration of the annuity or guaranteed interest contract is the calendar year valuation interest rate for the year of issue or year of purchase of the annuity or guaranteed interest contract, and the change in fund basis of valuation refers to a valuation basis under which the interest rate used to determine the minimum valuation standard applicable to each change in the fund held under the annuity or guaranteed interest contract is the calendar year valuation interest rate for the year of the change in the fund.

d. The reference interest rate referred to in paragraph b. of this subdivision shall be defined as follows:

1. For all life insurance, the lesser of the average over a period of 36 months and the average over a period of 12 months, ending on June 30 of the calendar year next preceding the year of issue, of Moody's Corporate Bond Yield Average — Monthly Average Corporates, as published by Moody's Investors Service, Inc.

2. For single premium immediate annuities and for annuity benefits involving life contingencies arising from other annuities with cash settlement options and guaranteed interest contracts with cash settlement options, the average over a period of 12 months, ending on June 30 of the calendar year of issue or year of purchase, of Moody's Corporate Bond Yield Average — Monthly Average Corporates, as published by Moody's Investors Service, Inc.

3. For other annuities with cash settlement options and guaranteed interest contracts with cash settlement options, valued on a year of issue basis, except as stated in subparagraph 2. of this paragraph, with guarantee duration in excess of 10 years, the lesser of the average over a period of 36 months and the average over a period of 12 months, ending on June 30 of the calendar year of issue or purchase, of Moody's Corporate Bond Yield Average — Monthly Average Corporates as published by Moody's Investors Service, Inc.

4. For other annuities with cash settlement options and guaranteed interest contracts with cash settlement options, valued on a year of

issue basis, except as stated in subparagraph 2. of this paragraph, with guarantee duration of 10 years or less, the average over a period of 12 months, ending on June 30 of the calendar year of issue or purchase, of Moody's Corporate Bond Yield Average — Monthly Average Corporates as published by Moody's Investors Service, Inc.

5. For other annuities with no cash settlement options and for guaranteed interest contracts with no cash settlement options, the average over a period of 12 months, ending on June 30 of the calendar year of issue or purchase, of Moody's Corporate Bond Yield Average — Monthly Average Corporates, as published by Moody's Investors Service, Inc.

6. For other annuities with cash settlement options and guaranteed interest contracts with cash settlement options, valued on a change in fund basis, except as stated in subparagraph 2. of this paragraph, the average over a period of 12 months, ending on June 30 of the calendar year of the change in the fund, of Moody's Corporate Bond Yield Average — Monthly Average Corporates as published by Moody's Investors Service, Inc.

e. In the event that Moody's Corporate Bond Yield Average — Monthly Average Corporates is no longer published by Moody's Investors Service, Inc. or in the event that the National Association of Insurance Commissioners determines that Moody's Corporate Bond Yield Average — Monthly Average Corporates, as published by Moody's Investors Service, Inc., is no longer appropriate for the determination of the reference interest rate, then an alternative method for determination of the reference interest rate, which is adopted by the National Association of Insurance Commissioners and approved by regulation promulgated by the commissioner, may be substituted.

(e)(1) Except as otherwise provided in subdivisions (3) and (4) of this subsection and in subsection (i) of this section, reserves, according to the commissioner's reserve valuation method, or reserves for the life insurance and endowment benefits of policies providing for a uniform amount of insurance and requiring the payment of uniform premiums, shall be the excess, if any, of the present value, at the date of valuation, of such future guaranteed benefits provided for by such policies over the then present value of any future modified net premiums therefor. The modified net premiums for any such policy shall be such uniform percentage of the respective contract premiums for such benefits, excluding extra premiums on a substandard policy, that the present value at the date of issue of the policy, of all such modified net premiums shall be equal to the sum of the then present value of such benefits provided for by the policy and the excess of paragraph a. over paragraph b. of this subdivision as follows:

a. A net level annual premium equal to the present value, at the date of issue, of such benefits provided for after the first policy year divided by the present value, at the date of issue, of an annuity of one percent per annum payable on the first and each subsequent anniversary of such policy on which a premium falls due; provided, however, that such net level annual premium shall not exceed the net level annual premium on the 19-year premium whole life plan for insurance of the same amount at an age one year higher than the age at issue of such policy; and

    b. A net one-year term premium for such benefits provided for in the first policy year;

provided, that for any life insurance policy issued on or after January 1, 1985 for which the contract premium in the first policy year exceeds that of the second year and for which no comparable additional benefit is provided in the first year for such excess and which provides an endowment benefit or a cash surrender value or a combination thereof in an amount greater than such excess premium, the reserve according to the commissioner's reserve valuation method as of any policy anniversary occurring on or before the assumed ending date defined herein as the first policy anniversary on which the sum of any endowment benefit and any cash surrender value then available is greater than such excess premium shall, except as otherwise provided in subsection (i) of this section, be the greater of the reserve as of such policy anniversary calculated as described in the preceding paragraph and the reserve as of such policy anniversary calculated as described in that paragraph, but with (i) the value defined in subparagraph a. of that paragraph being reduced by 15 percent of the amount of such excess first year premium, (ii) all present values of benefits and premiums being determined without reference to premiums or benefits provided for by the policy after the assumed ending date, (iii) the policy being assumed to mature on such date as an endowment and (iv) the cash surrender value provided on such date being considered as an endowment benefit. In making the above comparison the mortality and interest bases stated in subsection (d) of this section, shall be used.

    (2) Reserves according to the commissioner's reserve valuation method for:

    a. Life insurance policies providing for a varying amount of insurance or requiring the payment of varying premiums;

    b. Group annuity and pure endowment contracts purchased under a retirement plan or a plan of deferred compensation, established or maintained by an employer (including a partnership or sole proprietorship) or by an employee organization, or by both, other than a plan providing individual retirement accounts or individual retirement annuities under section 408 of the Internal Revenue Code, as now or hereafter amended;

    c. Disability and accidental death benefits in all policies and contracts; and

    d. All other benefits, except life insurance and endowment benefits in life insurance policies and benefits provided by all other annuity and pure endowment contracts

shall be calculated by a method consistent with the principles of subdivision (1) of this subsection.

(3) Subdivision (4) of this subsection shall apply to all annuity and pure endowment contracts other than group annuity and pure endowment contracts purchased under a retirement plan or plan of deferred compensation, established or maintained by an employer (including a partnership or sole proprietorship) or by an employee organization, or by both, other than a plan providing individual retirement accounts or individual retirement annuities under section 408 of the Internal Revenue Code, as now or hereafter amended.

(4) Reserves, according to the commissioner's annuity reserves method for benefits under annuity or pure endowment contracts, excluding any disability and accidental death benefits in such contracts, shall be the greatest of the respective excesses of the present values at the date of valuation, of the future guaranteed benefits, including guaranteed nonforfeiture benefits, provided for by such contracts at the end of each respective contract year, over the present value, at the date of valuation, of any future valuation considerations derived from future gross considerations, required by the terms of such contract, that become payable prior to the end of such respective contract year. The future guaranteed benefits shall be determined by using the mortality table, if any, and the interest rate, or rates, specified in such contracts for determining guaranteed benefits. The valuation considerations are the portions of the respective gross considerations applied under the terms of such contracts to determine nonforfeiture values.

(f) In no event shall an insurer's aggregate reserves for all life insurance policies, excluding disability and accidental death benefits, issued on or after January 1, 1972, be less than the aggregate reserves calculated in accordance with the methods set forth in subsections (e), (i) and (j) of this section and the mortality table, or tables, and rate, or rates, of interest used in calculating nonforfeiture benefits for such policies.

(g)(1) Reserves for all policies and contracts issued prior to January 1, 1972 may be calculated, at the option of the insurer, according to any standards which produce greater aggregate reserves for all such policies and contracts than the minimum reserves required by the laws in effect immediately prior to such date; and

(2) For any category of policies, contracts or benefits specified in subsection (d) of this section issued on or after January 1, 1972, reserves may be calculated, at the option of the insurer, according to any standard, or standards, which produce greater aggregate reserves for such category than those calculated according to the minimum standard provided in this section, but the rate, or rates, of interest used for such policies and contracts, other than annuity and pure endowment contracts, shall not be higher than the corresponding rate, or rates, of interest used in calculating any nonforfeiture benefits provided for therein.

(h) An insurer which at any time had adopted any standard of valuation producing greater aggregate reserves than those calculated according to the minimum standard provided in this section may, with written notice thereof to the commissioner, adopt any lower standard of valuation, but not lower than the minimum provided in this section.

(i) If in any contract year the gross premium charged by any life insurer on any policy or contract issued on or after January 1, 1972 is less than the valuation net premium for the policy or contract calculated by the method used in calculating the reserve thereon, but using the minimum valuation standards of mortality and rate of interest, the minimum reserve required for such policy or contract shall be the greater of either the reserve calculated according to the mortality table, rate of interest and method actually used for such policy or contract, or the reserve calculated by the method actually used for such policy or contract but using the minimum valuation standards of mortality and rate of interest and replacing the valuation net premium by the actual gross premium in each contract year for which the valuation net premium exceeds the actual gross premium. The minimum valuation standards of mortality and rate of interest referred to in this subsection are those standards stated in subsections (c) and (d) of this section.

Provided that for any life insurance policy issued on or after January 1, 1985 for which the gross premium in the first policy year exceeds that of the second year and for which no comparable additional benefit is provided in the first year for such excess and which provides an endowment benefit or a cash surrender value or a combination thereof in an amount greater than such excess premium, the foregoing provisions of this subsection shall be applied as if the method actually used in calculating the reserve for such policy were the method described in subdivisions (1) and (2) of subsection (e) of this section, ignoring the second paragraph of subdivision (1) of subsection (e) of this section. The minimum reserve at each policy anniversary of such policy shall be the greater of the minimum reserve calculated in accordance with subsection (e) of this section, including the second paragraph of subdivision (1) of subsection (e) of this section, and the minimum reserve calculated in accordance with this subsection.

(j) In the case of any plan of life insurance which provides for future premium determination, the amounts of which are to be determined by the insurer based on then estimates of future experience, or in the case of any plan of life insurance or annuity which is of such a nature that the minimum reserves cannot be determined by the methods described in subsections (e) and (i) of this section, the reserves which are held under any such plan must:

(1) Be appropriate in relation to the benefits and the pattern of premiums for that plan, and

(2) Be computed by a method which is consistent with the principles of this standard valuation law, as determined by regulations promulgated by

the commissioner. (Acts 1971, No. 407, p. 707, § 744; Acts 1976, No. 370, p. 459, § 2; Acts 1979, No. 79-661, p. 1142, § 2; Acts 1981, No. 81-783, p. 1347, § 2.)

U.S. Code. — For § 408 of the Internal Revenue Code, see 26 U.S.C. § 408.

CHAPTER 37.

ASSETS.

Sec.
27-37-1. Assets — Generally.
27-37-2. Same — Exclusions.
27-37-3. Assets and liabilities as deductions.
27-37-4. Disallowance of assets or credits for deception.
27-37-5. Valuation — Bonds and other evidences of debt.
27-37-6. Same — Other securities; preferred or guaranteed stocks or shares.

Sec.
27-37-7. Same — Real property and personal property acquired pursuant to chattel mortgages.
27-37-8. Same — Funeral supplies and equipment.
27-37-9. Same — Purchase money mortgages.

§ 27-37-1. Assets — Generally.

In any determination of the financial condition of an insurer, there shall be allowed as assets only such assets as are owned by the insurer and which consist of:

(1) Cash in the possession of the insurer or in transit under its control, and including the true balance of any deposit in a solvent bank or trust company;

(2) Investments, securities, properties and loans acquired, or held, in accordance with this title and in connection therewith the following items:

a. Interest due or accrued on any bond or evidence of indebtedness which is not in default and which is not valued on a basis including accrued interest;

b. Declared and unpaid dividends on stock and shares, unless such amount has otherwise been allowed as an asset;

c. Interest due or accrued upon a collateral loan in an amount not to exceed one year's interest thereon;

d. Interest due or accrued on deposits in solvent banks and trust companies, and interest due or accrued on other assets, if such interest is in the judgment of the commissioner a collectible asset;

e. Interest due or accrued on a mortgage loan, in an amount not exceeding in any event the amount, if any, of the excess of the value of the property less delinquent taxes thereon over the unpaid principal; but in no event shall interest accrued for a period in excess of 18 months be allowed as an asset;

f. Rent due or accrued on real property if such rent is not in arrears for more than three months and rent more than three months in arrears if the payment of such rent is adequately secured by property held in the name of the tenant and conveyed to the insurer as collateral; and

g. The unaccrued portion of taxes paid prior to the due date on real property;

(3) Premium notes, policy loans and other policy assets and liens on policies and certificates of life insurance and annuity contracts, and accrued interest thereon, in an amount not exceeding the legal reserve and other policy liabilities carried on each individual policy;

(4) The net amount of uncollected and deferred premiums and annuity considerations in the case of a life insurer;

(5) Premiums in the course of collection, other than for life insurance, not more than three months past due, less commissions payable thereon. The foregoing limitation shall not apply to premiums payable, directly or indirectly, by the United States government or by any of its instrumentalities;

(6) Installment premiums other than life insurance premiums to the extent of the unearned premium reserve carried on the policy to which premiums apply;

(7) Notes and like written obligations not past due taken for premiums, other than life insurance premiums, on policies permitted to be issued on such basis, to the extent of the unearned premium reserves carried thereon;

(8) The full amount of reinsurance recoverable by a ceding insurer from a solvent reinsurer and which reinsurance is authorized under section 27-5-12;

(9) Amounts receivable by an assuming insurer representing funds withheld by a solvent ceding insurer under a reinsurance treaty;

(10) Deposits or equities recoverable from underwriting associations, syndicates and reinsurance funds or from any suspended banking institution, to the extent deemed by the commissioner available for the payment of losses and claims and at values to be determined by him;

(11) Electronic and mechanical machines constituting a data processing and accounting system if the cost of such system is at least $10,000.00, which costs shall be amortized in full over a period not to exceed 10 calendar years;

(12) All assets, whether or not consistent with the provisions of this section, as may be allowed pursuant to the annual statement form approved by the commissioner for the kinds of insurance to be reported upon therein; and

(13) Other assets, not inconsistent with the provisions of this section, deemed by the commissioner to be available for the payment of losses and claims, at values to be determined by him. (Acts 1965, No. 572, p. 1056; Acts 1971, No. 407, p. 707, § 745.)

§ 27-37-2. Same — Exclusions.

In addition to assets impliedly excluded by the provisions of section 27-37-1, the following expressly shall not be allowed as assets in any determination of the financial condition of an insurer:

(1) Good will, trade names and other like intangible assets;

(2) Advances to officers, directors and controlling stockholders, other than policy loans, unless the same are secured by collateral satisfactory to the commissioner, and advances to employees, agents and other persons on personal security only;

(3) Stock of such insurer owned by it, or any equity therein, or loans secured thereby or any material proportionate interest in such stock acquired, or held, through the ownership by such insurer of an interest in another firm, corporation or business unit;

(4) Furniture, fixtures, furnishings, safes, vehicles, libraries, stationery, literature and supplies, except:

a. Such personal property as is required through foreclosure of chattel mortgages under loans insured or guaranteed under provisions of the National Housing Act or any act of congress relating to veterans benefits;

b. Such as is reasonably necessary for the maintenance and operation of real estate held by it other than real estate for home office, branch office and similar purposes; and

c. In the case of title insurers, abstract plant and equipment not to exceed 50 percent of the paid-in capital stock of such title insurer; and

(5) The amount, if any, by which the aggregate book value of investments as carried in the ledger assets of the insurer exceeds the aggregate value thereof, as determined under this title. (Acts 1971, No. 407, p. 707, § 747.)

§ 27-37-3. Assets and liabilities as deductions.

Assets may be allowed as deductions from corresponding liabilities, and liabilities may be charged as deductions from assets and deductions from assets may be charged as liabilities in accordance with the form of an annual statement applicable to the insurer as prescribed by the commissioner or otherwise in his discretion. (Acts 1971, No. 407, p. 707, § 746.)

§ 27-37-4. Disallowance of assets or credits for deception.

(a) The commissioner shall disallow as an asset or as a credit against liabilities any reinsurance found by him after a hearing thereon to have been arranged for on a temporary basis for the purpose principally of deception as to the ceding insurer's financial condition as at the date of any financial statement of the insurer. Reinsurance of any substantial part of the insurer's outstanding risks contracted for in fact within 90 days prior to the date of any such financial statement and cancelled in fact within 90 days after the date of such statement shall prima facie be deemed to have been arranged for the purpose of deception within the intent of this section.

(b) The commissioner shall disallow as an asset any deposit, funds or other assets of the insurer found by him after a hearing thereon:

(1) Not to be in good faith the property of the insurer;

(2) Not freely subject to withdrawal or liquidation by the insurer at any time for the payment or discharge of claims or other obligations arising under its policies; and

(3) To be resulting from arrangements made principally for the purpose of deception as to the insurer's financial condition as at the date of any financial statement of the insurer.

(c) No such disallowance of assets or credits shall be valid unless made by the commissioner after a hearing of which notice was given the insurer within six months after the date the financial statement of the insurer as to which such deception is claimed was filed with the commissioner.

(d) The commissioner may suspend or revoke the certificate of authority of any insurer which has knowingly been a party to any such deception or attempt thereat. (Acts 1971, No. 407, p. 707, § 748.)

§ 27-37-5. Valuation — Bonds and other evidences of debt.

(a) All bonds or other evidences of debt having a fixed term and rate of interest held by an insurer shall, if amply secured and not in default as to principal or interest, be valued as follows:

(1) If purchased at par, at the par value;

(2) If purchased above or below par, on the basis of the purchase price adjusted so as to bring the value to par at maturity and so as to yield in the meantime the effective rate of interest at which the purchase was made or, in lieu of such method, according to such accepted method of valuation as is approved by the commissioner;

(3) Purchase price shall in no case be taken at a higher figure than the actual market value at the time of purchase, plus actual brokerage, transfer, postage or express charges paid in the acquisition of such securities; and

(4) Unless otherwise provided by valuation established or approved by the commissioner, no such security shall be carried at above the call price for the entire issue during any period within which the security may be so called.

(b) The commissioner shall have full discretion in determining the method of calculating values according to the rules set forth in this section, but no such method or valuation shall be inconsistent with any applicable valuation or method currently accepted and in use among insurers in general. (Acts 1971, No. 407, p. 707, § 749.)

§ 27-37-6. Same — Other securities; preferred or guaranteed stocks or shares.

(a) Securities, other than those referred to in section 27-37-5, held by an insurer shall be valued, in the discretion of the commissioner, at their market value, or at their appraised value or at prices determined by him as representing their fair market value.

(b) Preferred or guaranteed stocks or shares, while paying full dividends, may be carried at a fixed value in lieu of market value, at the discretion of the commissioner and in accordance with such method of valuation as he may approve.

(c) No valuation under this section shall be inconsistent with any applicable valuation or method currently accepted and in use among insurers in general. (Acts 1971, No. 407, p. 707, § 750.)

§ 27-37-7. Same — Real property and personal property acquired pursuant to chattel mortgages.

(a) Real property acquired pursuant to a mortgage loan or contract for sale, in the absence of a recent appraisal deemed by the commissioner to be reliable, shall not be valued at an amount greater than the unpaid principal of the defaulted loan or contract at the date of such acquisition, together with any taxes and expenses paid or incurred in connection with such acquisition, and the cost of improvements thereafter made by the insurer and any amounts thereafter paid by the insurer on assessments levied for improvements in connection with the property.

(b) Other real property held by an insurer shall not be valued at an amount in excess of fair value as determined by recent appraisal. If valuation is based on an appraisal more than three years old, the commissioner may at his discretion call for and require a new appraisal in order to determine fair value.

(c) Personal property acquired pursuant to chattel mortgages shall not be valued at an amount greater than the unpaid balance of principal on the defaulted loan at the date of acquisition, together with taxes and expenses incurred in connection with such acquisition or the fair value of such property, whichever amount is the lesser. (Acts 1971, No. 407, p. 707, § 751.)

§ 27-37-8. Same — Funeral supplies and equipment.

Funeral supply inventories owned by the insurer shall be valued at an amount not exceeding cost to the insurer or market value, whichever is lower. Funeral equipment owned by the insurer shall be valued at an amount not in excess of cost to the insurer reduced by depreciation at the rate of not less than 18 percent per annum from date of acquisition of such equipment. (Acts 1971, No. 407, p. 707, § 752.)

§ 27-37-9. Same — Purchase money mortgages.

Purchase money mortgages on real property shall be valued in an amount not exceeding the acquisition cost of the real property covered thereby or the unpaid balance of the debt secured by such mortgage, whichever is less. (Acts 1971, No. 407, p. 707, § 753.)

CHAPTER 38.

SEPARATE ACCOUNTS AND VARIABLE ANNUITIES.

Sec.
27-38-1. Establishment of separate accounts by life insurers to provide for life insurance or annuities and benefits incidental thereto.
27-38-2. Variable contracts — Statement of procedures for determining benefits; death benefit provision.

Sec.
27-38-3. Same — Licensing of insurer.
27-38-4. Same — Rules and regulations.
27-38-5. Reserve liability for variable contracts.
27-38-6. Applicability of title.

§ 27-38-1. Establishment of separate accounts by life insurers to provide for life insurance or annuities and benefits incidental thereto.

A life insurer organized under the laws of this state may, by or pursuant to a resolution of its board of directors, establish one or more separate accounts and may allocate thereto amounts, including without limitation proceeds applied under optional modes of settlement or under dividend options, to provide for life insurance or annuities, and benefits incidental thereto, payable in fixed or variable amounts or both, subject to the following:

(1) The income, gains and losses, realized or unrealized, from assets allocated to a separate account shall be credited to, or charged against, the account, without regard to other income, gains or losses of the insurer;

(2) Except as provided in this section, amounts allocated to any separate account, and accumulations thereon, may be invested and reinvested without regard to any requirements or limitations prescribed by the laws of this state governing the investments of life insurers; provided, however, that to the extent that the insurer's reserve liability with regard to:

a. Benefits guaranteed as to dollar amount and duration; and

b. Funds guaranteed as to principal amount or stated rate of interest are maintained in any separate account, a portion of the assets of such separate account at least equal to such reserve liability shall be, except as the commissioner may otherwise approve, invested in accordance with the laws of this state governing the investments of life insurers.

The investments in such separate account or accounts shall not be taken into account in applying the investment limitations otherwise applicable to the investments of the insurer;

(3) With respect to 75 percent of the market value of the total assets in a separate account, no insurer shall purchase or otherwise acquire the securities of any issuer, other than securities issued or guaranteed as to principal or interest by the United States, if immediately after such purchase or acquisition the market value of such investment, together with prior investments of such separate account in such security taken at market, would exceed 10 percent of the market value of the assets of said separate account; provided, however, that the commissioner may waive such limitation if, in his opinion, such waiver will not render the operation

535

of such separate account hazardous to the public or the policyholders in this state;

(4) Unless otherwise approved by the commissioner, no insurer shall purchase or otherwise acquire for its separate accounts:

a. Any securities of any subsidiary of the insurer; or

b. More than 10 percent of the total issued and outstanding voting securities of any other single issuer; provided, however, that the foregoing shall not apply with respect to securities held in separate accounts, the voting rights in which are exercisable only in accordance with instructions from persons having interests in such accounts;

(5) The limitations provided in subdivisions (3) and (4) of this section shall not apply to the investment with respect to a separate account in the securities of an investment company registered under the Investment Company Act of 1940, provided that the investments of such investment company comply in substance with subdivisions (3) and (4) of this section.

(6) Unless otherwise approved by the commissioner, assets allocated to a separate account shall be valued at their market value on the date of valuation or, if there is no readily available market, then as provided under the terms of the contract, or the rules or other written agreement applicable to such separate account; provided, however, that, unless otherwise approved by the commissioner, the portion of the assets of such separate account equal to the insurer's reserve liability with regard to the guaranteed benefits and funds referred to in paragraphs (2) a and (2) b of this section, if any, shall be valued in accordance with the rules otherwise applicable to the insurer's assets;

(7) Amounts allocated to a separate account in the exercise of the power granted by this section shall be owned by the insurer, and the insurer shall not be, nor hold itself out to be, a trustee with respect to such amounts. That portion of the assets of any such separate account equal to the reserves and other contract liabilities with respect to such account shall not be chargeable with liabilities arising out of any other business the insurer may conduct;

(8) To the extent such insurer deems it necessary to comply with any applicable federal or state laws, such insurer, with respect to any separate account, including, without limitation, any separate account which is a management investment company or a unit investment trust, may provide for persons having an interest therein appropriate voting and other rights and special procedures for the conduct of the business of such account, including, without limitation, special rights and procedures relating to investment policy, investment advisory services, selection of independent public accountants and the selection of a committee, the members of which need not be otherwise affiliated with such insurer, to manage the business of such account; and

(9) No sale, exchange or other transfer of assets may be made by an insurer between any of its separate accounts or between any other investment account and one or more of its separate accounts unless, in case

of a transfer into a separate account, such transfer is made solely to establish the account or to support the operation of the contracts with respect to the separate account to which the transfer is made and unless such transfer, whether into or from a separate account, is made:

a. By a transfer of cash; or

b. By a transfer of securities having a readily determinable market value, provided that such transfer of securities is approved by the commissioner.

The commissioner may approve other transfers among such accounts if, in his opinion, such transfers would not be inequitable. (Acts 1969, No. 565, p. 1045; Acts 1971, No. 407, p. 707, § 754; Acts 1985, 2nd Ex. Sess., No. 85-993, § 1.)

The 1985 amendment, effective September 30, 1985, inserted "including without limitation proceeds applied under optional modes of settlement or under dividend options" and "life insurance or" in the introductory language.

§ 27-38-2. Variable contracts — Statement of procedures for determining benefits; death benefit provision.

(a) Any variable contract providing benefits payable in variable amounts delivered, or issued for delivery, in this state shall contain a statement of the essential features of the procedures to be followed by the insurer in determining the dollar amount of such variable benefits. Any such contract, including a group contract, and any certificate in evidence of variable benefits issued thereunder shall state that such dollar amount will vary to reflect investment experience and shall contain on its first page a statement to the effect that the benefits thereunder are on a variable basis.

(b) Variable annuity contracts delivered, or issued for delivery, in this state may include as an incidental benefit provision for payment on death during the deferred period of an amount not in excess of the greater of the sum of the premiums or stipulated payments paid under the contract or the value of the contract at time of death. Any such provision shall not be deemed to be life insurance and therefore shall not be subject to the provisions of this title governing life insurance contracts. A provision for any other benefit on death during the deferred period shall be subject to this title. (Acts 1969, No. 565, p. 1045; Acts 1971, No. 407, p. 707, § 755.)

§ 27-38-3. Same — Licensing of insurer.

(a) No insurer shall deliver, or issue for delivery, within this state variable contracts unless it is licensed to do a life insurance or annuity business in this state and the commissioner is satisfied that its condition or method of operation in connection with the issuance of such contracts will not render its operation hazardous to the public or its policyholders in this state. In this connection, the commissioner shall consider among other things:

(1) The history and financial condition of the insurer;

(2) The character, responsibility and fitness of the officers and directors of the insurer; and

(3) The law and regulation under which the insurer is authorized in the state of domicile to issue variable contracts.

(b) If the company is a subsidiary of an admitted life insurer or affiliated with such insurer through common management or ownership, it may be deemed to have met the provisions of the section if either it or the parent or affiliated company meets the requirements of this section. (Acts 1971, No. 407, p. 707, § 756.)

§ 27-38-4. Same — Rules and regulations.

Notwithstanding any other provision of law, the commissioner shall have sole authority to regulate the issuance and sale of variable contracts and the licensing of persons selling such contracts and to issue reasonable rules and regulations as may be appropriate to carry out the purposes and provisions of this chapter. (Acts 1969, No. 565, p. 1045; Acts 1971, No. 407, p. 707, § 757.)

§ 27-38-5. Reserve liability for variable contracts.

The reserve liability for variable contracts shall be established in accordance with actuarial procedures that recognize the variable nature of the benefits provided and any mortality guarantees. (Acts 1971, No. 407, p. 707, § 758; Acts 1985, 2nd Ex. Sess., No. 85-993, § 2.)

The 1985 amendment, effective September 30, 1985, substituted "contracts" for "annuities."

§ 27-38-6. Applicability of title.

Except for sections 27-15-16, 27-15-17, 27-15-22, 27-15-23 and 27-15-28.1 of this title, in the case of a variable annuity contract, and sections 27-15-2, 27-15-3, 27-15-8.1, 27-15-9, 27-15-10, 27-15-11 and 27-15-28 of this title, in the case of a variable life insurance policy, and except as otherwise provided in this chapter, all pertinent provisions of this title shall apply to separate accounts and contracts relating thereto. Any individual variable life insurance contract, delivered or issued for delivery in this state shall contain grace, reinstatement and nonforfeiture provisions appropriate to such a contract. (Acts 1969, No. 565, p. 1045; Acts 1971, No. 407, p. 707, § 759; Acts 1985, 2nd Ex. Sess., No. 85-993, § 3.)

The 1985 amendment, effective September 30, 1985, substituted the language beginning "sections 27-15-16" and ending "in the case of a variable life insurance policy" for "sections 27-38-1 through 27-38-5" near the beginning of the first sentence and added the second sentence.

CHAPTER 39.

AUTOMOBILE CLUBS AND ASSOCIATIONS.

Sec.
27-39-1. Definitions.
27-39-2. Applicability of chapter.
27-39-3. Incorporation and license require-
          ments.
27-39-4. Clubs and associations to be under
          authority, etc., of commissioner.
27-39-5. Powers of commissioner.

Sec.
27-39-6. Application for certificate of author-
          ity; issuance thereof.
27-39-7. Licensing of agents and representa-
          tives; control over same by com-
          missioner.
27-39-8. Penalty for violation of chapter.

§ 27-39-1. Definitions.

For the purposes of this chapter, the following terms shall have the meanings respectively ascribed to them by this section:

(1) AUTOMOBILE CLUB OR ASSOCIATION. A legal entity which, in consideration of dues, assessments or periodic payments of money, promises its members or subscribers to assist them in matters relating to the ownership, operation, use or maintenance of a motor vehicle; provided, however, that the definition of automobile clubs shall not include persons or associations or corporations which are organized and operated solely for the purpose of conducting, sponsoring or sanctioning motor vehicle races, exhibitions or contests upon race tracks or upon race courses established and marked as such for the duration of such particular event.

(2) COMMISSIONER. The commissioner of insurance of the state of Alabama. (Acts 1971, No. 407, p. 707, § 798.)

§ 27-39-2. Applicability of chapter.

This chapter shall be deemed and held exclusive authority for the organization and operation of automobile clubs and associations within this state, and such clubs and associations shall not be subject to any other laws respecting insurance companies of any class, kind or character except as to the conduct of hearings by the commissioner and appeals therefrom; provided, however, that this chapter shall not affect the validity of any membership certificate of any automobile club or association issued and outstanding prior to January 1, 1972. Notwithstanding the aforementioned, nothing in this chapter shall be construed as authority for a licensed automobile club or association to provide or furnish insurance coverage unless such clubs shall have complied with all the laws and regulations required of insurance companies authorized to do business in this state. (Acts 1971, No. 407, p. 707, § 805.)

§ 27-39-3. Incorporation and license requirements.

No automobile club or association shall do, or offer to do, business in the state unless the same shall be organized as a domestic or foreign corporation and shall be licensed by the commissioner. (Acts 1971, No. 407, p. 707, § 799.)

Collateral references. — 7 Am. Jur. 2d,
Automobiles & Highway Traffic, § 48.

§ 27-39-4. Clubs and associations to be under authority, etc., of commissioner.

All automobile clubs and associations now organized and/or operating in the state of Alabama and all automobile clubs and associations hereafter organized and/or operating in the state of Alabama shall be under the authority, supervision and control of the commissioner. (Acts 1971, No. 407, p. 707, § 801.)

§ 27-39-5. Powers of commissioner.

(a) The commissioner shall have full and complete authority to grant certificates of authorization to automobile clubs and associations, to revoke such certificates and to prescribe such rules and regulations as are reasonably necessary for the conduct of the business of such clubs and associations within the state and for carrying out the objects and purposes of this chapter. In determining if a certificate of authorization shall be issued, the commissioner shall take into consideration, along with all other factors, the name of the automobile club or association; and, if such name, emblem or trademark is distinctive and not likely to mislead the public as to the nature or identity of the corporation using it or interfere with the transactions of any other automobile club already doing business in the state, it shall be entitled to be approved.

(b) The commissioner shall also have the authority to conduct hearings as provided under this title. (Acts 1971, No. 407, p. 707, § 800.)

§ 27-39-6. Application for certificate of authority; issuance thereof.

(a) Within 30 days after January 1, 1972, every automobile club or association organized and/or operating in the state of Alabama shall file with the commissioner an application for a certificate of authority to continue said operations within the state, and every automobile club or association desiring to commence operations within the state shall, prior to the commencement of said operation, file application with and receive a certificate of authority from the commissioner. No certificate of authority shall be issued until the automobile club or association has paid to the commissioner $200.00 as an annual license fee, which fee shall not be returnable. Licenses shall be issued for the period beginning January 1 of each year and shall expire on the following December 31. The commissioner shall deposit all fees collected in the state treasury to the credit of the general fund.

(b) The following documents and information shall be filed with the application of all such clubs and associations:

(1) The sum of $25,000.00 in cash or securities, as approved by the commissioner and deposited in trust with the state treasurer or, in lieu thereof, a surety bond payable to the commissioner in the amount of $25,000.00 of a surety company authorized to do business in this state, conditioned upon the full compliance with this chapter and the faithful performance of the obligations of such club or association to its members. The bonds shall be approved by the commissioner and shall not be cancelled without 30 days' notice to the commissioner. If such bond is filed, any person defrauded or injured by any wrongful act, misrepresentation or failure on the part of a motor club with respect to selling or rendering of any service may maintain an action on such bond in his own name. Upon receipt of notice of the intended dissolution of such automobile club or association and upon receipt of notice of evidence satisfactory to the commissioner that all obligations of the club or association to its members and creditors have been satisfied, the state treasurer, upon written authorization from the commissioner, shall refund said money or securities and the obligations of said bond shall terminate;

(2) Appointment of an agent for service of process who shall be a resident of the state of Alabama or, in lieu thereof, the commissioner; and

(3) A copy of the proposed form of membership application, membership certificate, bylaws, contracts for service and any other material, including advertising matter, requested by the commissioner.

(c) If the commissioner shall be satisfied that the applicant is competent and trustworthy and possesses the professional ability to perform the services and that he meets all the requirements of this chapter, he shall issue to the applicant a certificate of authority to conduct the business of such automobile club or association within this state. (Acts 1971, No. 407, p. 707, § 802.)

Collateral references. — 7 Am. Jur. 2d, Automobiles & Highway Traffic, § 48.

§ 27-39-7. Licensing of agents and representatives; control over same by commissioner.

(a) Before any agent or representative shall or may represent any automobile club or association in this state, he, or she, shall first apply to the commissioner for a license, and the commissioner shall have full power and authority to issue such license upon proof satisfactory to him that such person is capable of soliciting automobile club or association memberships and is of good moral character and recommended by the club or association in behalf of which such membership solicitations are to be made; provided, however, that no such license shall be issued by the commissioner until the applicant has paid to the commissioner an annual license fee of $10.00.

(b) No employee or salesman of an automobile club shall, directly or indirectly, be licensed to solicit, negotiate or hold himself out in any manner to be an insurance agent or solicitor to effect insurance contracts unless it is in accordance with the provisions of the insurance laws.

(c) The commissioner may reject the application of any person who does not meet the requirements set out in this section and shall have the same powers with respect to the suspension, revocation, renewal and reinstatement of such licenses as are conferred with respect to insurance agents, other than life, by section 27-7-19. (Acts 1971, No. 407, p. 707, § 803.)

§ 27-39-8. Penalty for violation of chapter.

It shall be unlawful for any person, firm, association, copartnership, corporation, company or other organization to organize, operate or in any way solicit members for an automobile club or association or to offer any of the motor club services as defined in section 27-39-1 except in the manner provided in this chapter and under the rules and regulations promulgated by the commissioner. Any person, firm, association, copartnership, corporation, company or other organization violating the provisions of this chapter shall be guilty of a misdemeanor and, upon conviction, shall be punished by a fine not exceeding $500.00, or be imprisoned not exceeding six months or punished by both fine and imprisonment, in the discretion of the court. (Acts 1971, No. 407, p. 707, § 804.)

CHAPTER 40.

INSURANCE PREMIUM FINANCE COMPANIES.

Sec.
27-40-1. Definitions.
27-40-2. Exemptions from chapter.
27-40-3. Licenses — Required; fees; information to be furnished commissioner.
27-40-4. Same — Investigation and qualifications of applicant; issuance.
27-40-5. Same — Suspension or revocation.
27-40-6. Books and records.
27-40-7. Promulgation and enforcement of rules and regulations.
27-40-8. Contents and style of premium finance agreement.
27-40-9. Service charges; prepayment of obligation.
27-40-10. Delinquency and cancellation charges.
27-40-11. Procedure for cancellation of insurance contract upon default.

Sec.
27-40-12. Return of gross unearned premiums upon cancellation of contract.
27-40-13. Filing of agreement.
27-40-14. Exclusive jurisdiction of department of insurance.
27-40-15. Premium financed to be sent to insurance company; designation of agents; issuance of drafts, etc.; recovery of unearned premiums; duties with respect to cancellation.
27-40-16. Payment of rebates or inducements prohibited; purchase of premium finance agreement.
27-40-17. Notification of existence of premium finance agreement.
27-40-18. Delivery of copy of premium finance agreement to insured.

§ 27-40-1. Definitions.

For the purposes of this chapter, the following words and phrases shall have the meanings respectively ascribed to them by this section:

(1) INSURANCE PREMIUM FINANCE COMPANY. A person engaged in the business of entering into premium finance agreements.

(2) PREMIUM FINANCE AGREEMENT. An agreement by which an insured or prospective insured promises to pay to a premium finance company the amount advanced or to be advanced under the agreement to an insurer or to an insurance agent or broker in payment of premiums on an insurance contract together with a service charge, as authorized and limited by this chapter.

(3) LICENSEE. A premium finance company holding a license issued under this chapter.

(4) PERSON. An individual, partnership, association, business corporation, nonprofit corporation, common law trust, joint-stock company or any other group of individuals however organized.

(5) INSURANCE CONTRACT. The policy or contract of insurance which is the subject of premium financing under this chapter.

(6) DESIGNATED AGENT. An insurance agent or managing general agent designated by an insurance company to act on its behalf on matters pertaining to the financing of premiums on insurance contracts issued by such company. (Acts 1975, No. 1042, p. 2088, § 2; Acts 1986, No. 86-400, § 1.)

The 1986 amendment, which became effec-   § 125 of the Constitution on April 28, 1986,
tive without the governor's signature under   added subdivisions (5) and (6).

§ 27-40-2. Exemptions from chapter.

The provisions of this chapter shall not apply with respect to:

(1) Any insurance company licensed to do business in this state;

(2) Any banking or other financial institution regulated by the state, or savings and loan association, or credit union authorized to do business in this state, or any national banking institution or federal savings and loan association incorporated under the laws of the United States and located within this state;

(3) The inclusion of a charge for insurance in connection with an installment sale of a motor vehicle or boat or mobile home; or

(4) The financing of insurance premiums in this state in accordance with the provisions of this title relating to rates of insurance. (Acts 1975, No. 1042, p. 2088, § 1.)

§ 27-40-3. Licenses — Required; fees; information to be furnished commissioner.

(a) No person shall engage in the business of financing insurance premiums in this state without first having obtained a license as a premium finance company from the commissioner. Any person who shall engage in the business of financing insurance premiums in this state without first having obtained a license as provided herein shall be guilty of a misdemeanor and upon conviction shall be punished by a fine of not more than $1,000.00 or by imprisonment for not more than one year, or both.

(b) The annual license fee shall be $200.00; provided, that an insurance agency which finances its own business of less that $150,000.00 in premiums annually shall pay a fee of $50.00. The fee for said license shall be paid into the insurance department examination revolving fund and the same is hereby appropriated for that use.

(c) The person to whom the license or the renewal thereof may be issued shall file sworn answers subject to the penalties of perjury to such interrogatories as the commissioner may require. The commissioner shall have authority at any time to require the applicant fully to disclose the identity of all stockholders, partners, officers and employees and he may in his discretion refuse to issue or renew a license in the name of any firm, partnership or corporation if he is not satisfied that any officer, employee, stockholder or partner thereof who may materially influence the applicant's conduct meets the standards of this section. (Acts 1975, No. 1042, p. 2088, § 3.)

§ 27-40-4. Same — Investigation and qualifications of applicant; issuance.

(a) Upon the filing of an application and the payment of the license fee the commissioner shall make an investigation of each applicant and shall issue a license if the applicant is qualified in accordance with this section. If the commissioner does not so find, he shall, within 30 days after he has received such application, at the request of the applicant, give the applicant a full hearing.

(b) The commissioner shall issue or renew a license as may be applied for when he is satisfied that the person to be licensed:

(1) Is competent and trustworthy and intends to act in good faith in the capacity involved by the license applied for;

(2) Has a good business reputation and has had experience, training or education, so as to be qualified in the business for which the license is applied for; and

(3) If a corporation, is a corporation incorporated under the laws of this state or a foreign corporation authorized to transact business in this state. (Acts 1975, No. 1042, p. 2088, § 4.)

§ 27-40-5. Same — Suspension or revocation.

(a) The commissioner may revoke or suspend the license of any premium finance company when, and if, after complaint and investigation, it appears to the commissioner that:

(1) Any license issued to such company was obtained by fraud;

(2) There were any misrepresentations in the application for the license;

(3) The holder of such license has otherwise shown himself untrustworthy or incompetent to act as a premium finance company;

(4) Such company has violated any of the provisions of this chapter; or

(5) No license shall issue or remain in force if any principal of the licensee has been convicted of a crime involving moral turpitude.

(b) Before the commissioner shall revoke, suspend or refuse to renew the license of any premium finance company, the aggrieved person shall be entitled to a hearing in accord with administrative procedures in effect in this state or if no such administrative procedures are set out, then in the same manner as provided in section 27-2-28 et seq. In lieu of revoking or suspending the license for any of the causes enumerated in this section, after hearing as herein provided, the commissioner may subject such company to a penalty of not more than $200.00 for each offense but not more than a maximum of $5,000.00 in the event multiple violations occurred, when in his judgment he finds that the public interest would not be harmed by the continued operation of such company. The amount of any such penalty shall be paid by such company to the commissioner.

(c) If the commissioner refuses to issue to any person a license as a premium finance company, or he revokes, suspends or refuses to renew the license of any premium finance company or he imposes a penalty on such company, after a hearing as provided under subsection (b), the applicant or licensee may appeal from such refusal to issue a license or from such adjudication in accordance with section 27-2-32 et seq. (Acts 1975, No. 1042, p. 2088, § 5.)

§ 27-40-6. Books and records.

(a) Every licensee shall maintain records of its premium finance transactions and the said records shall be open to examination and investigation by the commissioner. The commissioner may at any time require any licensee to bring such records as he may direct to the commissioner's office for examination.

(b) Every licensee shall preserve its records of such premium finance transactions including cards used in a card system, if any, for at least three years after making the final entry in respect to any premium finance agreement. The preservation of records in photographic form shall constitute compliance with this requirement. (Acts 1975, No. 1042, p. 2088, § 6.)

§ 27-40-7. Promulgation and enforcement of rules and regulations.

The commissioner shall have authority to make and enforce such reasonable rules and regulations as may be necessary in making effective the provisions of this chapter, but such rules and regulations shall not be contrary to nor inconsistent with the provisions of this chapter. (Acts 1975, No. 1042, p. 2088, § 7.)

§ 27-40-8. Contents and style of premium finance agreement.

(a) The contents and style of the premium finance agreement shall be as follows:

(1) It shall be dated, signed by the insured or an authorized representative and the printed portion thereof shall be in at least eight-point type;

(2) Contain the name and place of business of the insurance agent negotiating the related insurance contract, the name and residence, or place of business, of the insured as specified by him, the name and place of business of the premium finance company to which payments are to be made, a description of the insurance contracts involved and the amount of the premium therefor; and

(3) Set forth the following items where applicable:

a. The total amount of the premiums;

b. The amount of the down payment;

c. The principal balance (the difference between items a and b);

d. The amount of the service charge;

e. The balance payable by the insured (sum of items c and d); and

f. The number of installments required, the amount of each installment expressed in dollars, and the due date or period thereof.

(b) The items set out need not be stated in the sequence or order in which they appear, and additional items may be included to explain the computations made in determining the amount to be paid by the insured. (Acts 1975, No. 1042, p. 2088, § 8; Acts 1986, No. 86-400, § 1.)

The 1986 amendment, which became effective without the governor's signature under § 125 of the Constitution on April 28, 1986, substituted "signed by the insured or an authorized representative" for "signed by or on behalf of the insured" in subdivision (a)(1).

§ 27-40-9. Service charges; prepayment of obligation.

(a) For the purpose of this section, "consumer insurance premium finance agreement" means an insurance premium finance agreement as defined in section 27-40-1 wherein the insurance contracts which are the subject of the premium finance agreement are for personal, family or household purposes or where the premiums for those agreements are $2,000.00 or less. For the purpose of this section, "commercial premium finance agreement" means any insurance premium finance agreement other than a consumer premium finance agreement.

(b) A premium finance company shall not charge, contract for, receive, or collect a service charge other than in accordance with the following provisions:

(1) The service charge is to be computed on the balance of the premium due, after subtracting the down payment made by the insured in accordance with the premium finance agreement, from the effective date of the insurance for which the premiums are being advanced, to and including the date when the final installment of the premium finance agreement is payable.

(2) The service charge per consumer insurance premium finance agreement shall be a maximum of $9.00 per $100.00 per annum plus an additional charge, which shall not exceed $15.00 per premium finance agreement, which additional charge need not be refunded.

(3) The service charge for a commercial insurance premium finance agreement shall be a maximum $9.00 per $100.00 per annum plus an additional charge, which shall not exceed $15.00 per premium finance agreement, which additional charge need not be refunded.

(c) Notwithstanding the provisions of any premium finance agreement, any insured may prepay the obligation in full at any time. In such event he shall receive a credit or refund under the rule of 78ths or the sum of the digits principle as follows: The amount of the refund or credit shall be as great a proportion of the finance charge originally contracted for as the sum of the periodic time balances of the debt scheduled to follow the date of prepayment bears to the sum of all the periodic time balances of the debt, both sums to be determined according to the scheduled payment originally contracted for. No refund of less than $1.00 need be made. If such prepayment is made by the debtor other than on a scheduled payment date, the nearest scheduled payment date shall be used in such computation. If, in addition to the service charge, an additional charge was imposed, such additional charge need not be refunded, nor taken into consideration in computing the credit refund. (Acts 1975, No. 1042, p. 2088, § 9; Acts 1986, No. 86-400, § 1.)

The **1986 amendment,** which became effective without the governor's signature under § 125 of the Constitution on April 28, 1986, substituted present subsections (a) and (b) for former subsection (a), and redesignated former subsection (b) as present subsection (c).

§ 27-40-10. Delinquency and cancellation charges.

A premium finance agreement may provide for the payment by the insured of the delinquency charge of $1.50 to a maximum of five percent of the delinquent installment which is in default for a period of five days or more. If the default results in the cancellation of any insurance contract listed in the agreement, the agreement may provide for the payment by the insured of a cancellation charge of $5.00 in the case of a consumer insurance premium finance agreement and $15.00 in the case of a commercial insurance premium finance agreement. (Acts 1975, No. 1042, p. 2088, § 10; Acts 1986, No. 86-400, § 1.)

The **1986 amendment,** which became effective without the governor's signature under § 125 of the Constitution on April 28, 1986, substituted "$1.50" for "$.50" in the first sentence and substituted "charge of $5.00 in the case of a consumer insurance premium finance agreement and $15.00 in the case of a commercial insurance premium finance agree-ment" for "charge equal to the difference between any delinquency charge imposed in respect to the installment in default and $5.00" at the end of the second sentence.

Collateral references. — Actual receipt or cancellation notice mailed by insurer as prerequisite to cancellation of insurance. 40 ALR4th 867.

§ 27-40-11. Procedure for cancellation of insurance contract upon default.

(a) When a premium finance agreement contains a power of attorney enabling the premium finance company to cancel any insurance contract or contracts listed in the agreement, the insurance contract or contracts shall not be cancelled by the premium finance company unless such cancellation is effectuated in accordance with this section.

(b) Not less than 10-day written notice shall be mailed to the insured, at his last known address as shown on the records of the premium finance company, of the intent of the premium finance company to cancel the insurance contract unless the default is cured within such 10-day period.

(c) After the notice in subsection (b) of this section has expired, the premium service company may thereafter request, in the name of the insured, cancellation of such insurance contract by mailing to the insurer a notice of cancellation, and the insurance contract shall be cancelled as if such notice of cancellation had been submitted by the insured himself, but without requiring the return of the insurance contract. The premium service company shall also mail a notice of cancellation to the insured at his last address as set forth in its records, and such mailing shall constitute sufficient proof of delivery.

(d) All statutory, regulatory and contractual restrictions providing that the insurance contract may not be cancelled unless notice is given to a governmental agency, mortgagee or other third party shall apply where cancellation is effected under the provisions of this section. The insurer shall give the prescribed notice in behalf of itself or the insured to any governmental agency, mortgagee or other third party on or before the second business day after the day it receives the notice of cancellation from the premium finance company and shall determine the effective date of cancellation taking into consideration the number of days' notice to complete the cancellation. (Acts 1975, No. 1042, p. 2088, § 11.)

Collateral references. — Actual receipt of cancellation notice mailed by insurer as pre- requisite to cancellation of insurance. 40 ALR4th 867.

§ 27-40-12. Return of gross unearned premiums upon cancellation of contract.

(a) Whenever a financed insurance contract is cancelled, the insurer or its designated agent, upon written notice of such financing, shall return whatever gross unearned premiums are due under the insurance contract to the premium finance company, either directly or via the agent, agency or broker placing the insurance, for the account of the insured or insureds. Provided, however, that if the insurer or its designated agent elects to return such unearned premiums to the premium finance company for the account of the insured or insureds, via the agent, agency or broker placing such insurance, the insurer shall be directly responsible to the premium finance company for any and all unearned premiums due to the premium finance company under the contract which are not properly returned to the premium finance company; and provided, further, that regardless of the method of the routing of the return of such unearned premiums to the insured or insureds, the insurer, the premium finance company and any agent or broker involved in the return of such unearned premiums shall be jointly and severally liable to the insured or insureds for any and all unearned premiums due to the insured or insureds under the insurance contract which are not properly returned to the insured or insureds.

(b) In the event that the crediting of return premiums to the account of the insured results in a surplus over the amount due from the insured, the premium finance company shall refund such excess to the insured or his insurance agent, agency or broker, provided that no such refund shall be required if it amounts to less than $1.00.

(c) All refunds of unearned premiums shall be made to the insured as soon as reasonably possible but in any event within 60 days of the date of cancellation of the insurance contract regardless of the method of routing of such unearned premiums.

(d) Notwithstanding anything to the contrary contained in this section:

(1) The insurance company or its designated agent shall have the right to credit to the account of or refund to the agent, agency or broker placing the insurance any or all unearned premiums on cancelled insurance contracts whose premiums were financed but which were not disbursed in accordance with the provisions of section 27-40-15; and, thereafter the premium finance company shall have no right to recover such unearned premiums except from the agent, agency or broker to whom refund was made or credit allowed in account.

(2) The insurance company shall not be relieved of its duty or obligation to return to the insured any unearned premium in excess of the balance owed by the insured to the premium finance company on any cancelled insurance contract issued by said insurance company. (Acts 1975, No. 1042, § 12; Acts 1986, No. 86-400, § 1.)

The 1986 amendment, which became effective without the governor's signature under § 125 of the Constitution on April 28, 1986, rewrote this section.

Collateral references. — Actual receipt of cancellation notice mailed by insurer as prerequisite to cancellation of insurance. 40 ALR4th 867.

§ 27-40-13. Filing of agreement.

No filing of the premium finance agreement shall be necessary to perfect the validity of such agreement as a secured transaction as against creditors, subsequent purchasers, pledges, encumbrances, successors or assigns. (Acts 1975, No. 1042, p. 2088, § 13.)

§ 27-40-14. Exclusive jurisdiction of department of insurance.

When a premium finance company has complied with the licensing provisions of this chapter, it shall not be subject to any other licensing or regulatory agency of the state of Alabama other than the department of insurance. (Acts 1975, No. 1042, p. 2088, § 14.)

§ 27-40-15. Premium financed to be sent to insurance company; designation of agents; issuance of drafts, etc.; recovery of unearned premiums; duties with respect to cancellation.

(a) The amount of premium financed, more specifically referred to as "the principal balance" in paragraph (3)c of section 27-40-8, shall be sent directly to the insurance company or companies whose premium for an insurance contract is the subject of financing under any premium finance agreement. The insurance company may, however, designate any insurance agent or managing general agent duly licensed by the insurance department of the state of Alabama, or any number of such agents, to receive such funds on its behalf by filing in writing the name and business address of such agent or agents with the insurance department. Thereafter, the agent or managing general agent so designated shall act with full authority on behalf of the insurance company on all matters pertaining to the acceptance of premiums financed, cancellation of the insurance contract and refund of unearned premiums. It shall be the duty of the premium finance company to ascertain from the insurance department the name of all agents, if any, so designated by the company.

(b) All drafts, checks or other orders of payment issued for premiums financed shall be issued by the premium finance company and shall be mailed, delivered, or otherwise transmitted directly to the insurance company or its designated agent. No insurance agent, insurance broker, managing general agent or any person employed by any of the aforementioned may be authorized or permitted to issue or sign any draft, check or other order of payment on behalf of such premium finance company unless the premium finance company is owned by or under the financial control of the agent, broker or managing general agent or an insurance agency operated by such agent, broker or managing general agent. The premium finance company shall not make available any presigned check, draft or other order or form of payment to any insurance agent, insurance broker, managing general agent or other person.

(c) With respect to any premiums financed which are not disbursed in accordance with this section, the right of recovery by the premium finance company of any unearned premiums shall be limited as provided in section 27-40-12.

(d) Notwithstanding anything to the contrary contained in this section, the insurance company shall not be relieved of any of its duties or responsibilities with respect to the cancellation of any insurance contract which is subject to the premium finance agreement. (Acts 1986, No. 86-400, § 2.)

Effective date. — The act which added this section became effective without the governor's signature under § 125 of the Constitution on April 28, 1986.

§ 27-40-16. Payment of rebates or inducements prohibited; purchase of premium finance agreement.

No premium finance company and no employee of such a company shall pay, allow, or offer to pay or allow in any manner whatsoever to the insurance agent, insurance broker, or managing general agent, or any employee of any of the aforesaid, or to any other person, either as an inducement to the financing of any insurance contract with the premium finance company, or, after any such contract has been financed, any rebate whatsoever, either from the service charge for financing specified in the premium finance agreement or otherwise, or shall give or offer to give any valuable consideration or inducement of any kind directly, but a premium finance company may purchase or otherwise acquire a premium finance agreement, provided that it conforms to the provisions of this chapter, in all respects, from another premium finance company on such terms and conditions as may be mutually agreed upon. (Acts 1986, No. 86-400, § 3.)

Effective date. — The act which added this section became effective without the governor's signature under § 125 of the Constitution on April 28, 1986.

§ 27-40-17. Notification of existence of premium finance agreement.

Any premium finance company which enters into a premium finance agreement under the provisions of this chapter shall notify the insurer or its designated agent, whose premiums are being financed, of the existence of such agreement within a reasonable period of time, not to exceed 30 days after the date such agreement is signed. (Acts 1986, No. 86-400, § 4.)

Effective date. — The act which added this section became effective without the governor's signature under § 125 of the Constitution on April 28, 1986.

§ 27-40-18. Delivery of copy of premium finance agreement to insured.

Prior to the due date of the first installment payable under a premium finance agreement, the premium finance company holding the agreement shall deliver to the insured, or mail to him at his or her address as shown in the agreement, a copy thereof. (Acts 1986, No. 86-400, § 5.)

Effective date. — The act which added this section became effective without the governor's signature under § 125 of the Constitution on April 28, 1986.

CHAPTER 41.

INVESTMENTS OF LIFE, DISABILITY AND BURIAL INSURANCE COMPANIES.

Sec.
27-41-1. Applicability of chapter.
27-41-2. Definitions.
27-41-3. Investments which may be counted as admitted assets generally; investments and obligations for investments deemed eligible investments under chapter generally; filing with commissioner of certified statements as to investments or obligations for investments not deemed eligible under chapter; assets or funds to which investment limitations based upon amounts of insurers assets or particular funds relate.
27-41-4. General requirements as to eligibility of investments.
27-41-5. Authorization of investments by board of directors, etc.
27-41-6. Limitations upon investments generally.
27-41-7. Particular investments — Bonds, notes, etc., of United States.
27-41-8. Same — Loans guaranteed by United States.
27-41-9. Same — Bonds, etc., of states or counties, municipalities, school districts, etc., therein generally.
27-41-10. Same — Bonds, etc., issued by states, counties, municipalities, etc., to provide funds for public projects, etc.
27-41-11. Same — Bonds, etc., of local public housing authorities.
27-41-12. Same — Obligations issued or guaranteed by certain federal agencies.
27-41-13. Same — Bonds, etc., issued, etc., by Canadian government, provinces thereof, etc.
27-41-14. Same — Obligations issued, etc., by international bank for reconstruction and development and National Mortgage Association.
27-41-15. Same — Obligations of American and Canadian institutions generally.
27-41-16. Same — Preferred or guaranteed stocks or shares of American corporations.
27-41-17. Same — Common stocks or shares and capital stocks of American and Canadian corporations.
27-41-18. Same — American insurance stocks.

Sec.
27-41-19. Same — Transportation equipment trust obligations; notes, etc., secured by leases, agreements, etc., relating to manufacturing, mining, etc., machinery, etc.
27-41-20. Same — Leased line obligations of railroads; terminal obligations of railroads and other common carriers.
27-41-21. Same — Obligations of religious institutions or societies.
27-41-22. Same — Loans secured by liens on interests in oil, gas or condensate properties, etc.
27-41-23. Same — Certificates, etc., issued by trustees or receivers of institutions being administered under court direction.
27-41-24. Same — Loans secured by pledges of securities or pledges or assignments of life insurance policies.
27-41-25. Same — Policy loans.
27-41-26. Same — Shares or savings accounts of savings and loan associations.
27-41-27. Same — Securities of foreign countries.
27-41-28. Same — Bonds, etc., guaranteed or insured by United States under federal law or secured by mortgages on ships, barges, etc.
27-41-29. Same — Bonds, etc., secured by mortgages or deeds of trust on real property, etc., generally.
27-41-30. Same — Loans, notes, etc., secured by mortgages and leases on real property.
27-41-31. Same — Data processing and accounting systems.
27-41-32. Same — Investments relating to agricultural property securing evidences of indebtedness held by insurers and subject to mortgage foreclosure or insolvency proceedings.
27-41-33. Same — Loans on personal property; chattel mortgages.
27-41-34. Same — Real estate.
27-41-34.1. Same — Oil and gas producing properties and facilities.
27-41-35. Miscellaneous investments.
27-41-36. Prohibited investments; underwriting, etc., of offerings of securities or property.
27-41-37. Investments of mutual aid associations — Generally.

Sec.
27-41-38. Same — Funeral supply inventories and funeral equipment.
27-41-39. Investments of foreign and alien insurers.
27-41-40. Effect of failure to dispose of real estate, personal property, securi-

Sec.
ties, etc., within prescribed period of time.
27-41-41. Only eligible investments to be counted as admitted assets; treatment of investments partially qualifying as eligible investments.

§ 27-41-1. Applicability of chapter.

Except as provided in section 27-41-39, this chapter shall apply to domestic life, disability and burial insurers only. (Acts 1977, No. 408, p. 530, § 1.)

§ 27-41-2. Definitions.

As used in this chapter, the following terms shall have the respective meanings herein set forth, unless the context shall otherwise require:

(1) ALABAMA INSURANCE CODE. Title 27 of this Code.

(2) INSURER. Such term shall have the meaning ascribed in section 27-1-2, but as used in this chapter shall apply only to domestic insurers engaged in whole or in part in the life, disability or burial insurance business.

(3) PERSON. Such term shall have the meaning ascribed in section 27-1-2.

(4) COMMISSIONER and DEPARTMENT. Such terms, respectively, shall have the meanings ascribed in section 27-1-2.

(5) INVESTMENT. Any asset owned by an insurer.

(6) ELIGIBLE INVESTMENT. Any investment permitted by sections 27-41-7 through 27-41-35, provided the investment meets all the other requirements of this chapter.

(7) DOMESTIC INSURER, FOREIGN INSURER, and ALIEN INSURER. Such terms shall have the meanings ascribed in section 27-1-2.

(8) ADMITTED ASSET. Any asset of an insurer permitted by the commissioner of insurance to be taken into account in any determination of the financial condition of such insurer. (Acts 1977, No. 408, p. 530, § 2.)

§ 27-41-3. Investments which may be counted as admitted assets generally; investments and obligations for investments deemed eligible investments under chapter generally; filing with commissioner of certified statements as to investments or obligations for investments not deemed eligible under chapter; assets or funds to which investment limitations based upon amounts of insurers assets or particular funds relate.

(a) Only eligible investments may be counted as admitted assets.

(b) Every investment lawfully held by an insurer on January 1, 1978, and every investment which the insurer became obligated to make prior to

January 1, 1978, which was a lawful investment for such insurer at the time made or at the time the insurer became obligated to make it shall be an eligible investment.

(c) The insurer shall within 90 days after January 1, 1978 file with the commissioner a written statement certified by its treasurer or chief investment officer, listing in such manner as to readily identify the same, all such investments or obligations for investments not otherwise eligible under this chapter, identifying each such investment and stating the terms and conditions of acquisition or proposed acquisition thereof.

(d) Eligibility of an investment shall be determined as of the date of its making or acquisition, except as stated in subsection (b) of this section.

(e) Any investment limitation based upon the amount of the insurer's assets or particular funds shall relate to the value of such assets or funds as shown by the insurer's annual statement as of December 31 next preceding the date of the investment by the insurer or as shown by a current financial statement filed with and accepted as to content in writing by the commissioner. (Acts 1977, No. 408, p. 530, § 3.)

Cross references. — As to assets of insurers generally, see § 27-37-1 et seq.

Collateral references. — 44 C.J.S., Insurance, §§ 72, 86.

43 Am. Jur. 2d, Insurance, §§ 33, 51, 52, 62.

§ 27-41-4. General requirements as to eligibility of investments.

No investment (other than in common stocks allowed under section 27-41-17, in insurance stocks allowed under section 27-41-18, in loans or investments allowed under section 27-41-35, in real property allowed under section 27-41-34, or in funeral supply inventories and equipment allowed under section 27-41-38) shall be an eligible investment unless it is interest-bearing or interest-accruing or dividend or income-paying, is not then in default and the insurer is entitled to receive for its account and benefit the interest or income accruing thereon.

An investment may be eligible notwithstanding that part of the interest or income accruing thereon is paid by the insurer to a third party in consideration of services rendered by the third party with respect to the investment or that part of the interest or income accruing thereon is shared by the insurer with one or more joint venturers or others participating in the same investment.

Any investment authorized may be deposited in a clearing corporation as defined in section 7-8-102(3), Code of Alabama, 1975, or in a federal reserve bank under book-entry system. When such securities are so deposited, certificates representing securities of the same class of the same issuer may be merged and held in bulk in the name of the nominee of such clearing corporation with any other securities deposited in such clearing corporation by any person, regardless of the ownership of such securities, and securities of small denominations may be merged into one or more certificates of larger denominations. Title to such securities may be transferred by bookkeeping entry on the books of such clearing corporation or federal reserve bank without physical delivery or certificates representing such securities. (Acts 1977, No. 408, p. 530, § 4; Acts 1981, No. 81-541, p. 904, § 4.)

§ 27-41-5. Authorization of investments by board of directors, etc.

An insurer shall not make any investment or loan, other than loans on policies or annuity contracts, unless the same be authorized, approved or ratified by the board of directors of the insurer or by such committee or person as the board of directors shall expressly authorize. The action of the board of directors, the committee or other persons so authorized shall be recorded and regular reports thereof shall be submitted to the board of directors. This requisite shall not apply to funeral supplies authorized for mutual aid associations under section 27-41-38 which are purchased in the regular course of business under the general supervision of the association's board of directors. (Acts 1977, No. 408, p. 530, § 5.)

§ 27-41-6. Limitations upon investments generally.

(a) An insurer shall not have at any one time any single investment or combination of investments in or loans upon the security of the obligations, property or securities of any one person aggregating in cost to the insurer in excess of the greater of 10 percent of such insurer's assets or the total of its capital and surplus, as shown in the latest annual report of the insurer filed pursuant to subsection (a) of section 27-3-26 of the Alabama insurance code, less the minimum capital and surplus required of said insurer for authority to transact insurance by sections 27-3-7 and 27-3-8 of the Alabama insurance code.

The restriction of this subsection shall not apply to evidences of indebtedness issued, assumed or guaranteed by the United States of America or any department, agency or instrumentality thereof or by any state of the United States.

(b) An insurer shall at all times invest and maintain invested funds in cash and assets allowed in the following sections of this chapter in an amount not less than the capital required of it to transact insurance by section 27-3-7 of the Alabama insurance code:

    (1) Section 27-41-7 (United States government obligations).

    (2) Section 27-41-9 (state, county, municipal and school obligations).

    (3) Section 27-41-29 (mortgage loans).

(c) An insurer shall at all times invest and maintain invested funds in cash and the investments prescribed in this chapter in an amount not less than the amount of the reserves under its policies and annuity contracts in force.

(d) Limits as to investments shall apply as stated in specific sections relating to particular kinds of investments. (Acts 1977, No. 408, p. 530, § 6.)

§ 27-41-7. Particular investments — Bonds, notes, etc., of United States.

An insurer may invest in bonds, notes, warrants, debentures and other evidences of indebtedness which are direct obligations of the United States of America for which the full faith and credit of the United States of America is pledged for the payment of principal and interest. (Acts 1977, No. 408, p. 530, § 7.)

§ 27-41-8. Same — Loans guaranteed by United States.

An insurer may invest in loans guaranteed as to principal and interest by the United States of America or by any agency or instrumentality of the United States of America to the extent of such guaranty. (Acts 1977, No. 408, p. 530, § 8.)

§ 27-41-9. Same — Bonds, etc., of states or counties, municipalities, school districts, etc., therein generally.

An insurer may invest in bonds or other evidences of indebtedness which are general obligations of or are adequately secured as to both principal and interest by irrevocable pledge of specific revenues by this state or any other state of the United States or any county, incorporated city or town or duly organized school district or other civil division, governmental unit or public instrumentality of any such state. Obligations payable solely out of special assessments on properties benefited by local improvements shall not be eligible under this section. (Acts 1977, No. 408, p. 530, § 9.)

§ 27-41-10. Same — Bonds, etc., issued by states, counties, municipalities, etc., to provide funds for public projects, etc.

An insurer may invest in bonds and other evidences of indebtedness which are obligations of any state, county, city, town, village, municipality, district or other political subdivision of any state or of any instrumentality or board thereof or of the United States of America issued to provide funds for public projects, or for refunding of bonds issued for such purposes, which are revenue producing and self-supporting if such obligations are secured by a lien on such revenues to pay principal and interest and the issuing body is required to charge adequate rates for the services so provided to pay all charges against the project, including principal and interest on all indebtedness outstanding against the project. (Acts 1977, No. 408, p. 530, § 10.)

§ 27-41-11. Same — Bonds, etc., of local public housing authorities.

An insurer may invest in bonds, debentures or other evidences of indebtedness of local public housing authorities existing under the laws of the United States or of any state if such obligations are:

(1) Secured by a pledge of annual contributions unconditionally payable under the annual contributions contract between the department of housing and urban development and the local agencies issuing the bonds;

(2) Unconditionally guaranteed by the state, municipality or political subdivision creating the authority, if the tax supported obligations of such state, municipality or political subdivision so guaranteeing would be eligible for investment under this chapter; or

(3) Secured by payments to be made sufficient to pay principal and interest on the bonds under an "assistance contract" between the local authority and the state, municipality or other political subdivision creating the authority; provided, the tax supported obligations of the assisting state, municipality or political subdivision would be eligible for investment under this chapter. (Acts 1977, No. 408, p. 530, § 11.)

§ 27-41-12. Same — Obligations issued or guaranteed by certain federal agencies.

An insurer may invest in obligations issued or guaranteed by the following agencies of the United States of America:

(1) Commodity Credit Corporation;

(2) Federal intermediate credit banks;

(3) Federal land banks;

(4) Central bank for cooperatives;

(5) Federal home loan banks;

(6) Federal National Mortgage Association;

(7) Federal Home Loan Mortgage Corporation;

(8) Tennessee Valley Authority; and

(9) Any other similar agency of the government of the United States of America having similar financial quality. (Acts 1977, No. 408, p. 530, § 12.)

§ 27-41-13. Same — Bonds, etc., issued, etc., by Canadian government, provinces thereof, etc.

An insurer may invest in bonds or other evidences of indebtedness issued, assumed or guaranteed by Canada or any province thereof or issued by any municipality in Canada having a population of 25,000 or more. (Acts 1977, No. 408, p. 530, § 13.)

§ 27-41-14. Same — Obligations issued, etc., by international bank for reconstruction and development and National Mortgage Association.

(a) An insurer may invest in obligations issued, assumed or guaranteed by the International Bank for Reconstruction and Development.

(b) An insurer may invest in the obligations of the Federal National Mortgage Association. (Acts 1977, No. 408, p. 530, § 14.)

§ 27-41-15. Same — Obligations of American and Canadian institutions generally.

An insurer may invest in secured and unsecured obligations bearing interest at a fixed rate, with mandatory principal and interest being due at specified times, of any solvent institution engaged in any lawful business and existing under the laws of the United States or any state of the United States or Canada or any province thereof if the issuing institution has not defaulted in the payment of principal and interest on any of its fixed interest obligations during the five years preceding the date of investment; provided, that the obligations of an institution which has not been in existence for a period of five years shall be deemed eligible for investment under this section if the institution has not defaulted in the payment of principal and interest on any of its fixed obligations during the period of its existence and if such institution meets the other requisites of this chapter. (Acts 1977, No. 408, p. 530, § 15.)

§ 27-41-16. Same — Preferred or guaranteed stocks or shares of American corporations.

An insurer may invest in the preferred or guaranteed stocks or shares of any solvent corporation engaged in any lawful business and existing under the laws of the United States or any state thereof if the prior obligations of the issuing company or the guarantor, if any, would be eligible for investment under the provisions of section 27-41-15 and if the company has continuously paid the dividends provided for by outstanding preferred stock, if any, during the five years preceding the acquisition of the investment. (Acts 1977, No. 408, p. 530, § 16.)

§ 27-41-17. Same — Common stocks or shares and capital stocks of American and Canadian corporations.

(a) An insurer may invest in common stocks or shares of any solvent corporation engaged in any lawful business and existing under the laws of the United States or any state thereof or of Canada or any province thereof if the prior obligations of such corporation, if any, would be eligible for investment under the provisions of section 27-41-15.

(b) An insurer may invest in and own all or a controlling part of the capital stock of any corporation organized under the laws of the United States or any state thereof if the stock of such corporation is eligible for investment under subsection (a) of this section.

(c) The total amount of the insurer's investments under this section shall not at any time exceed the greater of 10 percent of assets of the insurer or the amount of the insurer's capital and surplus less the minimum capital and surplus required of said insurer to transact insurance by sections 27-3-7 and 27-3-8 of the Alabama insurance code. The limitations contained in this section shall not prevent an insurer from making eligible investments in common stock in excess of said limitations pursuant to the provisions of section 27-41-35. (Acts 1977, No. 408, p. 530, § 17.)

§ 27-41-18. Same — American insurance stocks.

An insurer may invest in the stocks of other solvent insurers formed under the laws of the United States or any state thereof, provided that the total amount of the insurer's investments in excess of the net asset value of the stock acquired shall not at any time exceed the greater of 10 percent of assets of the insurer or the insurer's capital and surplus less the minimum capital and surplus required of said insurer to transact insurance by sections 27-3-7 and 27-3-8 of the Alabama insurance code. (Acts 1977, No. 408, p. 530, § 18.)

§ 27-41-19. Same — Transportation equipment trust obligations; notes, etc., secured by leases, agreements, etc., relating to manufacturing, mining, etc., machinery, etc.

(a) An insurer may invest in equipment trust obligations or certificates which are adequately secured evidencing an interest in transportation equipment wholly or in part within the United States and a right to receive determined portions of rental, purchase or other fixed obligatory payments for the use or purchase of such transportation equipment.

(b) An insurer may invest in notes, bonds, debentures or other evidences of indebtedness secured by an interest in manufacturing, mining or generating machinery and equipment located wholly within the United States evidencing a right to receive determined portions of rental, purchase or other fixed obligatory payments for the use or purchase of such machinery and equipment.

(c) An insurer may invest in notes, bonds, debentures or evidences of indebtedness secured by a lease of manufacturing, mining, computer equipment or generating machinery and equipment or a lease of other tangible personal property or by a contract or by an agreement requiring aggregate payments sufficient to pay all fixed charges, including maintenance, upkeep and repair, insurance charges and taxes, and to pay the installments of principal and interest and any other payments required by the instrument evidencing the indebtedness.

(d) The lessee or party contracting or agreeing to make such payments under subsections (a), (b) or (c) of this section must be the United States or an agency thereof, a state of the United States or a civil division or governmental unit thereof or a solvent institution whose fixed interest obligations, if any, would be eligible investments under section 27-41-15. (Acts 1977, No. 408, p. 530, § 19.)

§ 27-41-20. Same — Leased line obligations of railroads; terminal obligations of railroads and other common carriers.

An insurer may invest in:

(1) Leased line obligations of railroads where all of the fixed interest-bearing obligations of the lessee meet the standards prescribed in section 27-41-15.

(2) Terminal obligations of railroads and other common carriers where all of the fixed interest-bearing obligations of the obligor meet the standards prescribed in section 27-41-15. (Acts 1977, No. 408, p. 530, § 20.)

§ 27-41-21. Same — Obligations of religious institutions or societies.

An insurer may invest in secured and unsecured obligations of religious institutions or societies located within the United States if the institution or society has not defaulted in payment of principal or interest on any of its obligations during the five years preceding the investment. (Acts 1977, No. 408, p. 530, § 21.)

§ 27-41-22. Same — Loans secured by liens on interests in oil, gas or condensate properties, etc.

An insurer may invest in adequately secured loans secured by first liens on interests in oil, gas or condensate properties or leaseholds in the United States and Canada on which there are fully completed commercially producing wells. (Acts 1977, No. 408, p. 530, § 22.)

§ 27-41-23. Same — Certificates, etc., issued by trustees or receivers of institutions being administered under court direction.

An insurer may invest in certificates, notes or other obligations issued by trustees or receivers of any institution created or existing under the laws of the United States or of any state thereof which, or the assets of which, are being administered under the direction of any court having jurisdiction if any such obligation is adequately secured as to principal and interest. (Acts 1977, No. 408, p. 530, § 23.)

§ 27-41-24. Same — Loans secured by pledges of securities or pledges or assignments of life insurance policies.

An insurer may invest in loans with a maturity not in excess of five years from the date thereof which are secured by pledge of securities eligible for investment under this chapter or by the pledge or assignment of life insurance policies issued by insurers authorized to transact insurance in this state. On the date made, no such loan shall exceed in amount 75 percent of the market value of the collateral pledged; except, that loans upon the pledge of United States government bonds and loans upon the pledge or assignment of life insurance policies shall not exceed 95 percent of the market value of the bonds or the cash surrender value of the policies pledged. The amount so loaned shall be included in the maximum amount of funds permitted under this chapter to be invested in a single person. (Acts 1977, No. 408, p. 530, § 24.)

§ 27-41-25. Same — Policy loans.

A life insurer may lend to its policyholder upon the security of the policy any sum not exceeding the cash surrender value of the policy or may lend against pledge or assignment of any of its supplementary contracts or other contracts or obligations so long as the loan is adequately secured by such policy contracts. (Acts 1977, No. 408, p. 530, § 25.)

§ 27-41-26. Same — Shares or savings accounts of savings and loan associations.

An insurer may invest in shares or savings accounts of savings and loan associations insured by the federal savings and loan insurance corporation. (Acts 1977, No. 408, p. 530, § 26.)

§ 27-41-27. Same — Securities of foreign countries.

An insurer authorized to transact insurance in a foreign country may make investments, in an aggregate amount not exceeding its obligations incurred in such country, in securities of or in such country possessing characteristics similar to like investments required pursuant to this chapter for investments in the United States of America. Canadian securities eligible for investment under other provisions of this chapter are not subject to this section. (Acts 1977, No. 408, p. 530, § 27.)

§ 27-41-28. Same — Bonds, etc., guaranteed or insured by United States under federal law or secured by mortgages on ships, barges, etc.

An insurer may invest in bonds, debentures, notes or other evidences of indebtedness which are:

(1) Guaranteed by the United States of America, represented by the secretary of commerce acting pursuant to Title 11 of the Merchant Marine Act, 1936, as amended, and the Federal Ship Financing Act of 1972;

(2) Insured by the United States of America, represented by the secretary of commerce acting pursuant to Title 11 of the Merchant Marine Act, 1936, as amended, and the Federal Ship Mortgage Insurance Act, as amended; provided, that such indebtedness is secured by mortgages on ships, barges, tugboats or other shipping vessels; or

(3) Secured by mortgages on ships, barges, tugboats or other shipping vessels which are under lease or charter to the United States government or an agency or department of the United States government or to a solvent institution whose fixed interest obligations, if any, would be eligible investments under section 27-41-15, if such lease or charter is assigned as additional security for such bonds, debentures, notes or other evidences of indebtedness and requires aggregate payments sufficient to pay all fixed charges, including maintenance, upkeep and repair, insurance charges and taxes, and to pay the installments of principal and interest and any other payments required by the instrument evidencing the indebtedness. (Acts 1977, No. 408, p. 530, § 28.)

U.S. Code. — As to Merchant Marine Act of 1936, see 46 U.S.C. § 1101 et seq. As to Federal Ship Financing Act of 1972, see 46 U.S.C. § 1271 et seq. As to Federal Ship Mortgage Insurance Act, see 46 U.S.C. § 1271 et seq.

§ 27-41-29. Same — Bonds, etc., secured by mortgages or deeds of trust on real property, etc., generally.

An insurer may invest in:

(1) Bonds, notes or other evidences of indebtedness which are secured by a first mortgage lien or deed of trust upon unencumbered improved real property located in the United States or Canada, including leasehold estates in such real estate having an unexpired term (inclusive of the term or terms which may be provided by options of renewal) of not less than 10 years beyond the final maturity of the loan. Unless guaranteed or insured by the administrator of veterans affairs, the secretary of housing and urban development or by a mortgage guaranty insurance policy issued by an insurance company licensed and authorized to do business by and in the state of Alabama, no such mortgage loan or loans when made shall exceed 75 percent of the fair value of the real estate or leasehold, except that loans made on single family dwellings shall not exceed 80 percent of the fair value of the property. "Fair value" shall be determined by a competent appraiser or appraisers. For the purposes of this section and section 27-41-30, real estate shall not be deemed to be encumbered by reason of the existence of taxes or assessments that are not delinquent, instruments creating or reserving mineral, oil or timber rights, rights-of-way, joint driveways, sewer rights, public utility easements, rights in walls, nor by

reason of building restrictions or other restrictive covenants, nor when such real estate is subject to lease in whole or in part whereby rents or profits are reserved to the owner; provided, that the security created by the mortgage or trust deed on the real estate is a first lien upon such real estate and that there is no condition or right of re-entry or forfeiture under which such lien can be cut off, subordinated or otherwise disturbed.

(2) Bonds, notes or other evidences of indebtedness which are secured by mortgage or deed of trust on real estate or an interest in real estate in the United States, if payment of such indebtedness or part thereof is guaranteed or insured by the administrator of veterans affairs in accordance with the Servicemen's Readjustment Act of 1944, as amended. Any portion of a mortgage loan referred to in this subdivision which is not guaranteed as herein provided must not exceed 75 percent of the fair value of the property as defined in subdivision (1) above.

(3) Bonds, notes or other evidences of indebtedness which are secured by mortgage or deed of trust insured by the secretary of housing and urban development under the terms of the National Housing Act, as amended.

(4) Purchase money mortgages shall be valued as provided in section 27-37-9.

(5) Bonds, notes or other evidences of indebtedness which are secured by a first mortgage lien or deed of trust upon unencumbered improved or income bearing real property located in the United States or Canada, including leasehold estates in such real estate having an unexpired term of not less than 10 years beyond the final maturity of the loan where the borrower is a solvent corporation engaged in any lawful business and existing under the laws of the United States or any real estate of the United States or Canada, or any province thereof, if such corporation has not defaulted in the payment of principal and interest on any of its fixed interest obligations during five years preceding the date of investment and the amount of indebtedness does not exceed 100 percent of the value of the property. (Acts 1977, No. 408, p. 530, § 29; Acts 1979, No. 79-687, p. 1216.)

Code commissioner's note. — Subdivision (5) of this section is set out above as enacted by the legislature.

U.S. Code. — As to Servicemen's Readjust-ment Act of 1944, see 38 U.S.C. § 1801 et seq. As to National Housing Act, see 12 U.S.C. § 1701 et seq.

§ 27-41-30. Same — Loans, notes, etc., secured by mortgages and leases on real property.

An insurer may invest in loans, notes, bonds or other evidences of indebtedness of any person up to the fair value of real property securing said indebtedness, upon compliance with the following conditions and provisions:

(1) The indebtedness must be secured by a first mortgage lien on real property having a fair value of not less than the principal amount of the loan, except as provided in subdivision (8) of this section;

(2) The indebtedness must be additionally secured by a lease on said real property, which lease must be assigned and transferred by the lessor to the lender or to a trustee of the lender under a trust instrument;

(3) The lease so assigned as additional security must be noncancellable and may be terminated only upon such conditions as are generally provided in commercial leases, such as, for example, destruction by fire, tornado or similar hazard or condemnation or taking by power of eminent domain;

(4) Rental payments under such lease must be payable monthly, quarterly or semi-annually and the aggregate rental payments required to be paid during the initial term of any such lease must be sufficient to pay the fixed charges against the leased property, including expenses of maintenance, upkeep and repair, insurance charges and taxes, and to pay the installments of principal and interest and any other payments required by the instrument evidencing the indebtedness;

(5) The lease additionally securing such indebtedness shall be a so-called "net lease," except as otherwise provided in subdivision (8) of this section. "Net lease" shall mean a lease under the terms of which the lessee is required to pay, in addition to the rental payments, all other charges for the maintenance, upkeep and repair of the leased property and all taxes, insurance and other charges provided under the terms of the lease;

(6) The indebtedness must be payable in full, both as to principal and interest, during the initial term of the lease assigned or transferred as additional security. The required payments of principal and interest on such indebtedness must be made in substantially equal periodic installments in an aggregate amount sufficient to retire or pay the loan in full upon or prior to the expiration of the initial term of such lease; except, that if the substantially equal periodic installments are at a rate sufficient to retire or pay the loan in full as amortized over the initial term of the lease, balloon payments may be permitted to pay the remaining balance due on the indebtedness if, by the terms of the instruments evidencing the same, the entire indebtedness matures prior to the expiration of the initial term of the lease. In addition to the required payments of principal and interest, the evidences of indebtedness may also provide for payment of additional moneys to the holder thereof based upon excess rentals, volume of sales or other events or factors which the parties may agree upon;

(7) The lessee, or any obligor under any such lease, must be a person, corporation or other legal entity or government agency, unit or subdivision whose obligations, at the time the lender commits in writing to make a loan, are or would be an eligible investment under this chapter and are or would be amortizable under the rules and regulations promulgated by the commissioner (ordinarily the same as promulgated by the National Association of Insurance Commissioners); and

(8) If the lease additionally securing such indebtedness is not a "net lease," then, and in such event, the indebtedness shall not exceed 90 percent of the fair value of the real property mortgaged to secure the payment of such indebtedness.

Where the words "lease," "lessor" or "lessee" appear in this section, the singular shall include the plural. (Acts 1977, No. 408, p. 530, § 30.)

§ 27-41-31. Same — Data processing and accounting systems.

An insurer may invest in electronic and mechanical machines constituting a data processing and accounting system if the cost of such system is not less than $10,000.00 and cost for such machines is amortized in full over a period not to exceed ten calendar years. (Acts 1977, No. 408, p. 530, § 32.)

§ 27-41-32. Same — Investments relating to agricultural property securing evidences of indebtedness held by insurers and subject to mortgage foreclosure or insolvency proceedings.

(a) If real property securing any evidence of indebtedness held by an insurer is used for agricultural purposes and a proceeding to foreclose the mortgage or an insolvency proceeding relating to the mortgagor has been commenced or if the mortgagor has made an assignment for the benefit of creditors, the insurer may, for the purpose of preserving or enhancing the earnings of such property:

(1) Purchase agricultural livestock or equipment and utilize the same or cause the same to be utilized in the operation of the property by the mortgagor or by a receiver or trustee or by the insurer; or

(2) Lend up to the value of any agricultural equipment or livestock which may be utilized in the operation of the property on the security of such equipment and livestock as a first lien.

(b) Nothing in this section shall be deemed to limit any right which the insurer may otherwise have under or with respect to any such loan, mortgage or investment. (Acts 1977, No. 408, p. 530, § 33.)

§ 27-41-33. Same — Loans on personal property; chattel mortgages.

In connection with mortgage loans made under subdivisions (2) and (3) of section 27-41-29, an insurer may loan on the value of personal property items listed in the department of housing and urban development commitment for insurance or the veterans administration certificates of reasonable value. Nothing in this section shall be deemed to prevent an insurer from taking liens on personal property items as additional security for any investment eligible for investment under this chapter.

Domestic life insurance companies are authorized to invest, within the limitations set forth in this section, in chattel mortgages resulting from the financing of tangible personal property, which mortgages must constitute valid first liens on the chattels mortgaged. The maximum amount of such mortgages to be admitted as assets shall not exceed one half of the amount of surplus remaining after deducting from capital and surplus an amount equal to the statutory minimum capital and surplus required of a newly organized life insurance company. In addition, an adequate reserve for losses, based on past and prospective experience of the company, shall be maintained at all times. (Acts 1977, No. 408, p. 530, § 34.)

§ 27-41-34. Same — Real estate.

(a)(1) An insurer may acquire, invest in, own, maintain, alter, furnish and improve the following real estate:

    a. Land and buildings used for home office and branch office purposes, together with such other real estate as is required for the convenient transaction of its business; and

    b. Funeral home buildings used in the servicing of burial insurance policies.

(2) An insurer may lease to others part of the real property otherwise occupied by it for home office and other purposes under paragraphs a. and b. of subdivision (1) of this subsection, except that the value of the parts so leased must be included in subdivision (2) of subsection (b) of this section.

(3) Except as provided in subsection (e) of this section, an insurer may not carry, as an admitted asset, real estate acquired under this subsection following 10 years from the date when such real estate ceases to be necessary for the convenient accommodation of the insurer in the transaction of its business.

(4) The cost of the aggregate amount of real estate owned under this subsection, less encumbrances and less depreciation where applicable, shall not exceed five percent of the insurer's admitted assets.

(b)(1) An insurer may acquire, invest in, own, maintain, alter, furnish and improve the following real estate:

    a. Real estate acquired as payment or part payment in the sale of other real estate owned by the insurer;

    b. Real estate acquired by a gift or devise;

    c. Real estate necessary for the protection or enhancement of the value of other real estate owned by the insurer;

    d. Real estate acquired through a lawful merger or consolidation with another insurance company and not required for its accommodation as provided in subsection (a) of this section; and

    e. Real estate under lease or being constructed under a definite agreement providing for lease to a solvent person for industrial or commercial purposes. The fixed interest obligations, if any, of any such lessee under this paragraph must be eligible for investment under section 27-41-15.

(2) The cost of the aggregate amount of real estate owned under this subsection, less depreciation, where applicable, shall not exceed 10 percent of the insurer's admitted assets.

(c) An insurer may acquire, own, maintain, alter, furnish and improve real estate acquired in satisfaction of loans, mortgages, liens or other evidences of indebtedness previously owing to the insurer in the regular course of its business. Except as stated in subsection (e) of this section, an insurer may not carry as an admitted asset real estate acquired under this subsection following 10 years from the date of acquisition.

(d) An insurer may acquire, invest in, own, maintain, alter, furnish and improve real estate acquired to be improved or developed as an investment for the production of income. The cost of the aggregate amount of real estate owned under this subsection, including the cost of improvement and development, less depreciation, where applicable, shall not exceed 10 percent of the insurer's admitted assets.

(e) Upon evidence satisfactory to him that the interest of an insurer will suffer materially if it is not permitted to carry a particular parcel of real estate as an admitted asset after expiration of the period set out in subsections (a) and (c) of this section, the commissioner may, by order in writing, grant a reasonable extension of the period, as specified in said order, during which time the insurer may continue to carry such real estate as an admitted asset.

(f) Real estate permitted to be carried as an admitted asset of the insurer under this section shall be so carried at an amount equal to its cost at the time of acquisition together with the actual cost of improvements made thereon, less encumbrances and less depreciation where applicable.

(g) The limitations provided in this section with respect to real estate investments under this section shall not apply where the total amount invested by an insurer in such investments does not exceed the total capital and surplus of such insurer, less the minimum capital and surplus required to be maintained by such insurer under the provisions of sections 27-3-7 and 27-3-8 of the Alabama insurance code. (Acts 1977, No. 408, p. 530, § 35.)

§ 27-41-34.1. Same — Oil and gas producing properties and facilities.

(a) An insurer may invest in properties and facilities, and any interest and rights in such properties and facilities, for the development and production of fossil or synthetic fuel or other minerals, whether or not the extraction would deplete the surface of such properties, including, but not limited to, investments relating to:

(1) The exploration for and development and producton of such fuel and minerals, and

(2) Ownership and control of such property, facilities, interest, and rights.

(b) An insurer shall not have at any one time any single investment or combination of investments permitted under subsection (a) of this section aggregating in cost to the insurer in excess of five percent of the amount by which the admitted assets of such insurer exceed $50,000,000.00 (excluding in the computation of assets investments permitted under subsection (a) above). (Acts 1983, No. 83-522, p. 810, § 1; Acts 1983, No. 83-669, p. 1034, § 1.)

§ 27-41-35. Miscellaneous investments.

(a) An insurer may make investments not otherwise expressly permitted by this chapter which may be counted as admitted assets, except as expressly prohibited under section 27-41-36, provided that:

(1) The aggregate of all such investments shall not exceed 10 percent of the insurer's admitted assets;

(2) The insurer's capital and surplus shall not be less than twice the total capital and surplus required of the insurer to transact insurance under sections 27-3-7 and 27-3-8 of the Alabama insurance code; and

(3) Such investments are sound investments.

(b) No investment shall be an eligible investment under this section if the investment is in an asset not allowed under the provisions of section 27-37-2 of the Alabama insurance code or is otherwise expressly prohibited or is eligible under any other provision of this chapter; except, that an insurer may invest in common stocks up to the limits imposed by this section in excess of the limits imposed by section 27-41-17.

(c) The insurer shall keep a separate record of all investments made under this section.

(d) If an investment made under this section subsequently qualifies as an eligible investment under any other provision of this chapter, the investment shall thereafter not be eligible under this section. (Acts 1977, No. 408, p. 530, § 31.)

§ 27-41-36. Prohibited investments; underwriting, etc., of offerings of securities or property.

(a) After January 1, 1978, an insurer shall not invest in nor lend its funds upon the security of any note or other evidence of indebtedness of any director, officer or controlling stockholder of the insurer, except as to policy loans authorized under section 27-41-25 and except as provided in sections 27-1-2, 27-27-26 and 27-37-2 of the Alabama insurance code.

(b) No insurer shall underwrite or participate in the underwriting of an offering of securities or property by any other person; provided, that nothing in this subsection shall prevent an insurer from purchasing securities or property directly from any person so long as the purchase is made for investment purposes and not for the purpose of resale through public distribution. (Acts 1977, No. 408, p. 530, § 39.)

§ 27-41-37. Investments of mutual aid associations — Generally.

(a) The funds of a mutual aid association shall be in cash or shall be invested as provided in sections 27-41-3 through 27-41-36 and section 27-41-38 as applicable to life insurers, except that:

(1) Funds of the association to the extent of its reserve liabilities resulting from valuation of its contracts providing for benefits, aid or

services payable or to be rendered other than in cash may, at the option of the association, be invested in securities or assets eligible for investment of the funds of life insurers in general, but with category limits as follows in lieu of limits otherwise applicable thereto under sections 27-41-3 through 27-41-36:

a. Not to exceed 25 percent of the reserves of the association in the aggregate may be invested in preferred and guaranteed stocks authorized in section 27-41-16 and common stocks authorized under section 27-41-17;

b. Not to exceed 10 percent of such reserves may be invested in insurance stock authorized under section 27-41-18; and

c. Not to exceed 40 percent of such reserves may be invested in real estate for production of income authorized under section 27-41-34.

(2) In addition to the investment of particular reserves in designated categories of investments as provided in subdivision (1) of this subsection, the association may invest additional funds in the same categories, but within the percentage limitations otherwise applicable under sections 27-41-3 through 27-41-36 as computed upon all of the assets of the association after deduction of the reserves mentioned in subdivision (1) of this subsection.

(b) This section shall not apply to mutual aid corporations that received a certificate of authority prior to July 31, 1967. The moneys derived by such corporations from the payment of subscriptions to its capital stock, and the payment of sales of stock (contributed surplus for mutual) may be invested in bonds of the United States or of this state or of the cities or counties of this state, estimated at their market value, or in notes or mortgages secured by real estate collateral worth twice the amount of said mortgages or notes.

(c) Mutual aid corporations, both stock and mutual, organized prior to July 31, 1967, shall be solvent so long as their assets exceed their liabilities. (Acts 1977, No. 408, p. 530, § 41.)

Cross references. — As to mutual aid associations generally, see § 27-30-1 et seq.

§ 27-41-38. Same — Funeral supply inventories and funeral equipment.

In addition to other investments permitted under this chapter, mutual aid associations may invest in funeral supply inventories, consisting of caskets, suits, robes, dresses and embalming supplies, and funeral equipment, consisting of automobiles, hearses, ambulances, funeral cars and other motor vehicle equipment, to the extent reasonably necessary to the full performance by the association of its outstanding contracts and policies. Such funeral supply inventories shall not exceed 25 percent of the association's assets. (Acts 1977, No. 408, p. 530, § 38.)

§ 27-41-39. Investments of foreign and alien insurers.

The investments of a foreign or alien insurer shall be as permitted by the laws of its domicile but shall be of a quality and diversity substantially equivalent to that required of like domestic insurers under this chapter. (Acts 1977, No. 408, p. 530, § 40.)

Collateral references. — 44 C.J.S., Insurance, §§ 75-84.
43 Am. Jur. 2d, Insurance, §§ 74-82.

§ 27-41-40. Effect of failure to dispose of real estate, personal property, securities, etc., within prescribed period of time.

Any real estate, personal property, securities or other investment lawfully acquired and held by an insurer shall not be allowed as an admitted asset of the insurer after expiration of the period for disposal thereof or any extension of such period granted by the commissioner pursuant to the provisions of section 27-41-34. (Acts 1977, No. 408, p. 530, § 36.)

Cross references. — As to assets of insurers generally, see § 27-37-1 et seq.

§ 27-41-41. Only eligible investments to be counted as admitted assets; treatment of investments partially qualifying as eligible investments.

Except as expressly prohibited in section 27-41-36, an insurer may make any investment without limit as to kind, time or amount, but only eligible investments shall be included or counted as admitted assets of the insurer in the determination of its financial condition.

If part of an investment qualifies as an eligible investment under any provision of this act and part does not, then only the part of the investment so qualifying shall be counted as an admitted asset. (Acts 1977, No. 408, p. 530, § 37.)

Cross references. — As to assets of insurers generally, see § 27-37-1 et seq.

CHAPTER 42.

INSURANCE GUARANTY ASSOCIATION.

Sec.
27-42-1. Short title.
27-42-2. Purpose of chapter.
27-42-3. Applicability of chapter.
27-42-4. Construction of chapter.
27-42-5. Definitions.
27-42-6. Association created; member insurers; accounts.
27-42-7. Board of directors; selection; vacancies; expenses.
27-42-8. Powers and duties of the association.
27-42-9. Plan of operation.
27-42-10. Duties and powers of the commissioner; judicial review.
27-42-11. Effect of paid claims; filing of paid claims and estimates with receiver or liquidator.
27-42-12. Exhaustion of rights; nonduplication of recovery.

Sec.
27-42-13. Prevention of insolvencies; examinations of insurers; reports.
27-42-14. Examination of the association; financial report.
27-42-15. Tax exemption.
27-42-16. Credits for assessments paid; disposition of refunds previously offset.
27-42-17. Immunity.
27-42-18. Stay of proceedings; access of board to records of insurers.
27-42-19. Association, policyholders, beneficiaries and insureds to have preferred creditor status.
27-42-20. Access to assets of insolvent insurer; application for court approval of plan to disburse assets; notice of application.

§ 27-42-1. Short title.

This chapter shall be known and may be cited as the "Alabama Insurance Guaranty Association Act." (Acts 1980, No. 80-806, p. 1639, § 1.)

Collateral references. — Validity, construction, and effect of statute establishing compensation for claims not paid because of insurer's insolvency. 30 ALR4th 1110.

Apportionment of payments of no-fault (personal injury protection) benefits between insurers providing coverage to same insured under policies covering different vehicles. 34 ALR4th 374.

§ 27-42-2. Purpose of chapter.

The purpose of this chapter is to provide a mechanism for the payment of covered claims under certain insurance policies, to avoid excessive delay in payments and to avoid financial loss to claimants or policyholders because of the insolvency of an insurer, to assist in the detection and prevention of insurer insolvencies and to provide an association to assess the cost of such protection among insurers. (Acts 1980, No. 80-806, p. 1639, § 2.)

§ 27-42-3. Applicability of chapter.

This chapter shall apply to all kinds of direct insurance, except life, annuities, disability, accident and health, title, surety, credit, mortgage guaranty and ocean marine insurance. (Acts 1980, No. 80-806, p. 1639, § 3.)

§ 27-42-4. Construction of chapter.

This chapter shall be liberally construed to effect the purpose under section 27-42-2 which will constitute an aid and guide to interpretation. (Acts 1980, No. 80-806, p. 1639, § 4.)

§ 27-42-5. Definitions.

As used in this chapter, the following terms shall have the following meanings, respectively, unless the context clearly indicates otherwise:

(1) ACCOUNT. Any one of the three accounts created by section 27-42-6.

(2) ASSOCIATION. The Alabama Insurance Guaranty Association created under 27-42-6.

(3) COMMISSIONER. The commissioner of insurance of the state of Alabama.

(4) COVERED CLAIM. An unpaid claim, including one of unearned premiums, which arises out of and is within the coverage and not in excess of the applicable limits of an insurance policy to which this chapter applies issued by an insurer, if such insurer becomes an insolvent insurer after January 1, 1981 and (i) the claimant or insured is a resident of this state at the time of the insured event; or (ii) the property from which the claim arises is permanently located in this state. "Covered claim" shall not include any amount due any reinsurer, insurer, insurance pool, or underwriting association, as subrogation recoveries or otherwise.

(5) INSOLVENT INSURER. An insurer licensed to transact insurance in this state, either at the time the policy was issued or when the insured event occurred, and against whom an order of liquidation with a finding of insolvency has been entered after January 1, 1981 by a court of competent jurisdiction in the insurer's state of domicile or of this state under the provision(s) of chapter 32 of Title 27, which order of liquidation has not been stayed or been the subject of a writ of supersedeas bonds or other comparable order.

(6) MEMBER INSURER. Any person who (i) writes any kind of insurance to which this chapter applies under section 27-42-3, including the exchange of reciprocal or interinsurance contracts, and (ii) is licensed to transact insurance in this state.

(7) NET DIRECT WRITTEN PREMIUMS. Direct gross premiums written in this state on insurance policies to which this chapter applies, less return premiums thereon and dividends paid or credited to policyholders on such direct business. "Net direct written premiums" does not include premiums on contracts between insurers or reinsurers.

(8) PERSON. Any individual, corporation, partnership, association or voluntary organization. (Acts 1980, No. 80-806, p. 1639, § 5.)

§ 27-42-6. Association created; member insurers; accounts.

There is created a nonprofit unincorporated legal entity to be known as the Alabama Insurance Guaranty Association. All insurers defined as member insurers in subdivision (6) of section 27-42-5 shall be and remain members of the association as a condition of their authority to transact insurance in this state. The association shall perform its functions under a plan of operation established and approved under section 27-42-9 and shall exercise its powers through a board of directors established under section 27-42-7. For purposes of administration and assessment, the association shall be divided into three separate accounts: (a) the workmen's compensation insurance account; (b) the automobile insurance account; and (c) the account for all other insurance to which this chapter applies. (Acts 1980, No. 80-806, p. 1639, § 6.)

Collateral references. — 43 Am. Jur. 2d,
Insurance, § 70.

§ 27-42-7. Board of directors; selection; vacancies; expenses.

(a) The board of directors of the association shall consist of not less than five nor more than nine persons serving terms as established in the plan of operation. The members of the board shall be selected by member insurers subject to the approval of the commissioner. Vacancies on the board shall be filled for the remaining period of the term by a majority vote of the remaining board members subject to the approval of the commissioner. If no members are selected within 60 days after January 1, 1981, the commissioner may appoint the initial members of the board of directors.

(b) In approving the selections to the board, the commissioner shall consider among other things whether all member insurers are fairly represented.

(c) Members of the board may be reimbursed from the assets of the association for expenses incurred by them as members of the board of directors. (Acts 1980, No. 80-806, p. 1639, § 7.)

§ 27-42-8. Powers and duties of the association.

(a) The association shall:

(1) Be obligated to the extent of the covered claims existing prior to the determination of insolvency and arising within 30 days after the determination of insolvency, or before the policy expiration date if less than 30 days after the determination, on or before the insured replaces the policy or causes its cancellation, if he does so within 30 days of the determination, but such obligation shall include only that amount of each covered claim which is in excess of $100.00 and is less than $150,000.00, except that the association shall pay the full amount of any covered employee benefit claim arising under Section A of workmen's compensation policy. In no event

shall the association be obligated to a policyholder or claimant in an amount in excess of the obligation of the insolvent insurer under the policy from which the claim arises. Notwithstanding any other provisions of this chapter, a covered claim shall not include any claim filed with the guaranty fund after the final date set by the court for the filing of claims against the liquidator or receiver of an insolvent insurer.

(2) Be deemed the insurer to the extent of its obligation on the covered claims and to such extent shall have all rights, duties, and obligations of the insolvent insurer as if the insurer had not become insolvent.

(3) Allocate claims paid and expenses incurred among the three accounts separately, and assess member insurers separately for each account amounts necessary to pay the obligations of the association under subdivision (1) of this subsection subsequent to an insolvency, the expenses of handling covered claims subsequent to an insolvency, the cost of examinations under section 27-42-13 and other expenses authorized by this chapter. The assessments of each member insurer shall be in the proportion that the net direct written premiums of the member insurer for the calendar year preceding the assessment on the kinds of insurance in the account bears to the net direct written premiums of all member insurers for the calendar year preceding the assessment on the kinds of insurance in the account. Each member insurer shall be notified of the assessment not later than 30 days before it is due. No member insurer may be assessed in any one year on any account an amount greater than one percent of that member insurer's net direct written premiums for the calendar year preceding the assessment on the kinds of insurance in the account. If the maximum assessment, together with the other assets of the association in any account, does not provide in any one year in any account an amount sufficient to make all necessary payments from that account, the funds available shall be prorated and the unpaid portion shall be paid as soon thereafter as funds become available. The association shall pay claims in any order which it may deem reasonable, including the payment of claims as such are received from the claimants or in groups or categories of claims. The association may exempt or defer, in whole or in part, the assessment of any member insurer, if the assessment would cause the member insurer's financial statement to reflect amounts of capital or surplus less than the minimum amounts required for a certificate of authority by any jurisdiction in which the member insurer is authorized to transact insurance; provided, however, that during the period of deferment, no dividends shall be paid to shareholders or policyholders. Deferred assessments shall be paid when such payment will not reduce capital or surplus below required minimums. Such payments shall be refunded to those companies receiving larger assessments by virtue of such deferment or, at the election of any such company, credited against future assessments. Each member insurer may set off against any assessment, authorized payments made on covered claims and expenses incurred in the payment of such claims by the member insurer if they are chargeable to the account for which the assessment is made.

(4) Investigate claims brought against the association and adjust, compromise, settle and pay covered claims to the extent of the association's obligation and deny all other claims and may review settlements, releases and judgments to which the insolvent insurer or its insureds were parties to determine the extent to which such settlements, releases and judgments may be properly contested.

(5) Notify such persons as the commissioner directs under subdivision (1) of subsection (b) of section 27-42-10.

(6) Handle claims through its employees or through one or more insurers or other persons designated as servicing facilities. Designation of a servicing facility is subject to the approval of the commissioner, but such designation may be declined by a member insurer.

(7) Reimburse each servicing facility for obligations of the association paid by the facility and for expenses incurred by the facility while handling claims on behalf of the association and shall pay the other expenses of the association authorized by this chapter.

(b) The association may:

(1) Employ or retain such persons as are necessary to handle claims and perform other duties of the association.

(2) Borrow funds necessary to effect the purposes of this chapter in accord with the plan of operation.

(3) Sue or be sued.

(4) Negotiate and become a party to such contracts as are necessary to carry out the purpose of this chapter.

(5) Perform such other acts as are necessary or proper to effectuate the purpose of this chapter.

(6) Refund to the member insurers in proportion to the contribution of each member insurer to that account that amount by which the assets of the account exceed the liabilities if, at the end of any calendar year, the board of directors finds that the assets of the association in any account exceed the liabilities of that account as estimated by the board of directors for the coming year. (Acts 1980, No. 80-806, p. 1639, § 8.)

Collateral references. — 46 C.J.S., Insurance, §§ 1410, 1412, 1413, 1415-1421.
43 Am. Jur. 2d, Insurance, §§ 113-119.

§ 27-42-9. Plan of operation.

(a) The association shall submit to the commissioner a plan of operation and any amendments thereto necessary or suitable to assure the fair, reasonable and equitable administration of the association. The plan of operation and any amendments thereto shall become effective upon approval in writing by the commissioner.

If the association fails to submit a suitable plan of operation within 90 days following January 1, 1981 or if at any time thereafter the association fails to submit suitable amendments to the plan, the commissioner shall, after notice and hearing, adopt and promulgate such reasonable rules as are necessary or advisable to effectuate the provisions of this chapter. Such rules shall continue in force until modified by the commissioner or superseded by a plan submitted by the association and approved by the commissioner.

(b) All member insurers shall comply with the plan of operation.

(c) The plan of operation shall:

(1) Establish procedures whereby all the powers and duties of the association under section 27-42-8 will be performed.

(2) Establish procedures for handling assets of the association.

(3) Establish the amount and method of reimbursing members of the board of directors under section 27-42-7.

(4) Establish procedures by which claims may be filed with the association and establish acceptable forms of proof of covered claims. Notice of claims to the receiver or liquidator of the insolvent insurer shall be deemed notice to the association or its agent and a list of such claims shall be periodically submitted to the association or similar organization in another state by the receiver or liquidator.

(5) Establish regular places and times for meetings of the board of directors.

(6) Establish procedures for records to be kept of all financial transactions of the association, its agents, and the board of directors.

(7) Provide that any member insurer aggrieved by any final action or decision of the association may appeal to the commissioner within 30 days after the action or decision.

(8) Establish the procedures whereby selections for the board of directors will be submitted to the commissioner.

(9) Contain additional provisions necessary or proper for the execution of the powers and duties of the association.

(d) The plan of operation may provide that any or all powers and the duties of the association, except those under subdivision (3) of subsection (a) and subdivision (2) of subsection (b) of section 27-42-8 are delegated to a corporation, association or other organization which performs or will perform functions similar to those of this association, or its equivalent in two or more states. Such a corporation, association or organization shall be reimbursed as a servicing facility would be reimbursed and shall be paid for its performance of any other functions of the association. A delegation under this subsection shall take effect only with the approval of both the board of directors and the commissioner and may be made only to a corporation, association or organization which extends protection not substantially less favorable and effective than that provided by this chapter. (Acts 1980, No. 80-806, p. 1639, § 9.)

Collateral references. — 46 C.J.S., Insurance, §§ 1410, 1412, 1413, 1415-1421.
43 Am. Jur. 2d, Insurance, §§ 113-119.

§ 27-42-10. Duties and powers of the commissioner; judicial review.

(a) The commissioner shall:

(1) Notify the association of the existence of an insolvent insurer not later than three days after he receives notice of determination of the insolvency. The association shall be entitled to a copy of any complaint seeking an order of liquidation with a finding of insolvency against a member company at the time that such complaint is filed with a court of competent jurisdiction.

(2) Upon request of the board of directors, provide the association with a statement of the net direct written premiums of each member insurer.

(b) The commissioner may:

(1) Require that the association notify the insureds of the insolvent insurer and any other interested parties of the determination of insolvency and of their rights under this chapter. Such notification shall be by mail at their last known address, where available, but if sufficient information for notification by mail is not available, notice by publication in a newspaper of general circulation shall be sufficient.

(2) Suspend or revoke, after notice and hearing, the certificate of authority to transact insurance in this state of any member insurer which fails to pay an assessment when due or fails to comply with the plan of operation. As an alternative, the commissioner may levy a fine on any member insurer which fails to pay an assessment when due. Such fine shall not exceed five percent of the unpaid assessment per month, except that no fine shall be less than $100.00 per month.

(3) Revoke the designation of any servicing facility if he finds claims are being handled unsatisfactorily.

(c) Any final action or order of the commissioner under this chapter shall be subject to judicial review in a court of competent jurisdiction. (Acts 1980, No. 80-806, p. 1639, § 10.)

Collateral references. — 46 C.J.S., Insurance, §§ 1410, 1412, 1413, 1415-1421.
43 Am. Jur. 2d, Insurance, §§ 113-119.

§ 27-42-11. Effect of paid claims; filing of paid claims and estimates with receiver or liquidator.

(a) Any person recovering under this chapter shall be deemed to have assigned his rights under the policy to the association to the extent of his recovery from the association. Every insured or claimant seeking the protection of this chapter shall cooperate with the association to the same extent as such person would have been required to cooperate with the insolvent insurer. The association shall have no cause of action against the insured of the insolvent insurer for any sums it has paid out except such causes of action as the insolvent insurer would have had if such sums had been paid by the insolvent insurer. In the case of an insolvent insurer operating on a plan with assessment liability, payments of claims of the association shall not operate to reduce the liability of insureds to the receiver, liquidator, or statutory successor for unpaid assessments.

(b) The receiver, liquidator, or statutory successor of an insolvent insurer shall be bound by settlements of covered claims by the association or a similar organization in another state. The court having jurisdiction shall grant such claims priority equal to that which the claimant would have been entitled in the absence of this chapter against the assets of the insolvent insurer. The expenses of the association or similar organization in handling claims shall be accorded the same priority as the liquidator's expenses.

(c) The association shall periodically file with the receiver or liquidator of the insolvent insurer statements of the covered claims paid by the association and estimates of anticipated claims on the association which shall preserve the rights of the association against the assets of the insolvent insurer. (Acts 1980, No. 80-806, p. 1639, § 11.)

§ 27-42-12. Exhaustion of rights; nonduplication of recovery.

(a) Any person having a claim against an insurer under any provision in an insurance policy other than a policy of an insolvent insurer which is also a covered claim, shall be required to exhaust first his rights under such policy. Any amount payable on a covered claim under this chapter shall be reduced by the amount of any recovery under such insurance policy.

(b) Any person having a claim which may be recovered under more than one insurance guaranty association or its equivalent shall seek recovery first from the association of the place of residence of the insured except that if it is a first party claim for damage to property with a permanent location, he shall seek recovery first from the association of the location of the property and if it is a workmen's compensation claim, he shall seek recovery first from the association of the residence of the claimant. Any recovery under this chapter shall be reduced by the amount of recovery from any other insurance guaranty association or its equivalent. (Acts 1980, No. 80-806, p. 1639, § 12.)

§ 27-42-13. Prevention of insolvencies; examinations of insurers; reports.

(a) To aid in the detection and prevention of insurer insolvencies, it shall be the duty of the board of directors, upon majority vote, to notify the commissioner of any information indicating any member insurer may be insolvent or in a financial condition hazardous to the policyholders or the public.

(b) The board of directors may, upon majority vote, request that the commissioner order an examination of any member insurer which the board in good faith believes may be in a financial condition hazardous to the policyholders or the public. Within 30 days of the receipt of such request, the commissioner shall begin such examination. The examination may be conducted as a national association of insurance commissioners examination or may be conducted by such persons as the commissioner designates. The cost of such examination shall be paid by the association and the examination report shall be treated as are other examination reports. In no event, shall such examination report be released to the board of directors prior to its release to the public, but this shall not preclude the commissioner from complying with subsection (c) of this section. The commissioner shall notify the board of directors when the examination is completed. The request for an examination shall be kept on file by the commissioner, but it shall not be open to public inspection prior to the release of the examination report to the public.

(c) It shall be the duty of the commissioner to report to the board of directors when he has reasonable cause to believe that any member insurer examined or being examined at the request of the board of directors may be insolvent or in a financial condition hazardous to the policyholders or the public.

(d) The board of directors may, upon majority vote, make reports and recommendations to the commissioner upon any matter germane to the solvency, liquidation, rehabilitation or conservation of any member insurer. Such reports and recommendations shall not be considered public documents.

(e) The board of directors may, upon majority vote, make recommendations to the commissioner for the detection and prevention of insurer insolvencies.

(f) The board of directors shall, at the conclusion of any insurer insolvency in which the association was obligated to pay covered claims, prepare a report on the history and causes of such insolvency, based on the information available to the association and submit such report to the commissioner. (Acts 1980, No. 80-806, p. 1639, § 13.)

§ 27-42-14. Examination of the association; financial report.

The association shall be subject to examination and regulation by the commissioner. The board of directors shall submit, not later than March 30 of each year, a financial report for the preceding calendar year in a form approved by the commissioner. (Acts 1980, No. 80-806, p. 1639, § 14.)

§ 27-42-15. Tax exemption.

The association shall be exempt from payment of all fees and all taxes levied by this state or any of its subdivisions except taxes levied on real or personal property. (Acts 1980, No. 80-806, p. 1639, § 15.)

§ 27-42-16. Credits for assessments paid; disposition of refunds previously offset.

(a) A member insurer may offset against its premium tax liability to this state an assessment described in subdivision (3) of subsection (a) of section 27-42-8 to the extent of 20 percent of the amount of such assessment for each of the five calendar years following the year in which such assessment was paid. In the event a member insurer should cease doing business, all uncredited assessments may be credited against its premium tax liability for the year it ceases doing business.

(b) Any sums acquired by refund, pursuant to subdivision (7) of subsection (a) of section 27-42-8, from the association which have theretofore been written off by contributing insurers and offset against premium taxes as provided in subsection (a) of this section, and are not then needed for purposes of this chapter, shall be paid by the association to the commissioner and by him deposited with the state treasurer for credit to the general fund of this state. (Acts 1980, No. 80-806, p. 1639, § 16.)

§ 27-42-17. Immunity.

There shall be no liability on the part of and no cause of action of any nature shall arise against any member insurer, the association or its agents or employees, the board of directors or the commissioner or his representatives for any action taken by them in the performance of their powers and duties under this chapter. (Acts 1980, No. 80-806, p. 1639, § 17.)

§ 27-42-18. Stay of proceedings; access of board to records of insurers.

All proceedings in which the insolvent insurer is a party or is obligated to defend a party in any court in this state shall be stayed for up to six months and such additional time thereafter as may be determined by the court from the date the insolvency is determined or an ancillary proceeding is instituted in the state, whichever is later, to permit proper defense by the association of all pending causes of action as to any covered claims arising from a judgment under any decision, verdict or finding based on the default of the insolvent insurer or its failure to defend an insured, the association either on its own behalf or on behalf of such insured may apply to have such judgment, order or administrator that made such judgment, order, decision, verdict or finding and shall be permitted to defend such claim on the merits.

The liquidator, receiver or statutory successor of an insolvent insurer covered by this chapter shall permit access by the board or its authorized representative to such of the insolvent insurer's records which are necessary for the board in carrying out its functions under this chapter with regard to covered claims. In addition, the liquidator, receiver or statutory successor shall provide the board or its representative with copies of such records upon the request by the board and at the expense of the board. (Acts 1980, No. 80-806, p. 1639, § 18.)

Code commissioner's note. — The first paragraph of this section is set out as enacted by the legislature.

§ 27-42-19. Association, policyholders, beneficiaries and insureds to have preferred creditor status.

Upon the issuance of a proper court order placing a domestic insurer in receivership or placing a foreign insurer in ancillary receivership for rehabilitation or liquidation, all policyholders, beneficiaries and insureds of such insolvent insurer, with respect to claims arising from and within the coverages of and not in excess of the applicable limits of insurance policies and contracts issued by the insolvent insurer, and liability claims against insureds which claims are within the coverage of and not in excess of the applicable limits of insurance policies and insurance contracts issued by the insolvent insurer, and the Alabama Insurance Guaranty Association and any similar organization in another state shall be preferred creditors of said insolvent insurer. (Acts 1980, No. 80-806, p. 1639, § 19.)

§ 27-42-20. Access to assets of insolvent insurer; application for court approval of plan to disburse assets; notice of application.

(a) Within 120 days of a final determination of insolvency of an insurance company by a court of competent jurisdiction the receiver shall make application to the said court for approval of a proposal to disburse assets out of such company's marshalled assets, from time to time as such assets become available, to the Alabama Insurance Guaranty Association and to any entity or person performing a similar function in another state. (The Alabama Insurance Guaranty Association and any entity or person performing a similar function in other states shall hereinafter be referred to collectively as the associations.)

(b) Such proposal shall at least include provisions for:

(1) Reserving amounts for the payment of expenses of administration and claims falling within the priorities established in the Alabama Uniform Insurers Liquidation Act but only with respect to such priorities higher than that of the associations;

(2) Disbursement of the assets marshalled to date and subsequent disbursement of assets as they become available;

(3) Equitable allocation of disbursements to each of the associations entitled thereto;

(4) The securing by the receiver from each of the associations entitled to disbursements pursuant to this section of an agreement to return to the receiver such assets previously disbursed as may be required to pay claims of secured creditors and claims with a higher priority than those of the associations. No bond shall be required of any such association.

(c) The receiver's proposal shall provide for disbursements to the associations in amounts at least equal to the payments made or to be made thereby for which such associations could assert claims against the receiver, and shall further provide that if the assets available for disbursement from time to time do not equal or exceed the amount of such payments made or to be made by the associations then disbursements shall be in the amount of available assets.

(d) Notice of such application shall be given to the associations in and to the commissioners of insurance of each of the states. Any such notice shall be deemed to have been given when deposited in the United States certified mails, first-class postage prepaid, at least 30 days prior to submission of such application to the said court. Action on the application may be taken by the said court provided the above required notice has been given and provided further that the receiver's proposal complies with subdivisions (1) and (4) of subsection (b) of this section. (Acts 1980, No. 80-806, p. 1639, § 20.)

Code commissioner's note. — The Alabama Uniform Insurers Liquidation Act is codified as subdivisions (2) through (13) of § 27-32-1, together with §§ 27-32-4, 27-32-5 and 27-32-15 through 27-32-22.

CHAPTER 43.

LEGAL EXPENSE INSURANCE.

Sec.
27-43-1. Short title.
27-43-2. Purpose of chapter.
27-43-3. Definitions.
27-43-4. Applicability of chapter.
27-43-5. Authorization of prepaid legal expense insurance business required.
27-43-6. Insurers deemed eligible to transact legal expense insurance.
27-43-7. Procedure for incorporation of legal services insurance corporation generally.
27-43-8. Filing of application for certificate of authority; contents of application; issuance of certificate.
27-43-9. Bond or deposit requirements.
27-43-10. Types of legal expense insurance; policy and certificate forms; issuance of policies and certificates.
27-43-11. Premium rates.
27-43-12. Filing, approval, etc., of contracts between insurers and attorneys, etc.
27-43-13. Fees and taxes required of legal service insurance corporations; applicability of general insurance laws to legal service insurance corporations.

Sec.
27-43-14. Registration requirements — Generally.
27-43-15. Same — Sales agents.
27-43-16. Grounds for compulsory refusal, suspension, revocation, etc., of registration of contracting sales agents.
27-43-17. Grounds for discretionary refusal, suspension, revocation, etc., of registration of contracting sales agents.
27-43-18. Procedure for refusal, suspension, revocation, etc., of registration of contracting sales agent.
27-43-19. Imposition of administrative penalty in lieu of suspension, revocation, etc., of registration.
27-43-20. Funds belonging to legal service insurance corporations received by agents to be held in trust; accounting for and disposition of funds by agents; appropriation of funds, etc., by agent.
27-43-21. Disposition of moneys received from licenses and fees.
27-43-22. Promulgation of rules and regulations.
27-43-23. Construction of chapter.

Collateral references. — Liability insurance coverage as extending to liability for punitive or exemplary damages. 16 ALR4th 11.

§ 27-43-1. Short title.

This chapter shall be known and may be cited as the "Legal Expense Insurance Act". (Acts 1981, No. 81-719, p. 1214, § 1.)

§ 27-43-2. Purpose of chapter.

The purpose of this chapter is to authorize state certification and regulation of organizations which provide programs for the payment of the costs of legal services. (Acts 1981, No. 81-719, p. 1214, § 1.)

Collateral references. — 7 C.J.S., Attorney and Client, § 56.

§ 27-43-3. Definitions.

As used in this chapter, the following terms shall have the following meanings, respectively, unless the context requires otherwise:

(1) DEPARTMENT. The department of insurance;

(2) COMMISSIONER. The commissioner of insurance of this state;

(3) INSURER. Any person authorized to do a casualty insurance business or life, accident and sickness insurance business as an insurer in this state and organizations authorized to transact legal expense insurance under section 27-43-8;

(4) LEGAL EXPENSE INSURANCE. Such term means, irrespective of the definition of insurance in other chapters under this title, the assumption of a contractual obligation to pay for specific legal services or to reimburse for specific legal expenses, in consideration of a specified payment in advance for an interval of time, regardless of whether the payment is made by the beneficiaries individually or by a third person for them, but does not include the provision of or reimbursement for legal services incidental to other insurance coverages. (Acts 1981, No. 81-719, p. 1214, § 1; Acts 1984, No. 84-243, p. 374, § 1.)

Collateral references. — 44 C.J.S., Insurance, § 24.

§ 27-43-4. Applicability of chapter.

The insurance laws of this state, including this chapter, do not apply to:

(1) Retainer contracts made by attorneys-at-law with individual clients with fees based on estimates of the nature and amount of services to be provided to the specific client and similar contracts made with a group of clients involved in the same or closely related legal matters;

(2) Any lawyer referral services authorized by the state bar of Alabama;

(3) The furnishing of legal assistance by labor unions and other employee organizations to their members in matters relating to employment or occupations;

(4) The furnishing of legal assistance to members and/or dependents by churches, cooperatives, educational institutions, credit unions, labor unions or other organizations of employees, where such organizations contract with and pay directly a lawyer or law firm(s) for the provision of legal services, where the assistance is provided as an incident to membership and not on the basis of an optional fee or charge and the administration of such program of legal assistance is wholly conducted by the organization; and

(5) Employee welfare benefit plans to the extent that state laws are superseded by section 514 of the Employee Retirement Income Security Act of 1974, provided evidence of exemption from state laws is shown to the department. (Acts 1981, No. 81-719, p. 1214, § 1.)

§ 27-43-5. Authorization of prepaid legal expense insurance business required.

(a) No person or organization may do a prepaid legal expense insurance business in this state unless authorized to do so by the commissioner.

(b) This section does not apply to organizations exempt pursuant to section 27-43-4, Code of Alabama, 1975. (Acts 1981, No. 81-719, p. 1214, § 1.)

Collateral references. — 44 C.J.S., Insurance, §§ 56, 64(a).
43 Am. Jur. 2d, Insurance, §§ 52, 56.

§ 27-43-6. Insurers deemed eligible to transact legal expense insurance.

(a) Any domestic, foreign or alien insurer authorized to transact casualty insurance or life, accident and sickness insurance in this state may transact legal expense insurance in this state.

(b) Legal service insurance corporations possessing a valid certificate of authority may transact legal expense insurance in this state. (Acts 1981, No. 81-719, p. 1214, § 1; Acts 1984, No. 84-243, p. 374, § 1.)

§ 27-43-7. Procedure for incorporation of legal services insurance corporation generally.

(a) Any number of corporate or adult natural persons may organize a legal service insurance corporation under this section.

(b) The articles of incorporation shall conform to the requirements applicable to corporations, except that:

(1) The name of the corporation shall indicate that payment for legal services or indemnity for legal expenses is to be provided; and

(2) The purposes of the corporation shall be limited to payment for legal services or indemnity for legal expenses and business expenses reasonably related thereto. (Acts 1981, No. 81-719, p. 1214, § 1.)

§ 27-43-8. Filing of application for certificate of authority; contents of application; issuance of certificate.

(a) The incorporators shall file with the commissioner an application for a certificate of authority to do business upon a form to be furnished by the department, which shall include or have attached the following:

(1) The names and, for the preceding 10 years, all addresses and all occupations of all incorporators and proposed directors and officers;

(2) A certified copy of the corporate articles and bylaws and a list of the names, addresses and occupations of all directors and principal officers and, if previously incorporated, for the three most recent years, the corporation annual statements and reports;

(3) All agreements relating to the corporation to which any incorporator or proposed director or officer is a party;

(4) A statement of the amount and sources of the funds available for organization expenses and the proposed arrangements for reimbursement and compensation of incorporators or other persons;

(5) A statement of compensation of directors and officers;

(6) The forms to be used for any proposed contracts between the corporation and providers of legal services and any corporations which perform administrative, marketing or management services, concerning the provision of services to insureds;

(7) The plan for conducting the insurance business, including all of the following:

a. The geographical area in which business is intended to be done in the first five years;

b. The types of insurance intended to be written in the first five years, including specification whether and to what extent indemnity rather than service benefits are to be provided;

c. The proposed marketing methods;

d. Actuarial data or other similar statistical data, documented and verified in such manner as the department may reasonably require, affirmatively demonstrating the anticipated income and expenses in the first five years, including, without limitation, the projected expenditure for legal services and projected source of funds to make up any anticipated deficits.

(8) A current statement of the assets and liabilities of the applicant;

(9) Forms of all prepaid legal service contracts the applicant proposes to offer showing the rates to be charged for each form of contract; and

(10) Such other documents or information as the department may reasonably require;

(b) Copies of the documents filed pursuant to subdivisions (6) and (9) of subsection (a) of this section shall be filed with the state bar of Alabama within five days of filing with the commissioner;

(c) The commissioner shall issue a certificate of authority if he is satisfied that:

(1) All requirements of law have been met;

(2) All natural persons who are incorporators, the directors and principal officers of corporate incorporators and the proposed directors and officers of the corporation being formed are trustworthy and competent and collectively have the competence and experience to engage in the particular insurance business proposed; and

(3) The business plan is consistent with the interests of the corporation's potential insureds and of the public. (Acts 1981, No. 81-719, p. 1214, § 1.)

§ 27-43-9. Bond or deposit requirements.

(a) To assure the faithful performance of its obligations in the event of insolvency, each corporation authorized under section 27-43-8 shall, through the commissioner, deposit and maintain with the treasurer of the state securities of the type eligible for deposit by insurers under section 27-6-3, which securities shall have at all times a market value as follows:

(1) An insurer which has transacted no legal expense insurance in this state prior to January 1, 1982, shall, prior to the issuance of its certificate of authority and before receiving any premiums, place in trust with the treasurer of the state, through the commissioner an initial amount of $50,000.00;

(2) An insurer transacting a legal expense insurance business in this state prior to January 1, 1982 and having in force in this state less than $300,000.00 of gross written premiums, membership fees or similar charges shall place in trust with the treasurer of the state, through the commissioner, a sum equal to 50 percent of the gross premiums in force or $50,000.00, whichever is less;

(3) An insurer transacting a legal expense insurance business in this state prior to January 1, 1982 and having in force in this state more than $300,000.00 but less than $750,000.00 of gross written premiums, membership fees or similar charges in this state shall place in trust with the treasurer of the state, through the commissioner, an amount not less than $75,000.00; and

(4) An insurer transacting a legal expense insurance business in this state prior to January 1, 1982 and having in force in this state $750,000.00 or more of gross written premiums, membership fees or similar charges in this state shall place in trust with the treasurer of the state, through the commissioner, an amount equal to $100,000.00.

(b) In lieu of any deposit of securities required under subsection (a) of this section and subject to the commissioner's approval, a legal service insurance corporation may file with the treasurer of the state a surety bond issued by a surety insurer authorized to serve as surety under the provisions of chapter 24 of this title. The bond shall be for the same purpose as the deposit in lieu of which it is filed. The department shall not approve any bond under the terms of which the protection afforded against insolvency is not equivalent to the protection afforded by those securities provided for in subsection (a) of this section.

(c) Securities or bonds posted pursuant to this section shall be for the benefit of and subject to action thereon in the event of insolvency or impairment of any legal service insurance corporation by any person or persons sustaining an actionable injury due to the failure of the corporation to faithfully perform its obligations to its insureds.

(d) The state shall be responsible for the safekeeping of all securities deposited with the treasurer of the state under this chapter. Such securities shall not, on account of being in this state, be subject to taxation, but shall be held exclusively and solely to guarantee the legal service insurance corporation's performance of its obligations to its insureds.

(e) Such deposit or bond shall be maintained unimpaired as long as the legal service insurance corporation continues in business in this state. Whenever the corporation ceases to do business in this state and furnishes the commissioner proof satisfactory to the commissioner that it has discharged or otherwise adequately provided for all its obligations to its insureds in this state, the treasurer of the state shall release the deposited securities to the parties entitled thereto, on presentation of the treasurer's receipts for such securities, or shall release any bond filed with it in lieu of such deposit.

(f) The commissioner may at any time enter an order increasing the amount of the deposit or bond specified under subsections (a) and (b) of this section if he finds that there has been a substantial change in the facts, including an increase in the amounts of premiums, membership fees or similar charges in force in this state on which the original determination was based. The commissioner shall hold a hearing within 30 days after receiving a request from the corporation submitted within 30 days after being notified of the modification order. Failure to meet the new requirements within 30 days after final decision or after the expiration of the 30-day period for submitting the hearing request constitutes a ground for rehabilitation. (Acts 1981, No. 81-719, p. 1214, § 1.)

Collateral references. — 43 Am. Jur. 2d, Insurance, § 63.

§ 27-43-10. Types of legal expense insurance; policy and certificate forms; issuance of policies and certificates.

(a) Legal expense insurance may be written as individual, group, blanket or franchise insurance. Each contractual obligation for legal expense insurance must be evidenced by a policy. Each person insured under a group policy must be issued a certificate of coverage.

(b) No policy or certificate of legal expense insurance may be issued in this state unless a copy of the form has been filed and approved by the commissioner.

(c) The commissioner may not approve any form that does not meet the following requirements:

(1) Policies must contain a list and description of the legal service payments promised or the legal matters for which expenses are to be reimbursed and any limits on the amounts to be paid or reimbursed;

(2) Policies and certificates must indicate the name of the insurer and the full address of its principal place of business;

(3) Certificates issued under group policies must contain a full statement of the benefits provided and exceptions thereto, but may summarize the other terms of the master policy;

(4) Policies promising payment for legal services to be provided by a limited number of attorneys who have concluded provider contracts with the insurer, whether the attorney in an individual case is to be selected by the insured or by the insurer, must provide for alternative benefits in the case where the insured is unable to find a participating attorney willing to perform the promised services or the attorney selected by the insurer is disqualified or otherwise unable to perform the promised services. The alternative benefit may consist of furnishing the services of an attorney selected and paid by the insurer or paying the fee of an attorney selected by the insured. The policy must also provide a procedure that includes impartial review for settling disagreements about the grounds for demanding an alternative benefit;

(5) No policy except one issued by a mutual or reciprocal insurance company may provide for assessments on policyholders or for reduction of benefits for the purpose of maintaining the insurer's solvency;

(6) Policies must contain a statement that the subscriber has a right to complain to the state bar of Alabama about attorney conduct pursuant to the plan; and

(7) Policies must contain a statement that the individual beneficiary has the right to retain, at his own expense, except where the policy provides otherwise, any attorney authorized to practice law in the state;

(d) The department may disapprove a policy or certificate form if it finds that it:

(1) Is unfair, unfairly discriminatory, misleading, ambiguous or encourages misrepresentation or misunderstanding of the contract;

(2) Provides coverage or benefits or contains other provisions that would endanger the solvency of the insurer; or

(3) Is contrary to law. (Acts 1981, No. 81-719, p. 1214, § 1.)

Collateral references. — 43 Am. Jur. 2d,
Insurance, § 65.

§ 27-43-11. Premium rates.

(a) No policy of legal expense insurance may be issued in this state unless the premium rates for the insurance have been filed with and approved by the commissioner.

(b) Premium rates must be established and justified in accordance with generally accepted insurance principles, including, but not limited to, the experience or judgment of the insurer making the rate filing or actuarial computations.

(c) The commissioner may disapprove rates that are excessive, inadequate or unfairly discriminatory. Rates are not unfairly discriminatory because they are averaged broadly among persons insured under group, blanket or franchise policies.

(d) The commissioner may require the submission of whatever relevant information is deemed necessary in determining whether to approve or disapprove a filing made under this section or section 27-43-10, Code of Alabama, 1975. (Acts 1981, No. 81-719, p. 1214, § 1.)

§ 27-43-12. Filing, approval, etc., of contracts between insurers and attorneys, etc.

(a) Contracts made between the insurer and participating attorneys, management contracts and contracts with other providers of services by the legal expense insurance policy must be filed with and approved by the commissioner.

(b) Insurers must annually report to the commissioner, in such detail as is reasonably required, the number and geographical distribution of attorneys and other providers of services covered by the legal expense insurance policy with whom it maintains contractual relations and the nature of the relations. For individual insurers or groups of insurers, the commissioner may require more frequent reports. (Acts 1981, No. 81-719, p. 1214, § 1.)

§ 27-43-13. Fees and taxes required of legal service insurance corporations; applicability of general insurance laws to legal service insurance corporations.

(a) A legal service insurance corporation will pay the prescribed fees and taxes required of a domestic casualty insurer.

(b) The following provisions of the insurance laws of this state apply to legal service insurance corporations authorized under section 27-43-8, Code of Alabama, 1975, to the extent that they are not inconsistent with the provisions of this chapter:

(1) Chapters 27-1 and 27-2, Code of Alabama, 1975 — Administration and General Provisions;

(2) Chapter 27-4, Code of Alabama, 1975 — Fees and Taxes;

(3) Chapter 27-6, Code of Alabama, 1975 — Administration of Deposits;

(4) Chapter 27-11 [27-12], Code of Alabama, 1975 — Unfair Trade Practices; and

(5) Chapter 27-32, Code of Alabama, 1975 — Insurer Insolvency; Rehabilitation and Liquidation.

(c) The commissioner may by rule modify or waive any requirements referred to in subsection (b) of this section for legal service insurers if it is necessary to avoid unreasonable hardship, expense or inconvenience and if the interests of policyholders continue to be adequately protected. (Acts 1981, No. 81-719, p. 1214, § 1.)

§ 27-43-14. Registration requirements — Generally.

No person shall solicit, negotiate, advertise or effectuate legal expense insurance contracts in this state unless such person is registered as a contracting sales agent or is utilized by a contracting sales agent. (Acts 1981, No. 81-719, p. 1214, § 1.)

Collateral references. — 43 Am. Jur. 2d, Insurance, § 66.

§ 27-43-15. Same — Sales agents.

Every legal service insurance corporation shall, on forms prescribed by the commissioner, register, on or before October 1 of each year, the name and business address of each contracting sales agent utilized by it in Alabama and shall, within 30 days after termination of the contract, notify the commissioner of such termination. At the time of said annual registration, a $10.00 filing fee for each contracting sales agent shall be paid by the legal service insurance corporation to the commissioner. Any contracting sales agent utilized subsequent to the October 1 filing date shall be registered with the department within 10 days after such utilization. Such contracting sales agents shall be subject to the same regulations and controls as provided for casualty insurance representatives in chapter 7 of this title or the same regulations and controls as provided for life and/or accident and sickness insurance companies. (Acts 1981, No. 81-719, p. 1214, § 1; Acts 1984, No. 84-243, p. 374, § 1.)

Collateral references. — 43 Am. Jur. 2d, Insurance, § 66.

§ 27-43-16. Grounds for compulsory refusal, suspension, revocation, etc., of registration of contracting sales agents.

The commissioner shall deny, suspend, revoke or refuse to renew or continue the registration of any contracting sales agent if it is found that as to the agent, any one or more of the following applicable grounds exist:

(1) Material misstatement, misrepresentation or fraud in registration;

(2) The registration is willfully used or is to be used to circumvent any of the requirements or prohibitions of this chapter;

(3) Willful misrepresentation of any legal service expense contract or willful deception with regard to any such contract, done either in person or by any form of dissemination of information or advertising;

(4) In the adjustment of claims he has materially misrepresented to a contract holder or other interested party the terms and coverage of a contract, with the intent and for the purpose of effecting settlement of such claim on less favorable terms than those provided in and contemplated by the contract;

(5) For demonstrated lack of fitness or trustworthiness to engage in the business of legal service insurance;

(6) For demonstrated lack of adequate knowledge and technical competence to engage in the transactions authorized by the registration;

(7) Fraudulent or dishonest practices in the conduct of business under the registration;

(8) Misappropriation, conversion or unlawful withholding of moneys belonging to a legal service corporation, or to others, and received in the conduct of business under the registration;

(9) For rebating, or attempting to rebate, or for unlawfully dividing, or offering to divide his commission with another; and

(10) Willful failure to comply with, or willful violation of, any proper order or rule of the department or willful violation of any provision of this chapter. (Acts 1981, No. 81-719, p. 1214, § 1.)

§ 27-43-17. Grounds for discretionary refusal, suspension, revocation, etc., of registration of contracting sales agents.

The commissioner may, in his discretion, deny, suspend, revoke or refuse to renew or continue the registration of any contracting sales agent if it is found, after notice and hearing thereon as provided in section 27-43-18, that, as to the agent, any one or more of the following applicable grounds exist under circumstances for which such denial, suspension, revocation or refusal is not mandatory under section 27-43-16:

(1) Any cause for which granting of the registration could have been refused had it then existed and been known to the department;

(2) Violation of any provision of this chapter, or of any other law applicable to the business of legal service insurance, in the course of dealings under the registration;

(3) Violation of any lawful order or rule of the commissioner;

(4) Failure or refusal to pay over, upon demand, to any legal service insurer he represents or has represented, any money coming into his hands, belonging to the legal service insurance corporation;

(5) In the conduct of business under the registration, he has engaged in unfair methods of competition or in unfair or deceptive acts or practices, as such methods, acts or practices are or may be defined under section 27-7-19 or the Alabama Insurance Code, or has otherwise shown himself to be a source of injury or loss to the public or detrimental to the public interest; and

(6) Conviction of a felony. (Acts 1981, No. 81-719, p. 1214, § 1.)

Collateral references. — 44 C.J.S., Insurance, §§ 87, 89.

43 Am. Jur. 2d, Insurance, § 68.

§ 27-43-18. Procedure for refusal, suspension, revocation, etc., of registration of contracting sales agent.

(a) If any contracting sales agent is convicted by a court of a violation of any provision of this chapter, the registration of such individual shall thereby be deemed to be immediately revoked without any further procedure relative thereto by the commissioner.

(b) As to a registration denied, suspended or revoked by the commissioner, the persons aggrieved thereby shall have the right to a hearing thereon as provided in section 27-7-37.

(c) If, after an investigation or upon other evidence, the department has reason to believe that there may exist any one or more grounds for the suspension or revocation of, or refusal to renew or continue, the registration of any contracting sales agent, as such grounds are specified in sections 27-43-16 and 27-43-17, the department may proceed to suspend, revoke or refuse to renew or continue the registration as the case may be.

(d) Whenever it appears that any licensed insurance agent has violated the provisions of this chapter, the commissioner may take such action relative thereto as is authorized by the Alabama Insurance Code as for a violation of the Alabama Insurance Code by such agent. (Acts 1981, No. 81-719, p. 1214, § 1.)

Collateral references. — 44 C.J.S., Insurance, §§ 87, 89.
43 Am. Jur. 2d, Insurance, § 68.

§ 27-43-19. Imposition of administrative penalty in lieu of suspension, revocation, etc., of registration.

(a) If, pursuant to procedures provided for in this chapter, it is found that one or more grounds exist for the suspension or revocation of, or refusal to renew or continue, any registration issued under this chapter, except when such suspension, revocation or refusal is mandatory, an order may be entered imposing upon the registrant, in lieu of such suspension, revocation or refusal, an administrative penalty for each violation in the amount of $100.00 or, in the event of willful misconduct or willful violation on the part of the registrant, an administrative fine of $500.00. The administrative penalty may be augmented in amount by an amount equal to any commissions received by or accruing to the credit of the registrant in connection with any transaction to which the grounds for suspension, revocation or refusal related.

(b) The order may allow the registrant a reasonable period, not to exceed 30 days, within which to pay to the commissioner the amount of the penalty so imposed. If the registrant fails to pay the penalty in its entirety to the commissioner at his office in Montgomery within the period so allowed, the registration of the registrant shall stand suspended or revoked, or renewal or continuation may be refused, as the case may be, upon expiration of such period and without any further proceedings. (Acts 1981, No. 81-719, p. 1214, § 1.)

Collateral references. — 44 C.J.S., Insurance, § 86.

§ 27-43-20. Funds belonging to legal service insurance corporations received by agents to be held in trust; accounting for and disposition of funds by agents; appropriation of funds, etc., by agent.

(a) All funds belonging to legal service insurance corporations or others received by a contracting sales agent in transactions under his registration shall be trust funds so received by such agent in a fiduciary capacity, and the agent, in the applicable regular course of business, shall account for and pay the same to the legal service insurance corporation or other person entitled thereto.

(b) Any contracting sales agent who, not being entitled thereto, diverts or appropriates such funds or any portion thereof to his own use shall, upon conviction, be guilty of theft of property, punishable as provided in sections 13A-8-2 through 13A-8-5 of the Alabama Criminal Code. (Acts 1981, No. 81-719, p. 1214, § 1.)

Collateral references. — 44 C.J.S., Insurance, § 86.

§ 27-43-21. Disposition of moneys received from licenses and fees.

All moneys received from licenses and fees shall be deposited to the credit of the examiners' revolving fund of the department of insurance. (Acts 1981, No. 81-719, p. 1214, § 1.)

§ 27-43-22. Promulgation of rules and regulations.

The commissioner shall devise and promulgate rules and regulations, not inconsistent with the provisions of this chapter, as he deems advisable for effectuating its orderly administration. (Acts 1981, No. 81-719, p. 1214, § 1.)

§ 27-43-23. Construction of chapter.

Nothing contained in this chapter shall be construed to regulate the practice of law or limit the powers or authority of the supreme court of Alabama or state bar of Alabama in the regulation of the conduct of attorneys. (Acts 1981, No. 81-719, p. 1214, § 1.)

CHAPTER 44.

LIFE AND DISABILITY INSURANCE GUARANTY ASSOCIATION.

Sec.
27-44-1. Short title.
27-44-2. Purpose of chapter.
27-44-3. Scope of chapter.
27-44-4. Construction of chapter.
27-44-5. Definitions.
27-44-6. Creation of association; membership; accounts; supervision.
27-44-7. Board of directors; selection of members; vacancies; organizational meeting; reimbursement for expenses.
27-44-8. Powers and duties of association.
27-44-9. Assessments.
27-44-10. Submission of plan of operation and amendments; promulgation of rules in absence of plan.
27-44-11. Duties and powers of commissioner; appeal to commissioner from action of board or association; judicial review; notification of interested persons by liquidator, etc., of impaired insurer.
27-44-12. Duties of commissioner and board with regard to detection and pre-

Sec.
          vention of insolvencies or impairment.
27-44-13. Credits for assessments paid.
27-44-14. Liability of unpaid assessments; records of negotiations and meetings; association deemed creditor of impaired or insolvent insurer; judicial distribution of ownership rights of insolvent insurer; recovery by receiver of certain distributions from controlling affiliates.
27-44-15. Examination and regulation of association; annual report.
27-44-16. Tax exemptions.
27-44-17. Immunity under chapter.
27-44-18. Stay of proceedings; reopening default judgments.
27-44-19. Repealed.
27-44-20. Association, policyholders, beneficiaries and insureds to have preferred creditor status.
27-44-21. Immediate access of associations in this and other states to assets of insolvent insurer; application to court; contents of proposal; notice.

Collateral references. — Liability insurance coverage as extending to liability for punitive or exemplary damages. 16 ALR4th 11.

§ 27-44-1. Short title.

This chapter shall be known and may be cited as the "Alabama Life and Disability Insurance Guaranty Association Act." (Acts 1982, No. 82-561, p. 922, § 1.)

§ 27-44-2. Purpose of chapter.

The purpose of this chapter is to protect policyowners, insureds, beneficiaries, annuitants, payees, and the assignees of life insurance policies, disability insurance policies, annuity contracts, and supplemental contracts, subject to certain limitations, against failure in the performance of contractual obligations due to the impairment or insolvency of the insurer issuing such policies or contracts. To provide this protection, (1) an association of insurers is created to enable the guaranty of payment of benefits and of continuation of coverages, (2) members of the association are subject to assessment to provide funds to carry out the purpose of this chapter, and (3) the association is authorized to assist the commissioner, in the prescribed manner, in the detection and prevention of insurer impairments or insolvencies. (Acts 1982, No. 82-561, p. 922, § 2.)

§ 27-44-3. Scope of chapter.

(a) This chapter shall apply to direct life insurance policies, disability insurance policies, annuity contracts, and contracts supplemental to life and disability insurance policies, annuity contracts, and contracts supplemental to life and disability insurance policies and annuity contracts issued by persons licensed to transact insurance in this state at any time.

(b) This chapter shall not apply to:

(1) That portion or part of a variable life insurance or variable annuity contract not guaranteed by an insurer;

(2) That portion or part of any policy or contract under which the risk is borne by the policyholder;

(3) Any policy or contract or part thereof assumed by the impaired or insolvent insurer under a contract of reinsurance, other than reinsurance for which assumption certificates have been issued;

(4) Any such policy or contract issued by non-profit hospital and medical service plans, fraternals, cooperative hospital associations or health maintenance organizations. (Acts 1982, No. 82-561, p. 922, § 3.)

§ 27-44-4. Construction of chapter.

This chapter shall be liberally construed to effect the purpose under section 27-44-2 which shall constitute an aid and guide to interpretation. (Acts 1982, No. 82-561, p. 922, § 4.)

§ 27-44-5. Definitions.

As used in this chapter, the following terms shall have the following meanings, respectively, unless the context clearly indicates otherwise:

(1) ACCOUNT. Either of the three accounts created under section 27-44-6.

(2) ASSOCIATION. The Alabama life and disability insurance guaranty association created under section 27-44-6.

(3) COMMISSIONER. The commissioner of insurance of this state.

(4) CONTRACTUAL OBLIGATION. Any obligation under covered policies.

(5) COVERED POLICY. Any policy or contract within the scope of this chapter under section 27-44-3.

(6) IMPAIRED INSURER. A member insurer deemed by the commissioner after January 1, 1983 to be potentially unable to fulfill its contractual obligations and not an insolvent insurer.

(7) INSOLVENT INSURER. A member insurer which after January 1, 1983, becomes insolvent and is placed under a final order of liquidation, rehabilitation or conservation by a court of competent jurisdiction.

(8) MEMBER INSURER. Any insurer licensed to transact in this state any kind of insurance to which this chapter applies under section 27-44-3.

(9) PREMIUMS. Direct gross insurance premiums and annuity consider-ations received on covered policies, less return premiums and consider-

ations thereon and dividends paid or credited to policyholders on such direct business. "Premiums" do not include premiums and considerations on contracts between insurers and reinsurers.

(10) PERSON. Any individual, corporation, partnership, association or voluntary organization.

(11) RESIDENT. Any person who resides in this state at the time a member insurer is determined to be an impaired or insolvent insurer and to whom contractual obligations are owed. (Acts 1982, No. 82-561, p. 922, § 5.)

§ 27-44-6. Creation of association; membership; accounts; supervision.

(a) There is created a nonprofit unincorporated legal entity to be known as the Alabama life and disability insurance guaranty association. All member insurers shall be and remain members of the association as a condition of their authority to transact insurance in this state. The association shall perform its functions under the plan of operation established and approved under section 27-44-10 and shall exercise its powers through a board of directors established under section 27-44-7. For purposes of administration and assessment the association shall maintain three accounts:

(1) The disability insurance account;

(2) The life insurance account; and

(3) The annuity account.

(b) The association shall come under the immediate supervision of the commissioner and shall be subject to the applicable provisions of the insurance laws of this state. (Acts 1982, No. 82-561, p. 922, § 6.)

§ 27-44-7. Board of directors; selection of members; vacancies; organizational meeting; reimbursement for expenses.

(a) The board of directors of the association shall consist of not less than five nor more than nine member insurers serving terms as established in the plan of operation. At all times, at least one member of the board shall be a domestic insurer as defined in section 27-1-2(6). The members of the board shall be selected by member insurers subject to the approval of the commissioner. Vacancies on the board shall be filled for the remaining period of the term by a majority vote of the remaining board members, subject to the approval of the commissioner. To select the initial board of directors, and initially organize the association, the commissioner shall give notice to all member insurers of the time and place of the organizational meeting. In determining voting rights at the organizational meeting, each member insurer shall be entitled to one vote in person or by proxy. If the board of directors is not selected within 60 days after notice of the organizational meeting, the commissioner may appoint the initial members.

(b) In approving selections or in appointing members to the board, the commissioner shall consider, among other things, whether all member insurers are fairly represented.

(c) Members of the board may be reimbursed from the assets of the association for expenses incurred by them as members of the board of directors, but members of the board shall not otherwise be compensated by the association for their services. (Acts 1982, No. 82-561, p. 922, § 7.)

§ 27-44-8. Powers and duties of association.

In addition to the powers and duties enumerated in other sections of this chapter:

(1) If a domestic insurer is an impaired insurer, the association may subject to any conditions imposed by the association other than those which impair the contractual obligations of the impaired insurer, and approved by the impaired insurer and the commissioner:

a. Guarantee or reinsure, or cause to be guaranteed, assumed, or reinsured, any or all of the covered policies of the impaired insurers;

b. Provide such moneys, pledges, notes, guarantees, or other means as are proper to effectuate paragraph a, and assure payment of the contractual obligations of the impaired insurer pending action under paragraph a;

c. Loan money to the impaired insurer.

(2) If a domestic insurer is an insolvent insurer, the association shall, subject to the approval of the commissioner:

a. Guarantee, assume, or reinsure, or cause to be guaranteed, assumed, or reinsured the covered policies of the insolvent insurer;

b. Assure payment of the contractual obligations of the insolvent insurer; and

c. Provide such moneys, pledges, notes, guarantees, or other means as are reasonably necessary to discharge such duties.

(3) If a foreign or alien insurer is an insolvent insurer, the association shall, subject to the approval of the commissioner:

a. Guarantee, assume, or reinsure or cause to be guaranteed, assumed, or reinsured the covered policies of residents;

b. Assure payment of the contractual obligations of the insolvent insurer to residents; and

c. Provide such moneys, pledges, notes, guarantees, or other means as are reasonably necessary to discharge such duties.

Provided, however, that this subdivision shall not apply where the commissioner has determined that the foreign or alien insurer's domiciliary jurisdiction or state of entry provides, by statute, protection substantially similar to that provided by this chapter for residents of this state.

(4) a. In carrying out its duties under subdivisions (2) and (3), permanent policy liens, or contract liens may be imposed in connection with any guarantee, assumption or reinsurance agreement, if the court:

1. Finds that the amounts which can be assessed under this chapter are less than the amounts needed to assure full and prompt performance of the insolvent insurer's contractual obligations, or that the

599

economic or financial conditions as they affect member insurers are sufficiently adverse to render the imposition of policy or contract liens, to be in the public interest; and

2. Approves the specific policy liens or contract liens to be used.

b. Before being obligated under subdivisions (2) and (3) the association may request that there be imposed temporary moratoriums or liens on payments of cash values and policy loans in addition to any contractual provisions for deferral of cash or policy loan values, and such temporary moratoriums and liens may be imposed if they are approved by the court.

(5) If the association fails to act within a reasonable period of time as provided in subdivisions (2) and (3) of this section, the commissioner shall have the powers and duties of the association under this chapter with respect to insolvent insurers.

(6) The association may render assistance and advice to the commissioner, upon his request, concerning rehabilitation, payment of claims, continuance of coverage, or the performance of other contractual obligations of any impaired or insolvent insurer.

(7) The association shall have standing to appear before any court in this state with jurisdiction over an impaired or insolvent insurer concerning which the association is or may become obligated under this chapter. Such standing shall extend to all matters germane to the powers and duties of the association, including, but not limited to, proposals for reinsuring or guaranteeing the covered policies of the impaired or insolvent insurer and the determination of the covered policies and contractual obligations.

(8) a. Any person receiving benefits under this chapter shall be deemed to have assigned the rights under the covered policy to the association to the extent of the benefits received because of this chapter whether the benefits are payments of contractual obligations or continuation of coverage. The association may require an assignment to it of such rights by any payee, policy or contract owner, beneficiary, insured or annuitant as a condition precedent to the receipt of any rights or benefits conferred by this chapter upon such person. The association shall be subrogated to these rights against the assets of any insolvent insurer.

b. This subrogation rights of the association under this subdivision shall have the same priority against the assets of the insolvent insurer as that possessed by the person entitled to receive benefits under this chapter.

(9) The contractual obligations of the insolvent insurer for which the association becomes or may become liable shall be as great as but no greater than the contractual obligations of the insolvent insurer would have been in the absence of an insolvency unless such obligations are reduced as permitted by subdivision (4) but the aggregate liability of the association shall not exceed $100,000.00 in cash values, or $300,000.00 for all benefits, including cash values, with respect to any one life.

(10) The association may:

a. Enter into such contracts as are necessary or proper to carry out the provisions and purposes of this chapter;

b. Sue or be sued, including taking any legal actions necessary or proper for recovery of any unpaid assessments under section 27-44-9;

c. Borrow money to effect the purposes of this chapter. Any notes or other evidence of indebtedness of the association not in default shall be legal investments for domestic insurers and may be carried as admitted assets;

d. Employ or retain such persons as are necessary to handle the financial transactions of the association, and to perform such other functions as become necessary or proper under this chapter;

e. Negotiate and contract with any liquidator, rehabilitator, conservator, or ancillary receiver to carry out the powers and duties of the association;

f. Take such legal action as may be necessary to avoid payment of improper claims;

g. Exercise, for the purpose of this chapter, and to the extent approved by the commissioner, the powers of a domestic life or health insurer, but in no case may the association issue insurance policies or annuity contracts other than those issued to perform the contractual obligations of the impaired or insolvent insurer. (Acts 1982, No. 82-561, p. 922, § 8.)

§ 27-44-9. Assessments.

(a) For the purpose of providing the funds necessary to carry out the powers and duties of the association, the board of directors shall assess the member insurers, separately for each account, at such time and for such amounts as the board finds necessary. Assessments shall be due not less than 30 days after prior written notice to the member insurers and shall accrue interest at six percent per annum on and after the due date.

(b) There shall be three classes of assessments, as follows:

(1) Class A assessments shall be made for the purpose of meeting administrative costs and other general expenses and examinations conducted under the authority of section 27-44-12(5) not related to a particular impaired or insolvent insurer.

(2) Class B assessments shall be made to the extent necessary to carry out the powers and duties of the association under section 27-44-8 with regard to an impaired or insolvent domestic insurer.

(3) Class C assessments shall be made to the extent necessary to carry out the powers and duties of the association under section 27-44-8 with regard to an insolvent foreign or alien insurer.

(c)(1) The amount of any Class A assessment shall be determined by the board and may be made on a non-pro rata basis. Such assessment shall not exceed $50.00 per company in any one calendar year. The amount of any Class B or C assessment shall be allocated for assessment purposes among the accounts in the proportion that the premiums received by the impaired or insolvent insurer on the policies covered by each account for the last calendar year preceding the assessment in which the impaired or insolvent insurer received premiums bears to the premiums received by such insurer for such calendar year on all covered policies.

(2) Class C assessments against member insurers for each account shall be in the proportion that the premiums received on business in this state by each assessed member insurer on policies covered by each account for the calendar year preceding the assessment bears to such premiums received on business in this state for the calendar year preceding the assessment by all assessed member insurers.

(3) Class B assessments for each account shall be made separately for each state in which the impaired or insolvent domestic insurer was authorized to transact insurance at any time, in the proportion that the premiums received on business in such state by the impaired or insolvent insurer on policies covered by such account for the last calendar year preceding the assessment in which the impaired or insolvent insurer received premiums bears to such premiums received in all such states for such calendar year by the impaired or insolvent insurer. The assessments against member insurers shall be in the proportion that the premiums received on business in each such state by each assessed member insurer on policies covered by each account for the calendar year preceding the assessment bears to such premiums received on business in each state for the calendar year preceding assessment by all assessed member insurers.

(4) Assessments for funds to meet the requirements of the association with respect to an impaired or insolvent insurer shall not be made until necessary to implement the purposes of this chapter. Classification of assessments under subsection (b) and computation of assessments under this subsection shall be made with a reasonable degree of accuracy, recognizing that exact determinations may not always be possible.

(d) The association may abate or defer, in whole or in part, the assessment of a member insurer if, in the opinion of the board, payment of the assessment would endanger the ability of the member insurer to fulfill its contractual obligations. In the event an assessment against a member insurer is abated, or deferred in whole or in part, the amount by which such assessment is abated or deferred may be assessed against the other member insurers in a manner consistent with the basis for assessments set forth in this section.

(e) The total of all assessments upon a member insurer for each account shall not in any one calendar year exceed one percent of such insurer's premiums received in this state during the calendar year preceding the assessment on the policies covered by the account. If the maximum assessment, together with the other assets of the association in either account, does not provide in any one year in either account an amount sufficient to carry out the responsibilities of the association, the necessary additional funds shall be assessed as soon thereafter as permitted by this chapter.

(f) The board may, by an equitable method as established in the plan of operation, refund to member insurers, in proportion to the contribution of each insurer to that account, the amount by which the assets of the account exceed the amount the board finds is necessary to carry out during the coming year the obligations of the association with regard to that account, including assets accruing from net realized gains and income from investments. A reasonable amount may be retained in any account to provide funds for the continuing expenses of the association and for future losses if refunds are impractical.

(g) The association shall issue to each insurer paying an assessment under this chapter, other than a Class A assessment, a certificate of contribution, in a form prescribed by the commissioner, for the amount of the assessment so paid. All outstanding certificates shall be of equal dignity and priority without reference to amounts or dates of issue. A certificate of contribution may be shown by the insurer in its financial statement as an asset in such form and for such amount, if any, and period of time as the commissioner may approve. (Acts 1982, No. 82-561, p. 922, § 9.)

§ 27-44-10. Submission of plan of operation and amendments; promulgation of rules in absence of plan.

(a)(1) The association shall submit to the commissioner a plan of operation and any amendments thereto necessary or suitable to assure the fair, reasonable, and equitable administration of the association. The plan of operation and any amendments thereto shall become effective upon approval in writing by the commissioner.

(2) If the association fails to submit a suitable plan of operation within 180 days following January 1, 1983 or if at any time thereafter the association fails to submit suitable amendments to the plan, the commissioner shall, after notice and hearing, adopt and promulgate such reasonable rules as are necessary or advisable to effectuate the provisions of this chapter. Such rules shall continue in force until modified by the commissioner or superseded by a plan submitted by the association and approved by the commissioner.

(b) All member insurers shall comply with the plan of operation.

(c) The plan of operation shall, in addition to requirements enumerated elsewhere in this chapter:

(1) Establish procedures for handling the assets of the association.

(2) Establish the amount and method of reimbursing members of the board of directors under section 27-44-7.

(3) Establish regular places and times for meetings of the board of directors.

(4) Establish procedures for records to be kept of all financial transactions of the association, its agents, and the board of directors.

(5) Establish the procedures whereby selections for the board of directors will be made and submitted to the commissioner.

(6) Establish any additional procedures for assessments under section 27-44-9.

(7) Contain additional provisions necessary or proper for the execution of the powers and duties of the association.

(d) The plan of operation may provide that any or all powers and duties of the association, except those under sections 27-44-8 (10) c and 27-44-9, are delegated to a corporation, association, or other organization which performs or will perform functions similar to those of this association, or its equivalent, in two or more states. Such a corporation, association, or organization shall be reimbursed for any payments made on behalf of the association and shall be paid for its performance of any functions of the association. A delegation under this subsection shall take effect only with the approval of both the board of directors and the commissioner, and may be made only to a corporation, association, or organization which extends protection not substantially less favorable and effective than that provided by this chapter. (Acts 1982, No. 82-561, p. 922, § 10.)

§ 27-44-11. Duties and powers of commissioner; appeal to commissioner from action of board or association; judicial review; notification of interested persons by liquidator, etc., of impaired insurer.

In addition to the duties and powers enumerated elsewhere in this chapter:
(1) The commissioner shall:
a. Upon request of the board of directors, provide the association with a statement of the premiums in the appropriate states for each member insurer.

b. When an impairment is declared and the amount of the impairment is determined, serve a demand upon the impaired insurer to make good the impairment within a reasonable time. Notice to the impaired insurer shall constitute notice to its shareholders, if any. The failure of the insurer to promptly comply with such demand shall not excuse the association from the performance of its powers and duties under this chapter.

c. In any liquidation or rehabilitation proceeding involving a domestic insurer, petition the court of competent jurisdiction to have the chief of the receivership division appointed as the liquidator or rehabilitator. If a foreign or alien member insurer is subject to a liquidation proceeding in its domiciliary jurisdiction or state of entry, the chief of the receivership division shall be appointed conservator.

(2) The commissioner may suspend or revoke, after notice and hearing, the certificate of authority to transact insurance in this state of any member insurer which fails to pay an assessment when due or fails to comply with the plan of operation. As an alternative the commissioner may levy a forfeiture on any member insurer which fails to pay an assessment when due. Such forfeiture shall not exceed five percent of the unpaid assessment per month but no forfeiture shall be less than $100.00 per month.

(3) Any action of the board of directors or the association may be appealed to the commissioner by any member insurer if such appeal is taken within 30 days of the action being appealed. Any final action or order of the commissioner shall be subject to judicial review in a court of competent jurisdiction.

(4) The liquidator, rehabilitator, or conservator of any impaired insurer may notify all interested persons of the effect of this chapter. (Acts 1982, No. 82-561, p. 922, § 11.)

§ 27-44-12. Duties of commissioner and board with regard to detection and prevention of insolvencies or impairment.

To aid in the detection and prevention of insurer insolvencies or impairment:

(1) It shall be the duty of the commissioner:

a. To notify the commissioners of those states, territories of the United States and the District of Columbia where such member company is licensed when he takes any of the following actions against a member insurer:

1. Revocation of license;

2. Suspension of license;

3. Makes any formal order that such company restrict its premium writing or obtain additional contributions to capital or surplus.

Such notice shall be mailed to all commissioners within 30 days following the action taken or the date on which such action occurs.

b. To report to the board of directors when he has taken any of the actions set forth in paragraph a of this subdivision or has received a report from any other commissioner indicating that any such action has been taken in another state. Such report to the board of directors shall contain all significant details of the action taken on the report received from another commissioner.

c. To report to the board of directors when he has reasonable cause to believe from any examination, whether completed or in process, of any member company that such company may be an impaired or insolvent insurer.

d. To furnish to the board of directors upon its request the insurance regulatory information system ratios developed by the National Association of Insurance Commissioners, and the board may use the information contained therein in carrying out its duties and responsibilities under this section. Such report and the information contained therein shall be kept confidential by the board of directors until such time as made public by the commissioner or other lawful authority.

(2) The commissioner may seek the advice and recommendations of the board of directors concerning any matter affecting his duties and responsibilities regarding the financial condition of member companies and companies seeking admission to transact insurance business in this state.

(3) The board of directors may, upon majority vote, make reports and recommendations to the commissioner upon any matter germane to the solvency, liquidation, rehabilitation or conservation of any member insurer or germane to the solvency of any company seeking to do insurance business in this state. Such reports and recommendations shall not be considered public documents.

(4) It shall be the duty of the board of directors, upon majority vote, to notify the commissioner of any information indicating any member insurer may be an impaired or insolvent insurer.

(5) The board of directors may, upon majority vote, request that the commissioner order an examination of any member insurer which the board in good faith believes may be an impaired or insolvent insurer. Within 30 days of the receipt of such request, the commissioner shall begin such examination. The examination may be conducted as a National Association of Insurance Commissioners' examination or may be conducted by such persons as the commissioner designates. The cost of such examination shall be paid by the association and the examination report shall be treated as are other examination reports. In no event shall such examination report be released to the board of directors prior to its release to the public, but this shall not preclude the commissioner from complying with subdivision (1). The commissioner shall notify the board of directors when the examination is completed. The request for an examination shall be kept on file by the commissioner but it shall not be open to public inspection prior to the release of the examination report to the public.

(6) The board of directors may, upon majority vote, make recommendations to the commissioner for the detection and prevention of insurer insolvencies.

(7) The board of directors shall, at the conclusion of any insurer insolvency in which the association was obligated to pay covered claims, prepare a report to the commissioner containing such information as it may have in its possession bearing on the history and causes of such insolvency. The board shall cooperate with the boards of directors of guaranty associations in other states in preparing a report on the history and causes for insolvency of a particular insurer, and may adopt by reference any report prepared by such other associations. (Acts 1982, No. 82-561, p. 922, § 12.)

§ 27-44-13. Credits for assessments paid.

(a) A member insurer may offset against its premium tax liability to this state an assessment described in section 27-44-9(g) to the extent of 20 percent of the amount of such assessment for each of the five calendar years following the year in which such assessment was paid.

(b) Any sums acquired by refund, pursuant to section 27-44-9(f), from the association which have theretofore been written off by contributing insurers and offset against premium taxes as provided in subsection (a) above, and are not then needed for purposes of this chapter, shall be paid by the association to the commissioner and by him deposited with the state treasurer for credit to the general fund of this state. (Acts 1982, No. 82-561, p. 922, § 13.)

§ 27-44-14. Liability of unpaid assessments; records of negotiations and meetings; association deemed creditor of impaired or insolvent insurer; judicial distribution of ownership rights of insolvent insurer; recovery by receiver of certain distributions from controlling affiliates.

(a) Nothing in this chapter shall be construed to reduce the liability for unpaid assessments of the insureds on an impaired or insolvent insurer operating under a plan with assessment liability.

(b) Records shall be kept of all negotiations and meetings in which the association or its representatives are involved to discuss the activities of the association in carrying out its powers and duties under section 27-44-8. Records of such negotiations or meetings shall be made public only upon the termination of a liquidation, rehabilitation, or conservation proceeding involving the impaired or insolvent insurer, upon the termination of the impairment or insolvency of the insurer, or upon the order of a court of competent jurisdiction. Nothing in this subsection shall limit the duty of the association to render a report of its activities under section 27-44-15.

(c) For the purpose of carrying out its obligations under this chapter, the association shall be deemed to be a creditor of the impaired or insolvent insurer to the extent of assets attributable to covered policies reduced by any amounts to which the association is entitled as subrogee pursuant to section 27-44-8(8). Assets of the impaired or insolvent insurer attributable to covered policies shall be used to continue all covered policies and pay all contractual obligations of the impaired or insolvent insurer as required by this chapter. Assets attributable to covered policies, as used in this subsection, are that proportion of the assets which the reserves that should have been established for such policies bear to the reserves that should have been established for all policies of insurance written by the impaired or insolvent insurer.

(d)(1) Prior to the termination of any liquidation, rehabilitation, or conservation proceeding, the court may take into consideration the contributions of the respective parties, including the association, the shareholders and policyowners of the insolvent insurer, and any other party with a bona fide interest, in making an equitable distribution of the ownership rights of such insolvent insurer. In such a determination consideration shall be given to the welfare of the policyholders of the continuing or successor insurer.

(2) No distribution to stockholders, if any, of an impaired or insolvent insurer shall be made until and unless the total amount of valid claims of the association for funds expended in carrying out its powers and duties under section 27-44-8 with respect to such insurer have been fully recovered by the association.

(e) (1) If an order for liquidation or rehabilitation of an insurer domiciled in this state has been entered, the receiver appointed under such order shall have a right to recover on behalf of the insurer, from any affiliate that controlled it, the amount of distributions, other than stock dividends paid by the insurer on its capital stock, made at any time during the five years preceding the petition for liquidation or rehabilitation subject to the limitations of subdivisions (2) to (4) of this subsection.

(2) No such dividend shall be recoverable if the insurer shows that when paid the distribution was lawful and reasonable, and that the insurer did not know and could not reasonably have known that the distribution might adversely affect the ability of the insurer to fulfill its contractual obligations.

(3) Any person who was an affiliate that controlled the insurer at the time the distributions were paid shall be liable up to the amount of distributions he received. Any person who was an affiliate that controlled the insurer at the time the distributions were declared, shall be liable up to the amount of distributions he would have received if they had been paid immediately. If two persons are liable with respect to the same distributions, they shall be jointly and severally liable.

(4) The maximum amount recoverable under this subsection shall be the amount needed in excess of all other available assets of the insolvent insurer to pay the contractual obligations of the insolvent insurer.

(5) If any person liable under subdivision (3) of this subsection is insolvent, all its affiliates that controlled it at the time the dividend was paid, shall be jointly and severally liable for any resulting deficiency in the amount recovered from the insolvent affiliate. (Acts 1982, No. 82-561, p. 922, § 14.)

§ 27-44-15. Examination and regulation of association; annual report.

The association shall be subject to examination and regulation by the commissioner. The board of directors shall submit to the commissioner, not later than May 1 of each year, a financial report for the preceding calendar year in a form approved by the commissioner and a report of its activities during the preceding calendar year. (Acts 1982, No. 82-561, p. 922, § 15.)

§ 27-44-16. Tax exemptions.

The association shall be exempt from payment of all fees and all taxes levied by this state or any of its subdivisions, except taxes levied on real or personal property. (Acts 1982, No. 82-561, p. 922, § 16.)

§ 27-44-17. Immunity under chapter.

There shall be no liability on the part of and no cause of action of any nature shall arise against any member insurer or its agents or employees, the association or its agents or employees, members of the board of directors, or the commissioner or his representatives, for any action taken by them in the performance of their powers and duties under this chapter. (Acts 1982, No. 82-561, p. 922, § 17.)

§ 27-44-18. Stay of proceedings; reopening default judgments.

All proceedings in which the insolvent insurer is a party in any court in this state shall be stayed 60 days from the date an order of liquidation, rehabilitation, or conservation is final to permit proper legal action by the association on any matters germane to its powers or duties. As to judgment under any decision, order, verdict, or finding based on default the association may apply to have such judgment set aside by the same court that made such judgment and shall be permitted to defend against such suit on the merits. (Acts 1982, No. 82-561, p. 922, § 18.)

§ 27-44-19. Repealed by Acts 1983, 2nd Ex. Sess., No. 83-125, p. 133, effective February 22, 1983.

§ 27-44-20. Association, policyholders, beneficiaries and insureds to have preferred creditor status.

Upon the issuance of a proper court order placing a domestic insurer in receivership or placing a foreign insurer in ancillary receivership for rehabilitation or liquidation, all policyholders, beneficiaries and insureds of such insolvent insurer, with respect to claims arising from and within the coverage of and not in excess of the applicable limits of insurance policies and contracts issued by the insolvent insurer and the Alabama life and disability insurance guaranty fund shall be preferred creditors of said insolvent insurer. (Acts 1982, No. 82-561, p. 922, § 20.)

§ 27-44-21. Immediate access of associations in this and other states to assets of insolvent insurer; application to court; contents of proposal; notice.

(a) Within 120 days of a final determination of insolvency of an insurance company by a court of competent jurisdiction the receiver shall make application to the said court for approval of a proposal to disburse assets out of such company's marshalled assets, from time to time as such assets become available, to the Alabama life and disability insurance guaranty association and to any entity or person performing a similar function in another state. (The Alabama life and disability insurance guaranty association and any

609

entity or person performing a similar function in other states shall hereinafter be referred to collectively as associations.)

(b) Such proposal shall at least include provisions for:

(1) Reserving amounts for the payment of expenses of administration and claims falling within the priorities established in the Alabama Uniform Insurers Liquidation Act (subdivisions (2) through (13) of section 27-32-1 and sections 27-32-4, 27-32-5, 27-32-15 through 27-32-22) but only with respect to such priorities higher than that of the associations;

(2) Disbursement of the assets marshalled to date and subsequent disbursements of assets as they become available;

(3) Equitable allocation of disbursements to each of the associations entitled thereto;

(4) The securing by the receiver from each of the associations entitled to disbursements pursuant to this section of an agreement to return to the receiver such assets previously disbursed as may be required to pay claims of secured creditors and claims with a higher priority than those of the associations. No bond shall be required of any such association; and

(c) The receiver's proposal shall provide for disbursements to the associations in amounts at least equal to the payments made or to be made thereby for which such associations could assert claims against the receiver, and shall further provide that if the assets available for disbursement from time to time do not equal or exceed the amount of such payments made or to be made by the associations then disbursements shall be in the amount of available assets.

(d) Notice of such application shall be given to the associations in and to the commissioners of insurance of each of the states. Any such notice shall be deemed to have been given when deposited in the United States certified mails, first class postage prepaid, at least 30 days prior to submission of such application to the said court. Action on the application may be taken by the said court provided that above required notice has been given and provided further that the receiver's proposal complies with subdivisions (1) and (4) of subsection (b) hereof. (Acts 1982, No. 82-561, p. 922, § 21.)

TITLE 28.

INTOXICATING LIQUOR, MALT BEVERAGES AND WINE.

Chap. 1. General Provisions, §§ 28-1-1 through 28-1-5.
2. Elections as to Sale and Distribution of Alcoholic Beverages Within Counties, §§ 28-2-1 through 28-2-25.
2A. Elections as to Sale and Distribution of Alcoholic Beverages Within Municipalities, §§ 28-2A-1 through 28-2A-4.
3. Regulation and Control of Alcoholic Beverages in Wet Counties, §§ 28-3-1 through 28-3-286.
3A. Alcoholic Beverage Licensing Code, §§ 28-3A-1 through 28-3A-26.
4. Regulation and Control of Alcoholic Beverages in Dry Counties And Dry Municipalities, §§ 28-4-1 through 28-4-326.
5. Regulation of Manufacture, Sale, etc., of Industrial Alcohol, §§ 28-5-1 through 28-5-14.
6. Regulation of Production, Sale, etc., of Native Farm Wine, §§ 28-6-1 through 28-6-6.
7. Importation, Distribution and Sale of Table Wine, §§ 28-7-1 through 28-7-24.
8. Exclusive Sales Territories and Wholesalers, §§ 28-8-1 through 28-8-8.

CHAPTER 1.

GENERAL PROVISIONS.

Sec.
28-1-1. Possession of still, etc., or illegally manufactured, transported or imported alcoholic beverages.
28-1-2. Admissibility of evidence obtained by illegal searches in prosecutions under title; when search deemed illegal.
28-1-3. Repealed.

Sec.
28-1-4. Delivery of alcoholic beverages to persons, corporations, etc., within state by out-of-state manufacturers, suppliers, etc.
28-1-5. Minimum age for purchasing, consuming, possessing, etc., alcohol; employment of underage persons in places licensed to serve alcohol; penalty; exemption.

Cross references. — As to authority of cities and towns to adopt ordinances to promote temperance and suppress intemperance, see § 11-47-112. As to drunkenness or intoxication in public, see § 13A-11-10.

Collateral references. — Validity of statutory classifications based on population — intoxicating liquor statutes. 100 ALR3d 850.

§ 28-1-1. Possession of still, etc., or illegally manufactured, transported or imported alcoholic beverages.

In all counties of the state it shall be unlawful for any person, firm or corporation to have in his or its possession any still or apparatus to be used for the manufacture of any alcoholic beverage of any kind or any alcoholic beverage of any kind illegally manufactured or transported within the state or imported into the state from any other place without authority of the alcoholic control board of the state, and any person, firm or corporation violating this provision or who transports any illegally manufactured alcoholic beverages or who manufactures illegally any alcoholic beverages shall, upon conviction, be punished as provided by law. (Acts 1936-37, Ex. Sess., No. 66, p. 40; Code 1940, T. 29, § 68.)

Construction with other sections. — Section 28-4-52, prescribing penalty for unlawful possession of stills, and § 28-4-115, relating to transportation in quantities of five gallons or more, may be applicable to the offenses denounced by this section which defines in general the elements of the several offenses, which section must be construed in connection with the sections fixing the penalty for a misdemeanor or a felony as the case may be, and those sections read into this section as to the quantity transported when that is material. Hardin v. State, 241 Ala. 151, 3 So. 2d 93 (1941). See also Shirley v. State, 38 Ala. App. 104, 76 So. 2d 787 (1954).

Transportation in interstate or intrastate commerce. — Qualified agents or agencies, complying with this title and the board's rules and regulations, may legally and in good faith transport liquors or beverages, duly authorized to be sold and transported under the title, rules and regulations, in interstate commerce from without state through dry county in state to wet county therein or in intrastate commerce from wet county within state to another wet county therein, though such transportation must proceed through dry county or counties of state. Newton v. State, 241 Ala. 1, 200 So. 428, conformed to in 30 Ala. App. 42, 200 So. 431 (1941).

Accused was held not to come within the exceptions of Newton v. State, 241 Ala. 1, 200 So. 428 (1941), where he was found transporting liquor through a dry county and he was not a licensed dealer or carrier, or the agent of either, authorized to engage in such transportation. Stephens v. State, 33 Ala. App. 469, 34 So. 2d 508 (1948).

Amendment of complaint. — A complaint initiating prosecution for violation of prohibition law is amendable so as to charge illegal transportation or importation without regard to the quantity within the purview of this section or a nol pros may be taken and the case referred to the grand jury. Hardin v. State, 241 Ala. 151, 3 So. 2d 93 (1941).

Jury has authority to assess fine for violation of this section, notwithstanding no penalty for violation thereof is provided, in view of § 13A-5-12 providing punishment for public offense which is a misdemeanor and the punishment of which is not particularly specified. Turner v. State, 29 Ala. App. 142, 193 So. 325 (1940).

Sufficiency of indictment. — Indictment following wording of this section is sufficient to charge defendant with offense as therein denounced. Turner v. State, 29 Ala. App. 142, 193 So. 325 (1940).

Cited in Donoghue v. Bunkley, 247 Ala. 423, 25 So. 2d 61 (1946); Smothers v. State, 38 Ala. App. 553, 89 So. 2d 277 (1956); City of Birmingham v. Samford, 274 Ala. 367, 149 So. 2d 271 (1963); McDonald v. Brewer, 295 F. Supp. 1135 (N.D. Ala. 1968); Graham v. Brewer, 295 F. Supp. 1140 (N.D. Ala. 1968); State ex rel. Kernells v. Ezell, 291 Ala. 440, 282 So. 2d 266 (1973).

Collateral references. — 48 C.J.S., Intoxicating Liquors, §§ 60, 71-95.

45 Am. Jur. 2d, Intoxicating Liquors, § 79 et seq.

§ 28-1-2. Admissibility of evidence obtained by illegal searches in prosecutions under title; when search deemed illegal.

No evidence obtained by means of an illegal search of the private dwelling of any person shall be admissible in any court in the prosecution of any person for violating any of the provisions of this title. A search is deemed illegal, unless a valid search warrant has been issued in full compliance with law, including section 28-4-255, and such warrant is executed according to law. (Acts 1909, No. 191, p. 63; Acts 1915, No. 2, p. 8; Code 1923, § 4741; Code 1940, T. 29, § 210; Acts 1951, No. 905, p. 1544.)

Constitution. — For constitutional provision pertaining to unreasonable searches and seizures and search warrants, see Const., § 5.

Section is constitutional. — This section is not violative of Constitution, § 45. Toole v. State, 170 Ala. 41, 54 So. 195 (1910).

This section pertains to rights affected by Constitution, § 5. Dennis v. State, 40 Ala. App. 182, 111 So. 2d 21 (1959).

What is a search. — A search implies a probing into secret places for that which is hidden; it implies force, actual or constructive, or a forcible dispossession of the property of the owner by exploratory acts. A mere observation of that which is in full view is not a search. Kelley v. State, 39 Ala. App. 572, 105 So. 2d 687 (1958).

Where there was some evidence tending to show that an officer was within the curtilage of defendant's dwelling house, and that he had gone there in search of whiskey, an illegal search did not result when the whiskey was obtained by subterfuge and trickery, since the circumstance that the officer may have been within the curtilage of defendant's home could not affect the fact that the whiskey was produced by defendant himself, without any invasion, force or exploration by the officer. Kelley v. State, 39 Ala. App. 572, 105 So. 2d 687 (1958).

This section applies only to evidence obtained by means of illegal search of private dwelling. Oldham v. State, 37 Ala. App. 251, 67 So. 2d 52 (1953).

An illegal search of a person within his private dwelling house, or its curtilage, compounds the injury to the sanctity of the home, and is clearly a search controlled by this section. Dennis v. State, 40 Ala. App. 182, 111 So. 2d 21 (1959).

Term "private dwelling" as used in this section must be deemed to be synonymous with "dwelling," the word "private" being merely an epithetical surplusage, adding nothing to the term "dwelling." Dennis v. State, 40 Ala. App. 182, 111 So. 2d 21 (1959).

Is deemed to include the curtilage. — The term "private dwelling," as used in this section, is deemed to include the curtilage of a private dwelling rather than merely the area enclosed by its walls. Dennis v. State, 40 Ala. App. 182, 111 So. 2d 21 (1959).

A mailbox was not within the curtilage of a dwelling house so as to make this section applicable. Parker v. State, 40 Ala. App. 244, 112 So. 2d 493 (1959).

Search of automobile. — The general standard of reasonableness of search of an automobile or truck without a warrant is one of "probable cause;" that is, upon a belief, reasonably arising out of circumstances known to the seizing officer, that an automobile or other vehicle contains that which by law is subject to seizure and destruction. Yeager v. State, 281 Ala. 651, 207 So. 2d 125 (1967).

There is nothing unreasonable about observing whiskey which is plainly visible to the naked eye and thereafter seizing it. Yeager v. State, 281 Ala. 651, 207 So. 2d 125 (1967).

Section is limited to prosecution for violation of this title. — By its very terms the operation of this section is limited to prosecutions for violations of this title, relating to intoxicating liquors. It has no application to a prosecution for vagrancy. Morales v. State, 38 Ala. App. 400, 85 So. 2d 153 (1956).

It does not apply to prosecution for violation of municipal ordinance. — This section does not apply to a prosecution for the violation of a municipal ordinance. Perry v. City of Birmingham, 38 Ala. App. 460, 88 So. 2d 577 (1956).

A provision of the 1944 city code of Birmingham that it shall be unlawful for any person to violate within the city or within the police jurisdiction any law of the state the violation of which is a misdemeanor, and a provision of the Birmingham ordinance governing the sale of intoxicating liquor that the term "liquor" shall have the same meaning as in § 28-3-1, did not operate to make a prosecution for violation of the latter ordinance a prosecution for violation of this title of the Code so as to render this section applicable. Perry v. City of Birmingham, 38 Ala. App. 460, 88 So. 2d 577 (1956).

Nor in a prosecution for criminal assault; thus the trial court properly refused instructions for defendant which stated that search warrant under this section was issued without lawful authority. Ott v. State, 35 Ala. App. 219, 46 So. 2d 226 (1950).

Evidence procured by illegal search should be excluded. — The state's evidence procured by an illegal search contrary to this section should be excluded. Weldon v. State, 39 Ala. App. 286, 97 So. 2d 825 (1957).

Evidence of whiskey held inadmissible under this section. Dennis v. State, 40 Ala. App. 182, 111 So. 2d 21 (1959).

Evidence inadmissible where obtained under warrant supported by unsigned affidavit. — Where affidavit supporting purported search warrant was unsigned, a search of defendant's person was illegal and evidence obtained thereby was inadmissible under Mapp v. Ohio, 367 U.S. 643, 81 S. Ct. 1684, 6 L. Ed. 2d 1081 (1961). Lawson v. State, 42 Ala. App. 172, 157 So. 2d 226 (1963).

Evidence inadmissible before trial still inadmissible at trial if circumstances unchanged. — If illegally obtained evidence is inadmissible before the trial, it is still inadmissible at the trial if the circumstances have not changed. Brown v. State, 277 Ala. 108, 167 So. 2d 291 (1964).

Section as basis for motion to suppress evidence. — This section would, to the limited conditions of such section, that is, search of a private dwelling for prohibited liquors, serve as a basis for the introduction and use of a motion to suppress evidence obtained by illegal search. Green v. State, 38 Ala. App. 189, 79 So. 2d 555 (1955); Porch v. State, 38 Ala. App. 565, 89 So. 2d 694 (1956).

The court did not hold in Green v. State, 38 Ala. App. 189, 79 So. 2d 555 (1955), that an accused, in any and all events, would be entitled to a preliminary hearing on a motion to suppress. Kelley v. State, 39 Ala. App. 572, 105 So. 2d 687 (1958).

Motion to suppress evidence is ordinarily the proper remedy. — A motion to suppress the evidence so as to forbid use of the fruit of an illegal search in a criminal trial is ordinarily the proper remedy available to a defendant. Brown v. State, 42 Ala. App. 429, 167 So. 2d 281 (1964).

But such motion is not necessary. — A pretrial motion to suppress is not improper, but such motion is not necessary and objection may be made for the first time when the illegally obtained evidence is offered at the trial. Brown v. State, 277 Ala. 108, 167 So. 2d 291 (1964).

Nor incumbent upon defendant where affidavit appears valid on surface. — Because of the surface appearance of validity of the affidavit and warrant which led to the search, it was not incumbent upon the defendant to make a pretrial motion to suppress. Brown v. State, 42 Ala. App. 429, 167 So. 2d 281 (1964).

Cited in Thomas v. State, 37 Ala. App. 118, 66 So. 2d 103 (1953); Simpson v. State, 37 Ala. App. 465, 70 So. 2d 542 (1954); Smith v. State, 40 Ala. App. 600, 119 So. 2d 202 (1960); Beam v. State, 41 Ala. App. 401, 137 So. 2d 762 (1961); Duncan v. State, 278 Ala. 145, 176 So. 2d 840 (1965); Oliver v. State, 46 Ala. App. 118, 238 So. 2d 916 (1970); Funches v. State, 53 Ala. App. 330, 299 So. 2d 771 (1974); Griffith v. State, 386 So. 2d 771 (Ala. Crim. App. 1980).

Collateral references. — 48 C.J.S., Intoxicating Liquors, § 394.

---

§ 28-1-3. Repealed by Acts 1986, No. 86-334, effective April 24, 1986.

§ 28-1-4. Delivery of alcoholic beverages to persons, corporations, etc., within state by out-of-state manufacturers, suppliers, etc.

(a) The words and phrases used in this section shall have the meanings ascribed to them in section 28-3-1, Code of Alabama 1975, and any acts amendatory thereof, supplementary thereto or substituted therefor.

(b) It shall be unlawful for common or permit carriers, operators of trucks, buses or other conveyances or out-of-state manufacturers or suppliers to make delivery of any alcoholic beverage from without the state of Alabama to any person, association or corporation within the state, except to the Alabama alcoholic beverage control board and to manufacturers, importers, wholesalers and warehouses licensed by the Alabama alcoholic beverage control board to receive the alcoholic beverages so delivered.

(c) Any violation of subsection (a) of this section shall be a misdemeanor, punishable as provided in paragraph (1) of subsection (b) of section 28-3A-25, Code of Alabama 1975.

(d) All laws or parts of law which conflict or are inconsistent with this section are hereby repealed, provided, however, the provisions of section 28-1-3 are excluded. (Acts 1981, No. 81-768, p. 1320.)

Collateral references. — 48 C.J.S., Intoxicating Liquors, §§ 29, 33, 38, 192, 208.   45 Am. Jur. 2d, Intoxicating Liquors, §§ 23, 41, 118.

§ 28-1-5. Minimum age for purchasing, consuming, possessing, etc., alcohol; employment of underage persons in places licensed to serve alcohol; penalty; exemption.

Notwithstanding the provisions of section 26-1-1, it shall be unlawful for a person less than 21 years of age to purchase, consume, possess or to transport any alcohol, liquor or malt or brewed beverages within the state of Alabama. Notwithstanding any other provision of this section, it shall not be unlawful for any alcoholic beverage control board licensee to employ any person under the legal drinking age to work, provided there is an adult in attendance at all times. It shall be permissible to employ persons in an on-premise licensed establishment under legal drinking age such as professional entertainers, show people, musicians, cashiers, hostesses, ushers, waiters and waitresses, busboys or girls, and the like, provided they do not serve, dispense or consume alcoholic beverages and there is an adult in attendance at all times.

Whoever violates this section shall be fined not less than $25.00 nor more than $100.00, or imprisoned in the county jail for not more than 30 days or both; provided further, that juvenile offenders shall not be held in the county jail, but shall be held, either before or after sentencing, in a juvenile detention facility pursuant to the guidelines of the department of youth services, which shall be separate and apart from adult offenders.

Persons 19 years of age or older prior to October 1, 1985, are hereby expressly exempt from the provisions of this section. (Acts 1985, No. 85-687, p. 1102.)

Effective date. — The act which added this section became effective May 29, 1985.

Code commissioner's note. — Section 4 of Acts 1985, No. 85-687 provides that the act shall remain in effect only so long as section 6 of Public Law 98-363, 98th Congress, July 17, 1984, 98th Stat. 437 et seq., 23 U.S.C. section 158, shall be in effect.

CHAPTER 2.

ELECTIONS AS TO SALE AND DISTRIBUTION OF ALCOHOLIC
BEVERAGES WITHIN COUNTIES.

Article 1.

General Provisions.

Sec.
28-2-1.   Procedure for elections to determine
           classification of counties as wet or
           dry counties; laws applicable in
           dry counties.

Article 2.

Special Method Referendum.

28-2-20.   Short title.
28-2-21.   Petitioners for election under section
           28-2-1 may request election on
           adoption of this article; question
           to be asked voters.

Sec.
28-2-22.   Conditions governing sale of alco-
           holic beverages in county and
           municipalities therein where ma-
           jority of voters approve sale and
           distribution under article; penalty
           for violation of section.
28-2-23.   Levy and collection of tax upon sale
           of malt beverages by counties or
           municipalities permitting sale
           under article; disposition of pro-
           ceeds from tax.
28-2-24.   Counties not authorized to conduct
           referenda under provisions of sec-
           tion 28-2-21.
28-2-25.   Applicability of other provisions of
           title, etc., in county adopting arti-
           cle.

ARTICLE 1.

GENERAL PROVISIONS.

§ 28-2-1. Procedure for elections to determine classification of counties
as wet or dry counties; laws applicable in dry counties.

(a) In every county where a majority of the electors voting in an election,
called by the governor to determine whether chapter 3 of this title shall be
adopted in the county, vote "Yes," chapter 3 and all of its provisions shall be
immediately put into operation in such county, but in every county where a
majority of the electors voting in said election vote "No," chapter 3 shall not
go into effect in such county and all laws prohibiting the manufacture and
sale of alcoholic liquors or beverages now in force and effect in Alabama shall
remain in full force and effect in every such county. For the purpose of this
chapter the term "wet county" shall mean any county which by a majority of
those voting voted in the affirmative in the election provided for in this
section, and "dry counties" shall be construed to mean all counties which by a
majority of those voting voted in the negative in the election provided for in
this section. Any county in the state may change its classification from wet to
dry or from dry to wet under this section in the following manner: Upon the
petition of 25 percent of the number of voters voting in the last preceding
general election being filed with the probate judge of said county, said probate
judge must call an election for said county to determine the sentiment of the
people as to whether or not alcoholic beverages can be legally sold or
distributed in said county. Said election shall be held and the officers
appointed to hold same in the manner provided by law for holding other
county elections and the returns thereof tabulated and results certified as

616

provided by law for such elections. Said election shall be held within not less than 30 days, nor more than 45 days, from the date of filing of said petition and notice thereof shall be given by the probate judge by publication at least three weeks before the date of said election, in a newspaper in the county or, if there be none, by posting such notice at the courthouse apprising the voters of the county that an election will be held in the several precincts thereof to determine whether such county shall be wet or dry under the laws regulating alcoholic beverages. The cost of said election, including the cost of notice by publication, shall be paid out of the general funds of the county. On the ballot to be used for such election the question shall be in the following form: "Do you favor the legal sale and distribution of alcoholic beverages within this county? Yes . . . . . No . . . ." Only qualified voters shall vote in said election. If a majority of the voters voting in said election vote "Yes," said county shall be wet or remain wet under the terms of this section until said county shall in a subsequent election held under this section change to a dry county. If a majority of the electors voting in said election vote "No," said county shall be a dry county under the terms of chapter 4 until it shall by a subsequent election, held under this section, vote wet. Said elections in said counties may be held at any time; provided, that a period of not less than two years must elapse between the dates of such elections.

(b) In all dry counties, as defined in subsection (a) of this section, the statutes of Alabama prohibiting the manufacture, sale or distribution of alcoholic beverages shall remain in full force and effect, and any person, firm or corporation convicted of violating any of the provisions of law regulating or defining the illegal manufacture, sale or distribution of alcoholic beverages shall be punished as provided by such laws. (Acts 1936-37, Ex. Sess., No. 66, p. 40; Code 1940, T. 29, § 68.)

Cross references. — As to regulation and control of alcoholic beverages in dry counties, see § 28-4-1 et seq.

Prohibition laws apply in dry counties. — The prohibition laws, formerly in force for the entire state, are still in full force and effect in counties which voted dry in election under this chapter. Humphries v. State, 28 Ala. App. 307, 183 So. 685 (1938). See also Haire v. State, 28 Ala. App. 91, 178 So. 897 (1938).

This chapter does not preclude maintenance of prosecutions in dry counties for selling prohibited liquors, since alcoholic, spirituous or malt liquors containing more than one-half of one percent cannot lawfully be manufactured or sold in any dry county of state. Nerland v. State, 28 Ala. App. 137, 179 So. 921 (1938).

The sections of the prohibition law not repealed by the Alcoholic Beverage Control Act, and which still have a field of operation in wet counties consistent with the Act, are still effective. Lovett v. State, 244 Ala. 601, 14 So. 2d 838 (1943).

Differences in prosecutions for violations in dry or wet counties. — Where violation of prohibition or temperance laws is alleged to have been committed in a wet county, prosecution therefor should be instituted and based as for violation of state Alcoholic Beverage Control Act; but, where such offense is alleged to have been committed in a dry county, prosecution should be begun under provisions of state prohibition laws as they existed before such Act was enacted. Hardin v. State, 30 Ala. App. 204, 3 So. 2d 83 (1940).

There can be no legal possession of prohibited liquors for any purpose in any dry county. Broadfoot v. State, 28 Ala. App. 260, 182 So. 411 (1938).

The possession of whiskey or beer in a "dry" county, as defined in the Alcoholic Beverage Control Act, which would have been unlawful before the passage of that Act is unlawful although the whiskey or beer has been legally purchased from a legally authorized selling agency in a "wet" county. Williams v. State, 28 Ala. App. 73, 179 So. 915 (1938).

The possession of beer which was found stored in a room not used exclusively for a dwelling, in a "dry" county, was prima facie evidence that the beer was kept for sale or with intent to sell. Sinbeck v. State, 28 Ala. App. 118, 179 So. 645 (1938).

Instruction that accused had right to keep liquor in dwelling house in dry county for his own personal use was erroneous. Gibbs v. State, 29 Ala. App. 113, 192 So. 514 (1939).

Possession of whiskey in a dry county is illegal, though it was lawfully purchased from a state liquor store in a wet county. Hall v. State, 30 Ala. App. 373, 6 So. 2d 30 (1941); Stephens v. State, 33 Ala. App. 469, 34 So. 2d 508 (1948).

Allegation as to violation before or after enactment of this chapter is unnecessary.

— In prosecution for the illegal possession of prohibited liquors, where it was charged that offense was committed in a county which had retained the prohibition law after enactment of this chapter, allegation as to whether violation was committed before or after enactment of chapter was unnecessary. Haire v. State, 28 Ala. App. 91, 178 So. 897 (1938).

Cited in Jones v. State, 401 So. 2d 322 (Ala. Crim. App. 1981).

Collateral references. — Nonregistration as affecting one's qualification as signer of petition for election. 100 ALR 1308.

Withdrawal of name from petition, and time therefor. 126 ALR 1031, 27 ALR2d 604.

Operation and effect, in dry territory, of general state statute making sale or possession for sale of intoxicating liquor, without a license, an offense. 8 ALR2d 750.

Change of "wet" or "dry" status fixed by local option election by change of name, character, or boundaries of voting unit, without later election. 25 ALR2d 863.

ARTICLE 2.

SPECIAL METHOD REFERENDUM.

§ 28-2-20. Short title.

This article shall be known and cited as the Special Method Referendum Act of 1971. (Acts 1971, No. 1266, p. 2195, § 1.)

§ 28-2-21. Petitioners for election under section 28-2-1 may request election on adoption of this article; question to be asked voters.

Whenever petitioners for an election under section 28-2-1 shall so desire, the petition shall contain the following: "It is requested that the election herein requested be on the adoption of the Special Method Referendum Act of 1971."

In an election called for the above-stated act, the voters of the county shall be asked the question: "Do you favor the legal sale and distribution of alcoholic beverages within this county under the Special Method Referendum Act of 1971? Yes . . . ., No . . . .." (Acts 1971, No. 1266, p. 2195, § 2.)

§ 28-2-22. Conditions governing sale of alcoholic beverages in county and municipalities therein where majority of voters approve sale and distribution under article; penalty for violation of section.

(a) If the majority of the voters in any county approve the sale and distribution of alcoholic beverages under this article as provided in section 28-2-21, the sale of alcoholic beverages in such county shall be governed by the following conditions:

(1) Within 90 days after the affirmative vote of the voters of a county, each governing body of any incorporated municipality within such county may vote to exclude the sale of alcoholic beverages within its limits as provided for in this article. If the governing body does not take such action 90 days after the affirmative election, the provisions of this article shall apply for a period of 10 years, after which the municipality shall again have 90 days to exclude said municipality. Should a municipality choose to exclude the application of this article from its limits, it may, by its own action, include the municipality under the provisions of this article at any subsequent time for a period of 10 years and, after said 10-year period, shall have 90 days to continue or discontinue its applicability. A municipality may, within the 90-day period, submit the decision on the applicability of this article to its voters by a special election, said election being binding on the governing body.

(2) The governing body of any county which has adopted the special method as provided in section 28-2-21 may from time to time vote to exclude the sale of alcoholic beverages within all or any part of its unincorporated areas, but if a municipality annexes any unincorporated area, that area shall be subject to the rules of the municipality with regard to the sale and distribution of alcoholic beverages.

(3) Only nonrefrigerated malt beverages may be sold in any area in the county.

(4) Spirituous or vinous liquors may only be sold at stores operated by the Alabama alcoholic beverage control board.

(5) Possession of alcoholic beverages in any area in a county where their sale has not been legalized is prohibited.

(6) The consumption of alcoholic beverages on the premises where sold or in any public place is prohibited.

(b) Any person who violates any provision of this section shall be deemed guilty of a misdemeanor. (Acts 1971, No. 1266, p. 2195, § 3.)

§ 28-2-23. Levy and collection of tax upon sale of malt beverages by counties or municipalities permitting sale under article; disposition of proceeds from tax.

Any county or municipality which allows the sale of malt beverages under the provisions of this article shall be authorized to levy and collect a tax upon the sale of such beverages in an amount not to exceed $.05 on each 12 fluid ounces or fraction thereof; provided, that the county shall not have authority to impose such tax within any incorporated municipality within such county.

A minimum of 60 percent of the proceeds of such tax shall be used solely for the purpose of public education, with the remainder to be allocated by the county commission or municipal governing body levying and collecting the tax for any other public use. The county commission shall distribute the proceeds of this tax for public education to school systems within the county under the average daily attendance calculation used by the state department of education. (Acts 1971, No. 1266, p. 2195, § 4.)

§ 28-2-24. Counties not authorized to conduct referenda under provisions of section 28-2-21.

No county which, as of September 22, 1971, authorized the sale and distribution of alcoholic beverages shall be authorized to conduct a referendum under the provisions of section 28-2-21. (Acts 1971, No. 1266, p. 2195, § 6.)

§ 28-2-25. Applicability of other provisions of title, etc., in county adopting article.

All other provisions of this title and other laws and regulations of the state associated with the sale, taxing and regulation of alcoholic beverages shall apply to a county adopting this article except when in conflict with the special provisions of this article. (Acts 1971, No. 1266, p. 2195, § 5.)

CHAPTER 2A.

ELECTIONS AS TO SALE AND DISTRIBUTION OF ALCOHOLIC BEVERAGES WITHIN MUNICIPALITIES.

Sec.
28-2A-1. Procedure for elections to determine classification of municipalities as wet or dry municipalities.
28-2A-2. Distribution of funds pursuant to chapters 3 and 28 of Title 40.

Sec.
28-2A-3. Legislative intent.
28-2A-4. Elections in municipalities in same county with populations of 4,000 or more.

Cross references. — As to regulation and control of alcoholic beverages in dry counties, see ch. 4, T. 28.

§ 28-2A-1. Procedure for elections to determine classification of municipalities as wet or dry municipalities.

(a) Any municipality having a population of 7,000 or more may change its classification from dry to wet or wet to dry by a municipal option election, in the following manner:

(b) Upon petition of 25 percent of the number of voters voting in the last preceding general election of the municipality being filed with the city or town clerk or governing body of said municipality, said governing body must call a municipal option election for said municipality to determine the sentiment of the people as to whether or not alcoholic beverages can be legally sold or distributed in said municipality. Said petition for municipal option election shall contain the following: "It is petitioned that a municipal option election be held to permit the legal sale and distribution of alcoholic beverages within this municipality." On the ballot to be used for such municipal option election, the question shall be in the following form: "Do you favor the legal sale and distribution of alcoholic beverages within this municipality? Yes ____ No ____."

(c) Said municipal option election shall be held and the officers appointed to hold same in the manner provided by law for holding other municipal elections and the returns thereof tabulated and the results certified as provided by law for such municipal elections. Said municipal option election shall be held at the time of the primary, general, county-wide or municipal election next succeeding the date of the filing of said petition, provided, however, said election shall not be held within less than 30 days from the date of the filing of said petition. Notice of said municipal option election shall be given by the governing body of the municipality by publication at least three weeks before the date of election, in a newspaper in the municipality, or, if there be none, in a newspaper in the county, or, if there be neither, by posting such notice at the town or city hall, apprising the voters of the municipality that a municipal option election shall be held to determine whether such municipality shall be wet or dry under this chapter. The cost of said municipal option election, including the cost of notice by publication, shall be paid out of the general fund of the municipality.

(d) Only qualified voters shall vote in said municipal option election. If a majority of the voters in said municipal option election vote "yes," said municipality shall be wet, and alcoholic beverages can be legally sold, distributed and consumed within the corporate limits of said municipality, and all of the provisions of Title 28, relating to alcoholic beverages in wet counties, including chapters 3, 3A, 6 and 7, shall be immediately put into operation with respect to and effective within the corporate limits of said municipality. Said municipality shall remain wet until said municipality shall be in subsequent municipal option election held under this chapter changed to a dry municipality, notwithstanding the results of any subsequent county election or special method referendum. All other laws to the contrary notwithstanding, the electors residing within the corporate limits of any such municipality that has become wet pursuant to a municipal option election held under this chapter shall not be entitled to vote in any subsequent county election or special method referendum held to determine if the county in which such municipality is located shall become wet. The question of whether such county shall become wet shall be decided by the electors of such county residing outside the corporate limits of such wet municipality as otherwise provided by law.

(e) If a majority of the voters voting in said municipal option election vote "no," said municipality shall be a dry municipality under the terms of this chapter until the county shall by subsequent election or special referendum, vote wet, or the municipality shall by a subsequent municipal option election held under this chapter, vote wet.

(f) Said municipal option election in said municipality may be held at the time of any primary, general, county-wide or municipal election, provided a period of not less than 720 days must elapse between the dates of such municipal option elections; provided further, that a county wet-dry election or special method referendum may be held at any time without regard to the lapse of time between the dates of any municipal option elections. (Acts 1984, No. 84-408, p. 955, § 1.)

Constitutionality. — For case upholding the constitutionality and the validity of the enactment of Act No. 84-408, codified as §§ 28-2A-1 through 28-2A-4 and § 28-4-5, see Alabama Citizens Action Program v. Kennamer, 479 So. 2d 1237 (Ala. 1985).

General law. — Act No. 84-408 (codified as §§ 28-2A-1 through 28-2A-4 and 28-4-5) is so framed as to be reasonably susceptible of interpretation as a general law, and therefore the Supreme Court was bound not to construe it as a local law. Alabama Citizens Action Program v. Kennamer, 479 So. 2d 1237 (Ala. 1985).

Determination of population. — In drafting Act No. 84-408 (codified as §§ 28-2A-1 through 28-2A-4 and 28-4-5), the legislature did not refer to any class of municipalities under § 11-40-12 or to any census. In the absence of any such designation, in view of § 11-40-6, which states that the last census, whether federal or taken as authorized in Title 11, shall be used in determining the population of a city or town, and in view of the fact that another chapter of Title 28 (chapter 3A) defines "population" as the population according to the last preceding or any subsequent decennial census of the United States, the population of cities for the purposes of Act No. 84-408 would be determined by the last preceding federal decennial census. Alabama Citizens Action Program v. Kennamer, 479 So. 2d 1237 (Ala. 1985).

§ 28-2A-2. Distribution of funds pursuant to chapters 3 and 28 of Title 40.

The distribution of funds pursuant to chapter 28, Title 40, and chapter 3, Title 40, both Code of Alabama 1975, as amended, shall not be affected by this chapter. County school systems may receive revenue from the sale of alcoholic beverages upon approval by the city council of said municipality or by the sale of alcoholic beverages authorized by a municipal option election pursuant to this chapter. (Acts 1984, No. 84-408, p. 955, § 2.)

Constitutionality. — For case upholding the constitutionality and the validity of the enactment of Act No. 84-408, codified at §§ 28-2A-1 through 28-2A-4 and 28-4-5, see Alabama Citizens Action Program v. Kennamer, 479 So. 2d 1237 (Ala. 1985).

General law. — Act No. 84-408 (codified as §§ 28-2A-1 through 28-2A-4 and 28-4-5) is so framed as to be reasonably susceptible of interpretation as a general law, and therefore the Supreme Court was bound not to construe it as a local law. Alabama Citizens Action Program v. Kennamer, 479 So. 2d 1237 (Ala. 1985).

§ 28-2A-3. Legislative intent.

It is hereby declared the intention and the purpose of this chapter to permit an election by the citizens of certain municipalities to determine the wet or dry status of such municipalities with regard to the sale, distribution and consumption of alcoholic beverages within the corporate limits of such municipalities; and further that such election shall be provided only in those municipalities which can provide safeguards for the protection of the public welfare, health, peace and morals of the people. In the furtherance of the protection of the public welfare, health, peace and morals, the legislature has determined that a population classification should be established to provide this method of municipal option election only in those municipalities with a population of 7,000 or more people within a county, it being the judgment of the legislature that municipalities with a lesser population would be unable to support and maintain such protection where such municipality is located in a dry county, whereas a municipality of 7,000 or more population would have the resources and ability to support and maintain such safeguards. (Acts 1984, No. 84-408, p. 955, § 3.)

Constitutionality. — For case upholding the constitutionality and the validity of the enactment of Act No. 84-408, codified as §§ 28-2A-1 through 28-2A-4 and 28-4-5, see Alabama Citizens Action Program v. Kennamer, 479 So. 2d 1237 (Ala. 1985).

General law. — Act No. 84-408 (codified as §§ 28-2A-1 through 28-2A-4 and 28-4-5) is so framed as to be reasonably susceptible of interpretation as a general law, and therefore the Supreme Court was bound not to construe it as a local law. Alabama Citizens Action Program v. Kennamer, 479 So. 2d 1237 (Ala. 1985).

Determination of population. — In drafting Act No. 84-408 (codified as §§ 28-2A-1 through 28-2A-4 and 28-4-5), the legislature did not refer to any class of municipalities under § 11-40-12 or to any census. In the absence of any such designation, in view of § 11-40-6, which states that the last census, whether federal or taken as authorized in Title 11, shall be used in determining the population of a city or town, and in view of the fact that another chapter of Title 28 (chapter 3A) defines "population" as the population according to the last preceding or any subsequent decennial census of the United States, the population of cities for the purposes of Act No. 84-408 would be determined by the last preceding federal decennial census. Alabama Citizens Action Program v. Kennamer, 479 So. 2d 1237 (Ala. 1985).

§ 28-2A-4. Elections in municipalities in same county with populations of 4,000 or more.

If any municipality having a population of 7,000 or more, of any county, votes to allow the sale of alcoholic beverages in its corporate limits pursuant to this chapter, then every other municipality having a population of 4,000 or more in the county shall be likewise authorized to petition for and hold an election on whether to legalize the sale of such beverages in the same manner, and under the same conditions, as municipalities of 7,000 or more. (Acts 1984, No. 84-408, p. 955, § 4.)

Constitutionality. — For case upholding the constitutionality and the validity of the enactment of Act No. 84-408, codified as §§ 28-2A-1 through 28-2A-4 and 28-4-5, see Alabama Citizens Action Program v. Kennamer, 479 So. 2d 1237 (Ala. 1985).

General law. — Act No. 84-408 (codified as §§ 28-2A-1 through 28-2A-4 and 28-4-5) is so framed as to be reasonably susceptible of interpretation as a general law, and therefore the Supreme Court was bound not to construe it as a local law. Alabama Citizens Action Program v. Kennamer, 479 So. 2d 1237 (Ala. 1985).

Determination of population. — In drafting Act No. 84-408 (codified as §§ 28-2A-1 through 28-2A-4 and 28-4-5), the legislature did not refer to any class of municipalities under § 11-40-12 or to any census. In the absence of any such designation, in view of § 11-40-6, which states that the last census, whether federal or taken as authorized in Title 11, shall be used in determining the population of a city or town, and in view of the fact that another chapter of Title 28 (chapter 3A) defines "population" as the population according to the last preceding or any subsequent decennial census of the United States, the population of cities for the purposes of Act No. 84-408 would be determined by the last preceding federal decennial census. Alabama Citizens Action Program v. Kennamer, 479 So. 2d 1237 (Ala. 1985).

CHAPTER 3.

REGULATION AND CONTROL OF ALCOHOLIC BEVERAGES IN WET COUNTIES.

Article 1.

General Provisions.

Sec.
28-3-1. Definitions.
28-3-2. Purpose and construction of chapter generally.
28-3-3. Applicability of provisions of chapter to ethyl alcohol intended or used for certain purposes.
28-3-4. Provisions for maintenance of separation of financial and business interests between classes of businesses regulated by chapter.
28-3-5. Retail dealers to furnish duplicate invoices for shipments of alcoholic beverages received from without state to board.
28-3-6. Furnishing of statements of consignments and deliveries of alcoholic beverages to board by common carriers, contract carriers, etc.; carriers, etc., to permit examination of records by board.
28-3-7. Persons, firms, etc., receiving, storing, selling or handling alcoholic beverages to preserve invoices, books, papers, etc., relating thereto; audit and inspection of invoices, books, etc., by board.
28-3-8. Shipment, delivery, etc., within state of articles taxed by chapter by wholesale dealers or distributors generally; shipment, etc., of same to federal, military, etc., reservations within state by wholesale dealers or distributors.
28-3-9. Wholesalers and distributors to file monthly reports of alcoholic beverages purchased or received.
28-3-10. Wholesale dealers or distributors to file monthly reports as to orders of alcoholic beverages purchased by persons, firms, etc., without state.
28-3-11. Invoices and receipts to be maintained by persons, firms, etc., selling or shipping goods, merchandise, etc., to persons, firms, etc., in another state or to federal government for army, navy or marine purposes; audit and inspection of invoices and receipts by board; promulgation of rules and regulations by board for enforcement of section.

Sec.
28-3-12. Report of purchase, receipt, etc., of alcoholic beverages not having revenue, etc., stamps, crowns or lids affixed thereto.
28-3-13. Sale within state of alcoholic liquors or beverages manufactured within states discriminating against alcoholic liquors or beverages manufactured, etc., in this state.
28-3-14. Procedure for collection of due and unpaid taxes and penalties imposed by chapter; lien for taxes and penalties.
28-3-15. Acquisition, dispensing, etc., of alcoholic beverages, wine, etc., for medicinal, scientific, etc., purposes by physicians, dentists, etc.; acquisition, etc., of wine for sacramental or religious purposes by ministers, pastors, etc.
28-3-16. Advertising of alcoholic beverages.
28-3-17. Location of state liquor store or sale of intoxicating liquors, malt beverages, wine, etc., in establishments within certain distances of grounds, etc., of state teachers colleges, eleemosynary institutions, etc.
28-3-18. Laws as to manufacture or possession of illicit distilled liquor or apparatus for manufacture of same, etc., not repealed by chapter.
28-3-19. Engaging in prohibited practices, refusing to permit, etc., inspections of premises, interfering with confiscation of contraband alcoholic beverages, etc., by persons, firms, etc., subject to taxes under chapter.
28-3-20. Penalties for violations of provisions of chapter or rules and regulations of boards generally.
28-3-21. Imposition of sentence to hard labor for county in lieu of jail sentence for violations of provisions of chapter.
28-3-22. Remittance of part of prescribed penalties by board; board not to accept less than minimum penalties.
28-3-23. Repealed.

Article 2.

Alcoholic Beverage Control Board.

Sec.

28-3-40. Composition; qualifications, appointment, term of office and bond of members; conflicts of interest of members, employees, etc., of board; suspension or removal of members; office; meetings; quorum.

28-3-41. Compensation of board.

28-3-42. Administrator; annual report of board to governor as to administration of chapter; possession by officers, members, employees, etc., of board of liquor or malt or brewed beverages for personal use.

28-3-43. Functions, powers and duties of board generally; examination of board by examiners of public accounts.

28-3-44. Lease of trucks, etc., for transportation of alcoholic beverages purchased, sold or stored by board; employment of operators of leased equipment.

28-3-45. Supervision of sale and distribution of malt or brewed and vinous beverages; collection of licenses and taxes accruing from sale, distribution, etc., of malt and vinous beverages generally.

28-3-46. Powers as to administration and enforcement of taxes imposed by chapter generally.

28-3-47. Temporary closings of licensed places in municipalities during emergencies.

28-3-48. Design and promulgation of form, etc., of stamps, crowns or lids generally; designation of same.

28-3-49. Promulgation, amendment, etc., of regulations by board generally; introduction in evidence of regulations, etc.

28-3-50. Promulgation of rules and regulations as to breaking of packages, affixing of stamps, inspections, etc., generally.

28-3-51. Promulgation of rules and regulations as to affixing of stamps, crowns or lids on articles, etc., handled by persons, firms, etc., operating on interstate common carriers.

28-3-52. Maintenance, examination and audit of books, records and accounts of board.

28-3-53. Disposition of moneys received by board from licenses, taxes and earnings; procedure as to claims against said moneys generally.

Sec.

28-3-53.1. Delay in distribution of certain funds; use of moneys realized; distribution of funds accumulated as working capital.

28-3-53.2. "Board" and "mark up" defined; additional mark up credited to general fund.

28-3-54. Refund on overpayment or erroneous payment of taxes or licenses and of prepaid taxes where loss sustained prior to sale at retail; petition.

28-3-55. Cost of evidence fund; creation; aid in drug law enforcement; appropriation.

Article 3.

State Liquor Stores.

28-3-70 through 28-3-73. Repealed.

28-3-74. Distribution of net profits from proceeds of stores.

Article 4.

Licenses.

DIVISION 1.

GENERAL PROVISIONS.

28-3-90 through 28-3-95. Repealed.

DIVISION 2.

LICENSING OF MANUFACTURERS, DISTILLERS, PRODUCERS, ETC., SELLING TO STATE OR ALCOHOLIC BEVERAGE CONTROL BOARD.

28-3-110 through 28-3-115. Repealed.

DIVISION 3.

LICENSING OF HOTELS, RESTAURANTS, RAILROAD COMPANIES, ETC.

28-3-130 through 28-3-148. Repealed.

DIVISION 4.

SALE, ETC., OF LIQUOR, WINE AND MALT OR BREWED BEVERAGES BY LICENSEES GENERALLY.

28-3-160 through 28-3-167. Repealed.

28-3-168. Sale of table wine by wine retailers in certain counties.

Article 5.

Taxes on Sale of Malt or Brewed Beverages.

28-3-180 through 28-3-182. Repealed.

Article 5A.

Excise Taxes on Malt or Brewed Beverages.

Sec.
28-3-183. Definitions.
28-3-184. Tax levied; collection; disposition of funds.
28-3-185. Transactions between wholesalers exempt; reports.
28-3-186. Penalties for failure to pay taxes collected; possession of unidentified malt or brewed beverages; execution issued for unpaid taxes, etc.
28-3-187. Identification on containers; procedures; penalties.

Article 5B.

Excise Tax on Beer.

28-3-190. Levy of tax; collection; disposition of proceeds by localities; enforcement and administration; penalties; exclusive nature of tax.
28-3-191. Transactions between wholesalers and/or distributors exempt from article.
28-3-192. Unlawful acts and offenses; penalties.
28-3-193. Penalties on failure of wholesaler licensee to timely pay tax due; execution and levy; lien.
28-3-194. County and municipal license fees.
28-3-195. Legislative intent.
28-3-196. Revenue loss phase-out system.
28-3-197. Supplemental revenue loss phase-out system.
28-3-198. Meaning of words and phrases.
28-3-199. Repeal of certain local taxes and licenses.

Article 6.

Taxes on Sale of Spirituous or Vinous Liquors.

28-3-200. Additional 10 percent tax — Alcoholic beverage control board store fund.
28-3-201. Same — Alcoholic beverage control board store fund and general welfare purposes.
28-3-202. Same — Special mental health fund and general welfare purposes.
28-3-203. Additional five percent tax.
28-3-204. Additional three percent tax.
28-3-205. Additional 10 percent tax.
28-3-206. Limitation on additional tax on collector's bottles of liquor or gift packs of wine.
28-3-207. Exemption of sales to certificated or

Sec.
licensed air carrier with hub operation in state from this article.

Article 7.

Tax and Identification Stamps, Crowns or Lids.

28-3-220. Affixing of stamps, crowns or lids to original containers in which alcoholic beverages marketed, received, sold, etc., prior to sale, offer for sale, etc., by manufacturers, etc., required generally.
28-3-221. Board to design stamps, crowns or lids and require manufacturers, distillers, wholesalers, etc., to affix same to beer, wines or liquors sold in state.
28-3-222. Stamps, crowns or lids in amount of tax to be affixed to bottles, cans, etc., in which taxed articles sold; taxable articles offered for sale without stamps, crowns or lids subject to confiscation.
28-3-223. Manner and time for affixing of stamps, crowns or lids by wholesalers, distributors or retail dealers generally.
28-3-224. Stamping of alcoholic beverages by wholesalers, distributors or retail dealers; presumption as to sale of alcoholic beverages without proper stamps.
28-3-225. Board to provide for manufacture, sale and distribution of stamps, crowns or lids; sale of same by persons not designated and bonded by board; purchase of stamps, crowns or lids by manufacturers, etc.; persons, firms, etc., using tax-paid crowns or lids to pay costs of quarterly examinations of records by board examiners.
28-3-226. Penalty for failure to properly affix required stamps, crowns or lids; notification and right to trial of person, firm, etc., charged with same; lien for judgment in favor of state and issuance of execution thereupon.
28-3-227. Removal, restoration, etc., for use or reuse, unauthorized sale, etc., of revenue, etc., stamps, crowns or lids.
28-3-228. Manufacture, purchase, sale, possession, etc., of reproduction or counterfeit revenue, etc., stamps, crowns or lids.
28-3-229. Unauthorized possession of unat-

Sec.

tached revenue stamps, crowns or
lids.

Article 8.

Confiscation and Sale of Contraband Goods, Merchandise, etc.

28-3-240. Goods, etc., subject to confiscation
and sale generally; procedure for
confiscation and sale of goods,
etc., generally.
28-3-241. Additional beverages subject to confiscation and sale; punishment of
persons having contraband beverages in their possession.
28-3-242. Procedure for confiscation and sale
of goods, etc.; nature of proceedings against goods, etc.; court proceedings for collection of tax due
and assessed.
28-3-243. Return of confiscated goods.
28-3-244. Condemnation and delivery to board
of liquors seized upon which fed-

Sec.

eral tax has been paid and containers of which are unbroken or
unopened.

Article 9.

Miscellaneous Offenses.

28-3-260 through 28-3-268. Repealed.

Article 10.

Additional State Sales Tax on Alcoholic Beverages.

28-3-280. Additional state sales tax levied.
28-3-281. Collection and distribution of proceeds.
28-3-282. Use of tax proceeds.
28-3-283. Rules and regulations.
28-3-284. Levy of additional local taxes or fees
prohibited.
28-3-285. Article cumulative.
28-3-286. Effective date.

**The emasculation of the dram shop stat-
ute** by the passage of the new alcohol licensing
act (Title 38, chapter 3A) was the result of
legislative oversight, not legislative wisdom.
The legislature may have intended for the
A.B.C. board to promulgate regulations governing the sale of alcohol. It does not follow
from that premise, however, that it intended to
legalize the sale of alcohol to visibly intoxicated persons, to minors, and to insane persons. Buchanan v. Merger Enters., Inc., 463 So.
2d 121 (Ala. 1984).

ARTICLE 1.

GENERAL PROVISIONS.

Cross references. — As to names, marks,
etc., on beer, ale, etc., containers, see § 8-12-20
et seq.

§ 28-3-1. Definitions.

The following words or phrases, whenever they appear in this chapter, and
in Alcoholic Beverage Licensing Code, being Act No. 80-529, Acts of Alabama,
1980, as amended, appearing as chapter 3A, Title 28, as amended, and the
Alabama Table Wine Act, being Act 80-382, Acts of Alabama 1980, as
amended, appearing as chapter 7, Title 28, as amended, unless the context
clearly indicates otherwise, shall have the meaning ascribed to them in this
section:

(1) ALCOHOLIC BEVERAGES. Any alcoholic, spirituous, vinous, fermented
or other alcoholic beverage, or combination of liquors and mixed liquor, a
part of which is spirituous, vinous, fermented or otherwise alcoholic, and all
drinks or drinkable liquids, preparations or mixtures intended for beverage

purposes, which contain one-half of one percent or more of alcohol by volume, and shall include liquor, beer, and wine, both fortified and table wine.

(2) ASSOCIATION. A partnership, limited partnership, or any form of unincorporated enterprise owned by two or more persons.

(3) BEER, or MALT or BREWED BEVERAGES. Any beer, lager beer, ale, porter, malt or brewed beverage or similar fermented malt liquor containing one-half of one percent or more of alcohol by volume and not in excess of four percent alcohol by weight and five percent by volume, by whatever name the same may be called.

(4) BOARD. The alcoholic beverage control board.

(5) CARTON. The package or container or containers in which alcoholic beverages are originally packaged for shipment to market by the manufacturer or its designated representatives or the importer.

(6) CONTAINER. The single bottle, can, keg, bag or other receptacle, not a carton, in which alcoholic beverages are originally packaged for the market by the manufacturer or importer and from which the alcoholic beverage is consumed by or dispensed to the public.

(7) CLUB.

a. Class I. A corporation or association organized or formed in good faith by authority of law and which must have at least 150 paid-up members. It must be the owner, lessee or occupant of an establishment operated solely for the objects of a national, social, patriotic, political or athletic nature or the like, but not for pecuniary gain, and the property as well as the advantages of which, belong to all the members and which maintains an establishment provided with special space and accommodations where, in consideration of payment, food with or without lodging is habitually served. The club shall hold regular meetings, continue its business through officers regularly elected, admit members by written application, investigation and ballot and charge and collect dues from elected members.

b. Class II. A corporation or association organized or formed in good faith by authority of law and which must have at least 100 paid-up members. It must be the owner, lessee or occupant of an establishment operated solely for the objects of a national, social, patriotic, political or athletic nature or the like. The club shall hold regular meetings, continue its business through officers regularly elected, admit members by written application, investigation and ballot and charge and collect dues from elected members.

(8) CORPORATION. A corporation or joint stock association organized under the laws of this state, the United States, or any other state, territory or foreign country, or dependency.

(9) DRY COUNTY. Any county which by a majority of those voting voted in the negative in an election heretofore held under the applicable statutes at the time of said election or may hereafter vote in the negative in an election or special method referendum hereafter held in accordance with the

provisions of chapter 2, Title 28, or held in accordance with the provisions of any act hereafter enacted permitting such election.

(10) DRY MUNICIPALITY. Any municipality within a wet county which has, by its governing body or by a majority of those voting in a municipal election heretofore held in accordance with the provisions of section 28-2-22, or in a municipal option election heretofore or hereafter held in accordance with the provisions of Act 84-408, Acts of Alabama 1984, appearing as chapter 2A, Title 28, Code of Alabama 1975, as amended, or any act hereafter enacted permitting municipal option election, voted to exclude the sale of alcoholic beverages within the corporate limits of said municipality.

(11) GENERAL WELFARE PURPOSES.

a. The administration of public assistance as set out in sections 38-2-5 and 38-4-1;

b. Services, including supplementation and supplementary services under the federal Social Security Act, to or on behalf of persons to whom such public assistance may be given under said sections 38-2-5 and 38-4-1;

c. Service to and on behalf of dependent, neglected or delinquent children; and

d. Investigative and referral services to and on behalf of needy persons.

(12) HEARING COMMISSION. A body appointed by the board to hear and decide all contested license applications and all disciplinary charges against any licensee for violation of this title or the regulations of the board.

(13) HOTEL. A building or buildings held out to the public for housing accommodations of travelers or transients, and shall include motel, but shall not include a rooming house or boarding house.

(14) IMPORTER. Any person, association or corporation engaged in importing alcoholic beverages, liquor, wine or beer, manufactured outside of the United States of America into this state or for sale or distribution in this state, or to the board or to a licensee of the board.

(15) LIQUOR. Any alcoholic, spirituous, vinous, fermented, or other alcoholic beverage, or combination of liquors and mixed liquor, a part of which is spirituous, fermented, vinous or otherwise alcoholic, and all drinks or drinkable liquids, preparations or mixtures intended for beverage purposes, which contain one-half of one percent or more of alcohol by volume, except beer and table wine.

(16) LIQUOR STORE. A liquor store operated by the board, where alcoholic beverages other than beer are authorized to be sold in unopened containers.

(17) MANUFACTURER. Any person, association or corporation engaged in the producing, bottling, manufacturing, distilling, rectifying or compounding of alcoholic beverages, liquor, beer or wine in this state or for sale or distribution in this state or to the board or to a licensee of the board.

(18) MINOR. Any person under 21 years of age, except a person 19 years of age or older prior to October 1, 1985, is not a minor; provided, however, in the event section 28-1-5, shall be repealed or otherwise shall be no longer in effect, thereafter the provisions of section 26-1-1, shall govern.

(19) MUNICIPALITY. Any incorporated city or town of this state to include its police jurisdiction.

(20) PERSON. Every natural person, association or corporation. Whenever used in a clause prescribing or imposing a fine or imprisonment, or both, such term as applied to "association" shall mean the partners or members thereof and as applied to "corporation" shall mean the officers thereof, except as to incorporated clubs the term "person" shall mean such individual or individuals who, under the bylaws of such clubs, shall have jurisdiction over the possession and sale of liquor therein.

(21) POPULATION. The population according to the last preceding or any subsequent decennial census of the United States, except where a municipality is incorporated subsequent to the last census, in which event, its population until the next decennial census shall be the population of said municipality as determined by the judge of probate of said county as the official population on the date of its incorporation.

(22) RESTAURANT. A reputable place licensed as a restaurant, operated by a responsible person of good reputation and habitually and principally used for the purpose of preparing and serving meals for the public to consume on the premises.

(23) MEAL. A diversified selection of food some of which is not susceptible of being consumed in the absence of at least some articles of tableware and which cannot be conveniently consumed while one is standing or walking about.

(24) RETAILER. Any person licensed by the board to engage in the retail sale of any alcoholic beverages to the consumer.

(25) SALE or SELL. Any transfer of liquor, wine or beer for a consideration, and any gift in connection with, or as a part of, a transfer of property other than liquor, wine or beer for a consideration.

(26) SELLING PRICE. The total marked-up price of spirituous or vinous liquors sold by the board, exclusive of taxes levied thereon.

(27) UNOPENED CONTAINER. A container containing alcoholic beverages, which has not been opened or unsealed subsequent to filling and sealing by the manufacturer or importer.

(28) WET COUNTY. Any county which by a majority of those voting voted in the affirmative in an election heretofore held in accordance with the statutes applicable at the time of said election or may hereafter vote in the affirmative in an election or special method referendum held in accordance with the provisions of chapter 2, of Title 28, or other statutes applicable at the time of said election.

(29) WET MUNICIPALITY. Any municipality in a dry county which by a majority of those voting voted in the affirmative in a municipal option election heretofore or hereafter held in accordance with the provisions of Act 84-408, Acts of Alabama 1984, appearing as chapter 2A, Title 28, as amended, or any act hereafter enacted permitting municipal option election, or any municipality which became wet by vote of the governing body or by the voters of the municipality heretofore or hereafter held under

631

the special method referendum provisions of section 28-2-22, or as hereafter provided, where the county has become dry subsequent to the elected wet status of the municipality.

(30) WHOLESALER. Any person licensed by the board to engage in the sale and distribution of table wine and beer, or either of them, within this state, at wholesale only, to be sold by export or to retail licensees or other wholesale licensees or others within this state lawfully authorized to sell table wine and beer, or either of them, for the purpose of resale only.

(31) WINE. All beverages made from the fermentation of fruits, berries, or grapes, with or without added spirits, and produced in accordance with the laws and regulations of the United States, containing not more than 24 percent alcohol by volume, and shall include all sparkling wines, carbonated wines, special natural wines, rectified wines, vermouths, vinous beverages, vinous liquors, and like products, including restored or unrestored pure condensed juice.

(32) FORTIFIED WINE or VINOUS LIQUOR. Any wine containing more than 14 percent alcohol by volume but not more than 24 percent. Fortified wine is vinous liquor.

(33) TABLE WINE. Any wine containing not more than 14 percent alcohol by volume. Table wine is not liquor, spirituous or vinous. (Acts 1936-37, Ex. Sess., No. 66, p. 40; Code 1940, T. 29, §§ 1, 60; Acts 1967, No. 301, p. 839; Acts 1986, No. 86-212, § 1.)

The 1986 amendment, which became law without the governor's signature under § 125 of the Constitution on April 1, 1986, repealed and reenacted this section.

Code commissioner's note. — Acts 1986, No. 86-212, § 2 provides: "It is hereby declared the intention and purpose of this Act to make uniform the definitions applicable to Chapter 3, Title 28, Code of Alabama 1975, as amended, and to the Alcoholic Beverage Licensing Code being Act No. 80-529, Acts of Alabama 1980, as amended, appearing as Chapter 3A, Title 28, Code of Alabama 1975, as amended, and to the Alabama Table Wine Act, being Act No. 80-382, Acts of Alabama 1980, as amended, appearing as Chapter 7, Title 28, Code of Alabama 1975, as amended. It is the intention and the purpose of the legislature by this Act to resolve the problem of any conflict in definitions by the adoption of uniform definitions to appear as § 28-3-1, Code of Alabama 1975, as amended, which was previously repealed by Act No. 80-529, Acts of Alabama 1980."

Cross references. — For additional definition of "board" and definition of "mark up," see § 28-3-53.2.

This section must be construed in pari materia with § 28-4-1, where and to the extent pertinent. Kennedy v. State, 39 Ala. App. 676, 107 So. 2d 913 (1958).

Transaction whereby an incorporated social club sells alcoholic beverages to one of its members is a sale technically, and is within the meaning of a statute prohibiting the sale of vinous, spirituous or malt liquors without a license. Tarrant v. City of Birmingham, 39 Ala. App. 55, 93 So. 2d 925 (1957).

Proper subject for police regulation. — Traffic in intoxicating beverages is universally recognized as a proper subject for police regulation. Tarrant v. City of Birmingham, 39 Ala. App. 55, 93 So. 2d 925 (1957).

Cited in Tuscaloosa County v. Walker, 235 Ala. 293, 178 So. 543 (1938); Armstrong v. State ex rel. Embry, 248 Ala. 124, 26 So. 2d 874 (1946); Ekornes v. City of Mobile, 34 Ala. App. 159, 37 So. 2d 433 (1948); State ex rel. Morrow v. Santa Cruz, 252 Ala. 130, 39 So. 2d 786 (1949); Alabama ABC Bd. v. City of Birmingham, 253 Ala. 402, 44 So. 2d 593 (1950); Marks v. State, 35 Ala. App. 361, 46 So. 2d 854 (1950); State v. Ben R. Goltsman & Co., 261 Ala. 318, 74 So. 2d 414 (1954); Keene v. State, 37 Ala. App. 713, 76 So. 2d 180 (1954); Gulas v. City of Birmingham, 39 Ala. App. 86, 94 So. 2d 767 (1957); City of Mobile v. Madison, 40 Ala. App. 713, 122 So. 2d 540 (1960);

Loggins v. State, 52 Ala. App. 204, 290 So. 2d 665 (1974); Yessick v. State, 364 So. 2d 365 (Ala. Crim. App. 1978); Buchanan v. Merger Enters., Inc., 463 So. 2d 121 (Ala. 1984).

Collateral references. — 48 C.J.S., Intoxicating Liquors, §§ 1-19.

45 Am. Jur. 2d, Intoxicating Liquors, § 4 et seq.

What constitutes hotel or inn within meaning of liquor statute. 19 ALR 531, 53 ALR 988.

What amounts to restaurant or restaurant business within liquor law. 105 ALR 566.

What constitutes a "sale" of liquor in violation of a statute or ordinance. 89 ALR3d 551.

§ 28-3-2. Purpose and construction of chapter generally.

(a) This chapter shall be deemed an exercise of the police power of the state of Alabama for the protection of the public welfare, health, peace and morals of the people of the state and to prohibit forever the open saloon, and all of the provisions of this chapter shall be liberally construed for the accomplishment of this purpose.

(b) Except as otherwise expressly provided in this chapter, the purpose of this chapter is to prohibit transactions in liquor and alcohol and malt or brewed beverages which take place wholly within the state, except by and under the control of the board as specifically provided in this chapter, and every section and provision of this chapter shall be construed accordingly. The provisions of this chapter, through the instrumentality of the board and otherwise, provide the means by which such control shall be made effective. This chapter shall not be construed as forbidding, affecting or regulating any transaction which is not subject to the legislative authority of this state. (Acts 1936-37, Ex. Sess., No. 66, p. 40; Code 1940, T. 29, § 2.)

This section emphasizes the fact that the Alcoholic Beverage Control Act is an exercise of the police power of the state for the protection of the public welfare, health, peace and morals of the people of the state, and should be liberally construed. Subsection (b) of this section prohibits all transactions in liquor within the state except by and under the control of the board as herein specifically provided. Ott v. Moody, 283 Ala. 288, 216 So. 2d 177 (1968).

Cited in Lovett v. State, 244 Ala. 601, 14 So. 2d 838 (1943); State ex rel. Krasner v. Alabama ABC Bd., 246 Ala. 198, 19 So. 2d 841 (1944); Alabama ABC Bd. v. State ex rel.

Krasner, 247 Ala. 469, 25 So. 2d 30 (1945); Alabama ABC Bd. v. City of Birmingham, 253 Ala. 402, 44 So. 2d 593 (1950); Tarrant v. City of Birmingham, 39 Ala. App. 55, 93 So. 2d 925 (1957); Broughton v. Alabama Alcoholic Beverage Control Bd., 348 So. 2d 1059 (Ala. Civ. App. 1977); Rivers v. State, 406 So. 2d 1021 (Ala. Crim. App.), cert. denied, 406 So. 2d 1023 (Ala. 1981).

Collateral references. — 48 C.J.S., Intoxicating Liquors, §§ 35-44.

45 Am. Jur. 2d, Intoxicating Liquors, §§ 22-25.

Saloons or taverns as nuisance. 5 ALR3d 989.

§ 28-3-3. Applicability of provisions of chapter to ethyl alcohol intended or used for certain purposes.

The provisions of this chapter shall not apply to ethyl alcohol intended for use or used for the following purposes:

(1) For scientific, chemical, mechanical, industrial, medicinal and culinary purposes;

(2) For use by those authorized to procure the same tax-free as provided by acts of congress and regulations promulgated thereunder;

(3) In the manufacture of denatured alcohol produced and used as provided by acts of congress and regulations promulgated thereunder;

(4) In the manufacture of patented, patent, proprietary, medicinal, pharmaceutical, antiseptic, toilet, scientific, chemical, mechanical and industrial preparations or products unfit for beverage purposes; or

(5) In the manufacture of flavoring extracts and syrups unfit for beverage purposes. (Acts 1936-37, Ex. Sess., No. 66, p. 40; Code 1940, T. 29, § 1; Acts 1967, No. 301, p. 839.)

§ 28-3-4. Provisions for maintenance of separation of financial and business interests between classes of businesses regulated by chapter.

(a) No manufacturer and no officer or director of any manufacturer shall at the same time be a distributor, wholesaler or retail dispenser or an officer, director or stockholder or creditor of any distributor, wholesaler or retail dispenser, nor, except as provided in this section, be the owner, proprietor or lessor of any place covered directly or indirectly by any distributor's or wholesaler's malt or brewed beverage liquor license.

(b) No distributor or wholesaler and no officer or director of any distributor or wholesaler shall at the same time be a manufacturer or retailer or be an officer, director, stockholder or creditor of a manufacturer or retailer or be the owner, proprietor or lessor of any place covered by any other malt or brewed beverage or liquor license.

(c) No licensee licensed under this chapter shall directly or indirectly own any stock of, or have any financial interest in, any other class of business licensed under this chapter.

(d) Except as provided in this section, no manufacturer, wholesaler or distributor shall in any wise be interested, either directly or indirectly, in the ownership or leasehold of any property or in any mortgage against the same for which a liquor or retail dispensers' license is granted, nor shall a manufacturer, wholesaler or distributor, either directly or indirectly, lend any moneys, credit or equivalent thereof to any retailer in equipping, fitting out or maintaining and conducting, either in whole or in part, an establishment or business operated under a liquor retail dispensers' license, excepting only the usual and customary credits allowed for returning packages or containers in which malt or brewed beverages were packed for market by the manufacturer.

(e) Except as provided in this section no manufacturer shall in any wise be interested, directly or indirectly, in the ownership or leasehold of any property or any mortgage lien against the same, for which a distributor's or wholesaler's license is granted nor shall a manufacturer, either directly or indirectly, lend any moneys, credit or their equivalent to any distributor or wholesaler in equipping, fitting out or maintaining and conducting, either in whole or in part, an establishment or business where malt or brewed beverages are licensed for sale by a distributor or wholesaler, excepting only the usual credits allowed for the return of packages or containers in which malt or brewed beverages were originally packed for the market by the manufacturer.

(f) No distributor, wholesaler or retail dispenser shall in any wise, either directly or indirectly, receive any credit, loan, moneys or the equivalent thereof from any other licensee or from or through a subsidiary or affiliate of another licensee or from any firm, association or corporation, except a banking institution, in which another licensee or any officer, director or firm member of another licensee has a substantial interest or exercises a control of its business policy for equipping, fitting out, payment of license fee or maintaining and conducting, either in whole or in part, an establishment or business operated under a distributor's, wholesaler's or retail dispenser's license, excepting only the usual and customary credits allowed for the return of packages or containers in which malt or brewed beverages were packed for the market by the manufacturer.

(g) The purpose of this section is to require a separation of the financial and business interest between the various classes of business regulated by this chapter, and no person or corporation shall by any device whatsoever directly or indirectly, evade the provisions of this section. (Acts 1936-37, Ex. Sess., No. 66, p. 40; Code 1940, T. 29, § 41.)

Enforcement. — See Sterling Distribs., Inc. v. Patterson, 236 F. Supp. 479 (N.D. Ala. 1964).

Collateral references. — 45 Am. Jur. 2d, Intoxicating Liquors, § 123.

Statutes designed to prevent or limit control of retail liquor dealers by manufacturers, wholesalers, or importers. 136 ALR 1238.

§ 28-3-5. Retail dealers to furnish duplicate invoices for shipments of alcoholic beverages received from without state to board.

Any retail dealer of alcoholic beverages enumerated and defined in this chapter purchasing or receiving such commodities from without the state, whether the same shall have been ordered or purchased through a wholesaler or jobber in this state or by drop shipment or otherwise, shall, within 12 hours of receipt of such alcoholic beverages, mail by registered or certified mail a true duplicate invoice of all such purchases or receipts to the board at Montgomery, Alabama, said invoice carrying the name of the person or firm from whom or through whom such purchases or shipments of the alcoholic beverages were received and showing kinds and quantities.

Any retail dealer failing or refusing to furnish duplicate invoices in both the manner and time allowed shall be guilty of a misdemeanor and, upon conviction, shall be punished by a fine of not less than $50.00 for each offense or by imprisonment in the county jail for a period not exceeding 60 days. (Acts 1936-37, Ex. Sess., No. 66, p. 40; Code 1940, T. 29, § 48.)

§ 28-3-6. Furnishing of statements of consignments and deliveries of alcoholic beverages to board by common carriers, contract carriers, etc.; carriers, etc., to permit examination of records by board.

All common carriers, contract carriers, buses and trucks transporting alcoholic beverages may be required under regulations to be prescribed by the board to transmit to said board a periodic statement of such consignments or deliveries of alcoholic beverages, showing date, point of origin, point of delivery, to whom delivered and time of delivery.

All common carriers, contract carriers, buses or trucks shall permit the examination by the board or its agents of their records relating to shipment or receipt of alcoholic beverages at any time and place the board or its agents may deem it advisable and necessary to the enforcement of this chapter. Inspectors or any duly authorized agents of the board, on proper identification, may make such examination.

Any person, firm, corporation, partnership or association of persons who refuses to transmit to the board the statements provided for in this section or who refuses to permit the examination of his records by the board or its duly authorized agent shall be guilty of a misdemeanor and, upon conviction, shall be punished by a fine of not less than $100.00 nor more than $500.00 for each offense. (Acts 1936-37, Ex. Sess., No. 66, p. 40; Code 1940, T. 29, § 53.)

§ 28-3-7. Persons, firms, etc., receiving, storing, selling or handling alcoholic beverages to preserve invoices, books, papers, etc., relating thereto; audit and inspection of invoices, books, etc., by board.

It shall be the duty of every person, firm, corporation, club or association of persons, receiving, storing, selling or handling alcoholic beverages enumerated in this chapter in any manner whatsoever to keep and preserve all invoices, books, papers, cancelled checks or other memoranda touching the purchase, sale, exchange or receipt of any and all such alcoholic beverages for a period of three years.

All such invoices, books, papers, cancelled checks or other memoranda shall be subject to audit and inspection by any duly authorized representative of the board at any and all times.

Any person, firm, corporation, club or association of persons who fails or refuses to keep and preserve the records as required by this section or who upon request by a duly authorized agent of the board fails or refuses to allow an audit or inspection of records as provided in this section shall be guilty of a misdemeanor and shall, upon conviction, be punished by a fine of not less than $50.00 nor more than $200.00, or by imprisonment in the county jail for a period not to exceed 90 days for each offense. (Acts 1936-37, Ex. Sess., No. 66, p. 40; Code 1940, T. 29, § 55.)

§ 28-3-8. Shipment, delivery, etc., within state of articles taxed by chapter by wholesale dealers or distributors generally; shipment, etc., of same to federal, military, etc., reservations within state by wholesale dealers or distributors.

(a) Every wholesale dealer or distributor in this state shall, before shipping, delivering or sending out any one or more articles taxed in this chapter to any dealer in this state or for sale in this state, cause the same to have the requisite denominations and amount of stamps, crowns or lids to represent the tax affixed as stated in this chapter and, in the case of stamps, shall cause the same to be cancelled by writing or stamping across the face thereof the number of such wholesale dealer or distributor, said number to be applied by the board, and every wholesale dealer or distributor shall at the time of shipping or delivering any one or more articles taxed in this chapter make a true duplicate invoice of the same showing the date, amount and value of each class of articles shipped or delivered and retain a duplicate thereof, subject to the audit and inspection of the board, its authorized agents and representatives for three years.

(b) Wholesale dealers or distributors in this state who ship, deliver or send any one or more articles taxed in this chapter to the United States government for sale or distribution to any military, naval or marine reservation owned by the United States government within this state shall be required to carry out the provisions set out in this chapter for such sales or deliveries. (Acts 1936-37, Ex. Sess., No. 66, p. 40; Code 1940, T. 29, § 61.)

§ 28-3-9. Wholesalers and distributors to file monthly reports of alcoholic beverages purchased or received.

Each and every wholesaler or distributor qualifying as such with the board shall be required to file a report between the first and tenth of each month, covering the purchase or receipt by them of all alcoholic beverages enumerated and defined in this chapter during the preceding month. Said report shall give in detail the different kinds and quantities of alcoholic beverages so purchased or received by them during the preceding month.

Any wholesaler or distributor failing or refusing to file the above report in the manner and time allowed shall be guilty of a misdemeanor and, upon conviction, shall be fined not less than $100.00 nor more than $500.00 for each offense. (Acts 1936-37, Ex. Sess., No. 66, p. 40; Code 1940, T. 29, § 56.)

§ 28-3-10. Wholesale dealers or distributors to file monthly reports as to orders of alcoholic beverages purchased by persons, firms, etc., without state.

Every wholesale dealer or distributor shall furnish to the board a monthly report between the first and tenth of each month for the preceding month of all orders for alcoholic beverages enumerated and defined in this chapter purchased through said wholesale dealer or distributor from without the state on a drop shipment and consigned directly to the person, firm, corporation or association of persons ordering such alcoholic beverages from without this state through such wholesale dealer or distributor.

Any wholesale dealer or distributor who fails or refuses to comply with the provisions of this section shall be guilty of a misdemeanor and, upon conviction, shall be punished by a fine of not less than $500.00 nor more than $1,000.00 or imprisonment in the county jail for a period of six months or both at the discretion of the court. (Acts 1936-37, Ex. Sess., No. 66, p. 40; Code 1940, T. 29, § 47.)

§ 28-3-11. Invoices and receipts to be maintained by persons, firms, etc., selling or shipping goods, merchandise, etc., to persons, firms, etc., in another state or to federal government for army, navy or marine purposes; audit and inspection of invoices and receipts by board; promulgation of rules and regulations by board for enforcement of section.

(a) Where goods, wares or merchandise enumerated in this chapter are sold or shipped to any person, firm, corporation or association of persons in another state, the seller or shipper in this state shall make and preserve for three years a duplicate invoice bill, giving the name of the person, firm, corporation or association of persons to whom shipped, delivered or sold, the date of sale or shipment and the quantity of such merchandise so sold or shipped. Said seller in this state must have on file a freight, express or postal receipt for such merchandise showing that the same was turned over to a common carrier engaged in interstate commerce. If said merchandise is delivered by a conveyance belonging to a seller in this state, said seller must have on file a receipt signed by the purchasers showing such goods, wares or merchandise were received by him in another state. All of the above records shall at all times be subject to the inspection and audit of any duly authorized agent of the board.

(b) Any goods, wares or merchandise enumerated in this chapter that are sold to the United States government for army, navy or marine purposes and which shall be shipped from a point within this state to a place which has been lawfully ceded to the United States government for army, navy or marine purposes shall be subject to the same provisions as mentioned in subsection (a) of this section for goods, wares or merchandise sold or shipped to another state. Goods, wares or merchandise enumerated in this chapter which shall be sold or delivered to ships belonging to the United States navy for distribution and sale to members of the military establishment only or sold and delivered to ships regularly engaged in foreign or coastwise shipping between points in this state and points outside this state, shall be subject to the same provisions as mentioned in subsection (a) of this section for goods, wares or merchandise sold or shipped to another state.

(c) The board may promulgate rules and regulations from time to time to prevent any abuse of the provisions contained in this section.

(d) Any person, firm, corporation or association of persons who shall be found guilty of violating any of the provisions of this section or who receives or stores any of the articles of alcoholic beverages enumerated in this chapter for sale within the state of Alabama shall be guilty of a misdemeanor and, upon conviction, shall be punished by a fine of not less than $200.00 nor more than $500.00 or by imprisonment in the county jail for a period not to exceed six months or both at the discretion of the court. (Acts 1936-37, Ex. Sess., No. 66, p. 40; Code 1940, T. 29, § 59.)

§ 28-3-12. Report of purchase, receipt, etc., of alcoholic beverages not having revenue, etc., stamps, crowns or lids affixed thereto.

Any person, firm, corporation, club or association of persons who purchases or receives or who brings into the state in any manner whatsoever any of the articles of alcoholic beverages enumerated in this chapter which does not have affixed revenue stamps, crowns or lids or stamps or identification as described in this chapter shall, within three days of the receipt of such articles of alcoholic beverages, report the receipt or purchase of said alcoholic beverages to the board, giving the date of purchase or receipt, the name of person or firm from whom purchased or received and a list describing the articles of alcoholic beverages so purchased or received. This report must be made by registered or certified mail or in person.

Any person, firm, corporation, club or association of persons who fails or refuses to make the report as required in this section shall be guilty of a misdemeanor and, upon conviction, shall be fined not less than $5.00 nor more than $100.00 or imprisoned in the county jail not to exceed 30 days for each offense. (Acts 1936-37, Ex. Sess., No. 66, p. 40; Code 1940, T. 29, § 66.)

Unlicensed person bringing untaxed liquors into state. — One purchasing, outside state, alcoholic liquors bearing proper federal internal revenue stamps, but no state tax stamps, and transporting them into state, without having license or permit from the board to deal in, transport or import such liquors, is not guilty of violating this section as the section is inapplicable to unlicensed persons bringing untaxed liquors into state, but is guilty, if at all, of violating subsection (b) of § 28-2-1. Hardin v. State, 241 Ala. 4, 3 So. 2d 89 (1941).

§ 28-3-13. Sale within state of alcoholic liquors or beverages manufactured within states discriminating against alcoholic liquors or beverages manufactured, etc., in this state.

No alcoholic liquors or beverages of any kind shall be sold in this state which are manufactured in any state which by its laws or, in the opinion of the board, by its practices, discriminates with respect to the sale within such state against alcoholic liquors or beverages manufactured, distributed or sold at wholesale in Alabama. (Acts 1936-37, Ex. Sess., No. 66, p. 40; Code 1940, T. 29, § 77.)

§ 28-3-14. Procedure for collection of due and unpaid taxes and penalties imposed by chapter; lien for taxes and penalties.

If any taxes or penalties imposed by this chapter remain due and unpaid for a period of 10 days, the board shall issue a warrant of execution directed to any sheriff of the state of Alabama, commanding him to levy upon and sell the real and personal property of the taxpayer found within his county for the payment of the amount thereof, with penalties, if any, and the cost of executing the warrant and to return such warrant to the board and to pay it the money collected by virtue thereof.

Upon receipt of such execution, the sheriff shall file with the clerk of the circuit court of his county a copy thereof and thereupon the clerk of the circuit court shall enter in his abstract of judgments the name of the taxpayer mentioned in the warrant and in proper columns the amount of tax with penalties and costs for which the warrant is issued and the date and hour when such copy is filed and shall index the warrant upon the index of judgments.

The sheriff shall thereupon proceed upon the warrant in all respects with like effect and in the same manner prescribed by law in respect to executions issued against the property upon judgments of a court of record and shall be entitled to the same fees for services in executing the warrant to be collected in the same manner. He shall make return of such execution to the board within 30 days of issuance thereof.

The taxes and penalties imposed by this chapter shall be deemed a debt owing to the state by the party against whom the same shall be charged and shall be a preferred lien upon all property of the party against whom the same shall be charged. (Acts 1936-37, Ex. Sess., No. 66, p. 40; Code 1940, T. 29, § 67.)

Collateral references. — 48 C.J.S., Intoxicating Liquors, § 301.

§ 28-3-15. Acquisition, dispensing, etc., of alcoholic beverages, wine, etc., for medicinal, scientific, etc., purposes by physicians, dentists, etc.; acquisition, etc., of wine for sacramental or religious purposes by ministers, pastors, etc.

(a) Regularly licensed physicians, dentists or any person holding a license to practice medicine or to engage in any profession wherein the treatment of the human body or of an animal body is necessarily involved, clinics, noncommercial laboratories, manufacturing establishments, hospitals or sanatoria may acquire, own and dispense for medicinal, mechanical, scientific or other nonbeverage purposes only any alcoholic beverage, wine or ethyl alcohol.

(b) Any minister, pastor or officer of a regularly organized religious congregation or church and any other person who, under the ritual of any recognized religious denomination is authorized or required to use wine for sacramental or religious purposes in the ceremonies or ritual of such religious denominations, may acquire, own and use wine for such purposes only. (Acts 1936-37, Ex. Sess., No. 66, p. 40; Code 1940, T. 29, § 74; Acts 1943, No. 257, p. 229, § 1.)

Collateral references. — 48 C.J.S., Intoxicating Liquors, § 210.

§ 28-3-16. Advertising of alcoholic beverages.

There shall be no electric signs, painted signs or signs of any kind displayed outside any place of business advertising alcoholic beverages, as enumerated and defined in this chapter. There shall be no advertising of alcoholic beverages, as enumerated and defined in this chapter, except through newspapers, magazines, radio broadcasting stations, commercial vehicles used for transportation of alcoholic beverages and billboards located in "wet" counties, as defined in this chapter; provided, that there shall be no advertising of alcoholic beverages by means of billboards located in "dry" counties, as defined in this chapter. (Acts 1936-37, Ex. Sess., No. 66, p. 40; Code 1940, T. 29, § 12; Acts 1978, No. 434, p. 442.)

Collateral references. — 48 C.J.S., Intoxicating Liquors, §§ 194, 197, 220, 267.

Validity, construction, and effect of statutes, ordinances, or regulations prohibiting or regulating advertising of intoxicating liquors. 20 ALR4th 600.

§ 28-3-17. Location of state liquor store or sale of intoxicating liquors, malt beverages, wine, etc., in establishments within certain distances of grounds, etc., of state teachers colleges, eleemosynary institutions, etc.

It shall be unlawful to locate any state liquor store within one mile of the boundary of the campus or grounds of any state teachers college or any institution of higher learning or of any eleemosynary institution in this state, unless such store is within 400 feet of the courthouse, and it shall be unlawful to sell any intoxicating, spirituous, vinous, malt liquors or beverages or wine or beer in any establishment located within one mile of the boundary of the campus grounds of such institutions or college, unless such establishment is within 400 feet of the courthouse; provided, that the provisions of this section shall not apply to or be operative within the limits of any county having a population of 500,000 or more, except as provided in the next following sentence, or within the corporate limits or the police jurisdiction of cities having a population of more than 50,000 according to the last federal census or which shall have such population according to any federal census which may be taken hereafter; provided further, that within the corporate limits of any city having population of more than 20,000 and less than 30,000, which city is located within a county having a population of 500,000 or more, all according to the last or any subsequent federal decennial census, the foregoing provisions of this sentence shall not apply, but in lieu thereof the provisions of the next following sentences shall apply.

Within the corporate limits of any city having population of more than 20,000 and less than 30,000, which city is located within a county having a population of 500,000 or more, all according to the last or any subsequent federal decennial census, it shall be unlawful to locate any state liquor store within 4,200 feet of the principal administration building of any state teachers college or any institution of higher learning or of any eleemosynary institution in this state, unless such store is within 400 feet of the courthouse, and it shall be unlawful to sell any intoxicating, spirituous, vinous, malt liquors or beverages or wine or beer in any establishment located within 4,200 feet of the principal administration building of such institution or college, unless such establishment is within 400 feet of the courthouse.

Notwithstanding anything to the contrary contained above in this section, the removal or relocation of the said principal administration building of such institution or college to a new location shall not make unlawful the sale of intoxicating, spirituous, vinous, malt liquors or beverages or wine or beer in any place of business where, prior to the removal or relocation of said principal administration building, the sale of said liquors, beverages, wine or beer was not violative of the provisions of this section. (Acts 1936-37, Ex. Sess., No. 66, p. 40; Code 1940, T. 29, § 73; Acts 1971, No. 975, p. 1741.)

Cross references. — As to state liquor stores generally, see § 28-3-74 et seq.

Refusal to issue privilege business license to sell alcoholic beverages under this section held violation of equal protection. — See City of Hueytown v. Jiffy Chek Co., 342 So. 2d 761 (Ala. 1977).

Cited in Liger v. State, 28 Ala. App. 504, 188 So. 693 (1939); Broughton v. Alabama Alcoholic Beverage Control Bd., 348 So. 2d 1059 (Ala. Civ. App. 1977).

Collateral references. — 48 C.J.S., Intoxicating Liquors, § 263.

45 Am. Jur. 2d, Intoxicating Liquors, § 140 et seq.

Reasonableness of statutory regulation prohibiting license for sale of intoxicating liquors within prescribed distance from church, school, or other institution. 119 ALR 643.

"School," "schoolhouse," or the like within statute prohibiting liquor sales within specified distance thereof. 49 ALR2d 1103.

Measurement of distances for purposes of enactment prohibiting sale, or license for sale, of intoxicating liquor within given distance from church, university, school, or other institution or property as base. 4 ALR3d 1250.

§ 28-3-18. Laws as to manufacture or possession of illicit distilled liquor or apparatus for manufacture of same, etc., not repealed by chapter.

Nothing contained in this chapter shall be construed as repealing any of the laws of Alabama relating to the manufacture or possession of illicit distilled liquor or apparatus for the manufacture of same nor any law now fixing fees to officials for the enforcement of any and all laws, but the same shall remain in full force and effect. (Acts 1936-37, Ex. Sess., No. 66, p. 40; Code 1940, T. 29, § 75.)

Sections adopted by reference. — This section evinces a legislative intent to adopt by reference the provisions of §§ 28-4-50 and 28-4-52, which respectively make it unlawful for any person to have, sell, give away or manufacture a still to be used for manufacturing illicit liquors, and fixes the punishment for such offense at imprisonment at hard labor in the penitentiary for not less than one nor more than five years. Shirley v. State, 38 Ala. App. 104, 76 So. 2d 787 (1954).

Possession of "illicit distilled liquor" is prohibited by law, even in counties where legal liquors are authorized to be sold, and in that respect the prohibition law is preserved by this section. Boyd v. State, 239 Ala. 578, 195 So. 767 (1940).

The possession of "illicit distilled liquor" is prohibited by law even in counties where legal liquors are authorized to be sold, and in that respect the prohibition law is preserved by the repealing clause in the Alcoholic Beverage Control Act. Griffin v. State, 39 Ala. App. 671, 106 So. 2d 36 (1958).

Section 28-4-115 not repealed. — Section 28-4-115, which prohibits the transportation of prohibited beverages in quantities of five gallons or more, has not been repealed by implication because of the omission from this section of any reference to transportation of prohibited beverages. Griffin v. State, 39 Ala. App. 626, 106 So. 2d 182 (1958).

There was no merit in the contention that the transportation statute, § 28-4-115, was repealed by this section. Dixon v. State, 39 Ala. App. 575, 105 So. 2d 354 (1958).

§ 28-3-19. Engaging in prohibited practices, refusing to permit, etc., inspections of premises, interfering with confiscation of contraband alcoholic beverages, etc., by persons, firms, etc., subject to taxes under chapter.

Any person, firm or corporation subject to any of the taxes levied under the provisions of this chapter who engages in or permits any practices prohibited by the rules and regulations of the board or who by any other practice makes it difficult to enforce the provisions of this chapter or who, upon demand of the board or of any officer or agent of the board, refuses to allow full inspection of the premises or any part thereof or who shall hinder or in any wise delay or prevent any such inspection when demand is made therefor or who in any way interferes with any agent of the board in the performance of his duties in enforcing any of the provisions of this chapter relating to the confiscation of alcoholic beverages deemed by such agent of the board to be contraband as provided in this chapter shall be guilty of a misdemeanor and, upon conviction, shall be fined not less than $100.00 nor more than $200.00 for each offense, or may be imprisoned in the county jail for a period not exceeding 90 days, or both, in the discretion of the court. (Acts 1936-37, Ex. Sess., No. 66, p. 40; Code 1940, T. 29, § 54.)

Collateral references. — 48 C.J.S., Intoxicating Liquors, § 203.

Inspection, entry, or search of places where intoxicating liquors are sold, to facilitate determination of whether conditions of license are being complied with. 116 ALR 1098.

§ 28-3-20. Penalties for violations of provisions of chapter or rules and regulations of boards generally.

Any person who violates any of the provisions of this chapter for which a penalty is not provided or any rule or regulation promulgated in conformity with this chapter shall be guilty of a misdemeanor and, upon conviction, shall be fined not more than $500.00 for each offense and, in addition, may be imprisoned in the county jail for a period not to exceed six months. (Acts 1936-37, Ex. Sess., No. 66, p. 40; Code 1940, T. 29, § 44.)

Collateral references. — Criminal liability of member or agent of private club or association, or of owner or lessor of its premises, for violation of state or local liquor or gambling laws thereon. 98 ALR3d 694.

§ 28-3-21. Imposition of sentence to hard labor for county in lieu of jail sentence for violations of provisions of chapter.

Wherever in this chapter a jail sentence is provided as alternative punishment for a violation of any of its provisions, the court trying such case may, in lieu of and instead of said jail sentence, sentence one convicted for violation of any provisions of this chapter to hard labor for the county for the same period of time as provided for the jail sentence. (Acts 1936-37, Ex. Sess., No. 66, p. 40; Code 1940, T. 29, § 76.)

§ 28-3-22. Remittance of part of prescribed penalties by board; board not to accept less than minimum penalties.

The board, upon good cause shown, may in its discretion remit a part of the penalties prescribed in this chapter, but in no case shall it accept less than the minimum penalty provided for each offense. (Acts 1936-37, Ex. Sess., No. 66, p. 40; Code 1940, T. 29, § 62.)

§ 28-3-23. Repealed by Acts 1980, No. 80-529, p. 806, § 27, effective September 30, 1980.

ARTICLE 2.

ALCOHOLIC BEVERAGE CONTROL BOARD.

§ 28-3-40. Composition; qualifications, appointment, term of office and bond of members; conflicts of interest of members, employees, etc., of board; suspension or removal of members; office; meetings; quorum.

The alcoholic beverage control board shall consist of three persons, appointed by the governor with the advice and consent of the senate, one of whom shall be designated by the governor to be the chairman of said board.

Each member of said board at the time of his appointment and qualification shall be a resident of the state of Alabama and shall have resided in said state for a period of at least 10 years next preceding his appointment and qualification, and he shall also be a qualified voter therein.

The term of office of each member appointed shall be six years from the time of his appointment and qualification and until his successor shall qualify. In case any member shall be allowed to hold over after the expiration of his term, his successor shall be appointed for the balance of the unexpired term. Vacancies in said board shall be filled by the governor for the unexpired term. Each member shall be eligible for reappointment in the discretion of the governor.

No person shall be eligible for appointment or shall hold the office of member of the board or be appointed by the board or hold any office or position under the board who has any connection with any association, firm, person or corporation engaged in or conducting any alcoholic liquor business of any kind or who holds stocks or bonds therein or who has pecuniary interest therein, nor shall any such person receive any commission or profit whatsoever from, or have any interest whatsoever in any purchase or sales of any alcoholic liquors; provided, however, that if any member of the board is appointed when the senate is not in session, such member shall hold office until the senate has had an opportunity to reject or confirm his appointment.

Members of the board may be suspended or removed by the governor at his pleasure.

Each member of the board shall, before entering upon the discharge of his duties, give bond payable to the state of Alabama, in form approved by the attorney general, in such penalty as shall be fixed from time to time by the governor, with some surety or guaranty company duly authorized to do business in Alabama and approved by the governor, as security, conditioned upon the faithful discharge of his duties. The premium of such bond shall be paid by the state and the bonds shall be filed as bonds of other state officers.

The office of the board shall be in the city of Montgomery, Alabama. The said board shall meet at such times within the city of Montgomery, Alabama, as the board shall determine and the members thereof shall be entitled to their reasonable expenses and per diem for each meeting so attended. A majority of the members shall constitute a quorum for the transaction of any business, for the performance of any duty or for the exercise of any power of the board. (Acts 1936-37, Ex. Sess., No. 66, p. 40; Code 1940, T. 29, § 3.)

Venue. — Any action filed in the courts of this state to review a decision of the board should be filed in the county of their official residence, which is Montgomery county, and when this is not done, the trial court errs to reversal when it does not grant the motion to transfer venue to the circuit court of Montgomery county. Alabama ABC Bd. v. Owen, 54 Ala. App. 419, 309 So. 2d 459 (1975).

Cited in Alabama ABC Bd. v. City of Birmingham, 253 Ala. 402, 44 So. 2d 593 (1950); James v. Wallace, 533 F.2d 963 (5th Cir. 1976).

Collateral references. — 48 C.J.S., Intoxicating Liquors, §§ 187, 191, 212.

§ 28-3-41. Compensation of board.

Each member of the board shall be entitled to receive $25.00 for each day actually engaged in the performance of his duties, not to exceed $2,500.00 for any year. The governor, at his discretion, however, may at any time issue an executive order that any member of said board shall serve without compensation. In such event, and until such executive order is rescinded, any such member shall not be entitled to any compensation whatsoever for the performance of his duties as a member of said board, but he shall be entitled to the expenses provided by law for members of said board while engaged in the performance of their duties. (Acts 1951, Ex. Sess., No. 4, p. 167, § 3.)

Cross references. — As to travel expenses, see § 36-7-20 et seq.

§ 28-3-42. Administrator; annual report of board to governor as to administration of chapter; possession by officers, members, employees, etc., of board of liquor or malt or brewed beverages for personal use.

(a) The board shall appoint an administrator who, under the supervision of the board, shall administer the provisions of this chapter. Before entering upon the duties of his office, the administrator shall execute to the state of Alabama a bond, to be approved by the governor, in the amount of $25,000.00, for the faithful performance of his duties. The premiums on the bond of the administrator shall be paid out of moneys derived from any operation under the provisions of this chapter.

The administrator, with the approval of the board and subject to the provisions of the merit system, shall appoint all necessary clerks, stenographers, inspectors and chemists and other employees to enforce properly the provisions of this chapter. No person shall be eligible for any appointment who has any financial connection whatever with any person engaged in or conducting any liquor business of any kind or who holds stock or bonds therein and who has any pecuniary interest therein, nor shall any such person receive any commission or profit whatever from or have any interest whatsoever in the purchase or sales made by persons authorized by this chapter to manufacture, purchase, sell or otherwise deal in the liquor business.

The administrator shall act as manager, secretary and custodian of all records unless the board shall otherwise order.

The administrator shall devote his entire time to said office.

The administrator, with the approval of the board, shall fix the duties of all employees authorized by this chapter.

The administrator shall be at the time of his appointment a resident of the state of Alabama, and he shall have resided in the state for at least five years continuously prior to his appointment. He shall be a man of good moral character and not less than 35 years of age.

(b) It shall be the duty of the board, during the month of October of each year, to make a report to the governor concerning its administration of this chapter.

(c) The provisions of this chapter shall not prevent any officer, member, agent or employee of the board from purchasing and keeping in his possession for the personal use of himself, members of his family or guests, liquor or malt or brewed beverages which may be purchased or kept by any person by virtue of this chapter. (Acts 1936-37, Ex. Sess., No. 66, p. 40; Acts 1939, No. 107, p. 139; Code 1940, T. 29, § 4; Acts 1951, No. 614, p. 1060, § 1; Acts 1967, Ex. Sess., No. 172, p. 221.)

Cross references. — As to merit system, see § 36-26-1 et seq.

§ 28-3-43. Functions, powers and duties of board generally; examination of board by examiners of public accounts.

(a) The functions, duties and powers of the board shall be as follows:

(1) To buy, manufacture and sell alcoholic beverages and to have alcoholic beverages in its possession for sale, as defined and enumerated in this chapter.

(2) To control the possession, sale, transportation and delivery of alcoholic beverages as enumerated and defined in this chapter.

(3) To determine the localities within which any state store shall be established and operated and the location of such store. No store shall be established in and neither the board nor any other person may legally buy, manufacture or sell alcoholic beverages in any county which has voted in the negative in any election called as provided in chapter 2 of this title for determining the said issue unless and until said county has at a subsequent similar election voted in the affirmative. The board shall have the power to establish and maintain state stores for the sale of liquors as defined in this chapter; provided, that municipalities may by proper zoning ordinances establish zones or districts within which such liquor stores may or may not be established; provided further, that the number of liquor stores in any municipality shall be limited to two such stores for municipalities of 25,000

population or less according to the last or any subsequent federal census and, in municipalities having more than 25,000 population, such additional stores as the board, in its discretion, may determine.

(4) To make provision for the maintenance of warehouses for alcoholic beverages and to control the delivery of alcoholic beverages to and from such warehouses and the keeping of the same therein.

(5) To operate distilleries and to manufacture alcoholic beverages if, in the opinion of the board, the purposes of this chapter can be thereby promoted. The price of all spiritous and vinous liquors dispensed by the board shall be fixed by the board, and the location of liquor stores shall not be adjacent to schools or churches or in a neighborhood which is exclusively residential. Neither the board nor any state store operated by it shall in any manner advertise its wares for sale.

(6) To appoint, subject to the provisions of the merit system, every officer, agent, inspector, investigator and employee, in accordance with the qualifications specifically set out in this chapter, required for the operation of the business of said board, commission such agents, inspectors or investigators as necessary to make arrests and execute search warrants and have the same authority as designated to peace officers as now authorized by law, assign all employees their official positions and titles, define their respective duties and powers, require them or any of them to give bonds payable to the state in such penalty as shall be fixed by the board and engage the services of experts and persons engaged in the practice of a profession.

(7) To control the manufacture, possession, sale, consumption, importation, use and delivery of liquor, alcohol and malt and brewed beverages in accordance with the provisions of this chapter and to fix the wholesale and retail prices at which liquor shall be sold at Alabama liquor stores. The board shall require each Alabama manufacturer and each nonresident manufacturer of distilled liquors selling distilled liquors to the board to make application for and be granted a permit by the board before distilled liquors shall be purchased from such manufacturer. The board before issuing such permit shall collect from each applicant a permit fee of $15.00, which sum shall be paid annually thereafter on application. In the event that any such manufacturer shall, in the opinion of the board, sell distilled liquors to the board through another person for the purpose of evading this provision relating to permits, the board shall require such person before purchasing distilled liquors from him or it to take out a permit and pay the same fee as hereinbefore required to be paid by such manufacturer. All permit fees so collected shall be paid into the state stores fund.

(8) To grant, issue and suspend or revoke for cause liquor licenses and alcohol permits as provided in this chapter.

(9) To grant, issue and suspend or revoke for cause malt or brewed and vinous beverages licenses as provided in this chapter.

(10) To lease and furnish and equip such buildings, rooms and other accommodations as shall be required for the operation of this chapter. To

determine the nature, form and capacity of all packages to be used for containing liquor, alcohol or malt or brewed beverages to be kept or sold under this chapter and to prescribe the form and contents of all labels and seals to be placed thereon.

(11) To purchase from time to time the necessary stamps, crowns or lids, in a quantity sufficient for a period not to exceed six months, for identifying each article sold or distributed by or through the said state liquor stores. All liquors, vinous beverages and alcohol sold or distributed by the board or any licensee of said board shall be stamped or endorsed in such characteristic way or manner to be determined by the board as shall clearly indicate that it has been dispensed by the board, and all such liquors, vinous beverages or alcohol not containing such label shall be contraband and subject to forfeiture as other contraband liquors.

(12) To require all wholesalers who make sales of alcoholic beverages of any kind as defined in this chapter to any state store to forward, when the shipments of such alcoholic beverages are made, to the board an invoice setting out the quantities of beverages purchased, and the price quotation showing at what price such beverages were sold and such invoice and quotation to be placed on record in the records of the alcoholic beverage control board of the state of Alabama and to be held for a period of not less than 18 months.

(b) The alcoholic beverage control board shall be subject to regular examinations by the examiners of public accounts the same as all other state agencies. (Acts 1936-37, Ex. Sess., No. 66, p. 40; Code 1940, T. 29, § 5; Acts 1957, No. 373, p. 501; Acts 1961, No. 869, p. 1362.)

Cross references. — For functions and duties of the board under the Alcoholic Beverage Licensing Code, see chapter 3A of this title.

Board has a wide discretion in issuance of original licenses for sale of malt or brewed beverages. State ex rel. Krasner v. Alabama ABC Bd., 246 Ala. 198, 19 So. 2d 841 (1944).

The board has a wide discretion in the granting or refusing to grant original licenses, but not an unbridled discretion, and must find and assign some reason of greater weight than merely giving effect to some long-standing custom of the board. Reams v. State, ex rel. Clokey, 45 Ala. App. 614, 234 So. 2d 893 (1970).

Authority of municipality to enact proper zoning ordinance. — Neither in this section nor in any part of this chapter is the power and authority vested in the board in any way given to a municipality, except that by a proper zoning ordinance a city may limit the power of the board as to the location of the store. Alabama ABC Bd. v. City of Birmingham, 253 Ala. 402, 44 So. 2d 593 (1950).

With regard to interpretation of the words "proper zoning ordinance," which appear in this section, it must be noted that a city has no inherent power to enact and enforce zoning regulations. Alabama ABC Bd. v. City of Birmingham, 253 Ala. 402, 44 So. 2d 593 (1950).

Board has no authority to license operation of still in dry county. — Where a county had been dry for over a year the court, in trial of defendant for distilling and for possession of still, could judicially notice that the county had been dry and it was proper for the court to instruct the jury that the beverage control board did not have the authority to give permission to anyone to operate a still for the purpose of making prohibited liquors in a dry county. Smothers v. State, 38 Ala. App. 553, 89 So. 2d 277 (1956).

Cited in Williams v. State, 28 Ala. App. 73, 179 So. 915 (1938); State ex rel. Morrow v. Santa Cruz, 252 Ala. 130, 39 So. 2d 786 (1949); Sterling Distribs., Inc. v. Patterson, 236 F. Supp. 479 (N.D. Ala. 1964); Yeager v. State, 44 Ala. App. 263, 207 So. 2d 122 (1967); Livingston v. State, 44 Ala. App. 579, 217 So. 2d 90 (1968); USA Oil Corp. v. City of Lipscomb, 293 Ala. 103, 300 So. 2d 362 (1974); Broughton v. Alabama Alcoholic Beverage Control Bd., 348 So. 2d 1059 (Ala. Civ. App. 1977); Rivers v. State, 406 So. 2d 1021 (Ala. Crim. App.), cert. denied, 406 So. 2d 1023 (Ala. 1981).

Collateral references. — 48 C.J.S., Intoxicating Liquors, §§ 191-213.

45 Am. Jur. 2d, Intoxicating Liquors, §§ 114 et seq., 228 et seq.

State's power to regulate price of intoxicating liquors. 14 ALR2d 699.

Validity of state statute or regulation fixing minimum prices at which alcoholic beverages may be sold at retail. 96 ALR3d 639.

§ 28-3-44. Lease of trucks, etc., for transportation of alcoholic beverages purchased, sold or stored by board; employment of operators of leased equipment.

(a) The board is hereby authorized and empowered to lease trucks, road tractors and trailers and similar equipment when needed for the transportation of alcoholic beverages purchased, stored or sold by it, but only on condition that such equipment will be maintained by the lessor. The consideration for any such leased equipment to be paid by the board shall be based on fair rental value of the equipment leased, and the cost of transportation with leased equipment shall not be in excess of the cost of transportation by common motor carrier service.

(b) The board is also authorized and empowered to employ drivers or operators of any equipment leased by it, without regard to the provisions of the Merit System Act. (Acts 1955, No. 193, p. 478.)

Collateral references. — 48 C.J.S., Intoxicating Liquors, § 208.

§ 28-3-45. Supervision of sale and distribution of malt or brewed and vinous beverages; collection of licenses and taxes accruing from sale, distribution, etc., of malt and vinous beverages generally.

(a) The board is authorized, empowered and directed to supervise the conduct, management and operation of the sale and distribution within this state of all malt or brewed beverages as defined in this chapter and vinous beverages of an alcoholic content of not to exceed 24 percent by volume.

(b) The board is authorized and directed to collect all licenses and taxes levied in this chapter accruing from the sale, distribution, receipt or storing for the purpose of sale within this state any and all malt and vinous beverages enumerated and defined in this chapter. (Acts 1936-37, Ex. Sess., No. 66, p. 40; Code 1940, T. 29, § 42.)

§ 28-3-46. Powers as to administration and enforcement of taxes imposed by chapter generally.

The board shall administer and enforce the taxes imposed by this chapter. It shall have the power to enter upon the premises of any taxpayer to examine, or cause to be examined by any agent or representative designated by it for that purpose, any books, papers, records or memoranda, bearing upon the amount of taxes payable, and to secure other information directly or indirectly relating to the enforcement of this chapter. (Acts 1936-37, Ex. Sess., No. 66, p. 40; Code 1940, T. 29, § 65.)

§ 28-3-47. Temporary closings of licensed places in municipalities during emergencies.

The board may, with the approval of the governor, temporarily close all licensed places within any municipality during any period of emergency proclaimed to be such by the governor. (Acts 1936-37, Ex. Sess., No. 66, p. 40; Code 1940, T. 29, § 21.)

Collateral references. — 48 C.J.S., Intoxicating Liquors, §§ 237-268.
45 Am. Jur. 2d, Intoxicating Liquors, § 259.
Criminal responsibility of club authorized generally to sell intoxicating liquors for particular illegal sale thereof by employee or agent. 139 ALR 306.

§ 28-3-48. Design and promulgation of form, etc., of stamps, crowns or lids generally; designation of same.

The board shall design the form and kind of stamps, crowns or lids to be used and shall duly adopt and promulgate such form of stamps, crowns or lids. Such stamps, crowns or lids so adopted and promulgated shall be known and termed as "Alabama Revenue Stamps, Crowns or Lids" and in any information or indictment, it shall be sufficient to describe the stamps, crowns or lids as "Alabama Revenue Stamps, Crowns or Lids." (Acts 1936-37, Ex. Sess., No. 66, p. 40; Code 1940, T. 29, § 60.)

Cross references. — As to stamps, crowns and lids generally, see § 28-3-220.

§ 28-3-49. Promulgation, amendment, etc., of regulations by board generally; introduction in evidence of regulations, etc.

(a) The board shall have authority to promulgate rules and regulations not inconsistent with this chapter for carrying out the provisions of this chapter and to alter, repeal or amend such regulations. Such rules and regulations shall have the full force and effect of law.

(b) Prima facie evidence of any such regulation may be given in all courts and proceedings by the production of what purports to be an official printed copy of such regulation, alteration, repeal or amendment. (Acts 1936-37, Ex. Sess., No. 66, p. 40; Code 1940, T. 29, §§ 6, 44, 52.)

Regulations have force and effect of law. — All reasonable rules and regulations of the board have the force and effect of law. Lovett v. State, 30 Ala. App. 334, 6 So. 2d 437 (1941); Cowan v. State, 32 Ala. App. 161, 22 So. 2d 917 (1945).

And the court will take judical notice of rules and regulations promulgated by the board within the scope of its authority. Lovett v. State, 30 Ala. App. 334, 6 So. 2d 437 (1941); Cowan v. State, 32 Ala. App. 161, 22 So. 2d 917 (1945).

Hours of sale. — The legislature has acted to prohibit sales of alcoholic beverages only at certain times. Promulgation of any other regulations regarding hours of sale is left to the Alabama alcoholic beverage control board. Gadsden Motel Co. v. City of Attalla, 378 So. 2d 705 (Ala. 1979).

Cited in State ex rel. Krasner v. Alabama ABC Bd., 246 Ala. 198, 19 So. 2d 841 (1944); State ex rel. Morrow v. Santa Cruz, 252 Ala. 130, 39 So. 2d 786 (1949); Sterling Distribs., Inc. v. Patterson, 236 F. Supp. 479 (N.D. Ala. 1964); Reams v. State ex rel. Clokey, 45 Ala. App. 614, 234 So. 2d 893 (1970); Buchanan v. Merger Enters., Inc., 463 So. 2d 121 (Ala. 1984).

Collateral references. — 48 C.J.S., Intoxicating Liquors, §§ 191, 212, 403.

§ 28-3-50. Promulgation of rules and regulations as to breaking of packages, affixing of stamps, inspections, etc., generally.

The board shall provide by rules and regulations the methods of breaking packages, the forms and kinds of containers, the methods of affixing the stamps required for the payment of the tax imposed by the provisions of this chapter and also for such inspection as may be necessary to enforce effectively the payment of such taxes. (Acts 1936-37, Ex. Sess., No. 66, p. 40; Code 1940, T. 29, § 54.)

Cross references. — As to stamps, crowns and lids generally, see § 28-3-220.

Collateral references. — Validity and construction of statute or ordinance making it offense to have possession of open unsealed alcoholic beverage in public place. 39 ALR4th 668.

§ 28-3-51. Promulgation of rules and regulations as to affixing of stamps, crowns or lids on articles, etc., handled by persons, firms, etc., operating on interstate common carriers.

The board may promulgate rules and regulations governing the affixing of stamps, crowns or lids on any articles or commodities handled by persons, firms or corporations operating on interstate common carriers. (Acts 1936-37, Ex. Sess., No. 66, p. 40; Code 1940, T. 29, § 52.)

Cross references. — As to stamps, crowns and lids generally, see § 28-3-220.

§ 28-3-52. Maintenance, examination and audit of books, records and accounts of board.

The books and records of the board shall at all times be subject to examination and audit by the department of finance. The board shall keep a complete and accurate record of all its actions and devise and install a system of accounts as the department of finance shall approve and direct. All records of the board shall be public records. The cost of such installation, examinations and audits by the department of finance shall be a charge against the moneys collected under this chapter. At least one audit of the operations of the board shall be made each year by the examiner of public accounts. (Acts 1936-37, Ex. Sess., No. 66, p. 40; Acts 1936-37, Ex. Sess., No. 204, p. 244; Code 1940, T. 29, § 9; Acts 1943, No. 391, p. 361.)

Acts 1936-37, Ex. Sess., No. 204, p. 244 was not invalid as a local law not constitutionally enacted. Baumhauer v. State ex rel. Smith, 240 Ala. 10, 198 So. 272 (1940); See also Baumhauer v. State ex rel. Smith, 29 Ala. App. 470, 198 So. 275 (1940).

§ 28-3-53. Disposition of moneys received by board from licenses, taxes and earnings; procedure as to claims against said moneys generally.

All moneys received by said board from licenses, taxes and earnings shall be paid, as directed by the provision of law under which such moneys are received, into either the general fund of the state or the appropriate trust funds of the state, and all claims against said moneys shall be handled by said board as provided by law. (Acts 1936-37, Ex. Sess., No. 66, p. 40; Code 1940, T. 29, § 71.)

Cross references. — As to licenses generally, see § 28-3A-1 et seq. As to excise taxes on malt or brewed beverages, see § 28-3-183 et seq. As to excise taxes on beer, see § 28-3-190 et seq. As to taxes on sale of spirituous or vinous liquors, see § 28-3-200 et seq.

Collateral references. — 48 C.J.S., Intoxicating Liquors, § 188.

§ 28-3-53.1. Delay in distribution of certain funds; use of moneys realized; distribution of funds accumulated as working capital.

(a) There shall be no distribution of any taxes collected on alcoholic beverages sold by the Alabama alcoholic beverage control board or of any funds distributed as net profits by said board for at least 25 days beginning October 1, 1983, for at least 55 days by September 30, 1984, for at least 85 days by September 30, 1985, for at least 115 days by September 30, 1986, for at least 120 days by September 30, 1987, and thereafter, from the close of the month in which the said taxes or said funds are realized. The moneys so realized are intended for use by said board for inventory purposes.

(b) Any funds accumulated as working capital under section 28-3-74(d) shall be distributed to the several beneficiaries on the same basis as withheld on the next distribution of profits to such beneficiaries by the Alabama alcoholic beverage control board after October 1, 1984. (Acts 1982, No. 82-436, p. 686, §§ 1, 2.)

Code commissioner's note. — Subsection (d) of § 28-3-74, referred to in subsection (b) above, was repealed by Acts 1982, No. 82-436, § 3.

§ 28-3-53.2. "Board" and "mark up" defined; additional mark up credited to general fund.

(a) The word "board," wherever used in this section, shall mean the Alabama alcoholic beverage control board provided for in chapter 3, Title 28. The term "mark up," wherever used in this section shall mean the percentage amount added to cost plus freight on spirituous or vinous liquors sold by the "board," exclusive of taxes heretofore levied with respect thereto.

(b) The total amount of the additional "mark up" on cost of merchandise, levied by the alcoholic beverage control board subsequent to June 30, 1983, shall be designated to the credit of the general fund of the state. (Acts 1983, No. 83-427, p. 607, §§ 1, 2.)

§ 28-3-54. Refund on overpayment or erroneous payment of taxes or licenses and of prepaid taxes where loss sustained prior to sale at retail; petition.

Where any licensee of the alcoholic beverage control board in the payment of taxes or licenses which are paid directly to the board, and where, by a mistake of fact or law, has paid an amount in excess of the amount due or has made an erroneous payment, or where taxes have been prepaid to the board and the alcoholic beverages upon which the tax has been prepaid is, prior to the sale of the same at retail, lost or destroyed by fire, theft or casualty or is damaged by fire or other casualty resulting in destruction of or damage to the beverages or beverage containers, the comptroller is authorized to draw his warrant on the treasurer in favor of such licensee, and the treasurer is authorized to pay such warrant for the amount of such overpayment or erroneous payment or prepayment of taxes or licenses. Provided, however, claims for less than $250.00 must be accumulated until a total claim of at least $250.00 has been reached or for a period of three years, whichever first occurs.

Before any refund under this section can be made the licensee, its heirs, successors or assigns, shall file in duplicate, petition directed to the board, setting up the fact relied on to procure the refunding of the money erroneously paid or prepaid. Such application must be made within three years from the date of such payment. The board shall examine said petition and the records of the licensee and the board, and if the facts set forth in the petition are such as to entitle the petitioner to the refunding of the money as prayed for and the board, upon the evidence adduced, is satisfied that the petitioner is entitled to the refund as prayed for, it shall so certify to the comptroller stating the amount to be refunded by the state and the particular fund on which such warrant shall be drawn, and forward to the comptroller a copy of the petition with the certificate attached, and if the comptroller shall be satisfied that the petition is in form required by law, he shall draw his warrant on the treasurer as hereinbefore provided for the amount certified to him by the board. (Acts 1979, No. 79-309, p. 462.)

Collateral references. — 48 C.J.S., Intoxicating Liquors, §§ 181, 189.

45 Am. Jur. 2d, Intoxicating Liquors, § 212.

§ 28-3-55. Cost of evidence fund; creation; aid in drug law enforcement; appropriation.

(a) The law enforcement division of the Alabama alcoholic beverage control board, for the procurement of evidence to aid in drug and narcotic criminal enforcement of the laws of this state, is hereby authorized to establish a fund known as the "cost of evidence fund" in the amount of $50,000.00. This fund is to be administered by the administrator of the alcoholic beverage control board, and upon his approval the state comptroller shall draw a warrant on the state treasury to create this fund. It shall be the responsibility of the administrator of the alcoholic beverage control board to insure that the fund is maintained at $50,000.00, or as nearly thereto as possible, and upon presentation to the comptroller of the properly documented expenditures the comptroller shall cause his warrant to be drawn to replenish this fund. Said fund shall be managed by the administrator of the alcoholic beverage control board to make such distributions from this fund to alcoholic beverage control board agents as he deems necessary.

(b) The Alabama alcoholic beverage control board is hereby authorized to expend moneys for the purposes authorized in subsection (a), which moneys shall be paid from the funds appropriated to the law enforcement division of the alcoholic beverage control board for "other expenses." (Acts 1979, No. 79-699, p. 1243.)

ARTICLE 3.

STATE LIQUOR STORES.

Cross references. — As to location of state liquor stores near colleges, eleemosynary institutions, etc., see § 28-3-17.

Article is constitutional. — This article, providing for state liquor stores, does not infringe the due process clause or any other provision of the federal Constitution. State ex rel. Wilkinson v. Murphy, 237 Ala. 332, 186 So. 487 (1939).

State liquor stores are not "works of internal improvement," within Constitution 1901, art. 4, § 93, prohibiting state from engaging in such works or lending money or credit in aid thereof. State ex rel. Wilkinson v. Murphy, 237 Ala. 332, 186 So. 487 (1939).

§§ 28-3-70 through 28-3-73. Repealed by Acts 1980, No. 80-528, p. 805, § 27, effective September 30, 1980.

§ 28-3-74. Distribution of net profits from proceeds of stores.

(a) The net profits derived from the proceeds of the Alabama liquor stores in each fiscal year, including all tax levied upon the selling price of all spirituous or vinous liquors, less all cost and expense of collecting said tax, up to and including $2,000,000.00, shall be paid out and applied as follows:

(1) Fifty percent shall be covered into the general fund of the treasury of the state;

(2) Nineteen percent shall be covered into the treasury of the state to the credit of the state department of human resources to be used, and the same is hereby appropriated exclusively, for old age assistance and for other purposes of the state department of human resources;

(3) Ten percent shall be covered into the treasury of the state to the credit of the wet counties of the state and shall be divided equally among each of said counties and shall be paid to them and shall be covered by them into their respective general funds;

(4) One percent shall be paid into the treasury of the state to the credit of the wet counties of the state and shall be divided equally among each of said counties and shall be paid to them to be used by them exclusively for the purposes of public health; and

(5) Twenty percent shall be covered into the treasury of the state and shall be paid to the incorporated municipalities in which Alabama liquor stores are located on the following basis: Each municipality in which an Alabama liquor store is located shall receive as its percentage or portion of said 20 percent an amount equal to the ratio of the profits earned by such municipality's Alabama liquor store or stores to the total net profits of all Alabama liquor stores.

(b) If the net profits derived from the proceeds of said Alabama liquor stores in any such fiscal year, including all tax levied upon the selling price of all spirituous or vinous liquors, less all cost and expense of collecting said tax, shall exceed the sum of $2,000,000.00, such excess, up to and including $200,000.00, shall be apportioned among and paid to the several incorporated cities and towns in the wet counties, in the state on the basis of the ratio of the population of each such city or town to the total population of all such cities and towns.

Any remainder of such excess over said $200,000.00 shall be apportioned and paid out as follows:

(1) Ten percent of such remainder for each fiscal year thereafter shall be apportioned among and paid to the wet counties in the state for general purposes on the basis of the ratio of the population of each such county of the population of all such counties;

(2) Sixteen and two-thirds percent of such remainder for each fiscal year thereafter shall be apportioned among and paid to the aforesaid incorpo-

rated cities and towns in the wet counties in the state on the basis of the ratio of the population of each such city or town to the total population of such cities and towns;

(3) Three and one-third percent of such remainder for each fiscal year thereafter shall be apportioned among and paid to such of said several cities and towns as may have one or more Alabama liquor stores therein upon the basis of the ratio of the population of each such liquor store city or town to the total population of all such liquor store cities and towns. Each and every amount received by any city or town out of said remainder shall be for general purposes;

(4) Ten percent of such remainder shall be covered into the treasury of the state to the credit of the state department of human resources to be used for general welfare purposes; and

(5) Sixty percent of such remainder for each fiscal year thereafter shall be paid to the state for general purposes.

Populations shall be ascertained for the purposes of distribution under this subsection according to the last decennial federal census preceding commencement of the fiscal year for which distribution is to be made.

(c) Distribution of net profits (including all taxes levied upon the selling price of spirituous or vinous liquors) under subsections (a) and (b) of this section shall be made from time to time during the fiscal year for which net profits (including all taxes levied upon the selling price of spirituous liquors) are to be ascertained according to reasonable estimates of profits (including all taxes levied upon the selling price of spirituous or vinous liquors) for such year and such amounts to be paid beneficiaries or recovered from beneficiaries at the end of the year as will net beneficiaries the correct amounts for the year prescribed for them by subsections (a) and (b) of this section. Payments to counties and municipalities will be made semiannually on or before February 1 and August 1 of each year.

(d) Repealed by Acts 1982, No. 82-436, § 3.

(e) The board shall, on receipt of proof that a county has changed its status from a dry county to a wet county, accept such county as a beneficiary for participation in the ABC system profits as provided by law at the beginning of the next fiscal quarter of the board's fiscal year. The board shall, on receipt of proof of the incorporation of a newly created municipality in a wet county and the population thereof, accept the municipality as a beneficiary for participation in the ABC system profits as provided by law at the beginning of the next fiscal quarter of the board's fiscal year.

(f) No wet county which receives funds under the provisions of this section shall receive less than it received in the fiscal year beginning October 1, 1977. (Acts 1943, No. 255, p. 226; Acts 1951, No. 526, p. 915; Acts 1978, 2nd Ex. Sess., No. 92, p. 1786, § 4; Acts 1981, 3rd Ex. Sess., No. 81-1137, p. 411, § 1; Acts 1982, No. 82-436, p. 686, § 3.)

ARTICLE 4.

LICENSES.

Division 1.

General Provisions.

Code commissioner's note. — Section 29, Acts 1980, No. 80-529, p. 806, which added chapter 3A, provides that any license granted prior to September 30, 1980, shall remain in effect until its expiration.

§§ 28-3-90 through 28-3-95. Repealed by Acts 1980, No. 80-529, p. 806, § 27, effective September 30, 1980.

Division 2.

Licensing of Manufacturers, Distillers, Producers, etc., Selling to State or Alcoholic Beverage Control Board.

Code commissioner's note. — Section 29, Acts 1980, No. 80-529, p. 806, which added chapter 3A, provides that any license granted prior to September 30, 1980, shall remain in effect until its expiration.

§§ 28-3-110 through 28-3-115. Repealed by Acts 1980, No. 80-529, p. 806, § 27, effective September 30, 1980.

Division 3.

Licensing of Hotels, Restaurants, Railroad Companies, etc.

Code commissioner's note. — Section 29, Acts 1980, No. 80-529, p. 806, which added chapter 3A, provides that any license granted prior to September 30, 1980, shall remain in effect until its expiration.

§§ 28-3-130 through 28-3-148. Repealed by Acts 1980, No. 80-529, p. 806, § 27, effective September 30, 1980.

Division 4.

Sale, etc., of Liquor, Wine and Malt or Brewed Beverages by Licensees Generally.

Code commissioner's note. — Section 29, Acts 1980, No. 80-529, p. 806, which added chapter 3A, provides that any license granted prior to September 30, 1980, shall remain in effect until its expiration.

§§ 28-3-160 through 28-3-167. Repealed by Acts 1980, No. 80-529, p. 806, § 27, effective September 30, 1980.

§ 28-3-168. Sale of table wine by wine retailers in certain counties.

(a) For the purposes of this section, the following words and phrases shall have the following meanings:

(1) MANUFACTURER. Any person, association or corporation engaged in the producing, bottling, manufacturing, distilling, rectifying or compounding of liquor, alcohol, malt and brewed beverages or vinous beverages.

(2) WINE WHOLESALER, DISTRIBUTOR or JOBBER. Any person, association or corporation licensed by the board to engage in the sale and distribution of table wine within counties in which this chapter applies, at wholesale only, to be sold for export or to licensees within this state authorized by their licenses to sell wine.

(3) WINE RETAILER. Persons, corporations or associations licensed by the board to engage in the retail sale of table wine to be consumed off the premises and who do not possess a state liquor license.

(4) TABLE WINE. Any wine containing not more than 14 percent alcohol by volume.

(b) In all counties having a population of not less than 300,000 nor more than 500,000 according to the 1970 or any subsequent federal decennial census, table wines may be sold at retail by any licensed wine retailer for off-premises consumption only. A wine wholesaler may sell to a wine retailer table wines that have been purchased from a licensed manufacturer.

(c) In all counties having a population of not less than 500,000 according to the 1970 or any subsequent federal decennial census, table wines may be sold at retail by any licensed wine retailer for off-premises consumption only. A wine wholesaler may sell to a wine retailer table wines that have been purchased from a licensed manufacturer.

(d) In all counties having a population of not less than 115,000 nor more than 130,000 according to the 1970 or any subsequent federal decennial census, table wines may be sold at retail by any licensed wine retailer for off-premises consumption only. A wine wholesaler may sell to a wine retailer table wines that have been purchased from a licensed manufacturer. (Acts 1936-37, Ex. Sess., No. 66, p. 40; Code 1940, T. 29, § 24; Acts 1951, No. 614, p. 1060, § 4; Acts 1973, No. 863, p. 1351, § 2; Acts 1973, No. 1053, p. 1688, § 2; Acts 1973, No. 1054, p. 1693, § 2.)

Cross references. — As to the importation, distribution and sale of table wine, see chapter 7, Title 28.

ARTICLE 5.

TAXES ON SALE OF MALT OR BREWED BEVERAGES.

Code commissioner's note. — Acts 1979, No. 79-802, p. 1475, § 6(a), which repeals this article effective October 1, 1980, provides that no person shall be relieved of any tax liability, penalty or forfeiture incurred prior to October 1, 1980.

§§ 28-3-180 through 28-3-182. Repealed by Acts 1979, No. 79-802, p. 1475, § 6(a), effective October 1, 1980.

ARTICLE 5A.

EXCISE TAXES ON MALT OR BREWED BEVERAGES.

Collateral references. — 84 C.J.S., Taxation, §§ 19, 121 to 125, 229, 253. 45 Am. Jur. 2d, Intoxicating Liquors, §§ 203 to 221. 71 Am. Jur. 2d, State and Local Taxation, §§ 28 to 30, 94, 335.

§ 28-3-183. Definitions.

The words and phrases used in this article shall have the meanings ascribed to them in section 28-3-1. (Acts 1979, No. 79-802, p. 1475, § 5.)

§ 28-3-184. Tax levied; collection; disposition of funds.

(a) *Levy.* — In addition to the licenses provided for by chapter 3A, Title 28, there is hereby levied a privilege or excise tax on every person licensed under the provisions of said chapter 3A who sells, stores or receives for the purpose of distribution, to any person, firm, corporation, club or association within the state of Alabama any malt or brewed beverages. The tax levied hereby shall be measured by and graduated in accordance with the volume of sales by such person of malt or brewed beverages, and shall be an amount equal to $.05 for each 12 fluid ounces or fractional part thereof.

(b) *Collection.* — The tax levied by subsection (a) of this section shall be collected by the Alabama alcoholic beverage control board and said tax shall be added to the sales price of all malt or brewed beverages sold, and shall be collected from the purchasers. It shall be unlawful for any person, firm, corporation, club or association who is required to pay the tax in the first instance to fail or refuse to add to the sales price and collect from the purchaser the required amount of tax, it being the intent and purpose of this provision that the tax levied is in fact a tax on the consumer, with the person, firm, corporation, club or association who pays the tax in the first instance acting merely as an agent of the state for the collection and payment of the tax.

Except as hereinafter provided, the tax levied by subsection (a) of this section shall be collected by a return which shall be filed by the wholesaler or distributor with the alcoholic beverage control board postmarked not later than the last day of the month following the month of receipt of the malt or brewed beverages by the wholesaler or distributor from the manufacturer, which return shall be accompanied by the remittance of the tax due. Provided, however, for malt or brewed beverages received during the month of October, 1979, the return and remittance of tax shall be filed with the board postmarked not later than November 10, 1979, and for malt or brewed beverages received during the month of November, 1979, the return and remittance of tax shall be filed with the board postmarked not later than December 20, 1979.

All malt or brewed beverages sold, received or stored in this state shall have affixed by the manufacturer to each original container, an Alabama crown, lid or identification as designed in accordance with the rules and regulations promulgated by the board, which crown, lid or identification shall constitute prima facie proof that the appropriate tax as provided for in this article is paid at the time of the sale of the beverages.

The board shall have the authority to examine the books and records of any person, firm, corporation, club or association who sells, stores or receives for the purpose of distribution, any malt or brewed beverages, to determine the accuracy of any return required to be filed with the board.

(c) *Disposition of proceeds.* — The proceeds of the tax levied by subsection (a) of this section shall be paid into the state treasury to be distributed as follows:

(1) One-half cent of said proceeds shall be paid into the state treasury to the credit of the wet counties in the state and shall be divided and distributed equally on or before the fifteenth day of each month to said counties;

(2) One cent of said proceeds shall be paid into the state treasury to the credit of the state public welfare trust fund and shall be used for general welfare purposes. As used in this section, the phrase "general welfare purposes" means:

a. The administration of public assistance as set out in sections 38-2-5 and 38-4-1;

b. Services, including supplementation and supplementary services under the federal Social Security Act, to or on behalf of persons to whom such public assistance may be given under sections 38-2-5 and 38-4-1;

c. Services to and on behalf of dependent, neglected or delinquent children; and

d. Investigative and referral services to and on behalf of needy persons.

(3) Two cents of said proceeds shall be paid into the state treasury to the credit of the Alabama special educational trust fund, and so much thereof as may be necessary for the purpose if hereby appropriated to pay the principal of and interest on bonds not exceeding $30,000,000.00 in aggregate principal amount, issued and sold by the public corporation known as the Alabama Trade School and Junior College Authority.

(4) The residue of one and one-half cents shall be paid into the state treasury credited to the general fund of the state. (Acts 1979, No. 79-802, p. 1475, § 1.)

U.S. Code. — For the Social Security Act, see 42 U.S.C. § 401 et seq.

§ 28-3-185. Transactions between wholesalers exempt; reports.

The tax levied by subsection (a) of section 28-3-184 shall not be imposed upon the sale, trade or barter of malt or brewed beverages by one licensed wholesaler or distributor to another wholesaler or distributor licensed to sell and handle malt or brewed beverages in this state, which transaction is hereby made exempt from said tax; provided, however, that the board may require written reporting of any such transaction in such form as the board may prescribe. (Acts 1979, No. 79-802, p. 1475, § 2.)

§ 28-3-186. Penalties for failure to pay taxes collected; possession of unidentified malt or brewed beverages; execution issued for unpaid taxes, etc.

(a) Every wholesaler licensee collecting taxes on malt or brewed beverages levied by this article shall timely pay the same to the board as provided in this article.

(b)(1) If any taxes levied by this article remain due and unpaid for a period of 10 days beyond the due date, the wholesaler licensee serving as collection agent for the board shall be required to pay as part of the taxes so levied a penalty of not less than $50.00 nor more than $500.00 to be assessed and collected by the board.

(2) Any person found with possession of malt or brewed beverages without the required Alabama identification as set forth in this article shall pay to the board the tax levied on such malt or brewed beverages by this article and shall be further required to pay as a part of the taxes so levied a penalty of not less than $50.00 nor more than $500.00 to be assessed and collected by the board.

(c) Any wholesaler who fails timely to pay any tax levied by this article or any wholesaler or retailer who, upon discovery of absence of required Alabama identification on malt or brewed beverages in his possession, fails immediately to notify the board shall be subject to disciplinary action by the hearing commission and, upon being adjudged guilty, shall be subject to revocation or suspension of license.

(d) If any taxes or penalties imposed by this article remain due and unpaid for a period of 10 days, the board shall issue a warrant or execution directed to any sheriff of the state of Alabama, commanding him to levy upon and sell the real and personal property of the taxpayer found within his county for the payment of the amount thereof, with penalties, if any, and the cost of executing the warrant, and to return such warrant to the board and to pay it the money collected by virtue thereof. Upon receipt of such execution, the sheriff shall file with the clerk of the circuit court of his county a copy thereof and thereupon the clerk of the circuit court shall enter in his abstract of judgments the name of the taxpayer mentioned in the warrant and in proper columns the amount of tax, with penalties, and costs for which the warrant is issued and the date and hour when such copy is filed, and shall index the warrant upon the index of judgments. The sheriff shall thereupon proceed upon the warrant in all respects with like effect and in the same manner prescribed by law in respect to executions issued against the property upon judgments of a court of record and shall be entitled to the same fees for services in executing the warrant to be collected in the same manner. He shall make return of such execution to the board within 30 days of issuance thereof. The taxes and penalties imposed by this article shall be deemed a debt owing to the state by the party against whom the same shall be charged and shall be a preferred lien upon all property of the party against whom the same shall be charged. (Acts 1979, No. 79-802, p. 1475, § 3.)

§ 28-3-187. Identification on containers; procedures; penalties.

(a) For the protection of the public welfare, health, peace and morals of the people of this state, including without limitation regulation of the quality of malt or brewed beverages sold, offered for sale or held for sale within this state, and for the protection of the tax revenues accruing to the state by virtue of taxes levied on malt or brewed beverages, it is hereby declared the intention and purpose of this article that the board shall require all manufacturer licensees, or in lieu thereof, all importer licensees to affix Alabama identification, as will be prescribed by the board, to all original containers in which malt or brewed beverages is normally placed and prepared for market, received, sold or handled, before such beverages are sold, offered for sale or held for sale within this state. Provided, however, a wholesaler licensee may, subject to the rules and regulations promulgated by the board, prepay the tax and affix Alabama identification to certain malt or brewed beverages which come into the state without such identification being affixed by the manufacturer or importer licensee, where the wholesaler licensee was by court order permitted to do so prior to October 1, 1980; but this special permission shall apply only with respect to a brand or brands of malt or brewed beverages sold or distributed by the wholesaler licensee within this state during the period of six months first succeeding said court order.

(b)(1) The board is hereby authorized to design and have prepared and distributed Alabama identification to be affixed by the manufacturer or importer licensee to all malt or brewed beverages sold, offered for sale or held for sale in the state of Alabama.

(2) The board is authorized to enter into a contract on behalf of the state with one or more manufacturers for the manufacture, sale and distribution of such identification and shall require of each such manufacturer a bond or bonds in an amount and with sureties satisfactory to the board.

(3) Such identification prescribed by the board shall be purchased from the board or from such person designated by the board by the licensed manufacturer or importer of malt or brewed beverages to be sold within this state.

(4) Any person other than the board or its designated and bonded identification manufacturer or agent who sells such Alabama identification not affixed to malt or brewed beverages sold and delivered by them, whether genuine or counterfeit, shall be guilty of a felony and shall be punished as such as provided in section 28-3-227.

(5) Any person who manufactures, sells, offers for sale, buys or has in his or its possession any reproduction or counterfeit of Alabama malt or brewed beverage identification provided for in this article shall be guilty of a felony and shall be punishable as such as provided in section 28-3-228.

(6) Any person who removes or otherwise prepares Alabama malt or brewed beverage identification, with intent to use or caused to be used after such identification has already been used, or buys, sells, offers for sale, gives away or has in his or its possession any such previously used Alabama identification for the purpose of identifying malt or brewed beverages shall be guilty of a felony and shall be punishable as such as provided in section 28-3-227.

(c)(1) All malt or brewed beverages when possessed in this state by a person other than its manufacturer or importer licensee, without having required identification affixed in the manner required by the board, shall be subject to confiscation in the manner provided for contraband goods as set out in article 8 of this chapter.

(2) A licensed wholesaler may possess malt or brewed beverages in this state without Alabama identification affixed by the manufacturer or importer licensee which malt or brewed beverages (a) due to error of the manufacturer or importer was misdirected or missent to Alabama or (b) due to temporary inability of manufacturer or importer to affix identification because of equipment problems or malfunction, lack of supply of approved identification or other problem made known to the board in advance of shipment into this state; provided, the licensed wholesaler receiving malt or brewed beverages without Alabama identification affixed by the manufacturer or importer shall inform the board immediately upon the wholesaler's discovery of the absence of Alabama identification affixed by the manufacturer or importer and the board or its designated agent shall sell to such licensed wholesaler a sufficient quantity of identification to affix to the malt or brewed beverages transported into the state under such circumstances. (Acts 1979, No. 79-802, p. 1475, § 4.)

Cited in Flack v. State, 440 So. 2d 1177 (Ala. Crim. App. 1983).

Collateral references. — Criminal liability of member or agent of private club or association, or of owner or lessor of its premises, for violation of state or local liquor or gambling laws thereon. 98 ALR3d 694.

ARTICLE 5B.

EXCISE TAX ON BEER.

§ 28-3-190. Levy of tax; collection; disposition of proceeds by localities; enforcement and administration; penalties; exclusive nature of tax.

(a) *Levy.* — In addition to the excise tax levied by article 5A of chapter 3 of this title and the licenses provided for by chapter 3A of this title and by section 28-3-194, and any acts amendatory thereof, supplementary thereto or substituted therefor, and municipal and county licenses, there is hereby levied a privilege or excise tax on every person licensed under the provisions of said chapter 3A who sells, stores, or receives for the purpose of distribution, to any person, firm, corporation, club or association within the state of Alabama any beer. The tax levied hereby shall be measured by and graduated in accordance with the volume of sales by such person of beer, and shall be an amount equal to one and six hundred twenty-five thousands cents (1.625¢) for each four fluid ounces or fractional part thereof.

(b) *Collection.* — The tax levied by subsection (a) of this section shall be added to the sales price of all beer sold, and shall be collected from the purchasers. It shall be unlawful for any person who is required to pay the tax in the first instance to fail or refuse to add to the sales price and collect from the purchaser the required amount of tax, it being the intent and purpose of this provision that the tax levied is in fact a tax on the consumer, with the person, firm, corporation, club or association who pays the tax in the first instance acting merely as an agent of the county or municipality for the collection and payment of the tax.

The tax levied by subsection (a) of this section shall be collected by a return in the form as prescribed or approved by the collecting authority of the county or municipality, which shall be filed by the wholesaler with the wet county and wet municipality where sold postmarked not later than the 15th day of the month following the month during which the beer is sold, which return shall be accompanied by the remittance of the tax due; provided, where the taxes are timely paid, the tax due shall be discounted by two and one-half percent, which discount shall, subject to the provisions of section 28-3-195, be retained by said wholesaler for collecting the tax.

The county and municipality each shall have the authority to inspect, examine and audit the books and records of any person, firm, corporation, club or association who sells, stores, or receives for the purpose of distribution, any beer, to determine the accuracy of any return required to be filed with it.

The county shall have the authority to require any beer wholesaler not having a place of business within that county, who makes any sale, distribution or delivery of beer within the county to first obtain a permit from the beer tax collection authority of the county collecting the tax levied by this article.

665

The county and municipality shall have the authority to require any wholesale beer licensee, who sells, distributes or delivers beer within the county, to file with the tax collection authority a bond in the penal sum not to exceed twice the amount of the average monthly tax due by the licensee to such authority estimated by such tax collection authority, conditioned upon the payment of the tax on beer levied by this article to become due by the licensee.

(c) *Disposition of proceeds.* — The proceeds of the tax levied by subsection (a) of this section shall be paid and distributed as follows:

(1) Except as hereinafter provided in subdivision (2) or (3) of this subsection (c), one and six hundred twenty-five thousandths cents (1.625¢) per four fluid ounces or fractional part thereof shall be paid by wholesale licensees on their sales either into the treasury of the wet municipality in which the beer was sold or delivered by a wholesaler to a retailer within its corporate limits, or, where sold outside the corporate limits of any municipality, into the treasury of the wet county in which the beer was sold or delivered by the wholesaler to a retailer.

(2) Provided, however, such tax shall otherwise be paid and disposed of in the following counties, as hereinafter set forth:

a. Autauga county: The entire amount of the tax collected on sales outside of the area comprised by the corporate limits and police jurisdictions of the cities of Prattville and Autaugaville shall be paid to the Autauga county commission. Outside the corporate limits but within the police jurisdictions of said municipalities, two-thirds of the amount of the tax shall be paid to the county commission and one-third shall be paid to the respective municipality. Within the actual corporate limits of Autaugaville and Prattville, two-thirds of the tax shall be paid to the governing body of the respective municipality and one-third shall be paid to the county commission.

b. Baldwin county: The taxes shall be paid as follows:

1. All the taxes collected on sales within the corporate limits of any municipality shall be paid to said municipality.

2. One-half the taxes collected on sales within the police jurisdiction of any municipality shall be paid to said municipality and the remaining one-half shall be paid to the county.

3. All of the taxes on sales outside the corporate limits of any municipality and outside of any police jurisdiction shall be paid to the county board of education with the funds to be used for capital outlay, maintenance of existing buildings and instructional materials.

c. Calhoun county: The entire amount of the tax shall be collected by the Calhoun county probate judge and paid to the Calhoun county commission. All such taxes, after first reimbursing the county general fund for expenses incurred in administration and enforcement of the tax, shall be distributed as follows:

1. Sixth-ninths of the total amount of the tax shall be turned over by it to the custodian of county school funds. The county board of education

666

shall immediately divide the funds with the city boards of education within the county pro rata in the same manner as the public school funds from the state are apportioned in said county under the minimum program fund law.

2. One-ninth of the total amount of the tax or $150,000.00, which-ever is greater, shall be paid to the Calhoun county economic development council.

3. The balance of the total amount of the tax shall be distributed to certain municipalities as follows:

Anniston	28½%
Oxford	21½%
Jacksonsville	28%
Piedmont	17%
Hobson City	2%
Ohatchee	2%
Weaver	1%

4. All reference in the general bill to county or municipalities shall apply to the probate judge or his designated agent in Calhoun county.

d. Chambers county: The entire amount of the tax shall be paid to the Chambers county commission or like governing body of Chambers county, which, after the payment of all cost of collection and enforcement, shall distribute the net proceeds as follows:

1. Fifty percent be prorated among the city and county boards of education for educational purposes on the basis of the previous year's net enrollment of pupils;

2. Fifty percent be prorated among the Chambers county commission general fund and the municipalities within the county, with each municipality receiving the amount that its population bears to the entire population of the county, and the general fund of the county receiving the amount that the population of the county outside the corporate limits of the municipalities bears to the entire population of the county according to the latest federal census. In the event of the incorporation of any new municipalities, the proration shall be based on the official population of the municipality at the time of incorporation. Any annexation shall accrue to the city annexing according to the population annexed.

3. Fifteen percent of the amount prorated to the county general fund in subparagraph 2 of this paragraph shall be prorated among the fire and rescue squads located within the county.

e. Choctaw county: The entire amount of tax shall be paid to the probate judge and, after reimbursement of two and one-half percent for services distributed as follows:

1. One-ninth to the county general fund from which $7,000.00 shall be credited to:

(i) One-third to the Choctaw county rescue cquad.

(ii) One-third to the Choctaw county historical society.

(iii) One-third to the Choctaw county library system.

2. Of remainder, $20,000.00 to Choctaw county board of education.

3. Remainder up to $90,000.00 to the county and municipalities on the basis of population.

4. Of revenue in excess of $90,000.00, 20 percent to the county board of education and remainder to the county and municipalities on the basis of population.

f. Colbert county: One cent per twelve fluid ounces or fractional part thereof on all beer sold, within the county shall be paid to the probate judge and the proceeds shall be distributed by him as follows:

Two-fifths to the hospital fund of the county;

One-fifth to the county board of education for the benefit of the schools outside of the cities of Sheffield and Tuscumbia;

One-tenth to the Tuscumbia board of education for the benefit of the schools of the city of Tuscumbia;

One-tenth to the Sheffield board of education for the benefit of the schools of Sheffield; and

One-fifth to the general fund of the county.

For such services, the probate judge shall be entitled to commissions of two and one-half percent of all taxes collected.

The remainder of the tax shall be paid to the municipalities where sold.

g. Conecuh county: The entire amount of the tax shall be paid to the treasurer of Conecuh county, who, after first reimbursing the county general fund for all expenses incurred in the administration and enforcement of the tax, shall distribute the remainder of the proceeds of said tax as follows: one-third to be prorated between the municipalities of Evergreen, Repton and Castleberry upon the basis of their respective populations; one-third to be paid over to the general fund of the county; and one-third to be paid to the Conecuh county board of education to be expended for educational purposes.

h. Coosa county: The tax proceeds shall be paid by wholesalers as follows:

1. One cent per container sold within the corporate limits of the municipalities within the county shall be paid directly to the municipalities where sold.

2. The remainder of the tax shall be paid to the Coosa county commission and shall be distributed as follows:

(i) Fifty percent shall be deposited in the public school fund of the county to be used solely for public school purposes of Coosa county.

(ii) Fifty percent shall be deposited in the general fund of the county for general purposes of the county.

i. Dale county: The entire amount of the tax shall be paid to the county commission or like governing body and shall be distributed as follows:

County	44.17%
Ariton	0.53%
Clayhatchee	0.30%

County	44.17%
Daleville	7.59%
Grimes	0.30%
Level Plains	15.62%
Midland City	3.08%
Napier Field	0.28%
Newton	3.48%
Ozark	24.16%
Pinckard	0.49%

j. Dallas county: The entire amount of the tax collected on sales outside of the area comprised by the corporate limits and police jurisdiction of the city of Selma shall be paid to the Dallas county commission.

The tax collected on sales inside the corporate limits of the city of Selma and its police jurisdiction shall be paid as follows: 72.23 percent to be paid to the city and its board of education, with one-third of such 72.23 percent to be paid to the city and two-thirds of such 72.23 percent to be paid to the city board of education (the board of education of the city of Selma); and 27.77 percent to be paid to the Dallas county commission.

k. Elmore county: The entire amount of tax shall be paid to the Elmore county commission or other governing body of Elmore county and the net revenue, after first reimbursing the county general fund for all expenses incurred in the administration and enforcement of the tax, shall be distributed as follows: One-half of the net revenue from the tax shall be paid to Elmore county board of education; one-half the tax collected on sales inside the corporate limits of any municipality within the county and one-fourth of the taxes collected on sales made within the police jurisdiction of any municipality in the county shall be paid to such municipality; and the balance shall be paid into the Elmore county general fund.

l. Escambia county: The entire amount of tax shall be paid to the judge of probate of Escambia county and the net revenue, after first reimbursing the county general fund for all expenses incurred in the administration and enforcement of the tax, shall be distributed, as follows: Two and one-half percent to the judge of probate; 60 percent of the remainder to be prorated among the municipalities within the county upon the basis of their respective populations; and 40 percent of the remainder to be prorated among the city and county boards of education for educational purposes on the basis of the previous year's net enrollment of pupils.

m. Etowah county: The entire amount of tax shall be paid to the Etowah county commission and the net revenue, after first reimbursing the county general fund for all expenses incurred in the administration and enforcement of the tax, shall be distributed, as follows:

1. For beer delivered for retail sale within the corporate limits of a municipality having a board of education, all such proceeds shall be distributed according to the following percentages: 20.83$\frac{1}{3}$ percent to the Etowah county general fund; 20.38$\frac{1}{3}$ percent to the city and county boards of education of Etowah county, to be divided pro rata among

669

them in accordance with the most recent average daily attendance figures, to be used only for capital outlay purposes, renovation and repairs; 58.33⅓ percent to the general fund of the municipality.

2. For beer delivered for retail sale outside the city or town limits, but within the police jurisdiction, of a municipality having a board of education, all such proceeds shall be distributed according to the following percentages: 12.50 percent to the Etowah county board of education, to be used for capital outlay purposes, renovation and repairs; 20.83⅓ percent to the city and county boards of education in Etowah county to be divided pro rata among them in accordance with the most recent average daily attendance figures, to be used for capital outlay purposes, renovation, and repairs; 29.16⅔ percent to the general fund of the municipality; 37.50 percent to the Etowah county general fund.

3. For beer delivered for retail sale within the city or town limits of a municipality not having a board of education, all such proceeds shall be distributed according to the following percentages: 20.83⅓ percent to the Etowah county general fund; 20.83⅓ percent to the city and county boards of education in Etowah county, to be divided pro rata among them in accordance with the most recent average daily attendance figures, to be used for capital outlay purposes, renovation and repairs; 33.33⅓ percent to the general fund of the municipality; 25.00 percent to the Etowah county board of education to be used for capital outlay purposes, renovation and repairs;

4. For beer delivered for retail sale outside the city or town limits, but within the police jurisdiction of a municipality not having a board of education, all such proceeds shall be distributed according to the following percentages: 16.66⅔ percent to the general fund of the municipality; 20.83⅓ percent to the city and county boards of education within Etowah county to be divided pro rata among them in accordance with the most recent average daily attendance figures, to be used for capital outlay purposes, renovation and repairs; 25.00 percent to the Etowah county board of education, to be used for capital outlay purposes, renovation and repairs, 37.50 percent to the Etowah county general fund.

5. For beer delivered for retail sale in locations which are within the boundaries of Etowah county, Alabama, but not within the corporate limits or police jurisdiction of any municipality, all such proceeds shall be distributed according to the following percentages: 20.83⅓ percent to the city and county boards of education in Etowah county divided in accordance with the most recent average daily attendance figures to be used for capital outlay purposes, renovation or repairs; 25.00 percent to the Etowah county board of education, to be used for capital outlay purposes, renovation or repairs; 54.16⅔ percent to the Etowah county general fund.

6. For draft beer sold and delivered within all areas in Etowah county, all proceeds shall be distributed according to the following percentage: 83.33⅓ percent to the city and county boards of education in Etowah county to be divided pro rata among them in accordance with the most recent average daily attendance figure to be used for capital outlay purposes, renovation and repairs; 16.66⅔ percent to the municipalities in Etowah county within which draft beer is sold at retail, to be divided among them pro rata according to the population.

n. Greene county: The entire amount of the tax shall be paid to the judge of probate of Greene county and distributed by him as follows: two and one-half percent to the probate judge as commission for collection and administration; two-fifths of the remainder to the general fund of the county; two-fifths of the remainder to the county board of education; and one-fifth prorated among the municipalities within the county upon the basis of their respective populations.

o. Hale county: The entire amount of tax shall be paid to the Hale county commission or like governing body of Hale county and the net revenue, after first reimbursing the county general fund for all expenses incurred in the administration and enforcement of the tax, shall be prorated among the county and municipalities therein upon the basis of their respective populations.

p. Jefferson county: The tax as provided in subsection (a) of this section shall be paid by wholesalers to the director of revenue of Jefferson county. The tax received by the director of revenue shall be divided into Funds A, B and C. Fund A shall receive four-ninths of the tax received; Fund B shall receive two-ninths of the tax received; and Fund C shall receive three-ninths of the tax received. Funds A, B and C shall be distributed by the director of revenue on a monthly basis as follows:

1. Two percent of the net tax collected and placed in Fund A shall be paid to the general treasury of the county for the collection and distribution of said tax, and for the enforcement of the provisions of this article. The remaining amount in Fund A shall be distributed as follows:

(i) Two-eighths shall be paid to the county board of education for the payment of salaries of public school teachers.

(ii) Three-eighths shall be retained in the general treasury of the county.

(iii) Three-eighths shall be distributed to the incorporated municipalities within the county upon the basis of their respective populations, according to the federal census at the time the distribution is made.

2. Fund B shall be distributed to the municipalities in the county on the basis of the percentage of the beer taxed which was delivered to a retailer within the respective corporate limits of each municipality in the county.

3. Fund C shall be distributed as follows:

(i) Fifty percent, or $2,000,000.00 annually, whichever is the greater, shall be paid to the Birmingham-Jefferson county transit authority or its successor.

(ii) The balance shall be divided between the county and the incorporated municipalities within the county upon a population basis with the municipal share determined by the respective populations of said municipalities, and the county share by the population of the unincorporated areas thereof, according to the last federal census at the time the distribution is made.

Of the total amount of the county share, five percent shall be allocated for fire protection and paramedic services and equipment in fire districts in the unincorporated areas of the county. Such distribution shall be made to each such fire district on a pro rata basis that the number of homes and businesses served in that district bears to the total number of homes and businesses served in all such fire districts in the unincorporated areas.

q. Lee county: The entire amount of tax shall be paid to the Lee county commission or like governing body of Lee county and shall be distributed to the custodian of the county school fund, the custodian of the Opelika city school fund and the custodian of the Auburn city school fund in the same manner and at the same rate that the state minimum school program funds are distributed. Provided however that any subsidy received shall be paid to the city of Auburn.

r. Lowndes county: The tax proceeds shall be paid by wholesalers as follows:

1. One cent shall be distributed to municipalities in the following manner:

(i) One-third to municipalities that have an existing beer tax distributed on a population basis.

(ii) Two-thirds to go to all municipalities including those that have an existing beer tax distributed on a population basis.

2. One cent to be distributed as follows:

(i) One-twelfth to the county board of education and three-twelfths to the probate judge for services rendered.

(ii) Two-thirds to the county commission for the performance of services.

3. The remainder to be equally divided between the public school fund and the juvenile service trust fund account.

s. Macon county: The entire amount of tax shall be paid to the Macon county commission or like governing body of Macon county and the net revenue, after first reimbursing the county general fund for all expenses incurred in the administration and enforcement of the tax, shall be distributed by it as follows: Six-twelfths of the net proceeds shall be paid into the general fund of said county to be used for governmental purposes of the county as other moneys in the general fund; four-twelfths shall be apportioned and distributed to the city of Tuskegee and shall be deposited into its general fund to be used for governmental purposes of the city as other moneys in the general fund of said city are used; one-twelfth shall be apportioned and distributed to the town of Notasulga and deposited into the general fund of said town to be used for governmental purposes of the town as are other moneys in the general fund of said town; one-twelfth shall be apportioned and distributed to the town of Franklin and deposited into the general fund of said town to be used for governmental purposes of the town as are other moneys in the general fund of said town.

t. Madison county: The proceeds of the tax shall be paid by wholesalers to the county commission or like governing body and shall be distributed as follows:

1. One-eighteenth to the county general fund.

2. The remainder of the tax shall be distributed to the municipality where sold, including its police jurisdiction. Provided, however, that the following municipalities shall receive a dollar amount no less than the dollar amount actually received during the base year 1982:

Gurley

New Hope

Owens Crossroads

Triana

Madison

u. Marengo county: The entire amount of the tax shall be paid to the probate judge of Marengo county, who shall receive two and one-half percent of all taxes collected as compensation for administering this article and the remainder of the net revenue, after first reimbursing the county general fund for all expenses incurred in the administration and enforcement of the tax, shall be distributed by him as follows: The municipalities shall receive the taxes paid on all sales within the corporate limits and police jurisdiction of each municipality, and the county shall receive the tax on all sales made outside the corporate limits and police jurisdictions of all municipalities within the county.

v. Mobile county: The entire amount of tax shall be paid to the license commissioner of Mobile county and the net revenue, after first reimbursing the county general fund for all expenses incurred in the administration and enforcement of the tax, shall be distributed by him as follows: One-half to the governing body of the municipality where the malt or brewed beverages are sold within its corporate limits; and the remainder to the board of school commissioners of Mobile county.

w. Perry county: The tax shall be paid to the county governing body and be distributed as follows:

1. Except as hereinafter provided in subparagraph 2 of this paragraph, the proceeds shall be distributed as follows:

(i) The taxes collected on sales within the corporate limits of the municipality of Marion shall be paid to said municipality.

(ii) The taxes collected on sales within the corporate limits of the municipality of Uniontown shall be paid to said municipality.

(iii) The taxes collected on sales outside the police jurisdiction of a municipality and outside the corporate limits of any municipality shall be retained by the county.

(iv) The taxes collected on sales outside of a municipality's corporate limits but within said municipality's police jurisdiction shall be distributed in the following manner:

Three-fourths of the tax proceeds shall be retained by the county.

One-fourth of the tax proceeds shall be paid to the municipality controlling said police jurisdiction.

2. Until the conditions set forth in this subparagraph 2 have been satisfied, one-ninth shall be deducted from each of the foregoing distributions and retained by Perry county and earmarked for the purpose of purchasing mechanical voting machines with lever action and curtain and creating an election expense fund in the amount of $20,000.00. Said voting machines shall be purchased by May 1, 1982, and said election expense fund shall be used to pay board of registrars members' compensation and for election supplies and materials, election handling, storage and other expense. When the cost of the voting machines and election expense fund have been collected by the county, the right to deduct pursuant to this subparagraph 2 shall expire and the entire proceeds shall be distributed pursuant to and in accordance with subparagraph 1 hereof.

x. Russell county: The taxes shall be paid and distributed as follows:

1. Payment of taxes collected by wholesalers.

(i) All the taxes collected on sales within the corporate limits of the municipality of Phenix City shall be paid to said municipality.

(ii) All the taxes collected on sales within the corporate limits of the municipality of Hurtsboro shall be paid to said municipality.

(iii) One-half the taxes collected on sales within the police jurisdiction of Phenix City and Hurtsboro shall be paid to the respective municipality and the remaining one-half shall be paid to the county.

(iv) All of the taxes on sales outside the corporate limits of any municipality and outside of any police jurisdiction shall be paid to the county.

2. Distribution of county proceeds. All such taxes, after first reimbursing the county general fund for all expenses incurred in administration and enforcement of the tax, shall be used equally for the county school system and the county general fund. Of the moneys going to the county general fund, half of said amount shall be distributed to the volunteer fire departments in Russell county on a per department basis, who are recognized as legal fire districts.

y. St. Clair county: The entire amount of tax shall be paid to the St. Clair county commission or like governing body of St. Clair county and the net revenue, after reimbursing the county general fund for all expenses incurred in the administration and enforcement of the tax, shall be distributed by it as follows: One-third cent per four fluid ounces or fraction thereof to the governing body of each municipality where beer is sold within its corporate limits and one-sixth cent per four fluid ounces or fraction thereof to the governing body of each municipality where beer is sold within its police jurisdiction; the remainder to be distributed as follows: 25 percent to be paid to the road and building fund of the general fund of St. Clair county, which money shall be used for the operation of the St. Clair county road department, in the building and maintenance of all public roads and bridges in the county; 20.83$\frac{1}{3}$ percent of the remainder to the St. Clair county board of education; 8.33$\frac{1}{3}$ percent of the remainder to the St. Clair county library board to be used by the board for the use of libraries and/or book mobiles throughout the county; and 45.83$\frac{1}{3}$ percent to the general fund of St. Clair county to be disbursed by the St. Clair county governing body as other funds of the county are disbursed.

z. Shelby county: The entire amount of tax shall be paid to the Shelby county commission or like governing body of Shelby county to the credit of its county general fund and the net revenue, after first reimbursing the county general fund for all expenses incurred in the administration and enforcement of the tax, shall be disbursed as follows: Two-ninths of the net proceeds of such tax shall be paid to the Shelby county board of education; three-ninths of the net proceeds of such tax shall, on or before the 25th day of each month, be paid to the municipalities of Shelby county in the same ratio as the population of each municipality bears to the total population of all municipalities in Shelby county; two-ninths shall be paid into the Shelby county law enforcement personnel board fund to be used for the purposes set forth in Act No. 79-524, Acts of Alabama 1979; and the remaining two-ninths of the net proceeds shall remain in the Shelby county general fund to be disbursed by the county governing body.

aa. Sumter county: The entire proceeds of the tax shall be paid to the county treasurer. After the payment of all cost of collection and enforcement of the tax, the treasurer shall pay into the general fund of each incorporated municipality four-ninths of the revenue produced within the corporate limits of said municipality and the remainder shall be paid into the general fund of the county, from which $7,000.00 shall be credited to a legislative delegation fund to be controlled by the legislative delegation of Sumter county.

bb. Talladega county: The tax shall be paid to the probate judge and, after deduction of all expenses of collecting and administering the tax, the proceeds of the tax shall be distributed as follows: After determining net revenue received in the base year (county plus all municipalities), distribution of future revenue to each entity presently receiving beer tax distributions shall be in the same proportion as each entity's revenue to the total net revenue was during the base year.

The following entities shall be entitled to a share of beer tax revenue:

Talladega County   Community of Munford

Talladega County Board	Community of Eastaboga
of Education	North Talladega County Association
City of Talladega	for Retarded Citizens, Inc.
City of Sylacauga	South Talladega County Association
City of Childersburg	for Retarded Citizens, Inc.
City of Lincoln	

Provided, however, that from the county share, the sum of $6,500.00 shall be spent as follows:

1. The sum of $1,500.00 per annum shall be spent in the unincorporated community of Eastaboga for public projects for the benefit of said community;

2. The sum of $2,500.00 per annum shall be spent in the unincorporated community of Munford to provide rural health care in the existing rural health clinic in said community; and

3. The sum of $2,500.00 per annum shall be spent in the unincorporated community of Munford for youth activities, including the construction, improvement, lighting and maintenance of athletic playing fields.

The North and South Talladega County Associations for Retarded Citizens, Inc. shall receive from the county the same proportion of revenue received during the base year (1982).

Provided further, that the Talladega county board of education shall divide its share of the beer tax revenue between itself and the city boards of education now existing within the county pro rata in the same manner as public school funds from the state are apportioned in said county under the minimum program fund law.

cc. Tallapoosa county: The tax, after converting all sales to cases equivalent to 24 12-ounce containers and after deducting the two and one-half percent discount authorized by this article, shall be paid by wholesalers as follows:

1. Two cents per equivalent 12-ounce container sold or delivered to retail licensees within the county shall be paid to the custodian of public school funds of Tallapoosa county and shall be used and expended for public school purposes. Such funds shall be apportioned among the county and city school systems on the basis of the current ratio distribution formula used in apportionment of minimum program funds within the county.

2. The remainder of the tax shall be paid to the county commission or like governing body and distributed as follows:

56.4 percent to Alexander City

43.6 percent to the county for distribution, based on sales, either into the treasury of the municipalities (except Alexander City) in which the beer was sold or delivered by a wholesaler to a retailer within its corporate limits, or, where sold outside the corporate limits of any municipality into the treasury of the county.

3. Any subsidy received under the provisions of this article shall be distributed as provided for in subparagraph 2 above.

dd. Tuscaloosa county:

1. Forty-five percent of the tax shall be paid to the probate judge of Tuscaloosa county and shall by him be distributed in the same manner as provided in Act 556 of the 1953 Regular Session of the Alabama Legislature; and 55 percent shall be paid to the probate judge of Tuscaloosa county and shall by him be distributed in accordance with Act 81-739 of the 1981 Regular Session of the Alabama Legislature.

2. Any subsidy received by Tuscaloosa county pursuant to section 28-3-196 shall be paid and distributed among the county, municipalities and the Tuscaloosa county parks and recreation authority in accordance with the ratio of any net revenue loss of each such entity to the total subsidy paid to the county.

ee. Wilcox county: The entire tax revenue shall be paid to the Wilcox county commission or like governing body of Wilcox county and disbursed as follows: Two and one-half percent of the gross tax receipts to be paid as to the probate judge of Wilcox county as a fee for the administration and enforcement; the remainder shall be disbursed as follows: 50 percent to be prorated between the incorporated municipalities in Wilcox county upon the basis of their respective populations; and 50 percent to be paid over to the general fund of the county. Provided, however, prior to the distribution provided for in this subsection, the sum of $400.00 per month shall be paid to the Wilcox county civil defense agency.

(3) Or, such tax shall otherwise be paid and disposed of in accordance with and pursuant to any local act or general act of local application hereafter enacted with respect to any county directing a different disposition or apportionment of the proceeds of the tax.

(d)(1) For all purposes of enforcement of the provisions of this article, it is a prima facie presumption of law that any wholesaler or jobber subject to the article has accrued a liability for the taxes levied herein for the total amount of alcoholic beverages handled by it during any tax period under the article. The burden of proof is upon any such person to prove that any such alcoholic beverages disposed of in such a manner as not to become subject to the taxes imposed in this article were so disposed of in such a manner. It shall be the duty of any person subject to the privilege or license tax imposed by this article to keep full and complete records of all purchases, sales, receipts, inventories and of all other matters from which the correct amount of privilege or license tax to which such person is subject may be ascertained; and, in the event that such person shall discontinue his business, he shall not destroy or dispose of such records until he shall have given the probate judge of the county 30 days notice in writing of his intent to destroy or dispose of such records. The failure of such person to keep such records, or his destruction or disposition of such records without giving such notice, shall constitute a misdemeanor.

(2) Upon demand by the probate judge or his authorized deputy, auditor, or representative, it shall be the duty of any such person subject to the privilege or license tax imposed by this article to furnish such demanding person, without delay, all such information as may be required for determination of the correct amount of privilege or license tax to which such person is subject, and to that end it shall be the duty of such person to submit to such demanding person, for inspection and examination, during reasonable hours, at such person's place of business within the county, all books of accounts, invoices, papers, reports, memoranda containing entries showing the amount of purchases, sales, receipts, inventories, and any other information from which the correct amount of privilege or license tax to which such person is subject may be determined including exhibition of bank deposit books and bank statements; and any person failing or refusing to submit such records for such inspection and examination upon such demand, shall be guilty of a misdemeanor.

(3) If any person subject to the provisions of this article does not have in such person's control or possession, within the county, true and intelligible books of account, invoices, papers, reports or memoranda correctly showing the data and information necessary for determination of the correct amount of the privilege or license tax due, or if, having in such person's possession or under such person's control such books, invoices, papers, reports or memoranda, such person shall fail or refuse to submit and exhibit the same for inspection and examination as herein required, then, in either event, it shall be the duty of the probate judge of the county to ascertain, from such information and data as he may reasonably obtain, the correct amount of license tax due from such person and immediate payment of the amount of such privilege or license tax shall be made.

(4) All records and reports filed in the probate office under this article shall be public records and shall be open to inspection by any person during all probate office hours.

(5) The probate judge of the county shall provide rules and regulations and administrative machinery for the enforcement and collection of the privilege or license taxes authorized by this article. Each municipality within the county shall provide aid and assistance in collecting the taxes herein provided for within its territory. The probate judge may employ a person or persons to act as inspectors and otherwise to assist in the enforcement of the provisions of this article. The salary and expenses of such inspectors shall be paid out of the county general fund in such manner as is provided by law. Such inspectors shall have the same powers relative to enforcement of the taxes hereby levied that law enforcement officers employed by the Alabama alcoholic beverage control board have relative to enforcing the state tax on spirituous liquors and on malt and brewed beverages. Any municipality in the county may also employ a special alcoholic beverage law enforcement officer for such municipality whose chief duty shall be enforcement of this article.

(6) In addition to all other records and reports required under this article, each wholesale distributor shall, by the twentieth day of each month, file a report with the probate judge showing his inventory of beer on the first day of the preceding month, by brand and type of container, his inventory of beer on the last day of the preceding month, an accounting for all beer broken or damaged during the preceding month, proof of state authorization for transfers to other wholesale distributors, and a record of all beer in transit to such distributor from breweries.

(7) In addition to all other records and reports required under this article, each private club shall file with the probate judge on or before the twentieth day of each month detailed inventory of all alcoholic beverages on hand on the first day and the last day of the preceding month, and a record of all purchases of alcoholic beverages made by it during the preceding month.

(8) In addition to all other reports and records required under this article, each retail beer seller shall file with the probate judge on or before the twentieth day of each month a detailed inventory of all beer on hand on the first day and the last day of the preceding month.

(9) The license of any wholesale distributor, private club, or retail seller failing or refusing to file the reports shall be suspended forthwith by the probate judge pending receipt of such report.

(e) The tax herein levied is exclusive and shall be in lieu of all other or additional local taxes and licenses, county or municipal, imposed on or measured by the sale or volume of sale of beer; provided that nothing herein contained shall be construed to exempt the retail sales of beer from the levy of a tax on general retail sales by the county or municipality in the nature of, or in lieu of, a general sales tax. (Acts 1982, No. 82-344, p. 473, § 1; Acts 1983, No. 83-641, p. 989.)

Cross references. — As to minimum program fund for public schools referred to in this section, see article 3 of chapter 13 of Title 16.

This section is a general rather than local law, and it does not violate Ala. Const., art. IV, §§ 104(15), 105, or 106. Crosslin v. City of Muscle Shoals, 436 So. 2d 862 (Ala. 1983).

This section is a general law and the fact that the law permits or directs differences in matters of administration suited to the particular needs of the localities affected does not make it any less a general law. Crosslin v. City of Muscle Shoals, 436 So. 2d 862 (Ala. 1983).

A uniform tax was levied by the legislature to be collected from every purchaser of beer in all "wet counties" in the state. This tax is exclusive throughout the state. It is in lieu of every other local tax or license fee, measured by the sale, or volume of sale, of beer except a general sales tax. This tax is statewide because it applies everywhere within the state where beer is legally sold. Crosslin v. City of Muscle Shoals, 436 So. 2d 862 (Ala. 1983).

§ 28-3-191. Transactions between wholesalers and/or distributors exempt from article.

The tax levied by subsection (a) of section 28-3-190 shall not be imposed upon the sale, trade or barter of malt or brewed beverages by one licensed wholesaler or distributor to another wholesaler or distributor licensed to sell and handle malt or brewed beverages in this state, which transaction is hereby made exempt from said tax; provided, however, that the board shall and the county or municipality may require written reporting of any such transaction in such form as the board may prescribe, or if no form is prescribed by the board, in such form as may be prescribed by the county or municipality. (Acts 1982, No. 82-344, p. 473, § 2.)

§ 28-3-192. Unlawful acts and offenses; penalties.

(a) It shall be unlawful:

(1) For any licensee to sell, give away or otherwise dispose of beer taxable under this article within this state on which the taxes required by this article have not been paid within 10 days after the date upon which they were due.

(2) For any wholesale beer licensee to fail to keep for a period of at least three years, complete and truthful records covering the operation of his license and particularly showing all purchases and sales of beer and the name and address of the vendor or vendee, or to refuse the governing authority of any county or municipality in which beer sales are made or any authorized employee or agent of the county or municipality, access to such records or the opportunity to make inspection, examination, audit or copies of the same when the request is made at any time during which the licensed premises are open for the transaction of business.

(3) For any wholesale beer licensee to refuse the governing authority of any county or municipality in which he sells beer, or any authorized employee or agent thereof or any duly commissioned law enforcement officer thereof the right to completely inspect the entire licensed premises at any time during which such premises are open for the transaction of business.

(4) For any person to knowingly or willfully make, exhibit or file a falsified return or any information upon which said return is based for the purpose of defrauding any county or municipality by evading the payment of the tax levied by this article.

(b) Any violation of subsection (a) of this section shall be a misdemeanor punishable by a fine of not less than $100.00 nor more than $1,000.00, to which, at the discretion of the court or judge trying the case, may be added imprisonment in the county jail or at hard labor for the county for not more than three months for the first conviction; and, on the second conviction of a violation of said subsection, the offense may, in addition to a fine within the limits above named, be punishable by imprisonment or at hard labor for the county for not less than three months nor more than six months to be imposed by the court or judge trying the case; and, on the third and every subsequent conviction of a violation of said subsection, the offense may, in addition to a fine within the limits above named, be punishable by imprisonment or at hard labor for the county for not less than six months nor more than 12 months. (Acts 1982, No. 82-344, p. 473, § 3.)

§ 28-3-193. Penalties on failure of wholesaler licensee to timely pay tax due; execution and levy; lien.

(a) Every wholesaler licensee collecting tax on beer levied by this article shall timely pay the same as provided in this article. Every such wholesaler licensee failing for a period of 10 days beyond the due date to pay the said tax due pursuant to this article shall be required to pay as part of the taxes imposed under this article a penalty of not less than $50.00, nor more than $250.00, to be assessed and collected by the authority to whom the taxes are to be paid. In addition to such penalty, any wholesaler licensee failing for a period of 10 days beyond the due date to pay all or any part of the tax due pursuant to this article shall not be entitled to deduct and retain the two and one-half percent discount prescribed in section 28-3-190(b) hereof upon any portion of the tax which is not timely paid.

(b) If any taxes or penalties imposed by this article remain due and unpaid for a period of 10 days, the presiding officer of the affected governing body may issue a warrant or execution directed to any sheriff of the state of Alabama, commanding him to levy upon and sell the real and personal property of the taxpayer found within his county for the payment of the amount thereof, with penalties, if any, and the cost of executing the warrant, and to return such warrant to the governing body of the county or municipality and pay to it the money collected by virtue thereof. Upon receipt of such execution, the sheriff shall file with the clerk of the circuit court of his county a copy thereof and thereupon the clerk of the circuit court shall enter in his abstract of judgments the name of the taxpayer mentioned in the warrant and in proper columns the amount of tax, with penalties, and costs for which the warrant is issued and the date and hour when such copy is filed, and shall index the warrant upon the index of judgments. The sheriff shall thereupon proceed upon the warrant in all respects with like effect and in the same manner prescribed by law in respect to executions issued against the property upon judgments of a court of record and shall be entitled to the same fees for services in executing the warrant to be collected in the same manner. He shall make return of such execution to said governing body within 30 days of issuance thereof. The taxes and penalties imposed by this article shall be deemed a debt owing to the county or municipality by the party against whom the same shall be charged and shall be a preferred lien on all property of the party against whom the same shall be charged. (Acts 1982, No. 82-344, p. 473, § 4.)

§ 28-3-194. County and municipal license fees.

Each county and municipality is authorized to fix a reasonable privilege or license fee on retail, importer and wholesale licensees, for the purpose of covering the cost of administration, but not to generate revenue. Provided, however, that a county or municipality shall levy no license or privilege tax or other charge for the privilege of doing business as a beer wholesaler, importer or retailer which shall exceed one-half the amount of the state license fee. (Acts 1982, No. 82-344, p. 473, § 5.)

§ 28-3-195. Legislative intent.

(a) It is hereby declared the intention and purpose of this article to prescribe and levy an exclusive statewide local tax on the sale of beer for the protection of the public welfare, health, peace and morals of the people of this state and for the protection of revenues of the counties and municipalities in this state from avoidance and evasion.

(b) It is further declared to be the intention and purpose of this article to establish a system to phase out the projected loss of net revenue which would be experienced by those eligible counties, in which were imposed, as of October 1, 1981, a combined local tax rate on beer which exceeds the rate of the uniform tax levied on beer by this article. (Acts 1982, No. 82-344, p. 473, § 6.)

§ 28-3-196. Revenue loss phase-out system.

(a) When used in this section and in section 28-3-195(b) and section 28-3-197, the following words and phrases shall have the following meanings, respectively, unless the context clearly indicates otherwise:

(1) BEER TAX ESCROW FUND, or FUND. A fund established with the alcoholic beverage control board as escrow agent funded by payments made by wholesale beer licensees collecting the tax imposed by this article, such payments being made from the discount provided by section 28-3-190(b). From the fund, the board shall pay to each eligible county the amount or amounts provided by this section for the purpose of phasing out the net revenue loss which would be experienced by eligible counties.

(2) ELIGIBLE COUNTY. Any wet county in which was imposed, as of November 1, 1981, a combined local tax rate on beer in that county which exceeded the uniform tax levied on beer by this article and which would, as a result thereof, experience a decrease in its net local tax revenue collected on beer. In order for any county to become eligible, it must timely file a claim for its loss of net revenue, which claim must be certified by the board as provided in subsection (e) of this section.

(3) BASE YEAR. The year commencing October 1, 1981, and ending September 30, 1982.

(4) BASE YEAR CASES. The number of cases of beer sold within a county during the base year upon which local beer taxes were paid in that county, which number shall be determined by the board.

(5) BASE YEAR NET REVENUE. The actual net revenue realized within a county from combined local beer taxes collected on the sale of the base year cases. Net revenue shall be revenue received from combined local beer taxes, less administrative expenses including but not limited to cost of stamps, discounts or rebates to wholesalers, salary and expenses of beer tax inspectors, and such other costs of collection and administration rendered unnecessary by the provisions of this article.

(6) PROJECTED REVENUE. The amount of revenue derived from the base year cases multiplied by the rate of tax per case levied by this article, after deducting the discount of two and one-half percent prescribed in section 28-3-190(b). (Base year cases x rate of tax per case — two and one-half percent discount = projected revenue). The foregoing formula is a one-time calculation.

(7) NET REVENUE LOSS, or LOSS OF NET REVENUE. The excess of base year net revenue over projected revenue. (Base year net revenue — projected revenue = net revenue loss).

(8) SUBSIDY. The sum of money paid from the beer tax escrow fund by the board to each eligible county in installments as hereinafter provided totaling 400 percent of its net revenue loss.

(b) There is hereby established a beer tax escrow fund into which shall be paid the total amount of 400 percent of the annual net revenue loss as herein defined and calculated, which loss would be experienced by those eligible counties. This beer tax escrow fund shall be funded by payments from funds provided by the discount permitted by section 28-3-190(b) made by wholesale beer licensees who collect the uniform tax levied by this article.

(c) All wholesale beer licensees collecting the tax imposed by this article shall pay into the beer tax escrow fund. Such payments are to total a sum equal to 400 percent of the net revenue loss of eligible counties, as determined by the board, and are to be made from the two and one-half percent discount prescribed for wholesale licensees in section 28-3-190(b), as follows: Wholesale beer licensees collecting the tax imposed by this article shall pay monthly to the board for deposit in and credit to the beer tax escrow fund the sum of two and one-half cents per case for each case of beer received during the preceding month upon which beer tax is paid in this state. Such monthly payments shall commence on November 30, 1982, and shall be paid not later than the last day of each succeeding month and shall continue monthly until the total of the payments made into the fund shall be equal to or exceed the total subsidies to be paid to all eligible counties. The board shall cease collecting payments and shall so notify promptly each participating beer wholesaler when the total of the payments made to the board shall be equal to or exceed the total subsidies to be paid. Upon the payment of subsidies to all eligible counties, any moneys remaining in the fund shall be paid into the supplement beer tax escrow fund, if any, as authorized by section 28-3-197, or if there is no supplement beer tax escrow fund, then paid into the general fund of this state.

(d) Each eligible county shall be paid 400 percent of its net revenue loss (the difference between base year net revenue and projected revenue) by the board from the fund, as follows:

For the fiscal year commencing October 1, 1982, and ending September 30, 1983, the payment to each eligible county shall be 100 percent of its net revenue loss, or difference between base year net revenue and projected revenue; and for each of the three succeeding fiscal years thereafter, 100 percent of its net revenue loss.

The board shall pay the subsidy to each eligible county on the 15th day of the months of March, June and September of each year an amount equal to one-third of the total annual subsidy payment to be made during that fiscal year; provided, should the fund not contain sufficient money to make any given payment, any deficiency shall be made up in the next succeeding payment or payments.

(e) Any county desiring to assert a claim of eligibility for the subsidy under this section must file its claim with the board within 60 days after September 30, 1982. Upon the filing of such claim, the board shall, within 60 days after the filing of a claim, investigate and determine the eligibility of the claim of said county for subsidy and, if eligible, the amount of its subsidy. The decision of the board on eligibility and the subsidy amount shall be final and binding. No dry county shall be eligible to receive a subsidy on or after the effective date of its becoming a dry county. (Acts 1982, No. 82-344, p. 473, § 7.)

§ 28-3-197. Supplemental revenue loss phase-out system.

(a) When used in this section, the following words and phrases shall have the following meanings, respectively, unless the context clearly indicates otherwise:

(1) SUPPLEMENT BEER TAX ESCROW FUND. A fund established with the alcoholic beverage control board as escrow agent funded by payments made by wholesale beer licensees collecting the tax imposed by this article, such payments being made from the discount provided by section 28-3-190(b). From the fund, the board shall pay to each supplement eligible county the amount or amounts provided by this section for the purpose of phasing out the supplement net revenue loss, if any, which would be experienced by supplement eligible counties.

(2) SUPPLEMENT ELIGIBLE COUNTY. Any eligible county which would, as a result of the uniform tax levied on beer by this article, continue to experience a decrease in its net local tax revenue collected on beer beyond the end of the subsidy provided in section 28-3-196. In order for any county to become eligible for the supplement, it must have been an eligible county under section 28-3-196 and must timely file a claim for its supplement net revenue loss, which claim must be certified by the board as provided in subsection (e) of this section. Provided, however, that no county will be a supplement eligible county if any adjoining dry county or municipality shall have become wet between September 30, 1982 and October 1, 1985.

(3) SUPPLEMENT BASE YEAR. The year commencing October 1, 1985, and ending September 30, 1986.

(4) SUPPLEMENT BASE YEAR CASES. The number of cases of beer sold within an eligible county during the supplement base year upon which the uniform tax levied on beer by this article was paid in that county, which number shall be determined by the board.

(5) SUPPLEMENT BASE YEAR NET REVENUE. The actual revenue realized within a county from uniform local beer taxes collected on the sale of the supplement base year cases pursuant to this article. The amount of revenue derived from supplement base year cases multiplied by the rate of tax per case levied by this article, after deducting the discount of two and one-half percent prescribed in section 28-3-190(b). (Supplement base year cases x rate of tax per case — two and one-half percent discount = supplement base year net revenue).

(6) SUPPLEMENT NET REVENUE LOSS. The excess of base year net revenue over supplement base year net revenue. (Base year net revenue — supplement base year net revenue = supplement net revenue loss).

(7) SUPPLEMENT, or SUPPLEMENTAL SUBSIDY. The sum of money paid from the supplement beer tax escrow fund by the board to each supplement eligible county in installments as hereinafter provided totaling 200 percent of its supplement net revenue loss.

(b) There is hereby established a supplement beer tax escrow fund into which shall be paid the total amount of 200 percent of the annual supplement net revenue loss as herein defined and calculated, which loss would be experienced by those supplement eligible counties. This supplement beer tax escrow fund shall be funded by payments from funds provided by the discount permitted by section 28-3-190(b) made by wholesale beer licensees who collect the uniform tax levied by this article.

(c) All wholesale beer licensees collecting the tax imposed by this article shall pay into the supplement beer tax escrow fund. Such payments are to total a sum equal to 200 percent of the supplement net revenue loss of supplement eligible counties, as determined by the board, and are to be made from the two and one-half percent discount prescribed for wholesale licensees in section 28-3-190(b), as follows: Wholesale beer licensees collecting the tax imposed by this article shall pay monthly to the board for deposit in and credit to the supplement beer tax escrow fund the sum of two and one-half cents per case for each case of beer received during the preceding month upon which beer tax is paid in this state. Such monthly payments shall commence on October 31, 1986, and shall be paid not later than the last day of each succeeding month and shall continue monthly until the total of the payments made into the fund shall be equal to or exceed the total supplements to be paid to all supplement eligible counties. The board shall cease collecting payments and shall so notify promptly each participating beer wholesaler when the total of the payments made to the board shall be equal to or exceed the total supplements to be paid. Upon the payment of supplements to all supplement eligible counties, any moneys remaining in the fund shall be paid into the general fund of this state.

685

(d) Each supplement eligible county shall be paid 200 percent of its supplement net revenue loss (the excess of base year net revenue as defined in section 28-3-196 over supplement base year revenue) by the board from the fund from the supplement beer escrow fund, as follows:

For the fiscal year commencing October 1, 1986, and ending September 30, 1987, the payment to each supplement eligible county shall be 100 percent of its supplement net revenue loss, or excess of base year net revenue over supplement base year revenue, and for the fiscal year October 1, 1987 through September 30, 1988, 100 percent of its supplement net revenue loss.

The board shall pay the supplement to each supplement eligible county on the 15th day of the months of March, June and September of the years, 1987 and 1988, an amount equal to one-third of the total annual supplement payment to be made during that fiscal year; provided, should the supplement beer tax escrow fund not contain sufficient money to make any given payment, any deficiency shall be made up in the next succeeding payment or payments.

(e) Any eligible county desiring to assert a claim of eligibility for the supplement under this section must file its claim with the board within 60 days after September 30, 1986. Upon the filing of such claim, the board shall, within 60 days after the filing of a claim, investigate and determine the eligibility of the claim of said eligible county for supplement and, if eligible for the supplement, the amount of its supplement. The decision of the board on supplement eligibility and the supplement amount shall be final and binding. No dry county shall be eligible to receive a supplement on or after the effective date of its becoming a dry county. (Acts 1982, No. 82-344, p. 473, § 8.)

§ 28-3-198. Meaning of words and phrases.

The words and phrases used in this article shall have the meanings ascribed to them in section 28-3-1, and any acts amendatory thereof, supplementary thereto or substituted therefor. (Acts 1982, No. 82-344, p. 473, § 9.)

§ 28-3-199. Repeal of certain local taxes and licenses.

This article supersedes and repeals all local taxes and licenses, county or municipal, authorized, levied or imposed on or measured by the sale or volume of sale of beer, except the authorization, levy or imposition of a tax on general retail sales by the county or municipality in the nature of, or in lieu of, a general sales tax; provided, however, nothing herein shall be construed to relieve any person from any tax liability, penalty or forfeiture incurred thereunder, nor construed to repeal any provision of law respecting the enforcement of any such tax liability, penalty or forfeiture. (Acts 1982, No. 82-344, p. 473, § 10.)

ARTICLE 6.

TAXES ON SALE OF SPIRITUOUS OR VINOUS LIQUORS.

§ 28-3-200. Additional 10 percent tax — Alcoholic beverage control board store fund.

In addition to all other taxes of every kind now imposed by law and in addition to any marked-up price authorized or required by law, there is hereby levied and shall be collected a tax at the rate of 10 percent upon the selling price of all spirituous or vinous liquors sold by the Alabama alcoholic beverage control board.

The tax imposed by this section shall be computed at the time the sale is made to the purchaser and shall be collected by the board from said purchaser at the time the purchase price is paid; provided, however, that if said tax shall not be $.05 or a multiple of $.05 it shall be adjusted up or down to the nearest multiple of $.05.

Said tax, when collected, shall be paid to the state treasurer by the Alabama alcoholic beverage control board and shall be by said treasurer credited to the Alabama alcoholic beverage control board store fund to be distributed as provided by law. (Acts 1943, No. 99, p. 104.)

Collateral references. — 48 C.J.S., Intoxicating Liquors, §§ 181-190.

§ 28-3-201. Same — Alcoholic beverage control board store fund and general welfare purposes.

In addition to all other taxes of every kind now imposed by law and in addition to any marked-up price authorized or required by law, there is hereby levied and shall be collected a tax at the rate of 10 percent upon the selling price of all spirituous or vinous liquors sold by the Alabama alcoholic beverage control board. The tax hereby imposed shall be collected by the board from the purchaser at the time the purchase price is paid. In computing the proceeds of this tax, the board shall divide the total sales of spirituous and vinous liquors made by it by a factor of 110 and multiply the quotient by 100 and by 10. An amount equal to the quotient multiplied by 100 shall be deposited in the state treasury to the credit of the alcoholic beverage control board store fund and an amount equal to the quotient multiplied by 10 shall be deposited in the state treasury to the credit of the public welfare trust fund and shall be used for general welfare purposes and is hereby appropriated therefor. (Acts 1955, 2nd Ex. Sess., No. 78, p. 199; Acts 1973, No. 824, p. 1291; Acts 1986, No. 86-212, § 3.)

The **1986 amendment,** which became effective without the governor's signature under § 125 of the Constitution on April 1, 1986, deleted the definition of "general welfare purposes" at the end of this section.

Cross references. — As to the definition of "general welfare purposes", see now § 28-3-1.

§ 28-3-202. Same — Special mental health fund and general welfare purposes.

(a) Repealed by Acts 1986, No. 86-212, § 3.

(b) *Levy; collection; disposition of proceeds.* — In addition to all other taxes of every kind now imposed by law and in addition to any marked-up price authorized or required by law, there is hereby levied and shall be collected a tax at the rate of 10 percent upon the selling price of all spirituous or vinous liquors sold by the board. The tax imposed by this subsection shall be collected by the board from the purchaser at the time the purchase price is paid. One half of the proceeds derived from the tax shall be deposited in the state treasury to the credit of the public welfare trust fund and shall be used for general welfare purposes and is hereby appropriated therefor. The remainder of such proceeds from the tax levied by this subsection shall be deposited in the state treasury to the credit of a special fund which shall be designated the Alabama special mental health fund and shall be used only for mental health purposes, including the prevention of mental illness, the care and treatment of the mentally ill and the mentally deficient and the acquisition, equipment, operation and maintenance of facilities for mental health purposes.

The markup as currently established by the board on spirituous or vinuous liquors shall not be reduced by the board for the purpose of absorbing the tax levied by this subsection, it being the intention of this provision that the said tax shall be passed on to the purchaser. (Acts 1959, No. 312, p. 889; Acts 1973, No. 815, p. 1260; Acts 1986, No. 86-212, § 3.)

The **1986 amendment,** which became effective without the governor's signature under § 125 of the Constitution on April 1, 1986, deleted the definitions of "selling price" and "general welfare purposes" formerly appearing in subsection (a) of this section.

Cross references. — As to the definition of "selling price" and "general welfare purposes", see now § 28-3-1.

§ 28-3-203. Additional five percent tax.

(a) Repealed by Acts 1986, No. 86-212, § 3.

(b) *Levy and collection.* — In addition to all other taxes of every kind now imposed by law and in addition to any marked-up price authorized or required by law, there is hereby levied and shall be collected a tax at the rate of five percent upon the selling price of all spirituous or vinous liquors sold by the board. The tax imposed by this subsection shall be collected by the board from the purchaser at the time the purchase price is paid.

The markup as currently established by the board on spirituous or vinous liquors shall not be reduced by the board for the purpose of absorbing the tax levied by this subsection, it being the intention of this provision that the said tax shall be passed on to the purchaser.

(c) *Disposition of proceeds.* — All revenues collected under the provisions of subsection (b) of this section shall be paid into the state treasury to the credit of the general fund. (Acts 1969, No. 550, p. 1033; Acts 1986, No. 86-212, § 3.)

The 1986 amendment, which became effective without the governor's signature under § 125 of the Constitution on April 1, 1986, deleted the definition of "selling price" which was formerly found in subsection (a).

Cross references. — As to the definition of "selling price", see now § 28-3-1.

§ 28-3-204. Additional three percent tax.

(a) Repealed by Acts 1986, No. 86-212, § 3.

(b) *Levy and collection.* — In addition to all other taxes of every kind now imposed by law and in addition to any marked-up price authorized or required by law, there is hereby levied and shall be collected a tax at the rate of three percent upon the selling price of all spirituous or vinous liquors sold by the board.

The board shall have the authority to examine the books and records of any wine wholesaler to determine the accuracy of any return required to be filed with the board.

The markup as currently established by the board on spirituous or vinous liquors shall not be reduced by the board for the purpose of absorbing the tax levied in this subsection, it being the intention of this provision that the said tax shall be passed on to the purchaser.

(c) *Distribution of proceeds.* — One half of the proceeds derived from the tax shall be deposited in the state treasury to the credit of the public welfare trust fund and shall be used for general welfare purposes and is hereby appropriated therefor. The remainder of such proceeds from the tax levied by this section shall be deposited in the state treasury to the credit of a special fund which shall be designated the special mental health fund and shall be used only for mental health purposes, including the prevention of mental illness, the care and treatment of the mentally ill and the mentally deficient and the acquisition, equipment, operation and maintenance of facilities for mental health purposes. (Acts 1979, No. 79-761, p. 1360, §§ 4-6; Acts 1986, No. 86-212, § 3.)

The 1986 amendment, which became effective without the governor's signature under § 125 of the Constitution on April 1, 1986, deleted subsection (a), which defined "board," "general welfare purposes," "selling price," "table wine," "wine retailer," and "wine wholesaler."

U.S. Code. — For the Social Security Act, see 42 U.S.C. § 401 et seq.

§ 28-3-205. Additional 10 percent tax.

(a) Repealed by Acts 1986, No. 86-212, § 3.

(b) *Levy and collection of tax.* — In addition to all other taxes of every kind now imposed by law, and in addition to any marked-up price authorized or required by law, there is hereby levied and shall be collected a tax at the rate of 10 percent upon the selling price of all spirituous or vinous liquors sold by the board. The tax hereby imposed shall be collected by the board from the purchaser at the time the purchase price is paid.

(c) *Tax to be passed on to purchaser.* — The mark-up as currently established by the board on spirituous or vinous liquors shall not be reduced by the board for the purpose of absorbing the tax herein levied; it being the intention hereof that the said tax shall be passed on to the purchaser.

(d) *Disposition of proceeds.* — All revenues collected under the provisions of this section shall be paid into the state treasury to the credit of the general fund. (Acts 1980, No. 80-478, p. 749; Acts 1986, No. 86-212, § 3.)

The 1986 amendment, which became effective without the governor's signature under § 125 of the Constitution on April 1, 1986, deleted the definitions of "board" and "selling price" which were formerly found in subsection (a).

Cross references. — As to the definitions of "board" and "selling price", see now § 28-3-1.

Collateral references. — 48 C.J.S., Intoxicating Liquors, §§ 181 et seq.

45 Am. Jur. 2d, Intoxicating Liquors, §§ 203-208.

§ 28-3-206. Limitation on additional tax on collector's bottles of liquor or gift packs of wine.

It is hereby prohibited to levy an increased amount of alcoholic beverage tax on the increased amount that a "collector's" bottle of liquor as defined by the alcoholic beverage control board or "gift pack" of wine sells for over the amount a regular bottle of the same size and kind of liquor or wine sells for. (Acts 1981, No. 81-656, p. 1072.)

Collateral references. — 48 C.J.S., Intoxicating Liquors, §§ 40, 185.

45 Am. Jur. 2d, Intoxicating Liquors, §§ 23, 24, 208.

§ 28-3-207. Exemption of sales to certificated or licensed air carrier with hub operation in state from this article.

There is hereby exempted from the provisions of this article and from the computation of the amount of tax levied, assessed or payable under such article, the sale of all spirituous or vinous liquors sold by the Alabama alcoholic beverage control board to a certificated or licensed air carrier with a hub operation within this state, for use in conducting intrastate, interstate or foreign commerce for transporting people or property by air. For the purpose of this section the words "hub operation within this state" shall be construed to have all of the following ciriteria:

(1) There originates from the location 15 or more flight departures and five or more different first-stop destinations five days per week for six or more months during the calendar year; and

(2) Passengers and/or property are regularly exchanged at the location between flights of the same or a different certificated or licensed air carrier. (Acts 1986, No. 86-214, § 2.)

Effective date. — The act which added this section became law April 3, 1986, without the governor's signature under § 125 of the Constitution, effective May 1, 1986.

Code commissioner's note. — Acts 1986, No. 86-214, § 1 provides that the act shall be known and may be cited as the Alabama Air Transportation Development Act of 1986.

ARTICLE 7.

TAX AND IDENTIFICATION STAMPS, CROWNS OR LIDS.

Code commissioner's note. — Acts 1979, No. 79-802, p. 1475, § 6(a), effective October 1, 1980, provides that §§ 28-3-220 through 28-3-229 are repealed insofar as they relate to malt or brewed beverages, except with respect to the penalties set forth in §§ 28-3-227 and 28-3-228, but that no person shall be relieved from any tax liability, penalty or forfeiture incurred prior to October 1, 1980.

§ 28-3-220. Affixing of stamps, crowns or lids to original containers in which alcoholic beverages marketed, received, sold, etc., prior to sale, offer for sale, etc., by manufacturers, etc., required generally.

It is the intention and purpose of this chapter to require all manufacturers and other persons as provided in this chapter to affix stamps, crowns or lids as will be prescribed by the board to all original containers in which alcoholic beverages are normally placed and prepared for market, received, sold or handled before such beverages are sold, offered for sale or held for sale within this state. (Acts 1936-37, Ex. Sess., No. 66, p. 40; Code 1940, T. 29, § 58.)

Code commissioner's note. — Acts 1979, No. 79-802, p. 1475, § 6(a), effective October 1, 1980, provides that this section is repealed insofar as it relates to malt or brewed beverages.

§ 28-3-221. Board to design stamps, crowns or lids and require manufacturers, distillers, wholesalers, etc., to affix same to beer, wines or liquors sold in state.

The board is hereby authorized to design stamps, crowns or lids to be affixed to alcoholic beverages as defined in this chapter and sold in the state of Alabama and shall require breweries, vendors or manufacturers of wine and distillers or wholesalers of all other alcoholic commodities to affix such stamps, crowns or lids on beer, wines or liquors sold within the state. (Acts 1936-37, Ex. Sess., No. 66, p. 40; Code 1940, T. 29, § 57.)

§ 28-3-222. Stamps, crowns or lids in amount of tax to be affixed to bottles, cans, etc., in which taxed articles sold; taxable articles offered for sale without stamps, crowns or lids subject to confiscation.

Stamps, crowns or lids in denominations to the amount of the tax shall be affixed to the bottles, cans or containers from or in which articles taxed in this chapter are normally sold at retail.

All taxable articles enumerated in this chapter, when offered for sale, either at wholesale or retail, without having stamps, crowns or lids affixed in the manner set out in this chapter shall be subject to confiscation in the manner provided for contraband goods as set out in this chapter. (Acts 1936-37, Ex. Sess., No. 66, p. 40; Code 1940, T. 29, § 45.)

§ 28-3-223. Manner and time for affixing of stamps, crowns or lids by wholesalers, distributors or retail dealers generally.

The license taxes imposed by this chapter shall be paid by affixing stamps, crowns or lids in the manner and at the time set forth in this section. The stamps, crowns or lids shall be affixed to the bottle or container, in which or from which the taxed article is normally sold at retail. Time allowed for affixing stamps, crowns or lids shall be as follows: Every wholesaler, distributor or retail dealer in this state shall, immediately after receipt of any unstamped taxable articles enumerated and defined in this chapter, unless sooner offered for sale, cause the same to have the requisite denominations and amount of stamp, crown or lid or stamps, crowns or lids to represent the taxes affixed as stated herein and shall cause same to be cancelled by writing or stamping across the face of each stamp the registered number of such wholesaler, distributor or retailer, said number to be furnished by the board. (Acts 1936-37, Ex. Sess., No. 66, p. 40; Code 1940, T. 29, § 46.)

§ 28-3-224. Stamping of alcoholic beverages by wholesalers, distributors or retail dealers; presumption as to sale of alcoholic beverages without proper stamps.

(a) The stamping of alcoholic beverages as enumerated and defined in this chapter shall actually begin within one hour after receipt of said alcoholic beverages in the premises of the wholesaler, distributor or retail dealer, and said stamping shall be continued with reasonable diligence by the wholesaler, distributor or retail dealer until all of the unstamped alcoholic beverages as enumerated and defined in this chapter have been stamped and the stamps cancelled as provided by law; provided, that any wholesaler or distributor engaged in interstate business who shall furnish surety bond in an amount and with sureties satisfactory to the board shall be permitted to set aside such part of his stock as may be necessary for the conduct of such interstate business without affixing the stamps required by this chapter. Said interstate stock shall be kept in an entirely separate part of the building separate and apart from the stamped stock. Wholesalers, distributors and retail dealers shall also keep a record of purchasers of all alcoholic beverages enumerated and defined in this chapter and hold all books, records and memoranda pertaining to the purchase and sale of such alcoholic beverages enumerated and defined in this chapter open to the inspection of the board or its duly authorized agents at any and at all times.

(b) If, upon examination of invoices of any wholesaler or distributor or retail dealer, he is unable to furnish evidence to the board of sufficient stamp purchases to cover unstamped alcoholic beverages as enumerated and defined in this chapter purchased by him, the presumption shall arise that such alcoholic beverages were sold without the proper stamps affixed thereto.

(c) Any wholesaler, distributor or retailer who fails or refuses to comply with the provisions of this section shall be guilty of a misdemeanor and, upon conviction, shall be punished by a fine of not less than $500.00 nor more than $1,000.00 or imprisonment in the county jail for a period of six months or both at the discretion of the court. (Acts 1936-37, Ex. Sess., No. 66, p. 40; Code 1940, T. 29, § 47.)

Code commissioner's note. — Acts 1979, No. 79-802, p. 1475, § 6(a), effective October 1, 1980, provides that this section is repealed insofar as it relates to malt or brewed beverages.

§ 28-3-225. Board to provide for manufacture, sale and distribution of stamps, crowns or lids; sale of same by persons not designated and bonded by board; purchase of stamps, crowns or lids by manufacturers, etc.; persons, firms, etc., using tax-paid crowns or lids to pay costs of quarterly examinations of records by board examiners.

(a) The board is hereby authorized and directed to have prepared and distributed stamps, tax-paid crowns and lids suitable for denoting taxes on all articles enumerated in this chapter.

The board is authorized to enter into a contract on behalf of the state with one or more manufacturers for the manufacture, sale and distribution of such stamps, crowns or lids and shall require of such persons, firms or corporations so manufacturing, selling and distributing such stamps, crowns or lids a bond or bonds with a company authorized to do business in the state as surety, payable to the state of Alabama, in such penalty and upon such conditions as in the opinion of the board will adequately protect the state. The stamps, crowns or lids shall be manufactured, sold and distributed at the cost of the taxpayer.

(b) Any person, firm, corporation or association of persons other than the board or persons, firms, corporations or associations of persons designated and bonded by the board who sell stamps, tax-paid crowns or lids not affixed to alcoholic beverages sold and delivered by them, whether the said stamps, tax-paid crowns or lids be genuine or counterfeit, shall be guilty of a felony and punishable as set out in section 28-3-227.

(c) All stamps, crowns or lids provided for in this chapter shall be prescribed by the board, and under rules and regulations prescribed by the board they shall be purchased by the manufacturer or other person after the payment of the taxes imposed by this chapter.

(d) Any person, firm, corporation or association of persons who desires to use tax-paid crowns or lids and having been qualified by the board to use said tax-paid crowns or lids, as provided in this section, shall be required to pay the cost of the examination of their records by examiners of the board to determine the amount of taxes due and paid to the state by said person, firm or corporation, said examination to be made at least quarterly by the examiners of the board. (Acts 1936-37, Ex. Sess., No. 66, p. 40; Code 1940, T. 29, § 58.)

Code commissioner's note. — Acts 1979, No. 79-802, p. 1475, § 6(a), effective October 1, 1980, provides that this section is repealed insofar as it relates to malt or brewed beverages.

§ 28-3-226. Penalty for failure to properly affix required stamps, crowns or lids; notification and right to trial of person, firm, etc., charged with same; lien for judgment in favor of state and issuance of execution thereupon.

Persons failing to properly affix the required stamps, crowns or lids to any alcoholic beverages enumerated and defined in this chapter shall be required to pay as part of the taxes imposed under this chapter a penalty of not less than $50.00, nor more than $500.00, to be assessed and collected by the board as other taxes are collected. Each article or commodity not having proper stamps, crowns or lids affixed thereto as required in this chapter shall be deemed a separate offense. Any alcoholic beverages enumerated and defined in this chapter within the place of business of any person required by the provisions of this chapter to stamp the same shall be prima facie evidence that they are intended for sale.

Within 10 days, and not thereafter, after notification in writing by the board or its duly authorized agent to the person, firm or corporation of its failure to properly affix the required stamps, crowns or lids to any article or commodity or within 10 days after written notificiation to him that he has sold or offered for sale any article or commodity requiring stamps, crowns or lids without having the stamps, crowns or lids properly attached thereto as required by this chapter, the party charged with such omission as provided in this section shall have the right within said time, and not thereafter, to demand a trial of the issue before a court of competent jurisdiction in the manner now provided by law for the trial of civil actions.

The written notice required by this section may be served by mail. When it is so served, the paper must be deposited in the post office addressed to the person on whom it is to be served at his last known place of residence and the postage paid, and the 10 days provided for in this section shall begin to run from the date of the mailing. Said notice may also be personally served by any agent of the board or any other person by delivering the same to person or corporation charged or by leaving the same in the place of business of such person or corporation.

Any judgment entered in favor of the state in any civil action shall be a first preferred lien for taxes upon all property of the taxpayer and in the event of nonpayment shall be filed in the office of the clerk of the circuit court in the county where taken, and execution may be issued as provided by law. (Acts 1936-37, Ex. Sess., No. 66, p. 40; Code 1940, T. 29, § 62.)

Code commissioner's note. — Acts 1979, No. 79-802, p. 1475, § 6(a), effective October 1, 1980, provides that this section is repealed insofar as it relates to malt or brewed beverages.

§ 28-3-227. Removal, restoration, etc., for use or reuse, unauthorized sale, etc., of revenue, etc., stamps, crowns or lids.

Whoever removes or otherwise prepares any Alabama revenue stamps, crowns or lids or stamps, crowns or lids used to identify alcoholic beverages sold or distributed by state liquor stores with intent to use or cause the same to be used after they have already been used or buys, sells, offers for sale or gives away any such washed or removed and restored stamps, crowns or lids to any person for using or who used the same or has in his possession any washed or restored or removed or altered stamp, crown or lid for the purpose of indicating the payment of any tax provided for in this chapter or reuses any stamp, crown or lid which has heretofore been used for the purpose of paying any tax provided in this chapter or identifying any articles enumerated and defined in this chapter or whoever, except the board or persons, firms, corporations or associations of persons designated and bonded by the board, sells any Alabama revenue stamps, crowns or lids not affixed to taxable alcoholic beverages as provided in this chapter, shall be guilty of a felony and, upon conviction, shall be punished by imprisonment in the penitentiary for not less than a year and a day, nor more than five years, and in addition may be fined not less than $1,000.00, nor more than $5,000.00. (Acts 1936-37, Ex. Sess., No. 66, p. 40; Code 1940, T. 29, § 63.)

§ 28-3-228. Manufacture, purchase, sale, possession, etc., of reproduction or counterfeit revenue, etc., stamps, crowns or lids.

Whoever manufactures, buys, sells, offers for sale or has in his or its possession any reproduction or counterfeit of the Alabama revenue stamps, crowns or lids provided for in this chapter or stamps, crowns or lids used to identify articles sold or distributed by state liquor stores shall be guilty of a felony and, upon conviction, shall be punished by imprisonment in the penitentiary for not less than a year and a day nor more than 10 years and, in addition, may be fined not less than $2,000.00 nor more than $10,000.00. (Acts 1936-37, Ex. Sess., No. 66, p. 40; Code 1940, T. 29, § 64.)

Section applies to dry counties. — This section, declaring possession of counterfeit state revenue stamps a felony, is effective in dry counties. Holt v. State, 238 Ala. 2, 193 So. 89 (1939).

The supreme court's opinion in Holt v. State, 238 Ala. 2, 193 So. 89 (1939), that this section applies in all counties, including dry counties, was not erroneous as contrary to holding of court of appeals in Williams v. State, 28 Ala. App. 73, 179 So. 915 (1938).

The supreme court's decision in answer to question certified by court of appeals that this section is effective in dry counties precludes further discussion of such question by court of appeals. Holt v. State, 29 Ala. App. 100, 193 So. 98 (1939).

§ 28-3-229. Unauthorized possession of unattached revenue stamps, crowns or lids.

Any person other than a wholesaler, distributor or dealer or other person authorized by the Alabama alcoholic beverage control board who shall have in his possession any unattached Alabama revenue stamps, crowns or lids used for the purpose of identifying alcoholic beverages sold or distributed pursuant to this chapter shall be guilty of a felony and, upon conviction, may be fined not more than $5,000.00 and shall be imprisoned in the penitentiary for not less than one nor more than five years. (Acts 1955, No. 88, p. 336.)

Code commissioner's note. — Acts 1979, No. 79-802, p. 1475, § 6(a), effective October 1, 1980, provides that this section is repealed insofar as it relates to malt or brewed beverages.

ARTICLE 8.

CONFISCATION AND SALE OF CONTRABAND GOODS, MERCHANDISE, ETC.

§ 28-3-240. Goods, etc., subject to confiscation and sale generally; procedure for confiscation and sale of goods, etc., generally.

All alcoholic beverages enumerated and defined in this chapter or other products taxable under this chapter found at any point within the state of Alabama when said alcoholic beverages or products shall have been within the state of Alabama for a period of two hours or longer in possession of any retailer or for a period of 36 hours or longer in possession of any wholesaler or distributor not having affixed to the package, as defined in this chapter, the stamps, crowns or lids as provided by law are hereby declared to be contraband goods, and the same may be seized by the board or its agents or by any peace officer of the state of Alabama without a warrant, and the said goods shall be delivered to the board for sale at public auction to the highest bidder after due advertisement, but the board, before delivering any of said goods so seized, shall require the purchaser to affix the proper amount of stamps, crowns or lids to the individual package as defined in this chapter. The proceeds of sale of any goods sold under this article shall be turned over to the state treasurer by the board as other funds collected by said board. The cost of confiscation and sale shall be paid out of the proceeds derived from such sales before making remittance to the state treasurer.

Any of the goods, wares or merchandise enumerated in this chapter and all such goods, wares or merchandise when offered for sale, either at wholesale or retail, without the stamps, crowns or lids having been first affixed shall be subject to confiscation as hereinbefore provided.

Any vehicle not a common carrier which may be used for the transportation for the purpose of sale of unstamped articles as enumerated in this chapter shall likewise be subject to confiscation and sale in the manner as above provided for goods, wares or merchandise without stamps, crowns or lids. Should any alcoholic beverages without stamps, crowns or lids as enumerated and defined in this chapter be found in any vehicle which is engaged in the sale, distribution or delivery of taxable alcoholic beverages, the same shall be prima facie evidence that it was there for sale. (Acts 1936-37, Ex. Sess., No. 66, p. 40; Code 1940, T. 29, § 49.)

Burden of proof. — In an action to condemn a truck and beer it was carrying, intervenors who owned the truck and beer had the burden of proving the transportation was not illegal, and where there was a failure to show that the beer bore the stamps required by former § 28-3-260, or was exempt therefrom, a judgment of condemnation was not erroneous. Maddox v. State, 272 Ala. 683, 133 So. 2d 889 (1961).

Collateral references. — 48 C.J.S., Intoxicating Liquors, §§ 384-404.

45 Am. Jur. 2d, Intoxicating Liquors, § 490.

§ 28-3-241. Additional beverages subject to confiscation and sale; punishment of persons having contraband beverages in their possession.

Any alcoholic beverages as enumerated and defined in this chapter to be sold or distributed by and through state liquor stores found within this state in the possession of or on the premises of any person, firm, corporation or association of persons not having affixed thereto such mark of identification showing that said alcoholic beverages were sold or distributed by a state liquor store shall be subject to confiscation and sale in the same manner as set forth in this chapter for malt or brewed beverages as defined in this chapter and vinous beverages not exceeding 24 percent by volume which do not have affixed thereto the required revenue stamps as provided for in this chapter.

Persons who are found guilty of having in their possession any such contraband liquors shall be subject to the same fines and imprisonment as set forth in this chapter for persons having in their possession any malt or vinous beverages without the proper stamps affixed thereto as required by this chapter. (Acts 1936-37, Ex. Sess., No. 66, p. 40; Code 1940, T. 29, § 50.)

§ 28-3-242. Procedure for confiscation and sale of goods, etc.; nature of proceedings against goods, etc.; court proceedings for collection of tax due and assessed.

(a) In all cases of seizure of any goods, wares, merchandise or other property made as being subject to forfeiture under provisions of this chapter which, in the opinion of the officer or person making the seizure, are of the appraised value of $50.00 or more, the said officer or person shall proceed as follows. He shall cause a list containing a particular description of the goods, wares, merchandise or other property seized to be prepared in duplicate and appraisement thereof, to be made by three sworn appraisers to be selected by him, who shall be respectable and disinterested citizens of the state of Alabama, residing within the county wherein the seizure was made. Said list and appraisement shall be properly attested by said officer or persons, and said appraisers, for which service each of said appraisers shall be allowed the sum of $1.00 per day, not exceeding two days, to be paid by the board out of any revenue received by it from the sale of the confiscated goods or the compromise which may be effected. If the said goods are believed by the officer making the seizure to be of value of less than $50.00, no appraisement shall be made.

The said officer or person shall proceed to post a notice in writing for three weeks at three places in the county where the seizure was made, describing the articles and stating the time and place and cause of their seizure and requiring any person claiming them to appear and make such claim in writing within 30 days from the date of the first posting of such notice.

Any person claiming the said goods, wares or merchandise, or other property so seized as contraband within the time specified in the notice may file with the board a claim in writing, stating his interest in the articles seized, and may execute a bond to the board in a penal sum equal to double the value of said goods so seized, but in no case less than the sum of $200.00, with sureties to be approved by the clerk of the circuit court in the county in which the goods are seized, conditioned that in the case of condemnation of the articles so seized, the obligors shall pay to the board the full value of the goods so seized and all costs and expense of the proceedings to obtain such condemnation, including a reasonable attorney's fee. Upon the delivery of such bond to the board, it shall transmit the same with the duplicate list or description of the goods seized to the district attorney of the circuit in which such seizure was made, and the said district attorney shall file a complaint in the circuit court of the county where the seizure was made to secure the forfeiture of said goods, wares, merchandise or other property. Upon the filing of the bonds aforesaid, the said goods shall be delivered to the claimant pending the outcome of said case. Said goods must have the proper stamps, crowns or lids affixed to each such article of alcoholic beverage enumerated and defined in this chapter before turning same over to claimant, the stamps, crowns or lids so affixed to be paid for by claimant when goods properly stamped are delivered by the board.

If no claim is interposed and no bond given within the time above specified, such goods, wares, merchandise or other property shall be forfeited without further proceedings and the same shall be sold as provided in this article, and the proceeds of sale when received by the board shall be turned in to the treasury as other revenues collected by said board.

(b) In seizure in quantities of less value than $50.00, the same may be advertised with other quantities at Montgomery, Alabama by the board and disposed of as provided in subsection (a) of this section.

(c) The proceedings against goods, wares, merchandise or other property, pursuant to the provisions of this chapter, shall be considered as proceedings in rem unless otherwise provided.

(d) Should the board have to resort to the courts for collection of the tax due and assessed, no advertisement shall be made, and the confiscated alcoholic beverages may be held as evidence pending the result of court action. (Acts 1936-37, Ex. Sess., No. 66, p. 40; Code 1940, T. 29, § 51.)

Cited in Alabama ABC Bd. v. Roberts, 274 Ala. 256, 147 So. 2d 822 (1962).

Collateral references. — 45 Am. Jur. 2d, Intoxicating Liquors, § 501 et seq.

Lawfulness of seizure of property used in violation of law as prerequisite to forfeiture action or proceeding. 8 ALR3d 473.

§ 28-3-243. Return of confiscated goods.

The board may in its discretion return any goods confiscated under this chapter or any part thereof when it is shown that there was no intention to violate the provisions of this chapter; provided, that when any goods, merchandise or other property are confiscated under the provisions of this chapter, the board may, in its discretion, return such goods to the parties from whom they are confiscated if and when such parties shall pay to the board or its duly authorized representative an amount equal to the tax due under this chapter on the goods confiscated and, in such cases, no advertisement shall be made or notices posted in connection with said confiscation. (Acts 1936-37, Ex. Sess., No. 66, p. 40; Code 1940, T. 29, § 52.)

§ 28-3-244. Condemnation and delivery to board of liquors seized upon which federal tax has been paid and containers of which are unbroken or unopened.

Any liquors and beverages that are prohibited to be sold or otherwise disposed of in this state, including malt or brewed beverages, together with the vessels or other receptacles in which they are contained, that have been heretofore or may hereafter be seized by any officer of the state, county or municipal government, regardless of whether seized under the authority of a search warrant or not, upon which it appears that the federal tax has been paid, the federal stamp being located on the container being prima facie evidence thereof, and the containers of which appear to be unbroken or which appear to have never been opened after the placing thereon of the federal stamp or seal shall, upon a court order of forfeiture, be delivered immediately to the alcoholic beverage control board at Montgomery, Alabama, or to a properly designated representative of the Alabama alcoholic beverage control board, whereupon said board or its representative shall determine the reasonable value thereof, and the amounts so determined by said board or its representative to be the reasonable value thereof shall be paid by the board to the clerk of the court in which such order of forfeiture was made. Any funds paid into court, as provided in this section, shall be applied first to the payment of the court costs in such case, and the balance, if any, shall be paid into the general fund of the municipality or county in which said case arose.

Condemnation proceedings against such liquors and beverages may be instituted in the circuit court of the county in which such liquors or beverages were seized by the state of Alabama, on the relation of the district attorney, and notice shall be given of the institution of such proceedings and of the day and place set for the hearing thereof to "all persons claiming any right, title or interest in such liquors and beverages" either by publication once a week for three successive weeks in some newspaper published in the county or by posting one notice at the courthouse door in said county for three weeks, at the discretion of the court; provided, that in the case of malt or brewed beverages, the provisions of this section shall apply only where a minimum of 100 cases of such beverages are seized and where the proceedings provided for in this section may be completed within 90 days after the brewing date of such beverages. (Acts 1953, No. 835, p. 1126.)

ARTICLE 9.

MISCELLANEOUS OFFENSES.

§§ 28-3-260 through 28-3-268. Repealed by Acts 1980, No. 80-529, p. 806, § 27, effective September 30, 1980.

ARTICLE 10.

ADDITIONAL STATE SALES TAX ON ALCOHOLIC BEVERAGES.

§ 28-3-280. Additional state sales tax levied.

In addition to all other taxes levied and collected on the sale of any alcoholic beverage, there is hereby levied an additional state sales tax in the amount of two percent of the retail price, excluding taxes, on the sales of alcoholic beverages sold at retail by alcoholic beverage control board stores. Such tax shall be in addition to any and all other taxes collected on sales. (Acts 1982, No. 82-427, p. 675, § 1.)

§ 28-3-281. Collection and distribution of proceeds.

(a) The alcoholic beverage control board shall collect the revenues generated by this article in the same manner as other taxes and fees collected by it. The sales taxes as collected by the alcoholic beverage control board on retail sales shall be paid to the department of revenue. The department of revenue shall redistribute the proceeds therefrom in the following manner unless distribution is otherwise provided by local act:

(1) The department shall withhold any reasonable charges incurred by the department in handling such taxes which charges shall be prorated on the basis of the sum collected; provided, however, such charges shall not exceed a sum equal to five percent of the amount collected;

(2) An amount equal to 25 percent of the tax proceeds shall be distributed to the respective counties in which the taxes are collected, less costs as provided in subdivision (1) above; and

(3) An amount equal to 75 percent of the tax proceeds shall be distributed to the respective municipalities in which the taxes are collected, less costs as provided in subdivision (1) above.

(b) The department of revenue shall prepare and distribute such reports, forms and other information as may be necessary for the collection and distribution of the said taxes. (Acts 1982, No. 82-427, p. 675, § 2.)

§ 28-3-282. Use of tax proceeds.

The tax proceeds distributed to counties under the provisions of this article shall be used by those counties exclusively for law enforcement purposes unless otherwise provided by local act. (Acts 1982, No. 82-427, p. 675, § 3.)

§ 28-3-283. Rules and regulations.

The commissioner of the department of revenue is authorized to promulgate all reasonable rules and regulations necessary to implement the provisions of this article. (Acts 1982, No. 82-427, p. 675, § 4.)

§ 28-3-284. Levy of additional local taxes or fees prohibited.

Any county or municipality receiving any additional taxes pursuant to the provisions of this article shall be prohibited from levying any additional taxes or fees on the sale of alcoholic beverages which would be collected by the Alabama alcoholic beverage control board or its stores. (Acts 1982, No. 82-427, p. 675, § 5.)

§ 28-3-285. Article cumulative.

The provisions of this article are cumulative and shall not be construed to repeal or supersede any laws not directly in conflict herewith. (Acts 1982, No. 82-427, p. 675, § 6.)

§ 28-3-286. Effective date.

The taxes to be collected by the alcoholic beverage control board under this article shall begin with the next regular price change by the alcoholic beverage control board which occurs at least 60 days after this Article becomes law. (Acts 1982, No. 82-427, p. 675, § 8.)

CHAPTER 3A.

ALCOHOLIC BEVERAGE LICENSING CODE.

Sec.
28-3A-1. Short title.
28-3A-2. Repealed.
28-3A-3. Authority of board to issue licenses to engage in alcoholic beverage transactions.
28-3A-4. License application; fees.
28-3A-5. Issuance and renewal of licenses; penalty for delinquent renewal.
28-3A-6. Manufacturer license; issuance; restrictions on sales; registration of labels; seizure of unregistered goods; monthly reports; daily records; inspections.
28-3A-7. Importer license; issuance; restrictions on sales; registration of labels; seizure of unregistered goods; monthly reports; inspections.
28-3A-8. Liquor wholesaler license.
28-3A-9. Wholesaler license for beer or table wine.
28-3A-10. Warehouse license.
28-3A-11. Lounge retail liquor license; approval of municipality; entertainment; minors.
28-3A-12. Club liquor retail license; approval of municipality.
28-3A-13. Restaurant retail liquor license; approval of municipality.
28-3A-14. Retail table wine license for on-premises and off-premises consumption.

Sec.
28-3A-15. Retail table wine license for off-premises consumption.
28-3A-16. Retail beer license for on-premises and off-premises consumption.
28-3A-17. Retail beer license for off-premises consumption.
28-3A-18. Retail common carrier liquor license.
28-3A-19. Special retail license.
28-3A-20. Special events retail license.
28-3A-21. License fees for licenses issued by the board; local license taxes.
28-3A-22. Disposition of proceeds of filing fees and license taxes.
28-3A-23. Regulation of grant of licenses; to whom issued; display thereof; local approval of retail licenses; separate retail licenses; place of retail sales; beer and wine containers; place of sale of draft or keg beer and special permits therefor; place of wholesale operations; transfer of licenses; effect of insolvency of licensee.
28-3A-24. Suspension or revocation of licenses; appointment of hearing commission; notice, hearing and findings; fines.
28-3A-25. Unlawful acts and offenses; penalties.
28-3A-26. Revocation of license or permit upon second or subsequent conviction.

Code commissioner's note. — Section 29, Acts 1980, No. 80-529, p. 806, which added this chapter, provides that any license granted prior to September 30, 1980, shall remain in effect until its expiration.

Cross references. — As to the alcoholic beverage control board, generally, see § 28-3-40, et seq. As to the functions and duties of the board, see § 28-3-43.

Legislative intent. — Legislature intended the Alcoholic Beverage Licensing Code to provide a uniform and comprehensive body of liquor licensing law. City of Tuscaloosa v. Alabama Retail Ass'n, 466 So. 2d 103 (Ala. 1985).

The passage of the Alcoholic Beverage Licensing Code demonstrates a clear intention on the part of the legislature to revise the law as to the licensing and regulation of all alcoholic beverages. City of Tuscaloosa v. Alabama Retail Ass'n, 466 So. 2d 103 (Ala. 1985).

Table Wine Act is a specific statute. — The Alcoholic Beverage Licensing Code is a comprehensive statute which deals with the licensing of those engaged in transactions involving alcoholic beverages; and, while it is comprehensive, it is, by the very nature of its own broad scope, a general statute. The Table Wine Act (chapter 7 of Title 28), however, is a statute enacted to further a specific legislative intent and deals exclusively with transactions involving table wine; thus, it is a specific statute. City of Tuscaloosa v. Alabama Retail Ass'n, 466 So. 2d 103 (Ala. 1985).

Table Wine Act (ch. 7, T. 28) is neither repealed nor modified, either expressly or impliedly, by provisions of the Alcoholic Beverage Licensing Code. The statutes should be construed in pari materia, and where there exists a conflict between the two, the more specific provisions of the Table Wine Act will control. City of Tuscaloosa v. Alabama Retail Ass'n, 466 So. 2d 103 (Ala. 1985).

The general repealing clause found in § 27 of the act creating the Alcoholic Beverage Licensing Code cannot operate to repeal the Table Wine Act except to repeal by implication any conflicting portions of the Table Wine Act, and it has been consistently held that repeal by implication is never favored by the courts. City of Tuscaloosa v. Alabama Retail Ass'n, 466 So. 2d 103 (Ala. 1985).

Conflict between chapter 3A and chapter 7 not irreconcilable. — Because the "conflict" between chapter 3A and chapter 7 of this title does not rise to the degree of irreconcilability, each statute may be given a reasonable field of operation, which will, when they are construed together, give effect to the legislative intent and purpose of both enactments. Although the specific will control the general, the overall purpose of the general statute will not be thwarted by giving effect to the specific statute. City of Tuscaloosa v. Alabama Retail Ass'n, 466 So. 2d 103 (Ala. 1985).

The emasculation of the dram shop statute by the passage of this chapter was the result of legislative oversight, not legislative wisdom. The legislature may have intended for the A.B.C. board to promulgate regulations governing the sale of alcohol. It does not follow from that premise, however, that it intended to legalize the sale of alcohol to visibly intoxicated persons, to minors, and to insane persons. Buchanan v. Merger Enters., Inc., 463 So. 2d 121 (Ala. 1984).

Regulation of the liquor traffic is subject to the intrinsic police power of the state, a broad and plenary power. Ott v. Everett, 420 So. 2d 258 (Ala. 1982).

Section 28-3A-11 expressly provides that the governing authority of a municipality must give its consent and approval before a retail liquor license can be issued by the ABC board if the premises sought to be licensed are located within a municipality. Such requirement is within the legislature's authority to regulate traffic in liquors which power is considerably broader than the state's power to regulate a business not dealing in alcoholic beverages and a public officer exercising a quasi-judicial function in granting or refusing to grant a permit or license may not be liable for damages absent a corrupt or malicious motive in the exercise of that function. Ott v. Everett, 420 So. 2d 258 (Ala. 1982).

A license to engage in the sale of intoxicants is merely a privilege with no element of property right or vested interest of any kind. Selection of the beneficiaries of a mere privilege may be committed to the discretion of the body created for that purpose. Ott v. Everett, 420 So. 2d 258 (Ala. 1982).

The discretion of a licensing authority is broad regarding issuance or denial of a liquor license. Their discretion, however, is not irreversible if it is shown that the denial of that license is a result of arbitrary action on the part of the licensing authority. Ott v. Everett, 420 So. 2d 258 (Ala. 1982).

§ 28-3A-1. Short title.

This chapter shall be known and may be cited as the "Alcoholic Beverage Licensing Code." (Acts 1980, No. 80-529, p. 806, § 1.)

Cross references. — For definitions applicable to this chapter, see § 28-3-1.

City ordinance cannot restrict what legislature has granted. — The legislature had by act (Act No. 80-529), now codified as this section, given lounge licensees the right to sell for off-premises consumption. It is this construction of the legislative act that allows the appellant to legally do what it does—sell alcoholic beverages for off-premises consumption. It cannot escape the license fee required by not also selling alcoholic beverages for on-premises consumption. The city could not restrict by ordinance what the legislature has granted by legislative act and, where the general act of the legislature conflicts with a pre-existing ordinance, it would repeal it by necessary implication. Berryville Cent., Inc. v. City of Tuscaloosa, 474 So. 2d 688 (Ala. 1985).

Court not bound by administrative agency construction of statute. — Where the administrative agency charged with the responsibility of enforcing this chapter has construed both sections of the original version to allow sale for off-premises consumption, the court is not bound by its construction, but is obligated to give due consideration to its interpretation of statutes it must administer. In this case, the court agrees with its construction. Broadwater v. Blue & Gray Patio Club, 403 So. 2d 209 (Ala. 1981).

This chapter gives lounge licensees, for all intents and purposes, the right to sell for off-premises consumption the same as the club licensees. Broadwater v. Blue & Gray Patio Club, 403 So. 2d 209 (Ala. 1981).

Cited in Merrell v. City of Huntsville, 460 So. 2d 1248 (Ala. 1984); City of Tuscaloosa v.

Alabama Retail Ass'n, 466 So. 2d 103 (Ala. 1985).

§ 28-3A-2. Repealed by Acts 1986, No. 86-212, § 3, which became law without the governor's signature under § 125 of the Constitution on April 1, 1986.

Cross references. — For definitions applicable to this chapter, see now § 28-3-1.

§ 28-3A-3. Authority of board to issue licenses to engage in alcoholic beverage transactions.

(a) Subject to the provisions of this chapter and regulations promulgated thereunder, the board is authorized and empowered to issue and renew licenses to reputable and responsible persons for the following purposes:

(1) To manufacture, brew, distill, ferment, rectify, bottle or compound any or all alcoholic beverages within or for sale within this state.

(2) To import any or all alcoholic beverages manufactured outside the United States of America into this state or for sale or distribution within this state.

(3) To distribute, wholesale or act as jobber for the sale of alcoholic liquor.

(4) To distribute, wholesale or act as jobber for the sale of table wine and beer or either of them, to licensed retailers within the state and others within this state lawfully authorized to sell table wine or beer.

(5) To store or warehouse any or all alcoholic beverages for transshipment inside and outside the state.

(6) To sell and dispense at retail in a lounge, liquor and other alcoholic beverages.

(7) To sell and dispense at retail in an establishment habitually and principally used for the purpose of providing meals for the public, liquor and other alcoholic beverages for on-premises consumption.

(8) To sell liquor and wine at retail for off-premises consumption.

(9) To sell and dispense at retail in a club, liquor and other alcoholic beverages for on-premises consumption.

(10) To sell table wine at retail for off-premises consumption.

(11) To sell table wine at retail for on-premises and off-premises consumption.

(12) To sell beer at retail for on-premises and off-premises consumption.

(13) To sell beer at retail for off-premises consumption.

(14) To sell liquor and other alcoholic beverages at retail by retail common carrier with a passenger capacity of at least 10 people.

(15) To sell any or all alcoholic beverages at retail under special license issued conditioned upon terms and conditions and for the period of time prescribed by the board.

(16) To sell any or all alcoholic beverages at retail under a special event retail license issued for three days upon the terms and conditions prescribed by the board.

Provided, however, that such licenses may not be issued in dry counties where traffic in alcoholic beverages is not authorized by law therein. Provided the restriction of this paragraph shall not apply to the issuance of a renewal of a license under subdivisions (1), (2), (3), (4) and (5) where the county or municipality was wet when the initial license was issued and the county or municipality subsequently votes dry; however, no importer or wholesaler licensee may sell or distribute alcoholic beverages within a dry county (except in a wet municipality therein) or within a dry municipality.

(b) The board is granted discretionary powers in acting upon license applications under the provisions of this chapter.

(c) Licenses issued under this chapter shall, unless revoked or suspended in the manner provided in this chapter, be valid for the license year which shall begin on the first day of October of each year, unless otherwise established by this chapter or by the board. Licenses may be issued at any time during the year. (Acts 1980, No. 80-529, p. 806, § 3; Acts 1985, No. 85-547, p. 800.)

The 1985 amendment, which became law without the governor's signature under § 125 of the Constitution on May 16, 1985, rewrote the second sentence of the last paragraph of subsection (a).

When off-premises beer license may be denied. — An off-premises beer license may be properly denied within the broad discretion which is granted to the ABC board when the proposed location is not fit because of its surroundings. Delta Oil, Inc. v. Potts, 479 So. 2d 1273 (Ala. Civ. App. 1985).

Board's letter of denial of a beer license met minimum requirements of §§ 41-22-15 and 41-22-16 by apprising the applicant of its findings and conclusions denying the application for stated permissible reasons, i.e., that the applicant's establishment for which the beer license was sought was too close to a

school crossing, would be detrimental to the safety of the school children and would create a traffic hazard, and further by noting the opposition which had been voiced to the application. Spivey v. City of Florence, 480 So. 2d 598 (Ala. Civ. App. 1985).

Denial of license upheld. — The ABC board did not arbitrarily and capriciously deny an off-premises beer license to applicant where his store in Fairhope was situated directly across a 50 foot wide street from a church, and in close proximity to a public school and playground. Delta Oil, Inc. v. Potts, 479 So. 2d 1273 (Ala. Civ. App. 1985).

Collateral references. — 48 C.J.S., Intoxicating Liquors, §§ 102, 121, 123, 125, 128.

45 Am. Jur. 2d, Intoxicating Liquors, §§ 124, 125, 127, 128, 130-132, 185.

§ 28-3A-4. License application; fees.

Every applicant for an original license issued under this chapter shall file a written application with the board in such form and containing such information as the board may prescribe, which shall be accompanied by a nonrefundable filing fee of $50.00, and by the appropriate license fee as prescribed by this chapter, together with the amount or amounts of the prescribed license fee or fees, if any, levied or imposed by the county governing body. (Acts 1980, No. 80-529, p. 806, § 4.)

Collateral references. — 48 C.J.S., Intoxicating Liquors, §§ 143-147.

45 Am. Jur. 2d, Intoxicating Liquors, § 153.

Liquor license as subject to execution or attachment. 40 ALR4th 927.

§ 28-3A-5. Issuance and renewal of licenses; penalty for delinquent renewal.

(a) Upon receipt of the application, the proper fees, the bond if required, and upon being satisfied of the truth of the statements in the application and that the applicant is a person of good repute, the board shall grant and issue to applicant the appropriate license entitling the applicant to engage in the alcoholic beverage transactions authorized by such license as set forth in this chapter. All applications for licenses and accompanying statements shall be kept in the office of the board for a period of three years and shall be open for public inspection.

(b) Licenses issued under the provisions of this chapter shall be renewed annually upon the filing of applications, in such form as the board shall prescribe, at least 60 days before the expiration and upon payment to the board of the appropriate license fees, unless the board has good cause for not renewing or reissuing the license. Unless within one month prior to the scheduled date of expiration of such licenses the applicant shall have been notified by the board of objections to the granting thereof signed by persons authorized to do so, and upon payment of the required fees, the board shall issue such renewal of licenses.

(c) Licenses shall become due and payable on or before October first of each year or on the date established by this chapter or the board for the ensuing year, and shall be delinquent if not secured each year by October twentieth or the twentieth day of the first month of the license year established by this chapter or the board. If the license is not secured by October twentieth or by the twentieth day of the first month of the license year established by this chapter or by the board, such person or firm failing or refusing to file application and obtain said license, as provided in this chapter, while continuing to enjoy the privilege allowed under said license, shall be subject to a penalty of 50 percent of the state and county licenses and filing fees, which penalty must be collected at the time of issuance of license or permit, and shall be paid into the license fund of the board. Unless previously revoked, every license issued by the board under this chapter shall expire, and terminate on the thirtieth day of September in the year or on the last day of the month ending the license year established by this chapter or by the board for which the license is issued.

(d) No license shall be issued or renewed by the board until the filing and license fees fixed by this chapter shall have been paid to the board; provided no filing fee is required for renewal. (Acts 1980, No. 80-529, p. 806, § 5.)

Collateral references. — 48 C.J.S., Intoxicating Liquors, §§ 116, 157.   45 Am. Jur. 2d, Intoxicating Liquors, §§ 157, 159, 174-176.

§ 28-3A-6. Manufacturer license; issuance; restrictions on sales; registration of labels; seizure of unregistered goods; monthly reports; daily records; inspections.

(a) Upon applicant's compliance with the provisions of this chapter and the regulations made thereunder, the board shall issue to applicant a manufacturer license which shall authorize the licensee to manufacture or otherwise distill, produce, ferment, brew, bottle, rectify or compound alcoholic beverages within this state or for sale or distribution within this state. No person shall manufacture or otherwise distill, produce, ferment, brew, bottle, rectify or compound alcoholic beverages within this state or for sale or distribution within this state or to the state, the board, or any licensee of the board, unless such person or his authorized representative shall be granted a manufacturer license issued by the board.

(b) No manufacturer licensee shall sell any alcoholic beverages direct to any retailer or for consumption on the premises where sold, nor sell or deliver any such alcoholic beverages in other than original containers approved as to capacity by the board and in accordance with standards of fill prescribed by the U. S. treasury department, nor maintain or operate within the state any place or places, other than the place or places covered by the manufacturer license, where alcoholic beverages are sold or where orders are taken.

(c) Each manufacturer licensee shall be required to file with the board, prior to making any sales in Alabama a list of its labels to be sold in Alabama and shall file with the board its federal certificate of label approvals or its certificates of exemption as required by the U. S. treasury department. All liquors and wines whose labels have not been registered as herein provided for shall be considered contraband and may be seized by the board or its agents, or any peace officer of the state of Alabama without a warrant and said goods shall be delivered to the board and disposed of as provided by law.

(d) All such manufacturer licensees shall be required to mail to the board prior to the twentieth day of each month a consolidated report of all shipments of beer and table wine made to each wholesaler during the preceding month. Such reports shall be in such form and containing such information as the board may prescribe.

(e) Every manufacturer shall keep at his or its principal place of business within the state, daily permanent records which shall show the quantities of raw materials received and used in the manufacture of alcoholic beverages, and the quantities of alcoholic beverages manufactured and stored, the sale of alcoholic beverages, the quantities of alcoholic beverages stored for hire or transported for hire by or for the licensee and the names and addresses of the purchasers or other recipients thereof.

(f) Every place licensed as a manufacturer shall be subject to inspection by members of the board or by persons duly authorized and designated by the board at any and all times of the day or night as they may deem necessary, for the detection of violations of this chapter, of any law, or of the rules and regulations of the board, or for the purpose of ascertaining the correctness of the records required to be kept by the licensees. The books and records of such licensees shall, at all times, be open to inspection by members of the board, or by persons duly authorized and designated by the board. Members of the board and its duly authorized agents shall have the right, without hindrance, to enter any place which is subject to inspection hereunder, or any place where such records are kept for the purpose of making such inspections and making transcripts thereof.

(g) Licenses issued under this section shall, unless revoked in the manner provided in this chapter, be valid for the license year commencing January 1 of each year. (Acts 1980, No. 80-529, p. 806, § 6.)

Collateral references. — 48 C.J.S., Intoxicating Liquors, §§ 39, 99, 104, 203, 205, 209 et seq.

45 Am. Jur. 2d, Intoxicating Liquors, §§ 38, 56, 127, 185, 245, 479-485.

Products liability: alcoholic beverages. 42 ALR4th 253.

§ 28-3A-7. Importer license; issuance; restrictions on sales; registration of labels; seizure of unregistered goods; monthly reports; inspections.

(a) Upon applicant's compliance with the provisions of this chapter and the regulations made thereunder, the board shall issue to applicant an importer license which shall authorize the licensee to import alcoholic beverages manufactured outside the United States of America into this state or for sale or distribution within this state of liquor and wine to the board or the state, and table wine and beer to wholesaler licensees of the board. No person shall import alcoholic beverages manufactured outside the United States into this state or for sale or distribution within this state or to the state, the board or any licensee of the board, unless such person shall be granted an importer license issued by the board.

(b) An importer licensee shall not sell any alcoholic beverages for consumption on the premises where sold; nor, unless issued a wholesale license, sell or deliver to any retailer; nor deliver any such alcoholic beverages in other than original containers approved as to capacity by the board, and in accordance with standards of fill prescribed by the U. S. treasury department; nor maintain or operate within the state any place or places, other than the place or places covered by his or its importer license, where alcoholic beverages are sold or where orders are taken.

(c) Each importer licensee shall be required to file with the board, prior to making any sales in Alabama, a list of its labels to be sold in Alabama and shall file with the board its federal certificate of label approvals or its certificates of exemption as required by the U. S. treasury department. All liquors and wines whose labels have not been registered as herein provided for shall be considered contraband and may be seized by the board or its agents, or any peace officers of the state of Alabama, without a warrant and said goods shall be delivered to the board and disposed of as provided by law.

(d) All such importer licensees shall be required to mail to the board prior to the twentieth day of each month a consolidated report of all shipments of beer and table wine made to each wholesaler during the preceding month and of all shipments of alcoholic beverages received during the preceding month. Such reports shall be in such form and containing such information as the board may prescribe.

(e) The books and records of such licensee shall, at all times, be open to inspection by members of the board, or by persons duly authorized and designated by the board. Members of the board and its duly authorized agents shall have the right, without hindrance, to enter any place which is subject to inspection hereunder, or any place where such records are kept for the purpose of making such inspections and making transcripts thereof.

(f) Licenses issued under this section shall, unless revoked or suspended in the manner provided in this chapter, be valid for the license year commencing January 1 of each year. (Acts 1980, No. 80-529, p. 806, § 7.)

Collateral references. — 48 C.J.S., Intoxicating Liquors, §§ 104, 203, 205, 208.   45 Am. Jur. 2d, Intoxicating Liquors, §§ 55, 56, 128, 185, 479, 482, 483.

§ 28-3A-8. Liquor wholesaler license.

Upon applicant's compliance with the provisions of this chapter and the regulations made thereunder, the board shall issue to applicant a liquor wholesale license which shall authorize the licensee to import and receive shipments of liquor or wine from outside the state from licensed manufacturers and to sell at wholesale or distribute liquor or wine to the board or as authorized by the board except a liquor wholesale licensee may not sell liquor or fortified wine to retail licensees of the board. Sales shall be in original packages or containers as prepared for the market by the manufacturer or bottler. No person shall sell at wholesale or distribute liquor or wine within this state to the board or as authorized by the board unless such person shall be issued a liquor wholesale license by the board. (Acts 1980, No. 80-529, p. 806, § 8.)

Collateral references. — 48 C.J.S., Intoxicating Liquors, § 128.   45 Am. Jur. 2d, Intoxicating Liquors, §§ 38, 127, 128, 245.

§ 28-3A-9. Wholesaler license for beer or table wine.

Upon applicant's compliance with the provisions of this chapter and the regulations made thereunder, the board shall issue to applicant a wholesale license which shall authorize the licensee to import and receive shipments of beer and table wine from outside the state from licensed manufacturers, to purchase beer and table wine from licensed manufacturers or other licensed wholesalers within the state and to sell at wholesale or distribute beer and table wine to all licensees or others within this state lawfully authorized to sell beer and wine within said state, and to export beer and wine from the state. Sales to all authorized persons shall be in original packages or containers as prepared for the market by the manufacturer or bottler. No person shall sell at wholesale or distribute beer or table wine within this state or to licensees of the board unless such person shall be issued a wholesale license by the board. (Acts 1980, No. 80-529, p. 806, § 9.)

Collateral references. — 48 C.J.S., Intoxicating Liquors, § 128.   45 Am. Jur. 2d, Intoxicating Liquors, §§ 38, 127, 128, 245.

§ 28-3A-10. Warehouse license.

Upon applicant's compliance with the provisions of this chapter and the regulations made thereunder, the board shall issue to applicant a warehouse license which will authorize the licensee to receive, store or warehouse alcoholic beverages within the state for transshipment inside and outside the state. No person other than a manufacturer or wholesaler licensee shall receive, store or warehouse alcoholic beverages with the state for transshipment inside and outside the state without first obtaining a warehouse license from the board. (Acts 1980, No. 80-529, p. 806, § 10.)

Collateral references. — 48 C.J.S., Intoxicating Liquors, § 121.

§ 28-3A-11. Lounge retail liquor license; approval of municipality; entertainment; minors.

Upon applicant's compliance with the provisions of this chapter and the regulations made thereunder, the board shall, where the application is accompanied by a certificate from the clerk or proper officer setting out that the applicant has presented his application to the governing authority of the municipality, if the licensed premises is to be located therein, and has obtained its consent and approval, issue a retail liquor license which will authorize the licensee to purchase liquor and wine from the board or as authorized by the board and to purchase table wine, and beer, including draft or keg beer in any county or municipality in which the sale thereof is permitted, from any wholesaler licensee of the board and to sell at retail liquor and wine, dispensed from containers of any size, and beer, including draft or keg beer in any county or municipality in which the sale thereof is permitted, to patrons. A lounge liquor licensee may permit dancing or provide other lawful entertainment on the licensed premises. No person under 19 years of age shall be admitted on the premises of any lounge liquor licensee as a patron or employee, and it shall be unlawful for any such licensee to admit any minor to the premises as a patron or employee. (Acts 1980, No. 80-529, p. 806, § 11.)

A license to engage in the sale of intoxicants is merely a privilege with no element of property right or vested interest of any kind. Selection of the beneficiaries of a mere privilege may be committed to the discretion of the body created for that purpose. Ott v. Everett, 420 So. 2d 258 (Ala. 1982).

State's power to regulate liquor sales is broad. — This section expressly provides that the governing authority of a municipality must give its consent and approval before a retail liquor license can be issued by the ABC board if the premises sought to be licensed are located within a municipality. Such requirement is within the legislature's authority to regulate traffic in liquors which power is considerably broader than the state's power to regulate a business not dealing in alcoholic beverages and a public officer exercising a quasi-judicial function in granting or refusing to grant a permit or license may not be liable for damages absent a corrupt or malicious motive in the exercise of that function. Ott v. Everett, 420 So. 2d 258 (Ala. 1982). State's power to regulate sale of liquor is much broader than its power to regulate an ordinary lawful business. Possession of this broad regulatory power made former § 28-3-133, relating to hotel, restaurant, and club liquor licenses,

constitutional on its face. Black v. Pike County Comm'n, 375 So. 2d 255 (Ala. 1979).

Regulation of the liquor traffic is subject to the intrinsic police power of the state, a broad and plenary power. Ott v. Everett, 420 So. 2d 258 (Ala. 1982).

The discretion of a licensing authority is broad regarding issuance or denial of a liquor license. Their discretion, however, is not irreversible if it is shown that the denial of that license is a result of arbitrary action on the part of the licensing authority. Ott v. Everett, 420 So. 2d 258 (Ala. 1982).

City's arbitrary action with respect to liquor by drink licenses reviewable. — City, which was asserted to have withheld its approval of all applications for licenses for sale of liquor by the drink within city for purpose of keeping city "dry," did not have irrevisable discretion to deny approval of liquor licenses, but, rather, any arbitrary action in that regard was subject to judicial review. Inn of Oxford, Inc. v. City of Oxford, 366 So. 2d 690 (Ala. 1978), decided under former alcoholic beverage law.

Collateral references. — 48 C.J.S., Intoxicating Liquors, §§ 121, 259.

45 Am. Jur. 2d, Intoxicating Liquors, §§ 131, 267, 271, 273.

§ 28-3A-12. Club liquor retail license; approval of municipality.

Upon applicant's compliance with the provisions of this chapter and the regulations made thereunder, the board may, where the application is accompanied by a certificate from the clerk or proper officers setting out that the applicant has presented his application to the governing authority of the municipality, if the licensed premises is to be located therein, and has obtained its consent and approval, issue a club liquor license for a club which will authorize the licensee to purchase liquor and wine from the board or as authorized by the board and to purchase table wine and beer, including draft or keg beer in any county or municipality in which the sale thereof is permitted, from any wholesale licensee of the board and to sell liquor and wine, dispensed from containers of any size, and beer, including draft or keg beer, in any county or municipality in which the sale thereof is permitted, to the members of the club or their guests for on-premises consumption and to sell all of the above for off-premises consumption except on Sunday. (Acts 1980, No. 80-529, p. 806, § 12.)

Constitutionality. — This section does not allow a club retail liquor licensee to sell alcoholic beverages on Sunday for off-premises consumption. Rather than being a prohibitive statute, this section is a beneficial statute since it allows a club liquor retail licensee to sell

alcoholic beverages on Sunday when no other alcoholic beverage licensee may legally sell alcoholic beverages. Thus, this restriction of not allowing alcoholic beverage sales for off-premises consumption on Sunday is a reasonable classification and not a violation of the due process and equal protection clause of the Fourteenth Amendment. Historic Whse., Inc. v. Alabama ABC Bd., 423 So. 2d 211 (Ala. 1982).

State's power to regulate liquor sales is broad. — State's power to regulate sale of liquor is much broader than its power to regulate an ordinary lawful business. Possession of this broad regulatory power made former § 28-3-133, relating to hotel, restaurant, and club liquor licenses, constitutional on its face. Black v. Pike County Comm'n, 375 So. 2d 255 (Ala. 1979).

City's arbitrary action with respect to liquor by drink licenses reviewable. — City, which was asserted to have withheld its approval of all applications for licenses for sale of liquor by the drink within city for purpose of keeping city "dry," did not have irrevisable discretion to deny approval of liquor licenses, but, rather, any arbitrary action in that regard was subject to judicial review. Inn of Oxford, Inc. v. City of Oxford, 366 So.2d 690 (Ala. 1978), decided under former alcoholic beverage law.

Collateral references. — 48 C.J.S., Intoxicating Liquors, § 123.

45 Am. Jur. 2d, Intoxicating Liquors, § 130.

Validity, construction, and effect of "Sunday closing" or "blue" laws — modern status. 10 ALR4th 246.

§ 28-3A-13. Restaurant retail liquor license; approval of municipality.

Upon applicant's compliance with the provisions of this chapter and the regulations made thereunder, the board shall, where the application is accompanied by a certificate from the clerk or proper officer setting out that the applicant has presented his application to the governing authority of the municipality, if the licensed premises is to be located therein, and has obtained its consent and approval issue a restaurant liquor license for a hotel, restaurant, civic center authority or dinner theater which will authorize the licensee to purchase liquor and wine from the board or as authorized by the board and to purchase table wine and beer, including draft or keg beer in any county or municipality in which the sale thereof is permitted, from any wholesale licensee of the board and, in that part of the hotel, restaurant, club or dinner theater set out in the license, to sell liquor and wine, dispensed from containers of any size, and beer, including draft or keg beer, in any county or municipality in which the sale thereof is permitted, to the patrons, guests or members for on-premises consumption in any part of the civic center or in that part of the hotel, restaurant or dinner theater habitually used for serving meals to patrons, guests or members, or other public or private rooms of the building in accordance with the provisions of this chapter and the regulations made thereunder, and where a restaurant located in a hotel, but not operated by the owner of the hotel, is licensed to sell alcoholic beverages in the restaurant, it may also sell alcoholic beverages to guests in private rooms in the hotel. (Acts 1980, No. 80-529, p. 806, § 13.)

State's power to regulate liquor sales is broad. — State's power to regulate sale of liquor is much broader than its power to regulate an ordinary lawful business. Possession of this broad regulatory power made former § 28-3-133, relating to hotel, restaurant, and club liquor licenses, constitutional on its face. Black v. Pike County Comm'n, 375 So. 2d 255 (Ala. 1979).

City's arbitrary action with respect to

liquor by drink licenses reviewable. — City, which was asserted to have withheld its approval of all applications for licenses for sale of liquor by the drink within city for purpose of keeping city "dry," did not have irrevisable discretion to deny approval of liquor licenses, but, rather, any arbitrary action in that regard was subject to judicial review. Inn of Oxford, Inc. v. City of Oxford, 366 So. 2d 690 (Ala. 1978), decided under former alcoholic beverage law.

Collateral references. — 48 C.J.S., Intoxicating Liquors, §§ 121, 124.
45 Am. Jur. 2d, Intoxicating Liquors, § 131.

§ 28-3A-14. Retail table wine license for on-premises and off-premises consumption.

Upon applicant's compliance with the provisions of this chapter and the regulations made thereunder, the board shall issue to applicant a retail table wine license which will authorize the licensee to purchase table wine from the board or from a licensed wholesaler in counties and municipalities where authorized, and to sell at retail, in unopened original containers or dispense from containers of any size, for on-premises consumption in a room or rooms or place on the licensed premises at all times accessible to the use and accommodation of the general public, and in original unopened containers for off-premises consumption, where such use of the proposed location is not, at the time of the original application, prohibited by a valid zoning ordinance or other ordinance in the valid exercise of police power by the governing body of the municipality or county in which the outlet is located. (Acts 1980, No. 80-529, p. 806, § 14.)

Collateral references. — 48 C.J.S., Intoxicating Liquors, §§ 121, 123, 124.   45 Am. Jur. 2d, Intoxicating Liquors, §§ 130, 131.

§ 28-3A-15. Retail table wine license for off-premises consumption.

Upon applicant's compliance with the provisions of this chapter and the regulations made thereunder, in counties and municipalities where authorized, the board shall issue a retail table wine license for any retail outlet, which license will authorize the licensee to purchase table wine in packaged form from the board, or from licensed wholesalers and to sell such table wines in original unopened containers at retail for off-premises consumption, where such use of the proposed location of the retail outlet is not, at the time of original application, prohibited by a valid zoning ordinance or other ordinance in the valid exercise of police power by the governing body of the municipality or county in which the retail outlet is located. (Acts 1980, No. 80-529, p. 806, § 15.)

Collateral references. — 48 C.J.S., Intoxicating Liquors, § 121.   45 Am. Jur. 2d, Intoxicating Liquors, §§ 124, 125.

§ 28-3A-16. Retail beer license for on-premises and off-premises consumption.

Upon applicant's compliance with the provisions of this chapter and the regulations made thereunder, the board shall issue to applicant a retail beer license which will authorize the licensee to purchase beer, including draft beer in counties or municipalities where the sale thereof is permitted, from a licensed wholesaler and to sell at retail for on-premises consumption in a room or rooms or place on the licensed premises at all times accessible to the use and accommodation of the general public, and in original unopened containers for off-premises consumption, where such use of the proposed location is not, at the time of the original application, prohibited by a valid zoning ordinance or other ordinance in the valid exercise of police power by the governing body of the municipality or county in which the outlet is located. (Acts 1980, No. 80-529, p. 806, § 16.)

Collateral references. — 48 C.J.S., Intoxicating Liquors, §§ 121, 123, 124.

45 Am. Jur. 2d, Intoxicating Liquors, §§ 130, 131.

§ 28-3A-17. Retail beer license for off-premises consumption.

Upon applicant's compliance with the provisions of this chapter and the regulations made thereunder, the board shall issue to applicant a retail beer license which will authorize the licensee to purchase beer, including draft beer in counties or municipalities where the sale thereof is permitted, in original unopened containers from licensed wholesalers and to sell such beer in packaged form at retail for off-premises consumption, where such use of the proposed location is not, at the time of the original application, prohibited by a valid zoning ordinance or other ordinance in the valid exercise of police power by the governing body of the municipality or county in which the retail outlet is located. (Acts 1980, No. 80-529, p. 806, § 17.)

A license to sell intoxicants is a privilege, not a property right or vested interest. Therefore, the ABC board, within its broad discretion, may properly deny an off-premises beer license when "the proposed location is improper by reason of location and its surroundings." Mims v. Russell Petroleum Corp., 473 So. 2d 507 (Ala. Civ. App. 1985).

The ABC board is specifically vested with authority to grant and deny licenses for sale of beer for off-premises consumption. The ABC board has a broad discretion in the granting or denial of such licenses. Mims v. Russell Petroleum Corp., 473 So. 2d 507 (Ala. Civ. App. 1985).

An off-premises beer license may be properly denied within the broad discretion which is granted to the ABC board when the proposed location is not fit because of its location and its surroundings. Delta Oil, Inc. v. Potts, 479 So. 2d 1273 (Ala. Civ. App. 1985).

Discretion of board in granting license in near proximity to church, school, etc. — To say that a license must be granted to a particular licensee within a certain number of feet of a school, church, or other eleemosynary institution because there are other licensees in the same town, or another town, in a "near proximity," i.e., certain number of feet, of such institution, thwarts the discretion of the ABC board. Mims v. Russell Petroleum Corp., 473 So. 2d 507 (Ala. Civ. App. 1985).

Denial of license upheld. — The ABC board did not arbitrarily and capriciously deny an off-premises beer license to applicant where store in Fairhope was situated directly across a 50 foot wide street from a church, and in close proximity to a public school and playground. Delta Oil, Inc. v. Potts, 479 So. 2d 1273 (Ala. Civ. App. 1985).

Collateral references. — 48 C.J.S., Intoxicating Liquors, § 121.

45 Am. Jur. 2d, Intoxicating Liquors, §§ 125, 130.

§ 28-3A-18. Retail common carrier liquor license.

Upon applicant's compliance with the provisions of this chapter and the regulations made thereunder, the board shall issue a retail common carrier liquor license for a railroad, airline, bus line, ship line, vessel or other common carrier entity operating passenger vehicles with a passenger seating capacity of at least 10 people, which will authorize the licensee to sell, whenever operated in Alabama, alcoholic beverages, liquor, wine and beer, including draft beer, to passengers for consumption while aboard such licensee. No railroad, airline, bus line, ship line, vessel or common carrier entity shall sell alcoholic beverages to passengers for consumption within this state without first obtaining a retail common carrier liquor license from the board.

Sales within Alabama of alcoholic beverages by retail common carrier liquor licensees shall be made in accordance with and shall be subject to the provisions of this chapter and regulations promulgated thereunder. (Acts 1980, No. 80-529, p. 806, § 18.)

Collateral references. — 48 C.J.S., Intoxicating Liquors, § 121.

45 Am. Jur. 2d, Intoxicating Liquors, § 132.

§ 28-3A-19. Special retail license.

Upon applicant's compliance with the provisions of this chapter and the regulations made thereunder, the board shall issue a special retail license in wet counties for a state park, racing commission, fair authority, airport authority, or civic center authority, or the franchises or concessionaire of such park, commission or authority, and may, in its discretion, issue a special retail license to any other valid responsible organization of good reputation for such period of time not to exceed one year and upon such terms and conditions as the board shall prescribe, which will authorize the licensee to purchase, where the retail sale thereof is authorized by the board, liquor and wine from the board or as authorized by the board and table wine and beer from any wholesale licensee of the board and to sell at retail and dispense such alcoholic beverages as are authorized by the board at such locations authorized by the board upon such terms and conditions as prescribed by the board. Provided, however, no sale of alcoholic beverages shall be permitted on any Sunday after the hour of 2:00 A.M. (Acts 1980, No. 80-529, p. 806, § 19.)

Collateral references. — 48 C.J.S., Intoxicating Liquors, §§ 39, 121, 123, 206, 207.

45 Am. Jur. 2d, Intoxicating Liquors, §§ 125, 130, 276, 279.

§ 28-3A-20. Special events retail license.

Upon applicant's compliance with the provisions of this chapter and the regulations made thereunder, and upon application made on a form provided by the board at least 120 days in advance of the event for which a license is granted, the board shall issue a special events license for a valid, responsible organization of good reputation, for a period not to exceed seven days, and upon such terms and conditions as the board may prescribe, which will authorize the licensee to purchase, where the retail sale thereof is authorized by the board, liquor and wine from the board or as authorized by the board and table wine and beer from any wholesale licensee of the board and to sell at retail and dispense such alcoholic beverages as are authorized by the board to the patrons, guests or members of the organization at such locations or areas as shall be authorized by the board upon such terms and conditions as prescribed by the board. Provided, however, no sale of alcoholic beverages shall be permitted on any Sunday after the hour of 2:00 A.M. (Acts 1980, No. 80-529, p. 806, § 20.)

§ 28-3A-21. License fees for licenses issued by the board; local license taxes.

(a) The following annual license fees are levied and prescribed for licenses issued and renewed by the board pursuant to the authority contained in this chapter:

(1) Manufacturer license, license fee of $500.00.

(2) Importer license, license fee of $500.00.

(3) Liquor wholesale license, license fee of $500.00.

(4) Wholesaler license, beer license fee of $500.00 or wine license fee of $550.00; license fee for beer and wine of $750.00; plus $200.00 for each warehouse in addition to the principal warehouse.

(5) Warehouse license, license fee of $200.00.

(6) Lounge retail liquor license, license fee of $300.00.

(7) Restaurant retail liquor license, license fee of $300.00.

(8) Club liquor license, Class I license fee of $300.00, Class II license fee of $750.00.

(9) Retail table wine license for off-premises consumption, license fee of $150.00.

(10) Retail table wine license for on-premises and off-premises consumption, license fee of $150.00.

(11) Retail beer license for on-premises and off-premises consumption, license fee of $150.00.

(12) Retail beer license for off-premises consumption, license fee of $100.00.

(13) Retail common carrier liquor license, license fee of $150.00 for each railroad, airline, bus line, ship line, vessel or other common carrier entity with a vehicle passenger capacity of at least 10 people.

(14) Special retail license, license fee of $100.00 for 30 days or less; license fee of $250.00 for more than 30 days.

(15) Special events retail license, license fee of $150.00.

(b) The license fees levied and fixed by this section shall be paid before the license is issued or renewed.

(c) In addition to the foregoing filing fee and license taxes or fees, any county or municipality in which the sale of alcoholic beverages is permitted shall be authorized to fix and levy privileges or license taxes on any of the foregoing licenses located or operated therein, conditioned on a permit or license being issued by the board.

(d) No county or municipality shall have any authority to levy a license or tax of any nature on any liquor store. (Acts 1980, No. 80-529, p. 806, § 21; Acts 1981, No. 81-701, p. 1178, § 2.)

Collateral references. — 48 C.J.S., Intoxicating Liquors, §§ 181-190.

45 Am. Jur. 2d, Intoxicating Liquors, § 203 et seq.

§ 28-3A-22. Disposition of proceeds of filing fees and license taxes.

The revenue derived from filing fees, license fees or taxes levied under section 28-3A-4 and section 28-3A-21 shall be deposited upon receipt by the board in the state treasury to the credit of the beer tax and license fund and each month's receipts shall be distributed to the state general fund no later than the end of the following month.

County license fees authorized by and levied pursuant to section 28-3A-21 shall be collected by the board and the proceeds of such collections shall be paid by the board into the state treasury to the credit of the county levying said license fee and paid semiannually to the governing body of said county. (Acts 1980, No. 80-529, p. 806, § 22.)

Collateral references. — 48 C.J.S., Intoxicating Liquors, § 188.
45 Am. Jur. 2d, Intoxicating Liquors, § 217.

§ 28-3A-23. Regulation of grant of licenses; to whom issued; display thereof; local approval of retail licenses; separate retail licenses; place of retail sales; beer and wine containers; place of sale of draft or keg beer and special permits therefor; place of wholesale operations; transfer of licenses; effect of insolvency of licensee.

(a) No license prescribed in this Code shall be issued or renewed until the provisions of this Code have been complied with and the filing and license fees other than those levied by a municipality are paid to the board.

(b) Licenses shall be granted and issued by the board only to reputable individuals who are citizens of the United States or to associations whose members are reputable individuals who are citizens of the United States, or to reputable corporations organized under the laws of the state of Alabama or duly qualified thereunder to do business in Alabama, or, in the case of manufacturers, duly registered under the laws of Alabama, and then only when it appears that all officers and directors of the corporation are reputable individuals and are citizens of the United States, and that at least 51 percent of the capital stock is actually owned by individuals who are citizens of the United States; provided, the residence or citizenship requirements of this subsection do not apply to manufacturer licensees.

(c) Every license issued under this Code shall be constantly and conspicuously displayed on the licensed premises.

(d) Each retail liquor license application must be approved by the governing authority of the municipality if the retailer is located in a municipality, or by the county commission if the retailer is located in the county and outside the limits of the municipality before the board shall have authority to grant the license.

(e) Any retailer may be granted licenses to maintain, operate or conduct any number of places for the sale of alcoholic beverages, but a separate license must be secured for each place where alcoholic beverages are sold. No retail license issued under this Code shall be used for more than one premise, nor for separate types of operation on the same premise. Each premise must have a separate retail license. Where more than one retail operation is located within the same building, each such operation under a separate or different ownership is required to obtain a separate retail license; and where more than one type of retail operation located within the same building is operated by the same licensee, such licensee must have a license for each type of retail operation. Provided, there shall be no licenses issued by the board for the sale of liquor, beer or wine by rolling stores.

(f) No retailer shall sell any alcoholic beverages for consumption on the licensed premises except in a room or rooms or place on the licensed premises at all times accessible to the use and accommodation of the general public; but this section shall not be interpreted to prevent a hotel or club licensee from selling such beverages in any room of such hotel or club house occupied by a bona fide registered guest or member or private party entitled to purchase the same.

(g) All beer, except draft or keg beer, sold by retailers must be sold or dispensed in bottles, cans or other containers not to exceed one pint or 16 ounces. All wine sold by retailers for off-premise consumption must be sold or dispensed in bottles or other containers in accordance with the standards of fill specified in the then effective standards of fill for wine prescribed by the U. S. treasury department.

(h) Draft or keg beer may be sold or dispensed within this state within those counties in which and in the manner in which the sale of draft or keg beer was authorized by law on September 30, 1980 or in which the sale of draft or keg beer is hereafter authorized by law; provided in rural communities with a predominantly foreign population, after the payment of the tax imposed by this title, draft or keg beer may be sold or dispensed by special permit from the board, when, in the judgment of the board, the use and consumption of draft or keg beer is in accordance with the habit and customs of the people of any such rural community; provided further, the board may, in its discretion, grant to any civic center authority or its franchisee or concessionaire, to which the board may have issued or may simultaneously issue a retail license under the provisions of this Code, a revocable temporary permit to sell or dispense in any part of its civic center, for consumption therein, draft or keg beer. Either such permit shall be promptly revoked by the board if, in its judgment, the same tends to create intemperance or is prejudicial to the welfare, health, peace, temperance and safety of the people of the community or of the state.

(i) No wholesaler shall maintain or operate any place where sales are made other than that for which the wholesale license is granted; provided, however, a wholesaler may be licensed to sell and distribute liquor, wine and beer. No wholesaler shall maintain any place for the storage of liquor, wine or beer unless the same has been approved by the board. No wholesaler license shall be issued for any premises in any part of which there is operated any retail license for the sale of alcoholic beverages.

(j) Licenses issued under this Code may not be assigned. The board is hereby authorized to transfer any license from one person to another, or from one place to another within the same governing jurisdiction, or both, as the board may determine; but no transfers shall be made to a person who would not have been eligible to receive the license originally, nor for the transaction of business at a place for which the license could not originally have been issued lawfully.

(k) Every applicant for a transfer of a license shall file a written application with the board within such time as the board shall fix in its regulations. Whenever any license is transferred, there shall be collected a filing fee of $50.00, to be paid to the board, and the board shall pay such fee into the state treasury to the credit of the beer tax and license fund of the board.

(l) In the event that any person to whom a license shall have been issued under the terms of this Code shall become insolvent, make an assignment for the benefit of creditors, be adjudicated a bankrupt by either voluntary or involuntary action, the license of such person shall immediately terminate and be cancelled without any action on the part of the board, and there shall be no refund made, or credit given, for the unused portion of the license fee for the remainder of the license year for which said license was granted. Thereafter no license shall be issued by the board for the premises, wherein said license was conducted, to any assignee, committee, trustee, receiver or successor of such licensee until a hearing has been held by the board as in the case of a new application for license. In all such cases, the board shall have the sole and final discretion as to the propriety of the issuance of a license for such premises, and the time it shall issue, and the period for which it shall be issued, and shall have the further power to impose conditions under which said licensed premises shall be conducted. (Acts 1980, No. 80-529, p. 806, § 23; Acts 1981, No. 81-808, p. 1434.)

State's power to regulate liquor sales is broad. — State's power to regulate sale of liquor is much broader than its power to regulate an ordinary lawful business. Possession of this broad regulatory power made former § 28-3-133, relating to hotel, restaurant and club liquor licenses, constitutional on its face. Black v. Pike County Comm'n, 375 So. 2d 255 (Ala. 1979).

Decisions of county commissions in denying liquor licenses are subject to judicial review and such commissions do not have irreversible discretion to deny approval. If the applicant can prove the commission acted arbitrarily then its decision can be reversed; however, the burden of proof is on the applicant. Black v. Pike County Comm'n, 375 So. 2d 255 (Ala. 1979), decided under former § 28-3-133, relating to hotel, club, and restaurant liquor licenses.

As is city's arbitrary action with respect to liquor by drink licenses. — City, which was asserted to have withheld its approval of all applications for licenses for sale of liquor by the drink within city for purpose of keeping city "dry," did not have irreversible discretion to deny approval of liquor licenses, but, rather, any arbitrary action in that regard was subject to judicial review. Inn of Oxford, Inc. v. City of Oxford, 366 So. 2d 690 (Ala. 1978), (decided under former alcoholic beverage law).

Collateral references. — 48 C.J.S., Intoxicating Liquors, §§ 39, 51, 53, 100, 101, 109, 114, 128, 130, 135, 136, 138, 174-180, 195, 209, 214-285.

45 Am. Jur. 2d, Intoxicating Liquors, §§ 78, 118, 123, 137, 139, 148, 177-194, 313 et seq.

Liquor license as subject to execution or attachment. 40 ALR4th 927.

§ 28-3A-24. Suspension or revocation of licenses; appointment of hearing commission; notice, hearing and findings; fines.

(a) The board shall have full and final authority as to the suspension or revocation of any license issued under this chapter and to levy a fine against a licensee in lieu of such suspension or revocation. The board shall have the full right and authority to suspend any retail license issued by it for any reason which it may deem sufficient and proper.

Provided, however, the board may appoint a hearing commission of not less than three members to hear and decide all contested applications of licenses under this chapter, and hear and decide all charges against any licensee for violation of this chapter, the law or the regulations of the board and shall have the power and authority to revoke or suspend for cause licenses and permits, or to fine licensees provided in this chapter. Provided, no member of the hearing commission shall participate in the hearing or disposition of any application for license or charge against a licensee if he has an interest therein or he was involved in the investigation.

(b) The board or a hearing commission appointed by the board, upon sufficient cause being shown or proof being made that any licensee holding a license issued by the board, or any partners, members, officers, or directors of the licensee has or have violated any of the laws of this state or regulations of the board relating to the manufacture, sale, possession or transportation of alcoholic beverages, or where the licensed premises has been conducted in a manner prejudicial to the welfare, health, peace, temperance and safety of the people of the community or of the state, may upon due notice and proper hearing being given to the person so licensed, suspend or revoke the license issued by the board. In all such cases where the board or hearing commission shall suspend or revoke a license, it shall set forth its findings of fact, the evidence from which such findings of fact are made, and the reasons upon which its actions are based.

(c) When, in the opinion of the board or hearing commission, a fine is deemed more appropriate than suspending or revoking a license, the board or hearing commission is authorized to fine the licensee for any cause that could result in suspension or revocation. Such fines may not exceed the sum of $1,000.00. The licensee must remit the fine to the administrator within one week of the day that such fine is levied. Failure to pay the fine within this period shall result in an automatic suspension of the license until such fine is paid. All fines collected by the board shall be paid by the administrator into the treasury of the state and credited to the general fund.

(d) The maximum length of suspension of a license under these provisions shall be one year, and any licensee whose license is suspended by the board or hearing commission shall be, at the discretion of the board or hearing commission, ineligible to have any license under this chapter until the expiration or removal of the suspension. Any licensee whose license is revoked by the hearing commission or the board shall be, at the discretion of the board or hearing commission, ineligible to have any license under this chapter until the expiration of one year from the date such license is revoked. The board or hearing commission is hereby granted broad discretionary powers in exercising its authority under this section. (Acts 1980, No. 80-529, p. 806, § 24.)

Collateral references. — Tavernkeeper's liability to patron for third person's assault. 43 ALR4th 281.

§ 28-3A-25. Unlawful acts and offenses; penalties.

(a) It shall be unlawful:

(1) For any manufacturer, importer or wholesaler, or the servants, agents or employees of the same, to sell, trade or barter in alcoholic beverages between the hours of nine o'clock P.M. of any Saturday and two o'clock A.M. of the following Monday.

(2) For any wholesaler or the servants, agents or employees of the same to sell alcoholic beverages, to other than wholesale or retail licensees or others within this state lawfully authorized to sell alcoholic beverages or to sell for export.

(3) For any licensee or the board either directly or by the servants, agents or employees of the same, or for any servant, agent, or employee of the same, to sell, deliver, furnish or give away alcoholic beverages to any minor, or to permit any minor to drink or consume any alcoholic beverages on licensee's premises.

(4) For any person to consume alcoholic beverages on the premises of any state liquor store or any off-premises licensee, or to allow alcoholic beverages to be consumed on the premises of any state liquor store or any off-premises licensee.

(5) For any licensee to fail to keep for a period of at least three years, complete and truthful records covering the operation of his license and

particularly showing the date of all purchases of alcoholic beverages, the actual price paid therefor and the name of the vendor, or to refuse the board or any authorized employee of the board access thereto or the opportunity to make copies of the same when the request is made during business hours.

(6) For any licensee or the servants, agents or employees of the same to refuse the board, any of its authorized employees or any duly commissioned law enforcement officer the right to completely inspect the entire licensed premises at any time during which the premises are open for the transaction of business.

(7) For any licensee or the servants, agents or employees of the same to be directly or indirectly employed by any other licensee engaged in the manufacture, storage, transportation or sale of alcoholic beverages.

(8) For any person to knowingly sell any alcoholic beverages to any person engaged in the business of illegally selling alcoholic beverages.

(9) For any person to manufacture, transport or import alcoholic beverages into this state, except in accordance with the reasonable rules and regulations of the board. Provided, however, that this provision shall not be construed to prohibit the transportation of alcoholic beverages through the state or any dry county and not for delivery therein if such transportation is done in accordance with the reasonable rules and regulations of the board.

(10) For any person to fortify, adulterate, contaminate or in any wise change the character or purity of alcoholic beverages from that as originally marketed by the manufacturer, except for a retail licensee on order from a customer to mix a chaser or other ingredients necessary to prepare a cocktail or mixed drink for on-premises consumption.

(11) For any person licensed to sell alcoholic beverages to offer to give any thing of value as a premium for the return of caps, stoppers, corks, stamps or labels taken from any bottle, case, barrel or package containing such alcoholic beverages, or to offer to give any thing of value as a premium or present to induce the purchase of such alcoholic beverages or for any other purpose whatsoever in connection with the sale of such alcoholic beverages. Provided, however, this provision shall not apply to the return of any moneys specifically deposited for the return of the original containers to the owners thereof.

(12) For any licensee or transporter for hire, servant, agent or employee of the same, to transport any alcoholic beverages except in the original container, and for any transporter for hire to transport any alcoholic beverages within the state, unless such transporter shall hold a permit issued by the board.

(13) For any manufacturer, importer or wholesaler, servant, agent or employee of the same, to deliver any alcoholic beverages, excepting in vehicles bearing the name and address and permit number of such manufacturer, importer or wholesaler painted or affixed on each side of such vehicle in letters no smaller than four inches in height.

(14) For any person to sell alcoholic beverages within any dry county or county where the electors have voted against such sales, except in wet municipalities or as authorized by section 28-3A-18.

(15) For any person, firm, corporation, partnership or association of persons as such terms are defined in section 28-3-1, including any civic center authority, racing commission, fair authority, airport authority, public or quasi-public board, agency or commission, any agent thereof, or otherwise, who has not been licensed to do so under the appropriate provisions of this chapter to sell, offer for sale or have in possession for sale, any alcoholic beverages. Any alcoholic beverages so possessed, maintained, or kept shall be contraband and subject to condemnation and confiscation as provided by law.

(16) For any manufacturer, distiller, producer, importer or distributor of alcoholic beverages to employ and maintain any person not its full-time bona fide employee as its resident sales agent, broker or other like representative, for the purpose of promoting a sale, purchase or acquisition of alcoholic beverages to or by the state or the board, or for any person not a full-time bona fide employee to act as such agent, broker or representative of any manufacturer, distributor, producer, importer or distiller for that purpose.

(17) For any person to sell, give away, or otherwise dispose of taxable alcoholic beverages within this state on which the required taxes have not been paid as required by law.

(18) For any wholesaler or retailer, or the servant, agent or employee of the same, to sell, distribute, deliver or to receive or store for sale or distribution within this state any alcoholic beverages unless there first has been issued by the board a manufacturer's license to the manufacturer of such alcoholic beverages or its designated representative or an importer license to the importer of such alcoholic beverages.

(19) For a minor to attempt to purchase, to purchase, consume, possess or to transport any alcoholic beverages within the state; provided, however, it shall not be unlawful for a minor employee of a wholesale licensee or an off-premises retail licensee of the board to handle, transport or sell any beer or table wine if such minor is acting within the line and scope of his employment while so acting. There must be an adult licensee, servant, agent or employee of the same present at all times a licensed establishment is open for business.

(20) For any person, except where authorized by a local act or general act of local application, to buy, give away, sell, or serve for consumption on or off the premises, or drink or consume any alcoholic beverages in any cafe, lunchroom, restaurant, hotel dining room, or other public place on Sunday after the hour of two o'clock A.M.

(21) Except where authorized by a local act or general act of local application, for the proprietor, keeper or operator of any cafe, lunchroom, restaurant, hotel dining room, or other public place to knowingly permit any person to give away, sell, or serve for consumption on or off the premises, or drink or consume any alcoholic beverages on the premises of such cafe, lunchroom, restaurant, hotel dining room, or other public place on Sunday after the hour of two o'clock A.M.

(b) (1) Any violation of subdivisions (1) through (18) of subsection (a) of this section shall be a misdemeanor punishable by a fine of not less than $100.00 nor more than $1,000.00, to which, at the discretion of the court or judge trying the case, may be added imprisonment in the county jail or at hard labor for the county for not more than six months for the first conviction; and, on the second conviction of a violation of said subdivisions, the offense shall, in addition to a fine within the limits abovenamed, be punishable by imprisonment or at hard labor for the county for not less than three months nor more than six months to be imposed by the court or judge trying the case; and, on the third conviction and every subsequent conviction of a violation of said subdivisions, the offense shall, in addition to a fine within the limits abovenamed, be punishable by imprisonment or at hard labor for the county for not less than six months nor more than 12 months.

(2) Any violation of any of subdivisions (19), (20), and (21) of subsection (a) of this section shall be a misdemeanor punishable by a fine of not less than $50.00 nor more than $500.00, to which, at the discretion of the court or judge trying the case, may be added imprisonment in the county jail or at hard labor for the county for not more than three months. (Acts 1980, No. 80-529, p. 806, § 25; Acts 1984, No. 84-469, p. 1084; Acts 1986, No. 86-563, § 1.)

The 1986 amendment, effective April 30, 1986, rewrote this section, substituting references to alcoholic beverages for references to beer and wine, inserting references to servants, agents, employees and importers, and making additional changes.

Hours of sale. — Legislature has acted to prohibit sales of alcoholic beverages only at certain times; promulgation of any other regulations regarding hours of sale is left to Alabama alcoholic beverage control board. Gadsden Motel Co. v. City of Attalla, 378 So. 2d 705 (Ala. 1979), (decided under former § 28-3-260.)

A city has authority to regulate hours of sale of alcoholic beverages, as long as the hours of sale are reasonable. Gadsden Motel Co. v. City of Attalla, 378 So. 2d 705 (Ala. 1979), (decided under § 11-45-1 and former § 28-3-260.)

Principle of dram shop liability effectuated by common law negligence action. — Legislatively created principles of dram shop liability, not fully implemented by the acts themselves, can be effectuated by a common law negligence action. Under the common law doctrine of respondeat superior, a principal is liable for the negligence of his agents committed within the scope of their employment. Thus, the summary judgment granted by the trial court in favor of a licensee, on grounds that the alcoholic beverages were sold by his employee rather than the licensee himself, was reversed. Putman v. Cromwell, 475 So. 2d 524 (Ala. 1985) (decided prior to amendment of § 28-3A-25 by Acts No. 84-469).

Cited in Historic Whse., Inc. v. Alabama ABC Bd., 423 So. 2d 211 (Ala. 1982).

Collateral references. — Criminal liability of member or agent of private club or association, or of owner or lessor of its premises, for violation of state or local liquor or gambling laws thereon. 98 ALR3d 694.

Validity and construction of statute or ordinance making it offense to have possession of open or unsealed alcoholic beverage in public place. 39 ALR4th 668.

§ 28-3A-26. Revocation of license or permit upon second or subsequent conviction.

Any person who has been found guilty of violating any of the provisions of this chapter and who, after being punished by fine, penalty, assessment or imprisonment shall be guilty of a second or subsequent violation of this chapter, shall upon being found guilty of such second or subsequent offense, have the license or permit as provided in this chapter revoked by the board, and no further license or permit shall be issued or granted to such person for a period of one year from the date the license or permit shall have been revoked. (Acts 1980, No. 80-529, p. 806, § 26.)

Collateral references. — 48 C.J.S., Intoxicating Liquors, § 175.

45 Am. Jur. 2d, Intoxicating Liquors, §§ 150, 187, 190.

Tavernkeeper's liability to patron for third person's assault. 43 ALR4th 281.

CHAPTER 4.

REGULATION AND CONTROL OF ALCOHOLIC BEVERAGES IN DRY COUNTIES AND DRY MUNICIPALITIES.

Article 1.

General Provisions.

Sec.
28-4-1. Definitions.
28-4-2. Unauthorized possession, sale, delivery, use, etc., of wine or alcohol generally.
28-4-3. Applicability of laws as to possession, transportation or delivery of prohibited liquors to possession or receipt of wine, pure alcohol, etc., for sacramental purposes, domestic use, etc., generally.
28-4-4. Applicability of chapter.
28-4-5. Applicability to dry municipalities.

Article 2.

Manufacture, Sale, Offer for Sale, Possession, Distribution, etc., of Prohibited Liquors and Beverages.

28-4-20. Sale, offer for sale, possession, barter, exchange, etc., of prohibited liquors and beverages.
28-4-21. Penalties for violations of section 28-4-20.
28-4-22. Conduct of business of brewer, rectifier of spirits or retail or wholesale dealer in liquors or malt liquors.
28-4-23. Keeping, etc., of prohibited liquors and beverages in lockers, rooms, etc., of social clubs, etc.; duty of officers of such clubs, etc., to prevent violations of section.
28-4-24. Distillation or manufacture of prohibited liquors and beverages.
28-4-25. Allowance of reward to sheriff or other person furnishing evidence to support conviction for violation of section 28-4-24.
28-4-26. Sale, barter, exchange, etc., of prohibited liquors or beverages by person concealing self in house, room, etc.
28-4-27. Enforcement of section 28-4-26.
28-4-28. Storage, etc., of prohibited liquors or beverages by person, etc., engaged in business of selling beverages.
28-4-29. Solicitation or receipt of order for prohibited liquors or beverages.
28-4-30. Punishment of agents or assisting

Sec.
friends of buyers or sellers of prohibited liquors and beverages.
28-4-31. Exhibition of signs containing names of prohibited liquors or beverages or employment of certain words in designating business by dealers in beverages; use of evidence thereof in prosecutions against dealers for sale, offer for sale, etc., of prohibited liquors and beverages.

Article 3.

Manufacture, Possession, Allowance of Operation by Another, etc., of Still, etc., for Manufacture of Prohibited Liquors or Beverages.

28-4-50. Manufacture, sale, possession, etc., of still, etc., for manufacture of prohibited liquors or beverages.
28-4-51. Unexplained possession of part or parts of still, etc., deemed prima facie evidence of violation of section 28-4-50.
28-4-52. Penalty for violations of section 28-4-50.
28-4-53. Possession of still, etc., by sheriff, etc., enforcing law not deemed violation of section 28-4-50.
28-4-54. Allowance of reward to sheriff, etc., furnishing evidence to support convictions for violations of section 28-4-50.
28-4-55. Allowance, etc., of operation, etc., of still, etc., upon premises by another.

Article 4.

Maintenance, etc., of Unlawful Drinking Places.

28-4-70. Prohibited.
28-4-71. Unlawful drinking places deemed common nuisances; abatement thereof.
28-4-72. Forfeiture of charters of clubs or incorporated associations violating provisions of sections 28-4-70 or 28-4-71.
28-4-73. Sufficiency of charges in informations, indictments, etc.; admissibility of evidence.

727

Article 5.

Renting or Permitting Use of Premises for Sale, Manufacture, etc., of Prohibited Liquors or Beverages.

Sec.
28-4-90. Prohibited.
28-4-91. Forfeiture of rights of lessee under lease or rent contract.
28-4-92. Keeping of prohibited liquors or beverages in building not used exclusively for dwelling deemed prima facie evidence of possession for sale.
28-4-93. Delivery of prohibited liquors or beverages to stores, shops, dwellings, etc., from which sale prohibited deemed prima facie evidence of sale, etc.

Article 6.

Transportation, Delivery and Receipt Generally of Prohibited Liquors and Beverages.

28-4-110. Carriage, delivery, etc., into state by common carrier, etc., of prohibited liquors and beverages generally.
28-4-111. Receipt or acceptance from common carrier, etc., of prohibited liquors or beverages generally.
28-4-112. Receipt, etc., of prohibited liquors and beverages for storage, distribution, etc., for another.
28-4-113. Acceptance for or shipment, transportation, delivery, etc., of prohibited liquors or beverages from point to point or along public streets or highways within state.
28-4-114. Transportation and delivery of prohibited liquors and beverages C.O.D.
28-4-115. Transportation of prohibited liquors or beverages in quantities of five gallons or more.
28-4-116. Conduct of business of delivering, transporting, storing or warehousing prohibited liquors and beverages by transfer, warehouse, etc., companies; forfeiture of charter of corporations violating provisions of section.
28-4-117. Procedure for shipment, delivery, etc., of alcohol and wine to persons for sacramental or nonbeverage use — Preparation of affidavit by person desiring to receive shipment; copy of affidavit to be attached to container in which wine or alcohol shipped.

Sec.
28-4-118. Same — Maintenance of record of delivery by carrier generally; certificate to be filed with alcoholic beverage control board stating name of receiver, quantity and character of wine or alcohol, purposes for which received, etc.; inspection of books and records of carrier generally.
28-4-119. Same — Labeling of packages or containers of wine or alcohol for sacramental use.
28-4-120. Transportation from another state, foreign country, etc., or delivery within state of liquors intended to be used in violation of laws of state.
28-4-121. Delivery from another state, etc., of liquors consigned to fictitious person, firm, etc., or person, firm, etc., under fictitious name.
28-4-122. Giving of order for receipt, etc., of liquors consigned from another state, etc., to another person by consignee.
28-4-123. Acceptance of delivery from common carrier, etc., of liquors from another state, etc., with intent to use, etc., same in violation of laws of state.
28-4-124. Delivery by common carrier, etc., of liquors from another state, etc., to person, etc., other than consignee without written order of consignee therefor.
28-4-125. Delivery by common carrier, etc., to minor of liquors from another state, etc.
28-4-126. Presentation, collection, etc., by bank, etc., of draft, bill of exchange, etc., attached to, connected with, etc., bill of lading, order, etc., for prohibited liquors or beverages.
28-4-127. Duty of common carrier, etc., to file with alcoholic beverage control board statement showing date of delivery, name and address of consignee and consignor, kind and amount, etc., of liquor delivered.
28-4-128. Alcoholic beverage control board to make written demand for statement upon failure of common carrier, etc., to file same; notification of attorney general of further refusal or neglect to file statement; institution of proceedings for mandamus or injunction by attorney general.

Sec.
28-4-129. Filing of statement by board; inspection of statement by district attorney or police officers.
28-4-130. Board to furnish certified copies of statements to officers, etc.; admissibility in evidence of statements or copies.
28-4-131. Duty of common carriers, etc., to maintain current record of date of delivery, name and address of consignee and consignor, kind and amount, etc., of liquors delivered.
28-4-132. Inspection of record by enforcement officers, etc.; acquisition and admissibility in evidence of record.
28-4-133. Duty of common carriers, etc., to permit examination of books, records, papers, etc., in connection with prosecutions under article, etc.
28-4-134. Persons not to be excused from testifying before grand juries or at trials for violations of article; immunity from prosecution as to matters disclosed.
28-4-135. Where certain offenses deemed committed.
28-4-136. Penalties for violations of provisions of article by railroad companies, express companies, etc.; duties of district attorney in cases of grand jury indictments.
28-4-137. Applicability of article to interstate transportation of prohibited liquors or beverages.

Article 7.

Sale, Purchase and Prescription of Alcohol by Druggists and Physicians.

28-4-150. Sales by wholesale druggists generally; said druggists to file monthly statements as to sales with alcoholic beverage control board.
28-4-151. Sales by retail druggists generally; use of alcohol by such druggists for compounding of prescriptions, etc.
28-4-152. Sales by retail druggists of alcohol for use in arts or for scientific or mechanical purposes; execution of statement by persons desiring to purchase alcohol for said purposes.
28-4-153. Purchase and use of alcohol by physicians.
28-4-154. Sale of pure alcohol for medicinal

Sec.
purposes to be made only upon prescription of physician; physician to conduct examination prior to issuing prescription.
28-4-155. Prescription to be based upon professional opinion of physician that alcohol will be used by patient for medicinal purposes.
28-4-156. Physicians to file affidavit with probate judge before authorized to prescribe alcohol for medicinal purposes; form of affidavit; fee of probate judge for filing and recordation of affidavit.
28-4-157. Prescription — Contents.
28-4-158. Same — Form.
28-4-159. Physician to file copy of prescription with probate judge; probate judge to preserve same and deliver to next grand jury for examination.
28-4-160. Time for filling of prescription; limitation as to amount of alcohol sold and delivered on prescription; disposition of prescription when filled by druggist; filling of prescription at certain drugstores in which prescribing physician has financial, etc., interest.
28-4-161. Recordation, etc., by probate judge of statements or prescriptions required to be filed by article; fee of probate judge; evidentiary effect of certified copy of statement or prescription.
28-4-162. Prescription of whiskey, rum, gin, etc., for medicinal purposes.
28-4-163. Prescription, sale, dispensing, etc., of Jamaica ginger.
28-4-164. Failure to comply with requirements as to issuance of prescriptions for alcohol, unauthorized use of alcohol, etc., by physicians.
28-4-165. Sale, delivery, etc., of liquors, etc., to prisoners by persons in charge of jails.
28-4-166. Penalties for violations of article.

Article 8.

Purchase, Receipt, Possession, Use, etc., of Wine for Sacramental or Religious Purposes.

28-4-180. Persons authorized to purchase, have shipped, receive, possess and use wine for sacramental or religious purposes.
28-4-181. Purchase and sale of wine for sacramental purposes.
28-4-182. Permit from alcoholic beverage control board to have wine shipped

Sec.

from outside the state — Required.

28-4-183. Same — Permit to be used for one shipment only; expiration.

28-4-184. Carrier, etc., to maintain record of deliveries.

Article 9.

Possession, etc., of Certain Quantities of State Tax-Paid Alcoholic Beverages for Private Use.

28-4-200. Possession of certain quantities of state tax-paid alcoholic beverages for private use permitted; storage, possession, etc., of alcoholic beverages in passenger area of vehicles or in view of passengers.

28-4-201. Sale or offer for sale or possession in excess of quantity permitted of such alcoholic beverages; penalties for violations of article.

Article 10.

Abatement of Liquor Nuisances.

28-4-220. Authorization and procedure generally; filing of petition generally.

28-4-221. Persons, etc., against whom petition may be filed.

28-4-222. Contents and verification of petition.

28-4-223. Issuance of preliminary injunction generally.

28-4-224. Requirement of bond as condition precedent to issuance of preliminary injunction.

28-4-225. Application for and issuance of writ directing seizure of prohibited liquors and beverages, movable property, etc., used in connection with nuisance pending hearing of action.

28-4-226. Contents of writ.

28-4-227. Disposition of liquor and beverages, etc., seized upon final judgment generally — Destruction.

28-4-228. Same — Restoration to owner.

28-4-229. Fees and allowances of officers executing writs of seizure; payment of costs in proceedings.

28-4-230. Persons who may be joined as parties defendant in proceedings and who may be enjoined from maintaining, etc., nuisance.

28-4-231. Powers of court as to maintenance of jurisdiction and enforcement of judgments generally; rules of evidence, practice and procedure.

28-4-232. Entry of judgment for abatement of nuisance and destruction of all

Sec.

prohibited liquors and beverages, movable property, etc., used in connection with nuisance.

Article 11.

Forfeiture and Condemnation of Contraband Liquors and Beverages, etc.

28-4-250. Authorization and procedure generally.

28-4-251. Search warrant for seizure of prohibited liquors and beverages, etc., generally — Issuance — Authorization and procedure generally.

28-4-252. Same — Same — Persons authorized.

28-4-253. Same — Same — Grounds.

28-4-254. Same — Same — Standard for issuance; contents of affidavit supporting determination of probable cause.

28-4-255. Same — Same — Examination of and taking of depositions from complainant and witnesses; contents of depositions.

28-4-256. Same — Same — Issuance by judge.

28-4-257. Same — Form.

28-4-258. Same — Execution — Persons authorized.

28-4-259. Same — Same — Time.

28-4-260. Same — Same — Giving of receipt for prohibited liquors and beverages, etc., seized under warrant.

28-4-261. Same — Limitation period for execution and return of warrant.

28-4-262. Same — Return of warrant; furnishing of copies thereof to applicant for warrant, etc.

28-4-263. Issuance, etc., of warrants for search of steamboats, watercraft, depots, railway cars, etc.

28-4-264. Disposition of property seized by officer under warrant generally.

28-4-265. Liquors and beverages, etc., seized not to be recovered by writ of replevin or detinue during pendency of proceedings under article; final judgment of condemnation to bar actions to recover liquors and beverages, etc., seized, etc.

28-4-266. Issuance of general notice to persons claiming right, title, etc., in liquors and beverages, etc., seized to appear and show cause why same should not be forfeited and destroyed.

28-4-267. Delivery to certain persons and posting of copies of notice.

Sec.

28-4-268. Answer by persons claiming right, title, etc., in liquors and beverages, etc., seized.

28-4-269. Forfeiture and condemnation proceedings generally — Issues and parties generally; style of action; trial of action generally.

28-4-270. Same — Issues, etc., where more than one claimant to liquors and beverages seized.

28-4-271. Same — Prosecution of action.

28-4-272. Same — Persons not to be excused from attending and testifying or producing books, papers, etc., at hearing or trial; immunity from prosecution as to transactions, etc., as to which testimony or documents produced.

28-4-273. Same — Conduct of hearing or trial generally; entry of judgment of forfeiture and delivery of liquors and beverages to alcoholic beverage control board generally; destruction of nonfederal tax-paid liquors and beverages; disposition of funds paid into court by alcoholic beverage control board.

28-4-274. Same — Entry of judgment of dismissal and return of liquors and beverages, etc., to place or person from which or from whom taken generally.

28-4-275. Same — Apportionment and taxing of costs.

28-4-276. Same — Appeals from judgment of district court — Authorization and procedure generally.

28-4-277. Same — Same — Persons entitled to appeal; bond for costs of appeal required; right to jury trial; proceedings in circuit court.

28-4-278. Same — Same — Issuance of order for delivery of liquors and beverages, etc., to alcoholic beverage control board or for restoration of same to place or person from which or from whom seized upon entry of final judgment in proceedings under article.

28-4-279. Forfeiture and condemnation proceedings in circuit courts.

28-4-280. Allowances and fees of officers executing search warrants and attending and prosecuting forfeiture and condemnation actions for state.

28-4-281. Correction of defects or irregularities in notice, etc., in forfeiture and condemnation proceedings.

28-4-282. Appliances used, etc., for distillation

Sec.

or manufacture of prohibited liquors and beverages declared contraband; said appliances and products thereof to be summarily destroyed by sheriffs, etc., finding same; property, etc., where distillery, etc., found forfeited to state.

28-4-283. Enforcement of forfeiture.

28-4-284. Sale of property and disposition of proceeds therefrom.

28-4-285. Conveyances, vehicles of transportation or animals used for illegal conveyance of prohibited liquors and beverages declared contraband and forfeited to state; seizure of said conveyances, etc., and reporting thereof by sheriffs, etc., finding same; confiscation and condemnation generally.

28-4-286. Institution of proceedings for condemnation of vehicles, etc.; seized property not to be retaken by replevin or detinue during pendency of action; intervention by parties claiming superior right to seized property; powers of court to regulate proceedings to permit parties claiming vehicles, etc., to assert rights.

28-4-287. Execution of bond by defendant or claimant for recovery of seized vehicle, etc., pending condemnation action; proceedings upon failure of defendant or claimant to deliver said vehicle, etc., upon entry of judgment of condemnation.

28-4-288. Execution of bond by defendant or claimant for recovery of seized vehicle, etc., pending appeal; proceedings upon failure of bondsmen to deliver said vehicle, etc., upon affirmance of judgment upon appeal, etc.

28-4-289. Payment of costs in actions for condemnation of vehicles, etc., used in transportation of prohibited liquors or beverages where judgment entered against state.

28-4-290. Advertisement and sale by sheriff, etc., of vehicle, animal, etc., seized for illegal transportation of liquor or beverages where owner, etc., cannot be ascertained; rights in seized vehicles, animals, etc., disposed of upon such sale by sheriff or sale by court in condemnation proceedings.

28-4-291. Disposition of proceeds from sale of such property forfeited to state.

731

Sec.
28-4-292. Advertisement and sale of receptacles, etc., of prohibited liquors and beverages.
28-4-293. Property rights in prohibited liquors and beverages, vessels, vehicles, etc., kept, used, etc., for purpose of violating temperance laws, etc.; seizure, forfeiture, disposition, etc., of same generally.
28-4-294. Preparation of return by officer seizing prohibited liquors and beverages; officer to report delivery to any person, destruction, etc., of same.
28-4-295. Disposition of prohibited liquors and beverages held for use as evidence upon conviction of person possessing, etc., same.
28-4-296. Deposit with alcoholic beverage control board for sale of certain confiscated liquors and beverages; payment to county or municipality by board of reasonable value of liquors and beverages received.
28-4-297. Unlawful disposition, etc., of contraband liquors and beverages by custodian.
28-4-298. Article not intended to secure search of premises of bona fide druggists or physicians.
28-4-299. Forfeiture, sale and distribution of proceeds of sale of contraband generally.

Article 12.

Enforcement of Chapter.

28-4-310. Governor charged with supervision, etc., of enforcement of prohibition laws; governor may require reports from officers charged with duty of enforcing laws; failure of officer to make report, etc.
28-4-311. Appointment of inspectors, etc., to detect and report violations of prohibition laws; offer and payment of rewards for convictions of persons violating laws.
28-4-312. Governor may require attorney general to prepare instructions for officers of state, etc., for enforcement of laws; publication and distribution of same.
28-4-313. Prosecutions for violations of chapter, etc., begun by affidavit or indictment; right of person charged to demand grand jury indictment; continuation of prosecution upon original affidavit;

Sec.
    amendment of affidavit or complaint.
28-4-314. District attorneys to institute prosecutions for or make reports to grand juries as to violations of prohibition laws.
28-4-315. Sheriffs to cooperate with district attorneys in prosecutions, etc.
28-4-316. Grand jury proceedings generally — Effect of failure of person to attend and testify in obedience to summons.
28-4-317. Same — Offenses as to which witnesses may be required to testify; initial interrogation of witnesses to particular offense not required.
28-4-318. Same — Exemption from prosecution of witnesses.
28-4-319. Same — Duty of grand jury to present indictments for violations of laws.
28-4-320. Servants, agents, etc., and principals not to be excused from testifying against each other on grounds of self-incrimination; immunity of said persons from prosecution for offenses disclosed, etc.
28-4-321. Contents and sufficiency of charges in indictments, complaints, affidavits, etc., for sale, offer for sale, possession, etc., of prohibited liquors and beverages, etc., generally; proof of charges generally; admissibility in evidence of testimony of persons purchasing, etc., prohibited liquors and beverages, etc.; immunity from prosecution of persons testifying as to violations of chapter, etc.
28-4-322. Several charges may be set out in separate counts in indictments, complaints, etc.; judgment entered and punishment imposed upon each count.
28-4-323. Admissibility and effect of evidence showing similarity in color, odor and general appearance between prohibited liquor or beverage and beverage shown to be manufactured, sold, kept, etc., by defendant; applicability of rule as to admissibility, etc., of said evidence in proceedings for abatement of liquor nuisances, etc.
28-4-324. Issuance of injunctions to prevent violations of chapter, etc.
28-4-325. Fees of officers making seizures of prohibited liquors.
28-4-326. Penalties for violations of chapter.

Cross references. — As to authorization of municipal option elections to determine classi- fication of municipalities as wet or dry munici- palities, see ch. 2A, T. 28.

ARTICLE 1.

GENERAL PROVISIONS.

This article is not offensive to Constitution, § 45, requiring each law to contain but one subject, which shall be clearly expressed in the title. State v. T.J. Mattox Cigar & Tobacco Co., 201 Ala. 229, 77 So. 755 (1918). See also Jones v. State, 17 Ala. App. 444, 85 So. 839 (1920); Clements v. State ex rel. Sanford, 206 Ala. 377, 89 So. 545 (1921).

Prohibition laws apply to dry counties. — The prohibition laws already obtaining at time of enactment of the Alabama Alcoholic Beverage Control Act remained in effect in those counties to which the Act did not by its terms apply. Golden v. State, 28 Ala. App. 196, 180 So. 733 (1938).

§ 28-4-1. Definitions.

When used in this chapter, the following words and phrases shall have the following meanings, respectively, unless the context clearly indicates otherwise:

(1) BREWER. Every person, firm, association or corporation that manufactures fermented liquors of any name or description from malt, wholly or in part, or from any substitute therefor.

(2) DISTILLER. Every person, firm, association or corporation that produces distilled spirits or who brews or makes mash, wort or wash fit for distillation or for the production of spirits or who, by any process of evaporation, separates alcoholic spirits from any fermented substance or who, making or keeping mash, wort or wash, has also in possession or use a still.

(3) LIQUOR NUISANCES.

a. Any rooms or structures used for the unlawful manufacture, sale, furnishing, distilling, rectifying, brewing or keeping of liquors or beverages that are prohibited by the laws of Alabama to be manufactured, sold or otherwise disposed of in this state;

b. All houses, shops or places where such prohibited liquors and beverages or any of them are sold, bartered, exchanged or otherwise disposed of to be drunk on or near the premises or where such prohibited liquors, liquids or beverages are kept for the purpose of sale or other disposition thereof in violation of law;

c. All places of resort where persons are permitted to resort for the purpose of drinking such liquors or beverages on or about the premises;

d. Any unlawful drinking place that is kept or maintained in violation of the law of the state;

e. All restaurants, hotels and public eating places where the prohibited liquors and beverages or any of them are sold or served for beverage purposes;

f. All places where business is carried on by a wholesale or retail dealer in liquors or by a wholesale or retail dealer in malt liquors or by a brewer or distiller or rectifier of spirits in violation of the law of the state; and

g. All warehouses or storage places where the prohibited liquors and beverages or any of them are kept or stored or received on consignment or for distribution or delivery contrary to the law of the state.

(4) OTHERWISE DISPOSE OF. Such term, following the words sell, offer for sale or keep for sale, and following the words sold, offered for sale or kept for sale, when employed in any warrant, process, affidavit, indictment, information or complaint or other pleading in any judicial proceeding or in any judgment shall include and be deemed to include barter, exchange, giving away, furnishing or any manner of disposition by which said liquors and beverages may pass unlawfully from one person to another.

(5) PERSON or PARTY. Such terms, when employed alone, shall include a firm, corporation or association of persons.

(6) PROHIBITED LIQUORS AND BEVERAGES.

a. Alcohol, alcoholic liquors, spirituous liquors and all mixed liquors any part of which is spirituous;

b. Foreign or domestic spirits or rectified or distilled spirits, absinthe, whiskey, brandy, rum and gin;

c. Vinous liquors and beverages;

d. Malt, fermented or brewed liquors of any name or description manufactured from malt wholly or in part or from any substitute therefor;

e. Beer, lager beer, porter and ale and other brewed or fermented liquors and beverages by whatever name called;

f. Hop jack, hop ale, hop weiss, hop tea, malt tonic or any other beverage which is the production of maltose or glucose or in which maltose or glucose is a substantial ingredient;

g. Any intoxicating bitters or beverages by whatever name called; and

h. All liquors, liquids, drinks or beverages made in imitation of or intended as a substitute for beer, ale, rum, gin, whiskey or for any other alcoholic, spirituous, vinous or malt liquor and any liquor, drink or liquid made or used for beverage purposes containing any alcohol.

(7) RETAIL DEALER IN LIQUORS. Every person, firm, association or corporation that sells or offers for sale any foreign or domestic distilled spirits or wines in lesser quantities than five gallons at the same time.

(8) RETAIL DEALER IN MALT LIQUORS. Every person, firm, association or corporation that sells or offers for sale malt liquors in lesser quantities than five gallons at one time.

(9) UNLAWFUL DRINKING PLACES.

a. Any place or resort where the prohibited liquors or beverages or any of them are kept to be drunk upon or about the premises by persons resorting there for that purpose;

b. Any club room or other place in which are received or kept for the purpose of barter or sale or use or gift as a beverage or for distribution or division among or furnishing to or for use by members of any club or association of persons by any means whatsoever the prohibited liquors and beverages or any of them, referred to in subdivision (6) of this section; and

c. Any club room or room of any association of persons in which said prohibited liquors or beverages or any of them are kept or stored for the purpose of being drunk or consumed by the members of such club or other association of persons or their guests or others on the premises or at or near the place where such liquors or beverages or any of them, are kept or stored; and any place adjacent to or near the premises of any club, corporation or association or other combination of persons to which members or their guests or others, by the permission of members, resort for the purpose of drinking the prohibited liquors and beverages, or any of them that are kept at or near such place.

(10) WHOLESALE DEALER IN LIQUORS. Every person, firm, association or corporation that sells or offers for sale foreign or domestic distilled spirits or wine in quantities of not less than five gallons at the same time.

(11) WHOLESALE DEALER IN MALT LIQUORS. Every person, firm, corporation or association who sells or offers for sale malt liquors in quantities of not less than five gallons at the same time. (Acts 1909, No. 191, p. 63; Acts 1915, No. 1, p. 1; Acts 1915, No. 2, p. 8; Acts 1919, No. 7, p. 6; Code 1923, §§ 4615-4619; Code 1940, T. 29, §§ 93-97.)

I. General Consideration.
II. Liquor Nuisances.
III. Prohibited Beverages.
IV. Unlawful Drinking Places.

I. GENERAL CONSIDERATION.

Section 28-3-1 must be construed in pari materia with this section, where and to the extent pertinent. Brown v. State, 32 Ala. App. 406, 26 So. 2d 536 (1946); Kennedy v. State, 39 Ala. App. 676, 107 So. 2d 913 (1958).

Cited in Smith v. State, 55 Ala. 1 (1876); State ex rel. Garber v. Abraham, 165 Ala. 201, 51 So. 788 (1910); Fulton v. State, 171 Ala. 572, 54 So. 688 (1911); In re State ex rel. Attorney Gen., 179 Ala. 639, 60 So. 285 (1912); Broylan v. State, 17 Ala. App. 403, 86 So. 164 (1920); Whaley v. State, 17 Ala. App. 661, 88 So. 24 (1921); Booker v. City of Birmingham, 23 Ala. App. 312, 125 So. 603 (1929); Grimes v. State, 23 Ala. App. 511, 128 So. 120 (1930); Moore v. State, 25 Ala. App. 71, 140 So. 764 (1932); Noltey v. State, 25 Ala. App. 229, 144 So. 455 (1932); Noltey v. State, 225 Ala. 584, 144 So. 457 (1932); Slater v. State, 230 Ala. 320, 162 So. 130 (1935); Garrett v. State ex rel. Matthews, 235 Ala. 457, 179 So. 636 (1938); Klein v. State ex rel. Evans, 238 Ala. 148, 189

So. 771 (1939); Gandy v. City of Birmingham, 31 Ala. App. 313, 17 So. 2d 421 (1943); Smith v. State, 253 Ala. 365, 44 So. 2d 759 (1950); Walker v. State, 35 Ala. App. 167, 44 So. 2d 798 (1950); Stephens v. State ex rel. Ward, 257 Ala. 375, 59 So. 2d 69 (1952); Billingsley v. State, 261 Ala. 211, 73 So. 2d 541 (1954); Thompson v. State ex rel. Waid, 263 Ala. 463, 83 So. 2d 70 (1955); Thompson v. State, 267 Ala. 22, 99 So. 2d 198 (1957).

Collateral references. — 48 C.J.S., Intoxicating Liquors, §§ 1-19, 408.

45 Am. Jur. 2d, Intoxicating Liquors, § 4 et seq., § 429 et seq.

Test of intoxicating character of liquor. 4 ALR 1137, 11 ALR 1233, 19 ALR 512, 36 ALR 725, 91 ALR 513.

Charge of maintaining a liquor nuisance predicated on permitting guests to bring and consume their own liquor. 49 ALR 1451.

Sale and use of intoxicating liquors at public dance as nuisance. 44 ALR2d 1401.

Admissibility, in prosecution for maintaining liquor nuisance, of evidence of general reputation of premises. 68 ALR2d 1300.

Saloons or taverns as nuisance. 5 ALR3d 989.

II. LIQUOR NUISANCES.

Subdivision (3) was not repealed by Acts 1936-37, Ex. Sess., p. 85, § 61, repealing all laws and parts of laws in conflict with the act except as otherwise specially provided. Harvell v. State ex rel. Sanford, 235 Ala. 329, 179 So. 233 (1938).

Bare possession does not in and of itself amount to a nuisance as defined by this section. Cooley v. State, 262 Ala. 136, 77 So. 2d 488 (1955).

Possession of intoxicating liquors or beverages in a building used exclusively for a dwelling is not prima facie evidence that they are kept for sale. Johnson v. State ex rel. Johnson, 270 Ala. 470, 119 So. 2d 884 (1960).

Social drinking in home. — This section does not contemplate the inclusion of social drinking within the confines of one's own home as a "liquor nuisance," in the absence of evidence showing, or from which there can be a reasonable inference, that the persons who resort there do so for the main purpose of drinking unlawful liquors or beverages. Cooley v. State, 262 Ala. 136, 77 So. 2d 488 (1955).

Resort for drinking. — Where people who went to cafe and dance hall did so principally for legitimate recreation and refreshments served in the cafe, and to dance in the dance hall; the fact that some of them who went for that purpose carried their liquor and drank it in and around their automobiles, not in the house, did not make the place a resort for drinking. Lambert v. State ex rel. Hunter, 248 Ala. 487, 28 So. 2d 412 (1946).

III. PROHIBITED BEVERAGES.

Liquid must be beverage. — Possession of a liquid which is not appropriate for use as a beverage is not a violation of this section. Moody v. State, 23 Ala. App. 431, 126 So. 495 (1930).

In prosecution for violating prohibition laws based upon possession of an alleged intoxicating beverage, it was incumbent upon the state to prove not only that beverage contained alcohol, but that it was suitable to be used for a beverage purpose. Williams v. State, 30 Ala. App. 395, 6 So. 2d 525 (1942).

Possession of a liquid which is not suitable to be used as a beverage is not a violation of this section. Brown v. State, 32 Ala. App. 406, 26 So. 2d 536 (1946); Bevels v. State, 38 Ala. App. 198, 84 So. 2d 382 (1955).

Where the only evidence was that liquid in the possession of the defendant looked and smelled like home brew, and there was no evidence that it was suitable to be used as a beverage or that it contained alcohol sufficient to bring it within the terms of this section, a conviction of violation of the prohibition law could not be sustained. Brown v. State, 32 Ala. App. 406, 26 So. 2d 536 (1946).

And section cannot be extended by implication to include liquids not clearly described as prohibited liquors. Grant v. State, 22 Ala. App. 475, 117 So. 1 (1928); Wright v. State, 37 Ala. App. 689, 74 So. 2d 727 (1954).

"Whiskey" and "liquor" defined. — Whiskey is alcohol diluted with water and mixed with other elements or ingredients. The term "liquor" or "liquors" commonly includes all kinds of intoxicating decoctions, liquors or beverages, whether spirituous, vinous, malt or alcoholic. Marks v. State, 159 Ala. 71, 48 So. 864 (1909).

Moonshine whiskey. — The term "prohibited liquors and beverages" includes "moonshine whiskey." Griffin v. State, 39 Ala. App. 671, 106 So. 2d 36 (1958).

"Whiskey," "moonshine whiskey" or "corn whiskey" are within the expression "prohibited liquors and beverages." State v. Merrill, 203 Ala. 686, 85 So. 28 (1920).

Not all compounds containing alcohol included. — The term "alcoholic liquors," as used in the prohibition law, does not necessarily, ex vi termini, include every article or compound which contains alcohol. Marks v. State, 159 Ala. 71, 48 So. 864 (1909).

Just those that may be used as intoxicating beverage. — This section does embrace all articles which contain alcohol or malt in such proportions or form or state, which are or may be used as an intoxicating beverage, no matter what it is called or what else it contains, or for what other purposes it was intended or is used, or for which it may be used, and although the vendor or disposer did not know that it contained such ingredients or could be used as an intoxicating beverage, unless the law expressly excepts such article or such disposition. Adler v. State, 55 Ala. 16 (1876); Watson v. State, 55 Ala. 158 (1876); Carson v. State, 69 Ala. 235 (1881); Ryall v. State, 78 Ala. 410 (1885); Wall v. State, 78 Ala. 417 (1885); Knowles v. State, 80 Ala. 9 (1885); Allred v. State, 89 Ala. 112, 8 So. 56 (1889); Hinton v. State, 132 Ala. 29, 31 So. 563 (1902).

Sale of beer containing 3.2 percent alcohol held illegal under statutes and ordinances predicated thereon prohibiting sale of cereal beverages containing more than one-half of one percent alcohol. Ex parte Harduvel, 25 Ala. App. 561, 150 So. 808 (1933).

Beer is a prohibited beverage and the question of its alcoholic content is immaterial as an issue in the case, nor need it contain alcohol at all. It is a prohibited liquor or beverage if within the description and classification of this section. Woods v. State ex rel. Key, 247 Ala. 155, 22 So. 2d 901 (1945).

Home brew. — On trial for violating prohibition laws, evidence that bottles found contained home brew was permissible as preliminary evidence, though home brew is not included in this section, as further proof concerning its nature or ingredients could bring it within the section. Sharp v. State, 22 Ala. App. 562, 118 So. 238 (1928).

Evidence in prosecution for violating prohibition law by illegally possessing liquors contrary to § 28-4-20, tending to prove that defendant was in possession of home brew, held insufficient to sustain conviction without evidence that the home brew had been fermented or contained alcohol (which the courts do not judicially know), within meaning of "prohibited liquor" defined by this section. Grant v. State, 22 Ala. App. 475, 117 So. 1 (1928); Moody v. State, 23 Ala. App. 431, 126 So. 495 (1930); Wright v. State, 37 Ala. App. 689, 74 So. 2d 727 (1954).

Defendant's intent to use home brew as substitute for beer was immaterial, since only questions were whether it was such a substitute as was condemned by law and whether defendant was in possession. Moody v. State, 23 Ala. App. 431, 126 So. 495 (1930).

Where defendant in prosecution for possessing prohibited liquor in violation of city ordinance referred in testimony to liquid as "home brew," thus showing it to be beer, it was not essential that liquid be shown to be alcoholic, since, under this section, beer is prohibited liquor. Grant v. State, 23 Ala. App. 54, 120 So. 465 (1929); Booker v. City of Birmingham, 23 Ala. App. 312, 125 So. 603 (1929).

The court properly left to the jury the question of whether home brew was or was not prohibited liquid within the scope of this section. Hendrix v. State, 39 Ala. App. 155, 96 So. 2d 313 (1957).

Mead or metheglin. — The court does not judicially know that mead or metheglin is an alcoholic, spirituous, vinous, malt or intoxicating liquor or beverage, or that, if it is drunk to excess, it will produce intoxication. Marks v. State, 159 Ala. 71, 48 So. 864 (1909).

Imitations and substitutes. — The beverage known as "Besto," containing an enzyme, which is an unorganized ferment, and containing either maltose or glucose or a substitute therefor, is prohibited as a device or substitute for a prohibited beverage. State v. T.J. Mattox Cigar & Tobacco Co., 201 Ala. 229, 77 So. 755 (1918).

"Budweiser" made in imitation of beer is prohibited by this section. Wise v. State, 20 Ala. App. 145, 101 So. 155 (1924).

If the drink does not have the "kick" of beer or liquor but resembles it in every other respect it is prohibited by this section. Patterson v. State, 18 Ala. App. 55, 88 So. 360 (1921).

If the liquid is intended as a substitute for beer it is prohibited although containing less than one percent alcohol. Dettra v. State, 18 Ala. App. 259, 91 So. 500 (1921).

Lemon and vanilla extracts. — Under this section and § 28-4-20, lemon and vanilla extracts, made or used for beverage purposes, containing alcohol, are "alcoholic liquors" within section. Brandon v. State, 24 Ala. App. 289, 134 So. 890 (1931).

Merchant's sale and possession of lemon and vanilla extracts, as ordinarily sold and possessed as articles of legitimate commerce, and used for legitimate purposes, is not violation of section. Brandon v. State, 24 Ala. App. 289, 134 So. 890 (1931).

Vinegar. — Technical violation of prohibition law by defendant and his wife in making vinegar for domestic purposes held not to warrant conviction on liquor charge. Jones v. State, 23 Ala. App. 30, 120 So. 304 (1929).

Rotten peaches. — Conviction was improper where the only testimony concerning nature of alleged intoxicating beverage in defendant's possession was that it consisted only of rotten peaches which he used to feed his hogs. Williams v. State, 30 Ala. App. 395, 6 So. 2d 525 (1942).

Whiskey legally purchased in wet county. — Where according to the uncontradicted evidence all the whiskey found on premises was duly labeled with stamps and had been purchased from one of the state stores in a wet county, defendant could not be convicted of maintaining or aiding or abetting in maintaining an unlawful drinking place where "prohibited liquors or beverages" were kept to be drunk upon or about the premises. Harvey v. State, 30 Ala. App. 216, 3 So. 2d 142 (1941).

Indictment charging defendant with unlawfully having in his possession "intoxicating bitters or beverages" was sufficient, as the adjective "intoxicating" qualifies both "bitters" and "beverages," in view of the use of the term "prohibited liquors or beverages," in this section. Ex parte State ex rel. Attorney Gen., 207 Ala. 585, 93 So. 382 (1922).

IV. UNLAWFUL DRINKING PLACES.

Accused must be shown to have maintained or aided in maintenance of unlawful drinking place. — To sustain a charge of maintaining an unlawful drinking place, the state must show the accused's maintenance of the unlawful drinking place, or his aid and abetment therein. Davis v. State, 40 Ala. App. 609, 119 So. 2d 236 (1960).

Union hall not unlawful drinking place. — Under the definition contained in subdivision (9) of this section, union hall premises is not an unlawful drinking place. Johnson v. I.B.E.W. Local 558 Properties, Inc., 418 So. 2d 885 (Ala. 1982).

Cited in Sargent v. State, 351 So. 2d 666 (Ala. Crim. App. 1977); Allen v. State ex rel. Simpson, 377 So. 2d 942 (Ala. 1979).

§ 28-4-2. Unauthorized possession, sale, delivery, use, etc., of wine or alcohol generally.

Any person who shall sell any wine or alcohol in this state for any purpose other than allowed by law or who shall fail to comply with any regulation respecting the sale, delivery or use of alcohol or wine or who shall receive, have in possession or possess any alcohol or wine, except as authorized by law and for the purposes as prescribed by law, shall be guilty of a misdemeanor. (Acts 1919, No. 7, p. 6; Code 1923, § 4734; Code 1940, T. 29, § 202.)

Collateral references. — Revocation of license of physician, surgeon, or dentist because of violation of law regarding intoxicating liquor. 82 ALR 1188.

Charge of illegal sale predicated upon physician's issuance of prescription for intoxicating liquors otherwise than in the course of his professional practice. 133 ALR 1140.

§ 28-4-3. Applicability of laws as to possession, transportation or delivery of prohibited liquors to possession or receipt of wine, pure alcohol, etc., for sacramental purposes, domestic use, etc., generally.

The laws against possession, transportation or delivery of prohibited liquors shall not apply to the possession of wine or cordial made from grapes or other fruit when the grapes or other fruit are grown by the person making the same for his own domestic use upon his own premises in this state and when such person keeps such wine or cordial for his own domestic use on his own premises in any quantity not exceeding five gallons for one family in 12 months, nor shall such laws apply to the receipt or possession of pure or grain alcohol in nonprohibited quantities by persons who are permitted to buy, sell, use or possess the same under existing laws of the state nor to the receipt or possession of wine for sacramental purposes when received and possessed by an authorized person in accordance with the rules and regulations prescribed by law and when not exceeding the quantity so prescribed. (Acts 1919, No. 7, p. 6; Code 1923, § 4706; Code 1940, T. 29, § 175.)

§ 28-4-4. Applicability of chapter.

Pursuant to the provisions of sections 28-2-1 and 28-3-18, this chapter shall be applicable in all "dry counties" as the same are defined in section 28-2-1 and shall apply to the manufacture or possession of illicit distilled liquors or apparatus for the manufacture of the same, as specified in section 28-3-18, in this state. (Code 1940, T. 29, § 92.)

Cross references. — As to authorization of municipal option elections to determine Cited in Rogers v. State, 34 Ala. App. 617, 42 So. 2d 642 (1949); Copeland v. State, 377 So. 2d 1 (Ala. Crim. App. 1979).

§ 28-4-5. Applicability to dry municipalities.

This chapter as amended, is hereby amended to make the same consistent with the provisions of chapter 2A of this title, so that this chapter shall be applicable in all "dry counties" (but not in "wet municipalities") and in all "dry municipalities," as the terms are used in chapter 2A of this title. (Acts 1984, No. 84-408, p. 955, § 6.)

Constitutionality. — For case upholding the constitutionality and the validity of the enactment of Act No. 84-408, codified at §§ 28-2A-1 through 28-2A-4 and 28-4-5, see Alabama Citizens Action Program v. Kennamer, 479 So. 2d 1237 (Ala. 1985).

General law. — Act No. 84-408 (codified at §§ 28-2A-1 through 28-2A-4 and 28-4-5) is so framed as to be reasonably susceptible of interpretation as a general law, and therefore the Supreme Court was bound not to construe it as a local law. Alabama Citizens Action Program v. Kennamer, 479 So. 2d 1237 (Ala. 1985).

ARTICLE 2.

MANUFACTURE, SALE, OFFER FOR SALE, POSSESSION, DISTRIBUTION, ETC., OF PROHIBITED LIQUORS AND BEVERAGES.

§ 28-4-20. Sale, offer for sale, possession, barter, exchange, etc., of prohibited liquors and beverages.

It shall be unlawful for any person, firm or corporation or association within this state to sell, offer for sale, keep or have in possession, barter, exchange or to give away, furnish at a public place or elsewhere or otherwise dispose of the prohibited liquors and beverages described in this chapter or any of them in any quantity, except as provided in this chapter, or to accept the delivery of or to receive or to have in possession or possess in this state any of said prohibited liquors and beverages as defined by the laws of the state of Alabama in any quantity whatsoever. (Acts 1915, No. 1, p. 1; Acts 1919, No. 7, p. 6; Code 1923, § 4621; Code 1940, T. 29, § 98.)

I. General Consideration.
II. Pleading and Evidence.

I. GENERAL CONSIDERATION.

State may decline to consider intoxicating liquor as a legitimate article of commerce and may prohibit its possession or sale either absolutely or under such reasonable conditions as the state may prescribe. McDonald v. Brewer, 295 F. Supp. 1135 (N.D. Ala. 1968).

This section remains the law in "dry" counties. McDonald v. Brewer, 295 F. Supp. 1135 (N.D. Ala. 1968).

And is not repealed by the Beverage Control Act. — The Alabama Alcoholic Beverage Control Act applies solely to the wet counties of the state insofar as possession of prohibited liquor in dry counties is concerned and does not repeal this section making possession of prohibited liquors illegal as applied to dry counties. Williams v. State, 28 Ala. App. 73, 179 So. 915 (1938); Carroll v. State, 28 Ala. App. 108, 179 So. 397 (1938); Golden v. State, 28 Ala. App. 196, 180 So. 733 (1938).

Possession of liquor merely for purpose of destroying it is not a crime. Ex parte Christopher, 223 Ala. 19, 135 So. 420 (1931).

Alabama courts recognize two kinds or conditions of possession as applied to the violation of the prohibition laws: (1) actual or manucaptional possession; (2) constructive or possession by physical dominion or control. Pate v. State, 32 Ala. App. 365, 26 So. 2d 214 (1946); Wright v. State, 39 Ala. App. 289, 97 So. 2d 835 (1957).

Constructive possession cases under this section are reviewed in Grimes v. State, 38 Ala. App. 94, 76 So. 2d 684 (1954); Spencer v. State, 40 Ala. App. 93, 109 So. 2d 756 (1958).

Possession in "dry" county of legally purchased beer is unlawful. Williams v. State, 28 Ala. App. 73, 179 So. 915, cert. denied, 235 Ala. 520, 179 So. 920 (1938).

Where locus in quo is de jure dry, the possession of beer (which legally denotes an alcoholic beverage) is a misdemeanor. Owens v. State, 45 Ala. App. 227, 228 So. 2d 841 (1969).

Possession in "dry" county of legally purchased whiskey. — It is not violative of the fourteenth amendment to the federal Constitution for Alabama to prohibit persons who buy legal taxpaid whiskey in the state's "wet" counties from possessing such whiskey for their own personal use or otherwise in the state's "dry" counties. McDonald v. Brewer, 295 F. Supp. 1135 (N.D. Ala. 1968).

Because it lacks any element of fraud, larceny or criminal intent, the misdemeanor of possessing taxpaid alcoholic beverages in a "dry" county is not a crime involving moral turpitude. United States v. Smith, 420 F.2d 428 (5th Cir. 1970).

Defendant who legally bought whiskey in a wet county but took it to his home in a dry county was properly arrested and convicted under this section. Graham v. State, 45 Ala. App. 79, 224 So. 2d 905 (1969).

Transporting a pint of whiskey in a dry county (state store or wildcat) is only a misdemeanor flowing from possession, either moving or stationary. Wright v. State, 40 Ala. App. 263, 111 So. 2d 588 (1958).

One who purchases intoxicating liquor from a bootlegger is not an accomplice of the seller. He is guilty of no offense under this section unless after purchasing the liquor he should transport it or should have possession of it with intent to violate the law. These are independent offenses from the sale. Brown v. State, 44 Ala. App. 135, 203 So. 2d 700 (1967).

"Receiving" prohibited liquor. — Fact that defendant merely engaged in drinking bout with party of friends after procuring whiskey for such purpose did not affect his guilt of "receiving" prohibited liquor. Qualls v. State, 27 Ala. App. 159, 167 So. 610 (1936).

Throwing whiskey away is not "disposal" thereof. — Throwing a bottle of whiskey away while being pursued by officers did not constitute a disposal of the liquor, within the terms of this section. Smith v. State, 39 Ala. App. 673, 107 So. 2d 575 (1958).

Near beer. — Having and selling near beer containing less than one-half of one percent of alcohol is a violation of this section Dettra v. State, 18 Ala. App. 259, 91 So. 500 (1921). See also notes to § 28-4-1.

Storing. — The offenses denounced by this section and § 28-4-28 are separate and distinct and under an indictment charging an offense under this section it is error to admit evidence that will show an offense of storing intoxicants as denounced by § 28-4-28. Tidwell v. State, 21 Ala. App. 315, 108 So. 76 (1926).

"Larceny" of money given in hope of illegally obtaining whiskey. — Where evidence showed that state's witness parted willingly with both possession and title to his money in vain expectation that defendant would violate law by delivering to him a quantity of whiskey, defendant was not guilty of "larceny" of the money. Murchinson v. State, 30 Ala. App. 15, 199 So. 897 (1940).

Where an indictment charges a violation of section 28-4-115, defendant cannot be convicted on a plea of guilty of possession of prohibited liquors in violation of this section. Ryan v. State, 41 Ala. App. 340, 132 So. 2d 264 (1961).

Violation of this section is made a misdemeanor by § 28-4-21. Brown v. State, 44 Ala. App. 135, 203 So. 2d 700 (1967).

Cited in Jinright v. State, 220 Ala. 268, 125 So. 606 (1929); Noltey v. State, 225 Ala. 584, 144 So. 457 (1932); Warren v. State, 25 Ala. App. 29, 140 So. 177 (1932); McMillan v. State, 25 Ala. App. 31, 140 So. 183 (1932); Pate v. State, 25 Ala. App. 217, 145 So. 500 (1932); Ex parte Harduvel, 25 Ala. App. 561, 150 So. 808 (1933); Lewis v. State, 28 Ala. App. 429, 186 So. 187 (1939); Eason v. State, 31 Ala. App. 212, 14 So. 2d 255 (1943); Yates v. State, 245 Ala. 490, 17 So. 2d 777 (1944); Yates v. State, 31 Ala. App. 404, 17 So. 2d 594 (1944); Dodd v. State, 32 Ala. App. 307, 26 So. 2d 273 (1946); Black v. State, 35 Ala. App. 67, 43 So. 2d 759 (1950); Dotson v. State, 35 Ala. App. 373, 48 So. 2d 534 (1950); Henderson v. State, 36 Ala. App. 143, 53 So. 2d 624 (1951); Wright v. State, 37 Ala. App. 106, 63 So. 2d 733 (1953); Hunter v. State, 39 Ala. App. 214, 96 So. 2d 820 (1957); Roach v. State, 39 Ala. App. 271, 97 So. 2d 837 (1957); Kelley v. State, 39 Ala. App. 572, 105 So. 2d 687 (1958); Scruggs v. State, 39 Ala. App. 630, 106 So. 2d 275 (1958); Pearson v.

State, 39 Ala. App. 633, 106 So. 2d 267 (1958); Kennedy v. State, 39 Ala. App. 676, 107 So. 2d 913 (1958); Cunningham v. State, 40 Ala. App. 114, 108 So. 2d 192 (1959); Parker v. State, 40 Ala. App. 244, 112 So. 2d 493 (1959); Evans v. State, 40 Ala. App. 282, 112 So. 2d 355 (1959); Griggs v. State, 40 Ala. App. 675, 121 So. 2d 926 (1960); Beam v. State, 41 Ala. App. 401, 137 So. 2d 762 (1961); Brown v. State, 41 Ala. App. 565, 140 So. 2d 371 (1962); Harris v. State, 42 Ala. App. 208, 158 So. 2d 684 (1963); Brown v. State, 42 Ala. App. 429, 167 So. 2d 281 (1964); Denson v. State, 43 Ala. App. 243, 187 So. 2d 574 (1966); Livingston v. State, 44 Ala. App. 579, 217 So. 2d 90 (1968); Blackmon v. State, 45 Ala. App. 44, 222 So. 2d 374 (1969); Loggins v. State, 52 Ala. App. 204, 290 So. 2d 665 (1974); Sargent v. State, 351 So. 2d 666 (Ala. Crim. App. 1977); Walker v. State, 356 So. 2d 672 (Ala. 1977); Malone v. State, 406 So. 2d 1060 (Ala. Crim. App. 1981); Johnson v. State, 406 So. 2d 1063 (Ala. Crim. App. 1981); Todd v. State, 406 So. 2d 1065 (Ala. Crim. App. 1981).

Collateral references. — 48 C.J.S., Intoxicating Liquors, §§ 37, 234, 248.

45 Am. Jur. 2d, Intoxicating Liquors, § 313 et seq.

Evidence of other offenses in prosecution for violation of liquor law to prove identity of defendant. 3 ALR 1555, 22 ALR 1016, 27 ALR 357, 63 ALR 602.

Criminal responsibility of purchaser of liquor sold in violation of law. 5 ALR 786, 74 ALR 1110, 131 ALR 1322.

Admissibility, in prosecution for illegal sale of liquor, of evidence as to other sales. 40 ALR2d 817.

Serving liquor to minor in home as unlawful sale or gift. 14 ALR3d 1186.

What constitutes "sale" of liquor in violation of statute or ordinance. 89 ALR3d 551.

II. PLEADING AND EVIDENCE.

Court adheres to high standard of proof in "constructive possession cases". — To impute knowledge of the presence of liquor, the court of appeals has consistently adhered to a high standard of proof in what are termed "constructive possession cases." This is because the court is, in effect, saying, "the liquor was found in such a place that the defendant ought to have known of it being there," and thus it is making this conclusion serve as proof that he had the liquor in possession. Evans v. State, 39 Ala. App. 404, 103 So. 2d 40 (1958).

State must show guilty knowledge in addition to constructive possession. — Where the possession is constructive, to sustain a conviction the state must show, in addition to the constructive possession, a guilty knowledge or scienter on the part of defendant. Such guilty knowledge may be established by circumstantial evidence. Wright v. State, 39 Ala. App. 289, 97 So. 2d 835 (1957); Leashore v. State, 41 Ala. App. 128, 124 So. 2d 273 (1960).

Constructive possession may arise where prohibited liquor is found on premises owned or controlled by the accused, provided the state further shows facts enabling a jury to conclude beyond a reasonable doubt that the accused knew of the presence of the prohibited beverage. Davis v. State, 40 Ala. App. 609, 119 So. 2d 236 (1960).

Circumstances presenting question for jury as to guilty knowledge. — In a prosecution for the illegal possession of prohibited liquors the facts and circumstances shown presented a question for the jury as to defendant's guilty knowledge of the presence of the whiskey, and there was sufficient evidence from which the jury might infer guilty knowledge. Wright v. State, 39 Ala. App. 289, 97 So. 2d 835 (1957).

Circumstances of constructive possession coupled with evidence of actual possession. — Circumstances of constructive possession did not exclude the hypothesis of innocence standing alone. However, when coupled with evidence of actual possession — which the jury could have inferred from the sheriff's testimony that he found defendant's fingerprints on the bottles of prohibited liquor — there was a prima facie case, even though the time and place of actual possession did not appear. Evans v. State, 39 Ala. App. 404, 103 So. 2d 40 (1958).

Fingerprints as evidence of actual possession. — Evidence that defendant's fingerprints were on bottles of prohibited liquor, if believed, was evidence of actual possession, though at an unspecified time and place. Hence, constructive possession cases did not apply. Evans v. State, 39 Ala. App. 404, 103 So. 2d 40 (1958).

Circumstantial evidence may support a conviction under this section. Walton v. State, 39 Ala. App. 103, 96 So. 2d 311, cert. denied, 266 Ala. 701, 96 So. 2d 312 (1957); Hubert v. State, 41 Ala. App. 269, 128 So. 2d 527 (1961).

Charge of unlawfully possessing whiskey may be established by circumstantial as well as by direct testimony. Wilson v. State, 27 Ala. App. 38, 166 So. 715 (1935); Roughton v. State, 38 Ala. App. 17, 77 So. 2d 666, cert. denied, 262 Ala. 703, 77 So. 2d 667 (1954).

Circumstantial evidence found sufficient to sustain conviction for possession of prohibited liquors. Leashore v. State, 41 Ala. App. 128, 124 So. 2d 273 (1960).

Inference from possession. — A jury may

infer from the fact of possession of a large quantity of illegal liquor that a defendant had it for the purpose of sale, and not for private use. Peppers v. State, 36 Ala. App. 468, 59 So. 2d 685 (1952).

Defendant's own testimony is sufficient to support conviction for violating prohibition laws by having whiskey in his possession. Christopher v. State, 24 Ala. App. 335, 135 So. 419 (1931).

Evidence of possession. — Small amount of whiskey in pint bottle found in home of accused is sufficient to support conviction for unlawful possession of whiskey. Wilson v. State, 27 Ala. App. 38, 166 So. 715 (1935).

Evidence that accused had bottle containing half pint of whiskey and gave state's witness drink of whiskey held sufficient to sustain conviction for unlawful possession of prohibited liquor. Murphy v. State, 27 Ala. App. 204, 169 So. 24 (1936).

Evidence that defendant had in his hand a pint bottle of whiskey which he broke after seeing officer approaching warranted conviction for unlawfully possessing liquor. Slaughter v. State, 27 Ala. App. 39, 167 So. 333 (1935).

Evidence of defendant's guilt of unlawfully possessing whiskey in Calhoun county held insufficient for jury. Carroll v. State, 28 Ala. App. 108, 179 So. 397 (1938).

In prosecution for violating prohibition law, evidence that officers found several bottles of home brew in possession of defendant and that home brew contained alcohol sustained conviction. Howard v. State, 26 Ala. App. 103, 153 So. 781 (1934).

Evidence held to make jury question concerning guilt of unlawful possession of whiskey. Horton v. State, 30 Ala. App. 271, 4 So. 2d 477 (1941); Hubbert v. State, 41 Ala. App. 269, 128 So. 2d 527 (1961).

Evidence of receiving. — Defendant's admission that he received one quart of whiskey and state's testimony that he had possession of three fourths of a pint of whiskey held sufficient to support conviction of "receiving" prohibited liquor. Qualls v. State, 27 Ala. App. 159, 167 So. 610 (1936).

Sale and delivery. — Evidence sustained conviction of sale and delivery of prohibited liquor. Fairbanks v. State, 29 Ala. App. 376, 196 So. 746 (1940); Robinson v. State, 37 Ala. App. 320, 67 So. 2d 318 (1953).

Transporting. — Evidence held amply sufficient to support the verdict of guilty of transporting prohibited liquors. Peppers v. State, 36 Ala. App. 468, 59 So. 2d 685 (1952).

Evidence going to show a lending of liquor will support a conviction for sale, barter and exchange. Clark v. State, 167 Ala. 101, 52 So. 893 (1910).

Evidence of aiding an unlawful purchase will authorize a conviction of illegal sale. Rayfield v. State, 167 Ala. 94, 52 So. 833 (1910); Miller v. State, 168 Ala. 100, 53 So. 278 (1910); Johnson v. State, 172 Ala. 424, 55 So. 226 (1911).

Evidence as to alcoholic beverages. — Evidence introduced by the state held sufficient to show that the contents of the receptacles were alcoholic beverages. Peppers v. State, 36 Ala. App. 468, 59 So. 2d 685 (1952).

Uncontroverted testimony of officers held sufficient proof of illegal character of contents of jug. Roughton v. State, 38 Ala. App. 17, 77 So. 2d 666, cert. denied, 262 Ala. 703, 77 So. 2d 667 (1954).

Evidence held sufficient to be jury question where jug containing prohibited whiskey and allegedly thrown from defendant's car was recovered. Mott v. State, 40 Ala. App. 144, 109 So. 2d 309 (1959).

Admission in evidence of a former judgment showing only that defendant had pleaded guilty to the offense of violating the prohibition laws and had been convicted thereof was error, since such judgment fails to state an offense. Amerson v. State, 40 Ala. App. 540, 117 So. 2d 406 (1960).

Where the complaint contained an allegation that accused had previously been convicted of illegal possession of prohibited liquors, it was not error for the court to allow proof, properly made, of the prior conviction. Cheatham v. State, 40 Ala. App. 691, 122 So. 2d 554 (1960).

Bottle of whiskey allegedly purchased from the defendant was properly admitted in evidence though there had been attached to the bottle a label showing the names of the officers who made the purchase, and the time and place of purchase, the price and the defendant's name. Reynolds v. State, 32 Ala. App. 418, 26 So. 2d 626 (1946).

Hearsay reputation. — Admission of testimony of police officer who testified that he knew defendant and where defendant lived and that defendant was known as a whiskey seller and gambler was reversible error and the effect thereof could not be erased from minds of jury by sustaining objection to such testimony. Emerson v. State, 30 Ala. App. 248, 4 So. 2d 183 (1941).

Admission of testimony of deputy sheriff containing implied admission of guilt by the accused was error where there was a contradiction between the state's evidence and that of the accused as to whether any admission of ownership of prohibited beverages had been made. Dalrymple v. State, 41 Ala. App. 223, 127 So. 2d 385 (1961).

Burden of proof. — In prosecution for unlawfully possessing whiskey in Calhoun county, state had burden to prove beyond reasonable doubt that accused knowingly possessed the whiskey as charged. Carroll v. State, 28 Ala. App. 108, 179 So. 397 (1938).

Jury question. — Whether defendant illegally possessed prohibited liquor held for jury under conflicting evidence. Pate v. State, 25 Ala. App. 217, 145 So. 500 (1932); Roughton v. State, 38 Ala. App. 17, 77 So. 2d 666, cert. denied, 262 Ala. 703, 77 So. 2d 667 (1954).

Indictment. — In prosecution for possessing prohibited liquor, affidavit which ended with words "according to law," and complaint which charged that accused "within twelve months before the commencement of this prosecution did have prohibited beer in possession contrary to law, etc.," held sufficient where charge as stated in affidavit and complaint charged an offense under this section. Kiker v. State, 27 Ala. App. 306, 172 So. 288 (1936).

Where from the record it appeared that lower court's jurisdiction to try criminal prosecution was based merely on an "unsworn complaint" filed by the district attorney on the day of trial, which was entirely insufficient, judgment of conviction was erroneous. Jemison v. State, 28 Ala. App. 228, 181 So. 911 (1938).

There was no merit to a contention that because the warrant for possessing (attached to the originating complaint or affidavit) referred to the "offense of violating intoxicating liquor law," that such abbreviated language rendered the charge fatally vague. Stinson v. State, 41 Ala. App. 575, 142 So. 2d 897 (1962).

Failure to exclude district attorney's emotional remarks. — In a prosecution of a violation of this section by a grocery store clerk who allegedly sold whiskey to an alcoholic beverage control enforcement officer, the district attorney's shedding of tears in front of the jury and stating, "A kid could have got it" and "It could go uncontrolled in the hands of children and we can form our reasonable inference of the testimony," should not have been permitted, and the court's attempt to instruct the jury on the subject of "inference from the evidence" instead of correcting the error, added to the injury. Williams v. State, 42 Ala. App. 563, 171 So. 2d 474 (1965).

Joinder of counts. — While it is proper to join count charging the defendant with unlawfully possessing a still, etc., and count charging the unlawful manufacture of prohibited liquors in the same indictment, they were each subject to a separate verdict. Grayson v. State, 28 Ala. App. 210, 182 So. 579 (1938).

Exemption of section 28-4-3 must be pleaded. — A person may be convicted under this section for having intoxicants exempted by § 28-4-3 if the exemptions of such section are not pleaded. Tidwell v. State, 21 Ala. App. 315, 108 So. 76 (1926).

Use of previous convictions in setting penalty. — Notwithstanding that indictment does not aver former conviction for violating prohibition law, court may consider previous conviction in exercising statutory discretion to increase penalty. Johnson v. State, 222 Ala. 90, 130 So. 777 (1930).

§ 28-4-21. Penalties for violations of section 28-4-20.

Any violation of section 28-4-20 shall be a misdemeanor punishable by a fine of not less than $50.00 nor more than $500.00, to which, at the discretion of the court or judge trying the case, may be added imprisonment in the county jail or at hard labor for the county for not more than six months for the first conviction. On the second conviction of a violation of said section 28-4-20, the offense shall, in addition to a fine within the limits above named, be punishable by imprisonment at hard labor for the county for not less than three months nor more than six months, such imprisonment to be imposed by the court or judge trying the case. On the third and every subsequent conviction of a violation of said section 28-4-20, the offense shall, in addition to a fine within the limits above named, be punishable by imprisonment at hard labor for the county for not less than six months nor more than 12 months. (Acts 1915, No. 1, p. 1; Code 1923, § 4622; Acts 1927, No. 623, p. 714; Code 1940, T. 29, § 99.)

Violation of § 28-4-20 is made a misdemeanor by this section. Brown v. State, 44 Ala. App. 135, 203 So. 2d 700 (1967).

Averment as to prior conviction of violating prohibition laws relates to punishment only, under this section, and is addressed to court, whose sole duty it is to sentence defendant to hard labor on second conviction of such offense. Mitchell v. State, 22 Ala. App. 300, 115 So. 149 (1928).

Previous conviction may be called to court's attention. — In prosecution for violating the prohibition law, it was proper to bring to the attention of the court the fact of a previous conviction in order that there might be a compliance with this section. Fendley v. State, 36 Ala. App. 149, 53 So. 2d 397 (1951).

Where it was not clear whether prior convictions testified to were for violations of municipal ordinances or state statutes, the trial judge removed any error by excluding all of the evidence relating to other convictions at the close of the case, and fixed the hard labor punishment at six months, the maximum allowable for a first conviction under § 28-4-20, as prescribed by this section, so that the fact that the prior convictions might have been for breach of a municipal ordinance rather than of § 28-4-20 was harmless error. Mott v. State, 40 Ala. App. 144, 109 So. 2d 309 (1959).

Where there is no averment in the indictment or complaint as to a former conviction, it is discretionary with the trial judge whether he will inquire into the matter and impose the more severe sentence. Griggs v. State, 40 Ala. App. 675, 121 So. 2d 926 (1960).

When punishment deemed for first offense. — Where there was no recital in the judgment that the court ascertained from the evidence that defendant was a second offender, and no hard labor sentence was imposed, it must be deemed that the punishment imposed was for a first offense, and if such action of the court constituted error, it was error without injury to defendant. Griggs v. State, 40 Ala. App. 675, 121 So. 2d 926 (1960).

Cited in May v. State, 22 Ala. App. 239, 114 So. 423 (1927); Hardin v. State, 31 Ala. App. 303, 15 So. 2d 632 (1943); Yates v. State, 245 Ala. 490, 17 So. 2d 777 (1944); Yates v. State, 31 Ala. App. 362, 17 So. 2d 776 (1944); Pinkerton v. State, 246 Ala. 540, 22 So. 2d 113 (1945); Shealey v. State, 36 Ala. App. 70, 54 So. 2d 311 (1951); Pearson v. State, 39 Ala. App. 633, 106 So. 2d 267 (1958); Adkins v. State, 40 Ala. App. 87, 109 So. 2d 747 (1958); Cunningham v. State, 40 Ala. App. 114, 108 So. 2d 192 (1959); Evans v. State, 40 Ala. App. 282, 112 So. 2d 355 (1959); Harris v. State, 42 Ala. App. 208, 158 So. 2d 684 (1963); Edwards v. State, 42 Ala. App. 307, 162 So. 2d 894 (1964); United States v. Smith, 420 F.2d 428 (5th Cir. 1970); United States v. Poole, 434 F.2d 1021 (5th Cir. 1970); Loggins v. State, 52 Ala. App. 204, 290 So. 2d 665 (1974); Malone v. State, 406 So. 2d 1060 (Ala. Crim. App. 1981); Johnson v. State, 406 So. 2d 1063 (Ala. Crim. App. 1981); Todd v. State, 406 So. 2d 1065 (Ala. Crim. App. 1981).

Collateral references. — 48 C.J.S., Intoxicating Liquors, §§ 286-304.

45 Am. Jur. 2d, Intoxicating Liquors, § 406 et seq.

§ 28-4-22. Conduct of business of brewer, rectifier of spirits or retail or wholesale dealer in liquors or malt liquors.

It shall be unlawful within this state to carry on the business of a brewer, rectifier of spirits or retail or wholesale dealer in liquors or retail or wholesale dealer in malt liquors, and any violation of this section, whether a first or subsequent offense, shall be punishable as prescribed in section 28-4-21.

The carrying on of business as such brewer or rectifier of spirits or retail or wholesale dealer in liquors or retail or wholesale dealer in malt liquors shall, for each separate day that it is carried on, constitute a separate offense, to be punished as prescribed in section 28-4-21. (Acts 1915, No. 1, p. 1; Code 1923, § 4623; Code 1940, T. 29, § 100.)

§ 28-4-23. Keeping, etc., of prohibited liquors and beverages in lockers, rooms, etc., of social clubs, etc.; duty of officers of such clubs, etc., to prevent violations of section.

No prohibited liquors and beverages shall be kept or permitted to be kept by members or others in any locker or room of or on the premises of any social club or of any other association or organization of persons, whether of a fraternal or social nature or otherwise, and whether incorporated or not, and such club or club room shall not be deemed to be at the home or private premises of any member thereof.

It shall be the duty of all officers of any such club or association of persons, and especially of the secretary, manager or other officer in charge of the premises, to prevent the violation of this section by the members or by others resorting thereto. The presence of prohibited liquor in any locker or any other place on the premises or about the rooms of any such club or association of persons shall constitute prima facie evidence that the said officers in charge and the officers and directors of the club or of the organization are unlawfully permitting the possession of said prohibited liquors and beverages at such place and are guilty of violation of this section. (Acts 1919, No. 7, p. 6; Code 1923, § 4624; Code 1940, T. 29, § 101.)

Collateral references. — 48 C.J.S., Intoxicating Liquors, § 274.

Possession of intoxicating liquor as evidence of violation of law under statute. 31 ALR 1222.

§ 28-4-24. Distillation or manufacture of prohibited liquors and beverages.

Any person, firm or corporation who shall, within this state, distill, make or manufacture any alcoholic, spirituous, malted or mixed liquors or beverages, any part of which is alcohol, shall be guilty of a felony and, upon conviction thereof, shall be punished by imprisonment at hard labor in the penitentiary for not less than one year nor longer than five years, such imprisonment to be fixed within these limits by the court. (Acts 1919, No. 7, p. 6; Code 1923, § 4627; Code 1940, T. 29, § 103.)

Illegal manufacture of intoxicating liquor is a felony. Surrett v. United States, 421 F.2d 403 (5th Cir. 1970).

Attempting to make liquor. — A person may be convicted of attempting to make liquor. Mote v. State, 17 Ala. App. 526, 87 So. 628 (1920).

An indictment charging the offense of manufacturing prohibited liquors will support a conviction of an attempt to manufacture such prohibited liquors, where the evidence fails to make out the charge in the higher degree but is sufficient to make out the lesser offense. Bentley v. State, 41 Ala. App. 282, 131 So. 2d 426 (1961).

Aiders and abettors. — One can be an aider and abettor in making an alcoholic beverage without evidence tending to show that he has actual or constructive possession of the apparatus. Oden v. State, 41 Ala. App. 212, 127 So. 2d 380 (1961).

No federal assistance in enforcement of state prohibition laws. — In providing for registration provisions to protect the collection of revenue congress did not direct any federal officer to assist in enforcing any state's prohibition laws, and there are no established procedures in force for notifying state authorities of the names of registrants. United States v. Richardson, 284 F. Supp. 419 (M.D. Ala. 1968).

Corroboration by coconspirator. — In prosecution for possessing a still and distilling, that witness did not know accused's name at time witness saw accused at the still engaged in distilling whiskey, and that witness procured accused's name from accused's coconspirator, did not preclude conviction of accused because of lack of corroboration of coconspirator in view of other testimony. Hill v. State, 30 Ala. App. 332, 5 So. 2d 651 (1942).

Evidence of illicit distilling held sufficient. — Evidence that several officers observed defendant working at a still, which was complete and in full operation, and that the defendant ran when the officers made their presence known, and that after his arrest defendant made a voluntary statement, admitting that he was connected with the operation of the still, was sufficient to justify a conviction of illicit distilling. Reese v. State, 32 Ala. App. 449, 26 So. 2d 723 (1946); Wood v. State, 38 Ala. App. 368, 83 So. 2d 619 (1955).

Accepting verdict of guilty under indictment in two counts charging distinct offenses of possessing a still for purpose of manufacturing or distilling prohibited liquors and distilling or manufacturing such liquors was not error, where sentence pronounced did not impose a greater punishment than that prescribed for one of offenses charged in indictment. Hill v. State, 30 Ala. App. 332, 5 So. 2d 651 (1942).

Appeal of punishment. — Where trial court acted within limit provided by this section in imposing punishment for possessing a still unlawfully and distilling prohibited liquors, on appeal the court of appeals was unauthorized to review or revise the action of trial court on such matter. Wood v. State, 28 Ala. App. 464, 187 So. 250 (1939).

Complaint and argument as to severity of punishment imposed upon defendant by trial court would not be considered by court of appeals where nothing appeared in the record to sustain such complaint. Wood v. State, 28 Ala. App. 464, 187 So. 250 (1939).

Cited in Laminack v. State, 18 Ala. App. 399, 92 So. 502 (1922); Ex parte Lawrence, 21 Ala. App. 537, 109 So. 615 (1926); Murphy v. State, 22 Ala. App. 370, 115 So. 771 (1928); Tinker v. State, 24 Ala. App. 601, 139 So. 575 (1932); Dickerson v. State, 32 Ala. App. 432, 26 So. 2d 627 (1946); Roberson v. United States, 249 F.2d 737 (5th Cir. 1957), cert. denied, 356 U.S. 919, 78 S. Ct. 704, 2 L. Ed. 2d 715 (1958); United States v. Smith, 420 F.2d 428 (5th Cir. 1970).

Collateral references. — 48 C.J.S., Intoxicating Liquors, § 36.

§ 28-4-25. Allowance of reward to sheriff or other person furnishing evidence to support conviction for violation of section 28-4-24.

Whenever any person is convicted in the circuit court under section 28-4-24 of unlawfully distilling or manufacturing or making any of the prohibited liquors or beverages as defined in this chapter, there shall be charged to the Alabama alcoholic beverage control board to be paid by them the sum of $50.00 out of the funds used by the board for the purchase of alcoholic beverages to be allowed the sheriff or other officer or person who furnished the evidence and brought about the conviction. Said sheriff or other officer or person must satisfy the presiding judge that he is the person entitled to said sum and shall receive from the judge a certificate to that effect. (Acts 1919, No. 7, p. 6; Code 1923, § 4626; Code 1940, T. 29, § 102; Acts 1953, No. 699, p. 954.)

Reference to statutory reward. — Where deputy sheriff, who was state's only witness in prosecutions for unlawfully possessing still, would have been entitled to statutory reward if convictions were obtained, excluding defense argument disclosing such fact held error. Little v. State, 27 Ala. App. 119, 166 So. 618 (1936).

It is always permissible to show the pecuni-ary interest of a witness in the result of a trial, for the purpose of affecting the credibility and weight of his evidence. However, in a prosecution for distilling and possessing a still, questions as to the sheriff's usual procedure and arrangements with informers other than the informer in the case at hand were not material to any issue. Anderson v. State, 39 Ala. App. 400, 103 So. 2d 796 (1957).

Reward allowed by this section is a reward to spur individual initiative and diligence, whether the individual acts in an official or private capacity. It is not a fee allowed a sheriff or other officer because he is an officer. This statement of principle includes a chief deputy, as he too is an officer. Mosely v. Kennedy, 245 Ala. 448, 17 So. 2d 536 (1944).

This section gives a field of operation for a distinction between the performances of a deputy sheriff as they relate to his individual and his official acts. Jefferson County v. Dockerty, 33 Ala. App. 30, 30 So. 2d 469 (1947).

Charge held properly refused. — A charge stated, in effect, that anyone furnishing proof of possession of a still, etc., is entitled to a fee whether there is a conviction or not. Such is not the law and the trial court should not be put in error for refusing to so charge the jury. Dixon v. State, 269 Ala. 548, 115 So. 2d 270 (1959).

Cited in Dallas County v. Kennedy, 246 Ala. 558, 21 So. 2d 678 (1945); Jefferson County v. Dockerty, 249 Ala. 196, 30 So. 2d 474 (1947).

§ 28-4-26. Sale, barter, exchange, etc., of prohibited liquors or beverages by person concealing self in house, room, etc.

Any person who conceals himself in any house, room, booth, enclosure or other place and sells, gives away, barters, exchanges or otherwise disposes of spirituous, vinous or malt liquors or any other prohibited liquors or beverages or who, by any device or subterfuge, sells, gives away or otherwise disposes of any of said prohibited liquors or beverages in violation or evasion of law or who, in any house, room, booth, enclosure or other place, in such manner and under such circumstances as that he cannot be seen by persons from the exterior, sells, gives away or otherwise disposes of any such prohibited beverages, contrary to law, shall be fined not less than $50.00 nor more than $500.00 and may also be imprisoned in the county jail or sentenced to hard labor for the county for not less than three months nor more than six months, at the discretion of the court. (Acts 1909, No. 191, p. 63; Code 1923, § 4629; Code 1940, T. 29, § 105.)

§ 28-4-27. Enforcement of section 28-4-26.

If any person violates a provision of section 28-4-26, upon complaint being made on oath before a judge of any court having jurisdiction of misdemeanors that spirituous, vinous or malt liquors, or other beverages or liquors, prohibited by law to be sold, given away or otherwise disposed of have been sold, given away or otherwise disposed of in violation of law and that the person committing such offense comes within the terms of section 28-4-26 and that such person is known or unknown to the person making the complaint and that other parties present and participating in the tippling or drinking of liquors at such place are unknown to the person making the complaint, it shall be the duty of such judge to issue forthwith a warrant of arrest for such party for the offense charged in the complaint and immediately to place such warrant in the hands of the sheriff or other lawful officer. (Acts 1909, No. 191, p. 63; Code 1923, § 4630; Code 1940, T. 29, § 106.)

§ 28-4-28. Storage, etc., of prohibited liquors or beverages by person, etc., engaged in business of selling beverages.

It shall be unlawful for any person, firm or corporation engaged in the business of selling beverages to keep or store on the premises where said beverage business is conducted any prohibited liquors or beverages, the sale, offering for sale or other disposition of which is prohibited by the law of Alabama, and any person violating this section shall be guilty of a misdemeanor. (Acts 1909, No. 191, p. 63; Acts 1915, No. 2, p. 8; Code 1940, T. 29, § 114.)

Offense denounced by this section is separate and distinct from the offense denounced by § 28-4-20, and in proving an offense under § 28-4-20 it is error to admit evidence that will tend to prove an offense under this section. Tidwell v. State, 21 Ala. App. 315, 108 So. 76 (1926).

Collateral references. — 48 C.J.S., Intoxicating Liquors, § 222.

§ 28-4-29. Solicitation or receipt of order for prohibited liquors or beverages.

Any person who within this state solicits or receives any order for any spirituous, vinous or malt liquors or any other liquors or beverages prohibited by the law of the state to be sold or offered for sale or otherwise disposed of in this state in any quantity to be shipped into this state or to be shipped from one point in this state to another point in this state shall be guilty of a misdemeanor. The taking or soliciting of such orders is within the inhibition of this section, although the orders are subject to approval by some other person and no part of the price is paid nor any part of the goods delivered when the orders are taken.

If such order is in writing, parol evidence thereof is admissible without producing or accounting for the absence of the original. (Acts 1909, No. 191, p. 63; Acts 1915, No. 2, p. 8; Code 1923, § 4640; Code 1940, T. 29, § 115.)

Collateral references. — 48 C.J.S., Intoxicating Liquors, §§ 267, 353.

§ 28-4-30. Punishment of agents or assisting friends of buyers or sellers of prohibited liquors and beverages.

Any person who shall act as agent or assisting friend of the seller or buyer in procuring an unlawful sale of any prohibited liquors and beverages shall be punishable as if he had sold said prohibited liquors and beverages, and conviction may be had of such agent or assisting friend upon an indictment, affidavit or complaint against him for selling prohibited liquors and beverages contrary to law. (Acts 1909, No. 191, p. 63; Acts 1915, No. 2, p. 8; Code 1923, § 4651; Code 1940, T. 29, § 126.)

Collateral references. — 45 Am. Jur. 2d,
Intoxicating Liquors, § 244.

§ 28-4-31. Exhibition of signs containing names of prohibited liquors or beverages or employment of certain words in designating business by dealers in beverages; use of evidence thereof in prosecutions against dealers for sale, offer for sale, etc., of prohibited liquors and beverages.

No dealer in beverages shall post or place about the premises any sign or signs containing the name of any prohibited liquors or beverages or indicating that any prohibited liquors or beverages are kept on or about the premises for sale or other disposition, nor shall any dealer in beverages employ the words "saloon," "buffet" or "bar" in designating the business or the place where the beverage business is conducted. Any person violating any provision of this section shall be guilty of a misdemeanor.

In case of any charge or prosecution against any dealer in beverages for violating the law against selling, offering for sale or keeping for sale or otherwise disposing of prohibited liquors and beverages, it shall be competent to make proof in the action that said party had posted such signs on or about the premises or that the word saloon, buffet, or bar was employed to designate the business or the place where the business was conducted. (Acts 1909, No. 191, p. 63; Code 1915, No. 2, p. 8; Code 1923, § 4652; Code 1940, T. 29, § 127.)

Collateral references. — 48 C.J.S., Intoxicating Liquors, § 39, n. 58.

ARTICLE 3.

MANUFACTURE, POSSESSION, ALLOWANCE OF OPERATION BY ANOTHER, ETC., OF STILL, ETC., FOR MANUFACTURE OF PROHIBITED LIQUORS OR BEVERAGES.

§ 28-4-50. Manufacture, sale, possession, etc., of still, etc., for manufacture of prohibited liquors or beverages.

It shall be unlawful for any person, firm or corporation in this state to manufacture, sell, give away or have in possession any still, apparatus, appliance or any device or substitute therefor to be used for the purpose of manufacturing any prohibited liquors or beverages. (Acts 1919, No. 737, p. 1086; Code 1923, § 4656; Code 1940, T. 29, § 131.)

I. General Consideration.
II. Proof and Procedure.

I. GENERAL CONSIDERATION.

Section is constitutional. — This section and § 28-4-54 are not contrary to Constitution, § 45, requiring laws to contain but one subject which shall be clearly expressed in the title. McNeal v. State, 18 Ala. App. 311, 92 So. 95 (1921).

And is not repealed. — That indictment for unlawful possession of still was returned before passage of Alabama Alcoholic Beverage Control Act is immaterial, in view of express provision of such Act (see § 28-3-18) that law under which defendant was prosecuted was not repealed. Slayton v. State, 28 Ala. App. 494, 188 So. 273 (1939).

Evil sought to be suppressed in all of the Alabama liquor statutes is the making, possession and transportation, etc., of illegal liquors or beverages. The possession of a still or substitute therefor has a reasonable relationship to the evil sought to be suppressed. Bolin v. State, 266 Ala. 256, 96 So. 2d 582 (1957).

It is the possession of a complete still, and not merely part or parts thereof, that is essential to the crime of having possession of still for the purpose of manufacturing liquor, denounced by this section. McCormick v. State, 22 Ala. App. 577, 117 So. 911 (1928); Bowden v. State, 23 Ala. App. 215, 123 So. 107 (1929). See also Murphy v. State, 22 Ala. App. 163, 113 So. 623 (1927); Young v. State, 28 Ala. App. 491, 188 So. 270 (1939).

It is the possession of a still coupled with the fact that it is to be used for the purpose of manufacturing prohibited liquors or beverages, which constitutes the crime. German v. State, 429 So. 2d 1138 (Ala. Crim. App. 1982).

Mere possession of only a part or parts of a still, apparatus or device for making liquors is no offense under this section. Pate v. State, 19 Ala. App. 642, 99 So. 833 (1924).

The offense denounced by this section is the possession of a still to be used for the purpose of manufacturing prohibited beverages. If one possesses a complete still, it matters not if it be generally or commonly used, or suitable for the manufacture of prohibited beverages, if the still is possessed for the purpose of such manufacture. Johnson v. State, 38 Ala. App. 590, 90 So. 2d 164 (1956).

Coupled with the fact that it is to be used for manufacturing which constitutes the crime. — The mere possession of a still is not made a violation of this section; it is the possession of a still, apparatus or appliance, or any device or substitute therefor, coupled with the fact that it is to be used for the purpose of manufacturing prohibited liquors or beverages, which constitutes the crime. Brock v. State, 19 Ala. App. 124, 95 So. 559 (1923);

Young v. State, 28 Ala. App. 491, 188 So. 270 (1939); Bradley v. State, 31 Ala. App. 475, 18 So. 2d 702 (1944).

Proof that still found by officers was to be used to manufacture prohibited liquor, or was suitable to be so used, is essential to conviction, under this section, for unlawfully possessing still. Funderberg v. State, 22 Ala. App. 363, 115 So. 765 (1928).

It is the possession coupled with the fact that it is to be used for the purpose of manufacturing prohibited liquors, which constitutes the crime under this section, and when the two facts coexist the crime is complete and when so charged in an indictment all of the constituents of the crime are sufficiently described. Franklin v. State, 52 Ala. 414 (1875); Jenkins v. State, 97 Ala. 66, 12 So. 110 (1892); Holloway v. State, 18 Ala. App. 392, 92 So. 78 (1922); Griggs v. State, 18 Ala. App. 467, 93 So. 499 (1922); Masters v. State, 18 Ala. App. 614, 94 So. 249 (1922).

Section makes no distinction in the size of an apparatus prohibited under this section or § 28-4-51. Parker v. State, 41 Ala. App. 463, 135 So. 2d 169 (1961).

Possession of any appliances is prohibited. — This section would be violated if defendant possessed any articles to manufacture prohibited liquors, whether or not generally used for such purpose. Ex parte State ex rel. Davis, 211 Ala. 574, 100 So. 917 (1924); Pate v. State, 19 Ala. App. 642, 99 So. 833 (1924); Scott v. State, 20 Ala. App. 360, 102 So. 152 (1924).

But the words, "still, apparatus appliance," are in themselves insufficient as a description of the article, the possession of which is condemned. It is only when specifically described as "to be used for the purpose of manufacturing any prohibited liquors or beverages" that the description becomes certain and informs the defendant of what he is charged. Morris v. State, 18 Ala. App. 456, 93 So. 61 (1922).

Separate offense from possessing liquors. — In a prosecution for possessing a still, an answer of a prior conviction for possessing liquors made by defendant at this still is not a valid defense, as possessing liquor and possessing a still are different offenses. Day v. State, 19 Ala. App. 286, 97 So. 117 (1923).

Joinder of counts. — While it is proper to join count charging the defendant with unlawfully possessing a still, etc., in violation of this section and count charging the unlawful manufacture of prohibited liquors in violation of § 28-4-20 in the same indictment, they were each subject to a separate verdict. Grayson v. State, 28 Ala. App. 210, 182 So. 579 (1938).

When an offense denounced by this section is joined with another offense in the same indictment, but in separate counts, a conviction on one of the counts only is an acquittal on the other. Parris v. State, 18 Ala. App. 240, 90 So. 808 (1921).

Accepting verdict of guilty under indictment in two counts charging distinct offenses of possessing a still for purposes of manufacturing or distilling prohibited liquors and distilling or manufacturing such liquors was not error, where sentence pronounced did not impose a greater punishment than that prescribed for one of offenses charged in indictment. Hill v. State, 30 Ala. App. 332, 5 So. 2d 651 (1942).

Judicial notice. — Court is without authority to take judicial notice that oil tank, barrel, flakestand, condenser, furnace and two pieces of worm were complete still to be used for purpose of manufacturing liquor, as contemplated by this section. Murphy v. State, 22 Ala. App. 163, 113 So. 623 (1927).

Cited in Weaver v. State, 18 Ala. App. 47, 88 So. 362 (1921); McReynolds v. State, 18 Ala. App. 173, 89 So. 825 (1921); Frazier v. State, 18 Ala. App. 203, 89 So. 836 (1921); Isbell v. State, 18 Ala. App. 223, 90 So. 55 (1921); Savage v. State, 18 Ala. App. 299, 92 So. 19 (1921); Laminack v. State, 18 Ala. App. 399, 92 So. 502 (1922); Floyd v. State, 18 Ala. App. 647, 94 So. 192 (1922); Martin v. State, 22 Ala. App. 307, 115 So. 149 (1928); Funderberg v. State, 22 Ala. App. 363, 115 So. 765 (1928); Murphy v. State, 22 Ala. App. 370, 115 So. 771 (1928); Bowden v. State, 23 Ala. App. 215, 123 So. 107 (1929); Clay v. State, 23 Ala. App. 222, 123 So. 110 (1929); Tinker v. State, 24 Ala. App. 601, 139 So. 575 (1932); Statham v. State, 25 Ala. App. 135, 141 So. 915 (1932); Allen v. State, 25 Ala. App. 181, 142 So. 777 (1932); Berry v. State, 28 Ala. App. 446, 186 So. 781 (1939); In re Upshaw, 247 Ala. 221, 23 So. 2d 861 (1945); Shewbart v. State, 33 Ala. App. 199, 32 So. 2d 241 (1947); Barger v. State, 34 Ala. App. 62, 37 So. 2d 235 (1948); Clark v. State, 35 Ala. App. 60, 43 So. 2d 431 (1949); Bradberry v. State, 36 Ala. App. 681, 62 So. 2d 802 (1953); Stover v. State, 36 Ala. App. 696, 63 So. 2d 386 (1953); Smothers v. State, 38 Ala. App. 153, 83 So. 2d 374 (1954); Robinson v. State, 38 Ala. App. 315, 82 So. 2d 815 (1955); Clements v. State, 39 Ala. App. 386, 101 So. 2d 640 (1958); Barbour v. City of Montgomery, 39 Ala. App. 490, 104 So. 2d 300 (1958); Davis v. State, 41 Ala. App. 339, 132 So. 2d 265 (1961); Richardson v. State, 41 Ala. App. 556, 139 So. 2d 627 (1962); Godwin v. State, 279 Ala. 286, 184 So. 2d 374 (1965); Devaney v. State, 55 Ala. App. 408, 316 So. 2d 239 (1975).

Collateral references. — 48 C.J.S., Intoxicating Liquors, §§ 220, 221, 235.

Constitutionality of statute prohibiting manufacture of liquor. 3 ALR 285.

II. PROOF AND PROCEDURE.

Elements of proof. — Where the state relies on the rule of evidence established by § 28-4-51 for a conviction under this title, it is necessary to prove beyond a reasonable doubt: (1) Possession by the defendant of the articles designated; and (2) that such article or articles are commonly or generally used for or suitable to be used in the manufacture of prohibited liquors or beverages, and unless both of said elements are established the defendant is entitled to a directed verdict. Kizziah v. State, 42 Ala. App. 303, 162 So. 2d 889 (1964).

Under § 28-4-51, establishing rule of evidence for prosecution under this section for possessing still for purpose of manufacturing liquor, state had burden of showing beyond a reasonable doubt possession by accused of article or articles designated, and that such article or articles in possession of accused were commonly or generally used for manufacture of prohibited liquors and beverages, or were suitable for use for such purposes. Pouncey v. State, 22 Ala. App. 455, 116 So. 803 (1928).

For the state to be successful in a prosecution under this section, it is incumbent upon it to prove that accused was in possession of a complete still, apparatus, etc., which was to be used for the purpose of manufacturing prohibited liquor or beverages. Williams v. State, 45 Ala. App. 138, 227 So. 2d 135 (1969).

Mere presence of a defendant at a still, without more, will not support a conviction for its possession, but any acts of the defendant in and about the still showing dominion over it, or which indicate an interest therein, or that he is aiding or abetting in the possession, may be taken as sufficient upon which to base a verdict of guilt. Williams v. State, 45 Ala. App. 138, 227 So. 2d 135 (1969).

Proof of possession. — If a still is found, whether on defendant's premises or not, and it is proven beyond a reasonable doubt that the defendant was present, exercising acts of domain over it, the jury is warranted in the inference that he had the possession. Berry v. State, 20 Ala. App. 102, 100 So. 922 (1924).

The mere presence of a defendant at a still, without more, will not warrant a conviction for its possession, but courts hold that any act of the defendant in and about a still which indicates an interest in, or that he is aiding or abetting in the possession, may be taken as sufficient upon which to base a verdict of guilt. Vandiver v. State, 37 Ala. App. 526, 73 So. 2d 566 (1953); Thomas v. State, 41 Ala. App. 674, 149 So. 2d 290 (1963).

Evidence that accused was present at and

exercising acts of ownership over a "still" and that he fled when officers appeared, and that the "still" was connected to defendant's nearby house by a well-defined and constantly used path, sustained conviction for unlawful possession of a "still," notwithstanding the worm to the "still" was not connected in such way as to manufacture whiskey. Morgan v. State, 28 Ala. App. 516, 189 So. 85 (1939).

Of location. — A still in the vicinity of a man's home (in this case from 400 yards to one-half mile), a path leading from that still in the direction of the home of accused, without more, is in no sense the requisite proof necessary to sustain a conviction under this section. Wheat v. State, 19 Ala. App. 538, 98 So. 698 (1924).

Evidence, showing that a still was found about 200 yards from the defendant's house and there was a path leading from his house to the still, is not sufficient to sustain a conviction under this section. Clark v. State, 18 Ala. App. 217, 90 So. 16 (1921).

Of still components. — In prosecution for possessing a still, evidence that a lard can was found with hole cut in top, and a trough with a hole at each end, and a pipe about 100 yards away hanging in a tree, without any evidence that any of such articles were commonly used in manufacture of liquor, held insufficient to make out prima facie case, under this section. Martin v. State, 20 Ala. App. 593, 104 So. 287 (1925).

Evidence was sufficient to justify a conviction of the offense of illegal possession of a still where the evidence showed that all of the necessary parts of the still were present though not assembled. Johnson v. State, 38 Ala. App. 590, 90 So. 2d 164 (1956).

Evidence that arresting officers found "copper worm" and "copper connections" on wagon defendant was driving made prima facie case, under indictment charging possession of still for manufacturing prohibited liquors, though such articles were not alone sufficient with which to manufacture liquor, in view of this section and § 28-4-51. Horton v. State, 22 Ala. App. 114, 113 So. 279 (1927).

Evidence that officers found in defendant's cabin parts of a still consisting of one worm, a piece of copper pipe about three feet long, a beer barrel with about one inch of beer in the bottom of the barrel, and several pints of liquor, sustained conviction for unlawfully possessing a still. Austin v. State, 29 Ala. App. 164, 193 So. 874 (1940).

In prosecution under this section for violating the liquor law by reason of possessing a still, evidence not showing that articles in defendant's possession were generally used for or suitable to be used in the manufacture of intoxicating liquor, when measured in accordance with rule established by § 28-4-51, held insufficient to sustain conviction. Pouncey v. State, 22 Ala. App. 455, 116 So. 803 (1928). See also Atchley v. State, 22 Ala. App. 125, 113 So. 625 (1927).

Where the officers testified they found a complete still, except for a condenser, which is an essential part of a still when it is in actual operation, and the parts of the still present were such as are commonly or generally used for or suitable to be used in the manufacture of prohibited liquors or beverages, it was held that under § 28-4-51, this evidence made out a prima facie case of a violation of this section. Hood v. State, 42 Ala. App. 286, 161 So. 2d 154 (1964).

Of use. — Where a state witness saw defendant testing the mash, moving the fuel and connecting the fuel feeder lines, a reasonable jury could infer that a still was about to be put to work. Kizziah v. State, 42 Ala. App. 303, 162 So. 2d 889 (1964).

"Sell" under this section involves the sale of any apparatus, appliance or device used for manufacturing prohibited liquors and not the sale of whiskey. Gavin v. State, 52 Ala. App. 469, 294 So. 2d 169, cert. denied, 292 Ala. 722, 294 So. 2d 170 (1974).

Admissibility of photograph of defendant on still after arrest. — In prosecution for manufacturing whiskey, admission in evidence of a photograph of defendant on top of a still handcuffed to officers was error where there was no evidence tending to show defendant had posed voluntarily or had been advised as to his rights against self-incrimination and where no witness saw defendant closer than 150 to 200 feet from the still before he was arrested and taken there. Bates v. State, 40 Ala. App. 549, 117 So. 2d 258 (1959).

Admissibility of voluntary confession. — Where corpus delicti of offense of unlawfully possessing a still was proven by evidence without dispute in accordance with this section and § 28-4-51, a voluntary confession of defendant was admissible. Burchfield v. State, 23 Ala. App. 231, 123 So. 281 (1929).

Of former conviction for distilling. — In trial for unlawful possession of still, admission of defendant's testimony on cross-examination that he had been twice convicted of distilling was error requiring reversal of conviction. Slayton v. State, 28 Ala. App. 494, 188 So. 273 (1939).

Of attempt to secure compromise. — In prosecution for unlawfully possessing still, evidence that defendant on different occasions after his arrest undertook to secure compromise of case by making certain designated settlement held error, especially where at no time did defendant admit his guilt. Brunson v. State, 26 Ala. App. 255, 157 So. 678 (1934).

Evidence was sufficient to support verdict and judgment of conviction. Harris v. State, 39 Ala. App. 99, 94 So. 2d 884 (1957); Payne v. State, 40 Ala. App. 493, 115 So. 2d 670 (1959).

Possession question for jury. — When one charged with violating this section, on proof that a still was found in his home, shows that he had been away from home most of the time for the past few months, and that his home was occupied by his family and a cousin, possession of the still by the defendant becomes a question for the jury. Tyre v. State, 20 Ala. App. 483, 103 So. 91 (1925).

Evidence that defendant and another were present and exercising dominion over and possession of an incomplete still, other component parts thereof, and mash therein held sufficient to raise issue for jury as to defendant's guilt of possessing a still to be used for manufacturing prohibited liquors. McFarland v. State, 22 Ala. App. 609, 118 So. 500 (1928).

Evidence, including testimony of possession of parts of still commonly used for manufacturing prohibited liquors, held sufficient to take accused's guilt of possessing still to jury. Allen v. State, 26 Ala. App. 195, 155 So. 721 (1934).

Ownership and dominion over a still may be shown to prove possession, the offense denounced by this section, but ownership and dominion being evidentiary they are questions of fact for the jury. Hope v. State, 21 Ala. App. 491, 109 So. 521 (1926).

Accused's guilt of possessing still and distilling prohibited liquors was for jury. Hill v. State, 30 Ala. App. 332, 5 So. 2d 651 (1942); Rikard v. State, 31 Ala. App. 374, 18 So. 2d 435 (1944).

Whether the defendant unlawfully possessed the parts of a still presented a question for the jury. Hood v. State, 42 Ala. App. 286, 161 So. 2d 154 (1964).

As is question of whether device or substitute is part of still. — In a prosecution for possessing a still, whether a tub, trough, pans or buckets and wet meal constituted a part or parts of a still or device or substitute therefor to be used in manufacture of liquors, is for the jury. Arthur v. State, 19 Ala. App. 311, 97 So. 158 (1923).

And question of use. — In a prosecution for possessing a still, evidence that about 30 gallons of beer, adaptable for making moonshine whiskey, were found in defendant's home, was a circumstance to be considered by the jury in determining whether the still found in his possession was to be used for making prohibited liquors or beverages. Brock v. State, 19 Ala. App. 124, 95 So. 559 (1923).

Issue raised by plea of former jeopardy. — In prosecution for possessing still, issue raised by plea of former jeopardy held for jury under evidence. Statham v. State, 25 Ala. App. 135, 141 So. 915 (1932).

§ 28-4-51. Unexplained possession of part or parts of still, etc., deemed prima facie evidence of violation of section 28-4-50.

The unexplained possession of any part or parts of any still, apparatus, appliance or any device or substitute therefor commonly or generally used for or that is suitable to be used in the manufacture of prohibited liquors and beverages shall be prima facie evidence of a violation of section 28-4-50. (Acts 1919, No. 737, p. 1086; Code 1923, § 4657; Code 1940, T. 29, § 132.)

Constitutional. — The section making the unexplained possession of any part of a still, etc. prima facie evidence of a violation of law infringes no constitutional right. Coats v. State, 257 Ala. 406, 60 So. 2d 261 (1952), rev'g 36 Ala. App. 515, 60 So. 2d 257 (1951).

In effect this section merely creates a rule of evidence. Barger v. State, 34 Ala. App. 62, 37 So. 2d 235 (1948).

This section has been held to be constitutional apparently as a rule of evidence and not as an ipse dixit, making possession of part the possession of the whole. Parker v. State, 41 Ala. App. 463, 135 So. 2d 169 (1961).

This section has been construed to state a

rule of evidence. Kizziah v. State, 42 Ala. App. 303, 162 So. 2d 889 (1964).

Nevertheless, burden of proof remains throughout on the state. Kizziah v. State, 42 Ala. App. 303, 162 So. 2d 889 (1964).

"Prima facie evidence" means that which brings about a measure of proof which, unless it is self-contradictory or is contradicted by the defense, would support the jury's inferring the existence of one or more elements of a crime. Kizziah v. State, 42 Ala. App. 303, 162 So. 2d 889 (1964).

Question of what is possession can only be worked out from case to case rather than be deducible from the statement of an abstract general rule. Etheridge v. State, 42 Ala. App. 77, 152 So. 2d 689 (1963).

It is no offense to possess a part of still except under section 28-4-50. — Section 28-4-50 contemplates a complete still, and although this section makes possession of a part of a still prima facie evidence of the possession of a complete still, there is no statute making it an offense to possess a part of a still. Hence there can be no conviction for possessing only a part of a still, but conviction must be under § 28-4-50. Pate v. State, 19 Ala. App. 642, 99 So. 833 (1924); Berry v. State, 20 Ala. App. 102, 100 So. 922 (1924).

This section is a rule of evidence fixed by the legislature in its efforts to suppress the liquor traffic. It creates no crime and fixes no penalty, but simply fixes what will be prima facie evidence of a violation of § 28-4-50 when certain facts are proven, which are the unexplained possession of any part or parts of any still, apparatus or appliance, or any device or substitute therefor, commonly or generally used for, or that is suitable to be used in, the manufacture of prohibited liquors and beverages. Little v. State, 27 Ala. App. 119, 166 So. 618 (1936); Mitchell v. State, 38 Ala. App. 546, 89 So. 2d 238 (1956).

The possession of the articles named in this section is not made unlawful but their unexplained possession is merely an evidentiary presumption so that when taken in connection with other evidence would authorize a judge or jury to find that a defendant had committed the crime of possessing a complete still or substitute therefor, to be used for the purpose of manufacturing prohibited liquors or beverages. Bolin v. State, 266 Ala. 256, 96 So. 2d 582 (1957).

Under this section evidence of possession of lard can, cap and mash ready for distillation, warranted inference of possession of complete still, in violation of the preceding section. Whigham v. State, 21 Ala. App. 454, 109 So. 281 (1926).

To support conviction for possessing still, evidence must show complete still. But possession of any part of still commonly used in manufacture of prohibited liquors is prima facie evidence of possession of complete still. McNeel v. State, 25 Ala. App. 36, 140 So. 185 (1932). See also Jones v. State, 25 Ala. App. 346, 146 So. 424 (1933). This is not true of possession of incomplete still not shown as commonly used in manufacture of liquors or as suitable to such use. Allen v. State, 25 Ala. App. 181, 142 So. 777 (1932).

The possession of any parts of a still is sufficient to sustain a conviction under § 28-4-50, in view of this section, if the parts so found in the defendant's possession were com-

monly or generally used or suitable to be used in the manufacture of liquor, although liquor could not be made with the parts found. Lindsey v. State, 18 Ala. App. 494, 93 So. 331 (1922).

Section makes no distinction in the size of an apparatus prohibited under this section or § 28-4-50. Parker v. State, 41 Ala. App. 463, 135 So. 2d 169 (1961).

There is no such offense within the purview of the prohibition laws as an attempt to possess a still. Bentley v. State, 41 Ala. App. 339, 131 So. 2d 426 (1961). See also Clements v. State, 39 Ala. App. 386, 101 So. 2d 640 (1958).

Before possession shall make prima facie case evidence must show beyond reasonable doubt the possession of articles designated. Little v. State, 27 Ala. App. 119, 166 So. 618 (1936); Nugent v. State, 28 Ala. App. 182, 181 So. 707 (1938).

The possession of any part of a still, etc., is prima facie evidence of guilt and would authorize a conclusion by the jury that the defendant possessed the whole still or apparatus, etc., without additional proof. Maisel v. State, 17 Ala. App. 12, 81 So. 348 (1919); Lindsey v. State, 18 Ala. App. 494, 93 So. 331 (1922); Gamble v. State, 19 Ala. App. 82, 95 So. 202 (1922).

An accused rebuts the statutory prima facie case of unlawful possession of still made against accused when state proves that accused was found in possession of parts of still, when accused offers testimony of sufficient weight to raise in minds of jury a reasonable doubt of a guilty possession. Nugent v. State, 28 Ala. App. 182, 181 So. 707 (1938).

That articles were generally used for or suitable to be used in the manufacture of liquor. — See Ex parte State ex rel. Davis, 211 Ala. 574, 100 So. 917 (1924); Echols v. State, 24 Ala. App. 352, 135 So. 410 (1931); Little v. State, 27 Ala. App. 119, 166 So. 618 (1936).

Under this section the state must show beyond a reasonable doubt that the articles designated are commonly or generally used for manufacture of prohibited liquors and that they are suitable for such purpose. Young v. State, 28 Ala. App. 491, 188 So. 270 (1939).

The expression "can be used for making or manufacturing whiskey" is synonymous with and means the same as being "suitable to be used in the manufacture," etc., as used in this section. Wilson v. State, 2 Ala. App. 203, 56 So. 114 (1911); Bell v. State, 20 Ala. App. 150, 101 So. 158 (1924).

When the prosecution relies upon the rule of evidence created by this section to show a violation of § 28-4-50, it is encumbent upon the state to show: (1) That the articles designated, i.e., a part or parts of a still, were in the possession of the defendant; and (2) that such article or articles were commonly or generally used or suitable for the manufacture of prohibited beverages, and in the absence of evidence tending to establish either of said elements the defendant is entitled to a directed verdict. Hudson v. State, 33 Ala. App. 217, 31 So. 2d 771, rev'd, 249 Ala. 372, 31 So. 2d 774 (1947), on the ground that the evidence was insufficient to support the conviction; Barger v. State, 34 Ala. App. 62, 37 So. 2d 235 (1948); Stover v. State, 36 Ala. App. 696, 63 So. 2d 386 (1953); Robinson v. State, 38 Ala. App. 315, 82 So. 2d 815 (1955); Johnson v. State, 38 Ala. App. 590, 90 So. 2d 164 (1956).

That there is no satisfactory explanation of such possession. — See Little v. State, 27 Ala. App. 119, 166 So. 618 (1936).

Where it has been proven beyond reasonable doubt that an accused is found in possession of parts of a still and no explanation is offered, a prima facie case is made out that accused was in unlawful possession of a complete still. Nugent v. State, 28 Ala. App. 182, 181 So. 707 (1938); Robinson v. State, 38 Ala. App. 315, 82 So. 2d 815 (1955); Mitchell v. State, 38 Ala. App. 546, 89 So. 2d 238 (1956).

Unlawful possession question for jury. — Whether defendant unlawfully possessed still, parts of which were found on his premises, held for jury. Lowrey v. State, 26 Ala. App. 159, 155 So. 313 (1934). See also Jackson v. State, 22 Ala. App. 409, 117 So. 156 (1928).

When the testimony proves to the jury, beyond a reasonable doubt, that the defendant was in possession of the articles described in this section, a presumption of law arises, as fixed by this section, making the question of possession one for the jury rather than a case for a directed verdict. Nugent v. State, 28 Ala. App. 182, 181 So. 707 (1938); Robinson v. State, 38 Ala. App. 315, 82 So. 2d 815 (1955).

Under this section evidence connecting defendant with unlawful possession of part of still suitable for whiskey manufacture is sufficient to take case to jury. Davis v. State, 24 Ala. App. 190, 132 So. 458 (1931).

Question for jury when possession denied. — When parts of a still are found in a person's house there is a presumption of constructive possession, but if he denies possession showing that the still was there without his knowledge it becomes a question for the jury. Watford v. State, 21 Ala. App. 428, 109 So. 174 (1926); Whigham v. State, 21 Ala. App. 454, 109 So. 281 (1926).

Charge to the jury. — In prosecution for possessing a still, instruction that jury might find that defendant had possession of a whole still, if he possessed a part of an apparatus

used or suitable for use in manufacturing prohibited liquors, and such possession was unexplained, being in accordance with this section was not error. Arthur v. State, 19 Ala. App. 311, 97 So. 158 (1923); Freeman v. State, 21 Ala. App. 629, 111 So. 188 (1927).

The statement, "if he is in possession of a part of a still, it is prima facie evidence that he is in possession of the whole," without more, is not sufficient to state the rule of evidence made by this section. Notwithstanding the proof beyond a reasonable doubt that defendants were in possession of a part of a still suitable to be used in the manufacture of whiskey and such possession was unexplained, yet, if the facts and circumstances disclosed that in fact no completed still was in possession of defendants, there could be no conviction in spite of the prima facie case made by the state. This point should be made clear to the jury in explaining the legislative rule of evidence. Little v. State, 27 Ala. App. 119, 166 So. 618 (1936).

Charge that burden is on state to prove possession of complete still and to acquit if one essential part of still was missing held properly refused, as invasion of province of jury, under this section. Smallwood v. State, 21 Ala. App. 468, 109 So. 387 (1926).

Judicial notice. — The court of appeals cannot take judicial knowledge of whether or not certain articles are commonly used for or are suitable to be used in the manufacture of prohibited liquors. Young v. State, 28 Ala. App. 491, 188 So. 270 (1939).

The court of appeals in the case of Dabbs v. State, 20 Ala. App. 167, 101 So. 220 (1924), decided that whether certain articles are commonly used for, or are suitable to be used in the manufacture of intoxicating liquors, is a matter of which the court may not take judicial knowledge, and hence the court will not assume that certain articles are parts of a still, are commonly used, or are suitable to be used in, the manufacture of liquor. See also Ex parte State ex rel. Davis, 211 Ala. 574, 100 So. 917 (1924).

Evidence sufficient to make out prima facie case. — Testimony of an ATU agent that the wooden and metal still pot on which he saw the defendant standing "was a device to be used for the manufacture of whiskey," was sufficient for the state to make out a prima facie case under the evidentiary rule of this section. Parker v. State, 41 Ala. App. 463, 135 So. 2d 169 (1961).

Where the officers testified they found a complete still, except for a condenser, which is an essential part of a still when it is in actual operation, and the parts of the still present were such as are commonly or generally used for or suitable to be used in the manufacture of prohibited liquors or beverages, it was held that under this section, this evidence made out a prima facie case of a violation of § 28-4-50. Hood v. State, 42 Ala. App. 286, 161 So. 2d 154 (1964).

Evidence held sufficient to sustain conviction under this section. Sherman v. State, 38 Ala. App. 106, 77 So. 2d 495 (1954), cert. denied, 262 Ala. 704, 77 So. 2d 499 (1955); Anderson v. State, 39 Ala. App. 400, 103 So. 2d 796 (1957).

Cited in Allen v. State, 26 Ala. App. 195, 155 So. 721 (1934); Cantrell v. State, 29 Ala.

App. 614, 199 So. 742 (1941); Barger v. State, 34 Ala. App. 62, 37 So. 2d 235 (1948); Traffenstedt v. State, 34 Ala. App. 273, 38 So. 2d 619 (1949); Coats v. State, 257 Ala. 406, 60 So. 2d 261 (1952); Harris v. State, 39 Ala. App. 99, 94 So. 2d 884 (1957); Payne v. State, 40 Ala. App. 493, 115 So. 2d 670 (1959); Thomas v. State, 41 Ala. App. 674, 149 So. 2d 290 (1963).

Collateral references. — 48 C.J.S., Intoxicating Liquors, §§ 339, 348, 376.

45 Am. Jur. 2d, Intoxicating Liquors, §§ 362, 363.

§ 28-4-52. Penalty for violations of section 28-4-50.

Any person, firm or corporation who shall violate any provision of section 28-4-50 shall be guilty of a felony and, upon conviction thereof, shall be punished by imprisonment at hard labor in the penitentiary, for not less than one year nor more than five years, such punishment to be fixed within these limits by the court. (Acts 1919, No. 737, p. 1086; Code 1923, § 4658; Code 1940, T. 29, § 133.)

This section is mandatory. Conner v. State, 20 Ala. App. 613, 104 So. 554 (1925).

Construction of section. — This section and § 28-4-115, relating to transportation in quantities of five gallons or more, may be applicable to the offenses denounced by § 28-1-1 which defines in general the elements of the several offenses, which section must be construed in connection with the sections fixing the penalty for a misdemeanor or a felony as the case may be, and those sections read into § 28-1-1 as to the quantity transported when that is material. Hardin v. State, 241 Ala. 151, 3 So. 2d 93 (1941).

Punishment for distilling is prescribed

by the judge, but where the court erroneously charges the jury that its verdict of guilt should include punishment, this is treated as surplusage not affecting the power of the court. Harris v. State, 39 Ala. App. 99, 94 So. 2d 884 (1957).

Sentence of five years for possession of illegal still was not too severe. Latham v. State, 38 Ala. App. 92, 77 So. 2d 499 (1954).

Cited in Walters v. State, 19 Ala. App. 92, 95 So. 207 (1923); Farley v. State, 20 Ala. App. 105, 101 So. 69 (1924); Brunson v. State, 26 Ala. App. 255, 157 So. 678 (1934); Devaney v. State, 55 Ala. App. 408, 316 So. 2d 239 (1975).

Collateral references. — 48 C.J.S., Intoxicating Liquors, §§ 286-304.

§ 28-4-53. Possession of still, etc., by sheriff, etc., enforcing law not deemed violation of section 28-4-50.

The possession of any still, apparatus or appliance taken by the sheriff or other person in enforcing the laws of this state shall not be in violation of section 28-4-50. (Acts 1919, No. 737, p. 1086; Code 1923, § 4660; Code 1940, T. 29, § 135.)

§ 28-4-54. Allowance of reward to sheriff, etc., furnishing evidence to support convictions for violations of section 28-4-50.

When any person is convicted of violating the provisions of section 28-4-50, there shall be charged in the bill of cost the sum of $25.00, to be allowed the person who furnished the evidence and brought about the conviction of any person or persons for the violation of the said section; provided, that only one such amount shall be paid under this section for a conviction of any number of persons or for more than one conviction for a violation of said section where the evidence shows that the still, apparatus or appliance is one and the same. Such person may be the sheriff of the county, deputy or any other person furnishing the evidence necessary for conviction. The person so claiming said sum shall satisfy the presiding judge that he is the person entitled to same and shall receive from the judge a certificate to that effect. (Acts 1919, No. 737, p. 1086; Code 1923, § 4659; Acts 1933, Ex. Sess., No. 183, p. 200; Code 1940, T. 29, § 134.)

Conviction necessary. — A charge stated, in effect, that anyone furnishing proof of possession of a still, etc., is entitled to a fee whether there is a conviction or not. Such is not the law and the trial court should not be put in error for refusing to so charge the jury. Dixon v. State, 269 Ala. 548, 115 So. 2d 270 (1959).

Right to disclose fee in defense argument. — Where deputy sheriff, who was state's only witness in prosecutions for unlawfully possessing still, would have been entitled to statutory reward if convictions were obtained, excluding defense argument disclosing such fact held error. Little v. State, 27 Ala. App. 119, 166 So. 618 (1936).

Cross-examination. — In prosecution for manufacturing whiskey and possessing a still, sheriff may be cross-examined as to whether he claims fee under this section, for securing conviction and as to knowledge that law provides fee, but, where he answers that he does not claim fee, sustaining objection to question whether he knows that fee goes to party securing conviction is not prejudicial error. Cox v. State, 22 Ala. App. 102, 112 So. 898 (1927).

State may not recover costs of prosecution. — Where a judgment of conviction for possession of a still, sentencing the defendant to the penitentiary, included a provision that the state recover costs of prosecution, the provision for costs was void, but on appeal was regarded as mere surplusage and not considered a part of the sentence. Thomas v. State, 41 Ala. App. 674, 149 So. 2d 290 (1963).

Cited in Dixon v. State, 40 Ala. App. 465, 115 So. 2d 262 (1957).

§ 28-4-55. Allowance, etc., of operation, etc., of still, etc., upon premises by another.

It shall be unlawful for any person, firm or corporation to permit or allow anyone to have, possess, operate or locate on his premises any apparatus, plant or structure for the distilling or manufacturing of prohibited liquors or beverages or any of them. When such apparatus, plant or structure is found upon said premises, the fact shall be prima facie evidence that the tenant or owner in actual possession of the premises has knowledge of the existence of the same and of the purpose for which the same were to be used. Upon conviction of permitting or allowing the same to be upon his premises, such tenant or owner shall be punished by a fine of not less than $50.00 nor more than $500.00 and may also be imprisoned in the county jail or sentenced to hard labor for the county for not more than six months for the first conviction, at the discretion of the court. On the second and every subsequent conviction, in addition to the fine which may be imposed, the convicted party shall be imprisoned at hard labor for not less than three nor more than six months, such punishment to be fixed by the judge or court trying the case. (Acts 1919, No. 7, p. 6; Code 1923, § 4661; Code 1940, T. 29, § 136.)

Actual legal title to the premises is not required to be proved by the state. Jones v. State, 40 Ala. App. 419, 114 So. 2d 575 (1959).

Cited in Davis v. State, 44 Ala. App. 476, 213 So. 2d 581 (1968).

ARTICLE 4.

MAINTENANCE, ETC., OF UNLAWFUL DRINKING PLACES.

§ 28-4-70. Prohibited.

It shall be unlawful for any person, firm, association or corporation, directly or indirectly, to keep or maintain or in any manner to aid or abet in keeping or maintaining any of the places declared by this chapter to be unlawful drinking places. The act of keeping or maintaining any such room or place shall be deemed a separate offense for each day that it continues. Any violation of this section, whether a first or subsequent offense, shall be punished by a fine of not less than $50.00 nor more than $500.00, to which, at the discretion of the judge or court trying the case, may be added imprisonment in the county jail or imprisoned at hard labor for the county for not more than six months. (Acts 1915, No. 1, p. 1; Code 1923, § 4662; Code 1940, T. 29, § 137.)

Cited in Johnson v. I.B.E.W. Local 558 Properties, Inc., 418 So. 2d 885 (Ala. 1982).

§ 28-4-71. Unlawful drinking places deemed common nuisances; abatement thereof.

Any place or room kept or maintained in violation of the provisions of this chapter defining unlawful drinking places shall be deemed to be a common nuisance and may be abated by injunction issued out of a circuit court upon a petition filed in the name of the state by the state attorney general or any district attorney whose duties require him to prosecute criminal actions on behalf of the state in the county wherein the nuisance is maintained or by any citizen or citizens of such county, such petition to be filed in the county in which the nuisance exists. All rules of evidence and the practice and procedure that pertain to circuit courts generally in this state may be invoked and applied in any injunction procedure hereunder. (Acts 1915, No. 1, p. 1; Code 1923, § 4663; Code 1940, T. 29, § 138.)

Cross references. — As to rules of supreme court relative to injunctions, see ARCP, Rule 65.

Petition for temporary injunction, alleging that defendant maintained and operated tourist camp as resort for selling and drinking prohibited liquors, held to authorize injunction under this section, irrespective of whether defendants were selling liquors at time of injunction. West v. State ex rel. Matthews, 223 Ala. 588, 173 So. 46 (1937).

§ 28-4-72. Forfeiture of charters of clubs or incorporated associations violating provisions of sections 28-4-70 or 28-4-71.

Any chartered club or incorporated association of persons under the laws of Alabama guilty of violating any of the provisions of section 28-4-70 or maintaining or keeping any such place as is described in section 28-4-71 shall forfeit its charter, and such forfeiture may be declared by a proceeding in quo warranto against the club or incorporated association in a court of competent jurisdiction in the county where the unlawful act is committed. (Acts 1915, No. 1, p. 1; Code 1923, § 4664; Code 1940, T. 29, § 139.)

§ 28-4-73. Sufficiency of charges in informations, indictments, etc.; admissibility of evidence.

In all affidavits, informations, complaints or indictments against any party or parties for maintaining an unlawful drinking place as defined by this chapter, it shall be sufficient to charge that the defendant maintained an unlawful drinking place contrary to the statutes applicable in such cases, and under such charge it shall be competent to prove any act of the defendant which, under the law of the state, constitutes the keeping of an unlawful drinking place. (Acts 1909, No. 191, p. 63; Acts 1915, No. 2, p. 8; Code 1923, § 4665; Code 1940, T. 29, § 140.)

Maintenance is continuous act. — Under an indictment charging maintenance of an unlawful drinking place, proof of acts showing the character of defendant's place of business covering the time included by the indictment was competent, since crime was continuous in its nature. Holt v. State, 28 Ala. App. 287, 184 So. 205 (1938).

ARTICLE 5.

RENTING OR PERMITTING USE OF PREMISES FOR
SALE, MANUFACTURE, ETC., OF PROHIBITED
LIQUORS OR BEVERAGES.

§ 28-4-90. Prohibited.

If any person shall willfully let or suffer any other person, firm or corporation to use any premises which he owns or controls for the illegal sale or manufacture or other unlawful disposition of spirituous, vinous or malt liquors or any other liquors, liquids or beverages prohibited by the laws of Alabama to be manufactured, sold or otherwise disposed of for use by a wholesale or retail dealer in liquors or by a wholesale or retail dealer in malt liquors or by a rectifier of spirits or distiller or for the illegal storage or warehousing of such liquors and beverages, he shall be guilty of a misdemeanor. (Acts 1909, No. 191, p. 63; Acts 1915, No. 2, p. 8; Code 1923, § 4683; Code 1940, T. 29, § 153.)

Cited in Johnson v. I.B.E.W. Local 558 Properties, Inc., 418 So. 2d 885 (Ala. 1982).

Collateral references. — 48 C.J.S., Intoxicating Liquors, § 233.

§ 28-4-91. Forfeiture of rights of lessee under lease or rent contract.

The unlawful manufacture, sale, keeping for sale, giving away or otherwise disposing of any prohibited liquors or beverages contrary to the law of the state or the carrying on of the business of a retail or wholesale dealer in liquors or retail or wholesale dealer in malt liquors or the business of a brewer, distiller or rectifier of spirits shall, at the option of the landlord or lessor, work a forfeiture of all the rights of any lessee or tenant under any lease or contract of rent of the premises where such unlawful act is performed or such unlawful business is conducted by the lessee or tenant or by any agent, servant, clerk or employee of the lessee or tenant with the latter's knowledge or permission. (Acts 1909, No. 191, p. 63; Acts 1915, No. 2, p. 8; Code 1923, § 4684; Code 1940, T. 29, § 154.)

§ 28-4-92. Keeping of prohibited liquors or beverages in building not used exclusively for dwelling deemed prima facie evidence of possession for sale.

The keeping of liquors or beverages that are prohibited by the law of the state to be manufactured, sold or otherwise disposed of in any building not used exclusively for a dwelling shall be prima facie evidence that they are kept for sale or with intent to sell the same contrary to law. (Acts 1909, No. 191, p. 63; Acts 1915, No. 2, p. 8; Code 1923, § 4685; Code 1940, T. 29, § 155.)

This section is constitutional. Toole v. State, 170 Ala. 41, 54 So. 195 (1910).

Legislature has power to declare such a rule of evidence as declared by this section. Fitzpatrick v. State, 169 Ala. 1, 53 So. 1021 (1910).

And it is not repealed. — The Alabama Alcoholic Beverage Control Act does not repeal this section. Sinbeck v. State, 28 Ala. App. 118, 179 So. 645 (1938).

It may not be applicable to possession in dwelling. — Under this section the mere possession of prohibited liquors in a building used exclusively for a dwelling is not prima facie evidence that the whiskey was kept for sale. Strickland v. State, 20 Ala. App. 600, 104 So. 351 (1925); Cowan v. State, 32 Ala. App. 161, 22 So. 2d 917 (1945); Cooley v. State, 262 Ala. 136, 77 So. 2d 488 (1955).

Prohibited possession of beer. — The possession of a number of bottles of beer in a "dry" county as defined by § 28-2-1 subsequent to passage of that section, authorized conviction for unlawful possession of prohibited liquor. Sinbeck v. State, 28 Ala. App. 118, 179 So. 645 (1938).

Any "prevailing idea" or "general understanding" that beer could be legally possessed in dry county under the Alcoholic Beverage Control Act did not preclude conviction for the possession of eight cases of beer in an icebox adjoining a storekeeper's place of business in a dry county. Broadfoot v. State, 28 Ala. App. 260, 182 So. 411 (1938).

Insufficient proof for prima facie case. — The provisions of this section are without application to make out a prima facie case where the evidence disclosed that a jug of whiskey was hidden in a patch of weeds back of the garden at the home of defendant's brother, whom defendant was visiting at the time. Willingham v. State, 11 Ala. App. 205, 65 So. 847 (1914).

Presumption of section inapplicable. — In prosecution for illegal possession in a wet county of liquors for purpose of sale, where husband of accused testified without substantial contradiction that liquor involved was purchased from state liquor store, presumption of this section could not be applied so as to relieve state from burden of proving, circum-

stantially or otherwise, the guilty connection of accused with the liquor for illegal purposes charged in affidavit. Walls v. State, 29 Ala. App. 466, 198 So. 151 (1940).

Cited in Stokes v. State, 5 Ala. App. 159, 59 So. 310 (1912); Hauser v. State, 6 Ala. App. 31, 60 So. 549 (1912); Salley v. State, 9 Ala. App. 82, 64 So. 185 (1914); Carmichael v. State, 11 Ala. App. 209, 65 So. 694 (1914); Hall v. State, 30 Ala. App. 373, 6 So. 2d 30 (1941); Lawler v. State, 31 Ala. App. 458, 18 So. 2d 469 (1944); Tillison v. State, 32 Ala. App. 397, 27 So. 2d 41 (1946).

§ 28-4-93. Delivery of prohibited liquors or beverages to stores, shops, dwellings, etc., from which sale prohibited deemed prima facie evidence of sale, etc.

The delivery of liquors or beverages prohibited by the law of the state to be manufactured, sold or otherwise disposed of in or from any store, shop, warehouse, boat or other vessel or vehicle of any kind or any shanty or tent or any building or place used for the purpose of traffic or any dwelling house or dependency thereof, if any part of the same is used as a public eating house, grocery or other place of common resort, shall be deemed prima facie evidence of a sale or other unlawful disposition. (Acts 1909, No. 191, p. 63; Acts 1915, No. 2, p. 8; Code 1923, § 4686; Code 1940, T. 29, § 156.)

ARTICLE 6.

TRANSPORTATION, DELIVERY AND RECEIPT GENERALLY
OF PROHIBITED LIQUORS AND BEVERAGES.

§ 28-4-110. Carriage, delivery, etc., into state by common carrier, etc., of prohibited liquors and beverages generally.

It shall be unlawful for any common or other carrier or any other person, corporation or association or combination of persons to carry, bring or introduce into this state or to deliver to any person whomsoever in this state any of the prohibited liquors and beverages as defined by the laws of the state of Alabama in any quantity whatsoever, whether in original packages or otherwise and although brought from a point without the state of Alabama. (Acts 1919, No. 7, p. 6; Code 1923, § 4705; Code 1940, T. 29, § 174.)

Collateral references. — 48 C.J.S., Intoxicating Liquors, § 234.

§ 28-4-111. Receipt or acceptance from common carrier, etc., of prohibited liquors or beverages generally.

No person shall receive or accept any prohibited liquors or beverages from a common carrier or other carrier, except alcohol in accordance with regulations and restrictions of the laws of Alabama and for the purposes prescribed by said laws and except wine for sacramental or religious purposes as permitted under law and then only if there is permanently pasted or attached to the container a copy of the prescription or affidavit upon authority of which it was prescribed or obtained. (Acts 1919, No. 7, p. 6; Code 1923, § 4707; Code 1940, T. 29, § 176.)

Cited in State ex rel. Holcombe v. Stone, 229 Ala. 357, 157 So. 454 (1934).

§ 28-4-112. Receipt, etc., of prohibited liquors and beverages for storage, distribution, etc., for another.

It shall be unlawful for any person, firm, association or corporation to receive for storage, distribution or on consignment for another prohibited liquors and beverages or any of them or to have or maintain any warehouse or other place for the receipt, storage or distribution of liquors for another. Any person violating this section shall be guilty of a misdemeanor. (Acts 1909, No. 191, p. 63; Acts 1915, No. 2, p. 8; Code 1923, § 4713; Code 1940, T. 29, § 182.)

Cited in Toole v. State, 170 Ala. 41, 54 So. 195 (1910).

§ 28-4-113. Acceptance for or shipment, transportation, delivery, etc., of prohibited liquors or beverages from point to point or along public streets or highways within state.

It shall be unlawful for any person, firm, corporation or association, whether a common carrier or not, to accept from another for shipment, transportation or delivery or to ship, transport or deliver for another said prohibited liquors or beverages or any of them when received at one point, place or locality in this state to be shipped or transported to or delivered to another person, firm or corporation at another point, place or locality in this state, or to convey or transport over or along any public street or highway any of such prohibited liquors for another. The provisions of this section shall not apply to those transporting and delivering to the persons, firms or corporations authorized by law to receive said prohibited liquors or beverages or any of them. Any person violating any provision of this section shall be guilty of a misdemeanor. (Acts 1909, No. 191, p. 63; Acts 1915, No. 2, p. 8; Code 1923, § 4714; Code 1940, T. 29, § 183.)

§ 28-4-114. Transportation and delivery of prohibited liquors and beverages C.O.D.

If any prohibited liquors and beverages are delivered to a carrier to be by the carrier transported and delivered C.O.D. to any person at a point in this state, meaning thereby to collect on delivery by the carrier for the consignor the amount of the purchase money for such liquors, then and in every case the carrier shall be deemed and held the agent of the consignor, and all such prohibited liquors and beverages shall remain the property of the consignor until actually delivered and the money paid to the carrier therefor; and the servant or agent of the carrier who knowingly delivers any such liquors or receives pay therefor within the state shall be guilty of a misdemeanor. (Acts 1909, No. 191, p. 63; Acts 1915, No. 2, p. 8; Code 1923, § 4716; Code 1940, T. 29, § 185.)

§ 28-4-115. Transportation of prohibited liquors or beverages in quantities of five gallons or more.

It shall be unlawful for any person, firm or corporation or association within this state to transport in quantities of five gallons or more any of the liquors or beverages, the sale, possession or transportation of which is prohibited by law in Alabama. Any person convicted of violating this section shall be guilty of a felony and, upon conviction, shall be imprisoned in the penitentiary of this state for a period of not less than one year, nor more than five years. (Acts 1927, No. 605, p. 704; Code 1940, T. 29, § 187.)

I. General Consideration.
II. Pleading and Evidence.

I. GENERAL CONSIDERATION.

Section does not apply to interstate transportation. — A conviction under this section for transporting prohibited liquor is not authorized for a carrying or possession of such goods for the sole purpose of interstate transportation. Hill v. State, 27 Ala. App. 573, 176 So. 805 (1937).

The "interstate transportation" of liquor to which this section does not apply may be by automobile and over the public highways as well as by any other method. Hill v. State, 27 Ala. App. 573, 176 So. 805 (1937).

Strict construction against state. — The five-gallon law, because a felony, is strictly construed against the state. Livingston v. State, 44 Ala. App. 579, 217 So. 2d 90 (1968).

Construction with other statutes. — To warrant the imposition of the penalty prescribed by this section the indictment should charge illegal transportation or importation in quantities of five gallons or more of liquor,

and, if the indictment or complaint charges illegal transportation or importation without specifying quantity and a conviction follows, the penalty prescribed by § 28-4-136 only is applicable. Hardin v. State, 241 Ala. 151, 3 So. 2d 93 (1941).

Section 28-4-52, prescribing penalty for unlawful possession of stills, and this section may be applicable to the offenses denounced by § 28-1-1 which defines in general the elements of the several offenses, which section must be construed in connection with the statutes fixing the penalty for a misdemeanor or a felony as the case may be, and those statutes read into § 28-1-1 as to the quantity transported when that is material. Hardin v. State, 241 Ala. 151, 3 So. 2d 93 (1941).

This section has not been changed to a misdemeanor by §§ 28-4-200 and 28-4-201. Bryan v. State, 398 So. 2d 404 (Ala. Crim. App. 1981). But see, Copeland v. State, 377 So. 2d 1 (Ala. Crim. App. 1979).

There is no conflict between the scope of

§§ **28-4-200 and 28-4-201 and the operation of this section.** Johnston v. State, 54 Ala. App. 100, 304 So. 2d 918 (1974); Jones v. State, 401 So. 2d 322 (Ala. Crim. App. 1981). But see, Copeland v. State, 377 So. 2d 1 (Ala. Crim. App. 1979).

As each is mutually exclusive. Johnston v. State, 54 Ala. App. 100, 304 So. 2d 918 (1974); Jones v. State, 401 So. 2d 322 (Ala. Crim. App. 1981). But see, Copeland v. State, 377 So. 2d 1 (Ala. Crim. App. 1979).

Section not repealed. — This section, which prohibits the transportation of prohibited beverages in quantities of five gallons or more, has not been repealed by implication because of the omission from § 28-3-18 of any reference to transportation of prohibited beverages. Griffin v. State, 39 Ala. App. 626, 106 So. 2d 182 (1958).

There was no merit in the contention that this section was repealed by the adoption of § 28-3-18. Dixon v. State, 39 Ala. App. 575, 105 So. 2d 354 (1958).

Whiskey is liquor or beverage contemplated by this section. Jones v. State, 23 Ala. App. 339, 125 So. 382 (1929).

Whiskey is a spirituous liquor within the common knowledge of all men, and juries may so find without specific proof. Griffin v. State, 39 Ala. App. 626, 106 So. 2d 182 (1958).

"Shinney" is intoxicating and is but another name for a homemade, intoxicating whiskey. Yeager v. State, 44 Ala. App. 263, 207 So. 2d 122, rev'd on other grounds, 281 Ala. 651, 207 So. 2d 125 (1967).

Five-gallon limit marks point between felony and misdemeanor. — The five-gallon limit marks the line of a penitentiary offense, the critical point between a felony and, at most, a misdemeanor for possession. Blackwell v. State, 42 Ala. App. 246, 160 So. 2d 493 (1964).

This section makes transporting prohibited liquors in a quantity of five gallons or more a felony. Yeager v. State, 44 Ala. App. 263, 207 So. 2d 122, rev'd on other grounds, 281 Ala. 651, 207 So. 2d 125 (1967).

"Transportation" defined. — Under this section "transportation" of five or more gallons of liquors includes transportation by automobile, wagon, buggy, by hand or otherwise. Fitts v. State, 24 Ala. App. 405, 135 So. 654 (1931).

But mere presence in automobile, with knowledge of five or more gallons of liquor being transported therein, constitutes no felony under this section. Fitts v. State, 24 Ala. App. 405, 135 So. 654 (1931).

Carrying keg of illicit liquor on shoulder was within prohibition of this section making it unlawful to "transport" illicit liquor, since primary meaning of "transport" is to carry or convey from one place to another. Boyd v. State, 239 Ala. 578, 195 So. 767 (1940).

Accused is not required to own whiskey allegedly transported in violation of this section to be guilty. Whisenant v. State, 24 Ala. App. 458, 137 So. 456 (1931).

In a prosecution under this section, ownership of the cargo was immaterial. Miller v. State, 39 Ala. App. 584, 105 So. 2d 711 (1958).

"Violating the prohibition law" is not criminal charge. — Where, to an indictment charging the defendant with transporting in quantities of five gallons or more, prohibited liquors, etc., defendant being duly arraigned upon the said charge, for his plea thereto pleaded "guilty of violating the prohibition law," a judgment of conviction must be reversed, since the charge to which the defendant pleaded guilty was not included in the charge of transporting laid in the indictment, and in fact, "violating the prohibition law" is not any charge at all. Champion v. State, 266 Ala. 283, 95 So. 2d 801 (1957).

Offense of an attempt is embraced in the charge of transporting prohibited liquors in violation of this section. Champion v. State, 266 Ala. 283, 95 So. 2d 801 (1957).

Possession not lesser included offense. — Where an indictment charges a violation of this section, defendant cannot be convicted on a plea of guilty of possession of prohibited liquors, § 28-4-20, since an indictment under this section charges an indivisible crime which admits of no lesser included offense. Ryan v. State, 41 Ala. App. 340, 132 So. 2d 264 (1961).

Offense of transporting prohibited liquors under this section may be jointly committed by two or more parties, all of whom, whether directly committing, aiding or abetting, would be equally guilty, and indictable, triable, and punishable as principals. Dotson v. State, 24 Ala. App. 216, 135 So. 159 (1931).

Accused who employed other men to go into dry county in accused's automobile to purchase and return to accused 30 gallons of corn whiskey, and who furnished money with which to make the purchase, was a principal in the second degree in the commission of the offense and thus was liable to indictment, trial and punishment as though a principal in the first degree. Harris v. State, 32 Ala. App. 519, 27 So. 2d 794 (1946).

Pending misdemeanor prosecution held not to require abatement of prosecution. — That misdemeanor prosecution for possession of prohibited liquor which was pending in court at time indictment charging the commission of a felony by transporting prohibited liquors in quantities of five gallons or more was procured, held not to require abatement of felony prosecution. Jackson v. State, 27 Ala. App. 468, 174 So. 540 (1937).

Cited in Williamson v. State, 31 Ala. App. 360, 18 So. 2d 742 (1944); Hemphill v. State, 31 Ala. App. 625, 21 So. 2d 123 (1945); Stephens v. State, 36 Ala. App. 444, 58 So. 2d 644 (1952); Oldham v. State, 259 Ala. 507, 67 So. 2d 55 (1953); Steel v. State, 37 Ala. App. 621, 73 So. 2d 573 (1954); Mattison v. State, 37 Ala. App. 678, 75 So. 2d 682 (1954); Welch v. State, 38 Ala. App. 239, 81 So. 2d 897 (1954); Ray v. State, 39 Ala. App. 257, 97 So. 2d 594 (1957); Barbour v. City of Montgomery, 39 Ala. App. 490, 104 So. 2d 300 (1958); Downey v. City of Bay Minette, 39 Ala. App. 619, 106 So. 2d 32 (1958); Kennedy v. State, 39 Ala. App. 676, 107 So. 2d 913 (1958); Shaneyfelt v. State, 40 Ala. App. 13, 109 So. 2d 146 (1958), aff'd, 268 Ala. 520, 109 So. 2d 149 (1959); Orr v. State, 40 Ala. App. 45, 111 So. 2d 627 (1958), aff'd, 269 Ala. 176, 111 So. 2d 639 (1959); Maloney v. State, 41 Ala. App. 251, 130 So. 2d 359 (1961); Thompson v. State, 41 Ala. App. 353, 132 So. 2d 386 (1961); Roberts v. State, 41 Ala. App. 505, 137 So. 2d 59 (1962); York v. State, 43 Ala. App. 54, 179 So. 2d 330 (1964); Yelder v. State, 44 Ala. App. 122, 203 So. 2d 687 (1967); Eaton v. State, 45 Ala. App. 464, 231 So. 2d 918 (1970); Mayes v. State, 47 Ala. App. 672, 260 So. 2d 403 (1972); Shaneyfelt v. State, 48 Ala. App. 26, 261 So. 2d 445 (1972); Mars v. State, 339 So. 2d 104 (Ala. Crim. App.), cert. denied, 339 So. 2d 110 (Ala. 1976); Roberson v. State, 340 So. 2d 459 (Ala. Crim. App. 1976); Mars v. State, 348 So. 2d 541 (Ala. Crim. App. 1977); Sargent v. State, 351 So. 2d 666 (Ala. Crim. App. 1977); Whitener v. State, 390 So. 2d 1136 (Ala. Crim. App. 1980); Robinson v. State, 451 So. 2d 355 (Ala. Civ. App. 1984).

Collateral references. — What amounts to transportation of intoxicating liquor. 65 ALR 983.

Transporting liquor and possessing liquor as a single offense or as separate offenses. 74 ALR 411.

Unlawful transportation of intoxicating liquor in airplane. 99 ALR 210.

Validity of penal statutes relative to transportation of intoxicating liquor within states having "wet" and "dry" districts. 134 ALR 426.

II. PLEADING AND EVIDENCE.

Section 28-4-323 is applicable to prosecution under this section. — Section 28-4-323 setting up the evidential rule that evidence to the effect that a liquor which smells, tastes and has the general appearance of an alcoholic beverage shall constitute evidence that such liquor is a prohibited beverage, is applicable to a prosecution under this section. Austin v. State, 36 Ala. App. 690, 63 So. 2d 283 (1953).

Proof of quantity transported. — Where defendant was indicted for transporting prohibited liquor contrary to this section it is requisite to prove that the amount transported was five gallons or more, since this amount is the statutory metewand. The mode of so proving can come from a measuring done in the presence of the jury or elsewhere; the act of measurement is a relevant fact in issue and may be testified to. Miller v. State, 39 Ala. App. 584, 105 So. 2d 711 (1958).

Where defendant is indicted for transporting prohibited liquor contrary to this section a nonexpert may give an opinion on quantity based on personal observation, even though his evidence is but an approximate estimate. Miller v. State, 39 Ala. App. 584, 105 So. 2d 711 (1958).

It is essential to a conviction for a violation of this section that the state prove that the amount of liquors transported was five gallons or more. McCurdy v. State, 41 Ala. App. 546, 143 So. 2d 185 (1962); Blackwell v. State, 42 Ala. App. 246, 160 So. 2d 493 (1964).

The testimony of the officers, together with the jugs and the liquid contained therein, was sufficient to support a finding that the quantity of the whiskey was five gallons or more. Ledbetter v. State, 41 Ala. App. 323, 136 So. 2d 904 (1961).

Despite lack of statutory standard size for bottle or can of beer, presentation of four cases of beer seized in alleged crime to jury with a resulting opportunity to ascertain amount of beer, afforded jury opportunity to determine whether statutory amount was present. Clark v. State, 53 Ala. App. 495, 301 So. 2d 258 (1974).

Stricter proof of quantity required than that permissible in possession cases. — Cases under this section all show a marked difference in requiring stricter proof of quantity from that permissible in mere possession cases. Blackwell v. State, 42 Ala. App. 246, 160 So. 2d 493 (1964).

Opinion of witness as to whether liquid was whiskey. — Where it appears that the witness inspected the bottle, and smelled or tasted the contents thereof, no reason appears why he may not state his judgment as to whether the contents is whiskey, the characteristics of which is a matter of such common knowledge that courts take judicial knowledge thereof. Griffin v. State, 39 Ala. App. 626, 106 So. 2d 182 (1958).

It was not required that the witnesses be shown to be qualified as to sense of smell in order to state their judgment as to whether the jugs found in defendant's car contained whiskey. Griffin v. State, 39 Ala. App. 671, 106 So. 2d 36 (1958).

Accomplices' uncorroborated testimony insufficient. — Conviction for transporting five or more gallons of whiskey under this section cannot be based on accomplices' uncorroborated testimony. Fitts v. State, 24 Ala. App. 405, 135 So. 654 (1931).

Burden of showing that liquor was unfit for beverage purposes. — The state having presented evidence from which the jury could reasonably infer that the defendant was transporting prohibited whiskey in quantities of five gallons or more, had met its burden in establishing its prima facie case. If the whiskey so being transported was unfit for beverage purposes, such fact was a defensive matter to be shown by the defendant, in the absence of evidence by the state to such effect. Griffin v. State, 39 Ala. App. 626, 106 So. 2d 182 (1958).

"You caught me fair and square," cannot be treated as inculpatory of transporting since it is equivocal. It could denote possession or transporting. Blackwell v. State, 42 Ala. App. 246, 160 So. 2d 493 (1964).

Evidence as res gestae. — Everything said or done at time and place defendant was arrested for transporting intoxicants under this section is admissible as res gestae. Mattison v. State, 37 Ala. App. 678, 75 So. 2d 682 (1954).

Evidence showing prohibited liquor. — The arresting officer's testimony that the liquor found in defendant's car in five-gallon glass jars tasted like moonshine whiskey, together with the sheriff's testimony that the state alcoholic beverage control stores did not sell whiskey in five-gallon demijohns nor without revenue stamps, sufficed to show a prohibited liquor. Dixon v. State, 39 Ala. App. 575, 105 So. 2d 354 (1958).

In a prosecution under this section, where the arresting officers described liquid found in defendant's car as "untaxed bootleg whiskey," "homemade whiskey," "white whiskey" and "moonshine whiskey," and testified that it "smelled like whiskey," this uncontroverted testimony was sufficient proof of the illegal character of the liquid. Griffin v. State, 39 Ala. App. 671, 106 So. 2d 36 (1958).

The uncontroverted testimony of officers that whiskey was "moonshine" or "wildcat" whiskey and that it smelled like whiskey was sufficient proof of its illegal character. Ledbetter v. State, 41 Ala. App. 323, 136 So. 2d 904 (1961).

Testimony as to location. — In prosecution for transporting prohibited liquors in quantities of five gallons or more, testimony of witnesses for state who knew the locus in quo as to offense being committed within county in which charge was prosecuted, held admissible. Jackson v. State, 27 Ala. App. 468, 174 So. 540 (1937).

Transportation may be proved by circumstantial evidence. — The transportation feature or element of this section can be established by circumstantial evidence and it is not essential to a conviction to prove that the transporting vehicle was actually seen in motion. Green v. State, 37 Ala. App. 509, 72 So. 2d 107 (1954).

Where there is no evidence of whiskey in moving car. — Where no evidence is presented from which it could be reasonably inferred that whiskey was in the automobile while it was in motion, prior to being stopped, it is error to deny defendant's request for a directed verdict. Parker v. State, 41 Ala. App. 329, 132 So. 2d 267 (1961).

Evidence showing unlawful sales is irrelevant. — Defendant having been charged with unlawful transportation of alcoholic beverages, evidence tending to show unlawful sales of whiskey by him would be irrelevant to the issues charged by the indictment. Whitman v. State, 41 Ala. App. 124, 124 So. 2d 275 (1960).

Indictment form. — Indictment in § 15-8-150, held sufficient to charge violation of this section. Grimes v. State, 24 Ala. App. 392, 135 So. 644 (1931).

This section became the law of this state in 1927, and where a statute creates a new offense unknown to the common law, and describes its constituents, the offense may be charged in the statutory language. Cusimano v. State, 33 Ala. App. 62, 31 So. 2d 139 (1947).

Indictment charging transportation of prohibited liquors which substantially followed the language of this section was held sufficient. Harris v. State, 32 Ala. App. 519, 27 So. 2d 794 (1946).

An indictment substantially following the language of this section is sufficient. Oldham v. State, 37 Ala. App. 251, 67 So. 2d 52 (1953).

No form is prescribed for an indictment drawn under this section, and where no form is prescribed, the provisions of § 15-8-25, are applicable. Cusimano v. State, 33 Ala. App. 62, 31 So. 2d 139 (1947).

An indictment which substantially followed the language of this section was not fatally defective on the ground that it failed to allege that the transportation was "contrary to law" and that the transportation was in a dry county. Waldrop v. State, 39 Ala. App. 412, 104 So. 2d 567 (1957).

Examples of sufficient indictments. — See Ray v. State, 23 Ala. App. 357, 127 So. 799 (1929); Grimes v. State, 23 Ala. App. 518, 128 So. 122 (1930); Hayes v. State, 23 Ala. App. 524, 128 So. 774 (1930); Mars v. State, 23 Ala. App. 569, 129 So. 314 (1930); Alexander v. State, 24 Ala. App. 156, 132 So. 64 (1930); Dotson v. State, 223 Ala. 229, 135 So. 160

(1931); Dotson v. State, 24 Ala. App. 216, 135 So. 159 (1931); Jackson v. State, 27 Ala. App. 468, 174 So. 540 (1937); Harris v. State, 32 Ala. App. 519, 27 So. 2d 794 (1946); Mattison v. State, 37 Ala. App. 678, 75 So. 2d 682 (1954).

Admissibility of evidence. — Evidence that earlier in the day on which a raid was made defendant was stopped while driving another and different car, and as to his statements to officers that he was then going for a load, held irrelevant and incompetent as relating to a different offense than that charged. Chandler v. State, 23 Ala. App. 376, 125 So. 791 (1930).

Instructions. — In prosecution for transporting prohibited liquors in quantities of five gallons or more under this section, charge requiring conviction if defendant transported liquors, regardless of quantity, should have been refused, and giving of such charge was error, especially where there were inferences to be drawn from testimony whereby jury in absence of charge might have concluded venue was in different section of county. Fox v. State, 23 Ala. App. 371, 125 So. 783 (1930).

In prosecution for illegal transportation of prohibited liquors, court properly charged that any moving of the whiskey, in quantities of five gallons or more, whether "on your back, in your hands, or by vehicle," was a violation of the law. Boyd v. State, 29 Ala. App. 241, 195 So. 766 (1940).

In prosecution for transporting five gallons or more of prohibited liquor in violation of this section, accused could not complain on appeal that certain excerpts of court's oral charge were erroneous, where such portions were highly favorable to him and authorized jury to return verdict, if they so found, for misdemeanor, and undisputed evidence showed that five or more gallons of whiskey was being transported. Jones v. State, 23 Ala. App. 339, 125 So. 382 (1929).

Instruction that indictment charging violation of this section authorized conviction of lesser offense of violating prohibition law, if evidence failed to show liquor transported was less than five gallons, held erroneous. Overton v. State, 24 Ala. App. 8, 132 So. 50 (1930).

From flight the inference of guilt was legitimate; this coupled with defendant's being the driver of a car undisputedly carrying moonshine whiskey in a quantity which the state showed to be over five gallons all made a prima facie case. Miller v. State, 39 Ala. App. 584, 105 So. 2d 711 (1958).

Sufficiency of evidence. — Evidence of finding copper tank containing more than five gallons of whiskey deposited between back of front seat and upholstering of automobile held sufficient to sustain conviction for transporting

prohibited liquors in quantity of five gallons or more. Wells v. State, 23 Ala. App. 234, 123 So. 289 (1929).

Cumulative evidence as to exact date when automobile containing contraband whiskey was seized held insufficient to require new trial. Williams v. State, 25 Ala. App. 186, 142 So. 841 (1932).

In a prosecution for transporting prohibited liquors in quantities of five gallons or more, the court properly denied the defendant's motion to exclude the state's evidence on the ground that the state had failed to make out a case against the defendant. Shields v. State, 39 Ala. App. 57, 94 So. 2d 226 (1957).

Evidence held sufficient to sustain conviction. Pockrus v. State, 29 Ala. App. 391, 197 So. 81 (1940); Clayton v. State, 36 Ala. App. 610, 63 So. 2d 564 (1952); Austin v. State, 36 Ala. App. 690, 63 So. 2d 283 (1953); Oldham v. State, 37 Ala. App. 251, 67 So. 2d 52 (1953); Lee v. State, 37 Ala. App. 321, 69 So. 2d 467 (1953); King v. State, 37 Ala. App. 443, 69 So. 2d 898 (1954).

Jury determines guilt. — In prosecution for transporting five gallons or more of prohibited liquor, defendant's guilt held for jury. Jones v. State, 23 Ala. App. 339, 125 So. 382 (1929); Dotson v. State, 24 Ala. App. 216, 135 So. 159 (1931); Fulton v. State, 24 Ala. App. 356, 135 So. 414 (1931); Jackson v. State, 27 Ala. App. 468, 174 So. 540 (1937).

And whether transporting was in interstate commerce. — In prosecution for transporting prohibited liquor in quantity of five gallons or more, whether accused had whiskey in his possession merely in interstate commerce for which he could not be convicted was for the jury under the evidence. Hill v. State, 27 Ala. App. 573, 176 So. 805 (1937).

And whether accused was driver. — Evidence as to whether accused was driver of automobile containing contraband whiskey held for jury. Williams v. State, 25 Ala. App. 186, 142 So. 841 (1932).

And weight of alibi. — Evidence of defendant's guilt as against claim of alibi presented a question for jury's determination. McElroy v. State, 30 Ala. App. 404, 7 So. 2d 508 (1942).

And whether accused knew of presence of whiskey. — Where defendant was indicted for transporting prohibited liquor contrary to this section, whether or not he knew there was whiskey in the car was a jury question. Miller v. State, 39 Ala. App. 584, 105 So. 2d 711 (1958).

Where whiskey was found in the trunk of automobile being driven by accused and allegedly purchased by him only the evening before his arrest, accused's denial of any knowledge that whiskey was in the trunk and assertion that he had never looked in the trunk presented a question for the jury. McAllister v. State, 30 Ala. App. 366, 6 So. 2d 32 (1942).

§ 28-4-116. Conduct of business of delivering, transporting, storing or warehousing prohibited liquors and beverages by transfer, warehouse, etc., companies; forfeiture of charter of corporations violating provisions of section.

No transfer company, traffic company, transportation company, warehouse company or other like corporation chartered under or by the laws of Alabama shall have any right or power to engage in or carry on the business of delivering, transporting, storing or warehousing any prohibited liquors and beverages except under the supervision of and on permit from the alcoholic beverage control board.

Any corporation of this state offending against this provision or engaging in such business shall forfeit its charter, which forfeiture may be declared upon an action in quo warranto before a court of competent jurisdiction if any person or officer wishes to institute the action. (Acts 1909, No. 191, p. 63; Acts 1915, No. 2, p. 8; Code 1923, § 4715; Code 1940, T. 29, § 184.)

§ 28-4-117. Procedure for shipment, delivery, etc., of alcohol and wine to persons for sacramental or nonbeverage use — Preparation of affidavit by person desiring to receive shipment; copy of affidavit to be attached to container in which wine or alcohol shipped.

Any person desiring to have shipped to him under the laws of Alabama alcohol or wine for sacramental use, or for any nonbeverage use specified in section 28-3-15, shall make an affidavit before an officer in Alabama authorized to administer oaths, stating the quantity of such alcohol or such wine that the said party desires to receive, the use to which either the wine or the alcohol is to be put and that the person seeking the shipment is authorized under the laws of Alabama to have, receive and possess such quantity of alcohol or wine as is shipped and that the shipment is sought of a legal quantity and for a bona fide legal purpose permitted under the laws of Alabama, and for no other purpose.

A copy of said affidavit shall be pasted or permanently attached to the container of the alcohol or wine when the same is shipped into the state of Alabama and is received by said applicant from the carrier. (Acts 1919, No. 7, p. 6; Code 1923, § 4708; Code 1940, T. 29, § 177.)

Cross references. — As to purchase, possession, etc., of wine for sacramental or religious purposes generally, see § 28-4-180 et seq.

§ 28-4-118. Same — Maintenance of record of delivery by carrier generally; certificate to be filed with alcoholic beverage control board stating name of receiver, quantity and character of wine or alcohol, purposes for which received, etc.; inspection of books and records of carrier generally.

The common carrier delivering such wine or alcohol shall keep a record thereof and shall file in the office of the alcoholic beverage control board within 10 days after the receipt thereof a certificate stating the name of the shipper, the name of the receiver, the quantity and character of the alcohol or wine, and the purposes for which shipped and received and that it conforms to the requirements of law as to its preparation and as to the presence of the affidavit. The said delivery shall be made by the carrier to the consignee only, who shall sign and receipt therefor on the record.

The books and records of the carrier shall at all times be open during office hours to any prosecuting attorney or to the sheriff or chief of police of a municipality or county or to any other officer having the duty to enforce the execution of the law and to require conformity to the statutory regulations. (Acts 1919, No. 7, p. 6; Code 1923, § 4709; Code 1940, T. 29, § 178.)

§ 28-4-119. Same — Labeling of packages or containers of wine or alcohol for sacramental use.

On the outside of each package or container of alcohol or of wine shipped or sold for sacramental or religious purposes to be shipped, carried or delivered to any person in this state there shall be printed or written in the English language the name and address of the consignee or purchaser, the name and address of the consignor or seller and the kind and quantity of liquor, whether alcohol or wine. (Acts 1919, No. 7, p. 6; Code 1923, § 4711; Code 1940, T. 29, § 180.)

§ 28-4-120. Transportation from another state, foreign country, etc., or delivery within state of liquors intended to be used in violation of laws of state.

It shall be unlawful for any railroad company, express company or other common carrier or any officer, agent or employee of any of them or any other person to ship or to transport into or to deliver in this state in any manner or by any means whatsoever any spirituous, vinous, malted, fermented or other intoxicating liquors of any kind from any other state, territory or district of the United States or place noncontiguous to but subject to the jurisdiction of the United States or from any foreign country to any person, firm or corporation within the territory of this state, when the said spirituous, vinous, malted, fermented or other intoxicating liquors, or any of them, are intended by any person interested therein to be received, possessed, sold or in any manner used, either in the original package or otherwise, in violation of any law of this state. (Acts 1915, No. 10, p. 39; Code 1923, § 4687; Code 1940, T. 29, § 157.)

This section is constitutional. Howard v. State, 15 Ala. App. 411, 73 So. 559 (1916); Moragne v. State, 16 Ala. App. 26, 74 So. 862 (1917).

And does not interfere with interstate commerce. State v. Pensacola, St. Andrews & Gulf S.S. Co., 200 Ala. 144, 75 So. 892 (1917).

Shipment of seized liquor. — This section does not apply to shipments, of seized liquor, made by the state. Central of G. Ry. v. State, 197 Ala. 389, 72 So. 555 (1916).

§ 28-4-121. Delivery from another state, etc., of liquors consigned to fictitious person, firm, etc., or person, firm, etc., under fictitious name.

It shall be unlawful for any railroad company, express company or any other common carrier or any officer, agent or employee of any of them or any other person to deliver any liquors of the kind mentioned in section 28-4-120, when brought into the state from any of the points or places mentioned in section 28-4-120, to any person whomsoever, where said liquor has been consigned to a fictitious person, firm or corporation or to a person, firm or corporation under a fictitious name. (Acts 1915, No. 10, p. 39; Code 1923, § 4688; Code 1940, T. 29, § 158.)

§ 28-4-122. Giving of order for receipt, etc., of liquors consigned from another state, etc., to another person by consignee.

It shall be unlawful for any person, firm or corporation to whom any such liquor mentioned in section 28-4-120 has been consigned from any of the points or places mentioned in section 28-4-120, whether consigned to the party by the right name or by a fictitious name, to give to any other person an order for such liquor to any railroad company, express company or other common carrier or any officer, agent or employee of any of them or to any other person, where the purpose of such order is to enable such person to obtain or receive such liquors for himself or for any other person, firm or corporation than the consignee. (Acts 1915, No. 10, p. 39; Code 1923, § 4689; Code 1940, T. 29, § 159.)

§ 28-4-123. Acceptance of delivery from common carrier, etc., of liquors from another state, etc., with intent to use, etc., same in violation of laws of state.

It shall be unlawful for any person, firm or corporation to accept from any railroad company, express company or other common carrier or any officer, agent or employee of any of them or from any other person any delivery of the liquors mentioned in section 28-4-120, or any of them, when transported into this state or delivered in this state in any manner or by any means whatsoever from the points or places mentioned in section 28-4-120, where the said person, firm or corporation so accepting such delivery intends to receive, possess or sell or in any manner use, either in the original package or otherwise, the said liquors, or any of them, in violation of any law of this state. (Acts 1915, No. 10, p. 39; Code 1923, § 4690; Code 1940, T. 29, § 160.)

§ 28-4-124. Delivery by common carrier, etc., of liquors from another state, etc., to person, etc., other than consignee without written order of consignee therefor.

It shall be unlawful for any railroad company, express company or other common carrier or any officer, agent or employee of any of them or any other person to deliver any of the liquors mentioned in section 28-4-120, when brought into the state from any of the points or places mentioned in section 28-4-120, to any person other than the person to whom such liquors are consigned without a written order in each instance by said consignee therefor, or to make such delivery of said liquors as aforesaid, when consigned to a firm or corporation, except to a member of said firm or an officer or agent of such corporation or upon a written order in each instance by the consignee therefor. (Acts 1915, No. 10, p. 39; Code 1923, § 4691; Code 1940, T. 29, § 161.)

§ 28-4-125. Delivery by common carrier, etc., to minor of liquors from another state, etc.

It shall be unlawful for any railroad company, express company or other common carrier or any person, agent or employee thereof or any other person to deliver to any minor in this state any of the liquors mentioned in section 28-4-120 that may be brought into this state from any point or place mentioned in section 28-4-120. (Acts 1915, No. 10, p. 39; Code 1923, § 4698; Code 1940, T. 29, § 168.)

§ 28-4-126. Presentation, collection, etc., by bank, etc., of draft, bill of exchange, etc., attached to, connected with, etc., bill of lading, order, etc., for prohibited liquors or beverages.

It shall be unlawful for any bank incorporated under the laws of this state or a national bank or private banker or any individual, firm or association to present, collect or in any way handle any draft, bill of exchange or order to pay money, to which is attached a bill of lading or order or receipt for any spirituous, vinous, malted, fermented or other intoxicating liquors of any kind or any liquor, liquids or beverages prohibited by the laws of this state to be manufactured or sold or otherwise disposed of or which is enclosed with, connected with or in any way related to, directly or indirectly, any bill of lading, order or receipt for the said liquors or any of them. Any person, firm, corporation or bank or banker violating the provisions of this section shall be guilty of a misdemeanor. (Acts 1915, No. 10, § 39; Code 1923, § 4699; Code 1940, T. 29, § 169.)

§ 28-4-127. Duty of common carrier, etc., to file with alcoholic beverage control board statement showing date of delivery, name and address of consignee and consignor, kind and amount, etc., of liquor delivered.

It shall be the duty of every railroad company, express company or other common carrier and of every person, firm or corporation who shall carry or transport any of the liquors mentioned in section 28-4-120 into this state from any of the points or places mentioned in section 28-4-120 and who shall deliver such liquors or any of them to any person, firm or corporation in this state to file with the alcoholic beverage control board a statement, either printed or plainly written or typewritten on stout paper, correctly stating the date on which the liquor was delivered, the name and post office address of the consignee and consignor, the place of delivery and to whom delivered and the kind and amount of such liquor delivered. Such statement shall be filed within three days after the date of delivery of such liquor. If said statement is in writing, it shall be in a fair and legible hand, and the names of the consignee and consignor and of the party obtaining delivery shall be truly ascertained and furnished in such way as to avoid mistakes in names. (Acts 1915, No. 10, p. 39; Code 1923, § 4692; Code 1940, T. 29, § 162.)

§ 28-4-128. Alcoholic beverage control board to make written demand for statement upon failure of common carrier, etc., to file same; notification of attorney general of further refusal or neglect to file statement; institution of proceedings for mandamus or injunction by attorney general.

If any person, firm or corporation within the terms of this article shall neglect or refuse to file with the alcoholic beverage control board such statement or statements as required by section 28-4-127, then it shall be the duty of the said board to make written demand upon such person, firm or corporation to comply with the requirements of section 28-4-127, such demand to be served by any agent or officer of the board and return made to the board upon a copy of the original demand.

Upon further refusal or noncompliance, it shall be the duty of the board to inform promptly the attorney general of the state of such failure or refusal, and it shall then be the duty of the attorney general to file a petition in the name of the state on the relation of the office, filing same in an appropriate court to secure a mandamus to compel compliance with section 28-4-127 or to file a petition for a mandatory injunction restraining the further noncompliance with section 28-4-127 on the part of the delinquent person, firm or corporation. (Acts 1915, No. 10, p. 39; Code 1923, § 4693; Code 1940, T. 29, § 163.)

§ 28-4-129. Filing of statement by board; inspection of statement by district attorney or police officers.

It shall be the duty of the board to file immediately the statement required by section 28-4-127 as a part of the files of its office and to permit any sheriff, deputy sheriff, constable, chief of police or other police officer of a municipality, district attorney whose duty it is to prosecute crime in the county in which delivery is made and any other peace officer of the county or officer charged with the duty of prosecuting violations of the law to inspect the said statements as they may desire at any time and especially to permit inspection thereof by any officer or other duly authorized person seeking information for the prosecution of persons charged with or suspected of crime, especially the crime of selling, giving away, bartering, keeping for sale or otherwise disposing of liquors or any beverages prohibited by the laws of the state to be sold, given away, kept for sale or otherwise disposed of, and to permit any and all other persons so desiring to inspect the said statements to do so at any time. (Acts 1915, No. 10, p. 39; Code 1923, § 4694; Code 1940, T. 29, § 164.)

§ 28-4-130. Board to furnish certified copies of statements to officers, etc.; admissibility in evidence of statements or copies.

The alcoholic beverage control board shall give a certified copy of such statements to any of the officers mentioned in section 28-4-129 without charge or to other persons requesting or demanding the same upon the payment of lawful fees therefor.

The said original statements or certified copies thereof shall be competent evidence upon the trial of any action whatever in any of the courts of this state in which the same may be relevant or material to the issue or issues involved. (Acts 1915, No. 10, p. 39; Code 1923, § 4695; Code 1940, T. 29, § 165.)

§ 28-4-131. Duty of common carriers, etc., to maintain current record of date of delivery, name and address of consignee and consignor, kind and amount, etc., of liquors delivered.

It shall be the duty of every railroad company, express company or other common carrier and of every person, firm or corporation that shall carry or transport any of the liquors mentioned in section 28-4-120 into the state from any of the points or places mentioned in section 28-4-120 for the purpose of delivery and who shall deliver such liquors, or any of them, to any person, firm or corporation in this state to currently keep, in a fair and legible hand or typewritten or otherwise so that the same may be easily read, a record of such liquors and of the delivery thereof, which shall set forth the date on which such liquors were received and delivered, the name and post-office address of the consignor and consignee, the place of delivery and the person to whom delivered and the kind and amount of such liquor delivered. (Acts 1915, No. 10, p. 39; Code 1923, § 4696; Code 1940, T. 29, § 166.)

§ 28-4-132. Inspection of record by enforcement officers, etc.; acquisition and admissibility in evidence of record.

The record required by section 28-4-131 to be kept by common carriers or persons, firms or corporations making delivery of said liquors or any of them in this state from any point or place mentioned in section 28-4-120 shall also be open to the inspection of any enforcement officer and of the duly authorized person seeking information for the prosecution of persons charged with or suspected of crime, and when application is made by any of the said officers or persons for permission to examine and take copies of such record, they shall be allowed to do so during the office or business hours of the persons or corporations keeping said record, and in such reasonable manner as not to interfere with the business of the corporation or person keeping said record.

The said record may be secured to be produced in court by any lawful process issued by any court of the state, to be used as evidence, and said record shall be competent evidence upon the trial of any action whatsoever in any court, in which the record may be material or relevant to the issues involved. (Acts 1915, No. 10, p. 39; Code 1923, § 4697; Code 1940, T. 29, § 167.)

§ 28-4-133. Duty of common carriers, etc., to permit examination of books, records, papers, etc., in connection with prosecutions under article, etc.

In the prosecutions of violations of this article or any law for the suppression of the evils of intemperance or the promotion of temperance, any common carrier doing business in the state of Alabama or any person engaged in the transportation in the state or making deliveries in this state of the liquors mentioned in section 28-4-120 or of other prohibited liquors and beverages is required to permit an examination of all his books, records, papers, bills of lading and accounts pertaining to the shipment of such liquors by any officer in this state whose duty it is to prosecute crime or ferret out criminals, when such information is sought for the prosecution of persons charged with or suspected of crime. (Acts 1915, No. 10, p. 39; Code 1923, § 4701; Code 1940, T. 29, § 170.)

§ 28-4-134. Persons not to be excused from testifying before grand juries or at trials for violations of article; immunity from prosecution as to matters disclosed.

No person shall be excused from testifying before the grand jury or at the trial in any prosecution for any violation of provisions contained in this article, but no disclosure or discovery made by such person is to be used against him in any penal or criminal prosecution for and on account of the matters disclosed. (Acts 1915, No. 10, p. 39; Code 1923, § 4702; Code 1940, T. 29, § 171.)

§ 28-4-135. Where certain offenses deemed committed.

In all prosecutions under this article for unlawful shipments of the liquors mentioned in section 28-4-120 into this state, the offense shall be held to have been committed in any county of the state through which or into which said liquors have been carried or transported or in which they have been unloaded or to which they have been conveyed for delivery. (Acts 1915, No. 10, p. 39; Code 1923, § 4703; Code 1940, T. 29, § 172.)

§ 28-4-136. Penalties for violations of provisions of article by railroad companies, express companies, etc.; duties of district attorney in cases of grand jury indictments.

(a) Any railroad company, express company or other carrier or any person or corporation violating any of the provisions of this article or failing to comply with any requirements thereof shall be guilty of a misdemeanor, punishable by a fine of not less than $50.00 nor more than $500.00, to which, at the discretion of the court, may be added imprisonment in the county jail or confinement at hard labor for the county for not more than six months for the first conviction.

On the second and every subsequent conviction of a violation of any provisions of this article, the offense shall, in addition to a fine within the limitations above named, be punishable by imprisonment in the county jail or at hard labor for the county for not less than three nor more than six months, to be imposed by the court.

(b) It shall be the duty of the district attorney in all cases of indictment by the grand jury to ascertain whether or not the charge made by the grand jury is the first or subsequent offense and, if the latter, it shall be so stated in the indictment and returned, and he shall introduce proper evidence before the trial court showing that it is a subsequent offense and shall not be permitted to use his discretion in charging said second offense or in introducing evidence and proving the same on trial. (Acts 1915, No. 10, p. 39; Acts 1915, No. 491, p. 553; Code 1923, § 4704; Code 1940, T. 29, § 173.)

Prerequisites to application of other penalty. — To warrant the imposition of the penalty prescribed by § 28-4-115 the indictment should charge illegal transportation or importation in quantities of five gallons or more of liquor, and if the indictment or complaint charges illegal transportation or importation without specifying quantity and a conviction follows, the penalty prescribed by this section only is applicable. Hardin v. State, 241 Ala. 151, 3 So. 2d 93 (1941).

Cited in Ex parte State ex rel. Davis, 206 Ala. 546, 90 So. 278 (1921).

§ 28-4-137. Applicability of article to interstate transportation of prohibited liquors or beverages.

The provisions of this article in respect to the transportation of prohibited liquors into the state shall not apply to shipments transported by any railroad company or other common carrier of unbroken packages in sealed cars or vehicles in continuous transit through the state from one point outside of the state to another point outside of the state, but this article shall be construed to prohibit any person, firm or corporation from bringing into or transporting through this state any prohibited liquors or beverages except as provided by law. (Acts 1919, No. 7, p. 6; Code 1923, § 4717; Code 1940, T. 29, § 186.)

Collateral references. — State's right to interfere with shipment of liquor through its territory. 27 ALR 108.

ARTICLE 7.

SALE, PURCHASE AND PRESCRIPTION OF ALCOHOL
BY DRUGGISTS AND PHYSICIANS.

§ 28-4-150. Sales by wholesale druggists generally; said druggists to file monthly statements as to sales with alcoholic beverage control board.

Wholesale druggists may sell in wholesale quantities to retail druggists, public or charitable hospitals and medical or pharmaceutical colleges pure alcohol for medicinal purposes only and grain alcohol to be used by chemists or bacteriologists actually engaged in scientific work for such purposes only.

Such wholesale druggists shall, at the end of each month in which any such sales have been made, file with the alcoholic beverage control board a statement in writing giving the name of the purchaser, the price paid, the date of sale and the quantity and character of the alcohol sold. (Acts 1915, No. 1, p. 1; Code 1923, § 4718; Code 1940, T. 29, § 188.)

Collateral references. — 48 C.J.S., Intoxicating Liquors, § 210. 45 Am. Jur. 2d, Intoxicating Liquors, §§ 254-256.

§ 28-4-151. Sales by retail druggists generally; use of alcohol by such druggists for compounding of prescriptions, etc.

Any retail druggist in this state who is himself a registered or licensed pharmacist or who regularly employs a licensed or registered pharmacist may sell in the manner set out in this article pure alcohol for medicinal purposes only and grain alcohol to chemists and bacteriologists actually engaged in scientific work for such purposes only.

Nothing in this section shall prevent such druggist from using alcohol in the compounding of prescriptions or other medicines, the sale of which would not subject him to the payment of the special tax required of liquor dealers by the United States. (Acts 1915, No. 1, p. 1; Code 1923, § 4719; Code 1940, T. 29, § 189.)

Collateral references. — 45 Am. Jur. 2d, Intoxicating Liquors, §§ 254-256.

§ 28-4-152. Sales by retail druggists of alcohol for use in arts or for scientific or mechanical purposes; execution of statement by persons desiring to purchase alcohol for said purposes.

The retail druggists may sell, in quantities not greater than five gallons, alcohol to be used in the arts or for scientific or mechanical purposes and such druggists may sell in like quantities grain alcohol to chemists and bacteriologists engaged in scientific work and for such purposes only.

Any person desiring to purchase alcohol for the purposes set out in this section shall sign a written or printed statement, giving his name, residence and occupation and the purpose for which he intends to use said alcohol, and he shall certify that said alcohol is purchased in good faith for such purpose and no other. (Acts 1915, No. 1, p. 1; Code 1923, § 4720; Code 1940, T. 29, § 190.)

Collateral references. — Forbidding prescription, or restricting the amount, of intoxicating liquor for medicinal purposes. 49 ALR 588.

§ 28-4-153. Purchase and use of alcohol by physicians.

Regularly licensed and practicing physicians may purchase grain alcohol or pure alcohol in quantities of not more than one gallon at one time from wholesale or retail druggists and may use the same in compounding and dispensing remedies in the practice of their profession only. (Acts 1915, No. 1, p. 1; Code 1923, § 4721; Code 1940, T. 29, § 191.)

§ 28-4-154. Sale of pure alcohol for medicinal purposes to be made only upon prescription of physician; physician to conduct examination prior to issuing prescription.

No sale of pure alcohol for medicinal purposes shall be made by any person authorized by the law under proper circumstances to make sale of such liquor for medicinal purposes except upon the prescription of a regularly authorized practicing physician of this state, who, before writing such prescription, shall make an actual examination of the person for whom the prescription is issued. (Acts 1919, No. 7, p. 6; Code 1923, § 4722; Code 1940, T. 29, § 192.)

Collateral references. — 45 Am. Jur. 2d,
Intoxicating Liquors, § 262.

§ 28-4-155. Prescription to be based upon professional opinion of physician that alcohol will be used by patient for medicinal purposes.

No physician shall prescribe alcohol for any patient simply upon the affirmation or statement or promise of said patient that he will use the same for medicinal purposes, but the said prescription must be based upon the professional opinion of the physician after a careful examination of the person seeking the prescription and upon his opinion, derived from such examination, that the said party is bona fide applying for said alcohol to be used as a medicine and not as a drink or beverage. (Acts 1919, No. 7, p. 6; Code 1923, § 4724; Code 1940, T. 29, § 194.)

§ 28-4-156. Physicians to file affidavit with probate judge before authorized to prescribe alcohol for medicinal purposes; form of affidavit; fee of probate judge for filing and recordation of affidavit.

(a) Before any physician shall be authorized to prescribe alcohol for medicinal purposes, he shall first file with the probate judge of the county in which he practices an affidavit in the following form: "I, ..., a regularly authorized practicing physician, do solemnly swear or affirm that I am such regularly practicing physician in . . . . county; and that I will not prescribe or furnish alcohol to any one except it be in my judgment a necessity in the alleviation or cure of the disease with which the patient shall be at the time afflicted and I will strictly comply with all the legal requirements pertaining to the furnishing of said prescriptions and will give no prescription for an amount exceeding one-half pint of alcohol; and I will comply with all the laws of the state of Alabama, with respect to the giving of prescriptions of alcohol for sickness; that I will not prescribe alcohol to one who is afflicted with the habit of taking narcotics or who is a person of intemperate habits nor will I prescribe alcohol merely upon the promise or statement of the patient that the same will be used for medicinal purposes, but it shall be prescribed only upon my judgment as a physician that the same is necessary in the treatment of a disease or sickness, which I shall find upon personal examination of the patient to exist in his case."

(b) For the filing and recording of said affidavit by the probate judge in a book kept for that purpose, he may receive $.25 for each affidavit from the physician filing the same. (Acts 1919, No. 7, p. 6; Code 1923, § 4729; Code 1940, T. 29, § 199.)

§ 28-4-157. Prescription — Contents.

Said prescription shall state the disease or ailment from which the patient is suffering and shall prescribe the method of the use or administration of said alcohol and the quantity of the dose or doses to be taken and the intervals between doses or the time when the same are to be administered. The prescription shall state and certify that the use of such alcohol, in the opinion of the physician, is necessary to alleviate or cure the illness or disease from which such patient is suffering. Every such prescription shall contain the name and address of the physician giving the prescription, the name and address of the person for whom the alcohol is prescribed and the date on which the prescription is written and shall state the number of prescriptions for alcohol which the physician has written for said patient within 12 months or that he has not written any within that period for said patient. (Acts 1919, No. 7, p. 6; Code 1923, § 4723; Code 1940, T. 29, § 193.)

§ 28-4-158. Same — Form.

The following form of prescription shall be used: "State of Alabama, ... county. I, ..., a regularly licensed and practicing physician under the laws of said state, do hereby certify that I have examined ...., a patient under my charge, and I do hereby prescribe for the use of said patient, ... of alcohol (not exceeding one-half pint), and I further certify that the said patient is suffering from the following illness, sickness or disease, ... and that, in my opinion, the use of such alcohol is necessary to alleviate or cure the illness or disease or sickness from which such patient is suffering, and that I believe that the patient is seeking said prescription in good faith, to use said alcohol for medicinal purposes and not as a beverage, and in writing this prescription I am not relying upon his promise or affirmation that he or she will use the alcohol for medicinal purposes, but upon my own opinion, based upon an examination, that the alcohol is necessary to alleviate or cure the sickness of which he or she is suffering. And I further certify that he or she has been suffering from said sickness as far as I can ascertain for the following period of time (to be stated in months, weeks or days) .... The alcohol is to be administered or used as follows: (here state dose, etc., as above directed). Then state address of patient and doctor. (Signed) .... M. D. Date: ...." (Acts 1919, No. 7, p. 6; Code 1923, § 4725; Code 1940, T. 29, § 195.)

§ 28-4-159. Physician to file copy of prescription with probate judge; probate judge to preserve same and deliver to next grand jury for examination.

The physician shall immediately file a copy of the prescription, signed by himself, in the office of the probate judge, who shall preserve the same and deliver all such prescriptions to the next grand jury for examination. (Acts 1919, No. 7, p. 6; Code 1923, § 4728; Code 1940, T. 29, § 198.)

§ 28-4-160. Time for filling of prescription; limitation as to amount of alcohol sold and delivered on prescription; disposition of prescription when filled by druggist; filling of prescription at certain drugstores in which prescribing physician has financial, etc., interest.

(a) No prescription shall be filled under this article except upon the day upon which it is issued or the following day.

(b) No more than one-half pint of alcohol shall be sold and delivered on any one prescription.

(c) When any such prescription is filled, it shall not be refilled but shall be delivered to the druggist filling the same and, at the end of the month in which the same is filled, it shall be filed by such druggist with the alcoholic beverage control board.

(d) In towns having a population of 2,000 or more, no physician's prescription shall be filled at any drugstore of which he is the proprietor or in which said physician has a financial interest, either as partner, stockholder or otherwise. (Acts 1915, No. 1, p. 1; Code 1923, § 4726; Code 1940, T. 29, § 196.)

Collateral references. — Forbidding prescription, or restricting the amount, of intoxicating liquor for medicinal purposes. 49 ALR 588.

§ 28-4-161. Recordation, etc., by probate judge of statements or prescriptions required to be filed by article; fee of probate judge; evidentiary effect of certified copy of statement or prescription.

All statements or prescriptions required by this article to be filed in the office of the probate judge shall be recorded and properly indexed by him in a book kept for that purpose which shall at all times be open to public inspection, and a certified copy of such record or the original statement or prescription with the certificate of the probate judge endorsed thereon showing it has been recorded shall be prima facie evidence of the facts therein recited. For making such record, the probate judge shall be entitled to charge and collect for each prescription a fee of $.10 and, for all statements other than prescriptions, a fee of $.25, which shall be paid by the party filing the same. (Acts 1915, No. 1, p. 1; Code 1923, § 4730; Code 1940, T. 29, § 200.)

§ 28-4-162. Prescription of whiskey, rum, gin, etc., for medicinal purposes.

No physician shall prescribe whiskey, rum, gin or brandy or any prohibited liquor for medicinal purposes, except alcohol as provided by law. (Acts 1919, No. 7, p. 6; Code 1923, § 4727; Code 1940, T. 29, § 197.)

§ 28-4-163. Prescription, sale, dispensing, etc., of Jamaica ginger.

It shall be unlawful for any person to give away the essence, extract or tincture of Jamaica ginger for beverage purposes or for any person, except a druggist or proprietor of a drugstore, who is entitled by law to sell alcohol for medicinal purposes upon prescription of a physician, to sell or dispense the essence, extract or tincture of Jamaica ginger, and the said druggist or proprietor of a drugstore shall act only upon the prescription of a regularly authorized practicing physician, all in accordance with the rules and regulations prescribed by law for the furnishing of prescriptions of alcohol for medicinal purposes, with the same limitations and restrictions in all details and particulars. (Acts 1919, No. 7, p. 6; Code 1923, § 4731; Code 1940, T. 29, § 201.)

Jamaica ginger as prohibited liquor. — The fact that this section provides that it shall be unlawful to sell or dispose of Jamaica ginger except by a druggist on the conditions named does not militate against a construction of §§ 28-4-1 and 28-4-20, whereby Jamaica ginger may be shown as a fact to be a prohibited liquor, when so alleged, and, as such, those sections would apply with the exception of the right conferred by the instant section, which would relieve the transaction of being unlawful. Noltey v. State, 225 Ala. 584, 144 So. 457 (1932).

§ 28-4-164. Failure to comply with requirements as to issuance of prescriptions for alcohol, unauthorized use of alcohol, etc., by physicians.

Any physician who issues any prescription containing any false statement or who fails to comply with any requirement of the law in regard to the giving of prescription for alcohol to patients or who uses alcohol except for authorized purposes shall be guilty of a misdemeanor and shall be, by the judgment of the court, disbarred from the practice of his profession in this state upon conviction in addition to the other penalties prescribed. (Acts 1919, No. 7, p. 6; Code 1923, § 4734; Code 1940, T. 29, § 202.)

§ 28-4-165. Sale, delivery, etc., of liquors, etc., to prisoners by persons in charge of jails.

No sheriff, jailer, police officer, marshal or other person in charge of any jail or lockup, under any pretense whatever, shall give, sell or deliver to any prisoner therein any spirituous, vinous or malt liquors or any other liquor or beverage prohibited by law to be sold, given away or otherwise disposed of, unless a reputable physician certifies in writing that the health of such prisoner or inmate requires it, and, in case of such certification, the prisoner may be allowed the use of the prescribed quantity of pure alcohol and no more. Any of said officers violating any provision of this section shall be guilty of a misdemeanor. (Acts 1909, No. 191, p. 63; Acts 1915, No. 2, p. 8; Code 1923, § 4735; Code 1940, T. 29, § 203.)

§ 28-4-166. Penalties for violations of article.

Any person who violates any provision of this article shall be guilty of a misdemeanor, when not otherwise expressed, and shall be punished as prescribed in this section.

Such person, except in cases where other punishment is prescribed, shall, on conviction, be punished by a fine of not less than $50.00 nor more than $500.00 and may also be imprisoned in the county jail or sentenced to hard labor for the county for not more than six months for the first conviction, at the discretion of the court. On the second and every subsequent conviction, in addition to the fine which may be imposed, the convicted party shall be imprisoned at hard labor for the county for not less than three nor more than six months, such imprisonment to be fixed by the court. (Acts 1919, No. 7, p. 6; Code 1923, § 4734; Code 1940, T. 29, § 202.)

ARTICLE 8.

PURCHASE, RECEIPT, POSSESSION, USE, ETC., OF WINE FOR SACRAMENTAL OR RELIGIOUS PURPOSES.

Cross references. — As to procedure for shipment, delivery, etc., of alcohol and wine to persons for sacramental or nonbeverage use, see §§ 28-4-117 through 28-4-119.

§ 28-4-180. Persons authorized to purchase, have shipped, receive, possess and use wine for sacramental or religious purposes.

The following persons are authorized to purchase, have shipped from outside of the state, receive, accept delivery of, possess and use wines for sacramental or religious purposes: any minister, pastor or officer of a regularly organized religious congregation or church and any other person who, under the ritual of any recognized religious denomination, is authorized or required to use wine for sacramental or religious purposes in the ceremonies or ritual of such religious denominations. (Acts 1919, No. 653, p. 906; Code 1923, § 4736; Code 1940, T. 29, § 204.)

Collateral references. — 48 C.J.S., Intoxicating Liquors, § 364.

§ 28-4-181. Purchase and sale of wine for sacramental purposes.

It shall be unlawful to sell wine for sacramental purposes, except to a minister, pastor, priest or officer of a regularly organized religious congregation or church. Any such person desiring to make such purchase in quantities not exceeding one gallon from a druggist shall sign a written or printed statement giving his name and residence and the name and location of the church for which such wine is purchased, and he shall certify that said wine is purchased in good faith to be used for sacramental or religious purposes and no other. The statements provided for in this section shall be filed at the end of each month by the druggist making the sale with the alcoholic beverage control board. (Acts 1915, No. 1, p. 1; Code 1923, § 4732; Code 1940, T. 29, § 205.)

Collateral references. — 45 Am. Jur. 2d, Intoxicating Liquors, §§ 31, 77.

§ 28-4-182. Permit from alcoholic beverage control board to have wine shipped from outside the state — Required.

When any such person desires to have shipped from outside of the state wine for sacramental purposes in the usual religious exercises of his denomination, he may apply to the alcoholic beverage control board for a permit, stating the amount desired, during what period and for what purpose; and said board, if satisfied of the good faith of the application, shall grant a written permit to the applicant, permitting the shipment of such amount as is shown to be reasonably necessary, to be stated in the permit, for the time stated for such purpose. Said permit shall be attached to the package when shipped into the state. (Acts 1919, No. 653, p. 906; Code 1923, § 4737; Code 1940, T. 29, § 206; Acts 1963, 2nd Ex. Sess., No. 142, p. 328.)

§ 28-4-183. Same — Permit to be used for one shipment only; expiration.

The permit provided for in section 28-4-182 may be used for only one shipment and shall be void 20 days after the date of issuance. (Acts 1919, No. 653, p. 906; Code 1923, § 4738; Code 1940, T. 29, § 207.)

§ 28-4-184. Carrier, etc., to maintain record of deliveries.

The carrier or party making delivery must keep a record of all such deliveries of wine for such purposes, subject to the conditions applicable to other shipments of liquor. (Acts 1919, No. 653, p. 906; Code 1923, § 4739; Code 1940, T. 29, § 208.)

ARTICLE 9.

POSSESSION, ETC., OF CERTAIN QUANTITIES OF STATE TAX-PAID ALCOHOLIC BEVERAGES FOR PRIVATE USE.

There is no conflict between scope of this article and section 28-4-115. Johnston v. State, 54 Ala. App. 100, 304 So. 2d 918 (1974).

Each is mutually exclusive. — There is a full scope for the operation of this article and § 28-4-115 without conflict. Each is mutually exclusive. Johnston v. State, 54 Ala. App. 100, 304 So. 2d 918 (1974).

This article does not purport to make any provision that deals with transportation, or transportation of more than five gallons of prohibited liquors. It purports only to make an exception, allowing the possession of a prescribed amount of less than five gallons tax paid alcoholic beverages in dry counties for personal use. Heretofore, the possession of any quantity was a violation and would have prompted a prosecution and confiscation upon conviction. Thus, this article nowhere encroaches upon the field of operation of, § 28-4-115, and does not even contain the word "transport." Johnston v. State, 54 Ala. App. 100, 304 So. 2d 918 (1974).

§ 28-4-200. Possession of certain quantities of state tax-paid alcoholic beverages for private use permitted; storage, possession, etc., of alcoholic beverages in passenger area of vehicles or in view of passengers.

Any person 19 years of age or over shall be entitled to have in his possession in his motor vehicle or a private residence or place of private residence or the curtilage thereof in any dry county in this state for his own private use and not for resale not more than the following quantity of alcoholic beverages, as enumerated and defined in section 28-3-1, when such beverages have been sold or distributed by and through a state liquor store operated by the Alabama alcoholic beverage control board or a licensee of such board, and the containers of such beverages have affixed thereto such mark or identification and sufficient revenue stamps as to show that such alcoholic beverages were sold or distributed by a state liquor store or a licensee of the Alabama alcoholic beverage control board and that the required tax has been paid: three quarts of liquor and one case of malt or brewed beverages or three quarts of wine and one case of malt or brewed beverages; provided, however, that no alcoholic beverages shall be kept, stored or possessed in the passenger area of any vehicle or in the view of any passenger. (Acts 1971, No. 1265, p. 2194, § 1.)

This section does not purport to make any provision that deals with transportation, or transportation of more than five gallons of prohibited liquors. It purports only to make an exception, allowing the possession of a prescribed amount of less than five gallons tax paid alcoholic beverages in dry counties for personal use. Heretofore, the possession of any quantity was a violation and would have prompted a prosecution and confiscation upon conviction. Jones v. State, 401 So. 2d 322 (Ala. Crim. App. 1981).

Section 28-4-115 has not been changed to a misdemeanor by this section and § 28-4-201. Bryan v. State, 398 So. 2d 404 (Ala. Crim. App. 1981). But see, Copeland v. State, 377 So. 2d 1 (Ala. Crim. App. 1979).

There is no conflict between the scope of § 28-4-115 and this section. Jones v. State, 401 So. 2d 322 (Ala. Crim. App. 1981). But see,

Copeland v. State, 377 So. 2d 1 (Ala. Crim. App. 1979).

As they are mutually exclusive. Jones v. State, 401 So. 2d 322 (Ala. Crim. App. 1981). But see, Copeland v. State, 377 So. 2d 1 (Ala. Crim. App. 1979).

Cited in Hughes v. State, 52 Ala. App. 244, 291 So. 2d 331 (1974); Welden v. State, 57 Ala. App. 379, 328 So. 2d 630 (1976); Kean v. State, 340 So. 2d 102 (Ala. Crim. App. 1976); Mars v. State ex rel. Black, 340 So. 2d 1131 (Ala. Civ. App. 1976).

§ 28-4-201. Sale or offer for sale or possession in excess of quantity permitted of such alcoholic beverages; penalties for violations of article.

(a) It shall be unlawful for any person residing in or traveling through any dry county in this state to sell or offer to sell such alcoholic beverages to another or to have in his possession at any one time any amount of alcoholic beverages in excess of the quantity stipulated in section 28-4-200.

(b) Any person violating the provisions of this article shall be guilty of a misdemeanor and shall be fined not less than $50.00 nor more than $500.00 or imprisoned in the county jail for a period not to exceed six months or both, at the discretion of the court. (Acts 1971, No. 1265, p. 2194, § 2.)

Section 28-4-115 has not been changed to a misdemeanor by § 28-4-200 and this section. Bryan v. State, 398 So. 2d 404 (Ala. Crim. App. 1981). But see, Copeland v. State, 377 So. 2d 1 (Ala. Crim. App. 1979).

Cited in Hughes v. State, 52 Ala. App. 244, 291 So. 2d 331 (1974).

ARTICLE 10.

ABATEMENT OF LIQUOR NUISANCES.

Constitutionality. — The constitutionality of the provisions of this article, as to abatement of liquor nuisances, and the issuance of the writ of seizure in aid thereof, was fully discussed in the case of Fulton v. State, 171 Ala. 572, 54 So. 688 (1911); their validity being there upheld. In re State ex rel. Attorney Gen., 179 Ala. 639, 60 So. 285 (1912).

§ 28-4-220. Authorization and procedure generally; filing of petition generally.

The nuisances named in this chapter as liquor nuisances may be abated by a proceeding in a circuit court. The attorney general or the district attorney or deputy district attorney where his official duties require him to prosecute criminal cases on behalf of the state may, upon their relation, file a petition in the name of the state of Alabama in the circuit court in the county where the nuisance exists to abate and perpetually enjoin the same. (Acts 1909, No. 191, p. 63; Acts 1915, No. 2, p. 8; Code 1923, § 4671; Code 1940, T. 29, § 141.)

Jurisdiction. — The circuit court has power to set down action to abate liquor nuisance for trial after sufficient time for preparation. Garrett v. State ex rel. Matthews, 235 Ala. 457, 179 So. 636 (1938).

Nuisance in wet county. — Contention by defendant that intoxicating beverages were not being illegally sold at defendant's place of business since the beverages were all duly taxed and labeled and purchased from a state store could not be sustained, since such beverages can be "prohibited liquors" in a wet county if put to an illegal use. Smith v. State ex rel. Sullinger, 265 Ala. 138, 90 So. 2d 225 (1956).

Direct evidence required. — In a proceeding under this section to abate a liquor nuisance, the state was required to prove by direct, affirmative and admissible evidence that the defendants were maintaining a liquor nuisance. The state cannot support its complaint by indirect evidence of the general reputation of the place of business operated by the defendants. Thompson v. State ex rel. Waid, 263 Ala. 463, 83 So. 2d 70 (1955).

Padlocking. — Judgment padlocking defendant's place of business for maintaining a liquor nuisance was too severe in the absence of a showing that defendant was a persistent violator of the law, and judgment was modified to permit defendant to use his property for lawful purposes upon posting of bond for $2,000.00 that he would not use property to maintain a liquor nuisance. Smith v. State ex rel. Sullinger, 265 Ala. 138, 90 So. 2d 225 (1956).

In a proceeding by the state to abate a liquor nuisance in a garage, the padlocking of the garage was not justified where there was no evidence of the maintenance of a liquor nuisance in the garage after the issuance of the preliminary injunction. Livingston v. State ex rel. Wright, 264 Ala. 331, 86 So. 2d 876 (1956).

Padlocking is a severe remedy depriving one of the use of his property for lawful purposes, and should be exercised only as a necessary measure to enforce the law. But where the party is shown by his conduct to be a persistent violator of the law, determined to evade it, padlocking is proper, but is to be modified where it sufficiently appears the property will not be again employed in the conduct of a liquor nuisance. Espey v. State ex rel. Nicol, 268 Ala. 109, 105 So. 2d 93 (1958); Allen v. State ex rel. Simpson, 377 So. 2d 942 (Ala. 1979).

Cited in Ex parte Hill, 229 Ala. 501, 158 So. 531 (1935); Greenwood v. State ex rel. Bailes, 229 Ala. 630, 159 So. 91 (1935); Chandler v. State ex rel. Killcrease, 237 Ala. 407, 187 So. 189 (1939); Klein v. State ex rel. Evans, 238 Ala. 148, 189 So. 771 (1939); Gorman v. State ex rel. Embry, 240 Ala. 175, 198 So. 3 (1940); Stephens v. State ex rel. Ward, 257 Ala. 375, 59 So. 2d 69 (1952); Billingsley v. State, 261 Ala. 211, 73 So. 2d 541 (1954); Cooley v. State, 262 Ala. 136, 77 So. 2d 488 (1955); Taylor v. State ex rel. Adams, 275 Ala. 430, 155 So. 2d 595 (1963); Isbell v. State ex rel. Rayburn, 276 Ala. 351, 162 So. 2d 240 (1964).

Collateral references. — 48 C.J.S., Intoxicating Liquors, §§ 414, 426.

45 Am. Jur. 2d, Intoxicating Liquors, § 434 et seq.

Constitutionality of statute conferring on chancery courts power to prevent sale of liquors as a nuisance. 5 ALR 1474, 22 ALR 542, 75 ALR 1298.

Saloons or taverns as nuisance. 5 ALR3d 989.

§ 28-4-221. Persons, etc., against whom petition may be filed.

The petition to be filed to abate such nuisances may be filed against any person, firm or corporation who maintains or aids in maintaining such nuisance, including agents, servants and employees, as well as officers, of corporations. (Acts 1909, No. 191, p. 63; Acts 1915, No. 2, p. 8; Code 1923, § 4619; Code 1940, T. 29, § 97.)

Cited in Harvell v. State ex rel. Sanford, 235 Ala. 329, 179 So. 233 (1938); Cooley v. State, 262 Ala. 136, 77 So. 2d 488 (1955).

§ 28-4-222. Contents and verification of petition.

The petition shall state the facts upon which the application is based and shall be verified by the affidavit of the officer or citizen filing the action, either upon knowledge or information and belief, as the circumstances may warrant, and, in case the petition is filed by any one of the officers named and he is unwilling to make the affidavit, the verification may be made by any citizen or citizens in the same manner and terms as if the petition had been filed by him or them. (Acts 1909, No. 191, p. 63; Acts 1915, No. 2, p. 8; Code 1923, § 4672; Code 1940, T. 29, § 142.)

Section is not unconstitutional insofar as section prescribed such verification for issuance of temporary writ restraining further violation of criminal law. Greenwood v. State ex rel. Bailes, 230 Ala. 405, 161 So. 498 (1935).

Whole purpose of the affidavit is precautionary, a pledge of good faith in the commencement of the action. It could serve no other purpose than to put the judicial power in motion. Worthen v. State ex rel. Verner, 189 Ala. 395, 66 So. 686 (1914); Greenwood v. State ex rel. Bailes, 230 Ala. 405, 161 So. 498 (1935); Barnett v. State ex rel. Simpson, 235 Ala. 326, 179 So. 208 (1938).

Sufficiency of petition. — Where a petition averred that the respondents, for a period of six months before the filing of the petition, on premises occupied by respondents, had maintained the premises as headquarters for the selling, storing, or consuming of illegal beverages, a part of which was alcohol, and that police officers had had numerous complaints concerning the premises, it was held that the averments of the petition complied with the statutory requirements and were sufficient to invoke the jurisdiction of the circuit court. Isbell v. State ex rel. Rayburn, 276 Ala. 351, 162 So. 2d 240 (1964).

Sufficiency of verification. — A petition is sufficiently verified by relator's affidavit that he has probable cause to believe, and does believe, that allegations thereof are true. Garrett v. State ex rel. Matthews, 235 Ala. 457, 179 So. 636 (1938).

Verification of petition in proceeding to abate liquor nuisance on information or belief as provided by this section held sufficient where temporary writ issued merely restrained defendants from further violation of criminal law of state. Greenwood v. State ex rel. Bailes, 230 Ala. 405, 161 So. 498 (1935).

Waiver of irregularity. — The filing of answer by defendant denying allegations of petition to abate a liquor nuisance and his permitting case to proceed to trial on merits waived irregularity consisting of failure of constable verifying petition to state that prosecuting officers were unwilling to make the required affidavit, notwithstanding that answer stated that it was filed without waiving defendant's motion to discharge temporary injunction because of such irregularity. Barnett v. State ex rel. Simpson, 235 Ala. 326, 179 So. 208 (1938).

Cited in In re State ex rel. Attorney Gen., 179 Ala. 639, 60 So. 285 (1912); Auburn Sales Co. v. State, 223 Ala. 184, 134 So. 867 (1931); Ivey v. State ex rel. Orme, 231 Ala. 232, 164 So. 291 (1935).

Collateral references. — 48 C.J.S., Intoxicationg Liquors, § 419.

§ 28-4-223. Issuance of preliminary injunction generally.

When a petition making a prima facie case and properly verified is presented to the judge of the court wherein the petition is filed or is to be filed or other judge authorized by the law of the state to grant a preliminary injunction, such judge may, after notice to the adverse party and a hearing, issue a preliminary injunction, and the judge shall direct the terms of the preliminary injunction so as to carry out the purposes of the law, which is to secure the restraint and abatement of such liquor nuisances on the premises. (Acts 1909, No. 191, p. 63; Acts 1915, No. 2, p. 8; Code 1923, § 4674; Code 1940, T. 29, § 144.)

Cross references. — As to rules of supreme court relative to injunctions, see A.R.C.P., Rule 65.

Application of section. — In Ex parte Hill, 229 Ala. 501, 158 So. 531 (1935), it was observed that the padlock provisions of §§ 6-5-147 and 6-5-148 were in all reason applicable to abatement of liquor nuisances, and embraced within the broad powers of this section. Ex parte Harvell, 235 Ala. 63, 177 So. 345 (1937).

Erroneous issuance of temporary injunction, without notice and hearing, padlocking defendant's place of business pending trial of proceeding to abate liquor nuisance was cured by court order restoring property to the owner, who was defendant's wife. Barnett v. State ex rel. Simpson, 235 Ala. 326, 179 So. 208 (1938).

Cited in Greenwood v. State ex rel. Bailes, 230 Ala. 405, 161 So. 498 (1935).

Collateral references. — 48 C.J.S., Intoxicating Liquors, § 418.

§ 28-4-224. Requirement of bond as condition precedent to issuance of preliminary injunction.

No bond shall be required as a condition precedent to the issuance of a preliminary injunction when the action is brought by the attorney general of the state or a district attorney or deputy district attorney. (Acts 1909, No. 191, p. 63; Acts 1915, No. 2, p. 8; Code 1923, § 4673; Code 1940, T. 29, § 143.)

Collateral references. — 48 C.J.S., Intoxicating Liquors, §§ 418, 424.

§ 28-4-225. Application for and issuance of writ directing seizure of prohibited liquors and beverages, movable property, etc., used in connection with nuisance pending hearing of action.

If the petition shall request a writ of seizure authorizing the sheriff to seize all prohibited liquors and beverages on the premises, together with all signs, screens, bars, bottles, glasses and other movable property used in keeping and maintaining said nuisance, the officer, or citizen or citizens filing the petition may, at the time they apply for a preliminary injunction, make application to the judge who grants the preliminary injunction or to the judge of the court in which the petition is or is to be filed or they may, at any time pending the hearing, make such application to said judge for such writ of seizure, and said writ may be ordered to issue when probable cause is shown, supported by oath or affirmation for the issuance of said writ, that the officer or person making the application or filing the petition has probable cause to believe and does believe that said prohibited liquors and beverages are manufactured, sold, furnished, given away, kept or offered for sale in violation of law on or about said premises. The officer or citizen or citizens making the application may support the same by the production of affidavits in writing sworn to and subscribed by the person making them, and the judge may issue said writ of seizure when he is satisfied from the affidavit of the officer or citizen or citizens or of others that facts have been produced affording probable cause for believing the grounds of the application to exist. (Acts 1909, No. 191, p. 63; Acts 1915, No. 2, p. 8; Code 1923, § 4678; Code 1940, T. 29, § 148.)

Cited in In re State ex rel. Attorney Gen., 179 Ala. 639, 60 So. 285 (1912).

Collateral references. — 45 Am. Jur. 2d, Intoxicating Liquors, § 486 et seq.

§ 28-4-226. Contents of writ.

The writ shall name or describe the person or other party whose premises are to be searched and shall describe as nearly as possible the liquors or beverages that are to be seized and the place where said liquors and beverages are to be seized, as prescribed in this chapter for other search warrants. (Acts 1909, No. 191, p. 63; Acts 1915, No. 2, p. 8; Code 1923, § 4679; Code 1940, T. 29, § 149.)

§ 28-4-227. Disposition of liquor and beverages, etc., seized upon final judgment generally — Destruction.

Whenever it shall be finally decided in the action that the liquors seized as aforesaid are forfeited and that they were kept or stored for an illegal purpose, the judgment of the court shall order the officer having said liquors in custody to forthwith destroy the same, together with the vessels containing the same, and other movable property used in keeping and maintaining the nuisance and immediately thereafter to make return of said order to the court whence it issued, with his action endorsed thereon. (Acts 1909, No. 191, p. 63; Acts 1915, No. 2, p. 8; Code 1940, T. 29, § 150.)

Cited in Davis v. City of Birmingham, 278 Ala. 391, 178 So. 2d 547 (1965).

Collateral references. — 48 C.J.S., Intoxicating Liquors, §§ 423, 424.

§ 28-4-228. Same — Restoration to owner.

If it shall be finally decided that any liquors or beverages so seized are not liable to forfeiture, the court shall order the officer having the same in custody to restore said liquors, with the vessels containing the same, to the place where they were seized, as nearly as practicable, and to the person entitled to receive them, which order the officer shall obey and make return to the court of his acts thereunder. (Acts 1909, No. 191, p. 63; Acts 1915, No. 2, p. 8; Code 1923, § 4861; Code 1940, T. 29, § 151.)

§ 28-4-229. Fees and allowances of officers executing writs of seizure; payment of costs in proceedings.

There shall be allowed the officer making the seizure under a writ issued under sections 28-4-225 and 28-4-226 in an injunction proceeding the sum of $3.00 and the sum of $.10 for every mile traveled in making the seizure, together with such reasonable sum as the court may deem just for necessary expenses incurred in transporting and providing storage for liquors and beverages and other movable property seized, all which costs shall be taxed in the bill of costs and, if not collected from a defendant, then shall be taxed and paid as in criminal prosecutions in which the state fails.

The costs in such injunction proceedings, unless charged against some party defendant by the court and collected from him, shall be paid as in criminal actions in which the state fails, upon the court making an order to that effect. (Acts 1909, No. 191, p. 63; Acts 1915, No. 2, p. 8; Code 1923, § 4682; Code 1940, T. 29, § 152.)

§ 28-4-230. Persons who may be joined as parties defendant in proceedings and who may be enjoined from maintaining, etc., nuisance.

The owner of and all persons interested in the building or premises where the nuisance exists or any agent renting the same, as well as the keeper thereof, may be joined with the keeper as parties defendant to the proceedings, and all such owners, keepers, parties interested or agents who may be found to have knowingly assented to the keeping or maintaining of such nuisance on the premises at any time within six months prior to the commencement of the action and their servants, lessees and tenants shall be perpetually enjoined from maintaining and keeping or suffering to be kept and maintained such nuisance or any liquor nuisance upon the said premises. (Acts 1909, No. 191, p. 63; Acts 1915, No. 2, p. 8; Code 1923, § 4675; Code 1940, T. 29, § 145.)

Injunction against owner of rental property. — Where court under evidence was warranted in finding that tenants were guilty of maintaining liquor nuisance on rented premises with knowledge and acquiescence of owners, injunction enjoining owners from maintaining liquor nuisance held properly granted. Joiner v. State, 232 Ala. 522, 168 So. 885 (1936).

But operator may be enjoined without making owner a party. — Under this section the operator or keeper of a public nuisance may be enjoined, either with or without making the owner a party. Taylor v. State ex rel. Adams, 275 Ala. 430, 155 So. 2d 595 (1963).

An order permanently enjoining the manager of a tavern from operating the tavern as a public nuisance would not be reversed on appeal, even though the owner had not been made a party to the proceeding, where the petition was not against the owner nor had the owner intervened, nor was the illegal use of the property within the knowledge, assent and connivance of the owner, and thus, as to the parties joined, the order was regular. Taylor v. State ex rel. Adams, 275 Ala. 430, 155 So. 2d 595 (1963).

Six-month requirement. — This section clearly requires proof that the establishment was a liquor nuisance within six months preceding the filing of the petition for injunction, but an express averment that the liquor nuisance existed for six months prior to institution of proceeding is not required. Thompson v. State ex rel. Waid, 263 Ala. 463, 83 So. 2d 70 (1955).

Evidence held not sufficient to support finding that respondents maintained on the premises a liquor nuisance "within six months prior to the commencement of the suit [action now]." Cooley v. State, 262 Ala. 136, 77 So. 2d 488 (1955).

Cited in Billingsley v. State, 261 Ala. 211, 73 So. 2d 541 (1954); Johnson v. State ex rel. Johnson, 270 Ala. 470, 119 So. 2d 884 (1960).

§ 28-4-231. Powers of court as to maintenance of jurisdiction and enforcement of judgments generally; rules of evidence, practice and procedure.

The court shall have full power and authority to maintain its jurisdiction and by all suitable orders and writs to enforce its judgments in respect to the subject matter of the action and to so shape and mould its judgments as to accomplish the purpose of the petition. All the rules of evidence, practice and

procedure, except as otherwise provided in this article, that pertain to circuit courts generally or that exist by virtue of any law of this state may be invoked and applied in any such injunction proceeding instituted under this article. (Acts 1909, No. 191, p. 63; Acts 1915, No. 2, p. 8; Code 1923, § 4676; Code 1940, T. 29, § 146.)

Evidence as to purchase and drinking on premises admissible. — In action by state against owners of premises to abate liquor nuisance, testimony of witnesses that they purchased and drank whisky on such premises held admissible as tending to show that prohibited liquors were there sold with knowledge of owners. Joiner v. State, 232 Ala. 522, 168 So. 885 (1936).

Forfeiture of bond. — Where defendant illegally maintained liquor nuisance, and such nuisance was duly ordered abated by order of circuit court, and bond was required, conditioned on defendant's abating the nuisance pursuant to such order and to prevent nuisance from being thereafter actively maintained, circuit court had authority to declare bond forfeited for violation of order. Collier v. State ex rel. Powell, 241 Ala. 459, 3 So. 2d 17 (1941).

Cited in Ex parte Hill, 229 Ala. 501, 158 So. 531 (1935).

Collateral references. — 48 C.J.S., Intoxicating Liquors, § 420.

§ 28-4-232. Entry of judgment for abatement of nuisance and destruction of all prohibited liquors and beverages, movable property, etc., used in connection with nuisance.

Upon the final hearing of the action instituted to abate a liquor nuisance, if it shall appear that the petition has been sustained by the evidence or has been admitted, the court shall enter a judgment ordering abatement of the nuisance, which judgment shall order the destruction of all such prohibited liquors and beverages as are found upon the premises, together with all signs, screens, bars, bottles, glasses and other movable property used in keeping and maintaining said nuisance, and the destruction of all such liquors and beverages and such movable property as may have been seized under authority of the court pending the hearing of the action. (Acts 1909, No. 191, p. 63; Acts 1915, No. 2, p. 8; Code 1923, § 4677; Code 1940, T. 29, § 147.)

Cited in Davis v. City of Birmingham, 278 Ala. 391, 178 So. 2d 547 (1965); Walker v. State ex rel. Baxley, 285 Ala. 315, 231 So. 2d 882 (1970).

Collateral references. — 48 C.J.S., Intoxicating Liquors, §§ 421, 423, 424.

ARTICLE 11.

FORFEITURE AND CONDEMNATION OF CONTRABAND LIQUORS AND BEVERAGES, ETC.

Alcoholic Beverage Control Act did not repeal this article. Lovett v. State, 30 Ala. App. 334, 6 So. 2d 437 (1941).

Rules of evidence in civil actions govern in condemnation proceedings. State ex rel. Hooper v. 50 Cases of 12 Oz. Miller Beer, 384 So. 2d 120 (Ala. Civ. App. 1980).

§ 28-4-250. Authorization and procedure generally.

Prohibited liquors and beverages kept, stored or deposited in any place in this state for the purpose of sale or unlawful disposition or unlawful furnishing or distribution and the vessels and receptacles in which such liquors are contained are declared to be contraband and are forfeited to the state when seized and may be condemned for destruction as provided in this article, and prohibited liquors and beverages may be searched for, seized and ordered to be destroyed as set forth in this article. In all criminal prosecutions against any person for violating the provisions of the prohibition laws of this state, the court, upon a conviction, may order the destruction of such prohibited liquors or beverages as had been sold, offered for sale, had, kept in possession for sale or otherwise disposed of by the defendant, or had been employed by him for use or disposition at any unlawful drinking place or had been kept or used in conducting the business of a liquor dealer or malt liquor dealer when such liquors or beverages have been seized for use as evidence in the case, and such court shall have the same power, upon conviction, in case of the seizure for use as evidence of such prohibited liquors and beverages and prosecutions against any person for unlawfully storing, accepting on consignment or delivering, transporting or shipping such prohibited liquors and beverages. (Acts 1909, No. 191, p. 63; Acts 1915, No. 2, p. 8; Code 1923, § 4740; Code 1940, T. 29, § 209.)

What constitutes contraband. — Contraband has been judicially defined as alcoholic beverages illegally possessed, sold or otherwise disposed of contrary to law. State ex rel. Hooper v. 50 Cases of 12 Oz. Miller Beer, 384 So. 2d 120 (Ala. Civ. App. 1980).

Where operator of filling station, who did not have liquor license, kept liquor which had been purchased from state store and duly stamped and labeled with all taxes paid thereon for sale in wet county, the liquors were subject to confiscation as "contraband." Lovett v. State, 30 Ala. App. 334, 6 So. 2d 437 (1941).

Liquors passing through Alabama destined for dry state. — The federal constitutional amendment prohibiting transportation or importation of intoxicating liquors into any state for delivery or use therein in violation of its laws does not render such liquors "contraband" while passing through Alabama into another dry state for disposition in violation of its laws, nor authorize seizure and condemnation of such liquors and transporting vehicle under state statutes. Barnett v. State ex rel. Milner, 243 Ala. 410, 9 So. 2d 267 (1942).

Cited in Cabler v. Mobile County, 230 Ala. 118, 159 So. 692 (1935); Davis v. City of Birmingham, 278 Ala. 391, 178 So. 2d 547 (1965).

Collateral references. — 48 C.J.S., Intoxicating Liquors, § 403.

45 Am. Jur. 2d, Intoxicating Liquors, § 490.

Forfeiture of property used in connection with intoxicating liquor, before trial of individual offender. 3 ALR2d 742.

Lawfulness of seizure of property used in violation of law as prerequisite to forfeiture action or proceeding. 8 ALR3d 473.

§ 28-4-251. Search warrant for seizure of prohibited liquors and beverages, etc., generally — Issuance — Authorization and procedure generally.

Search warrants for the seizure of liquors and beverages that are prohibited to be sold or otherwise disposed of in this state, together with the vessel or other receptacle in which they are contained, may be issued as prescribed in this article, and proceedings may be had to secure the destruction of such liquors, beverages, vessels and receptacles upon the grounds and in the manner provided in this article. (Acts 1909, No. 191, p. 63; Acts 1915, No. 2, p. 8; Code 1923, § 4741; Code 1940, T. 29, § 210; Acts 1951, No. 905, p. 1544.)

Constitution. — For constitutional provision pertaining to unreasonable searches and seizures and search warrants, see Const., § 5.

Cross references. — As to search warrants generally, see § 15-5-1 et seq.

Search warrant issues by judicial act. Knox v. State, 42 Ala. App. 578, 172 So. 2d 787 (1964).

Proof required for issuance need not be such as would support conviction. — Search warrants being issued ex parte without notice, the proof before the judge need not be such as would support a conviction of guilt, but should, in all events, produce an independent judicial determination. Brown v. State, 42 Ala. App. 429, 167 So. 2d 281 (1964).

The facts, information and circumstances within the knowledge of the arresting officers need not amount to evidence which would suffice to convict; but the quantum of information which constitutes probable cause — evidence which would warrant a man of reasonable caution in the belief that a felony had been committed — must be measured by the facts of the particular case. Yeager v. State, 281 Ala. 651, 207 So. 2d 125 (1967).

"Probable cause" does not mean that the officers must possess enough evidence in admissible form to convict the person whom they arrest or search. The cases have discussed at least five factors, for example, which may be considered by the officers in establishing probable cause for a search: (1) The reputation of, or informant's reports concerning, the occupants; (2) a like reputation of the vehicle or owners; (3) the condition of the vehicle (e.g., heavily loaded); (4) information from reputable informers as to the existence and illegal purpose of the trip; and (5) the reputation of the location in which they are found. Yeager v. State, 281 Ala. 651, 207 So. 2d 125 (1967).

Proceedings are quasi criminal. — Though a proceeding for search and seizure is not "in any exact sense a criminal prosecution," as observed in Toole v. State, 170 Ala. 41, 54 So. 195 (1910), yet it is strictly penal in its character, and substantially resembles a criminal prosecution; the only practical differences being that it acts in rem instead of in personam, and is conclusive against the whole world. Like a bastardy proceeding, it is sui generis, and may be properly designated as quasi-criminal. Certainly it is not an action according to the courts of the common law, and would not, either in ordinary or technical language, be classed among civil actions. Edmunds v. State ex rel. Dedge, 199 Ala. 555, 74 So. 965 (1917).

Rules of evidence in civil actions govern in proceeding for forfeiture and destruction of liquors which are being kept or used for illegal sale. Lovett v. State, 30 Ala. App. 334, 6 So. 2d 437 (1941).

Evidence without search warrant. — There was no error in allowing the state to show that the officers searched the home of defendant and found whisky in his home, even though they had no search warrant. Banks v. State, 18 Ala. App. 376, 93 So. 293 (1921); Clements v. State, 19 Ala. App. 177, 95 So. 831 (1923); Thomasson v. State, 21 Ala. App. 562, 110 So. 563 (1926).

Cited in Griffith v. State, 386 So. 2d 771 (Ala. Crim. App. 1980).

§ 28-4-252. Same — Same — Persons authorized.

The warrant may be issued by a judge of a district court. (Acts 1909, No. 191, p. 63; Acts 1915, No. 2, p. 8; Code 1923, § 4742; Code 1940, T. 29, § 211; Acts 1955, 2nd Ex. Sess., No. 45, p. 151.)

Cited in Smith v. State, 51 Ala. App. 349, 285 So. 2d 512 (1973); Funches v. State, 53 Ala. App. 330, 299 So. 2d 771 (1974).

§ 28-4-253. Same — Same — Grounds.

The warrant may be issued on any one of the following grounds:

(1) When any person, firm, association of persons or corporation or unknown person or other party keeps a place where prohibited liquors and beverages, or any of them, are manufactured, sold, kept for sale or otherwise disposed of contrary to law or when such liquors and beverages, or any of them, are stored for sale, delivery or distribution contrary to law or for other illegal purposes in any warehouse or other place;

(2) When such prohibited liquors or beverages, or any of them, are in the possession of any person, firm, association of persons or corporation conducting on the premises an unlawful drinking place or maintaining a liquor nuisance thereon by means thereof; or

(3) When any person, firm, association or corporation is carrying on at a place the business of a retail or wholesale dealer in liquors (except bona fide druggists who sell and keep for sale alcohol only under the regulations prescribed by law) or the business of a retail or wholesale dealer in malt liquors and said liquors are kept for sale by such dealer. (Acts 1909, No. 191, p. 63; Acts 1915, No. 2, p. 8; Code 1923, § 4748; Code 1940, T. 29, § 217.)

Scope of this section. — The provisions of this section clearly show it is directed to places where liquors are manufactured, sold, kept for sale or storage contrary to law, etc. It does not deal with the matter of searching and seizing automobiles and liquors transported therein. Tranum v. Stringer, 216 Ala. 522, 113 So. 541 (1927).

Collateral references. — 48 C.J.S., Intoxicating Liquors, § 386.

Propriety of considering hearsay or other incompetent evidence in establishing probable cause for issuance of search warrant. 10 ALR3d 359.

Propriety of execution of search warrant at nighttime. 26 ALR3d 951.

§ 28-4-254. Same — Same — Standard for issuance; contents of affidavit supporting determination of probable cause.

Said warrants shall be issued only on probable cause supported by affidavit naming or describing the person or other party whose premises are to be searched, if known, and describing as nearly as possible the liquors and beverages to be searched for and the place to be searched. The liquors or beverages may be described as prohibited liquors and beverages or spirituous, vinous or malt liquors if more specific description is not obtainable, and the affidavit may show that more specific description is not obtainable. (Acts 1909, No. 191, p. 63; Acts 1915, No. 2, p. 8; Code 1923, § 4743; Code 1940, T. 29, § 212.)

This section is constitutional. McGill v. Varin, 213 Ala. 649, 106 So. 44 (1925).

Conduct of defendants in filling in blank search warrant previously signed by mayor and proceeding to a search of plaintiff's premises was completely without the pale of legal warrant. Bull v. Armstrong, 254 Ala. 390, 48 So. 2d 467 (1950).

Minimum degree of proof for issuance of state search warrants. — Inasmuch as Mapp v. Ohio, 367 U.S. 643, 81 S. Ct. 1684, 6 L. Ed. 2d 1081 (1961) brings the fourth amendment of the federal Constitution to bear upon state trials, it would seem that the minimum degree of proof established under the fourth amendment would necessarily be the minimum for the issuance of a state search warrant. Brown v. State, 42 Ala. App. 429, 167 So. 2d 281 (1964).

Issuance of warrant based on hearsay not sufficient probable cause to justify search. — Under the federal cases, the issuance of a search warrant based on hearsay information furnished by an anonymous informer is alone not sufficient reasonable probable cause within the fourth amendment of the U.S. Constitution to justify search or seizure. Brown v. State, 42 Ala. App. 429, 167 So. 2d 281 (1964).

To allow scant proof (anonymous phone calls) for the issuance of warrants would give pranksters or meddlers occasion for harassment as much as occurs when a false fire alarm is given. Brown v. State, 42 Ala. App. 429, 167 So. 2d 281 (1964).

Affidavit does not establish probable cause which merely states the affiant's belief that there is cause to search, without stating facts upon which that belief is based. A fortiori this is true of an affidavit which states only the belief of one not the affiant. Brown v. State, 42 Ala. App. 429, 167 So. 2d 281 (1964).

An affidavit which recites the affiant's belief of the matters contained therein, without supporting facts or circumstances upon which a finding of probable cause could be based, is insufficient to support a search warrant. Knox v. State, 42 Ala. App. 578, 172 So. 2d 787 (1964).

The affidavit upon which the search warrant was issued was insufficient to support the warrant for the reason that it went upon the affiant's belief of the matters contained therein, without facts or circumstances upon which such a belief could be based. Therefore, as the record did not reveal that any other information was before the judge, the articles seized as a result of the warrant should have been excluded. Knox v. State, 42 Ala. App. 578, 172 So. 2d 787 (1964).

Evidence seized as result of search warrant issued upon insufficient affidavit must be excluded in the absence of a showing by the state that, in addition to the matters contained in the affidavit, other information was before the judge from which a finding of probable cause could be based. Knox v. State, 42 Ala. App. 578, 172 So. 2d 787 (1964).

Evidence inadmissible where obtained under warrant supported by unsigned affidavit. — Where affidavit supporting purported search warrant was unsigned, a search of defendant's person was illegal and the evidence obtained thereby was inadmissible. Lawson v. State, 42 Ala. App. 172, 157 So. 2d 226 (1963).

Defendant may raise question of whether warrant issued upon probable cause. — Inasmuch as a defendant may now object to introduction of illegally seized evidence for the first time at the trial, a defendant would be denied his substantial rights if he could not raise the question of whether a search warrant under which evidence is seized was issued upon probable cause, supported by oath or affirmation. Knox v. State, 42 Ala. App. 578, 172 So. 2d 787 (1964).

Trial judge to determine if warrant supported by sufficient affidavit. — When a defendant objects to the introduction of evidence seized under a search warrant, on the ground that there was no probable cause for the issuance of the warrant, the trial judge should determine if the warrant is supported by a sufficient affidavit. Knox v. State, 42 Ala. App. 578, 172 So. 2d 787 (1964).

If the affidavit, on its face, is found by the trial judge to be insufficient to support a finding of probable cause, the state may then adduce testimony showing that sufficient evidence was, in fact, before the issuing judge upon which a finding of probable cause could be based. Knox v. State, 42 Ala. App. 578, 172 So. 2d 787 (1964).

Cited in Funches v. State, 53 Ala. App. 330, 299 So. 2d 771 (1974).

Collateral references. — 48 C.J.S., Intoxicating Liquors, § 393.

§ 28-4-255. Same — Same — Examination of and taking of depositions from complainant and witnesses; contents of depositions.

The judge of the district court, before issuing a warrant, must examine the complainant on oath and any other witnesses he may produce, take their depositions in writing and cause the same to be subscribed by the person or persons making them. The depositions must set forth facts and circumstances tending to establish the ground or grounds of the application or probable cause for believing that a ground exists authorizing a search warrant to issue.

(Acts 1909, No. 191, p. 63; Acts 1915, No. 2, p. 8; Code 1923, § 4745; Code 1940, T. 29, § 214.)

This section is constitutional. McGill v. Varin, 213 Ala. 649, 106 So. 44 (1925).

Its provisions are directory. — The omission of the requirements of this section has never been regarded as vitiative of the warrant when it is issued upon a sufficient affidavit. Edmunds v. State ex rel. Dedge, 199 Ala. 555, 74 So. 965 (1917); Porch v. State, 38 Ala. App. 565, 89 So. 2d 694 (1956).

This section and § 15-5-4 are almost identical and have been held to be considered in pari materia. Oliver v. State, 46 Ala. App. 118, 238 So. 2d 916 (1970).

Rule for issuing search warrant. — A judge of the district court must have sufficient evidence before him to support a finding of probable cause. Tyler v. State, 45 Ala. App. 155, 227 So. 2d 442 (1969).

Sworn statements before the issuing judge must be reduced to writing. Certainly this is a requisite at least as to the gist of the testimony of each witness who appears before the judge. Tyler v. State, 45 Ala. App. 155, 227 So. 2d 442 (1969).

All evidence need not be stated in affida- vit. — It is not necessary that all the evidence before the judge be stated in the affidavit. Tyler v. State, 45 Ala. App. 155, 227 So. 2d 442 (1969).

But enough must be stated to support requirement of probable cause. — Enough evidence must be stated in the affidavit to support the constitutional requirement of probable cause for issuing the search warrant or such warrant is insufficient. Tyler v. State, 45 Ala. App. 155, 227 So. 2d 442 (1969).

Sufficiency of petitory affidavit. — When the petitory affidavit is sufficient then the failure of the judge to take the depositions of complainant and other witnesses does not vitiate the search warrant. Brandies v. State, 44 Ala. App. 648, 219 So. 2d 404 (1968).

Cited in Weldon v. State, 39 Ala. App. 286, 97 So. 2d 825 (1957); Dennis v. State, 40 Ala. App. 182, 111 So. 2d 21 (1959); Brown v. State, 42 Ala. App. 429, 167 So. 2d 281 (1964); Knox v. State, 42 Ala. App. 578, 172 So. 2d 787 (1964); Funches v. State, 53 Ala. App. 330, 299 So. 2d 771 (1974).

§ 28-4-256. Same — Same — Issuance by judge.

If the judge of the district court is satisfied of the existence of ground or grounds for the application, or one of them, or that there is probable cause to believe the existence of them, or one of them, he must issue a search warrant, signed by him, directed to the sheriff or to any lawful officer, commanding him to forthwith search the place named for the prohibited liquors and beverages and to bring them before the judge. If the warrant is sought to search a place whose keeper or owner is unknown, the affidavit may so state and the warrant may issue accordingly. The judge of the district court may direct the warrant to the chief of police or any police officer of a municipality when the place to be searched is within a municipality or within the police jurisdiction thereof. (Acts 1909, No. 191, p. 63; Acts 1915, No. 2, p. 8; Code 1923, § 4746; Code 1940, T. 29, § 215.)

Collateral references. — 48 C.J.S., Intoxicating Liquors, § 394.

§ 28-4-257. Same — Form.

The warrant may be in substantially the form prescribed by law for other search warrants and must, except as otherwise specified in this article, be executed in the manner and with the authority of the officer as prescribed by law in respect to other search warrants. (Acts 1909, No. 191, p. 63; Acts 1915, No. 2, p. 8; Code 1923, § 4747; Code 1940, T. 29, § 216.)

Cited in State ex rel. Holcombe v. Stone, 233 Ala. 243, 171 So. 366 (1936).

§ 28-4-258. Same — Execution — Persons authorized.

The warrant may be executed by any one of the officers to whom it is directed, but by no other person, except in aid of the officer, he being present and acting in its execution. The complainant may accompany the officer who executes the warrant and give information and assist him in executing the writ. A writ addressed to a sheriff may be executed by any lawful officers. (Acts 1909, No. 191, p. 63; Acts 1915, No. 2, p. 8; Code 1923, § 4744; Code 1940, T. 29, § 213.)

Showing of warrant to defendant at the time of the search is a sufficient execution of the warrant. Porch v. State, 38 Ala. App. 565, 89 So. 2d 694 (1956).

Duly commissioned enforcement agents of the alcoholic beverage control board of the state are lawful officers of this state under § 28-4-311, and under the provisions of this section are authorized to execute a search warrant. Green v. State, 38 Ala. App. 189, 79 So. 2d 555 (1955).

Cited in Edmunds v. State ex rel. Dedge, 199 Ala. 555, 74 So. 965 (1917); State ex rel. Holcombe v. Stone, 233 Ala. 243, 171 So. 366 (1936); Ott v. State, 35 Ala. App. 219, 46 So. 2d 226 (1950); Funches v. State, 53 Ala. App. 330, 299 So. 2d 771 (1974).

Collateral references. — 48 C.J.S., Intoxicating Liquors, § 394.

§ 28-4-259. Same — Same — Time.

The warrant may be executed at any time between 8:00 A.M. and 6:00 P.M. or at any other time that the place or premises are open. (Acts 1909, No. 191, p. 63; Acts 1915, No. 2, p. 8; Code 1923, § 4751; Code 1940, T. 29, § 220.)

This section and sections 28-4-251, 28-4-252, 28-4-254, 28-4-255 and 28-4-258 and sections 15-5-2 — 15-5-8 are in pari materia. — Under the provisions of this section, a search warrant, issued under the provisions of §§ 28-4-251, 28-4-252, 28-4-254, 28-4-255 and 28-4-258, may be executed only between the hours of 8:00 a.m. and 6:00 p.m. However, under §§ 15-5-2 — 15-5-8 a search warrant may be executed at any time, day or night, if issued on an affidavit stating positively that the property is in the place to be searched, and the judge authorizes a search during the day or night. These two sets of statutes are in pari materia, and the one does not displace the other. Jordan v. State, 39 Ala. App. 469, 103 So. 2d 815 (1958).

This section and § 15-5-8 relate to the same subject matter, i.e., search warrants, and have the same general purpose, i.e., the discovery of property used in committing a public offense. They are therefore in pari materia, and the one does not displace the other. Funches v. State, 53 Ala. App. 330, 299 So. 2d 771, cert. denied, 293 Ala. 752, 299 So. 2d 778 (1974), cert. denied, 419 U.S. 1114, 95 S. Ct. 793, 42 L. Ed. 2d 813 (1975).

Failure to indicate hour of execution. —

Where the officers, in making their return on a search warrant, do not indicate the hour of its execution, the state's proof in parol must be clear and unequivocal to bring the execution within the time permitted by this section. Tyler v. State, 45 Ala. App. 155, 227 So. 2d 442 (1969).

Objection to nocturnal execution. — Where the defendant objects to the introduction of a warrant because of nocturnal execution, the burden is cast on the state to show timely execution. Tyler v. State, 45 Ala. App. 155, 227 So. 2d 442 (1969).

Burden on state to show that warrant was timely executed. — The defendant having objected to the introduction of the warrant on the ground that it was not executed before 6:00 p.m., the burden was cast upon the state to show that it was timely executed. Weldon v. State, 39 Ala. App. 286, 97 So. 2d 825 (1957).

"Open," as used in this section, must be construed to mean "open to the public," that is business, or quasi-business places or premises, or places or premises which have lost their status as private residences by virtue of the use made or permitted. Weldon v. State, 39 Ala. App. 286, 97 So. 2d 825 (1957).

A dwelling was not "open" within the meaning of this section in that the lights were on in the house and the owner, his wife and another woman were therein. Weldon v. State, 39 Ala. App. 286, 97 So. 2d 825 (1957).

Cited in Parker v. State, 40 Ala. App. 244, 112 So. 2d 493 (1959); Brown v. State, 42 Ala. App. 429, 167 So. 2d 281 (1964).

Collateral references. — 48 C.J.S., Intoxicating Liquors, § 394.

§ 28-4-260. Same — Same — Giving of receipt for prohibited liquors and beverages, etc., seized under warrant.

When an officer takes prohibited liquors and beverages under the warrant, he must, if required, give a receipt to the person from whom they were taken or in whose possession they were found and also a receipt for such receptacles or vessels as may be taken under the warrant. (Acts 1909, No. 191, p. 63; Acts 1915, No. 2, p. 8; Code 1923, § 4749; Code 1940, T. 29, § 218.)

Collateral references. — 48 C.J.S., Intoxicating Liquors, § 394.

§ 28-4-261. Same — Limitation period for execution and return of warrant.

The warrant must be executed and returned to the judge of the district court by whom it was issued within 10 days from the date of issuance. After that time, if it has not been executed, it is void. (Acts 1909, No. 191, p. 63; Acts 1915, No. 2, p. 8; Code 1923, § 4749; Code 1940, T. 29, § 218.)

§ 28-4-262. Same — Return of warrant; furnishing of copies thereof to applicant for warrant, etc.

The officer in his return of the warrant to the judge of the district court must specify with particularity the liquors and beverages and other articles taken, and the applicant for the warrant and the person from whose possession the liquors and articles were taken are entitled to a copy of the return, signed by the judge, which he must furnish them on their application therefor. (Acts 1909, No. 191, p. 63; Acts 1915, No. 2, p. 8; Code 1923, § 4750; Code 1940, T. 29, § 219.)

§ 28-4-263. Issuance, etc., of warrants for search of steamboats, water-craft, depots, railway cars, etc.

A search warrant may be obtained and prosecuted in accordance with the rules and regulations prescribed in this article in case there is probable cause to believe and it is made to appear to the judge issuing the warrant that there is probable cause to believe that prohibited liquors and beverages or some of them are kept or deposited in or on a watercraft of any kind or in a depot, railway car, carriage or vehicle of any kind for unlawful sale, furnishing, distribution or other unlawful disposition. The place where such search is to be made should be described as nearly as possible in the affidavit and warrant for purpose of identification. (Acts 1909, No. 191, p. 63; Acts 1915, No. 2, p. 8; Code 1923, § 4770; Code 1940, T. 29, § 239.)

Collateral references. — 48 C.J.S., Intoxicating Liquors, § 388.

§ 28-4-264. Disposition of property seized by officer under warrant generally.

When liquors and beverages and vessels and receptacles are seized by the officer, they shall be held by him subject to the order of the judge of the district court or the court to which the proceedings may be carried by appeal, and, upon final judgment in accordance with the procedure prescribed in this article, must be returned to the lawful owner or owners or be otherwise disposed of according to law. (Acts 1909, No. 191, p. 63; Acts 1915, No. 2, p. 8; Code 1923, § 4752; Code 1940, T. 29, § 221.)

Cited in State v. McCall, 232 Ala. 576, 169 So. 8 (1936); State ex rel. Hooper v. 50 Cases of 12 Oz. Miller Beer, 384 So. 2d 120 (Ala. Civ. App. 1980).

§ 28-4-265. Liquors and beverages, etc., seized not to be recovered by writ of replevin or detinue during pendency of proceedings under article; final judgment of condemnation to bar actions to recover liquors and beverages, etc., seized, etc.

Liquors and beverages seized and vessels and receptacles containing them shall not be taken from the custody of the officer by writ of replevin or detinue or other process while the proceedings under this article are pending.

A final judgment of condemnation in all proceedings under this article shall be a bar to all actions for the recovery of any liquors and beverages or vessels and receptacles seized or for the value of the same and for damages alleged to arise by reason of the seizure and detention thereof. (Acts 1909, No. 191, p. 63; Acts 1915, No. 2, p. 8; Code 1923, § 4753; Code 1940, T. 29, § 222.)

Section not applicable where no condemnation proceedings instituted. — In a proceeding by distributor to recover beer seized by sheriff, this section did not apply where at the time of hearing on motion to quash, no proceeding had been instituted seeking condemnation of the beer though there was a proceeding for condemnation of the truck. Ex parte Maddox, 265 Ala. 114, 89 So. 2d 916 (1956).

Cited in State v. McCall, 232 Ala. 576, 169 So. 8 (1936).

§ 28-4-266. Issuance of general notice to persons claiming right, title, etc., in liquors and beverages, etc., seized to appear and show cause why same should not be forfeited and destroyed.

Upon the return of the warrant to the judge of the district court showing a seizure thereunder, the judge shall issue a notice directed generally to all persons claiming any right, title or interests in such liquors and beverages and vessels and receptacles to appear before the judge issuing the warrant at a time and place therein specified not less than five nor more than 15 days after the issuance of said notice and show cause why such liquors and beverages and vessels and receptacles shall not be forfeited to the state and destroyed. (Acts 1909, No. 191, p. 63; Acts 1915, No. 2, p. 8; Code 1923, § 4754; Code 1940, T. 29, § 223.)

Cited in State v. McCall, 232 Ala. 576, 169 So. 8 (1936).

Collateral references. — 48 C.J.S., Intoxicating Liquors, § 398.

§ 28-4-267. Delivery to certain persons and posting of copies of notice.

A copy of such notice shall be delivered to the person or other party who kept the liquors and beverages or had possession of the liquors and beverages at the time of the seizure, and a copy shall also be delivered to the party named in the affidavit for the warrant if a different party from the one who kept or had possession of the liquors and beverages at the time of the seizure, and the officer shall place another copy of such notice in a conspicuous place upon said premises. (Acts 1909, No. 191, p. 63; Acts 1915, No. 2, p. 8; Code 1923, § 4755; Code 1940, T. 29, § 224.)

§ 28-4-268. Answer by persons claiming right, title, etc., in liquors and beverages, etc., seized.

At the time and place specified in the notice, any person claiming any right, title or interest in the liquors and beverages and vessels and receptacles seized under such warrant may interpose a verified answer controverting the allegations of the complaint upon which said warrant was issued and controverting the ground or grounds upon which the warrant was issued, and such person shall propound in such answer what right, title or interest he claims in the liquors and beverages or vessels and receptacles seized. (Acts 1909, No. 191, p. 63; Acts 1915, No. 2, p. 8; Code 1923, § 4756; Code 1940, T. 29, § 225.)

Allegation of interest. — The allegation by a claimant to intoxicating liquors that he was "interested in the property seized" is defective for failure to show that the claimant had such an interest as entitled him to defend. Toole v. State, 170 Ala. 41, 54 So. 195 (1910).

Burden of proof. — Claimant of liquors seized which were found in a building not used exclusively as a dwelling or a drug store had the burden of showing that he did not keep them for illegal purposes. Cheek v. State ex rel. Metcalf, 3 Ala. App. 646, 57 So. 108 (1911).

Cited in Toole v. State, 170 Ala. 41, 54 So. 195 (1910).

Collateral references. — 48 C.J.S., Intoxicating Liquors, § 397.

Disputation of truth of matters stated in affidavit in support of search warrant—modern cases. 24 ALR4th 1266.

§ 28-4-269. Forfeiture and condemnation proceedings generally — Issues and parties generally; style of action; trial of action generally.

The issue thus framed shall be deemed an action pending in the court of the judge who issued the warrant between the state of Alabama, on the relation of the complainant, and the liquor and beverages and vessels and receptacles so seized and against the party in possession of the liquors and beverages or against the party who interposes the claim, and may be entitled in the name of the state of Alabama against the said party so appearing, if any, and if no one appears, may be entitled as against said liquors and beverages adding for identification the name of the person or persons mentioned in the affidavit or warrant. The said action shall be tried in the district court as other actions are tried therein. (Acts 1909, No. 191, p. 63; Acts 1915, No. 2, p. 8; Code 1923, § 4757; Code 1940, T. 29, § 226.)

§ 28-4-270. Same — Issues, etc., where more than one claimant to liquors and beverages seized.

If different parties appear and claim separate portions of the liquor and beverages and vessels and receptacles seized, separate answers may be filed and separate issues may be framed and the trial had accordingly before the district court. (Acts 1909, No. 191, p. 63; Acts 1915, No. 2, p. 8; Code 1923, § 4760; Code 1940, T. 29, § 229.)

Safeguarding the legal rights of any person having a bona fide claim to seized liquors. — See State v. McCall, 232 Ala. 576, 169 So. 8 (1936).

§ 28-4-271. Same — Prosecution of action.

Where an officer seizes liquors and beverages and vessels and receptacles under a search warrant, he shall appear on the day fixed for the hearing. The district attorney or his deputy shall appear and prosecute said action on behalf of the state. (Acts 1909, No. 191, p. 63; Acts 1915, No. 2, p. 8; Code 1923, § 4767; Code 1940, T. 29, § 236.)

§ 28-4-272. Same — Persons not to be excused from attending and testifying or producing books, papers, etc., at hearing or trial; immunity from prosecution as to transactions, etc., as to which testimony or documents produced.

No person, except one who answers claiming some right, title or interest in the liquors so seized, shall be excused from attending and testifying or producing any books, papers or other documents before any court or judge upon any such hearing or trial upon the ground or for the reason that the testimony or evidence, documentary or otherwise, required of him may tend to convict him of a crime or to subject him to a penalty or forfeiture, but no person shall be prosecuted or subjected to any penalty or forfeiture for or on account of any transaction, matter or thing concerning which he may so testify or produce evidence, documentary or otherwise, and no testimony so given or produced shall be received against him upon any criminal investigation, trial or proceeding. (Acts 1909, No. 191, p. 63; Acts 1915, No. 2, p. 8; Code 1923, § 4765; Code 1940, T. 29, § 234.)

§ 28-4-273. Same — Conduct of hearing or trial generally; entry of judgment of forfeiture and delivery of liquors and beverages to alcoholic beverage control board generally; destruction of nonfederal tax-paid liquors and beverages; disposition of funds paid into court by alcoholic beverage control board.

If no party appears to make a claim at the time specified in the notice or if no verified answer controverting the allegations of the complaint and the grounds for issuance of the search warrant is interposed, the judge shall proceed to hear the testimony in support thereof. If it is established upon the hearing before said judge or upon the trial of the action, if issue be joined, that the liquors so seized are kept, stored or deposited for the purpose of unlawful sale or other disposition or for furnishing or distribution within this state or if it appears that the complainant has established a ground for the issuance of such search warrant, judgment of forfeiture of said liquors and beverages and vessels and receptacles shall be entered, which judgment shall order the immediate delivery of said liquors and beverages and vessels and receptacles to the alcoholic beverage control board at Montgomery, Alabama, whereupon said board shall determine the reasonable value thereof. The amounts so determined by said board to the reasonable value thereof shall be paid by the board to the clerk of the court in which such order or forfeiture was made. In the case of nonfederal tax-paid liquors and beverages, the court shall order the same to be publicly destroyed. Any funds paid into court, as provided in this section, shall be applied first to the payment of the court costs in such case, and the balance, if any, shall be paid into the general fund of the municipality or county in which said case arose. (Acts 1909, No. 191, p. 63; Acts 1915, No. 2, p. 8; Code 1923, § 4758; Code 1940, T. 29, § 227.)

Cited in State v. McCall, 232 Ala. 576, 169 So. 8 (1936).

Collateral references. — 48 C.J.S., Intoxicating Liquors, § 399.

Rights of innocent persons, and protection thereof, where property in which they are interested is seized because of its illegal use in connection with intoxicating liquor. 47 ALR 1055, 61 ALR 551, 73 ALR 1087, 82 ALR 607, 124 ALR 288.

§ 28-4-274. Same — Entry of judgment of dismissal and return of liquors and beverages, etc., to place or person from which or from whom taken generally.

If the testimony produced on the hearing before the judge or upon such trial before the judge or court shall fail to establish the complaint or that a ground existed for the issuance of the warrant or that the liquors and beverages and vessels and receptacles were kept, stored or deposited for the purpose of unlawful sale, distribution or delivery within this state, judgment shall be entered dismissing such complaint and providing that such liquors and beverages and the vessels and receptacles containing the same be returned to the place from which or to the person from whom they were taken. (Acts 1909, No. 191, p. 63; Acts 1915, No. 2, p. 8; Code 1923, § 4759; Code 1940, T. 29, § 228.)

Cited in State ex rel. Hooper v. 50 Cases of 12 Oz. Miller Beer, 384 So. 2d 120 (Ala. Civ. App. 1980).

Collateral references. — 48 C.J.S., Intoxicating Liquors, § 403.

§ 28-4-275. Same — Apportionment and taxing of costs.

If judgment shall be against only one party defendant appearing, he shall be charged to pay all the costs of the proceeding in the seizure and detention of the liquors and beverages and vessels and receptacles claimed by him and the costs of the trial. But if judgment shall be entered against more than one party claiming distinct parts of or interests in said liquors and beverages and vessels and receptacles, then the cost of the proceeding and trial may be equitably apportioned among the defendants for the amount of cost to be adjudged against them according to the discretion of the judge or court. In the event no one appears to contest the complaint or if the complaint is not sustained and no judgment of forfeiture is obtained, the costs shall be taxed and paid as costs are taxed and paid in criminal prosecutions wherein the state fails, and this rule shall apply as to any separate claim when several parties appear, claim and contest and such separate claim is sustained and there is failure to obtain judgment as to the part of the liquor and beverages and vessels and receptacles so claimed. (Acts 1909, No. 191, p. 63; Acts 1915, No. 2, p. 8; Code 1923, § 4761; Code 1940, T. 29, § 230.)

Cited in Cabler v. Mobile County, 230 Ala. 118, 159 So. 692 (1935); State ex rel. Holcombe v. Stone, 233 Ala. 243, 171 So. 366 (1936).

Collateral references. — 48 C.J.S., Intoxicating Liquors, § 401.

§ 28-4-276. Same — Appeals from judgment of district court — Authorization and procedure generally.

Any party may appeal within 14 days from the date of final judgment or denial of a post-trial motion, whichever is later, any judgment entered under the provisions of this article in any district court, such appeal to be taken in behalf of the state to the circuit court by the district attorney by filing a notice of appeal with the judge of the district court. (Acts 1909, No. 191, p. 63; Acts 1915, No. 2, p. 8; Code 1923, § 4762; Code 1940, T. 29, § 231.)

Collateral references. — 48 C.J.S., Intoxicating Liquors, § 400.

§ 28-4-277. Same — Same — Persons entitled to appeal; bond for costs of appeal required; right to jury trial; proceedings in circuit court.

Any person appearing and becoming a party defendant as provided in this article may appeal from the judgment of forfeiture and condemnation as to the whole or any part of the liquors and beverages and vessels and receptacles claimed by him and adjudged forfeited to the circuit court as in other cases appealed from a district court to a circuit court, the appeal to be granted upon parties giving bond for the cost of appeal, that will be incurred in the circuit court.

Upon written demand being made therefor endorsed on the appeal bond at the time said appeal is taken, the appellants may be entitled to a jury for the trial of the action in the circuit court. Said circuit court shall proceed with the case de novo and may cause suitable issues to be framed for the determination of the action. (Acts 1909, No. 191, p. 63; Acts 1915, No. 2, p. 8; Code 1923, § 4763; Code 1940, T. 29, § 232.)

Objections cannot be made for first time on appeal. — On appeal from a district court to the circuit court, where the case must be tried de novo, all objections to the proceedings, including the jurisdiction of the court, must be made before the district judge, and cannot be made for the first time in the court to which appeal is made. Edmunds v. State ex rel. Dedge, 199 Ala. 555, 74 So. 965 (1917).

Cited in State v. McCall, 232 Ala. 576, 169 So. 8 (1936).

§ 28-4-278. Same — Same — Issuance of order for delivery of liquors and beverages, etc., to alcoholic beverage control board or for restoration of same to place or person from which or from whom seized upon entry of final judgment in proceedings under article.

Whenever it shall be finally decided that the liquors and vessels seized as provided in this article are forfeited and ordered condemned, the judge or court entering final judgment of forfeiture shall issue to the officer having said liquors and beverages and vessels and receptacles in custody a written order directing him forthwith to deliver said liquors and beverages and vessels and receptacles to the alcoholic beverage control board as provided in section 28-4-273, except in the case of nonfederal tax-paid liquors or beverages, which shall be publicly destroyed, and the officer shall immediately thereafter make return of said order to the court whence issued with his actions in the premises endorsed thereon.

When it is finally decided that the liquors and beverages and vessels and receptacles so seized are not liable to forfeiture, the judge or the court entering the judgment shall issue a written order to the officer having the same in custody to restore the same to the place where seized, as nearly as possible, or to the persons who are entitled to receive them. (Acts 1909, No. 191, p. 63; Acts 1915, No. 2, p. 8; Code 1923, § 4764; Code 1940, T. 29, § 233.)

Collateral references. — 48 C.J.S., Intoxicating Liquors, § 403.

§ 28-4-279. Forfeiture and condemnation proceedings in circuit courts.

A search warrant may be issued by any judge of a circuit court, and on the return of the warrant, the same proceedings may be had before the judge sitting as a court as are prescribed in this article for the trial before district court judges issuing said warrants. Any defendant to the warrant in such circuit court may have a jury trial upon demanding the same at the time he files his verified answer and claim. (Acts 1909, No. 191, p. 63; Acts 1915, No. 2, p. 8; Code 1923, § 4766; Code 1940, T. 29, § 235.)

Collateral references. — 48 C.J.S., Intoxicating Liquors, § 397.

§ 28-4-280. Allowances and fees of officers executing search warrants and attending and prosecuting forfeiture and condemnation actions for state.

There shall be allowed the officer making the seizure under a search warrant the sum of $3.00 and also the additional sum of $2.00 for every day that such officer shall necessarily be employed in attending court for the purpose of causing liquors and beverages and vessels and receptacles seized to be forfeited or condemned and the sum of $.10 per mile for each mile he shall travel in executing the warrant, together with such reasonable sum as the court may deem just for necessary expenses incurred in transporting and providing storage for liquors and beverages and vessels and receptacles seized.

Where a warrant is issued to any peace officer to search a designated place for prohibited liquors and beverages and such officer executes such warrant and seizes such liquors or beverages, but fails to arrest any person or persons for having such prohibited liquors or beverages in his or their possession, then no fees, mileage or allowances shall be paid to anyone for any service under this article.

Where a warrant is issued to any peace officer to search a designated place for prohibited liquors or beverages and such officer executes said warrant, seizes such prohibited liquors or beverages, arrests one or more persons alleged to have had the possession of such liquors or beverages at the time of said seizure and said person is tried and acquitted of the charge or charges arising out of the possession, use or sale of said seized prohibited liquors or beverages by the court having jurisdiction of the action or the action is nol prossed by such court or withdrawn and filed, then the fees, mileage or allowances set out in this section shall be taxed and paid as in criminal prosecutions in which the state fails, upon the court or judge making an order to that effect. If, however, the arrest of one or more persons alleged to have had the possession of such liquors or beverages is made and the defendant or defendants are finally convicted, the costs or fees set out in this section shall be taxed in the bill of costs against such defendant or defendants and, if not collected from such defendant or defendants so convicted, shall be taxed and paid as in criminal prosecutions in which the state fails, upon the court or judge making an order to that effect. (Acts 1909, No. 191, p. 63; Acts 1915, No. 2, p. 8; Code 1923, § 4768; Acts 1935, No. 299, p. 727; Code 1940, T. 29, § 237.)

Fees intended to cover all incidental services required of sheriff. — Fees of three dollars for executing search warrant in liquor condemnation proceedings and of two dollars per day in each case during trial for looking after prosecution, and liberal allowance for mileage, haulage and storage of liquor seized, held intended to cover all incidental services required of sheriff in executing writ and preparing for trial, as well as during trial. State ex rel. Holcombe v. Stone, 233 Ala. 243, 171 So. 366 (1936).

Sheriff is entitled to charge two dollars for each case. — Sheriff is entitled to a charge of two dollars for attending court and looking after prosecution in each case, when more than one case is set for or tried on same date. State ex rel. Holcombe v. Stone, 229 Ala. 357, 157 So. 454 (1934).

Sheriff is entitled to three dollars for executing search warrant in liquor prosecution, and to two dollars per day for every day he is necessarily employed in attending court for purpose of causing liquors seized to be condemned, and such two dollars per day is for each case regardless of number heard in one day. State ex rel. Holcombe v. Stone, 233 Ala. 243, 171 So. 366 (1936).

Claim need not be presented to board of revenue. — Sheriff's claim for fees for attending and prosecuting liquor condemnation proceeding need not be presented to board of revenue for audit and approval. Stone v. State ex rel. Holcombe, 233 Ala. 583, 173 So. 63 (1937).

Sheriff who is paid statutory fee for attending and prosecuting liquor condemnation proceeding may not collect from county additional fees for service of notices and subpoenas in such proceeding. Stone v. State ex rel. Holcombe, 233 Ala. 583, 173 So. 63 (1937).

Approval of order of trial judge respecting allowance for officers attending and prosecuting condemnation proceedings would not be conclusive on county as to charges not authorized by law. State ex rel. Holcombe v. Stone, 229 Ala. 357, 157 So. 454 (1934).

Charge against fine and forfeiture fund. — Upon failure to make costs and fees, allowance for officers attending and prosecuting condemnation proceedings becomes charge against fine and forfeiture fund upon order of judge, or against general fund of county, where there is consolidation or merger of fine and forfeiture fund into general fund. State ex rel. Holcombe v. Stone, 229 Ala. 357, 157 So. 454 (1934).

Cited in State ex rel. Holcombe v. Stone, 26 Ala. App. 187, 155 So. 636 (1934).

§ 28-4-281. Correction of defects or irregularities in notice, etc., in forfeiture and condemnation proceedings.

Whenever in any proceedings for forfeiture and condemnation of liquors and beverages and vessels and receptacles it shall appear to the judge or court that there has been any irregularity in the service of any process or notice or any omission to post or serve notices required or any defect in the affidavit or notice or in the service or return of either, the judge or court may permit the same to be amended and may direct such further service of process or of notice as will, in the judgment of the judge or court, be most effectual in securing notice of the proceeding to those who may be entitled thereto and so that the proceeding may not fail for any irregularity or technicality. (Acts 1909, No. 191, p. 63; Acts 1915, No. 2; p. 8; Code 1923, § 4769; Code 1940, T. 29, § 238.)

§ 28-4-282. Appliances used, etc., for distillation or manufacture of prohibited liquors and beverages declared contraband; said appliances and products thereof to be summarily destroyed by sheriffs, etc., finding same; property, etc., where distillery, etc., found forfeited to state.

All appliances which have been used or are used or ready to be used for the purpose of distilling or manufacturing any prohibited liquors or beverages are contraband, and no person, firm or corporation or association of persons shall have any property rights in or to the same, and when said appliances or apparatus so used or ready to be used or that have been used for the manufacture of any prohibited liquors and beverages shall be found by any sheriff or other law officer, the same shall be by said officer at once summarily destroyed and rendered useless for service. The officer shall also summarily destroy any liquor or liquids, the product of a distillery or plant for the making of a prohibited liquor which he may find on the premises, and the owner of said distillery or plant or any person permitting the same to exist on the premises shall forfeit to the state of Alabama all property used in connection with said illegal plant, together with the buildings and lots or parcels of ground constituting the premises on which the unlawful act is performed or permitted to be performed. (Acts 1919, No. 7, p. 6; Code 1923, § 4775; Code 1940, T. 29, § 244.)

This section is constitutional. House & Lot v. State ex rel. Patterson, 204 Ala. 108, 85 So. 382 (1920).

Court order is not necessary. — It is not necessary, in view of this section, that there be a court order before contraband appliances and material used in the manufacture of liquor are destroyed. Thomasson v. State, 21 Ala. App. 562, 110 So. 563 (1926).

Particularity of allegation. — The burden is on the state to allege with accuracy the description of "the premises" or "the lots or parcels of ground constituting the premises" on which the still was illegally operated. If the state alleges the use of a large area and the proof shows the use of a small part thereof, then the state must by proof describe and carve out the smaller area from the larger tract and amend the complaint to correspond with the evidence. Johnson v. State, 205 Ala. 294, 87 So. 815 (1921). See also Dobbin's Distillery v. United States, 96 U.S. 395, 24 L. Ed. 637 (1877).

Burden of proof to show owner had notice. — Where it was shown that the owner had leased the premises, sought to be confiscated, to a tenant who was in actual possession, the burden was upon the state to show that the owner had actual or constructive notice of the unlawful use of the premises. State ex rel. Attorney Gen. v. Jebeles, 206 Ala. 161, 89 So. 547 (1921).

Constructive notice may be said to be a state of facts that would put a prudent owner upon inquiry and which would lead to the discovery of such facts as would lead to the knowledge of the existence of the apparatus or appliances used. State ex rel. Attorney Gen. v. Jebeles, 206 Ala. 161, 89 So. 547 (1921).

Cited in Hurvich v. State, 230 Ala. 578, 162 So. 362 (1935); Davis v. City of Birmingham, 278 Ala. 391, 178 So. 2d 547 (1965).

§ 28-4-283. Enforcement of forfeiture.

The forfeiture provided in section 28-4-282 may be enforced by a complaint filed in the circuit court of the county in which the property is located, the complaint to be filed in the name of the state of Alabama by the attorney general or by a district attorney in the county where the complaint is filed or by others as provided in the law for the filing of petitions for abatement of liquor nuisances. (Acts 1919, No. 7, p. 6; Code 1923, § 4776; Code 1940, T. 29, § 245.)

Cross references. — As to abatement of liquor nuisances, see § 28-4-220 et seq.

Cited in Hurvich v. State, 230 Ala. 578, 162 So. 362 (1935); Snyder v. State, 247 Ala. 278, 24 So. 2d 266 (1945).

§ 28-4-284. Sale of property and disposition of proceeds therefrom.

The property may be ordered sold and the proceeds, after paying the costs and expenses of the seizure and of the action, shall be paid into the law-enforcement fund to be used and applied on the enforcement of state laws under the supervision and control of the governor. (Acts 1919, No. 7, p. 6; Code 1923, § 4777; Code 1940, T. 29, § 246; Acts 1949, No. 669, p. 1032.)

Section does not violate Constitution. — This section does not violate Constitution, §§ 45 or 61. In re Opinion of the Justices, 252 Ala. 525, 41 So. 2d 758 (1949).

Cited in Robinson v. State, 451 So. 2d 355 (Ala. Civ. App. 1984).

Collateral references. — 48 C.J.S., Intoxicating Liquors, § 403.

§ 28-4-285. Conveyances, vehicles of transportation or animals used for illegal conveyance of prohibited liquors and beverages declared contraband and forfeited to state; seizure of said conveyances, etc., and reporting thereof by sheriffs, etc., finding same; confiscation and condemnation generally.

All conveyances and vehicles of transportation of any kind, whether on the waters of the state, under the waters, on land or in the air, including any animals that may be used in such transportation, whether hitched or not hitched to any vehicle so illegally used, together with all harness and other accessories employed in such illegal transportation, which have been or are used for the illegal conveying of any prohibited liquors or beverages into this state or from one point in the state to another point within the state shall be contraband and shall be forfeited to the state of Alabama, and shall be seized by any sheriff or any other person acting under authority of law in the enforcement of the prohibition laws of the state who becomes cognizant of the facts or who finds liquor being illegally transported as aforesaid in such vehicles or conveyances or on any such animal, and such officer or person shall report the seizure and the facts connected therewith to the district attorney in the county where seizure is made or, in default thereof, to the attorney general of the state.

In order to condemn and confiscate any of the above-mentioned conveyances or vehicles or animals, it shall not be necessary for the state to show any actual movement of said conveyances, vehicles or animals while loaded with any of said prohibited liquors or beverages; provided, that if said prohibited liquors or beverages shall have been purchased through the state liquor stores or shall bear the stamp of the Alabama alcoholic beverage control board, no such conveyance, vehicle or animal shall be confiscated or forfeited unless the court shall be convinced from the evidence that said prohibited liquors or beverages were being transported for the purpose of resale contrary to law, and the fact that the owner or operator of said conveyance or vehicle or animal has a reputation of being a seller of prohibited liquors shall be prima facie evidence that such liquors or beverages were being transported for resale. (Acts 1919, No. 7, p. 6; Code 1923, § 4778; Acts 1927, No. 624, p. 715; Code 1940, T. 29, § 247; Acts 1947, No. 129, p. 39.)

I. General Consideration.
II. Evidence.

I. GENERAL CONSIDERATION.

Purpose of the legislature in adopting the 1947 amendment to this section was to permit the transportation of intoxicating beverages purchased through the state liquor stores or bearing the stamps of the alcoholic beverage control board in dry counties except for the purpose of resale, and it was not the intention of the legislature to in anyway make the provisions of this section applicable to wet counties in regard to the transportation of intoxicating beverages purchased through the state liquor stores or which bear the stamps of the alcoholic beverage control board. Lyall v. State, 262 Ala. 96, 77 So. 2d 369 (1955).

This section is constitutional. In re One Ford Auto., 205 Ala. 193, 87 So. 842 (1921). See also Williams v. State, 179 Ala. 50, 60 So. 903 (1913); Tranum v. Stringer, 216 Ala. 522, 113 So. 541 (1927).

Provision of section that it shall not be necessary to show actual movement of vehicle while loaded with prohibited liquor to obtain confiscation thereof held constitutional. Parrish v. State, 221 Ala. 312, 128 So. 785 (1930).

This section does not violate the equal protection clause of the fourteenth amendment to the federal Constitution in that illegal transportation of liquor in a dry county subjects an automobile to confiscation, while in a wet county the automobile is only subject to such condemnation if the liquor is being transported for unlawful sale or is without the required stamps. Armstrong v. State ex rel. Embry, 248 Ala. 124, 26 So. 2d 874 (1946), appvd., 249 Ala. 40, 29 So. 2d 330 (1947).

And should be construed strictly. — The section is highly penal and should be strictly construed. Carey v. State ex rel. Almon, 206 Ala. 351, 89 So. 609 (1921); Thomas v. State, 241 Ala. 381, 2 So. 2d 772 (1941); Franklin v. State ex rel. Trammell, 275 Ala. 92, 152 So. 2d 158 (1963); Berryhill v. State, 372 So. 2d 355 (Ala. Civ. App. 1979).

The strict construction, referred to in cases holding that this section is highly penal and should be strictly construed, has reference to the substantive law and not to the sufficiency of pleading. Armstrong v. State ex rel. Embry, 248 Ala. 124, 26 So. 2d 874 (1946); Howell v.

State ex rel. Goodrich, 250 Ala. 243, 34 So. 2d 142 (1948).

Thus any transporting is a violation thereof. — Property may be seized under § 28-4-284 and condemned under this section when used in transporting prohibited liquors no matter how transported. It is not necessary that the transporting be along a public highway. See State v. Merrill, 203 Ala. 686, 85 So. 28 (1920).

Fourth amendment protection. — A forfeiture proceeding such as this is criminal in nature though civil in form and subject to the protection of the fourth amendment to the U.S. Constitution. Berryhill v. State, 372 So. 2d 355 (Ala. Civ. App. 1979).

Proceedings are in rem. — Proceedings under this section are in rem and the minority of the owner of the car does not render an order of condemnation defective. In re One Ford Auto., 205 Ala. 193, 87 So. 842 (1921); Koger v. State, 215 Ala. 319, 110 So. 573 (1926).

Ownership of automobile is immaterial. — That person claiming automobile, condemned as contraband under this section, as being used in transportation of intoxicating liquors, was not interested in such liquor as owner held immaterial, where he was aiding and assisting the owners of the liquor in knowingly and unlawfully transporting it for them in his car for unlawful purposes. Thrower v. State ex rel. Brickell, 213 Ala. 583, 105 So. 589 (1925).

As is the use of the liquor. — A vehicle is subject to condemnation and seizure under this section if whiskey is being transported, no matter if it be for sale or for private use. Koger v. State, 215 Ala. 319, 110 So. 573 (1926).

Once the state makes out a prima facie case to show violation of this section, the seizure, condemnation and forfeiture of the vehicle used is permitted. U-Haul Co. v. State, 294 Ala. 330, 316 So. 2d 685 (1975).

Truck found in wet county not subject to condemnation. — Truck which was found loaded with beer was not subject to condemnation where it was found in a wet county, notwithstanding fact that owner had no retail liquor dealer's license. Lyall v. State, 262 Ala. 96, 77 So. 2d 369 (1955).

Property may be confiscated whether liquor transported or not. — The effect of this section is to work a confiscation of any vehicle, or animal, into or upon which any prohibited liquor or beverage has been loaded for transportation, whether transported or not. The purpose of the 1927 amendment to this section is to meet and obviate the decision in Carey v. State ex rel. Almon, 206 Ala. 351, 89 So. 609 (1921), where it was decided that there could be no conveyance of intoxicating liquor by an automobile standing still. The effect of this amendment is to denounce, and punish by forfeiture of animal or vehicle, the placing on any animal, or in any vehicle, intoxicating liquor or beverage for transportation. Gibbs v. State, 259 Ala. 561, 67 So. 2d 836 (1953).

Transportation in interstate commerce. — Transportation of intoxicating liquors from one state through another state is within the protection of the commerce clause of the federal Constitution and not subject to state interference. This is true regardless of whether the state to which the liquor is being shipped prohibits the sale and traffic in such liquors. Alcohol Div. of Dep't of Fin. & Taxation v. State ex rel. Strawbridge, 258 Ala. 384, 63 So. 2d 358 (1953).

Where liquor is being transported from one state to another through Alabama fact that state to which liquor is being shipped prohibits the sale and traffic of such liquors does not authorize the seizure and condemnation of the liquors and the transporting vehicles under this section. Alcohol Div. of Dep't of Fin. & Taxation v. State ex rel. Strawbridge, 258 Ala. 384, 63 So. 2d 358 (1953).

If an automobile was being used for the transportation of intoxicating liquors in interstate commerce there can be no condemnation. Edison v. State ex rel. Burns, 263 Ala. 281, 82 So. 2d 218 (1955).

Liquor being shipped from another state for delivery into a dry county in this state is subject to seizure and condemnation, along with the transporting vehicles, by state authorities. Alcohol Div. & Dep't of Fin. & Taxation v. State ex rel. Strawbridge, 258 Ala. 384, 63 So. 2d 358 (1953).

Owner must have knowledge of illegal use. — It has been decided in State v. Hughes, 203 Ala. 90, 82 So. 104 (1919), and in Maples v. State, 203 Ala. 153, 82 So. 183 (1919), that this section does not contemplate the condemnation of property of those who do not aid or assist in the unlawful transporting of liquors, or who are not chargeable with notice or knowledge that their property is to be used for such unlawful purposes. The doctrine of the Hughes case has been followed in State ex rel. Tate v. One Lexington Auto., 203 Ala. 506, 84 So. 297 (1919); State v. Crosswhite, 203 Ala. 586, 84 So. 813 (1920); Briscoe Motor Car Co. v. State, 204 Ala. 231, 85 So. 475 (1920). See also Auburn Sales Co. v. State, 219 Ala. 360, 122 So. 463 (1929); Tittle v. State, 252 Ala. 377, 41 So. 2d 295 (1949); Shropshire v. State ex rel. Williams, 254 Ala. 470, 48 So. 2d 776 (1950).

If the owner of the automobile was not driving the car himself but had loaned it to another party who was driving at the time the automobile was seized, the evidence must show by positive proof that the owner knew or should have known or could have known by due diligence that the automobile was transporting illegal liquors in a dry county, or that the party he loaned the automobile to had such a reputation for handling and dealing in liquors that the owner should have known the said person was likely to illegally transport liquors in the automobile on the occasion the car was to be used and was used. Snyder v. State, 247 Ala. 278, 24 So. 2d 266 (1945).

Failure of an owner of a car to prosecute one for taking it without his consent, for the purpose of transporting liquor, does not imply that consent was given, nor will such omission be such a dereliction as to subject the property to condemnation when ignorance of the taking and using is shown by the owner. Briscoe Motor Car Co. v. State, 204 Ala. 231, 85 So. 475 (1920).

Bad character of illegal user is sufficient to impute notice to claimant. — The general bad character of person in possession of whiskey and vehicle in which it is being carried, in community of his residence or his place of business, is sufficient to impute notice to claimant, in state's proceedings to condemn vehicle. Parker v. State ex rel. Embry, 246 Ala. 372, 20 So. 2d 719 (1945); Modern Credit Co. v. State ex rel. Thetford, 265 Ala. 248, 90 So. 2d 756 (1956).

In a proceeding to condemn an automobile because of its use by the conditional vendee in the illegal transportation of intoxicating liquors, evidence of such conditional vendee's bad general reputation prior to the time of the sale as being a bootlegger or whiskey dealer either in the place of his residence or business, is admissible as tending to give notice to the conditional vendor of the probable future use of the automobile for the illegal transportation of intoxicating liquors. Alabama Disct. Corp. v. State ex rel. Stephens, 271 Ala. 338, 123 So. 2d 416 (1960).

Evidence of a purchaser-debtor's bad general reputation for bootlegging or dealing in prohibited liquors tends to give notice to a secured party of the probable future use of the vehicle for the illegal transportation of intoxicating liquors. Mars v. State ex rel. Black, 340 So. 2d 1131 (Ala. Civ. App. 1976).

For the purchaser-debtor's bad reputation to be notice or knowledge imputed to the party asserting a security interest in the vehicle so as to constitute culpable negligence in allowing the purchaser to obtain the vehicle, the bad reputation must be a general reputation, must exist at the purchaser's place of residence, or at his place of business or occupation, and must have existed at the time the car was sold. Mars v. State ex rel. Black, 340 So. 2d 1131 (Ala. Civ. App. 1976).

And failure to make inquiry results in forfeiture. — Where facts of bad reputation of purchaser were presumptively accessible to claimant, his failure to make inquiry is negligence which must result in forfeiture in state's proceeding to condemn automobile used to transport liquor. Parker v. State ex rel. Embry, 246 Ala. 372, 20 So. 2d 719 (1945).

Where a lessee is unknown to his lessor then the lessor should make reasonable inquiry as to lessee's reputation and character before completing the transaction. U-Haul Co. v. State, 294 Ala. 330, 316 So. 2d 685 (1975).

Duty to inquire not affected by enactment of section 28-4-200. — The enactment of § 28-4-200 in 1971 to permit the possession of small amounts of liquor and beer for private use in dry counties does not absolve a party asserting a security interest in a confiscated vehicle of any responsibility to inquire further in cases where it knows of charges against a purchaser-debtor for violating the prohibition laws prior to 1971. Mars v. State ex rel. Black, 340 So. 2d 1131 (Ala. Civ. App. 1976).

Procedure in forfeiture cases. — This section and § 28-4-286 relate to property seized while being used to transport alcoholic beverages in dry counties. There appears no substantive reason why the procedure in those cases would not be appropriate in other matters of forfeiture. Section 28-4-286 directs the action to be brought in the name of the state against either the property seized or against the person, if known, in possession when seized. The judge of the court where filed is authorized to make all orders of procedure necessary to regulate the proceedings so that all persons who claim an interest in the property may have the opportunity to appear and propound their claims to the property sought to be condemned. National Bank v. State, 403 So. 2d 258 (Ala. Civ. App. 1981).

Where the lessor took no action that reasonably could have been expected to prevent the proscribed use of the property, there is no constitutional objection to the forfeiture. U-Haul Co. v. State, 294 Ala. 330, 316 So. 2d 685 (1975).

Officer must have probable cause for search. — The officer who acts upon information which proves unreliable, resulting in the stoppage and search of the car of an innocent citizen, carries the full burden of showing probable cause. Tranum v. Stringer, 216 Ala. 522, 113 So. 541 (1927).

Before an officer has authority to seize and search a vehicle under this section, he "must become cognizant of the fact" that it is transporting liquor. Mere belief or a rash or undue suspicion cannot justify. There must come to him such facts as would to a reasonable man be probable cause. Tranum v. Stringer, 216 Ala. 522, 113 So. 541 (1927). See also In re One Ford Auto., 205 Ala. 193, 87 So. 842 (1921).

Amount transported is immaterial. — Automobile was held subject to condemnation, although amount of prohibited liquor was only a quart, and was on person of passenger. Morris v. State, 220 Ala. 418, 125 So. 655 (1930).

Meaning of "loaded". — This last clause of this section creates no presumption that automobile, found with pint of liquor therein, is subject to condemnation; "loaded" does not refer to quantity of liquors, but means loaded for movement. Kelly v. State, 219 Ala. 415, 122 So. 638 (1929).

Right of sellers and mortgagees. — In proceedings under this section, to condemn an automobile used in transporting prohibited liquor, seller and mortgagee of automobile held not to have acquitted itself of negligence sufficient to recover automobile, under evidence showing purchaser had reputation of being bootlegger, and frequented bootlegging joint near mortgagee's place of business, and that mortgagee merely investigated purchaser's moral character and court records for conviction for violating prohibition law. People's Auto Co. v. State, 218 Ala. 553, 119 So. 662 (1929).

Intervener in proceeding to condemn automobile used in unlawful transportation of prohibited liquors, in violation of this section, held not to have borne burden of showing valid claim to or ownership of automobile, where intervener claimed to be owner, but driver testified that intervener's claim was only mortgage which had not been foreclosed. Morris v. State, 220 Ala. 418, 125 So. 655 (1930).

Where a bona fide mortgagee or vendor in a conditional sales contract, by intervention, seeks to establish his superior right, title and ownership in property seized in an act that is prohibited and condemned by this section, he must not only aver in his pleading or claim, but must establish by evidence, that he did not have notice of the unlawful use of his property to which it was subjected when seized and by the exercise of reasonable diligence could not have obtained knowledge or notice of such illegal use and prevented the same. Alabama Disct. Corp. v. State ex rel. Stephens, 271 Ala. 338, 123 So. 2d 416 (1960).

Removal after seizure. — Assuming a seizure, the fact that defendant took the car off somewhere does not break the effect of such seizure as authority to proceed under this section and § 28-4-286. It does not allege that this was not done by permission of the sheriff, making him the sheriff's agent. Jackson v. State, 251 Ala. 226, 36 So. 2d 306 (1948).

This section does not require verification of the complaint. Howell v. State ex rel. Goodrich, 250 Ala. 243, 34 So. 2d 142 (1948).

Appropriate designation of complainant in a proceeding under this section is the state of Alabama on the relation of the named district attorney or named attorney general. Terry v. State ex rel. Pettus, 264 Ala. 133, 85 So. 2d 449 (1956).

Sufficiency of allegations. — A complaint which contained no allegation that the prohibited liquors or beverages were being transported into the state or from one point in the state to another point within the state, but the allegations of which were tantamount to an allegation that prohibited liquors were being transported from one point in the state to another point in the state, substantially complied with this section. Howell v. State ex rel. Goodrich, 250 Ala. 243, 34 So. 2d 142 (1948).

Complaint need not negative that transportation was from one wet county to another. — A complaint charging that defendant used and operated the automobile to be condemned in a dry county "in the transportation of illegal whiskey or beverages from one point in the state of Alabama to another point in the state of Alabama" makes out a prima facie case of illegal transportation of prohibited liquors and is not defective in failing to negate that the transportation was from one wet county to another wet county in the state through a dry county. Armstrong v. State ex rel. Embry, 248 Ala. 124, 26 So. 2d 874 (1946), appvd., 249 Ala. 40, 29 So. 2d 330 (1947).

And if this is a defense it should be brought forward by defendant. — In condemnation proceedings under this section, the defense that the vehicle to be condemned was being used to transport liquor from one wet county to another through a dry county, if a defense at all, is one to be brought forward by the defendant. Armstrong v. State ex rel. Embry, 248 Ala. 124, 26 So. 2d 874 (1946), appvd., 249 Ala. 40, 29 So. 2d 330 (1947).

No right to trial by jury in proceedings under this section and § 28-4-286 is afforded by Constitution, § 11. U-Haul Co. v. State, 294 Ala. 330, 316 So. 2d 685 (1975).

Cited in Byles v. State ex rel. Perry, 205 Ala. 286, 87 So. 856 (1921); In re One Chevrolet Auto., 205 Ala. 337, 87 So. 592 (1921); Eckl v. State, 205 Ala. 466, 88 So. 567 (1921); Fearn v. State ex rel. Almon, 205 Ala. 478, 88 So. 591 (1921); State ex rel. Seibels v. Farley, 206 Ala. 172, 89 So. 510 (1921); Snyder v. State ex rel. Elmore, 207 Ala. 147, 92 So. 170 (1922); State ex rel. Almon v. One Black Horse Mule, 207 Ala. 277, 92 So. 548 (1922); Standard Oil Co. v. State, 207 Ala. 303, 92 So. 894 (1922); State ex rel. Elmore v. Leveson, 207 Ala. 638, 93 So.

608 (1922); Armstrong v. Jefferson County, 208 Ala. 645, 95 So. 39 (1923); Hurvich v. State, 230 Ala. 578, 162 So. 362 (1935); Williamson v. State ex rel. Evans, 244 Ala. 609, 14 So. 2d 587 (1943); Woods v. State ex rel. Key, 247 Ala. 155, 22 So. 2d 901 (1945); Barnes v. State, 251 Ala. 489, 38 So. 2d 21 (1948); Speck v. State ex rel. Key, 254 Ala. 485, 48 So. 2d 529 (1950); Burt v. State ex rel. Burns, 262 Ala. 22, 76 So. 2d 676 (1954); Davis v. City of Birmingham, 278 Ala. 391, 178 So. 2d 547 (1965); Burnett v. State ex rel. Atkinson, 340 So. 2d 40 (Ala. Civ. App. 1976); Singleton v. State, 396 So. 2d 1050 (Ala. 1981); Murray v. State ex rel. Tidwell, 423 So. 2d 246 (Ala. Civ. App. 1982); Art Belew Chevrolet, Inc. v. State ex rel. Harris, 424 So. 2d 626 (Ala. Civ. App. 1982); Robinson v. State, 451 So. 2d 355 (Ala. Civ. App. 1984).

Collateral references. — 48 C.J.S., Intoxicating Liquors, §§ 42, 388.

45 Am. Jur. 2d, Intoxicating Liquors, §§ 496, 514 et seq.

Right to search or seize vehicle containing contraband as affected by the fact that it was stationary at the time. 61 ALR 1002.

Presence of liquor in vehicle at the time of search and seizure as condition of forfeiture for violating prohibition law. 71 ALR 911.

Relief to claimant of interest in motor vehicle subject to state forfeiture for use in violation of liquor laws. 14 ALR3d 221.

II. EVIDENCE.

Cross references. — See notes to § 28-4-286.

Civil rules of evidence apply in condemnation proceedings instituted under this section. Davis v. State ex rel. Pettus, 264 Ala. 233, 86 So. 2d 849 (1956).

Presumption that automobile is used for transportation. — Presumption that automobile, in which intoxicating liquor is found, is used for transportation thereof, so as to authorize condemnation of car, will not be indulged, unless such intent is clear and presumption does not infringe on constitutional rights. Kelley v. State, 219 Ala. 415, 122 So. 638 (1929); Gibbs v. State, 259 Ala. 561, 67 So. 2d 836 (1953).

Burden is on state to show transportation. — The burden is on the state to show that automobile, sought to be condemned, was used in transporting prohibited liquors. Kelley v. State, 219 Ala. 415, 122 So. 638 (1929); Lee v. State ex rel. Hare, 259 Ala. 455, 66 So. 2d 881 (1953); Gibbs v. State, 259 Ala. 561, 67 So. 2d 836 (1953).

Although the state is not required to prove actual movement of the vehicle, it does have the burden of proving that the prohibited liquor or beverage has been loaded for transportation. Gibbs v. State, 259 Ala. 561, 67 So. 2d 836 (1953).

The state has the burden of proving that the prohibited liquor or beverage has been loaded for transportation. Franklin v. State ex rel. Trammell, 275 Ala. 92, 152 So. 2d 158 (1963).

Burden then shifts to intervening owner or claimant. — The state proved without dispute that prohibited liquors were being illegally transported in the automobile at the time it was seized. The burden of proof was then shifted to the intervening owner or claimant: (1) To establish her superior title thereto; and (2) to prove that she had no knowledge or notice of the illegal use of the automobile or could not by reasonable diligence have obtained knowledge or notice thereof to prevent the illegal use. Lee v. State ex rel. Hare, 259 Ala. 455, 66 So. 2d 881 (1953); Brandon v. State, 261 Ala. 378, 74 So. 2d 606 (1954).

An owner-claimant to a vehicle must prove he had no knowledge of the illegal use of the vehicle and by the exercise of reasonable diligence could not have obtained knowledge of such intended use. U-Haul Co. v. State, 294 Ala. 330, 316 So. 2d 685 (1975).

In a case for condemnation of a contraband vehicle, once the state has met its burden of proof, the burden is on the party asserting a superior security interest in the vehicle to establish its superior claim and to show it had no knowledge or notice of the illegal use of the car and could not by reasonable diligence have obtained knowledge of the intended illegal use so as to prevent such use. Mars v. State ex rel. Black, 340 So. 2d 1131 (Ala. Civ. App. 1976).

It is only necessary for the evidence to show that the purpose of the transportation was for resale contrary to law when it is made to appear from the evidence that the prohibited liquors or beverages were purchased through the state liquor stores, or bore the stamps of the Alabama alcoholic beverage control board. Deerman v. State ex rel. Bains, 253 Ala. 632, 46 So. 2d 410 (1950).

Presumption from defendant's reputation. — If there was credible evidence that at the time of the alleged offense the defendant had a reputation of being a seller of prohibited liquors, this section writes into the case an inference on which a finding may be affirmed that the liquors or beverages were being transported for resale and warrants confiscation of the vehicle, if he were the owner and no interests of third parties are involved, unless satisfactory countervailing proof is adduced to overcome such inference. Tittle v. State, 252 Ala. 377, 41 So. 2d 295 (1949).

Where the owner of the vehicle is defendant's wife, no such presumption is indulged against her to warrant confiscation of her property. Tittle v. State, 252 Ala. 377, 41 So. 2d 295 (1949).

Under this section, when the state shows that the owner or operator of the car has a reputation among law enforcement officers as a seller of prohibited liquors, a prima facie case is established that the prohibited liquor contained in the car was being transported for resale. Bragg v. State, 253 Ala. 392, 44 So. 2d 591 (1949).

Admissibility of testimony taken at hearing on claim of conditional vendor. — A finance company filed a petition of intervention in a condemnation proceeding under this section, claiming title to the automobile under a conditional sales contract. Testimony on this claim was taken orally before the trial court, and the claim was denied, in advance of the hearing in the main action. On the hearing of the main action the state offered in evidence, over objection, the testimony taken at the hearing on the claim. It was held that the trial court did not err in considering this evidence. Whaley v. State ex rel. Bland, 263 Ala. 191, 82 So. 2d 187 (1955).

Sufficiency of evidence. — Evidence that officers saw owner reach into automobile, take out bottle of whiskey and walk away held sufficient for condemnation of automobile. Parrish v. State, 221 Ala. 312, 128 So. 785 (1930).

Conflicting evidence in confiscation proceedings as to whether whiskey was ever in automobile held for trial court. Parrish v. State, 221 Ala. 312, 128 So. 785 (1930).

Finding of intoxicating liquor in vehicle in such quantities and containers as to lead to natural inference that it was there to be transported or at time and place or under other circumstances warranting reasonable inference that it has been transported to place found or is there to be transported makes out state's case. Kelley v. State, 219 Ala. 415, 122 So. 638 (1929), wherein evidence was held insufficient. Gibbs v. State, 259 Ala. 561, 67 So. 2d 836 (1953).

Evidence in proceeding for forfeiture of auto-mobile used in delivery of prohibited intoxicating liquor held sufficient to sustain order of forfeiture. Willis v. State ex rel. Orme, 234 Ala. 642, 176 So. 612 (1937); Reno v. State ex rel. Johnson, 265 Ala. 60, 89 So. 2d 686 (1956).

Evidence was sufficient to show that defendant used car to take whiskey to smokehouse of witness, where witness stated to sheriff in presence of defendant that the defendant had brought the whiskey to the smokehouse in the car, and sheriff did not remember that defendant denied the accusation. Davis v. State ex rel. Pettus, 264 Ala. 233, 86 So. 2d 849 (1956).

Evidence held to show that motor truck was illegally used for transporting liquor between two points within state and to authorize condemnation of truck. Schefano v. State, 231 Ala. 391, 164 So. 902 (1935).

Evidence that deputy sheriff had telephoned defendant requesting him to bring two bottles of a particular whiskey to named place, that deputy sheriff and two others had met defendant's automobile and pursued it to another city, that whiskey bottle bearing label of brand ordered was thrown from automobile during chase, and that there were odor and traces of whiskey about automobile, held to justify condemnation of automobile under this section. Liger v. State ex rel. Orme, 232 Ala. 355, 168 So. 138 (1936).

Evidence warranted finding that owner knew of illegal use. — In state's proceeding to condemn automobile used to transport liquor, in which driver's brother filed a claim to automobile, evidence warranted assumption of knowledge on part of owner of automobile's use so as to bar claims to automobile. Parker v. State ex rel. Embry, 246 Ala. 372, 20 So. 2d 719 (1945).

Evidence warranted finding that liquors were being transported for resale. — Evidence clearly warranted the finding by the trial court that the liquors were being transported for resale, thus subjecting the automobile to condemnation. Whaley v. State ex rel. Bland, 263 Ala. 191, 82 So. 2d 187 (1955).

§ 28-4-286. Institution of proceedings for condemnation of vehicles, etc.; seized property not to be retaken by replevin or detinue during pendency of action; intervention by parties claiming superior right to seized property; powers of court to regulate proceedings to permit parties claiming vehicles, etc., to assert rights.

It shall be the duty of such officer in the county or the attorney general of the state to institute at once or cause to be instituted condemnation proceedings in the circuit court by filing a complaint in the name of the state against the property seized, describing the same, or against the person or persons in possession of said vehicles of transportation, if known, to obtain a judgment enforcing the forfeiture. No replevin or detinue writ may be employed to retake possession of such seized property pending the forfeiture action, but any party claiming a superior right may intervene by motion in said action and have his claim adjudicated.

The judge presiding in said circuit court or any division thereof may superintend and make all proper orders and orders of publication of notice to be published for all parties claiming the said vehicles to come in and assert their right thereto. The said court shall have authority to frame all orders of procedure so as to regulate the proceedings that persons may have an opportunity to come in and propound their claim to the vehicles and conveyances sought to be condemned. (Acts 1919, No. 7, p. 6; Code 1923, § 4779; Code 1940, T. 29, § 248.)

Proceeding under this section is not a criminal proceeding, but a civil action. Hence, it was not essential that the owner of the automobile be personally present when the testimony was being taken. Whaley v. State ex rel. Bland, 263 Ala. 191, 82 So. 2d 187 (1955).

Proceedings instituted in name of state on relation of district attorney. — Under the authority of this section and § 28-4-285, condemnation proceedings against the property seized are properly instituted in the name of the state on relation of the district attorney. Howell v. State ex rel. Goodrich, 250 Ala. 243, 34 So. 2d 142 (1948).

Procedure in forfeiture cases. — Section 28-4-285 and this section relate to property seized while being used to transport alcoholic beverages in dry counties. There appears no substantive reason why the procedure in those cases would not be appropriate in other matters of forfeiture. This section directs the action to be brought in the name of the state against either the property seized or against the person, if known, in possession when seized. The judge of the court where filed is authorized to make all orders of procedure necessary to regulate the proceedings so that all persons who claim an interest in the property may have the opportunity to appear and propound their claims to the property sought to be condemned. National Bank v. State, 403 So. 2d 258 (Ala. Civ. App. 1981).

Proceedings against person using automobile. — That state's proceedings to condemn automobile were brought against person allegedly using it in transporting liquor, and not against automobile itself, is proper under this section. Commercial Credit Co. v. State ex rel. Stewart, 224 Ala. 123, 139 So. 271 (1932); Parker v. State ex rel. Embry, 246 Ala. 372, 20 So. 2d 719 (1945).

Right to notice of taking of testimony. — Claimant of automobile sought to be condemned by state because used in liquor transportation, not having intervened by petition, is not entitled to notice of taking of testimony. Commercial Credit Co. v. State ex rel. Steward, 224 Ala. 123, 139 So. 271 (1932).

Right of intervention. — By this section a claimant is given the right to "intervene by motion in said action, and have his claim adjudicated." Such a claimant in intervention becomes a party to the action, and the hearing on its claim is a part of the condemnation proceeding. Whaley v. State ex rel Bland, 263 Ala. 191, 82 So. 2d 187 (1955).

Defense of laches is not available against the state in an action by it to enforce this section. Sisk v. State ex rel. Smith, 249 Ala. 279, 31 So. 2d 84 (1947).

Delay of five months in institution of action worked no estoppel against the state in the enforcement of this section. Sisk v. State ex rel. Smith, 249 Ala. 279, 31 So. 2d 84 (1947).

Burden of proof. — In view of this section and § 28-4-285, in petition to forfeit automobile engaged in the transportation of whiskey, burden was on petitioner to make out prima facie case for condemnation before claimant was required to offer proof of superior right. Carter Guar. Co. v. State, 214 Ala. 432, 108 So. 246 (1926).

The burden of proof is cast by this section on the intervening owner or claimant: (1) To establish his superior title thereto; and (2) to prove that he had "no knowledge or notice" of the illegal use of the vehicle or could not "by reasonable diligence have obtained knowledge or notice thereof" to prevent that illegal use. State ex rel. Tate v. One Lexington Auto., 203 Ala. 506, 84 So. 297 (1919), appvd. in State v.

Merrill, 203 Ala. 686, 85 So. 28 (1920); Parker v. State ex rel. Embry, 246 Ala. 372, 20 So. 2d 719 (1945); Anderson v. State ex rel. Dormon, 246 Ala. 468, 20 So. 2d 864 (1945); Shropshire v. State ex rel. Williams, 254 Ala. 470, 48 So. 2d 776 (1950); Modern Credit Co. v. State ex rel. Thetford, 265 Ala. 248, 90 So. 2d 756 (1956).

Where evidence showed that the owner of the car was not present at the time it was seized for transporting prohibited liquors or beverages in a dry county, the burden rested upon the owner to establish that he had no knowledge or notice of the illegal use of the vehicle, and could not by reasonable diligence have obtained notice to prevent that illegal use. Deerman v. State ex rel. Bains, 253 Ala. 632, 46 So. 2d 410 (1950).

Once the state makes out a prima facie case to show violation of the statute which prohibits the transportation of illegal liquors, the seizure, condemnation and forfeiture of the vehicle used is permitted. U-Haul Co. v. State, 294 Ala. 330, 316 So. 2d 685 (1975).

Evidence did not justify a condemnation where the defendant was not operating the car on the occasion complained of, and so far as the record showed did not know, nor was he chargeable with notice or knowledge, that his automobile was to be used for the purpose of transporting prohibited liquors. Shropshire v. State ex rel. Williams, 254 Ala. 470, 48 So. 2d 776 (1950).

No right to trial by jury in proceedings under § 28-4-285 and this section is afforded by Constitution, § 11. U-Haul Co. v. State, 294 Ala. 330, 316 So. 2d 685 (1975).

Usual presumption of verity attends the findings of the trial court on testimony taken ore tenus before it. But the rule will not be applied where there is no conflict in the evidence touching or bearing upon the issues presented. Shropshire v. State ex rel. Williams, 254 Ala. 470, 48 So. 2d 776 (1950).

Cited in Snyder v. State, 247 Ala. 278, 24 So. 2d 266 (1945); Armstrong v. State ex rel. Embry, 248 Ala. 124, 26 So. 2d 874 (1946), appvd. 249 Ala. 40, 29 So. 2d 330 (1947); Middlebrooks v. State ex rel. Dormon, 248 Ala. 402, 27 So. 2d 867 (1946); Barnes v. State, 34 Ala. App. 183, 38 So. 2d 21 (1948); State v. Le Croy, 254 Ala. 637, 49 So. 2d 553 (1950); Mosley v. State, 255 Ala. 130, 50 So. 2d 433 (1951); Nelson v. State, 255 Ala. 141, 50 So. 2d 401 (1951); Ferguson v. State ex rel. Bains, 273 Ala. 463, 142 So. 2d 260 (1962).

Collateral references. — Rights of innocent persons, and protection thereof, where property in which they are interested, is seized because of its illegal use in connection with intoxicating liquor. 47 ALR 1055, 61 ALR 551, 73 ALR 1087, 82 ALR 607, 124 ALR 288.

§ 28-4-287. Execution of bond by defendant or claimant for recovery of seized vehicle, etc., pending condemnation action; proceedings upon failure of defendant or claimant to deliver said vehicle, etc., upon entry of judgment of condemnation.

Whenever a conveyance, vehicle of any kind or animal used in drawing the same is seized by an officer of the state under the prohibition laws of this state, the defendant in the proceedings or the claimant of the property shall have the right to execute a bond in double the value of such property or of any item thereof, with good and sufficient surety, to be approved by the sheriff or the register or clerk of the circuit court and conditioned, in the event the said property is condemned, to deliver the same to the sheriff within 15 days from the date of such judgment of condemnation and to pay any difference between the value of said property at the time of the seizure and the time of the delivery to the sheriff after condemnation, such difference in value to be determined by the trial court upon motion of any party to said action. Upon the execution of such bond, the sheriff shall deliver said property to the defendant or claimant executing the same.

Upon the failure of the defendant or claimant to deliver the property condemned within 15 days after judgment of condemnation, the bond shall be returned forfeited to the register or clerk of the circuit court and execution may issue thereon against the principal and his sureties for the amount of the value of such property; or, in case of the return of the property to the sheriff and the failure to pay the difference in value as above set forth, execution may issue against the principal and his sureties for such difference in value. (Code 1923, § 4780; Code 1940, T. 29, § 249.)

Execution of bond was conclusive that the car was then in the custody of the law. Jackson v. State, 251 Ala. 226, 36 So. 2d 306 (1948).

And defendant executing the bond became estopped to deny the seizure on or prior to its date, and that the car was then held by the sheriff. Jackson v. State, 251 Ala. 226, 36 So. 2d 306 (1948).

Rule which relieves an obligor on account of impossibility of performance due to an "act of the law" does not contemplate an act precipitated solely by the subsequent unlawful use of the bonded vehicle. A contrary rule would enable an obligor to occupy the strange position of pleading the consequences of a subsequent unlawful use of the vehicle in exoneration of an obligation. Ferguson v. State ex rel Bains, 273 Ala. 463, 142 So. 2d 260 (1962).

Performance rendered impossible by obligor's own act. — Where the obligor's own act, or the act of some person or agency on his behalf, renders performance of the bond impossible, the principal could not in these circumstances exonerate himself, and what will not avail the principal cannot avail his sureties. Ferguson v. State ex rel Bains, 273 Ala. 463, 142 So. 2d 260 (1962).

Hazards assumed by surety. — When a surety pursuant to this section undertakes that the bonded vehicle shall be forthcoming within 15 days from an order of condemnation, he assumes the hazards of the use made of the vehicle by those to whom it is entrusted between the time of its release and the time it must be delivered in the event of an order of condemnation. If the vehicle be stolen or if it be retaken by a conditional vendor or if it be destroyed by the culpable act of the principal, it would hardly be contended that the surety is exonerated. Ferguson v. State ex rel. Bains, 273 Ala. 463, 142 So. 2d 260 (1962).

When sureties discharged. — Sureties on a forthcoming bond for property are discharged just as those on a personal recognizance bond are by an act of the obligee or of the law, without fault on the part of the obligors, which prevents performance. Ferguson v. State ex rel. Bains, 273 Ala. 463, 142 So. 2d 260 (1962).

Cited in Thompson v. State ex rel. Key, 247 Ala. 585, 25 So. 2d 671 (1946); Middlebrooks v. State ex rel. Dormon, 248 Ala. 402, 27 So. 2d 867 (1946); Sisk v. State ex rel. Smith, 249 Ala. 40, 31 So. 2d 84 (1947).

Collateral references. — 48 C.J.S., Intoxicating Liquors, § 403.

§ 28-4-288. Execution of bond by defendant or claimant for recovery of seized vehicle, etc., pending appeal; proceedings upon failure of bondsmen to deliver said vehicle, etc., upon affirmance of judgment upon appeal, etc.

Whenever a conveyance, vehicle of any kind or animal used in drawing the same is seized by an officer of the state under the prohibition laws of this state and has been condemned by the circuit court that tried the action, the defendant in the proceedings or the claimant of the property, pending an appeal to the supreme court or court of civil appeals, may, upon motion, have the court immediately appraise the value of said property and of the several items separately and shall have the right to execute a bond with two good sureties in double the appraised value of such property or of any item or items thereof, to be approved by the clerk or register of the circuit court, conditioned, in the event the appeal is affirmed or reversed and the conveyance, vehicle, animal or harness is subsequently condemned on another trial, to deliver the property for which a bond is given to the sheriff within 30 days from the date of such affirmance or reversal and subsequent condemnation on another trial, to be disposed of according to law and to pay any difference between any value thereof at the time of the original appraisal and at the time of the delivery to the sheriff, the difference in value to be determined by the circuit court. On the execution of such bond the sheriff shall deliver said property to the defendant or claimant executing such bond.

Upon the failure of the bondsmen to deliver the said property condemned within 30 days after the appeal has been affirmed or within 30 days after condemnation on another trial if the judgment is reversed, the bond shall be returned by the sheriff forfeited, and execution may issue thereon against the principal and sureties for the amount of the value of the property or, in case of the return of the property, for the difference between the value fixed by the court on the original appraisal and the final appraisal when it is returned after the appeal is affirmed. (Acts 1919, No. 683, p. 984; Code 1923, §§ 4786, 4787; Code 1940, T. 29, §§ 255, 256.)

§ 28-4-289. Payment of costs in actions for condemnation of vehicles, etc., used in transportation of prohibited liquors or beverages where judgment entered against state.

In all actions filed under this article for the purpose of condemning and selling conveyances and vehicles of transportation of any kind on account of their use in the transportation of prohibited liquors or beverages, if a judgment shall be entered against the state, the court costs shall be paid out of the law-enforcement fund provided for in this article, said payment to be made on warrant of the comptroller upon receipt by him of the bill of costs certified as being correct by the register or clerk of the circuit court in which such action shall have been tried, which cost bill should also bear the approval of the attorney general and the governor before a warrant shall be drawn. (Acts 1923, No. 567, p. 736; Code 1923, § 4785; Code 1940, T. 29, § 254.)

§ 28-4-290. Advertisement and sale by sheriff, etc., of vehicle, animal, etc., seized for illegal transportation of liquor or beverages where owner, etc., cannot be ascertained; rights in seized vehicles, animals, etc., disposed of upon such sale by sheriff or sale by court in condemnation proceedings.

Any sheriff or other officer who seizes or comes into possession of such vehicle, animal or property illegally used for the transportation of liquor or beverages within or into the state and does not know or cannot ascertain the possessor or owner thereof shall advertise and sell the same according to the rules for selling personal property under execution, and both the court in condemnation proceedings and the said officer on advertisement shall sell the right of all interested persons in and to said conveyances, vehicles and other property who aided or assisted in the illegal transportation or who had knowledge or notice thereof or could by reasonable diligence have obtained knowledge or notice thereof. (Acts 1919, No. 7, p. 6; Code 1923, § 4781; Code 1940, T. 29, § 250.)

In proceedings for condemnation and sale of an automobile for transporting prohibited liquor, person intervening and seeking to establish a claim to the automobile by reason of a mortgage has burden of proving that he had no knowledge or notice of the proposed illegal use of the automobile, and by reasonable diligence could not have had such notice. Middlebrooks v. State ex rel. Dormon, 248 Ala. 402, 27 So. 2d 867 (1946).

Where state condemns automobile used in transporting liquor, but claimant establishes equity in the automobile under a mortgage, the condemnation and sale will be only of the equity of redemption. The court has no authority to sell it free of the mortgage, and out of the proceeds settle the mortgage debt. Middlebrooks v. State ex rel. Dormon, 248 Ala. 402, 27 So. 2d 867 (1946).

Cited in State v. Dorrough, 342 So. 2d 781 (Ala. 1977).

Collateral references. — 48 C.J.S., Intoxicating Liquors, § 403.

§ 28-4-291. Disposition of proceeds from sale of such property forfeited to state.

Unless otherwise provided by law, the proceeds of the sale of any such property forfeited to the state, whether sold by court order or by an officer under advertisement, shall, after paying all expenses in the action, or of advertisement, as the case may be, including the costs of seizure and of keeping the property pending the proceedings, be applied as follows: One half of the proceeds shall be paid into the general fund of the county in which the property is seized, and the other one half shall be paid into the law-enforcement fund to be used and applied on the enforcement of state laws under the supervision and control of the governor; provided, that when such property shall be seized by an officer of a municipality, one half of the proceeds of the sale shall be paid into the general fund of the municipality, one quarter shall be paid into the general fund of the county, and the other one quarter shall be paid into the law-enforcement fund to be used and applied on the enforcement of state laws under the supervision and control of the governor. (Acts 1919, No. 7, p. 6; Code 1923, § 4782; Code 1940, T. 29, § 251; Acts 1947, No. 126, p. 38; Acts 1949, No. 669, p. 1032.)

Section is constitutional. — This section, as amended in 1949, does not violate Constitution, §§ 45 or 61. In re Opinion of the Justices, 252 Ala. 525, 41 So. 2d 758 (1949).

§ 28-4-292. Advertisement and sale of receptacles, etc., of prohibited liquors and beverages.

All vessels and receptacles of prohibited liquors and beverages such as handbags, suitcases or trunks, which have been seized in law enforcement and which are in the custody of any person or officer, after conviction of the parties from whom seized of the violation of the law in respect thereto, shall be sold after notice of sale by advertisement in a newspaper published in the county for 10 days in a daily paper or for two issues in a weekly paper.

The proceeds of the sale shall be paid into the municipal treasury, if sale is made by a municipal officer or custodian of such contraband seized by municipal officers, or to the law-enforcement fund in the state treasury if made by any other officer or custodian. (Acts 1919, No. 7, p. 6; Code 1923, § 4783; Code 1940, T. 29, § 252.)

§ 28-4-293. Property rights in prohibited liquors and beverages, vessels, vehicles, etc., kept, used, etc., for purpose of violating temperance laws, etc.; seizure, forfeiture, disposition, etc., of same generally.

No property rights of any kind shall exist in prohibited liquors and beverages, vessels, fixtures, furniture, implements or vehicles kept or used for the purpose of violating any law for the promotion of temperance or the suppression of the evils of intemperance, nor in any such liquors and beverages when received, possessed or stored in any forbidden place or anywhere forbidden by law. In all such cases the liquors and beverages are forfeited to the state of Alabama and may be searched for and seized and forfeited and disposed of under the rules prescribed by law concerning contraband liquors and beverages or by order of the judge or court, after a conviction, when such liquors and beverages have been seized for use as evidence. (Acts 1915, No. 491, p. 553; Code 1923, § 4771; Code 1940, T. 29, § 240.)

Liquor bearing tax stamps from another state. — Notwithstanding that liquor bears tax stamps from another state, unless it bears Alabama revenue stamps or identification as described in this title, or is exempt therefrom for one of the reasons set out in this title, it must be considered as contraband. Hodges v. Archer, 286 Ala. 457, 241 So. 2d 324 (1970).

Cited in Davis v. City of Birmingham, 278 Ala. 391, 178 So. 2d 547 (1965).

Collateral references. — 48 C.J.S., Intoxicating Liquors, § 42.

§ 28-4-294. Preparation of return by officer seizing prohibited liquors and beverages; officer to report delivery to any person, destruction, etc., of same.

When any officer shall seize or take possession of any prohibited liquors and beverages in the enforcement of the law, he shall at once, in writing, make a return of his acts, with a statement of the quantity and kind of liquors and beverages to the court that has or secures jurisdiction of the case. When any such liquor or beverage is destroyed, delivered to any person or otherwise disposed of, the officer acting in the matter shall in writing make a report of the facts to such court. (Acts 1915, No. 491, p. 553; Code 1923, § 4772; Code 1940, T. 29, § 241.)

§ 28-4-295. Disposition of prohibited liquors and beverages held for use as evidence upon conviction of person possessing, etc., same.

Whenever prohibited liquors and beverages, or any of them, are seized and held for use as evidence before any court on the trial of any person for a violation of the prohibitory laws of the state or the prohibitory ordinance of any municipality and the person is convicted for violating such law or ordinance in any way by his connection with or possession or ownership of the liquors and beverages, or any of them, then, within 10 days after conviction, without any order of the court to that effect, the custodian of the liquor or beverage is authorized to proceed and shall proceed to dispose of the same as provided in section 28-4-273. (Acts 1919, No. 7, p. 6; Code 1923, § 4773; Code 1940, T. 29, § 242.)

Provisions of this section are mandatory.
Nelson v. State, 23 Ala. App. 437, 126 So. 607 (1930).

§ 28-4-296. Deposit with alcoholic beverage control board for sale of certain confiscated liquors and beverages; payment to county or municipality by board of reasonable value of liquors and beverages received.

(a) All confiscated liquors and beverages which the alcoholic beverage control board will accept shall not be destroyed but shall be deposited with the alcoholic beverage control board for resale. All other liquors and beverages shall be disposed of as otherwise provided by law.

(b) The alcoholic beverage control board shall immediately upon receipt of such liquors or beverages determine the reasonable value of the amount thereof and issue its warrant for the payment of same to the custodian of the county funds in the county where seized or, if seized by municipal law-enforcement officers, then to the custodian of funds of the municipality, payable to the general fund of the county or the municipality as the case may be.

(c) Nothing in this section shall apply to liquors or beverages illegally made, manufactured or distilled in an unlicensed distillery, brewery or winery, and all such liquors or beverages shall be disposed of as otherwise provided by law. (Acts 1973, No. 1224, p. 2071.)

Collateral references. — 48 C.J.S., Intoxicating Liquors, § 403.

§ 28-4-297. Unlawful disposition, etc., of contraband liquors and beverages by custodian.

Any custodian of seized contraband liquor and beverages who shall permit the same to be improperly and unlawfully removed from his possession or shall give the same away to any person shall be punished, on conviction, by a fine of not less than $50.00 and by imprisonment at hard labor for the county for six months. (Acts 1919, No. 7, p. 6; Code 1923, § 4774; Code 1940, T. 29, § 243.)

§ 28-4-298. Article not intended to secure search of premises of bona fide druggists or physicians.

This article is not intended to secure the search of the premises of bona fide druggists who sell or keep for sale alcohol only for medical, scientific or mechanical purposes or wine for sacramental purposes as authorized by law or of bona fide physicians who sell and keep for sale pure alcohol only for medical purposes at the places that may be allowed and subject to the restrictions and regulations prescribed by law. (Acts 1909, No. 191, p. 63; Acts 1915, No. 2, p. 8; Code 1923, § 4751; Code 1940, T. 29, § 220.)

§ 28-4-299. Forfeiture, sale and distribution of proceeds of sale of contraband generally.

In cases of all contraband property, as provided in this article, there shall be a remedy by complaint filed in the name of the state by the officer or other person, in accordance with any provisions of the prohibition laws of the state, to secure a judgment of forfeiture, sale and distribution of the proceeds in accordance with the provisions of this article.

If the arrest and seizure of such property is made by an officer or employee of any municipality of this state, such municipality shall receive one half of the remainder of the proceeds derived from the sale of such property, after the costs and expenses (including payment to officers and informers provided for in this article) are paid. The said portion of the moneys derived from such proceeds shall be paid into the treasury of such municipality and used and applied as a law-enforcement fund, under the supervision and control of the governing body of such municipality, and the remaining half shall be paid to the law-enforcement fund in the state treasury. (Acts 1919, No. 7, p. 6; Code 1923, § 4784; Code 1940, T. 29, § 253.)

ARTICLE 12.

ENFORCEMENT OF CHAPTER.

§ 28-4-310. Governor charged with supervision, etc., of enforcement of prohibition laws; governor may require reports from officers charged with duty of enforcing laws; failure of officer to make report, etc.

In order for the governor to perform the duties imposed upon him by the Constitution, that he shall take care that the laws be faithfully executed, he is made the executive head of the law-enforcement machinery of the state and is charged with supervising and directing the enforcement of the laws of the state for the promotion of temperance and the suppression of the evils of intemperance and he is authorized to supervise, direct and give orders to any and all officers of the state or of any county in the state in regard to the exercise of their powers in the performance of their duties in respect to the enforcement of said laws.

The governor may, as he deems desirable, call upon said officers for reports to be made directly to him concerning any action they may have or may not have taken in enforcing said laws and for reports concerning conditions that may exist, calling for increased diligence in reference to said law enforcement, and all such officers shall strictly obey his orders and directions and make any reports called for and, in the event of a failure to do so or to carry out any instruction of the governor in respect to the enforcement of said laws, shall be guilty of a misdemeanor in office and may be punished, on conviction, by a fine not exceeding $50.00 and by imprisonment not exceeding 12 months at hard labor for the county, to be fixed in the discretion of the court or judge trying the case. (Acts 1919, No. 7, p. 6; Code 1923, § 4790; Code 1940, T. 29, § 259.)

§ 28-4-311. Appointment of inspectors, etc., to detect and report violations of prohibition laws; offer and payment of rewards for convictions of persons violating laws.

The governor may appoint and employ, subject to the provisions of the merit system, such inspectors or secret service men or such other persons as he may deem necessary for the purpose of detecting and reporting upon violations of the prohibition laws, or any of them, and contract with them for reasonable compensation to be paid by the state for their services. He may also offer a reward to all sheriffs, constables or other persons, in his discretion, who will bring about the conviction of any person for the violation of said laws and particularly for the violation of the laws against the manufacture of prohibited liquors, and may state the amount that will be paid out of the state treasury to any officer or person who may secure the conviction of anyone guilty of the offense of illicit distilling or other violation of said laws. In the

823

event such reward or rewards are earned, the same shall be paid by warrant drawn by the comptroller upon the state treasury or the law-enforcement fund therein provided by this chapter, as the governor decides, upon a bill presented against the state for the reward, stating the facts and circumstances which the claimant puts forward as entitling him to the reward, when the said bill is certified and approved as being correct by the attorney general of the state and is also approved by the governor. (Acts 1919, No. 7, p. 6; Code 1923, § 4791; Code 1940, T. 29, § 260.)

§ 28-4-312. Governor may require attorney general to prepare instructions for officers of state, etc., for enforcement of laws; publication and distribution of same.

The governor, in his discretion, may require the attorney general to prepare instructions to the officers of the state, counties or municipalities to aid them in enforcing the prohibition laws, to be published and distributed at the expense of the state, as directed by the governor. (Acts 1919, No. 7, p. 6; Code 1923, § 4792; Code 1940, T. 29, § 261.)

§ 28-4-313. Prosecutions for violations of chapter, etc., begun by affidavit or indictment; right of person charged to demand grand jury indictment; continuation of prosecution upon original affidavit; amendment of affidavit or complaint.

All prosecutions for a violation of any provision of this chapter or of any other law for the suppression of the evils of intemperance may be begun by affidavit as well as by indictment; and when begun by affidavit, the person charged shall not have the right to demand that a grand jury prefer an indictment for the alleged offense, except where such offense is a felony, but the prosecution may continue no matter in what court or before what judge the trial shall be had upon the affidavit upon which it was originally begun.

The said affidavit or any complaint that may be filed in such prosecution may be amended to meet the ends of justice and to prevent a dismissal of the case upon any informality, irregularity or technicality. (Acts 1909, No. 191, p. 63; Acts 1915, No. 2, p. 8; Code 1923, § 4646; Code 1940, T. 29, § 121.)

I. General Consideration.
II. Amendment.

I. GENERAL CONSIDERATION.

Affidavit or indictment is necessary to sustain conviction. — Under this section a conviction for violating prohibition law cannot be sustained, in absence of affidavit or indictment charging defendant with offense. Jacobs v. State, 24 Ala. App. 122, 130 So. 905 (1930).

Circuit court was without jurisdiction to try and determine liquor prosecution, in absence of indictment or affidavit upon which prosecution was begun. Woodham v. State, 28 Ala. App. 62, 178 So. 464 (1938).

Filing of complaint on appeal is unnecessary. — Under this section in prosecution for violating liquor laws, filing of complaint on appeal from inferior court to circuit court is unnecessary. Johnson v. State, 21 Ala. App. 623, 111 So. 50 (1926); Barlow v. State, 22 Ala. App. 288, 115 So. 73 (1928); Pappas v. City of Eufaula, 23 Ala. App. 485, 127 So. 263 (1930); Irwin v. State, 24 Ala. App. 181, 132 So. 69 (1931); St. John v. State, 24 Ala. App. 450, 137 So. 42 (1931); Aldridge v. State, 24 Ala. App. 582, 139 So. 119 (1932); Johnson v. State, 27 Ala. App. 190, 168 So. 602 (1936); Crooks v. State, 31 Ala. App. 308, 15 So. 2d 913 (1943).

All prosecutions for the violation of the prohibition laws may be begun by affidavit, and when begun by affidavit (in misdemeanor cases) the prosecution may continue no matter in what court or before what judge the trial shall be had upon the affidavit upon which it was originally begun. Cantor v. State, 27 Ala. App. 40, 165 So. 597 (1936).

Filing in circuit court of transcript showing conviction for violating prohibition law transferred case for trial de novo. Gilbert v. State, 25 Ala. App. 169, 142 So. 682 (1932).

In prosecution for selling intoxicating liquor on election day, where defendant was convicted in district court and again in circuit court on appeal, and affidavit in district court was in proper form and substantially followed language of section, complaint filed in circuit court was unnecessary and defendant was not prejudiced by misspelled word contained therein. Cusimano v. State, 31 Ala. App. 99, 12 So. 2d 418 (1943).

But may be done. — District attorney could, but was not required to, file complaint on appeal in circuit court from conviction in inferior court where liquor prosecution was had upon affidavit. McGee v. State, 25 Ala. App. 305, 145 So. 587 (1933).

Where accused who was convicted appealed, complaint in circuit court was unnecessary, by reason of this section, and omission in that complaint of date of alleged liquor violation contained in original affidavit and warrant did not constitute new charge against accused. Wilson v. State, 27 Ala. App. 38, 166 So. 715 (1935).

Venue. — Under this section the fact that complaint did not allege venue of offense could not be raised for first time on appeal. St. John v. State, 24 Ala. App. 477, 136 So. 862 (1931).

Cited in Hauser v. State, 6 Ala. App. 31, 60

So. 549 (1912); Hall v. State, 19 Ala. App. 178, 95 So. 904 (1923); Collins v. State, 22 Ala. App. 323, 118 So. 264 (1928); Hammons v. State, 25 Ala. App. 48, 140 So. 627 (1932); Pearson v. City of Huntsville, 42 Ala. App. 458, 168 So. 2d 24 (1964).

Collateral references. — 48 C.J.S., Intoxicating Liquors, § 306.

II. AMENDMENT.

Correction of informality or technicality on appeal. — In view of this section any informality or technicality in an affidavit, on which a prosecution is begun, may be corrected in the circuit court on appeal when no substantial rights of the defendant are affected. Richardson v. State, 21 Ala. App. 639, 111 So. 202 (1925).

Extent of amendment. — An affidavit cannot be amended to such an extent as to be a departure from the original affidavit. Broglan v. State, 17 Ala. App. 403, 86 So. 164 (1920).

Defect cured by amendment. — Defect in affidavit by which prosecution was commenced, in failing to charge substantive offense in certain alternative averments thereof, which defect was pointed out, was cured by amendment to affidavit eliminating defective alternative averments, under this section. Sadler v. State, 23 Ala. App. 269, 123 So. 294 (1929).

Name cannot be corrected after bar of limitations. — Under this section and § 15-3-2, failure to charge defendant with offense by correct name may not be corrected as matter of right over defendant's objection after bar of limitations. Lemley v. State, 24 Ala. App. 427, 136 So. 494 (1931).

When affidavit must be verified. — Under this section and § 15-3-2, where amendment of affidavit is made by insertion of material matter over defendant's objections, before bar of statute, affidavit must be verified. Lemley v. State, 24 Ala. App. 427, 136 So. 494 (1931).

Affidavit may be amended, being reverified by the original party making it, before the original officer before whom the affidavit was made. Spelce v. State, 17 Ala. App. 401, 85 So. 835 (1920).

It is not necessary to reverify a charge when an amendment to an affidavit is had under this section. Bell v. State, 21 Ala. App. 550, 109 So. 900 (1926).

§ 28-4-314. District attorneys to institute prosecutions for or make reports to grand juries as to violations of prohibition laws.

Any district attorney in the county whose duty it is to prosecute criminal cases on behalf of the state shall not be prohibited from commencing prosecution on his own affidavit against any party violating any provision of any law of the state of Alabama for the suppression of the evils of intemperance, and every such district attorney, upon receiving information giving him probable cause to believe that there has been a violation of any statute upon the subject named, shall proceed to lay the matter before the grand jury or to institute a criminal prosecution against said party by affidavit before a court or judge of competent jurisdiction, if he is willing and able to make such affidavit for the institution of a criminal prosecution. If he is not, he must superintend the preparation of the papers and the institution of the prosecution if any citizen is willing to make an affidavit for the institution of a criminal prosecution against any party for such violation; provided, that the district attorney is of opinion from the facts at hand that there is reasonable ground to believe that the offense has been committed. (Acts 1909, No. 191, p. 63; Acts 1915, No. 2, p. 8; Code 1923, § 4642; Code 1940, T. 29, § 117.)

§ 28-4-315. Sheriffs to cooperate with district attorneys in prosecutions, etc.

Sheriffs are charged with the duty of being on the alert for violations of any of the prohibition statutes and of cooperating with the district attorneys in bringing violators to justice. (Acts 1909, No. 191, p. 63; Code 1923, § 4643; Code 1940, T. 29, § 118.)

Sheriffs without search warrant were trespassers. — Charge that, if sheriff and deputy sheriff went onto defendant's premises to watch and see whether defendant was violating prohibition law, they were not trespassers, held prejudicially erroneous where officers had no search warrant. Wiggins v. State, 25 Ala. App. 192, 143 So. 188 (1932).

§ 28-4-316. Grand jury proceedings generally — Effect of failure of person to attend and testify in obedience to summons.

Any person who is summoned as a witness before the grand jury to answer as to any violation of law for the suppression of intemperance or prohibiting the manufacture, sale or other disposition of prohibited liquors or beverages or the keeping or maintaining of any unlawful drinking place, or liquor nuisance and who fails or refuses to attend and testify in obedience to such summons without good cause, to be determined by the court, is guilty of contempt and also of a misdemeanor and, on conviction of such misdemeanor, must be fined not less than $20.00 nor more than $300.00 and may also be imprisoned in the county jail or sentenced to hard labor for the county for not

more than three months, at the discretion of the court. (Acts 1909, No. 191, p. 63; Code 1923, § 4633; Code 1940, T. 29, § 109.)

Section limits and directs § 28-4-318. — Section 28-4-318 is addressed and limited to proceedings involving crimes of intemperance in dry counties by virtue of this section. Yarber v. State, 368 So. 2d 868 (Ala. Crim. App.), cert. denied, 368 So. 2d 871 (Ala. 1978).

§ 28-4-317. Same — Offenses as to which witnesses may be required to testify; initial interrogation of witnesses to particular offense not required.

The witnesses before the grand jury to give evidence may be required to answer generally as to any offense against the laws of Alabama for the promotion of temperance and the suppression of intemperance committed within their knowledge during the 12 months next preceding or as to any violation within said time of any law of the state prohibiting the manufacture, sale or other disposition of any of said prohibited liquors or beverages or the maintaining of any unlawful drinking place or liquor nuisance, and it shall not be necessary to first specially interrogate the witnesses to any particular offenses. (Acts 1909, No. 191, p. 63; Code 1923, § 4634; Code 1940, T. 29, § 110.)

§ 28-4-318. Same — Exemption from prosecution of witnesses.

A witness must not be prosecuted for any offense as to which he testifies before the grand jury, and the district attorney or any member of the grand jury may be a witness to prove that fact. (Acts 1909, No. 191, p. 63; Code 1923, § 4635; Code 1940, T. 29, § 111.)

This section is addressed and limited to proceedings involving crimes of intemperance in dry counties by virtue of § 28-4-316. Yarber v. State, 368 So. 2d 868 (Ala. Crim. App.), cert. denied, 368 So. 2d 871 (Ala. 1978).

Defendant, desiring to avail himself of immunity conferred by this section, must move to quash the indictment. Grace v. State, 22 Ala. App. 360, 115 So. 761 (1928).

Cited in Matson v. State, 27 Ala. App. 396, 173 So. 612 (1937); Gipson v. State, 375 So. 2d 504 (Ala. Crim. App. 1978).

§ 28-4-319. Same — Duty of grand jury to present indictments for violations of laws.

Grand juries shall have no discretion as to the finding of indictments for violations of the provisions of this chapter or for violations of the provisions of any law of the state for the promotion of temperance and the suppression of intemperance, and it shall be their duty, if the evidence justifies it, to find and present indictments for every such violation. (Acts 1909, No. 191, p. 63; Acts 1915, No. 2, p. 8; Code 1923, § 4637; Code 1940, T. 29, § 112.)

§ 28-4-320. Servants, agents, etc., and principals not to be excused from testifying against each other on grounds of self-incrimination; immunity of said persons from prosecution for offenses disclosed, etc.

No clerk, servant, agent or employee of any person accused of a violation of the laws to promote temperance and to suppress intemperance or prohibiting the sale, manufacture or other disposition of liquors or beverages shall be excused from testifying against his principal for the reason that he may thereby incriminate himself, nor shall any principal be excused for the same reason from testifying against any clerk, servant, agent or employee in such cases, but no testimony given by any of said parties shall in any manner in any prosecution be used as evidence, directly or indirectly, against him, nor shall the party testifying be thereafter prosecuted for any offense so disclosed by him. (Acts 1909, No. 191, p. 63; Acts 1915, No. 2, p. 8; Code 1923, § 4638; Code 1940, T. 29, § 113.)

Collateral references. — Necessity and sufficiency of assertion of privilege against self-incrimination as condition of statutory immunity of witness from prosecution. 145 ALR 1416.

§ 28-4-321. Contents and sufficiency of charges in indictments, complaints, affidavits, etc., for sale, offer for sale, possession, etc., of prohibited liquors and beverages, etc., generally; proof of charges generally; admissibility in evidence of testimony of persons purchasing, etc., prohibited liquors and beverages, etc.; immunity from prosecution of persons testifying as to violations of chapter, etc.

In an indictment, complaint or affidavit for selling, offering for sale, keeping for sale or otherwise disposing of spirituous, vinous or malt liquors, it is sufficient to charge that the defendant sold, offered for sale, kept for sale or otherwise disposed of spirituous, vinous or malt liquors contrary to law, and in an indictment, complaint or affidavit for selling, offering for sale, keeping for sale or otherwise disposing of prohibited liquors and beverages, it is sufficient to charge that the defendant sold, offered for sale, kept for sale or otherwise disposed of prohibited liquors and beverages. On the trial under a charge in either form, any act of selling in violation of law embraced in the charge may be proved and the charge in each of said forms shall be held to include any device or substitute for any of said liquors.

In any indictment, complaint or affidavit charging that prohibited liquors and beverages have been manufactured, sold, offered for sale, kept for sale or otherwise disposed of, it shall not be necessary to set out the kind or quantity of the prohibited liquors and beverages nor the person to whom such sale or offer to sell or other disposition was made, and in any prosecution for a second or subsequent offense, it shall not be requisite to set forth in the indictment, complaint or affidavit the record of a former conviction, but it shall be sufficient briefly to allege such conviction.

The person purchasing or to whom prohibited liquors and beverages or any of them have been sold or otherwise disposed of shall in all cases be a competent witness to prove the unlawful act.

No person who testifies with respect to any unlawful act under this chapter or other statute for the suppression of the evils of intemperance shall be prosecuted in respect to any act to which he testifies nor shall his evidence so given be used against him in any criminal proceeding. (Acts 1909, No. 191, p. 63; Code 1923, § 4644; Code 1940, T. 29, § 119.)

This section and § 28-4-322 do not authorize blanket charge of violating prohibition law, but require designation of offense, or of several related offenses, each sufficiently identified, in one indictment or affidavit. Slater v. State, 230 Ala. 320, 162 So. 130 (1935).

Sufficiency of affidavit. — An affidavit that substantially follows the section under which it is drawn is sufficient. Fitzpatrick v. State, 169 Ala. 1, 53 So. 1021 (1910); Armstrong v. State ex rel. Embry, 248 Ala. 124, 26 So. 2d 874 (1946).

Affidavit by which prosecution for violation of prohibition law was begun need not be signed. Bush v. State, 27 Ala. App. 30, 167 So. 335 (1935).

In McKinnon v. State, 24 Ala. App. 537, 137 So. 677 (1931), it was held that an affidavit in prosecution for possessing prohibited liquors was sufficient.

Sufficiency of indictment. — The term "otherwise dispose of" is specifically deemed by § 28-4-1 to include giving away and the indictment need not allege the name of the person to whom the gift was made. Grace v. State, 1 Ala. App. 211, 56 So. 25 (1911).

An indictment in the Code form is sufficient. Kelly v. State, 171 Ala. 44, 55 So. 141 (1911). See also Dillard v. State, 152 Ala. 86, 44 So. 537 (1907); Darrington v. State, 162 Ala. 60, 50 So. 396 (1909).

The statutes in regard to the prosecution of violators of the prohibition law are highly penal, but so far as the question of procedure is concerned the holding has been, in accordance with the language of this section, that the indictment or affidavit which substantially follows its provisions is sufficient. Armstrong v. State ex rel. Embry, 248 Ala. 124, 26 So. 2d 874 (1946).

An indictment charging in substantial conformity with section that accused did have in possession for sale whiskey contrary to law was sufficient. McPherson v. State, 29 Ala. App. 278, 196 So. 739 (1940).

When there is an allegation as to a former conviction in indictment for violation of prohibition laws, former conviction becomes an issue, evidence of it on trial is necessary for it to have operation, and a verdict of guilt justifies application of increased limits of punishment. Yates v. State, 245 Ala. 490, 17 So. 2d 777 (1944).

Cited in Noltey v. State, 225 Ala. 584, 144 So. 457 (1932); Slater v. State, 230 Ala. 320, 162 So. 130 (1935); Broadfoot v. State, 28 Ala. App. 260, 182 So. 411 (1938).

Collateral references. — 48 C.J.S., Intoxicating Liquors, §§ 307-338.

45 Am. Jur. 2d, Intoxicating Liquors, § 323 et seq.

Necessity of alleging in information or indictment that act was "unlawful." 169 ALR 166.

Evidence of identity for purposes of statute as to enhanced punishment in case of prior conviction. 11 ALR2d 870.

§ 28-4-322. Several charges may be set out in separate counts in indictments, complaints, etc.; judgment entered and punishment imposed upon each count.

Indictments, complaints or affidavits for any violation of this chapter or any provision thereof or of any other statute of the state for the suppression of the evils of intemperance may set out several charges in separate counts, and the accused may be convicted and punished upon each one as upon separate indictments, complaints or affidavits, and judgment shall be entered on each count under which there is a finding of guilty. (Acts 1909, No. 191, p. 63; Acts 1915, No. 2, p. 8; Code 1923, § 4645; Code 1940, T. 29, § 120.)

Sale or possession of prohibited liquors and of Jamaica ginger may be charged in same indictment in separate counts. Noltey v. State, 25 Ala. App. 229, 144 So. 455 (1932).

Cited in Slater v. State, 230 Ala. 320, 162 So. 130 (1935); Hill v. State, 30 Ala. App. 332, 5 So. 2d 651 (1942).

§ 28-4-323. Admissibility and effect of evidence showing similarity in color, odor and general appearance between prohibited liquor or beverage and beverage shown to be manufactured, sold, kept, etc., by defendant; applicability of rule as to admissibility, etc., of said evidence in proceedings for abatement of liquor nuisances, etc.

(a) In all prosecutions against any person for manufacturing, selling, offering for sale, keeping or having in possession for sale, bartering, exchanging, furnishing, giving away or otherwise disposing of prohibited liquors and beverages or for any one of the said acts, it shall be competent for the state to give in evidence the fact that the beverage which the evidence may tend to show the defendant had manufactured, sold, bartered, exchanged, furnished, given away or otherwise disposed of, possesses the same color, odor and general appearance or the same taste, color and general appearance of a prohibited liquor or beverage such as whiskey, rum, gin, ale, porter, beer and any other prohibited liquor or beverage. The fact that the beverage in question as above stated is of the same color, odor and general appearance or same taste, color and general appearance as beer shall constitute prima facie evidence that the beverage is a beer or a malt liquor or a substitute or device therefor and within the inhibition of the statutes of this state for the suppression of intemperance, and the like rule of evidence shall apply in respect to whiskey and the other beverages named, and, in the event the defendant claims that the beverage in question as above referred to is not within the inhibition of the statutes when it possesses the same color, odor and general appearance or the same taste, color and general appearance as a prohibited liquor or beverage, such as whiskey, beer or the other beverages named hereinabove, the burden of proof shall be upon him to establish to the reasonable satisfaction of the judge, court or jury trying the case that the beverage in question is not within the inhibition of the said statutes and that it is a beverage not prohibited by law to be manufactured, sold, offered for sale or otherwise disposed of.

(b) The same rule of evidence shall be applicable in all cases for the abatement of liquor nuisances and in all prosecutions for violations of statutes of the state for the suppression of the evils of intemperance when it becomes necessary to determine whether the liquor or beverage in question is a prohibited liquor or beverage. (Acts 1909, No. 191, p. 63; Acts 1915, No. 2, p. 8; Code 1923, § 4650; Code 1940, T. 29, § 125.)

Cross references. — As to abatement of liquor nuisances, see § 28-4-220.

Application of section to transportation of beverages. — This section applies to a prosecution for transporting alcoholic beverages in quantities of five gallons or more under § 28-4-115. Austin v. State, 36 Ala. App. 690, 63 So. 2d 283 (1953).

Sufficiency of proof of contents of bottles. — In prosecution for illegal possession of whiskey, evidence that defendant ran from officer and threw pint bottles of whiskey from his pockets, and that officer could tell from the smell that it was whiskey, was sufficient proof of illegal character of contents of the bottles. Gray v. State, 29 Ala. App. 568, 199 So. 255 (1940).

There was a prima facie case made out that the contents of bottles found in defendant's car were prohibited liquors, where an officer testified that he knew the smell and color of white and bonded whiskey and that he smelled the contents of the bottles and they were bonded whiskey. Kennedy v. State, 39 Ala. App. 676, 107 So. 2d 913 (1958).

Section affords no aid where liquor found in sealed can. — Cases under the five-gallon law all show a marked difference in requiring stricter proof of quantity from that permissible in mere possession cases. Nor does the "look like," "smell like," "taste like," statute (this section) afford any aid where the liquor claimed to be prohibited is found in an opaque unopened container, i.e., a sealed can. Blackwell v. State, 42 Ala. App. 246, 160 So. 2d 493 (1964).

Moral certainty of guilt of defendant. — Under this section state need not satisfy jury to moral certainty of defendant's guilt. Burrough v. State, 24 Ala. App. 374, 135 So. 651 (1931).

Cited in Dixon v. State, 39 Ala. App. 575, 105 So. 2d 354 (1958); Kennedy v. State, 39 Ala. App. 588, 106 So. 2d 257 (1958); Ivory v. State, 44 Ala. App. 91, 203 So. 2d 146 (1967).

Collateral references. — 48 C.J.S., Intoxicating Liquors, § 338.

45 Am. Jur. 2d, Intoxicating Liquors, § 375.

Test of intoxicating character of liquor. 4 ALR 1137, 11 ALR 1233, 19 ALR 512, 36 ALR 725, 91 ALR 513.

§ 28-4-324. Issuance of injunctions to prevent violations of chapter, etc.

When any violation of any provision of this chapter is threatened or shall have occurred, the doing of, or continuation or repetition of the unlawful act or any of like kind by the offending party may be prevented by injunction issued by a circuit court upon a petition filed in all respects as in cases of liquor nuisances.

In like manner the injunction may be employed to compel obedience to any rule or regulation prescribed by this chapter. (Acts 1915, No. 491, p. 553; Code 1923, § 4653; Code 1940, T. 29, § 128.)

Cross references. — As to abatement of liquor nuisances, see § 28-4-220. As to rules of supreme court relative to injunctions, see A.R.C.P., Rule 65.

§ 28-4-325. Fees of officers making seizures of prohibited liquors.

When an officer arrests any person in possession of an unlawful quantity or quantities of prohibited liquors or of such liquors under conditions prohibited by law, then, on the conviction of such party of a violation of a city ordinance or state law, whether in the municipal court or state court possessing jurisdiction, the following fee for making the seizure of the liquors shall be taxed against the defendant and paid to such officer as a part of the cost of the case:

(1) If a seizure is made of not less than one gallon nor more than five gallons of such liquors, the fee shall be $3.00;

(2) If the seizure is of more than five gallons and less than 20 gallons, the fee shall be $5.00; and

(3) If more than 20 gallons is seized, the fee shall be $10.00. (Acts 1915, No. 491, p. 553; Code 1923, § 4654; Code 1940, T. 29, § 129.)

Deputy sheriff's compensation. — When a deputy sheriff is performing the service for which this section provides compensation to the officer rendering same, he is acting in the name of the sheriff and performing a duty imposed by law upon the sheriff for which compensation is allowed. Jefferson County v. Dockerty, 249 Ala. 196, 30 So. 2d 474 (1947).

§ 28-4-326. Penalties for violations of chapter.

Any violation of any provision of this chapter for which no other penalty is provided shall be punishable by a fine of not less than $50.00 nor more than $500.00, to which may be added, in the discretion of the court, imprisonment in the county jail or at hard labor for the county for not less than six months nor more than 12 months. (Acts 1909, No. 191, p. 63; Acts 1915, No. 2, p. 8; Code 1923, § 4655; Code 1940, T. 29, § 130.)

Collateral references. — 48 C.J.S., Intoxicating Liquors, § 380.

CHAPTER 5.

REGULATION OF MANUFACTURE, SALE, ETC., OF INDUSTRIAL ALCOHOL.

Sec.
28-5-1. Definitions.
28-5-2. Authorization and procedure gener-
        ally for granting of permits for
        operation of alcohol distilleries
        and denaturing plants in connec-
        tion with sugar refineries.
28-5-3. Documents to be filed by applicants
        for permits.
28-5-4. Bonds of permittees.
28-5-5. Manufacture and sale of industrial
        alcohol by permittees generally.
28-5-6. Transportation of industrial alcohol
        manufactured and sold by permit-
        tees generally.
28-5-7. Sale, transportation, etc., of alcohol,
        etc., not authorized by federal or
        state permit; sale, transportation,
        etc., of denatured alcohol ren-
        dered unfit for beverage use.
28-5-8. Removal of denatured alcohol from
        industrial alcohol plant for pur-
        pose of recovering alcohol there-
        from for beverage purposes.
28-5-9. Governor to supervise enforcement of
        chapter; promulgation of regula-

Sec.
        tions, requirement of reports, etc.,
        suspension or revocation of per-
        mits, collection of penalties on
        bonds, etc., by governor; abate-
        ment of plant operating without
        permit.
28-5-10. Inspection and examination of plants
        and books and records of permit-
        tees; taking of samples for chemi-
        cal analysis.
28-5-11. Payment of fee by permittees to cover
        costs of inspection and supervi-
        sion; disposition of proceeds from
        fees; permittees to notify governor
        of changes in officers, directors,
        etc.
28-5-12. False statements in applications, etc.,
        forgery of permits, obstruction of
        enforcement of chapter, violation
        of terms of permits, etc.
28-5-13. Burden of proof as to existence of
        federal permit in prosecutions un-
        der chapter.
28-5-14. Penalties for violations of chapter.

§ 28-5-1. Definitions.

When used in this chapter, the following words and phrases shall have the following meanings, respectively, unless the context clearly indicates otherwise:

(1) INDUSTRIAL ALCOHOL. Ethyl alcohol and alcohol denatured as provided in this chapter.

(2) INDUSTRIAL ALCOHOL PLANT. The alcohol distillery, denaturing plant and all the premises used in connection therewith.

(3) PERMITTEE. The person, firm or corporation to whom the permit provided for in this chapter is issued. (Acts 1927, No. 474, p. 516; Code 1940, T. 29, § 79.)

§ 28-5-2. Authorization and procedure generally for granting of permits for operation of alcohol distilleries and denaturing plants in connection with sugar refineries.

Upon the filing with the governor of Alabama by any person, firm or corporation of an application to operate on any state-owned land that constitutes, in whole or in part, any plan of development by the state or its agency for the improvement or expansion of any of the harbors or seaports of the state an alcohol distillery and alcohol denaturing plant for the production of industrial alcohol solely for nonbeverage use, the governor may, in his discretion, grant a permit, as provided in this chapter, to such applicant to operate an alcohol distillery and alcohol denaturing plant, in connection with a sugar refinery, where the distillation of alcohol may be economically undertaken to conserve the by-product materials used in or incident to the operation of such sugar refinery; provided, that the applicant has or does secure, by lease, the right to occupy the premises described in the application.

No permit shall be granted to operate an alcohol denaturing plant away from the premises of the sugar refinery and the alcohol distillery where the alcohol is produced. (Acts 1927, No. 474, p. 516; Code 1940, T. 29, § 79.)

§ 28-5-3. Documents to be filed by applicants for permits.

The application filed with the governor for such permit shall be verified by affidavit and shall set forth the name and address of all parties having an interest in the proposed industrial alcohol plant or, if a corporation, shall set forth the name and address of its principal officers and directors and the names and addresses of the individuals owning 51 percent of the stock and the names and addresses of the individuals to be in charge of the plant.

Accompanying said application shall be an accurate plan and description of the premises and distilling apparatus, distinctly showing the location of every still, boiler, worm tub and receiving cistern, the course and construction of all pipes used or to be used in the distillery and every branch and every cock or joint thereof and of every valve therein, together with every place, vessel, tub or utensil from and to which any such pipe leads or with which it communicates and also the number and location and cubic content of every still, mash tub and fermenting tub, the cubic contents of every receiving cistern and the color of each fixed pipe.

There shall also be furnished a detailed description of the process employed at the plant, which will show the flow of material from the time received on the premises, through the various apparatus, into the locked receiving tanks and also a plat showing the line of the premises and location of buildings thereon; provided, that whenever the documents filed with the officers of the United States under the internal revenue laws and regulations pursuant thereto shall contain the foregoing information, the filing of a certified copy of such document or documents with the governor shall be deemed a sufficient compliance with this section. (Acts 1927, No. 474, p. 516; Code 1940, T. 29, § 80.)

§ 28-5-4. Bonds of permittees.

As a condition precedent to the granting of such permit, such person, firm or corporation shall file with the governor a bond payable to the state of Alabama, in the penal sum of $25,000.00, with surety to be approved by him, conditioned that such person, firm or corporation will not sell, barter, give away, deliver or remove any alcohol or liquid or compound containing alcohol or permit to be sold, bartered, given away, delivered or removed from such industrial alcohol plant any alcohol or liquid or compound containing alcohol in violation of the laws and regulations of the state and of the United States and will faithfully observe, keep, perform and be bound by any and all provisions, restraints and conditions of the laws of the state and of the United States concerning, affecting or regulating the manufacture, sale, transportation or delivery of alcohol and intoxicating liquors. This bond shall be renewed annually during the life of the permit provided for in this chapter. (Acts 1927, No. 474, p. 516; Code 1940, T. 29, § 81.)

§ 28-5-5. Manufacture and sale of industrial alcohol by permittees generally.

A permittee, as provided in this chapter, may manufacture and sell industrial alcohol solely for nonbeverage purposes to persons authorized by law to purchase the same, whether within or without the state, upon compliance with the laws of Alabama and of the United States and regulations issued thereunder relating to alcohol and intoxicating liquors. (Acts 1927, No. 474, p. 516; Code 1940, T. 29, § 82.)

§ 28-5-6. Transportation of industrial alcohol manufactured and sold by permittees generally.

Industrial alcohol manufactured and sold by a permittee, as provided by this chapter, may be transported and delivered to any person authorized by law to purchase the same for nonbeverage purposes upon compliance with the provisions of chapter 4 of this title. Whenever the consignee is without the state, the affidavit required by section 28-4-117 shall not be required. (Acts 1927, No. 474, p. 516; Code 1940, T. 29, § 83.)

§ 28-5-7. Sale, transportation, etc., of alcohol, etc., not authorized by federal or state permit; sale, transportation, etc., of denatured alcohol rendered unfit for beverage use.

It shall be unlawful for any permittee or for any officer, agent, employee or servant of such permittee or for any person to sell, deliver, transport or remove from the premises of an industrial alcohol plant any alcohol or liquid compound containing alcohol, except in compliance with a permit authorizing such sale, delivery, transportation or removal issued as required by the laws of the United States and the regulations issued thereunder and except as permitted by this chapter; provided, that no permit under this chapter shall be required for sale, delivery, transportation or removal from such industrial alcohol plant of denatured alcohol in accordance with formulas that may be provided by regulations of the United States government so as to render such alcohol unfit for beverage use. The container in which such denatured alcohol is transported shall be labeled "Denatured Alcohol." (Acts 1927, No. 474, p. 516; Code 1940, T. 29, § 87.)

§ 28-5-8. Removal of denatured alcohol from industrial alcohol plant for purpose of recovering alcohol therefrom for beverage purposes.

It shall be unlawful for any person to remove from an industrial alcohol plant any denatured alcohol for the recovery of the alcohol therefrom for beverage purposes or to redistill or by any other process to recover alcohol from denatured alcohol for beverage purposes. (Acts 1927, No. 474, p. 516; Code 1940, T. 29, § 88.)

§ 28-5-9. Governor to supervise enforcement of chapter; promulgation of regulations, requirement of reports, etc., suspension or revocation of permits, collection of penalties on bonds, etc., by governor; abatement of plant operating without permit.

It shall be the duty of the governor to supervise the enforcement of this chapter. The governor shall prescribe the form and fix the condition of all permits issued under this chapter and shall have authority to make regulations, require the keeping of the records and the filing of reports to give effect to the provisions of this chapter and shall have the right, after notice and hearing, to suspend or revoke such permit for the violation of any law or regulation by the permittee or by his or its officers, agents, employees or servants in connection with the privilege granted by such permit. Upon the breach of any of the conditions of the bond required by this chapter, the governor shall collect the penalty of the bond. No permit issued under this chapter shall grant any privilege inconsistent with the laws of the United States.

Any industrial alcohol plant operating without a valid permit issued by the governor, as required by this chapter, may be abated as a nuisance in a civil action brought in a court of competent jurisdiction. (Acts 1927, No. 474, p. 516; Code 1940, T. 29, § 84.)

§ 28-5-10. Inspection and examination of plants and books and records of permittees; taking of samples for chemical analysis.

The governor or any officer designated by him shall have the right, at any hour, to enter and inspect the premises of any industrial alcohol plant to examine the books and records of such permittee, to see that the laws relating to alcohol and intoxicating liquors are being observed and to take from the products found on the premises such samples as may be required for the purpose of chemical analysis. (Acts 1927, No. 474, p. 516; Code 1940, T. 29, § 85.)

§ 28-5-11. Payment of fee by permittees to cover costs of inspection and supervision; disposition of proceeds from fees; permittees to notify governor of changes in officers, directors, etc.

Every permittee, upon obtaining a permit under this chapter and annually thereafter, shall pay to the treasurer a fee of $1,000.00 to cover the cost of inspection and supervision of the operation of such industrial alcohol plant, which amount shall be accounted for as a separate fund, and the proceeds after the payment of all expenses of administration shall be paid into the general fund of the state.

Upon any change in the officers, directors or controlling interest of any permittee under this chapter, it shall be the duty of such permittee to promptly notify the governor of such change. (Acts 1927, No. 474, p. 516; Code 1940, T. 29, § 86.)

§ 28-5-12. False statements in applications, etc., forgery of permits, obstruction of enforcement of chapter, violation of terms of permits, etc.

It shall be unlawful for any permittee or for any officer, agent, employee or servant of such permittee to violate the terms of any permit or regulations issued under this chapter, or to make any false statement in any application, record or report required by the chapter, or to forge any permit required by this chapter, or to hinder or obstruct any officer charged with the duty of enforcing the provisions of this chapter, or to use any of the machinery, vats, pipes or other paraphernalia connected with such industrial alcohol plant, except as authorized by this chapter or the permit issued thereunder, or to remove or permit the removal of any mash, alcohol or liquid or compound containing alcohol from the premises of any alcohol manufacturing plant, except as provided in this chapter and in accordance with the regulations authorized in this chapter. (Acts 1927, No. 474, p. 516; Code 1940, T. 29, § 90.)

§ 28-5-13. Burden of proof as to existence of federal permit in prosecutions under chapter.

In any prosecution under this chapter where the defendant relies for justification upon a permit issued under the laws of the United States, the burden shall be upon him to prove the same. (Acts 1927, No. 474, p. 516; Code 1940, T. 29, § 89.)

§ 28-5-14. Penalties for violations of chapter.

Any officer, director, agent, servant or employee of any corporation or any other person who shall violate any of the provisions of this chapter shall be deemed guilty of a felony and, upon conviction, shall be punished by confinement in the penitentiary for not less than one nor more than three years. (Acts 1927, No. 474, p. 516; Code 1940, T. 29, § 91.)

CHAPTER 6.

REGULATION OF PRODUCTION, SALE, ETC., OF NATIVE FARM WINE.

Sec.
28-6-1. Definitions.
28-6-2. Sale of native farm wine lawful; license required.
28-6-3. To whom sales authorized.
28-6-4. Privilege license tax imposed; excise tax levied; exception; monthly re-

Sec.
    port and remittance; application to import fruit, etc., when not available; deposit of taxes.
28-6-5. Use of stamps authorized; rules and regulations.
28-6-6. Construction of chapter.

§ 28-6-1. Definitions.

When used in this chapter, the following words and phrases shall have the following meanings, respectively, unless the context clearly indicates otherwise:

(1) NATIVE FARM WINERY. A winery where the annual production does not exceed 100,000 gallons, and 75 percent or more of the berries, fruit, produce or honey used in the manufacture of such wine is grown and produced in Alabama by the native farm winery permit holder upon land owned or leased by the permit holder in the vicinity of his farm winery.

(2) NATIVE FARM WINE. Any product having an alcohol content not to exceed 14 percent by volume and made in accordance with the revenue laws of the United States, which is produced on a native farm winery.

(3) PERSON. One or more natural persons, or a corporation, partnership or association.

(4) BOARD. The Alabama alcoholic beverage control board. (Acts 1979, No. 79-182, p. 291, § 1.)

§ 28-6-2. Sale of native farm wine lawful; license required.

It shall be lawful to produce native farm wine in the state of Alabama and to sell such native farm wine within or without the state. Every native farm winery in the state of Alabama shall apply for a license as provided for in section 28-3A-6. (Acts 1979, No. 79-182, p. 291, § 2.)

§ 28-6-3. To whom sales authorized.

Every native farm winery is hereby authorized to make sales to the board, directly to consumers for off-premises consumption, to alcoholic beverage permit holders of the board, including but not limited to wholesale dealers and distributors, stores, hotels, restaurants, clubs, dining cars and to any producer, manufacturer, wholesaler, retailer or consumer located outside the state of Alabama. (Acts 1979, No. 79-182, p. 291, § 3.)

§ 28-6-4. Privilege license tax imposed; excise tax levied; exception; monthly report and remittance; application to import fruit, etc., when not available; deposit of taxes.

(a) Upon every manufacturer holding a license for the production of native farm wine, there is hereby levied and imposed for the privilege of engaging in the manufacture of native farm wine an annual privilege license tax in the amount of $25.00 which shall be paid to the board.

(b) There is hereby levied and assessed an excise tax upon each case of native farm wine sold by a manufacturer to any source to be collected from the manufacturer in an amount equal to $.05 per gallon. However, native farm wine produced in Alabama for export and sale without this state shall not be subject to said excise tax, but such tax shall accrue or be collected on native farm wines dispensed, as free samples in quantities of not more than six ounces, in the tasting room or wine cellar of a native farm winery. The excise tax provided for in this section shall be in lieu of all other taxes imposed.

(c) The privilege tax imposed by subsection (a) of this section shall be collected in the same manner as presently provided by law for the collection of other taxes on alcoholic beverages. The excise tax imposed by subsection (b) of this section shall be reported monthly by the producer to the board on all sales made in Alabama to the board, retailers, consumers or any alcoholic beverage permit holder of the board, along with a statement of gallonage produced during that month, and the producer shall remit the tax due and owing with each report. The producer shall also include in the report a statement of gallonage sold and exported for sale outside this state.

(d) Provided that such fruit, produce or honey used in the manufacture of native Alabama wine is not available in Alabama due to an act of God, the holder of a farm winery permit may apply to the Alabama alcoholic beverage control board for permission to import such produce.

(e) All taxes imposed, levied and collected under this section shall be deposited in the same manner as are other taxes collected by the board. (Acts 1979, No. 79-182, p. 291, § 4.)

§ 28-6-5. Use of stamps authorized; rules and regulations.

The board may in its discretion direct that stamps purchased at cost from the board be affixed to the cartons, bottles or containers as a means of identification. The board shall promulgate rules and regulations as needed to protect the revenue of Alabama derived from the excise tax on native farm wine. (Acts 1979, No. 79-182, p. 291, § 5.)

§ 28-6-6. Construction of chapter.

The provisions of this chapter are supplemental. It shall be construed in pari materia with other laws regulating this subject; however, those laws or parts of laws which are in direct conflict or inconsistent herewith are hereby repealed. (Acts 1979, No. 79-182, p. 291, § 7.)

CHAPTER 7.

IMPORTATION, DISTRIBUTION AND SALE OF TABLE WINE.

Sec.
28-7-1.   Short title.
28-7-2.   Legislative intent; purpose of chapter.
28-7-3.   Repealed.
28-7-4.   By and to whom table wine may be sold.
28-7-5.   Authority of board to issue licenses; county or municipal approval.
28-7-6.   Application for license; filing fee, license fee and bond.
28-7-7.   Issuance of license, generally.
28-7-8.   Wine retailer's license.
28-7-9.   Wine wholesaler's license; bond.
28-7-10. Wine importer license; restrictions on sale and operation; registration of labels; seizure of unregistered goods; monthly reports; inspection.
28-7-11. Wine manufacturers license; registration of labels; seizure of unregistered goods; monthly reports.
28-7-12. License renewal.
28-7-13. License fees; local license taxes; payment and distribution of license and filing fees.

Sec.
28-7-14. Regulation of grant of licenses; display thereof; separate retail licenses for each place of sale; restrictions on wholesaler's operations; transfer of licenses; filing fee for transfer; effect of insolvency of licensee.
28-7-15. Suspension or revocation of licenses and fines; notice, hearing and findings of fact.
28-7-16. Tax on sale of table wine; amount; collection; disposition of proceeds; exclusive; exemption.
28-7-17. Regulations of board; evidence thereof.
28-7-18. Sales by manufacturers.
28-7-19. Sales by wholesalers.
28-7-20. Sales by retailers.
28-7-21. Repealed.
28-7-22. Interlocking businesses and interests prohibited.
28-7-23. Advertising.
28-7-24. Repealer; application of certain taxes.

Cross references. — As to the sale of table wine by wine retailers in certain counties, see § 28-3-168.

The Table Wine Act (this chapter) is neither repealed nor modified, either expressly or impliedly, by the provisions of the Alcoholic Beverage Licensing Code. The statutes should be construed in pari materia, and where there exists a conflict between the two, the more specific provisions of the Table Wine Act will control. City of Tuscaloosa v. Alabama Retail Ass'n, 466 So. 2d 103 (Ala. 1985).

The general repealing clause found in section 27 of the act creating the Alcoholic Beverage Licensing Code cannot operate to repeal the Table Wine Act except to repeal by implication any conflicting portions of the Table Wine Act, and it has been consistently held that repeal by implication is never favored by the courts. City of Tuscaloosa v. Alabama Retail Ass'n, 466 So. 2d 103 (Ala. 1985).

Conflict between chapter 3A and chapter 7 not irreconcilable. — Because the "conflict" between chapter 3A and chapter 7 of this title does not rise to the degree of irreconcilability, each statute may be given a reasonable field of operation, which will, when they are construed together, give effect to the legislative intent and purpose of both enactments. Although the specific will control the general, the overall purpose of the general statute will not be thwarted by giving effect to the specific statute. City of Tuscaloosa v. Alabama Retail Ass'n, 466 So. 2d 103 (Ala. 1985).

The Alcoholic Beverage Licensing Code (chapter 3A) is a comprehensive statute which deals with the licensing of those engaged in transactions involving alcoholic beverages; and, while it is comprehensive, it is, by the very nature of its own broad scope, a general statute. The Table Wine Act (chapter 7), however, is a statute enacted to further a specific legislative intent and deals exclusively with transactions involving table wine; thus, it is a specific statute. City of Tuscaloosa v. Alabama Retail Ass'n, 466 So. 2d 103 (Ala. 1985).

Collateral references. — 48 C.J.S. Intoxicating Liquors, §§ 99-190.

45 Am. Jur. 2d, Intoxicating Liquors, §§ 114-219.

§ 28-7-1. Short title.

This chapter shall be known as and may be cited as the "Alabama Table Wine Act." (Acts 1980, No. 80-382, p. 505, § 1.)

Cross references. — As to the definitions applicable to this chapter, see § 28-3-1.

§ 28-7-2. Legislative intent; purpose of chapter.

The public interest lying in the promotion of temperance by and through the proper regulation of alcoholic beverages, through the instrumentality of the Alabama alcoholic beverage control board and otherwise, it is the intent of the legislature and declared to be the purpose and intent of this chapter to promote temperance and to further regulate the sale of alcoholic beverages in the state by distinguishing between fortified wine or vinous liquor having more than 14 percent alcohol by volume and table wine having not more than 14 percent alcohol by volume, which is hereby declared to be nonliquor and not vinous liquor, and specifically to authorize and regulate the sale and handling of table wine in Alabama by wine manufacturers, wholesalers and retailers licensed by the board. (Acts 1980, No. 80-382, p. 505, § 2.)

Collateral references. — 48 C.J.S., Intoxicating Liquors, §§ 12, 13.
45 Am. Jur. 2d, Intoxicating Liquors, § 13.

§ 28-7-3. Repealed by Acts 1986, No. 86-212, § 3, which became law without the governor's signature under § 125 of the Constitution on April 1, 1986.

Cross references. — As to the definitions applicable to this chapter, see now § 28-3-1.

§ 28-7-4. By and to whom table wine may be sold.

Table wine may be sold in any county in Alabama which is now wet or may hereafter be designated a wet county pursuant to law, as follows:

(1) A licensed wine manufacturer may sell table wine to any wine wholesaler or importer licensed to sell wine or to the board;

(2) A licensed wine importer may sell table wine to any wine wholesaler licensed to sell wine or to the board or state;

(3) A licensed wine wholesaler may sell, at wholesale only, table wine that has been purchased from a licensed manufacturer or importer to a licensed wine retailer or to a licensee of the board or other person lawfully authorized to sell wine in this state, or for export;

(4) A licensed wine retailer may sell table wine at retail for off-premises consumption only; provided, however, a licensee of the board authorized to sell at retail alcoholic beverages for on-premises consumption may sell table

wine at retail for consumption on-premises and off-premises. (Acts 1980, No. 80-382, p. 505, § 4.)

§ 28-7-5. Authority of board to issue licenses; county or municipal approval.

The board shall have full and final authority, with the approval of the county or municipal governing body, to issue and renew licenses of wine retailers, wholesalers, importers and manufacturers to sell and handle table wine in this state. Licenses issued under this chapter to wine retailers, wholesalers, importers or manufacturers shall, unless revoked in the manner provided in this chapter, be valid for the license year which shall begin on the 1st day of October of each year. (Acts 1980, No. 80-382, p. 505, § 5.)

§ 28-7-6. Application for license; filing fee, license fee and bond.

Every applicant for a wine retailer's or wholesaler's license shall file a written application with the board in such form as the board may prescribe, which shall be accompanied by the appropriate license fee as prescribed in this chapter and, in the case of an original application, by a filing fee of $50.00, together with the amount or amounts of the prescribed license fee or fees, if any, levied by the county or counties in which the licensee operates, and, in the case of a wholesaler, accompanied by the bond required by section 28-7-9. (Acts 1980, No. 80-382, p. 505, § 6.)

§ 28-7-7. Issuance of license, generally.

Upon receipt of the application, the proper fees, the bond, if required, and upon being satisfied of the truth of the statements in the application and the applicant is a person of good repute the board shall grant and issue to the applicant a wine retailer's or wine wholesaler's license entitling the applicant to sell or distribute table wine in this state as set forth in section 28-7-4. (Acts 1980, No. 80-382, p. 505, § 7.)

§ 28-7-8. Wine retailer's license.

Upon applicant's compliance with section 28-7-6, the board shall issue a wine retailer's license for any retail outlet kept or operated by a wine retailer for the retail sale of table wines for off-premises consumption. (Acts 1980, No. 80-382, p. 505, § 8.)

§ 28-7-9. Wine wholesaler's license; bond.

Upon applicant's compliance with section 28-7-6, the board shall issue to applicant a wine wholesaler's license which will authorize the licensee to import and receive shipments of table wine from outside the state from licensed wine manufacturers, to purchase table wine from licensed wine manufacturers or importers within the state, and to sell table wine to licensed wine retailers and all licensees or others within this state lawfully authorized to sell wine in this state, and to export table wine from the state. In addition, the applicant shall file with his original application a bond in the penal sum of not less than $1,000.00 nor more than $10,000.00 conditioned upon the payment of the taxes to be collected by the wine wholesaler and remitted to the board. (Acts 1980, No. 80-382, p. 505, § 9.)

§ 28-7-10. Wine importer license; restrictions on sale and operation; registration of labels; seizure of unregistered goods; monthly reports; inspection.

(a) Upon applicant's compliance with section 28-7-6, the board shall issue to applicant an importer license which shall authorize the licensee to import table wine manufactured outside the United States of America into this state or for sale or distribution within this state table wine to the board or the state, and table wine to wholesaler licensees of the board. No person shall import table wine manufactured outside the United States into this state or for sale or distribution within this state or to the state, the board or any licensee of the board, unless such person shall be granted an importer license issued by the board.

(b) An importer licensee shall not sell any table wine for consumption on the premises where sold; nor, unless issued a wholesale license, sell or deliver to any retailer; nor deliver any such table wine in other than original containers approved as to capacity by the board, and in accordance with standards of fill prescribed by the U. S. treasury department; nor maintain or operate within the state any place or places, other than the place or places covered by his or its importer license, where table wine is sold or where orders are taken.

(c) Each importer licensee shall be required to file with the board, prior to making any sales in Alabama, a list of its labels to be sold in Alabama and shall file with the board its federal certificate of label approvals or its certificates of exemption as required by the U. S. treasury department. All table wine whose labels have not been registered as herein provided for shall be considered contraband and may be seized by the board or its agents, or any peace officers of the state of Alabama without a warrant and said goods shall be delivered to the board and disposed of as provided by law.

(d) All such importer licensees shall be required to mail to the board prior to the twentieth day of each month a consolidated report of all shipments of table wine made to each wholesaler during the preceding month and of all shipments of table wine received during the preceding month. Such reports shall be in such form and containing such information as the board may prescribe.

(e) The books and records of such licensee shall, at all times, be open to inspection by members of the board, or by a person duly authorized and designated by the board. Members of the board and its duly authorized agents shall have the right, without hindrance, to enter any place which is subject to inspection hereunder, or any place where such records are kept for the purpose of making such inspections and making transcripts thereof.

(f) Licenses issued under this section shall, unless revoked or suspended in the manner provided in this chapter, be valid for the license year commencing January 1 of each year. (Acts 1980, No. 80-382, p. 505, § 10.)

§ 28-7-11. Wine manufacturers license; registration of labels; seizure of unregistered goods; monthly reports.

Every manufacturer, or its designated representative, desiring to sell table wines in or for resale in this state shall register with the board prior to making any such sales.

Each such manufacturer, or its designated representative, shall be required to file with the board, prior to making any sales in Alabama a list of its labels to be sold in this state and shall file with the board its federal certificate of label approvals or its certificates of exemption as required by the U.S. treasury department. All table wines whose labels have not been registered as herein provided for shall be considered contraband and may be seized by the board or its agents, or any peace officer of the state of Alabama without a warrant and said goods shall be delivered to the board and disposed of as contraband alcohol as provided by law.

All such manufacturers, or their designated representatives, shall be required to mail to the board prior to the tenth day of the month a consolidated report of all shipments of table wine made to each wine wholesaler or importer in Alabama during the preceding month. Such reports shall be certified as true and correct and shall be a complete listing of all items shipped, an invoice setting out the quantities purchased and the price quotation showing at what price such wines were sold, the size, type, brand label and point of destination and such other information as the board may prescribe. (Acts 1980, No. 80-382, p. 505, § 11.)

§ 28-7-12. License renewal.

The wine retailer's, wine wholesaler's and wine manufacturer's license herein provided for shall be required to be renewed annually and shall be reissued upon payment to the board of the appropriate license fee or fees, unless the board has good cause for not reissuing the license. (Acts 1980, No. 80-382, p. 505, § 12.)

§ 28-7-13. License fees; local license taxes; payment and distribution of license and filing fees.

(a) *License fees for licenses issued by the board.* — The following annual license fees are levied and prescribed for licenses issued and renewed by the board pursuant to the authority contained in this chapter:

(1) Wine retailer's license, license fee of $150.00.

(2) Wine wholesaler's license, license fee of $550.00.

(3) Wine importer's license, license fee of $500.00.

(4) Wine manufacturer's license, license fee of $500.00.

In addition, the county or municipality therein in which the wholesaler, importer or retailer sells or distributes table wine may fix a reasonable privilege or license tax on a wine wholesaler, importer or retailer located therein, conditioned on a permit or license being issued by the board. Provided, however, said county or municipality shall levy no license or privilege tax, or other charge for the privilege of doing business as a wine wholesaler, importer or retailer, which shall exceed one-half the amount of the state license fee levied under the provisions of this section for like privilege.

(b) *Payment, collection and administration.* — All license and filing fees levied or authorized by this chapter, other than those levied by a municipality, shall be paid to the board. All filing and license fees paid to the board shall be paid into the state treasury to the credit of the beer tax and license fund of the board and each month's receipts shall be distributed to the state general fund no later than the end of the following month. All license fees levied by any county and paid the board shall be paid not later than the last day of the month following the month of collection to the county governing body which shall distribute the proceeds thereof. (Acts 1980, No. 80-382, p. 505, § 13.)

§ 28-7-14. Regulation of grant of licenses; display thereof; separate retail licenses for each place of sale; restrictions on wholesaler's operations; transfer of licenses; filing fee for transfer; effect of insolvency of licensee.

(a) No license prescribed in this chapter shall be issued or renewed until the provisions of this chapter have been complied with and the filing and license fees other than those levied by a municipality are paid to the board.

(b) Every license issued under this chapter shall be constantly and conspicuously displayed on the licensed premises.

(c) Any wine retailer may be granted licenses to maintain, operate or conduct any number of places for the sale of table wine, but a separate license must be secured for each place where table wine is sold. Provided there shall be no licenses issued by the board for the sale of wine by rolling stores.

(d) A malt or brewed beverage wholesale licensee may also be granted a wine wholesaler's license. No wine wholesaler shall maintain or operate any place where sales are made other than that for which the license is granted. No wine wholesaler shall maintain any place for the storage of table wine unless the same has been approved by the board. No wine wholesaler's license shall be issued for any premises in any part of which there is operated any retail license for the sale of liquor, wine, malt or brewed beverages.

(e) Licenses shall be granted by the board only to reputable individuals, or to associations, partnerships and corporations whose members or officers and directors are reputable individuals.

(f) Licenses issued under this chapter may not be assigned. The board is hereby authorized to transfer any license from one person to another, or from one place to another within the same municipality, or both, as the board may determine; but no transfer shall be made to a person who would not have been eligible to receive the license originally, nor for the transaction of business at a place for which the license could not originally have been issued lawfully.

(g) Every applicant for a transfer of a license shall file a written application with the board within such time as the board shall fix in its regulations. Whenever any license is transferred, there shall be collected a filing fee of $10.00, to be paid to the board for the use of the state.

(h) In the event that any person to whom a license shall have been issued under the terms of this chapter shall become insolvent, make an assignment for the benefit of creditors, become a bankrupt by either voluntary or involuntary action, the license of such person shall immediately terminate and be cancelled without any action on the part of the board, and there shall be no refund made, or credit given, for the unused portion of the license fee for the remainder of the license year for which said license was granted. Thereafter no license shall be issued by the board for the premises, wherein said license was conducted, to any assignee, committee, trustee, receiver or successor of such licensee until a hearing has been held by the board as in the case of a new application for license. In all such cases, the board shall have the sole and final discretion as to the propriety of the issuance of a license for such premises, and to the time it shall issue, and the period for which it shall be issued, and shall have the further power to exact conditions under which said licensed premises shall be conducted. (Acts 1980, No. 80-382, p. 505, § 14.)

§ 28-7-15. Suspension or revocation of licenses and fines; notice, hearing and findings of fact.

(a) The board shall have full and final authority as to the suspension and revocation of any license issued hereunder. In lieu of suspension or revocation, the board shall have the authority, in the case of a wine retailer, to invoke a penalty of not less than $250.00 nor more than $500.00 for one or more of the following violations of this chapter:

(1) Selling wine other than during the legal hours of sale; or

(2) Selling wine to a minor.

(b) The board upon sufficient cause being shown or proof being made that any licensee holding a license issued by the board, or any partners, members, officers or directors of the licensee has or have violated any of the provisions of this chapter relating to the sale and handling of table wine and any of the laws of this state relating to the manufacture, sale, possession or transportation of malt or brewed beverages, alcohol or other alcoholic beverages, other than table wine, may upon due notice and proper hearing being given to the person so licensed, suspend or revoke the license issued by the board under the provisions of this chapter. In all cases where the board shall suspend or revoke a license, it shall set forth its findings of fact, the evidence from which such findings of fact are made, and the reasons upon which its action is based. Any licensee whose license is revoked by the board shall be ineligible to have a license under this chapter, until the expiration of one year from the date such license was revoked. (Acts 1980, No. 80-382, p. 505, § 15.)

Collateral references. — Criminal liability of member or agent of private club or association, or of owner or lessor of its premises, for violation of state or local liquor or gambling laws thereon. 98 ALR3d 694.

Tavernkeeper's liability to patron for third person's assault. 43 ALR4th 281.

§ 28-7-16. Tax on sale of table wine; amount; collection; disposition of proceeds; exclusive; exemption.

(a) *Levy.* — There is hereby levied in addition to the license taxes provided for by this chapter and municipal and county license taxes and in addition to any marked-up price made by the board on wine sold by the board a privilege or excise tax measured by and graduated in accordance with the volume of sales of table wine and shall be an amount equal to $.45 per liter of table wine sold to the wholesale licensee or board, to be collected from the purchaser by the board or by a licensed retailer.

(b) *Collection.* — The tax levied by subsection (a) of this section shall be added to the sales price of all table wine sold and shall be collected from the purchasers. The tax shall be collected in the first instance from the wholesaler where table wine is sold or handled by wholesale licensees, and by the board from whomever makes sales when table wine is sold by the board. It shall be unlawful for any person who is required to pay the tax in the first instance to fail or refuse to add to the sales price and collect from purchaser the required amount of tax, it being the intent and purpose of this provision that the tax levied is in fact a levy on the consumer. The person who pays the tax in the first instance is acting as an agent of the state for the collection and payment of the tax and as such may not collect a tax on table wine for any other level of government.

The tax hereby levied shall be collected by a monthly return, which shall be filed by the wholesale licensees as follows: a monthly return filed with the board not later than the fifteenth day of the second month following the month of receipt of table wine by the wholesaler on a form prescribed by the board showing receipts by the wholesalers from manufacturer, importer or other wholesaler licensees during the month of receipt and the taxes due thereon at the rate of $.38 per liter of table wine sold to the wholesale licensee or board; and the taxes due at such rate shall be remitted to the board along with the return; a monthly return filed with the county or municipality within which the wine is sold at retail filed not later than the fifteenth day of each month showing sales by wholesalers during the preceding month and the county or municipality in which sold and the taxes due thereon at the rate of $.07 per liter of table wine sold; and the taxes due at such rate shall be remitted to the county or municipality along with the return.

The tax hereby levied shall be collected by the board on the table wine sold by the board and shall be paid as follows: taxes at the rate of $.38 per liter of table wine sold shall be remitted by the board into the state treasury and taxes at the rate of $.07 per liter of table wine sold shall be remitted by the board to the county or municipality within which the wine was sold at retail not later than the last day of the month following the month of sale, as set forth in subsection (c) of this section.

The board and the governing body of each county and municipality served by the wholesaler shall have the authority to examine the books and records of any person who sells, stores or receives for the purpose of distribution any table wine, to determine the accuracy of any return required to be filed with it.

(c) *Disposition of proceeds.* — The proceeds of the tax levied by subsection (a) of this section shall be paid and distributed as follows:

(1) Thirty-eight cents per liter of table wine sold shall be collected by the board on its sales or paid to the board by wholesale licensees on their sales, and by the board paid into the state treasury to be credited as net profits from operation of the board to be distributed as provided by law.

(2) Seven cents per liter of table wine sold shall be paid by the board on its sales or by wholesale licensees on their sales, either into the treasury of the municipality in which the table wine was sold at retail within its corporate limits, or, where sold outside the corporate limits of any municipality, into the treasury of the county in which the table wine was sold at retail.

(d) *Tax exclusive.* — The tax herein levied is exclusive and shall be in lieu of all other and additional taxes and licenses of the state, county or municipality, imposed on or measured by the sale or volume of sale of table wine; provided, that nothing herein contained shall be construed to exempt the retail sale of table wine from the levy of tax on general retail sales by the state, county or municipality in the nature of, or in lieu of, a general sales tax.

(e) *Trade between wholesalers exempt.* — The tax levied by subsection (a) of this section shall not be imposed upon the sale, trade or barter of table wine by one licensed wholesaler to another wholesaler licensed to sell and handle table wine in this state, which transaction is hereby made exempt from said tax; provided, however, the board may require written reporting of any such transaction in such form as the board may prescribe. (Acts 1980, No. 80-382, p. 505, § 16; Acts 1983, No. 83-594, p. 927, § 1.)

§ 28-7-17. Regulations of board; evidence thereof.

The board may from time to time make such regulations not inconsistent with this chapter and the purpose and intention thereof as it shall deem necessary for carrying out the provisions of this chapter, and from time to time alter, repeal or amend such regulations, or any of them.

Prima facie evidence of any such regulation may be given in all courts and proceedings by the production of what purports to be an official printed copy of such regulation, alteration, repeal or amendment. (Acts 1980, No. 80-382, p. 505, § 17.)

§ 28-7-18. Sales by manufacturers.

No manufacturer shall sell any table wine direct to any retailer or for consumption on the premises where sold, nor sell or deliver any such table wine in other than original containers, nor shall any manufacturer maintain or operate within this state any place or places, other than the place or places covered by his or its license where table wine is sold or where orders therefor are taken. Provided, further, that table wine which is manufactured in Alabama where 75 percent or more of the fruit or produce used in the manufacture of such wine is grown in Alabama, may be sold directly at retail by the licensed manufacturer only on the manufacturer's premises, for on-premise or off-premise consumption. (Acts 1980, No. 80-382, p. 505, § 18.)

§ 28-7-19. Sales by wholesalers.

No wine wholesaler shall purchase, receive or resell any table wine except in the original container as prepared for the market by the manufacturer. (Acts 1980, No. 80-382, p. 505, § 19.)

§ 28-7-20. Sales by retailers.

No wine retailer shall purchase or receive any table wine except from the board or from wine wholesalers duly licensed under this chapter. All table wines must be received by the wine retailer in original containers as prepared for the market by the manufacturer. Wine retailers may sell or dispense at retail to be consumed off the premises only. On-premises retail licensees may break the bulk upon the licensed premises and sell or dispense at retail to be consumed on the premises, or sell or dispense at retail in original containers to be consumed on or off the premises. (Acts 1980, No. 80-382, p. 505, § 20.)

§ 28-7-21. Repealed by Acts 1986, No. 86-563, § 2, effective April 30, 1986.

Cross references. — As to unlawful acts
and offenses, see § 28-3A-25.

§ 28-7-22. Interlocking businesses and interests prohibited.

No manufacturer and no officer or director of any manufacturer shall, at the
same time, be a wine wholesaler or retailer, or an officer, director or
stockholder or creditor of any wine wholesaler or retailer, nor except as
hereinafter provided, be the owner, proprietor or lessor of any place covered
directly or indirectly by any wine wholesaler's license or wine retailer's
license or other retail license authorizing the sale of wine in this state.

No wine wholesaler and no officer or director of any wine wholesaler shall
at the same time be a manufacturer or wine retailer, or be an officer, director,
stockholder or creditor of a manufacturer or wine retailer, or be the owner,
proprietor or lessor of any place covered by any retail table wine license.

No licensee licensed under this chapter, shall directly or indirectly own any
stock of, or have any financial interest in, any other class of business licensed
under this chapter.

Excepting as hereinafter provided, no wine manufacturer or wholesaler
shall in anywise be interested, either directly or indirectly in the ownership or
leasehold of any property, or in any mortgage against the same, for which a
liquor or wine retailer's license is granted; nor shall a wine manufacturer or
wholesaler either directly or indirectly, lend any moneys, credit or equivalent
thereof to any retailer in equipping, fitting out or maintaining and conducting, either in whole or in part, an establishment or business operated under a
wine retailer's or liquor retail dispensers' license, excepting only the usual
and customary credits allowed for returning packages or containers in which
table wine was packed for market by the manufacturer.

Excepting as hereinafter provided, no manufacturer shall in anywise be
interested, directly or indirectly, in the ownership or leasehold of any
property, or any mortgage lien against the same, for which a wine wholesaler's license is granted, nor shall a manufacturer, either directly or
indirectly, lend any moneys, credit or their equivalent to any wine wholesaler
in equipping, fitting out, or maintaining and conducting, either in whole or in
part, an establishment or business where table wines are licensed for sale by a
wine wholesaler, excepting only the usual credits allowed for the return of
packages or containers in which table wines were originally packed for the
market by the manufacturer.

No wine wholesaler or retailer shall in anywise, either directly or
indirectly, receive any credit, loan, moneys or the equivalent thereof from any
other licensee, or from or through a subsidiary or affiliate of another licensee
or from a firm, association, or corporation, except banking institution in
which another licensee or any officer, director or firm member of another
licensee has a substantial interest or exercises a control of its business policy
for equipping, fitting out, payment of license fee, maintaining and conducting,

either in whole or in part, an establishment or business operated under a wine wholesaler's or retailer's license, excepting only the usual and customary credits allowed for the return of packages or containers in which table wines were packed for the market by the manufacturer.

The purpose of this section is to require a separation of the financial and business interest between the various classes of business regulated by this chapter, and no person or corporation shall by any device whatsoever, directly or indirectly, evade the provisions of this section. (Acts 1980, No. 80-382, p. 505, § 22.)

§ 28-7-23. Advertising.

No sign of any kind advertising table wine shall be displayed outside any retail place of business. Radio, television, newspaper, magazine, billboard and commercial vehicles used for transportation of table wine may be used to advertise table wine in accordance with rules and regulations issued by the board. No other advertising of table wine shall be permitted, except in accordance with rules and regulations issued by the board. Provided, however, that there shall be no advertising of table wine on billboards located in "dry" counties as defined in chapter 2 of this title. (Acts 1980, No. 80-382, p. 505, § 23.)

§ 28-7-24. Repealer; application of certain taxes.

All laws or parts of laws which conflict or are inconsistent with this chapter are hereby repealed. The taxes imposed by §§ 28-3-200, 28-3-201, 28-3-202, 28-3-203 and 28-3-204 do not apply to the sale of table wine; provided, that, nothing herein contained shall be construed to relieve any person from any tax liability, penalty or forfeiture incurred thereunder or under any local tax, county or municipal, hereby repealed, nor be construed to repeal any provision of law respecting the enforcement of any such tax liability, penalty or forfeiture incurred; provided further, that nothing herein contained shall be construed to repeal or as repealing chapter 6 of this title. (Acts 1980, No. 80-382, p. 505, § 25.)

CHAPTER 8.

EXCLUSIVE SALES TERRITORIES AND WHOLESALERS.

Sec.
28-8-1. Legislative policy and intent.
28-8-2. Designation of exclusive sales territory and exclusive wholesaler.
28-8-3. Territorial agreement may not establish or maintain resale price.
28-8-4. Modification of designated sales territory or territorial agreement.

Sec.
28-8-5. Wholesaler service and quality control.
28-8-6. Board verification of reporting and payment of taxes.
28-8-7. Definitions.
28-8-8. Unlawful acts and offenses; penalties.

§ 28-8-1. Legislative policy and intent.

Pursuant to the authority of this state under the Twenty-first Amendment to the United States Constitution, the policy and intent of the legislature in the enactment of this chapter are to further regulate and control alcoholic beverage transactions in Alabama under the control and supervision of the alcoholic beverage control board; to promote and assure the public's interest in fair and efficient distribution and quality control of alcoholic beverages in Alabama; to promote orderly marketing of alcoholic beverages; to promote vigorous inter-brand competition; and to facilitate collection of state and local revenue. (Acts 1984, No. 84-374, p. 876, § 1.)

§ 28-8-2. Designation of exclusive sales territory and exclusive wholesaler.

Each manufacturer or importer of alcholic beverages licensed by the board authorizing such licensee to sell its alcoholic beverages within the state of Alabama, whose alcoholic beverages are sold through wholesale licensees of the board to retail licensees of the board, shall designate exclusive sales territories for each of its brands sold in Alabama and shall name one licensed wholesaler for each such sales territory who, within such territory, shall be the exclusive wholesaler for said brand or brands; provided where a manufacturer or importer licensee has more than one brand of alcoholic beverages sold within this state, such licensee may designate the exclusive sales territory to a different wholesaler for the sale of each of its brands and may designate a different sales territory for each of its brands. Such manufacturer or importer licensee shall enter into a territorial agreement, in writing, designating the exclusive territory and authorizing the sale by a designated licensed wholesaler of that brand or brands within the designated territory. Such manufacturer or importer shall not designate more than one wholesaler for each brand for all or any part of a designated sales territory, and the written territorial agreement shall not provide for the distribution of a brand or brands to more than one licensed wholesaler for all or any part of the designated territory. All such territorial agreements shall be filed with the board. (Acts 1984, No. 84-374, p. 876, § 2.)

§ 28-8-3. Territorial agreement may not establish or maintain resale price.

No provision of any territorial agreement shall, expressly or by implication, or in its operation, establish or maintain the resale price of any brand or brands of alcoholic beverages by the wholesaler. (Acts 1984, No. 84-374, p. 876, § 3.)

§ 28-8-4. Modification of designated sales territory or territorial agreement.

No modification of either the designated sales territory or any territorial agreement shall be effective (i) until written notice thereof shall have been given by the manufacturer or importer to the wholesaler; (ii) until written notice thereof, together with the affidavit of the manufacturer stating that the level of service within the designated territory will not be adversely affected by the change, shall have been filed with the board; and (iii) until the board shall have verified that the level of service within the designated territory will not be adversely affected by the change. Provided, however, board verification shall not be required where the board has suspended or revoked the license of the wholesaler, shall not be unreasonably withheld and shall be completed within a reasonable time not to exceed 30 days from the date of filing with the board. The notice shall be given after recognizing all rights of the wholesaler and duties of the manufacturer or importer. Nothing in this chapter shall impair or alter contractual rights, duties or obligations of manufacturer, importer or wholesaler, including but not limited to the termination thereof. (Acts 1984, No. 84-374, p. 876, § 4.)

§ 28-8-5. Wholesaler service and quality control.

The wholesaler licensee designated as the exclusive wholesaler for a brand or brands within a designated territory must service retail licensees within that territory without discrimination, and shall service for the purpose of quality control all of the alcoholic beverages sold by that wholesaler to retailers within such territory. Each such wholesaler shall provide such additional quality control services and comply with such additional quality control standards as are specified in writing from time to time by the owner of the trademark of the brand or brands of alcoholic beverages, provided those activities or standards are reasonable and are reasonably related to the maintenance of quality control, and provided that the wholesaler has received written notice thereof. (Acts 1984, No. 84-374, p. 876, § 5.)

§ 28-8-6. Board verification of reporting and payment of taxes.

The board shall have the authority to inspect, examine and audit the books and records of any wholesaler licensee who sells, stores or receives for the purpose of distribution, any alcoholic beverages, to verify the proper filing and to determine the accuracy of any state or local tax return required to be filed by the wholesaler, and to determine the payment of all state and local taxes when and where due with respect to any state or local tax levied on alcoholic beverages by statute. In pursuance of said authority, the board shall have the further authority to inspect, examine and audit the books and records of any person, firm, corporation, club or association who sells at retail any alcoholic beverages. Provided, however, this section imposes no duty upon the board to inspect, examine and audit with respect to local taxes on alcoholic beverages. (Acts 1984, No. 84-374, p. 876, § 6.)

§ 28-8-7. Definitions.

The words and phrases used in this chapter shall have the meanings ascribed to them in section 28-3-1, and any acts amendatory thereof, supplementary thereto or substituted therefor. (Acts 1984, No. 84-374, p. 876, § 7.)

§ 28-8-8. Unlawful acts and offenses; penalties.

(a) *Unlawful acts and offenses.* — It shall be unlawful:

(1) For any manufacturer or importer licensed by the board to sell its brand or brands of alcoholic beverages in the state of Alabama to any person, except through the board in the case of spirituous liquor and wine, other than to a licensed wholesaler designated as the exclusive wholesaler for said brand or brands.

(2) For any wholesaler to sell to a retail licensee any brand of alcoholic beverages in the state of Alabama, except in the sales territory designated by the manufacturer or importer licensee and set forth in a written territorial agreement authorizing the sale by such wholesaler licensee of that brand within a designated territory; provided, however, a licensed wholesaler may, with the approval of the board, service a territory outside the territory designated to it during periods of temporary service interruptions when so requested by the manufacturer or importer and the designated wholesaler within such territory whose service is temporarily interrupted.

(3) For any wholesaler to sell to a retail licensee any brand of alcoholic beverages in the state of Alabama unless there is in effect a territorial agreement in writing between the licensed manufacturer or importer thereof and said licensed wholesaler authorizing the sale by such wholesaler of that brand within a designated territory.

(4) For any licensed retailer to purchase any brand of alcoholic beverages from any wholesaler which has not been designated by the licensed manufacturer or importer thereof as the wholesaler for such brand for the sales territory within which the retailer's place of business is located.

(b) *Penalties.* — Any violations of the provisions of this chapter subject the licensee to suspension or revocation of its license or to the levy of a fine in lieu of such suspension or revocation as set forth in section 28-3A-24. (Acts 1984, No. 84-374, p. 876, § 8.)

Code commissioner's note. — Acts 1985, No. 85-226 provides that the "legislative intent in enacting section 28-8-8, was to provide that it shall be unlawful for any wholesaler to sell to a retail licensee any brand of alcoholic beverages in the state of Alabama, except in, and for retail sale at the retailer's place of business in, the sales territory designated by the manufacturer or importer licensee and set forth in a written territorial agreement authorizing the sale of such wholesaler licensee of that brand within a designated territory (except in the case of temporary service interruptions); and for any licensed retailer to purchase any brand of alcoholic beverages from any wholesaler which has not been designated by the licensed manufacturer or importer thereof as the wholesaler for such brand for the sales territory within which is located the retailer's place of business where such purchased alcoholic beverages are to be sold at retail by the retailer to the consumer, or to purchase or acquire alcoholic beverages from another retail licensee or another licensed premises of the same retailer." The act further provides that the Alabama alcoholic beverage control board must carry out the legislative intent.

7759

CODE OF ALABAMA
1975

1995 Cumulative Supplement

ANNOTATED

Prepared by

The Editorial Staff of the Publishers

Under the Direction of

D. S. Tussey, R. W. Walter, W. L. Jackson, M. A. Sancilio,
J. H. Runkle, and L. A. Burckell

VOLUME 16

1986 REPLACEMENT VOLUME

*Including Acts through the 1995 Regular Session and
annotations taken through Southern Reporter,
Second Series, Volume 652, page 1133*

**Place in Pocket of Corresponding Volume of Main Set.
This Supersedes Previous Supplement, Which
May Be Retained for Reference Purposes.**

The Michie Company
Law Publishers
Charlottesville, Virginia
1995

Preface

The general and permanent laws of the State of Alabama, as enacted during the 1995 Regular Session of the Legislature which are contained in the 1995 Cumulative Supplement to certain volumes of the Code and in the 1995 Replacement Volumes of the Code, although operative on their effective dates, will not be adopted and incorporated into the Code of Alabama 1975 until the passage of the annual codification act. The annual codification act is usually passed the year following the current legislative session. As to previous years' codification acts, see Volume 1 of this set.

THIS SUPPLEMENT CONTAINS

Constitutions:

All amendments to the Alabama Constitution of 1901 ratified through September 1, 1995.

All amendments proposed to the Alabama Constitution of 1901 which are subject to referendum and which had not been voted upon as of September 1, 1995.

Statutes:

All laws of a general and permanent nature enacted by the Alabama Legislature through the 1995 Regular Session of the Legislature. Local laws and general laws of local application are not included in this supplement.

Rules of Alabama Supreme Court:

Rules promulgated by the Supreme Court of Alabama through September 1, 1995.

Annotations:

Annotations or constructions of Alabama statutes and the 1901 Constitution of Alabama and amendments thereto by the Alabama Supreme Court, the Alabama Courts of Appeal, the Supreme Court of the United States and other federal courts, taken from the following:

Southern Reporter, Second Series, through volume 652, p. 1133.
Federal Reporter, Third Series, through volume 51, p. 287.
Federal Supplement, through volume 879, p. 1340.
Federal Rules Decisions, through volume 160, p. 274.
Bankruptcy Reporter, through volume 179, p. 985.
Supreme Court Reporter, through volume 115, p. 1731.
Opinions of the Clerk of the Supreme Court of Alabama.

References to:

Corpus Juris Secundum.
American Jurisprudence, Second Edition.
American Law Reports, First Series.
American Law Reports, Second Series.
American Law Reports, Third Series.
American Law Reports, Fourth Series.
American Law Reports, Fifth Series.

Cross references to related provisions of the Code and the Alabama Constitution of 1901.

References to applicable or related federal statutes.

Tables:

Acts of Legislature to 1975 Code.

Index:

A supplement to the general index to the statutes, constitutional amendments and rules contained in this supplement and the bound volumes of the Code of Alabama.

User's Guide

In order to assist both the legal profession and the layman in obtaining the maximum benefit from the Code of Alabama, a User's Guide has been included in Volume 1. This guide contains comments and information on the many features found within the Code of Alabama intended to increase the usefulness of this set of laws to the user. See Volume 1 of this set for the complete User's Guide.

CODE OF ALABAMA

1995 Cumulative Supplement

TITLE 27.

INSURANCE.

TABLE OF CONTENTS

CHAPTER

3. Authorization of Insurers, §§ 27-3-1 through 27-3-33.
3A. Health Care Service Utilization Review Act, §§ 27-3A-1 through 27-3A-6.
4A. Insurance Premium Tax, §§ 27-4A-1 through 27-4A-7.
5A. Reinsurance Intermediaries, §§ 27-5A-1 through 27-5A-12.
6A. Managing General Agents, §§ 27-6A-1 through 27-6A-8.
6B. Business Transacted with Producer Controlled Property and Casualty Insurer Law, §§ 27-6B-1 through 27-6B-6.

CHAPTER

21B. Medical Support Health Care Access Act, §§ 27-21B-1 through 27-21B-9.
30. Mutual Aid Associations, §§ 27-30-1 through 27-30-34.
31A. Risk Retention Act, §§ 27-31A-1 through 27-31A-15.
45. Pharmaceutical Insurance Coverage, §§ 27-45-1 through 27-45-20.
46. Certified Registered Nurse Anesthetist Coverage, §§ 27-46-1 through 27-46-3.
47. Long-term Care Insurance Contracts, §§ 27-47-1 through 47-47-3.

Group insurer is required to notify participant of cancellation or modification of policy if the interests of the participant are adversely affected thereby. Newton v. United Chambers Insured Plans, 485 So. 2d 1147 (Ala. 1986).

Collateral references.

Liability insurance coverage for violations of antipollution laws. 87 ALR4th 444.

CHAPTER 1.

GENERAL PROVISIONS.

Sec.

27-1-10.1. Insurance coverage for drugs to treat life-threatening illnesses.
27-1-16. Standard health insurance claim form; electronic claims form; various claim forms.

Sec.

27-1-19. Reimbursement of health care providers.

§ 27-1-10. Payment for health services of chiropractor; insured to have exclusive right to select practitioner of healing arts.

Cited in Mullenix v. Aetna Life & Cas. Ins. Co., 912 F.2d 1406 (11th Cir. 1990).

§ 27-1-10.1. Insurance coverage for drugs to treat life-threatening illnesses.

(a) The Legislature finds and declares the following:

(1) The citizens of this state rely upon health insurance to cover the cost of obtaining health care and it is essential that the citizens' expectation that their health care costs will be paid by their insurance policies is not disappointed and that they obtain the coverage necessary and appropriate for their care within the terms of their insurance policies.

(2) Some insurers deny payment for drugs that have been approved by the Federal Food and Drug Administration, hereafter referred to as FDA, when the drugs are used for indications other than those stated in the labelling approved by the FDA, off-label use, while other insurers with similar coverage terms do pay for off-label use.

(3) Denial of payment for off-label use can interrupt or effectively deny access to necessary and appropriate treatment for a person being treated for a life-threatening illness.

(4) Equity among employers who obtain insurance coverage for their employees and fair competition among insurance companies require that insurance companies assure citizens reimbursement for drugs in the same way and in the way citizens expect.

(5) Off-label use of an FDA-approved drug is legal when prescribed in a medically appropriate manner and is often necessary to provide needed care. Approximately 50% of cancer drug treatment is for off-label indications. The FDA and the Federal Department of Health and Human Services recognize the wide variety of effective uses of FDA-approved drugs for off-label indications. Information on the appropriate off-label use of FDA-approved drugs is obtained from compendia published by the United States Pharmacopoeial Convention, the American Medical Association, and the American Society of Hospital Pharmacists. In addition, scientific studies of off-label use of drugs published in recognized peer-reviewed professional journals provide information on appropriate use of drugs for off-label indications. The Omnibus Budget Reconciliation Act of 1990 recognizes these three compendia and peer-reviewed literature as appropriate sources for reimbursement and requires Medicaid agencies to pay for off-label use of drugs prescribed for Medicaid patients if the use is stated in any of such sources. The Omnibus Budget Reconciliation Act of 1993 applies the same criteria and coverage to Medicare patients.

(6) Use of FDA-approved drugs for off-label indications provides efficacious drugs at a lower cost. To require that all appropriate uses of a drug undergo approval by the FDA would substantially increase the cost of drugs and delay or even deny patients' ability to obtain medically effective treatment. FDA approval for each use would require substantial expenditure and time to undergo the clinical trials necessary to obtain FDA approval. This is particularly the case when a drug is off-patent and in generic production, and consequently is available at a lower price. Once a drug is in

generic production by multiple manufacturers, it is not economically feasible for a manufacturer to incur the cost of FDA approval.

(7) Reimbursement for off-label indications of FDA-approved drugs is necessary to conform to the way in which appropriate medical treatment is provided, to make needed drugs available to patients, and to contain health care costs.

(b) The following words and phrases used in this section shall have the following meanings:

(1) CONTRAINDICATION. The potential for, or the occurrence of, an undesirable alteration of the therapeutic effect of a given prescription because of the presence, in the patient for whom it is prescribed, of a disease condition or the potential for, or the occurrence of, a clinically significant adverse effect of the drug on the patient's disease condition.

(2) INDICATION. Any symptom, cause, or occurrence in a disease which points out its cause, diagnosis, course of treatment, or prognosis.

(3) INSURANCE POLICY. An individual, group, blanket, or franchise insurance policy, insurance agreement, or group hospital service contract providing for hospital, medical, surgical, or pharmaceutical services.

(4) MEDICAL LITERATURE. Published scientific studies published in any peer-reviewed national professional journal.

(5) STANDARD REFERENCE COMPENDIA. Any of the following:

   a. The United States Pharmacopeia Drug Information.

   b. The American Medical Association Drug Evaluations.

   c. The American Hospital Formulary Service Drug Information.

(c)(1) Title 27, or any other provision of law, rule, or regulation to the contrary notwithstanding, it is specifically provided that:

   a. No insurance policy which provides coverage for drugs shall exclude coverage of a drug for a particular indication on the ground that the drug has not been approved by the Federal Food and Drug Administration for that indication, if the drug is recognized for treatment of that indication in one of the standard reference compendia, or in the medical literature, or by the Commissioner of Insurance.

   b. Coverage of a drug required by this section shall also include medically necessary services associated with the administration of the drug.

(2) This section shall not be construed to alter existing law with regard to provisions limiting the coverage of drugs that have not been approved by the Federal Food and Drug Administration.

(3) This section shall not be construed to require coverage for any drug when the Federal Food and Drug Administration has determined its use to be contraindicated.

(4) This section shall not be construed to require coverage for experimental drugs not otherwise approved for any indication by the Federal Food and Drug Administration.

(5) The Commissioner of Insurance may direct any person who issues an insurance policy to make payments required by this section.

(6) Nothing in this section shall be construed, expressly or by implication, to create, impair, alter, limit, modify, enlarge, abrogate, or prohibit reimbursement for drugs used in the treatment of any other disease or condition. (Acts 1994, 1st Ex. Sess., No. 94-805, p. 121, §§ 1-3.)

Effective date. — The act which added this section became effective May 6, 1994.

§ 27-1-12. Penalty for violation of title.

Cited in National Union Fire Ins. Co. v. Lomax Johnson Ins. Agency, Inc., 496 So. 2d 737 (Ala. 1986).

Collateral references. — Credit life insurer's punitive damage liability for refusing payment. 55 ALR4th 246.

§ 27-1-15. Payment for services of podiatrist.

Cited in Silver v. Baggiano, 804 F.2d 1211 (11th Cir. 1986).

§ 27-1-16. Standard health insurance claim form; electronic claims form; various claim forms.

(a)(1) The Commissioner of the Department of Insurance shall prescribe a standard health insurance claim form to be used by all hospitals. The forms shall be prescribed in a format which allows for the use of generally accepted diagnosis and treatment coding systems by providers of health care and payors. The standard form shall be accepted and used by all insurers doing business in the State of Alabama and by all state agencies which pay providers of health care for hospital services.

(2) The Commissioner of the Department of Insurance shall also prescribe a format for all health insurance claims transmitted or submitted for payment by electronic or electro-mechanical means. Such a format shall be used by all insurers doing business in the State of Alabama and by all state agencies which pay providers of health care for hospital services.

(b) An advisory committee of five persons, two appointed by the Alabama Hospital Association, two by the Health Insurance Association of America, and one by an Alabama nonprofit corporation which markets health insurance, shall advise the commissioner on an acceptable standard health insurance claim form and an electronic or electro-mechanical claims form no later than 60 days prior to January 1, 1982. If changes in the forms need to be made at any future time, the Commissioner of the Department of Insurance shall inform the advisory committee and the committee shall make recommendations as to the changes.

(c) All insurers doing business in Alabama and all state agencies shall accept, for services from physicians licensed to practice medicine, the Uniform Health Insurance Claim Form approved by the Council on Medical Service of the American Medical Association. Nothing in this section shall be construed to prohibit an insurer or state agency from accepting any other health insurance claim form for services provided by a physician licensed to practice medicine.

(d) Every third party prescription program serving patients in Alabama shall utilize the Universal Pharmacy Billing Claim form or format used by pharmacists billing for their services. Information required on the universal prescription claim form, either hard copy or electronic, shall be in compliance with the National Council on Pharmaceutical Drug Plan standards. If a provider, due to the location of the pharmacy, cannot comply with electronic claims submission requirements, then the prescription program shall allow the pharmacy to submit claims via hard copy. Pharmacy providers and recipients shall be given at least 45 days advance notice regarding changes in procedures and benefits.

(e) All insurers doing business in Alabama and all state agencies shall accept for services from dentists licensed to practice dentistry, the Uniform Dental Claim form approved by the Council on Dental Care Programs of the American Dental Association. Nothing in this section shall be construed to prohibit an insurer or state agency from accepting any other dental insurance claim form for services provided by a dentist licensed to practice dentistry.

(f) The foregoing provisions shall not apply to the Alabama Medicaid Agency. (Acts 1981, No. 81-292, p. 374; Acts 1993, No. 93-310, § 1.)

The **1993 amendment,** effective May 3, 1993, in subsection (a), in subdivision (1), substituted "The forms" for "Such forms" in the second sentence, and substituted "The standard" for "Such standard" in the third sentence; substituted "shall make" for "will make" in the second sentence of subsection (b); and added subsections (d) through (f).

§ 27-1-17. Limitation period for payment of claims under health and accident insurance policies; payment of interest; right of action for recovery of unpaid benefits.

This section does not apply where the insurer's reasons for denying the claim, although ultimately rejected by the court, are based on a "legitimately debatable dispute between the parties." Jordan v. National Accident Ins. Underwriters, Inc., 922 F.2d 732 (11th Cir. 1991).

Burden of proof. — An insured who successfully litigates is statutorily entitled to compensation for the insurer's detention of the policy proceeds. The insurer who denies a claim for "valid and proper" reasons does so at the risk that the judiciary will subsequently determine that those reasons were, in fact, not "valid and proper." Should there be such a judicial determination, this section places the burden on the insurer and provides the insured with the specified one and one-half percent per month rate of interest to compensate for the insurer's withholding of the policy proceeds. Jordan v. Reliable Life Ins. Co., 589 So. 2d 699 (Ala. 1991).

Validity of claim. — The legislature has not granted insurance companies the power to make conclusive decisions with regard to whether a claim is valid and proper. A grant of such a power would surely be contrary to what is the statute's policy of improving the insured's position relative to that of the insurer. Jordan v. Reliable Life Ins. Co., 589 So. 2d 699 (Ala. 1991).

Denial of health or accident claim. — The rate of interest specified in this section does apply when an insurer denies a health or accident claim based on a defensible interpretation of case law that is ultimately rejected by the court. Jordan v. Reliable Life Ins. Co., 589 So. 2d 699 (Ala. 1991).

After a loss is fixed, a policy of insurance becomes a contract for the payment. Georgia Cas. & Sur. Co. v. White, 582 So. 2d 487 (Ala. 1991).

Cited in Jordan v. National Accident Ins. Underwriters Inc., 948 F.2d 1218 (11th Cir. 1991).

§ 27-1-18. Contract providing for mental health services to entitle insured to reimbursement for outpatient and inpatient services by qualified psychiatrist or psychologist.

Collateral references. — What constitutes mental illness or disorder, insanity, or the like, within provision limiting or excluding coverage under health or disability policy. 19 ALR5th 533.

§ 27-1-19. Reimbursement of health care providers.

(a) All persons, firms, corporations, associations, health maintenance organizations, health insurance service, or preferred provider organizations, nonprofit health service organizations, and any employer sponsored health benefit company providing health, accident, dental, or workmen's compensation insurance coverage, either directly or indirectly through an agent, shall reimburse health care providers, including physicians, dentists, pharmacists, podiatrists, chiropractors, optometrists, durable medical equipment and home care providers, or subscribers for covered services within 25 working days of receipt of a proper claim or invoice at the office of the insurer or its designated office.

(b) If a provider of insurance coverage fails to comply with subsection (a), then interest shall be payable on the claim commencing on the 26th day of receipt of the claim at a rate of 1.5 percent per month or any part of a month thereof until the claim has been paid, without any further action by the provider being required except as provided in subsection (c).

(c) This section does not apply to claims where there is a dispute regarding the legitimacy of the claim, and the company or agency does both of the following:

(1) Notifies the provider within 2 weeks of the receipt of the claim that the claim is in dispute, and specifies which items of the claim are in dispute.

(2) Pays any undisputed portion of the claim within 30 days of receipt of the claim and makes a timely, good faith effort to resolve differences.

(d) The insured, or health or dental plan beneficiary may assign reimbursement for health or dental care services directly to the provider of services. Health benefits include medical, pharmacy, podiatric, chiropractic, optometric, durable medical equipment and home care services. The company or agency, when authorized by the insured, or health or dental plan beneficiary, shall pay directly to the health care provider the amount of the claim, under the same criteria and payment schedule that would have been reimbursed directly to the contract provider, and any applicable interest. This amount only applies to assigned claims. Any company or agency making a payment to the insured, or health or dental plan beneficiary, after the rights of reimbursement have been assigned to the provider of services, shall be liable to the provider for the payment. If the company or agency fails to reimburse the provider in accordance with the terms of the provider contract as provided in this section, then the provider shall be entitled to recover in the circuit or district courts of this state from the company or agency responsible for the payment of the claim an amount equal to the value of such claim plus interest and a reasonable attorney's fee to be determined by the court.

(e) Nothing in this section shall be construed to limit any insurer, health maintenance organization, preferred provider organization, health care service corporation, or other third party payor from determining the scope of its benefits or services or any other terms of its group and/or individual insured, subscriber or enrollee contracts nor from negotiating contracts with licensed providers on reimbursement rates or any other lawful provisions, except that the contract providing coverage to an insured may not exclude the right of assignment of benefits to any provider at the same benefit rate as paid to a contract provider.

(f) This section shall not apply to any persons covered under a state administered health benefit plan. (Acts 1994, No. 94-638, p. 1197, §§ 1-6.)

Effective date. — The act which added this section became effective April 26, 1994.

Code Commissioner's note. — In 1994, the Code Commissioner inserted "of" for "in" in subsection (a) to reflect the apparent meaning.

CHAPTER 2.

DEPARTMENT AND COMMISSIONER OF INSURANCE.

Article 1.

General Provisions.

Sec.
27-2-21. Examinations — Affairs, etc., of insurers and surplus line brokers.

ARTICLE 1.

GENERAL PROVISIONS.

§ 27-2-1. Department of Insurance.

Code Commissioner's note. — Section 2 of Acts 1989, No. 89-258 provides: "The existence and functioning of the insurance department, created and functioning pursuant to section 27-2-1 and Title 27, Code of Alabama 1975, is hereby continued, and said code sections are hereby expressly preserved."

Acts 1992, No. 92-126, § 2 provides: "The existence and functioning of the Department of Insurance, created and functioning pursuant to Section 27-2-1 specifically and Title 27, generally, Code of Alabama 1975, is hereby continued, and said code section and title are hereby expressly preserved."

§ 27-2-11. Assignment of assistant attorney general.

This section does not limit power given attorney general. — The power given to the attorney general to control "all litigation" in § 36-15-21 is not limited by the requirement of this section that the attorney general provide to the Insurance Department such legal services "as may be required." Ex parte Weaver, 570 So. 2d 675 (Ala. 1990).

Representation of commissioner of insurance not a violation of Rules of Professional Responsibility. — Where attorney general represented the commissioner of insurance in appellate proceedings, attorney general's representation did not violate the Rules of Professional Responsibility of the Alabama State Bar regarding conflicts of interest. Ex parte Weaver, 570 So. 2d 675 (Ala. 1990).

The attorney general has the authority

to move to dismiss the state department of insurance's proceedings in the Court of Civil Appeals over the objection of the commissioner

of insurance. Ex parte Weaver, 570 So. 2d 675 (Ala. 1990).

§ 27-2-17. Rules and regulations.

Commissioner of insurance must comply with all requirements of this section. — Pursuant to § 27-36-5, the commissioner of insurance may promulgate regulations to set the appropriate standards to be used in determining the reserve. However, the commissioner must comply with all notice and hearing requirements as set forth in this section. Old S. Life Ins. Co. v. State Dep't of Ins., 537 So. 2d 30 (Ala. Civ. App. 1988).

Order of commissioner of insurance re-

quiring the posting of additional reserves was error on the basis that it constituted a promulgation of a regulation without following proper procedural steps as authorized by § 27-36-5 and this section, since allowing the commissioner to adopt such requirements by ad hoc adjudication without notice or an opportunity to be heard in an administrative hearing could have a devastating effect on individual insurance companies. Old S. Life Ins. Co. v. State Dep't of Ins., 537 So. 2d 30 (Ala. Civ. App. 1988).

§ 27-2-19. Enforcement of insurance code.

Collateral references. — Credit life insurer's punitive damage liability for refusing payment. 55 ALR4th 246.

§ 27-2-21. Examinations — Affairs, etc., of insurers and surplus line brokers.

(a) For the purpose of determining its financial condition, ability to fulfill its obligations and compliance with the law, the commissioner shall examine the affairs, transactions, accounts, records, and assets of each authorized insurer, and the records of surplus line brokers restricted to those matters under Section 27-10-29, including the attorney-in-fact of a reciprocal insurer insofar as insurer transactions are involved as often as the commissioner deems appropriate but shall, at a minimum, conduct an examination of every insurer licensed in this state not less frequently than once every five years. In scheduling and determining the nature, scope, and frequency of the examinations, the commissioner shall consider such matters as the results of financial statement analyses and ratios, changes in management or ownership, actuarial opinions, reports of independent certified public accountants, and other criteria as set forth in the Examiners' Handbook adopted by the National Association of Insurance Commissioners and in effect when the commissioner exercises discretion under this section.

(b) The commissioner shall in like manner examine each insurer applying for an initial certificate of authority to transact insurance in this state.

(c) In lieu of an examination under this article of any foreign or alien insurer licensed in this state or applying for an initial certificate of authority, the commissioner may accept an examination report on the company as prepared by the Department of Insurance for the company's state of domicile or port-of-entry state until January 1, 1994. Thereafter, the reports may only be accepted if: (1) the Department of Insurance was at the time of the examination accredited under the National Association of Insurance Commissioners' Financial Regulation Standards and Accreditation Program, or (2) the exam-

14

ination is performed under the supervision of an accredited Department of Insurance or with the participation of one or more examiners who are employed by an accredited State Department of Insurance and who, after a review of the examination work papers and report, state under oath that the examination was performed in a manner consistent with the standards and procedures required by the accredited State Department of Insurance.

(d) As far as practical, the examination of a foreign or alien insurer shall be made in cooperation with the insurance supervisory officials of other states in which the insurer transacts business. (Acts 1915, No. 730, p. 834; Acts 1939, No. 527, p. 818; Acts 1965, No. 571, p. 1056; Acts 1971, No. 407, p. 707, § 35; Acts 1980, No. 80-774, p. 1608, § 1; Acts 1993, No. 93-675, § 2.)

The 1993 amendment, effective May 17, 1993, rewrote subsections (a) and (c).

Code Commissioner's note. — Acts 1993, No. 93-675, which amended this section, in § 1, provides: "The purpose of this section is to provide further for an effective and efficient system for examining the activities, operations, financial condition, and affairs of all persons transacting the business of insurance in this state and all persons otherwise subject to the jurisdiction of the Commissioner of Insurance by amending the current Alabama Insurance Code in such a way as to become substantially similar to the model law on examinations as adopted by the National Association of Insurance Commissioners. This title is intended to enable the commissioner to adopt a flexible system of examinations which directs resources as may be deemed appropriate and necessary for the administration of the insurance and insurance related laws of this state. These changes are made to meet the examination standards set by the National Association of Insurance Commissioners."

Acts 1993, No. 93-675, § 20, provides: "The Commissioner of Insurance may adopt reasonable rules and regulations necessary for the implementation and administration of this act."

Cross references. — As to provisions of rules and regulations necessary for the effectuation of this title, see § 27-2-17.

Cited in Old S. Life Ins. Co. v. State Dep't of Ins., 537 So. 2d 30 (Ala. Civ. App. 1988).

§ 27-2-25. Examinations — Expenses.

Code Commissioner's note. — Acts 1988, 1st Ex. Sess., No. 88-875, § 2 provides: "It is the legislative intent that nothing in this act [which amended §§ 27-4-2, 27-7-7, 27-8-5 and 27-39-6] shall be construed to affect the Special Examination Revolving Fund, as provided for in Section 27-2-25, Code of Alabama 1975, or the State Fire Marshal's Fund, as provided for in Section 24-5-10, Code of Alabama 1975."

§ 27-2-30. Hearings — How conducted.

Competitors of Blue Cross allowed to intervene on application for acquisition of life insurance company. — There was no doubt that the intervenors, competitors of Blue Cross, were properly permitted to become parties to the hearing before the commissioner on Blue Cross' application for approval for the acquisition of a life insurance company since, as competitors of Blue Cross, the intervenors had a direct financial interest that would be affected by the commissioner's order. Blue Cross & Blue Shield v. Protective Life Ins. Co., 527 So. 2d 125 (Ala. Civ. App. 1987).

§ 27-2-32. Hearings — Appeals.

Sections 27-29-9(b) and (c) did not apply when an appeal had already been taken under this section dealing with the same subject matter and parties, as the legislature could not have intended to have the same action pending in two distinct courts. National Sec. Ins. Co. v. Mutual Sav. Life Ins. Co., 536 So. 2d 1378 (Ala. 1988).

Competitors of Blue Cross held to have right of appeal. — Where intervenors were not simply competitors of Blue Cross, but were parties to the proceedings before the commissioner on Blue Cross' application to acquire United Trust, as such, they had the right to appeal from those proceedings under this section. Blue Cross & Blue Shield v. Protective Life Ins. Co., 527 So. 2d 125 (Ala. Civ. App. 1987).

On appeal, order taken as prima facie just and reasonable. — Order of the Commissioner of Insurance for the State of Alabama restraining the offering and selling of property insurance on poultry houses shall be taken as prima facie just and reasonable in action appealing such order. State Dep't of Ins. v. Arthur

J. Gallagher & Co., 622 So. 2d 370 (Ala. Civ. App. 1993).

Court shall reverse, vacate, or modify the decision or order of the commissioner of insurance in whole or in part if it finds that: (1) the commissioner erred to the prejudice of appellant's substantial rights in his application of the law; (2) the decision or order was procured by fraud or was based upon a finding of facts contrary to the weight of the evidence; or (3) the commissioner's action was arbitrary or capricious. Old S. Life Ins. Co. v. State Dep't of Ins., 537 So. 2d 30 (Ala. Civ. App. 1988).

CHAPTER 3.

AUTHORIZATION OF INSURERS.

Sec.
27-3-26.1. Annual statement to include statement of qualified independent loss reserve specialist.
27-3-28. Execution of contracts through countersigning resident agent; exceptions.
27-3-30. Foreign insurer may become domestic insurer; method; certificate and license eligibility; authority and jurisdiction of state; continuation of corporate existence and date of incorporation.
27-3-31. Domestic insurer may transfer domicile to another state and be admitted as foreign insurer if so qualified; approval of commissioner of

Sec.
 insurance; effect of interests of policyholders.
27-3-32. Domestic insurer may transfer domicile to another state and be admitted as foreign insurer if so qualified; approval of commissioner of insurance; effect of interests of policyholders; effect upon certificates of authority, agents, etc., including outstanding policies; insurer's duty to file new policy forms; insurer's duty to notify commissioner of details of transfer and file amendments required by law.
27-3-33. Rules and regulations.

Cross references. — As to provision of domestic life and disability insurance by mutual aid associations, see § 27-30-34.

§ 27-3-1. Certificate of authority — Requirement.

Cited in National Union Fire Ins. Co. v. Lomax Johnson Ins. Agency, Inc., 496 So. 2d 737 (Ala. 1986).

§ 27-3-26.1. Annual statement to include statement of qualified independent loss reserve specialist.

Every property or casualty insurer required to file an annual statement with the commissioner on March 1 of each year preceding, pursuant to Section 27-3-26, shall include a statement of a qualified independent loss reserve specialist setting forth his or her opinion relating to loss and loss adjustment expense reserves. For the purposes of this section, a qualified independent loss reserve specialist shall mean a person who is not a principal, director, or indirect owner of the insurer and is a member of the Casualty Actuarial Society, or has such other actuarial experience as is acceptable to the commissioner to assure a professional opinion on the adequacy of loss and loss adjustment expense reserves. (Acts 1993, No. 93-675, § 10; Acts 1994, 1st Ex. Sess., No. 94-789, p. 92, § 1.)

Effective date. — The act which added this section became effective May 17, 1993.

The 1994, 1st Ex. Sess., amendment, effective May 6, 1994, in the second sentence, substituted "a principal" for "an employee, principal," and inserted "actuarial."

Code Commissioner's note. — Acts 1993, No. 93-675, § 20, provides: "The Commissioner of Insurance may adopt reasonable rules and regulations necessary for the implementation and administration of this act."

Acts 1994, No. 94-789 provides that the provisions of this amendatory act shall apply retroactively to annual financial statements required to be filed pursuant to Section 27-3-26, due on March 1, 1994.

Cross references. — As to provisions of rules and regulations necessary for the effectuation of this title, see § 27-2-17.

§ 27-3-28. Execution of contracts through countersigning resident agent; exceptions.

(a) To assure the validity and construction of contracts according to the laws of this state and to facilitate the collection of privilege taxes and fees, all property, surety and casualty insurers doing business in this state shall execute all contracts upon property or risks in this state through a resident agent of the insurer, duly licensed under this title, who shall execute or countersign all such contracts.

(b) Each such agent shall keep a true record of all contracts thus executed or countersigned by him and shall, upon request, furnish a verified copy thereof to the commissioner to aid him in the collection of all privilege taxes due in this state.

(c) No such countersignature may be made by any solicitor, managing general agent or service representative, nor by any servant or employee thereof nor by any servant or employee of the insurer; except,

(1) That this provision shall not prevent any servant or employee of a direct-writing insurer from being licensed under this title as a resident insurance agent of the insurer to countersign contracts of insurance; and

(2) Residual-type insurance plans that have been approved by the commissioner may be countersigned by designated employees of the insurer or association sponsoring such plan.

(d) As to policies covering property or risks located in more than one state, the insurer may, in its discretion, use a countersignature endorsement thereon showing the policy to which attached and information in respect to such policy, including full premium information sufficient for the countersigning agent's records. Such endorsement shall be signed by the countersigning agent in lieu of countersignature of the original policy.

(e) No countersigning resident agent shall countersign a policy or countersignature endorsement in blank, except as to policy and endorsement forms of direct writing insurers reflecting same filed with and approved by the commissioner.

(f) This section shall not apply to:

(1) Insurance of the rolling stock, vessels or aircraft of any common carrier in interstate or foreign commerce or of any vehicle principally garaged and used in another state, or covering any liability or other risks incident to the ownership, maintenance or operation thereof;

(2) Insurance of property received for shipment or delivery or in transit while in the possession and custody of railroads or other common carriers;

(3) Wet marine and transportation insurance;

(4) Reinsurance contracts between insurers; or

(5) Bid bonds issued in connection with any public or private contracts. (Acts 1935, No. 194, p. 256; Acts 1971, No. 407, p. 707, §§ 73, 74; Acts 1988, No. 88-123, p. 159, § 1.)

§ 27-3-30. Foreign insurer may become domestic insurer; method; certificate and license eligibility; authority and jurisdiction of state; continuation of corporate existence and date of incorporation.

Any insurer which is organized under the laws of any other state and is admitted to do business in this state for the purpose of writing insurance may become a domestic insurer by complying with all of the requirements of law relative to the organization and licensing of a domestic insurer of the same type and by designating its principal place of business at a place in this state. Said domestic insurer will be entitled to like certificates and licenses to transact business in this state and shall be subject to the authority and jurisdiction of this state. Articles of incorporation of such domestic insurer may be amended to provide that the corporation is a continuation of the corporate existence of the original foreign corporation through adoption of this state as its corporate domicile and that the original date of incorporation in its original domiciliary state is the date of incorporation of such domestic insurer. (Acts 1991, No. 91-446, p. 816, § 1.)

§ 27-3-31. Domestic insurer may transfer domicile to another state and be admitted as foreign insurer if so qualified; approval of commissioner of insurance; effect of interests of policyholders.

Any domestic insurer may, upon the approval of the commissioner of insurance, transfer its domicile to any other state in which it is admitted to transact the business of insurance, and upon such a transfer shall cease to be a domestic insurer, and shall be admitted to this state if qualified as a foreign insurer. The commissioner of insurance shall approve any such proposed transfer unless he shall determine such transfer is not in the interest of the policyholders of this state. (Acts 1991, No. 91-446, p. 816, § 2.)

§ 27-3-32. Domestic insurer may transfer domicile to another state and be admitted as foreign insurer if so qualified; approval of commissioner of insurance; effect of interests of policyholders; effect upon certificates of authority, agents, etc., including outstanding policies; insurer's duty to file new policy forms; insurer's duty to notify commissioner of details of transfer and file amendments required by law.

The certificate of authority, agents appointments and licenses, rates, and other items which the commissioner of insurance allows, in his discretion, which are in existence at the time any insurer licensed to transact the business of insurance in this state transfers its corporate domicile to this or any other state by merger, consolidation or any other lawful method shall continue in full force and effect upon such transfer if such insurer remains duly qualified to transact the business of insurance in this state. All outstanding policies of any transferring insurer shall remain in full force and effect and need not be endorsed as to the new name of the company or its new location unless so ordered by the commissioner of insurance. Every transferring insurer shall file new policy forms with the commissioner of insurance on or before the effective date of the transfer, but may use existing policy forms with appropriate endorsements if allowed by and under such conditions as approved by the commissioner of insurance. However, every such transferring insurer shall notify the commissioner of insurance of the details of the proposed transfer, and shall file promptly any resulting amendments to corporate documents filed or required to be filed in accordance with sections 10-2A-90 through 10-2A-284, 27-3-17, 27-27-5 and 27-27-22. (Acts 1991, No. 91-446, p. 816, § 3.)

Code Commissioner's note. — Acts 1994, No. 94-245, § 3 repealed Sections 10-2A-90 through 10-2A-284 which are referred to in the last sentence. For present provisions, see Chapter 2B of Title 10.

§ 27-3-33. Rules and regulations.

The commissioner of insurance of this state may promulgate necessary rules and regulations to carry out the purposes of sections 27-3-30 through 27-3-32. (Acts 1991, No. 91-446, p. 816, § 4.)

CHAPTER 3A.

HEALTH CARE SERVICE UTILIZATION REVIEW ACT.

Sec.
27-3A-1. Short title.
27-3A-2. Purposes.
27-3A-3. Definitions.
27-3A-4. Duties of utilization review agents.

Sec.
27-3A-5. Standards for utilization review agents.
27-3A-6. Violations of chapter by utilization review agent.

Effective date. — The act which added this chapter became effective May 6, 1994.

§ 27-3A-1. Short title.

This chapter may be cited as the "Health Care Service Utilization Review Act." (Acts 1994, 1st Ex. Sess., No. 94-786, p. 80, § 1.)

§ 27-3A-2. Purposes.

The purposes of this chapter are to:

(1) Promote the delivery of quality health care in a cost-effective manner.

(2) Assure that utilization review agents adhere to reasonable standards for conducting utilization review.

(3) Foster greater coordination and cooperation between health care providers and utilization review agents.

(4) Improve communications and knowledge of benefit plan requirements among all parties concerned before expenses are incurred.

(5) Ensure that utilization review agents maintain the confidentiality of medical records in accordance with applicable laws. (Acts 1994, 1st Ex. Sess., No. 94-786, p. 80, § 2.)

§ 27-3A-3. Definitions.

As used in this chapter, the following words and phrases shall have the following meanings:

(1) DEPARTMENT. The Alabama Department of Public Health.

(2) ENROLLEE. An individual who has contracted for or who participates in coverage under an insurance policy, a health maintenance organization contract, a health service corporation contract, an employee welfare benefit plan, a hospital or medical services plan, or any other benefit program providing payment, reimbursement, or indemnification for health care costs for the individual or the eligible dependents of the individual.

(3) PROVIDER. A health care provider duly licensed or certified by the State of Alabama.

(4) UTILIZATION REVIEW. A system for prospective and concurrent review of the necessity and appropriateness in the allocation of health care resources and services given or proposed to be given to an individual within this state. The term does not include elective requests for clarification of coverage.

(5) UTILIZATION REVIEW AGENT. Any person or entity, including the State of Alabama, performing a utilization review, except the following:

a. An agency of the federal government.

b. An agent acting on behalf of the federal government, but only to the extent that the agent is providing services to the federal government.

c. The internal quality assurance program of a hospital.

d. An employee of a utilization review agent.

e. Health maintenance organizations licensed and regulated by the state, but only to the extent of providing a utilization review to their own members.

f. Any entity that has a current accreditation from the Utilization Review Accreditation Commission (URAC). However, entities with current URAC accreditation shall file a URAC certification with the department annually.

g. An entity performing utilization reviews or bill audits, or both, exclusively for workers' compensation claims pursuant to Section 25-5-312. If an entity also performs services for claims other than workers' compensation, it shall be considered a private review agent subject to this chapter for those claims.

h. An entity performing utilization reviews or bill audits, or both, exclusively for the Medicaid Agency.

i. A person performing utilization reviews or bill audits, or both, exclusively for their company's health plan, independent of a utilization review company.

j. An insurance company licensed by the State of Alabama performing utilization reviews or bill audits, or both, exclusively for their company's health plan, independent of a utilization review company.

k. The Peer Review Committee of the Alabama State Chiropractic Association. (Acts 1994, 1st Ex. Sess., No. 94-786, p. 80, § 3.)

§ 27-3A-4. Duties of utilization review agents.

(a) Utilization review agents shall adhere to the minimum standards set forth in Section 27-3A-5.

(b) On or after July 1, 1994, a utilization review agent shall not conduct a utilization review in this state unless the agent has certified to the department in writing that the agent is in compliance with Section 27-3A-5. Certification shall be made annually on or before July 1 of each calendar year. In addition, a utilization review agent shall file the following information:

(1) The name, address, telephone number, and normal business hours of the utilization review agent.

(2) The name and telephone number of a person for the department to contact.

(3) A description of the appeal procedures for utilization review determinations.

(c) Any material changes in the information filed in accordance with this section shall be filed with the State Health Officer within 30 days of the change.

(d) Unless exempted pursuant to paragraph f. of subdivision (5) of Section 27-3A-3, each utilization review agent, upon filing the certification, shall pay an annual fee in the amount of one thousand dollars ($1,000) to the department. All fees paid pursuant to this subdivision shall be held by the department as expendable receipts for the purpose of administering this chapter.

(e) The department may adopt rules pursuant to the Administrative Procedure Act necessary to implement this chapter. (Acts 1994, 1st Ex. Sess., No. 94-786, p. 80, § 4.)

Code Commissioner's note. — In 1994, the Code Commissioner inserted "Section 27-3A-3" for "subdivision (5) of this section" in subsection (d) to reference the apparent intended section.

§ 27-3A-5. Standards for utilization review agents.

(a) Except as provided in subsection (b), all utilization review agents shall meet the following minimum standards:

(1) Notification of a determination by the utilization review agent shall be mailed or otherwise communicated to the provider of record or the enrollee or other appropriate individual within two business days of the receipt of the request for determination and the receipt of all information necessary to complete the review.

(2) Any determination by a utilization review agent as to the necessity or appropriateness of an admission, service, or procedure shall be reviewed by a physician or determined in accordance with standards or guidelines approved by a physician.

(3) Any notification of determination not to certify an admission, service, or procedure shall include the principal reason for the determination and the procedures to initiate an appeal of the determination.

(4) Utilization review agents shall maintain and make available a written description of the appeal procedure by which the enrollee or the provider of record may seek review of a determination by the utilization review agent. The appeal procedure shall provide for the following:

a. On appeal, all determinations not to certify an admission, service, or procedure as being necessary or appropriate shall be made by a physician in the same or a similar general specialty as typically manages the medical condition, procedure, or treatment under discussion as mutually deemed appropriate. A chiropractor must review all cases in which the utilization review organization has concluded that a determination not to certify a chiropractic service or procedure is appropriate and an appeal has been made by the attending chiropractor, enrollee, or designee.

b. Utilization review agents shall complete the adjudication of appeals of determinations not to certify admissions, services, and procedures no later than 30 days from the date the appeal is filed and the receipt of all information necessary to complete the appeal.

c. When an initial determination not to certify a health care service is made prior to or during an ongoing service requiring review, and the attending physician believes that the determination warrants immediate appeal, the attending physician shall have an opportunity to appeal that determination over the telephone on an expedited basis. A representative of a hospital or other health care provider or a representative of the enrollee or covered patient may assist in an appeal. Utilization review agents shall complete the adjudication on an expedited basis. Utilization review agents shall complete the adjudication of expedited appeals within 48 hours of the date the appeal is filed and the receipt of all information necessary to complete the appeal. Expedited appeals that do not resolve a difference of opinion may be resubmitted through the standard appeal process.

(5) Utilization review agents shall make staff available by toll-free telephone at least 40 hours per week during normal business hours.

(6) Utilization review agents shall have a telephone system capable of accepting or recording incoming telephone calls during other than normal business hours and shall respond to these calls within two working days.

(7) Utilization review agents shall comply with all applicable laws to protect the confidentiality of individual medical records.

(8) Physicians, chiropractors, or psychologists making utilization review determinations shall have current licenses from a state licensing agency in the United States.

(9) Utilization review agents shall allow a minimum of 24 hours after an emergency admission, service, or procedure for an enrollee or representative of the enrollee to notify the utilization review agent and request certification or continuing treatment for that condition.

(b) Any utilization review agent that has received accreditation by the utilization review accreditation commission shall be exempt from this section. (Acts 1994, 1st Ex. Sess., No. 94-786, p. 80, § 5.)

§ 27-3A-6. Violations of chapter by utilization review agent.

(a) Whenever the department has reason to believe that a utilization review agent subject to this chapter has been or is engaged in conduct that violates this chapter, the department shall notify the utilization review agent of the alleged violation. The agent shall respond to the notice not later than 30 days after the notice is made.

(b) If the department finds that the utilization review agent has violated this chapter, or that the alleged violation has not been corrected, the department may conduct a contested case hearing on the alleged violation in accordance with the Administrative Procedure Act.

(c) If, after the hearing, the department determines that the utilization review agent has engaged in a violation, the department shall reduce the findings to writing and shall issue and cause to be served upon the agent a copy of the findings and an order requiring the agent to cease and desist from engaging in the violation.

(d) The department may also exercise either or both of the following disciplinary powers:

(1) Impose an administrative fine of not more than five thousand dollars ($5,000) for a violation that occurred with such frequency as to indicate a general business pattern or practice.

(2) Suspend or revoke the certification of a utilization review agent if the agent knew the act was in violation of this chapter and repeated the act with such frequency as to indicate a general business pattern or practice. (Acts 1994, 1st Ex. Sess., No. 94-786, p. 80, § 6.)

CHAPTER 4.

FEES AND TAXES.

Sec.
27-4-1. Repealed.
27-4-2. Advance fees, licenses and miscella-
      neous charges.

Sec.
27-4-3 through 27-4-7. Repealed.
27-4-9, 27-4-10. Repealed.

§ 27-4-1. Definitions. Repealed by Acts 1993, No. 93-679, p. 1291, § 12, effective at 12:01 a.m. on January 1, 1995.

Code Commissioner's note. — Acts 1993, No. 93-679, § 12, provides: "Except as provided in Section 14, Sections 27-4-1, 27-4-3 to 27-4-7, inclusive, 27-4-9 to 27-4-10, inclusive, and 27-30-31, Code of Alabama 1975, and all laws or parts of law which conflict with this act are repealed effective at 12:01 a.m. on the first day of January 1995."

Acts 1993, No. 93-679, § 14, provides: "Upon its passage and approval by the Governor, or upon its otherwise becoming a law, this act shall become effective at 12:01 a.m. on the first

day of January, 1995, with respect to insurance premiums received on or after January 1, 1995; provided, however, that (1) the determination and payment of taxes due on premiums received prior to January 1, 1995, shall be pursuant to the law in effect prior to January 1, 1995, and (2) the provisions of subsection (b) of Section 3 and the provisions of Section 11 shall become effective immediately upon passage of this act and approval by the Governor, or upon its otherwise becoming a law."

§ 27-4-2. Advance fees, licenses and miscellaneous charges.

(a) The commissioner of insurance shall collect in advance fees, licenses and miscellaneous charges as follows:

(1) Certificate of authority:

a. Initial application for original certificate of authority, including the filing with the commissioner of all documents incidental thereto $500.00

b. Issuance of original certificate of authority 500.00

c. Annual continuation or renewal fee 500.00

d. Reinstatement fee 500.00

(2) Charter documents, filing with the commissioner amendment to articles of incorporation or of association, or of other charter documents or to bylaws 25.00

(3) Solicitation permit, filing application and issuance 250.00

(4) Annual statement of insurer, except when filed as part of application for original certificate of authority, filing 25.00

(5) Agent Licenses and Appointments:

a. Property, casualty and surety agents (resident or nonresident):

1. Application fee (For filing of application for license or appointment) 20.00

2. Appointment fee (For appointment of agent by insurer and annual renewal of appointment, each insurer)

(i) All classification except comprehensive property, casualty and surety, each classification 7.50

(ii) Comprehensive property, casualty and surety 7.50

b. Life and disability resident agents

1. Application fee (For filing of application for license) 20.00

24

    2. License fee (For original license and each annual renewal, each insurer) ....$ 7.50

  c. Life and disability nonresident agents

    1. Application fee (For filing application for license) 20.00

    2. License fee (For original license and each annual renewal, each insurer) 30.00

  d. Examination fees (For filing application for examination or reexamination of resident agent or broker)

    1. Each classification of examination except comprehensive property, casualty and surety 10.00

    2. Comprehensive property, casualty and surety 30.00

  e. Each vending machine licensed under section 27-8-23, each year 25.00

(6) Broker's license (resident or nonresident brokers):

  a. Filing application for license 20.00

  b. Issuance of license 50.00

  c. Annual continuation of license 50.00

(7) Solicitor's license:

  a. Annual continuation of license 20.00

(8) General agent's license:

  a. Filing application for license 30.00

  b. Issuance of license, property and casualty, each insurer 25.00

  c. Annual continuation of license, each insurer 25.00

(9) Service representative's license:

  a. Filing application for license 20.00

  b. Issuance of license, property and casualty, each insurer 20.00

  c. Annual continuation of license, property and casualty, each insurer 20.00

(10) Surplus line broker license, each license year 50.00

(11) Adjusters:

  a. License 40.00

  b. Annual continuation of licenses 40.00

(12) Miscellaneous services:

  a. For copies of documents, records on file in insurance department, per page 1.00

  b. For each certificate of the commissioner under his seal, other than agent licenses 5.00

(13) The commissioner is hereby authorized and directed to collect a fee of $25.00 when, in acting as agent or attorney for any insurance company, fraternal benefit society, mutual aid association or credit union, he accepts the service of legal process as provided by the laws of this state. He shall refuse to receive and file or serve any process unless such process is accompanied by the aforementioned fee, which shall be taxed as costs in the action.

(b) The commissioner shall promptly pay all fees and licenses collected under this section into the state treasury to the credit of the general fund. (Acts

1935, No. 194, p. 256; Acts 1957, No. 598, p. 848, § 4; Acts 1971, No. 407, p. 707, § 76; Acts 1988, 1st Ex. Sess., No. 88-875, p. 410, § 1.)

Code Commissioner's note. — Acts 1988, 1st Ex. Sess., No. 88-875, § 2 provides: "It is the legislative intent that nothing in this act shall be construed to affect the Special Examination Revolving Fund, as provided for in Section 27-2-25, Code of Alabama 1975, or the State Fire Marshal's Fund, as provided for in Section 24-5-10, Code of Alabama 1975."

§§ 27-4-3 through 27-4-7. Repealed by Acts 1993, No. 93-679, p. 1291, § 12, effective at 12:01 a.m. on January 1, 1995.

Code Commissioner's note. — Acts 1993, No. 93-679, § 12, provides: "Except as provided in Section 14, Sections 27-4-1, 27-4-3 to 27-4-7, inclusive, 27-4-9 to 27-4-10, inclusive, and 27-30-31, Code of Alabama 1975, and all laws or parts of law which conflict with this act are repealed effective at 12:01 a.m. on the first day of January 1995."

Acts 1993, No. 93-679, § 14, provides: "Upon its passage and approval by the Governor, or upon its otherwise becoming a law, this act shall become effective at 12:01 a.m. on the first day of January, 1995, with respect to insurance premiums received on or after January 1, 1995; provided, however, that (1) the determination and payment of taxes due on premiums received prior to January 1, 1995, shall be pursuant to the law in effect prior to January 1, 1995, and (2) the provisions of subsection (b) of Section 3 and the provisions of Section 11 shall become effective immediately upon passage of this act and approval by the Governor, or upon its otherwise becoming a law."

§§ 27-4-9, 27-4-10. Repealed by Acts 1993, No. 93-679, p. 1291, § 12, effective at 12:01 a.m. on January 1, 1995.

Code Commissioner's note. — Acts 1993, No. 93-679, § 12 provides: "Except as provided in Section 14, Sections 27-4-1, 27-4-3 to 27-4-7, inclusive, 27-4-9 to 27-4-10, inclusive, and 27-30-31, Code of Alabama 1975, and all laws or parts of law which conflict with this act are repealed effective at 12:01 a.m. on the first day of January 1995."

Acts 1993, No. 93-679, § 14, provides: "Upon its passage and approval by the Governor, or upon its otherwise becoming a law, this act shall become effective at 12:01 a.m. on the first day of January, 1995, with respect to insurance premiums received on or after January 1, 1995; provided, however, that (1) the determination and payment of taxes due on premiums received prior to January 1, 1995, shall be pursuant to the law in effect prior to January 1, 1995, and (2) the provisions of subsection (b) of Section 3 and the provisions of Section 11 shall become effective immediately upon passage of this act and approval by the Governor, or upon its otherwise becoming a law."

CHAPTER 4A.

INSURANCE PREMIUM TAX.

Sec.
27-4A-1. Short title.
27-4A-2. Definitions.
27-4A-3. Premium taxation rates.
27-4A-4. Penalties.

Sec.
27-4A-5. Exclusive tax on premiums.
27-4A-6. Exemption from income and ad valorem taxes.
27-4A-7. Mutual aid associations.

Code Commissioner's note. — Acts 1993, No. 93-679, § 14, provides: "Upon its passage and approval by the Governor, or upon its otherwise becoming a law, this act shall become effective at 12:01 a.m. on the first day of January, 1995, with respect to insurance premiums received on or after January 1, 1995; provided, however, that (1) the determination and payment of taxes due on premiums received prior to January 1, 1995, shall be pursuant to the law in effect prior to January 1, 1995, and (2) the provisions of subsection (b) of Section 3 and the provisions of Section 11 shall become effective immediately upon passage of this act and approval by the Governor, or upon its otherwise becoming a law."

Acts 1993, No. 93-679, § 11, provides: "Each insurer who paid premium taxes to this state on business done during calendar year 1992 shall submit to the Department of Insurance a statement indicating the amount of premium taxes which would have been paid by that insurer on that business if the insurer's taxes had been determined under the provisions of this act which will apply to business done in this state during calendar year 1995, including, but not limited to, all provisions related to rates and credits. This information shall be submitted on a form to be developed and furnished by the commissioner, such form to be furnished by the department to insurers no later than August 1, 1993, and returned to the department by insurers no later than October 1, 1993. The statement shall be verified by the affidavit of an officer of the insurer having knowledge of the facts."

§ 27-4A-1. Short title.

This chapter shall be known and may be cited as "The Insurance Premium Tax Reform Act of 1993." (Acts 1993, No. 93-679, § 1.)

Code Commissioner's note. — Acts 1993, No. 93-679, § 14, provides: "Upon its passage and approval by the Governor, or upon its otherwise becoming a law, this act shall become effective at 12:01 a.m. on the first day of January, 1995, with respect to insurance premiums received on or after January 1, 1995; provided, however, that (1) the determination and payment of taxes due on premiums received prior to January 1, 1995, shall be pursuant to the law in effect prior to January 1, 1995, and (2) the provisions of subsection (b) of Section 3 and the provisions of Section 11 shall become effective immediately upon passage of this act and approval by the Governor, or upon its otherwise becoming a law."

§ 27-4A-2. Definitions.

For the purposes of this chapter only, the following terms, unless the context clearly indicates otherwise, shall have the meanings:

(1) ANNUITY CONSIDERATIONS. All sums received as consideration for annuity contracts.

(2) COMMISSIONER. The Commissioner of Insurance of the State of Alabama.

(3) DEPARTMENT. The Department of Insurance of the State of Alabama.

(4) DOMESTIC INSURER. Any insurer organized under the laws of the State of Alabama which maintains its principal office and chief place of business in the State of Alabama.

(5) FOREIGN INSURER. Any insurer organized under the laws of any country or of any state of the United States other than the State of Alabama and any insurer organized under the laws of Alabama which maintains its principal office or chief place of business outside the State of Alabama.

(6) INSURER. Every insurer as defined in Section 27-1-2, and every other insurance company or association charging a premium for contracts entered into by those companies, associations, or societies, which shall include every non-profit corporation organized pursuant to Sections 10-4-100 to 10-4-115, inclusive, every mutual aid association including those organized pursuant to Chapter 30, Title 27, and every health maintenance organization including those organized pursuant to Chapter 21A, Title 27. Notwithstanding the foregoing, societies exempt pursuant to Section 27-34-42, and self-insurance programs utilizing a trust fund or similar entity providing workers' compensation, health, and other insurance-like coverage shall not be included within this definition of insurer.

(7) MEDICAL LIABILITY INSURANCE. Liability insurance provided to hospitals, physicians, dentists, and other persons licensed by the State of Alabama to provide healthcare services against legal liability resulting from the failure of such insureds to comply with the standard of care applicable to them in rendering medical care to patients, including general liability insurance written as a part of such insurance.

(8) PREMIUMS. All amounts received in cash or otherwise on risks in this state as consideration for contracts of insurance, less all of the following:

a. Insurance premiums returned.

b. Reinsurance premiums from insurance companies authorized to do business in Alabama and subject to the premium tax provided for in Chapter 4 of Title 27.

c. Dividends paid, applied, or left with the company to accumulate at interest.

Premiums shall not include: (i) annuity considerations; or (ii) charges by title insurers for abstracting, record searching, certificates as to the record title, escrow and closing services and other related services, or the costs and expenses of examinations of title. (Acts 1993, No. 93-679, § 2; Acts 1993, 1st Ex. Sess., No. 93-847, p. 67, § 1.)

The 1993, 1st Ex. Sess., amendment, effective August 24, 1993, added subdivision (7), and redesignated former subdivision (7) as present subdivision (8).

Code Commissioner's note. — Acts 1993, No. 93-847, § 3, provides: "Upon its passage and approval by the Governor, or upon its otherwise becoming law, this act shall become effective at 12:01 a.m. on the first day of January, 1995."

Acts 1993, No. 93-679, § 14, provides: "Upon its passage and approval by the Governor, or upon its otherwise becoming a law, this act shall become effective at 12:01 a.m. on the first day of January, 1995, with respect to insurance premiums received on or after January 1, 1995; provided, however, that (1) the determination and payment of taxes due on premiums received prior to January 1, 1995, shall be pursuant to the law in effect prior to January 1, 1995, and (2) the provisions of subsection (b) of Section 3 and the provisions of Section 11 shall become effective immediately upon passage of this act and approval by the Governor, or upon its otherwise becoming a law."

§ 27-4A-3. Premium taxation rates.

(a) Subject to the exceptions and exemptions hereinafter set forth, for the year beginning on January 1, 1995, and for each year thereafter, every insurer shall pay to the commissioner a premium tax equal to the percentage, as set out in this subsection (a), of the premiums received by the insurer for business done in this state, whether the same was actually received by the insurer in this state or elsewhere:

(1) PREMIUM TAX ON LIFE INSURANCE PREMIUMS.

a. Except as hereinafter provided, the rates of taxation on life insurance premiums shall be those amounts set out in the following schedule:

Year	Foreign Insurers	Domestic Insurers
1995	2.9	1.3
1996	2.8	1.6
1997	2.7	1.8

Year	Foreign Insurers	Domestic Insurers
1998	2.5	2.1
Every Year Thereafter	2.3	2.3

b. Individual life insurance policies in a face amount of greater than $5,000 and up to and including $25,000, excluding group life insurance policies, shall be taxed at the rate of one percent per annum.

c. Individual life insurance policies in a face amount of $5,000 or less, excluding group life insurance policies, shall be taxed at the rate of one-half percent per annum.

d. For the purposes of computing the face amount of life insurance policies, all life insurance policies issued within 60 days of another on the life of the same applicant or applicants shall be treated as one policy.

(2) Premium Tax on Health Insurance Premiums.

a. Except as hereinafter provided, the rates of taxation on premiums for health insurance, and accident and health insurance for which a separate premium is charged, shall be those amounts set out in the following schedule:

Year	Foreign Insurers	Domestic Insurers
1995	2.9	1.3
1996	2.8	1.6
1997	2.4	1.6
1998	2.0	1.6
Every Year Thereafter	1.6	1.6

b. Premiums for hospital, medical, surgical, or other health care benefits provided pursuant to any employer sponsored plan for groups with less than 50 insured participants shall be taxed at the rate of one-half percent per annum.

c. Premiums for hospital, medical, surgical, or other health care benefits supplementary to Medicare and Medicaid, or provided pursuant to an employer sponsored plan for governmental employees, shall be exempt from the premium tax levied pursuant to this chapter.

(3) PREMIUM TAX ON OTHER INSURANCE PREMIUMS.

a. Except as hereinafter provided, the rate of taxation on insurance other than life insurance, health insurance, and accident health insurance shall be 3.6 percent per annum.

b. Premiums for all of the following types of insurance shall be taxed at the rate of one percent per annum:

1. All property and multi-peril insurance written in fire protection Classes 9 and 10.

2. Mobile homes, mobile homeowners, homeowners and low value dwelling policies in a face amount of $40,000 or less.

c. Premiums for medical liability insurance shall be taxed at the rate of 1.6 percent per annum.

d. The tax imposed at the rate specified in paragraph a of this subdivision (3) shall be reduced by the following credits for certain economic development activities pursued in the State of Alabama.

1. Alabama Insurance Offices Facilities Credit.

For each office owned or leased by an insurer in the State of Alabama and used for insurance operations, an insurer shall be entitled to a credit against the tax imposed by paragraph a. of this subdivision (3) according to the following schedule:

Number of Full Time Employees in Office	Credit as a % of Premiums Taxable Under Paragraph a.
1 — 3	0.0025%
4 — 10	0.0050%
11 — 50	0.0075%
51 or more	0.0100%

The total credit allowable for Alabama insurance office facilities shall not exceed one percent of an insurer's Alabama premiums taxable at the rate specified in paragraph a. of this subdivision (3).

2. Alabama Real Property Investment Credit.

For each $1,000,000 in value of real property investments in the State of Alabama, an insurer shall be entitled to a credit of 0.10 percent of its Alabama premiums taxable at the rate specified in paragraph a. of this subdivision (3). The total credit allowable for Alabama real property investments shall not exceed 1 percent of an insurer's Alabama premiums taxable at the rate specified in paragraph a. of this subdivision (3).

(i) Alabama real property investments which qualify for the Alabama real property investment credit include any improved Alabama real property owned by the insurer or an affiliate of the insurer on January 1, 1993, and any improved or unimproved Alabama real property acquired or new construction placed in service on or after January 1, 1993, by the insurer or an affiliate of the insurer.

(ii) For purposes of determining the Alabama real property investment credit, Alabama real property investments shall be valued at cost and not at book value or fair market value. The cost of capital improvements to existing Alabama real property investments, such as the renovation of shopping centers, hotels, or other buildings, completed and placed in service by the insurer or an affiliate of the insurer on or after January 1, 1993, shall be considered an Alabama real estate investment.

(iii) For purposes of determining the value of Alabama real property investments, funds borrowed to finance Alabama real property investments shall be subtracted from cost so that only the net cost in the investment properties borne from assets belonging to the insurer or an affiliate of the insurer qualifies for the Alabama real property investment credit. The cost of debt-financed Alabama real property investments of an insurer shall be increased pro tanto as the underlying debt is paid off by the insurer or an affiliate of the insurer.

(iv) The Alabama real property investment credit shall not be allowed for properties in the State of Alabama used in an insurer's insurance operations and for which the Alabama insurance office facilities credit is allowed or allowable, without regard to the 1 percent limitation on the credit. However, the cost of real property owned in the State of Alabama and used in part as an Alabama real property investment and in part for the insurer's insurance operations shall be allocated on a square-foot basis so that the cost allocated to that portion of the property not used for insurance operations shall qualify for the Alabama real property investment credit.

(v) Mortgages held by an insurer that are secured by real property located in the State of Alabama shall not be considered Alabama real property investments for purposes of the Alabama real property investment credit.

3. Special Rules.

The following special rules apply to the Alabama insurance office facilities credit and the Alabama real property investment credit.

(i) For purposes of determining the economic development credits allowed under this section, the term affiliate shall mean any business entity, other than a life or health insurance company, which is wholly owned by the insurer subject to tax under paragraph a. of this subdivision (3) or any other insurer and its wholly owned subsidiaries, other than a life or health insurance company, which is part of a group of companies, including the insurer, which are under common control and management. For an insurer having affiliates, all premiums of the insurer and its insurance company affiliates subject to tax at the rate specified in paragraph a. of this subdivision (3) may be aggregated; all Alabama insurance office facilities and all Alabama real property investments may be aggregated; and, subject to the specific credit limitations, the total allowable tax credits may be determined as if all the aggregated premiums, office facilities, and Alabama real property investments were owned by one insurer. Once the total allowable credits have been determined, the credits may be allocated to the insurer and its insurance company affiliates at the sole discretion of the insurer subject to the specific credit limitations on a per insurance company basis. The computation of allowable credits and their allocation to affiliates shall be made on forms to be supplied by the Alabama Department of Insurance, which forms shall be filed with the insurer's annual statement.

(ii) Economic development credits allowed to foreign insurers shall be treated as Alabama premium taxes paid by the insurers for purposes of calculating any retaliatory tax due under Section 27-3-29.

(b) Notwithstanding any provision of law to the contrary, including, but not limited to, Section 27-4-4 and Section 27-4-5, all premium tax payments made subsequent to passage of this chapter shall be remitted in accordance with this subsection (b). Beginning January 1, 1993, and all years thereafter, each insurer shall pay its premium taxes on a quarterly basis, as follows: on or before May 15, a payment estimated on the basis of 25 percent of its business done in this state during the preceding calendar year or, at the option of the insurer, on the basis of its actual business done in the state from January 1 through March 31 of the same calendar year; on or before August 15, a payment estimated on the basis of 45 percent of its business done in this state during the preceding calendar year or, at the option of the insurer, on the basis of 180 percent of its actual business done in this state from April 1 through June 30 of the same calendar year; on or before November 15, a payment estimated on the basis of five percent of its business done in this state during the preceding calendar year or, at the option of the insurer, on the basis of 20% of its actual business done in this state from July 1 through September 30 of the same calendar year; on or before March 1, a payment in the amount of the remainder of the actual premium taxes due on its business done in the state during the preceding calendar year. On or before March 1 of each year, every authorized insurer shall file with the commissioner a statement, on a form as furnished or approved by the commissioner, setting forth the total amount of premiums received by it for business done in this state during the preceding calendar year. The statement shall be verified by an affidavit of an officer of the insurer having knowledge of the facts. It is the intent and meaning of this subsection (b) that any taxes paid on an estimated quarterly basis during the calendar year shall be reconciled to actual premiums received on risks in this state for such calendar year on the March 1 payment date in the succeeding calendar year.

(c) The tax imposed by this section shall be subject to credit and deduction of the full amount, with 25 percent of the full amount paid, or estimated to be paid, being credited or deducted on each quarterly payment date, for all of the following:

(1) Ad valorem property taxes paid by an insurer on any building and real estate in this state which is owned and occupied, in whole or in part, by the insurer for the full period of the tax year as its principal office in the State of Alabama.

(2) All ad valorem taxes paid by an insurer during the calendar year on any other real estate and improvements thereon in this state which is owned and at least 50 percent occupied by the insurer for the full period of the tax year.

(3) Ad valorem property taxes paid by an insurer on the insurer's offices in this state during the calendar year, but with respect to the office apportioned to the square foot area occupied by the insured, whether the ad valorem taxes are paid directly by the insurer or in the form of rent to a third-party landlord.

(4) All license fees and taxes paid to any county in this state during the calendar year for the privilege of engaging in the business of insurance within the county.

(5) All expenses of examination of the insurer by the commissioner paid during the calendar year.

(6) All license or privilege taxes on lists of securities paid by the insurer under Section 40-24-8, during the calendar year.

(7) All franchise taxes paid by the insurer to the State of Alabama for the calendar year.

(8) All credits for assessments as provided under Sections 27-42-16 and 27-44-13, or assessments for any insurance guaranty fund or pool now or hereafter created by statute paid during the calendar year.

(9) It is the intent of this subsection (c) that any estimated allowable credits or deductions claimed on quarterly returns be reconciled to actual expenditures made during the calendar year on the return due for March 1 in the succeeding calendar year.

(d) The premium taxes collected under this section shall be deposited in the State Treasury and credited as follows:

(1) To THE CREDIT OF THE STATE GENERAL FUND:

a. One hundred percent of the premium tax paid by all health maintenance organizations, domestic and foreign.

b. Fifty percent of the premium tax paid by domestic life insurers.

c. No part of the premium tax paid by non-profit corporations organized pursuant to the provisions of Sections 10-4-100 to 10-4-115, inclusive.

d. Twenty-five percent of the premium tax paid by all other domestic insurers.

e. One hundred percent of the premium tax paid by foreign life insurers.

f. Sixty-two and one-half percent of the premium tax paid by all foreign property insurers.

g. Seventy-five percent of the premium tax paid by all other foreign insurers.

(2) To the credit of the Alabama Special Educational Trust Fund:

a. Fifty percent of the premium tax paid by domestic life insurers.

b. No part of the premium tax paid by non-profit corporations organized pursuant to the provisions of Sections 10-4-100 to 10-4-115, inclusive.

c. Seventy-five percent of the premium tax paid by all other domestic insurers.

d. Thirty-seven and one-half percent of the premium tax paid by foreign property insurers.

e. Twenty-five percent of the premium tax paid by all other foreign insurers.

(3) To the credit of the Alabama Special Mental Health Trust Fund 100 percent of the premium taxes paid by nonprofit corporations organized pursuant to Sections 10-4-100 to 10-4-115, inclusive.

(4) Any provision of this subsection (d) to the contrary notwithstanding, the amount credited to the Alabama Special Educational Trust Fund and the Alabama Special Mental Health Trust Fund for any fiscal year after the fiscal year ending September 30, 1992, under this subsection (d) shall be limited to no more than the amount so credited in the fiscal year ending September 30, 1992. Any premium tax that would have been credited to the

Alabama Special Educational Trust Fund or the Alabama Special Mental Health Trust Fund but for this limitation, shall be credited to the State General Fund. (Acts 1993, No. 93-679, § 3; Acts 1993, 1st Ex. Sess., No. 93-847, p. 67, § 1.)

The 1993, 1st Ex. Sess., amendment, effective August 24, 1993, in subsection (a)(3), added present paragraph c. and redesignated former paragraph c. as present paragraph d.

Code Commissioner's note. — Acts 1993, No. 93-847, § 3, provides: "Upon its passage and approval by the Governor, or upon its otherwise becoming a law, this act shall become effective at 12:01 a.m. on the first day of January, 1995, with respect to insurance premiums received on or after January 1, 1995."

Acts 1993, No. 93-679, § 14, provides: "Upon its passage and approval by the Governor, or upon its otherwise becoming a law, this act shall become effective at 12:01 a.m. on the first day of January, 1995, with respect to insurance premiums received on or after January 1, 1995; provided, however, that (1) the determination and payment of taxes due on premiums received prior to January 1, 1995, shall be pursuant to the law in effect prior to January 1, 1995, and (2) the provisions of subsection (b) of Section 3 and the provisions of Section 11 shall become effective immediately upon passage of this act and approval by the Governor, or upon its otherwise becoming a law."

Acts 1993, No. 93-679, § 12 repealed Sections 27-4-4 and 27-4-5 which are referred to in the first sentence of subsection (b).

§ 27-4A-4. Penalties.

Every insurer failing to comply with the requirements of this chapter shall be subject to a penalty of not less than $1,000 nor exceeding $10,000, recoverable in an action brought by the Attorney General for the Commissioner. Upon any violation, the Commissioner may suspend or revoke the insurer's certificate of authority. Penalties recovered under this section shall be paid to the State Treasury to the credit of the State General Fund. (Acts 1993, No. 93-679, § 4.)

Code Commissioner's note. — Acts 1993, No. 93-679, § 14, provides: "Upon its passage and approval by the Governor, or upon its otherwise becoming a law, this act shall become effective at 12:01 a.m. on the first day of January, 1995, with respect to insurance premiums received on or after January 1, 1995; provided, however, that (1) the determination and payment of taxes due on premiums received prior to January 1, 1995, shall be pursuant to the law in effect prior to January 1, 1995, and (2) the provisions of subsection (b) of Section 3 and the provisions of Section 11 shall become effective immediately upon passage of this act and approval by the Governor, or upon its otherwise becoming a law."

§ 27-4A-5. Exclusive tax on premiums.

The premium tax levied by this chapter is exclusive and shall be in lieu of all other and additional taxes and licenses of the state or county imposed on, based upon or measured by premiums received by the insurer for business done in this state. No license or privilege tax shall be charged any insurer paying the premium tax levied by this chapter by or on behalf of any county. (Acts 1993, No. 93-679, § 5.)

Code Commissioner's note. — Acts 1993, No. 93-679, § 14, provides: "Upon its passage and approval by the Governor, or upon its otherwise becoming a law, this act shall become effective at 12:01 a.m. on the first day of January, 1995, with respect to insurance premiums received on or after January 1, 1995; provided, however, that (1) the determination and payment of taxes due on premiums received prior to January 1, 1995, shall be pursuant to the law in effect prior to January 1, 1995, and (2) the provisions of subsection (b) of Section 3 and the provisions of Section 11 shall become effective immediately upon passage of this act and approval by the Governor, or upon its otherwise becoming a law."

§ 27-4A-6. Exemption from income and ad valorem taxes.

Nothing in this chapter shall be construed to repeal any existing laws or statutes which exempt or exclude insurers from the payment of fees, taxes, or licenses other than the tax imposed by this chapter. Without limiting the generality of the preceding sentence, insurers upon which this section imposes a tax upon their premium income or in lieu thereof, shall be exempt from income taxes imposed by the State of Alabama under the provisions of Chapter 18 of Title 40, or any other similar law; and the shares of domestic insurers shall be exempt from ad valorem taxes as provided by Section 40-14-70. (Acts 1993, No. 93-679, § 6.)

Code Commissioner's note. — Acts 1993, No. 93-679, § 14, provides: "Upon its passage and approval by the Governor, or upon its otherwise becoming a law, this act shall become effective at 12:01 a.m. on the first day of January, 1995, with respect to insurance premiums received on or after January 1, 1995; provided, however, that (1) the determination and payment of taxes due on premiums received prior to January 1, 1995, shall be pursuant to the law in effect prior to January 1, 1995, and (2) the provisions of subsection (b) of Section 3 and the provisions of Section 11 shall become effective immediately upon passage of this act and approval by the Governor, or upon its otherwise becoming a law."

§ 27-4A-7. Mutual aid associations.

Mutual aid associations shall be subject to the provisions of this chapter and subject to the annual premium tax to be paid by insurers on insurance premiums. (Acts 1993, No. 93-679, § 10.)

Code Commissioner's note. — Acts 1993, No. 93-679, § 14, provides: "Upon its passage and approval by the Governor, or upon its otherwise becoming a law, this act shall become effective at 12:01 a.m. on the first day of January, 1995, with respect to insurance premiums received on or after January 1, 1995; provided, however, that (1) the determination and payment of taxes due on premiums received prior to January 1, 1995, shall be pursuant to the law in effect prior to January 1, 1995, and (2) the provisions of subsection (b) of Section 3 and the provisions of Section 11 shall become effective immediately upon passage of this act and approval by the Governor, or upon its otherwise becoming a law."

CHAPTER 5.

KINDS OF INSURANCE; LIMITS OF RISK; REINSURANCE.

Sec.
27-5-12. Reinsurance.

§ 27-5-4. "Disability insurance" defined.

Disability insurance by definition insures "human beings," thus, where agreements between trusts and insurer concerned insurance for the funds in the trust and did not provide insurance for "human beings," the insurance was not "disability insurance" within the meaning of this section. Southtrust Bank v. Alabama Life & Disability Ins. Guar. Ass'n, 578 So. 2d 1302 (Ala. 1991).

§ 27-5-6. "Casualty insurance" defined.

Collateral references.

Livestock or animal insurance: risks and losses. 47 ALR4th 772.

Liability insurance: third party's right of action for insurer's bad-faith tactics designed to delay payment of claim. 62 ALR4th 1113.

What constitutes theft within automobile theft insurance policy—modern cases. 67 ALR4th 82.

Construction and effect of "rain insurance" policies insuring against rainfall on the date of concert, exhibition, game, or the like. 70 ALR4th 1010.

§ 27-5-10. "Title insurance" defined.

Closing service letter was not an insurance contract between loan company and title insurance company. The purpose of the closing service letter was to provide indemnity against loss due to a closing attorney's defalcation or failure to follow a lender's closing instructions. It was clear from a reading of the closing service letter that it stated Commonwealth's responsibility for the acts of its approved attorney. It was also clear that the closing letter was not a title insurance policy. Therefore, loan company presented no substantial evidence to support its bad faith claim. Metmor Fin., Inc. v. Commonwealth Land Title Ins. Co., 645 So. 2d 295 (Ala. 1993).

§ 27-5-12. Reinsurance.

(a) An insurer authorized under this title may accept reinsurance only of such risks and retain risk thereon within such limits as it is otherwise authorized to insure.

(b)(1) An insurer authorized under this title may reinsure all, or any part, of any particular risk with any solvent insurer.

(2)a. Credit for reinsurance shall be allowed a domestic ceding insurer as either an asset or a deduction from liability on account of reinsurance ceded to an assuming insurer which is licensed to transact insurance or reinsurance in this state.

b. Credit for reinsurance shall be allowed a domestic ceding insurer as either an asset or a deduction from liability on account of reinsurance ceded to an assuming insurer which is domiciled and licensed in or in the case of a U.S. branch of an alien assuming insurer is entered through a state which employs standards regarding credit for reinsurance substantially similar to those applicable under this statute and such assuming insurer or U.S. branch of an alien assuming insurer: (i) maintains a surplus as regards policyholders in an amount not less than twenty million dollars ($20,000,000); and (ii) submits to the authority of this state to examine its books and records. Provided, however, that the requirement of item (i) of this paragraph does not apply to reinsurance ceded and assumed pursuant to pooling arrangements among insurers in the same holding company system.

c.1. Credit for reinsurance shall be allowed a domestic ceding insurer as either an asset or a deduction from liability on account of reinsurance ceded to an assuming insurer which maintains a trust fund in a qualified United States financial institution, as defined in item (i) of subparagraph 4, for the payment of the valid claims of its United States policyholders and ceding insurers, their assigns and successors in interest. The assuming insurer shall report annually to the commissioner information substantially the same as that required to be reported on the NAIC annual statement form by licensed insurers to enable the commissioner to determine the sufficiency of the trust fund. In the case of a single assuming insurer, the trust shall consist of a trusteed account representing the assuming insurer's liabilities attributable to business written in the United States and, in addition, the assuming insurer shall maintain a trusteed surplus of not less than twenty million dollars ($20,000,000). In the case of a group including incorporated and individual unincorporated underwriters, the trust shall consist of a trusteed account representing the group's liabilities attributable to business written in the United States and, in addition, the group shall maintain a trusteed surplus of which one hundred million dollars ($100,000,000) shall be held jointly for the benefit of United States ceding insurers reinsured by any member of the group; the incorporated members of the group shall not be engaged in any business other than underwriting as a member of the group and shall be subject to the same level of solvency regulation and control by the group's domiciliary regulator as are the unincorporated members; and the group shall make available to the commissioner an annual certification by the group's domiciliary regulator and its independent public accountants of the solvency of each underwriter.

2. In the case of a group of incorporated insurers under common administration which complies with the filing requirements contained in subparagraph 1, and which has continuously transacted an insurance business outside the United States for at least three years; and submits to this state's authority to examine its books and records and bears the expense of the examination, and which has aggregate policyholders' surplus of ten billion dollars ($10,000,000,000); the trust shall be in an amount equal to the group's several liabilities attributable to business ceded by United States ceding insurers to any member of the group; plus the group shall maintain a joint trusteed surplus of which one hundred million dollars ($100,000,000) shall be held jointly for the benefit of United States ceding insurers of any member of the group as additional security for any such liabilities, and each member of the group shall make available to the commissioner an annual certification of the member's solvency by the member's domiciliary regulator and its independent public accountant.

3. The trust shall be established in a form approved by the Commissioner of Insurance. The trust instrument shall provide that contested claims shall be valid and enforceable upon the final order of any court of competent jurisdiction in the United States. The trust shall vest legal title to its assets in the trustees of the trust for its United States policyholders and ceding insurers, their assigns and successors in interest. The trust and the assuming insurer shall be subject to examination as determined by the commissioner. The trust described

herein must remain in effect for as long as the assuming insurer shall have outstanding obligations due under the reinsurance agreements subject to the trust.

4. No later than February 28 of each year the trustees of the trust shall report to the commissioner in writing setting forth the balance of the trust and listing the trust's investments at the preceding year end and shall certify the date of termination of the trust, if so planned, or certify that the trust shall not expire prior to the next following December 31.

d. Credit for reinsurance shall be allowed a domestic ceding insurer as either an asset or a deduction from liability when the reinsurance is ceded to an assuming insurer not meeting the requirements of paragraphs a, b or c, but only with respect to the insurance of risks located in jurisdictions where such reinsurance is required by applicable law or regulation of that jurisdiction.

e. If the assuming insurer is not licensed to transact insurance in this state, the credit permitted by paragraphs a, b and c of subdivision (b)(2) shall not be allowed unless the assuming insurer agrees in the reinsurance agreements:

1. That in the event of the failure of the assuming insurer to perform its obligations under the terms of the reinsurance agreement, the assuming insurer, at the request of the ceding insurer, shall submit to the jurisdiction of any court of competent jurisdiction in any state of the United States, will comply with all requirements necessary to give such court jurisdiction, and will abide by the final decision of such court or of any appellate court in the event of an appeal; and

2. To designate the commissioner or a designated attorney as its true and lawful attorney upon whom may be served any lawful process in any action, suit or proceeding instituted by or on behalf of the ceding company.

This provision is not intended to conflict with or override the obligation of the parties to a reinsurance agreement to arbitrate their disputes, if such an obligation is created in the agreement.

3. A reduction from liability for the reinsurance ceded by a domestic insurer to an assuming insurer not meeting the requirements of subdivision 2 of this subsection shall be allowed in an amount not exceeding the liabilities carried by the ceding insurer and such reduction shall be in the amount of funds held by or on behalf of the ceding insurer, including funds held in trust for the ceding insurer, under a reinsurance contract with such assuming insurer as security for the payment of obligations thereunder, if such security is held in the United States subject to withdrawal solely by, and under the exclusive control of, the ceding insurer; or, in the case of a trust, held in a qualified United States financial institution, as defined in subparagraph (4).

This security may be in the form of:

(i) Cash;

(ii) Securities listed by the securities valuation office of the National Association of Insurance Commissioners and qualifying as admitted assets;

(iii) Clean, irrevocable, unconditional letters of credit issued or confirmed by a qualified United States financial institution as defined in subparagraph (4) no later than December 31, in respect of the year for which filing is being made, and in the possession of the ceding company on or before the filing date of its annual statement.

As used herein, "clean" means that the letter of credit is not conditioned on the delivery of any other documents or materials. "Irrevocable" means that the letter of credit cannot be modified or revoked without the consent of the beneficiary, once the beneficiary is established.

Letters of credit meeting applicable standards of issuer acceptability as of the dates of their issuance (or confirmation) shall, notwithstanding the issuing (or confirming) institution's subsequent failure to meet applicable standards of issuer acceptability, continue to be acceptable as security until their expiration, extension, renewal, modification or amendment, whichever first occurs.

(iv) Any other form of security acceptable to the commissioner.

4.(i) For purposes of paragraph c of subdivision (2), a "qualified United States financial institution" means an institution that:

(I) Is organized or (in the case of a U.S. office of a foreign banking organization) licensed, under the laws of the United States or any state thereof;

(II) Is regulated, supervised and examined by U. S. federal or state authorities having regulatory authority over banks and trust companies; and

(III) Has been determined by either the commissioner, or the securities valuation office of the National Association of Insurance Commissioners, to meet such standards of financial condition and standing as are considered necessary and appropriate to regulate the quality of financial institutions whose letters of credit will be acceptable to the commissioner.

(ii) A "qualified United States financial institution" means, for purposes of those provisions of this law specifying those institutions that are eligible to act as a fiduciary of a trust, an institution that:

(I) Is organized, or (in the case of a U.S. branch or agency office of a foreign banking organization) licensed, under the laws of the United States or any state thereof and has been granted authority to operate with fiduciary powers; and

(II) Is regulated, supervised and examined by federal or state authorities having regulatory authority over banks and trust companies.

5. No credit shall be allowed to any ceding insurer for reinsurance placed with a reinsurer qualified under this section, unless the

reinsurance is payable by the assuming insurer on the basis of the liability of the ceding insurer under the contracts reinsured without diminution because of the insolvency of the ceding insurer.

(c) Upon request of the commissioner, an insurer shall promptly inform the commissioner in writing of the cancellation or any other material change of any of its reinsurance treaties or arrangements.

(d) This section shall not apply to wet marine and transportation insurance.

(e) The commissioner may adopt rules and regulations implementing the provisions of this section. (Acts 1971, No. 407, p. 707, § 96; Acts 1990, No. 90-767, p. 1566; Acts 1994, 1st Ex. Sess., No. 94-788, p. 87, § 1.)

The 1994, 1st Ex. Sess., amendment, effective May 6, 1994, in subdivision (2) of subsection (b), inserted the designation for paragraph a; in paragraph a, deleted "only when" following "ceded" and deleted "a. The reinsurance is ceded" preceding "to"; in paragraph b, substituted "Credit for reinsurance shall be allowed a domestic ceding insurer as either an asset or a deduction from liability on account of reinsurance" for "The reinsurance is"; in paragraph c, added subparagraph designations; in the first sentence of subparagraph 1, substituted "Credit for reinsurance shall be allowed a domestic ceding insurer as either an asset or a deduction from liability on account of reinsurance" for "The reinsurance is," in the fourth sentence substituted "including incorporated and" for "of" and inserted the language beginning "the incorporated members of the group" through the semicolon; added subparagraphs 2 and 4; inserted the first sentence in subparagraph 3; at the beginning of paragraph d, substituted "Credit for reinsurance shall be allowed a domestic ceding insurer as either an asset or a deduction from liability when the" for "The"; substituted "paragraph c of subdivision 2" for "item (iii) of subparagraph 3" in paragraph e; and made nonsubstantive changes.

Code Commissioner's note. — Acts 1990, No. 90-767, § 3 provides: "Subsection (b), (1) through (5), of this amendatory act shall apply to all cessions after the effective date of this act [May 3, 1990] under reinsurance agreements which have had an inception, anniversary, or renewal date not less than six months after the effective date of this act."

In 1994, the Code Commissioner substituted "paragraph c of subdivision (2)" for "paragraph c of subdivision (3)" in subparagraph 4 of paragraph e of subdivision 2 of subsection (b) to reflect, based on the context, the correct reference.

CHAPTER 5A.

REINSURANCE INTERMEDIARIES.

Sec.
27-5A-1. Short title.
27-5A-2. Definitions.
27-5A-3. Licensure.
27-5A-4. Required contract provisions; reinsurance intermediary-brokers.
27-5A-5. Books and records; reinsurance intermediary brokers.
27-5A-6. Duties of insurers utilizing the services of a reinsurance intermediary-broker.
27-5A-7. Required contract provisions;

Sec.
          reinsurance intermediary-managers.
27-5A-8. Prohibited acts.
27-5A-9. Duties of reinsurers utilizing services of reinsurance intermediary-manager.
27-5A-10. Examination authority.
27-5A-11. Penalties and liabilities.
27-5A-12. Rules and regulations.
27-5A-13. Utilization of services of reinsurance intermediary.

Effective date. — The act which added this chapter became effective May 17, 1993.

§ 27-5A-1. Short title.

This chapter may be cited as the Alabama Reinsurance Intermediary Act. (Acts 1993, No. 93-673, § 1.)

§ 27-5A-2. Definitions.

As used in this chapter, the following terms shall have the following meanings, respectively, unless the context clearly indicates otherwise:

(1) ACTUARY. A person who is a member in good standing of the American Academy of Actuaries.

(2) COMMISSIONER. The Alabama Commissioner of Insurance.

(3) CONTROLLING PERSON. Any person, firm, association, or corporation who directly or indirectly has the power to direct or cause to be directed, the management, control, or activities of the reinsurance intermediary.

(4) INSURER. Any person, firm, association, or corporation duly licensed in this state pursuant to the applicable provisions of the insurance law as an insurer.

(5) LICENSED PRODUCER. An agent, broker, or reinsurance intermediary licensed pursuant to the applicable provision of the insurance law.

(6) QUALIFIED U.S. FINANCIAL INSTITUTION. An institution that:

a. Is organized or, in the case of a U.S. office of a foreign banking organization, licensed, pursuant to the laws of the United States or any state.

b. Is regulated, supervised and examined by federal or state authorities having regulatory authority over banks and trust companies.

c. Has been determined by either the commissioner, or the Securities Valuation Office of the National Association of Insurance Commissioners, to meet the standards of financial condition and standing as are considered necessary and appropriate to regulate the quality of financial institutions whose letters of credit will be acceptable to the commissioner.

(7) REINSURANCE INTERMEDIARY. A reinsurance intermediary-broker or a reinsurance intermediary-manager as these terms are defined in subdivisions (8) and (9) of this section.

(8) REINSURANCE INTERMEDIARY-BROKER. Any person, other than an officer or employee of the ceding insurer, firm, association, or corporation who solicits, negotiates, or places reinsurance cessions or retrocessions on behalf of a ceding insurer without the authority or power to bind reinsurance on behalf of such insurer.

(9) REINSURANCE INTERMEDIARY-MANAGER. Any person, firm, association, or corporation who has authority to bind or manages all or part of the assumed reinsurance business of a reinsurer (including the management of a separate division, department or underwriting office) and acts as an agent for such reinsurer whether known as a reinsurance intermediary-manager, manager, or other similar term. Notwithstanding the above, the following persons shall not be considered a reinsurance intermediary-manager, with respect to such reinsurer, for the purposes of this chapter:

a. An employee of the reinsurer.

b. A U.S. manager of the United States branch of an alien reinsurer.

c. An underwriting manager which, pursuant to contract, manages all the reinsurance operations of the reinsurer, is under common control with the reinsurer, subject to Chapter 29, Title 27, and whose compensation is not based on the volume of premiums written.

d. The manager of a group, association, pool, or organization of insurers which engages in joint underwriting or joint reinsurance and who are subject to examination by the Commissioner of Insurance of the state in which the manager's principal business office is located.

(10) REINSURER. Any person, firm, association, or corporation duly licensed in this state pursuant to the applicable provisions of the insurance law as an insurer with the authority to assume reinsurance.

(11) TO BE IN VIOLATION. The reinsurance intermediary, insurer, or reinsurer for whom the reinsurance intermediary was acting failed to substantially comply with the provisions of this chapter. (Acts 1993, No. 93-673, § 2.)

§ 27-5A-3. Licensure.

(a) No person, firm, association, or corporation shall act as a reinsurance intermediary-broker in this state if the reinsurance intermediary-broker maintains an office either directly, or as a member or employee of a firm or association, or an officer, director, or employee of a corporation:

(1) In this state, unless the reinsurance intermediary-broker is a licensed producer in this state.

(2) In another state, unless the reinsurance intermediary-broker is a licensed producer in this state or another state having a law substantially similar to this law or the reinsurance intermediary-broker is licensed in this state as a nonresident reinsurance intermediary.

(b) No person, firm, association, or corporation shall act as a reinsurance intermediary-manager:

(1) For a reinsurer domiciled in this state, unless the reinsurance inter-mediary-manager is a licensed producer in this state.

(2) In this state, if the reinsurance intermediary-manager maintains an office either directly or as a member or employee of a firm or association, or an officer, director, or employee of a corporation in this state, unless the reinsurance intermediary-manager is a licensed producer in this state.

(3) In another state for a nondomestic insurer, unless the reinsurance intermediary-manager is a licensed producer in this state or another state having a law substantially similar to this law or the person is licensed in this state as a nonresident reinsurance intermediary.

(c) The commissioner may require a reinsurance intermediary-manager subject to subsection (b) to:

(1) File a bond in an amount from an insurer acceptable to the commissioner for the protection of the reinsurer.

(2) Maintain an errors and omissions policy in an amount acceptable to the commissioner.

(d)(1) The commissioner may issue a reinsurance intermediary license to any person, firm, association, or corporation who has complied with the requirements of this chapter. Any license issued to a firm or association shall authorize all the members of the firm or association and any designated employees to act as reinsurance intermediaries pursuant to the license, and all the persons shall be named in the application and any supplements to the application. Any license issued to a corporation shall authorize all of the officers, and any designated employees and directors of the corporation to act as reinsurance intermediaries on behalf of the corporation, and all the persons shall be named in the application and any supplements thereto.

(2) If the applicant for a reinsurance intermediary license is a nonresident, the applicant, as a condition precedent to receiving or holding a license, shall designate the commissioner as agent for service of process in the manner, and with the same legal effect, provided for by this chapter for designation of service of process upon unauthorized insurers; and also shall furnish the commissioner with the name and address of a resident of this state upon whom notices or orders of the commissioner or process affecting such nonresident reinsurance intermediary may be served. A licensee shall promptly notify the commissioner in writing of every change in its designated agent for service of process, and any change shall not become effective until acknowledged by the commissioner.

(e) The commissioner may refuse to issue a reinsurance intermediary license if, in his judgment, the applicant, any one named on the application, or any member, principal, officer, or director of the applicant, is not trustworthy, or that any controlling person of the applicant is not trustworthy to act as a reinsurance intermediary, or that any of the foregoing has given cause for revocation or suspension of such license, or has failed to comply with any prerequisite for the issuance of the license. Upon a refusal, the commissioner shall promptly give written notice to the applicant that the license is refused, stating the reasons for the refusal.

(f) Licensed attorneys at law of this state, when acting in their professional capacity, shall be exempt from this section. (Acts 1993, No. 93-673, § 3.)

§ 27-5A-4. Required contract provisions; reinsurance intermediary-brokers.

Transactions between a reinsurance intermediary-broker and the insurer it represents in that capacity shall only be entered into pursuant to a written authorization, specifying the responsibilities of each party. The authorization shall, at a minimum, provide that:

(1) The insurer may terminate the reinsurance intermediary-broker's authority at any time.

(2) The reinsurance intermediary-broker shall render accounts to the insurer accurately detailing all material transactions, including information necessary to support all commissions, charges, and other fees received by, or owing, to the reinsurance intermediary-broker, and remit all funds due to the insurer within 30 days of receipt.

(3) All funds collected for the insurer's account shall be held by the reinsurance intermediary-broker in a fiduciary capacity in a bank which is a qualified U.S. financial institution as defined herein.

(4) The reinsurance intermediary-broker shall comply with Section 27-5A-5.

(5) The reinsurance intermediary-broker shall comply with the written standards established by the insurer for the cession or retrocession of all risks.

(6) The reinsurance intermediary-broker shall disclose to the insurer any relationship with any reinsurer to which business will be ceded or retroceded. (Acts 1993, No. 93-673, § 4.)

§ 27-5A-5. Books and records; reinsurance intermediary brokers.

(a) For at least 10 years after expiration of each contract of reinsurance transacted by the reinsurance intermediary-broker, the reinsurance intermediary-broker shall keep a complete record for each transaction showing all of the following:

(1) The type of contract, limits, underwriting restrictions, classes, or risks and territory.

(2) Period of coverage, including effective and expiration dates, cancellation provisions, and notice required of cancellation.

(3) Reporting and settlement requirements of balances.

(4) Rate used to compute the reinsurance premium.

(5) Names and addresses of assuming reinsurers.

(6) Rates of all reinsurance commissions, including the commissions on any retrocessions handled by the reinsurance intermediary-broker.

(7) Related correspondence and memoranda.

(8) Proof of placement.

(9) Details regarding retrocessions handled by the reinsurance intermediary-broker including the identity of retrocessionaires and percentage of each contract assumed or ceded.

(10) Financial records, including, but not limited to, premium and loss accounts.

(11) When the reinsurance intermediary-broker procures a reinsurance contract on behalf of a licensed ceding insurer:

a. Directly from any assuming reinsurer, written evidence that the assuming reinsurer has agreed to assume the risk.

b. If placed through a representative of the assuming reinsurer, other than an employee, written evidence that the reinsurer has delegated binding authority to the representative.

(b) The insurer shall have access and the right to copy and audit all accounts and records maintained by the reinsurance intermediary-broker related to its business in a form usable by the insurer. (Acts 1993, No. 93-673, § 5.)

§ 27-5A-6. Duties of insurers utilizing the services of a reinsurance intermediary-broker.

(a) An insurer shall not engage the services of any person, firm, association, or corporation to act as a reinsurance intermediary-broker on its behalf unless the person is licensed as required by subsection (a) of Section 27-5A-3.

(b) An insurer may not employ an individual who is employed by a reinsurance intermediary-broker with which it transacts business, unless such reinsurance intermediary-broker is under common control with the insurer and subject to Chapter 29, Title 27.

(c) The insurer shall annually obtain a copy of statements of the financial condition of each reinsurance intermediary-broker with which it transacts business. (Acts 1993, No. 93-673, § 6.)

§ 27-5A-7. Required contract provisions; reinsurance intermediary-managers.

Transactions between a reinsurance intermediary-manager and the reinsurer it represents in that capacity shall only be entered into pursuant to a written contract, specifying the responsibilities of each party, which shall be approved by the reinsurer's board of directors. At least 30 days before a reinsurer assumes or cedes business through a producer, a true copy of the approved contract shall be filed with the commissioner for approval. The contract shall, at a minimum, provide that:

(1) The reinsurer may terminate the contract for cause upon written notice to the reinsurance intermediary-manager. The reinsurer may immediately suspend the authority of the reinsurance intermediary-manager to assume or cede business during the pendency of any dispute regarding the cause for termination.

(2) The reinsurance intermediary-manager shall render accounts to the reinsurer accurately detailing all material transactions, including information necessary to support all commissions, charges, and other fees received by, or owing to the reinsurance intermediary-manager, and remit all funds due under the contract to the reinsurer on not less than a monthly basis.

(3) All funds collected for the reinsurer's account shall be held by the reinsurance intermediary-manager in a fiduciary capacity in a bank which is a qualified U.S. financial institution as defined herein. The reinsurance intermediary-manager may retain no more than three months estimated claims payments and allocated loss adjustment expenses. The reinsurance intermediary-manager shall maintain a separate bank account for each reinsurer that it represents.

(4) For at least 10 years after expiration of each contract of reinsurance transacted by the reinsurance intermediary-manager, the reinsurance intermediary-manager shall keep a complete record for each transaction showing all of the following:

    a. The type of contract, limits, underwriting restrictions, classes, or risks and territory.

b. Period of coverage, including effective and expiration dates, cancellation provisions, and notice required of cancellation, and disposition of outstanding reserves on covered risks.

c. Reporting and settlement requirements of balances.

d. Rate used to compute the reinsurance premium.

e. Names and addresses of reinsurers.

f. Rates of all reinsurance commissions, including the commissions on any retrocessions handled by the reinsurance intermediary-manager.

g. Related correspondence and memoranda.

h. Proof of placement.

i. Details regarding retrocessions handled by the reinsurance intermediary-manager, as permitted by subsection (d) of Section 27-5A-9, including the identity of retrocessionaires and percentage of each contract assumed or ceded.

j. Financial records, including, but not limited to, premium and loss accounts.

k. When the reinsurance intermediary-manager places a reinsurance contract on behalf of a ceding insurer:

1. Directly from any assuming reinsurer, written evidence that the assuming reinsurer has agreed to assume the risk.

2. If placed through a representative of the assuming reinsurer, other than an employee, written evidence that the reinsurer has delegated binding authority to the representative.

(5) The reinsurer shall have access and the right to copy all accounts and records maintained by the reinsurance intermediary-manager related to its business in a form usable by the reinsurer.

(6) The contract cannot be assigned in whole or in part by the reinsurance intermediary-manager.

(7) The reinsurance intermediary-manager shall comply with the written underwriting and rating standards established by the insurer for the acceptance, rejection, or cession of all risks.

(8) Sets forth the rates, terms, and purposes of commissions, charges, and other fees which the reinsurance intermediary-manager may levy against the reinsurer.

(9) If the contract permits the reinsurance intermediary-manager to settle claims on behalf of the reinsurer:

a. All claims shall be reported to the reinsurer in a timely manner.

b. A copy of the claim file shall be sent to the reinsurer at its request or as soon as it becomes known that the claim:

1. Has the potential to exceed the lesser of an amount determined by the commissioner or the limit set by the reinsurer.

2. Involves a coverage dispute.

3. May exceed the reinsurance intermediary-manager's claims settlement authority.

4. Is open for more than six months.

5. Is closed by payment of the lesser of an amount set by the commissioner or an amount set by the reinsurer.

c. All claim files shall be the joint property of the reinsurer and reinsurance intermediary-manager. However, upon an order of liquidation of the reinsurer, the files shall become the sole property of the reinsurer or its estate; the reinsurance intermediary-manager shall have reasonable access to and the right to copy the files on a timely basis.

d. Any settlement authority granted to the reinsurance intermediary-manager may be terminated for cause upon the reinsurer's written notice to the reinsurance intermediary-manager or upon the termination of the contract. The reinsurer may suspend the settlement authority during the pendency of the dispute regarding the cause of termination.

(10) If the contract provides for a sharing of interim profits by the reinsurance intermediary-manager, that the interim profits shall not be paid until one year after the end of each underwriting period for property business and five years after the end of each underwriting period for casualty business (or a later period set by the commissioner for specified lines of insurance), and not until the adequacy of reserves on remaining claims has been verified pursuant to subsection (c) of Section 27-5A-9.

(11) The reinsurance intermediary-manager shall annually provide the reinsurer with a statement of its financial condition prepared by an independent certified accountant.

(12) The reinsurer shall periodically (at least semiannually) conduct an on-site review of the underwriting and claims processing operations of the reinsurance intermediary-manager.

(13) The reinsurance intermediary-manager shall disclose to the reinsurer any relationship it has with any insurer prior to ceding or assuming any business with such insurer pursuant to this contract.

(14) Within the scope of its actual or apparent authority the acts of the reinsurance intermediary-manager shall be deemed to be the acts of the reinsurer on whose behalf it is acting. (Acts 1993, No. 93-673, § 7.)

§ 27-5A-8. Prohibited acts.

The reinsurance intermediary-manager shall not:

(1) Cede retrocessions on behalf of the reinsurer, except that the reinsurance intermediary-manager may cede facultative retrocessions pursuant to obligatory facultative agreements if the contract with the reinsurer contains reinsurance underwriting guidelines for such retrocessions. The guidelines shall include a list of reinsurers with which any automatic agreements are in effect, and for each such reinsurer, the coverages and amounts or percentages that may be reinsured, and commission schedules.

(2) Commit the reinsurer to participate in reinsurance syndicates.

(3) Appoint any producer without assuring that the producer is lawfully licensed to transact the type of reinsurance for which the producer is appointed.

(4) Without prior approval of the reinsurer, pay or commit the reinsurer to pay a claim, net of retrocessions, that exceeds the lesser of an amount

specified by the reinsurer or one percent of the reinsurer's policyholder's surplus as of December 31 of the last complete calendar year.

(5) Collect any payment from a retrocessionaire or commit the reinsurer to any claim settlement with a retrocessionaire, without prior approval of the reinsurer. If prior approval is given, a report shall be promptly forwarded to the reinsurer.

(6) Jointly employ an individual who is employed by the reinsurer unless such reinsurance intermediary-manager is under common control with the reinsurer subject to the Chapter 29, Title 27.

(7) Appoint a sub-reinsurance intermediary-manager. (Acts 1993, No. 93-673, § 8.)

§ 27-5A-9. Duties of reinsurers utilizing services of reinsurance intermediary-manager.

(a) A reinsurer shall not engage the services of any person, firm, association, or corporation to act as a reinsurance intermediary-manager on its behalf unless such person is licensed as required by subsection (b) of Section 27-5A-3.

(b) The reinsurer shall annually obtain a copy of statements of the financial condition of each reinsurance intermediary-manager which such reinsurer has engaged prepared by an independent certified accountant in a form acceptable to the commissioner.

(c) If a reinsurance intermediary-manager establishes loss reserves, the reinsurer shall annually obtain the opinion of an actuary attesting to the adequacy of loss reserves established for losses incurred and outstanding on business produced by the reinsurance intermediary-manager. This opinion shall be in addition to any other required loss reserve certification.

(d) Binding authority for all retrocessional contracts or participation in reinsurance syndicates shall rest with an officer of the reinsurer who shall not be affiliated with the reinsurance intermediary-manager.

(e) Within 30 days of termination of a contract with a reinsurance intermediary-manager, the reinsurer shall provide written notification of such termination to the commissioner.

(f) A reinsurer shall not appoint to its board of directors, any officer, director, employee, controlling shareholder, or subproducer of its reinsurance intermediary-manager. This subsection shall not apply to relationships governed by Chapter 29, Title 27. (Acts 1993, No. 93-673, § 9.)

§ 27-5A-10. Examination authority.

(a) A reinsurance intermediary shall be subject to examination by the commissioner. The commissioner shall have access to all books, bank accounts, and records of the reinsurance intermediary in a form usable to the commissioner.

(b) A reinsurance intermediary-manager may be examined as if it were the reinsurer. (Acts 1993, No. 93-673, § 10.)

§ 27-5A-11. Penalties and liabilities.

(a) A reinsurance intermediary, insurer, or reinsurer found by the commissioner, after a hearing conducted in accordance with Section 27-2-28, to be in violation of this chapter, shall:

(1) For each separate violation, pay a penalty in an amount not exceeding $5,000.

(2) Be subject to revocation or suspension of its license.

(3) If a violation was committed by the reinsurance intermediary, the reinsurance intermediary shall make restitution to the insurer, reinsurer, rehabilitator, or liquidator of the insurer or reinsurer for the net losses incurred by the insurer or reinsurer attributable to such violation.

(b) The decision, determination, or order of the commissioner pursuant to subsection (a) of this section shall be subject to judicial review pursuant to Section 27-2-32.

(c) Nothing contained in this section shall affect the right of the commissioner to impose any other penalties provided in the insurance law.

(d) Nothing contained in this chapter is intended to or shall in any manner limit or restrict the rights of policyholders, claimants, creditors, or other third parties or confer any rights to those persons. (Acts 1993, No. 93-673, § 11.)

§ 27-5A-12. Rules and regulations.

The commissioner may adopt reasonable rules and regulations for the implementation and administration of the provisions of this chapter. (Acts 1993, No. 93-673, § 12.)

§ 27-5A-13. Utilization of services of reinsurance intermediary.

No insurer or reinsurer may continue to utilize the services of a reinsurance intermediary on and after May 17, 1993 unless utilization is in compliance with this chapter. (Acts 1993, No. 93-673, § 15.)

CHAPTER 6.

ADMINISTRATION OF DEPOSITS.

§ 27-6-13. Sale of surety insurers' special deposit to pay outstanding judgment.

Collateral references.
Liability of surety on private bond for statutory penalties imposed for nonpayment. 19 ALR5th 900.

CHAPTER 6A.

MANAGING GENERAL AGENTS.

Sec.
27-6A-1. Short title.
27-6A-2. Definitions.
27-6A-3. Licensure requirements.
27-6A-4. Contract requirements.

Sec.
27-6A-5. Duties of insurer.
27-6A-6. Acts of managing general agent.
27-6A-7. Penalties.
27-6A-8. Compliance.

Effective date. — The act which added this chapter became effective May 17, 1993.

Code Commissioner's note. — Acts 1993, No. 93-675, which enacted this chapter, in § 20, provides: "The Commissioner of Insurance may adopt reasonable rules and regulations neces-sary for the implementation and the adminis-tration of this act."

Cross references. — As to provisions of rules and regulations necessary for the effectu-ation of this title, see § 27-2-17.

§ 27-6A-1. Short title.

Sections 27-6A-2 through 27-6A-8, inclusive, of this chapter may be cited as the "Alabama Managing General Agents Act." (Acts 1993, No. 93-675, § 9.)

§ 27-6A-2. Definitions.

As used in this chapter, the following terms shall have the following meanings, respectively, unless the context clearly indicates otherwise:

(1) ACTUARY. A person who is a member in good standing of the American Academy of Actuaries.

(2) INSURER. A person defined in subsections (2) and (3) of Section 27-1-2.

(3) MANAGING GENERAL AGENT. In addition to the definition found in subdi-vision (a)(4) of Section 27-7-1, any person, firm, or association who does both of the following:

    a. Manages all or part of the insurance business of an insurer (including the management of a separate division, department, or underwriting office).

    b. Acts as an agent for an insurer whether known as a managing general agent, manager, or other similar term, who, with or without the authority, either separately or together with affiliates, produces, directly or indirectly, and underwrites an amount of gross direct written premium equal to or more than five percent of the policyholder surplus as reported in the last annual statement of the insurer in any one quarter or year together with one or more of the following activities related to the business produced:

      1. Adjusts or pays claims in excess of an amount determined by the commissioner.

      2. Negotiates reinsurance on behalf of the insurer.

    c. Notwithstanding the above, the following persons shall not be con-sidered as managing general agents for the purposes of this chapter:

      1. An employee of the insurer.

2. A United States manager of the United States branch of an alien insurer.

3. An underwriting manager who, pursuant to contract, manages all the insurance operations of the insurer, is under common control with the insurer, subject to the Alabama Insurance Holding Company Systems Regulatory Act, Chapter 29 (commencing with Section 27-29-1) of Title 27, and whose compensation is not based on the volume of premiums written.

4. The attorney-in-fact authorized by and acting for the subscribers of a reciprocal insurer or inter-insurance exchange under powers of attorney.

(4) POLICYHOLDER SURPLUS. The excess of assets over liabilities.

(5) UNDERWRITE. The authority to accept or reject risk on behalf of the insurer. (Acts 1993, No. 93-675, § 3.)

§ 27-6A-3. Licensure requirements.

(a) As to the kinds of insurance described in Section 27-7-2:

(1) No person, firm, association, or corporation shall act in the capacity of a managing general agent with respect to risks located in this state for an insurer licensed in this state unless then licensed in this state as a managing general agent of the insurer.

(2) No person, firm, association, or corporation shall act in the capacity of a managing general agent representing an insurer domiciled in this state with respect to risks located outside this state unless then licensed in this state as a managing general agent of the insurer. Where applicable, the license may be a nonresident license pursuant to this chapter.

(b) As to the kinds of insurance described in Section 27-8-2:

(1) No person, firm, association, or corporation shall act in the capacity of a managing general agent with respect to risks located in this state for an insurer licensed in this state unless then licensed as a managing general agent of the insurer and shall qualify and meet the requirements and qualifications of an agent pursuant to Chapter 8, Title 27. These managing general agents shall not be required to take and pass an examination or be a resident of Alabama.

(2) No person, firm, association, or corporation shall act in the capacity of a managing general agent representing an insurer domiciled in this state with respect to risks located outside this state unless then licensed in this state as a managing general agent of the insurer and shall qualify and meet the requirements and qualifications of an agent pursuant to Chapter 8 of Title 27. These managing general agents shall not be required to take and pass an examination or be a resident of Alabama.

(c) The fees required of general agents of property and casualty insurers under subdivision (a)(8) of Section 27-4-2, shall also apply to licenses required by this section.

(d) The commissioner may require the managing general agent to maintain a bond in an amount acceptable to the commissioner for the protection of the insurer.

(e) The commissioner may require the managing general agent to maintain an errors and omissions policy. (Acts 1993, No. 93-675, § 4.)

§ 27-6A-4. Contract requirements.

No person, firm, association, or corporation acting in the capacity of a managing general agent shall place business with an insurer unless there is in force a written contract between the parties that sets forth the responsibilities of each party and where both parties share responsibility for a particular function, specifies the division of such responsibilities, and that contains the following minimum provisions:

(a) The insurer may terminate the contract for cause upon written notice to the managing general agent. The insurer may suspend the underwriting authority of the managing general agent during the pendency of any dispute regarding the cause for termination.

(b) The managing general agent shall render accounts to the insurer detailing all transactions and remit all funds due under the contract to the insurer on not less than a monthly basis.

(c) All funds collected for the account of an insurer will be held by the managing general agent in a fiduciary capacity in a bank that is a member of the Federal Reserve System. This account shall be used for all payments on behalf of the insurer. The managing general agent may retain no more than three months estimated claims payments and allocated loss adjustment expenses.

(d) Separate records of business written by the managing general agent shall be maintained. The insurer shall have access and right to copy all accounts and records related to its business in a form usable by the insurer and the commissioner shall have access to all books, bank accounts, and records of the managing general agent in a form usable to the commissioner. The records shall be retained according to Section 27-7-33.

(e) The contract may not be assigned in whole or in part by the managing general agent.

(f) The contract shall contain appropriate underwriting guidelines including the following:

(1) The maximum annual premium volume.
(2) The basis of the rates to be charged.
(3) The types of risks that may be written.
(4) Maximum limits of liability.
(5) Applicable exclusions.
(6) Territorial limitations.
(7) Policy cancellation provisions.
(8) The maximum policy period.

(g) The insurer shall have the right to cancellation or non-renewal of any policy of insurance subject to the applicable laws and regulations concerning the cancellation and non-renewal of insurance policies.

(h) If the contract permits the managing general agent to settle claims on behalf of the insurer:

(1) All claims shall be reported to the company in a timely manner.

(2) A copy of the claim file shall be sent to the insurer at its request or as soon as it becomes known to the managing general agent that the claim:

a. Has the potential to exceed an amount determined by the commissioner or exceeds the limit set by the company, whichever is less.

b. Involves a coverage dispute.

c. May exceed the managing general agent's claims settlement authority.

d. Has been open for more than six months.

e. Is closed by payment of an amount set by the commissioner or an amount set by the company, whichever is less.

(3) All claim files shall be the joint property of the insurer and managing general agent. Upon an order of liquidation of the insurer, the files shall become the sole property of the insurer or its estate. The managing general agent shall have reasonable access to and the right to copy the files on a timely basis.

(4) Any settlement authority granted to the managing general agent may be terminated for cause upon the insurer's written notice to the managing general agent or upon the termination of the contract. The insurer may suspend the settlement authority during the pendency of any dispute regarding the cause for termination.

(i) Where electronic claims files are in existence, the contract shall address the timely transmission of the data.

(j) If the contract provides for a sharing of interim profits by the managing general agent, and the managing general agent has the authority to determine the amount of the interim profits by establishing loss reserves or controlling claim payments, or in any other manner, interim profits shall not be paid to the managing general agent until one year after they are earned for property insurance business and five years after they are earned on casualty business and not until the profits have been verified pursuant to Section 27-6A-5 of this chapter.

(k) The managing general agent shall not:

(1) Bind reinsurance or retrocessions on behalf of the insurer, except that the managing general agent may bind facultative reinsurance contracts pursuant to obligatory facultative agreements if the contract with the insurer contains reinsurance underwriting guidelines including, for both reinsurance assumed and ceded, a list of reinsurers with which such automatic agreements are in effect, the coverages and amounts or percentages that may be reinsured and commission schedules.

(2) Commit the insurer to participate in insurance or reinsurance syndicates.

(3) Appoint any agent without assuring that the agent is lawfully licensed to transact the type of insurance for which he or she is appointed.

(4) Without prior approval of the insurer, pay or commit the insurer to pay a claim over a specified amount, net of reinsurance, which shall not exceed one percent of the insurer's policyholder's surplus as of December 31 of the last completed calendar year.

(5) Collect any payment from a reinsurer or commit the insurer to any claim settlement with a reinsurer without prior approval of the insurer. If prior approval is given, a report shall be promptly forwarded to the insurer.

(6) Permit its subagent to serve on the insurer's board of directors.

(7) Jointly employ an individual who is employed by the insurer.

(8) Appoint a sub-managing general agent. (Acts 1993, No. 93-675, § 5.)

§ 27-6A-5. Duties of insurer.

Insurers shall have the following duties:

(1) The insurer shall have on file an independent financial examination, in a form acceptable to the commissioner, of each managing general agent with which it has done business.

(2) If a managing general agent establishes loss reserves, the insurer shall annually obtain the opinion of an actuary attesting to the adequacy of loss reserves established for losses incurred and outstanding on business produced by the managing general agent. This is in addition to any other required loss reserve certification.

(3) The insurer shall periodically, and at least semi-annually, conduct an on-site review of the underwriting and claims processing operations of the managing general agent.

(4) Binding authority for all reinsurance contracts or participation in insurance or reinsurance syndicate shall rest with an officer of the insurer, who shall not be affiliated with the managing general agent.

(5) Within 30 days of entering into or terminating a contract with a managing general agent, the insurer shall provide written notification of the appointment or termination to the commissioner. Notices of appointment of a managing general agent shall include a statement of duties which the applicant is expected to perform on behalf of the insurer, the lines of insurance for which the applicant is to be authorized to act, and any other information the commissioner may request.

(6) An insurer shall review its books and records each quarter to determine if any agent has become, by operation of subdivision (3) of Section 27-6A-2, a managing general agent as defined in that section. If the insurer determines that an agent has become a managing general agent, the insurer shall promptly notify the agent and the commissioner of the determination and the insurer and the agent shall fully comply with the provisions of this chapter within 30 days of the notification.

(7) An insurer shall not appoint to its board of directors an officer, director, employee, subagent, or controlling shareholder of its managing general agents. This subsection shall not apply to relationships governed by the Alabama Insurance Holding Company Act, Chapter 29 (commencing with Section 27-29-1) of Title 27. (Acts 1993, No. 93-675, § 6.)

§ 27-6A-6. Acts of managing general agent.

The acts of the managing general agent are considered to be the acts of the insurer on whose behalf it is acting. A managing general agent may be examined as if it were the insurer. (Acts 1993, No. 93-675, § 7.)

§ 27-6A-7. Penalties.

(a) If the commissioner finds after a hearing conducted in accordance with Section 27-2-28, that any person has violated this chapter, the commissioner may order:

(1) For each separate violation, a penalty in an amount of up to $5,000.

(2) Revocation or suspension of the managing general agent's license.

(3) The managing general agent to reimburse the insurer, the rehabilitator, or liquidator of the insurer for any losses incurred by the insurer caused by a violation of this chapter committed by the managing general agent.

(b) The decision, determination, or order of the commissioner pursuant to subsection (a) of this section shall be subject to judicial review pursuant to Section 27-2-31.

(c) No provision of this section shall affect the right of the commissioner to impose any other penalties provided for in the insurance law, rule, or regulation.

(d) No provision of this chapter is intended to or shall in any manner limit or restrict the rights of policyholders, claimants, and auditors. (Acts 1993, No. 93-675, § 8.)

§ 27-6A-8. Compliance.

No insurer may continue to use the services of a managing general agent after midnight December 31, 1993, unless the insurer is in compliance with this chapter. (Acts 1993, No. 93-675, § 9.)

CHAPTER 6B.

BUSINESS TRANSACTED WITH PRODUCER CONTROLLED PROPERTY AND CASUALTY INSURER LAW.

Sec.
27-6B-1. Short title.
27-6B-2. Definitions.
27-6B-3. Application of chapter to licensed insurer.

Sec.
27-6B-4. Contract requirements.
27-6B-5. Disclosure of relationship between producer and controlled insurer.
27-6B-6. Penalties.

Effective date. — The act which added this chapter became effective May 17, 1993.

Code Commissioner's note. — Acts 1993, No. 93-675, which enacted this chapter, in § 20, provides: "The Commissioner of Insurance may adopt reasonable rules and regulations neces-sary for the implementation and the administration of this act."

Cross references. — As to provisions of rules and regulations necessary for the effectuation of this title, see § 27-2-17.

§ 27-6B-1. Short title.

Sections 27-6B-2 to 27-6B-6, inclusive, of this chapter may be cited as the "Alabama Business Transacted With Producer Controlled Property and Casualty Insurer Law." (Acts 1993, No. 93-675, § 14.)

§ 27-6B-2. Definitions.

As used in this chapter, the following terms shall have the following meanings, respectively, unless the context clearly indicates otherwise:

(1) ACCREDITED STATE. A state in which the Department of Insurance meets the minimum financial qualifications and regulatory standards promulgated and established, from time to time, by the National Association of Insurance Commissioners.

(2) COMMISSIONER. The Commissioner of Insurance.

(3) CONTROL or CONTROLLED. The same as defined in subsection (3) of Section 27-29-1.

(4) CONTROLLED INSURER. A licensed insurer who is controlled, directly or indirectly, by a producer.

(5) CONTROLLING PRODUCER. A producer who, directly or indirectly controls an insurer.

(6) LICENSED INSURER or INSURER. Any person, firm, association, or corporation duly licensed to transact a property and casualty insurance business in this state. For the purposes of this chapter the following are not licensed insurers:

a. A risk retention group as defined in the Superfund Amendments Reauthorization Act of 1986, Pub. L. No. 99-499, 100 Stat. 1613 (1986) and the Risk Retention Act (commencing with Section 3901 of Title 15, U.S.C., 1982 and 1986 of Supp. to Title 15, U.S.C.).

b. A residual market pool and a joint underwriting authority or association.

c. A captive insurer, which, for the purposes of this chapter, is an insurance company owned by another organization whose exclusive purpose is to insure risks of the parent organization and any affiliated company or, in the case of any group and association, an insurance organization owned by the insured whose only purpose is to insure risks to any member-organization, group member or affiliate of the member.

(7) PRODUCER. An insurance broker or brokers or any other person, firm, association, or corporation, when, for any compensation, commission, or other thing of value, the person, firm, association, or corporation acts or aids in any manner in soliciting, negotiating, or procuring the making of any insurance contract on behalf of another insured person, firm, association, or corporation. The term is not intended to include an exclusive agent or any independent agent acting on behalf of the controlled insurer and any subagent or representative of the agent, who acts in the solicitation of, negotiation for, or procurement or making of an insurance contract, if the agent is not also acting in the capacity of an insurance broker in the transaction in question. (Acts 1993, No. 93-675, § 15.)

§ 27-6B-3. Application of chapter to licensed insurer.

This chapter shall apply to any licensed insurer as defined in Section 27-6B-2, either domiciled in this state or domiciled in a state that is not an accredited state but having in effect a substantially similar law. The Alabama Insurance Holding Company System Regulatory Act, Chapter 29 (commencing with Section 27-29-1) of Title 27, to the extent it is not superseded by this chapter, shall continue to apply to all parties within holding company systems subject to this chapter. (Acts 1993, No. 93-675, § 16.)

§ 27-6B-4. Contract requirements.

(a) Unless there is a written contract between the controlling producer and the insurer approved by the board of directors of the insurer and specifying the responsibilities of each party, a controlled insurer shall not accept business from a controlling producer and a controlling producer shall not place business with a controlled insurer. The contract between a controlling producer and a controlled insurer shall, as a minimum, contain the following:

(1) A provision that, upon written notice to the controlling producer, the controlled insurer may terminate the contract for cause. The controlled insurer shall suspend the authority of the controlling producer to write business during any pending dispute regarding the cause for the termination.

(2) A provision requiring the controlling producer to give a detailed accounting to the controlled insurer on any material transaction, including information necessary to support all commissions, charges, and other fees received by, or owing to, the controlling producer.

(3) A provision requiring the controlling producer to send all funds due, under the terms of the contract, to the controlled insurer on at least a monthly basis. The contract shall require the due date to be fixed so that premiums or any installment collected are remitted no later than ninety days after the effective date of any policy placed with the controlled insurer under the contract.

(4) A provision requiring all funds collected for the account of the controlled insurer to be held by the controlling producer in a fiduciary capacity, in one or more appropriately identified bank accounts in a bank that is a member of the Federal Reserve System, in accordance with any applicable insurance law. Funds of a controlling producer, not required to be licensed in this state, shall be maintained in compliance with the requirements of the domiciliary jurisdiction of the controlling producer.

(5) A provision requiring the controlling producer to maintain separate identifiable records of business written for the controlled insurer.

(6) A provision prohibiting the controlling producer from assigning the contract in whole or in part.

(7) A provision that the rates and terms of the commissions, charges, and other fees of the controlling producer shall be no greater than those applicable to comparable business placed with the controlled insurer by

57

producers other than controlling producers. For purposes of this subsection and subsection (d), examples of "comparable business" includes the same lines of insurance, the same kinds of insurance, the same kinds of risks, similar policy limits, and similar quality of business.

(8) A provision that if the contract provides that the controlling producer, on insurance business placed with the insurer, is to be compensated contingent upon the insurer's profits on that business, the compensation shall not be determined and paid until at least five years after the premiums on liability insurance are earned and at least one year after the premiums are earned on any other insurance. In no event may the commissions be paid until the adequacy of the controlled insurer's reserves on remaining claims has been independently verified pursuant to the reporting requirements of subsection (f).

(9) A provision that the insurer may establish a different limit for each line or sub-line of business written by the controlling producer. The controlled insurer shall notify the controlling producer when the limit is approached and shall not accept business from the controlling producer if the limit is reached. The controlling producer shall not place business with the controlled insurer if it has been notified by the controlled insurer that the limit has been reached.

(10) A provision that the controlling producer may negotiate but may not bind reinsurance on behalf of the controlled insurer on business the controlling producer places with the controlled insurer, except that the controlling producer may bind facultative reinsurance contracts pursuant to obligatory facultative agreements if the contract with the controlled insurer contains underwriting guidelines including, for both reinsurance assumed and ceded, a list of reinsurers with which the automatic agreements are in effect, the coverages, and amounts, or percentages that may be reinsured, and commission schedules.

(11) The controlled insurer shall provide the controlling producer with its underwriting standards, rules, and procedures, and manuals setting forth the rates to be charged, and the conditions for the acceptance or rejection of risks. The controlling producer shall adhere to the standards, rules, procedures, rates, and conditions. The standards, rules, procedures, rates, and conditions shall be the same as those applicable to comparable business placed with the controlled insurer by a producer other than the controlling producer.

(b) This section shall apply if, in any calendar year, the aggregate amount of gross written premium on business placed with a controlled insurer by a controlling producer is equal to or greater than five percent of the admitted assets of the controlled insurer, as reported by the controlled insurer in the quarterly statement filed as of September 30 of the year immediately preceding.

(c) This section shall not apply if:

(1) The controlling producer:

a. Places insurance only with the controlled insurer, or only with the controlled insurer and one or more members of the holding company system of the controlled insurer, or only with the parent, affiliate, or subsidiary of the controlled insurer and receives no compensation based upon the amount of premium written in connection with the insurance, and

b. Accepts insurance placements only from non-affiliated subproducers and not directly from insureds, and

(2) The controlled insurer, except for insurance business written through a residual market facility such as the Automobile Assigned Risk Plan, accepts insurance business only from a controlling producer, a producer controlled by the controlled insurer, or a producer that is a subsidiary of the controlled insurer.

(e) Each controlled insurer shall have an audit committee of the board of directors composed of independent directors. The audit committee shall annually meet with management, the insurer's independent certified public accountants, and an independent casualty actuary, or other independent loss reserve specialist acceptable to the commissioner to review the adequacy of the insurer's loss reserves.

(f) The controlled insurer shall report the following:

(1) In addition to any other required loss reserve certification, the controlled insurer shall annually, on April 1 of each year, file with the commissioner an opinion of an independent casualty actuary (or other independent loss reserve specialist acceptable to the commissioner) reporting loss ratios for each line of business written and attesting to the adequacy of loss reserves established for losses incurred and outstanding as of year-end (including incurred but not reported) on business placed by the producer.

(2) At least annually, the controlled insurer shall report to the commissioner, the amount of the commissions to be paid to the producer, the percentage the amount represents of the net premiums written, and comparable amounts and percentage paid to noncontrolling producers for placements of the same kinds of insurance. (Acts 1993, No. 93-675, § 17.)

§ 27-6B-5. Disclosure of relationship between producer and controlled insurer.

The producer, prior to the effective date of the policy, shall deliver written notice to the prospective insured disclosing the relationship between the producer and the controlled insurer. Except that, if the business is placed through a subproducer who is not a controlling producer, the controlling producer shall retain records of a signed commitment from the subproducer that the subproducer is aware of the relationship between the insurer and the producer and that the subproducer has or will notify the insured. (Acts 1993, No. 93-675, § 18.)

§ 27-6B-6. Penalties.

(a) If the commissioner believes that the controlling producer or any other person has not materially complied with this chapter, or any regulation or order promulgated hereunder, after notice and opportunity to be heard, the commissioner may order the controlling producer to cease placing business with the controlled insurer.

(b) If it was found that because of the material non-compliance that the controlled insurer or any policyholder thereof has suffered any loss or damage, the commissioner may maintain a civil action or intervene in an action brought by or on behalf of the insurer or policyholder for recovery of compensatory damages for the benefit of the insurer or policyholder, or other appropriate relief.

(c) If an order for liquidation or rehabilitation of the controlled insurer has been entered, pursuant to Chapter 32 of Title 27, and the receiver appointed under that order believes that the controlling producer or any other person has not substantially complied with this chapter, or any regulation or order promulgated under this chapter, and the insurer suffers any loss or damage because of the noncompliance, the receiver may maintain a civil action for recovery of damages or other appropriate sanctions or remedies for the benefit of the insurer.

(d) Nothing contained in this section shall affect the right of the commissioner to impose any other penalties provided for in the insurance law.

(e) This chapter shall be construed to preserve the rights of policyholders, claimants, creditors, or other third parties. (Acts 1993, No. 93-675, § 19.)

CHAPTER 7.

PROPERTY, CASUALTY AND SURETY INSURANCE REPRESENTATIVES.

Sec.
27-7-1. Definitions.
27-7-2. Applicability of chapter.
27-7-3. Applicability of provision on insurance vending machines.
27-7-4. Licenses — Requirement; forms.
27-7-5. Licenses — Qualifications.
27-7-6. Licenses — Artificial entities.
27-7-7. Licenses — Application — Generally; fees.
27-7-8. Licenses — Application — Statement of appointing insurer for agent.
27-7-9. Licenses — Application — Statement of appointing agent or broker for solicitor.
27-7-10. Licenses — Examination — Scope; notification; when given.
27-7-10.1. Licenses — Examination — Waiting period for person failing two examinations.
27-7-11. Licenses — Examination — Study materials; contents; conduct; grading.
27-7-13. Licenses — Examination — Exemptions; exception.

Sec.
27-7-14. Licenses — Examination — Consultations with experienced persons.
27-7-16. Repealed.
27-7-17. Licenses — Contents.
27-7-18. Licenses — Continuation and expiration; exception.
27-7-19. Licenses — Grounds for refusing to renew or to suspend or revoke.
27-7-26. Repealed.
27-7-28. Nonresident agents or brokers — License; commissions.
27-7-29. Nonresident agents or brokers — Service of process.
27-7-30. Filing of agent's appointment by insurer with commissioner of insurance; termination of such appointment; notice to agent of appointment or renewal.
27-7-31. Rights of agent following termination of appointment; exception.
27-7-33. Records.
27-7-34. Placing of insurance by agent not appointed or licensed.

§ 27-7-1. Definitions.

(a) For the purposes of this chapter, the following terms shall have the meanings respectively ascribed to them by this section:

(1) AGENT. A natural person, partnership or corporation appointed by an insurer to solicit and negotiate insurance contracts on its behalf, and if authorized to do so by the insurer, to effectuate, issue and countersign such contracts. An agent may not delegate the countersignature authority by appointing another person as his attorney-in-fact, except, that this provision shall not apply to agents for direct-writing insurers.

(2) BROKER. A natural person, partnership or corporation who, on behalf of the insured, for compensation as an independent contractor, for commission or fee and not being an agent of the insurer, solicits, negotiates or procures insurance or the renewal or continuance thereof, or in any manner aids therein, for insureds or prospective insureds other than himself or itself. Brokers cannot bind the insurer and all business produced must be countersigned by a resident agent of the insurer accepting the risk.

(3) SOLICITOR. A natural person appointed and authorized by a licensed agent or broker to solicit applications for insurance as a representative of such agent or broker and to collect premiums thereon when expressly so authorized by the agent or broker. A solicitor may not bind the insurer, accept risks or countersign policies of insurance. The solicitor must be domiciled in the same city or town as the sponsoring agent and must be under the direct supervision of the agent. An individual employed by and devoting full time to clerical work with incidental taking of insurance applications and receiving premiums in the office of the agent or broker shall not be deemed to be a solicitor if his compensation is not related to the volume of such applications, insurances or premiums.

(4) MANAGING GENERAL AGENT. An individual, firm or corporation appointed as an independent contractor by one or more insurers for the principal purpose of exercising general supervision over the business of the insurer in Alabama, with authority to appoint agents for such insurer and to terminate such appointments. The authority of a managing general agent shall not include countersignature privileges. A managing general agent shall otherwise qualify and be licensed as such as provided in this chapter, but shall not be required to take and pass an examination nor be a resident of Alabama. A managing general agent must be licensed for each insurer represented and for each class of insurance handled by the insurer in this state.

(5) SERVICE REPRESENTATIVE. A natural person, other than an officer, manager or managing general agent of the insurer, employed on salary by an insurer or managing general agent to work for, with or through agents in soliciting, negotiating and effectuating insurance in such insurer or in the insurers represented by the managing general agent. Officers and salaried nonresident traveling representatives of a mutual insurer operating on the premium deposit plan or of a reciprocal insurer not using resident agents for the solicitation of business who inspect risks or solicit insurance in this state and who receive no commissions from the insurer shall be deemed also to be

service representatives. A service representative shall otherwise qualify and be licensed as such under this chapter, but shall not be required to take and pass an examination nor be a resident of Alabama if he is qualified as a service representative in the state of his domicile. Service representatives are not authorized to countersign policies of insurance in the state of Alabama. The service representative must be licensed for each insurer or association of insurers represented and for each class of insurance handled by such insurer or insurers in this state.

(b) In addition to persons excluded by the terms thereof, the definition of an agent, broker, solicitor, managing general agent or service representative shall not be deemed to include any of the following:

(1) Salaried employees rendering solely clerical and administrative services in the office of the employer;

(2) Salaried administrative and clerical employees of agents and brokers performing any functions in the office and under the supervision of the employer and receiving no commissions;

(3) Salaried employees of insurers or organizations employed by insurers engaged in inspection, rating or classifying risks or in general supervision of agents and not in the solicitation or the writing of insurance;

(4) Officers of insurers or of an association of insurers engaged in the performance of their usual and customary executive duties, exclusive of field solicitation of insurance other than rendering assistance to, or on behalf of, a licensed agent but receiving no commission or other compensation directly dependent upon the amount of business transacted;

(5) Persons completing or delivering declarations or certificates of coverage under running inland marine insurance contracts evidencing coverage thereunder, if:

a. Such persons receive no commissions directly or indirectly on such insurance; and

b. Such persons or their employers have an insurable interest in the risk evidenced by the certificate or declaration; and

(6) Persons who secure and furnish information for the purpose of group life insurance, group or blanket health insurance or annuity coverages, or for enrolling individuals under such plans or issuing certificates thereunder or otherwise assisting in administering such plans where no commission is paid for such services. (Acts 1957, No. 530, p. 726, § 2; Acts 1971, No. 407, p. 707, § 114-118.1; Acts 1988, No. 88-123, p. 159, § 1.)

General agent.

A "general agent" is one who has authority to transact all the business of the principal, of a particular kind, or in a particular case. Washington Nat'l Ins. Co. v. Strickland, 491 So. 2d 872 (Ala. 1985).

A general agent has full power to bind the insurer to the agent's contract of insurance or to issue policies or to accept risks. Washington Nat'l Ins. Co. v. Strickland, 491 So. 2d 872 (Ala. 1985).

"Special agent," as distinguished from a "general agent," is authorized to act for the principal only in a particular transaction, or in a particular way. Washington Nat'l Ins. Co. v. Strickland, 491 So. 2d 872 (Ala. 1985).

Soliciting agent is different from a general agent in that he has no power to bind his insurer principal in contract. However, when a soliciting agent commits a fraud upon one who seeks insurance coverage, his insurer principal will be liable for that fraud, if the fraud was perpetrated by the agent within the scope of his employment. Washington Nat'l Ins. Co. v. Strickland, 491 So. 2d 872 (Ala. 1985).

Independent agent or broker is usually not agent for insurer at all; rather, he is the agent of the insured. Washington Nat'l Ins. Co. v. Strickland, 491 So. 2d 872 (Ala. 1985).

Independent agent may be agent for insurer for some purposes. — Although an independent agent or broker is normally an agent for the insured, for some purposes he may at the same time be an agent for the insurer as well. Washington Nat'l Ins. Co. v. Strickland, 491 So. 2d 872 (Ala. 1985).

Even though broker has not been formally appointed as an agent by company, he still may be deemed an agent of company if company retains a sufficient right of control over the details of his work. Wofford v. Safeway Ins. Co., 624 So. 2d 555 (Ala. 1993).

Insurer's liability for fraud of independent agent or broker is predicated upon actual or apparent authority conferred upon the agent/broker by the insurer to make representations on the insurer's behalf. Washington Nat'l Ins. Co. v. Strickland, 491 So. 2d 872 (Ala. 1985).

Rule book did not show company had control over broker. — Where broker was not formally appointed as an agent, company did not control broker's manner of performance by providing him with a "rule book" that described the prices of company's policies, who company would insure, and what types of vehicles company would insure. The "rule book" provided only general information as to the types and prices of company's products; therefore, the rule book did not provide substantial evidence that company exercised such control over broker as to make him its agent. Wofford v. Safeway Ins. Co., 624 So. 2d 555 (Ala. 1993).

Cited in Washburn v. Rabun, 487 So. 2d 1361 (Ala. 1986).

§ 27-7-2. Applicability of chapter.

This chapter applies only as to agents, brokers, solicitors and other insurance representatives, as defined in this chapter, transacting, or proposing to transact, as such representatives, any of the following kinds of insurance:

(1) Property insurance, except as to insurance of baggage or personal effects while in possession of a common carrier in connection with travel of the insured when such insurance is effectuated through ticket or transportation agencies selling tickets for such common carrier;

(2) Casualty insurance, except as to insurance of baggage or personal effects under the same circumstances as stated in subdivision (1) of this section;

(3) Surety insurance;

(4) Disability insurance when transacted by a casualty insurer; and

(5) For the purposes of this chapter "property" insurance includes also "wet marine and transportation" insurance as defined in section 27-5-9. (Acts 1957, No. 530, p. 726, § 1; Acts 1971, No. 407, p. 707, § 113; Acts 1988, No. 88-123, p. 159, § 1.)

§ 27-7-3. Applicability of provision on insurance vending machines.

Section 27-8-23, as to licensing of vending machines for the sale of personal travel accident insurance, shall also apply as to agents licensed under this chapter and appointed by any insurer authorized to transact disability insurance in this state. (Acts 1971, No. 407, p. 707, § 140; Acts 1988, No. 88-123, p. 159, § 1.)

§ 27-7-4. Licenses — Requirement; forms.

(a) No person shall in this state be, act as, hold himself out as or claim to be or act as an agent, broker, solicitor, managing general agent or service representative unless then licensed as such agent, broker, solicitor, managing general agent or service representative under this chapter. Any insurer accepting business directly from a person not licensed to transact such business and not appointed by such insurer shall be liable to a fine up to three times the premium received from such unlicensed person.

(b) No agent, broker or solicitor shall solicit or take application for, procure or place for others any kind of insurance as to which he is not then licensed.

(c) No agent shall place any business, other than coverage of his or its own risks, with any insurer for which an appointment is not held as agent under this chapter.

(d) The commissioner shall prescribe and furnish on request all forms required in connection with application for, issuance, continuation or termination of licenses and appointments. (Acts 1957, No. 530, p. 726, § 3; Acts 1971, No. 407, p. 707, § 119; Acts 1988, No. 88-123, p. 159, § 1.)

§ 27-7-5. Licenses — Qualifications.

For the protection of the people of this state, the commissioner shall not issue, continue or permit to exist any agent, broker, solicitor, managing general agent or service representative license for and on behalf of any natural person except in compliance with this chapter, or as to any individual not qualified therefor as follows:

(1) Must be 19 years or more of age, or be an individual whose disabilities of minority have been removed; except, that a managing general agent license may also be issued to a firm or corporation;

(2) Must be a citizen of the United States of America;

(3) Must be domiciled in and have been a bona fide resident of this state for not less than six months preceding the date of application for the license; except that this provision does not apply as to managing general agents or service representatives. The residence and domiciliary requirement may be waived upon determination by the commissioner that such waiver would be in the public interest and would prevent a hardship, if the applicant for a license:

a. Is a bona fide resident of and maintains an established office in a populous community lying partly in Alabama and partly in an adjoining state, which is composed of two or more contiguous cities, towns or villages not completely separated by a natural boundary;

b. Designates in writing the commissioner of insurance as his agent or attorney for acceptance of personal service of process in all actions involving matters connected with or arising out of his insurance business conducted in Alabama;

c. Agrees to keep like records, make similar reports and permit inspection of his records to the same extent as other licensees under this section; and

d. If the adjoining state by law or administrative action accords residents of Alabama a like waiver, benefit or privilege;

(4) Must be of good moral character and not have been convicted of a felony nor of any crime involving moral turpitude;

(5) Must intend to and, commencing immediately after issuance of such a license, shall, during the existence of the license, actively engage as to the general public in the business permitted under this license;

(6) If to be licensed as a broker, must have had experience either as an agent, solicitor, adjustor, managing general agent, broker or as an employee or special representative of an insurer, or insurers, or special education or training of sufficient duration and extent reasonably necessary for competence in fulfilling the responsibilities of a broker;

(7) Must not use, or intend to use, the license principally for the purpose of procuring insurance of his own risks or interests, or those of his relatives to the second degree or of his firm, corporation or employer;

(8) Must attend a pre-qualification course consisting of 40 classroom hours or equivalent individual instruction on the general principles of insurance, such course to be taught only by those educational institutions, junior or senior colleges, technical colleges, trade schools, insurance companies or insurance trade organizations which hold written authority from the commissioner to issue certificates of completion;

     a. Each such authority holder must apply annually for the continued authority to issue certificates under rules and regulations to be prescribed by the commissioner;

     b. Prior to writing the designated examination for license, the applicant must furnish a certificate of completion of the aforesaid pre-qualification course from the authorized educational institution, insurance company or insurance trade organization;

     c. All applicants under this chapter who are holders of the professional designation chartered property casualty underwriter (CPCU) or certified insurance counselor (CIC) or such other professional insurance designations as the commissioner may prescribe by regulation shall be deemed to have completed the pre-qualification course as prescribed in this subdivision;

     d. All applicants for license to transact only the following kinds of insurance shall be exempt from the requirements of this subdivision:

       1. automobile physical damage insurance,

       2. industrial fire (commonly known as debit fire) insurance, or

       3. physical damage coverage on household goods;

     e. An applicant who has been licensed under a like license in another state within 12 months prior to his application for a license in this state, and who files with the commissioner the certificate of the public official having supervision of insurance in such other state as to the applicant's license and good standing in such state shall be exempt from the requirements of this subdivision. A facsimile signature and seal of the certifying public official will be deemed sufficient.

     f. All agents, brokers, solicitors, managing general agents and service representatives who are lawfully licensed as such immediately prior to the effective date of the 1979 amendment, are exempt from the requirements of this section unless, after such effective date, any such license is permitted to expire or is otherwise terminated and remains out of effect for a period of 24 consecutive months, the exemption from a pre-qualification course shall no longer be applicable.

(9) Must pass any written examination for the license required under this chapter, except that no examination shall be required of an applicant whose license is limited to acting only as an agent with respect to personal property insurance sold to borrowers or debtors under a master group policy issued to a creditor, if such applicant is a full-time employee of the institution granting the credit. (Acts 1957, No. 530, p. 726, § 4; Acts 1959, 2nd Ex. Sess., No. 73, p. 250; Acts 1971, No. 407, p. 707, § 120; Acts 1971, 3rd Ex. Sess., No. 261, p. 4529; Acts 1979, No. 79-748, p. 1332; Acts 1988, No. 88-123, p. 159, § 1; Acts 1989, No. 89-815, p. 1629.)

The judgment of conviction in federal court constitutes a conviction under this section. The Commissioner is charged with the protection of the citizens of the state of Alabama, and part of that duty involves removing licenses from those agents who have been convicted of felonies. Alabama Ins. Dep't v. Shaw, 594 So. 2d 112 (Ala. Civ. App. 1991).

Introduction of criminal conviction does not stand for proof that acts were committed. — In an administrative proceeding, the introduction of the criminal conviction does not stand for proof that the acts underlying the conviction were committed, but rather simply that the conviction exists. Alabama Ins. Dep't v. Shaw, 594 So. 2d 112 (Ala. Civ. App. 1991).

§ 27-7-6. Licenses — Artificial entities.

(a) A partnership or corporation may be licensed as an insurance agent or broker provided:

(1) Every member of the partnership and every officer, director, stockholder and employee of the corporation personally engaged in this state in soliciting or negotiating policies of insurance shall be registered with the commissioner as to its license, and each such member, officer, director, stockholder or employee shall also qualify as an individual licensee; and

(2) The partnership or corporation is organized under the laws of this state and the transaction of the insurance business under the license is within the purposes stated in the partnership's agreement or the corporation's articles.

(b) The partnership or corporate licensee shall within 10 working days notify the commissioner of every change relative to the individuals registered with the corporate or partnership license. (Acts 1957, No. 530, p. 726, § 4; Acts 1959, 2nd Ex. Sess., No. 73, p. 250; Acts 1971, No. 407, p. 707, § 121; Acts 1988, No. 88-123, p. 159, § 1.)

§ 27-7-7. Licenses — Application — Generally; fees.

(a) The commissioner shall not issue any license except upon application therefor as in this chapter provided. Each applicant for a license shall file annually with the commissioner his written application therefor signed by him and showing:

(1) His name, age and place of residence;

(2) The kinds of insurance to be transacted under the license and the insurer or insurers he proposes so to represent;

(3) The person, firm or corporation by whom he expects to be employed or associated with as such licensee and his status as an officer or representative thereof;

(4) Whether he proposes to write or solicit insurance of his own risks and interest, or those of his relatives, any firm or corporation in which he is financially interested or connected, directly or indirectly, or of his employer;

(5) A short business history of the applicant and the name and nature of any business enterprise with which he may be associated;

(6) The extent of his formal education and business experience or apprenticeship;

(7) Whether he has ever applied previously for a license or been licensed to transact any kind of insurance business in this state or elsewhere and whether any such license was ever refused, suspended or revoked;

(8) Whether any insurer or managing general agent claims that he is in default as to premiums or other moneys collected and not accounted for and, if so, the details thereof and like information as to any member of his family who is then, or has theretofore been, engaged in the insurance business; and

(9) Any additional information reasonably required by the commissioner. Additional licenses shall require the applicant's full name, residence, age, place of business and certification whether he has had a license to solicit insurance contracts refused, suspended, or revoked since his last annual license; whether applicant has had any agency contract cancelled and, if so, when, by what insurer and the reason for the cancellation; and whether the applicant has been convicted of a felony since his last annual license.

(b) If the applicant for an agent's or broker's license is a partnership or corporation, the application shall show, in addition, names of every member of the partnership and every officer, director, stockholder and employee of the corporation personally engaged in this state in soliciting or negotiating policies of insurance. Each such member, officer, director, stockholder or employee shall furnish information with respect to himself as part of the application, as though for an individual license, and shall otherwise meet the requirements for an individual license.

(c) Partnerships and corporations shall file their organizational documents with the commissioner, accompanied by an initial filing fee of $50.00. The license shall continue in effect, subject to an annual fee of $50.00, unless cancelled, suspended or revoked. Each partnership and corporation shall file with the commissioner any change in its organization accompanied by a fee in the amount of $10.00.

(d) At the time of filing his original application for license, the applicant shall pay to the commissioner the application fee and the fees for any examinations required under section 27-7-10 as specified in section 27-4-2. Such fees shall not be returnable. Appointment fees, as required in section 27-4-2, shall be paid as to each individual included in the application for a partnership or corporation license.

(e) If the commissioner has contracted with a qualified testing institution as provided for in section 27-7-11(c), fees approved for such services by the commissioner may, at the commissioner's discretion, be paid directly to such testing institution and such fee shall be in lieu of but not in excess of the fees for the examination required under section 27-7-10 as specified in section 27-4-2. (Acts 1957, No. 530, p. 726, § 5; Acts 1971, No. 407, p. 707, § 122; Acts 1988, No. 88-123, p. 159, § 1; Acts 1988, 1st Ex. Sess., No. 88-875, p. 410, § 1; Acts 1990, No. 89-990, p. 35, § 1.)

Code Commissioner's note. — Acts 1988, 1st Ex. Sess., No. 88-875, § 2 provides: "It is the legislative intent that nothing in this act shall be construed to affect the Special Examination Revolving Fund, as provided for in Section 27-2-25, Code of Alabama 1975, or the State Fire Marshal's Fund, as provided for in Section 24-5-10, Code of Alabama 1975."

§ 27-7-8. Licenses — Application — Statement of appointing insurer for agent.

An insurer intending to appoint a person as its agent shall file with the commissioner its statement showing:

(1) The kind or kinds of insurance or classifications thereof as provided in section 27-7-11 it proposes to authorize the applicant to solicit or write;

(2) What investigation it has made of the applicant's qualifications, character and fitness for the duties to be assumed and the results of such investigation; and

(3) Such additional information as the commissioner reasonably requires. (Acts 1957, No. 530, p. 726, § 5; Acts 1971, No. 407, p. 707, § 123; Acts 1988, No. 88-123, p. 159, § 1.)

Even though broker has not been formally appointed as an agent by company, he still may be deemed an agent of company if company retains a sufficient right of control over the details of his work. Wofford v. Safeway Ins. Co., 624 So. 2d 555 (Ala. 1993).

Rule book provided by company did not exercise control over broker. — Where broker was not formally appointed as an agent, company did not control broker's manner of performance by providing him with a "rule book" that described the prices of company's policies, who company would insure, and what types of vehicles company would insure. The "rule book" provided only general information as to the types and prices of company's products; therefore, the rule book did not provide substantial evidence that company exercised such control over broker as to make him its agent. Wofford v. Safeway Ins. Co., 624 So. 2d 555 (Ala. 1993).

§ 27-7-9. Licenses — Application — Statement of appointing agent or broker for solicitor.

(a) No application for a license as solicitor shall be filed with the commissioner and no solicitors' licenses shall be granted by the commissioner after December 31, 1988.

(b) Persons holding a valid solicitor's license on December 31, 1988, may continue to renew such license after December 31, 1988, subject to those persons otherwise meeting the requirements of this chapter.

(c) If, after December 31, 1988, any such license is permitted to expire or is otherwise terminated and remains out of effect for a period of 12 consecutive months, it shall not be renewed by the commissioner or otherwise reactivated. (Acts 1957, No. 530, p. 726, § 5; Acts 1971, No. 407, p. 707, § 124; Acts 1988, No. 88-123, p. 159, § 1.)

§ 27-7-10. Licenses — Examination — Scope; notification; when given.

(a) After completion and filing of the application for license as required in sections 27-7-7 through 27-7-9, the commissioner shall give each applicant for license as agent, broker or solicitor, unless exempted from examination under section 27-7-13, a written examination of sufficient scope reasonably to test the applicant's knowledge relative to the kinds of insurance or classes thereof which may be dealt with under the proposed license and of the duties, responsibilities of and laws of this state applicable to such a licensee.

(b) If the applicant is a partnership or corporation, the examination shall be taken and initial educational requirements met by each individual who is to be designated in the license as having authority to act for the applicant under the license.

(c) Within 15 days after receipt of the application, the commissioner or any testing institution as authorized in section 27-7-11 shall notify the applicant by letter addressed to him at his address as shown on his application of the time and place of the examination for license. The examination shall be given, within not more than 60 nor less than three days after the giving of the notice, at the office of the commissioner at Montgomery or at such other place in Alabama as the commissioner reasonably designates; except, that the commissioner shall schedule an examination at least once in each calendar month, and any applicant otherwise eligible to take the examination shall be allowed at his request to take at that time all examinations relative to licenses for which he has applied, including examinations for license as an agent for life and disability insurances under chapter 8 of this title. (Acts 1957, No. 530, p. 726, § 6; Acts 1971, No. 407, p. 707, § 125; Acts 1988, No. 88-123, p. 159, § 1.)

§ 27-7-10.1. Licenses — Examination — Waiting period for person failing two examinations.

No person who has taken and failed to pass two examinations given pursuant to section 27-7-10 shall be entitled to take any further examination until after the expiration of three months from the date of the last examination which he failed to pass. If such person thereafter fails to pass two more such examinations, he shall not be eligible to take any further examination until after the expiration of six months from the date of his last unsuccessful examination. An examination fee shall be paid for each and every examination. (Acts 1991, No. 91-483, p. 875, § 2.)

§ 27-7-11. Licenses — Examination — Study materials; contents; conduct; grading.

(a) An applicant for license as agent, broker or solicitor shall be so examined as to any one or more of the following kinds of insurance or insurance classifications, as applied for:

(1) Automobile insurance;

(2) Industrial fire (commonly known as debit fire) insurance;

(3) Physical damage coverage on household goods;

(4) Comprehensive property, casualty and surety insurance;

(5) Bail bond insurance; and

(6) Any other reasonable classification prescribed by order of the commissioner.

(b) The rules and regulations of the commissioner shall designate textbooks, manuals and other materials to be studied by applicants in preparation for examinations in each classification designated by the commissioner pursuant to this section. Such textbooks, manuals or other materials may consist of matter available to applicants by purchase from the publisher or may consist of matter prepared at the direction of the commissioner and distributed to applicants upon request and payment of the reasonable cost thereof. If textbooks, manuals or other materials are so designated or prepared by the commissioner, all examination questions shall be prepared from the contents of such textbooks, manuals or other materials. Prior to the examination, the commissioner shall value each question to be asked therein and the sum of such values shall total 100. Each of the answers given shall correspondingly be valued proportionately to its correctness, and the sum of such values totaling 70 shall constitute a passing grade.

(c) The commissioner shall give, conduct and grade all examinations in a fair and impartial manner and without unfair discrimination as between individuals examined. The commissioner may contract with qualified educational testing institutions for preparation, analysis or grading of the written portion of the examinations.

(d) Within 15 days after the examination, the commissioner or testing institution shall inform the applicant and the appointing insurer, where applicable, as to whether the applicant has passed.

(e) His graded examination shall be available for review by the applicant for a period of not less than 90 days after the date of the examination. (Acts 1957, No. 530, p. 726, § 6; Acts 1971, No. 407, p. 707, § 126; Acts 1982, No. 82-401, p. 606, § 1; Acts 1988, No. 88-123, p. 159, § 1.)

§ 27-7-13. Licenses — Examination — Exemptions; exception.

(a) Except as provided in section 27-7-12, an agent, broker or solicitor lawfully licensed as such immediately prior to January 1, 1972, shall not be required to take an examination as to any kind of insurance or classification thereof as to which he is so licensed. This section does not apply to agents, solicitors or brokers who presently hold a temporary license, pending written examination.

(b) Except as provided in section 27-7-12 and in subsection (c) of this section, an agent, broker or solicitor lawfully licensed as such immediately prior to January 1, 1989, shall not be required to take an examination as to any kind of insurance or classification thereof to which this chapter applies.

(c) Subsection (b) of this section does not apply to:

(1) Agents, solicitors or brokers who presently hold a temporary license, pending written examination; or

(2) Agents, solicitors or brokers who presently hold licenses only for:

    a. automobile physical damage insurance;

    b. industrial fire (commonly known as debit fire) insurance; or

    c. physical damage coverage on household goods.

(d) If, after January 1, 1972, with respect to subsection (a) of this section, and after January 1, 1989, with respect to subsection (b) of this section, any such license is permitted to expire, or is otherwise terminated, and remains out of effect for a period of 24 consecutive months, the exemption from examination provided for in subsections (a) and (b), respectively, of this section shall no longer be applicable. (Acts 1957, No. 530, p. 726, § 6; Acts 1971, No. 407, p. 707, § 128; Acts 1988, No. 88-123, p. 159, § 1.)

§ 27-7-14. Licenses — Examination — Consultations with experienced persons.

The commissioner shall, from time to time as an aid to the efficient administration of this chapter, consult with individuals experienced in the property, casualty and miscellaneous casualty insurance business, to include officers, employees, managing general agents, managers and licensed agents of insurers engaged in such business, to the end that an orderly and effective program be developed as to scope, type and conduct of written examinations and the times and places in the state when and where they shall be held. (Acts 1957, No. 530, p. 726, § 7; Acts 1971, No. 407, p. 707, § 129; Acts 1988, No. 88-123, p. 159, § 1.)

§ 27-7-16. Licenses — Reapplication or reexamination upon denial; fees therefor. Repealed by Acts 1991, No. 91-483, p. 875, § 3, effective July 29, 1991.

§ 27-7-17. Licenses — Contents.

(a) The license of a managing general agent or service representative shall state the name and address of the licensee, the name of the insurer to be so represented, date of issue and of expiration and the general conditions of the license. The licensee must have a separate and additional appointment as to each insurer so represented.

(b) The single license of an agent shall state the name and address of the licensee, date of issue, general conditions relative to expiration or termination, the kinds of insurance or classifications thereof covered by the license, as classified under subsection (a) of section 27-7-11, and the general conditions of the license.

(c) The license of a broker shall state the licensee's name and address, the kinds of insurance or classifications thereof covered by the license, as classified under subsection (a) of section 27-7-11, date of issuance, conditions relative to expiration or termination and the general conditions of the license.

(d) The license of a solicitor shall state the licensee's name and address, the name and address of the agent or broker by whom he is appointed, the kinds of insurance or classifications thereof covered by the license, as classified under subsection (a) of section 27-7-11, conditions relative to expiration or termination and the general conditions of the license. (Acts 1971, No. 407, p. 707, § 132; Acts 1988, No. 88-123, p. 159, § 1.)

§ 27-7-18. Licenses — Continuation and expiration; exception.

(a) All agent appointments, broker, solicitor, managing general agent and service representative licenses issued under this chapter shall continue in force until expired, suspended, revoked or otherwise terminated, but subject to payment to the commissioner annually on or before December 31, of the applicable continuation fee, as stated in section 27-4-2, accompanied by written request for such continuation. Request for continuation shall be made as follows:

(1) As to broker's license, request for continuation signed by the licensee;

(2) As to solicitor's license, request for continuation signed by the appointing agent or broker;

(3) As to managing general agent's license, request signed by the insurer to be so represented;

(4) As to service representative's license, request signed by the insurer or managing general agent to be so represented; and

(5) As to agent's appointments, request signed by the insurer to be represented.

(b) Any license as to which the request for continuation and fee is not received by the commissioner as required under subsection (a) of this section shall be deemed to have expired at midnight December 31, above mentioned. Request for continuation of any such license or payment of the continuation fee therefor which is received by the commissioner after such December 31, and prior to the next following February 15, may be accepted and effectuated by the commissioner, in his discretion, if accompanied by an annual continuation fee in twice the amount otherwise required.

(c) The license of an agent shall be continuous until suspended or revoked; provided, however, the license shall expire automatically if the agent fails to hold a company appointment for a period of 24 consecutive months.

(d) This section does not apply to temporary licenses issued under sections 27-7-23 through 27-7-25. (Acts 1971, No. 407, p. 707, § 133; Acts 1988, No. 88-123, p. 159, § 1.)

§ 27-7-19. Licenses — Grounds for refusing to renew or to suspend or revoke.

(a) The commissioner may refuse to renew or continue or may suspend or revoke the license of any licensee under this chapter upon any of the following grounds:

(1) For any cause for which issuance of the license could have been refused had it then existed and been known to the commissioner;

(2) For the willful misrepresentation of any material fact in any application or in any communication to the commissioner;

(3) For intentional, material, misrepresentation with respect to any insurance policy;

(4) For rebating;

(5) For inducing, persuading or advising any policyholder to surrender or cause to be cancelled any policy of insurance issued to such policyholder by any authorized insurer in exchange for a policy offered by the licensee where such surrender or cancellation shall proximately result to the financial detriment of such policyholder, unless such policyholder shall have been fully advised of that fact by such licensee;

(6) For fraudulent or dishonest practices in the conduct of business under a license;

(7) For being in default, for a period of 60 days or more, in remitting to any insurer premiums collected by such applicant or licensee, after receiving demand, accompanied by proof and justification, from such insurer;

(8) For the misappropriation, conversion or unlawful withholding of any moneys belonging to the insurers, insureds or others received by the licensee in the exercise of his license;

(9) For willful failure to comply with, or willful violation of, any valid order, rule or regulation issued by the commissioner; or

(10) For willful violation of any provision of this title.

(b) The license of a partnership or corporation may be suspended, revoked or refused if the commissioner finds, after hearing, that an individual licensee's violation was known or should have been known by one or more of the partners, officers or managers acting on behalf of the partnership or corporation and such violation was not reported timely to the insurance department nor corrective action taken in relation thereto. (Acts 1957, No. 530, p. 726, § 8; Acts 1971, No. 407, p. 707, § 151; Acts 1988, No. 88-123, p. 159, § 1.)

§ 27-7-26. License — Apprentice solicitor. Repealed by Acts 1988, No. 88-123, p. 159, § 2.

§ 27-7-28. Nonresident agents or brokers — License; commissions.

(a) The commissioner may, upon written application made to him and payment of the license fee required under section 27-4-2, issue a license as a nonresident agent or nonresident broker to an individual otherwise qualified therefor under this chapter, but who is not a resident of this state, if by the laws of the state of his residence like licenses are granted to residents of this state.

(b) Any such licensing is also subject to the following conditions:

(1) The applicant must hold a license as an agent or broker in the state of his residence;

(2) The applicant or licensee must not have any direct or indirect pecuniary interest in any agent, insurance agency, broker or solicitor

licensed as a resident of this state nor shall he establish or maintain any kind of office or place of business in this state; and

(3) The licensee must not enter this state for the purpose of inspecting any risk or property without the written advance permission of the insured or that of a countersigning Alabama agent on such risk, nor shall the licensee directly or indirectly in this state solicit, negotiate or effect insurance policies unless accompanied by a resident agent of Alabama who is the countersigning agent on any insurance policy or policies so solicited, negotiated or effectuated. This provision shall not be deemed to apply to a service representative as defined in section 27-7-1.

(c) A countersigning resident agent cooperating with a nonresident agent or broker may share commissions as agreed between the two parties, if any commissions be paid, by the insurer. (Acts 1957, No. 530, p. 726, § 14; Acts 1971, No. 407, p. 707, § 141; Acts 1988, No. 88-123, p. 159, § 1.)

§ 27-7-29. Nonresident agents or brokers — Service of process.

(a) Each licensed nonresident agent and broker shall appoint the commissioner as his attorney to receive service of legal process issued against such agent or broker in this state upon causes of action arising within this state out of transactions under the nonresident agent's or broker's license. Service upon the commissioner as such attorney shall constitute effective legal service upon the nonresident agent or broker.

(b) The appointment shall be irrevocable for as long as there may be any such cause of action in this state against the nonresident agent or broker.

(c) Service of process under this section shall be made by leaving three copies of the summons and complaint, or other process, with the commissioner, and such service shall be sufficient service upon such nonresident if notice of the service and a copy of the summons and complaint or other process are forthwith sent by registered or certified mail to the defendant by the commissioner; and the defendant's return and the certificate of the commissioner certifying compliance herewith shall be filed in the office of the clerk of court, or in the court or tribunal wherein the action is pending. The certificate of the commissioner shall show the date of the mailing by registered or certified mail of the notice of the service and copy of the summons and complaint, or other process, to the nonresident defendant and the date of the receipt of the return card and shall be signed by the commissioner. The commissioner may give the nonresident defendant notice of such service upon him, in lieu of the notice of service hereinabove provided to be given by registered or certified mail, in the following manner:

(1) By having a notice of such service and a copy of the summons and complaint, or other process, served upon the nonresident defendant, if found within the state of Alabama, by any officer duly qualified to serve legal process within the state of Alabama or, if the nonresident defendant is found to be outside the state of Alabama, by a sheriff, deputy sheriff or United States marshal or deputy United States marshal or any duly constituted

officer qualified to serve like process in the state or the jurisdiction where the nonresident defendant is found; and

(2) The officer's return showing such service, when made, shall be filed in the office of the clerk of the court, or in the court or tribunal wherein the action is pending, on or before the return day of the process or within such further times as the court or tribunal may allow, and the court or tribunal in which the action is pending may order such continuance, or continuances, as may be necessary to afford the nonresident defendant reasonable opportunity to defend the action.

(d) The commissioner shall keep on file in his office for a period of not less than three years a copy of the summons and complaint or other process so served upon him, together with a record of all such process and of the day, hour and manner of service. (Acts 1957, No. 530, p. 726, § 14; Acts 1971, No. 407, p. 707, § 142; Acts 1988, No. 88-123, p. 159, § 1.)

§ 27-7-30. Filing of agent's appointment by insurer with commissioner of insurance; termination of such appointment; notice to agent of appointment or renewal.

(a) Each insurer appointing an agent in this state shall file with the commissioner the appointment, specifying the kinds of insurance or classifications thereof as specified in section 27-7-11 to be transacted by the agent for the insurer, and pay the appointment fee as specified in section 27-4-2. If the insurer also transacts disability insurance, the agent may be appointed by the same insurer also as to disability insurance without requiring an additional appointment or appointment fee.

(b) Subject to annual continuation by the insurer not later than December 31, each appointment shall remain in effect until the agent's license is revoked or otherwise terminated, unless written notice of earlier termination of the appointment is filed with the commissioner by the insurer or agent.

(c) Annually, prior to December 31, each insurer shall file with the commissioner an alphabetical list of the names and addresses of all its agents whose appointments in this state are to remain in effect, accompanied by payment of the annual continuation of appointment fee as provided in section 27-4-2. At the same time, the insurer shall also file with the commissioner an alphabetical list of the names and addresses of all of its agents whose appointments in this state are not to remain in effect and shall give written notice thereof to all such agents where reasonably possible. Any appointment not so continued and not otherwise expressly terminated shall be deemed to have expired at midnight on December 31.

(d) Subject to the agent's contract rights, if any, an insurer may terminate an agent's appointment at any time. The insurer shall promptly give written notice of such termination to the commissioner and to the agent where reasonably possible. The commissioner may require of the insurer reasonable proof that the insurer has given such notice to the agent, whether upon termination of the appointment by affirmative action of the insurer or by failure of the insurer to continue the appointment as provided for in subsection (c) of this section.

(e) As part of the notice of termination given the commissioner and in connection with the insurer's list of agent's appointments not to be continued as provided for in subsection (c) of this section, the insurer shall file with the commissioner a statement of the facts relative to the termination or noncontinuance and the cause thereof. Any such information, or statement and information or statements supplemental thereto shall be privileged and shall not form the basis of, or be admitted as evidence in, any action or proceeding against the insurer, or any director, officer, employee or representative of the insurer by, or on behalf of, any person affected by such termination.

(f) Each insurer shall give its agent timely written notice of all appointments and renewal of appointments. (Acts 1971, No. 407, p. 707, § 134; Acts 1988, No. 88-123, p. 159, § 1.)

Even though broker has not been formally appointed as an agent by company, he still may be deemed an agent of company if company retains a sufficient right of control over the details of his work. Wofford v. Safeway Ins. Co., 624 So. 2d 555 (Ala. 1993).

Rule book did not show company had control over broker. — Where broker was not formally appointed as an agent, company did not control broker's manner of performance by providing him with a "rule book" that described the prices of company's policies, who company would insure, and what types of vehicles company would insure. The "rule book" provided only general information as to the types and prices of company's products; therefore, the rule book did not provide substantial evidence that company exercised such control over broker as to make him its agent. Wofford v. Safeway Ins. Co., 624 So. 2d 555 (Ala. 1993).

§ 27-7-31. Rights of agent following termination of appointment; exception.

(a) Following termination of an agent's appointment as to an insurer, the agent may continue to service and receive from the insurer commissions or other compensation relative to policies written by him for the insurer during the existence of the appointment. The agent may countersign all certificates or endorsements necessary to continue such policies, including renewal option periods, and collect and remit premiums due thereon, but shall not otherwise change or modify any such policy in any way nor increase the hazards insured against therein; except, that the limited authority hereinabove provided for shall terminate altogether upon expiration or termination of the agent's license.

(b) This section does not apply as to agents of direct writing insurers or to agents and insurers between whom the relationship of employer and employee exists. (Acts 1957, No. 530, p. 726, § 3; Acts 1971, No. 407, p. 707, § 145; Acts 1988, No. 88-123, p. 159, § 1.)

§ 27-7-33. Records.

(a) The agent or broker shall keep for a period of not less than three years at his place of business complete records pertaining to transactions under his license and the licenses of his solicitors. If an agent, the licensee shall make and keep daily reports of all policies countersigned by him.

(b) The agent's records referred to in subsection (a) of this section shall include also record of all policies executed or countersigned by him and representing coverages handled by a nonresident agent or nonresident broker. Upon the commissioner's request, the agent shall furnish a verified copy of such record to the commissioner to aid him in the collection of all privilege taxes due in this state.

(c) The licensee shall exhibit to an insured, at any reasonable time during business hours, records in his office pertaining to policies of the insured upon the insured's demand. (Acts 1957, No. 530, p. 726, § 13; Acts 1971, No. 407, p. 707, § 144; Acts 1988, No. 88-123, p. 159, § 1.)

§ 27-7-34. Placing of insurance by agent not appointed or licensed.

(a) An agent may place with an insurer for which he is not an appointed agent only a kind of insurance or classification thereof for which he is licensed by placing such insurance through a duly appointed and licensed agent of the insurer.

(b) In addition to any other penalties provided for, the licenses of any licensee violating or participating in the violation of this section may be suspended or revoked in the discretion of the commissioner; and, if so suspended or revoked, the licenses shall not be restored for a period of at least one year. (Acts 1957, No. 530, p. 726, § 15; Acts 1971, No. 407, p. 707, § 146; Acts 1988, No. 88-123, p. 159, § 1.)

§ 27-7-36. Accounting for and payment of trust funds by licensees.

Agent not active in "fiduciary capacity" within meaning of 11 U.S.C. § 523(a)(4). — Under this section, agent was not acting in a "fiduciary capacity" for insurance company within the meaning of § 523(a)(4) of the Bankruptcy Code, nor was he guilty of embezzlement or larceny under § 523(a)(4), so as to preclude his discharge. Hartford Accident & Indem. Co. v. McCraney, 63 Bankr. 64 (Bankr. N.D. Ala. 1986).

Agent to account for premiums and pay them to person entitled thereto. — Where insurance was written in Alabama for an Illinois insurance company pursuant to a contract between its general agent in California and an Alabama corporation doing business as an insurance agency, and because § 27-7-1(a) requires agents and brokers to be natural persons, the Alabama corporation did business under the authority of a license issued to its sole stockholder, officer, and director. The Illinois company claimed that since § 27-7-1 and this section stated that all premiums belonging to others received by an agent or broker in transactions under his license shall be trust funds, it was entitled to a return of premiums to damages for loss or conversion of premiums; however, the claim did not state a cause of action against the individual Alabama licensee, since subsection (a) of this section required the Alabama agent to account for the premiums and to pay them, in the regular course of business, to the person entitled to them, and under their contract the person entitled to receive the funds from the Alabama agent was the California general agent, and nowhere in the contract was any mention made of an obligation upon the Alabama agent or his agency to remit funds to any insurer. Washburn v. Rabun, 487 So. 2d 1361 (Ala. 1986).

CHAPTER 8.

LIFE AND DISABILITY INSURANCE REPRESENTATIVES.

Sec.   Sec.
27-8-5. License — Application; certificate of   27-8-13. License — Content; number of li-
         insurer; fees; bond.   censes generally.
27-8-10. License — Examination — Reexami-
         nation; fee.

§ 27-8-5. License — Application; certificate of insurer; fees; bond.

(a) The commissioner shall not issue any license except upon application therefor as provided in this section. Each applicant for a license as an agent or broker shall file annually with the commissioner his written application therefor signed by him, verified by his oath and showing:

(1) Applicant's full name, residence, age, occupation and place of business for five years next preceding the date of the application;

(2) Whether applicant has ever held a license to solicit insurance contracts in any state;

(3) Whether applicant has ever been refused or has had suspended or revoked any license to solicit insurance contracts in any state;

(4) What insurance experience, if any, he has had;

(5) What instruction in insurance and in the insurance laws of this state he has had or expects to have;

(6) Whether any insurer claims that applicant is indebted to the insurer under any agency contracts or otherwise and, if so, the name of the claimant, nature of the claim and applicant's defense thereto;

(7) Whether applicant has had any agency contract cancelled and, if so, when, by what insurer and the reason for the cancellation;

(8) Whether applicant will devote all, or part of, his efforts to acting as an insurance agent and, if part time only, how much time he expects to devote to work as an agent or broker and in what other business, or businesses, he is engaged or employed;

(9) Whether, if applicant is married, the spouse has ever applied for or held a license to solicit insurance in any state and whether any such license has ever been refused, suspended or revoked; and

(10) Such other information as the commissioner may reasonably require.

Additional licenses shall require the applicant's full name, residence, age, place of business and certification whether he has had a license to solicit insurance contracts refused, suspended, or revoked since his last annual license; whether applicant has had any agency contract cancelled and, if so, when, by what insurer and the reason for the cancellation; and whether the applicant has been convicted of a felony since his last annual license.

(b) The application for an agent's license shall be accompanied by a certificate on forms furnished by the commissioner and signed by an officer or duly authorized representative of the insurer stating, if true, that the insurer has investigated the character and background of the applicant and is satisfied that he is trustworthy and qualified to act as its agent and to hold himself out in good faith to the general public as an agent and that the insurer desires that the applicant be licensed as an agent of the insurer as defined in subsection (a) of section 27-8-1.

(c) If the applicant for an agent's or broker's license is a partnership or corporation, the application shall show, in addition, names of every member of the partnership and every officer, director, stockholder and employee of the corporation personally engaged in this state in soliciting or negotiating policies of insurance. Each such member, officer, director, stockholder or employee shall furnish information with respect to himself as part of the application, as though for an individual license, and shall otherwise meet the requirements for an individual license.

(d) Partnerships and corporations shall file their organizational documents with the commissioner accompanied by an initial filing fee of $50.00. The license shall continue in effect, subject to an annual fee of $50.00, unless cancelled, suspended or revoked. Each partnership and corporation shall file with the commissioner any change in its organization accompanied by a fee in the amount of $10.00.

(e) When filed, the application shall be accompanied by the examination filing fee specified in section 27-4-2 if the applicant is subject to an examination under this chapter. Any such fee shall not be subject to refund, whether or not the applicant in fact takes an examination. An additional license fee shall be paid as to each individual included in the application for a partnership or corporation license.

(f) Prior to issuance of a license as an insurance broker, the applicant shall file with the commissioner and, thereafter for as long as the license remains in effect, shall keep in force a bond in the penal sum of not less than $20,000.00 with an authorized corporate surety approved by the commissioner. The aggregate liability of the surety for any and all claims on any such bond shall in no event exceed the penal sum thereof. No such bond shall be terminated unless at least 30 days' prior written notice thereof is given by the surety to the licensee and the commissioner. Upon termination of the license for which the bond was in effect, the commissioner shall notify the surety within 10 working days.

(g) All surety protection under this section is to inure to the benefit of the aggrieved parties. (Acts 1957, No. 598, p. 848, § 4; Acts 1971, No. 407, p. 707, § 159; Acts 1981, No. 81-862, p. 1635, § 1; Acts 1988, 1st Ex. Sess., No. 88-875, p. 410, § 1.)

Code Commissioner's note. — Acts 1988, 1st Ex. Sess., No. 88-875, § 2 provides: "It is the legislative intent that nothing in this act shall be const ued to affect the Special Examination Revolving Fund, as provided for in Section 27-2-25, Code of Alabama 1975, or the State Fire Marshal's Fund, as provided for in Section 24-5-10, Code of Alabama 1975."

Purpose. — This section, which requires that an insurer investigate the background and character of its perspective agents and certify in the application for the agents license that he or she is trustworthy and qualified to sell insurance to the public, is not intended to impose an additional burden of supervision on insurers, inuring to the benefit of the policyholders, beyond that existing under the common law. Ledbetter v. United Am. Ins. Co., 624 So. 2d 1371 (Ala. 1993).

§ 27-8-10. License — Examination — Reexamination; fee.

No person who has taken and failed to pass two examinations given pursuant to section 27-8-7 shall be entitled to take any further examination until after the expiration of three months from the date of the last examination in which he failed to pass. If such person thereafter fails to pass two more such examinations, he shall not be eligible to take any further examination until after the expiration of six months from the date of his last unsuccessful examination. An examination fee shall be paid for each and every examination; except, that an applicant shall be permitted to take a single examination covering all classes of insurance contracts as defined in section 27-8-7. (Acts 1957, No. 598, p. 848, § 6; Acts 1971, No. 407, p. 707, § 164; Acts 1991, No. 91-483, p. 875, § 1.)

§ 27-8-13. License — Content; number of licenses generally.

(a) Licenses shall state the name and address of the licensee, the kinds of insurance or classifications thereof covered by the license, date of issue and of expiration and the general conditions of the license.

(b) An agent with a license in force may solicit applications for policies of life and disability insurance on behalf of an insurer with respect to which he is not a licensed agent, provided that such agent submits an application for appointment as an agent of such insurer simultaneously with the submission to such insurer of the application for insurance solicited by him, and, provided further, that no commissions shall be paid by such insurer to the agent until such time as an additional license with respect to such insurer has been issued to the agent.

(c) The commissioner may, upon request, issue a single license covering all of the kinds of insurance and classifications thereof transacted by the same insurer. (Acts 1971, No. 407, p. 707, § 167; Acts 1981, No. 81-862, p. 1635, § 1; Acts 1989, No. 89-258, p. 373, § 4.)

§ 27-8-16. License — Refusal to renew or continue or suspension or revocation — Grounds.

Examination of agent's out-of-state actions. — The Alabama Insurance Department is not prevented from examining the out-of-state actions of an agent to determine whether he is fit for licensure in Alabama. State Ins. Dep't v. Howell, 614 So. 2d 1053 (Ala. Civ. App. 1992).

§ 27-8-27. Payment of commission or other valuable consideration to unlicensed persons not allowed; exceptions.

Applicability of subdivision (c)(1). — In dispute between insurance agent and insurer, subsection (a) controls because the contract between insured and insurer was an annual contract, because insured retained the right to change the agent of record and did designate another agent of record; thus, subdivision (c)(1) does not apply. Crockett v. Great-West Life Assurance Co., 578 So. 2d 1290 (Ala. 1991).

CHAPTER 10.

UNAUTHORIZED INSURERS AND SURPLUS LINES.

Article 2.
Surplus Line Insurance.

Sec.
27-10-24. Licensing of surplus line brokers.

Sec.
27-10-26. Eligibility of insurers for placement of surplus line insurance.
27-10-31. Annual tax of surplus line brokers.

ARTICLE 1.

GENERAL PROVISIONS.

§ 27-10-2. Liability of persons violating section 27-10-1; liability of adjusters.

Collateral references. — Liability of independent or public insurance adjuster to insured for conduct in adjusting claim. 50 ALR4th 900.

ARTICLE 2.

SURPLUS LINE INSURANCE.

§ 27-10-20. Procuring of surplus lines from unauthorized insurers.

Cited in Ex parte Dees, 594 So. 2d 77 (Ala. 1992).

§ 27-10-24. Licensing of surplus line brokers.

Any person, while licensed as a resident agent or broker of this state as to property, casualty, and surety insurance and who is deemed by the commissioner to have had sufficient experience in the insurance business to be competent for the purpose may be licensed as a surplus line broker for the types and kinds of insurance that he or she as a resident agent or broker is licensed to handle as follows:

(1) Application to the commissioner for the license shall be made on forms as designated and furnished by the commissioner.

(2) License fee in the amount stated in Section 27-4-2 shall be paid to the commissioner. The license shall expire on the first day of January next after its issue.

(3) Prior to the issuance of the license, the applicant shall file with the commissioner, and thereafter for as long as any license remains in effect he or she shall keep in force and unimpaired, a bond in favor of the State of Alabama in the penal sum of at least fifty thousand dollars ($50,000), aggregate liability, with authorized corporate sureties approved by the commissioner. The amount of the bond may be increased if deemed necessary by the commissioner, considering the amount of surplus lines tax paid

in previous years. The bond shall be conditioned that the broker will conduct business under the license in accordance with the provisions of the surplus line insurance law and that he or she will promptly remit the taxes as provided by the law. No bond shall be terminated unless at least 30 days' prior written notice thereof is given to the broker and the commissioner. (Acts 1963, No. 521, p. 1112, § 11; Acts 1971, No. 407, p. 707, § 199; Acts 1994, 1st Ex. Sess., No. 94-790, p. 92, § 2.)

The 1994, 1st Ex. Sess., amendment, effective May 6, 1994, in subdivision (3), substituted "at least fifty thousand dollars ($50,000)" for "$5,000.00" in the first sentence and inserted the second sentence; and made nonsubstantive changes throughout the section.

Code Commissioner's note. — Acts 1994, No. 94-790, which amended this section, in § 1 provides: "The Legislature declares that the purpose of this act is to provide for an effective and efficient system for the Commissioner of Insurance to regulate insurance transactions with nonadmitted insurers. The Legislature finds that insurance transactions are so affected with a public interest as to require regulation, taxation, supervision, and control under the Commissioner of Insurance. This act will increase the protection to insureds and claimants of this state in transactions involving the purchase of insurance from insurers not authorized to transact business in this state, and will protect revenues of this state."

§ 27-10-26. Eligibility of insurers for placement of surplus line insurance.

(a) A surplus line broker shall not knowingly place surplus line insurance with an insurer that is unsound financially, or that is ineligible under this section. The broker shall ascertain the financial condition of the unauthorized insurer before placing insurance therewith.

(b) The broker shall not so insure with any of the following:

(1) With any insurer which is not an authorized insurer in at least one state of the United States for the kind of insurance involved, and with capital or surplus, or both, amounting to at least five million dollars ($5,000,000); or guaranteed trust fund amounting to at least five million dollars ($5,000,000).

(2) With an alien insurer not authorized to transact insurance in at least one state of the United States, unless the insurer shall have established an effective trust fund of at least two million five hundred thousand dollars ($2,500,000) within the United States administered by a recognized financial institution and held for the benefit of all its policyholders or policyholders and creditors in the United States, and with capital or surplus, or both, amounting to at least fifteen million dollars ($15,000,000).

(3) With a foreign or alien insurer which has transacted insurance as an authorized insurer in its state or country of domicile for less than five years, unless it is a wholly owned subsidiary of an insurer authorized to transact insurance in this state.

(4) With an insurer the voting control of which is held in whole or substantial part by any government or governmental agency.

(5) In any insurer made ineligible as a surplus line insurer by order of the commissioner received by or known to the broker. The commissioner may issue an order of ineligibility if he or she finds that the insurer:

82

a. Does not meet the financial requirements of this section;

b. Has without just cause refused to pay valid claims arising under its contracts in this state or has otherwise conducted its affairs in a manner as to result in injury or loss to the insuring public of this state; or

c. Has conducted its affairs in a manner as to result in the avoidance of payment of tax as required by Sections 27-10-31 and 27-10-35. (Acts 1963, No. 521, p. 1112, § 13; Acts 1971, No. 407, p. 707, § 201; Acts 1975, No. 219, p. 746, § 1; Acts 1994, 1st Ex. Sess., No. 94-790, p. 92, § 2.)

The 1994, 1st Ex. Sess., amendment, effective May 6, 1994, in subsection (b), inserted in the introductory language "with any of the following"; in subdivision (1), substituted "or surplus, or both," for "and/or surplus," and substituted "five million dollars ($5,000,000)" for "$1,500,000.00" and for "$750,000.00"; in subdivision (2), substituted "two million five hundred thousand dollars ($2,500,000)" for "$750,000.00" and added the language beginning "and with capital or surplus"; and made nonsubstantive changes throughout the section.

Code Commissioner's note. — Acts 1994, No. 94-790, which amended this section, in § 1 provides: " The Legislature declares that the purpose of this act is to provide for an effective and efficient system for the Commissioner of Insurance to regulate insurance transactions with nonadmitted insurers. The Legislature finds that insurance transactions are so affected with a public interest as to require regulation, taxation, supervision, and control under the Commissioner of Insurance. This act will increase the protection to insureds and claimants of this state in transactions involving the purchase of insurance from insurers not authorized to transact business in this state, and will protect revenues of this state."

§ 27-10-28. Liability of insurer as to losses and unearned premiums.

Corporation did not meet premium due condition by paying premium to agency. — Where agency, an independent insurance broker, contacted employee of another insurance broker, who was authorized underwriter of surplus line insurer, to get insurance for corporation, where employee sent quote letter with net premium amount, where corporation paid agency the premium but agency never sent premium to insurance broker, corporation did not meet the net premium due condition by paying the net premium to agency. Surplus line insurer could have been bound to provide coverage to corporation even if it had never received the insurance premium, but only if it first accepted corporation as a surplus line risk and only if insurance broker that had placed the insurance also received the premium. These conditions were not met; thus, this section was inapplicable. Gulf Gate Mgt. Corp. v. St. Paul Surplus Lines Ins. Co., 646 So. 2d 654 (Ala. 1994).

§ 27-10-31. Annual tax of surplus line brokers.

(a) On or before the first day of March each year, the surplus line broker shall remit to the State Treasurer through the commissioner, as a tax imposed for the privilege of transacting business as a surplus line broker in this state, a tax of six percent on the direct premiums, less return premiums and exclusive of sums collected to cover state or federal taxes, on surplus line insurance subject to tax transacted by the broker during the preceding calendar year as shown by the annual statement filed with the commissioner.

(b) If a surplus line policy covers risks or exposures only partially in this state, the tax so payable shall be computed on the proportion of the premium which is properly allocable to the risks or exposures located in this state.

(c) The tax under the provisions of this section shall be subject to deduction of the full amount of all expenses of examination of the surplus line broker by the commissioner in the same manner as that allowed for domestic insurers for examination expenses under the provisions of subdivision (5) of subsection (c) of Section 27-4A-3. All taxes collected under this section shall be deposited in the State Treasury to the credit of the State General Fund. (Acts 1963, No. 521, p. 1112, § 18; Acts 1971, No. 407, p. 707, § 206; Acts 1980, No. 80-774, p. 1608, § 2; Acts 1993, No. 93-679, § 7.)

The 1993 amendment, in subsection (a), substituted "six percent" for "four percent," substituted "the broker" for "him," and substituted "the annual" for "his annual"; and in subsection (c), substituted "subdivision (5) of subsection (c) of Section 27-4A-3" for "subdivision (4) of subsection (b) of section 27-4-5" and added the second sentence. For effective date, see the Code commissioner's note.

Code Commissioner's note. — Acts 1993, No. 93-679, § 14, provides: "Upon its passage and approval by the Governor, or upon its otherwise becoming a law, this act shall become effective at 12:01 a.m. on the first day of Janu-

ary, 1995, with respect to insurance premiums received on or after January 1, 1995; provided, however, that (1) the determination and payment of taxes due on premiums received prior to January 1, 1995, shall be pursuant to the law in effect prior to January 1, 1995, and (2) the provisions of subsection (b) of Section 3 and the provisions of Section 11 shall become effective immediately upon passage of this act and approval by the Governor, or upon its otherwise becoming a law."

Collateral references. — 44 C.J.S., Insurance, § 85.

43 Am. Jur. 2d, Insurance, § 84.

CHAPTER 12.

TRADE PRACTICES LAW.

Sec.
27-12-17. Collection of premiums or charges when insurance not provided; excess premium or charge.

No section of the Trade Practices Law creates a private cause of action, as this chapter delegates its enforcement to an insurance commissioner by specifically granting the commissioner several remedies and establishing the procedures for pursuing such remedies. Farlow v. Union Cent. Life Ins. Co., 874 F.2d 791 (11th Cir. 1989).

§ 27-12-1. Purpose of chapter; short title.

Cited in Farlow v. Union Cent. Life Ins. Co., 874 F.2d 791 (11th Cir. 1989).

§ 27-12-6. "Twisting."

Section does not relate to employee benefit plan. — This section is simply and clearly a statute designed to regulate or to control one aspect of the insurance industry in Alabama and does not relate to an employee benefit plan under the Employee Retirement Income Security Act, 29 U.S.C. § 1001 et seq. Butler v. Fringe Benefits Plan, Inc., 701 F. Supp. 804 (N.D. Ala. 1988).

This section does not create a private cause of action, as this chapter delegates its enforcement to an insurance commissioner by specifically granting the commissioner several

remedies and establishing the procedures for pursuing such remedies. Farlow v. Union Cent. Life Ins. Co., 874 F.2d 791 (11th Cir. 1989).

The twisting statute does not create a private cause of action. Bryant v. Commonwealth Life Ins. Co., 767 F. Supp. 1120 (S.D. Ala. 1991), aff'd, 988 F.2d 1218 (11th Cir. 1993); Garris v. Pioneer Life Ins. Co., 768 F. Supp. 335 (S.D. Ala. 1991).

Implying private cause of action would duplicate existing fraud causes of action. — Because liability for fraud may exist even when one innocently or mistakenly misrepresents the coverage provided by an insurance policy, implying a private cause of action under this section would merely duplicate already existing fraud causes of action. Farlow v. Union Cent. Life Ins. Co., 874 F.2d 791 (11th Cir. 1989).

The trial court did not err in allowing plaintiff to amend his complaint after final judgment was entered, to allege a violation of the "twisting" statute, since every element underlying the "twisting" statute was included in the plaintiff's complaint stating a common law cause of action for fraud, therefore, the amendment to the complaint alleging violation of this section was redundant, and it could not have prejudiced the defendants in any way. HealthAmerica v. Menton, 551 So. 2d 235 (Ala. 1989), cert. denied, 493 U.S. 1093, 110 S. Ct. 1166, 107 L. Ed. 2d 1069 (1990).

Jury question as to statement that agent's statement was actionable. — Where defendant insurance company through its agent undertook to compare plaintiff's then-existing policy with defendant's policy and defendant agent advised plaintiff that defendant's

policy was "better," the question of whether agent's "better" statement constituted an actionable misrepresentation presented a question of fact for the jury to decide and defendants were not entitled to a summary judgment. Tribble v. Provident Life & Accident Ins. Co., 534 So. 2d 1096 (Ala. 1988).

Allegations dismissed since they were not materially different from fraud claims. — Where insured alleged in several counts that general agents for insurance company made false representations and comparisons regarding her existing policies and the policies that they wanted to sell her in violation of this section, since insured's allegations supported her claims of fraud, it did not appear that any of those counts stated a statutory claim for relief that was different in any material respect from a fraud claim; therefore, the trial court did not err in dismissing those counts. Guinn v. American Integrity Ins. Co., 568 So. 2d 760 (Ala. 1990).

Cited in Jarrard v. Nationwide Mut. Ins. Co., 495 So. 2d 584 (Ala. 1986).

§ 27-12-10. Financial inducements to purchase insurance.

Cited in Farlow v. Union Cent. Life Ins. Co., 874 F.2d 791 (11th Cir. 1989).

§ 27-12-12. Life, annuity and disability insurance — Agreements not expressed in contract, rebates and other inducements.

Cited in Farlow v. Union Cent. Life Ins. Co., 874 F.2d 791 (11th Cir. 1989).

Collateral references.
Insurance anti-rebate statutes: validity and construction. 90 ALR4th 213.

§ 27-12-13. Life, annuity and disability insurance — Exceptions to discrimination, rebates or special inducements.

Collateral references. — Insurance anti-rebate statutes: validity and construction. 90 ALR4th 213.

§ 27-12-14. Inducements as to property, casualty or surety insurance.

Collateral references.
Liability insurance: third party's right of ac-

tion for insurer's bad-faith tactics designed to delay payment of claim. 62 ALR4th 1113.

§ 27-12-15. Purchase of insurance as condition precedent to sale or loan on property.

Collateral references.
Propriety and prejudicial effect of trial counsel's reference or suggestion in medical mal-

practice case that defendant is insured. 71 ALR4th 1025.
Property damage insurance: what consti-

tutes "contamination" within policy clause excluding coverage. 72 ALR4th 633.

§ 27-12-17. Collection of premiums or charges when insurance not provided; excess premium or charge.

(a) No person shall willfully collect any sum as premium or charge for insurance which insurance is not then provided or is not in due course to be provided, subject to acceptance of the risk by the insurer, by an insurance policy issued by an insurer as permitted by this title.

(b) No person shall willfully collect as premium or charge for insurance any sum in excess of the premium or charge applicable to the insurance and as specified in the policy in accordance with the applicable classifications and rates as filed with, and approved by, the commissioner or, in cases where classifications, premiums, or rates are not required by this title to be so filed and approved. The premiums and charges shall not be in excess of those specified in the policy and as fixed by the insurer. This section shall not be deemed to prohibit the charging and collection by surplus line brokers licensed under Chapter 10 of this title of the amount of applicable state and federal taxes in addition to the premium required by the insurer; nor shall it be deemed to prohibit the charging and collection by a life insurer of amounts actually to be expended for medical examination of an applicant for life insurance or for reinstatement of a life insurance policy; nor shall it be deemed to prohibit an Alabama licensed agent from charging a collection fee of up to one and one-half percent per month on unpaid balances for insurance premiums.

(c) Each violation of this section shall be punishable under Section 27-1-12. (Acts 1971, No. 407, p. 707, § 243; Acts 1994, No. 94-118, p. 146, § 1.)

The 1994 amendment, effective February 25, 1994, added the language beginning "nor shall it be deemed" and ending "for insurance premiums" to the end of subsection (b); and made nonsubstantive changes.

Code Commissioner's note. — Subsection (c) was included in this section prior to the 1994

Act and appears to have been inadvertently omitted. Subsection (c) was restored by the Code Commissioner in 1994.

Cited in National Union Fire Ins. Co. v. Lomax Johnson Ins. Agency, Inc., 496 So. 2d 737 (Ala. 1986); State Ins. Dep't v. Howell, 614 So. 2d 1053 (Ala. Civ. App. 1992).

§ 27-12-18. Statement of charges; hearing, order and review thereon.

This section does not create a private cause of action, as this chapter delegates its enforcement to an insurance commissioner by specifically granting the commissioner several

remedies and establishing the procedures for pursuing such remedies. Farlow v. Union Cent. Life Ins. Co., 874 F.2d 791 (11th Cir. 1989).

§ 27-12-19. Service of statements, notices, orders and other processes.

Cited in Farlow v. Union Cent. Life Ins. Co., 874 F.2d 791 (11th Cir. 1989).

§ 27-12-20. Review of commissioner's cease and desist orders.

Cited in Farlow v. Union Cent. Life Ins. Co., 874 F.2d 791 (11th Cir. 1989).

§ 27-12-21. Proceedings on unfair competition, etc., not defined under chapter — Generally.

Cited in Farlow v. Union Cent. Life Ins. Co., 874 F.2d 791 (11th Cir. 1989).

§ 27-12-23. False statements, etc., in insurance application.

Collateral references.
Fraud actions: Right to recover for mental or emotional distress. 11 ALR5th 88.

§ 27-12-24. Refusal of insurer to pay or settle claims.

The plaintiff in a "bad faith refusal" case has the burden of proving, etc.
To prove a bad faith claim, a plaintiff must go beyond merely showing nonpayment; it is incumbent on the plaintiff to show that the insurance company had no legal or factual defense to the claim. Further, if the evidence produced by either side creates a fact issue with regard to the validity of the claim and, thus, the legitimacy of the denial thereof, the tort claim must fail and should not be submitted to the jury. Emanuelsen v. State Farm Auto. Ins. Co., 651 So. 2d 29 (Ala. Civ. App. 1994).

Entitlement to directed verdict on underlying contract claim is necessary. — In a normal case, to prevail on a claim based on bad faith refusal to pay, the plaintiff must be entitled to a directed verdict on the underlying contract claim. Hilley v. Allstate Ins. Co., 562 So. 2d 184 (Ala. 1990).

The standard adopted in National Sav. Life Ins. Co. v. Dutton, 419 So. 2d 1357 (Ala. 1982) is referred to as the "directed verdict on the contract claim standard." That standard is stated as follows: "In the normal case in order for a plaintiff to make out a prima facie case of bad faith refusal to pay an insurance claim, the proof offered must show that the plaintiff is entitled to a directed verdict on the contract claim, and, thus, entitled to recover on the contract claim as a matter of law." Emanuelsen v. State Farm Auto. Ins. Co., 651 So. 2d 29 (Ala. Civ. App. 1994).

Collateral references.
Emotional or mental distress as element of damages for liability insurer's wrongful refusal to settle. 57 ALR4th 801.

CHAPTER 13.

RATES AND RATING ORGANIZATIONS.

ARTICLE 1.

GENERAL PROVISIONS.

§ 27-13-1. Purpose of chapter; construction thereof.

Collateral references.
State regulation of insurer's right to classify

insureds for premium or other underwriting purposes by occupation. 57 ALR4th 625.

ARTICLE 2.

FIRE, ETC., AND INLAND MARINE INSURANCE.

§ 27-13-30. Filing of rating systems with department by insurers — Examination and approval or disapproval by commissioner.

Cited in National Fire Ins. Co. v. Housing Dev. Co., 827 F.2d 1475 (11th Cir. 1987).

CHAPTER 14.

THE INSURANCE CONTRACT.

Sec.
27-14-3. Insurable interest in personal insurance; insurable interest of corporations and charitable institutions.
27-14-6. Application for policy — Require-

Sec.
    ment; reliance by insurer; admissibility into evidence; alterations.
27-14-11.1. Contents of policies — Denial or reduction of benefits due to Medicaid eligibility void.

§ 27-14-3. Insurable interest in personal insurance; insurable interest of corporations and charitable institutions.

(a) Insurable interest with reference to personal insurance is an interest based upon a reasonable expectation of pecuniary advantage through the continued life, health, or bodily safety of another person and consequent loss by reason of his or her death or disability or a substantial interest engendered by love and affection in the case of individuals closely related by blood or by law.

(b) An individual has an unlimited insurable interest in his or her own life, health, and bodily safety and may lawfully take out a policy of insurance on his or her own life, health, or bodily safety and have the same made payable to whomsoever he or she pleases, regardless of whether the beneficiary so designated has an insurable interest.

(c) A corporation, foreign or domestic, has an insurable interest in the life or physical or mental ability of any of its directors, officers, or employees, or the directors, officers, or employees of any of its subsidiaries or any other person whose death or physical or mental disability might cause financial loss to the corporation; or, pursuant to any contractual arrangement with any shareholder concerning the reacquisition of shares owned by the shareholder at the time of his or her death or disability, on the life or physical or mental ability of that shareholder for the purpose of carrying out the contractual arrangement; or pursuant to any contract obligating the corporation as part of compensation arrangements or pursuant to a contract obligating the corporation as guarantor or surety, on the life of the principal obligor. The trustee of a trust established by a corporation for the sole benefit of the corporation has the same insurable interest in the life or physical or mental ability of any person as does the corporation. The trustee of a trust established by a corporation providing life, health, disability, retirement, or similar benefits to employees of the corporation or its affiliates and acting in a fiduciary capacity with respect to the employees, retired employees, or their dependents or beneficiaries has an insurable interest in the lives of employees for whom the benefits are to be provided.

(d) Any provision of this section and chapter to the contrary notwithstanding, a charitable organization that meets the requirements of Section 501(c)(3) of the Internal Revenue Code of 1986, as amended, may own or purchase life insurance on an individual who consents to the ownership of purchase of that insurance. The charitable organization shall be deemed to have a substantial interest in the individual insured and to have an insurable interest in the individual insured whether the charitable organization originally purchases the insurance or the insurance is later transferred to the charitable organization by the insured or another person. This subsection (d) is intended to clarify and declare existing law.

(e) An insurable interest shall exist at the time the contract of personal insurance becomes effective, but this requirement need not exist at the time the loss occurs.

(f) Any personal insurance contract procured, or caused to be procured, upon another individual is void unless the benefits under the contract are payable to the individual insured, or his or her personal representative, or to a person having, at the time when the contract was made, an insurable interest in the individual insured. In the case of a void contract, the insurer shall not be liable on the contract but shall be liable to repay to the person, or persons, who have paid the premiums, all premium payments without interest. (Acts 1971, No. 407, p. 707, § 316; Acts 1994, No. 94-576, p. 1049, § 1.)

The 1994 amendment, effective April 21, 1994, added present subsections (c) and (d) and made nonsubstantive changes.

Parent-foster child relationship. — Absent special circumstances, such as dependency or financial responsibility, the relationship between a foster parent and a foster child is not sufficient to create in the foster parent an insurable interest in the life of the foster child. Willingham v. United Ins. Co. of Am., 628 So. 2d 328 (Ala. 1993).

§ 27-14-4. Insurable interest — Property insurance.

Policy void if no insurable interest. — An insurance policy will be considered void if the insured has no insurable interest. Baldwin Mut. Ins. Co. v. Henderson, 580 So. 2d 574 (Ala. 1991).

Grantor of life estate justified in making claim for loss. — Insurance company was not justified in refusing to honor grantor's claim for loss, and summary judgment on the "insurable interest" issue was improperly granted to the defendant where, although grantor signed warranty deed transferring legal title to grantees, evidence supported grantor's claim that the conveyance was intended to create a life estate and where grantor continued to pay taxes on the home and kept most of her belongings in the house. Hunter v. State Farm Fire & Cas. Co., 543 So. 2d 679 (Ala. 1989), aff'd, 577 So. 2d 908 (Ala. 1991).

Vendors/mortgagors insurable interest. — Even though deed was executed before insurance policy was issued, vendors/mortgagors continued to have an insurable interest. Purchasers had assumed the mortgage, which made the purchasers primarily responsible and the vendors/mortgagors, sureties. Baldwin Mut. Ins. Co. v. Henderson, 580 So. 2d 574 (Ala. 1991).

Alabama, being a "title theory" state, allows the mortgagee to hold legal title to the property and the mortgagor to retain the equity of redemption in the property. Baldwin Mut. Ins. Co. v. Henderson, 580 So. 2d 574 (Ala. 1991).

Collateral references.
Insurable interest in property of lessee with
option to purchase property. 74 ALR4th 883.

§ 27-14-6. Application for policy — Requirement; reliance by insurer; admissibility into evidence; alterations.

(a) No life or disability insurance contract upon an individual, except a contract of group life insurance or of group or blanket disability insurance, shall be made or effectuated unless at the time of the making of the contract the individual insured, being of competent legal capacity to contract, applies therefor or has consented thereto, except in the following cases:

(1) A spouse may effectuate such insurance upon the other spouse;

(2) Any person having an insurable interest in the life of a minor or any person upon whom a minor is dependent for support and maintenance may effectuate insurance upon the life of, or pertaining to, such minor; and

(3) Family policies may be issued insuring any two or more members of a family on an application signed by either parent, a stepparent or by a husband or wife;

(b) An insurer shall be entitled to rely upon all statements, declarations and representations made by an applicant for insurance relative to the insurable interest which such applicant has in the insured, and no insurer shall incur any legal liability except as set forth in the policy by virtue of any untrue statements, declarations or representations so relied upon in good faith by the insurer.

(c) As to kinds of insurance other than life or disability insurance, no application for insurance signed by, or on behalf of, the insured shall be admissible in evidence in any action between the insured and the insurer arising out of the policy so applied for if the insurer has failed, at expiration of 30 days after receipt by the insurer of written demand therefor by, or on behalf of, the insured, to furnish to the insured a copy of such application reproduced by any legible means.

(d) No alteration of any written application for any life or disability insurance policy shall be made by any person other than the applicant without his written consent, except that insertions may be made by the insurer, for administrative purposes only, in such manner as to indicate clearly that such insertions are not to be ascribed to the applicant; provided, however, an insurer may prepare and attach to a contract of life or disability insurance a summary of the contents of the application therefor. (Acts 1971, No. 407, p. 707, § 319; Acts 1988, No. 88-545, p. 844, § 1.)

§ 27-14-7. Application for policy — Representations and misrepresentations, etc.

I. General Consideration.
II. Misrepresentation.
   A. In General.
   B. Health of Insured.
III. Bad Faith Refusal to Pay Claim.

I. GENERAL CONSIDERATION.

This section is excepted from ERISA preemption. — This section and the case law announced thereunder is plainly stated "law ... which regulates insurance" and thus is excepted from Employee Retirement Income Security Act preemption under 29 U.S.C. § 1144(b)(2)(A). Martin v. Pate, 749 F. Supp. 242 (S.D. Ala. 1990), aff'd, 934 F.2d 1265 (11th Cir. 1991).

Insurer may not complain of error by applicant where such was contributed to by agent's mistake. — Any mistake by insurer's agent, if it contributed to a technical error by the applicant, eliminated any right which insurer otherwise would have had to complain of the applicant's mistake. State Farm Gen. Ins. Co. v. Oliver, 658 F. Supp. 1546 (N.D. Ala. 1987), aff'd, 854 F.2d 416 (11th Cir. 1988).

Questions for jury.
Alabama courts have not yet held that every coronary occlusion increases the risk of loss to the insurance company as a matter of law. Until Alabama so declares the matter is inherently one of medical fact. As such it is properly one for the jury. Bennett v. Mutual of Omaha Ins. Co., 976 F.2d 659 (11th Cir. 1992).

The materiality of a misrepresentation is generally a jury question. Bennett v. Mutual of Omaha Ins. Co., 976 F.2d 659 (11th Cir. 1992).

The uncontradicted testimony of an insurance company's underwriter that a misrepresentation was material and that the company in good faith would not have issued the policy as written, is not necessarily dispositive. Bennett v. Mutual of Omaha Ins. Co., 976 F.2d 659 (11th Cir. 1992).

The question of "materiality" of high blood pressure to risk assumed is ordinarily one of fact. If the facts as to materiality are undisputed, then the question need not be submitted to the jury. Richerzhagen v. National Home Life Assurance Co., 523 So. 2d 344 (Ala. 1988).

Maladies that increase insurance risk. — It is true that Alabama courts recognize that there are some diseases which are commonly known to be of such serious consequences that the court will declare that they increase the risk of loss, without making a jury question. Alabama courts have been reluctant, however, to create broad categories of maladies that increase insurance risk as matters of law and thus that remove the risk of loss issue from the province of the jury. Richerzhagen v. National Home Life Assurance Co., 523 So. 2d 344 (Ala. 1988).

Evidence of notice. — Where there was evidence that insurer had previously paid one of claimant's losses and that this loss was one of those not disclosed on claimant's application, this evidence, if believed by the trier of fact, was sufficient to show that insurer should have been on notice that further inquiry was necessary, and having failed to so inquire, could not later void the policy when a new claim was filed. First Fin. Ins. Co. v. Tillery, 626 So. 2d 1252 (Ala. 1993).

Cited in Fard v. Omaha Indem. Co., 510 So. 2d 220 (Ala. 1987); Bird v. Auto Owners Ins. Co., 572 So. 2d 394 (Ala. 1990); Allstate Ins. Co. v. Swann, 27 F.3d 1539 (11th Cir. 1994).

Collateral references.
What constitutes "entering" or "alighting from" vehicle within meaning of insurance policy, or statute mandating insurance coverage. 59 ALR4th 149.

Fire insurance: failure to disclose prior fires affecting insured's property as ground for avoidance of policy. 4 ALR5th 117.

II. MISREPRESENTATION.

A. In General.

Subdivision (a)(3) strictly construed in favor of insured. — When the Alabama legislature provided that "misrepresentations, omissions, concealment of facts and incorrect statements shall not prevent a recovery ... unless," it obviously was mandating a strict interpretation of its subsequent language in favor of the insured. If literally construed, subdivision (a)(3) makes no reference to any "policy or contract" except a "policy or contract" issued in direct and immediate response to the false application. State Farm Gen. Ins. Co. v. Oliver, 658 F. Supp. 1546 (N.D. Ala. 1987), aff'd, 854 F.2d 416 (11th Cir. 1988).

Misrepresentation by insured in application for insurance contract addressed in this section. Hess v. Liberty Nat'l Life Ins. Co., 522 So. 2d 270 (Ala.), cert. denied, 489 U.S. 1100, 109 S. Ct. 1578, 103 L. Ed. 2d 944 (1988).

Insurance company does not normally have duty to inquire further into whether insured has told truth on her application. The misrepresentation by the insured supplied a defense, under this section, to a claim for payment on the policy. Hess v. Liberty Nat'l Life Ins. Co., 522 So. 2d 270 (Ala.), cert. denied, 489 U.S. 1100, 109 S. Ct. 1578, 103 L. Ed. 2d 944 (1988).

Insurer not allowed to avoid coverage in every case of misstatement by insured. — In every case where a loss occurs, whether after an innocent or after a deliberate misstatement in the insurance application, the insurance company cannot be allowed automatically to avoid coverage simply because its own employee testified that the company would not have undertaken the risk had it known the truth as to the particular fact. State Farm Gen. Ins. Co. v. Oliver, 658 F. Supp 1546 (N.D. Ala. 1987), aff'd, 854 F.2d 416 (11th Cir. 1988).

Court should not have submitted any issue under subdivision (a)(3) to the jury, where the undisputed evidence showed that neither the application nor the policy by its express terms required exact and full truth if a misstatement, no matter how innocent, might affect the risk. State Farm Gen. Ins. Co. v. Oliver, 658 F. Supp. 1546 (N.D. Ala. 1987), aff'd, 854 F.2d 416 (11th Cir. 1988).

A reason for not having submitted any question under subdivision (a)(3) to the jury is the statutory language which provides as an essential element that the insurer would not have issued the "policy or contract" but for the misinformation. The only "policy or contract" issued, in response to defendant's application of November 16, 1984, was not the "policy or contract" which was in force at the time of the fire. The policy involved was a renewal policy issued one year after November 16, 1984. State Farm Gen. Ins. Co. v. Oliver, 658 F. Supp. 1546 (N.D. Ala. 1987), aff'd, 854 F.2d 416 (11th Cir. 1988).

Innocent misrepresentation made by decedent. — Statute entitles insurer to void policy even if decedent made innocent misrepresentation. Duren v. Northwestern Nat'l Life Ins. Co., 581 So. 2d 810 (Ala. 1991).

No defense to innocent misrepresentation under subdivision (a)(3) where policy was voided only by intentional misrepresentation. — A reason why the insurance company never had a viable defense under subdivision (a)(3) is that its policy itself represented to its insured that "this policy is void . . . if [you] have intentionally concealed or misrepresented any material fact or circumstance." The insurance company, in effect, waived the statutory avenue of avoidance provided by subdivision (a)(3) by contracting for something different. It would not be fair for the insurance company to induce the sale of an insurance policy by holding out a more difficult avenue than subdivision (a)(3) for avoiding the policy and then avoiding its own inducement. The insurance company contractually excused innocent misrepresentations in the application. State Farm Gen. Ins. Co. v. Oliver, 658 F. Supp. 1546 (N.D. Ala. 1987), aff'd, 854 F.2d 416 (11th Cir. 1988).

Where insurance company had sufficient indications of true facts. — Where an insurance company has no knowledge or indications of a condition concealed by a misrepresentation in an application, it is entitled to void the policy, but where it knows the facts, knows the falsity of the statements on the application, or has sufficient indications that would put a

prudent person on notice so as to induce an inquiry which, if done with reasonable thoroughness, would reveal the truth, a question of fact is presented as to whether the insurer is entitled to void the policy. Duren v. Northwestern Nat'l Life Ins. Co., 581 So. 2d 810 (Ala. 1991).

Insurer waived defenses under subdivisions (a)(2) and (3). — By setting its own standards for avoiding a policy based only on insured's intentional misrepresentations and concealments, insurance company waived its defenses of innocent misrepresentation under subdivisions (a)(2) and (3) of this section. State Farm Fire & Cas. Co. v. Oliver, 854 F.2d 416, rehearing denied, 861 F.2d 1281 (11th Cir. 1988).

Intentional misrepresentation by applicant, etc.

An intentional misrepresentation of material fact by an applicant for insurance which is relied upon by the insurer to its prejudice provides an adequate ground for avoidance of a policy. Martin v. Pate, 749 F. Supp. 242 (S.D. Ala. 1990), aff'd, 934 F.2d 1265 (11th Cir. 1991).

Misrepresentations which are fault of insurance company, etc.

If insurance company's agent was responsible for wrong information on an application for health insurance then the company could not defend against the applicant's claim of misrepresentation. Union Bankers Ins. Co. v. McMinn, 541 So. 2d 494 (Ala. 1989).

B. Health of Insured.

Material question. — In order for the insurer to avoid liability on the ground of misrepresentation, it must appear that the misrepresentations relate to some serious ailment material to the question of the potential disability of the insured. State Farm Ins. Co. v. Whiddon, 515 So. 2d 1266 (Ala. Civ. App. 1987).

Life-threatening conditions material as a matter of law. — Alabama courts do take judicial notice that certain conditions are commonly known to be life threatening; their existence is material as a matter of law. Bennett v. Mutual of Omaha Ins. Co., 976 F.2d 659 (11th Cir. 1992).

Facts not sufficient indications to constitute notice. — Where deceased previously stated that he had been hospitalized for pneumonia, where he told paramedical examiner that he had taken chest X-rays, and he had had a CAT scan, these facts were not "sufficient indications" that he had cancer so as to constitute such notice as would prompt a prudent insurer to conduct further inquiries. Duren v. Northwestern Nat'l Life Ins. Co., 581 So. 2d 810 (Ala. 1991).

Questions for jury. — The issue of whether

a particular fact increases the risk of loss assumed by an insurance company — that is, whether it is material to the insurance coverage — is generally one for the jury. State Farm Ins. Co. v. Whiddon, 515 So. 2d 1266 (Ala. Civ. App. 1987).

III. BAD FAITH REFUSAL TO PAY CLAIM.

Prima facie case of bad faith refusal.
Usually for a plaintiff to make a prima facie case of bad faith, he must be entitled to a directed verdict on the underlying claim alleging breach of the insurance contract. Gillion v. Alabama Forestry Ass'n, 597 So. 2d 1315 (Ala. 1992).

The standard adopted in National Sav. Life Ins. Co. v. Dutton, 419 So. 2d 1357 (Ala. 1982) is referred to as the "directed verdict on the contract claim standard." That standard is stated as follows: "In the normal case in order for a plaintiff to make out a prima facie case of bad faith refusal to pay an insurance claim, the proof offered must show that the plaintiff is entitled to a directed verdict on the contract claim, and, thus, entitled to recover on the contract claim as a matter of law." Emanuelsen v. State Farm Auto. Ins. Co., 651 So. 2d 29 (Ala. Civ. App. 1994).

To prove a bad faith claim, a plaintiff must go beyond merely showing nonpayment; it is incumbent on the plaintiff to show that the insurance company had no legal or factual defense to the claim. Further, if the evidence produced by either side creates a fact issue with regard to the validity of the claim and, thus, the legitimacy of the denial thereof, the tort claim must fail and should not be submitted to the jury. Emanuelsen v. State Farm Auto. Ins. Co., 651 So. 2d 29 (Ala. Civ. App. 1994).

If any one of the reasons for denial of coverage is at least "arguable," the court need not look any further. Gillion v. Alabama Forestry Ass'n, 597 So. 2d 1315 (Ala. 1992).

Mere negligence or mistake not bad faith. — Since recognizing the tort of bad faith in Alabama, it has been held that mere negligence or mistake is not sufficient to support a claim of bad faith; there must be a refusal to pay, coupled with a conscious intent to injure. Georgia Cas. & Sur. Co. v. White, 582 So. 2d 487 (Ala. 1991).

An estate can maintain an action for bad faith refusal to pay a claim based upon a contract of insurance, to which the decedent was a party, when the bad faith occurs after the decedent's death in regard to the payment of a claim of the decedent that had matured into a contract to pay. Georgia Cas. & Sur. Co. v. White, 582 So. 2d 487 (Ala. 1991).

No finding of bad faith. — Insurance company possessed debatable reasons for denying insured's claim in each instance it was denied where, among other things, insured had been treated for epilepsy yet signed a "good health" statement indicating that she had not previously been under a doctor's care, and upon re-evaluating the claim, insurance company determined that none of the other physicians to whom it sent insured were able to affirmatively concur with her doctor's conclusion that plaintiff was totally disabled; therefore, insurance company could not be liable for bad faith. Burns v. MIC, 530 So. 2d 824 (Ala. Civ. App. 1987).

§ 27-14-8. Forms — Filing and approval or disapproval.

Cited in Aetna Ins. Co. v. Word, 611 So. 2d 266 (Ala. 1992).

§ 27-14-10. Standard or uniform provisions; waiver or substitution thereof.

Collateral references.
Policy provision limiting time within which action may be brought on the policy as applicable to tort action by insured against insurer. 66 ALR4th 859.

§ 27-14-11. Contents of policies — Generally.

Collateral references.
Validity, under insurance statutes, of coverage exclusion for injury to or death of insured's family or household members. 52 ALR4th 18.

Policy provision limiting time within which action may be brought on the policy as applicable to tort action by insured against insurer. 66 ALR4th 859.

§ 27-14-11.1. Contents of policies — Denial or reduction of benefits due to Medicaid eligibility void.

(a) For purposes of this section, "private insurer" is defined as any of the following:

(1) Any commercial insurance company offering health or casualty insurance to individuals or groups, including both experience-rated contracts and indemnity contracts.

(2) Any profit or nonprofit prepaid plan offering either medical services or full or partial payment for the diagnosis or treatment of an injury, disease, or disability.

(3) Any organization administering health or casualty insurance plans for professional associations, unions, fraternal groups, employer-employee benefit plans, and any similar organization offering these payments or services, including self-insured and self-funded plans.

(4) Any health insurer, including group health plans, as defined in Section 607(1) of the Employee Retirement Income Security Act of 1974, service benefit plan, or health maintenance organization.

(b) Any provision in an insurance contract issued or renewed after March 25, 1980, by a private insurer which denies or reduces benefits due to the eligibility of the insured to receive assistance under the Medicaid program is null and void.

(c) A private insurer may not deny enrollment to an individual because of Medicaid eligibility.

(d) The provisions of this section shall not be effective if they are found by a court of competent jurisdiction to contravene federal laws or federal regulations applicable to the Medicaid program. (Acts 1980, No. 80-124, p. 188; Acts 1994, No. 94-709, p. 1359, § 1.)

The 1994 amendment, effective May 4, 1994, in subsection (a), in the introductory language, added "any of the following" at the end, and added subdivision (4); added present subsection (c); and made nonsubstantive changes.

§ 27-14-13. Charter, bylaws, etc., of insurer as part of contract.

Cited in Superior Roofing Contractors v. Alabama Roofing, Sheet Metal, Heating & Air Conditioning Contractors' Ass'n Self Insurers Fund, 576 So. 2d 216 (Ala. 1991); Hyde v. Humana Ins. Co., 598 So. 2d 876 (Ala. 1992).

§ 27-14-17. Construction of policies.

Insurer's contesting status of wife's decedent as an employee within terms of group life insurance policy was the contesting of the policy's coverage, not its validity, and the contest was thus not barred by the incontestability clause. Miller v. Protective Life Ins. Co., 485 So. 2d 746 (Ala. Civ. App. 1986).

Collateral references.

Aviation insurance: causal link between breach of policy provisions and accident as requisite to avoid insurer's liability. 48 ALR4th 778.

Automobile liability insurance policy flight from police exclusion: validity and effect. 49 ALR4th 325.

Boiler and machinery insurance: risks and losses covered by policy or provision expressly covering boilers and machinery. 49 ALR4th 336.

Validity, under insurance statutes, of coverage exclusion for injury to or death of insured's family or household members. 52 ALR4th 18.

Partnership or joint venture exclusion in contractor's or other similar comprehensive general liability insurance policy. 57 ALR4th 1155.

What is "flood" within exclusionary clause of property damage policy. 78 ALR4th 817.

Construction and effect of provisional or monthly reporting inventory insurance. 81 ALR4th 9.

Rescission or cancellation of insurance policy for insured's misrepresentation or concealment of information concerning human immunodeficiency virus (HIV), acquired immunodeficiency syndrome (AIDS), or related health problems. 15 ALR5th 92.

§ 27-14-18. Binders.

Cited in Gray v. Great Am. Reserve Ins. Co., 495 So. 2d 602 (Ala. 1986).

§ 27-14-19. Delivery of policies.

Plaintiff provided no facts which qualified her as insured or entitled person. — Where plaintiff purchased car, and purchase contract said that if plaintiff did not obtain insurance or pay the premiums, finance company could do so for plaintiff or could purchase property damage insurance covering only finance company's interest in the collateral, and where because the plaintiff had not acquired any insurance, finance company took out a collateral single insurance policy to protect its financial interest in the car, and this policy was with insurance company, the plaintiff did not provide the court with a statute imposing a legal duty on the insurer to deliver a copy of the policy to the plaintiff. While insurers are required to provide the named insured or "the person entitled thereto" with a copy of the policy, the plaintiff had provided no facts which qualified her as either an insured or an entitled person. Although plaintiff paid the amount owed on the certificate of insurance, she paid the amount to finance company who had already paid the premium to insurance company. Surrett v. TIG Premier Ins. Co., 869 F. Supp. 919 (M.D. Ala. 1994).

Collateral references.

Insurer's duty, and effect of its failure, to provide insured or payee with copy of policy or other adequate documentation of its terms. 78 ALR4th 9.

§ 27-14-24. Effect of payments.

The phrase "in accordance with the terms of the policy" in this section and the phrase "according to the terms of the policy" in § 43-8-253(f) are not ambiguous and require a literal interpretation. In the context used by the legislature, they mean in "agreement" with or "consistent" with the terms of the policy. Pouncey v. New York Life Ins. Co., 577 So. 2d 433 (Ala. 1991).

Settlement agreement for amount less than that due under policy. — A settlement agreement between an insurer and a beneficiary for an amount less than that due under the policy did not constitute payment "in accordance with the terms of the policy" under this section or payment according to the terms of the insurers policy under § 43-8-253(f). Pouncey v. New York Life Ins. Co., 577 So. 2d 433 (Ala. 1991).

Collateral references.

Liability of insurer to insured for settling third-party claim within policy limits resulting in detriment to insured. 18 ALR5th 474.

§ 27-14-27. Acts not deemed waiver of provisions or defenses.

Collateral references.

Liability insurance: what is "claim" under deductibility-per-claim clause. 60 ALR4th 983.

§ 27-14-28. Effect of misrepresentations in proof of loss.

Public policy. — This section should be read as a clear statutory expression of the public policy of this state that, where an insured materially misrepresents to an insurer the proof of his loss with an intent to deceive, the insurer need not honor, and pay pursuant to, the contract of insurance. The statute, as worded, cannot be construed as a mere limitation on the enforceability of fraud and false swearing provisions that may appear in contracts of insurance. Martin Motors, Inc. v. State Farm Fire & Cas. Co., 523 So. 2d 119 (Ala. 1988).

Automobile insurer could void policy, regardless of whether policy contained any

"fraud or false swearing" provision, based on insured's fraudulent misrepresentations in proof of loss. Martin Motors, Inc. v. State Farm Fire & Cas. Co., 523 So. 2d 119 (Ala. 1988).

Cited in State Farm Fire & Cas. Co. v. Balmer, 672 F. Supp. 1395 (M.D. Ala. 1987); United Servs. Auto. Ass'n v. Wade, 544 So. 2d 906 (Ala. 1989).

Collateral references.

Estoppel of, or waiver by, issuer of life insurance policy to assert defense of lack of insurable interest. 86 ALR4th 828.

Requirement under property insurance policy that insured submit to examination under oath as to loss. 16 ALR5th 412.

CHAPTER 15.

LIFE INSURANCE AND ANNUITY CONTRACTS.

Sec.
27-15-5.　Life insurance policy provisions — Entire contract; representations.
27-15-19. Annuity and pure endowment con-
tract provisions — Entire contract.

§ 27-15-2. Life insurance policy provisions — Generally.

Collateral references. — Rescission or cancellation of insurance policy for insured's misrepresentation or concealment of information concerning human immunodeficiency virus

(HIV), acquired immunodeficiency syndrome (AIDS), or related health problems. 15 ALR5th 92.

§ 27-15-3. Life insurance policy provisions — Grace period.

Where the insured died within the grace period, and there was evidence that the insurer disregarded his cancellation letter, a genuine issue of material fact was presented as to

whether the policy was in effect on the day of his death. Gillespie v. Safeco Life Ins. Co., 565 So. 2d 150 (Ala. 1990).

§ 27-15-4. Life insurance policy provisions — Incontestability.

Collateral references.

Estoppel of, or waiver by, issuer of life insur-

ance policy to assert defense of lack of insurable interest. 86 ALR4th 828.

§ 27-15-5. Life insurance policy provisions — Entire contract; representations.

There shall be a provision that the policy, or the policy and the application or a summary of such application, if a copy of the application or a summary thereof is endorsed upon or attached to the policy when issued, shall constitute the entire contract between the parties and that all statements contained in the application shall, in the absence of fraud, be deemed representations and not warranties. In the event of discrepancies between the original application and the summary, the contents of the original application shall govern. When a summary of the application is attached to the policy, the insurer shall keep and maintain the original application for insurance or a copy thereof for a period of not less than three years from the date on which the policy was issued. (Acts 1935, No. 152, p. 194; Acts 1971, No. 407, p. 707, § 350; Acts 1988, No. 88-545, p. 844, § 2.)

§ 27-15-13. Life insurance policy provisions — Settlement of claims.

Collateral references.
Accident or life insurance: death by autoerotic asphyxiation as accidental. 62 ALR4th 823.

§ 27-15-18. Annuity and pure endowment contract provisions — Incontestability.

Collateral references.
Estoppel of, or waiver by, issuer of life insurance policy to assert defense of lack of insurable interest. 86 ALR4th 828.

§ 27-15-19. Annuity and pure endowment contract provisions — Entire contract.

In an annuity or pure endowment contract, other than a reversionary, survivorship or group annuity, there shall be a provision that the written contract shall constitute the entire contract between the parties or, if a copy of the application or a summary thereof is endorsed upon or attached to the contract when issued, a provision that the written contract and the application or summary thereof shall constitute the entire contract between the parties. In the event of discrepancies between the original application and the summary, the contents of the original application shall govern. When a summary of the application is attached to the policy, the insurer shall keep and maintain the original application for insurance or a copy thereof for a period of not less than three years from the date on which the policy was issued. (Acts 1935, No. 152, p. 194; Acts 1971, No. 407, p. 707, § 364; Acts 1988, No. 88-545, p. 844, § 3.)

§ 27-15-24. Exclusions and restrictions in life insurance policies.

This section applies to life insurance policies and not to accident insurance policies, and the accidental death policy in this case is a type of disability insurance specifically exempted from the requirements of this section. Duncan v. American Home Assurance Co., 747 F. Supp. 1418 (M.D. Ala. 1990).

Collateral references.
Accident or life insurance: death by autoerotic asphyxiation as accidental. 62 ALR4th 823.
Estoppel of, or waiver by, issuer of life insurance policy to assert defense of lack of insurable interest. 86 ALR4th 828.

§ 27-15-26. Power of life insurer to hold proceeds of policy.

Collateral references. — Accident or life insurance: death by autoerotic asphyxiation as accidental. 62 ALR4th 823.

CHAPTER 16.

INDUSTRIAL LIFE INSURANCE.

§ 27-16-1. "Industrial life insurance" defined.

Collateral references.
Estoppel of, or waiver by, issuer of life insur-

ance policy to assert defense of lack of insurable interest. 86 ALR4th 828.

§ 27-16-3. Policy provisions — Generally.

Collateral references. — Rescission or cancellation of insurance policy for insured's misrepresentation or concealment of information concerning human immunodeficiency virus

(HIV), acquired immunodeficiency syndrome (AIDS), or related health problems. 15 ALR5th 92.

CHAPTER 17.

BURIAL INSURANCE POLICIES.

§ 27-17-1. Applicability of chapter; "burial insurance" defined.

Collateral references.
Construction and effect of contracts or insur-

ance policies providing preneed coverage of burial expense or services. 67 ALR4th 36.

§ 27-17-14. Policy provisions — Title.

Collateral references. — Construction and effect of contracts or insurance policies provid-

ing preneed coverage of burial expense or services. 67 ALR4th 36.

CHAPTER 18.

GROUP LIFE INSURANCE.

§ 27-18-2. Policy provisions — Generally.

Collateral references. — Estoppel of, or waiver by, issuer of life insurance policy to

assert defense of lack of insurable interest. 86 ALR4th 828.

§ 27-18-4. Policy provisions — Incontestability.

Insurer's contesting status of wife's decedent as employee within terms of group life insurance policy was the contesting of the policy's coverage, not its validity, and the

contest was thus not barred by the incontestability clause. Miller v. Protective Life Ins. Co., 485 So. 2d 746 (Ala. Civ. App. 1986).

§ 27-18-6. Policy provisions — Insurability.

Collateral references.
Rescission or cancellation of insurance policy for insured's misrepresentation or concealment of information concerning human

immunodeficiency virus (HIV), acquired immunodeficiency syndrome (AIDS), or related health problems. 15 ALR5th 92.

§ 27-18-7. Policy provisions — Adjustment of premiums and/or benefits.

Collateral references.
Accident or life insurance: death by autoerotic asphyxiation as accidental. 62 ALR4th 823.

§ 27-18-9. Policy provisions — Payment of benefits.

Collateral references. — Accident or life insurance: death by autoerotic asphyxiation as accidental. 62 ALR4th 823.

§ 27-18-15. Employee life insurance.

Collateral references. — Accident or life insurance: death by autoerotic asphyxiation as accidental. 62 ALR4th 823.

CHAPTER 19.

DISABILITY INSURANCE POLICIES.

Article 2.

Medicare Supplement Policy Minimum Standards.

Sec.
27-19-57. Inclusion in policy of notice of right to return policy and receive refund of premium.

ARTICLE 1.

GENERAL PROVISIONS.

§ 27-19-19. Optional policy provisions — Other insurance in this insurer.

"Other insurance" clause in second policy did not void that policy. — Plaintiff cited no authority for the proposition that the "other insurance" clause contained in a second policy voided that policy and rendered that policy worthless by its own terms. This section specifically authorizes such a clause in an accident and sickness insurance contract. The presence of the "other insurance" clause in the second policy, without more, did not void that policy by its own terms. Howard v. Mutual Sav. Life Ins. Co., 650 So. 2d 868 (Ala. 1994).

§ 27-19-28. Exclusion of hospitalization benefits for mental patients in tax-supported institutions.

Collateral references. — What constitutes mental illness or disorder, insanity, or the like, within provision limiting or excluding coverage under health or disability policy. 19 ALR5th 533.

§ 27-19-35. Construction of policy provisions.

Collateral references.
Validity, under insurance statutes, of coverage exclusion for injury to or death of insured's
family or household members. 52 ALR4th 18.

ARTICLE 2.

MEDICARE SUPPLEMENT POLICY MINIMUM STANDARDS.

§ 27-19-54. Minimum standards for benefits generally.

Collateral references. — Liability insurance: third party's right of action for insurer's
bad-faith tactics designed to delay payment of
claim. 62 ALR4th 1113.

§ 27-19-57. Inclusion in policy of notice of right to return policy and receive refund of premium.

Medicare supplement policies or certificates, whether issued pursuant to direct response solicitation or otherwise, shall have a notice prominently printed on the first page of the policy, or attached thereto, stating in substance that the applicant shall have the right to return the policy or certificate within 30 days of its delivery and to have the premium refunded if, after examination of the policy or certificate, the applicant is not satisfied for any reason. (Acts 1981, No. 81-560, p. 940, § 8; Acts 1994, 1st Ex. Sess., No. 94-803, p. 108, § 1.)

The 1994, 1st Ex. Sess., amendment,
effective May 6, 1994, deleted the subsection (a)
designation from the beginning of the section;
substituted "whether" for "other than those,"
inserted "or otherwise" following "solicitation,"
substituted "30" for "10"; and deleted former
subsection (b) relating to Medicare supplement
policies or certificates issued pursuant to a
direct response solicitation."

CHAPTER 19A.

DENTAL CARE SERVICES.

§ 27-19A-7. Contracting directly with patient; distribution of information about policy or plan; payment and reimbursement procedures.

Collateral references. — Health provider's
agreement as to patient's copayment liability
after award by professional service insurer as
unfair trade practice under state law. 49
ALR4th 1240.

CHAPTER 20A.

ALCOHOLISM TREATMENT IN GROUP PLANS.

§ 27-20A-1. Definitions.

Collateral references. — Alcoholism or intoxication as ground for discharge justifying denial of unemployment compensation. 64 ALR4th 1151.

§ 27-20A-2. Chapter applicable to group, etc., policies.

Collateral references. — Alcoholism or intoxication as ground for discharge justifying denial of unemployment compensation. 64 ALR4th 1151.

§ 27-20A-3. Benefits required.

Collateral references. — Alcoholism or intoxication as ground for discharge justifying denial of unemployment compensation. 64 ALR4th 1151.

§ 27-20A-4. Extent of coverage.

Collateral references. — Alcoholism or intoxication as ground for discharge justifying denial of unemployment compensation. 64 ALR4th 1151.

CHAPTER 21.

ALABAMA HEALTH CARE PLAN.

Collateral references.
Coverage of artificial insemination procedures or other infertility treatments by health, sickness, or hospitalization insurance. 80 ALR4th 1059.

§ 27-21-2. Offering of insurance.

Collateral references. — Validity of state statute prohibiting health providers from the practice of waiving patients' obligation to pay health insurance deductibles or copayments, or advertising such practice. 8 ALR5th 855.

CHAPTER 21A.

HEALTH MAINTENANCE ORGANIZATIONS.

Sec.
27-21A-28. Taxes.

Collateral references. — Coverage of artificial insemination procedures or other infertility treatments by health, sickness, or hospitalization insurance. 80 ALR4th 1059.

§ 27-21A-25. Confidentiality of medical information.

Collateral references. — Physician's tort liability for unauthorized disclosure of confidential information about patient. 48 ALR4th 668.

§ 27-21A-28. Taxes.

Health maintenance organizations doing business in this state shall be subject to and pay the annual premium tax to be paid by insurers on insurance premiums. The same taxes and filing requirements applicable to life insurers under this title, shall apply to and shall be imposed upon each health maintenance organization licensed under the provisions of this chapter; and the organization shall also be entitled to the same tax deductions, reductions, abatements, and credits that life insurers are entitled to receive. (Acts 1986, No. 86-471, § 28; Acts 1993, No. 93-679, § 9.)

The 1993 amendment added the present first sentence, deleted "(a)" preceding "The same" in the present second sentence, deleted the former second sentence of subsection (a) which read: "All taxes collected hereunder shall be deposited to the credit of the general fund," and deleted former subsection (b) which read: "(b) As to health maintenance organizations doing business in this state as of May 29, 1986, the taxes imposed by this section shall not take effect until January 1, 1989, but on and after such date shall be payable in accordance with the provisions of sections 27-4-4 and 27-4-5." For effective date, see the Code commissioner's note.

Code Commissioner's note. — Acts 1993, No. 93-679, § 14, provides: "Upon its passage and approval by the Governor, or upon its otherwise becoming a law, this act shall become effective at 12:01 a.m. on the first day of January, 1995, with respect to insurance premiums received on or after January 1, 1995; provided, however, that (1) the determination and payment of taxes due on premiums received prior to January 1, 1995, shall be pursuant to the law in effect prior to January 1, 1995, and (2) the provisions of subsection (b) of Section 3 and the provisions of Section 11 shall become effective immediately upon passage of this act and approval by the Governor, or upon its otherwise becoming a law."

§ 27-21A-32. HMO enrollment requirements.

Collateral references. — Rescission or cancellation of insurance policy for insured's misrepresentation or concealment of information concerning human immunodeficiency virus (HIV), acquired immunodeficiency syndrome (AIDS), or related health problems. 15 ALR5th 92.

CHAPTER 21B.

MEDICAL SUPPORT HEALTH CARE ACCESS ACT.

Sec.
27-21B-1. Short title.
27-21B-2. Definitions.
27-21B-3. Power to conduct investigations.
27-21B-4. Enrollment of child.
27-21B-5. Health coverage through insurer.
27-21B-6. Health coverage through employer.

Sec.
27-21B-7. Imposition of additional requirements.
27-21B-8. Coverage through insurer of noncustodial parent.
27-21B-9. Garnishment of wages.

Effective date. — The act which added this chapter became effective May 4, 1994.

§ 27-21B-1. Short title.

This chapter shall be known as the "Medical Support Health Care Access Act." (Acts 1994, No. 94-710, p. 1377, § 1.)

§ 27-21B-2. Definitions.

As used in this chapter, the following terms shall have the following meanings:

(1) AGENCY. Any state agency responsible for administering programs under Title IV-D or Title XIX of the Social Security Act.

(2) INSURER. A health insurer, including a group health plan as defined in Section 607(1) of the Employee Retirement Income Security Act of 1974, a health maintenance organization, or an entity offering a service benefit plan. (Acts 1994, No. 94-710, p. 1377, § 2.)

§ 27-21B-3. Power to conduct investigations.

The Alabama Medicaid Agency is authorized and empowered to conduct investigations to determine whether a medical support order exists or eligibility for enrollment of a recipient in a parent's family health coverage exists. The parents of any child who is a recipient shall cooperate in this investigation. State agencies may share information regarding parentage and support orders. (Acts 1994, No. 94-710, p. 1377, § 3.)

§ 27-21B-4. Enrollment of child.

An insurer shall not deny enrollment of a child under the health coverage of the child's parent on any of the following grounds:

(1) That the child was born out of wedlock.

(2) That the child is not claimed as a dependent on the parent's federal income tax return.

(3) That the child does not reside with the parent or in the insurer's service area. (Acts 1994, No. 94-710, p. 1377, § 4.)

§ 27-21B-5. Health coverage through insurer.

When a parent is required by a court or administrative order to provide health coverage and the parent is eligible for family health coverage through an insurer, all of the following shall apply:

(1) The parent shall be able to enroll a child in family coverage without regard to open enrollment season restrictions.

(2) If the parent fails to enroll a child as required by court or administrative order, the child's other parent or the agency may make an enrollment.

(3) A child enrolled in health coverage pursuant to this section shall not be disenrolled unless the insurer is provided satisfactory written evidence of either of the following:

a. The court or administrative order is no longer in effect.

b. The child is or will be enrolled in comparable health coverage through another insurer which will take effect not later than the effective date of the disenrollment. (Acts 1994, No. 94-710, p. 1377, § 5.)

§ 27-21B-6. Health coverage through employer.

When a parent is required by a court or administrative order to provide health coverage and the parent is eligible for family health coverage through an employer doing business in the state, all of the following shall apply:

(1) The parent shall be able to enroll any child in family coverage without regard to open enrollment season restrictions.

(2) If the parent fails to enroll a child, the child's other parent or the agency can make the enrollment.

(3) The child shall not be disenrolled unless the employer is provided satisfactory written evidence of any of the following:

a. The court or administrative order is no longer in effect.

b. The child is or will be enrolled in comparable health coverage through another employer which will take effect not later than the effective date of the disenrollment.

c. The employer has eliminated family coverage for all of its employees.

(4) The employer shall withhold from the employee's compensation the employee's share, if any, of premiums for health coverage, so long as the amount does not exceed the maximum amount allowed by law. The employer shall then pay the employee's share of premiums to the insurer. (Acts 1994, No. 94-710, p. 1377, § 6.)

§ 27-21B-7. Imposition of additional requirements.

An insurer shall not impose any additional requirements on any state agency which has been assigned the rights of an individual eligible for medical assistance under this chapter and covered for health benefits from the insurer that are different from requirements applicable to an agent or assignee of a covered individual. (Acts 1994, No. 94-710, p. 1377, § 7.)

§ 27-21B-8. Coverage through insurer of non-custodial parent.

When a child has health coverage through the insurer of a non-custodial parent, the insurer shall do all of the following:

(1) Provide necessary information to the custodial parent in order for the child to obtain benefits through the coverage.

(2) Allow the custodial parent or the health provider, with the custodial parent's approval, to submit claims for covered services without approval from the non-custodial parent.

(3) Make payment on the submitted claims directly to the custodial parent, provider, or the agency. (Acts 1994, No. 94-710, p. 1377, § 8.)

§ 27-21B-9. Garnishment of wages.

(a) The Alabama Medicaid agency may garnish the wages, salary, or other employment income of any person who is required by a court or administrative order to provide coverage of the costs of health services to a child who is eligible for medical assistance and has received payment from a third party for the cost of services for the child but has not used the payments to reimburse the other parent or guardian of the child, the provider of services, or the Alabama Medicaid agency for its payments made. Current or past due child support shall have priority over claims for the costs of the services.

(b) In addition to the powers granted in subsection (a), the Alabama Medicaid agency may notify the State Department of Revenue of any amounts due under this section. Upon proper and timely notice, the department shall withhold any amount from any state tax refund due to the above-described person. (Acts 1994, No. 94-710, p. 1377, § 9.)

CHAPTER 22.

PROPERTY INSURANCE CONTRACTS.

Collateral references.
What is "flood" within exclusionary clause of property damage policy. 78 ALR4th 817.
Construction and effect of provisional or monthly reporting inventory insurance. 81 ALR4th 9.

Liability policy coverage for insured's injury to third party's investments, anticipated profits, goodwill, or the like, unaccompanied by physical property damage. 18 ALR5th 187.

CHAPTER 23.

CASUALTY INSURANCE CONTRACTS.

Article 1.

General Provisions.

§ 27-23-1. When insurer's liability absolute.

Cited in Mitchum v. Hudgens, 533 So. 2d 194 (Ala. 1988); Coates v. Universal Underwriters Ins. Co., 565 So. 2d 46 (Ala. 1990).

Collateral references.
Self-insurance against liability as other insurance within meaning of liability insurance policy. 46 ALR4th 707.

Liability insurance: what is "claim" under deductibility-per-claim clause. 60 ALR4th 983.

Liability insurance: third party's right of action for insurer's bad-faith tactics designed to delay payment of claim. 62 ALR4th 1113.

What constitutes single accident or occurrence within liability policy limiting insurer's liability to a specified amount per accident or occurrence. 64 ALR4th 668.

Theft and vandalism insurance: coinsured's misconduct as barring innocent coinsured's

right to recover on policy. 64 ALR4th 714.

Automobile insurance: umbrella or catastrophe policy automobile liability coverage as affected by primary policy "other insurance" clause. 67 ALR4th 14.

What constitutes theft within automobile theft insurance policy—modern cases. 67 ALR4th 82.

Liability insurer's postloss conduct as waiver of, or estoppel to assert, "no-action" clause. 68 ALR4th 389.

Liability of property owner for damages from spread of accidental fire originating on property. 17 ALR5th 547.

Liability of insurer to insured for settling third-party claim within policy limits resulting in detriment to insured. 18 ALR5th 474.

§ 27-23-2. Rights of judgment creditors.

Statutorily limited liability. — The insurance carrier of a hospital board was liable only

for $100,000.00 of a $500,000.00 wrongful death judgment against the board where the board's liability was statutorily limited. St. Paul Fire & Marine Ins. Co. v. Nowlin, 542 So. 2d 1190 (Ala. 1988).

Under Alabama law, the injured party acquires a vested interest, etc.

A judgment creditor's right under this section to proceed against the insurance company to satisfy a judgment obtained against the defendant/insured is dependent upon the rights of the insured against its insurer under the policy. Under Alabama law, the injured party acquires a vested interest (secondary) in the nature of a hypothecation of the insured's rights under the policy. St. Paul Fire & Marine Ins. Co. v. Nowlin, 542 So. 2d 1190 (Ala. 1988).

Cited in Langley v. Mutual Fire, Marine & Inland Ins. Co., 512 So. 2d 752 (Ala. 1987).

ARTICLE 2.

CANCELLATION OF AUTOMOBILE LIABILITY INSURANCE.

§ 27-23-20. Definitions.

Collateral references.

What constitutes "entering" or "alighting from" vehicle within meaning of insurance policy, or statute mandating insurance coverage. 59 ALR4th 149.

Validity and construction of automobile insurance provision or statute automatically terminating coverage when insured obtains another policy providing similar coverage. 61 ALR4th 1130.

Automobile insurance: umbrella or catastrophe policy automobile liability coverage as affected by primary policy "other insurance" clause. 67 ALR4th 14.

What constitutes "motor vehicle" for purposes of no-fault insurance. 73 ALR4th 1053.

§ 27-23-21. Reasons for cancellation.

Collateral references.

Validity and construction of automobile insurance provision or statute automatically terminating coverage when insured obtains another policy providing similar coverage. 61 ALR4th 1130.

§ 27-23-22. Effect of renewal.

Collateral references.

Validity and construction of automobile insurance provision or statute automatically terminating coverage when insured obtains another policy providing similar coverage. 61 ALR4th 1130.

§ 27-23-23. Notice of cancellation — Time; reasons.

Collateral references.

Validity and construction of automobile insurance provision or statute automatically terminating coverage when insured obtains another policy providing similar coverage. 61 ALR4th 1130.

§ 27-23-25. Notice of cancellation — Proof of notice.

Cited in Strickland v. Alabama Farm Bureau Mut. Cas. Ins. Co., 502 So. 2d 349 (Ala. 1987); Cornett v. Johnson, 578 So. 2d 1259 (Ala. 1991).

§ 27-23-27. Liability of insurer, etc., for statements, etc.

Collateral references.

Liability insurance: what is "claim" under deductibility-per-claim clause. 60 ALR4th 983.

§ 27-23-28. Applicability of article to nonrenewal.

Collateral references.
Validity and construction of automobile insurance provision or statute automatically terminating coverage when insured obtains another policy providing similar coverage. 61 ALR4th 1130.

CHAPTER 24.

SURETY INSURANCE CONTRACTS.

§ 27-24-6. Venue of actions on bonds or undertakings.

Cited in Morris v. Reliance Ins. Co., 484 So. 2d 414 (Ala. 1986).

CHAPTER 25.

TITLE INSURANCE.

§ 27-25-1. Enjoining of certain acts; revocation of charter for violating same.

Collateral references.
Title insurer's negligent failure to discover and disclose defect as basis for liability in tort. 19 ALR5th 786.

CHAPTER 26.

MEDICAL LIABILITY INSURANCE.

Article 1.

General Provisions.

Sec.
27-26-5. Reports of judgments and settlements; confidentiality; penalty.

ARTICLE 1.

GENERAL PROVISIONS.

§ 27-26-1. Definitions.

Collateral references.
Self-insurance against liability as other insurance within meaning of liability insurance policy. 46 ALR4th 707.

Medical malpractice: hospital's liability for injury allegedly caused by failure to have properly qualified staff. 62 ALR4th 692.

Liability insurance: third party's right of action for insurer's bad-faith tactics designed to delay payment of claim. 62 ALR4th 1113.

Liability for injury or death allegedly caused by activities of hospital "rescue team." 64 ALR4th 1200.

Tort liability of medical society or professional association for failure to discipline or investigate negligent or otherwise incompetent medical practitioner. 72 ALR4th 1148.

"Dual capacity doctrine" as basis for employee's recovery for medical malpractice from company medical personnel. 73 ALR4th 115.

What services, equipment, or supplies are "medically necessary" for purposes of coverage under medical insurance. 75 ALR4th 763.

§ 27-26-5. Reports of judgments and settlements; confidentiality; penalty.

(a) Any insurance company which sells medical liability insurance to Alabama physicians or their professional corporations or professional associations, or to hospitals or other health care providers shall be required to report to the state licensing agency which issues the license of the physician, hospital or other health care provider any final judgment or any settlement in or out of court resulting from a claim or action for damages for personal injuries caused by an error, omission or negligence in the performance of professional services with or without consent rendered by its policyholder within 30 days after entry of a judgment in court or agreement to settle a claim in or out of court.

(b) The report rendered to the appropriate state agency shall consist of the name of the policyholder, or if the policyholder is a professional corporation or professional association, the name of the physician or physicians against whom the claim was made, the name of the claimant, a summary of the allegations made in the lawsuit, the injuries incurred by the claimant and the terms of the judgment or settlement.

(c) The report rendered pursuant to the requirements of this section, and any and all information, interviews, reports, statements, memorandum, or other documents produced by the licensing board as a result of any investigation of the subject matter of the report are declared to be privileged and confidential. All such records, reports, proceedings or other documents and any findings, conclusions, recommendations or actions of the licensing board shall be confidential and shall not be public records nor available for court subpoena or for discovery proceedings. Nothing contained herein shall apply to records made in the regular course of business of a physician, hospital or other health care provider and information, documents or records otherwise available from original sources are not to be construed as immune from discovery or use in civil proceedings merely because they were presented to or considered by the licensing board.

(d) The failure to make the reports required by this section within the time periods which are provided shall be punishable under section 27-1-12. (Acts 1986, No. 86-441; Acts 1991, No. 91-663, p. 1271, § 1.)

ARTICLE 2.

JOINT UNDERWRITING ASSOCIATION.

§ 27-26-21. Creation; composition.

Collateral references. — Recovery in death action for failure to diagnose incurable disease which caused death. 64 ALR4th 1232.

§ 27-26-31. Insufficiency of funds.

Collateral references. — Liability insurance: third party's right of action for insurer's bad-faith tactics designed to delay payment of claim. 62 ALR4th 1113.

§ 27-26-32. Application for coverage.

Collateral references. — Liability insurance: what is "claim" under deductibility-per-claim clause. 60 ALR4th 983.

§ 27-26-37. Proration of participation in writings, expenses, etc.

Collateral references. — Liability insurance: third party's right of action for insurer's bad-faith tactics designed to delay payment of claim. 62 ALR4th 1113.

CHAPTER 27.

ORGANIZATION AND CORPORATE PROCEDURES OF STOCK AND MUTUAL INSURERS.

Sec.
27-27-37. Dividends — Domestic stock insurers.
27-27-38. Dividends — Domestic mutual insurers.

Sec.
27-27-49.1. Recovery.

§ 27-27-21. Domestic mutual insurers — Membership.

City or other public corporation is authorized to be a policyholder of a mutual insurance plan under this section. It would be imprudent for a small municipality, under most conditions, not to cover its exposure. Taxpayers & Citizens v. City of Foley, 527 So. 2d 1261 (Ala. 1988).

§ 27-27-37. Dividends — Domestic stock insurers.

(a) A domestic stock insurer shall not pay any cash dividend to stockholders except out of that part of its available surplus funds which is derived from realized net profits on its business.

(b) A stock dividend may be paid out of any available surplus funds in excess of the aggregate amount of surplus loaned to the insurer under Section 27-27-40.

(c) A dividend otherwise proper may be payable out of the insurer's surplus even though its total surplus is then less than the aggregate of its past contributed surplus resulting from issuance of its capital stock at a price in excess of the par value thereof if payment is conditioned upon receipt of the commissioner's approval and the insurer does not pay the dividend until the commissioner has done the following:

(1) Approved the payment of the dividend, or

(2) Not disapproved the payment of the dividend within 30 days after receipt of notice from the insurer of the declaration thereof. (Acts 1971, No. 407, p. 707, § 533; Acts 1994, No. 94-634, p. 1178, § 2.)

§ 27-27-38. Dividends — Domestic mutual insurers.

(a) The directors of a domestic mutual insurer may, from time to time, apportion and pay or credit to its members dividends only out of that part of its surplus funds which represents net realized savings and net realized earnings in excess of the surplus required by law to be maintained.

(b) A dividend otherwise proper may be payable out of the savings and earnings even though the insurer's total surplus is then less than the aggregate of its contributed surplus if payment is conditioned upon receipt of the commissioner's approval and the insurer does not pay the dividend until the commissioner has done the following:

(1) Approved the payment of the dividend, or

(2) Not disapproved the payment of the dividend within 30 days after receipt of notice from the insurer of the declaration thereof. (Acts 1971, No. 407, p. 707, § 534; Acts 1994, No. 94-634, p. 1178, § 2.)

§ 27-27-49.1. Recovery.

(a) If an order for liquidation or rehabilitation of a domestic insurer has been entered, the receiver appointed under such order shall have a right to recover on behalf of the insurer, (i) from any parent corporation or holding company or person or affiliate who otherwise controlled the insurer, the amount of distributions (other than distributions of shares of the same class of stock) paid by the insurer on its capital stock, or (ii) any payment in the form of a bonus, termination settlement, or extraordinary lump sum salary adjustment made by the insurer or its subsidiary to a director, officer, or employee, where the distribution or payment pursuant to (i) or (ii) is made at any time during the one year preceding the petition for liquidation, conservation, or rehabilitation, as the case may be, subject to the limitations of subsections (b), (c), and (d) of this section.

(b) No such distribution shall be recoverable if the parent or affiliate shows that when paid the distribution was lawful and reasonable, and that the insurer did not know and could not reasonably have known that the distribution might adversely affect the ability of the insurer to fulfill its contractual obligations.

(c) A person who was a parent corporation or holding company or a person who otherwise controlled the insurer or affiliate at the time such distributions were paid shall be liable up to the amount of distributions or payments under subsection (a) which the person received. A person who otherwise controlled the insurer at the time the distributions were declared shall be liable up to the amount of distributions he or she would have received if they had been paid immediately. If two or more persons are liable with respect to the same distributions, they shall be jointly and severally liable.

(d) The maximum amount recoverable under this section shall be the amount needed in excess of all other available assets of the impaired or insolvent insurer to pay the contractual obligations of the impaired or insolvent insurer and to reimburse any guaranty funds.

(e) To the extent that any person liable under subsection (c) of this section is insolvent or otherwise fails to pay claims due from it pursuant to the subsection, its parent corporation or holding company or person who otherwise controlled it at the time the distribution was paid, shall be jointly and severally liable for any resulting deficiency in the amount recovered from the parent corporation or holding company or person who otherwise controlled it. (Acts 1994, No. 94-634, p. 1178, § 3.)

Effective date. — The act which added this section became effective April 26, 1994.

CHAPTER 29.

INSURANCE HOLDING COMPANY SYSTEMS.

Sec.
27-29-1. Definitions.
27-29-2. Subsidiaries and affiliates of domestic insurers.
27-29-3. Acquisition of control of, or merger with, domestic insurers.

Sec.
27-29-4. Registration of insurers.
27-29-5. Transactions of insurers with affiliates; adequacy of surplus; dividends and other distributions.

§ 27-29-1. Definitions.

For purposes of this chapter, unless otherwise stated, the following terms shall have the meanings respectively ascribed to them by this section:

(1) AFFILIATE. The term shall include an "affiliate" of, or person "affiliated" with, a specific person, and shall mean a person that directly, or indirectly through one or more intermediaries, controls, or is controlled by, or is under common control with, the person specified.

(2) COMMISSIONER. The Commissioner of Insurance, his or her deputies, or the Insurance Department as appropriate.

(3) CONTROL. The term shall include "controlling," "controlled by," or "under common control with" and shall mean the possession, direct or indirect, of the power to direct or cause the direction of the management and policies of a person, whether through the ownership of voting securities, by

contract other than a commercial contract for goods or nonmanagement services, or otherwise, unless the power is the result of an official position with or corporate office held by the person. Control shall be presumed to exist if any person, directly or indirectly owns, controls, holds with the power to vote, or holds proxies representing five percent or more of the voting securities of any other person. This presumption may be rebutted by a showing made in the manner provided by subsection (i) of Section 27-29-4 that control does not exist in fact. Such "control" as used in this section shall not be deemed to exist where proxies have been obtained by management of such insurer solely in connection with voting at an annual or other regular meeting of the shareholders of such insurer. The commissioner may determine, after furnishing all persons in interest notice and opportunity to be heard and making specific finding of fact to support such determination, that control exists in fact, notwithstanding the absence of a presumption to that effect.

(4) INSURANCE HOLDING COMPANY SYSTEM. A system which consists of two or more affiliated persons, one or more of which is an insurer.

(5) INSURER. An insurance company as set forth in Section 27-1-2, except that it shall not include:

    a. Agencies, authorities, or instrumentalities of the United States, its possessions and territories, the Commonwealth of Puerto Rico, the District of Columbia, or a state or political subdivision of a state;

    b. Fraternal benefit societies; or

    c. Nonprofit medical and hospital service associations.

Notwithstanding the foregoing, for purposes of Section 27-29-3, a domestic insurer shall include any other person controlling a domestic insurer unless such other person is either directly or through its affiliates primarily engaged in business other than the business of insurance.

(6) PERSON. An individual, a corporation, a partnership, a limited partnership, an association, a joint-stock company, a trust, an unincorporated organization, or any similar entity or any combination of the foregoing acting in concert, but shall not include any securities broker performing no more than the usual and customary broker's function.

(7) SECURITYHOLDER. One who owns any security of such person, including common stock, preferred stock, debt obligations, and other security convertible into, or evidencing, the right to acquire any of the foregoing.

(8) SUBSIDIARY. An affiliate controlled by such person, directly or indirectly, through one or more intermediaries.

(9) VOTING SECURITY. The term shall include any security convertible into, or evidencing, a right to acquire a voting security. (Acts 1973, No. 1042, p. 1636, § 2; Acts 1982, No. 82-230, p. 280, § 1; Acts 1994, No. 94-634, p. 1178, § 2.)

The 1994 amendment, effective April 26, 1994, in subdivision (3), deleted the former third sentence, relating to persons controlling between five and 15 percent of the voting securities of another person; in paragraph b. of subdivision (5), substituted "benefit" for "bene-fits"; and made nonsubstantive changes.

Code Commissioner's note. — Acts 1994, No. 94-634, which amended this section, in § 1 provides: "The purpose of this act is to make Alabama law substantially similar to the Model Insurance Holding Company System Regulatory Act adopted by the National Association of Insurance Commissioners so as to make the Alabama Department of Insurance eligible for accreditation by the National Association of Insurance Commissioners."

Acts 1994, No. 94-634, § 27-27-49.1, provides: "(a) If an order for liquidation or rehabilitation of a domestic insurer has been entered, the receiver appointed under such order shall have a right to recover on behalf of the insurer, (i) from any parent corporation or holding company or person or affiliate who otherwise controlled the insurer, the amount of distributions (other than distributions of shares of the same class of stock) paid by the insurer on its capital stock, or (ii) any payment in the form of a bonus, termination settlement, or extraordinary lump sum salary adjustment made by the insurer or its subsidiary to a director, officer, or employee, where the distribution or payment pursuant to (i) or (ii) is made at any time during the one year preceding the petition for liquidation, conservation, or rehabilitation, as the case may be, subject to the limitations of subsections (b), (c), and (d) of this section.

"(b) No such distribution shall be recoverable if the parent or affiliate shows that when paid the distribution was lawful and reasonable, and that the insurer did not know and could not reasonably have known that the distribution might adversely affect the ability of the insurer to fulfill its contractual obligations.

"(c) A person who was a parent corporation or holding company or a person who otherwise controlled the insurer or affiliate at the time such distributions were paid shall be liable up to the amount of distributions or payments under subsection (a) which the person received. A person who otherwise controlled the insurer at the time the distributions were declared shall be liable up to the amount of distributions he or she would have received if they had been paid immediately. If two or more persons are liable with respect to the same distributions, they shall be jointly and severally liable.

"(d) The maximum amount recoverable under this section shall be the amount needed in excess of all other available assets of the impaired or insolvent insurer to pay the contractual obligations of the impaired or insolvent insurer and to reimburse any guaranty funds.

"(e) To the extent that any person liable under subsection (c) of this section is insolvent or otherwise fails to pay claims due from it pursuant to the subsection, its parent corporation or holding company or person who otherwise controlled it at the time the distribution was paid, shall be jointly and severally liable for any resulting deficiency in the amount recovered from the parent corporation or holding company or person who otherwise controlled it."

Cited in Elgin v. Alfa Corp., 598 So. 2d 807 (Ala. 1992).

§ 27-29-2. Subsidiaries and affiliates of domestic insurers.

(a) *Authorization.* — Any domestic insurer, either by itself or in cooperation with one or more persons, may organize or acquire one or more subsidiaries or affiliates in accordance with the provisions contained in this section. Such subsidiaries or affiliates may conduct any kind of business, or businesses, permitted by the Constitution and the laws of this state, and their authority to do so shall not be limited by reason of the fact that they are subsidiaries or affiliates of a domestic insurer.

(b) *Additional investment authority.* — In addition to investments in common stock, preferred stock, debt obligations, and other securities permitted under all other sections of this title, a domestic insurer may also:

(1) Invest, in common stock, preferred stock, debt obligations, and other securities of one or more subsidiaries or affiliates, including, without limitation, domestic or foreign insurance subsidiaries or affiliates, amounts which do not exceed the lesser of 10 percent of such insurer's assets or 50 percent of the total of the insurer's capital and surplus as shown in the latest annual report of the insurer filed pursuant to subsection (a) of Section 27-3-26, less the minimum capital and surplus required of said insurer for authority to transact insurance by Sections 27-3-7 and 27-3-8, provided that after such investments, the insurer's surplus as regards policyholders will be reasonable in relation to the insurer's outstanding liabilities and adequate to

its financial needs. In calculating the amount of such investments, investments in domestic and foreign insurance subsidiaries shall be excluded, and there shall be included:

a. Total net moneys or other consideration expended and obligations assumed in the acquisition or formation of a subsidiary or affiliate, including all organizational expenses and contributions to capital and surplus of such subsidiary or affiliate, whether or not represented by the purchase of capital stock or issuance of other securities; and

b. All amounts expended in acquiring additional common stock, debt obligations, and other securities and all contributions to the capital or surplus of a subsidiary or affiliate subsequent to its acquisition or formation;

(2) Invest any amount in common stock, preferred stock, debt obligations, and other securities of one or more subsidiaries engaged or organized to engage exclusively in the ownership and management of assets authorized as investments for the insurer provided that each such subsidiary agrees to limit its investments in any asset so that such investments will not cause the amount of the total investment of the insurer to exceed any of the investment limitations specified in subdivision (1) of this subsection or in Sections 27-41-15 through 27-41-18 and 27-41-35. For the purpose of this subdivision, "the total investment of the insurer" shall include:

a. Any direct investment by the insurer in an asset; and

b. The insurer's proportionate share of any investment in an asset by any subsidiary or affiliate of the insurer, which shall be calculated by multiplying the amount of the subsidiary's investment by the percentage of the insurer's ownership of such subsidiary or affiliate;

(3) With the approval of the commissioner, invest any amount in common stock, preferred stock, debt obligations, or other securities of one or more subsidiaries or affiliates, provided that after such investment the insurer's surplus as regards policyholders will be reasonable in relation to the insurer's outstanding liabilities and adequate to its financial needs.

(c) *Exemption from investment restrictions.* — Investments in common stock, preferred stock, debt obligations, or other securities of subsidiaries or affiliates made pursuant to subsection (b) of this section shall not be subject to any of the otherwise applicable restrictions or prohibitions contained in this title applicable to such investments of insurers.

(d) *Qualification of investment; when determined.* — Whether any investment pursuant to subsection (b) of this section meets the applicable requirements thereof is to be determined immediately after such investment is made, taking into account the then outstanding principal balance on all previous investments in debt obligations and the value of all previous investments in equity securities as of the date they were made.

(e) *Cessation of control.* — If an insurer ceases to control a subsidiary, it shall dispose of any investment therein made pursuant to this section within three years from the time of the cessation of control or within such further time as the commissioner may prescribe, unless at any time after such investment shall have been made such investment shall have met the requirements for investment under any other section of this title, and the insurer has notified the commissioner. (Acts 1973, No. 1042, p. 1636, § 3; Acts 1980, No. 80-199, p. 276; Acts 1981, No. 81-314, p. 446; Acts 1994, No. 94-634, p. 1178, § 2.)

The 1994 amendment, effective April 26, 1994, rewrote this section.

§ 27-29-3. Acquisition of control of, or merger with, domestic insurers.

(a) *Filing and approval requirements.* — No person other than the issuer shall make a tender offer for or a request or invitation for tenders of, or enter into any agreement to exchange securities for or acquire in the open market any voting security of a domestic insurer if, after the consummation thereof, such person would, directly or indirectly, or by conversion or by exercise of any right to acquire, be in control of such insurer, and no person shall enter into an agreement to merge with or otherwise to acquire control of a domestic insurer unless, at the time any such offer, request, or invitation is made or any such agreement is entered into, or prior to the acquisition of such securities if no offer or agreement is involved or within 15 days after any such offer, request, or invitation is made or any such agreement is entered into, such person has filed with the commissioner and has sent to such insurer a statement containing the information required by this section and such offer, request, invitation, agreement, or acquisition either:

(1) Has been approved by the commissioner in the manner prescribed in this section; or

(2) Expressly states that it is subject to approval by the commissioner in the manner prescribed in this section.

An offer, request, invitation, agreement, or acquisition which contains such a condition and which is approved by the commissioner in the manner so prescribed shall be effective and binding according to its terms from the date on which it was made.

(b) *Content of statement.* — The statement to be filed with the commissioner under this section shall be made under oath or affirmation and shall contain the following information:

(1) The name and address of each person by whom, or on whose behalf, the merger or other acquisition of control referred to in subsection (a) of this section is to be effected (hereinafter called "acquiring party"), and

    a. If such person is an individual, his or her principal occupation and all offices and positions held during the past five years, and any conviction of crimes other than minor traffic violations during the past 10 years; or

    b. If such person is not an individual, a report of the nature of its business operations during the past five years or for such lesser period as such person and any predecessors thereof shall have been in existence; an informative description of the business intended to be done by such person and such person's subsidiaries; and a list of all individuals who are, or who have been selected to become, directors or executive officers of such person or who perform, or will perform, functions appropriate to such positions. Such list shall include for each such individual the information required by paragraph a of this subdivision;

(2) The source, nature, and amount of the consideration used, or to be used, in effecting the merger or other acquisition of control, a description of any transaction wherein funds were, or are to be, obtained for any such purpose, and the identity of persons furnishing such consideration; provided, however, that where a source of such consideration is a loan made in the lender's ordinary course of business, the identity of the lender shall remain confidential if the person filing such statement so requests;

(3) Fully audited financial information as to the earnings and financial condition of each acquiring party for the preceding five fiscal years of each such acquiring party, or for such lesser period as such acquiring party and any predecessors thereof shall have been in existence, and similar unaudited information as of a date not earlier than 90 days prior to the filing of the statement; provided, however, that in the case of an acquiring party which is an insurer actively engaged in the business of insurance, the financial statements of such insurer need not be audited, except such audit may be required if the need therefor is determined by the commissioner;

(4) Any plans or proposals which each acquiring party may have to liquidate such insurer, to sell its assets, or to merge or consolidate it with any person or to make any other material change in its business or corporate structure or management;

(5) The number of shares of any security referred to in subsection (a) of this section which each acquiring party proposes to acquire, the terms of the offer, request, invitation, agreement, or acquisition referred to in subsection (a) of this section, and a statement as to the method by which the fairness of the proposal was arrived at;

(6) The amount of each class of any security referred to in subsection (a) of this section which is beneficially owned or concerning which there is a right to acquire beneficial ownership by each acquiring party;

(7) A full description of any contracts, arrangements, or understandings with respect to any security referred to in subsection (a) of this section in which any acquiring party is involved, including, but not limited to, transfer of any of the securities, joint ventures, loan or option arrangements, puts or calls, guarantees of loans, guarantees against loss or guarantees of profits, division of losses or profits, or the giving or withholding of proxies. Such description shall identify the persons with whom such contracts, arrangements, or understandings have been entered into;

(8) A description of the purchase of any security referred to in subsection (a) of this section during the 12 calendar months preceding the filing of the statement by any acquiring party, including the dates of purchase, names of the purchasers, and consideration paid, or agreed to be paid, therefor;

(9) A description of any recommendations to purchase any security referred to in subsection (a) of this section made during the 12 calendar months preceding the filing of the statement by any acquiring party or by anyone based upon interviews or at the suggestion of such acquiring party;

(10) Copies of all tender offers for, requests or invitations for tenders of, exchange offers for and agreements to acquire or exchange any securities referred to in subsection (a) of this section and, if distributed, of additional soliciting material relating thereto;

(11) The terms of any agreement, contract, or understanding made with any broker-dealer as to solicitation of securities referred to in subsection (a) of this section for tender and the amount of any fees, commissions, or other compensation to be paid to broker-dealers with regard thereto; and

(12) Such additional information as the commissioner may, by rule or regulation, prescribe as necessary or appropriate for the protection of policyholders and securityholders of the insurer or in the public interest.

If the person required to file the statement referred to in subsection (a) of this section is a partnership, limited partnership, syndicate, or other group, the commissioner may require that the information called for by subdivisions (1) through (12) of this subsection shall be given with respect to each partner of such partnership or limited partnership, each member of such syndicate or group, and each person who controls such partner or member. If any such partner, member or person is a corporation or the person required to file the statement referred to in subsection (a) of this section is a corporation, the commissioner may require that the information called for by subdivisions (1) through (12) of this subsection shall be given with respect to such corporation, each officer and director of such corporation, and each person who is, directly or indirectly, the beneficial owner of more than 15 percent of the outstanding voting securities of such corporation. If any material change occurs in the facts set forth in the statement filed with the commissioner and sent to such insurer pursuant to this section, an amendment setting forth such change, together with copies of all documents and other materials relevant to such change, shall be filed with the commissioner and sent to such insurer within two business days after the person learns of such change. Such insurer shall send such amendment to its shareholders.

(c) *Alternative filing materials.* — If any offer, request, invitation, agreement, or acquisition referred to in subsection (a) of this section is proposed to be made by means of a registration statement under the Securities Act of 1933, or in circumstances requiring the disclosure of similar information under the Securities Exchange Act of 1934, or under a state law requiring similar registration or disclosure, the person required to file the statement referred to in subsection (a) of this section may utilize such documents in furnishing the information called for by that statement.

(d) *Approval by commissioner; hearings.*

(1) The commissioner shall approve any merger or other acquisition of control referred to in subsection (a) of this section unless, after a public hearing thereon, he or she finds that:

a. After the change of control, the domestic insurer referred to in subsection (a) of this section would not be able to satisfy the requirements for the issuance of a license to write the line, or lines, of insurance for which it is presently licensed;

b. The effect of the merger or other acquisition of control would be substantially to lessen competition in insurance in this state or to create a monopoly therein;

c. The financial condition of any acquiring party is such as might jeopardize the financial stability of the insurer or prejudice the interest of its policyholders;

d. The plans or proposals which the acquiring party has to liquidate the insurer, to sell its assets, or to consolidate or merge it with any person or to make any other material change in its business or corporate structure or management are unfair and unreasonable to policyholders of the insurer and not in the public interest; or

e. The competence, experience, and integrity of those persons who would control the operation of the insurer are such that it would not be in the interest of policyholders of the insurer and of the public to permit the merger or other acquisition of control.

(2) The public hearing referred to in subdivision (1) of this subsection shall be held within 45 days after the statement required by subsection (a) of this section is filed, and at least 20 days' notice thereof shall be given by the commissioner to the person filing the statement. Not less than 15 days' notice of such public hearing shall be given by the person filing the statement to the insurer and to such other persons as may be designated by the commissioner. The insurer shall give such notice to its securityholders. The commissioner shall make a determination within 30 days after the conclusion of such hearing. At such hearing, the person filing the statement, the insurer, any person to whom notice of hearing was sent, and any other person whose interest may be affected thereby shall have the right to present evidence, examine and cross-examine witnesses and offer oral and written arguments and, in connection therewith, shall be entitled to conduct discovery proceedings in the same manner as is presently allowed in the circuit courts of this state. All discovery proceedings shall be concluded not later than five days prior to the commencement of the public hearing.

(e) *Mailings to stockholders; payments of expenses.* — All statements, amendments, or other material filed pursuant to subsections (a) or (b) of this section and all notices of public hearings held pursuant to subsection (d) of this section shall be mailed by the insurer to its stockholders within 10 business days after the insurer has received such statements, amendments, other material, or notices. The expenses of mailing shall be borne by the person making the filing. As security for the payment of such expenses, such person shall file with the commissioner an acceptable bond or other deposit in an amount to be determined by the commissioner.

(f) *Exemptions.* — The provisions of this section shall not apply to any offer, request, invitation, agreement, or acquisition which the commissioner by order shall exempt therefrom as:

(1) Not having been made or entered into for the purpose and not having the effect of changing or influencing the control of a domestic insurer; or

(2) As otherwise not comprehended within the purposes of this section.

(g) *Violations.* — The following shall be violations of this section:

(1) The failure to file any statement, amendment, or other material required to be filed pursuant to subsections (a) or (b) of this section; or

(2) The effectuation, or any attempt to effectuate, an acquisition of control of, or merger with, a domestic insurer unless the commissioner has given his or her approval thereto.

(h) *Jurisdiction; consent to service of process.* — The courts of this state are hereby vested with jurisdiction over every person not resident, domiciled, or authorized to do business in this state who files a statement with the commissioner under this section and over all actions involving such person arising out of violations of this section, and each such person shall be deemed to have performed acts equivalent to and constituting an appointment by such a person of the commissioner to be his or her true and lawful attorney upon whom may be served all lawful process in any action or proceeding arising out of violations of this section. Copies of all such lawful process shall be served on the commissioner and transmitted by registered or certified mail by the commissioner to such person at his or her last known address. (Acts 1973, No. 1042, p. 1636, § 4; Acts 1986, No. 86-464, § 1; Acts 1994, No. 94-634, p. 1178, § 2.)

The 1994 amendment, effective April 26, 1994, in paragraph (d)(1)d, inserted "to" preceding "sell its assets" and preceding "consolidate or merge"; deleted former subdivision (1) of subsection (f); and made nonsubstantive changes.

Code Commissioner's note. — In subdivision (10) of subsection (b), Acts 1994, No. 94-634 referred to "or" preceding "additional soliciting material". From the context, it appears that the correct reference should be "of".

Competitors of Blue Cross allowed to intervene on application for acquisition of life insurance company. — There was no doubt that the intervenors, competitors of Blue Cross, were properly permitted to become parties to the hearing before the commissioner on Blue Cross' application for approval for the acquisition of a life insurance company since, as competitors of Blue Cross, the intervenors had a direct financial interest that would have been affected by the commissioner's order. Blue Cross & Blue Shield v. Protective Life Ins. Co., 527 So. 2d 125 (Ala. Civ. App. 1987).

§ 27-29-4. Registration of insurers.

(a) *Registration.* — Every insurer which is authorized to do business in this state and which is a member of an insurance holding company system shall register with the commissioner, except a foreign insurer subject to registration requirements and standards adopted by statute or regulation in the jurisdiction of its domicile which are substantially similar to those contained in this section and Section 27-29-5. Any insurer which is subject to registration under this section shall register within 60 days after September 3, 1973, or 15 days after it becomes subject to registration, and annually thereafter by June 1 of each year for the previous calendar year, unless the commissioner for good cause shown extends the time for registration and, then, within such extended time. The commissioner may require any authorized insurer which is a member of a holding company system which is not subject to registration under this section to furnish a copy of the registration statement or other information filed by such insurance company with the insurance regulatory authority of domiciliary jurisdiction.

(b) *Information and form required.* — Every insurer subject to registration shall file a registration statement on a form provided by the commissioner which shall contain current information about:

(1) The capital structure, general financial condition, ownership, and management of the insurer and any person controlling the insurer;

(2) The identity of every member of the insurance holding company system;

(3) The following agreements in force, relationships subsisting, and transactions currently outstanding between such insurer and its affiliates:

a. Loans, other investments or purchases, sales or exchanges of securities of the affiliates by the insurer or of the insurer by its affiliates;

b. Purchases, sales, or exchanges of assets;

c. Transactions not in the ordinary course of business;

d. Guarantees or undertakings for the benefit of an affiliate which result in an actual contingent exposure of the insurer's assets to liability, other than insurance contracts entered into in the ordinary course of the insurer's business;

e. All management and service contracts and all cost-sharing arrangements;

f. Reinsurance agreements;

g. Dividends and other distributions to shareholders; and

h. Consolidated tax allocation agreements;

(4) Any pledge of the insurer's stock, including stock of any subsidiary or controlling affiliate, for a loan made to any member of the insurance holding company system;

(5) Other matters concerning transactions between registered insurers and any affiliates as may be included, from time to time, in any registration forms adopted or approved by the commissioner.

(c) *Materiality.* — No information need be disclosed on the registration statement filed pursuant to subsection (b) of this section if such information is not material for the purposes of this section. Unless the commissioner by rule, regulation, or order provides otherwise, sales, purchases, exchanges, loans or extensions of credit or investments involving one half of one percent or less of an insurer's admitted assets as of December 31, next preceding, shall not be deemed material for purposes of this section.

(d) *Amendments to registration statements.* — Each registered insurer shall keep current the information required to be disclosed in its registration statement by reporting all material changes or additions on amendment forms provided by the commissioner within 15 days after the end of the month in which it learns of each such change or addition, but at least annually, as provided in subsection (a); provided, however, that subject to Section 27-29-5, each registered insurer shall so report all dividends and other distributions to shareholders within five business days following the declaration thereof.

(e) *Termination of registration.* — The commissioner shall terminate the registration of any insurer which demonstrated that it no longer is a member of an insurance holding company system.

(f) *Consolidated filing.* — The commissioner may require or allow two or more affiliated insurers subject to registration under this section to file a consolidated registration statement or consolidated reports amending their consolidated registration statement or their individual registration statements.

(g) *Alternative registration.* — The commissioner may allow an insurer which is authorized to do business in this state and which is part of an insurance holding company system to register on behalf of any affiliated insurer which is required to register under subsection (a) of this section and to file all information and material required to be filed under this section.

(h) *Exemptions.* — The provisions of this section shall not apply to any insurer, information, or transaction if, and to the extent that, the commissioner by rule, regulation, or order shall exempt the same from the provisions of this section.

(i) *Disclaimer.* — Any person may file with the commissioner a disclaimer of affiliation with any authorized insurer or such a disclaimer may be filed by such insurer or any member of an insurance holding company system. The disclaimer shall fully disclose all material relationships and bases for affiliation between such person and such insurer as well as the basis for disclaiming such affiliation. After a disclaimer has been filed, the insurer shall be relieved of any duty to register or report under this section which may arise out of the insurer's relationship with such person, unless and until the commissioner disallows such a disclaimer. The commissioner shall disallow such a disclaimer only after furnishing all parties in interest with notice and opportunity to be heard and after making specific findings of fact to support such disallowance.

(j) *Violations.* — The failure to file a registration statement or any amendment thereto required by this section within the time specified for such filing shall be a violation of this section. (Acts 1973, No. 1042, p. 1636, § 5; Acts 1994, No. 94-634, p. 1178, § 2.)

The 1994 amendment, effective April 26, 1994, in subsection (a), in the first sentence, substituted "registration" for "disclosure" following "insurer subject to" and inserted "and Section 27-29-5" following "in this section" and in the second sentence, substituted "and annually thereafter by June 1 of each year for the previous calendar year" for "whichever is later"; in subsection (b), in subdivision (3), deleted "other than cost allocation arrangements based upon generally accepted accounting principles" following "cost-sharing arrangements" in paragraph e; deleted "covering all, or substantially all, of one or more lines of insurance of the ceding company; and" following "Reinsurance agreements" in paragraph f; added paragraphs g and h; inserted subdivision (4), redesignated former subdivision (4) as present subdivision (5); in subsection (d), inserted "but at least annually, as provided in subsection (a)" following "change or addition," deleted "subsection (c)" preceding "Section 27-29-5" and substituted "five business days" for "two business days"; and made nonsubstantive changes.

§ 27-29-5. Transactions of insurers with affiliates; adequacy of surplus; dividends and other distributions.

(a) *Transactions with affiliates.* — Material transactions by registered insurers with their affiliates shall be subject to the following standards:

(1) The terms shall be fair and reasonable;

(2) Charges or fees for services performed shall be reasonable;

(3) Expenses incurred and payment received shall be allocated to the insurer in conformity with customary insurance accounting practices consistently applied;

(4) The books, accounts, and records of each party will be so maintained as to clearly and accurately disclose the precise nature and details of the transactions; and

(5) The insurer's surplus as regards policyholders following any dividends or distributions to shareholder affiliates shall be reasonable in relation to the insurer's outstanding liabilities and adequate to its financial needs.

(b) The following transactions involving a domestic insurer and any person in its holding company system may not be entered into unless the insurer has notified the commissioner in writing of its intention to enter into such transaction at least 30 days prior thereto, or such shorter period as the commissioner may permit, and the commissioner has not disapproved it within that period.

(1) Sales, purchases, exchanges, loans or extensions of credit, guarantees, or investments provided the transactions are equal to or exceed:

    a. With respect to nonlife insurers, the lesser of three percent of the insurer's admitted assets or 25 percent of surplus as regards policyholders as of the 31st day of December next preceding;

    b. With respect to life insurers, three percent of the insurer's admitted assets as of the 31st day of December next preceding;

(2) Loans or extensions of credit to any person who is not an affiliate, where the insurer makes loans or extensions of credit with the agreement or understanding that the proceeds of the transactions, in whole or in substantial part, are to be used to make loans or extensions of credit to, to purchase assets of, or to make investments in, any affiliate of the insurer making the loans or extensions of credit provided the transactions are equal to or exceed:

    a. With respect to nonlife insurers, the lesser of three percent of the insurer's admitted assets or 25 percent of surplus as regards policyholders as of the 31st day of December next preceding;

    b. With respect to life insurers, three percent of the insurer's admitted assets as of the 31st day of December next preceding;

(3) Reinsurance agreements or modifications thereto in which the reinsurance premium or a change in the insurer's liabilities equals or exceeds five percent of the insurer's surplus as regards policyholders, as of the 31st day of December next preceding, including those agreements which may require as consideration the transfer of assets from an insurer to a nonaffiliate, if an agreement or understanding exists between the insurer and nonaffiliate that any portion of such assets will be transferred to one or more affiliates of the insurer;

(4) All management agreements, service contracts, and all cost-sharing arrangements; and

(5) Any material transactions, specified by regulation, which the commissioner determines may adversely affect the interests of the insurer's policyholders.

122

Nothing herein contained shall be deemed to authorize or permit any transactions which, in the case of an insurer not a member of the same holding company system, would be otherwise contrary to law.

(c) A domestic insurer may not enter into transactions which are part of a plan or series of like transactions with persons within the holding company system if the purpose of those separate transactions is to avoid the statutory threshold amount and thus avoid the review that would occur otherwise. If the commissioner determines that such separate transactions were entered into over any 12-month period for that purpose, he or she may exercise his or her authority under Section 27-29-10.

(d) The commissioner, in reviewing transactions pursuant to subsection (b), shall consider whether the transactions comply with the standards set forth in subsection (a) and whether they may adversely affect the interests of policyholders.

(e) The commissioner shall be notified within 30 days of any investment of the domestic insurer in any one corporation if the total investment in such corporation by the insurance holding company system exceeds 10 percent of the corporation's voting securities.

(f) *Adequacy of surplus.* — For purposes of this chapter in determining whether an insurer's surplus as regards policyholders is reasonable in relation to the insurer's outstanding liabilities and adequate to its financial needs, the following factors, among others, shall be considered:

(1) The size of the insurer as measured by its assets, capital and surplus, reserves, premium writings, insurance in force, and other appropriate criteria;

(2) The extent to which the insurer's business is diversified among the several lines of insurance;

(3) The number and size of risks insured in each line of business;

(4) The extent of the geographical dispersion of the insurer's insured risks;

(5) The nature and extent of the insurer's reinsurance program;

(6) The quality, diversification, and liquidity of the insurer's investment portfolio;

(7) The recent past and projected future trend in the size of the insurer's surplus as regards policyholders;

(8) The surplus as regards policyholders maintained by other comparable insurers;

(9) The adequacy of the insurer's reserves;

(10) The quality and liquidity of investments in subsidiaries made pursuant to Section 27-29-2. The commissioner may treat any such investment as a disallowed asset for purposes of determining the adequacy of surplus as regards policyholders whenever in his or her judgment such investment so warrants; and

(11) The quality of the company's earnings and the extent to which the reported earnings include extraordinary items.

(g) Dividends and other distributions.

(1) A domestic insurer shall not pay any extraordinary dividend or make any other extraordinary distribution to its shareholders until 30 days after the commissioner has received notice of the declaration of the dividend or distribution and has not disapproved such payment within the period, or until the time the commissioner has approved the payment within the 30-day period.

For purposes of this paragraph, an "extraordinary dividend or distribution" includes any dividend or distribution of cash or other property, whose fair market value together with that of other dividends or distributions made within the preceding 12 months exceeds the greater of the following:

a. Ten percent of the insurer's surplus as regards policyholders as of the 31st day of December next preceding; or

b. The net gain from operations of the insurer, if the insurer is a life insurer, or the net income, if the insurer is not a life insurer, for the 12-month period ending the 31st day of December next preceding.

An extraordinary dividend or distribution does not include pro rata distributions of any class of the insurer's own securities.

(2) A domestic insurer subject to registration under Section 27-29-4 shall report to the commissioner all dividends to shareholders within five business days following the declaration of the dividends and not less than 10 days prior to the payment of the dividends. This report shall also include a schedule setting forth all dividends or other distributions made within the previous 12 months.

(3) Notwithstanding any other provision of law, a domestic insurer may declare an extraordinary dividend or distribution which is conditional upon the commissioner's approval of the dividend or distribution. Such declaration does not confer any rights upon shareholders until the commissioner has approved the payment of the dividend or distribution or the commissioner has not disapproved the payment within the 30-day period as provided in subdivision (1).

(4) The commissioner shall assess such reasonable charges as he or she deems necessary for the review conducted pursuant to this section. All funds received shall be deposited in the State Treasury to the credit of the special examination revolving fund, from which the expenses incurred shall be paid. (Acts 1973, No. 1042, p. 1636, § 6; Acts 1994, No. 94-634, p. 1178, § 2.)

The 1994 amendment, effective April 26, 1994, rewrote the section.

§ 27-29-9. Injunctions; prohibitions against voting securities; sequestration of voting securities.

Subsections (b) and (c) did not apply when an appeal had already been taken under § 27-2-32 dealing with the same subject matter and parties, as the legislature could not have intended to have the same action pending in two distinct courts. National Sec. Ins. Co. v. Mutual Sav. Life Ins. Co., 536 So. 2d 1378 (Ala. 1988).

CHAPTER 30.

MUTUAL AID ASSOCIATIONS.

Sec.
27-30-31. Repealed.
27-30-34. Provision of domestic life and disability insurance pursuant to
chapter 3.

§ 27-30-16. Contracts — Annual valuation — Benefits payable in cash.

Mutual aid association which had calculated its reserves pursuant to the standard valuation law (§ 27-36-7) was not entitled to declaratory and injunctive relief to prevent the department of insurance from requiring it to comply with the mutual aid association statutory reserve requirements of this chapter. Security Sav. Life Ins. Co. v. Weaver, 579 So. 2d 1359 (Ala. Civ. App. 1991).

§ 27-30-17. Contracts — Annual valuation — Benefits, aid or services other than cash.

Mutual aid association which had calculated its reserves pursuant to the standard valuation law (§ 27-36-7) was not entitled to declaratory and injunctive relief to prevent the department of insurance from requiring it to comply with the mutual aid association statutory reserve requirements of this chapter. Security Sav. Life Ins. Co. v. Weaver, 579 So. 2d 1359 (Ala. Civ. App. 1991).

§ 27-30-31. Applicability of fee and taxation provisions. Repealed by Acts 1993, No. 93-679, p. 1291, § 12, effective at 12:01 a.m. on January 1, 1995.

Code Commissioner's note. — Acts 1993, No. 93-679, § 12, provides: "Except as provided in Section 14, Sections 27-4-1, 27-4-3 to 27-4-7, inclusive, 27-4-9 to 27-4-10, inclusive, and 27-30-31, Code of Alabama 1975, and all laws or parts of law which conflict with this act are repealed effective at 12:01 a.m. on the first day of January 1995."

Acts 1993, No. 93-679, § 14, provides: "Upon its passage and approval by the Governor, or upon its otherwise becoming a law, this act shall become effective at 12:01 a.m. on the first day of January, 1995, with respect to insurance premiums received on or after January 1, 1995; provided, however, that (1) the determination and payment of taxes due on premiums received prior to January 1, 1995, shall be pursuant to the law in effect prior to January 1, 1995, and (2) the provisions of subsection (b) of Section 3 and the provisions of Section 11 shall become effective immediately upon passage of this act and approval by the Governor, or upon its otherwise becoming a law."

§ 27-30-34. Provision of domestic life and disability insurance pursuant to chapter 3.

Mutual aid associations organized and authorized under the provisions of this chapter are, in addition to those authorizations and responsibilities stated in sections 27-17-16, 27-30-1, 27-30-31, 27-30-33 and 27-36-7, entitled to provide insurance policies and contracts as are authorized domestic life and disability insurers pursuant to chapter 3 of Title 27, subject to the limits on the size and types of risks to be insured as stated in section 27-30-15 and section 27-30-6.1. (Acts 1989, No. 89-686, p. 1351.)

Code Commissioner's note. — Acts 1993, No. 93-679, § 12 repealed Section 27-30-31 which is referred to in the section above.

CHAPTER 31A.

RISK RETENTION ACT.

Sec.
27-31A-1. Short title and purpose.
27-31A-2. Definitions.
27-31A-3. Risk retention groups chartered in this state.
27-31A-4. Risk retention groups not chartered in this state.
27-31A-5. Compulsory associations.
27-31A-6. Countersignatures not required.
27-31A-7. Purchasing groups — Exemption from certain laws.
27-31A-8. Notice and registration requirements of purchasing groups.

Sec.
27-31A-9. Restrictions on insurance purchased by purchasing groups.
27-31A-10. Purchasing group taxation.
27-31A-11. Administrative and procedural authority regarding risk retention groups and purchasing groups.
27-31A-12. Duty of agents or brokers to obtain license.
27-31A-13. Binding effect of orders issued in U.S. district court.
27-31A-14. County self-insurance funds.
27-31A-15. Rules and regulations.

Effective date. — The act which added this chapter became effective May 17, 1993.

§ 27-31A-1. Short title and purpose.

The purpose of this chapter is to regulate the formation and the operation of risk retention groups and purchasing groups in this state formed pursuant to the federal Liability Risk Retention Act of 1986, to the extent permitted by federal law. This chapter shall be known and may be cited as the "Alabama Risk Retention Act." (Acts 1993, No. 93-674, § 1.)

§ 27-31A-2. Definitions.

As used in this chapter, the following terms shall have the following meanings, respectively, unless the context clearly indicates otherwise:

(1) COMMISSIONER. The Insurance Commissioner of this state or the commissioner, director, or superintendent of insurance in any other state.

(2) COMPLETED OPERATIONS LIABILITY. Liability arising out of the installation, maintenance, or repair of any product at a site which is not owned or controlled by either of the following:

a. Any person who performs that work.

b. Any person who hires an independent contractor to perform that work, but shall include liability for activities which are completed or abandoned before the date of the occurrence giving rise to the liability.

(3) DOMICILE. For purposes of determining the state in which a purchasing group is domiciled:

a. For a corporation, the state in which the purchasing group is incorporated.

b. For an unincorporated entity, the state of its principal place of business.

(4) HAZARDOUS FINANCIAL CONDITION. Based on its present or reasonably anticipated financial condition, a risk retention group, although not yet financially impaired or insolvent, is unlikely to be able to do either of the following:

a. To meet obligations to policyholders with respect to their own claims and reasonably anticipated claims.

b. To pay other obligations in the normal course of business.

(5) INSURANCE. Primary insurance, excess insurance, reinsurance, surplus lines insurance, and any other arrangement for shifting and distributing risk which is determined to be insurance under the laws of this state.

(6) LIABILITY. a. Legal liability for damages (including costs of defense, legal costs and fees, and other claims expenses) because of injuries to other persons, damage to their property, or other damage or loss to other persons resulting from or arising out of either of the following:

1. Any business, whether profit or nonprofit, trade, product, services, including professional services, premises, or operations.

2. Any activity of any state or local government, or any agency, or political subdivision thereof.

b. Liability does not include personal risk liability and an employer's liability with respect to its employees other than legal liability under the Federal Employers' Liability Act, 45 U.S.C. 51 et seq.

(7) PERSONAL RISK LIABILITY. Liability for damages because of injury to any person, damage to property, or other loss or damage resulting from any personal, familial, or household responsibilities or activities, rather than from responsibilities or activities referred to in subdivisions (6)a. and b. of this section.

(8) PLAN OF OPERATION or FEASIBILITY STUDY. An analysis which presents the expected activities and results of a risk retention group including at a minimum all of the following:

a. Information sufficient to verify that its members are engaged in businesses or activities similar or related with respect to the liability to which the members are exposed by virtue of any related, similar, or common business, trade, product, services, premises, or operations.

b. For each state in which it intends to operate, the coverages, deductibles, coverage limits, rates, and rating classification systems for each line of insurance the group intends to offer.

c. Historical and expected loss experience of the proposed members and national experience of similar exposures to the extent that this experience is reasonably available.

d. Pro forma financial statements and projections.

e. Appropriate opinions by a qualified, independent casualty actuary, including a determination of minimum premium or participation levels required to commence operations and to prevent a hazardous financial condition.

f. Identification of management, underwriting and claims procedures, marketing methods, managerial oversight methods, investment policies, and reinsurance agreements.

g. Identification of each state in which the risk retention group has obtained, or sought to obtain, a charter and license, and a description of its status in each state.

h. Other matters as may be prescribed by the Commissioner of Insurance, or like official, in which the risk retention group is chartered for liability insurance companies authorized by the insurance laws of that state.

(9) PRODUCT LIABILITY. Liability for damages because of any personal injury, death, emotional harm, consequential economic damage, or property damage, including damages resulting from the loss of use of property, arising out of the manufacture, design, importation, distribution, packaging, labeling, lease, or sale of a product, but does not include the liability of any person for those damages if the product involved was in the possession of the person when the incident giving rise to the claim occurred.

(10) PURCHASING GROUP. Any group which meets all of the following:

a. Has as one of its purposes the purchase of liability insurance on a group basis.

b. Purchases the insurance only for its group members and only to cover their similar or related liability exposure, as described in subdivision (10)c.

c. Is composed of members whose businesses or activities are similar or related with respect to the liability to which members are exposed by virtue of any related, similar, or common business, trade, product, services, premises, or operations.

d. Is domiciled in any state.

(11) RISK RETENTION GROUP. Any corporation or other limited liability association which meets all of the following:

a. Its primary activity consists of assuming and spreading all, or any portion, of the liability exposure of its group members.

b. It is organized for the primary purpose of conducting the activity described under subdivision (11)a.

c. It is either of the following:

1. Chartered and licensed as a liability insurance company and authorized to engage in the business of insurance under the laws of any state.

2. Before January 1, 1985, it was chartered or licensed and authorized to engage in the business of insurance under the laws of Bermuda or the Cayman Islands and, before that date, had certified to the insurance commissioner of at least one state that it satisfied the capitalization requirements of the state, except that any such group shall be considered to be a risk retention group only if it has been engaged in business continuously since such date and only for the purpose of continuing to provide insurance to cover product liability or completed operations liability, as the terms were defined in the Product Liability Risk Retention Act of 1981 before the date of the enactment of the Liability Risk Retention Act of 1986.

d. It does not exclude any person from membership in the group solely to provide for their members a competitive advantage over the person denied.

e. It either:

1. Has as its owners only persons who comprise the membership of the risk retention group and who are provided insurance by the group.

2. Has as its sole owner an organization which has as:

(i) Its members only persons who comprise the membership of the risk retention group; and

(ii) Its owners only persons who comprise the membership of the risk retention group and who are provided insurance by that group.

f. Its members are engaged in businesses or activities similar, or related, with respect to the liability of which the members are exposed by virtue of any related, similar, or common business trade, product, services, premises, or operations.

g. Its activities do not include providing insurance other than both of the following:

1. Liability insurance for assuming and spreading all or any portion of the liability of its group members.

2. Reinsurance with respect to the liability of any other risk retention group, or any members of that other group, which is engaged in businesses or activities so that the group or member meets the requirement described in subdivision (6), a. and b. from membership in the risk retention group which provides the reinsurance.

h. The name of which includes the phrase "Risk Retention Group."

(12) STATE. Any state of the United States or the District of Columbia. (Acts 1993, No. 93-674, § 2.)

§ 27-31A-3. Risk retention groups chartered in this state.

(a) A risk retention group shall, pursuant to Title 27, be chartered and licensed to write only liability insurance pursuant to this chapter and, except as provided elsewhere in this chapter, shall comply with all of the laws, rules, regulations, and requirements applicable to the insurers chartered and licensed in this state and with Section 27-31A-4, to the extent the requirements are not a limitation on laws, rules, regulations, or requirements of this state.

(b) Before it may offer insurance in any state, each risk retention group shall also submit for approval to the Commissioner of Insurance a plan of operation or feasibility study. The risk retention group shall submit an appropriate revision in the event of any subsequent material change in any item of the plan of operation or feasibility study within 10 days of the change. The group shall not offer any additional kinds of liability insurance, in this state or in any other state, until a revision of the plan or study is approved by the commissioner.

(c) At the time of filing its application for charter, the risk retention group shall provide to the commissioner in summary form the following information:

the identity of the initial members of the group, the identity of those individuals who organized the group or who will provide administrative services, or otherwise influence or control the activities of the group, the amount and nature of initial capitalization, the coverages to be afforded, and the states in which the group intends to operate. Upon receipt of this information, the commissioner shall forward the information to the National Association of Insurance Commissioners. Notification to the National Association of Insurance Commissioners is in addition to and shall not be sufficient to satisfy the requirements of Section 27-31A-4 or any other sections of this chapter. (Acts 1993, No. 93-674, § 3.)

§ 27-31A-4. Risk retention groups not chartered in this state.

Risk retention groups chartered and licensed in states other than this state and seeking to do business as a risk retention group in this state shall comply with the laws of this state as follows:

(1) *Notice of operations and designation of commissioner as agent.*

a. Before offering insurance in this state, a risk retention group shall submit to the commissioner both of the following:

1. A statement identifying the state or states in which the risk retention group is chartered and licensed as a liability insurance company, charter date, its principal place of business, and other information, including information on its membership, as the commissioner of this state may require to verify that the risk retention group is qualified pursuant to subdivision (11) of Section 27-31A-2.

2. A copy of its plan of operations or feasibility study and revisions of the plan or study submitted to the state in which the risk retention group is chartered and licensed, provided that the provision relating to the submission of a plan of operation or feasibility study shall not apply with respect to any line or classification of liability insurance which was both:

(i) Defined in the Product Liability Risk Retention Act of 1981 before October 27, 1986.

(ii) Offered before that date by any risk retention group which had been chartered and operating for not less than three years before that date.

b. The risk retention group shall submit a copy of any revision to its plan of operation or feasibility study required by subsection (b) of Section 27-31A-3 at the same time that the revision is submitted to the commissioner of its chartering state.

c. The risk retention group shall designate the commissioner as its agent for the purpose of receiving service of legal documents or process with a statement of registration, for which a filing fee shall be determined by the commissioner.

(2) *Financial condition.* — Any risk retention group doing business in this state shall submit to the commissioner all of the following:

a. A copy of the group's financial statement submitted to the state in which the risk retention group is chartered and licensed which shall be certified by an independent public accountant and contain a statement of opinion on loss and loss adjustment expense reserves made by a member of the American Academy of Actuaries, or a qualified loss reserve specialist, under criteria established by the National Association of Insurance Commissioners.

b. A copy of each examination of the risk retention group as certified by the commissioner or public official conducting the examination.

c. Upon request by the commissioner, a copy of any information or document pertaining to any outside audit performed with respect to the risk retention group.

d. Information as may be required to verify its continuing qualification as a risk retention group pursuant to subdivision (11) of Section 27-31A-2.

(3) *Taxation.*

a. Each risk retention group shall be liable for the payment of premium taxes and taxes on premiums of direct business for risks resident or located within this state, and shall report to the commissioner the net premiums written for risks resident or located within this state. The risk retention group shall be subject to taxation, and any applicable fines and penalties related thereto, on the same basis as a foreign admitted insurer.

b. To the extent licensed agents or brokers are utilized pursuant to Section 27-31A-12, they shall report to the commissioner the premiums for direct business for risks resident or located within this state which the licensees have placed with or on behalf of a risk retention group not chartered in this state.

c. To the extent that insurance agents or brokers are utilized pursuant to Section 27-31A-12, any agent or broker shall keep a complete and separate record of all policies procured from each risk retention group, which record shall be open to examination by the commissioner, as provided in Section 27-2-20. These records shall, for each policy and each kind of insurance provided thereunder, include the following:

1. The limit of liability.
2. The time period covered.
3. The effective date.
4. The name of the risk retention group which issued the policy.
5. The gross premium charged.
6. The amount of return premiums, if any.

(4) *Compliance with Trade Practices Law.* — Any risk retention group, its agents, and representatives shall comply with the Trade Practices Law, Chapter 12 (commencing with Section 27-12-1), Title 27, regarding deceptive, false, or fraudulent acts or practices. If the commissioner seeks an injunction regarding that conduct, the injunction shall be obtained from a court of competent jurisdiction.

(5) *Examination regarding financial condition.* — Any risk retention group shall submit to an examination by the commissioner to determine its

financial condition if the commissioner of the jurisdiction in which the group is chartered and licensed has not initiated an examination or does not initiate an examination within 60 days after a request by the commissioner of this state. The examination shall be coordinated to avoid unjustified repetition and conducted in an expeditious manner and in accordance with the Examiner Handbook of the National Association of Insurance Commissioners.

(6) *Notice to purchasers.* — Every application form for insurance from a risk retention group, and every policy, on its front and declaration pages, issued by a risk retention group, shall contain in ten point type the following notice:

NOTICE

"This policy is issued by your risk retention group. Your risk retention group may not be subject to all of the insurance laws and regulations of your state. State insurance insolvency guaranty funds are not available for your risk retention group."

(7) *Prohibited acts regarding solicitation or sale.* — The following acts by a risk retention group are prohibited:

a. The solicitation or sale of insurance by a risk retention group to any person who is not eligible for membership in the group.

b. The solicitation or sale of insurance by, or operation of, a risk retention group that is in hazardous financial condition or financially impaired.

(8) *Prohibition on ownership by an insurance company.* — No risk retention group shall be allowed to do business in this state if an insurance company is directly or indirectly a member or owner of the risk retention group, other than in the case of a risk retention group all of whose numbers are insurance companies.

(9) *Prohibited coverage.* — The terms of any insurance policy issued by any risk retention group shall not provide, or be construed to provide, coverage prohibited generally by statute of this state or declared unlawful by the highest court of this state whose law applies to that policy.

(10) *Delinquency proceedings.* — A risk retention group not chartered in this state and doing business in this state shall comply with a lawful order issued in a voluntary dissolution proceeding or in a delinquency proceeding commenced by a state insurance commissioner if there has been a finding of financial impairment after an examination under subdivision (5) of this section.

(11) *Penalties.* — A risk retention group that violates this chapter will be subject to fines and penalties including revocation of its right to do business in this state, applicable to licensed insurers generally.

(12) *Operation prior to enactment of this chapter.* — In addition to complying with this section, any risk retention group operating in this state prior to enactment of this chapter shall, within 30 days after May 17, 1993, comply with subdivision (1)a of this section. (Acts 1993, No. 93-674, § 4.)

§ 27-31A-5. Compulsory associations.

(a) No risk retention group shall be required or permitted to join or contribute financially to any insurance insolvency guaranty fund, or similar mechanism, in this state, nor shall any risk retention group, or its insureds or claimants against its insureds, receive any benefit from any fund for claims arising under the insurance policies issued by that risk retention group.

(b) When a purchasing group obtains insurance covering its members' risks from an insurer, not authorized in this state or a risk retention group, no risk, wherever resident or located, shall be covered by any insurance guaranty fund or similar mechanism in this state.

(c) When a purchasing group obtains insurance covering its members' risks from an authorized insurer, only risks resident or located in this state shall be covered by the Alabama Insurance Guaranty Association, subject to Chapter 42 (commencing with Section 27-42-1), Title 27.

(d) Notwithstanding Article 2 (commencing with Section 27-26-20), Chapter 26, Title 27, the commissioner may require or exempt a risk retention group from participating in any mechanism established or authorized under the law of this state for the equitable apportionment among insurers of casualty insurance losses and expenses incurred on policies written through that mechanism. The risk retention group shall submit sufficient information to the commissioner to enable the commissioner to apportion on a nondiscriminatory basis the risk retention group's proportionate share of any losses and expenses. (Acts 1993, No. 93-674, § 5.)

§ 27-31A-6. Countersignatures not required.

A policy of insurance issued to a risk retention group, or any member of that group, shall not be required to be countersigned as otherwise provided in Section 27-3-28 or 27-7-28. (Acts 1993, No. 93-674, § 6.)

§ 27-31A-7. Purchasing groups — Exemption from certain laws.

A purchasing group and its insurer or insurers shall be subject to all applicable laws of this state, except that a purchasing group and its insurer or insurers shall be exempt, in regard to casualty insurance for the purchasing group, from any law that would do any of the following:

(1) Prohibit the establishment of a purchasing group.

(2) Make it unlawful for an insurer to provide or offer to provide insurance on a basis providing, to a purchasing group or its members, advantages based on their loss and expense experience not afforded to other persons with respect to rates, policy forms, coverages, or other matters.

(3) Prohibit a purchasing group or its members from purchasing insurance on a group basis described in subdivision (2) of this section.

(4) Prohibit a purchasing group from obtaining insurance on a group basis because the group has not been in existence for a minimum period of time or because any member has not belonged to the group for a minimum period of time.

(5) Require that a purchasing group must have a minimum number of members, common ownership or affiliation, or certain legal form.

(6) Require that a certain percentage of a purchasing group must obtain insurance on a group basis.

(7) Otherwise discriminate against a purchasing group or any of its members.

(8) Require that any insurance policy issued to a purchasing group or any of its members be countersigned by an insurance agent or broker residing in this state. (Acts 1993, No. 93-674, § 7.)

§ 27-31A-8. Notice and registration requirements of purchasing groups.

(a) A purchasing group which intends to do business in this state shall, prior to doing business, furnish notice to the commissioner which shall include all of the following:

(1) Identify the state in which the group is domiciled.

(2) Identify all other states in which the group intends to do business.

(3) Specify the lines and classifications of liability insurance which the purchasing group intends to purchase.

(4) Identify the insurance company or companies from which the group intends to purchase its insurance and the domicile of any company.

(5) Specify the method by which, and the person or persons, if any, through whom insurance will be offered to its members whose risks are resident or located in this state.

(6) Identify the principal place of business of the group.

(7) Provide other information as may be required by the commissioner to verify that the purchasing group is qualified under subdivision (10) of Section 27-31A-2.

(b) A purchasing group shall, within 10 days, notify the commissioner of any changes in any of the items set forth in subsection (a) of this section.

(c) The purchasing group shall register with and designate the commissioner, or other appropriate authority, as its agent solely for the purpose of receiving service of legal documents or process, for which a filing fee shall be determined by the commissioner, except that the requirements shall not apply in the case of a purchasing group which only purchases insurance that was authorized under the federal Products Liability Risk Retention Act of 1981, and:

(1) Which in any state of the United States:

   a. Was domiciled before April 1, 1986, and

   b. Is domiciled on and after October 27, 1986;

(2) Which:

   a. Before October 27, 1986, purchased insurance from an insurance carrier licensed in any state, and

   b. Since October 27, 1986, purchased its insurance from an insurance carrier licensed in any state; and

134

(3) Which was a purchasing group under the requirements of the Product Liability Risk Retention Act of 1981 before October 27, 1986.

(d) Each purchasing group that is required to give notice pursuant to subsection (a) of this section shall also furnish the information as may be required by the commissioner to do all of the following:

(1) Verify that the entity qualifies as a purchasing group.

(2) Determine where the purchasing group is located.

(3) Determine appropriate tax treatment.

(e) Any purchasing group which was doing business in this state prior to the enactment of this chapter shall, within 30 days after May 17, 1993, furnish notice to the commissioner pursuant to subsection (a) of this section and furnish information, as may be required, pursuant to subsections (b) and (c) of this section. (Acts 1993, No. 93-674, § 8.)

§ 27-31A-9. Restrictions on insurance purchased by purchasing groups.

(a) A purchasing group may not purchase insurance from a risk retention group that is not chartered in a state or from an insurer not admitted in the state in which the purchasing group is located, unless the purchase is effected through a licensed agent or broker acting pursuant to the surplus lines laws and regulations of the state.

(b) A purchasing group which obtains casualty insurance from an insurer not admitted in this state, or a risk retention group, shall inform each of the members of the group which have a risk resident or located in this state that the risk is not protected by an insurance insolvency guaranty fund in this state, and that the risk retention group or that insurer may not be subject to all insurance laws and regulations of this state.

(c) No purchasing group may purchase insurance providing for a deductible or self-insured retention applicable to the group as a whole. Coverage may provide for a deductible or self-insured retention applicable to individual members.

(d) Purchases of insurance by purchasing groups are subject to the same standards regarding aggregate limits which are applicable to all purchases of group insurance. (Acts 1993, No. 93-674, § 9.)

§ 27-31A-10. Purchasing group taxation.

Premium taxes and taxes on premiums paid for coverage of risks resident, or located in this state by a purchasing group, or any members of the purchasing groups shall be both:

(1) Imposed at the same rate and subject to the same interest, fines, and penalties as that applicable to premium taxes and taxes on premiums paid for similar coverage from a similar insurance source by other insureds.

(2) Paid first by the insurance source, and if not by that source, by the agent or broker for the purchasing group, and if not by the agent or broker then by the purchasing group, and if not by the purchasing group then by each of its members. (Acts 1993, No. 93-674, § 10.)

§ 27-31A-11. Administrative and procedural authority regarding risk retention groups and purchasing groups.

The commissioner is authorized to make use of any of the powers established under the Insurance Code of this state to enforce the laws of this state not specifically preempted by the Risk Retention Act of 1986, including the commissioner's administrative authority to investigate, issue subpoenas, conduct depositions and hearings, issue orders, impose penalties, and seek injunctive relief. With regard to any investigation, administrative proceedings, or litigation, the commissioner can rely on the procedural laws of this state. The injunctive authority of the commissioner, in regard to risk retention groups, is restricted by the requirement that any injunction be issued by a court of competent jurisdiction. (Acts 1993, No. 93-674, § 11.)

§ 27-31A-12. Duty of agents or brokers to obtain license.

(a) *Risk retention groups.* — No person, firm, association, or corporation shall act or aid in any manner in soliciting, negotiating, or procuring liability insurance in this state from a risk retention group unless the person, firm, association, or corporation is licensed as an insurance agent or broker in accordance with Chapter 7 (commencing with Section 27-7-1), Title 27.

(b) *Purchasing groups.*

(1) No person, firm, association, or corporation shall act or aid in any manner in soliciting, negotiating, or procuring liability insurance in this state for a purchasing group from an authorized insurer or a risk retention group chartered in a state unless the person, firm, association, or corporation is licensed as an insurance agent or broker in accordance with Chapter 7 (commencing with Section 27-7-1), Title 27.

(2) No person, firm, association, or corporation shall act or aid in any manner in soliciting, negotiating, or procuring liability insurance coverage in this state for any member of a purchasing group under a purchasing group's policy unless that person, firm, association, or corporation is licensed as an insurance agent or broker in accordance with Chapter 27 (commencing with Section 27-7-1), Title 27.

(3) No person, firm, association, or corporation shall act or aid in any manner in soliciting, negotiating, or procuring liability insurance from an insurer not authorized to do business in this state on behalf of a purchasing group located in this state unless the person, firm, association, or corporation is licensed as a surplus lines agent or excess line broker in accordance with Chapter 10 (commencing with Section 27-10-1), Title 27.

(c) *Residence requirement.* — For purposes of acting as an agent or broker for a risk retention group or purchasing group, pursuant to subsections (a) and (b) of this section, the requirement of residence in this state shall not apply.

(d) *Notice.* — Every person, firm, association, or corporation licensed, pursuant to the provisions of Chapter 7 (commencing with Section 27-7-1), Title 27, on business placed with risk retention groups or written through a purchasing group, shall inform each prospective insured of the provisions of the notice required by subdivision (6) of Section 27-31A-4 in the case of a risk retention group and subsection (b) of Section 27-31A-9 in the case of a purchasing group. (Acts 1993, No. 93-674, § 12.)

§ 27-31A-13. Binding effect of orders issued in U.S. district court.

An order issued by any district court of the United States enjoining a risk retention group from soliciting or selling insurance, or operating in any state, or in all states, or in any territory or possession of the United States, upon a finding that the group is in hazardous financial or financially impaired condition shall be enforceable in the courts of the state. (Acts 1993, No. 93-674, § 13.)

§ 27-31A-14. County self-insurance funds.

This chapter shall not apply to any liability self-insurance fund established by counties pursuant to Title 11, Chapter 30. (Acts 1993, No. 93-674, § 14.)

§ 27-31A-15. Rules and regulations.

The commissioner may promulgate and enforce, and from time to time amend, the rules and regulations relating to risk retention groups as may be necessary to carry out this chapter. (Acts 1993, No. 93-674, § 15.)

CHAPTER 32.

REHABILITATION, REORGANIZATION, CONSERVATION AND LIQUIDATION OF INSURERS.

§ 27-32-14. Conservation or liquidation of property.

Collateral references. — Property damage insurance: what constitutes "contamination" within policy clause excluding coverage. 72 ALR4th 633.

§ 27-32-26. Fixation of rights and liabilities on liquidation of insurer.

Collateral references. — What constitutes single accident or occurrence within liability policy limiting insurer's liability to a specified amount per accident or occurrence. 64 ALR4th 668.

§ 27-32-39. Priority of claims of policyholders and beneficiaries — Reinsuring of policies.

Cited in Washburn v. Rabun, 487 So. 2d 1361 (Ala. 1986).

CHAPTER 36.

LIABILITIES.

§ 27-36-1. Liabilities generally.

Word "incur" is best defined within the context of subsection (2) of this section as "become liable or subject to," or "to have liabilities cast upon one by act or operation of law." Old S. Life Ins. Co. v. Alabama Ins. Dep't, 503 So. 2d 852 (Ala. 1986).

Collateral references.
What constitutes single accident or occurrence within liability policy limiting insurer's liability to a specified amount per accident or occurrence. 64 ALR4th 668.

§ 27-36-5. Active life reserve for disability insurance.

Commissioner may promulgate regulations but must comply with notice and hearing requirements. — Pursuant to this section, the commissioner of insurance may promulgate regulations to set the appropriate standards to be used in determining the reserve; however, the commissioner must comply with all notice and hearing requirements as set forth in § 27-2-17. Old S. Life Ins. Co. v. State Dep't of Ins., 537 So. 2d 30 (Ala. Civ. App. 1988).

Order of the commissioner of insurance requiring the posting of additional reserves was error, as it constituted a promulgation of a regulation without following proper

procedural steps as authorized by this section and § 27-2-17, since to allow the commissioner to adopt such requirements by ad hoc adjudication without notice or an opportunity to be heard in an administrative hearing could have a devastating effect on individual insurance companies. Old S. Life Ins. Co. v. State Dep't of Ins., 537 So. 2d 30 (Ala. Civ. App. 1988).

Collateral references. — What constitutes single accident or occurrence within liability policy limiting insurer's liability to a specified amount per accident or occurrence. 64 ALR4th 668.

§ 27-36-7. Standard Valuation Law.

Mutual aid association, which had calculated its reserves pursuant to the standard valuation law, was not entitled to declaratory and injunctive relief to prevent the department of insurance from requiring it to comply with

the mutual aid association statutory reserve requirements of §§ 27-30-16 and 27-30-17. Security Sav. Life Ins. Co. v. Weaver, 579 So. 2d 1359 (Ala. Civ. App. 1991).

CHAPTER 37.

ASSETS.

§ 27-37-3. Assets and liabilities as deductions.

Collateral references. — What constitutes single accident or occurrence within liability policy limiting insurer's liability to a specified

amount per accident or occurrence. 64 ALR4th 668.

CHAPTER 39.

AUTOMOBILE CLUBS AND ASSOCIATIONS.

Sec.
27-39-6. Application for certificate of author-
         ity; annual license fee; issuance of
         license.

§ 27-39-6. Application for certificate of authority; annual license fee; issuance of license.

(a) Within 30 days after January 1, 1972, every automobile club or association organized and/or operating in the state of Alabama shall file with the commissioner an application for a certificate of authority to continue said operations within the state, and every automobile club or association desiring to commence operations within the state shall, prior to the commencement of said operation, file application with and receive a certificate of authority from the commissioner. No certificate of authority shall be issued until the automobile club or association has paid to the commissioner $250.00 as an annual license fee, which fee shall not be returnable. Licenses shall be issued for the period beginning January 1 of each year and shall expire on the following December 31. The commissioner shall deposit all fees collected in the state treasury to the credit of the general fund.

(b) The following documents and information shall be filed with the application of all such clubs and associations:

(1) The sum of $25,000.00 in cash or securities, as approved by the commissioner and deposited in trust with the state treasurer or, in lieu thereof, a surety bond payable to the commissioner in the amount of $25,000.00 of a surety company authorized to do business in this state, conditioned upon the full compliance with this chapter and the faithful performance of the obligations of such club or association to its members. The bonds shall be approved by the commissioner and shall not be cancelled without 30 days' notice to the commissioner. If such bond is filed, any person defrauded or injured by any wrongful act, misrepresentation or failure on the part of a motor club with respect to selling or rendering of any service may maintain an action on such bond in his own name. Upon receipt of notice of the intended dissolution of such automobile club or association and upon receipt of notice of evidence satisfactory to the commissioner that all obligations of the club or association to its members and creditors have been satisfied, the state treasurer, upon written authorization from the commissioner, shall refund said money or securities and the obligations of said bond shall terminate;

(2) Appointment of an agent for service of process who shall be a resident of the state of Alabama or, in lieu thereof, the commissioner; and

(3) A copy of the proposed form of membership application, membership certificate, bylaws, contracts for service and any other material, including advertising matter, requested by the commissioner.

(c) If the commissioner shall be satisfied that the applicant is competent and trustworthy and possesses the professional ability to perform the services and that he meets all the requirements of this chapter, he shall issue to the applicant a certificate of authority to conduct the business of such automobile club or association within this state. (Acts 1971, No. 407, p. 707, § 802; Acts 1988, 1st Ex. Sess., No. 88-875, p. 410, § 1.)

Code Commissioner's note. — Acts 1988, 1st Ex. Sess., No. 88-875, § 2 provides: "It is the legislative intent that nothing in this act shall be construed to affect the Special Examination Revolving Fund, as provided for in Section 27-2-25, Code of Alabama 1975, or the State Fire Marshal's Fund, as provided for in Section 24-5-10, Code of Alabama 1975."

CHAPTER 40.

INSURANCE PREMIUM FINANCE COMPANIES.

Sec.
27-40-1. Definitions.
27-40-2. Exemptions from chapter.
27-40-8. Contents and style of premium finance agreement.
27-40-9. Service charges; prepayment of obligation.
27-40-12. Return of gross unearned premiums upon cancellation of contract.

Sec.
27-40-15. Premium financed to be sent to insurance company, agent, or surplus lines broker; issuance of drafts, etc.; duties with respect to cancellation.
27-40-17. Notification of existence of premium finance agreement.

§ 27-40-1. Definitions.

For the purposes of this chapter, the following words and phrases shall have the following meanings:

(1) INSURANCE PREMIUM FINANCE COMPANY. A person engaged in the business of entering into premium finance agreements.

(2) PREMIUM FINANCE AGREEMENT. An agreement by which an insured or prospective insured promises to pay to a premium finance company the amount advanced or to be advanced under the agreement to an insurer or to an insurance agent or broker in payment of premiums on an insurance contract together with a service charge, as authorized and limited by this chapter.

(3) LICENSEE. A premium finance company holding a license issued under this chapter.

(4) PERSON. An individual, partnership, association, business corporation, nonprofit corporation, common law trust, joint-stock company, or any other group of individuals however organized.

(5) INSURANCE CONTRACT. The policy or contract of insurance which is the subject of premium financing under this chapter. (Acts 1975, No. 1042, p. 2088, § 2; Acts 1986, No. 86-400, § 1; Acts 1995, No. 95-309, § 1.)

The 1995 amendment, effective July 7, 1995, substituted "following meanings" for "meanings respectively ascribed to them by this section" in the introductory paragraph, and deleted former subdivision (6) which defined "designated agent."

§ 27-40-2. Exemptions from chapter.

The provisions of this chapter shall not apply with respect to any of the following:

(1) Any insurance company licensed to do business in this state.

(2) Any banking or other financial institution regulated by the state, or savings and loan association, or credit union authorized to do business in this state, or any national banking institution or federal savings and loan association incorporated under the laws of the United States and located within this state.

(3) A charge for insurance in connection with an installment sale of a motor vehicle or boat or mobile home.

(4) The financing of insurance premiums in this state in accordance with the provisions of this title relating to rates of insurance.

(5) Any insurance agent or agency licensed in Alabama that charges a collection fee on unpaid balances for insurance premiums under Section 27-12-17 or under the Alabama Consumer Credit Act. (Acts 1975, No. 1042, p. 2088, § 1; Acts 1994, No. 94-118, p. 146, § 1.)

The 1994 amendment, effective February 25, 1994, added "any of the following" to the end of the introductory language; substituted "A" for "The inclusion of a" in subdivision (3); added subdivision (5); and made nonsubstantive changes.

§ 27-40-8. Contents and style of premium finance agreement.

(a) The contents and style of the premium finance agreement shall be as follows:

(1) It shall be dated, signed by the insured or an authorized representative and the printed portion thereof shall be in at least eight-point type.

(2) It shall contain the name and place of business of the insurance agent negotiating the related insurance contract, the name and residence, or place of business, of the insured as specified by the insured, the name and place of business of the premium finance company to which payments are to be made, a description of the insurance contracts involved and the amount of the premium therefor.

(3) It shall set forth the following items where applicable:

  a. The total amount of the premiums.

  b. The amount of the down payment.

  c. The principal balance, that being the difference between items a and b.

  d. The amount of the service charge.

  e. The balance payable by the insured, that being the sum of items c and d.

  f. The number of installments required, the amount of each installment expressed in dollars, and the due date or period thereof.

  g. The annual percentage rate (APR) charged.

(b) The items set out need not be stated in the sequence or order in which they appear, and additional items may be included to explain the computations made in determining the amount to be paid by the insured. (Acts 1975, No. 1042, p. 2088, § 8; Acts 1986, No. 86-400, § 1; Acts 1995, No. 95-309, § 1.)

The **1995 amendment,** effective July 7, 1995, in subsection (a), in subdivision (2), added "It shall," and substituted "specified by the insured" for "specified by him," in subdivision (3), added "It shall" in the introductory language, inserted "that being" in paragraph c, inserted "that being the" in paragraph e, and added paragraph g; and made nonsubstantive changes.

§ 27-40-9. Service charges; prepayment of obligation.

(a) For the purpose of this section, "consumer insurance premium finance agreement" means an insurance premium finance agreement as defined in Section 27-40-1 wherein the insurance contracts which are the subject of the premium finance agreement are for personal, family, or household purposes or where the premiums for those agreements are two thousand dollars ($2,000) or less. For the purpose of this section, "commercial premium finance agreement" means any insurance premium finance agreement other than a consumer premium finance agreement.

(b) A premium finance company shall not charge, contract for, receive, or collect a service charge other than in accordance with the following provisions:

(1) The service charge is to be computed on the balance of the premium due, after subtracting the down payment made by the insured in accordance with the premium finance agreement, from the effective date of the insurance for which the premiums are being advanced, to and including the date when the final installment of the premium finance agreement is payable.

(2) The service charge per consumer insurance premium finance agreement shall be a maximum of nine dollars ($9) per one hundred dollars ($100) per annum plus an additional charge, which shall not exceed $15.00 per premium finance agreement, which additional charge need not be refunded.

(3) The service charge for a commercial insurance premium finance agreement shall be as agreed to by the parties to the agreement.

(c) Notwithstanding the provisions of any premium finance agreement, any insured may prepay the obligation in full at any time. In such event he shall receive a credit or refund under the rule of 78ths or the sum of the digits principle as follows: The amount of the refund or credit shall be as great a proportion of the finance charge originally contracted for as the sum of the periodic time balances of the debt scheduled to follow the date of prepayment bears to the sum of all the periodic time balances of the debt, both sums to be determined according to the scheduled payment originally contracted for. No refund of less than $1.00 need be made. If such prepayment is made by the debtor other than on a scheduled payment date, the nearest scheduled payment date shall be used in such computation. If, in addition to the service charge, an additional charge was imposed, such additional charge need not be refunded, nor taken into consideration in computing the credit refund. (Acts 1975, No. 1042, p. 2088, § 9; Acts 1986, No. 86-400, § 1; Acts 1995, No. 95-309, § 1.)

The 1995 amendment, effective July 7, 1995, substituted "as agreed to by the parties to the agreement" for "a maximum $9.00 per $100.00 per annum plus an additional charge, which shall not exceed $15.00 per premium finance agreement, which additional charge need not be refunded" in subdivision (b)(3); and made nonsubstantive changes.

§ 27-40-11. Procedure for cancellation of insurance contract upon default.

Collateral references.
What constitutes waiver by insured or in-sured's agent of required notice of cancellation of insurance policy. 86 ALR4th 886.

§ 27-40-12. Return of gross unearned premiums upon cancellation of contract.

(a) Whenever a financed insurance contract is cancelled, the insurer shall return whatever gross unearned premiums are due under the insurance contract to the premium finance company, either directly or via the agent or surplus lines broker placing the insurance, for the account of the insured or insureds as soon as reasonably possible, but in any event no later than 30 days after the effective date of cancellation.

(b) In the event that the crediting of return premiums to the account of the insured results in a surplus over the amount due from the insured, the premium finance company shall refund the excess to the insured or the agent or surplus lines broker, within 30 days after receipt by the premium finance company with the check or draft made payable to the agent or surplus lines broker and to the insured, provided that no refund shall be required if it amounts to less than one dollar ($1). (Acts 1975, No. 1042, § 12; Acts 1986, No. 86-400, § 1; Acts 1995, No. 95-309, § 1.)

The 1995 amendment, effective July 7, 1995, rewrote this section.

§ 27-40-15. Premium financed to be sent to insurance company, agent, or surplus lines broker; issuance of drafts, etc.; duties with respect to cancellation.

(a) The amount of premium financed, more specifically referred to as "the principal balance" in paragraph c. of subdivision (3) of subsection (a) of Section 27-40-8, shall be sent to the insurance company or companies, or the agent or surplus lines broker.

(b) All drafts, checks, or other orders of payment issued for premiums financed shall be issued by or on behalf of the premium finance company and shall be mailed, delivered, or otherwise transmitted directly to the insurance company or its agent, or surplus lines broker. Any check, draft, or other order or form of payment to any insurance agent, insurance broker, managing general agent, or other person, when issued shall be presumed to have been issued by the duly authorized agent of the premium finance company which provided the checks or drafts to the person issuing the same for the purpose of issuance of such instrument.

(c) Notwithstanding anything to the contrary in this section, the insurance company shall not be relieved of any of its duties or responsibilities with respect to the cancellation of any insurance contract which is subject to the premium finance agreement. (Acts 1986, No. 86-400, § 2; Acts 1995, No. 95-309, § 1.)

The 1995 amendment, effective July 7, 1995, rewrote this section.

Code Commissioner's note. — In 1995, the Code Commissioner inserted "of subsection (a)" after "subdivision (3)" in subsection (a) to properly complete the citation to the referenced paragraph.

§ 27-40-17. Notification of existence of premium finance agreement.

Any premium finance company which enters into a premium finance agreement under this chapter shall notify the insurer whose premiums are being financed of the existence of the agreement within a reasonable period of time, not to exceed 30 days after the date the agreement is accepted by the premium finance company. (Acts 1986, No. 86-400, § 4; Acts 1995, No. 95-309, § 1.)

The 1995 amendment, effective July 7, 1995, deleted "the provisions of" preceding "this chapter," deleted "or its designated agent" following "notify the insurer," substituted "agreement is accepted by the premium finance company" for "agreement is signed," and made nonsubstantive changes.

CHAPTER 41.

INVESTMENTS OF LIFE, DISABILITY AND BURIAL INSURANCE COMPANIES.

Sec.
27-41-1. Applicability of chapter.
27-41-2. Definitions.
27-41-3. Investments which may be counted as admitted assets generally; investments and obligations for investments deemed eligible investments under chapter generally; filing with commissioner of certified statements as to investments or obligations for investments not

Sec.
deemed eligible under chapter; assets or funds to which investment limitations based upon amounts of insurers assets or particular funds relate.
27-41-14. Particular investments — Obligations issued, etc., by international bank for reconstruction and development and National Mortgage Association.

§ 27-41-1. Applicability of chapter.

Except as provided in Section 27-41-39, this chapter shall apply to all domestic insurers and health maintenance organizations. (Acts 1977, No. 408, p. 530, § 1; Acts 1993, No. 93-675, § 13.)

The 1993 amendment, effective May 17, 1993, inserted "all," and inserted "and health maintenance organizations."

Code Commissioner's note. — Acts 1993, No. 93-675, § 12, provides: "The purpose of Sections 27-41-1, 27-41-2, and 27-41-3 are to provide further for the regulation of insurers to require all domestic insurers and health maintenance organizations to become subject to the investment limitations and qualifications of Chapter 41 of the Insurance Code, to allow the Alabama Insurance Department to be eligible to become accredited under the National Association of Insurance Commissioners' Financial

Regulation Standards and Accreditation Program."

Acts 1993, No. 93-675, § 20, provides: "The Commissioner of Insurance may adopt reasonable rules and regulations necessary for the

implementation and the administration of this chapter."

Cross references. — As to provisions of rules and regulations necessary for the effectuation of this title, see § 27-2-17.

§ 27-41-2. Definitions.

As used in this chapter, the following terms shall have the respective meanings herein set forth, unless the context shall otherwise require:

(1) ALABAMA INSURANCE CODE. Title 27 of this Code.

(2) INSURER. The term shall have the meaning ascribed in Section 27-1-2 and shall include health maintenance organizations.

(3) PERSON. The term shall have the meaning ascribed in Section 27-1-2.

(4) COMMISSIONER and DEPARTMENT. The terms, respectively, shall have the meanings ascribed in Section 27-1-2.

(5) INVESTMENT. Any asset owned by an insurer.

(6) ELIGIBLE INVESTMENT. Any investment permitted by Sections 27-41-7 to 27-41-35, inclusive, provided the investment meets all the other requirements of this chapter.

(7) DOMESTIC INSURER, FOREIGN INSURER, and ALIEN INSURER. The terms shall have the meanings ascribed in Section 27-1-2 and shall include health maintenance organizations.

(8) ADMITTED ASSET. Any asset of an insurer permitted by the Commissioner of Insurance to be taken into account in any determination of the financial condition of the insurer. (Acts 1977, No. 408, p. 530, § 2; Acts 1993, No. 93-675, § 13.)

The 1993 amendment, effective May 17, 1993, inserted "and shall include health maintenance organizations" following "section 27-1-2" in subdivisions (2) and (7); deleted "but as used in this chapter shall apply only to domestic insurers engaged in whole or in part in the life, disability or burial insurance business" at the end of subdivision (2); in subdivision (6), substituted "to" for "through" and inserted "inclusive"; substituted "the" for "such" in subdivision (8); and substituted "The" for "Such" at the beginning of subdivisions (2), (3), (4), and (7).

Code Commissioner's note. — Acts 1993, No. 93-675, § 12, provides: "The purpose of Sections 27-41-1, 27-41-2, and 27-41-3 are to provide further for the regulation of insurers to require all domestic insurers and health main-

tenance organizations to become subject to the investment limitations and qualifications of Chapter 41 of the Insurance Code, to allow the Alabama Insurance Department to be eligible to become accredited under the National Association of Insurance Commissioners' Financial Regulation Standards and Accreditation Program."

Acts 1993, No. 93-675, § 20, provides: "The Commissioner of Insurance may adopt reasonable rules and regulations necessary for the implementation and the administration of this chapter."

Cross references. — As to provisions of rules and regulations necessary for the effectuation of this title, see § 27-2-17.

§ 27-41-3. Investments which may be counted as admitted assets generally; investments and obligations for investments deemed eligible investments under chapter generally; filing with commissioner of certified statements as to investments or obligations for investments not deemed eligible under chapter; assets or funds to which investment limitations based upon amounts of insurers assets or particular funds relate.

(a) Only eligible investments may be counted as admitted assets.

(b) Every investment lawfully held by a life, disability, or burial insurer on January 1, 1978, and every investment which the life, disability, or burial insurer became obligated to make prior to January 1, 1978, which was a lawful investment for the insurer at the time made or at the time the insurer became obligated to make it shall be an eligible investment. Any particular investment held by an insurer on May 17, 1993, or any amendment thereto, which was a legal investment at the time it was made, and which the insurer was legally entitled to possess immediately prior to the effective date, shall be deemed to be an eligible investment; however, any investment made after May 17, 1993, shall be in compliance with the limitations and qualifications of this section.

(c) All life, disability, or burial insurers shall within 90 days after January 1, 1978 file with the commissioner a written statement certified by its treasurer or chief investment officer, listing in the manner as to readily identify the same, all the investments or obligations for investments not otherwise eligible under this chapter, identifying each nonconforming investment and stating the terms and conditions of acquisition or proposed acquisition thereof.

(d) All insurers, other than life, disability, or burial insurers, shall within 90 days after May 17, 1993, file with the commissioner a written statement certified by its treasurer or chief investment officer, listing in the manner as to readily identify the same, all the investments or obligations for investments not otherwise eligible under this chapter, identifying each nonconforming investment and stating the terms and conditions of acquisition or proposed acquisition thereof.

(e) Eligibility of an investment shall be determined as of the date of its making or acquisition, except as stated in subsection (b) of this section.

(f) Any investment limitation based upon the amount of the insurer's assets or particular funds shall relate to the value of the assets or funds as shown by the insurer's annual statement as of December 31 next preceding the date of the investment by the insurer or as shown by a current financial statement filed with and accepted as to content in writing by the commissioner. (Acts 1977, No. 408, p. 530, § 3; Acts 1993, No. 93-675, § 13.)

The 1993 amendment, effective May 17, 1993, in subsection (b), in the first sentence, inserted "life, disability, or burial" preceding "insurer" in two places and substituted "the insurer" for "such insurer," and added the second sentence; in subsection (c), substituted "All life, disability, or burial insurers" for "The insurer," substituted "the manner" for "such manner" substituted "the investments" for "such investments," and inserted "nonconforming";

added present subsection (d); redesignated former subsections (d) and (e) as present subsections (e) and (f); and substituted "the assets" for "such assets" in present subsection (f).

Code Commissioner's note. — Acts 1993, No. 93-675, § 12, provides: "The purpose of Sections 27-41-1, 27-41-2, and 27-41-3 are to provide further for the regulation of insurers to require all domestic insurers and health maintenance organizations to become subject to the investment limitations and qualifications of Chapter 41 of the Insurance Code, to allow the Alabama Insurance Department to be eligible to become accredited under the National Association of Insurance Commissioners' Financial Regulation Standards and Accreditation Program."

Acts 1993, No. 93-675, § 20, provides: "The Commissioner of Insurance may adopt reasonable rules and regulations necessary for the implementation and the administration of this chapter."

Cross references.

As to provisions of rules and regulations necessary for the effectuation of this title, see § 27-2-17.

§ 27-41-14. Particular investments — Obligations issued, etc., by international bank for reconstruction and development and National Mortgage Association.

(a) An insurer may invest in obligations issued, assumed or guaranteed by the International Bank for Reconstruction and Development.

(b) An insurer may invest in the obligations of the federal national mortgage association.

(c) An insurer may invest in obligations issued, assumed or guaranteed by the African Development Bank. (Acts 1977, No. 408, p. 530, § 14; Acts 1987, No. 87-594, p. 1033.)

CHAPTER 42.

INSURANCE GUARANTY ASSOCIATION.

§ 27-42-1. Short title.

Legislative intent. — It is apparent from the Alabama Insurance Guaranty Association Act, this section to § 27-42-20, that the legislature did not intend the AIGA stand in the stead of the insolvent insurer. Indeed, when the statutory limitations regarding payment of claims are read along with this avowed purpose, one sees that the effect of the Act is not necessarily to provide the claimant or insured the same coverage or dollar recovery he would have realized had his carrier not become insolvent. There are limits as to what type of claim will be paid. Windle v. Alabama Ins. Guar. Ass'n, 591 So. 2d 78 (Ala. 1991).

Reduction of covered claims. — Alabama Insurance Guaranty Association Act is entitled to reduce "covered claims" by amounts recovered under uninsured motorist policies. Windle v. Alabama Ins. Guar. Ass'n, 591 So. 2d 78 (Ala. 1991).

§ 27-42-2. Purpose of chapter.

Under this section, only a claim by an insured or a third party claimant is covered by the Act. Commercial Union Ins. Co. v. Sepco Corp., 918 F.2d 920 (11th Cir. 1990).

Act only provides protection from insolvent insurers licensed in state. — Where the named insurer on the policy had never been licensed to transact insurance business in Alabama, under the act, the guaranty association was not obligated to pay claims against named insurer, because the act only provides protection from the insolvency of insurers licensed to transact insurance in this State. Alabama Ins. Guar. Ass'n v. Pierce, 551 So. 2d 310 (Ala. 1989).

Legislative intent. — The legislature's purpose in enacting the Alabama Insurance Guaranty Association provisions was not to remedy the problem of inadequate insurance coverage, a problem not unique to the situation of insolvent insurers, but to alleviate the burden caused by a lack of coverage that occurs through no fault of the insured. Alabama Ins.

Guar. Ass'n v. Hamm, 601 So. 2d 419 (Ala. 1992); Dillard v. Alabama Ins. Guar. Ass'n, 601 So. 2d 894 (Ala. 1992).

It was clearly the intent of the legislature that there be no duplication of recovery, irrespective of whether the claimant has been made whole. Alabama Ins. Guar. Ass'n v. Hamm, 601 So. 2d 419 (Ala. 1992).

Cited in Alabama Ins. Guar. Ass'n v. Stephenson, 514 So. 2d 1000 (Ala. 1987).

§ 27-42-3. Applicability of chapter.

"Direct insurance" as used in the act refers to an insurance contract between an insured and an insurer that has accepted a designated risk of a designated loss to the insured. Alabama Ins. Guar. Ass'n v. Pierce, 551 So. 2d 310 (Ala. 1989).

Direct health insurance excepted. — The employee's plan of health insurance was a kind of direct insurance excepted by the provisions of this section, and thus benefits paid thereunder did not fall within the provisions of the Insurance Guaranty Association Act, in particular the nonduplication section, § 27-42-12. Alabama Ins. Guar. Ass'n v. Stephenson, 514 So. 2d 1000 (Ala. 1987).

Cited in Alabama Ins. Guar. Ass'n v. Magic City Trucking Serv., Inc., 547 So. 2d 849 (Ala. 1989).

§ 27-42-5. Definitions.

Act only provides protection from insolvent insurers licensed in state. — Where the named insurer on the policy had never been licensed to transact insurance business in Alabama, under the act, the guaranty association was not obligated to pay claims against named insurer, because the act only provides protection from the insolvency of insurers licensed to transact insurance in this State. Alabama Ins. Guar. Ass'n v. Pierce, 551 So. 2d 310 (Ala. 1989).

Definition of covered claim. — A "covered claim" is, by definition, limited to the amount of the policy issued by the now insolvent insurer. Windle v. Alabama Ins. Guar. Ass'n, 591 So. 2d 78 (Ala. 1991).

Cited in Alabama Ins. Guar. Ass'n v. Stephenson, 514 So. 2d 1000 (Ala. 1987); Commercial Union Ins. Co. v. Sepco Corp., 918 F.2d 920 (11th Cir. 1990).

§ 27-42-8. Powers and duties of the association.

Corporation may be resident in Alabama and other states at same time. — A finding by an arbitration panel that carrier was a resident of Tennessee because of its substantial contacts did not preclude a finding of residency in Alabama, since a corporation is a citizen, resident or inhabitant of the state under whose laws it was created; since the carrier was incorporated in Alabama, the carrier was a resident of Alabama. Alabama Ins. Guar. Ass'n v. Colonial Freight Sys., 537 So. 2d 475 (Ala. 1988).

Cited in Alabama Ins. Guar. Ass'n v. Magic City Trucking Serv., Inc., 547 So. 2d 849 (Ala. 1989).

§ 27-42-12. Exhaustion of rights; nonduplication of recovery.

Legislative intent. — The legislature intended, in enacting this section, that the claimant not be placed in a better position by the insurer's insolvency than the claimant would have occupied if the insurer had been solvent; conversely, where a claimant would not be placed in a better position by a recovery from the AIGA than the claimant would have occupied if the insolvent insurance company had been solvent, then the offset statute does not apply. Alabama Ins. Guar. Ass'n v. Hamm, 601 So. 2d 419 (Ala. 1992).

The legislature sought only to offer a measure of protection to remedy the problem of the nonexistence of coverage due to the insolvency of an insurer, not to redress the problem of inadequate existing coverage. Alabama Ins. Guar. Ass'n v. Hamm, 601 So. 2d 419 (Ala. 1992).

The legislature's purpose in enacting the Alabama Insurance Guaranty Association provisions was not to remedy the problem of inadequate insurance coverage, a problem not unique to the situation of insolvent insurers, but to alleviate the burden caused by a lack of coverage that occurs through no fault of the insured. Dillard v. Alabama Ins. Guar. Ass'n, 601 So. 2d 894 (Ala. 1992).

This section is sometimes referred to as the nonduplication provision of the Alabama Insurance Guaranty Association Act. Gibson v. Alabama Ins. Guar. Ass'n, 601 So. 2d 416 (Ala. 1992).

Underinsured motorist coverage defined. — Underinsured motorist coverage, by definition, does not duplicate liability coverage but is coverage in excess of liability coverage, and is available to a claimant only after the claimant has exhausted available liability coverages. Alabama Ins. Guar. Ass'n v. Hamm, 601 So. 2d 419 (Ala. 1992).

Construction of this section. — This section (the "offset statute"), entitled "Exhaustion of rights; nonduplication of recovery," provides that the amounts first recovered offset or reduce the "covered claim" with the Alabama Insurance Guaranty Association (AIGA); this has been construed to have a limited meaning: if recovery from the AIGA would be a duplication of amounts already recovered, the amount of the duplicated (windfall) sums cannot be recovered from the AIGA. Gibson v. Alabama Ins. Guar. Ass'n, 601 So. 2d 416 (Ala. 1992).

If the insolvent company issued liability coverage for the tort-feasor, a claimant can recover uninsured motorist coverages available to the claimant, but cannot then recover the full amount of the insolvent insurer's liability coverage from the Alabama Insurance Guaranty Association, irrespective of whether the claimant has been made whole. Alabama Ins. Guar. Ass'n v. Hamm, 601 So. 2d 419 (Ala. 1992).

One injured by a phantom driver is entitled to recover under the uninsured motorist provisions of his insurance policy or any policy under which he is an insured. Under this section, he is required to exhaust first his rights under such policy. Gibson v. Alabama Ins. Guar. Ass'n, 601 So. 2d 416 (Ala. 1992).

Underinsured motorists coverage, by definition, does not duplicate liability coverage but is coverage in excess of liability coverage, and is available to a claimant only after the claimant has exhausted available liability coverages; it differs from typical uninsured motorist coverage because uninsured motorist coverage takes the place of nonexistent liability coverage. Dillard v. Alabama Ins. Guar. Ass'n, 601 So. 2d 894 (Ala. 1992).

Underinsured motorist coverage, paid by the Alabama Insurance Guaranty Association on an insolvent insurer's underinsured policy, is not offset by a recovery against other liability insurance coverages, because underinsured motorist coverage does not duplicate the liability coverage. Dillard v. Alabama Ins. Guar. Ass'n, 601 So. 2d 894 (Ala. 1992).

When benefits are paid under the claimant's uninsured/underinsured motorist policy and the tort-feasor's liability insurer is insolvent, the benefits are paid as uninsured motorist benefits; such payments will offset the obligation of the Alabama Insurance Guaranty Association dollar for dollar up to the policy limits. Dillard v. Alabama Ins. Guar. Ass'n, 601 So. 2d 894 (Ala. 1992).

"Recovery" under uninsured motorist coverage policy. — The trial court correctly held that the appropriate amount by which to reduce carrier's reimbursement from Alabama Insurance Guaranty Association was $25,000, the amount of accident victim's recovery, for her injuries by carrier and not $50,000, the full coverage under her uninsured motorist coverage policy, since the language of subsection (a) clearly refers to "recovery" and not to full amounts potentially payable under the policy. Alabama Ins. Guar. Ass'n v. Colonial Freight Sys., 537 So. 2d 475 (Ala. 1988).

Direct health insurance excepted. — The employee's plan of health insurance was a kind of direct insurance excepted by the provisions of § 27-42-3, and thus benefits paid thereunder did not fall within the provisions of the Insurance Guaranty Association Act, in particular the nonduplication provisions of this section. Alabama Ins. Guar. Ass'n v. Stephenson, 514 So. 2d 1000 (Ala. 1987).

The employee's receipt of health insurance benefits placed her in no better position than she would have been in had the tortfeasor's insurer, which was under the supervision of the state insurance guaranty association, remained solvent; thus, no windfall situation was present, and the association was not entitled to deduct from its obligation any amount paid to the employee under the health insurance plan. Alabama Ins. Guar. Ass'n v. Stephenson, 514 So. 2d 1000 (Ala. 1987).

No reduction of obligation by amount of workmen's compensation benefits. — The Alabama Insurance Guaranty Association is not entitled to reduce its obligation to a policyholder or claimant by the amount paid to that person as workmen's compensation benefits. Alabama Ins. Guar. Ass'n v. Magic City Trucking Serv., Inc., 547 So. 2d 849 (Ala. 1989).

Recovery constituted a "covered claim" under Insurance Guaranty Association Act. — Where deceased estate recovered an amount as a result of uninsured/underinsured motorist coverage, his recovery was a "covered claim" pursuant to Insurance Guaranty Association Act, and therefore, the Guaranty Association should have been entitled to an offset up to that amount paid to the estate. Alabama Ins. Guar. Ass'n v. Hollingsworth, 613 So. 2d 1204 (Ala. 1991).

Cited in Alabama Ins. Guar. Ass'n v. Kinder-Care, Inc., 551 So. 2d 286 (Ala. 1989).

Collateral references. — Uninsured or underinsured motorist insurance: validity and construction of policy provision purporting to reduce recovery by amount of social security disability benefits or payments under similar disability benefits law. 24 ALR5th 766.

CHAPTER 44.

LIFE AND DISABILITY INSURANCE GUARANTY ASSOCIATION.

Sec.
27-44-3. Scope of chapter.

§ 27-44-2. Purpose of chapter.

Cited in Southtrust Bank v. Alabama Life & Disability Ins. Guar. Ass'n, 578 So. 2d 1302 (Ala. 1991).

§ 27-44-3. Scope of chapter.

(a) This chapter shall apply to direct life insurance policies, disability insurance policies, annuity contracts, and contracts supplemental to life and disability insurance policies, and annuity contracts issued by persons licensed to transact insurance in this state at any time, except as limited by this section.

(b) This chapter shall not apply to:

(1) That portion or part of a variable life insurance or variable annuity contract not guaranteed by an insurer.

(2) That portion or part of any policy or contract under which the risk is borne by the policyholder.

(3) Any policy or contract or part thereof assumed by the impaired or insolvent insurer under a contract of reinsurance, other than reinsurance for which assumption certificates have been issued.

(4) Any policy or contract issued by non-profit hospital and medical service plans, fraternal benefit societies, cooperative hospital associations, or health maintenance organizations.

(5) A policy or contract providing coverage to persons not specified in subsection (c).

(c) This chapter shall provide coverage for the policies and contracts specified in subsection (a) as follows:

(1) To persons who, regardless of where they reside (except for non-resident certificate holders under group policies or contracts), are the beneficiaries, assignees, or payees of the persons covered under subdivision (2).

(2) To persons who are owners of, or certificate holders under, covered policies or contracts, and who are residents, or are not residents, but only under all of the following conditions:

a. The insurers which issued the policies or contracts are domiciled in this state.

b. The insurers at the time of issuance of the policies or contracts did not hold licenses or certificates of authority in the state in which such persons reside.

150

c. The persons are not eligible for coverage by a guaranty association of another state providing protection substantially similar to that provided by this chapter for residents of this state.

(d) Any member insurer that has been declared insolvent and is placed under a final order of liquidation, rehabilitation, or conservation by a court of competent jurisdiction prior to May 17, 1993 shall be subject to this chapter as it existed prior to May 17, 1993. (Acts 1982, No. 82-561, p. 922, § 3; Acts 1993, No. 93-675, § 11.)

The 1993 amendment, effective May 17, 1993, in subsection (a), inserted "and" preceding "annuity contracts," deleted "and contracts supplemental to life and disability insurance policies and annuity contracts" preceding "issued by," and inserted "except as limited by this section" at the end of the subsection; in subsection (b), subdivision (4), deleted "such" preceding "policy" and substituted "fraternal benefit societies" for "fraternals," and added subdivision (5), and added subsections (c) and (d).

Code Commissioner's note. — Acts 1993, No. 93-675, § 20, provides: "The Commissioner of Insurance may adopt reasonable rules and regulations necessary for the implementation and the administration of this chapter."

Cross references. — As to provisions of rules and regulations necessary for the effectuation of this title, see § 27-2-17.

Cited in Southtrust Bank v. Alabama Life & Disability Ins. Guar. Ass'n, 578 So. 2d 1302 (Ala. 1991).

§ 27-44-8. Powers and duties of association.

Cited in Southtrust Bank v. Alabama Life & Disability Ins. Guar. Ass'n, 578 So. 2d 1302 (Ala. 1991).

CHAPTER 45.

PHARMACEUTICAL INSURANCE COVERAGE.

Article 1.

General Provisions.

Sec.
27-45-1. Applicability of article.
27-45-2. Definitions.
27-45-3. Choice of pharmaceutical services; right to participate as contracting provider.
27-45-4. Effect of policies or plans contrary to article.
27-45-5. Article does not mandate that pharmaceutical services be provided.

Sec.
27-45-6. Compliance with article.
27-45-7. Nonconforming policies and plans not to be approved for sale.
27-45-8. Duty to enforce article.
27-45-9. Violations.

Article 2.

Written Proof Pharmacy Registered with State Board.

27-45-20. No agreement for services until written verification of registration obtained.

ARTICLE 1.

GENERAL PROVISIONS.

§ 27-45-1. Applicability of article.

This article shall apply to health insurance and employee benefit plans providing for pharmaceutical services, including without limitation, prescription drugs. (Acts 1988, No. 88-379, p. 565, § 1.)

§ 27-45-2. Definitions.

As used in this article, the following terms shall have the respective meanings herein set forth, unless the context shall otherwise require:

(1) ALABAMA INSURANCE CODE. Title 27 of the Code of Alabama 1975.

(2) INSURER. Such term shall have the meaning ascribed in section 27-1-2.

(3) PERSON. Such term shall have the meaning ascribed in section 27-1-2.

(4) COMMISSIONER and DEPARTMENT. Such terms, respectively, shall have the meanings ascribed in section 27-1-2.

(5) CONTRACTUAL OBLIGATION. Any obligation under covered policies or employee benefit plans.

(6) COVERED POLICY or PLAN. Any policy, employee benefit plan or contract within the scope of this article.

(7) HEALTH INSURANCE POLICY. Any individual, group, blanket, or franchise insurance policy, insurance agreement, or group hospital service contract providing for pharmaceutical services, including without limitation, prescription drugs, incurred as a result of accident or sickness, or to prevent same.

(8) EMPLOYEE BENEFIT PLAN. Any plan, fund, or program heretofore or hereafter established or maintained by an employer or an employee organization, or by both, to the extent that such plan, fund, or program was established or is maintained for the purpose of providing for its participants or their beneficiaries, through the purchase of insurance or otherwise, pharmaceutical services, including without limitation, prescription drugs.

(9) PHARMACIST. Any person licensed by the Alabama state board of pharmacy to practice the profession of pharmacy in the state of Alabama and whose license is in good standing.

(10) PHARMACY. A place licensed by the Alabama state board of pharmacy in which prescriptions, drugs, medicines, chemicals and poisons are sold, offered for sale, compounded or dispensed, and shall include all places whose title may imply the sale, offering for sale, compounding or dispensing of prescriptions, drugs, medicines, chemicals or poisons.

(11) PHARMACEUTICAL SERVICES. Services ordinarily and customarily rendered by a pharmacy or pharmacist, including without limitation, the dispensing of prescriptions, drugs, medicines, chemicals or poisons.

(12) DRUGS. All medical substances, preparations and devices recognized by the United States Pharmacopoeia and National Formulary, or any revision thereof, and all substances and preparations intended for external and internal use in the cure, diagnosis, mitigation, treatment or prevention of disease in man or animal and all substances and preparations other than food intended to affect the structure or any function of the body of man or animal.

(13) PRESCRIPTION. Any order for drug or medical supplies, written or signed or transmitted by word of mouth, telephone, telegraph, closed circuit, television or other means of communication by a legally competent practitioner, licensed by law to prescribe and administer such drugs and medical

supplies intended to be filled, compounded or dispensed by a pharmacist. (Acts 1988, No. 88-379, p. 565, § 2.)

§ 27-45-3. Choice of pharmaceutical services; right to participate as contracting provider.

No health insurance policy or employee benefit plan which is delivered, renewed, issued for delivery, or otherwise contracted for in this state shall:

(1) Prevent any person who is a party to or beneficiary of any such health insurance policy or employee benefit plan from selecting the pharmacy or pharmacist of his choice to furnish the pharmaceutical services, including without limitation, prescription drugs, offered by said policy or plan or interfere with said selection provided the pharmacy or pharmacist is licensed to furnish such pharmaceutical services in this state; or

(2) Deny any pharmacy or pharmacist the right to participate as a contracting provider for such policy or plan provided the pharmacist is licensed to furnish pharmaceutical services, including without limitation, prescription drugs offered by said policy or plan. (Acts 1988, No. 88-379, p. 565, § 3.)

§ 27-45-4. Effect of policies or plans contrary to article.

Any provision in a health insurance policy or employee benefit plan which is delivered, renewed, issued for delivery, or otherwise contracted for in this state which is contrary to this article shall to the extent of such conflict be void. (Acts 1988, No. 88-379, p. 565, § 4.)

§ 27-45-5. Article does not mandate that pharmaceutical services be provided.

The provisions of this article do not mandate that any type of benefits for pharmaceutical services, including without limitation, prescription drugs, be provided by a health insurance policy or an employee benefit plan. (Acts 1988, No. 88-379, p. 565, § 5.)

§ 27-45-6. Compliance with article.

It shall be unlawful for any insurer or any person to provide any health insurance policy or employee benefit plan providing for pharmaceutical services, including without limitation, prescription drugs, that does not conform to the provisions of this article. (Acts 1988, No. 88-379, p. 565, § 6.)

§ 27-45-7. Nonconforming policies and plans not to be approved for sale.

The commissioner of insurance shall not approve for sale in this state any health insurance policy or employee benefit plan providing for pharmaceutical services, including without limitation, prescription drugs, which does not conform to the provisions of this article or to the provisions of sections 27-14-8 and 27-14-9. (Acts 1988, No. 88-379, p. 565, § 7.)

§ 27-45-8. Duty to enforce article.

It shall be the duty and responsibility of the commissioner of insurance to enforce the provisions of this article. (Acts 1988, No. 88-379, p. 565, § 8.)

§ 27-45-9. Violations.

Each willful violation of the provisions of this article shall be punishable as provided in section 27-1-12. (Acts 1988, No. 88-379, p. 565, § 9.)

ARTICLE 2.

WRITTEN PROOF PHARMACY REGISTERED WITH STATE BOARD.

§ 27-45-20. No agreement for services until written verification of registration obtained.

No insurance company, health maintenance organization (HMO), employer or organization offering a pharmaceutical prescription program to their employees or members in Alabama, shall enter into an agreement for services until they have obtained written verification that the provider pharmacies are registered with the Alabama state board of pharmacy. Such verification must be filed with the Alabama department of insurance within 10 days of initiating such agreement. Said department shall provide a copy of the verification to the Alabama state board of pharmacy. Failure to comply with such verification requirement shall result in a fine to the sponsor of such prescription program, of $100.00 per day, from the date that such agreement was signed until such verification requirement is satisfied. (Acts 1991, No. 91-595, p. 1098, § 1.)

Cross references. — As to third party prescription programs being required to comply with article 5, chapter 23, Title 34, see § 34-23-118.

CHAPTER 46.

CERTIFIED REGISTERED NURSE ANESTHETIST COVERAGE.

Sec.
27-46-1. Reimbursement or payment for services.
27-46-2. Hospitals not prohibited from prescribing policies, rules, etc.

Sec.
27-46-3. "Certified registered nurse anesthetist" defined.

§ 27-46-1. Reimbursement or payment for services.

Notwithstanding any other provision of law, when any contract or plan of health insurance, or any plan or agreement for health care services provides for the reimbursement or payment for services which are within the scope of practice of registered nurses who have passed or who are qualified to take the national certification examination for the specialty practice of nurse anesthetist as recognized by the Alabama board of nursing, then the insured, or any other person covered by the policy, plan, contract or certificate shall be entitled to reimbursement or payment for such services performed by the certified registered nurse anesthetist, and said certified registered nurse anesthetist shall be entitled to direct reimbursement by the insurer, unless the certified registered nurse anesthetist is employed by contract with a group practice of anesthesiologist or a hospital, then such services shall be reimbursed through the employer. (Acts 1989, No. 89-664, p. 1318, § 1.)

This section is preempted by the Employee Retirement Income Security Act of 1974, 29 U.S.C. §§ 1001, et seq. (ERISA) as to employee welfare benefit plans governed by ERISA. Hayden v. Blue Cross & Blue Shield, 843 F. Supp. 1427 (M.D. Ala. 1994).

Plaintiffs are precluded from contending that when a patient with an ERISA plan uses anesthesia services, the plaintiffs become a beneficiary, participant or assignee of the patient-beneficiary or patient-participant under the ERISA plan. Hayden v. Blue Cross & Blue Shield, 855 F. Supp. 344 (M.D. Ala. 1994).

Defendant Blue Cross and Blue Shield of Alabama was not subject to this section as to plans not governed by Employee Retirement Income Security Act (ERISA). Hayden v. Blue Cross & Blue Shield, 843 F. Supp. 1427 (M.D. Ala. 1994).

§ 27-46-2. Hospitals not prohibited from prescribing policies, rules, etc.

Nothing in this chapter shall prohibit a licensed hospital from prescribing in its bylaws, policies, rules, or regulations, the qualifications, training, experience, scope of permissible activities, and level or degree of supervision required of any certified registered nurse anesthetist employed by or performing services in such hospital. (Acts 1989, No. 89-664, p. 1318, § 2.)

§ 27-46-3. "Certified registered nurse anesthetist" defined.

For the purposes of this section, certified registered nurse anesthetist means any licensed registered nurse licensed under section 34-21-20, who is a graduate of a formal education program accredited by the council on accreditation of nurse anesthesia educational programs or its predecessor, the American association of nurse anesthetists, and is currently certified as a registered nurse anesthetist by the council on certification/recertification of nurse anesthetists. (Acts 1989, No. 89-664, p. 1318, § 3.)

CHAPTER 47.

LONG-TERM CARE INSURANCE CONTRACTS.

Sec.
27-47-1. Qualified long-term care services.
27-47-2. Deduction for premiums paid for long-term care insurance contract; treatment of contract; coverage.

Sec.
27-47-3. Premium tax for long-term care coverage to be deposited into Alabama Special Educational Trust Fund.

Effective date. — The act which added this chapter became effective August 7, 1995.

Cross references. — As to a deduction in state taxes for premiums paid for qualifying long-term care coverage, see § 40-18-15.

§ 27-47-1. Qualified long-term care services.

For purposes of this chapter, "qualified long-term care services" includes care for necessary diagnostic, preventive, therapeutic, and rehabilitative services and maintenance or personal care services which are required by a chronically ill individual in a qualified facility or services which are provided pursuant to a plan of care prescribed by a licensed health care practitioner. (Acts 1995, No. 95-738, § 1.)

§ 27-47-2. Deduction for premiums paid for long-term care insurance contract; treatment of contract; coverage.

(a) The premiums paid for a long-term care insurance contract are deductible pursuant to Section 40-18-15, if the contract meets the following requirements:

(1) Offers coverage only for qualified long-term care services and benefits incidental to the coverage.

(2) Guaranteed renewal.

(3) No cash surrender value.

(4) All refunds of premiums and all policyholder dividends or similar amounts under the contract are to be applied as a reduction in future premiums or to increase future benefits, except for a refund of premiums on surrender or cancellation of the policy.

(b) For purposes of this chapter, a long-term care insurance contract shall be treated as an accident or health insurance contract. The amount of coverage under the long-term care insurance contract shall be equal to or greater than Medicaid coverage for a period of at least three years.

(c) An insurance contract shall not fail to be treated as a long-term care contract by reason of the payments being made on a per diem or other periodic basis without regard to the expenses incurred during the period to which the payments relate.

(d) A long-term care insurance contract may cover Medicare reimbursable expenses where Medicare is a secondary payor.

(e) In the case of long-term care insurance coverage provided by a rider on a life insurance contract, this chapter shall apply as if the portion of the contract providing long-term care coverage was a separate contract.

(f) The deduction is available to the person or entity who pays the premiums. (Acts 1995, No. 95-738, § 2.)

§ 27-47-3. Premium tax for long-term care coverage to be deposited into Alabama Special Educational Trust Fund.

Any amounts of premium tax for long-term care coverage shall be deposited into the Alabama Special Educational Trust Fund. (Acts 1995, No. 95-738, § 3.)

TITLE 28.

INTOXICATING LIQUOR, MALT BEVERAGES AND WINE.

TABLE OF CONTENTS

CHAPTER
4A. Alabama Brewpub Act, §§ 28-4A-1 through 28-4A-6.
7A. Audit and Collection of Taxes on Beer or Table Wine by Board for Benefit of Local Governing Bodies, §§ 28-7A-1 through 28-7A-6.

CHAPTER
9. Business Relations Between Wholesalers and Suppliers of Beer, §§ 28-9-1 through 28-9-11.
10. Alabama Responsible Vendor Act, §§ 28-10-1 through 28-10-8.

CHAPTER 1.

GENERAL PROVISIONS.

Sec.
28-1-3. Repealed.
28-1-3.1. Possession of certain quantities of alcoholic beverages purchased from military liquor stores, etc., by eligible persons authorized; penalty for unauthorized sale or possession.

Sec.
28-1-6. Alcoholic Beverage Control Board prohibited from issuing licenses for sale of intoxicating beverages in Class 1 or 2 municipalities; exceptions.

As to community development districts, see Chapter 8B of Title 35.

§ 28-1-3. Possession of certain quantities of alcoholic beverages purchased from military liquor stores, etc., by eligible persons authorized; penalty for unauthorized sale or possession. Repealed by Acts 1986, No. 86-334, p. 507, effective April 24, 1986.

Cross references. — For provisions as to the purchase of alcoholic beverages from military liquor stores, see § 28-1-3.1.

§ 28-1-3.1. Possession of certain quantities of alcoholic beverages purchased from military liquor stores, etc., by eligible persons authorized; penalty for unauthorized sale or possession.

(a) Any person 21 years of age or over who is on active duty, in active reserve status or retired from the armed forces of the United States, or the dependent of such person, or is otherwise eligible to purchase alcoholic beverages from military package or liquor stores, shall be entitled to have in his possession, in his motor vehicle, or a private residence or place of private residence or the curtilage thereof in any county in this state, for his own private use and not for resale, not more than the following quantity of alcoholic beverages as defined in § 28-3-1, which beverages have been sold by a military liquor, package, class 6 or similar store or outlet: three liters of liquor and one case of beer; or three liters of wine and one case of beer; or two cases of beer; provided, however, that no alcoholic beverages shall be kept, stored or possessed in the passenger area of any vehicle, or in the view of any passenger; and further provided that the beer and table wine must first have been purchased by the military package or liquor stores from licensed Alabama wholesalers, and liquor and fortified wine must first have been purchased by the military package and liquor stores from the Alabama ABC board; and shall have sufficient identification, including but not limited to a sales receipt, to show that such alcoholic beverages were purchased in Alabama and sold by such military store or outlet; provided further that no rule or regulation of the board shall require a wholesaler to affix stamps or decals to beer or table wine.

(b) It shall be unlawful for any person in possession of alcoholic beverages as enumerated in subsection (a) of this section to sell or offer to sell such alcoholic beverages to anyone not authorized to purchase such state untaxed beverages himself or to have in his possession at any one time any amount of state untaxed alcoholic beverages in excess of the quantity set forth in subsection (a) of this section. Any person violating the provisions of this section shall be guilty of a misdemeanor and shall be fined not less than $50.00 nor more than $500.00, or imprisoned in the county jail for a period not to exceed six months, either or both, at the discretion of the court. (Acts 1986, Ex. Sess., No. 86-648, p. 29.)

Code Commissioner's note. — Section 28-1-3, pertaining to same subject matter as this section, was repealed by Acts 1986, No. 86-334, p. 507, effective April 24, 1986.

Collateral references. — Social host's liability for injuries incurred by third parties as a result of intoxicated guest's negligence. 62 ALR4th 16.

§ 28-1-5. Minimum age for purchasing, consuming, possessing, etc., alcohol; employment of underage persons in places licensed to serve alcohol; penalty; exemption.

Willful furnishing of alcohol to one under 18. — It is a misdemeanor for persons under the age of 21 to purchase, consume, possess or to transport any alcoholic beverage, and consequently, one who willfully furnishes alcoholic beverages to persons under the age of 18 clearly violates both the first and second alternatives of subsection (a) of § 28-3A-25. Senf v. State, 622 So. 2d 435 (Ala. Crim. App. 1993).

Legislative intent. — It was not the intent of the legislature to bar persons between the ages of 19 and 21 years from entering or being admitted to such premises which sells alcoholic beverages, either as a patron or an employee, so long as they do not consume, dispense, or transport alcoholic beverages. Swint v. State ABC Bd., 628 So. 2d 769 (Ala. Civ. App. 1993).

Collateral references. — Social host's liability for injuries incurred by third parties as a result of intoxicated guest's negligence. 62 ALR4th 16.

§ 28-1-6. Alcoholic Beverage Control Board prohibited from issuing licenses for sale of intoxicating beverages in Class 1 or 2 municipalities; exceptions.

(a) All other provisions of law, rules, or regulations to the contrary notwithstanding, the Alabama Alcoholic Beverage Control Board shall absolutely have no authority to issue any form of license in a Class 1 or Class 2 municipality, including, but not limited to, off-premise consumption licenses, restaurant licenses, or club licenses, for the retail sale of any form of intoxicating beverages, including, but not limited to, malt liquor, beer, wine, liquor, or other alcoholic beverage regulated by the board, unless one of the following requirements are satisfied:

(1) The application has first been approved by the governing body of the municipality in which the site of the license is situated.

(2) The denial of approval by the governing body has been set aside by order of the circuit court of the county in which the site is situated on the ground that the municipal approval was arbitrarily or capriciously denied without a showing of one of the following:

a. The creation of a nuisance.

b. Circumstances clearly detrimental to adjacent residential neighborhoods.

c. A violation of applicable zoning restrictions or regulations.

(b) Proceedings in the circuit courts to review an action of a municipal governing body denying approval of an application shall be expedited de novo proceedings heard by a circuit judge without a jury who shall consider any testimony presented by the city governing body and any new evidence presented in explanation or contradiction of the testimony. If a license applicant prevails in any judicial review on any basis other than new evidence presented to the court that was not presented to the municipal governing body, the applicant shall be entitled to an award of attorney fees against the municipality. Any proceeding to review the denial of approval of a license application shall be commenced within 14 days of the action by the municipal governing body and shall be set for hearing by the court within 30 days thereafter. (Acts 1995, No. 95-561, §§ 1, 2.)

Effective date. — The act which added this section became effective July 31, 1995.

Code Commissioner's note. — In 1995, a comma was deleted after "any form of license" in subsection (a) for clarity.

CHAPTER 2.

ELECTIONS AS TO SALE AND DISTRIBUTION OF ALCOHOLIC BEVERAGES WITHIN COUNTIES.

Article 2.

Special Method Referendum.

Sec.

28-2-23. Levy and collection of tax upon sale of

malt beverages by counties or municipalities permitting sale under article; disposition of proceeds from tax.

ARTICLE 2.

SPECIAL METHOD REFERENDUM.

§ 28-2-23. Levy and collection of tax upon sale of malt beverages by counties or municipalities permitting sale under article; disposition of proceeds from tax.

Any county or municipality which allows the sale of malt beverages under the provisions of this article shall be authorized to levy and collect a tax upon the sale of such beverages in an amount not to exceed $.05 on each 12 fluid ounces or fraction thereof; provided, that the county shall not have authority to impose such tax within any incorporated municipality within such county.

A minimum of 60 percent of the proceeds of such tax shall be used solely for the purpose of public education, with the remainder to be allocated by the county commission or municipal governing body levying and collecting the tax for any other public use. The county commission shall distribute the proceeds of this tax for public education to school systems within the county on the same basis as the total calculated costs of the Foundation Program for the local boards of education within the county. (Acts 1971, No. 1266, p. 2195, § 4; Acts 1995, No. 95-261, § 1.)

The **1995 amendment,** effective June 26, 1995, and to be implemented with the beginning of the 1995-96 fiscal year, substituted the language beginning "on the same basis as the total" for "under the average daily attendance calculation used by the state department of education" in the second sentence of the second paragraph.

CHAPTER 2A.

ELECTIONS AS TO SALE AND DISTRIBUTION OF ALCOHOLIC BEVERAGES WITHIN MUNICIPALITIES.

§ 28-2A-1. Procedure for elections to determine classification of municipalities as wet or dry municipalities.

Legislative intent. — In ascertaining the legislative intent of this section, the court can turn to § 28-2A-3, part of the statute itself. There, it is stated that the purpose of requiring that a municipality have a population of at least 7,000 in order to have a municipal motion election pursuant to this section, is that it is the judgment of the legislature that municipalities with a lesser population would be unable to support and maintain such necessary protection for public welfare, health, peace, and morals of the people. This shows no basis for requiring 10-year gaps between the times that the population may be determined. Dennis v. Pendley, 518 So. 2d 688 (Ala. 1987).

Determination of population.

This section does not require that only a decennial census conducted by the United States Department of Commerce, Bureau of the Census, be used to determine the population of a municipality. City of Bridgeport v. Citizens Action Comm., 571 So. 2d 1089 (Ala. 1990).

This section makes no provision for how population is to be determined and it is the court's function to make clear the intent of the legislature when some degree of ambiguity is found in a statute. Dennis v. Pendley, 518 So. 2d 688 (Ala. 1987).

Decennial census requirement. — The interim census conducted by the United States Department of Commerce, Bureau of the Census, which determined city's population served the function of meeting a preceding decennial census for purposes of this section. Dennis v. Pendley, 518 So. 2d 688 (Ala. 1987).

This section does not say that only decennial census can be used to determine population. Dennis v. Pendley, 518 So. 2d 688 (Ala. 1987).

§ 28-2A-3. Legislative intent.

Legislative intent. — In ascertaining the legislative intent of § 28-2A-1, the court can turn to this section. Here, it is stated that the purpose of requiring that a municipality have a population of at least 7,000 in order to have a municipal motion election pursuant to § 28-2A-1, is that it is the judgment of the legislature that municipalities with a lesser population would be unable to support and maintain such necessary protection for public welfare, health, peace, and morals of the people. This shows no basis for requiring 10-year gaps between the times that the population may be determined. Dennis v. Pendley, 518 So. 2d 688 (Ala. 1987).

§ 28-2A-4. Elections in municipalities in same county with populations of 4,000 or more.

Cited in City of Bridgeport v. Citizens Action Comm., 571 So. 2d 1089 (Ala. 1990).

CHAPTER 3.

REGULATION AND CONTROL OF ALCOHOLIC BEVERAGES IN WET COUNTIES.

Article 1.

General Provisions.

Sec.
28-3-1.   Definitions.
28-3-11. Invoices and receipts to be maintained by persons, firms, etc., selling or shipping goods, merchandise, etc., to persons, firms, etc., in another state or to federal government for army, navy or marine purposes; exemption from taxation goods purchased from Alcoholic Beverage Control Board for export to another country.

Article 5A.

Excise Taxes on Malt or Brewed Beverages.

Sec.
28-3-187.1. Exemption from labeling requirement.

Article 5B.

Excise Tax on Beer.

28-3-190. Levy of tax; collection; disposition of proceeds by localities; enforcement and administration; penalties; exclusive nature of tax.

Article 6.

Taxes on Sale of Spirituous or Vinous Liquors.

Sec.
28-3-203. Additional five percent tax.

Article 7.

Tax and Identification Stamps, Crowns or Lids.

Sec.
28-3-220 through 28-3-226. Repealed.

Cross references. — As to community development districts, see Chapter 8B of Title 35.

ARTICLE 1.

GENERAL PROVISIONS.

§ 28-3-1. Definitions.

The following words or phrases, whenever they appear in this chapter, and in Alcoholic Beverage Licensing Code, being Act No. 80-529, Acts of Alabama, 1980, as amended, appearing as chapter 3A, Title 28, as amended, and the Alabama Table Wine Act, being Act 80-382, Acts of Alabama 1980, as amended, appearing as chapter 7, Title 28, as amended, unless the context clearly indicates otherwise, shall have the meaning ascribed to them in this section:

(1) ALCOHOLIC BEVERAGES. Any alcoholic, spirituous, vinous, fermented or other alcoholic beverage, or combination of liquors and mixed liquor, a part of which is spirituous, vinous, fermented or otherwise alcoholic, and all drinks or drinkable liquids, preparations or mixtures intended for beverage purposes, which contain one-half of one percent or more of alcohol by volume, and shall include liquor, beer, and wine, both fortified and table wine.

(2) ASSOCIATION. A partnership, limited partnership, or any form of unincorporated enterprise owned by two or more persons.

(3) BEER, or MALT or BREWED BEVERAGES. Any beer, lager beer, ale, porter, malt or brewed beverage or similar fermented malt liquor containing one-half of one percent or more of alcohol by volume and not in excess of four percent alcohol by weight and five percent by volume, by whatever name the same may be called.

(4) BOARD. The alcoholic beverage control board.

(5) CARTON. The package or container or containers in which alcoholic beverages are originally packaged for shipment to market by the manufacturer or its designated representatives or the importer.

(6) CONTAINER. The single bottle, can, keg, bag or other receptacle, not a carton, in which alcoholic beverages are originally packaged for the market by the manufacturer or importer and from which the alcoholic beverage is consumed by or dispensed to the public.

(7) CLUB.

a. Class I. A corporation or association organized or formed in good faith by authority of law and which must have at least 150 paid-up members. It must be the owner, lessee or occupant of an establishment operated solely for the objects of a national, social, patriotic, political or athletic nature or

163

the like, but not for pecuniary gain, and the property as well as the advantages of which, belong to all the members and which maintains an establishment provided with special space and accommodations where, in consideration of payment, food with or without lodging is habitually served. The club shall hold regular meetings, continue its business through officers regularly elected, admit members by written application, investigation and ballot and charge and collect dues from elected members.

b. Class II. A corporation or association organized or formed in good faith by authority of law and which must have at least 100 paid-up members. It must be the owner, lessee or occupant of an establishment operated solely for the objects of a national, social, patriotic, political or athletic nature or the like. The club shall hold regular meetings, continue its business through officers regularly elected, admit members by written application, investigation and ballot and charge and collect dues from elected members.

(8) CORPORATION. A corporation or joint stock association organized under the laws of this state, the United States, or any other state, territory or foreign country, or dependency.

(9) DRY COUNTY. Any county which by a majority of those voting voted in the negative in an election heretofore held under the applicable statutes at the time of said election or may hereafter vote in the negative in an election or special method referendum hereafter held in accordance with the provisions of chapter 2, Title 28, or held in accordance with the provisions of any act hereafter enacted permitting such election.

(10) DRY MUNICIPALITY. Any municipality within a wet county which has, by its governing body or by a majority of those voting in a municipal election heretofore held in accordance with the provisions of section 28-2-22, or in a municipal option election heretofore or hereafter held in accordance with the provisions of Act 84-408, Acts of Alabama 1984, appearing as chapter 2A, Title 28, Code of Alabama 1975, as amended, or any act hereafter enacted permitting municipal option election, voted to exclude the sale of alcoholic beverages within the corporate limits of said municipality.

(11) GENERAL WELFARE PURPOSES.

a. The administration of public assistance as set out in sections 38-2-5 and 38-4-1;

b. Services, including supplementation and supplementary services under the federal Social Security Act, to or on behalf of persons to whom such public assistance may be given under said sections 38-2-5 and 38-4-1;

c. Service to and on behalf of dependent, neglected or delinquent children; and

d. Investigative and referral services to and on behalf of needy persons.

(12) HEARING COMMISSION. A body appointed by the board to hear and decide all contested license applications and all disciplinary charges against any licensee for violation of this title or the regulations of the board.

(13) HOTEL. A building or buildings held out to the public for housing accommodations of travelers or transients, and shall include motel, but shall not include a rooming house or boarding house.

(14) IMPORTER. Any person, association or corporation engaged in importing alcoholic beverages, liquor, wine or beer, manufactured outside of the United States of America into this state or for sale or distribution in this state, or to the board or to a licensee of the board.

(15) LIQUOR. Any alcoholic, spirituous, vinous, fermented, or other alcoholic beverage, or combination of liquors and mixed liquor, a part of which is spirituous, fermented, vinous or otherwise alcoholic, and all drinks or drinkable liquids, preparations or mixtures intended for beverage purposes, which contain one-half of one percent or more of alcohol by volume, except beer and table wine.

(16) LIQUOR STORE. A liquor store operated by the board, where alcoholic beverages other than beer are authorized to be sold in unopened containers.

(17) MANUFACTURER. Any person, association or corporation engaged in the producing, bottling, manufacturing, distilling, rectifying or compounding of alcoholic beverages, liquor, beer or wine in this state or for sale or distribution in this state or to the board or to a licensee of the board.

(18) MINOR. Any person under 21 years of age, except a person 19 years of age or older prior to October 1, 1985, is not a minor; provided, however, in the event section 28-1-5, shall be repealed or otherwise shall be no longer in effect, thereafter the provisions of section 26-1-1, shall govern.

(19) MUNICIPALITY. Any incorporated city or town of this state to include its police jurisdiction.

(20) PERSON. Every natural person, association or corporation. Whenever used in a clause prescribing or imposing a fine or imprisonment, or both, such term as applied to "association" shall mean the partners or members thereof and as applied to "corporation" shall mean the officers thereof, except as to incorporated clubs the term "person" shall mean such individual or individuals who, under the bylaws of such clubs, shall have jurisdiction over the possession and sale of liquor therein.

(21) POPULATION. The population according to the last preceding or any subsequent decennial census of the United States, except where a municipality is incorporated subsequent to the last census, in which event, its population until the next decennial census shall be the population of said municipality as determined by the judge of probate of said county as the official population on the date of its incorporation.

(22) RESTAURANT. A reputable place licensed as a restaurant, operated by a responsible person of good reputation and habitually and principally used for the purpose of preparing and serving meals for the public to consume on the premises.

(23) MEAL. A diversified selection of food some of which is not susceptible of being consumed in the absence of at least some articles of tableware and which cannot be conveniently consumed while one is standing or walking about.

(24) RETAILER. Any person licensed by the board to engage in the retail sale of any alcoholic beverages to the consumer.

(25) SALE or SELL. Any transfer of liquor, wine or beer for a consideration, and any gift in connection with, or as a part of, a transfer of property other than liquor, wine or beer for a consideration.

(26) SELLING PRICE. The total marked-up price of spirituous or vinous liquors sold by the board, exclusive of taxes levied thereon.

(27) UNOPENED CONTAINER. A container containing alcoholic beverages, which has not been opened or unsealed subsequent to filling and sealing by the manufacturer or importer.

(28) WET COUNTY. Any county which by a majority of those voting voted in the affirmative in an election heretofore held in accordance with the statutes applicable at the time of said election or may hereafter vote in the affirmative in an election or special method referendum held in accordance with the provisions of chapter 2, of Title 28, or other statutes applicable at the time of said election.

(29) WET MUNICIPALITY. Any municipality in a dry county which by a majority of those voting voted in the affirmative in a municipal option election heretofore or hereafter held in accordance with the provisions of Act 84-408, Acts of Alabama 1984, appearing as chapter 2A, Title 28, as amended, or any act hereafter enacted permitting municipal option election, or any municipality which became wet by vote of the governing body or by the voters of the municipality heretofore or hereafter held under the special method referendum provisions of section 28-2-22, or as hereafter provided, where the county has become dry subsequent to the elected wet status of the municipality.

(30) WHOLESALER. Any person licensed by the board to engage in the sale and distribution of table wine and beer, or either of them, within this state, at wholesale only, to be sold by export or to retail licensees or other wholesale licensees or others within this state lawfully authorized to sell table wine and beer, or either of them, for the purpose of resale only.

(31) WINE. All beverages made from the fermentation of fruits, berries, or grapes, with or without added spirits, and produced in accordance with the laws and regulations of the United States, containing not more than 24 percent alcohol by volume, and shall include all sparkling wines, carbonated wines, special natural wines, rectified wines, vermouths, vinous beverages, vinous liquors, and like products, including restored or unrestored pure condensed juice.

(32) FORTIFIED WINE or VINOUS LIQUOR. Any wine containing more than 14 percent alcohol by volume but not more than 24 percent. Fortified wine is vinous liquor.

(33) TABLE WINE. Any wine containing not more than 14 percent alcohol by volume. Table wine is not liquor, spirituous or vinous.

(34) BRANDY. All beverages which are an alcoholic distillate from the fermented juice, mash, or wine of fruit, or from the residue thereof, produced in such manner that the distillate possesses the taste, aroma, and charac-

teristics generally attributed to the beverage, as bottled at not less than 80 degree proof. (Acts 1936-37, Ex. Sess., No. 66, p. 40; Code 1940, T. 29, §§ 1, 60; Acts 1967, No. 301, p. 839; Acts 1986, No. 86-212, § 1; Acts 1991, No. 91-211, p. 393, § 1.)

Subdivision (15)'s definition of "liquor" is not determinative of the definition of the term "spirituous liquors" in § 6-5-70. Espey v. Convenience Marketers, Inc., 578 So. 2d 1221 (Ala. 1991).

Summary judgment proper for defendant where plaintiff injured by negligent driving of volunteer waiter who was served free drinks at chamber of commerce function.

Smoyer v. Birmingham Area Chamber of Commerce, 517 So. 2d 585 (Ala. 1987).

Cited in Swint v. State ABC Bd., 628 So. 2d 769 (Ala. Civ. App. 1993).

Collateral references.

Social host's liability for injuries incurred by third parties as a result of intoxicated guest's negligence. 62 ALR4th 16.

§ 28-3-11. Invoices and receipts to be maintained by persons, firms, etc., selling or shipping goods, merchandise, etc., to persons, firms, etc., in another state or to federal government for army, navy or marine purposes; exemption from taxation goods purchased from Alcoholic Beverage Control Board for export to another country.

(a) Where goods, wares, or merchandise enumerated in this chapter are sold or shipped to any person, firm, corporation, or association of persons in another state, the seller or shipper in this state shall make and preserve for three years a duplicate invoice bill, giving the name of the person, firm, corporation, or association of persons to whom shipped, delivered, or sold, the date of sale or shipment, and the quantity of the merchandise sold or shipped. The seller in this state shall have on file a freight, express, or postal receipt for the merchandise showing that the merchandise was turned over to a common carrier engaged in interstate commerce. If the merchandise is delivered by a conveyance belonging to a seller in this state, the seller shall have on file a receipt signed by the purchasers showing the goods, wares, or merchandise were received by him or her in another state. All of the above records shall at all times be subject to the inspection and audit of any duly authorized agent of the board.

Notwithstanding any law to the contrary, no tax levied pursuant to this chapter shall be collected on any goods, wares, or merchandise purchased from the Alcoholic Beverage Control Board for export to another country provided all of the following conditions are met:

(1) The exporter is approved by the board based on any reasonable criteria set by the board by rule.

(2) The goods, wares, or merchandise are picked up by the exporter from the central distribution location of the board.

(3) The exporter operates only in a duty free zone.

(4) The exporter is subject to audit and inspection by the board.

The board may adopt any rules necessary to carry out the intent of this provision.

(b) Any goods, wares, or merchandise enumerated in this chapter that are sold to the United States government for army, navy, or marine purposes and which are shipped from a point within this state to a place which has been lawfully ceded to the United States government for army, navy, or marine purposes shall be subject to the same provisions as mentioned in subsection (a) for goods, wares, or merchandise sold or shipped to another state. Goods, wares, or merchandise enumerated in this chapter sold or delivered to ships belonging to the United States Navy for distribution and sale to members of the military establishment only or sold and delivered to ships regularly engaged in foreign or coastwise shipping between points in this state and points outside this state, shall be subject to the same provisions as mentioned in subsection (a) for goods, wares, or merchandise sold or shipped to another state.

(c) The board may promulgate rules and regulations from time to time to prevent any abuse of the provisions contained in this section.

(d) Any person, firm, corporation, or association of persons found guilty of violating any of the provisions of this section or who receives or stores any of the articles of alcoholic beverages enumerated in this chapter for sale within the State of Alabama shall be guilty of a misdemeanor and, upon conviction, shall be punished by a fine of not less than two hundred dollars ($200) nor more than five hundred dollars ($500) or by imprisonment in the county jail for a period not to exceed six months or both at the discretion of the court. (Acts 1936-37, Ex. Sess., No. 66, p. 40; Code 1940, T. 29, § 59; Acts 1995, No. 95-546, § 1.)

The 1995 amendment, effective July 31, 1995, in subsection (a), substituted "merchandise" for "same" in the second sentence of the first paragraph, in the second paragraph, added the language beginning "Notwithstanding any law" and ending "the following conditions are met," added subdivisions (1) through (4), and added the last sentence; in subsection (b), in the first sentence, substituted "are shipped" for "shall be shipped" and deleted "of this section" following "in subsection (a)," and in the second sentence deleted "which shall be" following "in this chapter" and deleted "of this section" following "in subsection (a)"; deleted "who shall be" following "persons" in subsection (d); and made nonsubstantive changes.

§ 28-3-16. Advertising of alcoholic beverages.

Collateral references.
Construction and application of restrictive covenants to the use of signs. 61 ALR4th 1028.

ARTICLE 2.

ALCOHOLIC BEVERAGE CONTROL BOARD.

Code Commissioner's note. — Acts 1992, No. 92-120, § 2 provides: "The existence and functioning of the Alcoholic Beverage Control Board, created and functioning pursuant to Sections 28-3-40 to 28-3-55, inclusive, Code of Alabama 1975, is continued, and those Code sections are expressly preserved."

§ 28-3-43. Functions, powers and duties of board generally; examination of board by examiners of public accounts.

Code Commissioner's note. — Acts 1994, No. 94-220, provides: "That it is the will of the Legislature of Alabama that the Alcoholic Beverage Control Board take appropriate action to increase the markup on alcoholic beverages sold by the state from 30 percent to 40 percent."

§ 28-3-49. Promulgation, amendment, etc., of regulations by board generally; introduction in evidence of regulations, etc.

Restrictions on bottomless and topless dress. — City ordinances which prohibited the exposing of a woman's breasts in establishments within the city were reasonable restrictions falling within the scope of the city's police power to promote public morals and to protect the public welfare, and were not arbitrary and did not directly conflict with state statute; rather, the ordinances enlarged its scope by restricting not only bottomless dress, but topless and other specified dress. Smith v. City of Huntsville, 515 So. 2d 72 (Ala. Crim. App. 1986).

A sale of liquor to a visibly intoxicated person is contrary to the provision of law. Attalla Golf & Country Club, Inc. v. Harris, 601 So. 2d 965 (Ala. 1992).

Cited in Lackey v. HealthAmerica Ala., 514 So. 2d 883 (Ala. 1987); Lanier v. City of Newton, 518 So. 2d 40 (Ala. 1987); Lanier v. City of Newton, 842 F.2d 253 (11th Cir. 1988).

§ 28-3-50. Promulgation of rules and regulations as to breaking of packages, affixing of stamps, inspections, etc., generally.

Collateral references.
Social host's liability for injuries incurred by third parties as a result of intoxicated guest's negligence. 62 ALR4th 16.

§ 28-3-53.2. "Board" and "mark up" defined; additional mark up credited to general fund.

Code Commissioner's note. — Acts 1994, No. 94-220, provides: "That it is the will of the Legislature of Alabama that the Alcoholic Beverage Control Board take appropriate action to increase the markup on alcoholic beverages sold by the state from 30 percent to 40 percent."

ARTICLE 5A.

EXCISE TAXES ON MALT OR BREWED BEVERAGES.

§ 28-3-184. Tax levied; collection; disposition of funds.

Cited in Childree v. Hubbert, 524 So. 2d 336 (Ala. 1988).

§ 28-3-187.1. Exemption from labeling requirement.

Any laws or parts of laws to the contrary notwithstanding, no manufacturer, importer or wholesaler licensee of fortified wine and vinous liquor and brandy, as defined by section 28-3-1, shall be required to comply with the provisions of section 28-3-187, nor any other provisions of laws, rules or regulations relating to the state labeling of certain containers of alcoholic beverages by such manufacturer, importer or wholesaler licensees. (Acts 1990, No. 90-576, p. 981; Acts 1991, No. 91-211, p. 393, § 1.)

ARTICLE 5B.

EXCISE TAX ON BEER.

**§ 28-3-190. Levy of tax; collection; disposition of proceeds by locali-
ties; enforcement and administration; penalties; exclu-
sive nature of tax.**

(a) *Levy.* — In addition to the excise tax levied by Article 5A of Chapter 3 of
this title and the licenses provided for by Chapter 3A of this title and by Section
28-3-194, and any acts amendatory thereof, supplementary thereto or substituted therefor, and municipal and county licenses, there is hereby levied a
privilege or excise tax on every person licensed under the provisions of said
Chapter 3A who sells, stores, or receives for the purpose of distribution, to any
person, firm, corporation, club or association within the State of Alabama any
beer. The tax levied hereby shall be measured by and graduated in accordance
with the volume of sales by such person of beer, and shall be an amount equal
to one and six hundred twenty-five thousands cents (1.625 cents) for each four
fluid ounces or fractional part thereof.

(b) *Collection.* — The tax levied by subsection (a) of this section shall be
added to the sales price of all beer sold, and shall be collected from the
purchasers. It shall be unlawful for any person who is required to pay the tax
in the first instance to fail or refuse to add to the sales price and collect from
the purchaser the required amount of tax, it being the intent and purpose of
this provision that the tax levied is in fact a tax on the consumer, with the
person, firm, corporation, club or association who pays the tax in the first
instance acting merely as an agent of the county or municipality for the
collection and payment of the tax.

The tax levied by subsection (a) of this section shall be collected by a return
in the form as prescribed or approved by the collection authority of the county
or municipality, which shall be filed by the wholesaler with the wet county and
wet municipality where sold postmarked not later than the 15th day of the
month following the month during which the beer is sold, which return shall be
accompanied by the remittance of the tax due; provided, where the taxes are
timely paid, the tax due shall be discounted by two and one-half percent, which
discount shall, subject to the provisions of Section 28-3-195, be retained by said
wholesaler for collecting the tax.

The county and municipality each shall have the authority to inspect,
examine and audit the books and records of any person, firm, corporation, club
or association who sells, stores, or receives for the purpose of distribution, any
beer, to determine the accuracy of any return required to be filed with it.

The county shall have the authority to require any beer wholesaler not
having a place of business within that county, who makes any sale, distribution
or delivery of beer within the county to first obtain a permit from the beer tax
collection authority of the county collecting the tax levied by this article.

The county and municipality shall have the authority to require any
wholesale beer licensee, who sells, distributes or delivers beer within the

county, to file with the tax collection authority a bond in the penal sum not to exceed twice the amount of the average monthly tax due by the licensee to such authority estimated by such tax collection authority, conditioned upon the payment of the tax on beer levied by this article to become due by the licensee.

(c) *Disposition of proceeds.* — The proceeds of the tax levied by subsection (a) of this section shall be paid and distributed as follows:

(1) Except as hereinafter provided in subdivision (2) or (3) of this subsection (c), one and six hundred twenty-five thousandths cents (1.625 cents) per four fluid ounces or fractional part thereof shall be paid by wholesale licensees on their sales either into the treasury of the wet municipality in which the beer was sold or delivered by a wholesaler to a retailer within its corporate limits, or, where sold outside the corporate limits of any municipality, into the treasury of the wet county in which the beer was sold or delivered by the wholesaler to a retailer.

(2) Provided, however, such tax shall otherwise be paid and disposed of in the following counties, as hereinafter set forth:

a. Autauga County: The entire amount of the tax collected on sales outside of the area comprised by the corporate limits and police jurisdictions of the cities of Prattville and Autaugaville shall be paid to the Autauga County Commission. Outside the corporate limits but within the police jurisdictions of said municipalities, two-thirds of the amount of the tax shall be paid to the county commission and one-third shall be paid to the respective municipality. Within the actual corporate limits of Autaugaville and Prattville, two-thirds of the tax shall be paid to the governing body of the respective municipality and one-third shall be paid to the county commission.

b. Baldwin County: The taxes shall be paid as follows:

1. All the taxes collected on sales within the corporate limits of any municipality shall be paid to said municipality.

2. One-half the taxes collected on sales within the police jurisdiction of any municipality shall be paid to said municipality and the remaining one-half shall be paid to the county.

3. All of the taxes on sales outside the corporate limits of any municipality and outside of any police jurisdiction shall be paid to the local board of education with the funds to be used for capital outlay, maintenance of existing buildings and instructional materials.

c. Calhoun County: The entire amount of the tax shall be collected by the Calhoun County Probate Judge and paid to the Calhoun County Commission. All such taxes, after first reimbursing the county general fund for expenses incurred in administration and enforcement of the tax, shall be distributed as follows:

1. Six-ninths of the total amount of the tax shall be turned over by it to the custodian of county school funds. The county board of education shall immediately divide the funds with the city boards of education within the county on the same basis as the total calculated costs of the Foundation Program for the local boards of education within the county.

2. One-ninth of the total amount of the tax or $150,000.00, whichever is greater, shall be paid to the Calhoun County Economic Development Council.

3. The balance of the total amount of the tax shall be distributed to certain municipalities as follows:

Anniston	28½%
Oxford	21½%
Jacksonsville	28%
Piedmont	17%
Hobson City	2%
Ohatchee	2%
Weaver	1%

4. All reference in the general bill to county or municipalities shall apply to the probate judge or his designated agent in Calhoun County.

d. Chambers County: The entire amount of the tax shall be paid to the Chambers County Commission or like governing body of Chambers County, which, after the payment of all cost of collection and enforcement, shall distribute the net proceeds as follows:

1. Fifty percent be prorated among the local boards of education for educational purposes on the basis of the previous year's net enrollment of pupils;

2. Fifty percent be prorated among the Chambers County Commission General Fund and the municipalities within the county, with each municipality receiving the amount that its population bears to the entire population of the county, and the general fund of the county receiving the amount that the population of the county outside the corporate limits of the municipalities bears to the entire population of the county according to the latest federal census. In the event of the incorporation of any new municipalities, the proration shall be based on the official population of the municipality at the time of incorporation. Any annexation shall accrue to the city annexing according to the population annexed.

3. Fifteen percent of the amount prorated to the county general fund in subparagraph 2 of this paragraph shall be prorated among the fire and rescue squads located within the county.

e. Choctaw County: The entire amount of tax shall be paid to the probate judge and, after reimbursement of two and one-half percent for services distributed as follows:

1. One-ninth to the county general fund from which $7,000.00 shall be credited to:

(i)   One-third to the Choctaw County Rescue Squad.

(ii) One-third to the Choctaw County Historical Society.

(iii) One-third to the Choctaw County library system.

2. Of remainder, $20,000.00 to Choctaw County Board of Education.

3. Remainder up to $90,000.00 to the county and municipalities on the basis of population.

4. Of revenue in excess of $90,000.00, 20 percent to the county board of education and remainder to the county and municipalities on the basis of population.

f. Colbert County: One cent per twelve fluid ounces or fractional part thereof on all beer sold, within the county shall be paid to the probate judge and the proceeds shall be distributed by him or her as follows:

Two-fifths to the hospital fund of the county;

One-fifth to the county board of education for the benefit of the schools outside of the cities of Sheffield and Tuscumbia;

One-tenth to the Tuscumbia Board of Education for the benefit of the schools of the City of Tuscumbia;

One-tenth to the Sheffield Board of Education for the benefit of the schools of Sheffield; and

One-fifth to the general fund of the county.

For such services, the probate judge shall be entitled to commissions of two and one-half percent of all taxes collected.

The remainder of the tax shall be paid to the municipalities where sold.

g. Conecuh County: The entire amount of the tax shall be paid to the Treasurer of Conecuh County, who, after first reimbursing the county general fund for all expenses incurred in the administration and enforcement of the tax, shall distribute the remainder of the proceeds of said tax as follows: one-third to be prorated between the municipalities of Evergreen, Repton and Castleberry upon the basis of their respective populations; one-third to be paid over to the general fund of the county; and one-third to be paid to the Conecuh County Board of Education to be expended for educational purposes.

h. Coosa County: The tax proceeds shall be paid by wholesalers as follows:

1. One cent per container sold within the corporate limits of the municipalities within the county shall be paid directly to the municipalities where sold.

2. The remainder of the tax shall be paid to the Coosa County Commission and shall be distributed as follows:

(i) Fifty percent shall be deposited in the public school fund of the county to be used solely for public school purposes of Coosa County.

(ii) Fifty percent shall be deposited in the general fund of the county for general purposes of the county.

i. Dale County: Any law to the contrary notwithstanding, in Dale County, the proceeds of the beer tax collected pursuant to this article shall be paid to the county commission and distributed as follows:

1. 44.17 percent to the Dale County Commission;

2. The remaining 55.83 percent of the tax shall be distributed to each municipality according to beer sales in its respective corporate limits.

j. Dallas County: The entire amount of the tax collected on sales outside of the area comprised by the corporate limits and police jurisdiction of the City of Selma shall be paid to the Dallas County Commission.

The tax collected on sales inside the corporate limits of the City of Selma and its police jurisdiction shall be paid as follows: 72.23 percent to be paid to the city and its board of education, with one-third of such 72.23 percent to be paid to the city and two-thirds of such 72.23 percent to be paid to the city board of education (the Board of Education of the City of Selma); and 27.77 percent to be paid to the Dallas County Commission.

k. Elmore County: The entire amount of tax shall be paid to the Elmore County Commission or other governing body of Elmore County and the net revenue, after first reimbursing the county general fund for all expenses incurred in the administration and enforcement of the tax, shall be distributed as follows: One-half of the net revenue from the tax shall be paid to Elmore County Board of Education; one-half the tax collected on sales inside the corporate limits of any municipality within the county and one-fourth of the taxes collected on sales made within the police jurisdiction of any municipality in the county shall be paid to such municipality; and the balance shall be paid into the Elmore County General Fund.

l. Escambia County: The entire amount of tax shall be paid to the Judge of Probate of Escambia County and the net revenue, after first reimbursing the county general fund for all expenses incurred in the administration and enforcement of the tax, shall be distributed, as follows: Two and one-half percent to the judge of probate; 60 percent of the remainder to be prorated among the municipalities within the county upon the basis of their respective populations; and 40 percent of the remainder to be prorated among the local boards of education for educational purposes on the basis of the previous year's net enrollment of pupils.

m. Etowah County: The entire amount of tax shall be paid to the Etowah County Commission and the net revenue, after first reimbursing the county general fund for all expenses incurred in the administration and enforcement of the tax, shall be distributed, as follows:

1. For beer delivered for retail sale within the corporate limits of a municipality having a board of education, all such proceeds shall be distributed according to the following percentages: 20.83 ⅓ percent to the Etowah County General Fund; 20.38 ⅓ percent to the local boards of education of Etowah County, to be divided pro rata among them in accordance with the most recent average daily membership figures, to be used only for capital outlay purposes, renovation and repairs; 58.33 ⅓ percent to the general fund of the municipality.

2. For beer delivered for retail sale outside the city or town limits, but within the police jurisdiction, of a municipality having a board of education, all such proceeds shall be distributed according to the following percentages: 12.50 percent to the Etowah County Board of Education, to be used for capital outlay purposes, renovation and repairs; 20.83 ⅓ percent to the local boards of education in Etowah County to be divided pro rata among them in accordance with the most recent average daily membership figures, to be used for capital outlay purposes, renovation, and repairs; 29.16 ⅔ percent to the general fund of the municipality; 37.50 percent to the Etowah County General Fund.

3. For beer delivered for retail sale within the city or town limits of a municipality not having a board of education, all such proceeds shall be distributed according to the following percentages: 20.83 ⅓ percent to the Etowah County General Fund; 20.83 ⅓ percent to the local boards of education in Etowah County, to be divided pro rata among them in accordance with the most recent average daily membership figures, to be used for capital outlay purposes, renovation and repairs; 33.33 ⅓ percent to the general fund of the municipality; 25.00 percent to the Etowah County Board of Education to be used for capital outlay purposes, renovation and repairs;

4. For beer delivered for retail sale outside the city or town limits, but within the police jurisdiction of a municipality not having a board of education, all such proceeds shall be distributed according to the following percentages: 16.66 ⅔ percent to the general fund of the municipality; 20.83 ⅓ percent to the local boards of education within Etowah County to be divided pro rata among them in accordance with the most recent average daily membership figures, to be used for capital outlay purposes, renovation and repairs; 25.00 percent to the Etowah County Board of Education, to be used for capital outlay purposes, renovation and repairs, 37.50 percent to the Etowah County General Fund.

5. For beer delivered for retail sale in locations which are within the boundaries of Etowah County, Alabama, but not within the corporate limits or police jurisdiction of any municipality, all such proceeds shall be distributed according to the following percentages: 20.83 ⅓ percent to the local boards of education in Etowah County divided in accordance with the most recent average daily membership figures to be used for capital outlay purposes, renovation or repairs; 25.00 percent to the Etowah County Board of Education, to be used for capital outlay purposes, renovation or repairs; 54.16 ⅔ percent to the Etowah County General Fund.

6. For draft beer sold and delivered within all areas in Etowah County, all proceeds shall be distributed according to the following percentage: 83.33 ⅓ percent to the local boards of education in Etowah County to be divided pro rata among them in accordance with the most recent average daily membership figure to be used for capital outlay purposes, renovation and repairs; 16.66 ⅔ percent to the municipalities in Etowah County within which draft beer is sold at retail, to be divided among them pro rata according to the population.

n. Greene County: The entire amount of the tax shall be paid to the Judge of Probate of Greene County and distributed by him or her as follows: two and one-half percent to the probate judge as commission for collection and administration; two-fifths of the remainder to the general fund of the county; two-fifths of the remainder to the county board of education; and one-fifth prorated among the municipalities within the county upon the basis of their respective populations.

o. Hale County: The entire amount of tax shall be paid to the Hale County Commission or like governing body of Hale County and the net revenue, after first reimbursing the county general fund for all expenses incurred in the administration and enforcement of the tax, shall be prorated among the county and municipalities therein upon the basis of their respective populations.

p. Jefferson County: The tax as provided in subsection (a) of this section shall be paid by wholesalers to the Director of Revenue of Jefferson County. The tax received by the Director of Revenue shall be divided into Funds A, B and C. Fund A shall receive four-ninths of the tax received; Fund B shall receive two-ninths of the tax received; and Fund C shall receive three-ninths of the tax received. Funds A, B and C shall be distributed by the Director of Revenue on a monthly basis as follows:

1. Two percent of the net tax collected and placed in Fund A shall be paid to the general treasury of the county for the collection and distribution of said tax, and for the enforcement of the provisions of this article. The remaining amount in Fund A shall be distributed as follows:

(i) Two-eighths shall be paid to the county board of education for the payment of salaries of public school teachers.

(ii) Three-eighths shall be retained in the general treasury of the county.

(iii) Three-eighths shall be distributed to the incorporated municipalities within the county upon the basis of their respective populations, according to the federal census at the time the distribution is made.

2. Fund B shall be distributed to the municipalities in the county on the basis of the percentage of the beer taxed which was delivered to a retailer within the respective corporate limits of each municipality in the county.

3. Fund C shall be distributed as follows:

(i) Fifty percent, or $2,000,000.00 annually, whichever is the greater, shall be paid to the Birmingham-Jefferson County Transit Authority or its successor.

(ii) The balance shall be divided between the county and the incorporated municipalities within the county upon a population basis with the municipal share determined by the respective populations of said municipalities, and the county share by the population of the unincorporated areas thereof, according to the last federal census at the time the distribution is made.

(iii) Of the total amount of the county share, five percent shall be allocated for fire protection and paramedic services and equipment in fire districts in the unincorporated areas of the county. Such distribution shall be made to each such fire district on a pro rata basis that the number of homes and businesses served in that district bears to the total number of homes and businesses served in all such fire districts in the unincorporated areas.

q. Lee County: The entire amount of tax shall be paid to the Lee County Commission or like governing body of Lee County and shall be distributed to the custodian of the county school fund, the custodian of the Opelika City School Fund and the custodian of the Auburn City School Fund on the same basis as the total calculated costs of the Foundation Program for the local boards of education within the county. Provided however that any subsidy received shall be paid to the City of Auburn.

r. Lowndes County: The tax proceeds shall be paid by wholesalers as follows:

1. One cent shall be distributed to municipalities in the following manner:

(i) One-third to municipalities that have an existing beer tax distributed on a population basis.

(ii) Two-thirds to go to all municipalities including those that have an existing beer tax distributed on a population basis.

2. One cent to be distributed as follows:

(i) One-twelfth to the county board of education and three-twelfths to the probate judge for services rendered.

(ii) Two-thirds to the county commission for the performance of services.

3. The remainder to be equally divided between the public school fund and the juvenile service trust fund account.

s. Macon County: The entire amount of tax shall be paid to the Macon County Commission or like governing body of Macon County and the net revenue, after first reimbursing the county general fund for all expenses incurred in the administration and enforcement of the tax, shall be distributed by it as follows: Six-twelfths of the net proceeds shall be paid into the general fund of said county to be used for governmental purposes of the county as other moneys in the general fund; four-twelfths shall be apportioned and distributed to the City of Tuskegee and shall be deposited into its general fund to be used for governmental purposes of the city as other moneys in the general fund of said city are used; one-twelfth shall be apportioned and distributed to the Town of Notasulga and deposited into the general fund of said town to be used for governmental purposes of the town as are other moneys in the general fund of said town; one-twelfth shall be apportioned and distributed to the Town of Franklin and deposited into the general fund of said town to be used for governmental purposes of the town as are other moneys in the general fund of said town.

t. Madison County: The proceeds of the tax shall be paid by wholesalers to the county commission or like governing body and shall be distributed as follows:

1. One-eighteenth to the county general fund.

2. The remainder of the tax shall be distributed to the municipality where sold, including its police jurisdiction. Provided, however, that the following municipalities shall receive a dollar amount no less than the dollar amount actually received during the base year 1982:

177

Gurley
New Hope
Owens Crossroads
Triana
Madison

u. Marengo County: The entire amount of the tax shall be paid to the Probate Judge of Marengo County, who shall receive two and one-half percent of all taxes collected as compensation for administering this article and the remainder of the net revenue, after first reimbursing the county general fund for all expenses incurred in the administration and enforcement of the tax, shall be distributed by him or her as follows: The municipalities shall receive the taxes paid on all sales within the corporate limits and police jurisdiction of each municipality, and the county shall receive the tax on all sales made outside the corporate limits and police jurisdictions of all municipalities within the county.

v. Mobile County: The entire amount of tax shall be paid to the License Commissioner of Mobile County and the net revenue, after first reimbursing the county general fund for all expenses incurred in the administration and enforcement of the tax, shall be distributed by him or her as follows: One-half to the governing body of the municipality where the malt or brewed beverages are sold within its corporate limits; and the remainder to the Board of School Commissioners of Mobile County.

w. Perry County: The tax shall be paid to the county governing body and be distributed as follows:

1. Except as hereinafter provided in subparagraph 2 of this paragraph, the proceeds shall be distributed as follows:

(i) The taxes collected on sales within the corporate limits of the Municipality of Marion shall be paid to said municipality.

(ii) The taxes collected on sales within the corporate limits of the Municipality of Uniontown shall be paid to said municipality.

(iii) The taxes collected on sales outside the police jurisdiction of a municipality and outside the corporate limits of any municipality shall be retained by the county.

(iv) The taxes collected on sales outside of a municipality's corporate limits but within said municipality's police jurisdiction shall be distributed in the following manner:

Three-fourths of the tax proceeds shall be retained by the county.

One-fourth of the tax proceeds shall be paid to the municipality controlling said police jurisdiction.

2. Until the conditions set forth in this subparagraph 2 have been satisfied, one-ninth shall be deducted from each of the foregoing distributions and retained by Perry County and earmarked for the purpose of purchasing mechanical voting machines with lever action and curtain and creating an election expense fund in the amount of $20,000.00. Said voting machines shall be purchased by May 1, 1982, and said election expense fund shall be used to pay board of registrars members' compen-

sation and for election supplies and materials, election handling, storage and other expense. When the cost of the voting machines and election expense fund have been collected by the county, the right to deduct pursuant to this subparagraph 2 shall expire and the entire proceeds shall be distributed pursuant to and in accordance with subparagraph 1 hereof.

x. Russell County: The taxes shall be paid and distributed as follows:

1. Payment of taxes collected by wholesalers.

(i) All the taxes collected on sales within the corporate limits of the municipality of Phenix City shall be paid to said municipality.

(ii) All the taxes collected on sales within the corporate limits of the Municipality of Hurtsboro shall be paid to said municipality.

(iii) One-half the taxes collected on sales within the police jurisdiction of Phenix City and Hurtsboro shall be paid to the respective municipality and the remaining one-half shall be paid to the county.

(iv) All of the taxes on sales outside the corporate limits of any municipality and outside of any police jurisdiction shall be paid to the county.

2. Distribution of county proceeds. All such taxes, after first reimbursing the county general fund for all expenses incurred in administration and enforcement of the tax, shall be used equally for the county school system and the county general fund. Of the moneys going to the county general fund, half of said amount shall be distributed to the volunteer fire departments in Russell County on a per department basis, who are recognized as legal fire districts.

y. St. Clair County: The entire amount of tax shall be paid to the St. Clair County Commission or like governing body of St. Clair County and the net revenue, after reimbursing the county general fund for all expenses incurred in the administration and enforcement of the tax, shall be distributed by it as follows: One-third cent per four fluid ounces or fraction thereof to the governing body of each municipality where beer is sold within its corporate limits and one-sixth cent per four fluid ounces or fraction thereof to the governing body of each municipality where beer is sold within its police jurisdiction; the remainder to be distributed as follows: 25 percent to be paid to the Road and Building Fund of the General Fund of St. Clair County, which money shall be used for the operation of the St. Clair County Road Department, in the building and maintenance of all public roads and bridges in the county; 20.83 ⅓ percent of the remainder to the St. Clair County Board of Education; 8.33 ⅓ percent of the remainder to the St. Clair County Library Board to be used by the board for the use of libraries and/or book mobiles throughout the county; and 45.83 ⅓ percent to the General Fund of St. Clair County to be disbursed by the St. Clair County governing body as other funds of the county are disbursed.

z. Shelby County: The entire amount of tax shall be paid to the Shelby County Commission or like governing body of Shelby County to the credit of its county general fund and the net revenue, after first reimbursing the county general fund for all expenses incurred in the administration and enforcement of the tax, shall be disbursed as follows: Two-ninths of the net proceeds of such tax shall be paid to the Shelby County Board of Education; three-ninths of the net proceeds of such tax shall, on or before the 25th day of each month, be paid to the municipalities of Shelby County in the same ratio as the population of each municipality bears to the total population of all municipalities in Shelby County; two-ninths shall be paid into the Shelby County Law Enforcement Personnel Board Fund to be used for the purposes set forth in Act No. 79-524, Acts of Alabama 1979; and the remaining two-ninths of the net proceeds shall remain in the Shelby County General Fund to be disbursed by the county governing body.

aa. Sumter County: The entire proceeds of the tax shall be paid to the county treasurer. After the payment of all cost of collection and enforcement of the tax, the treasurer shall pay into the general fund of each incorporated municipality four-ninths of the revenue produced within the corporate limits of said municipality and the remainder shall be paid into the general fund of the county, from which $7,000.00 shall be credited to a legislative delegation fund to be controlled by the legislative delegation of Sumter County.

bb. Talladega County: The tax shall be paid to the probate judge and, after deduction of all expenses of collecting and administering the tax, the proceeds of the tax shall be distributed as follows: After determining net revenue received in the base year (county plus all municipalities), distribution of future revenue to each entity presently receiving beer tax distributions shall be in the same proportion as each entity's revenue to the total net revenue was during the base year.

The following entities shall be entitled to a share of beer tax revenue:

Talladega County	Community of Munford
Talladega County Board of Education	Community of Eastaboga
City of Talladega	North Talladega County Association for Retarded Citizens, Inc.
City of Sylacauga	
City of Childersburg	South Talladega County Association for Retarded Citizens, Inc.
City of Lincoln	

Provided, however, that from the county share, the sum of $6,500.00 shall be spent as follows:

1. The sum of $1,500.00 per annum shall be spent in the unincorporated community of Eastaboga for public projects for the benefit of said community;

2. The sum of $2,500.00 per annum shall be spent in the unincorporated community of Munford to provide rural health care in the existing rural health clinic in said community; and

3. The sum of $2,500.00 per annum shall be spent in the unincorporated community of Munford for youth activities, including the construction, improvement, lighting and maintenance of athletic playing fields. The North and South Talladega County Associations for Retarded Citizens, Inc. shall receive from the county the same proportion of revenue received during the base year (1982).

Provided further, that the Talladega County Board of Education shall divide its share of the beer tax revenue between itself and the city boards of education now existing within the county on the same basis as the total calculated costs of the Foundation Program for the local boards of education within the county.

cc. Tallapoosa County: The tax, after converting all sales to cases equivalent to 24 12-ounce containers and after deducting the two and one-half percent discount authorized by this article, shall be paid by wholesalers as follows:

1. Two cents per equivalent 12-ounce container sold or delivered to retail licensees within the county shall be paid to the custodian of public school funds of Tallapoosa County and shall be used and expended for public school purposes. Such funds shall be apportioned among the local boards of education on the same basis as the total calculated costs of the Foundation Program for the local boards of education within the county.

2. The remainder of the tax shall be paid to the county commission or like governing body and distributed as follows:

56.4 percent to Alexander City

43.6 percent to the county for distribution, based on sales, either into the treasury of the municipalities (except Alexander City) in which the beer was sold or delivered by a wholesaler to a retailer within its corporate limits, or, where sold outside the corporate limits of any municipality into the treasury of the county.

3. Any subsidy received under the provisions of this article shall be distributed as provided for in subparagraph 2 above.

dd. Tuscaloosa County:

1. Forty-five percent of the tax shall be paid to the Probate Judge of Tuscaloosa County and shall by him be distributed in the same manner as provided in Act 556 of the 1953 Regular Session of the Alabama Legislature; and 55 percent shall be paid to the Probate Judge of Tuscaloosa County and shall by him or her be distributed in accordance with Act 81-739 of the 1981 Regular Session of the Alabama Legislature.

2. Any subsidy received by Tuscaloosa County pursuant to Section 28-3-196 shall be paid and distributed among the county, municipalities and the Tuscaloosa County Parks and Recreation Authority in accordance with the ratio of any net revenue loss of each such entity to the total subsidy paid to the county.

ee. Wilcox County: The entire tax revenue shall be paid to the Wilcox County Commission or like governing body of Wilcox County and disbursed as follows: Two and one-half percent of the gross tax receipts to be paid as to the Probate Judge of Wilcox County as a fee for the administration and enforcement; the remainder shall be disbursed as follows: 50 percent to be prorated between the incorporated municipalities in Wilcox County upon the basis of their respective populations; and 50 percent to be paid over to the general fund of the county. Provided, however, prior to the distribution provided for in this subsection, the sum of $400.00 per month shall be paid to the Wilcox County Civil Defense Agency.

(3) Or, such tax shall otherwise be paid and disposed of in accordance with and pursuant to any local act or general act of local application hereafter enacted with respect to any county directing a different disposition or apportionment of the proceeds of the tax.

(d)(1) For all purposes of enforcement of the provisions of this article, it is a prima facie presumption of law that any wholesaler or jobber subject to the article has accrued a liability for the taxes levied herein for the total amount of alcoholic beverages handled by it during any tax period under the article. The burden of proof is upon any such person to prove that any such alcoholic beverages disposed of in such a manner as not to become subject to the taxes imposed in this article were so disposed of in such a manner. It shall be the duty of any person subject to the privilege or license tax imposed by this article to keep full and complete records of all purchases, sales, receipts, inventories and of all other matters from which the correct amount of privilege or license tax to which such person is subject may be ascertained; and, in the event that such person shall discontinue his or her business, he or she shall not destroy or dispose of such records until he or she shall have given the probate judge of the county 30 days' notice in writing of his or her intent to destroy or dispose of such records. The failure of such person to keep such records, or his or her destruction or disposition of such records without giving such notice, shall constitute a misdemeanor.

(2) Upon demand by the probate judge or his or her authorized deputy, auditor or representative, it shall be the duty of any such person subject to the privilege or license tax imposed by this article to furnish such demanding person, without delay, all such information as may be required for determination of the correct amount of privilege or license tax to which such person is subject, and to that end it shall be the duty of such person to submit to such demanding person, for inspection and examination, during reasonable hours, at such person's place of business within the county, all books of accounts, invoices, papers, reports, memoranda containing entries showing the amount of purchases, sales, receipts, inventories, and any other information from which the correct amount of privilege or license tax to which such person is subject may be determined including exhibition of bank deposit books and bank statements; and any person failing or refusing to submit such records for such inspection and examination upon such demand, shall be guilty of a misdemeanor.

(3) If any person subject to the provisions of this article does not have in such person's control or possession, within the county, true and intelligible books of account, invoices, papers, reports or memoranda correctly showing

the data and information necessary for determination of the correct amount of the privilege or license tax due, or if, having in such person's possession or under such person's control such books, invoices, papers, reports or memoranda, such person shall fail or refuse to submit and exhibit the same for inspection and examination as herein required, then, in either event, it shall be the duty of the probate judge of the county to ascertain, from such information and data as he may reasonably obtain, the correct amount of license tax due from such person and immediate payment of the amount of such privilege or license tax shall be made.

(4) All records and reports filed in the probate office under this article shall be public records and shall be open to inspection by any person during all probate office hours.

(5) The probate judge of the county shall provide rules and regulations and administrative machinery for the enforcement and collection of the privilege or license taxes authorized by this article. Each municipality within the county shall provide aid and assistance in collecting the taxes herein provided for within its territory. The probate judge may employ a person or persons to act as inspectors and otherwise to assist in the enforcement of the provisions of this article. The salary and expenses of such inspectors shall be paid out of the county general fund in such manner as is provided by law. Such inspectors shall have the same powers relative to enforcement of the taxes hereby levied that law enforcement officers employed by the Alabama Alcoholic Beverage Control Board have relative to enforcing the state tax on spirituous liquors and on malt and brewed beverages. Any municipality in the county may also employ a special alcoholic beverage law enforcement officer for such municipality whose chief duty shall be enforcement of this article.

(6) In addition to all other records and reports required under this article, each wholesale distributor shall, by the twentieth day of each month, file a report with the probate judge showing his or her inventory of beer on the first day of the preceding month, by brand and type of container, his or her inventory of beer on the last day of the preceding month, an accounting for all beer broken or damaged during the preceding month, proof of state authorization for transfers to other wholesale distributors, and a record of all beer in transit to such distributor from breweries.

(7) In addition to all other records and reports required under this article, each private club shall file with the probate judge on or before the twentieth day of each month detailed inventory of all alcoholic beverages on hand on the first day and the last day of the preceding month, and a record of all purchases of alcoholic beverages made by it during the preceding month.

(8) In addition to all other reports and records required under this article, each retail beer seller shall file with the probate judge on or before the twentieth day of each month a detailed inventory of all beer on hand on the first day and the last day of the preceding month.

(9) The license of any wholesale distributor, private club, or retail seller failing or refusing to file the reports shall be suspended forthwith by the probate judge pending receipt of such report.

(e) The tax herein levied is exclusive and shall be in lieu of all other or additional local taxes and licenses, county or municipal, imposed on or measured by the sale or volume of sale of beer; provided that nothing herein contained shall be construed to exempt the retail sales of beer from the levy of a tax on general retail sales by the county or municipality in the nature of, or in lieu of, a general sales tax. (Acts 1982, No. 82-344, p. 473, § 1; Acts 1983, No. 83-641, p. 989; 1988, 1st Ex. Sess., No. 88-950, p. 571; Acts 1995, No. 95-261, § 2.)

The 1995 amendment, effective June 26, 1995, and to be implemented with the beginning of the 1995-96 fiscal year, substituted "wholesale beer licensee" for "wholesale beer license" in the last paragraph of subsection (b); in subdivision (c)(2) substituted "local boards" for "city and county boards" and "membership figures" for "attendance figures" throughout the subdivision, substituted "local board" for "county board" in subparagraph b3, in subparagraph c1, substituted "Six-ninths" for "Sixth-ninths" in the first sentence, and substituted the language beginning "on the same basis as the total" for "pro rata in the same manner as the public school funds from the state are appointed in said county under the minimum program fund law," substituted "be prorated" for "by prorated" in subparagraph d1, substituted "municipal share" for "municipal shall" in item p3(ii), substituted the language beginning "on the same basis as the total" for "in the same manner and at the same rate that the state minimum school program funds are distributed" in the first sentence of paragraph q, inserted "actually" in subparagraph t2, substituted "into" for "in" preceding "the Shelby County law enforcement" in paragraph z, inserted "be" preceding "distributed as follows" in the first paragraph of paragraph bb, substituted the language beginning "on the same basis as the total" for "pro rata in the same manner as the public school funds from the state are appointed in said county under the minimum program fund law" in the last paragraph of paragraph bb, in subparagraph cc1, in the second sentence substituted "local boards of education" for "county and city school systems," inserted "same," and substituted "as the total calculated costs of the Foundation Program for the local boards of education" for "of the current ratio distribution formula used in apportionment of minimum program funds"; substituted "data and information" for "date and information" in subdivision (d)(3); and made nonsubstantive changes.

As to audit and collection of taxes on beer or table wine by alcoholic beverage control board for the benefit of local governing bodies under certain conditions, see § 28-7A-1 et seq.

The Uniform Beer Tax is an exclusive tax and is in lieu of all local taxes and license fees measured by the sale of beer except for a general sales tax. Danny's, Inc. v. City of Muscle Shoals, 620 So. 2d 8 (Ala. Civ. App. 1992).

Collateral references. — Social host's liability for injuries incurred by third parties as a result of intoxicated guest's negligence. 62 ALR4th 16.

§ 28-3-192. Unlawful acts and offenses; penalties.

Collateral references. — Social host's liability for injuries incurred by third parties as a result of intoxicated guest's negligence. 62 ALR4th 16.

ARTICLE 6.

TAXES ON SALE OF SPIRITUOUS OR VINOUS LIQUORS.

§ 28-3-200. Additional 10 percent tax — Alcoholic beverage control board store fund.

Legislative intent. — The intent of legislature in the use of the term "purchaser" in the section was for the liquor taxes, as it was for the beer and wine taxes, to be on the ultimate consumer, not the retail stores buying at wholesale for resale. Any other interpretation would lead to double taxation, which should be avoided whenever possible. Guthrie Enters., Inc. v. City of Decatur, 595 So. 2d 1358 (Ala. 1992).

The liquor taxes imposed by §§ 28-3-200 through 28-3-205 are consumer taxes and may properly be deducted from a retailer's gross receipts for purposes of computation and payment of the county license tax and sales tax. S & L Beverages & Blends, Inc. v. Ritchie, 567 So. 2d 341 (Ala. Civ. App. 1990).

State stores and package stores, in that they both sell liquor at retail, are engaged in the same business and any difference in treatment by the state department of revenue would violate the fourteenth amendment. State Dep't of Revenue v. B & B Beverage, Inc., 534 So. 2d 1114 (Ala. Civ. App. 1987).

§ 28-3-203. Additional five percent tax.

(a) Repealed by Acts 1986, No. 86-212, § 3.

(b) *Levy and collection.* — In addition to all other taxes of every kind now imposed by law and in addition to any marked-up price authorized or required by law, there is hereby levied and shall be collected a tax at the rate of 13 percent upon the selling price of all spirituous or vinous liquors sold by the board. The tax imposed by this subsection shall be collected by the board from the purchaser at the time the purchase price is paid.

The markup as currently established by the board on spirituous or vinous liquors shall not be reduced by the board for the purpose of absorbing the tax levied by this subsection, it being the intention of this provision that the said tax shall be passed on to the purchaser.

(c) *Disposition of proceeds.*

(1) 38.5 percent of the revenues collected under the provisions of subsection (b) of this section shall be paid into the state treasury to the credit of the general fund.

(2) 61.5 percent of the revenues collected under the provisions of subsection (b) of this section are hereby irrevocably pledged and hereby appropriated for the purposes of providing for payment of the principal of, premium, if any, and interest on, all bonds issued by the Alabama mental health finance authority, as authorized by Title 41, chapter 10, article 11, in the amount that may be necessary for such purposes to the extent and only to the extent that the revenues appropriated for such purposes under section 40-25-23 are not sufficient to pay at their respective maturities the principal of, premium, if any, and interest on, such bonds.

(d) Any portion of the aforesaid 61.5 percent of the revenues pledged and appropriated in subdivision (c)(2), above, not needed in any fiscal year shall be deposited in the state treasury to the credit of the state general fund. (Acts 1969, No. 550, p. 1033; Acts 1986, No. 86-212, § 3; Acts 1988, 1st Ex. Sess., No. 88-869, p. 380.)

ARTICLE 7.

TAX AND IDENTIFICATION STAMPS, CROWNS OR LIDS.

§§ 28-3-220 through 28-3-226. Repealed by Acts 1995, No. 95-755, § 1, effective August 7, 1995.

Code Commissioner's note. — Acts 1995, No. 95-755, § 2 provides: "All laws or parts thereof which are inconsistent with the repeal of these statutes enumerated herein are repealed; except, nothing herein contained shall be construed as amended or repealing Section 28-3-187, Code of Alabama 1975."

185

CHAPTER 3A.

ALCOHOLIC BEVERAGE LICENSING CODE.

Sec.
28-3A-23. Regulation of grant of licenses.
28-3A-25. Unlawful acts and offenses; penalties.

Cross references. — As to revocation of alcoholic beverage license for illegal possession of food stamps, see § 13A-9-92.

As to community development districts, see Chapter 8B of Title 35.

§ 28-3A-3. Authority of board to issue licenses to engage in alcoholic beverage transactions.

Due process afforded applicant for off-premises beer license. — An applicant for an off-premises beer license need not be given any more due process than is required by the Alabama Administrative Procedure Act and the Alcoholic Beverage Licensing Code. Potts v. Bennett, 487 So. 2d 919 (Ala. Civ. App. 1985).

Denial of license on basis of location not violation of equal protection. — Denial of off-premises license on the basis of store's location and surroundings did not constitute a denial to applicant of the equal protection of the law. Potts v. Bennett, 487 So. 2d 919 (Ala. Civ. App. 1985).

The language "upon applicant's compli- ance with the provisions of this chapter" in § 28-3A-17 is an express incorporation by the legislature of the discretionary power which it has bestowed upon the ABC Board in subsection (b) of this section. Potts v. Bennett, 487 So. 2d 919 (Ala. Civ. App. 1985).

Summary judgment proper for defendant where plaintiff injured by negligent driving of volunteer waiter who was served free drinks at chamber of commerce function. Smoyer v. Birmingham Area Chamber of Commerce, 517 So. 2d 585 (Ala. 1987).

Collateral references.
Zoning regulation of intoxicating liquor as pre-empted by state law. 65 ALR4th 555.

§ 28-3A-5. Issuance and renewal of licenses; penalty for delinquent renewal.

Alabama Alcoholic Beverage Control Board did not exceed discretionary power. — The trial court was correct in finding that the Alabama Alcoholic Beverage Control Board did not exceed its discretionary power in finding that the city's police department was an interested party as well as an agency of the city

which had authority to protest renewal of liquor license. Flowers v. Alabama ABC Bd., 627 So. 2d 415 (Ala. Civ. App. 1993).

Cited in Potts v. Bennett, 487 So. 2d 919 (Ala. Civ. App. 1985); Davis v. State ABC Bd., 636 So. 2d 448 (Ala. Civ. App. 1994).

§ 28-3A-11. Lounge retail liquor license; approval of municipality; entertainment; minors.

Cross references. — As to provisions relating to the Alcoholic Beverage Control Board being prohibited from issuing licenses for sale of intoxicating beverages in Class 1 or 2 municipalities unless given approval by the governing body, see § 28-1-6.

Minors on the premises. — It is not the intent of the legislature to bar persons between the ages of 19 and 21 years from entering or being admitted to premises which sells alcoholic beverages, either as a patron or an employee, so long as they do not consume, dispense, or transport alcoholic beverages. Swint v. State ABC Bd., 628 So. 2d 769 (Ala. Civ. App. 1993).

Collateral references.
Social host's liability for injuries incurred by third parties as a result of intoxicated guest's negligence. 62 ALR4th 16.

§ 28-3A-12. Club liquor retail license; approval of municipality.

Cross references. — As to provisions relating to the Alcoholic Beverage Control Board being prohibited from issuing licenses for sale of intoxicating beverages in Class 1 or 2 municipalities unless given approval by the governing body, see § 28-1-6.

Trial court did not have jurisdiction to restrict club's hours. — Where club was holder of valid club liquor license, trial court did not have jurisdiction to restrict club's Sunday hours of operation as the trial court's order was in conflict with a legislative enactment on the same subject; it was not within the jurisdiction of the court to modify a statute, as the court in the instant case had done by restricting

the right of a club operating under a valid club license to open on Sunday, which in effect, defeated the purpose of a club license; furthermore, club could not have supplied this jurisdiction by the agreement incorporated into the trial court's order. Lamplighter, Inc. v. Town of Littleville, 571 So. 2d 1157 (Ala. Civ. App. 1990).

Collateral references.
Social host's liability for injuries incurred by third parties as a result of intoxicated guest's negligence. 62 ALR4th 16.

Zoning regulation of intoxicating liquor as pre-empted by state law. 65 ALR4th 555.

§ 28-3A-13. Restaurant retail liquor license; approval of municipality.

Cross references. — As to provisions relating to the Alcoholic Beverage Control Board being prohibited from issuing licenses for sale

of intoxicating beverages in Class 1 or 2 municipalities unless given approval by the governing body, see § 28-1-6.

§ 28-3A-14. Retail table wine license for on-premises and off-premises consumption.

Cross references. — As to provisions relating to the Alcoholic Beverage Control Board being prohibited from issuing licenses for sale

of intoxicating beverages in Class 1 or 2 municipalities unless given approval by the governing body, see § 28-1-6.

§ 28-3A-15. Retail table wine license for off-premises consumption.

Cross references. — As to provisions relating to the Alcoholic Beverage Control Board being prohibited from issuing licenses for sale

of intoxicating beverages in Class 1 or 2 municipalities unless given approval by the governing body, see § 28-1-6.

§ 28-3A-16. Retail beer license for on-premises and off-premises consumption.

Cross references. — As to provisions relating to the Alcoholic Beverage Control Board being prohibited from issuing licenses for sale of intoxicating beverages in Class 1 or 2 municipalities unless given approval by the governing body, see § 28-1-6.

Collateral references.
Social host's liability for injuries incurred by third parties as a result of intoxicated guest's negligence. 62 ALR4th 16.

§ 28-3A-17. Retail beer license for off-premises consumption.

Cross references. — As to provisions relating to the Alcoholic Beverage Control Board

being prohibited from issuing licenses for sale of intoxicating beverages in Class 1 or 2 municipalities unless given approval by the governing body, see § 28-1-6.

Due process afforded applicant for off-premises beer license. — An applicant for an off-premises beer license need not be given any more due process than is required by the Alabama Administrative Procedure Act and the Alcoholic Beverage Licensing Code. Potts v. Bennett, 487 So. 2d 919 (Ala. Civ. App. 1985).

Denial of license on basis of location not violation of equal protection. — Denial of off-premises license on the basis of store's location and surroundings did not constitute a denial to applicant of the equal protection of the

law. Potts v. Bennett, 487 So. 2d 919 (Ala. Civ. App. 1985).

The language "upon applicant's compliance with the provisions of this chapter" in this section is an express incorporation by the legislature of the discretionary power which it has bestowed upon the ABC Board in § 28-3A-3(b). Potts v. Bennett, 487 So. 2d 919 (Ala. Civ. App. 1985).

Collateral references.
Social host's liability for injuries incurred by third parties as a result of intoxicated guest's negligence. 62 ALR4th 16.

§ 28-3A-18. Retail common carrier liquor license.

Collateral references.
Social host's liability for injuries incurred by

third parties as a result of intoxicated guest's negligence. 62 ALR4th 16.

§ 28-3A-19. Special retail license.

Cross references. — As to provisions relating to the Alcoholic Beverage Control Board being prohibited from issuing licenses for sale of intoxicating beverages in Class 1 or 2 municipalities unless given approval by the governing body, see § 28-1-6.

Collateral references.
Social host's liability for injuries incurred by third parties as a result of intoxicated guest's negligence. 62 ALR4th 16.

§ 28-3A-20. Special events retail license.

Cross references. — As to provisions relating to the Alcoholic Beverage Control Board being prohibited from issuing licenses for sale of intoxicating beverages in Class 1 or 2 municipalities unless given approval by the governing body, see § 28-1-6.

Collateral references. — Social host's liability for injuries incurred by third parties as a result of intoxicated guest's negligence. 62 ALR4th 16.

§ 28-3A-21. License fees for licenses issued by the board; local license taxes.

Cited in Gillespie v. Alabama ABC Bd., 572 So. 2d 493 (Ala. Civ. App. 1990).

Collateral references.
Social host's liability for injuries incurred by third parties as a result of intoxicated guest's negligence. 62 ALR4th 16.

§ 28-3A-23. Regulation of grant of licenses.

(a) No license prescribed in this code shall be issued or renewed until the provisions of this code have been complied with and the filing and license fees other than those levied by a municipality are paid to the board.

(b) Licenses shall be granted and issued by the board only to reputable individuals, to associations whose members are reputable individuals, or to reputable corporations organized under the laws of the State of Alabama or duly qualified thereunder to do business in Alabama, or, in the case of manufacturers, duly registered under the laws of Alabama, and then only when it appears that all officers and directors of the corporation are reputable individuals.

(c) Every license issued under this code shall be constantly and conspicuously displayed on the licensed premises.

(d) Each retail liquor license application must be approved by the governing authority of the municipality if the retailer is located in a municipality, or by the county commission if the retailer is located in the county and outside the limits of the municipality before the board shall have authority to grant the license.

(e) Any retailer may be granted licenses to maintain, operate or conduct any number of places for the sale of alcoholic beverages, but a separate license must be secured for each place where alcoholic beverages are sold. No retail license issued under this code shall be used for more than one premise, nor for separate types of operation on the same premise. Each premise must have a separate retail license. Where more than one retail operation is located within the same building, each such operation under a separate or different ownership is required to obtain a separate retail license; and where more than one type of retail operation located within the same building is operated by the same licensee, such licensee must have a license for each type of retail operation. Provided, there shall be no licenses issued by the board for the sale of liquor, beer or wine by rolling stores.

(f) No retailer shall sell any alcoholic beverages for consumption on the licensed premises except in a room or rooms or place on the licensed premises at all times accessible to the use and accommodation of the general public; but this section shall not be interpreted to prevent a hotel or club licensee from selling such beverages in any room of such hotel or club house occupied by a bona fide registered guest or member or private party entitled to purchase the same.

(g) All beer, except draft or keg beer, sold by retailers must be sold or dispensed in bottles, cans or other containers not to exceed one pint or 16 ounces. All wine sold by retailers for off-premise consumption must be sold or dispensed in bottles or other containers in accordance with the standards of fill specified in the then effective standards of fill for wine prescribed by the U.S. Treasury Department.

(h) Draft or keg beer may be sold or dispensed within this state within those counties in which and in the manner in which the sale of draft or keg beer was authorized by law on September 30, 1980 or in which the sale of draft or keg beer is hereafter authorized by law; provided in rural communities with a predominantly foreign population, after the payment of the tax imposed by this title, draft or keg beer may be sold or dispensed by special permit from the board, when, in the judgment of the board, the use and consumption of draft or keg beer is in accordance with the habit and customs of the people of any such rural community; provided further, the board may, in its discretion, grant to any civic center authority or its franchisee or concessionaire, to which the board may have issued or may simultaneously issue a retail license under the provisions of this code, a revocable temporary permit to sell or dispense in any part of its civic center, for consumption therein, draft or keg beer. Either such permit shall be promptly revoked by the board if, in its judgment, the same tends to create intemperance or is prejudicial to the welfare, health, peace, temperance and safety of the people of the community or of the state.

(i) No importer shall sell alcoholic beverages to any person other than a wholesaler licensee, or sell to a wholesaler licensee any brand or brands of alcoholic beverages for sale or distribution in this state, except where the importer has been granted written authorization from the manufacturer thereof to import and sell the brand or brands to be sold in the State of Alabama, which authorization is on file with the board.

(j) No wholesaler shall maintain or operate any place where sales are made other than that for which the wholesale license is granted; provided, however, a wholesaler may be licensed to sell and distribute liquor, wine and beer. No wholesaler shall maintain any place for the storage of liquor, wine or beer unless the same has been approved by the board. No wholesaler license shall be issued for any premises in any part of which there is operated any retail license for the sale of alcoholic beverages.

(k) Licenses issued under this code may not be assigned. The board is hereby authorized to transfer any license from one person to another, or from one place to another within the same governing jurisdiction, or both, as the board may determine; but no transfers shall be made to a person who would not have been eligible to receive the license originally, nor for the transaction of business at a place for which the license could not originally have been issued lawfully.

(l) Every applicant for a transfer of a license shall file a written application with the board within such time as the board shall fix in its regulations. Whenever any license is transferred, there shall be collected a filing fee of $50.00, to be paid to the board, and the board shall pay such fee into the State Treasury to the credit of the Beer Tax and License Fund of the board.

(m) In the event that any person to whom a license shall have been issued under the terms of this code shall become insolvent, make an assignment for the benefit of creditors, be adjudicated a bankrupt by either voluntary or involuntary action, the license of such person shall immediately terminate and be cancelled without any action on the part of the board, and there shall be no refund made, or credit given, for the unused portion of the license fee for the remainder of the license year for which said license was granted. Thereafter no license shall be issued by the board for the premises, wherein said license was conducted, to any assignee, committee, trustee, receiver or successor of such licensee until a hearing has been held by the board as in the case of a new application for license. In all such cases, the board shall have the sole and final discretion as to the propriety of the issuance of a license for such premises, and the time it shall issue, and the period for which it shall be issued, and shall have the further power to impose conditions under which said licensed premises shall be conducted. (Acts 1980, No. 80-529, p. 806, § 23; Acts 1981, No. 81-808, p. 1434; Acts 1994, 1st Ex. Sess., No. 94-791, p. 95, § 1.)

The 1994 amendment, 1st Ex. Sess., effective May 6, 1994, in subsection (b), deleted "who are citizens of the United States or" following "individuals" in two places, and deleted language beginning "and are citizens of the United States,"; added present subsection (i); and redesignated former subsections (i) through (k) as present subsections (j) through (m).

Cross references. — As to provisions relating to the Alcoholic Beverage Control Board being prohibited from issuing licenses for sale of intoxicating beverages in Class 1 or 2 municipalities unless given approval by the governing body, see § 28-1-6.

Cited in Stuart v. Historic Whse., Inc., 505 So. 2d 298 (Ala. 1986).

Collateral references.

Security interests in liquor licenses. 56 ALR4th 1131.

Social host's liability for injuries incurred by third parties as a result of intoxicated guest's negligence. 62 ALR4th 16.

§ 28-3A-25. Unlawful acts and offenses; penalties.

(a) It shall be unlawful:

(1) For any manufacturer, importer, or wholesaler, or the servants, agents, or employees of the same, to sell, trade, or barter in alcoholic beverages between the hours of nine o'clock P.M. of any Saturday and two o'clock A.M. of the following Monday.

(2) For any wholesaler or the servants, agents, or employees of the wholesaler to sell alcoholic beverages, to other than wholesale or retail licensees or others within this state lawfully authorized to sell alcoholic beverages, or to sell for export.

(3) For any person, licensee, or the board either directly or by the servants, agents, or employees of the same, or for any servant, agent, or employee of the same, to sell, deliver, furnish, or give away alcoholic beverages to any person under the legal drinking age, as defined in Section 28-1-5, or to permit any person under the legal drinking age, as defined in Section 28-1-5, to drink, consume, or possess any alcoholic beverages on any licensee's premises.

(4) For any person to consume alcoholic beverages on the premises of any state liquor store or any off-premises licensee, or to allow alcoholic beverages to be consumed on the premises of any state liquor store or any off-premises licensee.

(5) For any licensee to fail to keep for a period of at least three years, complete and truthful records covering the operation of his or her license and particularly showing the date of all purchases of alcoholic beverages, the actual price paid therefor, and the name of the vendor, or to refuse the board or any authorized employee of the board access to the records or the opportunity to make copies of the records when the request is made during business hours.

(6) For any licensee or the servants, agents, or employees of the same to refuse the board, any of its authorized employees, or any duly commissioned law enforcement officer the right to completely inspect the entire licensed premises at any time the premises are open for business.

(7) For any licensee or the servants, agents, or employees of the same to be directly or indirectly employed by any other licensee engaged in the manufacture, storage, transportation, or sale of alcoholic beverages.

(8) For any person to knowingly sell any alcoholic beverages to any person engaged in the business of illegally selling alcoholic beverages.

(9) For any person to manufacture, transport, or import alcoholic beverages into this state, except in accordance with the reasonable rules and regulations of the board. This subdivision shall not prohibit the transportation of alcoholic beverages through the state or any dry county so long as the beverages are not for delivery therein, if the transportation is done in accordance with the reasonable rules and regulations of the board.

(10) For any person to fortify, adulterate, contaminate, or in any manner change the character or purity of alcoholic beverages from that as originally marketed by the manufacturer, except that a retail licensee on order from a customer may mix a chaser or other ingredients necessary to prepare a cocktail or mixed drink for on-premises consumption.

(11) For any person licensed to sell alcoholic beverages to offer to give any thing of value as a premium for the return of caps, stoppers, corks, stamps, or labels taken from any bottle, case, barrel, or package containing the alcoholic beverages, or to offer to give any thing of value as a premium or present to induce the purchase of the alcoholic beverages, or for any other purpose whatsoever in connection with the sale of the alcoholic beverages. This subdivision shall not apply to the return of any moneys specifically deposited for the return of the original containers to the owners of the containers.

(12) For any licensee or transporter for hire, servant, agent, or employee of the same, to transport any alcoholic beverages except in the original container, and for any transporter for hire to transport any alcoholic beverages within the state, unless the transporter holds a permit issued by the board.

(13) For any manufacturer, importer, or wholesaler, servant, agent, or employee of the same, to deliver any alcoholic beverages, except in vehicles bearing the name, address, and permit number of the manufacturer, importer, or wholesaler painted or affixed on each side of the vehicle in letters no smaller than four inches in height.

(14) For any person to sell alcoholic beverages within any dry county or county where the electors have voted against the sales, except in wet municipalities or as authorized by Section 28-3A-18.

(15) For any person, firm, corporation, partnership, or association of persons as the terms are defined in Section 28-3-1, including any civic center authority, racing commission, fair authority, airport authority, public or quasi-public board, agency, or commission, any agent thereof, or otherwise, who or which has not been properly licensed under the appropriate provisions of this chapter to sell, offer for sale, or have in possession for sale, any alcoholic beverages. Any alcoholic beverages so possessed, maintained, or kept shall be contraband and subject to condemnation and confiscation as provided by law.

(16) For any manufacturer, distiller, producer, importer, or distributor of alcoholic beverages to employ and maintain any person, who is not a

full-time bona fide employee, as a resident sales agent, broker, or other like representative, for the purpose of promoting a sale, purchase, or acquisition of alcoholic beverages to or by the state or the board, or for any person who is not a full-time bona fide employee to act as an agent, broker, or representative of any manufacturer, distributor, producer, importer, or distiller for that purpose.

(17) For any person to sell, give away, or otherwise dispose of taxable alcoholic beverages within this state on which the required taxes have not been paid as required by law.

(18) For any wholesaler or retailer, or the servant, agent, or employee of the same, to sell, distribute, deliver, or to receive or store for sale or distribution within this state any alcoholic beverages unless there first has been issued by the board a manufacturer's license to the manufacturer of the alcoholic beverages or its designated representative or an importer license to the importer of the alcoholic beverages.

(19) For any person under the legal drinking age, as defined in Section 28-1-5, to attempt to purchase, to purchase, consume, possess, or to transport any alcoholic beverages within the state; provided, however, it shall not be unlawful for a person under the legal drinking age, as defined in Section 28-1-5, to be an employee of a wholesale licensee or an off-premises retail licensee of the board to handle, transport, or sell any beer or table wine if the person under the legal drinking age is acting within the line and scope of his or her employment while so acting. There must be an adult licensee, servant, agent, or employee of the same present at all times a licensed establishment is open for business.

(20) For any person, except where authorized by a local act or general act of local application, to buy, give away, sell, or serve for consumption on or off the premises, or to drink or consume any alcoholic beverages in any cafe, lunchroom, restaurant, hotel dining room, or other public place on Sunday after the hour of two o'clock A.M.

(21) Except where authorized by a local act or general act of local application, for the proprietor, keeper or operator of any cafe, lunchroom, restaurant, hotel dining room, or other public place to knowingly permit any person to give away, sell, or serve for consumption on or off the premises, or to drink or consume any alcoholic beverages on the premises of the cafe, lunchroom, restaurant, hotel dining room, or other public place on Sunday after the hour of two o'clock A.M.

(22) For a person under the age of 21 years to knowingly use or attempt to use a false, forged, deceptive, or otherwise nongenuine driver's license to obtain or attempt to obtain alcoholic beverages within this state.

(b)(1) Any violation of subdivisions (1) through (18) of subsection (a) of this section shall be a misdemeanor punishable by a fine of not less than one hundred dollars ($100) nor more than one thousand dollars ($1,000), to which, at the discretion of the court or judge trying the case, may be added imprisonment in the county jail or at hard labor for the county for not more than six months for the first conviction; and, on the second conviction of a violation of the subdivisions, the offense shall, in addition to the aforementioned fine, be punishable by imprisonment or at hard labor for the county for not less than three months nor more than six months to be imposed by the court or judge trying the case; and, on the third conviction and every subsequent conviction of a violation of the subdivisions, the offense shall, in addition to a fine within the limits abovenamed, be punishable by imprisonment or at hard labor for the county for not less than six months nor more than 12 months.

(2) Any violation of any provision of subdivisions (19), (20), (21), and (22) of subsection (a) of this section shall be a misdemeanor punishable by a fine of not less than fifty dollars ($50) nor more than five hundred dollars ($500), to which, at the discretion of the court or judge trying the case, may be added imprisonment in the county jail or at hard labor for the county for not more than three months.

In addition to the penalties otherwise provided for a violation of subdivisions (19) and (22) of subsection (a) of this section, upon conviction, including convictions in juvenile court or under the Youthful Offender Act, the offender's license to operate a motor vehicle in this state shall be surrendered by the offender to the judge adjudicating the case for a period of not less than three months nor more than six months. The judge shall forward a copy of the order suspending the license to the Department of Public Safety for enforcement purposes. (Acts 1980, No. 80-529, p. 806, § 25; Acts 1984, No. 84-469, p. 1084; Acts 1986, No. 86-563, § 1; Acts 1995, No. 95-766, § 1.)

The 1995 amendment, effective August 8, 1995, substituted "person under the legal drinking age, as defined in Section 28-1-5" for "minor" throughout this section; in subsection (a), substituted "wholesaler" for "same" in subdivision (2), in subdivision (3), inserted "person," deleted "or" following "drink," inserted "or possess," and inserted "any," in subdivision (5), substituted "to the records" for "thereto," and substituted "records" for "same," in subdivision (6), deleted "during which" following "any time," and deleted "the transaction of" preceding "business," in the second sentence of subdivision (9), substituted "This subdivision" for "Provided, however, that this provision," deleted "be construed to" preceding "prohibit," and substituted "so long as the beverages are" for "and," in subdivision (10), substituted "manner" for "wise," substituted "that" for "for," and substituted "may mix" for "to mix," in the second sentence of subdivision (11), substituted "This subdivision" for "Provided, however, this provision," and substituted "of the containers" for "thereof," substituted "holds" for "shall hold" in subdivision (12), in subdivision (13), substituted "except" for "excepting," and deleted "and" preceding "address," in the first sentence of subdivision (15), inserted "or which," and substituted "properly licensed" for "licensed to do so," in subdivision (16), inserted "who is" in two places, and substituted "a" for "its" in two places, in the first sentence of subdivision (19), substituted "any" for "a," inserted "to be an," and substituted "person under the legal drinking age," for "minor," inserted "to" preceding "drink" in subdivisions (20) and (21), and added subdivision (22); in subsection (b), substituted "the aforementioned fine" for "a fine within the limits abovenamed" in subdivision (1), and in subdivision (2), in the first paragraph, inserted "provision," deleted "and" following "(20)," and inserted "and (22)," and added the second paragraph; and made nonsubstantive changes.

Police power. — This section was enacted for the purpose of protecting the public welfare, health, peace, and morals of the people of this state and should be deemed a valid exercise of the state's police power. Funari v. City of Decatur, 563 So. 2d 54 (Ala. Crim. App. 1990).

Legislative intent. — The portion of the statute which prohibits the selling of alcohol to minors does not contain any language requiring knowledge or intent; and the legislature could easily have included the element of knowledge as it did in subdivision (a)(21) of this section; the very purpose of the statute clearly indicates a legislative intent to impose strict liability. Funari v. City of Decatur, 563 So. 2d 54 (Ala. Crim. App. 1990).

The purpose of the legislation prohibit-

ing the sale of alcohol to minors is to promote and protect the public welfare of minors. Funari v. City of Decatur, 563 So. 2d 54 (Ala. Crim. App. 1990).

"Totality of the circumstances test" not applicable under Dram Shop Act. — Totality of the circumstances test is applicable under the Civil Damages Act, and such test will not be extended to Dram Shop Statute claims for the language and, therefore, inferentially, the purpose of the Dram Shop Statute differs substantially from those of the Civil Damages Act; moreover, the list of potential claimants identified in the Civil Damages Act — parents, guardians, or those standing in loco parentis — is far smaller than the one set forth in the Dram Shop Statute, and to apply this test, the Dram Shop Act would subject a large number of this state's citizens to liability that is not only strict, but nearly absolute. Moreland v. Jitney Jungle, Inc., 621 So. 2d 285 (Ala. 1993).

Hours of sale.

Where club was holder of valid club liquor license, trial court did not have jurisdiction to restrict club's Sunday hours of operation as the trial court's order was in conflict with a legislative enactment on the same subject; it was not within the jurisdiction of the court to modify a statute, as the court in the instant case had done by restricting the right of a club operating under a valid club license to open on Sunday, which in effect, defeated the purpose of a club license; club could not have supplied this jurisdiction by the agreement incorporated into the trial court's order. Lamplighter, Inc. v. Town of Littleville, 571 So. 2d 1157 (Ala. Civ. App. 1990).

Without private club status, it would be illegal for a club to sell alcohol on a Sunday. Attalla Golf & Country Club, Inc. v. Harris, 601 So. 2d 965 (Ala. 1992).

Liability for civil conspiracy rests upon the existence of an underlying wrong, and if the underlying wrong provides no cause of action, then neither does the conspiracy. Jones v. BP Oil Co., 632 So. 2d 435 (Ala. 1993).

Supermarket not liable under Dram Shop Act for sale of beer to a 21-year-old, who gave the beer to her 19-year-old friend, "contrary to the provisions of law" in a suit by a motorcycle driver who suffered injuries when he collided with vehicle operated by the 19-year-old. Moreland v. Jitney Jungle, Inc., 621 So. 2d 285 (Ala. 1993).

Licensee seeking summary judgment on sale to minor allegation, must, if claiming the minor had an adult purchase the alcoholic beverage for him, make a prima facie showing that it did not have knowledge of and participate in the adult buyer scheme. Liao v. Harry's Bar, 574 So. 2d 775 (Ala. 1990).

Summary judgment proper for defendant where plaintiff injured by negligent driving of volunteer waiter who was served free drinks at chamber of commerce function. Smoyer v. Birmingham Area Chamber of Commerce, 517 So. 2d 585 (Ala. 1987).

Willful furnishing of alcohol to one under 18. — It is a misdemeanor for persons under the age of 21 to purchase, consume, possess or to transport any alcoholic beverage, and consequently, one who willfully furnishes alcoholic beverages to persons under the age of 18 clearly violates both the first and second alternatives of subsection (a) of this section. Senf v. State, 622 So. 2d 435 (Ala. Crim. App. 1993).

Cited in Martin v. Watts, 513 So. 2d 958 (Ala. 1987).

Collateral references.

Social host's liability for injuries incurred by third parties as a result of intoxicated guest's negligence. 62 ALR4th 16.

CHAPTER 4.

REGULATION AND CONTROL OF ALCOHOLIC BEVERAGES IN DRY COUNTIES AND DRY MUNICIPALITIES.

Cross references. — As to community development districts, see Chapter 8B of Title 35.

ARTICLE 1.

GENERAL PROVISIONS.

§ 28-4-2. Unauthorized possession, sale, delivery, use, etc., of wine or alcohol generally.

Chain of custody held unbroken although evidence left unattended for short time. — Where agent who had custody of bottle of whiskey had, before he locked it up in the evidence vault, left it in his car unattended for a short period of time, but at trial, the agent testified that the bottle of whiskey was in the same condition as it was at the time of the purchase, the city sufficiently proved an unbroken chain of custody of the bottle. Talley v. City of Clanton, 495 So. 2d 1165 (Ala. Crim. App. 1986).

§ 28-4-5. Applicability to dry municipalities.

Collateral references. — Zoning regulation of intoxicating liquor as pre-empted by state law. 65 ALR4th 555.

ARTICLE 2.

MANUFACTURE, SALE, OFFER FOR SALE, POSSESSION, DISTRIBUTION, ETC., OF PROHIBITED LIQUORS AND BEVERAGES.

§ 28-4-20. Sale, offer for sale, possession, barter, exchange, etc., of prohibited liquors and beverages.

I. GENERAL CONSIDERATION.

Twelve-month sentence erroneous absent proof of prior convictions. — Imposition of a 12-month sentence for the sale of prohibited liquor in violation of this section was error under § 28-4-21, where the state failed to provide an affirmative showing that defendant had any prior convictions under this section. Callahan v. State, 489 So. 2d 636 (Ala. Crim. App. 1985).

§ 28-4-21. Penalties for violations of section 28-4-20.

Twelve-month sentence erroneous absent proof of prior convictions. — Imposition of a 12-month sentence for the sale of prohibited liquor in violation of § 28-4-20, was error under this section, where the state failed to provide an affirmative showing that defendant had any prior convictions under § 28-4-20. Callahan v. State, 489 So. 2d 636 (Ala. Crim. App. 1985).

§ 28-4-30. Punishment of agents or assisting friends of buyers or sellers of prohibited liquors and beverages.

Collateral references.
Social host's liability for injuries incurred by third parties as a result of intoxicated guest's negligence. 62 ALR4th 16.

§ 28-4-31. Exhibition of signs containing names of prohibited liquors or beverages or employment of certain words in designating business by dealers in beverages; use of evidence thereof in prosecutions against dealers for sale, offer for sale, etc., of prohibited liquors and beverages.

Collateral references.
Construction and application of restrictive covenants to the use of signs. 61 ALR4th 1028.

ARTICLE 4.

MAINTENANCE, ETC., OF UNLAWFUL DRINKING PLACES.

§ 28-4-72. Forfeiture of charters of clubs or incorporated associations violating provisions of sections 28-4-70 or 28-4-71.

Collateral references. — Social host's liability for injuries incurred by third parties as a result of intoxicated guest's negligence. 62 ALR4th 16.

ARTICLE 6.

TRANSPORTATION, DELIVERY AND RECEIPT GENERALLY OF PROHIBITED LIQUORS AND BEVERAGES.

§ 28-4-115. Transportation of prohibited liquors or beverages in quantities of five gallons or more.

I. GENERAL CONSIDERATION.

Habitual Felony Offender Act is applicable to violation of section. — Because the Alabama Legislature has expressed no contrary intent, the Habitual Felony Offender Act is applicable to a conviction for a violation of this section. Callahan v. State, 644 So. 2d 1329 (Ala. Crim. App. 1994).

ARTICLE 9.

POSSESSION, ETC., OF CERTAIN QUANTITIES OF STATE TAX-PAID ALCOHOLIC BEVERAGES FOR PRIVATE USE.

§ 28-4-200. Possession of certain quantities of state tax-paid alcoholic beverages for private use permitted; storage, possession, etc., of alcoholic beverages in passenger area of vehicles or in view of passengers.

Cited in Martin v. Watts, 513 So. 2d 958 (Ala. 1987).

§ 28-4-201. Sale or offer for sale or possession in excess of quantity permitted of such alcoholic beverages; penalties for violations of article.

Evidence held insufficient for conviction. — The only evidence presented at trial to suggest that the defendant was in violation of this section was the deputy's testimony that he saw one open can of "Miller's Best" on the floorboard and two unopened cans behind the driver's seat of the defendant's vehicle. The deputy testified that he seized these cans; however, they were not presented at trial or offered into evidence. Furthermore, no testimony was offered to establish that any of the suspect cans actually contained beer or, in fact, whether "Miller's Best" is indeed a brand name for a line of malt or brewed beverages. Therefore, the evidence presented was insufficient to sustain the defendant's conviction for possessing alcoholic beverages in a dry county. Leverette v. State, 594 So. 2d 731 (Ala. Crim. App. 1992).

ARTICLE 10.

ABATEMENT OF LIQUOR NUISANCES.

§ 28-4-220. Authorization and procedure generally; filing of petition generally.

Collateral references.
Zoning regulation of intoxicating liquor as pre-empted by state law. 65 ALR4th 555.

ARTICLE 11.

FORFEITURE AND CONDEMNATION OF CONTRABAND LIQUORS AND BEVERAGES, ETC.

§ 28-4-285. Conveyances, vehicles of transportation or animals used for illegal conveyance of prohibited liquors and beverages declared contraband and forfeited to state; seizure of said conveyances, etc., and reporting thereof by sheriffs, etc., finding same; confiscation and condemnation generally.

I. GENERAL CONSIDERATION.

Section 20-2-93 compared. — Section 20-2-93, unlike this section and § 28-4-290, does not require reasonable diligence in inquiring as to the proposed use of the car or contain a provision that would impute notice of reputation as a matter of law. Metropolitan Toyota, Inc. v. State ex rel. Galanos, 496 So. 2d 25 (Ala. 1986).

§ 28-4-286. Institution of proceedings for condemnation of vehicles, etc.; seized property not to be retaken by replevin or detinue during pendency of action; intervention by parties claiming superior right to seized property; powers of court to regulate proceedings to permit parties claiming vehicles, etc., to assert rights.

Prompt action. — The necessity of prompt action to adjudicate the merits of the seizure and to effectuate the forfeiture is what is constitutionally required. Woods v. Reeves, 628 So. 2d 563 (Ala. 1993).

Condemnation proceedings must be

prompt. — The state has lost its right to a forfeiture where after more than four years has passed and no condemnation proceedings have been initiated. Woods v. Reeves, 621 So. 2d 672 (Ala. 1993).

§ 28-4-290. Advertisement and sale by sheriff, etc., of vehicle, animal, etc., seized for illegal transportation of liquor or beverages where owner, etc., cannot be ascertained; rights in seized vehicles, animals, etc., disposed of upon such sale by sheriff or sale by court in condemnation proceedings.

Section 20-2-93 compared. — Section 20-2-93, unlike § 28-4-285 and this section, does not require reasonable diligence in inquiring as to the proposed use of the car or contain a provision that would impute notice of reputation as a matter of law. Metropolitan Toyota, Inc. v. State ex rel. Galanos, 496 So. 2d 25 (Ala. 1986).

ARTICLE 12.

ENFORCEMENT OF CHAPTER.

§ 28-4-320. Servants, agents, etc., and principals not to be excused from testifying against each other on grounds of self-incrimination; immunity of said persons from prosecution for offenses disclosed, etc.

Collateral references.
Social host's liability for injuries incurred by third parties as a result of intoxicated guest's negligence. 62 ALR4th 16.

CHAPTER 4A.

ALABAMA BREWPUB ACT.

Sec.
28-4A-1. Short title.
28-4A-2. Definitions.
28-4A-3. Licensing of brewpubs to brew and sell beer on same premises for on-premises consumption only; annual license fee; applicability of Title 28 and §§ 28-3-4 and 28-3A-6(b).
28-4A-4. Privilege and excise taxes levied on

Sec.
  brewpub; maintenance of records; appointment of wholesaler designee; exemption from §§ 28-9-3 through 28-9-11.
28-4A-5. Violation of chapter constitutes unlawful act; automatic revocation of license.
28-4A-6. Legislative findings.

§ 28-4A-1. Short title.

This chapter shall be known as and may be cited as the "Alabama Brewpub Act." (Acts 1992, No. 92-535, p. 1078, § 1.)

Code Commissioner's note. — Acts 1992, No. 92-535, which enacted this chapter, in § 8 provides: "The provisions of this Act are cumulative and shall not be construed to repeal or supersede any laws or parts of laws not directly inconsistent herewith."

§ 28-4A-2. Definitions.

(a) The words and phrases used in this chapter shall have the meanings ascribed to them in Section 28-3-1, and any acts amendatory thereof, supplementary thereto or substituted therefor.

(b) The following words or phrases, whenever they appear in this chapter, unless the context clearly indicates otherwise, shall have the meaning ascribed to them in this subsection:

(1) BREWPUB. Any premises upon which beer is manufactured or brewed, subject to the barrel production limitation prescribed in this chapter, for consumption exclusively on the premises.

(2) PREMISES. Any building, structure or portion thereof designated as a historic building and site as defined in Section 40-8-1, in which is located the operations of a brewpub. (Acts 1992, No. 92-535, p. 1078, § 2.)

§ 28-4A-3. Licensing of brewpubs to brew and sell beer on same premises for on-premises consumption only; annual license fee; applicability of Title 28 and §§ 28-3-4 and 28-3A-6(b).

(a) In addition to the licenses authorized to be issued and renewed by the board pursuant to the Alcoholic Beverage Licensing Code codified as Chapter 3A, Title 28, the board, upon applicant's compliance with the provisions of this chapter and with Chapter 3A, Title 28, and the regulations made thereunder, is authorized to issue to a qualified applicant a brewpub license which shall authorize the licensee to manufacture or brew beer in a quantity not to exceed 10,000 barrels in any one year and to sell such beer in unpackaged form at retail for on-premises consumption only, and to purchase beer in original unopened containers from licensed wholesalers and to sell such beer at retail for on-premises consumption only, in a room or rooms or place on the licensed premises at all times accessible to the use and accommodation of the general public, subject to the following conditions:

(1) The brewpub premises must be located in an historic building or site as defined in Section 40-8-1, in a wet county or wet municipality, in which county beer was brewed for public consumption prior to the ratification of the Eighteenth Amendment to the U.S. Constitution in 1919.

(2) The proposed location of the premises shall not, at the time of the original application, be prohibited by a valid zoning ordinance or other ordinance in the valid exercise of police power by the governing body of the municipality or county in which the brewpub is located.

(3) Beer brewed by the brewpub licensee shall not be possessed, sold or dispensed except on the premises where brewed, and shall not be packaged or contained in other than barrels from which the beer is to be dispensed on the premises for consumption on the premises.

(4) The brewpub must contain and operate a restaurant with a seating capacity of not less than 80.

(b) The annual license fee levied and prescribed for a license as a brewpub issued or renewed by the board pursuant to the authority of this chapter is $1,000.

(c) Except as provided in this subsection, the provisions of Title 28 shall be applicable. The provisions of Section 28-3-4 and subsection (b) of Section 28-3A-6, shall not be applicable with regard to beer brewed by the brewpub and sold and dispensed on the brewpub premises. In all other respects, Section 28-3-4 and Section 28-3A-6(b) shall be applicable. (Acts 1992, No. 92-535, p. 1078, § 3.)

§ 28-4A-4. Privilege and excise taxes levied on brewpub; maintenance of records; appointment of wholesaler designee; exemption from §§ 28-9-3 through 28-9-11.

(a) In addition to the licenses provided for by this chapter and any county or municipal license, there is levied on the brewpub the privilege or excise taxes imposed by Sections 28-3-184 and 28-3-190. Every brewpub licensee shall file the tax returns, pay the taxes and perform all obligations imposed on wholesalers at the times and places set forth therein. It shall be unlawful for any brewpub licensee who is required to pay the taxes so imposed in the first instance to fail or refuse to add to the sales price and collect from the purchaser the required amount of tax, it being the intent and purpose of this provision that each of the taxes levied is in fact a tax on the consumer, with the brewpub licensee who pays the tax in the first instance acting merely as an agent of the State for the collection and payment of the tax levied by Section 28-3-184 and as an agent of the county or municipality for the collection and payment of the tax levied by Section 28-3-190.

(b) The brewpub shall be required to keep and maintain all of the records otherwise required to be kept and maintained by manufacturer, wholesaler, and retailer licensees.

(c) The brewpub shall appoint a licensed wholesaler designee in order to preserve Section 28-9-1. In addition, the brewpub shall be exempt from Sections 28-9-3 through 28-9-11. (Acts 1992, No. 92-535, p. 1078, § 4.)

§ 28-4A-5. Violation of chapter constitutes unlawful act; automatic revocation of license.

A violation of any provision of this chapter shall constitute an unlawful act. A finding by the Board that the brewpub licensee is guilty of violating any provision of this chapter shall effect an automatic revocation of the license. (Acts 1992, No. 92-535, p. 1078, § 5.)

§ 28-4A-6. Legislative findings.

The legislature finds that it is in the best interest of the public welfare of the State of Alabama to preserve and redevelop the original "downtown" municipal areas of this state and to further promote the preservation and redevelopment of historic buildings and sites. The legislature finds that an effective way of facilitating the urban redevelopment program and the preservation of historic buildings and sites is by creating a single exception to the existing alcoholic beverage laws to authorize and permit the establishment of brewpubs located in historic buildings and sites in urban redevelopment areas of those municipalities located within counties where the brewing of beer for consumption by the public had historically been located. The policy and intent of the legislature in the enactment of this chapter is to promote the public welfare by further regulating and controlling alcoholic beverage transactions in Alabama under the control and supervision of the Alabama Alcoholic Beverage Control Board to accomplish this legislative purpose set forth herein. (Acts 1992, No. 92-535, p. 1078, § 6.)

CHAPTER 6.

REGULATION OF PRODUCTION, SALE, ETC., OF NATIVE FARM WINE.

§ 28-6-1. Definitions.

Inability to meet full capacity production quota not bar to license grant. — Where nothing in the record indicated that licensee intended to operate at full capacity, this section did not set a minimum production to qualify for a farm winery license, and since there was ample testimony in the record to establish that licensee intended full compliance with the Alabama farm winery laws regarding the operation of a farm winery if allowed to operate the winery as such, license grant by the ABC Board was not to be reversed. Gillespie v. Alabama ABC Bd., 572 So. 2d 493 (Ala. Civ. App. 1990).

CHAPTER 7.

IMPORTATION, DISTRIBUTION AND SALE OF TABLE WINE.

§ 28-7-16. Tax on sale of table wine; amount; collection; disposition of proceeds; exclusive; exemption.

Cross references. — As to audit and collection of taxes on beer or table wine by alcoholic beverage control board for the benefit of local governing bodies under certain conditions, see § 28-7A-1 et seq.

CHAPTER 7A.

AUDIT AND COLLECTION OF TAXES ON BEER OR TABLE WINE BY BOARD FOR BENEFIT OF LOCAL GOVERNING BODIES.

Sec.
28-7A-1. Definitions.
28-7A-2. Authorization of board to audit and collect taxes levied upon sale of beer or table wine; retention or reclamation of authority by local governing body.
28-7A-3. Collection and disposition of moneys from taxes on beer or table wine; fee payable to board.

Sec.
28-7A-4. Receipt of fee or percentage of taxes by probate judge or officials.
28-7A-5. Reports, forms and other information; rules and regulations.
28-7A-6. Board authorized to inspect, examine and audit books and records of wholesaler licensees and retail sellers of alcoholic beverages.

Code Commissioner's note. — Acts 1988, 1st Ex. Sess., No. 88-723, § 7 provides: "The provisions of this act are supplemental. It shall be construed in pari materia with other laws regulating this subject; however, those laws or parts of laws which are in direct conflict or inconsistent herewith are hereby repealed."

§ 28-7A-1. Definitions.

For the purpose of this chapter, the following terms shall have the following meanings:

(1) BOARD. The alcoholic beverage control board.

(2) LOCAL GOVERNING BODY. Any county or municipal commission, council or other governing body or any official of any county or municipality that is authorized by sections 28-3-190 and 28-7-16, to collect taxes levied by the state of Alabama upon the sale of any beer or table wine. (Acts 1988, 1st Ex. Sess., No. 88-723, p. 118, § 1.)

§ 28-7A-2. Authorization of board to audit and collect taxes levied upon sale of beer or table wine; retention or reclamation of authority by local governing body.

Any local governing body may, prior to October 1, 1988 or at any time thereafter, elect to authorize the board to audit and collect any and all taxes levied pursuant to sections 28-3-190 and 28-7-16, upon the sale of any beer or table wine. Any local governing body may elect to retain, or at any time after October 1, 1988, by an appropriate resolution or ordinance duly adopted and spread upon its minutes, elect to retain or reclaim the power and authority granted to it by sections 28-3-190 and 28-7-16, to audit and collect any such taxes, whereupon said taxes shall be paid to and collected by the local governing body as provided in said sections. (Acts 1988, 1st Ex. Sess., No. 88-723, p. 118, § 2; Acts 1989, Ex. Sess., No. 89-990, p. 35, § 1.)

§ 28-7A-3. Collection and disposition of moneys from taxes on beer or table wine; fee payable to board.

The taxes on beer or table wine levied pursuant to sections 28-3-190 and 28-7-16, to be collected by any local governing body, except as provided in section 28-7A-2, shall be paid when due in accordance with the applicable law to the board for the use and benefit of such local governing body. The board shall collect the revenues generated by such tax at the same time and in the same manner as provided for collection by the local governing body. The taxes so collected shall be deposited into a special fund for the local governing body and paid by the board to the treasury of the local governing body for which they were collected within 25 days after the end of the month in which such funds are received by the board. Provided, however, that the board shall retain two and one-half percent of the tax due to the local governing body as a fee to the board for auditing, collecting, disbursing and administering the tax. The sum so retained by the board shall be deposited to the credit of the general fund of the state and dispersed therefrom according to law. Each such local governing body shall further distribute such proceeds in the manner provided by law. (Acts 1988, 1st Ex. Sess., No. 88-723, p. 118, § 3.)

§ 28-7A-4. Receipt of fee or percentage of taxes by probate judge or officials.

Any provisions of this chapter to the contrary notwithstanding, the probate judge or any official or agent of any local governing body or any other person who, by statute applicable on October 1, 1988, receives a fee as a percentage of the tax for collecting such tax on beer or table wine levied pursuant to sections 28-3-190 and 28-7-16, shall continue to receive the said fee or percentage. (Acts 1988, 1st Ex. Sess., No. 88-723, p. 118, § 4.)

§ 28-7A-5. Reports, forms and other information; rules and regulations.

The board shall prepare and distribute such reports, forms and other information as may be necessary for the collection and distribution of the said taxes. The board is authorized to promulgate all reasonable rules and regulations necessary to implement the provisions of this chapter. (Acts 1988, 1st Ex. Sess., No. 88-723, p. 118, § 5.)

§ 28-7A-6. Board authorized to inspect, examine and audit books and records of wholesaler licensees and retail sellers of alcoholic beverages.

The board shall have the authority to inspect, examine and audit the books and records of any wholesaler licensee who sells, stores or receives for the purpose of distribution, any alcoholic beverages, to verify the proper filing and to determine the accuracy of any state or local tax return required to be filed by the wholesaler, and to determine the payment of all state and local taxes when and where due with respect to any state or local tax levied on alcoholic beverages by statute. In pursuance of said authority, the board shall have the further authority to inspect, examine and audit the books and records of any person, firm, corporation, club or association who sells at retail any alcoholic beverages. (Acts 1988, 1st Ex. Sess., No. 88-723, p. 118, § 6.)

CHAPTER 8.

EXCLUSIVE SALES TERRITORIES AND WHOLESALERS.

§ 28-8-1. Legislative policy and intent.

Cited in Stuart v. Historic Whse., Inc., 505 So. 2d 298 (Ala. 1986).

§ 28-8-8. Unlawful acts and offenses; penalties.

Cited in Stuart v. Historic Whse., Inc., 505 So. 2d 298 (Ala. 1986).

CHAPTER 9.

BUSINESS RELATIONS BETWEEN WHOLESALERS AND SUPPLIERS OF BEER.

Sec.
28-9-1. Legislative intent and purpose.
28-9-2. Definitions.
28-9-3. Sales by beer suppliers through wholesalers; exclusive sales territory.
28-9-4. Prohibited acts — Suppliers.
28-9-5. Prohibited acts — Wholesalers.
28-9-6. Amendment, cancellation, etc., of agreements; proof of good faith; notice; good cause.
28-9-7. Transfer of wholesaler's business.
28-9-8. Liability of supplier for acts diminishing value of wholesaler's business;

Sec.
     arbitration procedures; determination of amount of compensation; cost of arbitration; default of arbitration procedures.
28-9-9. Waiver of rights; good faith dispute settlements.
28-9-10. Application, transferee of wholesaler's business; successor of supplier's business.
28-9-11. Liabilities and duties of supplier; action for damages; declaratory judgment and injunctive relief; remedies.

Code Commissioner's note. — Section 13 of Acts 1988, No. 88-80 provides that this chapter is cumulative and supplements and is in addition to §§ 28-8-1, 28-8-2, 28-8-3, 28-8-4, 28-8-5, 28-8-6, 28-8-7 and 28-8-8 of the Code of Alabama 1975, as interpreted by Acts 1985, Act No. 85-226.

Cross references. — For provisions as to exclusive sales territories and wholesalers of alcoholic beverages, see Title 28, chapter 8.

§ 28-9-1. Legislative intent and purpose.

The legislative intent and purpose of this chapter is to provide a structure for the business relations between a wholesaler and a supplier of beer. Regulation in this area is considered necessary for the following reasons:

(1) To maintain stability and healthy competition in the beer industry in this state.

(2) To promote and maintain a sound, stable, and viable three-tier system of distribution of beer to the public.

(3) To promote the public health, safety, and welfare. (Acts 1988, No. 88-80, p. 87, § 1.)

§ 28-9-2. Definitions.

(a) The following words or phrases, or the plural thereof, whenever they appear in this chapter, unless the context clearly requires otherwise, shall have the meanings ascribed to them in this section:

(1) AGREEMENT. Any agreement between a wholesaler and a supplier, whether oral or written, whereby a wholesaler is granted the right to purchase and sell a brand or brands of beer sold by a supplier.

(2) ANCILLARY BUSINESS. A business owned by a wholesaler, by a substantial stockholder of a wholesaler, or by a substantial partner of a wholesaler the primary business of which is directly related to the transporting, storing, or marketing of the brand or brands of beer of a supplier with whom the wholesaler has an agreement; or a business owned by a wholesaler, a substantial stockholder of a wholesaler or a substantial partner of a wholesaler which recycles empty beverage containers.

(3) DESIGNATED MEMBER. The spouse, child, grandchild, parent, brother or sister of a deceased individual who owned an interest, including a controlling interest, in a wholesaler; or any person who inherits the deceased individual's ownership interest in the wholesaler under the terms of the deceased individual's will, or under the laws of intestate succession of this state; or any person who or entity which has otherwise, by designation in writing by the deceased individual, succeeded the deceased individual in the wholesaler's business, or has succeeded to the deceased individual's ownership interest in the wholesaler pursuant to a written contract or instrument; and also includes the appointed and qualified personal representative and the testamentary trustee of a deceased individual owning an ownership interest in a wholesaler. Designated member also includes the person appointed by a court as the guardian or conservator of the property of an incapacitated individual owning an ownership interest in a wholesaler.

(4) GOOD FAITH. Honesty in fact and the observance of reasonable commercial standards of fair dealing in the trade, as defined in and interpreted under the uniform commercial code, section 7-2-103.

(5) REASONABLE QUALIFICATIONS. The standard of the reasonable criteria established and consistently used by the respective supplier for Alabama wholesalers that entered into, continued or renewed an agreement with the supplier during a period of 24 months prior to the proposed transfer of the wholesaler's business, or for Alabama wholesalers who have changed managers or designated managers during a period of 24 months prior to the proposed change in manager or successor manager of the wholesaler's business.

(6) RETALIATORY ACTION. Includes, but is not limited to, the refusal to continue an agreement, or a material reduction in the quality of service or quantity of products available to a wholesaler under an agreement, which refusal or reduction is not made in good faith.

(7) SALES TERRITORY. An area of exclusive sales responsibility for the brand or brands of beer sold by a supplier as designated by an agreement.

(8) SUBSTANTIAL STOCKHOLDER or SUBSTANTIAL PARTNER. A stockholder of or partner in the wholesaler who owns an interest of 25 percent or more of the partnership or of the capital stock of a corporate wholesaler.

(9) SUPPLIER. A manufacturer or importer of beer licensed by the board.

(10) TRANSFER OF WHOLESALER'S BUSINESS. The voluntary sale, assignment or other transfer of all or control of the business or all or substantially all of the assets of the wholesaler, or all or control of the capital stock of the wholesaler, including without limitation the sale or other transfer of capital

stock or assets by merger, consolidation or dissolution, or of the capital stock of the parent corporation, or of the capital stock or beneficial ownership of any other entity owning or controlling the wholesaler.

(11) WHOLESALER. A wholesaler of beer licensed by the board.

(b) Other words and phrases used in this chapter shall have the meanings ascribed to them in section 28-3-1, as amended, and any acts amendatory thereof, supplementary thereto or substituted therefor, unless the context clearly requires otherwise. (Acts 1988, No. 88-80, p. 87, § 2; Acts 1989, No. 89-525, p. 1074, § 1.)

§ 28-9-3. Sales by beer suppliers through wholesalers; exclusive sales territory.

Each supplier of beer licensed by the board authorizing such licensee to sell its beer within the state of Alabama shall sell its beer through wholesaler licensees of the board, and shall grant in writing to each of its wholesalers an exclusive sales territory in accordance with the provisions of Act No. 84-374 (Acts 1984), appearing as chapter 8, Title 28, as amended. (Acts 1988, No. 88-80, p. 87, § 3.)

§ 28-9-4. Prohibited acts — Suppliers.

A supplier is prohibited from doing the following:

(1) Fail to provide each wholesaler of the supplier's brand or brands with a written agreement which contains in total the supplier's agreement with each wholesaler, and designates a specific exclusive sales territory. Any agreement which is in existence on March 3, 1988, shall be renewed consistent with this chapter; provided, that this chapter may be incorporated by reference in the agreement. Provided, however, nothing contained herein shall prevent a supplier from appointing, one time for a period not to exceed 90 days, a wholesaler to temporarily service a sales territory not designated to another wholesaler, until such time as a wholesaler is appointed by the supplier; and such wholesaler who is designated to service the sales territory during this period of temporary service shall not be in violation of the chapter, and, with respect to the temporary service territory, shall not have any of the rights provided under sections 28-9-6 and 28-9-8.

(2) Fix, maintain, or establish the price at which a wholesaler shall sell any beer.

(3) Enter into an additional agreement with any other wholesaler for, or to sell to any other wholesaler, the same brand or brands of beer in the same territory or any portion thereof, or to sell directly to any retailer in this state.

(4) Coerce, or attempt to coerce, any wholesaler to accept delivery of any beer, or other commodity which has not been ordered by the wholesaler. Provided, however, a supplier may impose reasonable inventory requirements upon a wholesaler if the requirements are made in good faith and are generally applied to other similarly situated wholesalers having an agreement with the supplier.

(5) Coerce, or attempt to coerce, any wholesaler to accept delivery of any beer, or other commodity ordered by a wholesaler if the order was canceled by the wholesaler.

(6) Coerce, or attempt to coerce, any wholesaler to do any illegal act or to violate any law or regulation by threatening to amend, modify, cancel, terminate, or refuse to renew any agreement existing between the supplier and wholesaler.

(7) Require a wholesaler to assent to any condition, stipulation, or provision limiting the wholesaler's right to sell the brand or brands of beer or other products of any other supplier unless the acquisition of the brand or brands or products of another supplier would materially impair or adversely affect the wholesaler's quality of service, sales or ability to compete effectively in representing the brand or brands of the supplier presently being sold by the wholesaler; provided the supplier shall have the burden of proving that such acquisition of such other brand or brands or products would have such effect.

(8) Require a wholesaler to purchase one or more brands of beer or other products in order for the wholesaler to purchase another brand or brands of beer for any reason. Provided, however, a wholesaler that has agreed to distribute a brand or brands before March 3, 1988, shall continue to distribute the brand or brands in conformance with this chapter.

(9) Request a wholesaler to submit audited profit and loss statements, balance sheets, or financial records as a condition of renewal or continuation of an agreement.

(10) Withhold delivery of beer ordered by a wholesaler, or change a wholesaler's quota of a brand or brands if the withholding or change is not made in good faith.

(11) Require a wholesaler by any means directly to participate in or contribute to any local or national advertising fund controlled directly or indirectly by a supplier.

(12) Take any retaliatory action against a wholesaler that files a complaint regarding an alleged violation by the supplier of federal, state or local law or an administrative rule.

(13) Require or prohibit, without just and reasonable cause, any change in the manager or successor manager of any wholesaler who has been approved by the supplier as of or subsequent to March 3, 1988. Should a wholesaler change an approved manager or successor manager, a supplier shall not require or prohibit the change unless the person selected by the wholesaler fails to meet the nondiscriminatory, material and reasonable standards and qualifications for managers of Alabama wholesalers of the supplier which standards and qualifications previously have been consistently applied to Alabama wholesalers by the supplier. Provided, however, the supplier shall have the burden of proving that such person fails to meet such standards and qualifications which are nondiscriminatory, material and reasonable and have been consistently applied to Alabama wholesalers.

(14) Upon written notice of intent to transfer the wholesaler's business, interfere with, prevent, or unreasonably delay (not to exceed 30 days) the

transfer of the wholesaler's business if the proposed transferee is a designated member.

(15) Upon written notice of intent to transfer the wholesaler's business other than to a designated member, withhold consent to or approval of, or unreasonably delay (not to exceed 30 days after receipt of all material information reasonably requested) a response to a request by the wholesaler for, any transfer of a wholesaler's business if the proposed transferee meets the nondiscriminatory, material and reasonable qualifications and standards required by the supplier for Alabama wholesalers. Provided, however, the supplier shall have the burden of proving that the proposed transferee does not meet such standards and qualifications which are nondiscriminatory, material and reasonable and have been consistently applied to Alabama wholesalers.

(16) Restrict or inhibit, directly or indirectly, the right of free association among wholesalers for any lawful purpose. (Acts 1988, No. 88-80, p. 87, § 4.)

§ 28-9-5. Prohibited acts — Wholesalers.

A wholesaler is prohibited from doing the following:

(1) Fail to devote reasonable efforts and resources, within supplier's designated sales territory, to the sale and distribution of all the supplier's brands of beer which the wholesaler has been granted the right to sell or distribute.

(2) Sell or deliver beer to a retail licensee located outside the sales territory designated to the wholesaler by the supplier of a particular brand or brands of beer. Provided, however, during periods of temporary service interruptions impacting a particular sales territory, a wholesaler who normally services the impacted sales territory shall file with the board and give to the affected supplier written notice designating the specific licensed wholesaler or wholesalers, not disapproved by the supplier, who will service the sales territory during the period of temporary service interruption and the approximate length of time of the service interruption. Each wholesaler designated to temporarily service the sales territory shall be a wholesaler who has a current written agreement with a supplier for the brand or brands affected. When the temporary service interruption is over, the wholesaler who normally services the sales territory shall notify in writing the board, the supplier and the wholesaler, or wholesalers, servicing the sales territory on a temporary basis of this fact, and any wholesaler servicing the sales territory on a temporary basis shall cease servicing the sales territory upon receipt of the notice. A wholesaler who is designated to service the impacted sales territory during the period of temporary service shall not be in violation of this chapter, and, with respect to the temporary service territory, shall not have any of the rights provided under sections 28-9-6 and 28-9-8.

(3) Transfer the wholesaler's business without giving the supplier written notice of intent to transfer the wholesaler's business and, where required by this chapter, receiving the supplier's approval for the proposed transfer.

Provided, consent or approval for the supplier shall not be required of any transfer of the wholesaler's business to a designated member, or any transfer of less than control of the wholesaler's business. Provided, however, that the wholesaler shall give the supplier written notice of any change in ownership of the wholesaler. (Acts 1988, No. 88-80, p. 87, § 5; Acts 1989, No. 89-525, p. 1074, § 1.)

§ 28-9-6. Amendment, cancellation, etc., of agreements; proof of good faith; notice; good cause.

(a) Notwithstanding any agreement and except as otherwise provided for in this chapter, a supplier shall not: amend or modify an agreement; cause a wholesaler to resign from an agreement; or cancel, terminate, fail to renew, or refuse to continue under an agreement, unless the supplier has complied with all of the following:

(1) Has satisfied the applicable notice requirements of subsection (c) of this section.

(2) Has acted in good faith.

(3) Has good cause for the amendment, modification, cancellation, termination, nonrenewal, discontinuance, or forced resignation.

(b) For each amendment, modification, termination, cancellation, nonrenewal, or discontinuance, the supplier shall have the burden of proving that it has acted in good faith, that the notice requirements under this section have been complied with, and that there was good cause for the amendment, modification, termination, cancellation, nonrenewal, or discontinuance.

(c) Notwithstanding any agreement and except as otherwise provided in this section, and in addition to the time limits set forth in subdivision (d)(5) of this section, the supplier shall furnish written notice of the amendment, modification, termination, cancellation, nonrenewal, or discontinuance of an agreement to the wholesaler not less than 60 days before the effective date of the amendment, modification, termination, cancellation, nonrenewal, or discontinuance. The notice shall be by certified mail and shall contain all of the following:

(1) A statement of intention to amend, modify, terminate, cancel, not renew, or discontinue the agreement.

(2) A statement of the reason for the amendment, modification, termination, cancellation, nonrenewal, or discontinuance.

(3) The date on which the amendment, modification, termination, cancellation, nonrenewal, or discontinuance takes effect.

(d) Notwithstanding any agreement, good cause shall exist for the purposes of a termination, cancellation, nonrenewal, or discontinuance under subdivision (a)(3) of this section when all of the following occur:

(1) There is a failure by the wholesaler to comply with a provision of the agreement which is both reasonable and of material significance to the business relationship between the wholesaler and the supplier.

(2) The supplier first acquired knowledge of the failure described in subdivision (1) not more than 18 months before the date notification was given pursuant to subdivision (a)(1) of this section.

(3) The wholesaler was given notice by the supplier of failure to comply with the agreement.

(4) The wholesaler was afforded a reasonable opportunity to assert good faith efforts to comply with agreement within the time limits as provided for in subdivision (d)(5) of this section.

(5) The wholesaler has been afforded 30 days in which to submit a plan of corrective action to comply with the agreement and an additional 120 days to cure such noncompliance in accordance with the plan.

(e) Notwithstanding subsections (a) and (c) of this section, a supplier may terminate, cancel, fail to renew, or discontinue an agreement immediately upon written notice given in the manner and containing the information required by subsection (c) of this section if any of the following occur:

(1) Insolvency of the wholesaler, the filing of any petition by or against the wholesaler under any bankruptcy or receivership law, or the assignment for the benefit of creditors or dissolution or liquidation of the wholesaler which materially affects the wholesaler's ability to remain in business.

(2) Revocation or suspension of the wholesaler's state or federal license by the appropriate regulatory agency whereby the wholesaler cannot service the wholesaler's sales territory for more than 61 days.

(3) The wholesaler, or a partner or an individual who owns 10 percent or more of the partnership or stock of a corporate wholesaler, has been convicted of a felony under the United States code or the laws of any state which reasonably may adversely affect the good will or interest of the wholesaler or supplier. However, an existing stockholder or stockholders, or partner or partners, or a designated member or members, shall have, subject to the provisions of this chapter, the right to purchase the partnership interest or the stock of the offending partner or stockholder prior to the conviction of the offending partner or stockholder and if the sale is completed prior to conviction the provisions of this subdivision (3) shall not apply.

(f) Notwithstanding subsections (a), (c) and (e) of this section, upon not less than 15 days' prior written notice given in the manner and containing the information required by subsection (c) of this section, a supplier may terminate, cancel, fail to renew, or discontinue an agreement if any of the following events occur:

(1) There was intentional fraudulent conduct relating to a material matter on the part of the wholesaler in dealings with the supplier. Provided, however, the supplier shall have the burden of proving intentional fraudulent conduct relating to a material matter on the part of the wholesaler.

(2) The wholesaler failed to confine to the designated sales territory its sales of a brand or brands to retailers. Provided this subdivision does not apply if there is a dispute between two or more wholesalers as to the boundaries of the assigned territory, and the boundaries cannot be determined by a reading of the description contained in the agreements between the supplier and the wholesalers.

(3) A wholesaler who has failed to pay for beer ordered and delivered in accordance with established terms with the supplier fails to make full

payment within two business days after receipt of written notice of the delinquency and demand for immediate payment from the supplier.

(4) A wholesaler intentionally has made a transfer of wholesaler's business, other than a transfer to a designated member or pursuant to a loan agreement or debt instrument, without prior written notice to the supplier, and has failed, within 30 days from the receipt of written notice from the supplier of its intent to terminate on the ground of such transfer, to reverse said transfer of wholesaler's business.

(5) A wholesaler intentionally has made a transfer of wholesaler's business, other than a transfer to a designated member, although the wholesaler has prior to said transfer received from supplier a timely notice of disapproval of said transfer in accordance with this chapter.

(6) The wholesaler intentionally ceases, or ceases for a period of more than 61 days, to carry on business with respect to any of supplier's brand or brands previously serviced by wholesaler in its territory designated by the supplier, unless such cessation is due to force majeure or to labor dispute and the wholesaler has made good faith efforts to overcome such events. Provided, however, this shall affect only that brand or brands with respect to which the wholesaler ceased to carry on business.

(g) Notwithstanding subsections (a), (c), (e), and (f) of this section, a supplier may terminate, cancel, not renew, or discontinue an agreement upon not less than 30 days' prior written notice if the supplier discontinues production or discontinues distribution in this state of all the brands sold by the supplier to the wholesaler. Provided, however, nothing in this section shall prohibit a supplier from: (1) upon not less than 30 days' notice, discontinuing the distribution of any particular brand or package of beer; or (2) conducting test marketing of a new brand of beer or of a brand of beer which is not currently being sold in this state, provided that the supplier has notified the board in writing of its plans to test market, which notice shall describe the market area in which the test shall be conducted; the name or names of the wholesaler or wholesalers who will be selling the beer; the name or names of the brand of beer being tested; and the period of time, not to exceed 18 months, during which the testing will take place. (Acts 1988, No. 88-80, p. 87, § 6; Acts 1989, No. 89-525, p. 1074, § 1.)

Beer supplier's change in territorial maps and descriptions did not constitute an amendment of the territory transferred from seller of wholesale business to buyer; rather, the changes merely updated the maps and descriptions to formally reflect the actual area that seller served. Accordingly, the requirements of the statute were never invoked, and beer supplier was entitled to a judgment as a matter of law on the issue. Bama Budweiser of Montgomery, Inc. v. Anheuser-Busch, Inc., 611 So. 2d 238 (Ala. 1992).

§ 28-9-7. Transfer of wholesaler's business.

(a) Upon written notice of intent to transfer the wholesaler's business, any individual owning or deceased individual who owned an interest in a wholesaler may transfer the wholesaler's business to a designated member, or to any other person who meets the nondiscriminatory, material and reasonable qualifications and standards required by the supplier for Alabama wholesalers. The consent or approval of the supplier shall not be required of any transfer of the wholesaler's business, including the assignment of wholesaler's rights under the agreement, to a designated member or shall not be withheld or unreasonably delayed to a proposed transferee (other than a designated member) who meets such nondiscriminatory, material and reasonable qualifications and standards. Provided, however, the supplier shall have the burden of proving that the proposed transferee fails to meet such qualifications and standards which are nondiscriminatory, material and reasonable and consistently applied to Alabama wholesalers by the supplier. Provided, such designated member or transferee shall in no event be qualified as a transferee, without the written approval or consent of the supplier, where such proposed transferee shall have been involved in any of the following:

(1) Insolvency, filing of any voluntary or involuntary petition under any bankruptcy or receivership law, or execution of any assignment for the benefit of creditors; or

(2) Revocation or suspension of an alcoholic beverage license by the regulatory agency of the United States Government or any state, whereby service was interrupted for more than 61 days; or

(3) Convicted of a felony under the United States Code or the laws of any state, which reasonably may adversely affect the good will or interest of the wholesaler or supplier; or

(4) Had an agreement involuntarily terminated, cancelled, not renewed, or discontinued by a supplier for good cause.

(b) The supplier shall not interfere with, prevent or unreasonably delay the transfer of the wholesaler's business, including an assignment of wholesaler's rights under the agreement, if the proposed transferee is a designated member, or if the transferee other than a designated member meets such nondiscriminatory, material and reasonable qualifications and standards required by the supplier for Alabama wholesalers. Where the transferee is other than a designated member, the supplier may in good faith and for good cause related to the reasonable qualifications refuse to accept the transfer of wholesaler's business or the assignment of wholesaler's rights under the agreement. The supplier shall have the burden proving that it has acted in good faith and that there was good cause for failure to accept or consent to the transfer of the wholesaler's business or the assignment of wholesaler's rights under the agreement. (Acts 1988, No. 88-80, p. 87, § 7; Acts 1989, No. 89-525, p. 1074, § 1.)

§ 28-9-8. Liability of supplier for acts diminishing value of wholesaler's business; arbitration procedures; determination of amount of compensation; cost of arbitration; default of arbitration procedures.

(a) Except as provided for in this chapter, a supplier that has amended, modified, canceled, terminated, or refused to renew any agreement; or has caused a wholesaler to resign from an agreement; or has interfered with, prevented or unreasonably delayed, or where required by this chapter, has withheld or unreasonably delayed consent to or approval of, any assignment or transfer of a wholesaler's business, shall pay the wholesaler reasonable compensation for the diminished value of the wholesaler's business, including any ancillary business which has been negatively affected by the act of the supplier. The value of the wholesaler's business or ancillary business shall include, but not be limited to, any good will. Provided, however, nothing contained in this chapter shall give rise to a claim against the supplier or wholesaler by any proposed purchaser of wholesaler's business.

(b) Should either party, at any time, determine that mutual agreement on the amount of reasonable compensation cannot be reached, the supplier or the wholesaler may send by certified mail, return receipt requested, written notice to the other party declaring its intention to proceed with arbitration. Arbitration shall proceed only by mutual agreement of both parties.

(c) Not more than 10 business days after the notice to enter into arbitration has been delivered, the other party shall send written notice to the requesting party declaring its intention either to proceed or not to proceed with arbitration. Should the other party fail to respond within the 10 business days, it shall be conclusively presumed that said party shall have agreed to arbitration.

(d) The matter of determining the amount of compensation may, by agreement of the parties, be submitted to a three-member arbitration panel consisting of one representative selected by the supplier but unassociated with the affected supplier; one wholesaler representative selected by the wholesaler but unassociated with the wholesaler; and an impartial arbitrator.

(e) Not more than 10 business days after mutual agreement of both parties has been reached to arbitrate, each party shall designate, in writing, its one arbitrator representative and the party initiating arbitration shall request, in writing, a list of five arbitrators from the American arbitration association or its successor and request that the list shall be mailed to each party by certified mail, return receipt requested. Not more than 10 business days after the receipt of the list of five choices, the wholesaler arbitrator and the supplier arbitrator shall strike and disqualify up to two names each from the list. Should either party fail to respond within the 10 business days or should more than one name remain after the strikes, the American arbitration association shall make the selection of the impartial arbitrator from the names not stricken from said list.

(f) Not more than 30 days after the final selection of the arbitration panel is made, the arbitration panel shall convene to decide the dispute. The panel shall conclude the arbitration within 20 days after the arbitration panel convenes and shall render a decision by majority vote of the arbitrators within 20 days from the conclusion of the arbitration. The award of the arbitration panel shall be final and binding on the parties as to the amount of compensation for said diminished value.

(g) The cost of the impartial arbitrator, the stenographer, and the meeting site shall be equally divided between the wholesaler and the supplier. All other costs shall be paid by the party incurring them.

(h) After both parties have agreed to arbitrate should either party, except by mutual agreement, fail to abide by the time limitations as prescribed in subsections (c), (e) and (f) of this section, or fail or refuse to make the selection of any arbitrators, or fail to participate in the arbitration hearings, the other party shall make the selection of its arbitrator and proceed to arbitration. The party who has failed or refused to comply as prescribed in this section shall be considered to be in default. Any party considered to be in default pursuant to this subsection shall have waived any and all rights the party would have had in the arbitration and shall be considered to have consented to the determination of the arbitration panel. (Acts 1988, No. 88-80, p. 87, § 8; Acts 1989, No. 89-525, p. 1074, § 1.)

§ 28-9-9. Waiver of rights; good faith dispute settlements.

A wholesaler may not waive any of the rights granted in any provision of this chapter and the provisions of any agreement which would have such an effect shall be null and void. Nothing in this chapter shall be construed to limit or prohibit good faith dispute settlements voluntarily entered into by the parties. (Acts 1988, No. 88-80, p. 87, § 9.)

§ 28-9-10. Application, transferee of wholesaler's business; successor of supplier's business.

(a) This chapter shall apply to agreements in existence on March 3, 1988, as well as agreements entered into or renewed after March 3, 1988.

(b) A transferee of a wholesaler that continues in business as a wholesaler shall have the benefit of and be bound by all terms and conditions of the agreement with the supplier in effect on the date of the transfer; provided, however, a transfer of a wholesaler's business which requires supplier's consent or approval but is disapproved by the supplier shall be null and void.

(c) A successor to a supplier that continues in business as a supplier shall be bound by all terms and conditions of each agreement of the supplier in effect on the date of succession. (Acts 1988, No. 88-80, p. 87, § 10.)

§ 28-9-11. Liabilities and duties of supplier; action for damages; declaratory judgment and injunctive relief; remedies.

(a) If a supplier engages in conduct prohibited under this chapter, a wholesaler with which the supplier has an agreement may maintain a civil action against the supplier to recover actual damages reasonably incurred as the result of the prohibited conduct. If a wholesaler engages in conduct prohibited under this chapter, a supplier with which the wholesaler has an agreement may maintain a civil action against the wholesaler to recover actual damages reasonably incurred as the result of the prohibited conduct.

(b) A supplier that violates any provision of this chapter shall be liable for all actual damages and all court costs and, in the court's discretion, reasonable attorney fees incurred by a wholesaler as a result of that violation. A

215

wholesaler that violates any provision of this chapter shall be liable for all actual damages and all court costs and, in the court's discretion, reasonable attorney fees incurred by the supplier as a result of that violation.

(c) This chapter imposes upon a supplier the duty to deal fairly and in good faith with a wholesaler which has entered into an agreement with the supplier to purchase and sell a brand or brands of beer sold by the supplier. Except as otherwise provided in this chapter, if a court finds that a supplier has intentionally, consciously or deliberately acted or failed to act which was not in good faith or was in bad faith either in (1) effecting an amendment, modification, termination, cancellation, or nonrenewal of any agreement; or (2) unreasonably interfering with, preventing or unreasonably delaying the transfer of the wholesaler's business where approval of the proposed transferee is not required by this chapter; or (3) unreasonably withholding its consent to or approval of any assignment, transfer, or sale of a wholesaler's business, where approval of the proposed transferee is required by this chapter; it may, upon proof thereof by clear and convincing evidence as defined in section 6-11-20, award exemplary or punitive damages, as well as actual damages, court costs, and reasonable attorney fees to the wholesaler who has been damaged by the action or failure to act of the supplier. Such actions or failure to act on the part of the supplier shall constitute the tort of bad faith, and the amount of any award of punitive damages and the review thereof by the trial or appellate court shall be governed by the provisions of section 6-11-25.

(d) A supplier or wholesaler may bring an action for declaratory judgment for determination of any controversy arising pursuant to this chapter.

(e) Upon proper application to the court, a supplier or wholesaler may obtain injunctive relief against any violation of this chapter. If the court grants injunctive relief or issues a temporary restraining order, bond shall not be required to be posted.

(f) The remedies provided by this section are nonexclusive, and nothing contained herein shall abolish any cause of action or remedy available to the supplier or the wholesaler existing on March 3, 1988.

(g) Any legal action taken under this chapter, or in a dispute arising out of an agreement or breach thereof, or over the provisions of an agreement shall be filed in a court, state or federal, located in Alabama, which state court is located in, or which federal court has jurisdiction and venue of, the county in which the wholesaler maintains its principal place of business in this state. (Acts 1988, 88-80, p. 87, § 11.)

CHAPTER 10.

ALABAMA RESPONSIBLE VENDOR ACT.

Sec.
28-10-1. Short title.
28-10-2. Legislative intent.
28-10-3. Definitions.
28-10-4. Establishment of responsible vendors program.

Sec.
28-10-5. Evidence of compliance; certification; renewal; rules and regulations; enforcement personnel.
28-10-6. Requirements for certification.
28-10-7. Compliance as defense to license sus-

Sec.
    pension or revocation; mitigation
    of administrative penalties or
    fines.

Sec.
28-10-8. License fee.

§ 28-10-1. Short title.

This chapter may be cited as the "Alabama Responsible Vendor Act." (Acts 1990, No. 90-525, p. 767, § 1.)

§ 28-10-2. Legislative intent.

It is the intent of the legislature through the provisions of this chapter:

(1) To eliminate the sale of alcoholic beverages to, and consumption of alcoholic beverages by underaged persons;

(2) To reduce intoxication and to reduce accidents, injuries, and deaths in the state which are related to intoxication; and

(3) To encourage alcoholic beverage vendors to be prudent in their selling practices and to restrict or reduce the sanctions that may be imposed in administrative proceedings by the alcoholic beverage control board against those vendors who comply with responsible practices in accordance with this chapter. (Acts 1990, No. 90-525, p. 767, § 2.)

§ 28-10-3. Definitions.

The following terms shall have the following meanings unless the context clearly indicates otherwise:

(1) BOARD. The alcoholic beverage control board of the state of Alabama.

(2) VENDOR. A person who is licensed by the board to sell alcoholic beverages for on-the-premises consumption and/or for off-the-premises consumption. (Acts 1990, No. 90-525, p. 767, § 3.)

§ 28-10-4. Establishment of responsible vendors program.

The alcoholic beverage control board (the board) shall establish or cause to be established a responsible vendors program designed to encourage vendors and their employees and customers to treat alcoholic beverages in a responsible manner. The program must include, without limitation, comprehensive instruction on the prevention of the sale of alcoholic beverages to persons not of legal age. (Acts 1990, No. 90-525, p. 767, § 4.)

§ 28-10-5. Evidence of compliance; certification; renewal; rules and regulations; enforcement personnel.

(a) A vendor who seeks to qualify as a responsible vendor must provide to the board, pursuant to procedures adopted by the board, evidence of compliance with the requirements of this chapter. Upon satisfactory proof that the vendor has complied with the requirements, the board shall certify the vendor as a responsible vendor. Certification as a responsible vendor shall be renewed annually.

(b) The board shall adopt rules and regulations for monitoring compliance by certified vendors and for revoking or suspending a vendor's certification for noncompliance with this section. The board is hereby authorized to utilize nonlaw enforcement personnel to monitor and enforce compliance with this section. (Acts 1990, No. 90-525, p. 767, § 5.)

§ 28-10-6. Requirements for certification.

In order to qualify for certification, the vendor shall comply with the following requirements:

(1) Provide a course of instruction for its employees approved by the board which shall include subjects dealing with alcoholic beverages as follows:

a. Laws regarding the sale of alcoholic beverages for on-the-premises consumption and/or for off-the-premises consumption;

b. Methods of recognizing and dealing with underage customers; and

c. The development of specific procedures for refusing to sell alcoholic beverages to underage customers; for assisting employees in dealing with underage customers; and for dealing with intoxicated customers.

(2) Require each employee who is authorized to sell alcoholic beverages in the normal course of his or her employment to complete the employee training course set out in subdivision (1) hereof within 30 days of commencing employment;

(3) Require all such trained employees to attend additional meetings at least semiannually or such other schedule of meetings as may be approved by the board, which meetings shall include the dissemination of existing and new information covering the applicable subjects specified in this section and explaining the vendor's policies and procedures relating to those subjects;

(4) Maintain employment records of the training of its employees required by this section; and

(5) Post signs on the vendor's premises informing customers of the vendor's policy against selling alcoholic beverages to underaged persons. (Acts 1990, No. 90-525, p. 767, § 6.)

§ 28-10-7. Compliance as defense to license suspension or revocation; mitigation of administrative penalties or fines.

(a) The license of a vendor certified as a responsible vendor under this chapter may not be suspended or revoked for an employee's illegal sale of an alcoholic beverage to a person who is not of lawful drinking age if the employee had completed the applicable training prescribed by this chapter prior to committing such violation, unless the vendor had knowledge of the violation or should have known about such violation, or participated in or committed such violation. No vendor may use as a defense to decertification the fact that he was absent from the licensed premises at the time of noncompliance with this section.

(b) The board shall consider certification by a vendor in the responsible vendors program in mitigation of administrative penalties or fines for an employee's illegal sale of an alcoholic beverage to a person who is not of lawful drinking age. (Acts 1990, No. 90-525, p. 767, § 7.)

§ 28-10-8. License fee.

There is hereby imposed on each licensee of the board who is licensed and applies for certification as a responsible vendor for the sale of alcoholic beverages for on-the-premises consumption and/or off-the-premises consumption a fee of $35.00 payable upon the issuance or renewal of such license. This amount is appropriated in addition to the general appropriation for the ABC board. Any unexpended sums remaining at the end of the fiscal year shall not revert to the general fund, but shall continue to be preserved for the administration of the program. (Acts 1990, No. 90-525, p. 767, § 8.)